Contemporary Authors

ISSN 0010-7468

Contemporary

Authors

**A Bio-Bibliographical Guide to
Current Writers in Fiction, General Nonfiction,
Poetry, Journalism, Drama, Motion Pictures,
Television, and Other Fields**

HAL MAY
Editor

**DIANE L. DUPUIS
LILLIAN S. SIMS
SUSAN M. TROSKY**
Associate Editors

volume **115**

GALE RESEARCH COMPANY • BOOK TOWER • DETROIT, MICHIGAN 48226

STAFF

Hal May, *Editor, Original Volumes*

Diane L. Dupuis, Lillian S. Sims, and Susan M. Trosky, *Associate Editors*

Les Stone, *Senior Writer*

Nancy H. Evans and Michael L. LaBlanc, *Senior Assistant Editors*

Lori R. Clemens, Louise Mooney, Nancy Pear, and Susan Stefani, *Assistant Editors and Writers*

Barbara A. Cicchetti, Dean David Dauphinais, Zoran Minderovic, Joanne M. Peters,
Paulette Petrimoulx, and Polly A. Vedder, *Assistant Editors*

Arlene True, *Sketchwriter*

Peter Benjaminson, Fred Bornhauser, and Jean W. Ross, *Interviewers*

Frances C. Locher, *Consulting Editor*

Charity Anne Dorgan, Linda Hubbard,
Adele Sarkissian, and Curtis Skinner, *Contributing Editors*

Eunice Bergin, *Copy Editor*

Deborah A. Straub, *Index Coordinator*

Debra G. Hunter, *Research Supervisor*

Marian Gonsior, *Research Coordinator*

Betty Joan Best, Mary Rose Bonk, Reginald A. Carlton, Ellen Koral, Sara A. Lederer,
Timothy P. Loszewski, Christine Joan May, Mary Alice Rattenbury, Norma Sawaya,
Shirley Seip, Aida M. Smith, Tracey Head Turbett, and Peter Wehrli, *Research Assistants*

Special recognition is given to the staff of
Young People's Literature Department, Gale Research Company

Frederick G. Ruffner, *Publisher*

James M. Ethridge, *Executive Vice-President/Editorial*

Dedria Bryfonski, *Editorial Director*

Christine Nasso, *Director, Literature Division*

Ann Evory, *Senior Editor, Contemporary Authors*

Library of Congress Catalog Card Number 62-52046
ISBN 0-8103-1915-2
ISSN 0010-7468

Computerized photocomposition by
Typographics, Incorporated
Kansas City, Missouri

Contents

Authors and Media People
Featured in This Volume

Donald L. Barlett—American investigative journalist associated with the *Philadelphia Inquirer* since 1970; author of several award-winning news series with fellow reporter James B. Steele (see also Steele's sketch in this volume); in addition to earning the prestigious George Polk Memorial Award in both 1971 and 1973, the pair received a Pulitzer Prize in 1975 for national reporting; they also collaborated on the critically acclaimed book *Empire: The Life, Legend, and Madness of Howard Hughes.* (Sketch includes interview.)

Chuck Berry—American singer, musician, and composer; considered among the most influential figures in the development of rock and roll music; his first recording, "Maybelline," became an instant hit; other songs written and recorded by Berry include "Roll Over Beethoven," the rock anthem "Johnny B. Goode," and "My Ding-A-Ling," an extremely popular, risque tune.

Mary Chamberlain—British lecturer and historian; author of women's studies that focus on the role of ordinary women in human history, such as *Fenwomen* and *Old Wives' Tales.*

Sylvia Chase—Award-winning American broadcast journalist; best known for her work on the popular ABC-TV news magazine show "20/20"; widely esteemed in her field, Chase has won two Emmys and two Headliner Awards for reporting; before joining ABC, she was employed by CBS-TV, first as a correspondent for "The CBS Evening News With Walter Cronkite" and then as anchor of the network's morning news journal, "Magazine." (Sketch includes interview.)

Marion Chesney—British novelist; author of more than thirty romance novels, many of which are English Regency works; Chesney writes under her own name and under the pseudonyms Helen Crampton, Ann Fairfax, and Jennie Tremaine. (Sketch includes interview.)

Ian Dalrymple—British screenwriter, producer, and motion picture director; best known as the co-author of "Pygmalion," the Academy Award-winning screen adaptation of George Bernard Shaw's play, and of the film version of A. J. Cronin's novel *The Citadel.*

William H. Deverell—Canadian attorney-turned-novelist whose first book was published when the author was more than forty years old; the book, a psychological thriller titled *Needles,* won the $50,000 McClelland & Stewart/Seal First Novel Award in 1979; Deverell is also the author of *Mecca* and *High Crimes.*

Hedley Donovan—American journalist and publishing executive; associated with Time Inc. from 1945 to 1981, Donovan succeeded Henry R. Luce as editor in chief of all Time publications in 1964; under Donovan's direction the firm expanded its list of periodicals with the popular *Money* and *People* magazines; a colleague once described Donovan as "a boss of awesome intelligence, competence, and character." (Sketch includes interview.)

Ellen Douglas—Pseudonym of Josephine Haxton, an award-winning American novelist whose critically acclaimed works depict the southern experience in a fictional Mississippi county; her novels include *Apostles of Light,* which was nominated for a National Book Award, *The Rock Cried Out,* and *A Lifetime Burning.*

Sergei Dovlatov—Soviet emigre writer; a journalist in good standing in the U.S.S.R. until he began writing fiction for unauthorized publications as well as smuggling his works to the West; as a result Dovlatov was arrested and forced to emigrate; he now lives in the United States and has published short stories and such novels as *The Zone* and *The Compromise.*

Linda Ellerbee—American broadcast journalist; Ellerbee gained prominence during the 1982-83 television season as co-anchor of "NBC News Overnight," a program noted for its intelligent treatment of current events; she is currently serving as co-anchor of the weekly television news magazine "Summer Sunday U.S.A." (Sketch includes interview.)

Serge Klarsfeld—Anti-Nazi activist and writer; outraged when former Nazi Kurt Georg Kiesinger was elected chancellor of West Germany in 1967, Klarsfeld and his wife, Beate, decided to devote themselves to bringing other members of the Third Reich to justice; Klarsfeld has become a leading authority on the Holocaust and is known for his meticulous research; the evidence he unearths is considered vital in locating people like Klaus Barbie, the infamous "Butcher of Lyons," who was arrested in 1983; Klarsfeld's writings include *The Holocaust and the Neo-Nazi Mythomania.*

Ted Kotcheff—Canadian director, screenwriter, and producer of motion pictures; in 1974 he directed "The Apprenticeship of Duddy Kravitz," which *Newsweek* predicted would "become the first big movie to come out of Canada in living memory"; Kotcheff also directed the films "Fun With Dick and Jane," "North Dallas Forty," and "First Blood."

Mary Kuczkir—American writer; under the joint pseudonym Fern Michaels, Kuczkir and collaborator Roberta Anderson have written more then twenty best-selling romance novels, such as *Captive Passions, Valentina,* and *Cinders to Satin.* (Sketch includes interview.)

Robert C. Maynard—American journalist; in 1967 Maynard became the first full-time black national correspondent at the *Washington Post;* since 1979, he has been editor, publisher, and president of the Oakland, California, *Oakland Tribune.* (Sketch includes interview.)

Samuel Menashe—American minimalist poet acclaimed for his compact, precise poems; Stephen Spender has called the language of Menashe's verse "intense and clear as diamonds"; among his volumes of poetry are *To Open, Fringe on Fire,* and *No Jerusalem But This.* (Sketch includes interview.)

Jonathan Miller—British physician, actor, and producer and director of stage, opera, radio, and television productions; his first theatrical work, the immensely successful satirical review "Beyond the Fringe," was written in collaboration with Dudley Moore, Peter Cook, and Alan Bennett and received a special Tony Award in 1963; Miller left the medical profession for the performing arts but drew upon his background as a physician to create the thirteen-part television series "The Body in Question," which aired in England on the BBC and later in the United States on public television.

Richard Perry—American college professor and writer; in addition to short stories and articles, Perry is the author of two novels, *Changes* and the well-received *Montgomery's Children;* the *New York Times Book Review* deemed him "an extremely talented writer whose work bears watching."

Andre Previn—World-renowned German-born American symphony orchestra conductor, composer, film scorer, and pianist; dubbed MGM's "boy wonder" when he became the film company's composer and conductor at age eighteen, Previn subsequently received four Academy Awards and more than a dozen other Oscar nominations for his film scores; during the 1960's he turned to conducting classical music and eventually headed the London Symphony Orchestra and later the Pittsburgh Symphony Orchestra.

Peter Quennell—British biographer, historian, editor, and critic; esteemed as "one of England's radiant literary lights for more than half a century," he is known especially as an expert on Byron and Pope; Quennell is also the founder and longtime co-editor of *History Today,* a journal recognized for its "good scholarship and readability"; his books include *Byron in Italy, Alexander Pope: The Education of a Genius,* and *The Marble Foot,* an autobiography.

Diane K. Sawyer—American broadcast journalist; White House press secretary Ron Ziegler's assistant from 1970 to 1974, Sawyer assisted President Richard Nixon in the writing of his memoirs after he resigned from office; as a CBS-News journalist since 1978, Sawyer has been described as "the fastest-rising star in television news and its most intriguing personality"; Sawyer co-anchored the "CBS Morning News" from 1981 to 1984; she joined the "60 Minutes" investigative team in 1984. (Sketch includes interview.)

James B. Steele—Award-winning American investigative journalist; since 1970 he has worked for the *Philadelphia Inquirer* with fellow reporter Donald L. Barlett (see also Barlett's sketch in this volume); the team has received many awards for their stories, notably the Pulitzer Prize and the George Polk Memorial Award; Steele is also the author of *Oil: The Created Crisis* and *Forevermore: Nuclear Waste in America.* (Sketch includes interview.)

James Stevenson—American humorist and children's author; Stevenson began his writing career as a satirist of suburbia and later expanded his subject matter to encompass social criticism, nostalgia, and children's problems; among his award-winning books are *Monty, Howard,* and *Could Be Worse!*

Preface

The over 1,000 entries in *Contemporary Authors (CA)*, Volume 115, bring to more than 82,000 the number of authors now represented in the *Contemporary Authors* series. *CA* includes nontechnical writers in all genres—fiction, nonfiction, poetry, drama, etc.—whose books are issued by commercial, risk publishers or by university presses. Authors of books published only by known vanity or author-subsidized firms are ordinarily not included. Since native language and nationality have no bearing on inclusion in *CA*, authors who write in languages other than English are included in *CA* if their works have been published in the United States or translated into English.

Although *CA* focuses primarily on authors of published books, the series also encompasses prominent persons in communications: newspaper and television reporters and correspondents, columnists, newspaper and magazine editors, photojournalists, syndicated cartoonists, screenwriters, television scriptwriters, and other media people.

Starting with Volume 104, the editors of *CA* began to broaden the series' scope to encompass authors deceased since 1900 whose works are still of interest to today's readers. (Previously, *CA* covered only living writers and authors deceased 1960 or later.) Since the great poets, novelists, short story writers, and playwrights of the early twentieth century are popular writers for study in today's high school and college curriculums, and since their writings continue to be analyzed by today's literary critics, these writers are in many ways as contemporary as the authors *CA* has featured up to this point.

Therefore, *CA* now contains information on important authors who lived and wrote between 1900 and 1959. Numerous authors from this period, most of whom will receive longer treatment later, are presently represented in *CA* with short, succinct entries that summarize their lives and literary contributions. These brief entries are further explained in the section of the preface below headed "Brief Entries."

No charge or obligation is attached to a *CA* listing. Authors are included in the series solely on the basis of the above criteria and their interest to *CA* users.

Compilation Methods

The editors make every effort to secure information directly from the authors through questionnaires and personal correspondence. If writers of special interest to *CA* users are deceased or fail to reply to requests for information, material is gathered from other reliable sources. Biographical dictionaries are checked (a task made easier through the use of Gale's *Biography and Genealogy Master Index* and other volumes in the "Gale Biographical Index Series"), as are bibliographical sources such as *Cumulative Book Index* and *The National Union Catalog*. Published interviews, feature stories, and book reviews are examined, and often material is supplied by the authors' publishers. All sketches, whether prepared from questionnaires or through extensive research, are sent to the biographees for review prior to publication. Sketches on recently deceased authors are sent to family members, agents, etc., if possible, for a similar review.

Format

CA is designed to present, clearly and concisely, biographical and bibliographical information in three kinds of entries: sketches, brief entries, and obituary notices. In recent volumes the editors have introduced a number of improvements in the format of these listings. Sketches in Volume 114, for instance, contain individual paragraphs with rubrics identifying address, membership, and awards and honors information, permitting *CA* users to locate more easily the specific facts they need.

As part of *CA*'s continuing efforts to make the information in entries as accessible as possible, Volume 115 introduces a new format for title listings. In sketch sections headed "Writings," the title of each book, play, and other published or unpublished work appears on a separate line, clearly distinguishing one title from another. Now *CA* readers can quickly scan an author's bibliography to find the titles they need. This same convenient bibliographical presentation is featured in the "Biographical/Critical Sources" sections of sketches and brief entries and in the "Obituaries and Other Sources" sections of obituary notices where individual book and periodical titles are also listed on separate lines.

Brief Entries

CA users have indicated that having some information, however brief, on authors not yet in the series would be preferable to waiting until full-length sketches can be prepared as outlined above under "Compilation Methods." Since Volume 104, therefore, *CA* has included concise, condensed entries on both early twentieth-century and current writers who presently do not have sketches in *CA*. These short listings, identified by the heading "Brief Entry," highlight the author's career and writings and often provide a few sources where additional information can be found.

Brief entries are not intended to serve as sketches. Instead, they are designed to increase *CA*'s comprehensiveness and thus better serve *CA* users by providing pertinent information about a large number of authors, many of whom will be the subjects of full sketches in forthcoming volumes.

Informative Sidelights

Numerous *CA* sketches contain sidelights, which provide personal dimensions to the listings, supply information about the critical reception the authors' works have received, or both. Some authors listed in Volume 115 worked closely with *CA*'s editors to develop lengthy, incisive sidelights, such as the comments provided by Edgar E. MacDonald, a professor of English since 1957. The informed, educated reader, he argues, bears a responsibility towards the work he reads, a duty to think about and analyze the text objectively. "As a teacher," he says, "I have little interest in the subjective effusions of students, interpretations of a 'message' largely imagined. Leaving that area of appreciation to educationists and religious psychologists, I try instead to instill in a student a respect for an objective appraisal of a work, one based on a preliminary consideration of forms. If one is going to be made to feel, he ought to understand the techniques and processes by which he is made to feel. . . . Our subjective enjoyment is augmented by the cerebral pleasure of understanding how a poem or novel works. Every work of art is a commentary on life. For the unanalytical reader, the message is filtered through his neuroses; for the analytical, through his intellectual rationale."

CA's editors also compile sidelights when authors and media people of particular interest do not supply sidelights material, or when demand for information about the critical reception their books have received is especially high. Senior writer Les Stone's sidelights for Serge Klarsfeld, for example, describe the efforts of the famed anti-Nazi activist and his wife, Beate, to bring to trial accused war criminals such as former S.S. officer Herbert Hagan, ex-Gestapo agent Ernest Heinrichsohn, and Walter Rauff, inventor of the mobile gas vans that experts say were used by the Nazis to kill more than 250,000 prisoners. The Klarsfelds' investigations led to the arrest in 1983 of Klaus Barbie, "the infamous 'Butcher of Lyons,' who reportedly participated in countless tortures and authorized thousands of murders and deportations" during World War II.

One of *CA*'s assistant editors and writers, Lori R. Clemens, provides sidelights for internationally known composer-conductor Andre Previn, who once said, "I *like* the fact that music is so unpredictably quixotic— that it reflects the philosophy of everything that goes on in the whole world." In the opinion of Pittsburgh Symphony Orchestra manager Seymour Rosen: "There are other conductors who play and compose, but they don't do many things as brilliantly as Andre does. He's a true Renaissance man."

And senior assistant editor Nancy H. Evans notes the transformation of Donald L. Barlett from "traditional scandal-hunting" newsman to Pulitzer Prize-winning journalist in sidelights for the *Philadelphia Inquirer* reporter. Ms. Evans also offers sidelights for Barlett's partner, James B. Steele, a reporter for the *Kansas City Times* before he joined Barlett on the staff of the *Inquirer*. According to *Nation*'s Robert Sherrill, the two newsmen constitute "the finest team of investigative reporters west of *The Times of London*."

We hope these sketches, as well as others with sidelights compiled by *CA*'s editors, provide informative and enjoyable reading.

Writers of Special Interest

CA's editors make every effort to include a substantial number of entries in each volume on active authors and media people of special interest to *CA*'s readers. Since *CA* also includes sketches on noteworthy deceased writers, a significant amount of work on the part of *CA*'s editors goes into the compilation of full-length entries on important deceased authors. Some of the prominent writers whose sketches are contained in this volume are noted in the list on pages 7-8 headed "Authors and Media People Featured in This Volume."

Exclusive Interviews

CA provides exclusive, primary information on certain writers in the form of interviews. Prepared specifically for *CA,* the never-before-published conversations presented in the section of the sketch headed "*CA* Interview" give *CA* users the opportunity to learn the authors' thoughts, in depth, about their craft. Subjects chosen for interviews are, the editors feel, authors who hold special interest for *CA*'s readers.

Writers and journalists in this volume whose sketches include interviews are Donald L. Barlett, Sylvia Chase, Marion Chesney, Hedley Donovan, Linda Ellerbee, Mary Kuczkir, Robert C. Maynard, Samuel Menashe, Diane K. Sawyer, and James B. Steele.

Obituary Notices Make *CA* Timely and Comprehensive

To be as timely and comprehensive as possible, *CA* publishes obituary notices on deceased authors within the scope of the series. These notices provide date and place of birth and death, highlight the author's career and writings, and list other sources where additional biographical information and obituaries may be found. To distinguish them from full-length sketches, obituaries are identified with the heading "Obituary Notice."

CA includes obituary notices for writers who already have full-length entries in earlier *CA* volumes—28 percent of the obituary notices in this volume are for such authors—as well as for authors who do not yet have sketches in the series. Deceased writers of special interest currently represented only by obituary notices will be scheduled for full-length sketch treatment in forthcoming *CA* volumes.

Numerous *CA* users have commented favorably on the value of *CA*'s obituary notices. To continue to meet the need for concise obituary information on authors and media people, *CA*'s editors intend to maintain the emphasis on comprehensive obituary coverage.

Contemporary Authors New Revision Series

A major change in the preparation of *CA* revision volumes began with the first volume of *Contemporary Authors New Revision Series.* No longer are all of the sketches in a given *CA* volume updated and published together as a revision volume. Instead, entries from a number of volumes are assessed, and only those sketches requiring *significant change* are revised and published in a *New Revision Series* volume. This enables us to provide *CA* users with updated information about active writers on a more timely basis and avoids printing entries in which there has been little or no change. As always, the most recent *CA* cumulative index continues to be the user's guide to the location of an individual author's revised listing.

Contemporary Authors Autobiography Series

Designed to complement the information in *CA* original and revision volumes, the new *Contemporary Authors Autobiography Series* provides autobiographical essays written by important current authors. Each volume contains from twenty to thirty specially commissioned autobiographies and is illustrated with numerous personal photographs supplied by the authors. The range of contemporary writers who will be describing their lives and interests in the new *Autobiography Series* is indicated by the variety of authors who contributed to Volumes 1 and 2—writers such as Dannie Abse, Vance Bourjaily, Erskine Caldwell, John Ciardi, Doris Grumbach, Elizabeth Forsythe Hailey, Marge Piercy, Frederik Pohl, Alan Sillitoe, and Diane Wakoski. Though the information presented in the autobiographies is as varied and unique as the authors, common topics of discussion include their motivations for writing, the people and experiences that shaped their careers, the rewards they derive from their work, and their impressions of the current literary scene.

Autobiographies included in the *Contemporary Authors Autobiography Series* can be located through both the *CA* cumulative index and the *Contemporary Authors Autobiography Series* cumulative index, which lists not only personal names but also titles of works, geographical names, subjects, and schools of writing.

CA Numbering System

Occasionally questions arise about the *CA* numbering system. Despite numbers like "97-100" and "115," the entire *CA* series consists of only 59 physical volumes with the publication of *CA* Volume 115. The information below notes changes in the numbering system, as well as in cover design, to help *CA* users better understand the organization of the entire *CA* series.

CA First Revisions

- 1-4R through 41-44R (11 books)
  Cover: Brown with black and gold trim.
  There will be no further *First Revisions* because revised entries are now being handled exclusively through the more efficient *New Revision Series* mentioned below.

CA Original Volumes	• 45-48 through 97-100 (14 books)
	Cover: Brown with black and gold trim.
	• 101 through 115 (15 books)
	Cover: Blue and black with orange bands.
	The same as previous *CA* original volumes but with a new, simplified numbering system and new cover design.
CA New Revision Series	• *CANR*-1 through *CANR*-15 (15 books)
	Cover: Blue and black with green bands.
	Includes only sketches requiring extensive change; **sketches are taken from any previously published *CA* volume.**
CA Permanent Series	• *CAP*-1 and *CAP*-2 (2 books)
	Cover: Brown with red and gold trim.
	There will be no further *Permanent Series* volumes because revised entries are now being handled exclusively through the more efficient *New Revision Series* mentioned above.
CA Autobiography Series	• *CAA*-1 and *CAA*-2 (2 books)
	Cover: Blue and black with pink and purple bands.
	Presents specially commissioned autobiographies by leading contemporary writers to complement the information in *CA* original and revision volumes.

Retaining *CA* Volumes

As new volumes in the series are published, users often ask which *CA* volumes, if any, can be discarded. The Volume Update Chart on page 13 is designed to assist users in keeping their collections as complete as possible. All volumes in the left column of the chart should be retained to have the most complete, up-to-date coverage possible; volumes in the right column can be discarded if the appropriate replacements are held.

Cumulative Index Should Always Be Consulted

The key to locating an individual author's listing is the *CA* cumulative index bound into the back of alternate original volumes (and available separately as an offprint). Since the *CA* cumulative index provides access to *all* entries in the *CA* series, the latest cumulative index should always be consulted to find the specific volume containing an author's original or most recently revised sketch.

For the convenience of *CA* users, the *CA* cumulative index also includes references to all entries in these related Gale literary series: *Something About the Author, Dictionary of Literary Biography, Contemporary Literary Criticism, Twentieth-Century Literary Criticism,* and *Authors in the News.*

As always, suggestions from users about any aspect of *CA* will be welcomed.

Volume Update Chart

IF YOU HAVE:	YOU MAY DISCARD:
1-4 First Revision (1967)	1 (1962) 2 (1963) 3 (1963) 4 (1963)
5-8 First Revision (1969)	5-6 (1963) 7-8 (1963)
Both 9-12 First Revision (1974) AND *Contemporary Authors Permanent Series*, Volume 1 (1975)	9-10 (1964) 11-12 (1965)
Both 13-16 First Revision (1975) AND *Contemporary Authors Permanent Series*, Volumes 1 and 2 (1975, 1978)	13-14 (1965) 15-16 (1966)
Both 17-20 First Revision (1976) AND *Contemporary Authors Permanent Series*, Volumes 1 and 2 (1975, 1978)	17-18 (1967) 19-20 (1968)
Both 21-24 First Revision (1977) AND *Contemporary Authors Permanent Series*, Volumes 1 and 2 (1975, 1978)	21-22 (1969) 23-24 (1970)
Both 25-28 First Revision (1977) AND *Contemporary Authors Permanent Series*, Volume 2 (1978)	25-28 (1971)
Both 29-32 First Revision (1978) AND *Contemporary Authors Permanent Series*, Volume 2 (1978)	29-32 (1972)
Both 33-36 First Revision (1978) AND *Contemporary Authors Permanent Series*, Volume 2 (1978)	33-36 (1973)
37-40 First Revision (1979)	37-40 (1973)
41-44 First Revision (1979)	41-44 (1974)
45-48 (1974) 49-52 (1975) ↓ ↓ 115 (1985)	NONE: These volumes will not be superseded by corresponding revised volumes. Individual entries from these and all other volumes appearing in the left column of this chart will be revised and included in the *New Revision Series*.
Volumes in the *Contemporary Authors New Revision Series*	NONE: The *New Revision Series* does not replace any single volume of *CA*. All volumes appearing in the left column of this chart must be retained to have information on all authors in the series.

Indicates that a listing has been compiled from secondary sources believed to be reliable, but has not been personally verified for this edition by the author sketched.

AASHEIM, Ashley   1942-
(A. Ashley)

PERSONAL: Born March 8, 1942, in Middlesex, England; son of Leonard Mikal (an officer in the Norwegian navy) and Stella (a millinery shop manager; maiden name, Zeiderman) Aasheim. *Education:* Ruskin College, Oxford, Diploma, 1968; Sussex University, B.A. (honors), 1970; London School of Economics and Political Science, London, M.Sc., 1972.

ADDRESSES: Home—5 St. James Dr., London SW17 7RN, England. *Agent*—Al Zuckerman, Writers House, Inc., 21 West 26th St., New York, N.Y. 10010; and Jon Zackon, Bromley, Kent BRI 2HV, England.

CAREER: Worked as merchant seaman, salesman, factory worker, clerk, messenger, and shop assistant, 1957-66; Pitman College, London, England, teacher of English and commerce, 1973-84; writer.

WRITINGS:

NOVELS

The Artemis Sanction, Dell, 1981.
Vulcan Rising, Dell, 1982.
The Apostate, Frederick Muller, 1983.
A Stillness at Sea, Banbury Press, 1983.

OTHER

(Under pseudonym A. Ashley) *Handbook of Commercial Correspondence*, Oxford University Press, 1984.

Author of unproduced plays and television scripts, including "The Agents." Under pseudonym A. Ashley, author of textbooks.

WORK IN PROGRESS: Children of the Hosti, a fantasy novel; a thriller set in Stalin's Soviet Union; a commercial textbook.

SIDELIGHTS: Ashley Aasheim told *CA:* "I am half Norwegian, on my father's side, and half Austrian, on my mother's. Half Lutheran, father, and half Jewish, mother. I barely knew my father, a naval officer who returned to Bergen, Norway, when I was five, though I tracked him down some fifteen years later. I don't think I really knew my mother, who died when I was fifteen. But she was hard-working, practical, and tough and intellectually liberated long before the phrase 'women's

liberation' was coined. But then, weren't most working women of that era?

"It was my grandmother who had the most influence on me. As pragmatic as my mother, but with what seemed to me then, and even now, a voluminous knowledge of history and politics and a slap that had the force of fifty years of grim, hard work behind it. Did we love one another? I really don't know. They were austere post-war years for everyone around us. Monochrome years of rationing and doing without.

"Education, too, was 'rationed.' I was taught by ex-services teachers who probably knew their subjects but little of how to teach them. So even without qualifications I was pleased to get out of school at fifteen, but not pleased with the next nine years. They were years of drifting through a series of blue/white collar jobs as salesman, factory worker, laborer, merchant seaman, clerk, messenger, shop assistant—I once counted more than forty, but lost track after that. No aims, just meandering to the next factory or office—not colorful. 'Colorful' is getting experience. 'Not colorful' is getting by.

"But at twenty-four I was told about scholarships offered to people like me at Ruskin College, Oxford. They consisted of writing a five-thousand-word dissertation on given subjects. I chose 'delinquency,' something I knew about, and I got accepted. Six academic years and three qualifications later I got an M.Sc. from the London School of Economics and began teaching English and commerce. I was no longer meandering, but stagnant.

"The cliche, 'Writing is more from desperation than inspiration,' must have applied to me, as after five years of teaching I began to write television scripts, which were turned down, and plays, which were rejected. But fortunately one novel attempt got me an agent. He liked the writing, but not the novel. However, he had an idea for another and from that I wrote *The Artemis Sanction*, a spy thriller I followed with *Vulcan Rising* in the same genre. But I wanted to write a novel based on the knights of Malta and I began work on *The Apostate*, the story of a sixteenth-century knight of St. John who, excommunicated, becomes a mercenary, then fifteen war years later returns to Spain and embarks on a journey down to Seville to see his ex-wife before facing what he knows will be his last battle against the Turks in besieged Malta. It's the story of a man's changing character from young idealist to cynical heretic, then pathological killer, until he finally finds a redemption that comes from a God within himself.

"Soon after *The Apostate* I wrote *Stillness at Sea*—the story of the *Lusitania,* the ship sunk by Germans in 1915. Although there is a 'thriller' element in it, it is essentially a story about ideas and values locked in a ship making an almost certainly doomed voyage. The extraordinary and ordinary boarded her in New York despite German threats to sink her. I don't think I used a character in it that I hadn't known at one time in my life, including myself. And while researching the material, I was shocked to find the merchant marine I was in had hardly changed in conditions in the forty odd years since the *Lusitania.*

"I have just finished *Children of the Hosti,* a fantasy that blends New York gang life, the barbarism of ten thousand years ago, and the epitome of achievement a million years hence, all finding their existence on a plane known as parallax six. There are elements of fantasy in it, but no magic. Elements of science fiction, but no technology. It's a blend of ideas that lets me develop real characters and problems in an unreal world. Again there is the clash of ideas and values that I imagine is the generating force of all character writing. After all, they are what a person *is.* I like the book, as fantasy makes anything possible, but here it is restricted to the bounds of man's minds rather than the *hardware* he creates. And that gives the characters that 'third dimension' that makes them real.

"My motivation in writing was that of most authors—make money, be successful. And like 'most' I have done neither. But there is the huge compensation of creating existences you know as well as you know yourself. Where you are participant and observer, creator and visitor, but never intruder. It is that balance that gives me the most sense of achievement, when a character surprises me by a word or action—that's when I know s/he's real."

BIOGRAPHICAL/CRITICAL SOURCES

PERIODICALS

Times Literary Supplement, May 20, 1983.

* * *

ABAYAKOON, Cyrus D. F.   1912-

BRIEF ENTRY: Born in 1912 in Ceylon (now Sri Lanka). Astrologer and author. Abayakoon, who learned astrology from Buddhist priests, specializes in palmistry and healing through sound vibrations, or mantra yoga. He accurately predicted the assassinations of Mohandas Gandhi and John F. Kennedy and, more recently, foretold the Watergate scandal. Abayakoon is the author of *Astro-Palmistry: Signs and Seals of the Hand* (ASI Publishers, 1975).

* * *

ABDULLAH, Achmed   1881-1945

BRIEF ENTRY: Born in 1881 in Yalta, Crimea, Russia (now U.S.S.R.); naturalized British citizen; died of a heart attack, May 12, 1945, in New York, N.Y. Russian-born British novelist and playwright known almost exclusively under his pen name, Achmed Abdullah. Because of his parents' divorce and his subsequent adoption by his maternal grandfather, an Afghan Moslem, Abdullah was reared in Afghanistan and brought up in the Moslem faith. Although it is believed that he was

christened Alexander Nicholayevitch Romanoff, he became known as Syyed Shaykh Achmed Abdullah Nadir Kahn el-Idrissvieh el-Durani, or Prince Nadir Khan Durani. Abdullah later used only his Moslem given names as his nom de plume. One source cites his actual name as Nadir Khan-Romanoffski, combining his Christian and Moslem names.

Among Achmed Abdullah's best known writings are the plays "Toto" (1920) and "The Grand Duke" (1921); the screenplays "The Thief of Bagdad" (1924) and "The Lives of a Bengal Lancer" (1935); the novel *The Honourable Gentleman and Others* (1919); and an autobiography, *The Cat Had Nine Lives: Adventures and Reminiscences* (1933). Abdullah also contributed stories of romance, intrigue, and adventure to popular magazines both in the United States and abroad. In addition to his work as a writer, Abdullah served for seventeen years in the British and British-Indian armies, advancing from captain to colonel. For one year he served as a colonel in the Turkish Army as well. His distinctions include a doctorate from the College of El-Azar in Cairo and membership in the French Academy.

BIOGRAPHICAL/CRITICAL SOURCES:

BOOKS

Catholic Authors: Contemporary Biographical Sketches, Gale, 1981.
Current Biography, Wilson, 1945.
Twentieth-Century Authors: A Biographical Dictionary of Modern Literature, H. W. Wilson, 1942.

PERIODICALS

New York Times, May 13, 1945.

* * *

ABERCROMBIE, M(innie) L(ouie) J(ohnson) 1909(?)-1984
(M. L. Johnson Abercrombie, M. L. Johnson)

OBITUARY NOTICE: Born c. 1909 in Birmingham, England; died November 25, 1984. Biologist, educator, and author. Abercrombie began her career as a teacher at the University of Birmingham. She then joined the anatomy department of the University of London's University College, where she was involved in selecting and training medical students. As a result of her classroom experiences, she developed influential teaching methods that employed concepts of group-analytic psychotherapy and focused on the instruction of students in small groups. Abercrombie, who also conducted research on cerebral palsy and radiology, was a founding member and president of the Group-Analytic Society in London and with her husband Michael Abercrombie, edited the "New Biology" series. She also co-edited, under the name M. L. Johnson, the *Penguin Dictionary of Biology.* As M. L. Johnson Abercrombie she wrote *The Anatomy of Judgement: An Investigation Into the Processes of Perception and Reasoning* and, under the name M. L. J. Abercrombie, published *Aims and Techniques of Group Teaching* and *Talking to Learn: Improving Teaching and Learning in Small Groups.*

OBITUARIES AND OTHER SOURCES:

PERIODICALS

Times (London), December 11, 1984.

ABERCROMBIE, M. L. Johnson
See ABERCROMBIE, M(innie) L(ouie) J(ohnson)

*   *   *

ABERCROMBIE, Michael   1912-1979

OBITUARY NOTICE: Born August 14 (one source says August 16), 1912, in Ryton, Gloucestershire, England; died May 28, 1979, in Cambridge, England. Biologist, educator, and author. Credited with influential discoveries in cell behavior and cell population dynamics, Abercrombie received his education at Oxford University's Queen's College. He joined the faculty of the University of London's University College in 1947, serving in the anatomy department from 1947 to 1962 and as Jodrell Professor of Zoology from 1962-1970. In 1970 he moved to Cambridge University's Strangeway's Research Laboratory, where he worked as director until his death. With his wife, Minnie Louie Johnson Abercrombie, he was founder and editor of the Penguin "New Biology" series, as well as author of the *Penguin Dictionary of Biology*. Abercrombie also edited the *Journal of Embryology and Experimental Morphology* and served as co-editor of *Advances in Morphogenesis*.

OBITUARIES AND OTHER SOURCES:

BOOKS

International Who's Who, 43rd edition, Europa, 1979.
Twentieth-Century Culture: A Biographical Companion, Harper, 1983.
Who's Who in the World, 4th edition, Marquis, 1978.

*   *   *

ABRASHKIN, Raymond   1911-1960
(Ray Ashley)

PERSONAL: Born in 1911 in Brooklyn, N.Y.; died August 25, 1960, in Weston, Conn.; married wife, Evelyn; children: William H., John W. *Education:* Received degree from City College (now of the City University of New York).

ADDRESSES: Home—Weston, Conn.

CAREER: Film producer, teacher, and author of books for children. *Military service:* U.S. Maritime Service in World War II.

AWARDS, HONORS: Silver Lion Award for best American film from Venice International Film Festival and Academy Award nomination from Academy of Motion Picture Arts and Sciences, both 1954, both for "The Little Fugitive"; Young Reader's Choice Award from Pacific Northwest Library Association, 1961, for *Danny Dunn and the Homework Machine*, and 1963, for *Danny Dunn on the Ocean Floor*.

WRITINGS:

CHILDREN'S BOOKS

(With Jay Williams) *Danny Dunn and the Anti-Gravity Paint*, Whittlesey House, 1956.
(With Williams) *Danny Dunn on a Desert Island*, Whittlesey House, 1957.
(With Williams) *Danny Dunn and the Homework Machine*, McGraw, 1958.
(With Williams) *Danny Dunn and the Weather Machine*, McGraw, 1959.
(With Williams) *Danny Dunn on the Ocean Floor*, Whittlesey House, 1960.

(With Williams) *Danny Dunn and the Fossil Cave*, Whittlesey House, 1961.

OTHER

(Under pseudonym Ray Ashley; and producer) "The Little Fugitive" (screenplay), Little Fugitive Productions, 1953.

Composer of operas for children. Contributor to magazines, including *Ladies' Home Journal*. Education editor of newspaper, *PM*.

SIDELIGHTS: Raymond Abrashkin was the co-author of the first six "Danny Dunn" books. Other books in the series, often attributed to Abrashkin and Jay Williams, were actually written after Abrashkin's death. *Danny Dunn and the Homework Machine* was adapted for the stage by Julie Mandel in 1969 for Metromedia-on-Stage. In the same year the story was released as a recording by Golden Records.

Other recordings of Abrashkin's work include "Busy Policeman Joe" and "Tall Fireman Paul," RCA Victor, 1960; "On the Ranch: A Story-Song Record for Your Child to Grow On," RCA Victor, 1961; "Music for Ones and Twos," CMS Records, 1972; and "The Emperor's New Clothes."

OBITUARIES:

PERIODICALS

New York Times, August 26, 1960.
Publishers Weekly, September 12, 1960.*

*   *   *

ABRUZZO, Ben(jamin Lawrence)   1930-1985

OBITUARY NOTICE: Born June 9, 1930, in Rockford, Ill.; died in an airplane crash, February 11, 1985, in Albuquerque, N.M. Real estate developer, aviator, balloonist, and author. Abruzzo gained public recognition in 1978 as one of the first balloonists to make a trans-Atlantic balloon flight. He and two others, Maxie Anderson and Larry Newman, made the three-thousand-mile, six-day trip from Maine to Paris, France, aboard the helium craft *Double Eagle II*. In 1981 Abruzzo and a crew of three took another balloon, the *Double Eagle V*, from Nagashima, Japan, to northern California, making Abruzzo one of the first to fly a balloon across the Pacific Ocean. The balloonist, whose career included posts as chairman and president of the Sandia Peak Ski, Tram, and Utility companies as well as the Alvarado Realty Company, won a number of awards for his airborne activities, including a special gold medal from the U.S. Congress. Together with Anderson, Newman, and writer Charles McCarry, Abruzzo wrote a book on the historic 1978 flight titled *Double Eagle*.

OBITUARIES AND OTHER SOURCES:

BOOKS

Who's Who in the West, 20th edition, Marquis, 1984.

PERIODICALS

National Geographic, April, 1982.
Newsweek, February 25, 1985.
Time, February 25, 1985.
Times Literary Supplement, June 13, 1980.
Washington Post, February 11, 1985.

ADAM, Jan 1920-

PERSONAL: Born August 24, 1920, in Malcov, Czechoslovakia; married wife, Zuzana, 1945. children: Julie. *Education:* School for Political and Social Studies, Prague, Czechoslovakia, graduated, 1949, Dr. Rs., 1953.

ADDRESSES: Home—5855 Dalridge Hill S.W., Calgary, Alberta, Canada T3A 1M1. *Office*—Department of Economics, University of Calgary, 2500 University Dr. N.W., Calgary, Alberta, Canada T2N 1N4.

CAREER: Czechoslovak Ministry of Foreign Affairs, Czechoslovak Embassy, Vienna, Austria, 1949-51; Charles University, Prague, Czechoslovakia, assistant, 1959-63, docent in political economy, 1963-68; McGill University, Montreal, Quebec, visiting associate professor of economics, 1968-69; University of Calgary, Calgary, Alberta, professor of economics, 1969—.

MEMBER: American Association for the Advancement of Slavic Studies, Canadian Association of Slavists, British Association for Soviet and East European Studies.

WRITINGS:

Wage, Price, Taxation Policies in Czechoslovakia: 1948-1970, Duncker & Humbolt, 1974.
Wage Control and Inflation in Soviet Bloc Countries, Macmillan, 1979, Praeger, 1980.
(Editor) *Employment Policies in the Soviet Union and Eastern Europe,* St. Martin's, 1982.
Employment and Wage Policies in Poland, Czechoslovakia, and Hungary Since 1950, Macmillan (London), 1984.

WORK IN PROGRESS: Research on employment policies, income distribution, and economic reforms in the Soviet Union and Eastern Europe.

SIDELIGHTS: Jan Adam told *CA:* "The real socialist system in the Soviet Union and East European countries is not based on democratic institutions. The legitimacy of the system relies on the ability of the Communist leaders to make people believe that the system fulfills certain social functions that cannot be met by any other system, namely, ensuring full employment, a much more equal distribution of income, and relatively stable prices. On the other hand, the Soviet Union and East European countries were for a long time obsessed with economic growth geared primarily to the fast growth of heavy industry. Needless to say, economic and social objectives have necessarily clashed as a result. It has always been my ambition to examine the working of the real socialist system in the crucial aspects where the mentioned objectives clash: wages, price, employment, housing policies.

"Soviet bloc countries have managed to sustain full employment but at a high cost (overemployment, labor shortages, low labor discipline). They are trying to reduce these costs by improving labor economy but with no great success. The Soviet bloc countries have also achieved some success in price stability, though there is no uniform approach to this problem. Countries sticking to the old, traditional Soviet system pursue a more or less rigid price stability policy. (They are willing to maintain unchanged prices even at the cost of shortages, lines before the stores, and the black market.) Whereas countries with a more decentralized system follow a flexible price policy.

"During the postwar period there were two waves of economic reforms, and recently socialist countries have been going through a third one. In some countries there are attempts at far-reaching reforms, whereas in the U.S.S.R. and Czechoslovakia the reforms are only of a cosmetic nature. The economic reforms are a good indication of the possible trend in the systemic development of these countries.

"Politicians, economists, businessmen, and many ordinary people are undoubtedly interested in an unbiased analysis of the working of the socialist system and in how problems that cause great concern in the West are solved in socialist countries, particularly in the U.S.S.R., which is the second most powerful industrial country. Can one learn from socialist countries' experiences? The answer is very much influenced by ideological biases."

*　　*　　*

ADAMS, Herbert Mayow 1893-1985

OBITUARY NOTICE—See index for *CA* sketch: Born February 9, 1893, in Sydenham, London, England; died January 15, 1985. Librarian and bibliographer. Following a five-year association with the bookselling firm of Bernard Quaritch, Adams became the librarian of Cambridge University's Trinity College in 1924. He served in that post until his retirement in 1958 and counted among his professional achievements is the complete recataloguing of the Trinity library. Adams spent more than thirty years compiling the *Catalogue of Books Printed on the Continent of Europe, 1501-1600, in Cambridge Libraries,* which was published in 1967.

OBITUARIES AND OTHER SOURCES:

PERIODICALS

Times (London), February 5, 1985.

*　　*　　*

ADAMS, James Truslow 1878-1949

BRIEF ENTRY: Born October 18, 1878, in Brooklyn, N.Y.; died May 18, 1949, in Southport, Conn. American historian, business executive, and author. A prolific, popular author of works best known for their blend of scholarship and literary skill, Adams established his reputation as an important historical writer during the 1920's with his studies of early New England. In the middle of graduate studies in philosophy at Yale, Adams decided instead to pursue a career on Wall Street. Accepting a position in a bond office, he eventually advanced to a partnership in a stock exchange company and also served as a railroad official, a bank executive, and a manufacturing company director. At the age of thirty-four he retired from business and moved to Bridgehampton, Long Island, to devote his time to study and writing.

Adams spent the next year studying Persian language and literature and began writing history, at first on local subjects. His work was interrupted, however, by the entry of the United States into World War I. At the age of forty he joined the U.S. Army as a captain in the Military Intelligence Service and in 1919 was assigned to special duty at the Paris Peace Conference. Returning from France, Adams undertook to reexamine the old conceptions of New England history and, in particular, the role of Puritanism. His research culminated in a three-volume study of New England life, the first of which, *The Founding of New England* (1921), won the 1922 Pulitzer Prize in history. It was followed by *Revolutionary New England, 1691-1776* (1923) and *New England in the Republic,*

1776-1850 (1926). Also critically-acclaimed was his widely translated volume *The Epic of America* (1931), which headed the best-seller list in 1932. Adams was an authority on New England's Adams family, to whom he was not related. He wrote of the celebrated family in such volumes as *The Adams Family* (1930) and *Henry Adams* (1933). An associate of the publishing house of Charles Scribner's Sons, Adams served as co-editor and editor in chief of several standard reference works. A member of many literary and historical societies, including the American Academy of Arts and Letters, Adams received numerous honorary degrees and won an award from the *Yale Review* in 1933 for an article on politics. He was also one of the few Americans to be made a fellow of the Royal Society of Literature.

BIOGRAPHICAL/CRITICAL SOURCES:

BOOKS

Contemporary American Authors: A Critical Survey and 219 Bio-Bibliographies, AMS Press, 1970.
Current Biography, Wilson, 1941, July, 1949.
Dictionary of Literary Biography, Volume 17: *Twentieth-Century American Historians*, Gale, 1983.
The National Cyclopaedia of American Biography, Volume 36, James T. White, 1950.
Nevins, Allan, *James Truslow Adams: Historian of the American Dream*, University of Illinois Press, 1968.
Twentieth-Century Authors: A Biographical Dictionary of Modern Literature, H. W. Wilson, 1942, 1st supplement, 1955.

PERIODICALS

New York Times, May 19, 1949.

* * *

ADAMS, John D(avid) 1942-

PERSONAL: Born September 13, 1942, in Wooster, Ohio; son of Lyman Harry and Catherine Ruth (Whittlesey) Adams; married Sarah Jane Dalbey (a manager), August 15, 1964; children: Samantha Lee, Gillian Lindsey. *Education:* Wittenberg University, A.B., 1963; Case Western Reserve University, B.S., 1965, Ph.D., 1969.

ADDRESSES: Home and office—2914 27th St. N., Arlington, Va. 22207.

CAREER: University of Leeds, Leeds, England, visiting lecturer in social psychology, 1969-71; National Training Laboratories, Washington, D.C., director of Professional Development Division, 1971-75; independent consultant in human systems development, 1975-84; Resources for Human Systems Development, Arlington, Va., president, 1984—. Member of adjunct faculty at Bowling Green State University and American University. Member of board of governors of Potomac Rugby Union, 1975-80.

MEMBER: National Organizational Development Network, American Psychological Association, Association for Humanistic Psychology.

WRITINGS:

New Technologies in Organization Development, University Associates, 1974.
(With John Hays and Barrie Hopson) *Transition: Understanding and Managing Personal Change*, Allanheld, Osmun, 1976.

Understanding and Managing Stress, University Associates, 1980.
Organization Development in Health Care Organizations, Addison-Wesley, 1982.
(Editor) *Transforming Work*, Miles River Press, 1984.
Transforming Leadership, Miles River Press, 1985.

Editor of *TWG Newsletter*.

SIDELIGHTS: John D. Adams told *CA:* "It is essential that people take responsibility for themselves if they are to maximize their fulfillment and well-being. All of my work somehow reflects this theme and provides guidelines for individual self-employment.

"There is a fundamental shift underway in the field of organization development that is toward a more vision-based approach and away from a problem-solving approach. It is now generally recognized that a focus on problems reinforces the status quo; whereas a focus on what one *wants* to create in his or her life or organization makes true change more likely, and the problems get solved along the way. This changing trend arises from the limited impact of organization development over its first twenty years, plus the development of new, more powerful techniques that utilize leading-edge knowledge from brain research and other physical sciences.

"The fundamental shift that managers are undergoing is due to the recognition that management and leadership require quite different orientations of consciousness. Managers have been taught to regard and react to what the environment presents them with, while leaders are learning to 'make up' or create the environment they want."

* * *

ADKINS, Cecil (Dale) 1932-

PERSONAL: Born January 30, 1932, in Red Oak, Iowa; son of Edward Doyle (a construction worker) and Grace Elinor (Fram) Adkins; married Alis Dickinson (a musicologist and writer), May 27, 1967; children: Sean M., Lynne E., Elisabeth, Christopher D., Clare, Anthony, Alexandra, Madeline. *Education:* University of Omaha (now University of Nebraska at Omaha), B.F.A., 1953; State University of South Dakota (now University of South Dakota), Mus.M., 1959; University of Iowa, Ph.D., 1963.

ADDRESSES: Home—2227 Houston Pl., Denton, Tex. 76201. *Office*—School of Music, North Texas State University, Denton, Tex. 76203.

CAREER: Director of instrumental music at public schools in Paullina, Iowa, 1955-60; Mount Mercy College, Cedar Rapids, Iowa, instructor in music, 1960-63; North Texas State University, Denton, assistant professor, 1963-67, associate professor, 1967-69, professor of music, 1969—. Member of executive board of Southern Renaissance Conference, 1968-69; member of executive committee of Musica Antiquae Europae Orientalis, Bydgoszcz and Warsaw, Poland, 1978-81 and 1982-84. *Military service:* U.S. Army, 1953-55, assistant conductor of Fourth Armored Division Band, 1954-55.

MEMBER: International Musicological Society (chairman of Center for Musicological Works in Progress, 1969—), American Musicological Society (state president, 1965-67; member of council, 1971-73 and 1976-78; director of Placement Service, 1972-77), Music Teachers National Association (chairman of historical instruments committee, 1967-71), American

Musical Instrument Society (member of board of directors, 1976-79 and 1981-84; member of executive board, 1978—), Danske Selskab for Musikforskning, Texas Association of College Teachers (member of executive board, 1968-69).

AWARDS, HONORS: Grants from American Musicological Society, 1969, American Council of Learned Societies, 1969 and 1972, International Musicological Society, 1970, 1972, 1976, and 1977, and Pro Helvetia, 1978.

WRITINGS:

(Editor and translator) Joseph Haydn, *Philemon and Baucis,* Theodore Presser, 1968.

A Topical Index to Edmond de Coussemaker's Scriptores de Musica Medii Aevi, Nova Series, North Texas State University Press, 1968.

(With wife, Alis Dickinson) *An Index to Acta Musicologica,* Barenreiter, 1970.

Doctoral Dissertations in Musicology, 5th edition, American Musicological Society, 1971, 7th edition, 1984.

(Editor and translator) Orazio Vecchi, *L'Amfiparnaso: A New Edition of the Music With Historical and Analytical Essays,* University of North Carolina Press, 1977.

The "ab Yberg" Positive Organ: Basle, Historical Museum, 1927-258; Description and Technical Drawings, R. K. Lee, 1979.

(With Dickinson) *International Index of Dissertations and Musicological Works in Progress,* International Musicological Society, 1977, 2nd edition, 1984.

(With Dickinson) *A Trumpet by Any Other Name: A History of the Trumpet Marine,* Frits Knuf, 1985.

Editor of "Fretted String," a regular feature in *American Music Teacher,* 1967-71. Contributor to *New Grove Dictionary of Music and Musicians.* Contributor to music journals.

WORK IN PROGRESS: Research on the history of small positive organs, 1550-1800; research on the oboes of Henrik Richters and the zither in Omaha at the end of the nineteenth century.

*   *   *

AGRESTO, John   1946-

PERSONAL: Born January 7, 1946, in Brooklyn, N.Y.; son of John and Teresa (diBiagio) Agresto; married Catherine Murphy (a computer programmer), June 15, 1968; children: Molly, Meghan. *Education:* Boston College, A.B. (magna cum laude), 1967; Cornell University, Ph.D., 1974.

ADDRESSES: Home—Washington, D.C. *Office*—Room 502, National Endowment for the Humanities, 1100 Pennsylvania Ave. N.W., Washington, D.C. 20506.

CAREER: University of Toronto, Toronto, Ontario, visiting lecturer in political economy, 1971-72; Kenyon College, Gambier, Ohio, assistant professor of political science, 1972-78; National Humanities Center, Research Triangle Park, N.C., fellow, 1978-79, projects director, 1979-82; National Endowment for the Humanities, Washington, D.C., assistant chairman, 1982—. Visiting assistant professor at Duke University, autumn, 1981; public speaker. Member of Atlantic Council of the United States.

MEMBER: American Political Science Association, American Society for Political and Legal Philosophy.

WRITINGS:

(Editor with Peter Riesenberg, and contributor) *The Humanist as Citizen: Essays on the Uses of the Humanities,* University of North Carolina Press, 1981.

(Author of preface) Ian Barbour, Harvey Brooks, and others, *Energy and American Values,* Praeger, 1982.

(Contributor) Edward A. Wynne, editor, *Character Policy: An Emerging Issue,* University Press of America, 1982.

(Editor and contributor) *Liberty and Equality Under the Constitution,* American Political Science Association, 1983.

The Supreme Court and Constitutional Democracy, Cornell University Press, 1984.

Contributor to political science and education journals and newspapers.

WORK IN PROGRESS: "My next work will be on how our understanding of the Constitution can be said to 'grow' or develop."

SIDELIGHTS: John Agresto told *CA:* "Despite the diversity of the titles of my books, there is one question that animates them all: To what degree do *ideas* make *history*? The commonplace and misleading answer is always that history shapes ideas, people are 'products of their time,' ideas should be seen in the 'context' from which they grew. Yet the converse is probably truer—our ideas, our principles, our 'values' are most often the engines of change rather than the side-effects of change. So my work has been an attempt to ask: To what degree do our ideas of liberty, equality, democracy, virtue and vice, and so on, shape our culture, and how do ideas grow and develop?"

*   *   *

AHERN, Tim(othy James)   1952-

PERSONAL: Surname is pronounced *Ay*-hern; born July 27, 1952, in Seattle, Wash.; son of Robert E. (an engineer) and Ramona (Slowinski) Ahern; married Gabriele Koch (a teacher and feminist), October 29, 1982. *Education:* University of Washington, Seattle, B.A., 1975, B.S., 1975, Ph.D., 1980. *Politics:* Libertarian. *Religion:* "Nothingarian."

ADDRESSES: Home—263 Elm St., Cambridge, Mass. 02139. *Office*—Department of Applied Biological Science, 16-210, Massachusetts Institute of Technology, Cambridge, Mass. 02139.

CAREER: Kyoto University, Kyoto, Japan, research fellow, 1980-82; Massachusetts Institute of Technology, Cambridge, research associate, 1982—.

MEMBER: Amnesty International (group leader, 1979-80), American Association for the Advancement of Science, American Chemical Society.

WRITINGS:

(With Richard D. Freed) *Dracula,* Biseisha Press, 1982.

"Harry" (one-act play), first produced in Osaka, Japan, at Banana Hall, November 3, 1982.

The Illnestraited Colossick Idition of Finnegans Wake, University of Washington Press, 1983.

Contributor to scientific journals, *James Joyce Broadsheet,* and Japanese newspapers.

WORK IN PROGRESS: The Buddha Killer, a novel about meditation and East-West relations in Kyoto, Japan; *Pacifying,* a novel about the ocean, Heidegger, and Wittgenstein.

SIDELIGHTS: Tim Ahern told *CA:* "My motivation to write stems from a larger impulse of mine to play, to see all things as plastic manifestations of one another. This undoubtedly comes from contact with James Joyce's writings when I was at the impressionable age of sixteen. I've studied languages and litterature extensively but have chosen science as a career and reserve my unbounded speculative time for writing and illustration. I began work on *The Illnesstraited Colossick Idition of Finnegans Wake* when I realized that Joyce's last and unfathomably great work was perfect material for an illustrator such as myself who quickly tires of recreating the same characters frame after frame. Illustrated interpretation neatly sidesteps the offense of which many critics and explicators of Joyce's *Finnegans Wake* find themselves guilty—namely, rendering laborious and forbidding what is at the heart comic and exhilarating. I was invited to present the completed first chapter at the Seventh International James Joyce Symposium in Zurich in 1979, which in turn led to its publication in part in the early issues of *The James Joyce Broadsheet* and finally as a whole by the University of Washington Press (Seattle and London).

"Having completed my doctoral studies in applied biochemistry, I set off for Japan where I divided my time between the world of enzymes and seaweed in a dank basement laboratory at Kyoto University, and the intriguing yet ultimately inaccessible mysteries of the city itself. The latter adventures resulted in my work-in-progress, *The Buddha Killer,* a novel concerning three foreigners who by means of scholarship, nihilism, or meditation realize themselves in the mirror of Kyoto. Another, more ambitious work-in-the-making, *Pacifying,* sets against one another the perspectives of Heidegger and Wittgenstein from within a comic, muddled consciousness embodied by the northern Pacific Ocean. In the course of its currents' gyrations, the great body of water brushes up against and carries away bits and pieces of the neighboring continents' languages, garbage, and sensibilities, all eventually to commingle and resolve in a climax of philosophical-political-theological-sociological insight before ultimate dissolution. Among the elements of flotsam and jetsam are a Richard M. Nixon soliloquy from the shores of San Clemente Island, gamelan myths and ritual drama of Indonesia, the Vietnam War, Japanese fisherman viewing the bombing of Hiroshima, Siberian prison camps, the prehistoric crossing of the Bering Straits, and Alaskan gold diggers.

"I am presently a research associate at MIT engaged in recombinant DNA research and enzyme design which, I submit, is but another form of contemporary authorship."

BIOGRAPHICAL/CRITICAL SOURCES:

PERIODICALS

Los Angeles Times, March 13, 1983.
Times Literary Supplement, February 10, 1984.

* * *

AITKEN, Douglas 1933-

PERSONAL: Born November 14, 1933, in London, England; son of John (an engineer) and Marion (a seamstress; maiden name, Greig) Aitken; married Fiona Ritchie (a voluntary worker), June 25, 1960; children: Ewan, Stewart, Ronald. *Education:* University of Glasgow, M.A., 1959; Trinity College, Glasgow, Diploma in Divinity, 1961. *Politics:* Liberal.

ADDRESSES: Home—73 Scotland Dr., Dunfermline KY12 7TP, Scotland. *Office*—British Broadcasting Corp., 5 Queen St., Edinburgh EH2 1JF, Scotland.

CAREER: Ordained minister of Church of Scotland (Presbyterian); minister of Church of Scotland in Nairobi, Kenya, 1962-69; British Broadcasting Corp., Edinburgh, Scotland, senior radio producer, 1969—. Deputy clerk of General Assembly of the Presbyterian Church of East Africa, 1963-69. Member of Dunfermline District Council and leader of its Alliance Group, 1980—. *Military service:* British Army, Royal Artillery, 1956-57; became lieutenant.

WRITINGS:

Words for Living, St. Andrews Press, 1983.

Author of more than two hundred scripts for BBC-Radio. Contributor to *Life and Work.*

WORK IN PROGRESS: Research on the influence, place, and future of the church in East and Central Africa, for a series of radio programs and possibly a book.

SIDELIGHTS: Douglas Aitken told *CA:* "My interest is in the communication of Christian truth in a way that is acceptable to people inside and outside the church. The use of words in a 'poetic' manner—imagery and word-picture—is a fascination for me."

* * *

AKINS, Zoe 1886-1958

BRIEF ENTRY: Born October 30, 1886, in Humansville, Mo.; died October 29, 1958, in Los Angeles, Calif. American poet, novelist, screenwriter, and playwright. Akins was awarded the Pulitzer Prize for drama in 1935 for "The Old Maid," her adaptation of a story by Edith Wharton. Akins's earliest writings included contributions to the *St. Louis Mirror* and a verse collection, *Interpretations: A Book of First Poems* (1912). Her first theatrical success came in 1919 with *Declassee* (1923; first produced in 1919), whch revealed her flair for light comedy. Subsequent works, including *Daddy's Gone-a-Hunting* (1923; first produced in 1921) and "A Royal Fandango" (1923), served to strengthen her reputation as one of Broadway's finest comedic talents. Akins went to Hollywood in the late 1920's to work as a screenwriter. But in the ensuing decade, despite a prosperous career in film, Akins continued writing for the stage. Her production declined after she received the Pulitzer Prize in 1935. Among Akins' last works are two more plays and a novel, *Forever Young* (1941).

BIOGRAPHICAL/CRITICAL SOURCES:

BOOKS

Contemporary American Authors: A Critical Survey and 219 Bio-Bibliographies, AMS Press, 1970.
Dictionary of Literary Biography, Volume 26: *American Screenwriters,* Gale, 1984.
McGraw-Hill Encyclopedia of World Drama, 2nd edition, McGraw, 1984.
The Reader's Encyclopedia, 2nd edition, Crowell, 1965.
Twentieth-Century Authors: A Biographical Dictionary of Modern Literature, 1st supplement, H. W. Wilson, 1955.

PERIODICALS

New York Times, October 30, 1958.

ALCHEMY, Jack
  See GERSHATOR, David

*   *   *

ALEXANDER, Meena   1951-

PERSONAL: Born February 17, 1951, in Allahabad, India; came to the United States in 1979; daughter of George and Mary Alexander; married David Lelyveld; children: Adam Kuruvilla. *Education:* University of Khartoum, B.A. (with first-class honors), 1969; University of Nottingham, Ph.D., 1973.

ADDRESSES: Home—511 West 113th St., No. 82, New York, N.Y. 10025. *Office*—Department of English, Fordham University, Rose Hill, Bronx, N.Y. 10458.

CAREER: University of Khartoum, Khartoum, Sudan, tutor in English, 1969; University of Delhi, Delhi, India, lecturer in English, 1974; Jawaharlal Nehru University, Delhi, lecturer in English and French, 1975; Central Institute of English and Foreign Language, Hyderabad, India, lecturer in English, 1975-77; University of Hyderabad, Hyderabad, lecturer, 1977-79, reader in English, 1979; Fordham University, Bronx, N.Y., assistant professor of English, 1980—. Visiting fellow at Centre de Recherches en Litterature et Civilization Nord-Americaines, Sorbonne, University of Paris, autumn, 1979; visiting assistant professor at University of Minnesota—Twin Cities, summer, 1981; lecturer at University of Stirling, 1973, and Osmania University, 1978. Gives poetry readings.

WRITINGS:

The Bird's Bright Ring (poems), Writers Workshop (Calcutta, India), 1976.
Without Place (poems), Writers Workshop (Calcutta, India), 1977.
I Root My Name (poems), United Writers, 1977.
In the Middle Earth (one-act play), Enact, 1977.
The Poetic Self: Towards a Phenomenology of Romanticism, Arnold-Heinemann, 1979, Humanities, 1981.
Stone Roots (poems), Arnold-Heinemann, 1980.

Also contributor to *Encountering Jayanta Mahapatra: An Anthology of Critical Essays,* edited by Madhusudan Prasad, 1984. Contributor to scholarly journals.

WORK IN PROGRESS: Women in Romanticism: Mary Wollstonecraft, Dorothy Wordsworth, and Mary Shelley, publication by Macmillan expected in 1987; *Nampally Road,* a novel; *Searching for Heaven,* poems.

SIDELIGHTS: Meena Alexander commented on her manuscript of poems in progress, *Searching for Heaven:* ''While many of the poems are set in India, a few leap off from the landscape around me, including the streets of New York City. In the poems that hunt backwards, there's always, I think, the persistent need for a figure, an image that can suffice as the origin. My grandmother for instance: part fact, part made of that imaginative aura without which a poem couldn't be, she haunts my beginnings, a woman in and out of time, inextricable still from the landscape of Kerala in India, where she lived. All the poems, though, begin as a disturbance, a jostling in the soul, even a torment. I cannot go on as I am. I have to stop and make a poem, that fortuitous, fleeting meaning, so precious, so scanty.''

Alexander also described her novel in progress, *Nampally Road.* ''I am working on a novel set in Hyderabad. The contortions of the political scene after Indian independence are viewed by a young woman who teaches in a local college. One of the central scenes is based on an actual event—the rape of a woman by the police and the burning down of Gowliguda police station.''

*   *   *

ALEXANDER, Ralph (Holland)   1936-

PERSONAL: Born September 3, 1936, in Tyler, Tex.; son of Joe Barkley (a civil engineer) and Virginia Louise (a housewife; maiden name, Kinard) Alexander; married Myrna Jean Campbell (a housewife and author), 1964; children: David Campbell, Christina Louise, Jonathan Barkley. *Education:* William M. Rice Institute (now Rice University), A.B., 1959; Dallas Theological Seminary, Th.M., 1963, Th.D., 1968. *Religion:* Baptist.

ADDRESSES: Home—4815 Southeast 140th St., Portland, Ore. 97236. *Office*—Department of Old Testament Languages, Western Conservative Baptist Seminary, 5511 Southeast Hawthorne Blvd., Portland, Ore. 97215.

CAREER: Ordained minister, 1963; Wheaton College, Wheaton, Ill., instructor, 1966-69, assistant professor of Bible and archaeology, 1969-72; Western Conservative Baptist Seminary, Portland, Ore., associate professor of Old Testament language and exegesis, 1972-75, professor of Hebrew scripture, 1975—. Gresham Community Baptist Chruch, Gresham, Ore., pastor, 1975—. *Military service:* U.S. Army, chaplain, 1959-67; became first lieutenant.

MEMBER: National Association of Professor of Hebrew, Society of Biblical Literature, American Schools of Oriental Research, Evangelical Theological Society, Archaeological Institute of America, Near Eastern Archaeological Society (member of board of directors, 1976), Israel Exploration Society.

AWARDS, HONORS: Fulbright grant for Hebrew University of Jerusalem and grant from State of Israel, both 1964-65.

WRITINGS:

(Contributor) Alan Johnson, editor, *God Speaks to an X-Rated Society,* Moody, 1973.
Ezekiel, Moody, 1976.

Contributor to *Baker's Dictionary of Christian Ethics, Zondervan Pictorial Encyclopedia of the Bible,* and *Theological Wordbook of the Old Testament.*

WORK IN PROGRESS: Ezekiel, a commentary, for Zondervan; *A Beginning Hebrew Grammar for Students of the Old Testament.*

SIDELIGHTS: Ralph Alexander told *CA:* ''My concern is to provide more readily accessible aids for studying the Bible. The commentary on Ezekiel reveals the purpose of God in judgment—how he deals graciously with Israel according to his divine program. I have also written articles dealing with such subjects as the relevance of the fifth commandment (Honor your father and mother) for today, lying, pride, pity, and abstinence, and Hebrew word studies.

''At least once a year I conduct study tours to Israel and other Middle Eastern countries that are significant to biblical studies. The purpose of these tours is to relate the geography, history, and culture to understanding the Bible.

''I have also participated in a number of archaeological excavations, and I speak modern Hebrew.''

ALLANA, Ghulam Ali   1906-1985

OBITUARY NOTICE: Given name listed in some sources as Ghulamali; born August 22, 1906; died March 8, 1985, in Karachi, Sind, Pakistan. Public servant, editor, translator, poet, and author. During his public service career in Pakistan, Allana served as president of the Sind province Muslim League, as finance secretary of the All Pakistan Muslim League, and as a member of the West Pakistan Legislative Assembly. For twenty years he was active in the Karachi Municipal Corporation and in 1948 held the office of mayor of Karachi. A representative of Pakistan on numerous international committees and at conferences, Allana fought to make Pakistan an independent country when it was still a part of British-ruled India. His books of poems include *Incense and Echoes, Thus Spake Man,* and *The Silent Hour;* among his other books are *Reflections of Respect, Reverence, and Revolt, Some of My Yesterdays,* and *Eminent Muslim Freedom Fighters.* Allana also compiled and edited *A Rosary of Islamic Readings* and translated into Urdu a selection of poems titled *Bazgasht.*

OBITUARIES AND OTHER SOURCES:

BOOKS

Contemporary Poets, St. Martin's, 1970.
International Who's Who in Poetry, 5th edition, Melrose Press, 1977.

PERIODICALS

New York Times, March 11, 1985.

*   *   *

ALLANA, Ghulamali
See ALLANA, Ghulam Ali

*   *   *

ALLARD, William Albert   1937-

PERSONAL: Born September 30, 1937, in Minneapolis, Minn.; son of George A. and Wilhelmina A. (Dunbar) Allard; married Mary Kay Burns, October 5, 1957 (divorced March, 1983); married Ana Maria Baraybar, April 16, 1983; children: Scott, Christine, Teresa, David. *Education:* Attended Minneapolis School of Fine Art, 1959-60; University of Minnesota, B.S.A., 1964.

ADDRESSES: Home—Marsh Run Farm, Box 549, Somerset, Va. 22972.

CAREER: National Geographic, Washington, D.C., staff photographer, 1964-67; free-lance photographer and writer, 1967—.

AWARDS, HONORS: Vanishing Breed was nominated for the American Book Award in 1982 and won the Western Heritage Award from the National Cowboy Hall of Fame and Western Heritage Center, 1983.

WRITINGS:

(Illustrator) Bart McDowell, *The American Cowboy in Life and Legend* (photographs), National Geographic Society, 1972.
Vanishing Breed: Photographs of the Cowboy and the West, New York Graphic Society, 1982.

Contributor of articles and photographs to *National Geographic.*

WORK IN PROGRESS: A book about Peru.

SIDELIGHTS: William Albert Allard told *CA:* "I joined the staff of National Geographic the day after graduating from college in June, 1964. In the late 1960's I became deeply attracted to the American West and the American cowboy. I am now moving away from the West as a primary subject for my work and am gravitating toward Latin America—especially toward Peru, as my wife, Ani, is Peruvian."

BIOGRAPHICAL/CRITICAL SOURCES:

PERIODICALS

American Photographer, July, 1984.

OTHER

"Images of Man" (audio-visual program), released by Scholastic Magazines, 1973.

*   *   *

ALLEN, David   1939-

PERSONAL: Born January 9, 1939, in Harrow, England; son of Stanley Roy (a translator) and Eve (Poulton) Allen; married Gillian Lilias (a library researcher), August 11, 1965; children: Hugo Richard, Charlotte Luise. *Education:* Balliol College, Oxford, B.A., 1962. *Religion:* Church of England.

ADDRESSES: Home—19 Priory Rd., Richmond, Surrey TW9 3DQ, England. *Office*—BBC Television, 810 Villiers House, London W.5, England.

CAREER: Science teacher and department head at boys' private secondary school in Windsor, England, 1962-67, and in Blackburn, England, 1967-69; British Broadcasting Corporation (BBC-TV), London, England, 1969-75, began as assistant producer, became producer, senior producer, 1975—, editor of television series "The BBC Literacy Project," 1982—.

AWARDS, HONORS: Red ribbon from New York Film Festival, 1981, for "And What of the Future?"; judges' award from Royal Television Society, 1984, for series "The BBC Literacy Project."

WRITINGS:

(Editor) *The Computer Book,* Addison-Wesley, 1982.
(Editor) *Early Years at School,* BBC Publications, 1972.
(Editor) *That's the Way the Money Goes,* BBC Publications, 1978.
Microelectronics, Manpower Services Commission, 1980.

Contributor to computer journals and to newspapers.

WORK IN PROGRESS: "Microlive," a series of live television programs on information technology.

SIDELIGHTS: David Allen told *CA:* "Over the past five years I have been responsible for programs and policy on information technology. As one of the major architects of the BBC Computer Literacy Project I have helped to establish the world's first telesoftware service (by television), have edited a best-selling computer book, and have produced six television series. They include "The Silicon Factor," "Managing the Micro," "Making the Most of the Micro," "Electronic Office," "Computers in School," and "Microlive," and all have been addressed to a general, intelligent audience in the traditions of British educational broadcasting.

"We always provide materials that allow people who have been stimulated by the programs to carry their interest even further. Among these materials are a layman's computer guide, a postal referral service, home study courses, and the BBC microcomputer and related software (now used in over 75 percent of British schools).

"In addition, we offer the telesoftware service, which makes use of the existing broadcast teletext service that the BBC pioneered as long ago as 1975. It uses four lines of the television signal to transmit, digitally, a magazine of information. Most television sets in Britain are supplied with a decoder that can display the information on the screen as an alternative to the television picture. Telesoftware goes one stage further and consists of computer programs for the BBC microcomputer system, which needs a special adapter to receive and decode the software. This service is a world first.

"Materials from the project have sold well in various parts of the world, and the television series is shown on 150 Public Broadcasting Service (PBS) stations in the United States."

AVOCATIONAL INTERESTS: Singing, windsurfing, theatre.

*   *   *

ALLEN, David Grayson 1943-

PERSONAL: Born October 17, 1943, in Salt Lake City, Utah; son of David Grayson Allen and Blanche (Wilson) Allen Cottrell; married Julyann Westby (a lawyer), September 6, 1969; children: David Grayson III. *Education:* University of Utah, B.S., 1965; Michigan State University, M.S., 1967; attended Linacre College, Oxford, 1971-72; University of Wisconsin—Madison, Ph.D., 1974.

ADDRESSES: Home—Concord, Mass. 01742. *Office*—The Winthrop Group, Inc., 17 Dunster St., Cambridge, Mass. 02138.

CAREER: Dartmouth College, Hanover, N.H., assistant editor of *Papers of Daniel Webster,* 1972-75; Massachusetts Historical Society, Boston, associate editor of the *Adams Papers,* 1976-80; Abt Associates, Cambridge, Mass., consultant in law and public policy, 1980-81; The Winthrop Group, Inc. (management consulting firm), Cambridge, executive vice-president and director, 1981—. Adjunct professor of history at Northeastern and Harvard universities, 1978-80. Chairman of Records and Archives Committee for Concord, Mass.

MEMBER: American Historical Association, Organization of American Historians, American Society for Legal History, Academy of Management.

AWARDS, HONORS: American Bar Foundation fellow, 1971-72; Jamestown Prize for *In English Ways* from the Colonial Williamsburg Foundation, the Institute of Early American History and Culture, and the University of North Carolina Press, 1976; Charles Warren fellow at Harvard University, 1980-81; National Endowment for the Humanities fellow, 1980-81.

WRITINGS:

(Editor with Charles M. Wiltse) *Papers of Daniel Webster: Correspondence,* Volume III: *1830-1834,* University Press of New England, 1977.
(Editor with Robert J. Taylor, Marc Friedlaender, and Celeste Waler) *Diary of John Quincy Adams,* Volume I: *November 1779-March 1786,* Volume II: *March 1786-December 1788,* Harvard University Press, 1982.

In English Ways: The Movement of Societies and the Transferral of English Local Law and Custom to Massachusetts Bay in the Seventeenth Century, University of North Carolina Press, 1981.
(Contributor) Jonathan L. Fairbanks and Robert F. Trent, editors, *New England Begins: The Seventeenth Century* (exhibition catalog), three volumes, Museum of Fine Arts (Boston), 1982.
Technology and Enterprise, The Winthrop Group, 1984.
(Editor) *Seventeenth-Century New England,* University of Virginia Press, 1985.

Contributor of articles and reviews to periodicals, including the *William and Mary Quarterly, American Historical Review, American Journal of Legal History,* and *Journal of Social History.*

WORK IN PROGRESS: Articles on the history of management consulting and on contemporary changes in large law firms; research and writing on the development of the semiconductor for industry and on changes in the telecommunications-information and construction industries.

SIDELIGHTS: In his book *In English Ways* David Grayson Allen examines the diversity of culture within seventeenth-century England and then analyzes how that culture was transferred to five settlements in Massachusetts. He argues that Englishmen who immigrated to New England repeated the patterns of agricultural practice and administrative organization that characterized the English regions from which they came and, in so doing, essentially produced a lifestyle remarkably similar to that which they knew before their emigration.

Critic Lawrence Stone of the *New York Review of Books* questioned the "randomness" of the population sample Allen used in establishing such a repetition of pattern, yet praised *In English Ways* as an example of "vigorously written history that has relevance to our present conditions and future prospects." Bruce C. Daniels, contributor to the *American Historical Review,* called the book an "extraordinarily detailed and well-researched study" that "significantly advances our knowledge of English local life, Massachusetts towns, and the transmission of culture across the Atlantic."

David Grayson Allen told *CA:* "Certainly the most important development in my life in recent years was to move from an academic to a business environment. My background in the liberal arts and my interest and work in history—and the history backgrounds of others in the management consulting company I helped establish—have proved to be an important asset in helping large businesses discover their corporate cultures and in laying the foundations for their strategic planning. Historians possess an understanding of corporate strengths and constraints that are not always apparent to other consultants of management."

BIOGRAPHICAL/CRITICAL SOURCES:

PERIODICALS

American Historical Review, December, 1981.
Journal of American History, December, 1981.
New York Review of Books, February 5, 1981.
Times Literary Supplement, June 5, 1981, October 29, 1982.

*   *   *

ALLEY, Norman William 1895-1981

OBITUARY NOTICE: Born January 22, 1895, in Chicago, Ill.;

died of heart failure, April 1, 1981, in Woodland Hills, Calif. Photojournalist and author. Alley, who documented—on film—the Spanish Civil War, the Ethiopian War, and two world wars, is best remembered for his film footage of the Japanese bombing of the U.S.S. *Panay*. Its release in the United States is considered to have influenced the public in favoring war with Japan. He began his career as a copyboy with the *Chicago Tribune* and eventually worked as a news photographer for the paper. From 1917 to 1919 he served as an army photographer in France and his subsequent activities as a cameraman included a one-year stint as an editor at International Newsreel. Alley covered World War II in Europe from 1939 to 1940, after which he directed newsreel production in South America for Hearst Publications. He then served as a war correspondent in Australia and from 1943 to 1945 covered military maneuvers in Italy and the Pacific. A recipient of numerous awards for photojournalism, Alley also worked as a special camera correspondent for the Columbia Broadcasting System (CBS-TV) program "See It Now" and in 1954 became western manager of Hearst Newsreels. He contributed articles on photography and world events to magazines and wrote an autobiography titled *I Witness*.

OBITUARIES AND OTHER SOURCES:

BOOKS

Who Was Who in America, With World Notables, Volume VII: *1977-1981*, Marquis, 1981.

PERIODICALS

New York Times, April 3, 1981.

*   *   *

ALLIS, Frederick Scouller, Jr.   1913-

PERSONAL: Born November 21, 1913, in Amherst, Mass.; married Eleanor Gummere, 1939 (died, 1963); married Laura Reasor (a painter), 1965; children: Abigail, Samuel Gummere. *Education:* Amherst College, A.B., 1935; Harvard University, A.M., 1940.

ADDRESSES: Home—340 Long Pond Rd., R.F.D. 1, Harwich, Mass. 02645. *Office*—Colonial Society of Massachusetts, 87 Mount Vernon, Boston, Mass. 02108.

CAREER: History teacher at private boys' school in Andover, Mass., 1936-79, chairman of department of history and social science, 1971-79; Colonial Society of Massachusetts, Boston, editor of publications, 1978—. Member of visiting committee at Harvard University, 1963-69, and Harvard University Press, 1965-71.

MEMBER: Massachusetts Historical Society, Colonial Society of Massachusetts.

AWARDS, HONORS: Grant from the National Historical Publications Commission, during the 1950's; distinguished teaching award from Yale University, 1964; L.H.D. from Amherst College, 1965.

WRITINGS:

William Bingham's Maine Lands, 1790-1820, Colonial Society of Massachusetts, 1954.
Government Through Opposition, Macmillan, 1964.
Youth From Every Quarter: A Bicentennial History of Phillips Academy, Andover, University Press of New England, 1979.

(Editor) *Sibley's Heir: A Volume in Memory of Clifford Kenyon Shipton*, University Press of Virginia, 1981.
(Editor) *Law in Colonial Massachusetts*, Colonial Society of Massachusetts, 1984.
(Editor) *The Pynchon Papers*, Volume II, Colonial Society of Massachusetts, 1985.
(Editor) *Music in Colonial Massachusetts*, Volume II, Colonial Society of Massachusetts, 1985.

Also contributor to *Teachers of History: Festschrift for Professor Laurence B. Packard at Amherst College*, edited by Myron P. Gilmore and H. Stuart Hughes, 1954.

*   *   *

ALLISON, Penny
See KATZ, Carol

*   *   *

ALPERS, Svetlana (Leontief)   1936-

PERSONAL: Born February 10, 1936, in Cambridge, Mass.; daughter of Wassily (a professor of economics) and Estelle (a writer; maiden name, Marks) Leontief; married Paul Joel Alpers (a professor of English), 1958; children: Benjamin, Nicholas. *Education:* Radcliffe College, B.A., 1957; Harvard University, Ph.D., 1965.

ADDRESSES: Home—Berkeley, Calif. *Office*—Department of History of Art, University of California, Berkeley, Calif. 94720.

CAREER: University of California, Berkeley, instructor, 1962-65, assistant professor, 1965-69, associate professor, 1969-75, professor of history of art, 1975—. Fellow of Center for Advanced Study in the Behavioral Sciences, Stanford, Calif., 1975-76; member of Institute for Advanced Study, Princeton University, 1979-80. Consultant to National Public Radio and National Endowment for the Humanities.

MEMBER: College Art Association of America, Renaissance Society of America, Women's Caucus for Art, Phi Beta Kappa.

AWARDS, HONORS: Woodrow Wilson fellowship, 1957-58; American Association of University Women fellowship, 1961-62; Guggenheim fellowship, 1972-73; American Council of Learned Societies fellowship, 1979; *The Art of Describing* was nominated one of 1983's best books of criticism by the National Book Critics Circle.

WRITINGS:

The Decorations of the Torre de la Parada, Phaidon, 1970.
The Art of Describing: Dutch Art in the Seventeenth Century, University of Chicago Press, 1983.

Contributor to art and art history journals. Editor of *Raritan Review*, 1981—, and *Representations*, 1983—.

WORK IN PROGRESS: A book on Rembrandt; a book on G. B. Tiepolo, with Michael Baxardell.

SIDELIGHTS: In *The Art of Describing*, Svetlana Alpers examines the works of seventeenth-century Dutch artists, including Rembrandt, Vermeer, and ter Borch, and puts forth the thesis that, unlike Italian artists of the same period, "the Dutch present their pictures as describing the world seen rather than as imitations of significant human actions." According to *Times Literary Supplement* critic John Nash, "Alpers repeatedly contrasts the Italian 'picture considered as an object in the world, a framed window to which we bring our eyes' with the Dutch 'picture taking the place of the eye with the frame and our location thus left undefined.'" Nash upheld Alpers's work as "the most brilliant, erudite and provocative attempt to characterize seventeenth-century Dutch art that I have read for many years."

Alpers told *CA:* "My aim as historian, critic, and finally as a teacher of art is to practice informed looking at images and to help others to do so too."

BIOGRAPHICAL/CRITICAL SOURCES:

PERIODICALS

Times Literary Supplement, November 4, 1983.
Washington Post, December 16, 1983.

* * *

ANDERSON, Charles Burroughs 1905-1985

OBITUARY NOTICE—See index for *CA* sketch: Born March 4, 1905, in Washington, Iowa; died January 20 (one source says January 23), 1985, in Ormand Beach, Fla. Bookseller, editor, and author. Anderson was the owner and operator of Anderson's Bookshop in Larchmont, New York from 1946 to 1974. He also served as a member of the board of directors of the American Booksellers Association (ABA) from 1954 to 1962 and again from 1964 to 1974. He was president of that organization from 1958 to 1960, chairman of the board from 1960 to 1962, and editor in chief of ABA Publications from 1972 to 1975. Anderson was the author of *Common Errors in English Corrected, Rapid Vocabulary Builder,* and *Guide to Good Pronunciation.* He was also the editor of *A Manual on Bookselling* and *Bookselling in America and the World* and co-translator, with Bessie Schonberg, of Curt Sachs' *World History of the Dance.*

OBITUARIES AND OTHER SOURCES:

BOOKS

Who's Who in America, 42nd edition, Marquis, 1982.

PERIODICALS

ABA Newswire, January 28, 1985.
Publishers Weekly, February 8, 1985.

* * *

ANDERSON, Gary Lee 1939-

BRIEF ENTRY: Born October 8, 1939, in Holdrege, Neb. American clergyman, politician, and author. An ordained Presbyterian minister, Anderson was a pastor in Axtell, Nebraska, until 1970. In 1973 he became a Democratic member of the Nebraska Senate. Anderson, who won an Olympic gold medal in target shooting and several military marksmanship awards, wrote *Marksmanship* (Simon & Schuster, 1972).

BIOGRAPHICAL/CRITICAL SOURCES:

BOOKS

Who's Who in Government, 2nd edition, Marquis, 1975.

PERIODICALS

Senior Scholastic, May 6, 1965.

ANDERSON, Gerald Dwight 1944-

PERSONAL: Born November 18, 1944, in Hitterdal, Minn.; son of Wilferd Dean (a farmer) and Violet Caria Maria (Heigg) Anderson; married Barbara Thill (an artist), May 13, 1978; children: Carmen Nell, Karl August, Paul Martin. *Education:* Concordia College, Moorhead, Minn., B.A., 1965; North Dakota State University, M.A., 1966; University of Iowa, Ph.D., 1973. *Politics:* Democrat. *Religion:* Lutheran.

ADDRESSES: Home—208 Ohio St., Decorah, Iowa 52101. *Office*—Department of History, Luther College, Decorah, Iowa 52101.

CAREER: Waldorf College, Forest City, Iowa, assistant professor of history, 1966-70; Drake University, Des Moines, Iowa, assistant professor of history, 1973; Iowa Wesleyan College, Mount Pleasant, assistant professor of history, 1974; Austin Community College, Austin, Minn., instructor in history, 1975; Moorhead State University, Moorhead, Minn., associate director of Northwest Minnesota Regional History Center, 1976-77; Minnesota State Senate, St. Paul, Minn., research aide, 1977-79; Luther College, Decorah, Iowa, associate professor of history, 1979—, director of Nottingham Program, 1983—. Member of theatre group New Minowa Players.

MEMBER: American Historical Association, Pi Gamma Mu (president of Iota chapter, 1964-65), Phi Alpha Theta.

WRITINGS:

Fascists, Communists, and the National Government: Civil Liberties in Great Britain, University of Missouri Press, 1983.

WORK IN PROGRESS: The Egg Case, a historical novel set in rural America during the 1920's.

SIDELIGHTS: Gerald Dwight Anderson told *CA:* "In 1983-1984 I spent a year in England living in a communal setting with sixteen of my Luther College students. While they attended the University of Nottingham, I had the opportunity to observe the subjects of so many of my studies. I first became interested in British civil liberties when, as an undergraduate, I discovered that there had actually been a Fascist party in England during the 1930's. Why was fascism successful in gaining power in so much of Europe while fascism in Britain remained such a well kept secret? At the time, it was obvious that Britain had never experienced a real threat from the communists. Why had the British government been so successful in keeping such challenges to parliamentary democracy to a minimum? While my studies proved that there was a potential for the abuse of traditional civil liberties in Britain during the interwar years, those civil liberties were never seriously threatened. It seemed that British soil was a poor seed-bed for extremist politics.

"While living in Britain in the midst of the 1984 coal strike, this impression was only partly confirmed—there is now considerable extremism in a part of the Labour party. Nevertheless, there remains deep in the British psyche a deep respect for tradition, proper public behavior, and moderation.

"Such observations will, I hope, improve my teaching. Teaching is my life and career; writing is merely an outgrowth of that. This attitude is reflected in my writing, for I believe that even as a teacher's words must come alive in the classroom, so too must the written word reflect the living, human aspects of people moving through time."

ANDERSON, Maxie (Leroy)   1934-1983

OBITUARY NOTICE: Born September 10, 1934, in Sayre, Okla.; died in a ballooning accident, June 27, 1983, near Bad Brueckenau, West Germany. Business executive, balloonist, and author. Anderson is best remembered for making the first trans-Atlantic balloon flight in 1978 with Ben Abruzzo and Larry Newman. President and owner of Ranchers Exploration Development, a mining company in Albuquerque, New Mexico, Anderson made three attempts to travel around the world in the helium balloon *Jules Verne*. Anderson and another balloonist, Don Ida, had been competing in the Gordon Bennett Balloon Race that originated in Paris and had been trying to land the helium-filled craft when the balloon's basket, or gondola, detached from the balloon, causing the two men to fall to their deaths. With Abruzzo, Newman, and Charles McCarry, Anderson chronicled the famous 1978 trans-Atlantic balloon flight in the book *Double Eagle*.

OBITUARIES AND OTHER SOURCES:

BOOKS

McCarry, Charles, Ben Abruzzo, Maxie Anderson, and Larry Newman, *Double Eagle*, Little, Brown, 1979.
Who's Who in the West, 20th edition, Marquis, 1984.

PERIODICALS

National Geographic, December, 1983.
Newsweek, July 11, 1983.
New York Times, June 28, 1983.
Time, July 11, 1983.
Times Literary Supplement, June 13, 1980.

* * *

ANDERSON, Roberta   1942-
(Fern Michaels, a joint pseudonym)

PERSONAL: August 22, 1942, in New Jersey; daughter of John P. (in electronics) and Sophie F. (a retailer; maiden name, Kwityn) Cuomo; married Alfred P. Anderson (a teacher and research chemist); children: Arlene Lorraine, David Alan.

ADDRESSES: Home—14 West Side Ave., Avenel, N.J. 07001.

CAREER: Writer. Worked as supervisor and free-lance jobber in market research.

WRITINGS:

WITH MARY KUCZKIR UNDER JOINT PSEUDONYM FERN MICHAELS

Vixen in Velvet (romance), Ballantine, 1976.
Captive Passions (romance), Ballantine, 1977.
Valentina (romance), Ballantine, 1978.
Captive Embrace (romance), Ballantine, 1979.
Captive Splendors (romance), Ballantine, 1980.
The Delta Ladies (romance), Pocket Books, 1980.
Captive Innocence (romance), Ballantine, 1981.
Without Warning (thriller), Pocket Books, 1981.
Sea Gypsy (romance), Silhouette, 1981.
Golden Lasso (romance), Silhouette, 1981.
Whisper My Name (romance), Silhouette, 1981.
Beyond Tomorrow (romance), Silhouette, 1981.
Night Star (romance), Silhouette, 1982.
Panda Bear Is Critical (thriller), Macmillan, 1982.
Wild Honey Pocket Books, (romance), 1982.

Paint Me Rainbows (romance), G. K. Hall, 1982.
All She Can Be (romance), Ballantine, 1983.
Free Spirit (romance), Ballantine, 1983.
Tender Warrior (romance), Ballantine, 1983.
Nightstar (romance), G. K. Hall, 1983.
Cinders to Satin (romance), Ballantine, 1984.
Texas Rich (romance), Ballantine, 1985.

WORK IN PROGRESS: With Kuczkir under pseudonym Fern Michaels, *Ever the Empire,* for Ballantine.

SIDELIGHTS: Under the joint pseudonym Fern Michaels, Roberta Anderson and co-author Mary Kuczkir are creators of several best-selling romance novels. Their most successful works include *Captive Embraces,* in which the heroine is deserted by her husband after the death of their child and then marries a cruel fellow who threatens to commit her to an asylum, and *The Delta Ladies,* in which the hero returns to his hometown as an oil company executive after having fled years earlier for seducing the town tycoon's daughter.

As Fern Michaels, Anderson and Kuczkir have fashioned a remarkable literary partnership. In *Writer's Digest,* William J. Slattery wrote: "Neither Roberta nor Mary has a college education, neither owned a typewriter or knew how to type. Neither knew anything about the publishing business, how to go about getting a book published. They decided to forge ahead with a book anyhow." Anderson attributes much of her success with Kuczkir to their ability to portray sex as romantic instead of pornographic. "We get letters from readers all the time thanking us for making sex pretty," she told Slattery. "That's half the formula in a nutshell. The whole formula is violence and pretty sex."

BIOGRAPHICAL/CRITICAL SOURCES:

BOOKS

Falk, Kathryn, *Love's Leading Ladies*, Pinnacle Books, 1982.

PERIODICALS

New York Times Book Review, July 8, 1979.
Us, June 27, 1978.
Writer's Digest, December, 1978.

* * *

ANDERSON, William G(ary)   1945-

PERSONAL: Born March 13, 1945, in Rockville Centre, N.Y.; son of Francis J. (a government employee) and Lillian (Nelsen) Anderson; married Patricia Flannery, June 8, 1968 (divorced, 1983); children: Leanne Jean, Gary Nelsen. *Education:* University of Notre Dame, A.B. (cum laude), 1967; attended Cornell University, 1967; Hofstra University, M.A., 1968; State University of New York at Stony Brook, Ph.D., 1975.

ADDRESSES: Home—3 Appomattox Court, Coram, N.Y. 11727. *Office*—Department of History, Suffolk County Community College, Selden, N.Y. 11784.

CAREER: Suffolk County Community College, Selden, N.Y., instructor, 1968-71, assistant professor, 1971-75, associate professor, 1975-80, professor of history, 1980—.

MEMBER: American Numismatic Association.

AWARDS, HONORS: Heath Literary Award from American Numismatic Association, 1976, for article "The United States Experimental Cents of 1942."

WRITINGS:

John Adams and the Creation of the American Navy, University Microfilms, 1975.
The Price of Liberty: The Public Debt of the American Revolution, University Press of Virginia, 1983.

Contributor to *American Neptune, Numismatist, Paper Money,* and education journals.

SIDELIGHTS: William G. Anderson told *CA:* "Although numismatics and ancient history have long been linked in the field of scholarship, until *The Price of Liberty* the same had not been true of numismatics and American history. *The Price of Liberty* presents an illustrated and annotated listing of all the debt certificates issued by the Constitutional Congress and the revolutionary state governments to finance the Revolution. In addition, the book contains a detailed historical narrative of the controversies surrounding the origins of the national debt. Both the U.S. Constitution and the first national political parties were results of the disputes engendered by these certificates of public debt."

*   *   *

ANSON, Robert Sam   1945-

BRIEF ENTRY: American journalist and author. As a senior writer for *New Times* magazine, Anson earned recognition for his feature articles on the controversy surrounding the assassination of former U.S. President John F. Kennedy. Anson's research on the assassination formed the basis for his book *They've Killed the President!: The Search for the Murderers of John F. Kennedy* (Bantam, 1975). The work won critical praise for its thorough, rational treatment of the evidence and various theories pointing to a conspiracy rather than a single assassin as the cause of Kennedy's death. Anson also wrote three other nonfiction books: *McGovern: A Biography* (Holt, 1972); *Gone Crazy and Back Again: The Rise and Fall of the Rolling Stone Generation* (Doubleday, 1981), a chronicle of *Rolling Stone* magazine's changes in content, readership, societal role, and editorial outlook since its 1967 founding; and *Exile: The Unquiet Oblivion of Richard M. Nixon* (Simon & Schuster, 1984), an account of Nixon's life after the former president resigned from office in 1974.

Prior to writing for *New Times,* Anson spent several years as a reporter for *Time* magazine during the 1960's and early 1970's. As a *Time* correspondent, he traveled to Cambodia to cover the Vietnam War and was taken captive by North Vietnamese and Cambodian Kmer Rouge troops on August 3, 1970. He was released unharmed three weeks later and thereafter referred to his capture as a positive experience that led to understanding, even friendship, between his captors and himself. Anson's other journalistic activities have included starting a student newspaper while attending the University of Notre Dame, hosting a current events television program for New York's WNET-TV station, and contributing frequently to *Esquire* and *Mademoiselle* magazines.

BIOGRAPHICAL/CRITICAL SOURCES:

BOOKS

Dygert, James H., *The Investigative Journalist: Folk Heroes of a New Era,* Prentice-Hall, 1976.

PERIODICALS

Newsweek, September 7, 1970.

New York Times Book Review, January 4, 1976.
Time, September 7, 1970.

*   *   *

AOKI, Hisako   1942-

PERSONAL: Born July 27, 1942, in Japan; daughter of Shoichi (an importer) and Fumiko (Yamazaki) Aoki. *Education:* International Christian University, B.A., 1965.

ADDRESSES: Home and office—9-1-515 Sanban-Cho, Chiyoda-Ku, Tokyo 102, Japan.

CAREER: Shiko-Sha Co. Ltd., Tokyo, Japan, editor and foreign rights specialist, 1972-79; Neugebauer Press, Salzburg, Austria, editor and foreign rights specialist, 1979-80; Kado-Sobo, Tokyo, editor of picture books, 1980—. Free-lance editor, translator, and coordinator.

WRITINGS:

CHILDREN'S BOOKS

(Translator from the Japanese) Yumiko Kondo, *Moontoo the Cat,* Barron, 1978.
(Translator from the Japanese) Yutaka Sugita, *Casper and the Rainbow Bird,* Barron, 1978.
(Translator from the Japanese) Sugita, *Fly Hoops, Fly!,* Barron, 1979.
(Translator from the English) Fernando Krahn, *Santakurosu no Nagai Tabi* (title means "How Santa Claus Had a Long and Difficult Journey Delivering His Presents"), Kodansha, 1980.
(Editor) *Henzeru to Greteru* (title means "Hansel and Gretel"), Kado-Sobo, 1981.
(Editor) *Kenzo Kobayashi, Nohara no chiisana ie* (title means "A Little House in the Field"), Kado-Sobo, 1981.
(Translator from the English) *Arayat-san no Megami* (title means "The Trail of Animals"), Holp Shuppan, 1982.
(Editor) *Oyayubi-hime* (title means "Thumbelina"), Kado-Sobo, 1982.
Santa's Favorite Story, illustrated by Ivan Gantschev, Neugebauer Press (Natick, Mass.), 1982.

BIOGRAPHICAL/CRITICAL SOURCES:

PERIODICALS

Washington Post Book World, December 12, 1982.

*   *   *

APPLEGATH, John   1935-

PERSONAL: Born November 17, 1935, in Meriden, Conn.; son of Charles S. (a minister) and Edna (Lightle) Applegath; divorced; children: Molly. *Education:* Ohio Wesleyan University, B.A., 1957.

ADDRESSES: Home—Nahant, Mass.

CAREER: Rand McNally & Co. (publisher), Chicago, Ill., editor, 1958-66; Markham Publishing Co., Chicago, founder and president, 1966-74; Rand McNally & Co., editorial director of College Division, 1974-75; University of Chicago, Chicago, Ill., writer and media specialist in Public Information Office, 1977-78; Human Economy Center, Amherst, Mass., founder and director, 1979-82; writer.

AWARDS, HONORS: Ford Foundation grant, 1980; grant from E. L. Cabot Trust, 1981.

WRITINGS:

Human Economy: A Bibliography, Human Economy Center, 1981.
Working Free: Practical Alternatives to the Nine-to-Five Job, American Management Association, 1982.
Beating the VDT Blues, New American Library, 1985.

Contributor to newspapers. Editor of Human Economy Newsletter, 1980-82.

WORK IN PROGRESS: Editing Non-Economists on Economics, which will include sections by Gandhi and Albert Einstein.

SIDELIGHTS: John Applegath commented: "After many years as a publisher of academic books in the social sciences, I have become impressed with the sterility and inadequacy of economics in particular. In response to that, I've done a good deal of writing, organizing, and networking internationally, all aimed toward helping to develop a new economics with greater concern for basic human values and ecological realities."

BIOGRAPHICAL/CRITICAL SOURCES:

PERIODICALS

U.S. News and World Report, August 2, 1982.

*   *   *

ARATA, Luis O(scar) 1950-

PERSONAL: Born November 5, 1950, in Buenos Aires, Argentina; came to United States, 1968; naturalized U.S. citizen, 1982; son of Luis (a sculptor) and Maria (Guell) Arata; married Laurie Hernandez (in mental health), May 24, 1975; children: Julio Shannon. Education: University of Pittsburgh, B.S., 1971; State University of New York at Stony Brook, M.A., 1974; Cornell University, Ph.D., 1978.

ADDRESSES: Home—299 Greene St., New Haven, Conn. 06511.

CAREER: Colgate University, Hamilton, N.Y., visiting professor of Spanish, 1978; University of Wisconsin—Milwaukee, Milwaukee, lecturer in comparative literature, 1978-80; Paradox Studio Theatre, Inc., Milwaukee, founder and managing director, 1980-83; writer.

MEMBER: Dramatists Guild.

WRITINGS:

The Festive Play of Fernando Arrabal (criticism), University Press of Kentucky, 1982.

PLAYS

"The Temptation" (five-act), first produced in Milwaukee at Paradox Studio Theatre, 1977.
"Variations on Breakfast" (two-act), first produced in Milwaukee at Paradox Studio Theatre, 1979.
"The World and Other Inventions" (two-act), first produced in Milwaukee at Paradox Studio Theatre, 1983.
"Midnight Dream" (two-act), first produced in Milwaukee at Paradox Studio Theatre, 1983.

UNPRODUCED PLAYS

"Metamorphoses" (one-act), 1976.
"Pas de deux" (two-act), 1978.
"Perhaps" (one-act), 1978.

Also author of screenplay "A Second Wind," 1984. Contributor to journals, including Kansas Quarterly and Quarterly Review of Film Studies.

WORK IN PROGRESS: For a Child Who Lived One Day, a biographical novel.

SIDELIGHTS: Luis O. Arata's The Festive Play of Fernando Arrabal is a study of the Spanish playwright's pre-1972 dramas. Arata addresses Arrabal's contribution to the creation of Pan/Panic theatre, in which characteristics of the mythological figure Pan are prominent in the protagonists of the plays. Bettina L. Knapp, reviewing Arata's critical work, described it in World Literature Today as "fascinating and scholarly."

Arata told CA: "At heart I am an explorer. Writing has become my vehicle for this playful adventure of discovery. It is certainly a shared adventure. If I could give back even a tiny fraction of what Julio Cortazar, Gabriel Garcia Marquez, Octavio Paz, Jean Piaget, Arthur Koestler, Georges Brassens, and so many others have given me unknowingly through their work, I would be more than pleased. Writing—a craft—is a way of life, not a substitute for it. It has a lot to do with the imagination, particularly with that imaginary space called reality, where the human adventure gasps along."

AVOCATIONAL INTERESTS: Swimming, skiing, racing motorcycles.

BIOGRAPHICAL/CRITICAL SOURCES:

PERIODICALS

World Literature Today, summer, 1982.

*   *   *

ARCHERD, Armand
(Army Archerd)

PERSONAL: Professionally known as Army Archerd; born January 13th in New York. Education: Attended City College (now of the City University of New York), 1937-39; University of California, Los Angeles, 1941; graduate study at U.S. Naval Academy, 1944.

ADDRESSES: Office—Daily Variety, 1400 North Cahuenga Blvd., Hollywood, Calif. 90028.

CAREER/WRITINGS: Paramount Studios, Hollywood, Calif., worked in mail room and in production planning, 1941-42; Associated Press—Hollywood Bureau, Hollywood correspondent, 1945-47. Herald Express, Los Angeles, Calif., writer, 1947-53. Daily Variety, Hollywood, author of column "Just for Variety," 1953—. Entertainment broadcaster for Hollywood television news programs; master of ceremonies for Hollywood motion picture premieres, Academy Awards programs, and "The Movie Game" (television game show) series; co-host of "People's Choice" (annual television awards program). Appearances in numerous motion pictures, including "Wild in the Streets," "Escape From Planet of the Apes," "The Outfit," "California Suite," and "The Users." Military service: U.S. Navy, 1942-45; became lieutenant.

MEMBER: Hollywood Press Club (founder; president, 1960-62).

AWARDS, HONORS: Awards from Hollywood Foreign Press Club, 1962, Los Angeles Press Club, 1962, and Masquers, 1963; named newsman of the year by the Publicists Guild, 1970; received star on Hollywood Walk of Fame, 1984.

SIDELIGHTS: Asked to comment on his career as an entertainment journalist, Archerd told *CA* that he first became interested in motion pictures at a young age. "I used to go to the Saturday movies in the Bronx, where I grew up. I went to a theatre called the Park Plaza. I remember it vividly. I'd bring my lunch and sit through the series, the shorts, cartoons, features. My parents went to the neighborhood theatres when they had fish night during the Depression. I had an uncle who used to go out on stage shows in the grand days when the movie palaces in New York had big stage shows. I grew up going to the movie houses.

"As a navy officer on a destroyer I had about fifteen thousand duties, and one of them, as the movie officer, was to procure movies for the ship. I went off and traded some of our fresh vegetables with the bigger ships to get newer movies."

Archerd told *CA* that when he became a Hollywood columnist, "the first person I was sent out to interview was Barbara Stanwyck, and she kept me waiting for a very long time. I told her that I didn't think that was nice, and we've been the best of friends ever since. That was forty years ago. When people know you're writing for a reliable service like the Associated Press, that acts as an entree."

Archerd was one of the originators of "The Movie Game," a television game show. That series, Archerd explained to *CA,* "was the first to use celebrities in the game-show format. After we started it, of course, every game show in the world found that it could use celebrities. We had people like Bob Hope and John Wayne and Jimmy Stewart playing games. It was really a fun show."

Of his future writing plans, Archerd told *CA* that he'd like to write in a different genre if he ever stops writing his *Daily Variety* column. "It's a twenty-four-hour-a-day job, though it may not seem so when you read it. But I would like to write some fiction and a play, and also some nonfiction about Hollywood—when I decide to leave town, I guess!"

*   *   *

ARCHERD, Army
  See ARCHERD, Armand

*   *   *

ARDLEY, Neil (Richard)   1937-

PERSONAL: Born May 26, 1937, in Wallington, Surrey, England; son of Sydney Vivian (a clerk) and Alma Mary (Rutty) Ardley; married Bridget Mary Gantley (a researcher), September 3, 1960; children: Jane Catherine. *Education:* University of Bristol, B.Sc., 1959.

ADDRESSES: Home—Lathkill House, Youlgrave, Derbyshire DE4 1WL, England. *Office*—13a Priory Ave., London W4, England.

CAREER: World Book Encyclopedia, London, England, editor, 1962-66; Hamlyn Publishing Group, London, editor, 1967-68; full-time writer.

MEMBER: Royal Society of Arts (fellow).

WRITINGS:

(Editor) Arrigo Polillo, *Jazz: A Guide to the History and Development of Jazz and Jazz Musicians,* Hamlyn/American, 1969.

Birds of Towns, Almark Publishing, 1975.
Birds of the Country, Almark Publishing, 1975.
Birds of Coasts, Lakes, and Rivers, Almark Publishing, 1976.
(With Brian Hawkes) *Bird-Watching,* Macdonald Educational, 1978.
Bird Life, Sackett & Marshall, 1978.
Birds of Britain and Europe, Ward Lock, 1978.
(With Ian Ridpath) *The Universe,* Silver Burdett, 1978.
Illustrated Guide to Birds and Birdwatching, Kingfisher Books, 1980.
(With Robin Kerrod) *The World of Science,* Macdonald & Co., 1982.

JUVENILE

(Editor and adapter) *How Birds Behave* (adapted from John Sparks's *Bird Behaviour*), Hamlyn Publishing Group, 1969, Grosset, 1971.
Atlas of Space, Macdonald Educational, 1970.
Experiments With Heat, Wolfe Publishing, 1970.
What Do You Know?, Hamlyn Publishing Group, 1972.
(Editor) Elizabeth S. Austin and Oliver L. Austin, *The Look-It-Up Book of Birds,* revised edition, Collins, 1973.
The Earth and Beyond, Macmillan, 1974.
Countries and Homes, Macmillan, 1974.
Birds, Sampson Low, 1974, Warwick Press, 1976.
Atoms and Energy, Sampson Low, 1975, Warwick Press, 1976, revised edition, Warwick Press, 1982.
Purnell's Find Out About Wonders of the World, Purnell Books, 1976.
(Editor) Vaclav Kvapil, *Exploring the Universe,* Hamlyn Publishing Group, 1976.
The Amazing World of Machines, Angus & Robertson, 1977.
Let's Look at Birds, Ward Lock, 1977, Derrydale, 1979.
Man and Space, Macdonald Educational, 1978.
The Scientific World, Pan Books, 1978.
Know Your Underwater Exploration, Rand McNally, 1978 (published in England as *Underwater Exploration,* Purnell Books, 1978).
Musical Instruments, Macmillan (England), 1978, Silver Burdett, 1980.
People and Homes, Macmillan, 1978.
Guide to Birds, Pan Books, 1979.
Purnell's Find Out About Birds, Purnell Books, 1979.
Stars, Macdonald Educational, 1980, Silver Burdett, 1981.
Our World of Nature: A First Picture Encyclopedia, Purnell Books, 1981.
(With wife, Bridget Ardley) *One Thousand One Questions and Answers,* Kingfisher Books, 1981.
Nature, illustrated by Chris Shields, Pan Books, 1981.
Transport on Earth, F. Watts, 1981.
Out Into Space, F. Watts, 1981.
Tomorrow's Home, F. Watts, 1981.
At School, Work, and Play, F. Watts, 1981.
Our Future Needs, F. Watts, 1982.
Health and Medicine, F. Watts, 1982.
Future War and Weapons, F. Watts, 1982.
Fact or Fantasy, F. Watts, 1982.
Computers, Warwick Press, 1983.
Working With Water, F. Watts, 1983.
Using the Computer, F. Watts, 1983.
My Favourite Encyclopedia of Science, Hamlyn Publishing Group, 1983.
Hot and Cold, F. Watts, 1983.
Sun and Light, F. Watts, 1983.
First Look at Computers, F. Watts, 1983.

Making Metric Measurements (published in England as *Making Measurements*), F. Watts, 1984.
Exploring Magnetism, F. Watts, 1984.
Making Things Move, F. Watts, 1984.
Discovering Electricity, F. Watts, 1984.
Air and Flight, F. Watts, 1984.
Sound and Music, F. Watts, 1984.
Simple Chemistry, F. Watts, 1984.
Force and Strength, F. Watts, 1984.

Contributor to *Our World Encyclopedia, Joy of Knowledge Encyclopedia, Collins Music Encyclopedia, Caxton Yearbook, Children's Britannica,* and *The Biographical Dictionary of Scientists (Physicists).*

SIDELIGHTS: Neil Ardley told *CA:* "My experience with the *World Book Encyclopedia* gave me an appreciation of the necessity to express ideas clearly and concisely. In my information books, I've tried to link this to a sense of wonder at the marvels of the world."

AVOCATIONAL INTERESTS: Musical composition.

*   *   *

ARGENTI, John   1926-

PERSONAL: Born February 10, 1926, in London, England; son of Nicholas (a stockbroker) and Elfrida (Ionides) Argenti; married Mildred Marshall, December 29, 1948; children: Hilary Argenti De Marco, Matthew. *Education:* Trinity College, Oxford, M.A. (with honors), 1948.

ADDRESSES: Home—Pettistree Lodge, Woodbridge, Suffolk IP13 0HX, England.

CAREER: Fisons Fertilizers Ltd., Felixstowe, Suffolk, England, production manager, 1954-63, planning manager, 1963-68; independent writer and consultant, 1968—. *Military service:* Royal Air Force, trainee pilot, 1944-46.

MEMBER: Society for Strategic and Long Range Planning (London; co-founder).

AWARDS, HONORS: Metra Award from Metra Consultants Ltd., 1971, for *Management Techniques;* Tunku Abdel Rahman Award from Malaysian Institute of Management, 1982, for annual management lecture.

WRITINGS:

Corporate Planning: A Practical Guide, Allen & Unwin, 1968.
Management Techniques, Allen & Unwin, 1970.
Systematic Corporate Planning, Thomas Nelson, 1974, revised edition, Van Nostrand, 1976.
Corporate Collapse, McGraw (England), 1976.
Practical Corporate Planning, Allen & Unwin, 1980.

WORK IN PROGRESS: Revising *Corporate Collapse,* completion expected in 1987; *Organizations: What Are They For?*

SIDELIGHTS: John Argenti told *CA:* "My specialism seems to be finding patterns, or perhaps imposing them on previously unrelated facts. My books on corporate planning are essentially about the best sequence in which to arrange the well-known stages of planning, and my book on corporate collapse finds a pattern in the stages of failure.

"So far as I know, no one has suggested before that failure is a *process.* To most people failure is something that just happens to a company; usually it happens suddenly and quite unexpectedly, like an act of God, a flash of lightning, or a stroke of bad luck. But no one really believes that some huge company like Penn Central, with thousands of employees, goes bust in ten minutes. But if not in ten minutes, is it in ten weeks, ten months, ten years? I believe it is often ten years (it was twenty years with Penn Central). If failure does come gradually, then surely we can see the cracks appearing years before the final denouement.

"I believe, in fact, that failing companies move through three clearly visible stages on the route to collapse; the sequence is defects, mistakes, symptoms, and failures. The important points to notice about this sequence are: 1) Only a company with the defects associated with failure would make the mistakes that lead to failure; 2) Having made the mistakes, the company is set on the path to collapse; and 3) Many of the signs and symptoms of failure that follow the mistakes stage are financial in nature. The last point implies that the financial signs, which most accountants see as the first signs of failure, are actually among the last in the sequence.

"The early signs—the ones I call defects—include an autocratic chief executive, poor financial controls, and poor response to change, among others. The mistakes are well known, too, and so are the symptoms. I believe I have a pattern that links all these previously recognized, but hitherto disjointed, items into a predictive tool that tells you not only if a company is on the path to collapse, but how far down it has gone, and how it can get off. It even tells you how to avoid collapse.

"I have made many of the same discoveries with corporate planning. Everyone knows what the various constituent parts of the technique of corporate planning are (such as objectives, forecasts, and scanning the environment), but twenty years of experience has suggested to me that there is one particular sequence that works best. There is a remarkably simple and logical process used by hundreds of companies for many years, and it has become known as the 'Argenti System'."

*   *   *

ARMSTRONG, Charles B.   1923-1985

OBITUARY NOTICE: Born July 22, 1923, in Nashville, Tenn.; shot to death, March 25, 1985, in Chicago, Ill. Educator, political activist, editor, and publisher. Armstrong, founder of the Chicago *South Suburban News* (now the *Metro News*), served in the U.S. Army during World War II and earned degrees from Fisk and De Paul universities. From 1950 to 1963 he taught social sciences in Chicago public schools and later became an advertising manager for the Chicago *Courier.* He founded the *South Suburban News* in 1965 and became editor and publisher of the black-oriented weekly when it was renamed the *Metro News* in 1972. An advocate of black participation in Chicago politics, he served as regional director of the Committee to Re-Elect the President during former President Richard M. Nixon's campaign. In 1980, Armstrong was named most outstanding publisher by the National Newspaper Publishers Association. Armstrong's shooting death was the result of an ongoing argument. The alleged murderer had been forbidden to see Armstrong's youngest daughter.

OBITUARIES AND OTHER SOURCES:

BOOKS

Who's Who Among Black Americans, 3rd edition, Who's Who Among Black Americans, 1981.

PERIODICALS

Chicago Tribune, March 29, 1985.

* * *

ARNAU, Frank
See SCHMITT, Heinrich

* * *

ASHLEY, A.
See AASHEIM, Ashley

* * *

ASHLEY, Ray
See ABRASHKIN, Raymond

* * *

ATKINS, Burton M(ark) 1944-

BRIEF ENTRY: Born October 23, 1944, in Cambridge, Mass. American educator and author. Atkins began teaching government at Florida State University in 1971. He wrote *The Invisible Justice System: Discretion and the Law* (Anderson Publishing, 1982) with Mark Pogrebin. He co-edited *Prisons, Protests, and Politics* (Prentice-Hall, 1972). *Address:* Department of Government, Florida State University, Tallahassee, Fla. 32306.

BIOGRAPHICAL/CRITICAL SOURCES:

PERIODICALS

Washington Post Book World, November 26, 1972.

* * *

AUGARTEN, Stan 1952-

PERSONAL: Surname is pronounced *Ow*-gar-ten; born November 25, 1952, in New York, N.Y.; son of Abraham (a jeweler) and Clara (a dressmaker; maiden name, Hertzberg) Augarten. *Education:* State University of New York at Stony Brook, B.A., 1975; Columbia University, M.A., 1977. *Politics:* Independent. *Religion:* Atheist.

ADDRESSES: Home—Palo Alto, Calif. *Agent*—Michael Larsen/Elizabeth Pomada, 1029 Jones St., San Francisco, Calif. 94109.

CAREER: Associated Press, New York, N.Y., 1972-76, began as summer intern, became reporter, then editor; *Electronic Buyers' News*, San Francisco, Calif., West Coast editor, 1978; Lowry Russom & Leeper, San Francisco, staff writer, 1979; worked as news writer and producer for KRON-TV, San Francisco, and KTVU-TV, Oakland, Calif; *Peninsula Times Tribune*, Palo Alto, Calif., business reporter, 1983.

WRITINGS:

State of the Art: A Photographic History of the Integrated Circuit, Ticknor & Fields, 1983.
Bit by Bit: An Illustrated History of Computers, Ticknor & Fields, 1984.

WORK IN PROGRESS: "Footprints," a science fiction filmscript.

SIDELIGHTS: Stan Augarten commented: "I have many intellectual interests. Computers and electronics are only two of them. I write to satisfy my passions for the subjects. I will always write books—my first love, but I hope to move into television, film, and the theatre as a writer, director, and producer. Ideas are much more important, much more tangible to me than things."

* * *

AULETTA, Robert 1940-

BRIEF ENTRY: Born March 5, 1940, in New York, N.Y. American educator, author of poems, stories, and articles on the theatre, and playwright. A teacher of theatre at the School of Visual Arts in New York City since 1975, Auletta has written more than fifteen plays dealing with the confusion, conflicts, illusions, images, and neuroses of Americans. Several of these plays have been produced in Off-Broadway theatres, and in 1982 Auletta won a *Village Voice* Off-Broadway (Obie) Award for distinguished playwriting for "Stops," originally produced in 1972, and "Virgins" (1982).

Prior to his tenure at the School of Visual Arts, Auletta taught theatre at the University of Illinois for five years. His other academic posts include those as playwright in residence at Yale Repertory Theatre and Yale Divinity School and teacher of theatre at Southern Connecticut State College and the Eugene O'Neill Theatre Center in Waterford, Connecticut. In addition to "Stops" and "Virgins," Auletta's plays include "Red Mountain High" (1969), "Walk the Dog, Willie" (1976), "Hage: The Sexual History" (1981), and "Rundown," which was first produced by Harvard University's American Repertory Theatre and was cited by the American Theatre Critics Association as one of the eight most outstanding plays produced outside of New York City during the 1981-82 season. Auletta also contributes poems, short stories, and articles to periodicals. *Address:* 161 Prince St., No. 12, New York, N.Y. 10012.

BIOGRAPHICAL/CRITICAL SOURCES:

BOOKS

National Playwrights Directory, 2nd edition, Eugene O'Neill Theatre Center, 1981.

PERIODICALS

Boston Phoenix, April 13, 1982.
New York Times, May 2, 1982.

* * *

AUSMUS, Harry Jack 1937-

PERSONAL: Born June 14, 1937, in Lafollette, Tenn.; son of Harry L. (in insurance business) and Gretna C. (a homemaker) Ausmus; married Linda S. Dronsick, June 7, 1963; children: Bradley David, Laura Blaine. *Education:* East Tennessee State University, B.A., 1959, M.A., 1963; Drew University, B.D., 1963; Ohio State University, Ph.D., 1969.

ADDRESSES: Office—Department of History, Southern Connecticut State College, 501 Crescent St., New Haven, Conn. 06515.

CAREER: Southern Connecticut State College, New Haven, assistant professor, 1967-71, associate professor, 1971-77, professor of European intellectual history and historiography, 1977—.

MEMBER: American Historical Association, Society for Reformation Research.

WRITINGS:

The Polite Escape: On the Myth of Secularization, Ohio University Press, 1981.

Contributor to history journals.

WORK IN PROGRESS: Will Herberg: From Right to Right; Augustine and Modern Thought; translating *Christianity and Neoplatonism,* by Albert Camus.

SIDELIGHTS: Harry Jack Ausmus told *CA:* ''My writing is motivated by an avid desire to find someone with whom I can communicate.''

*   *   *

AUTRY, James Arthur   1933-

BRIEF ENTRY: Born March 8, 1933, in Memphis, Tenn. American journalist, educator, and editor. Autry was hired by *Better Homes and Gardens* in 1960 as a copy chief; in 1970 he became the editor of the magazine. He has also been editor and publisher of the magazine *New Orleans* and editorial director of Meredith Special Interest Publishers. *Address:* c/o *Better Homes and Gardens,* 1716 Locust St., Des Moines, Iowa 50303.

*   *   *

AVIAD, Janet   1942-

PERSONAL: Surname legally changed in 1980; born May 27, 1942, in Philadelphia, Pa.; daughter of Abbott C.. and Elizabeth (Rosenfeld) Koffler. *Education:* Barnard College, B.A., 1963; Jewish Theological Seminary, B.H.L., 1964; Columbia University, M.A., Ph.D., 1969.

ADDRESSES: Office—Van Leer Foundation, 43 Jabotinsky St., Jerusalem, Israel.

CAREER: Writer. Van Leer Foundation, Jerusalem, Israel, research fellow, 1978-81; Hebrew University of Jerusalem, Jerusalem, lecturer in education, 1981-84.

WRITINGS:

Return to Judaism: Religious Renewal in Israel, University of Chicago Press, 1983.

*   *   *

AXINN, Donald E(verett)   1929-

BRIEF ENTRY: Born July 13, 1929, in New York, N.Y. American real estate developer, academic administrator, and author. Founder and owner of his own real estate firm, Axinn is also a trustee of Hofstra University and a member of the board of directors of the New York Quarterly Review Foundation. He has been actively involved with numerous civic, educational, and cultural enrichment projects, for which he received a Humanitarian Award from the American Jewish Committee and a Brotherhood Award from the National Conference of Christians and Jews. Axinn was also honored as the Tennessee Williams fellow at the Bread Loaf Writer's Conference in 1979. His books include *Sliding Down the Wind* (Swallow Press, 1977) and *The Hawk's Dream and Other Poems* (Grove, 1982). *Address:* 131 Jericho Turnpike, Jericho, N.Y. 11753.

AYERS, Edward L(ynn)   1953-

PERSONAL: Born January 22, 1953, in Asheville, N.C.; son of Tom (an automobile salesman) and Billie L. (a teacher; maiden name, Buckner) Ayers; married Abby Brown, August 24, 1974; children: Nathaniel. *Education:* University of Tennessee, Knoxville, B.A., 1974; Yale University, M.A., 1977, Ph.D., 1980.

ADDRESSES: Home—2404 Angus Rd., Charlottesville, Va. 22901. *Office*—Department of History, 201 Randall Hall, University of Virginia, Charlottesville, Va. 22903.

CAREER: University of Virginia, Charlottesville, assistant professor of history, 1980—.

MEMBER: Organization of American Historians, American Historical Association, Southern Historical Association, Phi Beta Kappa.

AWARDS, HONORS: Grant from American Philosophical Society, 1984; fellow of National Endowment for the Humanities, 1985.

WRITINGS:

Vengeance and Justice: Crime and Punishment in the Nineteenth-Century American South, Oxford University Press, 1984.

WORK IN PROGRESS: The Gilded South: Culture and Society in the 1890's, publication by Oxford University Press expected in 1988.

SIDELIGHTS: Edward L. Ayers told *CA:* ''History appeals to me because it tries, at its best, to understand the totality of a society—something no other social science or humanistic study even attempts. I am drawn to American southern history in particular because the south is so complex and enigmatic, and because the southern past has been filled with so much suffering and triumph over suffering. Both of those conditions have a great deal to teach us.

''The project I am working on now is an attempt to combine kinds of materials that are usually kept separate—computer-generated data and love letters, photographs, and store ledgers—in order to get at the history between the lines during an especially crucial time in the South's cultural, political, and radical evolution.''

*   *   *

AYNESWORTH, Hugh G.   1931-

BRIEF ENTRY: Born August 2, 1931, in Clarksburg, W.Va. American private investigator, journalist, magazine editor, and author. Aynesworth has built his career on his investigative ability, both as a private detective and as a journalist. He served as Southwest bureau chief of *Newsweek* from 1967 to 1975, became investigative editor of the *Dallas Times Herald* in 1976 and, after three years in that position, left the newspaper to become an investigative reporter for the American Broadcasting Companies (ABC-TV) news program ''20/20.'' A former aviation and science editor for the *Dallas Morning News,* Aynesworth is considered a leading expert on the assassination of former U.S. President John F. Kennedy and has been nominated for the Pulitzer Prize four times for his stories on manned spaceflight and for his coverage of the Kennedy assassination. As a private investigator he has helped rescue kidnapping victims and has retrieved a number of young people from cults.

The Only Living Witness: A True Account of Homicidal Insanity (Linden Press, 1983), a book Aynesworth wrote with fellow journalist Stephen G. Michaud, contains the authors' research on convicted mass murderer Theodore Bundy, his victims, his arrest and conviction, and the forensic techniques used to indict him. Regarded as the most notable aspect of the book, however, is its extensive transcripts of Bundy's "speculative," third-person account of the murder spree that may have left nearly forty women dead during the 1970's. The narrative, which was taken from interviews Bundy gave to Aynesworth and Michaud, has been described as graphic, detailed, and chilling. Ostensibly, however, it is only a hypothetical account, as Bundy claims to be innocent of the murders. Aynesworth's other literary activities include serving as founding editor in chief of *Parkway* magazine in Dallas. *Address:* 6000 Hudson St., Dallas, Tex. 75206.

BIOGRAPHICAL/CRITICAL SOURCES:

PERIODICALS

Chicago Tribune, March 10, 1983.
Detroit News, February 27, 1983.
New York Times Book Review, April 24, 1983.
Washington Post, April 18, 1983.

B

BACH, Ira J(ohn)   1906-1985

PERSONAL: Born May 19, 1906, in Chicago, Ill.; died of cancer, March 6, 1985; son of Jacob Lester and Rachel (Rose) Bach; married Ruth Lackritz, May 22, 1934 (died, 1961); married Muriel Dunkleman Wolfson, April 14, 1963; children: (first marriage) John Lawrence, Caroline Ruth (Mrs. Dennis P. Marandos); (second marriage) Susan Wolfson (stepdaughter). *Education:* Attended University of Illinois at Urbana-Champaign, 1926-27, and Harvard University, 1929-30; Massachusetts Institute of Technology, B.S., 1932.

ADDRESSES: Home—Chicago, Ill.

CAREER: Lichtmann & Bach (architectural firm), Chicago, Ill., partner, 1935-42; Washington Terrace Housing Project, Ogden, Utah, project planner, 1942-44; Tri-County Regional Planning Commission, Denver, Colo., director, 1944-45; Chicago Housing Authority, Chicago, director of planning, 1946-47; Cook County Housing Authority, Chicago, executive director, 1947-48; Chicago Land Clearance Commission, Chicago, executive director, 1948-57; Department of City Planning, Chicago, commissioner of planning, 1957-67; Chicago Dwelling Association, Chicago, executive director, 1965-69; Urban Associates of Chicago, Inc., Chicago, president, 1969-75; Illinois-Indiana Bi-State Commission, Chicago, administrator, 1975-81; Office of the Mayor, Chicago, senior project adviser and director of city development, 1981-85.

Visiting lecturer at colleges and universities, including Yale University, 1960-75. Member of Northeastern Illinois Metropolitan Area Local Government Services Commission, 1958-62; president of Northeastern Illinois Metropolitan Area Planning Commission, 1968-75; co-chairman of Interstate Planning Commission, 1972-75; member of Chicago Urban Renewal Board and Commercial District Development Commission, 1980-85; chairman of Commission of Chicago Historical and Architectural Landmarks; member of board of directors of National Housing Conference; consultant to Organization of American States.

MEMBER: American Institute of Certified Planners (past president), American Institute of Architects, American Planning Association, National Association of Housing and Redevelopment Officials (past president), Chicago Association of Commerce and Industry, Lambda Alpha (president of Ely chapter, 1953-57), Sigma Alpha Mu, Tavern Club, Arts Club.

AWARDS, HONORS: Named "Man of the Year in Architecture and Engineering" by Chicago Junior Chamber of Commerce, 1960; City Planning Award from Municipal Art League of Chicago, 1960; Honor Award from Citizens of Greater Chicago, 1958; Distinguished Service Award from Chicago chapter of American Institute of Architects, 1981; Regional Statesman Award from Metropolitan and Planning Council, 1983; Neighborhood Award from Trust, Inc., 1984, for outstanding career in public service; city of Chicago named a section of Wacker Drive "Ira J. Bach Walk," 1984; a fund to establish an annual design contest in Bach's name was established by private citizens and the City of Chicago in 1984.

WRITINGS:

Chicago on Foot: An Architectural Walking Tour, Rand McNally, 1979, 4th edition, 1985.
(With stepdaughter, Susan Wolfson) *A Guide to Chicago's Historic Suburbs: On Wheels and on Foot,* Ohio University Press, 1981.
A Guide to Chicago's Public Sculpture, University of Chicago Press, 1983.
A Guide to Chicago's Train Stations: Past and Present, Ohio University Press, 1985.

Also author of *Uniform Building Code of Colorado, Uniform Sub-Division Regulation of Colorado,* and *Chicago's Famous Buildings.*

Contributor to *American People's Encyclopedia of Arts.* Contributor to planning and architecture journals.

WORK IN PROGRESS: From the Eye of the Urban Storm, memoirs of working under five Chicago mayors.

OBITUARIES:

PERIODICALS

Chicago Tribune, March 8, 1985.

[Sketch verified by wife, Muriel Bach.]

*   *   *

BACH, Marcus (Louis)   1906-

BRIEF ENTRY: Born December 15, 1906, in Sauk City, Wis. American educator and author. Bach became a professor of religion at the University of Iowa in 1942. He is also the founder and director of the Foundation for Spiritual Understanding International. Bach's many books and plays include *Major Religions of the World: Their Origins, Basic Beliefs, and Development* (Abingdon, 1959), *The Way of Life* (Unity Books, 1972), *I, Monty* (Island Heritage, 1977), *The Power of Total Living: A Holistic Approach to the Coming of the New Person for the New Age* (Dodd, 1977), *Questions on the Quest: Search and Discovery in the World Within, the World Around, and Worlds Beyond* (Harper, 1978), and *The World of Serendipity* (De Vorss, 1980). *Address:* P.O. Box 816, Palos Verde Estates, Calif. 90274.

BIOGRAPHICAL/CRITICAL SOURCES:

BOOKS

Who's Who in America, 42nd edition, Marquis, 1982.

PERIODICALS

New York Times Book Review, November 28, 1971.
Spectator, September 8, 1983.

*   *   *

BACH, Orville E(uing), Jr.   1946-

PERSONAL: Born October 27, 1946, in Montgomery, Ala.; son of Orville E. (a postal services representative) and Margaret (a claims examiner; maiden name, Knowlton) Bach; married Margaret Current (a homemaker and artist), June 1, 1969; children: Caroline, Alison. *Education:* Auburn University, B.S., 1969, M.A.C.T., 1976; University of Tennessee, Ed.D., 1984. *Politics:* Democrat. *Religion:* Presbyterian.

ADDRESSES: Home—915 Woodhaven Dr., Morristown, Tenn. 37814. *Office*—Walters State Community College, Davy Crockett Parkway, Morristown, Tenn. 37814.

CAREER: Walters State Community College, Morristown, Tenn., instructor, 1976-79, assistant professor, 1979-83, associate professor of business, 1984—. Ranger at Yellowstone National Park, 1974—. *Military service:* U.S. Air Force, Strategic Air Command, 1970-74; became first lieutenant.

AWARDS, HONORS: Award from Tennessee Outdoor Writers Association, 1982, for article "Death of the Little T."

WRITINGS:

Hiking the Yellowstone Backcountry, Sierra Books, 1973.

Contributor of more than a dozen articles to magazines, including *Outdoor Life, Canoe, Backpacker, Christian Science Monitor, Outdoor America,* and *Tennessee Conservationist,* and to newspapers.

WORK IN PROGRESS: Contemporary Issues in Business, an introductory collegiate textbook, publication expected in 1985 or 1986.

SIDELIGHTS: Orville E. Bach, Jr., told *CA:* "People often ask how I can be a business professor for nine months and a National Park Service ranger in Yellowstone the other three. Easy—I love working with people of all ages, which both jobs allow. Much of my educational background is in business and resource economics, so the mental transition between teaching business and conservation-related work is not really that difficult.

"*Hiking the Yellowstone Backcountry* reveals my great love for the outdoors and especially that magnificent park. Much

of the trail 'work' was done while working summers in Yellowstone during my college years and continued while I was stationed at Malmstrom Air Force Base in Montana from 1970 to 1974.

"During the last eleven summers I have worked in the interpretive division at Yellowstone, which mostly involves leading walks, presenting programs, and conducting field research."

*   *   *

BAECK, Leo   1873-1956

BRIEF ENTRY: Born May 23, 1873, in Lissa, Prussia, Germany (now Leseno, Poland); died November 2, 1956, in London, England. German religious leader, scholar, and author. A prominent rabbi in Berlin during the persecution of the Jews in Hitler's Germany, Baeck became known for his nonviolent resistance to the Nazis. Rejecting an offer of asylum in the United States, he chose to remain in Germany and use his influence as head of the German-Jewish community to aid in lessening or delaying the atrocities being perpetrated by the Nazis against the Jews. Imprisoned in 1943 at the Theresienstadt concentration camp in Czechoslovakia, he was one of only seven hundred survivors out of nearly fifty thousand persons sent there. Baeck was alternately criticized for not advocating physical resistance to the Nazis during the Holocaust and praised for the guidance and comfort he provided the Theresienstadt death camp inmates.

After the war Baeck resumed his position of leadership in the international Jewish community, serving as president of the Council for the Protection of the Rights and Interests of Jews from Germany, an organization dedicated to directing the activities of former German Jews who had immigrated to England, the United States, Israel, and other countries, and as president of the World Union of Progressive Judaism. A highly regarded scholar and author, Baeck served as visiting professor at the Hebrew Union College in Cincinnati, Ohio, until a few years before his death and wrote *The Essence of Judaism* (1905), a work considered a classic on Judaism. Another of his books, *The Pharisees and Other Essays* (1947), includes writings suppressed by the Nazis, and his last work, *This People Israel: The Meaning of Jewish Existence* (1955), chronicles Jewish life in the twentieth century. Baeck was also the subject of a book by Leonard Baker, *Days of Sorrow and Pain: Leo Baeck and the Berlin Jews* (1978), which won the Pulitzer Prize for biography in 1979.

BIOGRAPHICAL/CRITICAL SOURCES:

BOOKS

Baker, Leonard, *Days of Sorrow and Pain: Leo Baeck and the Berlin Jews,* Macmillan, 1978.
Friedlander, Albert H., *Leo Baeck: Teacher of Theresienstadt,* Holt, 1968.

PERIODICALS

New York Times, November 3, 1956.

*   *   *

BAIN, Kenneth Bruce Findlater   1921-1985
(Richard Findlater)

OBITUARY NOTICE—See index for *CA* sketch: Born December 21, 1921, in London, England; died January 5, 1985.

Journalist, critic, editor, poet, and author of a number of biographies and books on the theatre. Bain served as the theatre critic and literary editor for the London *Tribune* from 1946 until 1956, when he became editor of *Books and Art.* He also was editor of *Twentieth Century* from 1961 to 1965 and of *Author* beginning in 1961. In addition, Bain served as assistant editor of the London *Observer* for twenty-one years. Under the pen name Richard Findlater he wrote *The Unholy Trade, Grimaldi, Michael Redgrave, Actor, Banned,* and *The Player Kings.* He also edited several books, including *Comic Cuts.*

OBITUARIES AND OTHER SOURCES:

BOOKS

International Authors and Writers Who's Who, 9th edition, [and] *International Who's Who in Poetry,* 6th edition, Melrose, 1982.
The Writers Directory: 1984-1986, St. James Press, 1983.

PERIODICALS

Times (London), January 14, 1985.

*   *   *

BALLANTINE, David 1926-

PERSONAL: Born May 11, 1926, in Rochester, N.Y.; son of Edward James (an actor) and Stella (Commins) Ballantine; separated; children: Lucy. *Education:* Attended Columbia University, 1947-51. *Politics:* None. *Religion:* None.

ADDRESSES: Home—P.O. Box 67, Bearsville, N.Y. 12409.

CAREER: Armscraft House (mail order gun business), West Hurley, N.Y., owner and manager, 1954-68; construction worker, 1969-77; free-lance writer and book editor, 1977—. Gulf Coast shrimp fisherman, 1969—. Voting machine custodian of town of Woodstock, N.Y., 1977—. *Military service:* U.S. Army, 1944-46.

WRITINGS:

Lobo (novel), Ballantine, 1972.
(With Robert Haney) *Woodstock Handmade Houses* (photography by Jonathan Elliott), Ballantine, 1974.

Editor of Bantam's "War Book Series."

WORK IN PROGRESS: Captain Matapan, Chalk's Woman, and *A Child Is Gone,* all novels; a photo-essay book.

SIDELIGHTS: "Most of my thrust as a writer," David Ballantine commented, "is in the direction of my own brand of pacifism. *Lobo* is a novel opposed to war. It is perhaps the only western novel in which no one gets killed. A very dear and supportive friend said, in describing one of my unpublished novels, *Captain Matapan,* that he thought of it as an attempt to rewind the clock of hope."

*   *   *

BALOGH, Thomas 1905-1985

OBITUARY NOTICE—See index for *CA* sketch: Born November 2, 1905, in Budapest, Austria-Hungary (now Hungary); died January 20, 1985, in London, England. Educator, economist, government official, and author. A Hungarian exile, Balogh lived briefly in the United States before moving to England in 1930. He spent the 1930's as an economic adviser to various firms and as a lecturer at London University's University College. Following World War II Balogh concentrated

on aiding developing countries in achieving economic stability. He served as an adviser to Britain's Labour government from 1964 to 1967 and became a consultant to the British prime minister in 1968. From 1974 to 1976 Balogh was minister of state for energy and was instrumental in the development of the British National Oil Corporation. A fellow of Oxford University's Balliol College beginning in 1945, he began his forty-year association with Oxford in 1934. Balogh, who in 1968 was made a life peer of the British royal court as Baron Balogh of Hampstead, wrote and co-authored numerous books on economics and governmental economic policies, including *Studies in Financial Organization, The Dollar Crisis, Causes and Cure: A Report to the Fabian Society, Germany: An Experiment in 'Planning' by the 'Free' Price Mechanism, Some Aspects of Economic Growth of Under-Developed Areas: Three Lectures, The Economic Impact of Monetary and Commercial Institutions of a European Origin in Africa,* and *The Irrelevance of Conventional Economics.*

OBITUARIES AND OTHER SOURCES:

BOOKS

International Authors and Writers Who's Who, 9th edition, [and] *International Who's Who in Poetry,* 6th edition, Melrose, 1982.
The International Who's Who, 45th edition, Europa, 1981.
The Writers Directory: 1984-1986, St. James Press, 1983.

PERIODICALS

Times (London), January 21, 1985.

*   *   *

BALTENSPERGER, Peter 1938-

PERSONAL: Born May 30, 1938, in Winterthur, Switzerland; son of Otto (a draftsman) and Emmy (an accountant; maiden name, Matter) Baltensperger; married Brenda Krewen (a writer); children: Miriam, Angela, Rudy, Ted. *Education:* Technikum Winterthur, B.Sc., 1961; Carleton University, B.A., 1967; Brock University, B.A. (with honors), 1975.

ADDRESSES: Home—11 Dundas Cres., St. Catharines, Ontario, Canada L2T 1T4.

CAREER: Gore Bay Recorder, Gore Bay, Ontario, reporter, 1962-64; Adult Education Centre, Stephenville, Newfoundland, teacher, 1967-70; Governor Simcoe Secondary School, St. Catharines, Ontario, teacher of English, 1970—. Publisher of Moonstone Press.

MEMBER: Association of Canadian Publishers, Literary Press Group, Ontario Council of Teachers of English (executive member), Niagara Peninsula Writers.

AWARDS, HONORS: Editors Prize from *Pierian Spring,* 1982, for poem "Secret File," and 1983, for poem "Destinies"; Hilroy fellowship from Canadian Teachers' Federation, 1983.

WRITINGS:

Lost Season (poems), Three Trees Press, 1981.
This Place (poems), Highway Book Shop, 1982.
Saints and Sinners of Niagara, Belsten Publishing, 1982.
(Editor) *Magic Land* (fairy tales), Three Trees Press, 1983.
Inner Journeys (nonfiction), Three Trees Press, 1983.
Moonfires (poems), Pierian Press, 1984.
Mirror Mirror (poems), Moonstone Press, 1984.
Guardians of Time (novel), Three Trees Press, 1984.

Before Time and After (poems), Moonstone Press, in press.

Contributor to magazines, including *Antigonish Review, Quarry, Descant, Canadian Literature, Nebula,* and *Waves.* Editor of annual publication, *Souldust and Pearls.*

WORK IN PROGRESS: Stones for the River God, poems; *Tattles and Tales,* a collection of short stories.

SIDELIGHTS: Peter Baltensperger told *CA:* "Poetry (writing, editing, and publishing it) has been my major concern since adolescence, and it will always remain my primary and most important activity. In my poetry I explore the regions where reality and fantasy overlap, making use of subconscious images and archetypal and mythological symbolism to express my innermost thoughts and to reflect upon my experiences. Occasionally, I also deal with places and roots in attempts to affirm my existence in time and space and, again, to deal with and to make use of the subconscious layers, with their imagery and symbols.

"Moonstone Press was established in 1984 to encourage young and new poets in their careers, concentrating on the Niagara area where I have been living for the past fifteen years. We have published three such poets so far and will be adding two children's authors and two illustrators to our list in 1985. We will also be adding a Canadian annual anthology of poetry by students and teachers. There is a lot of talent among our young people that deserves to be recognized and encouraged. Moonstone Press hopes to be a key factor in this development of our young writers."

*   *   *

BANDEIRA (FILHO), Manuel (Carneiro de Sousa) 1886(?)-1968

OBITUARY NOTICE: Born April 19, 1886 (one source says 1885), in Recife, Pernambuco, Brazil; died October 13, 1968, in Rio de Janeiro, Brazil. Literary historian, essayist, journalist, translator, editor, poet, and author. Bandeira was stricken with tuberculosis in his youth and from 1913 to 1914 convalesced in a sanatorium in Switzerland. There he met the French surrealist poet Paul Eluard and began writing poetry. In 1917 he published *A cinza das horas,* his first collection of poems. He later became a columnist and music critic for newspapers in Rio de Janeiro and held teaching positions at the College of Pedro II and the University of Brazil. Though Bandeira's early work reflects the influences of symbolism after 1930, the author was generally identified with the modernist movement. His collections of poetry include *Carnaval, Libertinagem, Estrela de manha,* and *Belo belo.* Bandeira, who was elected to the Brazilian Academy of Letters in 1940, edited several major anthologies. His *Poesia e prosa,* a two-volume work consisting of literary essays, art criticism, verse translation, his autobiography, and a biography of the Brazilian poet Goncalves Dias, was published in 1958. English translations of Bandeira's work include *A Brief History of Brazilian Literature.*

OBITUARIES AND OTHER SOURCES:

BOOKS

Encyclopedia of Latin America, McGraw, 1974.
Encyclopedia of World Literature in the Twentieth Century, Ungar, 1981.
The Penguin Companion to American Literature, McGraw, 1971.

World Authors: 1950-1970, H. W. Wilson, 1975.

*   *   *

BANNISTER, Patricia V.   1923-
(Patricia Veryan)

BRIEF ENTRY: Born November 21, 1923, in London, England. Anglo-American secretary and author. Bannister has been a secretary for major organizations and institutions, including Columbia Pictures, the U.S. Army, Humble Oil & Refining Company, and, beginning in 1971, the University of California in Riverside. As a writer, she has concentrated on British historical romances. Her novels include *The Lord and the Gypsy* (Walker & Co., 1978), *Love's Duet* (Walker & Co., 1979), *Mistress of Willowvale* (Walker & Co., 1980), *Nanette* (Walker & Co., 1981), and *Feather Castles* (St. Martin's, 1982.). *Address:* 6111 Del Ray Court, Riverside, Calif. 92506; and c/o Richard Curtis, Richard Curtis Associates, 156 East 52nd St., New York, N.Y. 10022.

BIOGRAPHICAL/CRITICAL SOURCES:

BOOKS

The Writers Directory: 1984-1986, St. James Press, 1983.

*   *   *

BARACKMAN, Floyd Hays, Jr.   1923-

PERSONAL: Born March 20, 1923, in Youngstown, Ohio; son of Floyd Hays (a stationary engineer) and Velda Mary (a housewife; maiden name, Crom) Barackman; married Ella Myra Hayes (a housewife), December 29, 1944; children: Ruth Ann Barackman Shuey, Philip John. *Education:* Practical Bible Training School, Diploma, 1944; also attended Wheaton College, Wheaton, Ill., Buffalo Bible Institute, and Baptist Bible Seminary, Johnson City, N.Y. *Politics:* Republican.

ADDRESSES: Home—R.D. 3, Box 205, English Rd., Endicott, N.Y. 13760. *Office*—Practical Bible Training School, Bible School Park, N.Y. 13737.

CAREER: Ordained Baptist minister, 1944; pastor of Baptist churches in Meadville, Pa., 1944-49, Newfane, N.Y., 1951-59, and Maine, N.Y., 1959-68; Practical Bible Training School, Bible School Park, N.Y., assistant professor of systematic theology, 1968—.

WRITINGS:

Practical Christian Theology, Revell, 1984.

Author of adult Bible study guides.

WORK IN PROGRESS: Practical Bible Interpretation, "a book that will, in a simple way, help lay people interpret the Bible accurately for themselves."

SIDELIGHTS: Floyd Hays Barackman, Jr., told *CA:* "Begun in 1976, *Practical Christian Theology* is the outgrowth of class notes that developed while teaching systematic theology (since 1968) and from earlier doctrinal study. 'Practical' derives both from the name of the school in which I teach and the effort to relate theology to practical application in Christian life.

"My awareness of the need for such a book arose from my teaching experience and from the lack of market supply. The book surveys the cardinal doctrines of the Bible, including the Scriptures, God, Christ, the Holy Spirit, man, sin, salvation, the church, Christian life, and unfulfilled, future prophetic events. *Practical Christian Theology* is dispensational in its theological orientation as well as moderately Calvinistic. I believe that it is important not only to understand what it is that God wants us to do and be, but also to understand how these things are brought about in our lives. In addition, the book discusses those provisions that God makes available to us for the translation of biblical doctrine into life values and experience, which in turn leads to happiness, fulfillment, and fellowship with God.''

AVOCATIONAL INTERESTS: Photography, American Indian artifacts, firearms, woodworking.

*   *   *

BARBER, Noel (John Lysberg)   1909-

BRIEF ENTRY: Born September 9, 1909. British journalist and author. After first working for newspapers in Britain, Barber was appointed editor of Singapore's *Malaya Tribune* in 1937. A stint with the *Overseas Daily Mail* was followed by service as a navigator in the Royal Air Force during World War II. Barber next worked as editor of the *Continental Daily Mail* in Paris. He later was employed as foreign manager, syndication manager, and director of Associated Newspapers. During his career, which spanned more than thirty years, the journalist traveled to countries all over the world, including China, Russia, and France, and to the South Pole. He is the author of more than twenty history and travel books, most based on his observations and recollections: titles include *The Black Hole of Calcutta: A Reconstruction* (Collins, 1965), *The War of the Running Dogs: How Malaya Defeated the Communist Guerrillas, 1948-60* (Collins, 1971), *Seven Days of Freedom: The Hungarian Uprising, 1956* (Macmillan, 1973), and *The Fall of Shanghai* (Coward, 1979). Barber also wrote the novels *Tanamera* (Macmillan, 1981) and *A Farewell to France* (Macmillan, 1983). *Address:* 312a Kings Rd, London SW3, England.

BIOGRAPHICAL/CRITICAL SOURCES:

PERIODICALS

Atlantic Monthly, March, 1970.
Times (London), June 30, 1983.
Virginia Quarterly Review, summer, 1971.
Washington Post Book World, July 18, 1983.

*   *   *

BAR-HILLEL, Yehoshua   1915-1975

OBITUARY NOTICE: Born September 8, 1915, in Vienna, Austria-Hungary (now Austria); died September 25, 1975, in Jerusalem, Israel. Philosopher, educator, linguist, and author. Educated at the Hebrew University in Jerusalem, Bar-Hillel worked as a research associate at Massachusetts Institute of Technology from 1951 to 1953. He then returned to the Hebrew University where he taught logic and the philosophy of science, becoming full professor in 1961. Influential in bridging the gap between logicians and linguists, Bar-Hillel studied language from a variety of perspectives, including philosophical and mathematical. He wrote *Language and Information,* and *Aspects of Language,* and co-authored *Foundations of Set Theory.*

OBITUARIES AND OTHER SOURCES:

BOOKS

Kasher, A., editor, *Language in Focus: Foundations, Methods, and Systems: Essays in Memory of Yehoshua Bar-Hillel,* Dordrecht, 1976.
Twentieth-Century Culture: A Biographical Companion, Harper, 1983.
Who's Who in the World, 3rd edition, Marquis, 1976.
Who's Who in World Jewry: A Biographical Dictionary of Outstanding Jews, Olive Press, 1978.

*   *   *

BARKS, Carl   1901-

PERSONAL: Born March 27, 1901, near Merrill, Ore.; son of William and Arminta (Johnson) Barks; married third wife, Gare Williams (a painter).

ADDRESSES: Home—Grants Pass, Ore.

CAREER: Cartoonist. Held various jobs, including cowboy, logger, steelworker, carpenter, and railroad repairman before becoming a free-lance artist, c. 1927; *Eye-Opener* (magazine), Minneapolis, Minn., cartoonist, 1931-35; Walt Disney Studios, Burbank, Calif., 1935-42, began as apprentice animator, became story outliner; Dell Publishing Co., New York, N.Y., free-lance writer and illustrator for *Donald Duck* feature magazine, for "Donald Duck" segments in the monthly publication *Walt Disney Comics and Stories,* 1943-66, and for *Uncle Scrooge* feature magazine, beginning in 1947; free-lance comic strip writer, 1965-73; retired as illustrator, 1966.

WRITINGS:

SELF-ILLUSTRATED BOOKS

Donald Duck and the Magic Hourglass, Abbeville Press, 1981.
Uncle Scrooge and the Secret of the Old Castle, Abbeville Press, 1981.

SELF-ILLUSTRATED CARTOON COLLECTIONS

Donald Duck, Abbeville Press, 1978.
(With Piero Zanotto) *Walt Disney's Uncle Scrooge,* edited by Mark Greenberg, Abbeville Press, 1979.
Uncle Scrooge McDuck: His Life and Times, Celestial Arts, 1981.
The Fine Art of Walt Disney's Donald Duck, Another Rainbow, 1981.
The Carl Barks Library, edited by Bruce Hamilton and Russ Cochran, Another Rainbow, 1983.
Limited Edition Lithographs of Disney Duck Subjects, Another Rainbow, 1983.

Also author and illustrator of numerous Dell comic books, including *Donald Duck Finds Pirate Gold,* 1942; *Christmas on Bear Mountain,* 1947; and *Only a Poor Duck,* 1952.

WORK IN PROGRESS: With Piero Zanotto, *Huey, Dewey, and Louie,* edited by Michael Sonino, for publication by Abbeville Press.

SIDELIGHTS: Cartoonist Carl Barks is perhaps best known as the creator of the Walt Disney comic strip character Uncle Scrooge McDuck, whom he introduced in 1947. According to Barks, Uncle Scrooge "is by any measurements the richest character ever to live in the realm of fiction. He is also the stingiest." Scrooge first came into being as a foil for Donald Duck in the comic book story *Christmas on Bear Mountain.*

"I might never have used him again," Barks recalled, "except that about a year later I wanted to write a story about an old Scottish castle on a spooky moor, and Uncle Scrooge's wealth furnished an excuse for Donald and the kids to go there, accompanied of course by Uncle Scrooge."

Scrooge began as a minor character in the Donald Duck stories, but as his popularity grew he went on to star in his own comic books, such as *Only a Poor Old Man* and *Back to the Klondike*. At this time Barks fleshed out Scrooge's personality by adding "a little bit of humanity." He explained: "I wasn't sure just how I wanted to make Scrooge—just how much of an old tightwad, how cranky. I was afraid if I got him to be too softhearted, then he would be wishy-washy. So it was difficult to make him do what he did in this story and still keep that whole tightwad personality." The basis for Scrooge's character had been the "Robber Barons" of the turn of the century—men who had made their fortunes in railroads and mining, Barks observed, "by being just a little bit unscrupulous with the way they eliminated the competition." He further explained that "Scrooge had to be in that mold, or he couldn't have made it in an era when he was up against all those plutocrats."

According to Barks, in the mid 1950's he began "to lose interest in my duck work," and he entertained the idea of developing his own comic strips. That dream, however, was short-lived. "When I got to thinking up material for a strip," he said, "I soon realized that it would take months, even years, before I'd get enough polished material to have three weeks of continuity to show to a syndicate. In the meantime, I would have had to have something to buy groceries with. I couldn't leave the ducks for that long, so I decided to stick with those ducks and figure that sometime something's going to make the decision for me. I thought, 'It will either be that I go on to the end of my time with the ducks, or the ducks will lose their publisher, or something will happen so that there are no longer any duck comic books for me to do.'

Before retiring as an illustrator in 1966, Barks drew more than five hundred duck comics, and, although he never received a by-line or royalties for his work, he enjoyed his anonymity. "Actually," he said, "I was expressing myself more freely because I was anonymous than if I had had a lot of fame and a lot of people trying to influence my thinking. Guys like Walt Kelly were surrounded by swarms of people. Of course, he loved it, but it would have stagnated me. I needed privacy and my own little old hole in the earth where I could work in order to be productive and inspired."

Looking back on his career, Barks commented: "I've always wanted to promote a broader understanding of life as well as to entertain. As the world becomes more overpopulated, hatreds intensify. People have got to learn to be more patient and liberal about each other's views."

BIOGRAPHICAL/CRITICAL SOURCES:

BOOKS

Chalker, Jack, *An Informal Biography of Scrooge McDuck*, Mirage Press, 1974.
Lupoff, Dick and Don Thompson, *The Comic-Book Book*, Arlington House, 1974.
Overstreet, Bob, *Comic Book Price Guide*, Number 7, Harmony, 1977.

PERIODICALS

California Monthly, January/February, 1976.

Funnyworld, June, 1967, fall, 1979.
Graphic Story World, July, 1971.
Newsweek, June 28, 1982.
Panels, spring, 1981.
Time, May 17, 1982.

* * *

BARLETT, Donald L(eon) 1936-

PERSONAL: Born July 17, 1936, in DuBois, Pa.; son of James L. and Mary V. (Wineberg) Barlett; married Shirley A. Jones (a nurse); children: Matthew J. *Education:* Attended Pennsylvania State University, 1954-55.

ADDRESSES: Home—14 Woodland Dr., Churchville, Pa. 18966. *Office*—*Philadelphia Inquirer*, P.O. Box 8263, Philadelphia, Pa. 19101.

CAREER: Reading Times, Reading, Pa., general assignment and beat reporter, 1956-58, 1961-62; *Akron Beacon-Journal*, Akron, Ohio, general assignment and beat reporter, 1962-64; *Cleveland Plain Dealer*, Cleveland, Ohio, investigative reporter, 1965-66, 1969-70; *Chicago Daily News*, Chicago, Ill., investigative reporter, 1967-68; *Philadelphia Inquirer*, Philadelphia, Pa., investigative reporter, 1970—. *Military service:* U.S. Army, 1958-61; served as counterintelligence agent.

AWARDS, HONORS: George Polk Memorial Award for metropolitan reporting and Sigma Delta Chi Distinguished Service in Journalism award, 1971, for newspaper series on the Federal Housing Administration; George Polk Memorial Award for special reporting, Heywood Broun Award for public interest reporting, and Sidney Hillman Foundation Award, 1973, for newspaper series "Crimes and Injustice"; Overseas Press Club award and Sigma Delta Chi Distinguished Service in Journalism award for foreign correspondence, 1974, for newspaper series "Foreign Aid: The Flawed Dream"; Pulitzer Prize for national reporting, 1975, for newspaper series "Auditing the IRS"; Honor Medal for distinguished service to journalism from University of Missouri, 1983.

WRITINGS:

(With James B. Steele) *Oil: The Created Crisis* (pamphlet), Philadelphia Inquirer, 1973.
(With Steele) *Empire: The Life, Legend, and Madness of Howard Hughes* (biography), Norton, 1979.
(With Steele) *Forevermore: Nuclear Waste in America*, Norton, 1985.

Contributor to periodicals, including *Nation* and *New Republic*.

WORK IN PROGRESS: With Steele, a book on income tax: "it is hoped that this book, still untitled, will be the definitive work on the federal income tax—a catalogue of special interests and inequities the system has created and why it is so resistant to reform," publication by Norton expected in 1986.

SIDELIGHTS: Since the early 1970's, Donald L. Barlett and James B. Steele have collaborated as investigative reporters for the *Philadelphia Inquirer*, where their work together has garnered numerous awards, including a Pulitzer Prize. They also co-authored a highly acclaimed biography, *Empire: The Life, Legend, and Madness of Howard Hughes*, and have earned reputations for credible reporting by basing their stories on documentation rather than on scandal-hunting. According to reviewer Robert Sherrill in *Nation*, the pair constitutes "the finest team of investigative reporters west of *The Times of London*."

Before teaming up with Steele at the *Inquirer*, Barlett was "a traditional scandal-hunting investigative reporter," appraised Leonard Downie, Jr., in *The New Muckrakers*. But while he had worked on a variety of newspapers and specialized in uncovering local corruption, Barlett had not been permitted to do the kind of aggressive investigative work he found most exciting. As a result, he eventually sought employment with the Knight newspaper chain, whose editors were said to support enterprising reporting. Barlett began work at the chain's Philadelphia paper, the *Inquirer*, in 1970, on the same day as Steele, and was first assigned to write about narcotics traffic and phony business bankruptcies in the city. Before long, however, the two men were instructed to work together looking for evidence of fraud in a Federal Housing Administration (FHA) subsidy program for rehabilitating and selling slum houses. The pair found they worked well together and after months of painstaking research—which included examining deeds and mortgages and interviewing families living in the substandard homes—Barlett and Steele published a thoroughly documented series of articles detailing abuse in the FHA program.

The award-winning FHA articles were only the first of many successes for the two reporters. During subsequent investigations they disclosed inequities in Philadelphia's criminal courts and in tax law enforcement by the Internal Revenue Service; they revealed that the "oil crisis" of the early 1970's was largely the creation of policies designed by multinational firms and the U.S. government in order to control the supply of crude oil for their own ends; and they showed that funds of the U.S. Foreign Aid program more often ended up lining the pockets of the rich than helping the poor.

Especially fruitful for the two men was the time they spent systematically examining Howard Hughes's connections with the U.S. Government. For eight months they searched through all kinds of records, including contracts, corporation documents, and financial statements, and finally assembled ten thousand pages of notes and documents—enough material not just for a series of articles, but for a book as well. The critics greeted *Empire: The Life, Legend, and Madness of Howard Hughes* with considerable fanfare. Critiquing for the *New York Times Book Review*, Ted Morgan declared: "Of all the books written about Howard Hughes, 'Empire' is easily the best . . . the authors have assembled the first fully documented, cradle-to-grave account of a unique American life." And in *Newsweek*, reviewer Peter S. Presscot commented: "Donald L. Barlett and James B. Steele . . . have made an impressive use of documents to fashion this longest, most responsible and authoritative biography of Hughes to date."

Their use of documentation has particularly distinguished Barlett and Steele. They are among the "new breed of muckraker," declared Downie. Their journalism goes beyond the old reliance on stories from informants and looks to the public record for evidence. "It reveals with expert analysis and thorough documentation what has systematically gone wrong with the powerful, complex institutions that affect so much of life today," explained Downie. "The best of this work reaches far enough beneath the skin of those institutions to enlighten even those who run them, thus improving the chances for change."

Both men credit their success to teamwork and the support they received from the *Inquirer*. Downie noted that Barlett believes it is important to have someone else to discuss ideas with; Barlett also thinks that he and Steele help prevent one another from becoming too personally involved in what they're

reporting. Equally as important, the paper gives the two-man team the time and resources they need and has never yet killed a story because of pressure from its advertisers—even though that has occasionally meant losing advertisements. The journalists have also been given almost complete autonomy in their work. They might consult with an editor before embarking on a new project or when submitting their articles for final editing, but otherwise, they're pretty much on their own.

According to Barlett, this system suits him quite well. "When people ask me after each project we finish if I'm getting tired of this kind of work," he revealed to Downie, "I say, 'Are you kidding? How could I get tired of this?'" And from Barlett's point of view, it's just as well that he does like it. He believes that the kind of in-depth reporting he and Steele do on a single subject is "where newspaper circulation is going to be ten years from now."

See also *Steele, James B(ruce, Jr.)*

CA INTERVIEW

CA interviewed Donald L. Barlett by telephone at his office at the *Philadelphia Inquirer* on June 9, 1983.

CA: You seem to prefer stories based on documents to stories based on sources. Why?

BARLETT: We use sources, but not in the popular sense of someone providing a secret bit of information. The sources we do use are experts, particularly in the academic community. It's very helpful to pick up a phone and call a professor tucked away in some university who has devoted his life to a subject and can give you an enormous amount of background information on some esoteric point. Much of our work, though, is based on documents, especially government documents.

CA: Some people might consider some of what you do as an invasion of privacy of the people you're investigating. What do you think of that criticism?

BARLETT: I'm going to take a rather extreme position on that. I have a great deal of difficulty with the concept of privacy in an open society. The two are mutually exclusive. That doesn't mean that you go out and write about a person's sex life, unless it relates somehow to what that person's doing in a public position. On the other hand, I think anyone involved in spending public money really doesn't have much of a claim to any kind of privacy that relates to his making of or dealing with public policy.

If you go back to the early years of this country, privacy wasn't an issue, because everyone knew everything, not only involving the government but personal things, because such things were a matter of neighborhood gossip. It wasn't so much a case of anyone publishing it or printing it, but it was widespread. And the only difference today is that society has become very large and impersonal, and the word of mouth phenomenon doesn't exist so much anymore, so the idea that what is being done now is new isn't true.

CA: You're opposed to advocacy journalism but in favor of investigative journalism. What's the difference between the two, as you see it?

BARLETT: I think there are some newspaper people and some authors who take a subject and feel so passionately about it that they believe that something should be done to correct whatever wrong it is they're writing about. The early investigative reporters, the Lincoln Steffens and the Ida Tarbells, tried to pursue a subject until there was some kind of change. But both Jim [Steele] and I feel our only obligation is to lay it out. If the person reading it feels the obligation to do something, fine. If he doesn't, fine. A reporter, as opposed to an editorial writer, shouldn't champion a cause, because it hurts the reporter's credibility.

CA: Were you allowed to do investigative reporting on the other newspapers you worked for?

BARLETT: Yes, but it was a more traditional kind of reporting at those papers, aimed at organized crime and at wrongdoing not in the policy sense but in the criminal sense. At the *Inquirer* we mostly look at governments and institutions and compare what they say they're doing with what they really are doing.

CA: Many investigative reporters have problems working together as a team. Do you and Steele have such problems?

BARLETT: It just so happens that we work well together. Most other reporters don't, at least over an extended period. Neither of us has a real ego problem when it comes to writing, which is different than with many other teams. Most people have a writing style, and they want any story to reflect their writing style, and they quarrel over that. We have a style, but it's common to the two of us so it doesn't get in the way.

CA: You come from fairly different backgrounds. Is there any explanation of why you get along so well?

BARLETT: No. It's a total freak accident of nature.

CA: You don't find yourself doing work the other one already has done?

BARLETT: No. We look at something generally for an initial period. Then we break it down and one goes off one way and one the other way. We just keep exchanging information so that we don't cover the same ground. And whoever has concentrated in a particular area usually ends up writing about that part of it.

CA: Many of your stories concentrate on showing injustice through unequal treatment: of oil customers, defendants, taxpayers. Is that what angers you most?

BARLETT: That's a thing that bothers many people. And that's also what encourages so many problems to develop. One group sees another group getting a certain advantage and it tries to get its own. It's a kind of chain reaction that never seems to slow down.

CA: Some investigative reporters complain that nothing seems to change permanently as a result of their work.

BARLETT: I think that's probably true. There's a great example from our work. The first story we did together was a Federal Housing Authority (FHA) study back in 1971. A lot of fast-moving real estate people were buying ghetto houses very cheaply for one or two thousand dollars, spending five hundred or a thousand to repair them, and then selling them for $15,000-$20,000 under government-guaranteed financing programs. We did the first large series on the subject. Then

papers in Detroit and a number of other cities picked up on it and did their own. That law was gradually changed and the situation faded out. Now the [federal] Department of Housing and Urban Development (HUD), which ended up owning the houses after the people couldn't repair them and had to walk away from them, is trying to get rid of them under the Reagan program of getting rid of a lot of government properties. So HUD is going back to those real estate people and selling the houses back to them for, again, a small sum of money. This will enable the real estate people to resell the houses again and make their profits again. So the whole thing has come full circle, only this time the government is doing it. So some things don't change.

CA: Does that ever discourage you?

BARLETT: I think it's human nature that some things don't change, but I think the worst thing that could happen would be to accept it. It's difficult to believe people want it that way. I really don't think they do; I think they just don't know what's happening. There's always someone looking for a way to put a government program to his own personal use, to the disadvantage of the average person. But the average person, more often than not, isn't aware of it.

CA: Obviously you feel you're accomplishing quite a bit by making people aware of what's going on.

BARLETT: I think so. In newspapers these days you have a lot of emphasis on stories that aren't very long, yet our stories are the longest in the newspaper business, period. We occasionally get static on that from papers other than the *Inquirer.* "People don't read that," some editors say. So the reward for me comes whenever we run a series and one of the inner-city victims of that FHA scandal calls to ask a question about the series or to talk about it. These are people who aren't well educated but are well read. To me that's probably more important than anything else, because it shows up the pompous attitude some newspaper editors have, that no one out there is interested. The reason they're not interested is because no one presents it to them in a way that's understandable, nor do most newspapers really want to devote their resources to doing so. Let me give you an example of how interested people can be. The last series we did was printed in a number of newspapers around the country in abbreviated form. But in several cities the newspapers ran little coupons with the series saying, "If you'd like the entire series, send a quarter," and forty thousand people sent their quarters. That tells me that there's a lot of faulty thinking out there about the length of stories people will read and what people really are interested in. If a subject touches a person, he's going to read it. He's not going to stop because it's longer than thirty inches, assuming it's understandable.

CA: Do you think your stories would have more impact if you were working in, say, New York, rather than in Philadelphia?

BARLETT: I think that's totally true, without a doubt.

CA: That seems unfair to me. Does it bother you?

BARLETT: That's one of those things that, if you really let it get to you, you wouldn't get anything done. But neither the New York nor Washington papers do the kinds of things we do, so it wouldn't make any difference if we were there, since we wouldn't be doing them.

CA: Do your stories have more impact now than they did earlier in your joint career?

BARLETT: The one thing that has made a difference, and I think it showed up in the requests for reprints I mentioned, is that more papers are running at least abbreviated versions of our series. Some even come close to running the full series.

CA: Do you have a favorite story among the many you've done?

BARLETT: No. They've all been so different, which is another reason this sort of work is fun. You don't do the same story twice.

CA: Are there any stories you'd like to do twice?

BARLETT: One, that I did with a partner in Cleveland. It was a story about probate court. Every year there are a number of probate cases in which someone dies without any known heirs and the money ultimately goes to the state. But in the process a lot of lawyers make a lot of money searching for heirs and shuffling papers. We took about a dozen of the cases in which a person had died seemingly without heirs and the lawyers had collected $100,000 or more looking for heirs that they couldn't find. We went out and found the heirs. In one case we traced the heirs without leaving the Cleveland Public Library. It was like that old TV program "The Millionaire," although it was never that much money. That story was fun. I'd like to do it again, in Philadelphia.

CA: Do you plan to remain an investigative reporter indefinitely?

BARLETT: I really like it. I wouldn't trade jobs with anyone.

CA: Do you think investigative reporting in this country is as good as it used to be?

BARLETT: I have a theory that newspapers run in cycles on a couple of different levels. One level is that there's always a time to be at a certain newspaper. There was a time to work for the *New York World,* there was a time to work for the *New York Sun,* there was a time to work for the *New York Herald Tribune,* or the *St. Louis Post-Dispatch,* and lately the *Inquirer* has been the one to work for. The second level is that the same thing's true of investigative reporting. When I started out in the 1950's there wasn't very much, and much of what there was fell into the two categories of labor racketeering and crime and that was it: safe areas. It wasn't until the late 1960's that that began to change. Where it is right today I'm not sure. I'm not sure if we've peaked now or started back down as a profession or if we have leveled off. But all of that goes back to the management of the newspaper. If the reporter is going to make the commitment but the person at the top isn't, the reporter might as well forget it. The reporter might as well bang his head against the wall for the rest of his life.

CA: Do any of your Inquirer *colleagues give you any flack for all the time you spend on individual stories or series?*

BARLETT: That's another advantage of being at this newspaper. To my knowledge, anyone who has wanted to do investigative reporting here, and has had an idea and proposed it, has been given an opportunity. There are more than a dozen

people off right now doing projects they proposed. So we don't get any of the flack you're talking about.

On the other hand, most newspaper people who may think they want to do investigative reporting of the sort we do don't want to any more after they've done it once. The average reporter wants to see his name in the paper regularly. I know reporters here and in Chicago who would just about have apoplexy if they didn't have a byline in the newspaper every day. I think that's what attracts people to the business: the immediacy. But a story that takes more than three or four days to do gets a lot of people very nervous.

CA: What was your reaction to receiving the Pulitzer?

BARLETT: It was rewarding, for us and the paper. The *Inquirer* didn't have the greatest reputation when Walter Annenberg owned it. I started in the business in Reading, Pennsylvania, not far from here, and even in Reading, with a forty thousand circulation, we always looked down our noses at the *Inquirer.* The *Inquirer* was always trying to hire people from the Reading paper, and everybody would laugh. People would get a letter from the *Inquirer* once a year offering them a job, and no one would ever come.

CA: You've written books as well as newspaper stories and magazine articles. Did you have any trouble switching to book writing?

BARLETT: It was a little slow in the beginning, but after a while it worked out fairly well. There's a little bit more of a tendency to overexplain in a newspaper than is necessary in a book, and not overexplaining became our biggest challenge.

CA: Did you ever specify in your Howard Hughes book what he did to get the favorable treatment from the government that he and his companies received over the years?

BARLETT: Not really, although I think a lot of it was just his mystique. Although, in the case of the Hughes Aircraft Company, the company and the government needed one another, so a lot of the favorable tax treatment the Hughes Medical Institute received was without question a result of the government's need for Hughes Aircraft. There's no question in my mind that the IRS, which still hasn't ruled on the tax-exempt status of the Hughes Institute, hasn't done so because the Defense Department doesn't want turmoil at Hughes Aircraft, which does mostly military work.

CA: Are you now writing another book?

BARLETT: We're in the middle of one on the income tax. It will be finished next summer. We're trying to trace how the tax started out and how it ended up, and we're examining how the inequities in the tax laws cut across all classes.

CA: Do you have a title yet?

BARLETT: We're the world's worst title makers. We didn't have a title for the Hughes book until W. W. Norton, our publisher, said, "OK, you guys, we're printing it now." The Hughes title was a three-way creation put together by Jim [Steele] and me and our editor at Norton. We each contributed approximately two words to it.

BIOGRAPHICAL/CRITICAL SOURCES:

BOOKS

Downie, Leonard, Jr., *The New Muckrakers*, New Republic
    Books, 1976.
Dygert, James H., *The Investigative Journalist*, Prentice-Hall,
    1976.

PERIODICALS

Christian Science Monitor, May 21, 1979.
Maclean's, June 4, 1979.
Nation, May 5, 1979.
National Review, April 27, 1979.
Newsweek, December 30, 1974, April 23, 1979.
New West, May 21, 1979.
New York, May 7, 1979.
New York Review of Books, May 31, 1979.
New York Times Book Review, May 6, 1979, November 25,
    1979, March 22, 1981, March 17, 1985.
Publishers Weekly, April 26, 1976.
Washington Monthly, April, 1979.
Washington Post Book World, December 2, 1979.
West Coast Review of Books, July, 1979.

—*Sketch by Nancy H. Evans*

—*Interview by Peter Benjaminson*

*   *   *

BARLOW, Jane   1857-1917

BRIEF ENTRY: Born in 1857 in Clontarf, County Dublin,
Ireland; died April 17, 1917, in Bray, County Wicklow, Ireland. Irish poet and novelist. Known for her ability to capture
the dialect of the Irish peasant in her verse-narratives, Barlow
published more than a dozen volumes during her twenty-year
career as an author. Her writings focused on a gentler side of
Irish life than that portrayed by some of the author's contemporaries. Though they were very popular in their day, Barlow's books are now seldom read. The author, who was educated at home, received an honorary degree from Trinity
College for scholastic excellence. Among her writings are
Bogland Studies (1892), *Irish Idylls* (1892), *Kerrigan's Quality* (1893), *Ghost-Bereft* (1901), and *By Beach and Bogland*
(1905). Barlow's only novel, *Flaws*, was published in 1911.

BIOGRAPHICAL/CRITICAL SOURCES:

BOOKS

Dictionary of Irish Literature, Greenwood Press, 1979.
Dictionary of Irish Writers, Volume I, *Fiction*, Mercier Press,
    1967.
*Twentieth-Century Authors: A Biographical Dictionary of
    Modern Literature*, H. W. Wilson, 1942.

*   *   *

BARNES, Valerie

PERSONAL: Born in Morristown, N.J.; daughter of Francis J., Jr., and Imelda D. Barnes; married John L. Cavnar (a
magazine managing editor), June 8, 1971. *Education:* Received B.A. from Upsala College.

ADDRESSES: Home—Lloyd Rd., Bernardsville, N.J. 07924.

CAREER: Newark Evening News, Newark, N.J., staff correspondent, 1965-72; free-lance writer, 1972—. Member of board
of directors of Bernardsville Public Library, 1974—.

AWARDS, HONORS: Grant from New Jersey Historical Commission, 1974.

WRITINGS:

Behind the Scenes at Giralda Farms, Bernardsville Book Co.,
    1976.
(With Thomas Murray) *Seven Wonders of New Jersey . . . and
    Then Some*, Enslow Publishers, 1980.

Contributor to *New Jersey Monthly*.

WORK IN PROGRESS: Research for manuals about moving
to New Jersey; research on American art.

SIDELIGHTS: Valerie Barnes told *CA:* "New Jersey is a great
state, with its changing landscape and 350-year-old legacy
from the past. More than twenty thousand school students decided it was a wonder-filled state when they selected the Seven
Plus Seven Wonders. Students in the Jerseyman History Club,
the youth branch of the New Jersey Historical Society, selected
twenty-eight candidates. Ballots were distributed, and the seven
most popular natural and man-made sites were voted the 'wonders' of the state. Radio, television, and newspapers acclaimed
New Jersey's attractions. They discovered in the list a popular
site for almost everyone throughout the state.

"Why seven? In the sixth century B.C. Pythagoras, a Greek
philosopher and mathematician, maintained that the number
seven was associated with sacred things. New Jersey's seven
natural wonders are the Delaware Water Gap, the Great Falls
of the Pasaic River, High Point State Park, the New Jersey
Shoreline, Palisades, the Pine Barrens, and Sunfish Pond. The
seven man-made wonders of New Jersey are the Atlantic City
Boardwalk; Edison's electric light bulb; the George Washington Bridge; the Holland Tunnel; Lucy, the Margate elephant;
Meadowlands, the New Jersey sports complex; and the Twin
Lights Navesink Lighthouse.

"I am particularly fond of the diversity of New Jersey as
illustrated by the choice of the wonders. We have four seasons,
one hundred twenty-seven miles of shoreline, mountains, forests, and farmland. New Jersey is a microcosm. New Jersey
is the winter sports of the Rockies, the summer of the West
Coast, the spring of the South, and the autumn of New England. We are urban, suburban, and country—all in a major
metropolitan area with a superb highway system that enables
one to travel from High Point to the tip of Cape May in a
short time.

"New Jersey has matured to the point where it offers all major
professional sports at the Meadowlands, top entertainment in
Atlantic City, as well as major cultural and artistic activities
for adults and children at New Jersey's museums."

*   *   *

BARNETT, Vivian E(ndicott)   1944-

PERSONAL: Born July 8, 1944, in Putnam, Conn.; daughter
of George (an executive) and Vivian (Wood) Endicott; married
Peter Barnett (a philosopher), 1967; children: Sarah, Alexander. *Education:* Vassar College, A.B., 1965; New York
University, M.A., 1971.

ADDRESSES: Office—Solomon R. Guggenheim Museum, 1071
Fifth Ave., New York, N.Y. 10128.

CAREER: Solomon R. Guggenheim Museum, New York, N.Y.,
research assistant, 1973-77, curatorial associate, 1978-79, associate curator, 1980-81, research curator, 1981-82, curator,
1982—.

MEMBER: American Association of Museums, College Art Association of America.

WRITINGS:

The Guggenheim Museum: Justin K. Thannhauser Collection, Guggenheim Foundation, 1978.
Handbook: The Guggenheim Museum Collection, 1900-1980, Guggenheim Foundation, 1980.
Kandinsky Watercolors: A Selection From the Guggenheim and Rebay Collections, Guggenheim Foundation, 1982.
Kandinsky at the Guggenheim, Abbeville Press, 1983.
One Hundred Works by Modern Masters From the Guggenheim Museum, Abrams, 1984.

Contributor to art journals.

WORK IN PROGRESS: The Guggenheim Museum: Sculpture and Works on Paper, 1880-1945; Kandinsky: Catalogue Raisonne of Watercolors, Gouaches, and Temperas.

SIDELIGHTS: Vivian E. Barnett told *CA:* "Most of my publications are scholarly catalogues on twentieth-century works of art. Among the artists I have focused on is Vasily Kandinsky, and I have become a specialist in his work. As an art historian and museum curator, I find it essential to communicate, not only with scholars, but also with the public."

*　　*　　*

BARR, Jene
    See COHEN, Jene Barr

*　　*　　*

BARROW, John D(avid) 1952-

PERSONAL: Born November 29, 1952, in London, England; son of Walter Henry (a factory section manager) and Lois (a homemaker; maiden name, Tucker) Barrow; married Elizabeth East (a nurse), September 13, 1975; children: David Lloyd, Roger James, Louise Elizabeth. *Education:* University of Durham, England, B.Sc. (first class honors), 1974; Magdalen College, Oxford, D.Phil., 1977.

ADDRESSES: Office—Astronomy Centre, University of Sussex, Falmer, Brighton BN1 9QH, England.

CAREER: Oxford University, Christ Church, Oxford, England, junior research lecturer in astrophysics, 1977-80; University of Sussex, Astronomy Centre, Brighton, England, lecturer in astronomy, 1981—. Participated in "L'Homme et le cosmos," a radio interview series broadcast in France.

MEMBER: International Astronomical Association, Royal Astronomical Society (fellow), Victoria Institute (fellow).

AWARDS, HONORS: Collingwood Prize from University of Durham and London Mathematical Society, 1974, for work in mathematics; Johnson Memorial Prize from Oxford University, 1975, for work in astrophysics; Lindemann fellow at University of California, Berkeley, 1977-78; Wallace Prize from Magdalen College, Oxford, 1979, for work in astrophysics; gravity prizes from Gravity Research Foundation, 1979 and 1981; Miller fellow at University of California, Berkeley, 1980-81.

WRITINGS:

(With Joseph Silk) *The Left Hand of Creation: The Origin and Evolution of the Expanding Universe* (included in the As-

tronomical Society of the Pacific list of best nontechnical astronomy books for 1983; main selection of the Astronomy Book Club for March, 1984), Basic Books, 1983.
(With Frank Tipler) *L'Homme et le cosmos* (title means "Man and the Universe"), Editions Imago, 1984.
(With Tipler) *The Anthropic Cosmological Principle,* Oxford University Press, 1985.

Contributor of more than seventy research articles to professional journals, including *New Scientist, Scientific American, Nature,* and *Contemporary Physics.*

WORK IN PROGRESS: Research on galaxy formation cosmology, elementary particle physics, general relativity, chaotic dynamical systems, and related aspects of the history and philosophy of science.

SIDELIGHTS: In *The Left Hand of Creation: The Origins and Evolution of the Expanding Universe* John D. Barrow and Joseph Silk endeavor to provide a nontechnical explanation of particle physics—the study of nature on its smallest scale—and its application to the study of the creation and evolution of the universe. And, according to Timothy Ferris, critic for the *New York Times Book Review,* "by and large they succeed." Ferris commended the book for handling concepts important in physics but virtually unknown elsewhere with "clarity, poise, even wit." "The nourishment here is physics, not literature," concluded the critic, "and taken as such, 'The Left Hand of Creation' is a reliable and tough-minded guide to the latest scientific ideas about genesis."

Times Higher Education Supplement critic Paul Davies agreed, calling Barrow and co-author Silk "masters at communicating" their exciting insights about the birth of the universe "without falling prey to superficial sensationalism." In Davies's opinion, the "reader who demands a mind-stretching survey of the creation of the universe, without losing authority and accuracy, need look no further."

BIOGRAPHICAL/CRITICAL SOURCES:

PERIODICALS

American Scientist, May-June, 1984.
Mercury, May-June, 1984.
Nature, January 26, 1984.
New Scientist, May 24, 1984.
New York Times Book Review, November 20, 1983.
Physics Bulletin, July, 1984.
Times Higher Education Supplement, March 30, 1984.

*　　*　　*

BARRY, William A(nthony) 1930-

PERSONAL: Born November 22, 1930, in Worcester, Mass.; son of William (a steelworker) and Catherine (a housewife and mother; maiden name, McKenna) Barry. *Education:* Boston College, A.B., 1956; Fordham University, M.A., 1960; Weston School of Theology, S.T.L., 1963; University of Michigan, Ph.D., 1968.

ADDRESSES: Home—Jesuit Community, Boston College, Chestnut Hill, Mass. 02167. *Office*—Provincial Office of New England, Society of Jesus, 761 Harrison Ave., Boston, Mass. 02118.

CAREER: Entered Society of Jesus (Jesuits), 1950, ordained Roman Catholic priest, 1962; teacher of Latin, English, and German at private secondary school in Fairfield, Conn., 1956-

58; University of Michigan, Ann Arbor, staff psychologist and lecturer in psychology, 1968-69; Weston School of Theology, Cambridge, Mass., assistant professor, 1969-73, associate professor of pastoral psychology, 1973-78, member of staff at Center for Religious Development, 1971-78, director of center, 1971-75; Society of Jesus, Provincial Office of New England, Boston, Mass., vice-provincial, 1978—. Ecumenical Counseling Service, Melrose, Mass., staff psychologist, 1970-71, member of board of directors, 1971-81; member of board of directors of Weston School of Theology, 1979-84.

MEMBER: American Psychological Association, Society for the Scientific Study of Religion, Society for the Psychological Study of Social Issues.

AWARDS, HONORS: Grant from Association of Theological Schools, 1975-76.

WRITINGS:

(With Harold L. Rausch, Richard K. Hertel, and Mary Ann Swain) *Communication, Conflict, and Marriage: Explorations in the Theory and Study of Relationships,* Jossey-Bass, 1974.
(With William J. Connolly) *The Practice of Spiritual Direction,* Seabury, 1982.

Contributor to religious and psychology journals.

WORK IN PROGRESS: Research on the relationship between psychology and spirituality, especially in the development of a personal relationship with God.

SIDELIGHTS: William A. Barry told *CA:* "I originally decided on doctoral studies in clinical psychology because of a conviction that there is an intimate connection between human intra- and interpersonal dynamics and the human reaction to God. While at the University of Michigan I became part of a research project on interpersonal relationships headed by Harold L. Raush. We analyzed data from newlywed couples engaged in improvisational conflict. Our premise was that the inevitable conflict in intimate relationships could be handled in ways that were constructive or destructive depending on the strength of the affective bond between the couple and the flexibility of the personality structures of the individuals. If the bond was strong and both parties relatively flexible and adaptable as persons, then they could face conflict and communicate in ways that led to constructive resolution of the conflict. On the other hand, if the bond was not strong and/or each party had relatively inflexible personalities, then conflict would either be avoided entirely, leading to less and less intimacy, or escalate sooner or later into a pitched battle with destructive consequences for the individuals, their relationship, and probably their children.

"In the research and in my work as a psychotherapist I noted the strength of the resistance to newness, difference, and change, but I was also aware of the human capacity and desire for growth, health, freedom, and a less neurotic life. Few psychologists focus on the latter and fewer still wonder about the source of this capacity for transcendence. I certainly enjoyed doing psychotherapy and helping people uncover hidden, neurotic motivation, but I found myself more and more fascinated and deeply moved by the courage of people to face their own conflicts and darkness. I became convinced that whether they could name the source of such confidence or not, that source was a trust, a faith in the power of light over darkness, of love over fear and hate. As I helped people to look at this source, they became more articulate about experiences of transcendence, of a sense of hope in the midst of despair and darkness, of a Presence that promised life, of a wholeness that was possible and desirable. People were helped by talking about such experiences and found themselves more and more conscious of their relationship with God.

"All my training as a clinical psychologist became focused on helping people to develop that relationship through paying attention to their experiences of God in their daily lives and through trying to describe these experiences. We discovered together that such a focus not only gave more meaning to our lives but also gradually forced us to examine our other relationships, our work and the direction of our lives in the light of this relationship. Whereas psychology tends to reduce human experience to its explanation in past history, a laudable enterprise in itself, the type of pastoral counseling I call spiritual direction, and the theological reflection based on it, tend to expand the way of looking at human experience to include the mysterious Other we call God as participant in it.

"Consistently, through all my writing, I have tried to pay close attention to human experience and to tie theory to such experience."

*   *   *

BARTENBACH, Jean 1918-

PERSONAL: Born August 12, 1918, in Brooklyn, N.Y.; daughter of Mark (a musician) and Bertha (a singer; maiden name, Cooper) Marcus; married Lou Lewis (a musician and singer; marriage ended); married Allen Bartenbach (an actor), 1962; children: Julie Lewis Gray. *Education:* Attended Pratt Institute and Otis Art Institute (now Otis Institute of Parsons School of Design).

ADDRESSES: Home—Los Angeles, Calif.

CAREER: Artist and writer. Established and operated a silk screen and textile design business in Los Angeles, Calif., during the 1940's.

MEMBER: Southern California Society of Literature for Young People and Children, Eagle Rock Writers Panel, Pasadena Lunch Bunch.

WRITINGS:

Rockhound Trails (self-illustrated juvenile nonfiction), Atheneum, 1977.

Work represented in anthologies published by *Country Beautiful,* 1973, the Youth Division Series of the *Saturday Evening Post,* 1975, and the Boston Educational Series, 1977.

Contributor to magazines for adults and children, including *Highlights for Children, Jack and Jill, Humpty Dumpty, Children's Playmate, Good Housekeeping, Saturday Evening Post, National Federation of Wildlife,* and *Outdoor World.*

WORK IN PROGRESS: Rocks Came First, Animals in Trouble, and *Biographies of Authors and Illustrators,* all for Atheneum.

SIDELIGHTS: Jean Bartenbach told *CA:* "To support my education I worked as a waitress and assembly-line worker. I was a fork-lift operator at the army base in Brooklyn. When I was twenty-three and living in Los Angeles I started my own business in silk screen and textile design. I hired artists and contracted jobs from manufacturers. Business boomed for ten years. Then I built a rock house in the red rock country of Sedona, Arizona, and I took acting parts in many of the western movies filmed there. I painted, inspired by the magnificent scenery, and sold my paintings. I bought a trailer and traveled through the West, staying for a while in Colorado, where I continued to paint in oils and watercolor.

"I started to write thirteen years ago and went through the learning process by taking an adult evening course. I made wonderful, lasting friendships with writers and began selling stories to magazines. Everyone encouraged me to write a book, so I did. I wrote about my hobbies of rock collecting and camping and was able to combine my talents by illustrating the book I had written. The art was as difficult to do as the writing. Nothing comes easy.

"My greatest pleasure is to pack abundant food in dry ice, fill jugs with water, load my pickup that has a camper shell, and drive into the desert. I camp in a remote desert wash laced with palo verde and mesquite trees. I've learned to avoid treacherous sand traps and to keep the wheels on firm malpi. The wash teems with wildlife, green growing shrubs, and exotic birds.

"There I stay until food and water is gone. Then I head for home, taking with me the sweet smells of sage and creosote, the indelible colors of wildflowers spilling across the sand, great breaths of clean air, and the balm of quietness and solitude. I am ready to go back to work."

BIOGRAPHICAL/CRITICAL SOURCES:

PERIODICALS

Appraisal, winter, 1978.
Eagle Rock Star Review, August 13, 1977, November 22, 1980.
Enterprise Sun (Simi Valley), August 17, 1977.
Glendale News Press, June 24, 1977, July 7, 1977.
Long Beach Press Telegram, March 17, 1978.
Northeast News Herald, February 25, 1968, April 6, 1977, September 9, 1977, May 6, 1978.
Valley News, February 4, 1978.

*   *   *

BARTHEL, Diane L(ee)   1949-

PERSONAL: Born January 15, 1949, in Valley Stream, N.Y.; daughter of Henry C. (a teacher) and Lissette C. (a teacher; maiden name, Ehrmann) Barthel; married David Bouchier (a writer), April 16, 1983. *Education:* Duke University, B.A., 1971; Harvard University, M.A., 1973, Ph.D., 1977.

ADDRESSES: Office—Department of Sociology, State University of New York at Stony Brook, Stony Brook, N.Y. 11794.

CAREER: Boston College, Boston, Mass., assistant professor of sociology, 1975-77; State University of New York at Stony Brook, associate professor of sociology, 1977—. Visiting professor at University of Essex, 1980-81.

MEMBER: American Sociological Association, Eastern Sociological Society.

WRITINGS:

Amana: From Pietist Sect to American Community, University of Nebraska Press, 1984.

WORK IN PROGRESS: Gender Cultures, with husband, David Bouchier, publication by Prentice-Hall expected in 1987.

SIDELIGHTS: In *Amana: From Pietist Sect to American Community,* Diane L. Barthel records the history of members of a German Pietist sect who emigrated to the United States in the mid-1800's to escape religious persecution. She traces their movement from their first home in western New York State to their establishment of seven small villages in southeastern Iowa known as the Amana Colonies. Barthel discusses Amana's successful evolution from a religious haven to a commercial triumph known for the products of its woolen mills and farms—and for the appeal of its quaint villages as a tourist attraction. *New York Times Book Review* writer Diane Manuel called *Amana* "highly readable," assessing it "a thoughtful and at times wry examination of how the Amana Colonies . . . made the transition while still preserving [their] pietism."

BIOGRAPHICAL/CRITICAL SOURCES:

PERIODICALS

Kirkus Review, May 15, 1984.
New York Times Book Review, September 2, 1984.

*   *   *

BARTHOLOMEW, Bart
See BARTHOLOMEW, Frank H.

*   *   *

BARTHOLOMEW, Frank H.   1898-1985
(Bart Bartholomew)

OBITUARY NOTICE: Born October 5, 1898, in San Francisco, Calif.; died of cancer, March 26, 1985, in Sonoma, Calif. News agency executive and journalist. Bartholomew, who was known by the name Bart, was president of United Press International (formerly United Press) from 1955 until 1962, when he became chairman of the board. Educated at Oregon State University, he joined United Press in 1921 as a reporter in Portland, Oregon. In 1924 he became Pacific division manager and from 1942 to 1954 took various assignments as a war correspondent in the Pacific during World War II, and later in China, Korea, and Indo-China. Bartholomew retired as United Press International chairman emeritus in 1981.

OBITUARIES AND OTHER SOURCES:

BOOKS

International Who's Who, 48th edition, Europa, 1984.
Who's Who in the World, 6th edition, Marquis, 1982.

PERIODICALS

Chicago Tribune, March 29, 1985.
Los Angeles Times, March 28, 1985.
New York Times, March 28, 1985.
Washington Post, March 28, 1985.

*   *   *

BARTLETT, Basil Hardington   1905-1985

OBITUARY NOTICE: Born September 15, 1905, in London, England; died January 2, 1985. Actor, playwright, journalist, and author. After attending Cambridge University, Bartlett served for a time as a correspondent for the London *Evening News.* He first appeared on stage in the 1930 production of "Milestones" and his subsequent performances included roles in "Judas," "Musical Chairs," "No Surrender," "Within the Gates," "As You Like It," "Where the Rainbow Ends," "Frolic Wind," and "The Importance of Being Earnest." He also made motion picture, radio, and television appearances and from 1952 to 1955 was a drama script supervisor for the British Broadcasting Corporation Television Service. Bartlett wrote several plays, including "Policeman's Holiday," "This Seat of Mars," "The Jersey Lily," and "A Fish in the Family." Following World War II, he published two books chronicling his wartime experiences titled *My First War* and *Next of Kin*. His volume of memoirs, *Jam Tomorrow: Some Early Reminiscences,* was published in 1978.

OBITUARIES AND OTHER SOURCES:

BOOKS

Who Was Who in the Theatre, 1912-1976, Gale, 1978.

PERIODICALS

Times (London), January 4, 1985.

* * *

BARTLETT, F. C.
    See BARTLETT, Frederic Charles

* * *

BARTLETT, Frederic Charles   1886-1969
    (F. C. Bartlett)

OBITUARY NOTICE: One source lists given name as Frederick; born October 20, 1886, in Stow-on-the-Wold, Gloucestershire, England; died September 30, 1969, in Cambridge, England. Psychologist, educator, editor, and author. Best remembered for his influential studies on memory and social psychology, Bartlett graduated from the University of London in 1910. He then joined Cambridge University's laboratory of experimental psychology and in 1922 became its director. He later taught at the university from 1931 until his retirement in 1952. Bartlett served as editor of the *British Journal of Psychology* from 1924 to 1948, and his writings include *Remembering, The Mind at Work and Play,* and *Thinking: An Experimental and Social Study.*

OBITUARIES AND OTHER SOURCES:

BOOKS

Names in the History of Psychology: A Biographical Sourcebook, Wiley, 1975.
Twentieth-Century Culture: A Biographical Companion, Harper, 1983.

* * *

BASS, T. J.
    See BASSLER, Thomas J(oseph)

* * *

BASSLER, Thomas J(oseph)   1932-
    (T. J. Bass)

PERSONAL: Born July 7, 1932, in Clinton, Iowa; son of Louis (a shoe repairman) and Faustina (a registered nurse; maiden name, Slattery) Bassler; married Gloria Napoli, 1960; children: Sara, Tom, Joan, Mary, Karl, David. *Education:* St. Ambrose College, B.A., 1955; State University of Iowa, M.D., 1959. *Religion:* Catholic.

ADDRESSES: Home—27558 Sunnyridge Rd., Palos Verdes Peninsula, Calif. 90274.

CAREER: City of Los Angeles, Los Angeles, Calif., deputy medical examiner, 1961-64; pathologist in private practice in Los Angeles, 1964—; lecturer and writer. *Military service:* U.S. Army, 1964-66; became captain.

MEMBER: Science Fiction Writers of America, American Medical Joggers Association, National Joggers Association, Alpha Omega Alpha.

AWARDS, HONORS: Nominations for Nebula Awards from Science Fiction Writers of America, 1971, for *Half Past Human,* and 1974, for *The Godwhale.*

WRITINGS:

(Under pseudonym T. J. Bass) *Half Past Human* (science fiction), Ballantine, 1971.
(Under Bass pseudonym) *The Godwhale* (science fiction), Ballantine, 1974.
(With Robert E. Burger) *The Whole Life Diet: An Integrated Program of Nutrition and Exercise for a Lifestyle of Total Health,* M. Evans, 1979.

Contributor of articles to medical journals, including *Journal of the American Medical Association,* and, under Bass pseudonym, to science fiction periodicals, including *Galaxy* and *If.* Founder and editor of *American Medical Joggers Newsletter,* 1969—.

SIDELIGHTS: Under the pseudonym T. J. Bass, Bassler has written two novels that John Ower, in his essay in *Dictionary of Literary Biography Yearbook: 1981,* ranks among "the best works of science fiction to be published during the 1970s." Bassler's first work, *Half Past Human,* introduced a bleak environment called the Earth Society, or "big ES." This society of three trillion Nebishes—whose lives are dictated in part by a computer—thrive beneath an earth's surface congested with crops. The few real humans who live free of the ES constitute the salvation of the human race. They work with independent Nebishes to escape from earth and start a new society on another planet.

The Godwhale continues the gloomy depiction of the ES. The title of the novel comes from a massive machine used by sea humans in harvesting plankton. In this novel Bassler further explores the individual's relation with machinery. Commanding the godwhale are real humans who have adapted to sea life. The only other master of the huge machine is a super individual bred by the Nebishes. In *The Godwhale,* the real humans succeed in living at sea and thus, like their counterparts who escape earth in *Half Past Human,* offer hope in a world of subterranean Nebishes.

In both *Half Past Human* and *The Godwhale* Bassler juxtaposes the stifling and unproductive ways of the Nebishes with the positive, self-fulfilling lives of the real humans. He portrays the ES as dependent on mechanization and harmful chemicals—fertlizers and pesticides—while humans outside the ES rely on an essentially natural diet and use machinery only as means to an end. Ower wrote: "Bassler draws a clear-cut antithesis in *Half Past Human* and *The Godwhale* between the fulfillment of the positive potential of man's technology and the realization of its negative possibilities. . . . The latter outcome involves a pejorative contrast between the organic and the mechanical, together with a reduction of men to a subhuman level by the technological violation of their physical and psychic integrity."

Bassler's promotion of the organic over the synthetic is further evident in *The Whole Life Diet,* a health volume he wrote with

Robert E. Burger. In this book Bassler advocates a diet of natural, unprocessed foods—including eggs, fruits, and nuts—and a health regime of daily walking and running. Adopting this regime, Bassler and Burger insist, will insure a longer life. They contend, as Ower notes, that "the natural aging process can be greatly slowed by a person's keeping fit enough to walk as many miles as he is years old!"

Thomas J. Bassler told *CA:* "I like to take long walks when I am organizing my thoughts. There is nothing like a ten hour (thirty mile) hike to clear the mind. The mileage helps wash away trivia and leaves plenty of 'empty' mental space for growing fiction.

"Of course the routine chore of formatting lectures and examinations for my students in laboratory technology forces me to do a little 'storytelling' when I try to spark their interest in hematology, parasitology, and chemistry. Frequently a germ of an idea from a lecture grows into a larger piece of fiction during a long walk.

"I also use science fiction to rewrite history. My gut reaction to any tragedy is a bit of wishful thinking: 'This could have been avoided if . . .' Larry, the 'hemihuman' in *The Godwhale,* was based on an actual event in which an accident victim was cut in two and lived long enough to receive medical care at the scene. I realized all of the problems this man would have faced had he survived. However, I never thought for a moment that survival was not desirable. Life is always a better alternative than death! I stick to the scientific possibilities when I write (so-called 'hard science fiction') and my stories are always up-beat, looking at the bright side. *The Godwhale* has a hidden premise: 'It is better to be a hemihuman than to be no human at all.'"

AVOCATIONAL INTERESTS: Hiking, running, studying whales.

BIOGRAPHICAL/CRITICAL SOURCES:

BOOKS

Dictionary of Literary Biography Yearbook: 1981, Gale, 1982.

*   *   *

BASU, Kaushik   1952-

PERSONAL: Born January 9, 1952, in Calcutta, India; son of Keshab C. (a solicitor) and Usha (a housewife; maiden name, Ghosh) Basu; married Alaka Malwade (a demographer), July 21, 1977; children: Karna (son), Diksha (daughter). *Education:* University of Delhi, B.A. (with honors), 1972; London School of Economics and Political Science, London, M.Sc, 1974, Ph.D., 1976.

ADDRESSES: Office—Centre for Advanced Studies in Economic History and Economic Development, Delhi School of Economics, University of Delhi, Delhi, India 110 007.

CAREER: University of Delhi, Delhi, India, reader in economics, 1978-85, professor of economics, 1985—. Visiting associate professor at Centre for Operations Research and Econometrics (CORE), Louvain-la-Neuve, Belgium, 1981-82; visiting professor at Centre d'economie mathematique et d'econometrie (CEME), Brussels, Belgium, 1981-82. Joint managing editor of *Journal of Quantitative Economics.*

MEMBER: Econometric Society (United States), Royal Economic Society (England).

AWARDS, HONORS: Fellow of CORE, 1981.

WRITINGS:

Revealed Preference of Government, Cambridge University Press, 1980.
The Less Developed Economy: A Critique of Contemporary Theory, Basil Blackwell, 1984.

Author of "An Economist's Diary," a fortnightly column in the newspaper *Indian Express.* Contributor to economic journals. Member of board of editors of *Indian Economic Review.*

WORK IN PROGRESS: Agrarian Structure and Development Possibilities, to be part of the series "Fundamentals of Pure and Applied Economics," publication expected in 1986.

SIDELIGHTS: Kaushik Basu told *CA:* "The person whose writings have influenced me the most is Bertrand Russell. I have always enjoyed abstract reasoning and deductive logic. Like Russell, I believe that one should speak the truth as far as possible. It follows—and this is my advice to fellow human beings—that if you do not have enough courage to criticize an evil man to his face, at least have the courage to do it behind his back!"

*   *   *

BATOR, Robert   1939-

PERSONAL: Born January 3, 1939, in Chicago, Ill.; son of Stanley (a millwright) and Veronica (a factory worker) Bator; married Sheila Blondell (a lawyer), December 26, 1964; children: Miranda, Aaron. *Education:* Loyola University of Chicago, B.S., 1961, M.A., 1962, Ph.D., 1969.

ADDRESSES: Home—5420 South Blackstone Ave., Chicago, Ill. 60615. *Office*—Department of English, Olive-Harvey College of City Colleges of Chicago, 10001 South Woodlawn, Chicago, Ill. 60628.

CAREER: Loyola University of Chicago, Chicago, Ill., instructor in English, 1962-63; Olive-Harvey College of City Colleges of Chicago, Chicago, instructor, 1963-65, assistant professor, 1966-69, associate professor, 1970-73, professor of English, 1974—.

MEMBER: National Council of Teachers of English, Children's Literature Association.

WRITINGS:

(Editor) *Signposts to Criticism of Children's Literature,* American Library, 1983.
(Editor) *Masterworks of Children's Literature,* Volumes III and IV: *1740-1836,* Chelsea House, 1983-84.
Shared Prose: Process to Product, Holt, 1985.

Contributor to *Children's Literature, Research Studies,* and *ChLA Journal.*

WORK IN PROGRESS: Research on eighteenth-century fiction for children in England.

SIDELIGHTS: Robert Bator told *CA:* "I agree wholeheartedly with Frank Smith that writers are not more gifted people; they are just those who live with their uncertainties and write nonetheless. For teaching writing I am sold on conferencing as promulagated by Roger Garrison and the late Donald Murray. Conferencing intervenes when it counts—while the writing is still in process."

BAUMANN, Hans Felix S(iegismund)   1893-1985
(Felix H. Man)

OBITUARY NOTICE: Professionally known as Felix H. Man; born November 30, 1893, in Freiburg im Breisgau, Germany (now West Germany), immigrated to England, 1934, naturalized citizen, 1948; died January 30, 1985, in London, England. Photographer, photojournalist, and author. Man became a professional photographer in the late 1920's after serving in the German Army and taking documentary reportage photographs during World War I. He then worked for several German publications until 1934, when he went to London and founded, with Stephen Lorant, the *Weekly Illustrated* magazine. Thereafter he served as a special assignments photographer in London for Time-Life Publications, the *Daily Mirror, Harper's Bazaar,* the *Sunday Times,* and *Picture Post,* which he had helped found. Man's photographic works have appeared in individual and group shows throughout Europe, Canada, the United States, and Argentina. He also wrote several books, including *Eight European Artists, Lithography in England, 1801-1810,* a ten-volume work titled *Europaeische Graphik,* and *Artist's Lithographs: A World History From Senefelder to the Present Day.*

OBITUARIES AND OTHER SOURCES:

BOOKS

Coke, Van Deren, *Avant Garde Photography in Germany,* Pantheon, 1982.
Contemporary Photographers, St. Martin's, 1982.

PERIODICALS

New York Times, May 14, 1971, January 27, 1978.
Times (London), February 1, 1985.

* * *

BAVIER, Robert Newton (Jr.)   1918-

PERSONAL: Born March 10, 1918, in New Rochelle, N.Y.; son of Robert Newton and Grace M. (Pearson) Bavier; married Charlotte Whaley Small, March 26, 1946; children: Robert Newton III, Louise S., Anne, John S. *Education:* Williams College, A.B., 1940. *Politics:* Republican. *Religion:* Presbyterian.

ADDRESSES: Home—2423 Bent Twig Rd., Johns Island, S.C. 29455. *Office*—Ziff-Davis Publishing, 1 Park Ave., New York, N.Y. 10016.

CAREER: Ziff-Davis Publishing, New York, N.Y., associate editor of Yachting Publishing Co., 1941-52, advertising director, 1953-71, president and publisher, 1972-77, corporation vice-president, 1977—, past president and publisher of *Yachting.*

MEMBER: International Yacht Racing Union, North American Yacht Racing Union (president, 1967-71), U.S. Yacht Racing Union, Cruising Club of America, New York Yacht Club, Norton Yacht Club, Wee Burn Country Club.

WRITINGS:

Sailing to Win, Dodd, 1947, revised edition, 1983.
The New Yacht Racing Rules, Norton, 1948.
Faster Sailing, Dodd, 1955.
A View From the Cockpit, Dodd, 1966.
Americas Cup Fever, Ziff-Davis, 1980, revised edition published as *The Americas Cup: An Insider's View,* Dodd, in press.

Keys to Racing Success, Dodd, 1983.

SIDELIGHTS: Robert Newton Bavier told *CA:* "I have long felt that the key to successful writing is to have something to say. That's why I confine my writing to nautical subjects on which I am well informed.

"The highlight of my yacht racing career was successfully defending the America's Cup as helmsman of the *Constellation* in 1964. The sport has changed since I first began sailing; a greater intensity of effort is now required to excel. It used to be that having a great natural ability was enough. Now you need that plus constant training and practice."

* * *

BAYES, Marjorie   1934-

PERSONAL: Born December 1, 1934, in Chicago, Ill.; daughter of Allan Wallace (a citrus grower) and Mary (a citrus grower; maiden name, Nixon) Andress; married Andrew H. Bayes, August, 1957 (divorced, 1965); children: Stephen, Christopher. *Education:* University of Florida, B.A. (with honors), 1956; University of Kentucky, M.A., 1959; University of Miami, Ph.D., 1970. *Politics:* Democrat. *Religion:* Unitarian-Universalist.

ADDRESSES: Home—11 Revell Ave., Northampton, Mass. 01060. *Office*—25 Main St., Northampton, Mass. 01060.

CAREER: Homemaker, 1959-63; Montanari Residential Treatment Cener, Hialeah, Fla., psychologist, 1963-65; Yale University, School of Medicine New Haven, Conn., assistant professor, 1970-76, lecturer, 1976-80; private practice of psychotherapy and organizational consultant in Northampton, Mass., 1980—.

MEMBER: American Psychological Association, American Association of University Professors, Phi Beta Kappa, Sigma Xi, Phi Kappa Phi.

WRITINGS:

(Editor with Elizabeth Howell) *Women and Mental Health,* Basic Books, 1981.

WORK IN PROGRESS: A book on women and work.

SIDELIGHTS: Marjorie Bayes told *CA:* "My concern for women and mental health arose from my career as a psychologist—working with women students and clients and becoming concerned that they did not receive appropriate training or services. Discrimination against women pervades the educational and human services systems. Our book, *Women and Mental Health,* was an attempt to address issues of sexism and to contribute relevant ways of thinking about women's lives."

* * *

BEACH, David (Williams)   1938-

PERSONAL: Born September 5, 1938, in Hartford, Conn.; son of Raymond S. (an automotive executive) and Avis (Sugden) Beach; married Marcia Francesca Salemme (a teacher), June 20, 1964; children: Juliana, Matthew. *Education:* Brown University, B.A., 1961; Yale University, M.Mus., 1964, M.Phil., 1973, Ph.D., 1974.

ADDRESSES: Home—Fairport, N.Y. *Office*—Department of Theory, Eastman School of Music, University of Rochester, 26 Gibbs St., Rochester, N.Y. 14604.

CAREER: Yale University, New Haven, Conn., instructor, 1964-67, assistant professor of music and director of undergraduate studies in theory and composition, 1967-71; Brooklyn College of the City University of New York, Brooklyn, N.Y., assistant professor of music, 1971-72; University of Rochester, Eastman School of Music, Rochester, N.Y., associate professor of music theory, 1974—, chairman of department of theory, 1981—.

MEMBER: American Musicological Society, Society for Music Theory (chairman of publications committee, 1978-84; member of executive board, 1984—).

AWARDS, HONORS: Deems Taylor Award from American Society of Composers, Authors, and Publishers, 1983, for translating *The Art of Strict Musical Composition.*

WRITINGS:

(Contributor) Maury Yeston, editor, *Readings in Schenker Analysis,* Yale University Press, 1977.
(Translator with Jurgen Thym, and author of introduction and notes) Johann Philipp Kirnberger, *The Art of Strict Musical Composition,* Yale University Press, 1982.
(Editor and contributor) *Aspects of Schenkerian Theory,* Yale University Press, 1983.

Contributor of articles to music journals, including *Music Analysis* and *Journal of Music Theory.* Editor of *Journal of Music Theory,* 1967-71.

WORK IN PROGRESS: The Current Status of Schenkerian Research, for Acta Musicologica; a monograph, *Beethoven's Piano Sonata in A-Flat, Op. 110: An Analytic Study;* a monograph on concealed motivic repetition in selected works of the classsical period.

SIDELIGHTS: David Beach told *CA:* "I feel strongly about the emergence of music theory as a specialized area of research. My research and teaching is directed at the elucidation of musical structure through detailed and rigorous examination of musical works. My work has been most strongly influenced by the writings of Heinrich Schenker."

*   *   *

BEARD, Charles A(ustin)   1874-1948

BRIEF ENTRY: Born November 27, 1874, near Knightstown, Ind.; died September 1, 1948, in New Haven, Conn. American political scientist, historian, educator, and author. Beard is probably best known for his many works on American history. He taught at Columbia University from 1907 to 1917, when he resigned over a dispute on academic freedom. He then worked as a director of the Training School for Public Service and, in 1919, helped found the New School for Social Research. Beard's early writings on American history, including *An Economic Interpretation of the Constitution* (1913) and *The Economic Origins of Jeffersonian Democracy* (1915), focused on domestic capitalism and earned the educator a reputation in some quarters as an advocate of economic determinism. In 1927 Beard and his wife, Mary Ritter Beard, published their two-volume study *The Rise of American Civilization,* which has been described as a brilliant analysis of U.S. history as a conflict between agricultural and economic interests. During World War II Beard championed isolationism in foreign policy, and subsequent works, such as *American Foreign Policy in the Making, 1932-40* (1946) and *President Roosevelt and the Coming of War, 1941* (1948), were considered quite crit-

ical of President Franklin D. Roosevelt's prewar actions and policies.

BIOGRAPHICAL/CRITICAL SOURCES:

BOOKS

Dictionary of Literary Biography, Volume 17: *Twentieth-Century American Historians,* Gale, 1973.
The Oxford Companion to American Literature, Oxford University Press, 1966.
Twentieth-Century Authors: A Biographical Dictionary of Modern Literature, 1st supplement, H. W. Wilson, 1955.
Twentieth-Century Literary Criticism, Volume 15, Gale, 1985.

*   *   *

BEATON, M. C.
See CHESNEY, Marion

*   *   *

BEAVER, Paul (Eli)   1953-

PERSONAL: Born April 3, 1953, in Winchester, England; son of Norman (an engineer) and Olive (a horticulturalist) Beaver; married Ann Middleton (a researcher), 1978. *Education:* Attended Farnborough College of Technology, 1971-72, and Sheffield City Polytechnic, 1973-77.

ADDRESSES: Home—19 Bexmoor Way, Old Basing, near Basingstoke, Hampshire RG24 0BL, England.

CAREER: Free-lance writer and photographer, 1975—. Chartered surveyor.

MEMBER: Royal Institute of Chartered Surveyors (associate member), Fleet Air Army Officers Association, Airborne Law Enforcement Association, Army Aviation Association of America, Helicopter Club of Great Britain.

WRITINGS:

"Ark Royal": A Pictorial History of the Royal Navy's Last Conventional Aircraft Carrier, Patrick Stephens, 1979.
U-Boats in the Atlantic, Patrick Stephens, 1979.
German Capital Ships, Patrick Stephens, 1980.
E-Boats and Coastal Craft, Patrick Stephens, 1980.
German Destroyers, Patrick Stephens, 1981.
The British Aircraft Carrier, Patrick Stephens, 1982.
(Editor) *Encyclopaedia of the Modern Royal Navy, Including the Fleet Air Arm and Royal Marines,* Patrick Stephens, 1982, Naval Institute Press, 1983.
Carrier Air Operations Since 1945, Arms & Armour Press, 1983.
"Invincible Class," Ian Allan, 1984.
Fleet Command, Ian Allan, 1984.
Missile Systems, Ian Allan, 1985.
British Naval Air Power, Arms & Armour Press, 1985.
Encyclopaedia of the Fleet Air Arm, 1945-1985, Patrick Stephens, in press.
The Royal Navy in the 1980's, Arms & Armour Press, in press.
NATO Navies in the 1980's, Arms & Armour Press, in press.

Writer for British Broadcasting Corp. (BBC-Radio) series "Going Places," BBC-World Service, and British Forces Broadcasting. Editor of *Helicopter World* and *Defence Helicopter World,* both 1982—.

SIDELIGHTS: Paul Beaver told *CA:* "Those who wish to become specialist writers should know their subject and not worry about reading for degrees or diplomas in journalism."

BEAZLEY, John Davidson   1885-1970

OBITUARY NOTICE: Born September 13, 1885, in Glasgow, Scotland; died May 6, 1970, in Oxford, England. Archaeologist, educator, and author. Beazley was a recognized authority in the field of Greek vase painting and is credited with developing a method of identifying and classifying the many schools, artists, and styles of Attic red-figure vases. Beginning in 1908 he taught at Oxford University's Christ Church and in 1925 became Lincoln Professor of Archaeology. Beazley was a contributor to the *Journal of Hellenic Studies* and wrote *Attic Red-Figure Vase-Painters, Potter and Painter in Ancient Athens, Attic Black-Figure Vase-Painters,* and *Attic Vases in American Museums.*

OBITUARIES AND OTHER SOURCES:

BOOKS

Longman Companion to Twentieth Century Literature, Longman, 1970.
Twentieth-Century Culture: A Biographical Companion, Harper, 1983.
Who Was Who Among English and European Authors, 1931-1949, Gale, 1978.

*   *   *

BECKER, Howard Saul   1928-

BRIEF ENTRY: Born April 18, 1928, in Chicago, Ill. American sociologist, educator, and author. Becker, who became the editor of *Social Problems* in 1961, was appointed professor of sociology at Northwestern University in 1965. He has also taught at the University of Chicago and Stanford University, and he has worked as a research sociologist in Missouri for Community Studies, Incorporated. Becker wrote *Boys in White: Student Culture in Medical School* (University of Chicago Press, 1961), *Outsiders: Studies in the Sociology of Deviance* (Free Press, 1963), and *Art Worlds* (University of California Press, 1982). He edited *Social Problems: A Modern Approach* (Wiley, 1966), *Campus Power Struggle* (Aldine, 1970), and *Culture and Civility in San Francisco* (Aldine, 1971). *Address:* Department of Sociology, Northwestern University, 633 Clark St., Evanston, Ill. 60201.

*   *   *

BEITZELL, Robert (E.)   1930-

BRIEF ENTRY: Born May 24, 1930, in Elizabeth, N.J. American historian, educator, and author. Beitzell began teaching history at the University of Maine at Orono in 1967. He wrote *The Uneasy Alliance: America, Britain, and Russia, 1941-1943* (Knopf, 1972). Beitzell edited *Tehran, Yalta, and Potsdam: The Soviet Protocols* (Academic International, 1970).

BIOGRAPHICAL/CRITICAL SOURCES:

PERIODICALS

American Historical Review, June, 1974.
Political Science Quarterly, September, 1973.

*   *   *

BELK, Fred Richard   1937-

PERSONAL: Born March 13, 1937, in Kansas City, Mo.; son of Oliver W. and Crystal (Prock) Belk; married Nadine K. Rochon (a health administrator), November 22, 1961; children: Stephanie, Stephen, Christopher. *Education:* William Jewell College, B.A., 1959; Texas Christian University, M.A., 1965; San Francisco Theological Seminary, M.Div., 1965; Northwestern University, Certificate in African Studies, 1970; Oklahoma State University, Ph.D. 1973. *Politics:* Democrat.

ADDRESSES: Home—627 Moro, Manhattan, Kan. 66502. *Office*—Department of History, Eisenhower Hall, Kansas State University, Manhattan, Kan. 66506; and Native American Art, P.O. Box 19161, Topeka, Kan. 66619.

CAREER: Ordained Presbyterian minister, 1966; Young Men's Christian Association, Kansas City, Mo., youth program director, 1959-61; Young Men's Christian Association, Fort Worth, Tex., program director, 1962-64; minister of Presbyterian church in Perry, Okla., 1966-69; Sterling College, Sterling, Kan., assistant professor, 1969-75, associate professor, 1975-82; Kansas State University, Manhattan, assistant professor of history, 1984—. Instructor at Oklahoma State University, 1966-69; adjunct professor at Emporia State University, 1976—; visiting professor at College Ganado, 1976—; owner and operator of Native American Art (antique Indian art and artifact business).

MEMBER: American Historical Association, American Association of University Professors, Conference on Faith and History, Southwestern Social Science Association, Kansas Historical Association, Pi Gamma Mu, Phi Alpha Theta, Sigma Tau Delta.

WRITINGS:

The Great Trek of the Russian Mennonites to Central Asia, 1880-1884, Herald Press, 1976, revised edition, 1978.

Contributor to history journals.

WORK IN PROGRESS: Two books on Katherine Van Born, wife of Martin Luther; *Indian Anthropologist,* a book on American Indian history, completion expected in 1986; articles on Navajo and Hopi Indians and American military activities in Russia after World War I.

SIDELIGHTS: Fred Richard Belk told *CA:* "Working at Kansas State University has stimulated me to become involved in research on nineteenth-century Russian history and nineteenth-century American Indian history. It has also involved extensive writing and travel concerning the importance of American Indian art. Antique Indian art and artifacts have been an interest of mine for many years and the interest is growing. The art of the Indian and Russian civilizations is unique.

"The nineteenth century is a fascinating frontier time whether one studies Russia or America. Because the ancestors of the American Indian crossed the Bering Strait from Russian Asia, I have developed a close proclivity to emphasize Russian and American interrelationships. For example, imperialistic advance in Asia by the czars is similar to American 'winning of the West.' Amid the struggle of the imperial powers were native tribal people who were just trying to live out their lives. Many need to study the plight of minority native peoples, East and West. I believe they are not given enough significance in world history because it was the dominant society that wrote the history books. A re-evaluation is needed in our writing and research when we think of Russian national minorities or American Indian tribes."

BELL, Barbara Currier 1941-

PERSONAL: Born November 17, 1941, in New York, N.Y.; daughter of David Fletcher and Margaret (Brown) Currier; married Donald C. Bell (a physician), December 19, 1971; children: Meredith Currier. *Education:* Vassar College, B.A. (magna cum laude), 1963; Columbia University, M.A., 1965, Ph.D., 1972.

ADDRESSES: Home—160 Harbor Rd., Southport, Conn. 06490.

CAREER: Wesleyan University, Middletown, Conn., assistant professor of English, 1970-78, visiting lecturer in humanities, 1978-80, co-founder of College of Science in Society, 1973-75; independent scholar, 1980—. Vassar College, Poughkeepsie, N.Y., visiting lecturer in English, 1983—. Member of summer faculty at Virginia Union University, 1966; member of Center for Independent Study, New Haven, Conn. Member of board of trustees of St. Timothy's School, Stevenson, Md., 1971-76; volunteer worker for local civic groups.

MEMBER: Modern Language Association of America, American Association for the Advancement of Science, National Council of Teachers of English, American Association of University Women, Center for Independent Study.

AWARDS, HONORS: White House fellow, 1967-68.

WRITINGS:

Tools in the Learning Trade, Scarecrow, 1984.

CONTRIBUTOR

Josephine Donovan, editor, *Feminist Literary Criticism*, University Press of Kentucky, 1975.
Frederick O. Waage, editor, *Teaching Environmental Literature*, Modern Language Association of America, 1985.
James E. Ford, editor, *Teaching the Research Paper*, Modern Language Association of America, 1985.

Contributor of articles and reviews to literature journals.

WORK IN PROGRESS: Encountering Nature: Roles for Humankind to Play in the Natural World, completion expected in 1987.

SIDELIGHTS: Barbara Currier Bell told *CA:* "*Tools in the Learning Trade* reflects my work as a writing teacher. It discusses certain reference tools that are basic for college students to own, giving advice about how to use each kind of tool and which particular ones to buy. It offers self-help at the nitty-gritty level, and that is the kind of teaching I try to do in the classroom; so, indirectly the book implies a theory of education.

"*Encountering Nature* reflects my work as a scholar. It is comparative literary criticism covering a very wide range of works and following a very broad theme; it is the sort of work more appropriate to label 'humanities' than 'English.'

"My career has followed the same two lines my books do: I teach in, do administrative work for, and write about the educational system in America. I am also a scholar."

*   *   *

BELL, Robert S(tanley) W(arren) 1871-1921
(Hawksley Brett, Old Fag)

BRIEF ENTRY: Born in 1871; died September 26, 1921. British editor and author of boys' stories. Under the pseudonym

Old Fag, Bell edited the monthly boys' magazine *The Captain*, which published P. G. Wodehouse's early school stories. Many of Bell's books appeared in *The Captain* as serials before publication in book form. Bell's first attempt at writing boys' stories was "The Boys of Daneleigh College," written under the pseudonym of Hawksley Brett and serialized in *British Boys* magazine. Bell also launched and edited the short-lived magazine *Boys' Life*. In addition to editing and writing fiction for youths, Bell spent the last ten years of his life writing for the theatre. His comedy, "A Companion for George," was successfully produced in London in 1911. Among Bell's novels are *Tales of Greyhouse* (1901), *J. O. Jones* (1903), *The Duffer* (1906), and *Jim Mortimer* (1908).

BIOGRAPHICAL/CRITICAL SOURCES:

BOOKS

The Men Behind Boys' Fiction, Howard Baker, 1970.
The Who's Who of Children's Literature, Schocken, 1968.

*   *   *

BELLE, Pamela 1952-

PERSONAL: Born June 16, 1952, in Ipswich, England; daughter of Brian Henry (a teacher) and Sylvia (a housewife; maiden name, Wilkinson) Belle; married Alan David Fincher, July 3, 1976 (divorced, 1984). *Education:* University of Sussex, B.A. (with honors), 1975; Coventry College of Education, Postgraduate Certificate in Education, 1976. *Politics:* "Slightly left of center!" *Religion:* None.

ADDRESSES: Home—63 Prospect R., St. Albans, Hertfordshire, England. *Agent*—Vivienne Schuster, John Farquharson Ltd., 162-168 Regent St., London W.1, England.

CAREER: Northchurch St. Mary's First School, Berkhamsted, England, teacher, 1978-85; writer, 1985—.

MEMBER: National Union of Teachers, Richard III Society.

WRITINGS:

The Moon in the Water (novel), Berkley Publishing, 1984.
The Chains of Fate (novel), Berkley Publishing, 1984.
Alathea (novel), Berkley Publishing, 1985.

WORK IN PROGRESS: The Lodestar (working title), a novel set in the time of Richard III (the 1480's), publication by Pan Books expected in 1987.

SIDELIGHTS: Pamela Belle told *CA:* "Originally I wrote purely for my own enjoyment. Successful publication was a bonus! I have no particular viewpoint to put forth or axe to grind, although I tend to fill my books with all the things I find enjoyable: poetry, music, magic, food, animals, children, humor, and the fascination of entering a world long vanished. My characters also tend to reflect my own beliefs and prejudices on the equality of women and the importance of love, tolerance, and compassion, my distrust of organized religion, and my love of the world of imagination. Nevertheless, my main concern is to tell my story entertainingly and convincingly, and more serious considerations are by the way. I would rather have my books read and enjoyed by many and ignored by serious reviewers than write more difficult and obscure works that, like many 'classics,' people think they ought to read, but haven't.

"I do, however, place great importance on proper historical research. I think this is because my characters seem so real to me that I cannot bear to destroy the illusion by falsifying the picture. Everything I write about *could* have happened or existed, even if it never did in reality. I want my characters to be sufficiently real and alive to lead my readers into my own enjoyment and study of history.''

*　　*　　*

BELLOT, Leland J(oseph)　1936-

BRIEF ENTRY: Born December 10, 1936, in Port Arthur, Tex. American historian, educator, and author. Bellot began teaching history at California State University, Fullerton, in 1964; ten years later he was appointed dean of humanities and social science. His specialties include eighteenth-century British history and British-American studies. Bellot is the author of *William Knox: The Life and Thought of an Eighteenth-Century Imperialist* (University of Texas Press, 1977). *Address:* Department of History, California State University, Fullerton, Calif. 92634.

*　　*　　*

BELLOWS, Fiona (Ann)　1941-

PERSONAL: Born August 29, 1941, in Denver, Colo.; daughter of Clark (a salesman) and Jennifer (a homemaker; maiden name, Melton) Andrews; married Frank Bellows, 1966 (divorced); children: Anthony, Gloria.

ADDRESSES: Home and office—221 Lewiston Rd., Grosse Pointe Farms, Mich. 48236.

CAREER: Worked as secretary in Detroit, Mich., 1966-72; writer.

MEMBER: Wayne County Women's Cooperative, Summons Club.

WRITINGS:

CHILDREN'S BOOKS

The Angel on the Farm, Bugle Books, 1973.
All the Way From School, Golden Laurel Editions, 1974.
The Girls Are Thinking, Golden Laurel Editions, 1974.
Our Friend, the Water, Golden Laurel Editions, 1975.
Ben Grange and the Wrong Way Home: A True Story, Bugle Books, 1979.
What Is in the Kitchen?, Home Aid Publications, 1980.
(And illustrator) *Thor and the Thunder Boy,* Bugle Books, 1980.
Sarah's Wagon, Golden Laurel Editions, 1981.
Sarah's Puppy, Golden Laurel Editions, 1981.
Sarah's Adventure at Summer Camp, Golden Laurel Editions, 1982.
(And illustrator) *Hercules and the Girl From America,* Bugle Books, 1983.

WORK IN PROGRESS: Two more books in the ''Sarah'' series, for Golden Laurel Editions; an adult book about leukemia.

SIDELIGHTS: Fiona Bellows told *CA:* ''I don't consider myself a real writer yet, despite several publications. I began writing to supplement my income following my divorce and found it both an enjoyable and profitable pursuit. I have tested most of my books on my two children. If they like it, it goes. As they grow older this has become more difficult.

''I quit writing for five years when my daughter was stricken with leukemia. Her illness is in remission now, and I plan to write a serious book about her experience.''

*　　*　　*

BEMIS, Stephen Edward　1937-1985

OBITUARY NOTICE: Born August 1, 1937, in Providence, R.I.; died in an automobile accident, March 27, 1985, near Raleigh, N.C. Psychologist and author. Bemis held degrees from the University of Connecticut and Bowie State College and in 1961 became a psychologist with the U.S. Army Department in Washington, D.C. He later worked for the U.S. Labor Department, developing a general aptitude test and other testing materials. In 1981 he joined Psychological Services, a consulting firm, and eventually became vice-president. Bemis, a member of the American Psychological Association, was the founding president of the Personal Testing Council of Metropolitan Washington and was co-author of *Job Analysis: An Effective Management Tool.*

OBITUARIES AND OTHER SOURCES:

PERIODICALS

Washington Post, March 30, 1985.

*　　*　　*

BENN, John Andrews　1904-1984

OBITUARY NOTICE: Born January 28, 1904, in London, England; died December 19, 1984. Businessman, city official, publisher, and author. Benn, whose family's publishing enterprises included the companies of Benn Brothers and Ernest Benn Limited, attended Princeton and Cambridge universities. Following his education he worked in the family business supervising the library of adult education books. He then toured Latin America where, in 1931, he founded Industria Britanica, a firm that promoted British exports. After serving in World War II he again attended to the publishing affairs of his family, helping to revive the business that had suffered during the war. One result of his efforts was the publication of Winston Churchill's book *Painting as a Pastime.* In 1949 Benn became the chairman and managing director of the United Kingdom Temperance and General Provident Institution, a post he held until 1968. He served as chairman on the boards of both U.S. and British companies, including Technical Development Capital, which he founded in 1962. Benn was the author of *Adventurer in South America, Tradesman's Entrance, I Say Rejoice,* a book written in memory of his brother who was killed in World War II, and *Something In the City.*

OBITUARIES AND OTHER SOURCES:

BOOKS

Who's Who, 136th edition, St. Martin's, 1984.
Who Was Who Among English and European Authors, 1931-1949, Gale, 1978.

PERIODICALS

Times (London), December 22, 1984.

*　　*　　*

BENNETT, Betty T.

PERSONAL: Children—Peter, Matthew. *Education:* Brooklyn

College of the City University of New York, B.A. (magna cum laude), 1962; New York University, M.A., 1963, Ph.D., 1970.

ADDRESSES: Office—Office of the Dean of Liberal Arts and Sciences, Pratt Institute, 200 Willoughby Ave., Brooklyn, N.Y. 11205.

CAREER: State University of New York at Stony Brook, adjunct assistant professor, 1970-74, adjunct associate professor of English, 1975-79; Pratt Institue, Brooklyn, N.Y., dean of School of Liberal Arts and Sciences and associate professor of English, 1979—, Betty T. Bennett Professor of English, 1981—.

MEMBER: Modern Language Association of America, American Association of University Professors, American Association of University Women, Keats-Shelley Association, Byron Association, Brooklyn College Alumni Association, New York University Alumni Association, Phi Beta Kappa.

AWARDS, HONORS: Fellow of National Endowment for the Humanities, 1974-75, 1984-86, and of American Council of Learned Societies, 1977-78; grant from American Philosophical Society, 1979-80.

WRITINGS:

British War Poetry in the Age of Romanticism, 1793-1815, Garland Publishing, 1976.
(Author of introduction) Mary Shelley, *Perkin Warbeck,* Folcroft, 1976.
(Co-editor and contributor) *Evidence of the Imagination,* New York University Press, 1978.
The Critical Temper, Ungar, 1978.
(Editor) *The Letters of Mary Wollstonecraft Shelley,* Johns Hopkins University Press, Volume I, 1980, Volume II, 1983.

WORK IN PROGRESS: Editing *The Letters of Mary Wollstonecraft Shelley,* Volume III, publication by Johns Hopkins University Press expected in 1987; a critical biography of Mary Wollstonecraft Shelley.

*   *   *

BENNETT, Boyce McLean, Jr.   1928-

PERSONAL: Born July 19, 1928, in Brownwood, Tex.; son of Boyce McLean (a pharmacist) and Ruby (a housewife; maiden name, Kyle) Bennett; married Mildred Edwards, January 15, 1956 (divorced, 1981); children: Rebecca Ann Bennett Hellman. *Education:* Texas A & M University, B.S., 1949; General Theological Seminary, M.Div., 1953, Th.D., 1969; Nashotah House, S.T.M., 1963.

ADDRESSES: Home and office—General Theological Seminary, 175 Ninth Ave., New York, N.Y. 10011.

CAREER: Ordained Episcopal minister, 1953; vicar of Episcopal mission in Dallas, Tex., 1953-56; curate of Episcopal church in Philadelphia, Pa., 1957-59; rector of Episcopal church in Menomonie, Wis., 1959-63; General Theological Seminary, New York, N.Y., instructor, 1968-69, assistant professor, 1969-70, professor of Old Testament, 1970—, sub-dean for academic affairs, 1984—. Lecturer at Bronxville Adult School, 1973—, and Cathedral School of Theology, 1974—. Assistant field supervisor at Tel Hasi Archaeological Excavation in Israel, 1974—. General Board of Examining Chaplains of the Episcopal Church, vice-chairman, 1974-82, chairman, 1982-83.

MEMBER: Society of Biblical Literature, American Schools of Oriental Research.

AWARDS, HONORS: James Alan Montgomery fellow of American Schools of Oriental Research, Jerusalem, Israel, 1967-68; grant from Catholic Diocese of New York's Commission on Ministry, 1974.

WRITINGS:

(Editor with David H. Scott) *Harper's Encyclopedia of Bible Life,* Harper, 1978.
Bennett's Guide to the Bible: Graphic Aids and Outlines, self-illustrated, Seabury, 1982.

Also author of "The Genius of Anglicanism" (filmstrip), released by Rectory Publishers, 1963. Contributor to *Encyclopedia Americana.* Contributor to scholarly journals.

*   *   *

BENNETT, Linda L(eveque)   1946-

PERSONAL: Born Sepember 30, 1946, in Lake Charles, La.; daughter of James Howard (a newspaper editor) and Ocie (a bookkeeper; maiden name, Johnson) Leveque; married Steven Logan Bennett (a U.S. Air Force captain; deceased); children: one. *Education:* University of Southwestern Louisiana, B.A., 1969; Our Lady of the Lake College (now Our Lady of the Lake University of San Antonio), M.S.L.S., 1974; further graduate study at University of Texas at San Antonio, 1974-77, and Louisiana State University.

ADDRESSES: Home—512 East Tenth Ave., Oakdale, La. 71463. *Office*—Allen Parish Library, P.O. Box 400, Oberlin, La. 70655.

CAREER: Glenmora Branch Library, Glenmora, La., library assistant, 1956-64; Howard County Public Library, Big Spring, Tex., assistant librarian, 1969-70; St. Luke's Episcopal Elementary School, San Antonio, Tex., head librarian, 1976-81; Allen Parish Library, Oberlin, La., director, 1983—.

MEMBER: American Library Association, Public Library Association, Library Administration and Management Association, American Library Trustee Association, Southeast Library Association, Louisiana Library Association.

WRITINGS:

Volunteers in the School Media Center, Libraries Unlimited, 1984.

SIDELIGHTS: Linda L. Bennett told *CA:* "My motivation in writing *Volunteers in the School Media Center* was to provide a framework, a system, for those who already wished to work with volunteers. In no way did I set out to try to convince anyone that volunteer programs are beneficial and fun. By the time revisions were complete, however, I was mildly surprised to find that much of the book did cover pros and cons of volunteer programs.

"Working with volunteers has been a source of delight for me. I have met some of the nicest people and accomplished some splendid projects because of volunteer programs. It has always bothered me when a valid idea is approached haphazardly and allowed to fail so that it provides 'proof' that the idea itself isn't worthwhile. Usually, any drawbacks of working with volunteers can be overcome, and some even used to advantage.

"How did I begin my writing career? Well, it was like this. I decided that I, like many people, firmly believed that I was capable of writing, and that it was time to prove or disprove the theory. Being a good librarian, I researched the system to discover how one went about getting published. The one thing I didn't want was to spend five years writing a magnum opus which would be seen twice a year when I cleaned the closet.

"I discovered that I should write query letters. So I used *Writer's Market,* found the publishers of different types of materials, and wrote each a letter suggesting topics about which I could write for them. I got a nibble from a children's magazine, a nip from a children's book publisher, and two large bites, one from *McCall's* and one from a children's nonfiction editor. None of those 'took,' but my last positive response did: 'Send chapter and outline.' Needless to say, chapter and outline didn't exist at that point. So, for the first time, I tried to write. After receiving a contract (a great thrill, I must say, as well as assurance that any work I did would come to something in the end) I sat down with my typewriter.

"Advice to new writers? Read about writing and publishing, so you'll know what to expect. Limit outside contacts, or make a schedule for yourself. Most of all, don't put off the decision. Go ahead and try. *Now!*"

* * *

BENVENISTE, Emile   1902-1976

OBITUARY NOTICE: Born May 25, 1902, in Aleppo, Syria, Ottoman Empire (now Syria); died October 3, 1976, in Versailles, Yvelines, France. Linguist, educator, and author. Benveniste was educated at the University of Paris's Sorbonne and at Ecole des Hautes Etudes, where he later served as director of studies in comparative grammar of Indo-European languages. From 1937 to 1969 he was professor of comparative grammar at the College de France. Throughout his career Benveniste concentrated on both ancient and modern Indo-European languages, with a particular focus on Iranian languages. His writings include *Problems in General Linguistics* and *Indo-European Language and Society*.

OBITUARIES AND OTHER SOURCES:

BOOKS

Twentieth-Century Culture: A Biographical Companion, Harper, 1983.

* * *

BENZIGER, Barbara Field   1918-

BRIEF ENTRY: Born January 6, 1918, in New York, N.Y. American author. Benziger founded the North Shore Community Hospital in 1946 and remained on its board of trustees for ten years. When she became the victim of mental illness, Benziger discovered that not even the affluent are safe from institutional cruelty, the deprivation of legal rights, the withdrawal of family support because of misunderstanding and fear, and the greed and incompetence of some professionals. The story of her illness and the painful road to recovery is the subject of Benziger's book, *The Prison of My Mind* (Walker & Co., 1969). The author received an award from the National Association of Mental Health in 1969 for her writing and other activities on behalf of the mentally ill. She later conducted a series of interviews with mental health professionals and patients. These resulted in another book, *Speaking Out: Thera-*

pists and Patients; How They Cure and Cope With Mental Illness Today (Walker & Co., 1976).

BIOGRAPHICAL/CRITICAL SOURCES:

PERIODICALS

Washington Post Book World, March 9, 1969.

* * *

BERG, Richard F(rederick)   1936-

PERSONAL: Born December 1, 1936, in Portland, Ore.; son of Richard Frederick (a physician) and Elizabeth (a housewife; maiden name, Eastman) Berg. *Education:* University of Notre Dame, B.A., 1959; Pontifical Gregorian University, S.T.B., 1963; University of Portland, M.A., 1967, Ph.D., 1969.

ADDRESSES: Office—College of Arts and Sciences, University of Portland, 5000 North Willamette Blvd., Portland, Ore. 97203.

CAREER: Entered Congregation of the Holy Cross, 1954, ordained Roman Catholic priest, 1963; Purdue University, West Lafayette, Ind., postdoctoral researcher, 1969-71; St. Edward's University, Austin, Tex., assistant professor of psychology, 1971-74; University of Portland, Portland, Ore., religious superior, 1974-78, associate professor of psychology and dean of arts and sciences, 1978—.

MEMBER: American Psychological Association, Oregon Psychological Association.

WRITINGS:

(With Christine McCartney) *Depression and the Integrated Life: A Christian Understanding of Sadness and Inner Suffering,* Alba House, 1981.

WORK IN PROGRESS: Research on health psychology, the psychology of healing, and motivation and aggression.

SIDELIGHTS: Richard F. Berg told *CA:* "*Depression and the Integrated Life* was written to provide a holistic perspective on the causes and treatment of clinical depression. It treats psychological, medical, and spiritual aspects of this disorder.

"The book grew out of our work with those who suffer either from depression or from sadness that affects the lives of all of us from time to time. Our experience in ministry and counseling with depressed people and their families and friends has led to an acute awareness of the increasing frequency with which depression occurs today and the physical, mental, and spiritual pain it engenders. Particular complications arise for the depressed Christian, who often is not understood by those who believe that 'good Christians do not get depressed, and also by others who cannot understand how depression afflicts one's faith life. This climate of misunderstanding by others, together with spiritual emptiness, doubt, and guilt which often accompany depression, produce an inner burden which only serves to deepen and prolong depression or sadness. Our work with people convinced us of the need for a readable book that specifically addresses the problems of depression in a faith context, such as how depression affects the spiritual life, prayer in the midst of depression, and spiritual approaches to healing.

"We are not satisfied that a purely spiritual approach is enough. Although a number of books on depression have been written by and for Christians, we did not know of any that included the very valid information that modern medicine and psychology have to offer. In fact, we are dismayed by well-meaning

Christians who reject or are unaware of medical and psychological insights into the causes and healing of depression. Because depression touches virtually all areas of our lives, we are convinced that the more effective approaches to treatment will be those designed to heal the whole person. We wrote *Depression and the Integrated Life*, then, in an effort to provide a holistic approach to the understanding and treatment of depression. Without in any way compromising medical-biological and emotional-psychological approaches, we have incorporated within the entire context of this book a spiritual approach helpful to one professing the Christian faith.

"In the first half of the book, many causes of depression are described; in the remaining chapters and epilogue, we have presented several avenues for the alleviation of depression and sadness. Present throughout the book is the fundamental notion that each person is a unity of body, mind, and spirit. What we feel makes this volume unique is that it includes, with the assistance of scripture and case histories, the Christian self as a vital resource in one's struggle toward physical, mental, and spiritual wholeness. It is our hope that this book will be of help not only to those who suffer from depression but also to the family members, friends, and others who are striving to help those who are depressed. The book is also intended for priests, ministers, pastoral counselors, nurses, social workers, and those in the healing ministries of prayer communities."

*   *   *

BERGER, David 1943-

PERSONAL: Born June 24, 1943, in Brooklyn, N.Y.; son of Isaiah and Shirley (Kravitz) Berger; married Pearl Rabinowitz (a librarian), 1965; children: Miriam, Yitzhak, Gedalyah. *Education:* Yeshiva University, B.A., 1964; Columbia University, M.A., 1965, Ph.D., 1970. *Religion:* Jewish.

ADDRESSES: Home—Flushing, N.Y. *Office*—Department of History, Brooklyn College of the City University of New York, Brooklyn, N.Y. 11210.

CAREER: Yeshiva University, New York, N.Y., instructor in Jewish history, 1968-70; Brooklyn College of the City University of New York, Brooklyn, N.Y., assistant professor, 1970-75, associate professor, 1976-80, professor of history, 1981—.

MEMBER: American Historical Association, Mediaeval Academy of America, American Academy for Jewish Research, Association for Jewish Studies (member of board of directors).

AWARDS, HONORS: John Nicholas Brown Prize from Mediaeval Academy of America, 1983, for *The Jewish-Christian Debate in the High Middle Ages*.

WRITINGS:

(With Michael Wyschogrod) *Jews and "Jewish Christianity,"* Ktav, 1978.
The Jewish-Christian Debate in the High Middle Ages: A Critical Edition of the Nizzahon Vetus, With an Introduction, Translation, and Commentary, Jewish Publication Society, 1979.
(Editor) *The Legacy of Jewish Migration: 1881 and Its Impact*, Brooklyn College Press, 1983.
(Editor) *Anti-Semitism in Historical Perspective*, Jewish Publication Society, in press.

Contributor to scholarly journals.

WORK IN PROGRESS: Research on medieval Jewish polemic and exegesis; research on Jewish-Christian relations.

SIDELIGHTS: David Berger told *CA:* "Though my work is essentially scholarly, the little book on 'Jewish Christianity' was written for more popular consumption at the request of the Jewish Community Relations Council of New York as a response to the missionary activity of groups like 'Jews for Jesus.' While maintaining a consistently respectful attitude toward Christianity, it seeks to persuade Jews that missionary propaganda makes untenable claims that must be resisted. Since such propaganda repeats the same type of arguments that were current in the medieval works that I have studied as a historian, this is one of the few instances in which a medievalist can find his work 'relevant' in a strikingly direct sense."

*   *   *

BERNSTEIN, Gail Lee 1939-

PERSONAL: Born February 22, 1939, in Brooklyn, N.Y.; daughter of Bernard and Edna (Levy) Bernstein. *Education:* Barnard College, B.A., 1959; Radcliffe College, M.A., 1961; Harvard University, Ph.D., 1968.

ADDRESSES: Office—Department of Oriental Studies, University of Arizona, Tucson, Ariz. 85721.

CAREER: University of Arizona, Tucson, assistant professor, 1967-72, associate professor, 1972-84, professor of Oriental studies, 1984—.

MEMBER: Association for Asian Studies (member of executive committee and board of trustees, 1982-84; chairperson of Northeast Asia Council, 1982-84).

AWARDS, HONORS: John K. Fairbank Prize in East Asian History from American Historical Association, 1977, for *Japanese Marxist*.

WRITINGS:

Japanese Marxist: A Portrait of Kawakami Hajime, Harvard University Press, 1976.
(Contributor) Joyce Lebra and others, editors, *Women in Changing Japan*, Westview, 1976.
(Contributor) Margarita Kay, editor, *An Anthropology of Human Birth*, F. A. Davis, 1981.
Haruko's World: A Japanese Farm Woman and Her Community, Stanford University Press, 1983.

Contributor to Asian studies journals. Member of editorial board of *Journal of Asian Studies*, 1978-83.

WORK IN PROGRESS: A study of women's work in pre-industrial Japan; a study of women in the silk reel industry in the early years of industrialization in Japan.

SIDELIGHTS: Gail Lee Bernstein told *CA:* "People often ask me how I happened to get into the field of Asian studies. It was by accident. My interest in Japan was sparked during my college days, when I became friends with the daughter of the first Japanese ambassador to the United Nations. The study of Asia was still considered an exotic occupation in the late 1950's, even though the United States had already fought a major war with Japan, had become involved in another conflict with Korea, and was about to become embroiled in yet another war with Vietnam.

"The study of Asia continues to satisfy my intellectual life, but it is distressing to note that, despite the growing economic and political importance to the United States of countries like China, Korea, and Japan, Americans remain dangerously parochial in their understanding of life beyond their own national boundaries. In some parts of the country, the study of Asia remains as exotic as it was when I started out twenty-five years ago.

"In my career as a university teacher and scholar, I share with my colleagues in the field of Asian studies a sense of urgency about the need to disseminate knowledge of Asia that will make the richness of non-Western civilizations available to more persons and that will equip them to work and live in the twenty-first century."

BIOGRAPHICAL/CRITICAL SOURCES:

PERIODICALS

American Historical Review, February, 1979.

* * *

BERRY, Charles Edward Anderson 1931-
(Chuck Berry)

PERSONAL: Professionally known as Chuck Berry; born October 18, 1931 (some sources say October 18, 1926, or January 15, 1926), in St. Louis, Mo. (some sources say San Jose, Calif.); son of Henry (a carpenter) and Martha Berry; married wife, Thelmetta; children: three daughters, one son. *Education:* Educated in St. Louis, Mo.

ADDRESSES: Agent—Bob Astor Management, 23 Holly Dr., LaPlace, La. 70068.

CAREER: Entertainer, composer, and lyricist, 1955—. Appeared in motion pictures. Also worked as a hairdresser and factory worker.

WRITINGS:

COMPOSER AND LYRICIST

Songs include: "Maybelline," "Roll Over Beethoven," "Sweet Little Sixteen," "Johnny B. Goode," "Jo Jo Gunne," "Back in the U.S.A.," "Too Pooped to Pop," "Nadine," "My Ding-A-Ling," "Reelin' and Rockin'," "Memphis," "Come On," "Little Queenie," "The Promised Land," "Carol," "School Day," and "No Particular Place to Go."

RECORDINGS

After School Sessions, Chess, 1958.
One Dozen Berrys, Chess, 1958.
Chuck Berry on Stage, Chess, 1963.
St. Louis to Liverpool, Chess, 1964.
(With Bo Diddley) *Two Great Guitars*, Checker, 1964.
Chuck Berry in London, Chess, 1965.
Golden Decade, Chess, 1967.
Golden Hits, Chess, 1967.
Chuck Berry in Memphis, Chess, 1967.
Live at the Filmore, Chess, 1967.
From St. Louis to Frisco, Chess, 1968.
The London Chuck Berry Sessions, Chess, 1972.
St. Louis to Frisco to Memphis, Mercury/Phillips, 1972.
San Francisco Dues, Chess, 1972.
Bio, Chess, 1973.
Chuck Berry '75, Chess, 1975.
Rockit, Chess, 1979.

Also recorded *Chuck Berry Is on Top, Rockin' at the Hop, New Juke Box Hit, Twist, Chuck Berry's Greatest Hits, Golden*

Decade, Vol. II, Golden Decade, Volume III, Back Home, and others.

SIDELIGHTS: Singer, musician, and composer Chuck Berry is considered among the most influential figures in the development of rock and roll music. He was discovered in Chicago in 1955 when he sat in on a recording session with the legendary blues singer, Muddy Waters. Waters introduced Berry to Chess Records magnate Leonard Chess, who offered Berry a contract. Berry's first recording, "Maybelline," was an instant hit, and the single's flip side, "Wee Wee Hours," also fared well on the music charts.

Berry subsequently enjoyed only moderate commercial success until "Roll Over Beethoven" rose to number twenty-nine on the top hundred chart. Despite the unimpressive sales of his records, Berry was establishing a following of devotees who identified with his songs, many of which are credited with influencing the youth counter-culture of the fifties and sixties. "Roll Over Beethoven," for example, mocked high culture, while "Too Much Monkey Business" dealt with the pressures and problems of education, labor, and the military, whereas "Brown-Eyed Handsome Man" portrayed the plight of the black man in the fifties.

Berry's stage presence has brought him nearly as much fame as his tunes. His trademark is the "duck walk," a squatty, knees-bent walk that he uses to move about the stage. In a *Rolling Stone* interview Berry revealed that the duck walk was introduced in 1956 at New York's Paramount Theatre. "I had to outfit my trio, . . . and I always remember the suits cost me $66, $22 apiece. They were rayon, but looked like seersucker by the time we got there. I actually did the duck walk to hide the wrinkles in the suit—I got an ovation, so I figured I pleased the audience, so I did it again, and again."

Berry's career knew one of its better years in 1958, when "Sweet Little Sixteen," "Johnny B. Goode," "Reelin' and Rockin'," "Around and Around," "Beautiful Delilah," and several other songs made the top 100 chart in the United States. His popularity also brought him parts in four films: "Rock, Rock, Rock," "Mr. Rock and Roll," "Go Johnny Go," and "'Jazz on a Summer's Day." But his success waned in the following years—in 1959 and 1960 he recorded fewer tunes that made the "Hot Hundred" charts, and his image was damaged when he was arrested under the Mann Act for taking a fourteen-year-old girl across state lines for immoral purposes. A bitter two-year trial ensued, and Berry, found guilty, was sentenced to a two-year term in the Indiana State Penitentiary.

Upon his release from prison, Berry found the music industry dominated by British groups—primarily the Beatles and the Rolling Stones. Berry began touring Great Britain, where his musical style and expertise on the guitar influenced many British acts; both the Beatles and Stones recorded songs previously done by Berry. Many American musicians also recorded Berry's compositions; Elvis Presley, the Beach Boys, Buddy Holly, and Bob Dylan were among the artists who were inspired by Berry's music and made his songs hits. Although Berry had few hits of his own during this time, in 1972 his risque "My Ding-A-Ling" reached the number two spot in the United States.

To date Berry has never equaled the success of "My Ding-A-Ling," but his popularity as a performer has not diminished. He does many concerts for universities and appears frequently in nostalgic concerts with some of his contemporaries, including Chubby Checker and Bo Diddley.

BIOGRAPHICAL/CRITICAL SOURCES:

BOOKS

Contemporary Literary Criticism, Gale, Volume 17, 1981.
The Rolling Stone Interviews, Straight Arrow Books, 1971.*

* * *

BERRY, Chuck
    See BERRY, Charles Edward Anderson

* * *

BERTHOLF, Diana   1946-

PERSONAL: Born September 23, 1946; married Clifford L. Bertholf, Jr. (an attorney); children: Marlee Suzanne, Christopher Lee. *Education:* Ohio University, B.F.A., 1968; graduate study at University of Kansas, 1969-72. *Religion;* United Methodist.

ADDRESSES: Home—8229 Brookhollow Lane, Wichita, Kan. 67206.

CAREER: Preschool teacher, 1972-80, at First Presbyterian Church Preschool in Lawrence, Kan., and at Mt. Olivet Methodist Church in Wichita, Kan.; writer, 1981—. Public speaker. Member of Wichita Junior League and Hospice of Wichita; past member of board of directors of Kansas Dance Foundation, Kansas Humane Society, and Wichita Community Theater.

AWARDS, HONORS: Special award from Wichita Community Theater, 1982.

WRITINGS:

Diana's Star (autobiography), Tyndale, 1983.

Contributor to *Guidepost.*

WORK IN PROGRESS: With Doug Morphis, a book on divorce and grief recovery for United Methodist Board of Discipleship; a book on evangelism and church growth, for Abingdon; a novel about Korea in the 1950's; a novel about the aftermath of the Vietnam war.

SIDELIGHTS: Diana Bertholf is a Christian who was converted from Judaism as a young woman. She told *CA:* "I am in the process of writing two novels. They will both deal with the pain inherent in life and how human will can overcome great adversity. My viewpoint is Christian and is directed toward mainstream Christians. There is a need for good fiction in the Christian market.

"I especially love the Orient, Korea particularly, and I hope to travel there soon to watch, listen, and do research."

BIOGRAPHICAL/CRITICAL SOURCES:

PERIODICALS

Biblical Evangelist, March, 1984.
Christian Life, December, 1983.
United Methodist Reporter, December, 1983.

* * *

BERTHRONG, Evelyn Nagai
    See NAGAI BERTHRONG, Evelyn

BESSIE, Constance Ernst   1918(?)-1985

OBITUARY NOTICE: Born c. 1918 in New York, N.Y.; died of cancer, March 19, 1985, in New York, N.Y. Producer, director, journalist, and editor. Bessie, a graduate of Bennington College, began her career in London during World War II as a producer of radio programs for the Voice of America. She helped create and eventually became assistant producer of "Theatre U.S.A.," an American National Theatre and Academy radio program that was later moved to television. Bessie, one of the founders of Atheneum Publishers, also produced radio programs for the Columbia Broadcasting System (CBS-Radio) and served as a correspondent and editor of *Newsweek*'s letter column.

OBITUARIES AND OTHER SOURCES:

PERIODICALS

Newsweek, April 1, 1985.
New York Times, March 22, 1985.

* * *

BEST, Hugh   1920-

PERSONAL: Born May 16, 1920, in Rome, Ga.; son of Hugh H. (an automobile dealer and horseman) and Eliza (Patterson) Best; married Barbara Thornburgh (a manager), May 13, 1950; children: Donald Patterson, Barbara Kelsey, Christopher James. *Education:* Attended Washington and Lee University, 1937-39; University of Georgia, A.B.J., 1941; graduate study at Columbia University, 1946. *Religion:* Presbyterian.

ADDRESSES: Home—Wayne, Pa. *Office*—Chilton Book Co., 201 King of Prussia Rd., Radnor, Pa. 19089. *Agent*—Jacques de Spoelberch, J de S Associates, Inc., Shagbark Rd., Wilson Point, South Norwalk, Conn. 06854.

CAREER: House Beautiful, New York City, assistant publisher, 1946-48; *Holiday,* Philadelphia, Pa., advertising promotion, 1948-54; N.W. Ayer, Philadelphia, advertising copywriter, 1954-60; Arndt, Preston, Chapin, Lamb & Keen Advertising (APCL&K), New York City and Philadelphia, vice-president and creative director, 1960-73; *Homestyle,* Wayne, Pa., editor and publisher, 1974-75; Best Advertising & Promotion Co., Wayne, president, 1975—. Creator of corporate communications for Chilton Book Co.

WRITINGS:

Spirit of a Century: Biography of a Church, Jarratt Press, 1975.
Red Hot and Blue: An X-Rated History of the American Revolution, New Hope Publishing, 1976.
Debrett's Texas Peerage, Putnam, 1983.
Debrett's Southern Peerage, Putnam, 1985.

TELEVISION SCRIPTS

"Ranger Joe," first broadcast by WPVI-TV (Philadelphia), 1950.
"Willie," first broadcast by WCAU-TV (Philadephia), 1951.
"Action in the Afternoon," first broadcast by WCAU-TV, 1951.
"Vacation Ventures," first broadcast by WCAU-TV, 1953.

PLAYS

"Take It Off: A Burlesque of Burlesque" (two-act musical), first produced in Pampa, Tex., for U.S. Army Air Forces, February 14, 1945.

Also author of children's story "The Enchanted Mill," published in *Jack and Jill,* and of book inserts for ABC Sports. Contributor to magazines, including *Town and Country, Ultra,* and *Travel and Leisure,* and to newspapers.

WORK IN PROGRESS: A book, *Wonderful Weddings (and Some Not So): A Hundred Years of America's Legendary Nuptials;* articles for *Town and Country* and *Travel and Leisure.*

SIDELIGHTS: Hugh Best told *CA:* "Reviewers find my books 'a jolly good read' and say I have a 'bourbon-and-branch-water' style. My books for Debrett are not 'listings' like the social register. Debrett asked me to write its first book in America on the social history of various sections, for the publisher liked my work in *Town and Country.* Suddenly, I became a 'social arbiter' since I alone chose the families to appear in my Texas peerage and Southern peerage books and my *Town and Country* articles. Publishers ask me to write books on etiquette, thoroughbred horses, polo—all 'social.' I enjoy writing social history and travel pieces and do a lot of both."

BIOGRAPHICAL/CRITICAL SOURCES:

PERIODICALS

Barron's, June 14, 1984.
People, July, 1984.
Philadelphia Inquirer, March 12, 1984.
Time, May 30, 1983.
Ultra, November, 1983.
Vanity Fair, December, 1983.
Wilmington Times, October 13, 1983.

* * *

BETHE, H. A.
   See BETHE, Hans Albrecht

* * *

BETHE, Hans A.
   See BETHE, Hans Albrecht

* * *

BETHE, Hans Albrecht 1906-
   (H. A. Bethe, Hans A. Bethe)

BRIEF ENTRY: Born July 2, 1906, in Strassburg, Germany (now Strasbourg, France). American physicist, educator, and author. A Nobel laureate in physics in 1967, Bethe was a professor of physics at Cornell University from 1937 to 1975. During World War II he directed the Theoretical Physics Division at Los Alamos Scientific Laboratory, and before the war he taught at universities in Germany and England. Bethe's research on nuclear fusion led indirectly to the development of the hydrogen bomb, but it also directed scientific research toward the possibility of unlimited power supplies for the future, based on controlled nuclear fusion. In addition to the Nobel Prize, Bethe's honors include the Max Planck Medal, the Enrico Fermi Award of the Atomic Energy Commission, and the National Medal of Science. Among his numerous technical and scientific publications are *Elementary Nuclear Theory* (Wiley, 1947) and *Intermediate Quantum Mechanics* (W. A. Benjamin, 1964). Bethe also wrote *American Energy Choices Before the Year 2000* (Lexington Books, 1978). *Address:* c/o Laboratory of Nuclear Studies, Cornell University, Ithaca, N.Y. 14853.

BIOGRAPHICAL/CRITICAL SOURCES:

BOOKS

Bernstein, Jeremy, *Hans Bethe, Prophet of Energy,* Basic Books, 1980.
Current Biography, Wilson, 1950.
Who's Who in America, 42nd edition, Bowker, 1982.

* * *

BILEK, Arthur J(ohn) 1929-

PERSONAL: Surname is pronounced *Bee*-lick; born October 21, 1929, in Chicago, Ill.; son of Arthur John (a businessman) and Marcella (a homemaker; maiden name, Nohren) Bilek; married Angela Concetta Vignola (a homemaker), October 23, 1954; children: Mary Lucille Bilek Marcu, Arthur John III, Judy Ann Bilek Zoromski, Mark Joseph. *Education:* Loyola University of Chicago, B.S., 1951, M.S.W., 1953; Northwestern University, Diploma, 1962. *Religion:* Roman Catholic.

ADDRESSES: Office—First National Bank of Chicago, Chicago, Ill. 60670.

CAREER: Chicago Police Department, Chicago, Ill., 1953-62, began as patrolman, became training director; Cook County Sheriff's Police Department, Chicago, chief of police, 1962-67; University of Illinois at Chicago Circle, Chicago, professor of criminal justice and chairman of department, 1967-70; Illinois Law Enforcement Commission, Chicago, chairman, 1969-72; Hilton Hotels, Inc., Chicago, corporate security director, 1972-74; Pinkerton's, Inc., Chicago, corporate vice-president for development, 1974-76; independent security consultant in Chicago, 1976-77; CFS Continental, Inc., Chicago, corporate security director, 1977-78; First National Bank of Chicago, Chicago, director of security risk management and vice-president, 1978—. *Military service:* U.S. Army, special agent in Counter Intelligence Corps, 1953-55. U.S. Army Reserve, Civil Affairs/Military Government Corps, 1958-60; became first lieutenant.

MEMBER: International Banking Security Association (chairman, 1982—), American Society for Industrial Security, Asset Protection Executives.

WRITINGS:

(Editor) *Private Security,* Anderson Publishing, 1977.
(with R. Kegan Federal and John Klotter) *Legal Aspects of Private Security,* Anderson Publishing, 1979.

WORK IN PROGRESS: Research on organized crime in Chicago, frauds and deceptions, great myths, organized crime in the United States, and corruption in law enforcement.

* * *

BINYON, (Robert) Laurence 1869-1943

BRIEF ENTRY: Born August 10, 1869, in Lancaster, England; died March 10 (some sources say March 11), 1943, in Reading, England. British art historian, critic, translator, playwright, and poet. Binyon was a British Museum official for forty years, during which time he became a respected authority on Oriental art and English letters. He wrote numerous books on art, including *Painting in the Far East* (1908), and lectured throughout the world on art and literature. He succeeded T. S. Eliot as Norton Professor of Poetry at Harvard University, was named chevalier of the French Legion of Honor, and was appointed to the Byron Chair of Letters at the University of Athens.

In addition to writing books on art, Binyon published many collections of poetry and was best known for his poem about World War I, "For the Fallen," which appeared in his book *The Winnowing Fan: Poems on the Great War* (1914). He wrote several plays that were produced in London, and he frequently contributed to the *New York Times*. During the 1930's, Binyon translated Dante's *Divine Comedy*. Among his other works are two odes, *The Sirens* (1924) and *The Idols* (1928), and the two-volume *Collected Poems of Laurence Binyon* (1931). *Address:* Westridge Farm House, Streatly, Berkshire, England.

BIOGRAPHICAL/CRITICAL SOURCES:

BOOKS

Dictionary of Literary Biography, Volume 19: *British Poets, 1840-1914*, Gale, 1983.
Longman Companion to Twentieth Century Literature, Longman, 1970.
Twentieth-Century Authors: A Biographical Dictionary of Modern Literature, H. W. Wilson, 1942, 1st supplement, 1955.
Who Was Who in the Theatre, 1912-1976, Gale, 1978.

PERIODICALS

New York Times, March 11, 1943.

*   *   *

BIXLER, Julius Seelye   1894-1985

OBITUARY NOTICE: Born April 4, 1894, in New London, Connecticut; died of pneumonia, March 28 (one source says March 29), 1985, in Weston, Mass. Philosopher, educator, administrator, and author. Bixler, one of the first American scholars to explore European existentialism, German phenomenology, and German and Swiss crisis theology, was president of Colby College in Maine from 1942 to 1960. Among his achievements as president of Colby College was the establishment of a fine arts department. Bixler began his teaching career at the American College in Madura, India, where he was an instructor in Latin and English. He later taught at American University in Beirut, Lebanon, and served on the faculties of Smith College and Harvard University. During his scholarly career, Bixler maintained friendships with such eminent philosophers as Albert Schweitzer and Martin Heidegger. His last book, *German Recollections: Some of My Best Friends Were Philosophers*, is scheduled to be published posthumously. His other writings include *Religion in the Philosophy of William James*, *Immortality and the Present Mood*, *Conversations With an Unrepentant Liberal*, *A Faith That Fulfills*, and *Education for Adversity*.

OBITUARIES AND OTHER SOURCES:

BOOKS

American Authors and Books: 1640 to the Present Day, 3rd revised edition, Crown, 1962.
Who Was Who in Literature: 1906-1934, Gale, 1979.

PERIODICALS

New London Day (Connecticut), March 29, 1985.
New York Times, April 2, 1985.

BLACK, Dorothy   1899-1985

OBITUARY NOTICE: Born September 13, 1899, in Johannesburg, Transvaal (now Republic of South Africa); died February 19, 1985, in London, England. Actress and playwright. Black was best known for her 1933 portrayal of author Emily Bronte in a British stage production of "The Brontes." Following her London debut in "The Farmer's Wife" in 1925, Black performed for the next twenty years in such plays as "Six Characters in Search of an Author," "Rasputin," "Everyman," and "Love's Labours Lost." She was noted for her ability to play intense characters such as Lady Macbeth in "Macbeth," Gertrude in "Hamlet," and Mrs. Dearth in "Dear Brutus." Her writings include "The Edwardians" a stage adaptation that was produced in 1932.

OBITUARIES AND OTHER SOURCES:

PERIODICALS

Times (London), February 23, 1985.

*   *   *

BLACKER, Irwin R(obert)   1919-1985

OBITUARY NOTICE—See index for *CA* sketch: Born October 6, 1919, in Cleveland, Ohio; died of a heart attack, February 23, 1985, in Sherman Oaks, Calif. Educator, critic, and author of screenplays and books. Blacker taught English at Purdue University from 1949 to 1950 and then worked briefly for the Central Intelligence Agency. In 1954 he became staff director at the Jewish Theological Seminary and in 1956 went to work for the Columbia Broadcasting System (CBS-TV) as a writer. Blacker joined the faculty of the University of Southern California, Los Angeles, in the early 1960's, becoming professor of cinema and chairman of graduate studies at the university's School of Cinema and Television before his retirement in 1978.

During his tenure at Southern California Blacker taught a number of students who were to become noted writers, directors, and producers, including George Lucas, creator of the "Star Wars" film series. He also served as story consultant to CBS and the National Broadcasting Corporation (NBC-TV) and wrote numerous screenplays for television series, including "Bonanza," "Odyssey," and "Conquest." He wrote more than twenty books of fiction and nonfiction, including *Westering, Taos, The Old West in Fiction, The Old West in Fact, Chain of Command,* and *Search and Destroy.* In addition, he edited and co-edited a number of books, and he reviewed books for the *Los Angeles Times.*

OBITUARIES AND OTHER SOURCES:

PERIODICALS

Chicago Tribune, February 26, 1985.
Daily Variety, February 25, 1985.
Los Angeles Times, February 24, 1985.
New York Times, February 25, 1985.

*   *   *

BLACKWELL, Betsy Talbot   1905(?)-1985

OBITUARY NOTICE: Born c. 1905 in New York, N.Y.; died of cancer, February 4, 1985, in Norwalk, Conn. Editor. Blackwell was best known as editor in chief of *Mademoiselle*, a fashion and beauty magazine for young women that, under her leadership, became recognized for its role in expanding women's social consciousness and encouraging its readers to pursue their educational and career goals. Blackwell's career began in 1923 when she joined the staff of *The Breath of the Avenue* magazine as a fashion reporter. Within a year she moved to *Charm* magazine and served on its editorial staff until 1931. After working as an advertising manager and promoter of children's clothes, she joined the newly founded *Mademoiselle* in 1935 and two years later became its editor in chief, a position she held until her retirement in 1971. A recipient of the 1942 Neiman-Marcus Award for distinguished service in the field of fashion and the 1953 Junior Achievement Award for Inspiration to Youth, Blackwell sought to broaden *Mademoiselle*'s literary appeal by showcasing such authors as Dylan Thomas and William Faulkner and by establishing an annual writing competion and scholarship.

OBITUARIES AND OTHER SOURCES:

BOOKS

Current Biography, Wilson, 1954, April, 1985.
Rayner, William P., *Wise Women,* St. Martin's, 1983.
Who's Who in America, 38th edition, Marquis, 1974.

PERIODICALS

Newsweek, February 18, 1985.
New York Times, February 5, 1985.

* * *

BLACKWOOD, Easley 1903-

PERSONAL: Born June 25, 1903, in Birmingham, Ala.; son of Easley John and Eudora (Rutland) Blackwood; married Beatrice Overall, July 4, 1926 (died October 28, 1982); children: Easley. *Education:* Attended high school. *Politics:* Republican. *Religion:* "Deist."

ADDRESSES: Home and office—3801 North Meridian, Apt. 2008, Indianapolis, Ind. 46208.

CAREER: Metropolitan Life Insurance Company, Indianapolis, Ind., general manager of Riley Branch, 1934-64; Blackwood Bridge Enterprises, Indianapolis, founder and manager, 1964—.

MEMBER: American Contract Bridge League (executive secretary and general manager, 1968-71; honorary member, 1980—), American Bridge Teachers (honorary member, 1978—).

AWARDS, HONORS: Mayor of Indianapolis proclaimed October 28, 1977, Easley Blackwood Day.

WRITINGS:

Bridge Humanics: How to Play People as Well as the Cards, Droke House, 1949.
Blackwood on Bidding: Dynamic Point Count, Bobbs-Merrill, 1956.
Blackwood on Slams, Prentice-Hall, 1970.
Winning Bridge With Blackwood, Pinnacle Press, 1978.
Play of the Hand With Blackwood, Corwin, 1978.
The Complete Book of Opening Leads, Devyn Press, 1983.
Balance With the Odds, Devyn Press, 1985.
Signaling at Bridge, Devyn Press, in press.

Contributor of syndicated column in *Indianapolis News,* 1952—. Also contributor of monthly article to *American Contract Bridge League Bulletin.*

WORK IN PROGRESS: Third Hand Fear Play, publication by Devyn Press expected in 1987.

BIOGRAPHICAL/CRITICAL SOURCES:

BOOKS

Sue Emery, *No Passing Fancy,* American Contract Bridge League, 1977.
The Encyclopedia of Bridge, fifth edition, Crown, 1984.

* * *

BLAKISTON, Noel 1905-1984

OBITUARY NOTICE: Born in 1905; died December 22, 1984. Civil servant and author. Balkiston was considered an authority on the *Risorgimento,* the nineteenth-century Italian movement for political unity. Educated at Cambridge University's Magdalene College, he worked in the Research and Modern Records Department of the Public Records Office in Britain from 1928 until his retirement as principal assistant keeper in 1970. During his career Blakiston catalogued the documents and charters of Eton College dating back to the fourteenth century. His efforts were rewarded by Eton in 1974, when Blakiston was made an honorary fellow of the college. In addition to four volumes of short stories, he wrote *The Roman Question* and published a collection of letters from Cyril Connolly titled *A Romantic Friendship.*

OBITUARIES AND OTHER SOURCES:

PERIODICALS

Times (London), January 4, 1985.

* * *

BLONDELL, (Rose) Joan 1906(?)-1979

PERSONAL: Born August 30, c. 1906, in New York, N.Y; died of leukemia, December 25, 1979, in Santa Monica, Calif.; daughter of Edward (a vaudeville performer) and Kathryn (a vaudeville performer; maiden name, Cain) Blondell; married George S. Barnes (a cinematographer; divorced); married Dick Powell (an actor and singer), June, 1937 (divorced, 1944); married Mike Todd (a show business entrepreneur), 1946 (divorced, 1950); children: (first marriage) Norman Scott Powell; (second marriage) Ellen Powell. *Education:* Attended various public schools while traveling with family vaudeville troupe.

CAREER: Member of family vaudeville act, 1915-27, appearing in Europe, Australia, China, and the United States; actress, 1927-79; stage performances include "The Trial of Mary Dugan," 1927, "Maggie, the Magnificent," 1929, "Penny Arcade," 1930, "The Naked Genius," 1943, "Call Me Madam," 1952, "A Tree Grows in Brooklyn," 1952, "Come Back Little Sheba," "The Time of the Cuckoo," "Happy Birthday," "Copper and Brass," "The Rope Dancers," 1957, "Crazy October," "A Palm Tree in a Rose Garden," "The Dark at the Top of the Stairs," 1959-60, "Bye Bye Birdie," 1961, "Watch the Birdie," and "The Effect of Gamma Rays on Man-in-the-Moon Marigolds."

Motion picture performances include "Sinners' Holiday," 1930, "Steel Highway," 1930, "Office Wife," 1930, "Blonde Crazy," 1930, "God's Gift to Women," 1931, "Illicit," 1931, "Ex-Mistress," 1931, "Local Boy Makes Good," 1931, "Millie," 1931, "My Past," 1931, "Night Nurse," 1931, "Reckless Hour," 1931, "Men's Women," 1931, "Larceny Lane," 1931, "Public Enemy," 1931, "Central Park," 1932, "Crowd Roars," 1932, "Big City Blues," 1932, "Famous Ferguson Case," 1932, "Lawyer Man," 1932, "Make Me a

Star,'' 1932, ''Miss Pinkerton,'' 1932, ''Greeks Had a Word for Them,'' 1932, ''Three on a Match,'' 1932, ''Union Depot,'' 1932, ''Blondie Johnson,'' 1933, ''Convention City,'' 1933, ''Gold Diggers of 1933,'' 1933, ''Broadway Bad,'' 1933, ''Goodbye Again,'' 1933, ''Havana Widows,'' 1933, ''Dames,'' 1934, ''He Was Her Man,'' 1934, ''I've Got Your Number,'' 1934, ''Kansas City Princess,'' 1934, ''Merry Wives of Reno,'' 1934, ''Smarty,'' 1934, ''Broadway Gondolier,'' 1935, ''Maybe It's Love,'' 1935, ''Miss Pacific Fleet,'' 1935, ''Traveling Saleslady,'' 1935, ''We're in the Money,'' 1935.

''Stage Struck,'' 1936, ''Bullets or Ballots,'' 1936, ''Sons o' Guns,'' 1936, ''Colleen,'' 1936, ''Gold Diggers of 1937,'' 1936, ''Three Men on a Horse,'' 1936, ''Perfect Specimen,'' 1937, ''Stand In,'' 1937, ''Back in Circulation,'' 1937, ''The King and the Chorus Girl,'' 1937, ''There's Always a Woman,'' 1938, ''The Amazing Mr. Williams,'' 1939, ''East Side of Heaven,'' 1939, ''Good Girls Go to Paris,'' 1939, ''Kid From Kokomo,'' 1939, ''Off the Record,'' 1939, ''I Want a Divorce,'' 1940, ''Two Girls on Broadway,'' 1940, ''Lady for a Night,'' 1941, ''The Nurse's Secret,'' 1941, ''Model Wife,'' 1941, ''Three Girls About Town,'' 1941, ''Topper Returns,'' 1941, ''Cry Havoc,'' 1943, ''A Tree Grows in Brooklyn,'' 1945, ''Don Juan Quilligan,'' 1945, ''Adventure,'' 1945, ''Christmas Eve,'' 1947, ''The Corpse Came C.O.D.,'' 1947, ''Nightmare Alley,'' 1947, ''Without Honor,'' 1949, ''For Heaven's Sake,'' 1950, ''The Blue Veil,'' 1951, ''The Opposite Sex,'' 1956, ''Desk Set,'' 1957, ''Lizzie,'' 1957, ''This Could Be the Night,'' 1957, ''Will Success Spoil Rock Hunter?,'' 1957, ''Angel Baby,'' 1961, ''Company of Cowards,'' 1963, ''Advance to the Rear,'' ''The Cincinnati Kid,'' ''Ride for Vengeance,'' ''Paradise Road,'' ''Waterhole Number Three,'' ''Kona Coast,'' ''Stay Away Joe,'' ''The Phynx,'' ''Support Your Local Gunfighter,'' ''Won Ton Ton, The Dog Who Saved Hollywood,'' ''Grease,'' and ''The Champ,'' 1979.

Television performances include ''Studio One,'' ''Playhouse 90,'' ''Hallmark Hall of Fame,'' ''Here Come the Brides'' series, 1968-70, and ''Banyon,'' 1972, and guest appearances on weekly programs, including ''McCloud,'' ''Medical Center,'' and ''The Rookies''; radio performer.

MEMBER: Screen Actors Guild, American Federation of Television and Radio Artists, Actors' Equity Association, American Guild of Variety Artists (AGVA).

AWARDS, HONORS: Box Office award, 1930's; Academy Award nomination for best supporting actress from Academy of Motion Picture Arts and Sciences, 1951, for ''The Blue Veil''; Global award nomination, 1960's.

WRITINGS:

Center Door Fancy (autobiographical novel), Delacorte, 1972.

SIDELIGHTS: Veteran stage, motion picture, and television actress Joan Blondell made her show business debut at the age of four months in her parents' traveling vaudeville act. Daughter of Eddie Blondell, the original ''Katzenjammer Kid,'' Joan soon became an active member of the family variety troupe, touring in the United States, Europe, Australia, and China. In 1927 the young performer joined an acting stock company and by 1929 she had a major role on the New York stage in ''Maggie, the Magnificent''; a year later she and fellow newcomer James Cagney caught the attention of theatregoers in ''Penny Arcade'' and signed movie contracts with Warner Brothers Studios, moving to Hollywood to recreate their roles on the screen in ''Sinners' Holiday.''

As a contract actress at Warners, Blondell made dozens of films in quick succession, working with such Hollywood leading men as Cagney, Clark Gable, Robert Taylor, and Dick Powell. Originally stereotyped as a gun moll, the actress used her song-and-dance background to break into the era's musicals, like ''Footlight Parade'' and ''Dames.'' Most of the characters she portrayed were brassy, wisecracking, and self-reliant—secretaries, girl reporters, showgirls. Charles Higham wrote in the *New York Times* that Blondell ''croaking 'Remember My Forgotten Man' under the lamp-post in 'Gold Diggers of 1933' . . . symbolizes, in that superb sequence, the thirties, just as Crawford in broad-shouldered mink on a fog-cloaked wharf in 'Mildred Pierce' absolutely symbolizes the forties.'' Yet feeling that Warners was giving her largely undistinguished roles, Blondell joined Columbia Pictures in 1938 and later turned to Twentieth Century-Fox for more challenging parts.

''I've had a very long career,'' Blondell once said, ''with not very good material under me.'' Yet critics regarded her performances in later films—after she had outgrown her young, saucy image—as affecting character portrayals. Most notable were her roles in ''Adventure,'' ''Nightmare Alley,'' and as Aunt Cissy in ''A Tree Grows in Brooklyn,'' which Blondell considered ''the best piece of acting I have ever done.'' In 1951 the performer received an Academy Award nomination as best supporting actress in ''The Blue Veil.''

Blondell continued to perform frequently in films, on stage, and in television until her death in 1979. In 1972 the actress published an autobiographical novel, *Center Door Fancy*, in which her heroine, Nora, survives the twilight years of vaudeville and goes on to capture Hollywood stardom. Martin Levin wrote in the *New York Times Book Review* that ''in this lively, warm and funny novel by Joan Blondell . . . the particulars are recognizable.'' ''Any reader who is a stage-and-screen buff will enjoy Nora's journey, at all its hectic stages,'' he added. ''They don't make theater/picture careers like this anymore.''

AVOCATIONAL INTERESTS: Writing, painting.

BIOGRAPHICAL/CRITICAL SOURCES:

PERIODICALS

New York Times, August 20, 1972.
New York Times Book Review, October 22, 1972.
Variety, October 25, 1972.
Washington Post Book World, October 28, 1973.

OBITUARIES

New York Times, December 26, 1979.
Washington Post, December 26, 1979.*

*   *   *

BLOOM, Ken(neth) 1949-

PERSONAL: Born November 28, 1949, in Silver Spring, Md.; son of George (an accountant) and Florence (an accountant; maiden name, Berkowitz) Bloom. *Education:* Attended University of Maryland, 1969-72.

ADDRESSES: Home—532 West 50th St., No. 4AR, New York, N.Y. 10019. *Office*—Lucy Stille, Sanford J. Greenburger Associates, Inc., 55 Fifth Ave., New York, N.Y. 10003.

CAREER: New Playwrights Theatre, Washington, D.C., associate producer and director, 1970-79; *Washington Post*,

Washington, D.C., editor of "Washington Season," 1979-81; Broadway correspondent for Canadian Broadcasting and National Public Radio, 1981-83; Harbinger Records, New York, N.Y., president, 1983—. Assistant company manager of the Joffrey Ballet, spring, 1985. Consultant to Wolf Trap Farm Park, Smithsonian Institution's Division of Performing Arts, Theatre Collection of the Museum of the City of New York, Library of Performing Arts at Lincoln Center, Brooklyn Academy of Music, and American Society of Composers, Authors, and Publishers (ASCAP).

MEMBER: National Academy of Recording Arts and Sciences, Dramatists Guild.

WRITINGS:

American Song, Volume I: *The Complete Musical Theatre Companion, 1900-1984,* Facts on File, 1985.
Encyclopedia of Times Square and Broadway, Facts on File, 1985.

Also author of musical comedies.

WORK IN PROGRESS: Biographical Encyclopedia of the American Musical.

SIDELIGHTS: Ken Bloom told *CA* that he is especially interested in musical theatre and popular song. As the president of Harbinger Records, he co-produced the original cast album of Geraldine Fitzgerald's performance in "Streetsongs" and "Maxine Sullivan Sings the Songs of Harold Arlen and Ted Koehler." With his partner, Bill Rudman, he is producing "Maxine Sullivan Sings the Burton Lane Songbook." Also forthcoming is an album of rare types by Harold Arlen.

The author has directed musical revues based on the works of Arlen, Cole Porter, Dietz and Schwartz, and Jerome Kern. The Kern revue was adapted for a series of programs broadcast by Pennsylvania Public Television. Bloom has also directed original musical comedies, both in Washington and New York City.

*   *   *

BLUESTONE, Barry A(lan) 1944-

PERSONAL: Born December 27, 1944, in Brooklyn, N.Y.; son of Irving and Zelda (Fitch) Bluestone. *Education:* University of Michigan, B.A., 1966, M.A., 1968, Ph.D., 1974.

ADDRESSES: Office—Department of Economics, Boston College, 140 Commonwealth Ave., Chestnut Hill, Mass. 02167.

CAREER: Boston College, Chestnut Hill, Mass., instructor, 1971-74, assistant professor, 1974-77, associate professor, 1977-82, professor of economics, 1982—, director of Social Welfare Research Institute, 1977-84.

MEMBER: American Economics Association, Union for Radical Political Economics, Economic Policy Institute.

AWARDS, HONORS: Woodrow Wilson fellow, 1966-67; Osterweil Prize in Economics, 1966; John Eliot Parker Award in Labor Economics, 1971.

WRITINGS:

(With William M. Murphy and Mary Stevenson) *Low Wages and the Working Poor,* Institute of Labor and Industrial Relations, 1973.
(With Patricia Hanna, Sarah Kuhn, and Laura Moore) *The Retail Revolution: Market Transformation, Investment, and Labor in the Modern Department Store Industry,* Auburn House, 1981.
(With Peter Jordan and Mark Sullivan) *Aircraft Industry Dynamics: An Analysis of Competition, Capital, and Labor,* Auburn House 1981.
(With Bennett Harrison) *The Deindustrialization of America: Plant Closings, Community Abandonment, and the Dismantling of Basic Industry,* Basic Books, 1982.
(With Paula Rayman) *Skidding: Unemployment and Its Aftermath in the 80's,* Simon & Schuster, in press.

WORK IN PROGRESS: The Laissez-Faire Affair: Why the Conservative Economic Strategy Will Fail, with Bennett Harrison, publication by Basic Books expected in 1987.

SIDELIGHTS: According to authors Barry Bluestone and Bennett Harrison, an estimated thirty million jobs were lost due to plant closings, relocations, and contractions during the 1970's. In their book *The Deindustrialization of America,* the two economists extensively document the social and human costs of the industrial changes that marked that decade, analyze possible reasons for the economic decline that accompanied them, and suggest strategies for handling such change in the future.

The research statistics the authors gathered revealed that the price paid by workers displaced during the 1970's was high, including such hardships as the failure to find equally rewarding employment, the loss of savings, homes, pension rights, and health insurance coverage, serious emotional suffering, and even the dissolution of some families and communities. The authors also found, noted Robert B. Reich in his review for *New Republic,* that the decline of a major employer generates a total unemployment that is two or three times the number of employees originally affected and leaves entire communities without adequate tax bases, just when they have greatest need for the extra funds to provide health and welfare services.

Bluestone and Harrison cite several reasons for the economic decline of the seventies: the growth in foreign competition, the transportation and communications revolutions that made relocation relatively easy and cost-effective, and government tax and tariff policies that provided incentives to depreciate older capital and relocate production. They place the major blame, however, on American business strategies, rather than public policies, for the plight that ensued. Instead of investing in restructuring American industry and retraining workers, the authors argue, American management turned its back on the "social contract" it had entered into with organized labor decades earlier. Management policy and practice shifted, they continue, "from productive investment in our basic national industries into unproductive speculation, mergers and acquisitions and foreign investment." Consequently, they posit, American investment capital fled to other nations and to low-wage, nonunionized areas of the United States.

The plan for the reindustrialization of America which Bluestone and Harrison favor, and call "Reindustrialization with a Human Face," features the establishment of a national "industrial policy" to ease the transition from the older "sunset industries," predominantly heavy manufacturing, to the newer "hi-tech" ones. The authors' "strongest practical suggestion," according to *Washington Post Book World* contributor Jack Beatty, "is the passage of an Employment Priorities Act requiring companies to give communities notice of their plans to relocate or shut down operations and to help pay for retraining laid-off workers." It is a way to economic recovery that is, in Beatty's opinion, "a third path between the alternatives of protectionism or chronically high unemployment,'' an industrial policy that needs to be ''sold politically.'' The book, in Beatty's judgment, is ''an important one, based on a power of original research and a careful synthesis of other scholarship.'' Likewise, *New York Times* critic Alfred E. Kahn complimented the two economists on their ''genuine contribution'' to the debate on how to cope with industrial change ''by emphasizing the costs of change to the people, families and communities disadvantaged by it, many of them permanently.'' Additionally, Kahn noted: ''They persuade even the skeptical reader that the problem is real and enormous and that our prevailing institutions for dealing with it are grossly insufficient.''

Barry A. Bluestone told *CA*: ''My work is motivated by the desire to bring the latest in economic and sociological insights to bear on critical policy issues of employment, equity, and economic development.''

AVOCATIONAL INTERESTS: Bicycling, tennis.

BIOGRAPHICAL/CRITICAL SOURCES:

PERIODICALS

New Republic, November 15, 1982.
New York Times Book Review, December 12, 1982.
Washington Post Book World, December 12, 1982.

*   *   *

BLUMENTHAL, Susan
See TRIBICH, Susan

*   *   *

BOAS, Franz   1858-1942

BRIEF ENTRY: Born July 9, 1858, in Minden, North Rhine-Westphalia, Germany (now West Germany); immigrated to United States, 1887, naturalized citizen, 1892; died of a heart attack, December 21, 1942, in New York, N.Y. German-born American geographer, educator, linguist, anthropologist, editor, and author. Perhaps best remembered for his bitter opposition to racism, Boas is considered by many historians to be ''the founding father of American anthropology.'' He established culture—as opposed to heredity—as the basis for contemporary anthropological study, and he used the science to analyze many social problems. With his book *The Mind of Primitive Man* (1911), Boas succeeded in changing earlier beliefs about the mentality of primitive peoples. He became Columbia University's first professor of anthropology in 1896 and held that position until his retirement in 1936. He was professor emeritus until his death.

Before turning to anthropology Boas was a geographer, and this led to his becoming a member of a German expedition to study the Eskimos of Baffin Land in the Canadian Arctic. From the work performed on that expedition Boas wrote *The Central Eskimo* (1888). Later in his career he studied Indian tribes of the Pacific Northwest and edited *Handbook of American Indian Languages* (1911). Boas was also the editor of the *American Anthropologist* and the *Journal of American Folklore*. In addition, he founded and edited the *International Journal of American Linguistics* and served as an assistant editor of *Science* magazine. Some of his other writings are *The Growth of Children* (1896), *Anthropology and Modern Life* (1928), and *Race, Language, and Culture* (1940). *Address:* Grantwood, Bergen County, N.J.

BIOGRAPHICAL/CRITICAL SOURCES:

BOOKS

Dictionary of American Biography, Supplement Three: 1941-1945, Scribner, 1973.
Herskovits, Melville J., *Franz Boas: The Science of Man in the Making*, Scribner, 1953.
McGraw-Hill Encyclopedia of World Biography, McGraw, 1973.
Stocking, George W., Jr., editor, *The Shaping of American Anthropology, 1883-1911: A Franz Boas Reader*, Basic Books, 1974.
Twentieth-Century Authors: A Biographical Dictionary of Modern Literature, 1st supplement, H. W. Wilson, 1955.

PERIODICALS

New York Times, December 22, 1942.

*   *   *

BOEGEHOLD, Betty (Doyle)   1913-1985
(Donovan Doyle)

OBITUARY NOTICE—See index for *CA* sketch: Born September 15, 1913, in New York, N.Y.; died of an apparent heart attack, April 7, 1985, in Bronxville, N.Y. Educator, librarian, editor, and author. Boegehold, who has worked variously as a teacher, librarian, assistant principal, workshop director, and remedial reading specialist, has written numerous books for and about children, including *Three to Get Ready, Pippa Mouse*, and *In the Castle of Cats*. Under the pseudonym Donovan Doyle, she wrote *Gray Gull, Bugs*, and *The Old Woman Who Couldn't Keep a Secret*.

OBITUARIES AND OTHER SOURCES:

PERIODICALS

New York Times, April 9, 1985.

*   *   *

BOGER, Louise Ade   1909-

BRIEF ENTRY: Born December 24, 1909, in Williamsport, Pa. American antiques expert, columnist, and author. Boger, who writes a column on antiques for *House and Garden*, is the author of the highly acclaimed *Dictionary of World Pottery and Porcelain* (Scribner, 1971). Her book has been praised as an unusually comprehensive guide for both the collector and the general reader. It encompasses pottery terms spanning the entire history of the craft, an exhaustive list of ceramic manufacturers and manufacturing cities all over the world, and informative descriptions of individual potters and styles. Boger's magazine columns have been collected in *House and Garden Antiques: Questions and Answers* (Simon & Schuster, 1973). Her other books include *The Complete Guide to Furniture Styles* (Scribner, 1959) and *The Dictionary of Antiques and the Decorative Arts: A Book of Reference for Glass, Furniture, Ceramics, Silver, Periods, Styles, Technical Terms . . .* (Scribner, 1967). *Address:* c/o ''Antiques: Questions and Answers,'' *House and Garden*, Conde Nast Publications, Inc., 350 Madison Ave., New York, N.Y. 10017.

BIOGRAPHICAL/CRITICAL SOURCES:

PERIODICALS

New York Times Book Review, December 5, 1971.
Saturday Review, December 6, 1969.

Times Literary Supplement, December 20, 1969, April 14, 1972.

* * *

BOLTON, John Robert 1948-

PERSONAL: Born November 20, 1948, in Baltimore, Md.; son of Edward Jackson and Virginia (Godfrey) Bolton. *Education:* Yale University, B.A. (summa cum laude), 1970, J.D., 1974.

ADDRESSES: Home—1021 Arlington Blvd., Arlington, Va. 22209. *Office*—Covington & Burling, 1201 Pennsylvania Ave. N.W., Washington, D.C. 20044.

CAREER: Covington & Burling (law firm), Washington, D.C., attorney, 1974-81; Agency for International Development, Washington, D.C., general counsel, 1981-82, assistant administrator for program and policy coordination, 1982-83; Covington & Burling, partner, 1983—. Executive director of Republican National Committee's Committee on Resolutions (Platform), 1983-84. *Military service:* U.S. Army Reserve, 1970-76.

MEMBER: Phi Beta Kappa, Pi Sigma Alpha.

WRITINGS:

(With Ralph K. Winter, Jr.) *Campaign Financing and Political Freedom,* American Enterprise Institute for Public Policy Research, 1973.
The Hatch Act: A Civil Libertarian Defense, American Enterprise Institute for Public Policy Research, 1976.
The Legislative Veto: Unseparating the Powers, American Enterprise Institute for Public Policy Research, 1977.

Contributor to law journals. Editor of *Yale Law Journal,* 1972.

* * *

BONNER, William Hallam 1899-1980

OBITUARY NOTICE: Born May 13, 1899, in Lynn, Mass.; died April 22, 1980. Educator and author. Bonner began teaching English at Michigan State University in 1921 after earning a master's degree from Stanford University. A year later he joined the faculty of the State University of New York at Buffalo, where he was professor of English from 1922 to 1968. A member of Phi Beta Kappa, he received his doctorate from Yale University in 1931. In addition to contributing articles to magazines and scholarly journals, Bonner edited *De Quincey at Work* and wrote *Pirate Laureate: The Life and Legends of Captain Kidd* and *The Journals and Letters of Sarah and William Hazlitt, 1822-1831.*

OBITUARIES AND OTHER SOURCES:

BOOKS

Directory of American Scholars, Volume II: *English, Speech, and Drama,* 8th edition, Bowker, 1982.
Who Was Who, Volume VII, *1971-1980,* A. & C. Black, 1981.

* * *

BOR, Josef 1906-1979

OBITUARY NOTICE: Original name Josef Bondy; born July 2, 1906, in Maehrisch-Ostrau, Austria-Hungary (now Ostrava, Czechoslovakia); died in 1979. Legal adviser and author. Bor

graduated from the University of Brno in 1929 and is best remembered for his books *Terezin Requiem* and *Opustena panenka* (title means "The Derelict Doll"). He was also the author of "Appassionata," a television script, and a film script and teleplay of *Terezin Requiem.* (Date of death provided by agent, Ivana Mazalova.)

* * *

BOSSCHERE, Jean de 1878(?)-1953

BRIEF ENTRY: Born in 1878 (some sources say 1881) in Belgium; died in 1953. Belgian etcher, engraver, illustrator, and poet. Among the many books Bosschere illustrated are *The History of Don Quixote* (1922) and *The Decameron* (1930). Some of the books that he both wrote and illustrated have appeared in English translation, including *The Closed Door* (1917), *The City Curious* (1920), and *Marthe and the Madman* (1928). Bosschere also wrote *Weird Islands* (1921).

BIOGRAPHICAL/CRITICAL SOURCES:

BOOKS

Dictionary of British Artists Working 1900-1950, Eastbourne Fine Art, 1975.
Illustrators of Children's Books: 1744-1945, Horn Book, 1947.

* * *

BOULTON, Wayne G(ranberry) 1941-

PERSONAL: Born September 23, 1941, in Gaffney, S.C.; married, 1966; children: two. *Education:* Lafayette College, B.A., 1963; McCormick Theological Seminary, M.Div., 1967; Duke University, Ph.D., 1972.

ADDRESSES: Office—Department of Religion, Hope College, Holland, Mich. 48423.

CAREER: Hope College, Holland, Mich., assistant professor, 1974-78, associate professor of religion, 1978—. Member of United Presbyterian Church task force on morality, 1974-76.

MEMBER: American Academy of Religion, American Society for Christian Ethics.

WRITINGS:

Is Legalism a Heresy?: The Legacy of the Pharisees in the Christian Ethics, Paulist Press, 1983.

Contributor to magazines, including *Christian Century* and *Reformed Journal.*

WORK IN PROGRESS: Family Under Fire: Christian Observations on an Embattled Institution.

SIDELIGHTS: Wayne G. Boulton told *CA:* "At the heart of my first book is the Hebraic concept of law, a concept that continues to fascinate me. One of the only political commentators who operates with something like it is George F. Will, as I argued in *Reformed Journal* in December, 1983. After visiting Scotland during the summer of 1983, I'm convinced that much of Scottish Calvinism is dependent on it."

* * *

BOWEN, (Ivor) Ian 1908-1984
(Charles Hogarth, a joint pseudonym)

OBITUARY NOTICE—See index for *CA* sketch: Born December 3, 1908, in Cardiff, Wales; died November 20, 1984, at

Xalet Verena, La Massana, Andorra. Educator and author. Bowen taught at Oxford University from 1930 until 1947, except for the years between 1940 and 1945, during which time he served as the chief statistical officer for the British Ministry of Works. The educator taught economics at the University of Hull from 1947 until 1958, when he accepted a teaching post at the University of Western Australia. After Bowen left teaching in 1973 he became associated with the International Bank for Reconstruction and Development and the International Monetary Fund. His publications include *Cobden, Population, Seven Lectures on Manpower Planning With Special Reference to Thailand, Acceptable Inequalities, Economics and Demography*, and, with John Creasey under the joint pseudonym Charles Hogarth, *Largo Island.*

OBITUARIES AND OTHER SOURCES:

BOOKS

Who's Who, 136th edition, St. Martin's, 1984.

PERIODICALS

Times (London), December 12, 1984.

*   *   *

BOWMAN, Larry G(ene)   1935-

BRIEF ENTRY: Born June 11, 1935, in Hutchinson, Kan. American historian, educator, and author. Bowman taught at Kansas State College of Pittsburg (now Pittsburg State University) from 1962 until 1966; he then became a member of the history faculty of North Texas State University. His book, *Captive Americans: Prisoners During the American Revolution* (Ohio University Press), was published in 1976. *Address:* Department of History, North Texas State University, Denton, Tex. 76203.

BIOGRAPHICAL/CRITICAL SOURCES:

PERIODICALS

American Historical Review, October, 1977.
Times Literary Supplement, June 17, 1977.

*   *   *

BRACELAND, Francis J(ames)   1900-1985

OBITUARY NOTICE: Born July 22, 1900, in Philadelphia, Pa.; died of heart disease, February 23, 1985, in Sarasota, Fla.; buried in Arlington National Cemetery, Arlington, VA. Physician, educator, editor, and author. An internationally known psychiatrist, Braceland is probably best remembered for his long association with the Institute of Living, a psychiatric facility in Hartford, Connecticut, that under his direction became the largest private psychiatric hospital in the United States. Braceland joined the institute as psychiatrist in chief in 1951, remaining in that position until 1965. Thereafter he continued his affiliation with the hospital as a senior consultant and planning director. From 1951 to 1968 he also served as professor of psychiatry at Yale University, retiring as professor emeritus.

Before joining the Institute of Living, Braceland spent many years as a physician and professor in his native Philadelphia. He also held the posts of professor of psychiatry and dean of the medical school at Loyola University in Chicago for one year, leaving the university in 1941 for wartime service with the U.S. Navy's medical staff. While with the navy, Braceland was among President Franklin D. Roosevelt's attending physicians and attained the rank of rear admiral in the Naval Reserve. Following World War II Braceland testified as special witness at the Nuremburg war crimes trials and as such affirmed the insanity of Nazi leader Rudolph Hess. In 1946 the psychiatrist moved to Minnesota to organize and direct the psychiatric section of Mayo Clinic. He remained with the clinic for five years, concurrently working as professor of psychiatry at the University of Minnesota.

During his lengthy career Braceland was active in numerous professional organizations and worked on the editorial staffs of professional publications, among them the *American Journal of Psychiatry*, which he edited from 1965 until 1978, and the *Year Book of Psychiatry and Applied Mental Health*, for which he was the senior editor from 1968 until 1976. His books include *The Institute of Living: The Hartford Retreat, 1822-1972; Faith, Reason, and Modern Psychiatry: Sources for a Synthesis;* and *Modern Psychiatry: A Handbook for Believers*, written with Michael Stock.

OBITUARIES AND OTHER SOURCES:

BOOKS

Who's Who in America, 42nd edition, Marquis, 1982.

PERIODICALS

Los Angeles Times, February 28, 1985.
New York Times, February 27, 1985.
Washington Post, February 25, 1985.

*   *   *

BRACKEN, Paul   1948-

PERSONAL: Born March 12, 1948, in Philadelphia, Pa.; married Nanette Beattie (an attorney), May 25, 1974; children: Kathleen, James. *Education:* Columbia University, B.S., 1971; Yale University, Ph.D., 1982.

ADDRESSES: Home—14 Mulberry St., Ridgefield, Conn. 06877.

CAREER: Ketron, Inc., Arlington, Va., member of senior professional staff, 1972-74; Hudson Institute, Croton-on-Hudson, N.Y., director of research services, 1974-83; Yale University, New Haven, Conn., associate professor of political science and of organization and management, 1983—.

MEMBER: International Institute for Strategic Studies.

WRITINGS:

The Command and Control of Nuclear Forces, Yale University Press, 1983.

Contributor to periodicals, including *International Security, Survival*, and *New York Times Magazine*. Editor of *ORBIS, Defense Analysis*, and *Journal of Conflict Resolution*.

WORK IN PROGRESS: Researching "organizational aspects of the threat and use of force" and "international security dimensions of business and finance."

SIDELIGHTS: Paul Bracken's *The Command and Control of Nuclear Arms* offers an analysis of the United States-Soviet Union nuclear arms race and speculates on probable patterns of behavior following a possible collapse of deterence. McGeorge Bundy, reviewing the book in *New York Times Book Review*, described it as "a scrupulous and detailed account of the complex and secret world where men seek to meet the requirements that these dreadful systems set for those who hope to make them do—and not do—what the ultimate commanders choose.'' Bundy added: ''No one has fully mastered this arcane subject, but no one who wants to understand it better can afford to neglect this book. There is nothing superior in the declassified literature.'' Lawrence Freedman, a reviewer for *Washington Post Book World,* was similarly impressed with Bracken's work. ''Bracken has succeeded in putting the nuclear debate on to a new plane,'' wrote Freedman. ''He identifies instabilities in the system that many had suspected but nobody had pinned down so precisely and effectively. Fortunately, he has also identified sufficient stabilities to give us time for corrective action.''

BIOGRAPHICAL/CRITICAL SOURCES:

PERIODICALS

New York Times Book Review, October 9, 1983.
Times Literary Supplement, March 3, 1984.
Washington Post Book World, December 11, 1983.

*   *   *

BRADEN, Spruille   1894-1978

OBITUARY NOTICE: Born March 13, 1894, in Elkhorn, Mont.; died of a heart ailment, January 10 (some sources say January 11), 1978, in Los Angeles, Calif. Diplomat, government official, consultant, and author. Braden had been in mining and various other businesses before becoming U.S. ambassador to Columbia in 1939. He also served as ambassador to Cuba, and later, to Argentina, until 1945 when President Harry S. Truman appointed him assistant secretary of state. After his retirement in 1947 he acted for nearly three decades as a consultant to a number of U.S. businesses in their relations with South America. An outspoken anti-Communist and member of the ultra-conservative John Birch Society, Braden was nonetheless once accused of aiding South American Communists. Among the highlights of his career as an ambassador was his involvement in ending the Chaco war between Bolivia and Paraguay in the early 1930's. His book of memoirs, *Diplomats and Demagogues: The Memories of Spruille Braden,* was published in 1971.

OBITUARIES AND OTHER SOURCES:

BOOKS

Current Biography, Wilson, 1945, March, 1978.
Directory of American Diplomatic History, Greenwood Press, 1980.
Political Profiles: The Truman Years, Facts on File, 1978.

PERIODICALS

New York Times, January 12, 1978.
Time, January 23, 1978.

*   *   *

BRAGG, William Lawrence   1890-1971

OBITUARY NOTICE: Born April 30, 1890, in Adelaide, Australia; died July 1, 1971, in Walfringford, Suffolk, England. Physicist and author of scientific writings. Bragg gained prominence in his field at an early age. In 1912, while testing various theories concerning X rays with his father, physicist William Henry Bragg, William Lawrence Bragg formulated an equation—now known as Bragg's Law—that describes the quantitative relationship between X ray wavelengths, the spac-

ing of crystal planes, and the angle of the X rays' reflection by the crystal planes during diffraction. Three years later Bragg and his father shared the 1915 Nobel Prize in physics for their work in using X-ray diffraction for crystal-structure analysis. Bragg later conducted research to analyze the molecular and atomic structure of silicates, metals, and proteins. His findings contributed substantially to many fields, including physics, crystallography, mineralogy, metallurgy, inorganic chemistry, and molecular biology. His professional positions included those as Langworthy Professor of Physics at the University of Manchester, Cavendish Professor of Experimental Physics at Cambridge University, Fullerton Professor of Chemistry at the Royal Institution, London, and director of the Davy-Faraday Research Laboratory, a position his father had once filled. Among Bragg's writings are *X-rays and Crystal Structure,* which he wrote with his father, *Old Trades and New Knowledge, Electricity,* and *The Development of X-ray Analysis.* He also wrote volumes I and IV of *The Crystalline State* and edited volumes II, III, and IV.

OBITUARIES AND OTHER SOURCES:

BOOKS

Dictionary of Scientific Biography, Supplement I, Scribner, 1978.
Twentieth-Century Culture: A Biographical Companion, Harper, 1983.

*   *   *

BRAUN, Edward   1936-

BRIEF ENTRY: Born in 1936 in London, England. British educator and author. After eight years at St. John's College of Cambridge University, Braun joined the drama department at the University of Bristol in 1969. He wrote *The Theatre of Meyerhold: Revolution on the Modern Stage* (Drama Book Specialists, 1979). Braun also edited and translated *Meyerhold on Theatre* (Hill & Wang, 1969).

BIOGRAPHICAL/CRITICAL SOURCES:

PERIODICALS

New York Times Book Review, December 2, 1979.

*   *   *

BRAUN, Thomas (Felix Rudry Gerhart)   1935-

PERSONAL: Surname is pronounced like ''brown''; born August 30, 1935, in Berlin, Germany; son of Konrad (a judge of the Berlin Appeal Court and a college lecturer) and Hildburg (Weber) Braun. *Education:* Balliol College, Oxford, received degree in classics (with first class honors), 1957, received degree in Philosophy and ancient history (with first class honors), 1959; Merton College, Oxford, M.A., 1962. *Religion:* Society of Friends (Quakers).

ADDRESSES: Office—Merton College, Oxford University, Oxford, England.

CAREER: Friends' Ambulance Unit, member in International service in England and Greece, 1953-55; University of Leicester, Leicester, England, assistant lecturer in classics, 1962-63; Oxford University, Oxford, England, lecturer in ancient history and fellow and tutor of Merton College, 1963—, dean of Merton College, 1974—. Founding member of Oxford Civic Society, 1970—.

AWARDS, HONORS: Visiting fellow at John Carter Brown Library, Brown University, 1983.

WRITINGS:

(Editor) E.G.W. Bill, *Christ Church Meadow,* Oxford University Press, 1965, 2nd edition, 1968.
(Translator) K. Friedlaender (under pseudonym Conrad Peregrinus) *A Journey to Springistan,* Stockholm, 1971.
(Editor) Ilse Rosenthal-Schneider, *Reality and Scientific Truth: Discussions With Einstein, Von Laue, and Planck,* Wayne State University Press, 1980.

Also contributor of translations to *Digest;* contributor to *Cambridge Ancient History.* Contributor of articles and reviews to scholarly journals.

WORK IN PROGRESS: Research on Greek geography and exploration; research on Greek history of the early and classical periods.

SIDELIGHTS: Thomas Braun told *CA:* "Since spending nine months in Greece in 1953 and from 1954 to 1955, I have traveled extensively in classical lands, and I have been a guest lecturer on tours in the eastern Mediterranean region in 1979 and 1982. I have visited the Near East many times since 1958, including travel in India, from 1971 to 1972, and in China, following the silk route, in 1981."

AVOCATIONAL INTERESTS: Foreign languages (classical and modern Greek, German, French, Italian, Latin), reading literature and modern history, home improvement, gardening, classical music (plays clarinet), running, "real tennis."

*   *   *

BREMBECK, Winston Lamont 1912-

BRIEF ENTRY: Born September 28, 1912, in Urbana, Ill. American educator and author. In 1946 Brembeck began teaching at the University of Wisconsin—Madison, where he became a professor of communication and public address in 1958. He and William S. Howell collaborated on *Persuasion: A Means of Social Influence* (Prentice-Hall), which was published in 1976. *Address:* 3206 Leyton Lane, Madison, Wis. 53713; and Department of Communication Arts, University of Wisconsin—Madison, Madison, Wis. 53706.

BIOGRAPHICAL/CRITICAL SOURCES:

BOOKS

Directory of American Scholars, Volume II: *English, Speech, and Drama,* 8th edition, Bowker, 1982.

*   *   *

BREMNER, Geoffrey 1930-

PERSONAL: Born August 22, 1930, in London, England. *Education:* Oxford University, M.A., 1953; University of Reading, Ph.D., 1977.

ADDRESSES: Office—Department of Romance Languages, Hugh Owen Building, University College of Wales, University of Wales, Aberystwyth, Dyfed SY23 3DY, Wales.

CAREER: Schoolmaster in southern England, 1954-66; University of the West Indies, St. Augustine, Trinidad, lecturer in French, 1966-69; University of Khartoum, Khartoum, Sudan, senior lecturer in French, 1969-74; teacher at Reading University and Open University, 1974-78; University of Wales,

University College of Wales, Aberystwyth, lecturer in French, 1978—.

WRITINGS:

Order and Chance: The Pattern of Diderot's Thought, Cambridge University Press, 1983.

Contributor to learned journals.

WORK IN PROGRESS: A full-length study of the common factors in literature, art, aesthetic and political theory, and natural history, characterizing the structure and epistemological limits of eighteenth-century French thought.

SIDELIGHTS: Geoffrey Bremner told *CA:* "My book and most of the articles I have written are attempts to show how writers reflect in their works the concerns of their ages. I see these concerns as forming a largely unconscious, prerational pattern of thought which manifests itself in every area of conscious activity. In my studies of Diderot I have tried to show this process at work in one writer. In my next book I shall try to identify the dominant features of this pattern as they appear in a variety of representative writers and artists."

*   *   *

BRENGELMAN, Fred(erick Henry) 1928-

BRIEF ENTRY: Born March 31, 1928, in Farwell, Neb. American linguist, educator, and author. Brengelman became a member of the faculty of California State University, Fresno, in 1957; he was promoted to professor of linguistics in 1968. From 1965 to 1966 he directed a Fulbright English-language program in Athens, Greece. The linguist's writings include *The English Language: An Introduction for Teachers* (Prentice-Hall, 1970), *Contemporary English* (Silver Burdett, 1972), *Understanding Words: Systematic Spelling and Vocabulary Building* (Kendall/Hunt, 1980), and *Shaping Sentences and Paragraphs: A Systematic Approach to Sentence and Paragraph Construction* (Kendall/Hunt, 1980). *Address:* Department of Linguistics, California State University, 6241 North Maple Ave., Fresno, Calif. 93740.

*   *   *

BRESLOW, Lester 1915-

PERSONAL: Born March 17, 1915, in Bismarck, N.D.; son of Joseph (a pharmacist) and Mayme (Danziger) Breslow; married Devra J. R. Miller (an arts and health administrator), 1967; children: Norman, Jack, Stephen. *Education:* University of Minnesota, B.A., 1935, M.D., 1938, M.P.H., 1941.

ADDRESSES: Home—10926 Verano Rd., Los Angeles, Calif. 90077. *Office*—School of Public Health, University of California, Los Angeles, Calif. 90024.

CAREER: U.S. Public Health Service Hospital, Stapleton, N.Y., intern, 1938-40; Minnesota Department of Health, Rochester, district health officer, 1941-43; California Department of Public Health, Berkeley, chief of Bureau of Chronic Diseases, 1946-60, chief of Division of Preventive Medicine, 1960-65, director of department, 1965-68; University of California, Los Angeles, professor of public health, 1968—, chairman of department of preventive medicine and social medicine, 1969-72, dean of School of Public Health, 1972-80. Diplomate of American Board of Preventive Medicine and Public Health. Lecturer at University of California, Los Angeles, 1950-68. Study director of President's Commission on the Health Needs of the Nation, 1952—; consultant to National Cancer Institute. *Military service:* U.S. Army, 1943-46; became captain; received Bronze Star.

MEMBER: International Epidemiological Association (president, 1967-68), American Association for the Advancement of Science (fellow), American College of Physicians (fellow), American Public Health Association (president, 1968), American Epidemiological Society (president, 1967-68), American Cancer Society (member of national and state boards of directors; chairman of advisory committee on research etiology), Association of Schools of Public Health (president, 1973-74), National Institute of Medicine, National Academy of Sciences (member of council, 1978-80; chairman of board of health promotion and disease prevention, 1981-83).

AWARDS, HONORS: Lasker Award, 1960; Sedgwick Medal from American Public Health Association.

WRITINGS:

(With Lisa F. Berkman) *Health and Ways of Living: The Alameda County Study,* Oxford University Press, 1983.

Contributor of more than one hundred articles to scientific journals and of approximately twenty chapters to books on public health and preventative medicine. Co-editor of *Annual Review of Public Health,* 1979—.

WORK IN PROGRESS: Research on measurement of health, health promotion, and cancer control.

* * *

BRETT, Hawksley
    See BELL, Robert S(tanley) W(arren)

* * *

BREUER, Reinhard   1946-

PERSONAL: Born August 3, 1946, in Regensburg, West Germany. *Education:* Attended University of Michigan, 1969; University of Wuerzburg, M. H., 1971, Ph.D., 1974; attended University of Maryland at College Park, 1972, and Oxford University, 1973; University of Munich, habilitation, 1979.

ADDRESSES: Office—GEO Magazine, Postfach 30 20 40, D-2000 Hamburg 36, West Germany.

CAREER: Max-Planck-Institut fuer Astrophysik, Munich, West Germany, scientist, 1974-80; Max-Planck-Institut fuer Plasmaphysik, Munich, press officer, 1980-84; GEO Magazine, Hamburg, West Germany, editor, 1984—. Lecturer and astrophysicist at University of Munich; lecturer at Hamburg University, 1984.

MEMBER: Astronomical Society of West Germany.

WRITINGS:

Das anthropische Prinzip, Meyster, 1981, translation published as *The Anthropic Principle,* Birkhaeuser, 1984.
Contact With the Stars, W. H. Freeman, 1982.
Der lautlose Schlag (title means "The Silent Strike"), Meyster, 1982.
Die Pfeile der Zeit (title means "The Arrows of Time"), Meyster, 1984.

Also author of articles and of science features for television.

WORK IN PROGRESS: The End of the World: From Apocalypse to the Death of Matter.

SIDELIGHTS: Reinhard Breuer told *CA:* "Both books, *Contact With the Stars* and *The Anthropic Principle,* are concerned with the role of mankind and intelligence in the universe. There is the question of extraterrestrial life forms and communication with them if they exist, which seems unlikely, then the structure of the laws of nature and the universe, which seemingly had to be quite special in order to bring forward intelligence. The long-term prospects for intelligence in the universe—survival, influence—are investigated in my work in progress, presumably boiling down to the suspicion that life and intelligence have only a marginal role to play in the universe."

* * *

BREWER, (Lucie) Elisabeth   1923-

PERSONAL: Born January 16, 1923, in London, England; daughter of Basil (a clerk in holy orders) and Margaret (a teacher; maiden name, Cowell) Hoole; married Derek Stanley Brewer (an educator), August 17, 1951; children: Sarah, Michael, Helena, Adrian, Guy. *Education:* University of Birmingham, B.A. (with honors), 1950, teaching certificate, 1951, M.A., 1956. *Religion:* Church of England.

ADDRESSES: Home—Emmanuel College, Cambridge University, Cambridge, England. *Office*—Homerton College of Education, Cambridge, England.

CAREER: Teacher of English at schools in Birmingham, England, beginning in 1951; Homerton College of Education, Cambridge, England, began as part-time lecturer, became senior lecturer in English. Former part-time teacher of English at Hitotsubashi University and Tokyo Women's Christian College.

WRITINGS:

(Editor and translator) *From Cuchulainn to Gawain: Sources and Analogues of Sir Gawain and the Green Knight,* Boydell & Brewer, 1973.
York Notes: The Miller's Tale—Geoffrey Chaucer, Longman, 1982.
York Notes: Troilus and Criseyde—Geoffrey Chaucer, Longman, 1983.
(With Beverly Taylor) *The Return of King Arthur: British and American Arthurian Literature,* Boydell & Brewer, 1983.
York Handbooks: Studying Chaucer, Longman, 1984.

WORK IN PROGRESS: Fantasy Writing in Britian, 1880-1930; "Edward Burne-Jones and the Arthurian Legend," for a collection of essays for the University of Bonn, publication expected in 1986.

SIDELIGHTS: Elisabeth Brewer told *CA:* "I met Beverly Taylor, my co-author for *The Return of King Arthur,* quite by chance and found that we shared the same interests. We were both aware of the continuing interest in the Arthurian legend, particularly in the United States, as manifested in the various movies that have been produced of recent years, and in the myth 'Camelot.' We also knew that previous books on the subject needed updating in various ways.

"Our book provides a critical survey of British and American literature (novels, poetry, and drama written for adults) from 1800 to 1983, when the book came out. In it we discuss the ways in which authors have not merely retold Arthurian stories, but have used them as poetic and symbolic imagery by which to communicate their ideas. We try to account for the unflagging interest in this material that has been apparent since about 1800 and analyze what the various works reveal about the period that produced them. Our book also has a comprehensive bibliography of the Arthurian texts from 1800.

"My interest in fantasy has grown out of *The Return of King Arthur* because I have become increasingly aware of the fascination with fantasy, both on the part of writers and of the reading public at the end of the nineteenth century. This seems to be associated with interest in psychical research and scientific discovery, as well as with the decay of orthodox religious belief in the United Kingdom. This decay produced, on one hand, tales of the supernatural, and, on the other, science fiction. The enormous number of novels, many now forgotten, suggests the desire on the part of the literate public to read novels that transcend ordinary, everyday experience.

"I am also interested in medievalism in the nineteenth century, especially in the work of Pre-Raphaelite painters, and in the use of the Arthurian legend as a source of symbolic imagery, particularly by Edward Burne-Jones and Dante Gabriel Rossetti."

AVOCATIONAL INTERESTS: Italian life and art, long-distance running.

*   *   *

BRIEN, Raley
See McCULLEY, Johnston

*   *   *

BRITTEN, Milton R(eese)   1924-1985

OBITUARY NOTICE: Born December 17, 1924, in Wilkes-Barre, Pa.; died after an apparent heart attack, March 19, 1985, in Memphis, Tenn. Journalist and co-author of *The Foreign Aid Story: Where Did Your Money Go?,* a 1964 account of aid given by the United States to developing nations. After graduating from Yale University in 1949 Britten joined the *Memphis Press-Scimitar* newspaper as a reporter. Six years later he transferred to the Washington D.C., bureau of the Scripps-Howard News Service, of which the *Press-Scimitar* was a member, and in 1963 became night editor of the bureau. He served in this capacity until 1966, when he became the bureau's assistant managing editor, a post he held until becoming managing editor in 1974. Two years later Britten returned to Memphis as editor of the *Press-Scimitar.* He filled that position until the paper's demise in 1983.

OBITUARIES AND OTHER SOURCES:

BOOKS

Who's Who in America, 40th edition, Marquis, 1978.

PERIODICALS

Chicago Tribune, March 21, 1985.
New York Times, March 21, 1985.
Washington Post, March 25, 1985.

*   *   *

BRODIE, John (Riley)   1935-

BRIEF ENTRY: Born August 14, 1935, in San Francisco, Calif. American professional athlete, sports broadcaster, and author. A quarterback for the San Francisco Forty-niners from 1957 to 1973, Brodie was named National Football Conference player of the year by *Sporting News* in 1970. In 1974 he became a football commentator for the National Broadcasting Company (NBC-TV). Brodie is the co-author of *Open Field* (Houghton, 1974). *Address:* c/o Sports Press Department, National Broadcasting Co., 30 Rockefeller Plaza, New York, N.Y. 10020.

BIOGRAPHICAL/CRITICAL SOURCES:

BOOKS

Chass, Murray, *Power Football,* 1973.

*   *   *

BROOKS, Charles (Gordon)   1920-

PERSONAL: Born November 22, 1920, in Andalusia, Ala.; son of Gordie Motts (a restaurant owner) and Emily Elizabeth (a homemaker; maiden name, Smith) Brooks; married Virginia Matson (a medical records clerk), September 4, 1943; children: Barbara Jean Brooks Hynds, Charles Gordon, Jr. *Education:* Attended Birmingham Southern College, 1939-41, and Chicago Academy of Fine Arts, 1941-42. *Religion:* Methodist.

ADDRESSES: Home—1612 Cresthill Rd., Birmingham, Ala. 35213. *Office*—*Birmingham News,* 2200 Fourth Ave. N., Birmingham, Ala. 35202.

CAREER: Birmingham News, Birmingham, Ala., editorial cartoonist, 1948—. *Military service:* U.S. Army, Engineers, 1942-45; became first lieutenant; received four battle stars and Croix de Guerre.

MEMBER: Association of American Editorial Cartoonists (president, 1969-70), Sigma Delta Chi (president of Alabama professional chapter, 1968), Birmingham Press Club (founder and president, 1968-69), Birmingham Sailing Club, Friends of German Language and Culture Club.

AWARDS, HONORS: National Cartoon Award from Disabled American Veterans, 1951; Sigma Delta Chi distinguished service award, 1969, for editorial cartooning; Vigilant Patriot Award from All-American Conference to Combat Communism, 1968, for outstanding contribution to public awareness and understanding of the communist menace to the nation; first annual Grover C. Hall Award from Troy State University, 1974, for excellence in Alabama journalism; Hector Award from Troy State University, 1978, for editorial cartooning; fourteen awards from Freedoms Foundation.

WRITINGS:

(Illustrator) S. T. Agnew, *Real Spiro Agnew,* Pelican, 1970.
(Editor)"Best Editorial Cartoons of the Year" series, thirteen books, Pelican, first volume published in 1972.

Contributor of cartoons to more than fifty books, including encyclopedias, yearbooks, and high school and college textbooks on political science, economics, and history. Cartoons in permanent collections at libraries and universities and in university archives. Cartoons shown in exhibits, including the White House, National Portrait Gallery in London, and Smithsonian Institution.

WORK IN PROGRESS: Best Editorial Cartoons of the Year, 1986 edition.

BIOGRAPHICAL/CRITICAL SOURCES:

PERIODICALS

Los Angeles Times Book Review, July 11, 1982.

BROOKS, Hindi

BRIEF ENTRY: Born in Detroit, Mich. American author. Brooks, who became a free-lance writer in 1946, was a critic and columnist for *Places* from 1973 to 1978. Her plays include "That's No Lady" (1962), "What's His Name Gets All the Good Musicians" (1974), "A Minor Incident" (1975), and "An Appointment With the Principal" (1976).

* * *

BROWN, Daphne Faunce
See FAUNCE-BROWN, Daphne (Bridget)

* * *

BROWN, Rosemary (Eleanor) 1938-

BRIEF ENTRY: Born in 1938 in Sidmouth, Devon, England. British pianist, educator, and author. Brown is a licentiate of the Royal Academy of Music and an associate of the Royal College of Music. She has taught music and worked as a piano accompanist. Brown is best known, however, as a musical medium whose psychic performances are said to originate from such long-dead composers as Beethoven, Mozart, and Liszt. Her experiences have been recorded in *Unfinished Symphonies: Voices From the Beyond* (Souvenir Press, 1971) and *Immortals at My Elbow* (Bachman & Turner, 1974).

BIOGRAPHICAL/CRITICAL SOURCES:

PERIODICALS

New Statesman, June 18, 1971, November 29, 1974.
New York Times Book Review, September 12, 1971.
Spectator, July 10, 1971, December 14, 1974.

* * *

BRUNTON, Paul 1898-1981

OBITUARY NOTICE: Born in 1898 in England; died in 1981. Journalist and author. Brunton, who traveled in Egypt and India, became interested in the holy men of the East, particularly those known for working miracles. He subsequently became attracted to the metaphysical aspects of Yoga and mysticism. Brunton's well-known book *A Search in Secret India* appeared in 1934; two years later the author published *A Search in Secret Egypt.* In 1983 several of Brunton's works were published in revised editions, including *Discover Yourself: Inner Reality,* which was first published as *Inner Reality* in 1939; *The Wisdom of the Overself,* originally published in 1943; and *The Spiritual Crisis of Man,* previously published in 1952.

OBITUARIES AND OTHER SOURCES:

BOOKS

Encyclopedia of Occultism and Parapsychology, 2nd printing with revisions, Gale, 1979.
International Authors and Writers Who's Who, 9th edition [and] *International Who's Who in Poetry,* 6th edition, Melrose, 1982.

PERIODICALS

Library Journal, October 1, 1984.

BRUST, Steven K. (Zoltan) 1955-

PERSONAL: Born November 23, 1955, in St. Paul, Minn.; son of William Z. (a professor) and Jean (Tilsen) Brust; married wife, Reen, December 29, 1974; children: Corwin Edward, Aliera Jean and Carolyn Rozsa (twins), Antonia Eileen. *Education:* Control Data Institute, Programming Certificate (with honors), 1976; also attended University of Minnesota—Twin Cities.

ADDRESSES: Home—4880 106th Ave. N.E., Circle Pines, Minn. 55014. *Office*—Network Systems, 7600 Boone Ave. N., New Brighton, Minn. 55112. *Agent*—Valerie Smith, Virginia Kidd, 538 East Harford St., Milford, Pa. 18337.

CAREER: Employed as systems programmer, 1976—; Network Systems, New Brighton, Minn., systems programmer, 1983—. Actor for local community theater; drummer for rock 'n' roll and country/rock bands; folk guitarist and singer.

MEMBER: Science Fiction Writers of America, Interstate Writers Workshop, Minnesota Science Fiction Society (vice-president).

WRITINGS:

Jhereg (fantasy novel), Ace Books, 1983.
To Reign in Hell (fantasy novel), Steel Dragon, 1984.
Yendi (fantasy novel), Ace Books, 1984.
Teckla (fantasy novel), Ace Books, in press.

Work represented in anthologies, including *Liavek Anthology,* 1985.

WORK IN PROGRESS: Brokedown Palace, a fantasy novel, publication expected in 1985.

SIDELIGHTS: Steven K. Brust told *CA:* "It is clear to me that a novelist who is unwilling to tell a story is wasting his own and his reader's time. There is so much more that we, as writers, are able to do—but if we can't entertain we are in the wrong profession.

"It is very easy to cheat when writing fantasy—to say 'this is magic, it just works.' But if one is able to avoid this trap, one has the power to work real magic with the story. For me, magic must be either an alternate set of physical laws, used to express something about how we view our tools, or else a metaphor for Mystery, or the Unknown, or whatever. On the other hand, the metaphor itself can be a dangerous toy. There are many fantasy novels that are thinly disguised Christian metaphors. So I wrote *To Reign in Hell,* which is a Christian metaphor that is really a thinly disguised fantasy novel.

"Major influences in my work have been Mark Twain, Roger Zelazny, and my editor, Terri Windling. I admire writers, such as the above, who are able to write on several levels at once—*without* neglecting the most basic thing—telling a good story. It seems that, today, science fiction is one of the few areas where this is possible."

AVOCATIONAL INTERESTS: Shotokan karate, reading (Mark Twain, Roger Zelazny, Robert B. Parker, Robin McKinley, and Megan Lindholm).

* * *

BRYAN, Mina R(uese) 1908-1985

OBITUARY NOTICE: Born January 23, 1908, in Sidney, Ohio; died following a stroke, February 14, 1985, in Princeton, N.J. Librarian and editor. Bryan began her career as a librarian for the Scheide Library in Titusville, Pennsylvania, in 1930 and stayed with the library until 1944, when she moved to Princeton, New Jersey. From 1944 until 1957 she served as associate editor of the highly regarded *Papers of Thomas Jefferson,* a multi-volume collection published by Princeton University Press. In 1959 she resumed her affiliation with the Scheide Library, which had become part of Princeton University's rare books collection and had relocated to the Princeton campus.

OBITUARIES AND OTHER SOURCES:

BOOKS

A Biographical Directory of Librarians in the United States and Canada, 5th edition, American Library Association, 1970.

PERIODICALS

New York Times, February 17, 1985.

*   *   *

BRYAN, Sharon   1943-

PERSONAL: Born February 10, 1943, in Salt Lake City, Utah; daughter of Glen and Shirley (Storrs) Allen. *Education:* University of Utah, B.A., 1965; Cornell University, M.A., 1969; University of Iowa, M.F.A., 1977.

ADDRESSES: Home—845 Bellevue Pl. E., No. 206, Seattle, Wash. 98102. *Office*—Department of English, University of Washington, Seattle, Wash. 98195.

CAREER: Marlboro College, Marlboro, Vt., member of English faculty, 1977-78; manuscript editor of *Journal of Asian Studies,* 1978-80; University of Washington, Seattle, acting assistant professor of English, 1980—. Member of faculty of Creative Writing Workshop, Fort Worden, Wash., 1980, and Spectrum Writers Conference, Seattle, 1983.

MEMBER: Associated Writing Programs.

AWARDS, HONORS: Prize from Academy of American Poets, 1976, for poem "Big Sheep Knocks You About"; Discovery Award from *Nation,* 1977.

WRITINGS:

Salt Air (poems), Wesleyan University Press, 1983.
(Editor) *Intro 14,* Associated Writing Programs, 1983.

Work represented in anthologies, including *Bumbershoot Anthology,* Red Sky Press, 1984; *Selections From University and College Poetry Prizes, 1973-1978,* Academy of American Poets; *Morrow Anthology of Younger American Poets,* edited by Dave Smith and David Bottoms, 1984; and *Anthology of Magazine Verse and Yearbook of American Poetry,* edited by Alan F. Pater, 1984.

Contributor of poems to literary magazines, including *American Poetry Review, Atlantic Monthly, Georgia Review, Ironwood, Nation, Iowa Review, Ohio Review, Ploughshares, Poetry Northwest,* and *Seattle Review.*

WORK IN PROGRESS: Fallacies of Hope, a book of poems.

SIDELIGHTS: Writing in the *New York Times Book Review,* Alan Williamson remarked that "one may be grateful for the cool, clear eye Sharon Bryan brings to her native Utah in 'Salt Air.'" The critic, who favorably compared her work with that of late poet Elizabeth Bishop, further noted that Bryan is "a touching poet of domestic light and shade."

BIOGRAPHICAL/CRITICAL SOURCES:

PERIODICALS

New York Times Book Review, November 13, 1983.
Poetry, April, 1984.

*   *   *

BUEHLMANN, Walbert   1916-

PERSONAL: Born August 6, 1916, in Lucerne, Switzerland; son of Jacob (a butcher) and Elisabeth (Sigrist) Buehlmann. *Education:* Attended Capuchin Theological Union, 1935-43; University of Fribourg, D.D., 1949.

ADDRESSES: Home—Kapuzinerkloster, CH-6415 Arth, Switzerland.

CAREER: Entered Order of Franciscan Capuchins, 1935, ordained Roman Catholic priest, 1942; Roman Catholic missionary in Tanzania, 1950-53; University of Fribourg, Fribourg, Switzerland, professor of missiology, 1954-70; Generalate of Order of Franciscan Capuchins, Rome, Italy, general secretary for mission, 1970-82; writer, 1983—.

WRITINGS:

The Coming of the Third Church, Orbis, 1977.
Courage, Church, Orbis, 1977.
The Missions on Trial, Orbis, 1978.
The Search for God, Orbis, 1979.
God's Chosen Peoples, Orbis, 1982.
Church Model for the Year 2001, Orbis, 1985.

SIDELIGHTS: Walburt Buehlmann told *CA:* "Since I have been a missionary in Tanzania, under colonial rule and in the pre-conciliar church, mission has changed tremendously. In that time, we had 'our missions,' for which we were fully responsible. Now 'our missions' have become 'local churches' with the missionaries in their service. In that time we aimed first at the 'conversion of pagans.' Now we try to announce God's universal love for all people in all religions, and consequently to build up a better world, together with all people of good will. In that time we had the only European (Roman) model of Church. Now we stress on inculturation and hope to have—in the future—a more pluriform, more decentralized Church of six continents. After all, I try to show in my books a worldwide, open-minded, updated Church, for which it is worthwhile to be engaged."

BIOGRAPHICAL/CRITICAL SOURCES:

PERIODICALS

Commonweal, March 3, 1978.

*   *   *

BUHLMANN, Walbert
See BUEHLMANN, Walbert

*   *   *

BULL, George (Anthony)   1929-

PERSONAL: Born August 23, 1929, in London, England; son of George Thomas (a streetcar inspector and driver) and Bridget Philomena (a homemaker; maiden name, Nugent) Bull; married Doreen Marjorie Griffin (a nurse and counselor), March 2, 1957; children: Catherine Jane, Julian George, Jennifer

Elizabeth, Simon Richard. *Education:* Brasenose College, Oxford, B.A., 1952, M.A., 1955. *Religion:* Catholic.

ADDRESSES: Home—19 Hugh St., London SW1, England. *Office*—c/o Editorial Design Consultants, 4 Wedgwood Mews, Greek St., London WW1, England. *Agent*—Giles Gordon, Anthony Sheil Associates Ltd., 2-3 Morewell St., London WC1B 3AR, England.

CAREER: Writer, journalist, political and business consultant. *Financial Times*, London, England, reporter, 1952-56, foreign news editor, 1956-59; McGraw-Hill World News, London Bureau, London, news editor, 1959-60; *Director* (magazine), London, associate editor, 1960-68, editor, 1968-74, editor-in-chief, 1974-84; Penguin Books, London, consulting editor for the Business Book Library, 1985—. Trustee of the *Universe,* 1970—; Tablet Publishing Co., member of board of directors, 1971—, trustee, 1976; member of board of directors of Anvil Productions, Ltd., 1980—, of Editorial Design Consultants, and of Westminster and Overseas Consultants. Chairman of Comission for International Justice and Peace, Episcopal Conference of England and Wales, 1971-74. Governor of St. Mary's College, Strawberry Hill, 1976—.

MEMBER: Society for Renaissance Studies (honorary treasurer, 1967—), Royal Society of Literature of the United Kingdom (fellow, 1983—), Royal Society of Arts (fellow, 1984—).

AWARDS, HONORS: Knight of the Holy Sepulchre.

WRITINGS:

(With Anthony Vice) *Bid for Power*, Elek, 1958, 3rd revised edition, 1961.
Vatican Politics at the Second Vatican Council, 1962-1965, Oxford University Press, 1966.
The Renaissance (juvenile), illustrations by Elizabeth Hammond, John Day, 1968.
(Editor) *The Director's Handbook*, McGraw, 1969, 2nd edition, 1977.
(Editor with Eric Foster) *The Director, His Money, and His Job*, McGraw, 1970.
(Advisory editor) *Director's Guide to Management Techniques*, edited by Dennis Lock and Gerard Tavernier, foreword by Richard Powell, Directors Bookshelf, 1970, 2nd edition, edited by D. Lock, 1972.
(With Peter Hobday and John Hemway) *Industrial Relations: The Boardroom Viewpoint*, Bodley Head, 1972.
The Director's Guide to Pensions, Quartermaine House Ltd., 1978.
Venice: The Most Triumphant City, St. Martin's, 1981.
Inside the Vatican, Hutchinson, 1982, St. Martin's, 1983.

TRANSLATOR

(And author of introduction) Benvenuto Cellini, *Autobiography*, Penguin, 1956, published as *The Autobiography of Benvenuto Cellini*, 1961.
(And author of introduction) Niccolo Machiavelli, *The Prince*, Penguin, 1961, revised edition, 1975, also published with prelude by Benito Mussolini, Folio Society, 1970, 2nd edition, 1975.
Giorgio Vasari, *The Lives of the Artists: A Selection*, Penguin, 1965, abridged edition published as *Artists of the Renaissance: An Illustrated Selection*, Allen Lane, 1978.
(And author of introduction) Baldassare Castiglione, *The Book of the Courtier*, Penguin, 1967.

(And author of introduction) Vasari, *Life of Michelangelo Buonarroti*, Folio Society, 1971.
(And author of introduction) Pietro Aretino, *Selected Letters of Aretino*, Penguin, 1976.

Columnist for *CBI News* (fortnightly publication of Confederation of British Industry); writer on business affairs for the *Tablet* (Catholic news weekly). Contributor to magazines and newspapers, including *Times* (London) and *Het Parool*.

WORK IN PROGRESS: Translating *Life, Letters, and Poetry of Michelangelo: A Selection*, for publication by Oxford University Press; translating further selections from Giorgio Vasari's "Lives of the Artists" series, for publication by Penguin Books; a history of the international finance group, Mercantile House; a play about Niccolo Machiavelli.

SIDELIGHTS: Described variously as a travelogue, a history, and an anthology of remniscences, George Bull's 1981 publication, *Venice: The Most Triumphant City*, presents a collage of anecdotes, impressions, and insights from Venetian travelers throughout the years beginning with the Renaissance. Assessed "impressionistic in manner and casual in tone" by *New York Times* critic Michiko Kakutani, the book draws from the "memoirs of such famous visitors as John Ruskin, Lord Byron and Percy Bysshe Shelley" and "explains the British fascination for Venice by pointing out the historical parallels of empire-building and decline." Bull also includes his own impressions, based on experience, of the city he chronicles, admitting that "this is a very personal book . . . a first volume of autobiography." A *Spectator* reviewer called the work "a historical gondola ride through Venice with cultured travellers past and present organised by Mr. George Bull."

In his 1982 book, *Inside the Vatican*, Bull couples historical research and personal interviews to describe the organization and activities of various Vatican institutions and the men who run them. Topics covered include architectural innovations, diplomatic tradition, papal etiquette, and the structure of the curia. Although the "author is too loyal a Catholic to utter any serious criticisms," opined Kenneth Ballhatchet in *British Book News*, "he is too perceptive and honest a journalist to look the other way, and much can be learned by the attentive reader." Critic Michael Walsh of the *Times Literary Supplement* questioned Bull's reluctance to address the "major issues concerning the Vatican's relationship with the rest of the Catholic world," yet he too felt that "there is much between the elegant covers of this book which will entertain the reader." Reviewer Eugene K. Culhane of *America* lauded *Inside the Vatican* not only for its "thoroughness and readableness" but also for "the solidity of this book, written out of the author's balanced judgment and an obvious love of his subject matter."

Bull told *CA:* "Extensive travels and a variety of contacts are important to me as a journalist and translator. My interests are broad, ranging from the novel to the world of industry and finance. As a writer, I keep an occasional diary to jog my memory and to record events or ideas that strike me at the time as worth putting into words, if only for myself. But also, who knows, these notes can be capital for further output.

"My field of interest widens all the time—especially since I have become a consulting editor for Penguin Book's Business Book Library. I am also developing an interest in the literature of Japan, following my second visit to that country after a twenty-one-year gap. So the paper mountain grows."

BIOGRAPHICAL/CRITICAL SOURCES:

PERIODICALS

America, June 4, 1983.
British Book News, August, 1982.
New York Times, May 28, 1982.
Spectator, January 16, 1982, June 5, 1982.
Times (London), March 11, 1982, March 18, 1982.
Times Literary Supplement, May 28, 1982.

*   *   *

BULOFF, Joseph   1899(?)-1985

OBITUARY NOTICE: Born December 6, 1899 (some sources say 1907), in Vilnius, Lithuania (now U.S.S.R.); died after a long illness, February 27, 1985, in New York, N.Y. Actor, theatrical director, and adapter of plays. In 1928, after acting in Europe with the Vilna Troupe for several years, Buloff immigrated to the United States, where he later joined the Yiddish Art Theatre in New York City. He also formed his own troupe, the Folks Theatre. Known for his command of comic gesture and expression, Buloff acted in both Yiddish- and English-language productions and appeared in more than two hundred plays. Among them were the Broadway productions of "Don't Look Now," "Call Me Ziggy," and "The Man From Cairo" and the original production of "Oklahoma." In the course of his lengthy theatrical career Buloff acted in a number of stage productions that he simultaneously directed, including the Yiddish plays "Yoshke Musikant," which he adapted, and "Hard to Be a Jew," which he co-adapted. And in 1980 he directed and starred in "The Chekhov Sketchbook," which he co-adapted from three plays by Anton Chekhov. Buloff also ventured into television acting, and he appeared in the movies "Silk Stockings," "Somebody up There Likes Me," and "Let's Make Music."

OBITUARIES AND OTHER SOURCES:

BOOKS

*Who's Who in the Theatre: A Biographical Record of the Con-
    temporary Stage,* 16th edition, Pitman, 1977.

PERIODICALS

New York Times, February 28, 1985.

*   *   *

BUNTING, Basil   1900-1985

OBITUARY NOTICE—See index for *CA* sketch: Born March 1, 1900, in Scotswood, Northumberland, England; died April 17, 1985, in Hexham, England. Educator, journalist, and poet. Jailed as a conscientious objector during World War I, Bunting moved to Paris in the 1920's and became part of the literary group that included Ernest Hemingway. From 1929 to 1933 he lived in Italy, where he befriended poets W. B. Yeats and Ezra Pound. His relationship with Pound, a staunch supporter of Fascist dictator Benito Mussolini, is thought to have adversely affected the acceptance of Bunting's writings by the literary world, particularly in Europe. Judging Bunting by the company he kept, readers and critics alike mistakenly associated him with Mussolini and shunned his work. It was not until 1964, fourteen years after his first volume of commercially published poetry, *Poems: 1950,* appeared in the United States, that any of his work was published in England.

In addition to living in France and Italy, Bunting resided in the Canary Islands from 1933 to 1936 and in Iran from 1943 to 1951. He was financial sub-editor of Britain's Newcastle *Evening Chronicle* from 1953 to 1966, and he taught poetry at several universities in the United States, Canada, and England from 1966 to 1973. His poetry, characterized by its musical qualities, has been collected into a number of volumes, including *The Spoils, First Book of Odes, Ode II/2, Two Poems,* and what most critics feel to be Bunting's best work, *Briggflatts: An Autobiography.*

OBITUARIES AND OTHER SOURCES:

BOOKS

Who's Who, 136th edition, St. Martin's, 1984.
The Writers Directory: 1984-1986, St. James Press, 1983.

PERIODICALS

Los Angeles Times, April 20, 1985.

*   *   *

BURKHOLDER, John Richard   1928-

PERSONAL: Born December 19, 1928, in Lancaster, Pa.; son of Clarence A. (a contractor) and Blanche (a housewife; maiden name, Herr) Burkholder; married Susan Elizabeth Herr (a teacher), June 6, 1952; children: Evelyn Burkholder King, Lissa, Samuel, Rebecca, Peter. *Education:* Goshen College, B.A., 1952, B.D., 1955; Harvard University, Ph.D., 1969.

ADDRESSES: Home—1508 South 14th St., Goshen, Ind. 46526.

CAREER: Ordained Mennonite minister, 1954; Mennonite missionary and teacher in Goiania, Brazil, 1954-57; church administrator in Philadelphia, Pa., 1958-60; Goshen College, Goshen, Ind., assistant professor, 1963-67, associate professor, 1967-73, professor of religion, 1973-85, chairman of department of religion, 1975-77, director of peace studies, 1975-85. C. Henry Smith Lecturer at Bluffton and Goshen Colleges, 1984-85; director of Dallas Peace Center, Dallas, Tex., 1982-84.

MEMBER: American Academy of Religion, Society of Christian Ethics, Consortium for Peace Research, Education, and Development, Fellowship of Reconciliation (member of national council, 1965-73).

WRITINGS:

(Contributor) Irving Zaretsky and Mark Leone, editors, *Religious Movements in Contemporary America,* Princeton University Press, 1975.
(Editor with Calvin Redekop, and contributor) *Kingdom, Cross, and Community,* Herald Press, 1976.
(With John Bender) *Children of Peace,* Herald Press, 1982.

Contributor to academic and religious journals.

WORK IN PROGRESS: Research on current issues in religious freedom and church-state conflict, the church and revolution in Central America, personal transformation and action for social change, and alternatives to violence in social conflict.

SIDELIGHTS: J. R. Burkholder told *CA:* "Most of my writing has been done in fulfillment of assignments connected with my profession as teacher and churchman. All too often these have been routine academic chores, not very inspiring for either reader or writer.

"I am currently in a time of professional transition and want to rethink my personal priorities. I must admit that I am at heart a preacher and a proclaimer, that I want to write and speak—not just to inform, but to convince, to promote change in both persons and society.

"It has taken me a long time to learn that facts and logic probably don't go very far in bringing about genuine attitudinal change. Symbols and images and stories that appeal to elemental human experience are more effective. So I want to become a storyteller.

"I hope to build on the learnings from thirty years of involvement with religiously oriented justice and peace efforts as I write and speak and organize on behalf of the oppressed peoples of our planet. A 1984 trip to Central America, renewing personal acquaintances from previous experience there and gaining new insights into the social and political realities, has renewed my conviction that an alternative to the official position must be communicated to the American people."

*   *   *

BURNHAM, J. W.
See BURNHAM, Jack (Wesley)

*   *   *

BURNHAM, Jack (Wesley) 1931-
(J. W. Burnham)

PERSONAL: Born November 13, 1931, in New York, N.Y.; son of Jack Wesley (in advertising) and Dorothy (a housewife; maiden name, Fowler) Burnham. *Education:* Attended Boston Museum School, 1953-54 and 1956-57; Wentworth Institute, A.E., 1956; Yale University, B.F.A., 1959, M.F.A., 1961.

ADDRESSES: Office—Department of Art, University of Maryland, College Park, Md. 20782.

CAREER: Northwestern University, Evanston, Ill., professor of art, beginning 1962; Colgate University, Hamilton, N.Y., Dana Professor of Fine Arts, 1975-76; Williams College, Williamstown, Mass., Clark Professor of Art History, 1980; University of Maryland, College Park, Md., professor and chairman of art department, 1983—. *Military service:* U.S. Army Engineers, 1949-52.

AWARDS, HONORS: Fellowship from Guggenheim Foundation, 1973; critics awards from Chicago Art Awards Committee, 1977 and 1978.

WRITINGS:

Beyond Modern Sculpture: Effects of Science and Technology on Sculpture of This Century, Braziller, 1968.
Art in the Marcusean (monograph), Pennsylvania State University Press, 1969.
(Contributor under name J. W. Burnham) Edward F. Fry, editor, *On the Future of Art: Essays by Arnold J. Toynbee and Others,* Viking, 1970.
The Structure of Art, Braziller, 1971, revised edition, 1973.
Great Western Salt Works: Essays on the Meaning of Post-Formalist Art, Braziller, 1974.

Contributor to journals, including *Diacritics* and *Criteria.* Contributing editor of *Artforum,* 1971-72, and *New Art Examiner.* Associate editor of *Arts,* 1972-76.

WORK IN PROGRESS: Two books, *The Art and Writing of Marcel Duchamp* and *Deep Structure in Western Art.*

BURNS, Geoff 1954-

PERSONAL: Born April 5, 1954, in Invercargill, New Zealand; immigrated to United States, 1983; son of Bruce and Isla (Webb) Burns; married Jill Birse, January 19, 1974; children: Hannah. *Education:* University of Otago, B.Com., 1975.

ADDRESSES: Home—79C Avon Circle, Rye Brook, N.Y. 10573.

CAREER: Associated with Franklin Watts Ltd. (publisher), London, England, beginning in 1979, financial director, 1981-83; Franklin Watts, Inc. (publisher), New York, N.Y., controller, 1983—, director of telemarketing, 1984—.

WRITINGS:

Take a Trip to New Zealand (juvenile nonfiction), F. Watts, 1982.

Contributor to magazines, including *Field Hockey,* and newspapers.

WORK IN PROGRESS: Fiction and nonfiction about New Zealand.

SIDELIGHTS: Geoff Burns told *CA:* "I am developing fictional and nonfictional writing in order to present and explain New Zealand's place and its uniqueness to the world, particularly to Americans, who can be very insular in knowledge and outlook. My first book, *Take a Trip to New Zealand,* was a start to educate children about New Zealand and New Zealanders. I am also working on a pictorial guide (with a difference) to common sense travel in the 'developed' world."

*   *   *

BURNS, John Horne 1916-1953

BRIEF ENTRY: Born October 7, 1916, in Andover, Mass.; died of a cerebral hemorrhage (one source says sunstroke), August 10 (some sources say August 11), 1953, in Livorno, Italy. American teacher and novelist. Burns was best known for *The Gallery* (1947), a novel about the lives of soldiers in Naples, Italy, during World War II. The book was a best-seller and was chosen as "the best war book of the year" by the *Saturday Review of Literature.* Before becoming a full-time writer, Burns taught English at a boys' preparatory school in Connecticut and served in the U.S. Army during World War II. *The Gallery* was inspired by the year and a half Burns spent in Italy while in the military. His other published novels are *Lucifer With a Book* (1949) and *A Cry of Children* (1952). A fourth work, *The Stranger's Guise,* was left unpublished.

BIOGRAPHICAL/CRITICAL SOURCES:

BOOKS

American Novelists of Today, Greenwood Press, 1976.
Mitzel, John, *John Horne Burns: An Appreciative Biography,* Destiny Books, 1974.
Twentieth-Century Authors: A Biographical Dictionary of Modern Literature, 1st supplement, H. W. Wilson, 1955.
Webster's New World Companion to English and American Literature, World Publishing, 1973.

PERIODICALS

New York Times, August 14, 1953.

BURR, Keith 1946-

PERSONAL: Born August 5, 1946, in Jacksonville, Fla.; married Andrea Kopriua, May 2, 1970; children: Kevin. *Education:* University of Pittsburgh, B.A., 1968, J.D., 1973.

ADDRESSES: Home and office—935 Savannah Ave., Pittsburgh, Pa. 15221.

CAREER: Attorney in Pittsburgh, Pa., 1973-80; writer, 1980—.

WRITINGS:

(With Joseph Gillis) *The Screenwriters Guide*, New York Zoetrope, 1982.

Comedy writer for entertainers, including Rodney Dangerfield and Joan Rivers. Contributor to magazines, including *American Film* and *Film Quarterly*.

WORK IN PROGRESS: Three screenplays.

*   *   *

BUTCHER, Harry Cecil 1901-1985

OBITUARY NOTICE: Born November 15, 1901, in Springville, Iowa; died of Alzheimer's disease, April 20, 1985, in Santa Barbara, Calif. Broadcasting executive, naval officer, and author of the best-selling book *My Three Years With Eisenhower*. Butcher based his book on the official diary that he kept for Dwight D. Eisenhower while serving as his naval aide during World War II. The book was initially serialized in the *Saturday Evening Post* in 1945 and 1946. Prior to his three years of World War II service, Butcher opened the Washington, D.C., Columbia Broadcasting System (CBS) radio station. He directed the station from its opening in 1929 until he became a vice-president of CBS-Radio during the early 1930's. After World War II Butcher moved to Santa Barbara, California, where he founded KIST radio and television station and purchased KEY-TV cable news station.

OBITUARIES AND OTHER SOURCES:

BOOKS

The Reader's Encyclopedia of American Literature, Crowell, 1962.

PERIODICALS

New York Times, April 24, 1985.
Washington Post, April 24, 1985.
Washington Times, April 23, 1985.

*   *   *

BUTTINGER, Muriel Gardiner 1901-1985
(Muriel Gardiner)

OBITUARY NOTICE: See index for *CA* sketch: Professionally known as Muriel Gardiner; born November 23, 1901, in Chicago, Ill.; died of cancer, February 6, 1985, in Princeton, N.J. Educator, psychoanalyst, and author. Born into a wealthy Chicago family, Gardiner was studying English literature at Oxford University in 1926 when an interest in the work of famed psychoanalyst Sigmund Freud prompted her to seek him in Vienna, Austria. There Freud arranged for Gardiner to begin analysis with one of his students. In 1932 Gardiner entered the University of Vienna Medical School with the goal of becoming a psychoanalyst herself.

After witnessing Nazis throw Jewish students from the windows of a school in Vienna, Gardiner became active in the anti-Fascist Socialist underground. Using the code name Mary, she hid dissidents, dealt in forged documents, smuggled money, and facilitated the escape of people forced to flee the country. One of those she hid, Joseph Buttinger, head of the Austrian Revolutionary Socialists, became her second husband. The couple moved to Paris in 1938 and in the following year came to the United States, where Gardiner taught, lectured, and practiced psychoanalysis, specializing in treating disturbed children. She was influential in establishing the Freud Museum in England. When Gardiner's memoir, *Code Name Mary*, was published in 1983, some readers speculated that Gardiner had served as the model for Lillian Hellman's heroine Julia in the playwright's memoir, *Pentimento*, from which the 1977 motion picture "Julia" was adapted. Hellman, however, denied the connection. Gardiner also wrote *The Deadly Innocents: Portraits of Children Who Kill* and served as co-author and editor of *The Wolf-Man*.

OBITUARIES AND OTHER SOURCES:

PERIODICALS

American Medical News, February 22, 1985.
Chicago Tribune, February 8, 1985.
Detroit Free Press, February 8, 1985.
Los Angeles Times, February 8, 1985.
Newsweek, February 18, 1985.
Time, February 18, 1985.
Times (London), February 16, 1985.
Washington Post, February 10, 1985.

*   *   *

BUXTON, Anne (Arundel)
(Anne Maybury, Katherine Troy)

BRIEF ENTRY: British novelist. Buxton has written at least eighty gothic or romance novels, most under the pseudonym Anne Maybury. Among her most recent titles are *Walk in the Paradise Garden* (Random House, 1972), *The Midnight Dancers* (Random House, 1973), *Jessamy Court* (Random House, 1974), *The Jewelled Daughter* (Random House, 1976), *Dark Star* (Random House, 1977), and *Radiance* (Random House, 1979). *Address:* c/o A. M. Heath, 40-42 William IV St., London WC2N 4DD, England.

BIOGRAPHICAL/CRITICAL SOURCES:

BOOKS

The Writers Directory: 1984-1986, St. James Press, 1983.

C

CAGNEY, James 1904(?)-

BRIEF ENTRY: Born July 1, 1904 (some sources say July 17, 1904, or July 17, 1899), in New York, N.Y. American actor and author. Cagney, who became famous for his screen portrayals of tough, streetwise hoodlums in gangster films of the 1930's and 1940's, began his entertainment career in 1924 as a chorus boy in the Broadway musical comedy "Pitter Patter." He then worked in vaudeville, an experience that served him well when he later portayed vaudevillian George M. Cohan in the motion picture musical "Yankee Doodle Dandy." His performance in the film earned the actor an Academy Award in 1942. Cagney had made his motion picture debut in the 1931 film "Sinner's Holiday." He then appeared in a string of gangster films that included "Public Enemy," "The Roaring Twenties," and "White Heat." Cagney also portrayed a gangster in the film biography of singer Ruth Etting, "Love Me or Leave Me." The entertainer retired from acting in 1961 but made a brief comeback twenty years later when he appeared in "Ragtime," the movie adaptation of E. L. Doctorow's best-selling novel. Cagney published his autobiography, *Cagney by Cagney* (Doubleday), in 1976.

BIOGRAPHICAL/CRITICAL SOURCES:

BOOKS

Current Biography, Wilson, 1942.
Freedland, Michael, *Cagney: A Biography,* Stein & Day, 1975.
Parish, James Robert, *Tough Guys,* Arlington House, 1976.
Warren, Doug, *James Cagney: The Authorized Biography,* St. Martin's, 1983.

PERIODICALS

New York Times, November 17, 1981.

*   *   *

CALDWELL, Nat(han Green) 1912-1985

OBITUARY NOTICE: Born July 16, 1912, in St. Charles, Mo.; died following a car accident, February 11, 1985, near Gallatin, Tenn. Journalist and author. A reporter for the Nashville *Tennessean* newspaper for fifty-one years, Caldwell shared a 1962 Pulitzer Prize in national reporting with Gene S. Graham for "their exclusive disclosure and six years of detailed reporting of the undercover cooperation between management interests in the coal industry and the United Mine Workers." He also wrote *The Cotton Picker Moves People* and *The Strange Romance of John L. Lewis and Cyrus Eaton.*

OBITUARIES AND OTHER SOURCES:

BOOKS

Who's Who in the South and Southwest, 13th edition, Marquis, 1973.

PERIODICALS

New York Times, February 18, 1985.
Washington Post, February 18, 1985.

*   *   *

CAMERON, Neil 1920-1985

OBITUARY NOTICE: Born July 8, 1920, in Perth, Scotland; died January 29, 1985, in London, England. Military officer, college administrator, and author. Cameron joined the Volunteer Reserve of Britain's Royal Air Force (RAF) in 1939, shortly before the outbreak of World War II. Following the war he became a career officer and remained with the RAF until his 1979 retirement, attaining the rank of chief of the Air Staff in 1976 and chief of the Defense Staff in 1977. Known as an outspoken man, Cameron headed the Programme Evaluation Group at the Ministry of Defence from 1966 to 1968 and continued even after his retirement to voice his opinions on defense policy through the British Atlantic Committee. He was named principal of the University of London's King's College in 1980 and was created a life peer as Lord Cameron of Balhousie in 1983. His writings include articles for defense journals, the 1984 book *Diminishing the Nuclear Threat: Nato's Defense and New Technology,* and *What Hope in an Armed World?,* which he co-authored with Richard Harries.

OBITUARIES AND OTHER SOURCES:

BOOKS

Who's Who, 134th edition, St. Martin's, 1982.

PERIODICALS

Times (London), January 30, 1985.

CAMPBELL, (Mary) Jean 1943-

PERSONAL: Born May 14, 1943, in Alma, Mich.; daughter of Orley Theodore (a laborer) and Beulah (a housewife; maiden name, Goodwin) Marzolf; married second husband, Leonard Baker (an inventor). *Education:* Michigan State University, B.A., 1964; graduate study at University of Richmond, 1965-66, University of Pennsylvania, 1966-67, and Old Dominion University.

ADDRESSES: Home—443 Hill Meadow Dr., Virginia Beach, Va. 23451. *Office*—Poseidia Institute, Suite 216, The Sun Building, 138 Rosemont Rd., Virginia Beach, Va. 23452.

CAREER: Teacher of English and creative writing and drama coach at public high school in Eaton Rapids, Mich., 1964-65; American Friends Service Committee, Philadelphia, Pa., assistant to college coordinator for Mid-Atlantic Region, 1966-67; librarian and teacher of remedial English at public elementary school in Chiefland, Fla., 1967-68; *Raleigh Register,* Beckley, W.Va., reporter and feature writer, 1969-72; teacher of English, creative writing, and world literature at public high school in Virginia Beach, Va., 1973-75; Poseidia Institute, Virginia Beach, executive director, designer of classes, and instructor, 1976—. Associate editor for publisher, Donning Co., 1976—. Co-host of "Psychic Dimensions," a talk show on WNIS-AM Radio, 1980-81; coordinator of seminars; public speaker. Candidate for Virginia Beajch City Council, 1982; member of Oceana Civil League.

MEMBER: Association for the Study of Dreams.

WRITINGS:

Great Gardens of America, Putnam, 1970.
Dreams Beyond Dreaming, Donning, 1979.

Contributor to magazines, including *West Virginia, Grantsmanship News,* and *Dream Network Bulletin,* and newspapers. Creator of newsletter *Creative Consciousness,* 1984. Contributing member of editorial staff of *Pyramid: Quarterly Journal of Poseidia Institute* and *Pi-Line.*

WORK IN PROGRESS: Life Among the Psychics; Dreams[10]; The Powhatan Prophecies, cycle of four novels, tracing the metaphysical relationship between the British and the American Indian, Volume I: *Matoaka; So You Think You're the Only One* (tentative title), "aimed at giving the ordinary person hope that he/she isn't the only one ever to have 'psychic' experiences; research on the role of intuition in creativity, the nature of consciousness, relationships between parapsychology, psychology, physics, and medicine, and the practical applications of intuitive skills.

SIDELIGHTS: Jean Campbell told *CA:* "Directing a research organization, starting a newsletter or digest that will cover work in the field of consciousness studies, full-time graduate studies, ghostwriting one book while working on others of my own, helping with the production of an opera, and teaching classes at Poseidia Institute keep me pretty busy. My work in parapsychology keeps me traveling, lecturing, making media appearances, meeting interesting people, and hearing interesting stories. Since becoming involved in the operation of a nonprofit organization in 1976, I have also taken considerable interest in the workings of the nonprofit industry in general, particularly in the areas of community support and organizational funding. This has led me toward more political activity and community involvement.

"The thing I like best about Poseidia Institute is that it started from the basic assumption that extrasensory abilities exist, and that there is no need to prove their existence, as has been the direction of most parapsychology research in the country since the late 1800's. Further, we observed that *everyone* seemed to have psychic abilities, whether they were called 'hunches' or 'feelings' or 'women's intuition,' so the goal could become one of discovering how to develop these abilities and the practical application of them.

"I have almost never spoken before a group or addressed a radio or television audience in the past ten years without someone relating a psychic experience—generally starting with 'You'll probably think I'm crazy, but. . . .' So I have seen my own role as one of reintroducing people to what seems to be a very natural and useful part of themselves that is currently regarded with awe or superstition.

"A few years ago, after thinking about how many authors produced manuscripts in just a couple of weeks (whether they called it 'automatic writing' or not—and you'd be surprised at the number who do), I decided I should try it. The result was *Life Among the Psychics,* a manuscript of more than four hundred pages, written in two weeks' time.

"I'm not saying that there isn't work involved or no standard of quality to be observed. There is. I believe thoroughly that if it isn't quality work, it shouldn't be done. However, why shouldn't all people have regular, controlled access to the qualities of genius, or what, to date, has been considered only an occasional flash of brilliance or something available only to a few?

"What prompted me to begin my cycle of novels, *The Powhatan Prophecies,* was similar intuitive fact. While running for public office in 1982, I found myself extraordinarily busy. So to maintain my sanity I started 'writing to myself' every day. That is, I let my mind wander and my hand wander across the page for five or ten minutes every morning in order to pick up any unconscious thoughts or impressions I was missing.

"I had been thinking about returning to some fiction writing, an area that has been harder for me to master than nonfiction, and my 'self' said to myself, 'Here's what you're going to do.' It proceeded to outline four novels that crossed American history from the first British settlement to the present, and were based on a 'prophecy' given to Chief Powhatan before the first British settlers arrived.

"I have an interest in history, even a college minor in the subject, but had always steered away from American history, finding it generally distasteful. I certainly didn't know anything about any prophecy being given to Powhatan, but my curiosity got the better of me and before long I found myself in the library. Sure enough, there has been a story recorded of the coming of the white men being prophesied to Powhatan before the settlers arrived. Well, even I was impressed. This was pretty interesting.

"I began to weave a historical fantasy in which I asked the questions, 'What if the Indians had known 'psychically' the probable outcome of the British settlement? What if there had been a conflict over what direction to take, what attitude to take toward the settlers, with one side represented by Powhatan and his advisers, while the other side was represented by Pocahontas and her cohorts? What if one side represented the adversary position between cultures and the other side represented the Native American tradition or harmony, or teaching the British (or Westerners) about harmony or how to live peaceably with all life? And what if this battle were fought over time and space by shamans or Algonquin power figures who understood mastery?

"Well, I was hooked. Since then I have been studying American history, learning the Algonquin language, working with a friend on an opera based on part of the plot, and trying to figure out how to construct a coherent whole out of what seems at times like a totally unmanageable amount of material. I call it alternative history. That is, it takes actual historical people and events and reinterprets them in what I think is a believable, if alternate, way. My personal views about the nature of time and space and 'reality' are reflected, of course, by the Pocahontas figure (who appears, as do the others, as other people in various historical settings), but I have been amazed to find how close this might have been, could be, to a 'real' interpretation of history."

AVOCATIONAL INTERESTS: Reading (science fiction and fantasy), theatre, music, knitting, gardening, walking, bowling, cycling.

* * *

CANFIELD, Muriel 1935-

PERSONAL: Born May 14, 1935, in Oak Park, Ill.; daughter of Donald MacDonnell (in business) and Audrey (a homemaker; maiden name, Hinden) Hansen, married Eugene David Canfield (a civil engineer), September 7, 1956; children: Donald, Deborah Morgan, Douglas. *Education:* Miami University, Ohio, B.S. (summa cum laude), 1978. *Religion:* Christian.

ADDRESSES: Home—2591 California Rd., Okeana, Ohio 45053.

CAREER: Barnhorn Realtors, Cincinnati, Ohio, real estate agent, 1968-70; West Shell Realtors, Cincinnati, real estate agent, 1970-71, 1973, and 1975; writer, 1979—.

MEMBER: Harrison Writers' Group.

WRITINGS:

I Wish I Could Say I Love You (autobiography), Bethany House, 1983.
Anne (young adult romance), Bethany House, 1984.

WORK IN PROGRESS: A novel tentatively titled *A Victorian Marriage,* set in Chicago just prior to and including the Chicago fire, completion expected in 1986.

SIDELIGHTS: Muriel Canfield told *CA:* "After various jobs, such as selling real estate, waiting on tables, and selling china, at age forty-three I began writing. I quickly became intrigued with it, establishing a routine of writing six days a week between 7:00 A.M. and noon. I live in the country, and my den overlooks trees, hills, and a field—a beautiful part of God's creation and very inspiring to me. In fiction and nonfiction I pursue the theme of the sufficiency of God and the insufficiency of man. For technique and style I like best the novels of Joyce Cary, and I would advise new writers to study the classics of literature to learn the craft of writing. In the future I hope to write predominantly fiction, as I enjoy the process of setting up a fictional world."

AVOCATIONAL INTERESTS: Walking, birdwatching, playing bridge.

CAPRON, Alexander Morgan 1944-

PERSONAL: Born August 16, 1944, in Hartford, Conn.; son of William M. (a professor of economics) and Margaret (a specialist in problems of the elderly; maiden name, Morgan) Capron; divorced; children: Jared J. *Education:* Swarthmore College, B.A., 1966; Yale University, LL.B., 1969.

ADDRESSES: Office—Law Center, University of Southern California, Los Angeles, Calif. 90089-0071.

CAREER: U.S. Court of Appeals, Washington, D.C., law clerk to Chief Judge David L. Bazelon, 1969-70; Yale University, New Haven, Conn., lecturer in law and postdoctoral research associate, 1970-72; University of Pennsylvania, Philadelphia, assistant professor, 1972-75, associate professor, 1975-78, professor of law, 1978-82, professor of human genetics, 1976-82, vice-dean of Law School, 1975-76; Georgetown University, Washington, D.C., professor of law, ethics, and public policy, 1983-84; University of Southern California, Los Angeles, Topping Professor of Law, Medicine, and Public Policy, 1985—. Executive director of President's Commission for the Study of Ethical Problems in Medicine and Biomedical and Behavioral Research, 1980-83. Senior fellow at Joseph and Rose Kennedy Institute of Ethics, Georgetown University, 1983—; member of board of managers of Swarthmore College, 1982—. Consultant to National Institutes of Health and Office for Technology Assessment.

MEMBER: American Association of University professors (past member of University of Pennsylvania executive committee), Institute of Society, Ethics, and the Life Sciences (fellow; member of board of directors, 1975-80, 1982—), Institute of Medicine (member of council and executive committee, both 1985—), Society of American Law Teachers, American Society of Law and Medicine (member of board of directors, 1984—), Swarthmore College Alumni Society (vice-president, 1974-77), Coif.

AWARDS, HONORS: Rosenthal Foundation Award from American College of Physicians, 1984, for contributions made to health care with reports of the President's Commission; award from Association of College and Research Libraries, 1984, for President's Commission report "Making Health Care Decisions."

WRITINGS:

(With Jay Katz) *Catastrophic Diseases: Who Decides What?,* Russell Sage, 1975.
(With Marc Lappe, Robert F. Murray, Tabitha M. Powledge, and others) *Genetic Counseling: Facts, Values, and Norms,* Alan Liss, 1979.
(With Judith Areen, Patricia A. King, and Steven Goldberg) *Law, Science, and Medicine,* Foundation Press, 1984.

Contributor to medical and law journals.

WORK IN PROGRESS: A Moral Basis for Action in a Pluralistic Society, "a study of the mechanisms available for decisionmaking on difficult issues in medical ethics and public policy, including birth, illness, and death."

SIDELIGHTS: Alexander Morgan Capron told *CA:* "The ethical and legal issues generated by the life sciences, including health care delivery, are not arcane matters for consideration only by a few 'experts.' Rather, they enter into the lives of all Americans, as individuals, as family members, as members of various professions, and as citizens. I believe it is possible to address these issues in a way that is accessible to concerned lay people without oversimplification; moreover, I think it is important to do so.''

* * *

CARLETON, Will(iam McKendree) 1845-1912

BRIEF ENTRY: Born October 21, 1845, in Hudson, Mich.; died December 18, 1912, in Brooklyn, N.Y. American lecturer, journalist, editor, publisher, and poet. Carleton was best known for his ballads about common life, including ''Betsy and I Are Out'' and ''Over the Hill to the Poor House,'' which were published in his book *Farm Ballads* (1873). Early in his career Carleton served as editor of the Hillsdale *Standard* and Detroit *Weekly Tribune.* In 1894 he founded *Everywhere* magazine, which he published until his death. Carleton lectured throughout the United States and Canada and twice visited Europe as a lecturer. In addition, he was one of the first poets to give public readings from his own works. Among his other writings are *Farm Legends* (1875), *Young Folks' Centennial Rhymes* (1876), *Farm Festivals* (1881), *City Ballads* (1885), and *Rhymes of Our Planet* (1895).

BIOGRAPHICAL/CRITICAL SOURCES:

BOOKS

American Biographies, Gale, 1974.
Corning, A. Elwood, *Will Carleton: A Biographical Study,* Lanmere, 1917.
Everyman's Dictionary of Literary Biography, English and American, revised edition, Dutton, 1960.
The National Cyclopaedia of American Biography, Volume 2, James T. White, 1891.
Who Was Who in America, Volume I: *1897-1942,* Marquis, 1943.

* * *

CARMICHAEL, Carrie
See CARMICHAEL, Harriet

* * *

CARMICHAEL, Harriet
(Carrie Carmichael)

PERSONAL: Born in Plainfield, N.J.; daughter of William and Harriet (a teacher; maiden name, Wentlandt) Carmichael; married Jeff Greenfield (a writer and broadcaster), May 11, 1968; children: Casey (daughter), David. *Education:* Muhlenberg College, B.A., 1966; New York University, M.A., 1968.

ADDRESSES: Home—322 West 72nd St., Apt. 11B, New York, N.Y. 10023. *Agent*—Patricia Berens, Sterling Lord Agency Inc., 660 Madison Ave., New York, N.Y. 10022.

CAREER: United Press International, New York City, financial reporter, 1967-68; WNYC–TV, New York City, anchor of daily news broadcast ''News of New York,'' producer and anchor of weekly television program ''Women: New York Edition,'' 1977-80; National Broadcasting Co. (NBC Radio), New York City, broadcaster of daily radio program ''Workplace,'' 1978—. Member of board of directors of Rheedlan Foundation.

AWARDS, HONORS: Women at Work Broadcast Award from National Commission on Working Women, 1982, for excellence in broadcasting; first prize media award from Odyssey Institute Corporation, 1984, for five-part NBC-Radio series ''When a Child Is Missing.''

WRITINGS:

UNDER NAME CARRIE CARMICHAEL; NONFICTION

Non-Sexist Childraising, Beacon, 1977.
Big Foot: Myth, Man, or Monster? (juvenile), Raintree, 1978.
Secrets of the Great Magicians (juvenile), Raintree, 1978.
(With Marcia L. Storch) *How to Relieve Cramps and Other Menstrual Problems,* Workman Publishing, 1982.
(With Ruby Wright) *Mama Ruby's Book of Baby Knowledge,* Bantam, 1984.

SIDELIGHTS: Carrie Carmichael told *CA:* ''*Non-Sexist Childraising* sprang from an article in *Ms.* called 'How Feminists Are Raising Their Sons' that I wrote with Lindsy Van Gelder. MaryAnn Lash at Beacon Press thought there was more to how feminists were parenting than just how they were raising their sons. She was right. At first Beacon and I talked about writing a how-to guide on the nonsexist raising of children, but since none of the nonsexist-raised children were grown up at that point and I had only one child, a female toddler, we decided the book should be a progress report on how feminist families were doing. I hope our society reaches a stage of development where we can raise our children free of sex stereotypes so they are free to grow up and be themselves, but we are not there yet.

''I like print writing but prefer to combine it with something else. Since 1977 that something else has been broadcasting, both on radio and television. Sitting alone in a room with words and papers is too isolated for me as a steady diet. I like the mix of broadcasting—the studio and the people—with the solitary job of print writing.

'' 'Mama' Ruby Wright is a wonderful Honduran immigrant to the United States who has been a nurse to nearly one thousand babies. She lives in New York and has helped couples get over their trepidations about their newborn babies. She is a loving, total-care professional baby nurse whose no-nonsense approach has brought comfort and baby care skills to every family she has worked for. I was introduced to 'Mama' Ruby by literary agent-packager John Boswell.''

* * *

CARPENTER, J(ohn) D(avid) 1948-

PERSONAL: Born June 17, 1948, in Toronto, Ontario, Canada; son of Alan and Pat (Dodds) Carpenter; married Claudine Elisabeth Downes, 1972; children: Hadley, Reeves. *Education:* York University, B.A. (with honors), 1971; Queen's University, Kingston, Ontario, B.Ed., 1972.

ADDRESSES: Home—4 Ferris Rd., Toronto, Ontario, Canada M4B 1E8.

CAREER: Daily Racing Form, Windsor, Ontario, reporter, 1971, Montreal, Quebec, reporter, 1972; East York Board of Education, Toronto, Ontario, teacher, 1973—.

MEMBER: Federation of Ontario Naturalists.

WRITINGS:

Nightfall, Ferryland Head (poems), Missing Link Press, 1977.
Swimming at Twelve Mile (poems), Penumbra Press, 1979.

Contributor to magazines and newspapers.

WORK IN PROGRESS: Country Music, a novel, publication expected in 1985; *Men in Groups,* a novel, completion expected in 1986.

SIDELIGHTS: J. D. Carpenter told *CA:* "I began writing poetry when I was twenty; my first poem was a long ballad describing the gruesome deaths of various racehorses during a fogbound steeplechase. I quickly switched to free verse and wrote my way through periods of landscape poetry, dream poetry, and domestic poetry. After about twelve years the poetry stopped coming and I finally got down to the prose writing I had always wanted to do. Whereas the writing of poetry is a brief, impassioned business dependent on a 'gift' line or a 'gift' image, the writing of novels is a slower, friendlier, more constant process. Also, I write book reviews, which I find useful academic exercises in that they force me to study the writing styles of other writers, and I write short stories, which serve as effective conditioning for the larger writing of novels.''

*   *   *

CARR, Robyn 1951-

PERSONAL: Born July 25, 1951, in St. Paul, Minn.; daughter of Ronald E. and Bette (Crandall) Henrichs; married James R. Carr; children: Brian, Jamie. *Education:* Attended Arthur B. Anker School of Nursing, St. Paul, Minn., 1969-71.

ADDRESSES: Home—Tempe, Ariz. *Agent*—Ruth Cohen, Inc., P.O. Box 7626, Menlo Park, Calif. 94025.

CAREER: Writer, 1975—.

WRITINGS:

NOVELS

Chelynne, Little, Brown, 1980.
The Blue Falcon, Little, Brown, 1981.
The Bellerose Bargain, Little, Brown, 1982.
The Braeswood Tapestry, Little, Brown, 1984.
The Troubadour's Romance, Little, Brown, 1985.
The Chappington Affair, Pinnacle Books, 1985.
By Right of Arms, Little, Brown, in press.

Contributor to *Writer's Digest.*

SIDELIGHTS: Robyn Carr told *CA:* "It seems to me that writing is more of a lifestyle than a career. My family tells me that writers are strange, unpredictable people. They argue about when I'm the most difficult to live with—when I'm waiting for an offer on a proposal, or trying to finish the book on time, or waiting for the final manuscript to be read and accepted. Undoubtedly, I'm difficult at all those times.

"There is a space of time in the process that is my favorite to occupy. That is the brief point between the satisfactory (by my standards) completion of a manuscript and the very beginning of the next novel—the *very* end of one and the *very* beginning of the next. There is not much actual typing happening in this space of time. One book is gone and cannot be touched or improved any further, and the next exists only as a seedling, not even planted onto paper. It is during this time that I talk aloud to myself, page through phone books and maps, leave myself unintelligible notes, read voraciously, and daydream constantly. My family feels that I'm not really working, since I'm not stacking up pages or typing. This is the most important thing I do, though; and, this initial enthusiasm for the story, this first spark will, after a great deal of technical

and mechanical manipulation, become a novel. Writing, from beinning to end, might be a long, creative process. For me it is this flicker of excitement at the start that is creation. Then I do my work.

"What seems to make my books work well and maintain popularity has largely to do with the heroines. The women in my works adhere to the customs of their time but are possessed of some contemporary values. While they might indeed marry their father's choice or seem to hold their men as 'heads of households,' they regard their own strength, independence, and self-esteem highly. There were women in historical periods whose actions and values were far ahead of their time and who strongly resemble our most admired contemporary women. Eleanor of Aquitaine, for instance, endowed a convent as a shelter for abused women. My heroines are fun to create because of the delicate balance between the way they seem to fit the period into which they are drawn and the way they hold a strong identity with the contemporary woman in their strength of conviction, their determination to succeed despite the odds, their affirmation of their own power.''

*   *   *

CARROLL, Rosalynn
See KATZ, Carol

*   *   *

CARSON, Alan 1951-

PERSONAL: Born October 18, 1951, in Toronto, Ontario, Canada; son of Mervyn Shannon (an engineer) and Louise (Brigham) Carson; married Susan Martin, June 5, 1982. *Education:* University of Waterloo, B.S., 1975.

ADDRESSES: Home—257 Dewhurst Blvd., Toronto, Ontario, Canada M4J 3K7. *Office*—Carson, Dunlop & Associates Ltd., 597 Parliament St., Toronto, Ontario, Canada M4X 1W3.

CAREER: Lumbermans Mutual Casualty Co., Toronto, Ontario, fire protection engineer, 1975-78; Carson, Dunlop & Associates Ltd. (home inspection firm), Toronto, vice-president, 1978—.

MEMBER: Society of Fire Protection Engineers.

WRITINGS:

(With Robert Dunlop) *Inspecting a House: A Guide for Buyers, Owners, and Renovators,* Beaufort Books (New York, N.Y.), 1982.

SIDELIGHTS: Alan Carson told *CA:* "Bob Dunlop and I are involved in home inspection for prospective purchases. We believe strongly in the viability of older homes for providing high quality living environments. We started the home inspection firm after working as fire protection engineers, inspecting larger commercial and industrial buildings. We found that there was no one in the Toronto area who would provide an objective technical inspection report for people buying houses. In the same sense that when one buys a used automobile, it makes sense to take it to a mechanic for a physical checkup, we felt that it was important for people to be able to determine the physical condition of the home they were buying. The work of our certified engineering company puts our client in the position to make an educated buying decision.

"The book is intended primarily for the ordinary home buyer and although not technically exhaustive, it gives the lay person some insight into the workings of a home. We have attempted to help them determine the important and costly flaws and to distinguish them from the minor nuisance deficiencies. Typical home buyers often make the mistake of judging the home by the condition of the interior finishes. Many people will over-react to cracks in plaster or drywall (which are often entirely cosmetic) and overlook more major problems, such as advanced termite damage in the structure, an unsafe electrical system, or a heating plant at the end of its life cycle.

"Our book is intended to assist the home buyer in understanding what specialists will do and is not meant to replace the professional inspection process. In many cases, as we perform a home inspection, we are also acting as educators, showing the prospective purchaser how the home operates and how the various systems are controlled and maintained. Clients who have read our book find it easier to understand the big picture, having gained an understanding of the workings of a house.

"Our penchant for older homes comes from an appreciation of a time when labor-intensive work was not a prohibitive cost and when more time was devoted to architectural detail. While in some cases the lack of strict building controls meant that construction errors were made, there is a good deal of truth in the adage, 'They don't build them like they used to.' The quality of building materials was often higher in older houses although, of course, quality could be inconsistent. The modern building age of mass-production housing with more factory-produced and assembled components has both its advantages and disadvantages."

*   *   *

CARUSO, Enrico   1873-1921

BRIEF ENTRY: Born February 25 (one source says February 27), 1873, in Naples, Italy; died of pleurisy, August 2, 1921, in Naples, Italy. Italian opera singer, artist, and author. Considered one of the greatest tenors in the history of opera, Caruso made his operatic debut in 1894 at Teatro Nuovo in Naples. Six years later he gained wide public attention with his performance in *La Boheme* at Milan's prestigious opera house, La Scala, and he went on to perform there for four seasons before beginning a successful tour of Europe. With his 1902 London debut at Covent Garden, Caruso immediately won favor with British audiences. But it was in the United States, where he was attended with extensive publicity, that Caruso achieved his most spectacular successes. His American debut, singing in *Rigoletto,* also marked the beginning of Caruso's sixteen-year association with the Metropolitan Opera Company. He continued to live in Italy but made frequent trips to the United States as the leading male singer for the Met.

One of the first opera singers to make recordings, Caruso was lauded for his vocal power, resonance, and range. He was considered an awkward actor in the beginning of his career, but he later elicited enthusiastic praise for exemplary dramatic interpretations of such roles as Canio in *Pagliacci* and Radames in *Aida.* Caruso was also known as a talented caricaturist, and for many years he contributed weekly drawings to the Italian-language newspaper *La Follia di New York.* His artwork has been published in two collections, *Caruso's Book* (1906) and *Caricatures* (1908). With Louisa Tetrazzini he wrote *The Art of Singing* (1909). He was also the author of *How to Sing: Some Practical Hints* (1913).

Caruso suffered a throat hemorrhage while singing at the Brooklyn Academy of Music on December 11, 1920, and on Christmas Eve of that year he made his last performance in a Metropolitan Opera production of *La Juive.* His life was depicted in the 1950 motion picture *The Great Caruso,* starring Mario Lanza in the title role.

BIOGRAPHICAL/CRITICAL SOURCES:

BOOKS

Caruso, Dorothy and Torrance Goddard, *Wings of Song: The Story of Caruso,* Minton Balch, 1928.
Caruso, Dorothy, *Enrico Caruso: His Life and Death,* Laurie, 1946.
Donway, Philip and George DeKay, editors, *Turning Point,* Random, 1958.
Marek, George Richard, editor, *World Treasury of Grand Opera,* Harper, 1957.
Pleasants, Henry, *The Great Singers,* Simon & Schuster, 1966.
Taylor, Henry J., *Men and Moments,* Random, 1966.
Ybarra, Thomas Russell, *Caruso: The Man of Naples and the Voice of Gold,* Harcourt, 1953.

*   *   *

CASH, Kevin (Richard)   1926-1985

OBITUARY NOTICE—See index for *CA* sketch: Born February 22, 1926 in Manchester, N.H.; died of cancer, February 27, 1985, in Manchester, N.H. Public relations consultant, journalist, and author. Cash worked as a copyboy, reporter, and feature writer for the *Manchester Union Leader* and as an editor and writer for the *Journal of Commerce,* the *New York Herald Tribune,* and the *New York Journal-American.* He had served as the president of Amoskeag Press since 1973 and as a public affairs consultant since 1977. He was the author of *Who the Hell Is William Loeb?*

OBITUARIES AND OTHER SOURCES:

BOOKS

Who's Who in the East, 19th edition, Marquis, 1983.

PERIODICALS

Chicago Tribune, March 1, 1985.

*   *   *

CASTELLS, Manuel   1942-

PERSONAL: Born February 9, 1942, in Hellin, Spain. *Education:* University of Paris, LL.B., 1964, M.A., 1966, Ph.D., 1967.

ADDRESSES: Office—Department of City and Regional Planning, University of California, Berkeley, Calif. 94720.

CAREER: University of Paris, Paris, France, assistant professor of sociology, 1967-70; Sorbonne, University of Paris, associate professor of sociology, 1970-79; University of California, Berkeley, professor of city and regional planning, 1979—. Visiting professor, University of Chile, 1968, 1970, 1971, and 1972, University of Montreal, 1969, University of Wisconsin—Madison, 1975 and 1977, Boston University, 1976, University of Copenhagen, 1976, University of Mexico, 1976 and 1982, and University of Hong Kong, 1983.

MEMBER: International Sociological Association (president of urban research committee, 1978-82), American Planning Association, American Sociological Association.

AWARDS, HONORS: Guggenheim Memorial Fellow, 1982-83; C. Wright Mills Award, 1983, for *The City and the Grassroots.*

WRITINGS:

IN ENGLISH

The City and the Grassroots: A Cross-Cultural Theory of Urban Social Movements, University of California Press, 1983.

The Economic Crisis and American Society, Princeton University Press, 1980.

(Co-author and editor) *High Technology, Space, and Society,* Sage Publications, 1985.

IN ENGLISH TRANSLATION

The Urban Question: A Marxist Approach, MIT Press, 1977.
City, Class and Power, St. Martin's, 1978.

OTHER

Co-editor of *International Journal of Urban and Regional Research,* 1978—.

WORK IN PROGRESS: The Informational City: Technological Change, Economic Restructuring, and the Urban-Regional Process.

SIDELIGHTS: In *Economic Crisis and American Society* Manuel Castells maintains that we need to replace Keynesian economic theory with a new one that accounts for the stagnant productivity and simultaneous inflation and unemployment that plague our current world order. Taking an evolutionary perspective, the author adopts Karl Marx's theory that the advance of capitalism leads to a falling rate of profit.

Castells told *CA:* "I have recast the theory of the city and shown how scholarly research can contribute to the understanding of crucial dimensions of our everyday lives. Also, I have systematically worked in a variety of cultures and countries, giving to my work an international dimension. I have written books in French, English, and Spanish, which have been translated into other languages. I am focusing on the connection between the economic crisis, the city, and changes in culture."

BIOGRAPHICAL/CRITICAL SOURCES:

PERIODICALS

Journal of the American Planning Association, summer, 1984.

* * *

CATLING, Patrick Skene 1925-

BRIEF ENTRY: Born February 14, 1925, in London, England; immigrated to United States, naturalized citizen, 1956. American journalist and author. Before becoming a free-lance writer in 1964, Catling worked as a member of the editorial staff of the *Baltimore Sun,* the *Manchester Guardian, Punch,* and *Newsweek.* His books include *Exterminator* (Trident, 1969), *The Experiment* (Pocket Books, 1972), *Best Summer Job* (Hart-Davis, 1974), *Bliss Incorporated* (Weidenfeld & Nicolson, 1976), *Secret Ingredients* (Hart-Davis, 1976), and *Jazz, Jazz, Jazz* (Blond & Briggs, 1980).

BIOGRAPHICAL/CRITICAL SOURCES:

PERIODICALS

New York Times Book Review, August 24, 1969, March 14, 1971, June 30, 1974.

Punch, April 30, 1969, November 12, 1969, November 25, 1970, January 9, 1980.
Saturday Review, October 11, 1969.
Times Literary Supplement, May 22, 1969, January 8, 1970, May 19, 1972, April 2, 1976, August 20, 1976, February 29, 1980.

* * *

CAUGHEY, John L(yon) 1941-

PERSONAL: Born March 28, 1941, in New York, N.Y.; son of John Lyon (a physician) and Winnifred (a nurse; maiden name, Scott) Caughey; married Frances Blossom (an anthropologist), June 18, 1963; children: Thomas Dawson, Jack Scott, Sarah Marguerite. *Education:* Harvard University, B.A., 1963; University of Pennsylvania, M.A., 1967, Ph.D., 1970.

ADDRESSES: Home—6600 Van Dusen Rd., Laurel, Md. 20707. *Office*—Department of American Studies, University of Maryland at College Park, College Park, Md. 20742.

CAREER: University of Pennsylvania, Philadelphia, assistant professor of American studies, 1970-76; University of Islamabad, Islamabad, Pakistan, senior Fulbright lecturer in anthropology and U.S. studies, 1976-77; University of Maryland at College Park, assistant professor, 1978-83, associate professor of American studies, 1983—. Conducted anthropological field work among Old Order Mennonites of Lancaster County, Pa., 1967, in the Truk Islands of Micronesia, 1968, at an urban psychiatric ward in Philadelphia, 1972-75, at a Sufi shrine in the Margalla Hills, Pakistan, 1976-77, and among middle-class Americans in Maryland, 1978-82.

MEMBER: American Anthropological Association, American Studies Association, Society for Psychological Anthropology, Society for Medical Anthropology, University of Maryland Squash Racquets Club (president).

WRITINGS:

Faanakkar: Cultural Values in a Micronesian Society (monograph), Department of Anthropology, University of Pennsylvania, 1977.

Imaginary Social Worlds: A Cultural Approach, University of Nebraska Press, 1984.

(Contributor) Herve Varenne, editor, *Symbolizing America,* University of Nebraska Press, 1985.

Contributor to psychology, anthropology, and American studies journals.

WORK IN PROGRESS: Research on culture and imaginary experience; an ethnographic study on Eastern philosophy in the United States.

SIDELIGHTS: John L. Caughey told *CA:* "The step out into other cultural realities has proven most useful and exciting in my study of the cultural structuring of our own country's consciousness. It has helped me to see the extent to which our own dreams, memories, and daydreams are culturally shaped. It has also helped me to see our own taken-for-granted social worlds better and to learn about alternative ways of handling our lives."

BIOGRAPHICAL/CRITICAL SOURCES:

PERIODICALS

Baltimore Sun, March 27, 1979, March 29, 1984.
U. S. News and World Report, July 16, 1984.

Washington Post, October 30, 1984.
Washington Star, April 4, 1981.

*   *   *

CAUTHEN, Baker James   1909-1985

OBITUARY NOTICE: Born December 20, 1909, in Hunts-ville, Tex.; died April 15, 1985, in Virginia. Clergyman, mis-sionary, educator, and author. Licensed to preach by the Bap-tist church at the age of sixteen, Cauthen went on to become executive secretary and director of the Southern Baptist For-eign Mission Board in 1954. During his twenty-five-year ten-ure as leader of the board the number of Southern Baptist missionaries more than tripled, growing from 908 in 1954 to 3,000 in 1979, the year that Cauthen retired. Prior to heading the Foreign Mission Board, Cauthen taught at Southwestern Baptist Theological Seminary, worked as pastor of Polytechnic Baptist Church in Fort Worth, Texas, and served as a mis-sionary in the Far East beginning in 1939. His books include *Beyond the Call, Now Is the Day, By All Means,* and *Advance: A History of Southern Baptist Foreign Missions,* which he co-authored.

OBITUARIES AND OTHER SOURCES:

BOOKS

Fletcher, Jesse C., *Baker James Cauthen: A Man for All Na-tions,* Broadman Press, 1977.
Who's Who in America, 41st edition, Marquis, 1980.

PERIODICALS

Chicago Tribune, April 17, 1985.

*   *   *

CECIL, Henry
See LEON, Henry Cecil

*   *   *

CHAMBERLAIN, Mary (Christina)   1947-

PERSONAL: Born September 3, 1947, in London, England; daughter of Arthur and Gladys (Harris) Chamberlain; married Peter Lane, 1980; children: three daughters. *Education:* At-tended University of Edinburgh and London School of Eco-nomics and Political Science, London. *Politics:* Labour.

ADDRESSES: Home—21 Onslow Rd., Richmond, Surrey TW10 6QH, England. *Office*—London College of Printing, Elephant and Castle, London SE1 6SB, England. *Agent*—Anne McDermid, Curtis Brown Ltd., 162-168 Regent St., London W1R 5TA, England.

CAREER: Arms Control and Disarmament Research Unit, Foreign and Commonwealth Office, London, England, re-search officer, 1970-71; Richardson Institute for Peace and Conflict Research, London, research officer, 1972; Social Sci-ence Research Council, London, administrative officer, 1972; Norfolk College of Art and Technology, King's Lynn, Nor-folk, England, assistant lecturer in liberal studies, 1973-74; London College of Fashion, London, assistant lecturer in lib-eral studies, 1974-75; Ipswich Civic College, Ipswich, East Suffolk, England, lecturer in liberal studies, 1975-77; London College of Printing, London, senior lecturer in complementary studies, 1977—. Founding member and member of the council of management of London History Workshop Center; member of Television History Workshop's Council of Management.

MEMBER: Virago Advisory Group.

AWARDS, HONORS: Twenty Seven Foundation Award, 1984, for research for the book *Just Above the Breadline.*

WRITINGS:

Fenwomen: A Portrait of Women in an English Village, Vir-ago, 1975, Charles River Books, 1983.
Old Wives' Tales: Their History, Remedies, and Spells, Vir-ago, 1981, Merrimack Book Service, 1983.
Just Above the Breadline: Women in the Inner City, Virago, in press.

Contributor to historical journals. Editor of reviews for *Oral History.*

SIDELIGHTS: In her books *Fenwomen* and *Old Wives' Tales* Mary Chamberlain examines female aspects of human history. Her 1975 portrait, *Fenwomen,* records the experiences and life perspectives of three generations of women from Isleham, an isolated village on the British Fens. Told to the author under the promise of anonymity—even the name of the village was changed to Gislea in *Fenwomen*—the accounts detail the toil, pleasures, and dissatisfactions of the Fenwomen. They present what Elizabeth Thomas of *New Statesman* described as "a consistent picture of poverty and hard work, . . . brightened by harvest feasts, poaching, swimming, or skating on the river." Some of the women's comments, particularly those of the younger ones, concern intimate, even sexual, matters, a cir-cumstance that led to a scandal when the identity of the village became known.

But *Fenwomen* was not meant to be sensational or to exploit the villagers' confidences. Rather, as Chamberlain asserts, the book was intended to give attention to the roles of women in rural British history, roles that have not changed much in three generations, according to the author. This emphasis on women stems from Chamberlain's view that the focus of historians has been skewed in favor of men, women's lives having been traditionally seen as too insignificant to record. Chamberlain seeks to mitigate this situation in *Fenwomen.* She explained, as quoted by the London *Times:* "History is as much about women bringing up a family on nine shillings a week as about men's deeds and diplomatic decisions." And, concluded Chamberlain in a *Listener* quote, "The woman's story must be told."

Chamberlain's second book, *Old Wives' Tales,* approaches medical history as *Fenwomen* approaches rural community studies. It shifts the emphasis from the rise of the male-dom-inated medical profession to the part that women, specifically "old wives," played in human healing practices through the ages. And, according to the author, "What started out to be a history of alternative medicine ended up as an alternative history of medicine." In her book Chamberlain demonstrates that centuries before the onset of scientific medicine old wives' tales were considered valuable, as were the women who used them to care for the ill or injured. Today, however, old wives' tales are generally considered groundless or even superstitious remedies, and few people remember or use many of them. But Chamberlain managed to interview individuals who have re-tained the old ways and has entered their recollections in her book. As Anne Karpf of *New Statesman* explained, *Old Wives Tales* is "laced with fascinating quotations from senescent women, the last of the real old wives, and you can almost hear them whisper to [Chamberlain] their toothless confi-dences." She supports these accounts with research concern-ing the old wives' place in various societies throughout time and the reasons they were eventually displaced by doctors. "Chamberlain's analysis of these changes is illuminating," commented Karpf, who called the book a "shocking tale of misogyny and oppression." As Chamberlain reveals, the old wives' cures were not merely replaced by scientific medical ones; often replacements did not even exist. Rather, the wives themselves were persecuted as witches and conjurers by the male-dominated Church and medical practitioners eager to take over the old wives' patients. Chamberlain concludes with a collection of old wives' tales, complete with recipes and instructions. In doing so, as Karpf remarked, the author has "rescued centuries of once-common knowledge from oblivion" and performed a "most valuable feat."

Chamberlain told *CA:* "I want to record what G.D.H. Cole called 'The Common People,' the lives of ordinary men and women disenfranchised from history by class, education, or sex. I believe that history is a powerful tool for understanding the present and for helping shape and create the future. History has more than an antiquarian interest; it has a strong political purpose.

"My current research uses oral history to investigate and chronicle the lives of working-class women in North Lambeth, a poor area of central London. More than sixty women have been interviewed for my book, *Just Above the Breadline,* which should be completed late in 1984. This work will build on and supplement Maud Pember Reeves's pioneering survey of women in this area of London, which was first published in 1913 and entitled *Round About a Pound a Week.*"

MEDIA ADAPTATIONS: Chamberlain's book *Fenwomen* was adapted as a play, "Fen," by Caryl Churchill. Both *Fenwomen* and *Old Wives' Tales* have been translated into French and published in France.

AVOCATIONAL INTERESTS: Needlework and quilting.

BIOGRAPHICAL/CRITICAL SOURCES:

PERIODICALS

British Book News, May, 1982.
Listener, September 25, 1975.
New Statesman, September 12, 1975, November 13, 1981.
Times (London), July 20, 1983.

*   *   *

CHAMPE, Flavia Waters   1902-

PERSONAL: Born April 3, 1902, in Lincoln, Neb.; daughter of George L. (in insurance) and Ida (Parsons) Waters; married John L. Champe (an anthropologist and educator), December 27, 1924 (deceased). *Education:* University of Nebraska—Lincoln, B.A., 1940. *Religion:* Protestant.

ADDRESSES: Home—1917 South 27th, Lincoln, Neb. 68502.

CAREER: Toured as member of vaudeville group "Portia Mansfield Dancers," 1921-24; conductor of private classes at School of the Dance, 1924-78; writer, 1967—. Director and choreographer of community dance performances. Anthropological field researcher in New Mexico, 1947-80.

WRITINGS:

The Matachines Dance of the Upper Rio Grande: History, Music, and Choreography, University of Nebraska Press, 1983.
Contributor to *El Palacio* and *New Mexico.*

WORK IN PROGRESS: Innocents on Broadway, a collection of letters written to her mother during her years in vaudeville, 1921-24.

SIDELIGHTS: Flavia Waters Champe told *CA:* "My publication on the Matachines dance began on Christmas Day, 1947, when my husband and I saw a performance of the dance in San Ildefonso Pueblo. As a dancer I was intrigued by the balletic quality of the choreography and in the next twenty years we made numerous trips to New Mexico to see variations of the dance in other pueblos and Hispanic communities. In 1967 the International Folk Art Museum of Santa Fe asked me to write a book on the Matachines dance to be a part of a series they were planning on Spanish influences in New Mexico.

"By 1970 I had finished writing a description of the dance as performed at San Ildefonso—the characters, the costumes, the notation of the music, and the choreography. My husband planned to write a chapter on the history but had not done it at the time of his death in 1978. I completed the manuscript and, with the usual delays in finding a publisher, the book was published in 1983. It even has a recording of thirteen melodies played on violin and guitars which we recorded in 1954.

"My manuscript in progress, *Innocents on Broadway,* which I originally called *Mother, Dearie,* is a collection of letters to my mother written during three years in vaudeville, from 1921 to 1924, when I was a Portia Mansfield dancer. Four of us trained at the camp in Colorado and were barefoot dancers of the 'interpretive' or 'aesthetic' school of dancing, before 'modern' became a name. The youngest of the dancers was fifteen, and I at nineteen was in charge of the group. We were fortunate to be able to join an established act, a ballet-trained dancer and her husband, a concert violinist. With their reputation and experience our act was given excellent billing on Keith and Orpheum circuits. We even headlined at the Palace in New York.

"The letters to my mother are many as they were written over sixty years ago. They have the enthusiasm of youth as they describe each new city and each new experience. Radio was a novelty; travel was by train or boat. The insight into the world of vaudeville is unusual. The daily life of four girls living together is entertaining. Nevertheless, it is interesting how the writer matures and changes during the three years. Gradually the cities begin to look alike; the hotels and theatres are the same; and by the middle of the third season she is ready to leave the stage and go home.

"There is definitely a nostalgic quality in the letters as well as historical value. At age eighty-three I can look at them from a fairly impersonal point of view. I hope I can find a publisher."

*   *   *

CHANG, Chen-chi   1920-
(Ch'eng-chi Chang, Garma C. C. Chang)

BRIEF ENTRY: Born August 28, 1920, in Canton, China. American philosopher, theologian, educator, and author. Chang, who was educated at a Tibetan monastery, taught at the University of Nanking and the College of Chinese Culture in Taiwan before coming to the United States. He taught Oriental philosophy at the University of Nebraska in 1965, then moved to Pennsylvania State University, where he was appointed a professor of Buddhism in 1971. The educator is probably best known for a book review he wrote for *Tomorrow* magazine in 1958. In it Chang exposed Lobsang Rampa's book *The Third Eye* as "inaccurate and superficial" and its author as a fraud. One of Chang's special interests has been the question of life after death. His books include *The Practice of Zen* (Harper, 1959), *The Buddhist Teaching of Totality: The Philosophy of Hwa Yen Buddhism* (Pennsylvania State University Press, 1971), and *A Treasury of Mahayana Sutras* (Pennsylvania State University Press, 1983). *Address:* Department of Religious Studies, Pennsylvania State University, University Park, Pa. 16802.

BIOGRAPHICAL/CRITICAL SOURCES:

BOOKS

Directory of American Scholars, Volume IV: *Philosophy, Religion, and Law,* 7th edition, Bowker, 1978.

*   *   *

CHANG, Ch'eng-chi
  See CHANG, Chen-chi

*   *   *

CHANG, Garma C. C.
  See CHANG, Chen-chi

*   *   *

CHARANIS, Peter   1908-1985

OBITUARY NOTICE—See index for *CA* sketch: Born August 15, 1908, in Lemnos, Greece; died of a stroke, March 23, 1985, in New Brunswick, N.J. Educator and author. Charanis, who taught history at Rutgers University from 1938 until his retirement in 1976, was the author of *Church and State in the Later Roman Empire: The Religious Policy of Anastasius the First, Studies on the Demography of the Byzantine Empire: A Collection,* and *Social, Economic, and Political Life in the Byzantine Empire: Collected Studies.*

OBITUARIES AND OTHER SOURCES:

BOOKS

Directory of American Scholars, Volume I: *History,* 8th edition, Bowker, 1982.
Who's Who in America, 42nd edition, Marquis, 1982.

PERIODICALS

New York Times, March 27, 1985.

*   *   *

CHARLES, Nathanael
  See FRANKLIN, Benjamin V

*   *   *

CHARLES, Ray
  See ROBINSON, Ray Charles

*   *   *

CHARTHAM, Robert
  See SETH, Ronald (Sydney)

CHASE, James Hadley
  See RAYMOND, Rene (Brabazon)

*   *   *

CHASE, Sylvia (Belle)   1938-

PERSONAL: Born February 23, 1938, in St. Paul, Minn.; daughter of Kelsey David (a merchant) and Sylvia (Bennett) Chase. *Education:* University of California, Los Angeles, B.A., 1961.

ADDRESSES: Home—New York City. *Office*—ABC News, 77 West 66th St., New York, N.Y. 10023.

CAREER/WRITINGS: California State Assembly, Sacramento, aide to Senator Thomas Rees and the Finance Committee, 1961-65; worked on political campaigns in California, 1961-68; advance person for Attorney General Tom Lynch of California, 1966; coordinator of (Robert F.) Kennedy for President Campaign in Southern California, 1968; KNX-Radio, Los Angeles, Calif., reporter, 1969-71; CBS News, New York City, correspondent and anchorwoman, 1971-77; ABC News, New York City, correspondent and anchorwoman, 1977—.

AWARDS, HONORS: Public Service Award from American Trial Lawyers Association, 1970; Emmy Awards from National Academy of Television Arts and Sciences, 1978, and (for feature "VW Beatle: The Hidden Danger"), 1980; Headliner Awards from Women in Communications, Inc., 1979 and 1983; Front Page Award from Newswomen's Club of New York, 1979; Consumer Journalism Award from National Press Club, 1982; Pinnacle Award from American Women in Radio and TV, 1983, for "Throwaway Kids."

SIDELIGHTS: Sylvia Chase worked as a political aide and campaign organizer in California before embarking on a career in journalism in 1968. After serving a two-year stint as a reporter and ombudsman at a Los Angeles, California, radio station, where she showed a flair for investigative reporting that was stifled in the job, Chase joined the Columbia Broadcasting System (CBS-TV). During her six years with the network she worked as a correspondent on "The CBS Evening News With Walter Cronkite" and later anchored the morning news magazine show "Magazine," which, though acknowledged as a breakthrough in daytime programming, was never able to develop a steady audience because of its erratic scheduling.

Chase moved from CBS to the American Broadcasting Companies (ABC-TV) in 1977, where she first served as co-anchor of the "ABC Weekend News" and still appears intermittently on prime-time "ABC News Brief" spots. She is probably best known, however, for her work as a correspondent on the popular news magazine show "20/20," which she has been with since it first aired in 1978.

CA INTERVIEW

CA interviewed Sylvia Chase by phone, July 25, 1983, at her office in Manhattan.

CA: You once said that politics is good training for journalism. Why?

CHASE: Because so much of what you're reporting on involves politics and public policy issues. Even if you're going to be reporting on food, the way the food industry operates is basically politics. The way the co-ops operate and the way the markets are manipulated, everything boils down to all these little duchies. Also, because life is essentially politics, you need to have a good understanding of the political process. If you can understand how government works and how the bureaucracies can thwart the legislative intent of the elected officials of the people, then you can understand something very basic about the way life works.

CA: When you were working in politics, did you ever feel your candidate was being treated unfairly by the media?

CHASE: Yes. And I don't think the situation has improved much; it probably has gotten worse. Journalists travel around in packs. They horde after people, they follow them around, and they all report the same thing. What's the point? I'd far rather see us reporting on issues than on people. But issues don't seem as sexy as people, and that's really unfortunate because I think they can be made interesting.

CA: Was working in government and politics your first choice?

CHASE: It wasn't my first choice, but it was the first thing I did. Work in journalism was very difficult for women to get at the time I graduated from college.

CA: You've been quoted as saying that women don't move up as fast as men do in corporations because women aren't or weren't good at letting their bosses know they want promotions. Do you think that's still true?

CHASE: Much less so now. But I think women still have difficulty with aggression.

CA: Do you have that difficulty?

CHASE: Yes, but I don't know whether my problem with being assertive has to do with my being a woman or being a Midwesterner. It's the way I was raised and the way the people I grew up with acted. You didn't act in the way that's considered essential to progress in this world. You didn't toot your own horn.

CA: Did you ever feel that you had to work harder at broadcasting because you're a woman?

CHASE: I've always felt I had to work harder at everything because I'm a woman.

CA: Even these days?

CHASE: Yes. Now I've finally realized it's because it's me. But there was a time when I also did it for all the women who might come after me. And I still do, to some extent.

CA: Why did you move from governmental and political work into radio journalism?

CHASE: Because there was an opportunity, finally. It became clear that it was going to be possible for me to work in the profession to which I'd always aspired and that my sex was no longer going to stand in my way, nor would it consign me to the women's page or to writing about food.

CA: How did the KNX-Radio opportunity occur? Did someone notice your work in politics and government?

CHASE: Yes. I had been a pretty reliable source. I was one of the people at the assistant and consultant level who was frequently consulted by the press about policy and political issues in the State of California.

CA: What was your job at KNX-Radio?

CHASE: I was the ombudsman and did consumer reporting.

CA: Was the ombudsman job the same sort of job an ombudsman has at a newspaper?

CHASE: No. The role of ombudsman in the Ben Bagdikian sense seems to be providing a middle ground between a newspaper and its readers. I helped our listeners cope with the entanglements of red tape in the bureaucracies and sometimes with consumer matters.

CA: Including problems people may have had with the radio station?

CHASE: No. That was before people mistrusted journalism.

CA: Why did you move from radio to television?

CHASE: I got a much better offer. Also, in the course of my work as an ombudsman I had come across a few situations that required the kind of stories we now call investigative, and I very much wanted to do them for the station. But my boss and I agreed that that would not be proper use of my time. I was on the budget as the ombudsman and couldn't go off spending months investigating things. And he didn't have the money or the staff for that kind of thing anyway. We agreed that the thing for me to do was to move onward and upward, which he had always thought I would do anyway. He and I both wanted me to go someplace where I could do the kind of work for which I clearly had some skills.

CA: Did you have any problems adjusting to the move from radio to television?

CHASE: No. I thought it was going to be very difficult, but it really was only a matter of days.

CA: Many television reporters seem to emphasize footage of people who are emotionally distraught after tragic occurrences. Do you try to avoid that sort of shot?

CHASE: I certainly don't try to avoid it. Television is an emotional medium, and I don't think there's anything wrong with that. I think we're unfairly criticized for showing the emotional sides of things; those are the images that stick with us forever. But I think what's wrong is that reporters are also human beings, and they simply can't show bad manners, and bad taste, and bad humanity, by badgering people at times of great grief. At Frank Reynolds's funeral someone made note of the fact to President Reagan, who was in the church, that when Mr. Reagan had lost the nomination in 1976, Frank was within a few feet of him. But rather than pressing Mr. Reagan at that moment, Frank stepped back. And I think that good caliber reporters, although it's in our nature to be very curious, should temper our curiosity with humanity.

CA: Do you try to do that yourself?

CHASE: Oh, always. By the nature of the work that I do, I interview people who are in pretty bad straits sometimes: have been taken advantage of, have had relatives die through the carelessness of individuals or corporations, have been severely injured themselves. And I ask them all the questions I feel the viewers would want to have answered, even though sometimes it makes me uncomfortable to ask them. By the same token it makes me feel very sad when the answers come, and I sometimes cry in the course of doing an interview.

CA: What attracted you to the "Magazine" show?

CHASE: I thought it was important to do daytime news programming, even though going to the show was a great sacrifice for me. I was in the arena of the evening news, working for Walter Cronkite almost exclusively, and going to "Magazine" meant giving up exposure. That's a decision that's tough to make in a business like this, where exposure really counts for everything. But I felt it was very important to try to get news into daytime programming. I had faith that women wanted that as much as or more than some of the daytime fare that was offered. I think the proof that they did, even though we never received any promotion or publicity to speak of and were scheduled on a very erratic basis when we did appear, was that toward the end of the time that I was doing the show, we got better numbers, share points, and rating points than "The Price Is Right," which we were pre-empting.

CA: Was some of your attraction to "Magazine" the desire to have your own show?

CHASE: Oh, sure, to be in control of my own show, that was also a motivating thing. But you have to understand that the women at CBS had organized at that point, and the newswomen had asked for a greater contribution on the part of women and a greater emphasis on thinking about what it was that women wanted to see. I felt an ideological commitment. I kept putting myself in the place of women who are at home all day. They are the real heroes of this culture—the ones who are at home raising the future of this nation. And I thought, "Boy, they sure deserve something that I know I can give them, that they need, that they want, and that they should have for their children." I think mothers and motherhood are a much neglected area of our society. We don't seem to pay too much attention to it, almost as if it's going to happen without our bothering about it—the children are going to grow up and get fed, sent to school, and put to bed with a hug at night without us doing a thing. But they're not, and mothers need help.

CA: Didn't the "Magazine" show deal with many topics of interest to women that other shows didn't touch upon?

CHASE: Yes. I think those subjects appealed to men, too, but at the time we didn't think that way. A lot of the material on "20/20" at prime time now is the sort of thing that a few years ago we would have thought, "We can't do that. They're not going to be interested in stories about families, drug problems involving kids, or other similar stories." But now we're reporting those sorts of stories in prime time programming, thank goodness.

CA: You also did photo essays on "Magazine" about the lives of viewers who wrote to the program. Why?

CHASE: I wanted to figure out a different way to handle letters to the editor because CBS, in particular Dick Salant, the president of news at that time, had a real abiding interest in getting the viewers on the air. I chose photo essays because I happen to love still photographs. It was more a stylistic thing. You can do things with still photos and a tape recorder that you can't do with a television camera and clapsticks and those sorts of things. You can sit down, and it's cheap. You can sit down for four, five, six hours and talk to people or have two or three sessions over a period of days, and they get so used to you that they relax and they really say what's on their minds. And you can take still photos of them while they're busy doing something, and if you're around enough, and if you don't have one of those terrible drive motors, people just sort of lose consciousness that you're there. It was more of a technique than it was an idea. I was looking for a new way to use the medium.

CA: Why did you switch from CBS to ABC?

CHASE: A new prime-time magazine broadcast, "20/20," was going to be created here, and I was eager to be involved in it because I had created my own daytime magazine, "Magazine."

CA: It's said that television investigative reporting, the sort of reporting you do on "20/20," is difficult in part because people know your face and you can't really do any kind of undercover work. Also, you or someone else has to carry a lot of equipment around. Do those factors ever stand in your way?

CHASE: Nope. But I don't talk about how I do that. There are ways of getting around that. Let's put it that way.

CA: Do you have any problems doing investigative work on television that you can talk about?

CHASE: Well, I've never been sued, and I think that's the biggest problem facing the profession at this time.

CA: Has the threat of a large libel suit against you bothered you in your work?

CHASE: Well, knock on wood, I hope it's never going to happen to me. You have to be extraordinarily careful about what you say, and you have to be fair. You have to be fair. I always tell people that I start from the position that government operates in the best interests of the taxpayer and business operates in the best interests of the consumer. Now if you proceed from that position, you're not likely to get into very much trouble. When you find out that there are exceptions, you always start investigating them from ground zero. You start from the position of, "Well, I don't think this could have happened, because the rules say it's not supposed to be this way." So, in a sense you have to prove wrongdoing to yourself, rather than going around with a chip on your shoulder.

CA: Have you ever had any major failures as an investigative reporter, something you started investigating with great hopes that never produced a newsworthy story?

CHASE: There are no failures. You investigate something, and if it turns out that it's not what you thought, that's not a failure. It's never a failure when you learn the truth about something and decide that it isn't what you thought it was.

CA: I'd think your superiors might be upset if you spent a lot of time investigating and came up with no tangible results.

CHASE: I don't think I've ever had that problem. If you're worth your salt, you know when you get into something whether or not you've got the story. You know before you've invested a great deal of time. Also, sometimes you say, "Look, this is going to take me a lot of time, but it may not pan out." It's okay as long as everybody understands everybody. I've always called this "the no-surprises business." Don't let anybody who is relying on you to do your job be surprised. Warn them ahead of time.

CA: What's your future in television news? Do you plan to stay with "20/20" indefinitely?

CHASE: My five-year plan is to win every major journalism award there is.

CA: You've won quite a few already, haven't you?

CHASE: There are a few more out there I want to earn.

BIOGRAPHICAL/CRITICAL SOURCES:

PERIODICALS

TV Guide, June 19, 1976.

—*Interview by Peter Benjaminson*

* * *

CHELIUS, James R(obert) 1943-

PERSONAL: Born April 24, 1943, in Chicago, Ill.; son of Robert Edward (a printer) and Ruth (a nurse; maiden name, Anderson) Chelius; married Maureen O'Brien (an attorney), 1966; children: Karen, Lori. *Education:* University of Illinois at Urbana-Champaign, B.S., 1965, M.B.A., 1967; University of Chicago, Ph.D., 1973.

ADDRESSES: Home—Westfield, N.J. *Office*—Institute of Management and Labor Relations, Rutgers University, New Brunswick, N.J. 08903.

CAREER: Purdue University, West Lafayette, Ind., assistant professor, 1972-77, associate professor of industrial management, 1977-81; Rutgers University, New Brunswick, N.J., associate professor of industrial relations, 1981—, associate director of Institute of Management and Labor Relations, 1984—. *Military service:* U.S. Navy, 1969-71; served as lieutenant.

WRITINGS:

Workplace Safety and Health: The Role of Workers' Compensation, American Enterprise Institute for Public Policy Research, 1977.
(Editor) *Current Issues in Workers' Compensation,* Upjohn Institute for Employment Research, 1984.
Human Resources: A Managerial Perspective, Macmillan, 1985.

WORK IN PROGRESS: Research on workers' compensation, occupational safety and health, and collective bargaining.

* * *

CHERNENKO, Konstantin Ustinovich 1911-1985

OBITUARY NOTICE: Born September 24, 1911, in Bolshaya Tes, Siberia (now Novoselovo, U.S.S.R.); died of heart failure, March 10, 1985; buried in Red Square, Moscow, U.S.S.R. Government official and propagandist. In February, 1984, Chernenko was elected general secretary of the Communist party of the Soviet Union, becoming, at the age of seventy-two, the oldest person ever to assume leadership of the U.S.S.R. Shortly after he took office Chernenko's position was consolidated by his election to the largely honorary posts of chairman of the Defense Council and chairman of the Presidium of the Supreme Soviet. During his tenure as Party chairman he took steps to ease tensions in the Soviet Union's relationships to China and the United States, prompting trade negotiations with the former and renewed arms negotiations with the latter. But his rule was cut short by his death in 1985 and consisted mostly in perpetuating the policies of his predecessors.

Chenenko came to power after a long career as a propagandist for the Communist party, initially as a member of the Communist Youth League, then at the county and provincial levels, and finally, when his patron and mentor Leonid Brezhnev became influential in central party politics during the 1950's and 1960's, at the national level. He became a sector head in the Central Committee's Department of Propaganda and Agitation in Moscow in 1956 and in 1960 was named head of the Secretariat of the Presidium of the Supreme Soviet by Brezhnev, who had been elected chairman of the Presidium. Five years later Chernenko assumed the head post of the General Department of the Party's Central Committee when Brezhnev became Party chairman. Having joined the Communist Party in 1931, Chernenko became a full member of the Central Committee in 1971, its Secretary in charge of ideology in 1976, and a full member of the Politburo in 1978. He was devoted to maintaining the ideological purity of Soviet Communism and wrote numerous articles and speeches pertaining to Marxist-Leninist tenets, many of which were published in the Soviet Union. His books in English translation include *Human Rights in Soviet Society, Soviet Democracy: Principles and Practice,* and *Selected Speeches and Writings.*

OBITUARIES AND OTHER SOURCES:

BOOKS

Current Biography, Wilson, 1984, May, 1985.

PERIODICALS

Chicago Tribune, March 14, 1985.
New York Times, March 12, 1985.
Time, March 25, 1985.
Times (London), March 12, 1985.
Washington Post, March 12, 1985.

* * *

CHESNEY, Marion 1936-
(M. C. Beaton, Helen Crampton, Ann Fairfax, Jennie Tremaine, Charlotte Ward)

PERSONAL: Born June 10, 1936, in Glasgow, Scotland; married Harry Scott Gibbons (a writer and editor); children: Charlie.

ADDRESSES: Home—5 Clarges Mews, London W1, England.

CAREER: Worked as a fiction buyer for a bookseller; women's fashion editor for *Scottish Field* (magazine) in Glasgow, Scotland; theatre critic and reporter for *Scottish Daily Express* in Glasgow; chief reporter for *Daily Express* in London, England; writer.

WRITINGS:

HISTORICAL ROMANCE NOVELS

(Under pseudonym Ann Fairfax) *Henrietta,* Jove, 1979.
(Under pseudonym Jennie Tremaine) *Kitty,* Dell, 1979.
Regency Gold, Fawcett, 1980.
Lady Margery's Intrigue, Fawcett, 1980.
The Constant Companion, Fawcett, 1980.
(Under pseudonym Helen Crampton) *The Marquis Takes a Bride,* Pocket Books, 1980.
(Under Tremaine pseudonym) *Daisy,* Dell, 1980.
(Editor under Tremaine pseudonym) *Lucy,* Dell, 1980.
(Under Tremaine pseudonym) *Polly,* Dell, 1980.
(Under Tremaine pseudonym) *Molly,* Dell, 1980.
(Under Tremaine pseudonym) *Ginny,* Dell, 1980.
Quadrille, Fawcett, 1981.
My Lords, Ladies, and Marjorie, Fawcett, 1981.
(Under Crampton pseudonym) *The Highland Countess,* Pocket Books, 1981.
(Under Fairfax pseudonym) *Annabelle,* Jove, 1981.
(Under Fairfax pseudonym) *Penelope,* Jove, 1981.
(Under Tremaine pseudonym) *Tilly,* Dell, 1981.
(Under Tremaine pseudonym) *Susie,* Dell, 1981.
Love and Lady Lovelace, Fawcett, 1982.
(Under Tremaine pseudonym) *Poppy,* Dell, 1982.
(Under Tremaine pseudonym) *Sally,* Dell, 1982.
(Under pseudoym Charlotte Ward) *The Westerby Inheritance,* Pinnacle Books, 1982.
Duke's Diamonds, Fawcett, 1983.
The Westerby Sisters, Pinnacle Books, 1983.
Minerva: Being the First of Six Sisters, St. Martin's, 1983.
The Taming of Annabelle, St. Martin's, 1983.
The Viscount's Revenge, New American Library, 1983.
Deirdre and Desire, St. Martin's, 1984.
The Poor Relation, New American Library, 1984.
Daphne, St. Martin's, 1984.
The French Affair, Fawcett, 1984.
Diana the Huntress, St. Martin's, 1985.

WORK IN PROGRESS: A detective story, under pseudonym M. C. Beaton, for St. Martin's, 1985.

SIDELIGHTS: Marion Chesney is best known as the author of more than thirty romance novels, many of which take place during the English Regency, a period from 1811 to 1819 encompassing the regency of George, Prince of Wales (later King George IV). Popular in England and America as well as in Germany and Italy, Chesney's books are noted for their historical accuracy and reflect her fondness for such period details as clothing, decor, cuisine, manners, and idiosyncrasies of language.

CA INTERVIEW

CA interviewed Marion Chesney by telephone on September 14, 1984, at her home in London.

CA: You talked your way into some newspaper writing when you were nineteen by becoming a theatre critic. How did your career proceed from there?

CHESNEY: I was working in a bookshop as fiction buyer while I was a theatre critic; then I got a job as women's fashion editor of *Scottish Field* magazine. It was a very genteel job, but the money was not very good. Then I got an offer from the *Scottish Daily Express.* I mostly reported crime. Glasgow

at that time had some of the worst slums in Western Europe. I'd never seen such poverty, filth, incest, rape. So I got a transfer to London and eventually became chief reporter of the *London Daily Express.*

CA: According to Love's Leading Ladies *(Pinnacle Books, 1982), you began writing romances to pay your son's school tuition. Is that right?*

CHESNEY: Although that was a factor, the main factor was that my husband had a slight stroke. He was working on a newspaper in Connecticut when we lived in Brooklyn, and the strain of commuting between there and New York was too much. I really had to do something to help. If I'd only read Georgette Heyer, I don't know if I would have thought of Regency romances, but there were some others that were inaccurate enough to give me the courage to try writing one myself.

My husband knew a chap on the newspaper who wrote gothics under the name of Joy Anne Blackwood. He took a look at what I'd started; he was an ex-editor, and he said, "*I* would buy it. If she does the first fifty pages, I'll give it to my agent in New York." So I did the first fifty pages and an outline and it went to Barbara Lowenstein—she was just starting off as an agent then. She phoned me up and said, "In the first eleven pages, I don't understand who these pepole are. It's very confusing. If you change the first eleven pages, I'll sell it." I did, and I gave it to her on the Friday. On the Monday she'd sold it. That was very exciting.

Then other contracts began to come in. At that time writing was a bit like watching the stock market on Wall Street: Regencies are up, spies are down; mysteries are out, bodice-rippers are in. I think that's going, because the publishers seem to have realized that an author can't fake it. You can't cheat our reader; you must work awfully hard and never write down. It's no use looking at someone else making a lot of money writing something that just happens to be successful and thinking that you can do it and get the same money. All you'll do is turn out second best.

From then my husband was able to stop his job, and then *he* started writing books—he's not used to being unemployed. He's had three spy stories published and has a big historical book coming out from Bantam called *The Tall Woman.* It's based on Virginia Dare, who was the first English woman born in America.

CA: Was the English Regency a favorite period of yours before you began writing your books? You must have already known something about it.

CHESNEY: Yes. My mother was a great Regency fan, so I cut my teeth on Jane Austen and then she bought me Arthur Bryant's *The Age of Elegance.* She was so fascinated by it. Then she got Captain Gronow's *Recollections.* They were published around 1862. Captain Gronow described what the Regency was really like—the garments, the food, the people. My parents were perpetually curious about everything. They would drag us around to all these stately homes that are open to the public, and they read anything and everything. I can still see my mother bowed under two net shopping bags piled high with library books.

Added to that was my journalistic training. I had been working under pressure writing thousands and thousands of words, and although it wasn't Regency, the research I had to do in reporting was merely transferred to historical research. It's like detective work; you're always looking for new books or diaries.

CA: You have quite a collection of books now, don't you?

CHESNEY: Yes. We just had two thousand books shipped over from America. They're not strictly what I would call political and economic histories of the period because no one wants a history lecture. They're about clothes, food, hunting, old diaries, trees and flowers, the seasons, what the weather was like, what people talked about. I find you can't rely too much on anyone else's history book, or you get bogged down with their impressions. It's a good idea to buy a history book and then find the original source and go back to that.

CA: The clothing worn by your characters is especially fun to read about. Do you have a special interest in clothing design?

CHESNEY: Well, I'm an ex-fashion editor, and I still have a terrific appreciation of clothes and line—on someone else. I'm not a very good dresser, though I would like to be. The clothes are very much a part of the period, and I don't think there's another time in history when women have worn so little as they did then. Not only did they dress in thin, see-through muslins, but the most they often wore underneath was a scanty petticoat. There were an awful lot of deaths from pneumonia, influenza, and so on.

CA: Do you find it hard to draw a line between setting the scene with historical detail and, as you said earlier, giving a history lecture?

CHESNEY: Sometimes, yes. It's hard when you've done a lot of research and you have to throw much of it away because you know no one's going to be completely interested in it. For example, in one book I had to do this when it got to the Battle of Waterloo, which already has been described excellently by Georgette Heyer. It was a very grim battle; and it was not the most heroic of battles, because it was just a bloody slaughter on either side. So I simply wrote about before and after the battle.

The other thing that's difficult is that the Regency is a genre that's an escape for intelligent women and they expect an intelligent book. It's people under aspic—modes and manners. It's always very hard, particularly in the present day, not to have his Lordship running out founding orphanages—to give him a social conscience. People really believed that God had put them in their appointed place, no matter which stratum they were in. It's like when I was a child going to church on Sunday: I walked through horrendous slums where the children didn't even have any shoes, but I didn't stop to wonder what caused it—it was just part of the scenery. It is not part of the genre to bring in miserable social conditions, any more than you would in a frivolous operetta.

CA: You've written under other names besides Marion Chesney.

CHESNEY: Yes. Jennie Tremaine, which was the name I wrote Edwardian [novels] under, is not dead, I'm glad to say. There's a new one coming out from St. Martin's Press. And I've just written my first detective story, as M. C. Beaton. That's also St. Martin's Press. I was rather nervous, because I wondered

if I could move into the twentieth century. I went to a fishing school in Sutherland, way up in the north of Scotland, last summer to learn about salmon fishing, fly casting, simply because it was something I knew nothing about. While I was there, we were eleven people in this most beautiful setting—the hotel used to be a country house which belonged to the Duke of Sutherland in the last century—and I thought, here we are, eleven people of varying backgrounds isolated in a small community; what a lovely setting for a murder! That's what gave me the idea.

CA: Have the pseudonyms had any significance apart from designating the various periods you've written about?

CHESNEY: What happened with Jenny Tremaine, for example, was that they said they would like another name because the Marion Chesney name at that time was strictly run by Fawcett. I said, "Well, *Tremaine* is a very Edwardian-sounding name. What about Barbara Tremaine?" They said, "No, not Barbara." So I thought of Jennie Churchill and said, "What about Jennie Tremaine?" That's how that came about. Helen Crampton originally was Helen *Crompton* but was changed through a typing error or an artist's error. I simply looked up in a 1793 *Gentlemen's Sporting Annual* all the names of the people who owned racehorses and I saw *Crompton.* Ann Fairfax simply because it sounded English. M. C. Beaton came about because Hope Dellon, my editor at St. Martin's, said, "Oh, what about a Scottish name—but not a Mac." Then I thought of that old song that goes, "Yestreen the queen she had four Marys / The nicht she'll hae but three / There was Mary Seaton and Mary Beaton and Mary Carmichael and me." And she said, "Beaton sounds all right."

CA: Your books have been translated into several languages. Do they seem to be especially popular in certain countries? Where do you get most of your fan mail from?

CHESNEY: Italy and Germany. And I've just started to sell in Sweden.

CA: Do you try to answer all of your mail?

CHESNEY: Oh, yes. I answer it all myself.

CA: With your expertise in the Regency period and your collection of books on it, have you thought of doing something besides the kinds of things you've done—maybe a nonfiction book or acting as consultant for movie or television sets?

CHESNEY: No, I'm a Walter Mitty. I like telling stories.

CA: Are you concerned about the apparent slump in romance popularity?

CHESNEY: No, I was very lucky; I survived the Great Regency Slump of 1982. You see, what had been happening was this: Someone like John le Carre writes very good spy stories, and immediately the publishers and agents are apt to say, "We want something like John le Carre." But the John le Carre reader is getting not only le Carre's writing, but his life and experience. The same thing happened when Jack Higgins produced "The Eagle Has Landed." Suddenly it was: "We must have World War II."

I learned from other writers that it's better to stick to what you know best and hope it will work out in the end. I have a friend who writes detectives that are very popular. He was told that World War II was the thing when he wasn't doing well with detective stories. He said that his efforts to write on World War II were so bad that he had to have someone come in and help him finish. Then when he returnd to detective stories, he hit the top of the market. He just stuck to what he knew best.

I think there's been too much of publishers giving the public what they think they ought to have. In writing, the "good read" went out—you know, the nice book that you read on a wet day, the book with a beginning, a middle, and an end. So you either had very low category romance or, on the literary end, rather narcissistic, introverted writing—forgetting that Somerset Maugham, H. G. Wells, and Charles Dickens really did write stories to entertain. Therefore people read an awful lot of detective stories these days in order to get a good read and good writing.

CA: Don't you think the "good read" kind of book is coming back?

CHESNEY: Well, I was very pleased when an editor here asked me to do a book and said they wanted "a historical book with romance" rather than "a historical romance." They said because of the programs like "The Irish R. M." and "Upstairs, Downstairs," people are getting much wiser about history. Another thing is that they've made the great mistake of equating romance with sex. That's been done before in the 1930's. It lasts for a certain amount of time, and then people get a feeling of revulsion. What happened in the popular romance was it was becoming a vehicle for sex, whereas the more plot there is in a story, the less sex you need.

CA: Has your recent move back to England changed your writing patterns at all?

CHESNEY: It has because of getting settled—having the animals in quarantine, getting the child in school. But basically, no. I regret to say that my writing pattern is to wait until almost the last minute and then practically burst into tears. The thing that's so marvelous here is having the public libraries all about, with tremendous numbers of books.

CA: Better than in the States?

CHESNEY: Oh, much better because there are so many of them in such a small area. You can just walk to them. The Westminster Library, for example, has an archives section. You go in and tell them roughly what you want, and they bring you piles of books.

CA: Do you really not keep any kind of schedule when you're working on a specific book?

CHESNEY: I'm afraid not. I really wish I did. I attack the typewriter in panic. But somehow I write better under pressure, because I find if I leave it for too long, I forget what I really thought about the characters at the beginning.

CA: How does it work out having two writers in the family now?

CHESNEY: It works out very well. My husband's been helping me with the copy typing here, because it's very expensive to get it done—it's about the equivalent of eight hundred dollars

to get it really done properly. He pecks away and does a good job. He was once an editor himself and a foreign correspondent. It doesn't matter how hard you try, sometimes you make mistakes in the time factor; he's very good at picking up things like that.

CA: Do you read his work at some stage?

CHESNEY: We read each other's work, but we don't criticize much. We're completely different writers, with completely different styles, but we both admire each other's work. He's also marvelous at finding historical books for me, going around to second-hand bookshops.

CA: What will the new book be about?

CHESNEY: It will be a historical that isn't a Regency. It's set after the 1745 rebellion—the time of bonnie Prince Charlie—when the Highland men had one of their ears sliced off and were branded on the cheek and sent to America as slaves. The women and children were just drowned; bullets were too expensive. In the book, I have someone going to Virginia and then coming back to Scotland. My husband did such a lot of research in Virginia, so we've been all around and seen the plantations and gathered details and manuscripts of the time. One interesting thing was the attitude toward white slaves; they didn't like them very much. A white slave would only fetch about 14 pounds; a black slave would fetch 144 pounds.

CA: Any thoughts on your career at this point that you'd like to share with readers?

CHESNEY: Just generally that I feel very lucky in being with St. Martin's Press. I find them surprising because they're very well organized. And I'm lucky in my editors: Barbara Dicks at Fawcett, Hope Dellon at St. Martin's, and Hilary Ross at New American Library—my three angels. They work very hard at finding out what the public wants. And they know that you can't write down, that people want something readable. I find them all very encouraging.

BIOGRAPHICAL/CRITICAL SOURCES:

BOOKS

Kathryn Falk, *Love's Leading Ladies*, Pinnacle Books, 1982.

—*Interview by Jean W. Ross*

*   *   *

CHITTICK, Donald Ernest 1932-

PERSONAL: Born May 3, 1932, in Salem, Ore.; son of Ernest Stanley (an optical technician) and Laura (a bank clerk; maiden name, Jorgensen) Chittick; married Donna Wright (a secretary), 1957; children: Anna Laurene. *Education:* Williamette University, B.S., 1954; Oregon State College (now University), Ph.D., 1960.

ADDRESSES: Home—Route 2, Box 194, Newberg, Ore. 97132.

CAREER: University of Puget Sound, Tacoma, Wash., instructor, 1958-59, assistant professor, 1959-65, associate professor of chemistry, 1965-68; George Fox College, Newberg, Ore., professor of chemistry, 1968-79, chairman of department of science and mathematics, 1974-79; Pyrenco, Inc., Prosser, Wash., director of research, 1979-82; Alpha Tech,

Inc., Newberg, Ore., director of research and development, 1982—.

MEMBER: American Chemical Society, American Association for the Advancement of Science, Creation Research Society, New York Academy of Sciences.

WRITINGS:

(Contributor) *Symposium on Creation II,* Donald Patten, editor, Baker Book, 1970.
The Controversy: Roots of the Creation-Evolution Conflict, Multnomah, 1984.

WORK IN PROGRESS: Exploring religion and the age of the earth; research on alternate fuels.

SIDELIGHTS: Donald Ernest Chittick told *CA:* "I am an inventor and hold patents in the area of biomass gasification and programmed instruction. My present work is involved with research and development work in converting waste materials into useable fuels and energy. I have developed one of the world's smallest conversion devices for changing agricultural wastes into gaseous fuel suitable for running small engines to generate electricity or pump water.

"I also present seminars on the creation-evolution issue. These seminars are presented before a wide variety of audiences, schools, universities, scientific societies, churches, civic groups, etc.

"My approach to the creation-evolution issue is that the roots of the issue lie with basic philosophical differences or different and antithetical world views and not with science as such. The facts of science are interpreted differently within the creationist or evolutionist world views. Qualified scientists are found in both the creationist and evolutionist camps. My research on creation-evolution has shown that the issue of the age of the earth can also be traced to the same philosophical differences associated with creation-evolution."

*   *   *

CHOI Sunu 1916-1984

OBITUARY NOTICE: Born April 27, 1916, in Kaesong, Korea (now North Korea); died December 15, 1984. Curator and author of books on Korean art. Director-general of the Seoul National Museum of Korea from 1974 until his death, Choi began his affiliation with the museum in 1948. Prior to becoming director-general Choi served as head of the art department and chief curator of the museum, and during the Korean War he supervised various relocations of the museum's treasures. He was dedicated to stimulating an interest in and awareness of Korean cultural traditions, both among Koreans and people of other nations, and so worked to bring exhibits representing five thousand years of Korean art to various parts of the world. He also promoted the excavation and study of the kiln sites of Korea's Koryo dynasty, which produced what are considered the finest celadon wares in East Asia. His writings include the books *Ink Paintings of the Choson Dynasty, Five Thousand Years of Korean Art,* a volume on the Seoul National Museum for the series "Oriental Ceramics: The World's Great Collections," volumes on Korean art for the "Arts of Korea" series, and a chronology of Kim Hongdo, a painter of the Choson dynasty period.

OBITUARIES AND OTHER SOURCES:

PERIODICALS

Times (London), February 11, 1985.

CHRISTALLER, Walter 1893-1969

OBITUARY NOTICE: Born April 21, 1893, in Berneck, Baden-Wuerttemberg, Germany (now West Germany); died March 9, 1969, in Koenigstein, East Germany. Geographer and author of the book *Central Places of Southern Germany.* City planner for the Municipality of Berlin, Germany, during the 1920's, Christaller went on to develop theories about the structure of cities and their peripheral settlements and why they are established in certain locations. In his hypotheses Christaller emphasized the economic aspects of geographical location, including natural resources and the trading structure of an area. Though not given much recognition prior to the 1950's, when his work was circulated in the English-speaking world, Christaller came to be known as the father of theoretical geography, and his work is said to have contributed significantly to economic geography.

OBITUARIES AND OTHER SOURCES:

BOOKS

Twentieth-Century Culture: A Biographical Companion, Harper, 1983.
Who's Who in Economics: A Biographical Dictionary of Major Economists, 1700-1981, MIT Press, 1983.

*   *   *

CHRISTIAN, Glynn 1942-

PERSONAL: Born January 1, 1942, in Aukland, New Zealand; son of Claude Royce (a manager) and Enid Olwyn (a housewife; maiden name, Pitman) Christian. *Education:* Attended schools in New Zealand.

ADDRESSES: Office—BBC-TV, Lime Grove, London W12, England. *Agent*—Jo Gurnett Ltd., 45 Queens Gate Mews, London SW7, England.

CAREER: Writer for advertising agencies in New Zealand, 1960-65; travel writer in Great Britain, 1963-74; Mr. Christian's (delicatessen), London, England, proprietor, 1974-82; British Broadcasting Corporation (BBC-TV), London, food reporter and chef-presenter for "Breakfast Time," 1982—. Film, television, and radio scriptwriter; documentarist.

MEMBER: Royal Geographical Society (fellow), Guild of Foodwriters (member of steering committee).

WRITINGS:

Fragile Paradise: The Discovery of Fletcher Christian, Bounty Mutineer, Atlantic/Little, Brown, 1982.
The Delicatessan Food Handbook, MacDonald, 1982.
The Delicatessan Cookbook, MacDonald, 1984.
World Guide to Cheese, Ebury Press, 1984.
British Cooking at Its Best, Sainsbury, 1984.
Edible France: A Traveller's Guide to Eating in France, Ebury Press, 1985.
The New Classic Cookbook, Octopus Books, in press.

Also author of eleven other foodbooks, including *The No-Cook Cookbook,* Jupiter Books, *Cheese and Cheesemaking,* MacDonald, *Bread and Yeast Cookery,* MacDonald, and *The Radio and TV Cookbook,* Futura Publications.

SCREENPLAYS

"Her Private Hell," Piccadilly Pictures, 1967.

TELEVISION SCRIPTS

"Stop, Look, Listen" (series), Associated Television Ltd. (ATV), 1971.
"Words and Music" (series), British Broadcasting Corp. (BBC-TV).

OTHER

Contributor to *The Sunday Times Complete Cookbook, Last Suppers, Man in the Kitchen,* and *One Thousand More Recipes;* contributor of recipe and cooking features to *Over 21* and *Living.*

WORK IN PROGRESS: Food in an Eighteenth-Century Country House, publication expected in 1987.

SIDELIGHTS: In *Fragile Paradise: The Discovery of Fletcher Christian, Bounty Mutineer,* Glynn Christian examines the infamous 1789 mutiny of the crew of Her Majesty's Ship *Bounty.* Hoping to come to know his great-great-great-great-grandfather—mutiny leader Fletcher Christian—as well as uncover the real cause of the mutiny, the author employs known data and newly discovered family papers to reconsturct the drama; he also embarked on a three-month expedition that retraces the *Bounty*'s voyage to Tahiti, Tubuai, and Pitcairn. Barbara Bright noted in the *New York Times Book Review* that despite some disorganization, Glynn Christian "tells a fascinating tale." "His passages depicting Tahiti and Pitcairn, both 18th-century and modern, are among the best parts of the book," she added.

Glynn Christian told *CA:* "Besides working three times weekly as food reporter and chef for the BBC's 'Breakfast Time,' I have been working informally to improve the conditions on Pitcairn Island, home of *Bounty* descendents. I have also filmed five thirty-minute documentaries on life in New Zealand, approached through the country's food and the way it is grown, cooked, served, and eaten. Series in China and the United States are also planned. I strongly hold that food is the most reliable way to learn about any country, town, village, or individual."

BIOGRAPHICAL/CRITICAL SOURCES:

New York Times Book Review, December 26, 1982.
Times Literary Supplement, December 24, 1982.

*   *   *

CLARK, Garth (Reginald)   1947-

PERSONAL: Born May 15, 1947, in Pretoria, South Africa; immigrated to United States, 1976; son of Reginald and Johanna Clark; children: Mark Richard, Kellan Reginald. *Education:* Royal College of Art, M.A., 1976.

ADDRESSES: Home—170 South da Brea, Los Angeles, Calif. 90036.

CAREER: University of California, Los Angeles, art historian, 1978; Institute for Ceramic History, Los Angeles, director, 1979-81; Garth Clark Gallery, Los Angeles, founder and owner, 1981—. Morton Professor at Ohio University, 1981. Founder of Garth Clark Gallery, New York, N.Y., 1983; collections arranged include "The Contemporary American Potter," a touring exhibition of the Smithsonian Institution, 1980-82; member of overview committee of National Endowment for the Arts Visual Art Program, 1984.

MEMBER: Decorative Art Society.

AWARDS, HONORS: National Endowment for the Arts, Services to the Field Award, 1979; Art Critics Award, 1980.

WRITINGS:

(With Lynne Wagner) *Potters of Southern Africa,* G. Struik, 1973.
(Editor) *Ceramic Art: Comment and Review, 1882-1977,* Dutton, 1978.
(With Margie Hughto) *A Century of Ceramics in the United States, 1878-1978,* Dutton, 1979.
American Potters, Watson-Guptill, 1981.
Michael Cardew: An Intimate Account of a Potter Who Has Captured the Spirit of Country Craft, Kodansha, 1982.
(Editor) *Ceramic Echoes: Historical References in Contemporary Ceramic Art,* Contemporary Art Society, 1983.
Modern Ceramic Art: A History Since 1850, Thomas & Hudson, in press.

Author of *Ceramic Arts* newsletter; contributor of articles and essays to exhibition catalogs and magazines.

SIDELIGHTS: Garth Clark told *CA:* "My writing has been dedicated to developing an understanding and appreciation of ceramics since 1850 as an art form. To raise the levels of understanding has required both an improvement in the levels of scholarship and the evolution of an analytical language that encompasses the unique quality of this medium.

"My interest in ceramics developed while I was still living in South Africa. It was spurred on by the discovery that there was *very* little written about twentieth-century ceramics that was scholarly and art-critical in nature. Much of my writing has been directed toward exhibition catalogs and magazine reviews and articles—in this area I have more than seventy-five essays and reviews published. I now direct two galleries, one in Los Angeles and one in New York, and am still actively writing with one book on the way and a regular newsletter, *Ceramic Arts,* that is published by the galleries."

*   *   *

CLARKE, Richard (William Barnes)   1910-1975

OBITUARY NOTICE: Born August 13, 1910; died June 21, 1975. Civil servant, journalist, and author. Known to his colleagues as Otto, Clarke was educated at Cambridge University as a journalist and spent six years writing for the *Financial News* before joining Britain's Civil Service in 1939. He remained with the service for forty years, rising through the ranks to become assistant secretary to the Treasury in 1945, undersecretary in 1947, third secretary in 1955, and second secretary in 1962. In 1966 he left the Treasury to serve as permanent secretary to the Ministry of Aviation for a year and then spent four years as permanent secretary to the Ministry of Technology.

Among Clarke's most notable achievements during his civil service career were his efforts during World War II to adapt public administration to the demands of wartime Britain, his contributions to the postwar coordination of international economic recovery plans with British needs, and his collaboration on the reorganization of the Treasury, which was effected in 1962. Aside from his civil service duties, Clarke maintained an active interest in chess throughout his lifetime. A competitive player during his college years, Clarke later developed a rating system for the British Chess Federation (BCF) and became chairman of the BCF Grading Committee. In 1970 he was named committee chairman of the Friends of Chess organization. Among his official writings are the European report in response to the speech that introduced the Marshall Plan following World War II and *Economic Survey 1947,* considered a landmark in Keynesian economic planning. His other works include an index of share prices and the books *The Economic Effort of War, The Management of the Public Sector of the National Economy,* and *New Trends in Government.*

OBITUARIES AND OTHER SOURCES:

BOOKS

Who's Who, 126th edition, St. Martin's, 1974.

PERIODICALS

Times (London), June 23, 1975.
Times Literary Supplement, June 4, 1982.

*   *   *

CLAY, Diskin   1938-

PERSONAL: Born November 2, 1938, in Fresno, Calif.; son of Norman and Florence Patricia (a housewife; maiden name, Diskin) Clay; married Sara Christine Clark, October 28, 1978; children: Andreia. *Education:* Reed College, B.A., 1960; graduate study at University of Montpellier, 1960-61; University of Washington, Seattle, M.A., 1963, Ph.D., 1967; attended American School of Classical Studies, Athens, Greece, 1963-64. *Religion:* Roman Catholic.

ADDRESSES: Home—206 Hawthorn Rd., Baltimore, Md. 21210. *Office*—Department of Classics, Johns Hopkins University, Baltimore, Md. 21218.

CAREER: Reed College, Portland, Ore., assistant professor of classics and humanities, 1966-69; Harvard University, Center for Hellenic Studies, junior fellow, 1969-70; Haverford College, Haverford, Pa., assistant professor, 1970-73, associate professor of classics, 1973-76; Johns Hopkins University, Baltimore, Md., professor of classics, 1976—, Francis White Professor of Greek, 1980—, chairman of department of classics, 1976-82. Visiting professor at University of Lille, 1972.

MEMBER: American Philological Association, American Institute of Archaeology, Society for Ancient Greek Philosophy, Modern Greek Studies Association, Phi Beta Kappa.

AWARDS, HONORS: Fulbright fellow in France, 1960-61; Woodrow Wilson fellow, 1963-64; fellow of National Endowment for the Humanities, 1974-75.

WRITINGS:

Oxyrhynchan Poems, Press 22, 1973.
(Translator with Stephen Berg) Sophocles, *Oedipus the King,* Oxford University Press, 1978.
Lucretius and Epicurus, Cornell University Press, 1983.
(With Jenny Clay and Robert Horwitz) *John Locke: Questions Concerning the Law of Nature,* University Press of Virginia, 1985.

Contributor to classical journals. *American Journal of Philology,* member of editorial board, 1975—, editor, 1982—.

WORK IN PROGRESS: Two works on Plato; an introduction for Yale University Press and the Hermes Guides to Classical Masters; a study of Plato's portraits of Socrates; a translation of *De rerum natura* by Lucretius for Cornell University Press.

SIDELIGHTS: Diskin Clay told *CA:* "I have been attracted to the monuments of Greece, Cyprus, and Turkey. I worked as

an underwater archaeologist in Cyprus from 1968 to 1969 and an epigrapher in Turkey, at the site of the philosophical inscription of Oenoanda. I speak modern Greek, French, Italian, German, and some Turkish and Spanish. I continue, somehow, to write poetry."

BIOGRAPHICAL/CRITICAL SOURCES:

PERIODICALS

National Geographic, June, 1970.

*   *   *

CLEARMAN, Brian (Patrick Joseph)   1941-

PERSONAL: Born March 19, 1941, in Longview, Wash.; son of W. Wade (a carpenter and builder) and Ethel K. (a beautician and homemaker; maiden name, Sauers) Clearman. *Education:* Attended Lower Columbia College, 1959-60, 1964, and Saint Martin's College, 1960-62; Portland State University, B.S., 1965; graduate study at Western State College of Colorado, 1972; University of Oregon, M.S., 1975.

ADDRESSES: Home and office—Mount Angel Abbey, Saint Benedict, Ore. 97373.

CAREER: Entered Order of St. Benedict (Benedictines), 1964, made monastic vows, 1966; Mount Angel Abbey, Saint Benedict, Ore., teacher at preparatory school, 1968-76, staff member of Business Office, 1976—.

WRITINGS:

Transportation Markings: A Study in Communication, Volume I, Parts A-D, University Press of America, 1981, Volume II, Part E.: *International Traffic Control Devices,* Mount Angel Abbey, 1984, Part F: *International Railway Signals,* Mount Angel Abbey, in press.

SIDELIGHTS: Brian Clearman told *CA:* "Transportation markings are those devices—external to a means of transportation—that aid the safety of motorists, navigators, and engineers. They include buoys, lighthouses, fog signals, unlighted beacons, road and rail signals, safety signs, electronic mechanisms, aeronautical lights, and road and runway markings. My interest in them began more than twenty-five years ago with the lighthouses and river lights of the Washington and Oregon coasts and of the Columbia River and Puget Sound. Gradually it expanded to include all other forms of transportation markings. My writings survey markings less as technical phenomena and more as communications and as applied semiotics.

"The preparation of the studies has taken place, to a considerable extent, within a monastic context. That milieu has greatly influenced, not only the form, but also the content of the research and writing. Hopefully, the end product will provide an introductory compendium of the whole range of markings."

*   *   *

COBBS, John L(ewis)   1917-

BRIEF ENTRY: Born September 10, 1917, in Washington, D.C. American journalist and magazine editor. Cobbs joined the editorial staff of *Business Week* in 1942. He worked as finance editor, Washington, D.C., correspondent, business policy editor, and managing editor, then served as the magazine's editor from 1966 until he retired from that post in 1982. His association with *Business Week* has continued, however, with Cobbs writing business articles for the publication. He was honored with a distinguished service award from Sigma Delta Chi in 1959, a reporting award from the Overseas Press Club of America in 1972, and the Gerald Loeb Memorial Award from the Graduate School of Management at the University of California, Los Angeles, in 1972. *Address:* c/o *Business Week,* 1221 Avenue of the Americas, New York, N.Y. 10020.

BIOGRAPHICAL/CRITICAL SOURCES:

PERIODICALS

Business Week, November 29, 1982.

*   *   *

COCHRAN-SMITH, Marilyn   1951-

PERSONAL: Born March 31, 1951, in Washington, Pa.; daughter of James M. and Betty M. Cochran; married Walter K. Smith, July 7, 1973; children: Bradford, Michael, Karen. *Education:* College of Wooster, B.A. (with honors), 1973; Cleveland State University, M.Ed., 1978; University of Pennsylvania, Ph.D., 1981.

ADDRESSES: Home—310 Joy Lane, West Chester, Pa. 19380. *Office*—Graduate School of Education, University of Pennsylvania, 3700 Walnut St., Philadelphia, Pa. 19104.

CAREER: Elementary school teacher in Brecksville, Ohio, 1973-78; University of Pennsylvania, Philadelphia, lecture in teacher education, 1979—.

MEMBER: International Reading Association, National Council of Teachers of English, Phi Beta Kappa.

WRITINGS:

The Making of a Reader, Ablex Publishing, 1984.

*   *   *

COCKFIELD, Jamie (Hartwell)   1945-

PERSONAL: Born June 20, 1945, in Charleston, S.C.; son of Jamie H. (a dentist) and Pierrine (Le Prince) Cockfield. *Education:* University of South Carolina—Columbia, B.A., 1967, M.A., 1968; University of Virginia, Ph.D., 1972. *Religion:* Baptist.

ADDRESSES: Office—Department of History, Mercer University, 1400 Coleman Ave., Macon, Ga. 31207.

CAREER: Mercer University, Macon, Ga., assistant professor, 1972-77, associate professor of history, 1977—, chairman of department, 1979-82. Chairman of Bibb County Republican Party, 1977-79; member of Macon-Bibb County Board of Elections, 1979—.

MEMBER: American Association for the Advancement of Slavic Studies, Southern Conference for Slavic Studies.

WRITINGS:

(Editor) *Dollars and Diplomacy: Ambassador David Rowland Francis and the Fall of Tsarism, 1916-1917,* Duke University Press, 1981.

Contributor to history journals.

WORK IN PROGRESS: Snow on Their Boots: The Russian Expeditionary Force in France, 1916-1918, completion expected in 1988.

COFER, Judith Ortiz   1952-

PERSONAL: Born February 24, 1952, in Hormigueros, P.R.; immigrated to United States, 1956; daughter of J. M. (in U.S. Navy) and Fanny (Morot) Ortiz; married Charles John Cofer (a businessman), November 13, 1971; children: Tanya. *Education:* Augusta College, B.A., 1974; Florida Atlantic University, M.A., 1977; attended Oxford University, 1977.

ADDRESSES: Home—P.O. Box 2418, Athens, Ga. 30612. *Office*—Department of English, University of Georgia, Athens, Ga. 30602. *Agent*—Berenice Hoffman Literary Agency, 215 West 75th St., New York, N.Y. 10023.

CAREER: Bilingual teacher at public schools in Palm Beach County, Fla., 1974-75; Broward Community College, Fort Lauderdale, Fla., adjunct instructor in English, 1978-80, instructor in Spanish, 1979; University of Miami, Coral Gables, Fla., lecturer in English, 1980-84; University of Georgia, Athens, instructor in English, 1984—. Adjunct instructor at Palm Beach Junior College, 1978-80. Conducts poetry workshops and gives poetry readings. Member of regular staff of International Conference on the Fantastic in Literature, 1979-82; member of literature panel of Fine Arts Council of Florida, 1982; member of administrative staff of Bread Loaf Writers' Conference, 1983, 1984.

MEMBER: Poetry Society of America, Poets and Writers, Associated Writing Programs.

AWARDS, HONORS: Scholar of English Speaking Union at Oxford University, 1977; fellow of Fine Arts Council of Florida, 1980; Bread Loaf Writers' Conference, scholar, 1981, John Atherton Scholar in Poetry, 1982.

WRITINGS:

POETRY

Latin Women Pray, Florida Arts Gazette Press, 1980.
The Native Dancer, Pteranodon Press, 1981.
Among the Ancestors, Louisville News Press, 1981.
Reaching for the Mainland, Bilingual Review Press, 1984.

PLAYS

''Latin Women Pray'' (three-act play), first produced in Atlanta at Georgia State University, June, 1984.

OTHER

Work represented in anthologies, including *Hispanics in the U.S.,* Bilingual Review Press, 1982; *Latina Writers;* and *Revista Chicano-Riquena.* Contributor of poems to magazines, including *Southern Humanities Review, Poem, Prairie Schooner, Apalachee Quarterly, Kansas Quarterly,* and *Kalliope.* Poetry editor of *Florida Arts Gazette,* 1978-81; member of editorial board of *Waves.*

WORK IN PROGRESS: Letters From a Caribbean Island, poems; *The Line of the Sun,* a memoir.

SIDELIGHTS: Judith Ortiz Cofer told *CA:* ''The 'infinite variety' and power of language interest me. I never cease to experiment with it. As a native Puerto Rican, my first language was Spanish. It was a challenge, not only to learn English, but to master it enough to teach it and—the ultimate goal—to write poetry in it.

''My family is one of the main topics of my poetry; the ones left behind on the island of Puerto Rico, and the ones who came to the United States. In tracing their lives, I discover more about mine. The place of birth itself becomes a metaphor for the things we all must leave behind; the assimilation of a new culture is the coming into maturity by accepting the terms necessary for survival. My poetry is a study of this process of change, assimilation and transformation.''

* * *

COFFIN, Harold Glen   1926-

PERSONAL: Born April 9, 1926, in Nanning, China; U.S. citizen born abroad; son of Day D. (a physician) and Edyth (Gruber) Coffin; married Emma Pritel (a librarian), June 17, 1947; children: Glenda Coffin Hayward, Carolyn. *Education:* Walla Walla College, B.A., 1947, M.A., 1952; University of Southern California, Ph.D., 1955. *Religion:* Seventh-day Adventist.

ADDRESSES: Home—11314 La Verne Dr., Riverside, Calif. 92505. *Office*—Geoscience Research Institute, Loma Linda University, Loma Linda, Calif. 92350.

CAREER: Canadian Union College, Lacombe, Alberta, instructor in science, 1947-56, head of department of biology, 1947-52, head of Division of Science and Mathematics, 1954-56; Walla Walla College, Walla Walla, Wash., associate professor, 1956-58, professor and head of department of biology, 1958-64; Andrews University, Berrien Springs, Mich., professor of zoology, 1964-65, and paleontology, 1965-80; Loma Linda University, Loma Linda, Calif., senior research scientist at Geoscience Research Institute, 1980—.

MEMBER: American Association for the Advancement of Science, Geological Society of America, Sigma Xi.

WRITINGS:

Trails Unlimited (with own photographs), Pacific Press Publishing Association, 1955.
Creation: Accident or Design?, Review and Herald, 1969.
(With J. Kerby Anderson) *Fossils in Focus,* Zondervan, 1977.
(With Ruth Wheeler) *Dinosaurs,* Pacific Press Publishing Association, 1978.
Origin by Design, Review and Herald, 1984.

Contributor to scientific journals and religious magazines.

WORK IN PROGRESS: Research on petrified trees, particularly the Yellowstone petrified forests.

SIDELIGHTS: Harold Glen Coffin told *CA:* "My employing organization, the Geoscience Research Institute, is funded by the Seventh-day Adventist Church. As a conservative Christian I consider God to be the author of nature and Scripture; therefore, they will not conflict if both are correctly understood. My own research confirms the correctness of this view.''

* * *

COHEN, Edward H.   1941-

BRIEF ENTRY: Born November 6, 1941, in Washington, D.C. American educator and author. Cohen joined the faculty of Rollins College in 1967 and became a full professor of English in 1979. He has been a fellow of the Henry E. Huntington Library, the National Endowment for the Humanities, and the American Council on Education. Cohen's books include *Works and Criticism of Gerard Manley Hopkins: A Comprehensive Bibliography* (Catholic University of America Press, 1969), *The Henley-Stevenson Quarrel* (University Presses of Florida,

1974), and *Ebenezer Cooke: The Sot-Weed Canon* (University of Georgia Press, 1975). *Address:* Department of English, Rollins College, Winter Park, Fla. 32789.

* * *

COHEN, Jene Barr   1900-1985
(Jene Barr)

OBITUARY NOTICE—See index for *CA* sketch: Born July 28, 1900, in Kobrin, Russia (now U.S.S.R.); died April 5, 1985, in San Jose, Calif. Educator and author. Cohen, who wrote under the name Jene Barr, was a physical education instructor in the Chicago Public Schools for more than thirty years before her retirement in 1964. She was the prize-winning author of numerous books for children, including *Ben's Busy Service Station, Mike the Milkman, Texas Pete, Little Cowboy, Mr. Mailman, Little Circus Dog,* and *Baker Bill.*

OBITUARIES AND OTHER SOURCES:

PERIODICALS

Chicago Sun-Times, April 10, 1985.
Chicago Tribune, April 11, 1985.

* * *

COHEN, Paul Andrew   1934-

PERSONAL: Born June 2, 1934, in New York, N.Y.; son of Wilfred P. (a manufacturer) and Rose (Junger) Cohen; children: Joanna, Nathaniel, Lisa, Emily. *Education:* University of Chicago, B.A., 1955; Harvard University, M.A., 1957, Ph.D., 1961.

ADDRESSES: Office—Department of History, Wellesley College, Wellesley, Mass. 02181.

CAREER: University of Michigan, Ann Arbor, visiting lecturer in history, 1962-63; Amherst College, Amherst, Mass., assistant professor of history, 1963-65; Wellesley College, Wellesley, Mass., associate professor, 1965-71, Edith Stix Wasserman Professor of Asian Studies, 1971—. Associate at Fairbank Center for East Asian Research, Harvard University. Member of National Committee on United States-China Relations and China Council of Asian Society.

MEMBER: American Historical Association, Association for Asian Studies, Society for Ch'ing Studies, American Association of University Professors.

WRITINGS:

China and Christianity: The Missionary Movement and the Growth of Chinese Antiforeignism, 1860-1870, Harvard University Press, 1963.
(Contributor) Albert Fenerwerker, Rhoads Murphey, and Mary C. Wright, editors, *Approaches to Modern Chinese History,* University of California Press, 1967.
(Contributor) James B. Crowley, editor, *Modern East Asia: Essays in Interpretation,* Harcourt, 1970.
Between Tradition and Modernity: Wang Tao and Reform in Late Ch'ing China, Harvard University Press, 1974.
(Editor with John E. Schrecker, and contributor) *Reform in Nineteenth-Century China,* Harvard University Press, 1976.
Discovering History in China: American Historical Writing on the Recent Chinese Past, Columbia University Press, 1984.

Contributor to history and Asian studies journals.

WORK IN PROGRESS: "The Post-Mao Reforms in China From a Historian's Perspective," for inclusion in a conference volume; *The Boxer Rebellion.*

SIDELIGHTS: Paul Andrew Cohen told *CA:* "I backed into the professional study of China in 1955, when, about to finish college, I needed an excuse to stay in school (which at that time was the only way to keep from being drafted into the Army). As a graduate student at Harvard, I came under the influence of John K. Fairbank, an influence that is reflected—along with increasingly less muted signs of my struggle against it—in my first two books. My latest book, *Discovering History in China,* started out as a more explicit attempt to sort things out intellecutally for myself but quickly turned into a critical examination of the entire field of recent (nineteenth- and twentieth-century) Chinese history as it has been thought about and practiced in the United States since World War II. Writing it was alternately painful and great fun. I am hopeful that it will be of interest not only to students of the Chinese past but also to people interested in the evolution of American historical scholarship on non-Western societies other than China."

*　　*　　*

COKE, Tom S(tephen)   1943-

PERSONAL: Born January 19, 1943, in Wichita, Kan.; son of James Walter (a machinist) and Esther (a housewife; maiden name, Turley) Coke; married Barbara Kay Gardner (a housewife), November 21, 1965; children: Julie Ann, Christopher Thomas, Rebecca Leigh. *Education:* Attended Prairie Bible Institute, 1961-63; Wichita State University, B.A., 1968; Northern Baptist Theological Seminary, M.A., 1976. *Religion:* Christian.

ADDRESSES: Home—206 South Osage, Wichita, Kan. 67213.

CAREER: Dialogue, Berwyn, Ill., editorial staff writer, 1969-74; Oak Brook Limousine Co., Oak Brook, Ill., chauffeur, 1974-79; Evangelical Teacher Training Association, Wheaton, Ill., member of editorial staff, 1979; partner in James Coke and Sons, Inc., 1979—. Free-lance writer, 1974-79.

WRITINGS:

Life in a Fishbowl, Scripture Press, 1978.
More Than Just You, Scripture Press, 1979.

Contributor to *Reformed Journal.*

WORK IN PROGRESS: Major Words of the Bible.

SIDELIGHTS: Tom S. Coke told *CA:* "The more a person takes part in life, the better he or she can write about it. That's why I've tried to work at different jobs throughout my life, from limousine chauffeur to machinist. I've also learned much from other authors, particularly C. S. Lewis, Tom Wolfe, and Rudolf Flesch. Lewis's books show me how to use vivid illustrations, Wolfe prevents me from becoming too formal, and Flesch keeps me simple—I hope. I've tried to bring all these influences into play in my books on Christian faith and hope that its meaning becomes just a little better understood because of what I've written."

*　　*　　*

COLAIACO, James A(lfred)   1945-

PERSONAL: Born June 22, 1945, in New York, N.Y.; son of Alfred James and Helen Ann (McGrail) Colaiaco. *Education:*

Fordham University, B.A., 1967; Columbia University, M.A., 1968, Ph.D., 1976.

ADDRESSES: Home—145-81 Eighth Ave., Whitestone, N.Y. 11357. *Office*—Dalton School, 108 East 89th St., New York, N.Y. 10028.

CAREER: Association of the Bar of the City of New York, New York City, deputy night librarian, 1969-76, night librarian, 1976-80; New York University, New York City, adjunct lecturer, 1979-81, adjunct assistant professor, 1981-83, adjunct associate professor of humanities, 1984; Dalton School, New York City, teacher, 1984—. Member of national advisory board of *History Teacher.*

MEMBER: American Historical Association, American Association of Law Libraries, Society for History Education, Law Library Association of Greater New York, Phi Beta Kappa.

WRITINGS:

James Fitzjames Stephen and the Crisis of Victorian Thought, Macmillan, 1983.

Contributor to history and library journals.

WORK IN PROGRESS: A book tentatively titled *Martin Luther King, Jr., and the Politics of Crisis,* publication by Macmillan (London) expected in 1987.

SIDELIGHTS: James A. Colaiaco told *CA:* "James Fitzjames Stephen was a prominent Victorian thinker whose important contributions to his age have been underestimated or forgotten. Because Stephen's intellectual interests were so cosmopolitan—embracing politics, literature, law, religion, journalism, the British Empire—my book may be characterized as an intellectual history of the Victorian Age from the perspective of one of its great thinkers. Stephen was a formidable polemicist who engaged in controversy with several of the giants of his time, including Dickens, Carlyle, Arnold, Gladstone, Newman, and especially John Stuart Mill. Stephen's writings also shed valuable light on what I call the 'crisis of Victorian thought,' meaning the intellectual turmoil created by the growth of democracy and the decline of religion as an effective social sanction. Throughout his intellectual life, Stephen remained a classical liberal, skeptical of rule by the masses and opposed to big government. I hope that I have shown in my book that Stephen deserves to rank as one of the truly great Victorians.

"My book on Martin Luther King, Jr., will be both an analysis of King's tactic of nonviolent direct action and civil disobedience and a general assessment of his contribution to the civil rights movement. I plan to show how King was a brilliant strategist who perfected a technique for bringing about profound social change by nonviolent means. In view of the fact that the United States will be celebrating King's birthday as a national holiday beginning in 1986, it is fitting that we reflect on his enormous contributions to the movement for black equality in America."

*　　*　　*

COLE, Joanna   1944-
(Ann Cooke)

PERSONAL: Born August 11, 1944, in Newark, N.J.; daughter of Mario and Elizabeth (Reid) Basilea; married Philip A. Cole (a psychotherapist), October 8, 1965; children: Rachel Elizabeth. *Education:* Attended University of Massachusetts at Amherst and Indiana University—Bloomington; City College of New York (now City College of the City University of New York), B.A., 1967.

ADDRESSES: Home—New York, N.Y. *Office*—171 West 79th St., New York, N.Y. 10024.

CAREER: New York City Board of Education, New York City, elementary school librarian, 1967-68; *Newsweek,* New York City, letters correspondent, 1968-71; Scholastic, Inc., New York City, associate editor of See-Saw Book Club, 1971-73; Doubleday & Co., Garden City, N.Y., senior editor of books for young readers, 1973-80; writer, 1980—.

MEMBER: Authors Guild, Society of Children's Book Writers.

AWARDS, HONORS: All of Cole's science books have been named outstanding science trade books for children by the joint committee of the National Science Teachers Association and the Children's Book Council; *School Library Journal* selected *Fleas* to its Best Books of the Year list, 1973; *A Chick Hatches, A Frog's Body, A Horse's Body,* and *A Snake's Body* were all named notable children's books by the American Library Association, 1976, 1980, 1981, and 1981, respectively; *A Chick Hatches* was selected for the Children's Book Showcase, 1977; *A Snake's Body* was named a *Horn Book* Honor Book, 1981, and a New York Academy of Sciences Children's Science Honor Book, 1981; *A Snake's Body* was named a Children's Choice Book by the joint committee of the International Reading Association and the Children's Book Council, 1982.

WRITINGS:

JUVENILE FICTION

Cousin Matilda and the Foolish Wolf, Whitman Publishing, 1970.
The Secret Box, Morrow, 1971.
Fun on Wheels, Morrow, 1976.
The Clown-Arounds, Parents Magazine Press, 1981.
(Editor and author of introduction) *Best-Loved Folktales of the World,* Doubleday, 1982.
The Clown-Arounds Have a Party, Parents Magazine Press, 1982.
Golly Gump Swallowed a Fly, Parents Magazine Press, 1982.
Get Well, Clown-Arounds!, Parents Magazine Press, 1982.
The Clown-Arounds Go on Vacation, Parents Magazine Press, 1983.
Aren't You Forgetting Something, Fiona?, Parents Magazine Press, 1983.
Bony-Legs, Four Winds, 1983.
Sweet Dreams, Clown-Arounds, Parents Magazine Press, 1985.

JUVENILE NONFICTION

Cockroaches, Morrow, 1971.
(Under pseudonym Ann Cooke) *Giraffes at Home,* Crowell, 1972.
(With Madeleine Edmondson) *Twins: The Story of Multiple Births,* Morrow, 1972.
Plants in Winter, Crowell, 1973.
My Puppy Is Born (Children's Book Club choice), Morrow, 1973.
Fleas, Morrow, 1973.
Dinosaur Story, Morrow, 1974.
A Calf Is Born, Morrow, 1975.
A Chick Hatches, Morrow, 1976.
Saber-Toothed Tiger and Other Ice-Age Mammals, Morrow, 1977.
A Fish Hatches, Morrow, 1978.

Find the Hidden Insect, Morrow, 1979.
A Frog's Body, Morrow, 1980.
A Horse's Body, Morrow, 1981.
A Snake's Body, Morrow, 1981.
A Cat's Body (Junior Literary Guild selection), Morrow, 1982.
A Bird's Body (Junior Literary Guild selection), Morrow, 1982.
Cars and How They Go, Crowell, 1983.
How You Were Born, Morrow, 1983.
An Insect's Body, Morrow, 1984.
The New Baby at Your House, Morrow, 1985.
Cuts, Breaks, Bruises, and Burns: How Your Body Heals, Crowell, 1985.
A Dog's Body, Morrow, 1985.

OTHER

The Parents Book of Toilet Teaching (for adults), Ballantine, 1983.
(Editor) *A New Treasury of Children's Poetry,* Doubleday, 1983.

WORK IN PROGRESS: A nonfiction book on sharks, for Random House; a nonfiction book on evolution, for Crowell; editing, with Stephanie Calmenson, an anthology of humor, for Doubleday.

SIDELIGHTS: "As a child," Joanna Cole told *CA,* "my favorite subjects in school were science and writing. In my twenties I combined both by writing science books for children. Now my interest in parenting and child development has led me to write *about* children, as well as *for* them. I'm also writing more fiction. I feel I'm bringing more and more of my whole personality to my work every year."

BIOGRAPHICAL/CRITICAL SOURCES:

PERIODICALS

Horn Book, October, 1980, February, 1982.
Washington Post Book World, September 9, 1984.

*　　　*　　　*

COLES, Don　1928-

PERSONAL: Born April 12, 1928, in Woodstock, Ontario, Canada; son of John Langdon (a stockbroker) and Alice Margaret (Brown) Coles; married Heidi Goelnitz; children: Sarah, Luke. *Education:* University of Toronto, M.A., 1952; Cambridge University, M.A., 1954.

ADDRESSES: Home—122 Glenview Ave., Toronto, Ontario, Canada M4R 1P8. *Office*—Vanier College, York University, North York, Ontario, Canada.

CAREER: Worked as a translator in Scandinavia, Italy, and Germany, 1954-65; York University, North York, Ontario, instructor, 1965-66, lecturer, 1966-68, assistant professor, 1968-71, associate professor, 1971-81, professor of humanities and creative writing, 1981—, director of Programme in Creative Writing, 1979—.

MEMBER: League of Canadian Poets.

AWARDS, HONORS: Prize from Canadian Broadcasting Corporation Literary Competition, 1980, for poem "Landslides"; grants from Canada Council.

WRITINGS:

Sometimes All Over (poems), Macmillan, 1975.
Anniversaries (poems), Macmillan, 1979.

The Prinzhorn Collection (poems), Macmillan, 1982.

Work represented in anthologies, including *The Poets of Canada,* edited by John Robert Colombo, Hurtig, 1978; *The Oxford Book of Canadian Verse,* Oxford University Press, 1983; *Penguin Anthology of Canadian Poetry,* Penguin Books, 1984. Contributor to magazines, including *Saturday Night, Poetry, Canadian Forum, Ariel,* and *Arc.*

WORK IN PROGRESS: A book of new and selected poems, tentatively titled *Dark Fields,* completion expected in 1986.

* * *

COLLINGS, I. J(illie)

PERSONAL: Born in Adelaide, Australia; daughter of George Collings; married; children: Kean Christopher Buckley. *Education:* University of Adelaide, B.A., 1955; London School of Palmistry, F.S.S.P.P., 1968; Mayo School of Astrology, D.M.S. (with honors), 1978.

ADDRESSES: Home—6 Woodstock House, 11 Marylebone High St., London W.1, England. *Office*—14 Highbourne House, 13-15 Marylebone High St., London W.1, England.

CAREER: Woman, London, England, feature writer, 1969-70, deputy features editor, 1970—, author of "The *Woman Magazine* Astrology Column," during the 1980's. Television broadcaster; public speaker.

MEMBER: British Institute of Graphologists (founding member).

WRITINGS:

The Malevolent Despot (novel), Gollancz, 1986.
Astrology and Your Child, twelve volumes, Mayflower, 1980.

Also author of astrology columns in *Mother,* 1983—.

WORK IN PROGRESS: Research for a historical novel set in Australia c. 1900; *The Castle in the Air,* a children's fantasy.

* * *

COLLINS, Judith Graham 1942-

PERSONAL: Born March 4, 1942, in Chicago, Ill.; daughter of Joseph P. (an insurance agent) and Sophie R. (a homemaker) Graham; married George Patrick Collins, Jr. (in business), October 1, 1966; children: Robert, Kenneth, Margaret, John, Daniel. *Education:* Attended Elmhurst College, 1960-62; Rosary College, B.A., 1964.

ADDRESSES: Home—531 Oakwood Dr., Grayslake, Ill. 60030.

CAREER: Writer. *Chicago New World* (newspaper), Chicago, Ill., feature writer, 1964-66; Press Publications (newspaper chain), Elmhurst, Ill., reporter and editor, 1966-67; Round Lake Area Library, Round Lake, Ill., member of library staff and author of "Off the Shelf," a library column in *Round Lake News,* both 1976—.

MEMBER: Society of Children's Book Writers, Children's Reading Round Table.

WRITINGS:

Josh's Scary Dad (juvenile), Abingdon, 1983.

WORK IN PROGRESS: Hasty Retreat (tentative title), a novel for adults; a detective series for children, featuring Detective Dart and Dan.

SIDELIGHTS: Judith Graham Collins told *CA:* "As a child I was surrounded by books, mostly adult books from my father's extensive collection of fiction. I was guided from an early age into the Mark Twain classics, and I soon felt that a day without reading was truly not complete. From there it seemed but a short hop of the imagination to envision myself as an author some day, God willing.

"I feel the primary concern of an author should be to entertain, not preach. And I feel strongly that when a child or an adult chooses a fiction book he or she is looking for enjoyment instead of an education or a sermon. The best writers, however, have the ability to teach and to impart their moral view of the world while entertaining on a grand scale. But this must always be done as part of the story itself, not as tacked-on commentary.

"The first draft of *Josh's Scary Dad* was written in one sitting, immediately after I overheard my sons discussing a father in the neighborhood who had frightened them. The story went through several re-writings and a critique at a writer's conference and was then submitted to sixteen different publishers before I found the right one in Abingdon. Obviously, my advice to beginning writers is to keep submitting stories and never to give up. Seek expert advice from writers' groups if you feel something in your story is not quite right. But if you believe in your story, don't put it in a drawer to die. Keep it circulating."

BIOGRAPHICAL/CRITICAL SOURCES:

PERIODICALS

Bookstore Journal, April, 1984.
Chicago Catholic, February 10, 1984.
School Library Journal, November, 1983.

* * *

CONGER, (Seymour) Beach III 1912-1969

OBITUARY NOTICE: Born March 1, 1912, in Berlin, Germany; died January 6, 1969, in Pleasantville, N.Y.; buried in Wellfleet, Mass. Journalist. An American born abroad, Conger immigrated to the United States in 1926. He worked for the *New York Herald Tribune* from 1936 until its closing in 1966. Beginning as a reporter and rewrite man, Conger went on to serve the *Herald Tribune* in a number of capacities. During World War II he was a foreign correspondent for the paper and covered events in Germany, France, the Netherlands, and Hungary. He later held the posts of editorial writer, news editor, travel editor, assistant managing editor in charge of foreign news coverage, and Sunday news editor. After the *Herald Tribune*'s demise in 1966, Conger joined the *Reader's Digest* as editorial manager of the general books division, a position he held until his death. In addition to numerous articles for the *Herald Tribune* and other periodicals, Conger wrote *History of the Pleasantville Library.*

OBITUARIES AND OTHER SOURCES:

BOOKS

The National Cyclopaedia of American Biography, Volume 54, James T. White, 1973.
Who Was Who in America, With World Notables, Volume V: *1969-1973,* Marquis, 1973.

PERIODICALS

New York Times, January 7, 1969.

CONKLIN, Paul

PERSONAL: Education—Attended Wayne State University; received M.A. from Columbia University.

CAREER: Photographer and author of books for children.

AWARDS, HONORS: Touching Washington, D.C. was selected for the American Institute of Graphic Arts Book Show, 1976.

WRITINGS:

JUVENILE NONFICTION

(And photographer) *Cimarron Kid,* Dodd, 1973.
(And photographer) *Choctaw Boy,* Dodd, 1975.
(And photographer) *Michael of Wales,* Dodd, 1977.

PHOTOGRAPHER

Seymour Reit, *Child of the Navajos,* Dodd, 1971.
Reit, *Rice Cakes and Paper Dragons,* Dodd, 1973.
Grace E. Moremen, *Touching Washington, D.C.,* privately printed, 1976.
Brent K. Ashabranner, *Morning Star, Black Sun: The Northern Cheyenne Indians and America's Energy Crisis,* Dodd, 1982.
Ashabranner, *The New Americans: Changing Patterns in U.S. Immigration,* Dodd, 1983.

Contributor of photographs to magazines.

BIOGRAPHICAL/CRITICAL SOURCES:

PERIODICALS

Natural History, December, 1975.

*   *   *

CONOVER, David (Beals)   1919-1983

PERSONAL: Born June 26, 1919, in Kansas City, Mo.; died of cancer, December 21, 1983; son of John Austin (a business owner) and Dora (Beals) Conover; married Jean Faber, October 31, 1940 (divorced, 1969); married Barbara Mittendorf (an author), November 18, 1978; children: David B., Jr. *Education:* Attended University of Southern California.

CAREER: Wallace Island Resort, Wallace Island, British Columbia, owner and operator, 1946-67; writer, 1967-83.

WRITINGS:

Once Upon an Island (adventure), Crown, 1967.
One Man's Island (philosophy), Paper Jacks, 1971.
Sitting on a Salt Spring (humor), Paper Jacks, 1978.
Finding Marilyn, Grosset, 1981.
(With wife, Barbara Conover) *The Murder of Marilyn Monroe,* Springer (West Germany), 1984.

WORK IN PROGRESS—At time of death: *Come Live With Me,* a novel, publication expected in 1985; *Father to Son,* letters, edited by wife, Barbara Conover; a sequel to *Come Live With Me,* with B. Conover.

SIDELIGHTS: David Conover's wife, Barbara, told *CA:* "David was especially influenced by the writings of Thoreau and Goethe. For a man who lived a very solitary life, he had a positive influence on the lives of many people. He believed anyone could make their dreams come true and wrote *Once Upon an Island* not only to chronicle his adventures, but to inspire others. I still get letters about that book from all over the world.''

She added: "David was the photographer who first discovered Norma Jean Daugherty, who was later known as Marilyn Monroe. He remained her friend until her death.''

(Date of death verified by wife, Barbara Conover)

*   *   *

CONROY, (Francis) Hilary   1919-

PERSONAL: Born December 31, 1919, in Bloomington, Ill.; son of Francis Hilary, Sr. (in business) and Marguerite (Hall) Conroy; married Charlotte J. Alger (director of the International Classroom at University of Pennsylvania), September 4, 1943; children: Sharlie Conroy Ushioda, France H. (son). *Education:* Northwestern University, B.A., (with high honors), 1941; University of California, Berkeley, A.M., 1942, Ph.D., 1949.

ADDRESSES: Office—Department of History, 207 College Hall, University of Pennsylvania, Philadelphia, Pa. 19104.

CAREER: University of California, Berkeley, lecturer in Far Eastern history, 1949-51; University of Pennsylvania, Philadelphia, assistant professor, 1951-58, associate professor, 1959-64, professor of history, 1965—, past chairman of graduate studies in history, East Asian studies, and international relations, member of advisory board of International Classroom. Past member of part-time faculty at Swarthmore College, University of Colorado, University of Hawaii at Manoa, and International Christian University; director of Japan seminar program for American Friends Service Committee, 1958-59; senior specialist at East-West Center, University of Hawaii at Manoa, 1965-66; past chairman of Interchange for Pacific Scholarship. Past president of Media Fellowship, Media, Pa.; member of board of managers of Pendle Hill and International Christian University Foundation; member of advisory board of Balch Institute. *Military service:* U.S. Naval Reserve, Japanese language officer, 1944-46.

MEMBER: American Historical Association (chairman of committee on J. K. Fairbank Prize in East Asian History, 1980-81), American Association of University Professors, Association for Asian Studies, Conference on Peace Research in History (past president), Philadelphia Oriental Club (past president), Phi Beta Kappa.

AWARDS, HONORS: Mills traveling fellowship from University of California, Berkeley, 1949-50; fellow of Social Science Research Council, 1949-50; Fulbright fellow at University of Tokyo, 1953-54; American Historical Association prize in Pacific history for *The Japanese Frontier in Hawaii, 1868-1898.*

WRITINGS:

The Japanese Frontier in Hawaii, 1868-1898, University of California Press, 1953.
(With Woodbridge Bingham) *The History and Civilization of Asia,* University of California Press, 1953, revised edition, 1958.
(With Bingham and Frank W. Ilke) *Southwest Asia: A Brief History,* University of California Press, 1956, 3rd edition, revised, 1959.
The Japanese Seizure of Korea, 1868-1910: A Study of Realism and Idealism in International Relations, University of Pennsylvania Press, 1960.

(With Bingham and Ilke) *A History of Asia,* Volume I: *Formation of Civilizations, From Antiquity to 1600,* Volume II: *Old Empires, Western Penetration, and the Rise of New Nations Since 1600,* Allyn & Bacon, 1964-65, 2nd edition, 1974.

(Editor with Alvin D. Coox) *China and Japan: Search for Balance Since World War I,* ABC-Clio Books, 1978.

(Editor with Harry Wray) *Japan Examined: Perspectives on Modern Japanese History,* University of Hawaii Press, 1983.

(With Sandra T. W. Davis and Wayne Patterson) *Japan in Transition,* Associated University Presses, 1984.

(Editor with Roy Kim) *New Tides in the Pacific,* University of Alabama Press, in press.

Contributor to history journals. Editor of American Historical Association's bibliography, *Recently Published Articles: East Asia,* 1955—.

WORK IN PROGRESS: Pearl Harbor Reexamined: Was the Pacific War Inevitable?, with Harry Wray, completion expected in 1986; *America Views China: Then and Now,* with Jerry Israel and Jonathan Goldstein, completion expected in 1987; a volume of speculative essays in cosmic history, with others.

SIDELIGHTS: Hilary Conroy told *CA:* "People should get acquainted around the world: They might like each other. If we could get *Spaceship Earth* organized, we might also be able to explore the rest of the universe."

BIOGRAPHICAL/CRITICAL SOURCES:

PERIODICALS

American Historical Review, June, 1979.

*   *   *

COOK, Alice H(anson)   1903-

PERSONAL: Born November 28, 1903, in Alexandria, Va.; daughter of August T. and Flora Kays Hanson; married Wesley W. Cook, 1926 (divorced, 1950); children: Philip J., Thomas P. Bernstein (foster son). *Education:* Northwestern University, B.L., 1924; attended University of Frankfurt, 1929-31, and Hochschule fuer Politik, Berlin, Germany, 1930-31.

ADDRESSES: Home—766 Elm St., Ithaca, N.Y. 14850.

CAREER: Social worker in Indianapolis, Ind., 1924-25, and in St. Louis, Mo., 1925-26; Young Women's Christian Association, industrial secretary in Chicago, Ill., 1926-29, and in Philadelphia, Pa., 1931-38; employed in various union-related activities, 1938-47; High Commission, Berlin and Frankfurt, West Germany, adult educator, 1947, 1949-50; employed in adult and labor education, 1950-52; New York State School of Industrial and Labor Relations, Cornell University, Ithaca, N.Y., extension specialist, 1952-55, assistant professor, 1955, associate professor, 1956-64, professor of industrial relations, 1964-72, professor emerita, 1972—, university ombudsman, 1969-71. U.S. Information Agency lecturer in Germany, Asia, Austria, and England.

MEMBER: International Industrial Relations Association, International Sociological Association, Industrial Relations Research Association, Association of Asian Studies, American Association of University Professors, American Association of University Women, National Comission on Pay Equity.

AWARDS, HONORS: Fulbright scholar in Japan, 1962-63; visiting Mellon fellow at Wellesley College, 1979; LL.D. from Grand Valley State Colleges, 1980; Corinne Galvin Award in Civil Rights from government of Tompkins County, N.Y., 1983; named Woman of the Year in Education, 1984.

WRITINGS:

Union Democracy: Practice and Ideal, Industrial and Labor Relations Press, Cornell University, 1964.

An Introduction to Japanese Trade Unionism, Industrial and Labor Relations Press, Cornell University, 1966.

Public Employee Labor Relations in Japan, Institute of Labor and Industrial Relations, University of Michigan, 1971.

The Working Mother, Industrial and Labor Relations Press, Cornell University, 1978.

Equal Employment Opportunity, Industrial and Labor Relations Center, University of Hawaii at Manoa, 1979.

Working Women in Japan, Industrial and Labor Relations Press, Cornell University, 1980.

Women, Unions, and Equal Opportunity, Center for Women in Government, State University of New York at Albany, 1981.

Comparable Worth, Industrial and Labor Relations Center, University of Hawaii at Manoa, 1983.

(Editor and contributor) *Women and Trade Unions in Eleven Industrialized Countries,* Temple University Press, 1984.

Contributor of more than fifty articles to labor and industrial relations journals.

WORK IN PROGRESS: A report on states' activities in introducing comparable worth; a study of women in trade unions in the United States; a review and critique of research on women in the labor markets of industrialized countries.

SIDELIGHTS: Alice H. Cook told *CA:* "I went to Germany in 1929 as a graduate exchange student and chose the University of Frankfurt because the Academy of Labor (Akademie der Arbeit) was associated with the University and I would be able to continue my interest in workers' education. During my two-year stay in the country, I was able to visit all the residential schools associated at that time with the trade unions and the Social Democratic Party as well as a number of independent schools catering to workers.

"As a consequence, when the Army at the end of World War II wanted an expert on labor education to look at those problems and opportunities in the reorganized labor movement of Germany, I was asked to make a survey on a two-months' trip in 1947. A year-and-a-half later, when I was living in Vienna, the High Commission for Germany (which succeeded the Army as the administration for civilian affairs in Germany) employed me again to look at problems of working women, as well as to continue work with the unions and their labor education programs in various locations in the American Zone of Occupation. An offer to head the section of the Education Division that was responsible for all kinds of adult education in Germany followed.

"My interest in labor problems began with opportunities to visit the Hull House Settlement in Chicago where I met labor leaders and social workers concerned with problems of working people. Experience in social work in Indianapolis and St. Louis deepened that interest and a year at Commonwealth College (Mena, Arkansas) channeled it into labor education. Work in the industrial division of the YWCA in Chicago opened an opportunity to teach at the Bryn Mawr Summer School for Women Workers. All those experiences led me to use labor education as my field of study and investigation in Weimar Germany. These in turn took me into new fields of labor education back in the United States and to the return to Germany at the end of the war.

"When the High Commission was ending its work in Germany in the early 1950's, and I was ready to return to the U.S., friends told me of an opening at Cornell University on a project sponsored and funded by the Interuniversity Labor Education Committee (IULEC). I became a member of the labor education section of the newly founded New York State School of Industrial and Labor Relations at Cornell University which was operating an extension division offering education services to labor, management, and the public throughout New York State. Three years in extension work led to a professorship in trade union affairs that kept me at Cornell until my retirement.

"I had an early introduction to the women's movement through my mother and grandmother who were both suffragettes at the turn of the century. The work in the YWCA had focused this interest particularly on the problems of working women in and outside the unions. My first opportunity to turn fully to this field came with an offer from the Ford Foundation on my retirement in 1972 to do a study in a number of countries abroad on social policies developed in communist and non-communist countries in support of working mothers. I came home from eighteen months study of those problems determined to write and work entirely in that field and have done so ever since.

"I have continued making studies and reports on conditions in some twenty countries affecting women workers and tried to make available to American lawmakers and women's organizations this experience. The United States is behind most European countries in providing for maternity leave, parental leave, and child care for working parents, although our equal opportunity legislation goes considerably beyond the equality legislation of most other industrialized countries. The opportunity to exchange information and experience in this field has been greatly aided by the women's program of the German Marshall Fund, which sponsored my research with Val Lorwin on women in trade unions in eleven industrialized countries.

"I continue to welcome opportunities to travel and meet with working women of other countries. But in recent years, in connection with my annual trips to Hawaii, I have been drawn more and more into writing and consulting on the developing social policy in this country on equal pay as it is expressed in the comparable worth movement. Hawaii was one of the first states to attempt to write legislation in this field. To assist the scholars and legislators there, I began a study of other states' experience with comparable worth.

"I am now developing a case book of nation-wide experience in states and local governments, which already includes more than 125 examples of various approaches and stages of implementation. I hope to make this a regularly updated service to the many local governments and school districts now venturing into the field, for it not only records, insofar as I can obtain the information, steps in developing programs but my own critical analysis of those undertakings. A visit to the Center for the Study of Women in Society at the University of Oregon in the fall of 1984 has enabled me to observe the workings of the legislative task force in that state as it moves into full implementation of its comparable worth program."

BIOGRAPHICAL/CRITICAL SOURCES:

BOOKS

Farley, Jennie, editor, *Women Workers in Fifteen Countries: Essays in Honor of Alice Hanson Cook,* Cornell International Industrial and Labor Relations Reports Series, 1985.

PERIODICALS

In These Times, November 23-December 6, 1983.
Industrial Relations Report, spring, 1984.

*   *   *

COOK, W(illiam) Robert   1928-

PERSONAL: Born November 18, 1928, in Portland, Ore.; son of Floyd N. (a salesman) and Alice (a homemaker; maiden name, Schmidt) Cook; married Elaine Johnson (a homemaker), June 8, 1951; children: David Bryan, Kimberly Christine. *Education:* Westmont College, B.A., 1951; Dallas Theological Seminary, Th.M., 1955, Th.D., 1960; attended Hebrew University of Jerusalem, 1975. *Politics:* Republican. *Religion:* Conservative Baptist.

ADDRESSES: Home—12367 Southeast Ridgecrest Rd., Portland, Ore. 97236. *Office*—Western Conservative Baptist Seminary, 5511 Southeast Hawthorne Blvd., Portland, Ore. 97215.

CAREER: Ordained by Galvin Bible Chapel, 1956; pastor in Galvin, Washington, 1955-58; Northwestern College, Roseville, Minn., assistant professor, 1960-62, associate professor of Bible and Greek, 1963-65; Western Conservative Baptist Seminary, Portland, Ore., professor of biblical theology, 1965—, dean of student affairs, 1966-69, dean of faculty and academic vice-president, both 1969—.

MEMBER: Evangelical Theological Society.

WRITINGS:

Systematic Theology in Outline Form, Western Baptist Press, 1970-78.
(Contributor) William F. Kett, editor, *God: What Is He Like?,* Tyndale, 1977.
Theology of John, Moody, 1979.

Contributor to *Bibliotheca Sacra.*

WORK IN PROGRESS: The Christian Faith (tentative title), a systematic theology.

SIDELIGHTS: W. Robert Cook told *CA:* "The greatest motivation for me to write in my field, and the most authentic expression of ideas related thereto, have come after years of research and teaching. The most worthwhile statements of theological thought often follow many years of mature reflection and the extended stimulation of the classroom and interaction with colleagues.

"In the past, America has produced some outstanding Evangelical Protestant theology. Until the last half of the 1970's there was a marked hiatus in such production. While several fine evangelical writers have written or are now writing in this discipline, I believe there continues to be a need.

"I have also learned that I am most productive when removed temporarily from my usual vocational setting. Three-quarters of my manuscript on systematic theology was written while I was on sabbatical leave in Jerusalem. I have lived in Israel for extended periods on two separate occasions and have had the privilege of visiting various other parts of the Middle East. I am interested in the life of the Evangelical Protestant church in Europe, as well, and have had the opportunity to travel extensively in that part of the world.''

*   *   *

COOKE, Ann
See COLE, Joanna

*   *   *

COOKE, Deryck (Victor)   1919-1976

OBITUARY NOTICE: Born September 14, 1919, in Leicester, England; died October 26, 1976, in London, England. Musicologist and author. Music presentation editor for the British Broadcasting Corporation (BBC) beginning in 1964, Cooke was best known for his edition of nineteenth-century composer Gustav Mahler's unfinished Tenth Symphony, which was first performed in London on August 13, 1964. Prior to working as BBC's music presentation director, Cooke spent twelve years as an assistant in BBC's music division and five years as a free-lance writer. Among his writings are the 1959 book *The Language of Music* and the BBC-booklet *Mahler, 1860-1911,* which was revised, expanded, and published as the 1980 book *Gustav Mahler: An Introduction to His Music.*

OBITUARIES AND OTHER SOURCES:

BOOKS

Baker's Biographical Dictionary of Musicians, 6th edition, Schirmer, 1978.
International Who's Who in Music and Musicians Directory, 8th edition, Melrose Press, 1977.

PERIODICALS

Times Literary Supplement, October 24, 1980.

*   *   *

COOKE, James Francis   1875-1960

OBITUARY NOTICE: Born November 14, 1875, in Bay City, Mich.; died March 3, 1960, in Bala-Cynwyd, Pa. Music historian, educator, composer, editor, playwright, and author. An instructor in piano and voice for many years in New York, Cooke studied the systems of teaching music employed in various American and European colleges and conservatories and edited *Etude* music magazine for more than forty years. He also served as president of a number of organizations, among them the Theodore Presser Company, the Presser Foundation, the John Church Company, the Philadelphia Music Teachers' Association, and the Oliver Ditson Company. Cooke, who was decorated chevalier of the French Legion of Honor in 1930 for his contributions to ''art, education, and public affairs,'' wrote many books on music and musicians, including *Standard History of Music, Mastering the Scales and Arpeggios, Great Men and Famous Musicians,* and *A Historical Musical Pilgrimage.* He also wrote four plays that were professionally produced, a book of memoirs titled *Friends Everywhere,* and numerous stories, songs, and piano compositions.

OBITUARIES AND OTHER SOURCES:

BOOKS

Who Was Who in America, Volume III, *1951-1960,* Marquis, 1966.

PERIODICALS

New York Times, March 5, 1960.

*   *   *

COOKE, Thomas D(arlington)   1933-

PERSONAL: Born March 16, 1933, in Kansas City, Mo.; son of Sidney M. (a banker) and Thelma R. (a housewife) Cooke. *Education:* St. Louis University, A.B., 1957; Fordham University, M.A., 1961; University of Pittsburgh, Ph.D., 1970.

ADDRESSES: Office—Department of English, University of Missouri—Columbia, Columbia, Mo. 65211.

CAREER: Duquesne University, Pittsburgh, Pa., instructor in English, 1963-65; University of Missouri—Columbia, assistant professor, 1967-73, associate professor, 1973-80, professor of English, 1980—, director of graduate studies, 1977-82.

MEMBER: International Arthurian Society, Modern Language Association of America, Mediaeval Academy of America, New Chaucer Society.

WRITINGS:

(Editor with Benjamin L. Honeycutt, and contributor) *The Humor of the Fabliaux: A Collection of Critical Essays,* University of Missouri Press, 1974.
The Old French and Chaucerian Fabliaux: A Study of Their Comic Climax, University of Missouri Press, 1978.
(Editor) *The Present State of Scholarship in Fourteenth-Century Literature,* University of Missouri Press, 1983.

Contributor to literature and folklore journals.

WORK IN PROGRESS: ''Medieval English Tales,'' to be included in *A Manual of the Writings in Middle English, 1050-1500,* edited by Albert Hartung, publication by Connecticut Academy of Arts and Sciences expected in 1987.

*   *   *

COOLIDGE, Harold Jefferson   1904-1985

OBITUARY NOTICE: Born January 15, 1904, in Boston, Mass.; died of complications following a fall, February 15, 1985, in Beverly, Mass. Conservationist, zoologist, curator, and author. Internationally known for his conservationist efforts and his expertise in primate and fossil studies, Coolidge began his career in 1926 by participating in the Harvard African Expedition to Liberia and the Belgian Congo as an assistant mammologist. Two years later Coolidge served as leader of the Indochina division of the Kelley-Roosevelt Asian Expedition, which was conducted to gather specimens for the Field Museum of Natural History in Chicago. The expedition featured a one-thousand-mile raft and canoe trip down the Mekong River and its tributaries and resulted in the book *Three Kingdoms of Indochina,* which Coolidge wrote with Theodore Roosevelt, Jr., who had also participated in the journey.

Upon his return to the United States in 1929 Coolidge joined Harvard University's Museum of Comparative Zoology as assistant curator of mammals. He remained with the museum until 1946, when he became executive director of the Pacific Science Board of the National Academy of Sciences, a post he held until retiring in 1970. Coolidge was also active in numerous conservation and science organizations, including the International Union for the Conservation of Nature and the Natural Resources and the World Wildlife Fund, both of which he served as a founding director. He was also founder and trustee of the Darwin Foundation and served as secretary of the American National Parks Association. Among Coolidge's many awards were the J. Paul Getty Medal for wildlife conservation and the Browning Medal from the Smithsonian Institution.

OBITUARIES AND OTHER SOURCES:

BOOKS

Who's Who in America, 42nd edition, Marquis, 1982.

PERIODICALS

New York Times, February 16, 1985.
Washington Post, February 16, 1985.

*   *   *

COOLIDGE, Susan
   See WOOLSEY, Sarah Chauncy

*   *   *

COOMARASWAMY, A. K.
   See COOMARASWAMY, Ananda K(entish)

*   *   *

COOMARASWAMY, Ananda K(entish)   1877-1947
   (A. K. Coomaraswamy)

BRIEF ENTRY: Born August 22, 1877, in Colombo, Ceylon (now Sri Lanka); died of a heart attack, September 9, 1947, in Needham, Mass. Art historian, museum curator, religious scholar, and author. While conducting mineralogical research in Ceylon, Coomaraswamy grew concerned for the future of traditional culture in that part of the world. The result was *Mediaeval Sinhalese Art* (1908). Coomaraswamy then explored the art, religion, and mythos of India. He returned to his home in England and began a collection of Indian arts and crafts. From 1917 to 1933, he served as keeper of Indian and Muhammadan Art at the Museum of Fine Arts in Boston, his own collection forming the bulk of the museum's exhibit. During the early 1930's Coomaraswamy began a comparative study of the world's religions that interested him for the rest of his life. His metaphysical writings include *A New Approach to the Vedas* (1933), *Why Exhibit Works of Art?* (1947), *Time and Eternity* (1947), *Am I My Brother's Keeper?* (1947), and *The Dance of Shiva: Fourteen Indian Essays* (1948).

BIOGRAPHICAL/CRITICAL SOURCES:

BOOKS

Dictionary of American Biography, Supplement Four: 1946-1950, Scribner, 1974.

PERIODICALS

New York Review of Books, February 22, 1979.

*   *   *

COOMBS, Murdo
   See DAVIS, Frederick C(lyde)

*   *   *

COONEY, John   1942-

PERSONAL: Born May 17, 1942, in Philadelphia, Pa.; son of Edward P. (a merchant marine) and Margaret (a nurse; maiden name, Dougherty) Cooney; married wife, Lenore C. (a publicist), June 6, 1964; children: David, Glynis. *Education:* Villanova University, B.A., 1964.

ADDRESSES: Home—Brooklyn, N.Y. *Agent*—Dominick Abel, 498 West End Ave., New York, N.Y. 10024.

CAREER: Writer.

WRITINGS:

(With wife, Lenore Cooney) *The Most Natural Thing in the World,* Harper, 1972.
The Annenbergs: The Salvaging of a Tainted Dynasty, Simon & Schuster, 1982.
The American Pope: The Life and Times of Francis Cardinal Spellman, Times Books, 1984.

SIDELIGHTS: In *The Annenbergs: The Salvaging of a Tainted Dynasty,* John Cooney examines the lives of the father and son publishing duo Moses and Walter Annenberg. An emigrant from Eastern Europe, Moses Annenberg was trained as a newspaperman by William Randolph Hearst, later becoming circulation chief for Hearst's *Chicago Examiner* and a millionaire by the age of thirty-six. In 1922 the elder Annenberg bought the *Daily Racing Form,* which became the nation's primary source of racing news, and soon after he acquired the *Philadelphia Inquirer,* which he used as a forum for his Republican, anti-Roosevelt views. In turn, the Roosevelt administration investigated Annenberg's tax records. Moses Annenberg was imprisoned for tax evasion in 1940 and died two years later.

Following his father's conviction, Walter Annenberg assumed Moses's position as manager of the *Inquirer* and introduced such successful publications as *TV Guide* and *Seventeen,* thus reestablishing the Annenberg publishing empire. In 1969 the publisher was named ambassador to Britain, an event that, according to Cooney, made Annenberg "a most honorable name."

BIOGRAPHICAL/CRITICAL SOURCES:

PERIODICALS

Los Angeles Times Book Review, June 27, 1982.
New York Times Book Review, October 28, 1984.
Washington Post Book World, July 4, 1982.

*   *   *

CORBALLIS, Michael C(harles)   1936-

PERSONAL: Surname is accented on first syllable; born September 10, 1936, in Marton, New Zealand; son of Philip P.J. (a farmer) and Alice Elizabeth (Harris) Corballis; married Barbara Elizabeth Wheeler (a potter), May 8, 1962; children: two. *Education:* Victoria University of Wellington, B.Sc., 1958, M.Sc., 1959, B.A., 1961; University of Auckland, M.A., 1962; McGill University, Ph.D., 1965. *Religion:* None.

ADDRESSES: Home—86 Gladston Rd., Parnell, Auckland 1, New Zealand. *Office*—Department of Psychology, University of Auckland, Auckland, New Zealand.

CAREER: University of Auckland, Auckland, New Zealand, junior lecturer, 1961-63, lecturer in psychology, 1966-68; McGill University, Montreal, Quebec, assistant professor, 1968-71, associate professor, 1971-75, professor of psychology, 1975-77; University of Auckland, professor of psychology, 1978—.

MEMBER: American Association for the Advancement of Science (fellow), American Psychological Association (fellow), Royal Society of New Zealand (fellow), New Zealand Psychological Society (fellow), New York Academy of Sciences, Sigma Xi.

WRITINGS:

(With Ivan L. Beale)*The Psychology of Left and Right,* Lawrence Erlbaum, 1976.
Human Laterality, Academic Press, 1983.
The Ambivalent Mind: The Neuropsychology of Left and Right, Nelson-Hall, 1983.

Contributor to academic journals and popular magazines, including *Science, Nature,* and *Scientific American.*

WORK IN PROGRESS: Research on human neuropsychology.

SIDELIGHTS: Michael C. Corballis told *CA:* "My writing is motivated by an interest in human cognition and brain function and by a wish to communicate to a lay readership where possible. I am also a part-time potter and one-time cartoonist."

AVOCATIONAL INTERESTS: "I jog and play regular tennis and squash, and very irregular cricket."

*   *   *

CORNEBISE, Alfred E(mile) 1929-

PERSONAL: Surname is pronounced *Corn*-a-beeze; born May 3, 1929, in Brownfield, Tex.; son of Fred Marcel (a farmer) and Mattie Bell (a housewife; maiden name, Williams) Cornebise; married Jan Miller (a teacher and artist), August 9, 1957; children: Michael Wayne, Tanya Renee, Mark Alfred. *Education:* Wayland Baptist College (now University), B.A., 1955; Texas Technological College (now Texas Tech University), M.A., 1958; University of North Carolina at Chapel Hill, Ph.D., 1965; also attended University of Wyoming, 1959, and Oxford University, 1978. *Politics:* Democrat. *Religion:* Congregational.

ADDRESSES: Office—Department of History, University of Northern Colorado, Greeley, Colo. 80631.

CAREER: Wayland Baptist College (now University), Plainview, Tex., instructor in European history, 1959-60; Valdosta State College, Valdosta, Ga., associate professor of modern European history, 1965-67; University of Northern Colorado, Greeley, assistant professor, 1967-71, associate professor, 1971-75, professor of modern European history, 1975—, chairman of department of history, 1984—. *Military service:* U.S. Marine Corps, 1951-53; served in Korea; became sergeant. U.S. Naval Reserve, intelligence officer, 1958-68; became lieutenant.

MEMBER: German Studies Association.

WRITINGS:

The Weimar in Crisis: Cuno's Germany and the Ruhr Occupation, University Press of America, 1977.
The Amaroc News: The Daily Newspaper of the American Forces in Germany, 1919-1923, Southern Illinois University Press, 1981.
Typhus and Doughboys: The American Polish Typhus Relief Expedition, 1919-1921, University of Delaware Press, 1982.
The Stars and Stripes: Doughboy Journalism in World War I, Greenwood Press, 1984.

War as Advertised: The Four Minute Men and America's Crusade, 1917-1918, American Philosophical Society, 1984.

Contributor to history and philosophy journals.

WORK IN PROGRESS: Art Goes to War: The Official Artists of the American Expeditionary Force and Their Work, 1917-1919.

SIDELIGHTS: Alfred Cornebise told *CA:* "It is my belief that the historian should be particularly interested in developing a clear, coherent narrative which tells the story of the past, rather than over-analyzing historical events. In addition, emphasis needs to be placed upon what the common people were doing when documentary evidence exists to illustrate this. Newspapers are good sources that can be turned to this end. My books, especially those on the U.S. Army newspapers, are intended to be examples of this approach to history. I've attempted, in these cases, to make the American doughboy of the World War I era 'come alive' as a historical character. I have been concerned with his general attitudes, his loves, hates, and what his daily life was like. Many of these things are revealed in the soldier newspapers that he read. It has also been my intent to write history that can be read, understood, and appreciated by the general reader, while maintaining the scholarly mode and apparatus for the benefit of academics.

"My first book was based on research in several German archives, including the Bundesarchiv in Coblenz and the Berlin Document Center in West Berlin. Additional research was done in the Public Record Office and the British Library in London. I have a competency in the German language and used this in connection with my researches. I have traveled worldwide, including such places as Korea, Japan, Mexico, the United Kingdom, Denmark, Belgium, the Netherlands, France, West Germany, East Germany, Finland, and the Soviet Union."

*   *   *

CORNELIUS, Carol 1942-

PERSONAL: Born November 18, 1942, in St. Joseph, Mo.; daughter of James J. (a security officer) and Dorothy (Norene) Bokay; married Ronald D. Cornelius (a dairy farmer), December 16, 1966; children: Richard D., Ronda A. *Education:* Attended Mount St. Scholastica Junior College (now Benedictine College), 1961-62, and Missouri Western State College, 1981—.

ADDRESSES: Home—P.O. Box 62, Easton, Mo. 64443.

CAREER: Writer.

MEMBER: Missouri Writers Guild, Friends of Rolling Hills Library.

WRITINGS:

FOR CHILDREN

Polka Dots, Checks, and Stripes, illustrations by Diana Magnuson, Child's World, 1978.
Bobbin's Land, illustrations by Franz Altschuler, Child's World, 1978.
Isabella Wooly Bear Tiger Moth, illustrations by Altschuler, Child's World, 1978.
Hyla (Peep) Crucifer, illustrations by Altschuler, Child's World, 1978.

WORK IN PROGRESS: A traditional fairy tale; a "perception" book on similarities; an adult mystery novel.

SIDELIGHTS: Carol Cornelius told *CA:* "My interest in reading and its offshoot, writing, can be directly attributed to the fact that my parents, grandparents, aunts, and uncles took the time to sing to me, to tell me stories and, very importantly, to teach me nursery rhymes. My head is still full of nursery rhymes."

* * *

CORNELL, Tim 1946-

PERSONAL: Born May 11, 1946, in Halesworth, England; son of John Lister and Margaret (Levesley) Cornell; married Mary Burgess (a teacher), September 20, 1969; children: Katherine Margaret, David Michael. *Education:* University College, London, B.A. (first class honors), 1968, Ph.D., 1972. *Politics:* Socialist, *Religion:* Atheist.

ADDRESSES: Home—22 Park St., Tring, Hertfordshire HP23 6AW, England. *Office*—History Department, University College, University of London, London WCIE 6BT, England. *Agent*—John McLaughlin, 31 Newington Green, London N16 9PU, England.

CAREER: Cambridge University, Christ's College, Cambridge, England, research fellow in ancient history, 1973-75; British School at Rome, Rome, Italy, assistant director, 1975-77; University of London, University College, London, England, lecturer in ancient history, 1978—.

MEMBER: Society for Promotion of Roman Studies.

AWARDS, HONORS: Norman H. Baynes Prize from University of London, 1971, for dissertation.

WRITINGS:

(With John Matthews) *Atlas of the Roman World,* Facts on File, 1982.
(Contributor) *Cambridge Ancient History,* Volume III, 2nd edition, Cambridge University Press, 1984.
History of Rome: 753-264 B.C., Methuen, 1985.

Contributor of articles to journals on Roman history, including *Journal of Roman Studies, Museum Helveticum, Archaelogical Reports,* and *Annali delta Scuda Normale Superiore di Pisa.* Editor of *Classical Quarterly,* 1982—.

SIDELIGHTS: In *Atlas of the Roman World,* authors Tim Cornell and John Matthews present the Roman Republic in all its aspects from 800 B.C. to 500 A.D. The text is supported by fifty-four maps and many color illustrations. Writing in the *Times Literary Supplement,* book reviewer J. J. Wilkes praised this "splendid production," expressing his satisfaction with both the text and supporting materials. Wilkes also lauded the authors' discussion of early Italy and the Roman Republic through the dictatorship of Sulla as "a first-rate survey which presents succinctly the state of knowledge, or rather of the argument, concerning early Rome, its institutions, society and relations with other peoples in Italy."

BIOGRAPHICAL/CRITICAL SOURCES:

PERIODICALS

Chicago Tribune Book World, December 5, 1982.
Times Literary Supplement, June 4, 1982.

* * *

CORNEY, Estelle 1911-

PERSONAL: Born September 14, 1911, in Christchurch, New Zealand; daughter of Michael (a glass blower) and Maud (Mills) Cook; married Cedric Corney (a farmer), May 23, 1941; children: Andrew, Fleur Corney Beale, Michael, Christopher, Benjamin, Deborah. *Education:* University of Canterbury, B.A., 1932.

ADDRESSES: Home—Norfolk Rd., R.D.8, Inglewood, Taranaki, New Zealand. *Agent:* Butler Richards, P.O. Box 31240, Milford, Auckland, New Zealand.

CAREER: High school teacher of English and history, 1936-41.

AWARDS, HONORS: First prize from Stratford Centenary, Taranaki, New Zealand, 1981, for short story "The Place of Power."

WRITINGS:

Pa's Top Hat (juvenile), Deutsch, 1980.

Author of stories and scripts for Radio New Zealand, *Ashton Scholastic,* and *New Zealand School Journal.*

WORK IN PROGRESS: Research on early New Plymouth and Taranaki, New Zealand, 1840-1900.

SIDELIGHTS: Estelle Corney told *CA:* "The dearth of educational opportunity during my youth was an important factor for so many young people in a time of deep economic depression, but I was saved by two things: a) I lived in the university city of Christchurch, and so did not have to leave home for higher education, and b) if 'cleanliness is next to godliness,' my mother put education ahead of both! Even if you just about had to starve for it.

"New Plymouth, New Zealand (the object of my current research), is a thriving city near great oil and gas fields and in one of the most productive farming areas in the world. It has many schools and colleges and a polytechnic school. Although it has no university, it has easy access to universities in other cities.

"But in the year 1900 it was a different story. New Plymouth had been settled by white people for just sixty years and did not, in the beginning, progress as fast as most other settlements. At first, immigrants were slow to come because Taranaki was plagued by the Maori land wars (who owned this land we paid for in England—the Maoris or us?). Though these wars were over by 1900 New Plymouth suffered from isolation from other centers because it was on no major route to anywhere.

"If a girl in New Plymouth in 1900 had wanted a tertiary education and her family (father) were against it, her difficulties would have been colossal. As a matter of interest, the whole education system, up to the university level (I can't speak for university education), is in a state of change in New Zealand. The hotly debated issues are sex education in primary schools, placing more women in positions of authority (especially as heads of schools), smaller classrooms, elimination of old university entrance examinations, and the methods of assessing students, etc. There is also a great upsurge in activity in Maori culture—Maori language, songs, and dances are taught in many schools."

* * *

CORNWALL, John 1928-

PERSONAL: Born April 27, 1928, in Spencer, Iowa; son of

Morgan (a lawyer) and Inez (a housewife; maiden name, Lally) Cornwall. *Education:* University of Iowa, B.A., 1950; London School of Economics and Political Science, London, M.Sc., 1952; Harvard University, Ph.D., 1958.

ADDRESSES: Office—Department of Economics, Dalhousie University, Halifax, Nova Scotia, Canada B2H 3J3.

CAREER: Tufts University, Medford, Mass., assistant professor, 1959-63, associate professor, 1963-66, professor of economics, 1966-70; Southern Illinois University at Carbondale, professor of economics, 1970-76; Dalhousie University, Halifax, Nova Scotia, professor of economics, 1976—.

WRITINGS:

Growth and Stability in a Mature Economy, Wiley, 1972.
Modern Capitalism: Its Growth and Transformation, St. Martin's, 1977.
(With Wendy Maclean) *Economic Recovery for Canada,* Lorimer Press, 1983.
The Conditions for Economic Recovery: A Post-Keynesian Analysis, Basil Blackwell, 1983, M. E. Sharpe, 1984.
(Editor) *After Stagflation: Alternatives to Economic Decline,* Basil Blackwell, 1984.

WORK IN PROGRESS: Research on "incomes policy and stagflation policy."

SIDELIGHTS: John Cornwall told *CA:* "The basic aim of my writings is to explain some of the major developments and problems of the advanced capitalist economies over the past century. In the process, I have tried to show that properly-used macroeconomic theory has powerful explanatory capability, and that it is therefore a sound basis for the development of policies to relieve advanced economies of such problems as economic depression, inflation, and stagnation.

"Given these themes, my writing inevitably includes considerable criticism of 'mainstream' economics. I have increasingly come to believe that the dominant schools of economic thought, based on neoclassical economics, trivialize a respectable social science by sacrificing realism for the appearance of scientific rigor."

*   *   *

CORSON, Fred Pierce 1896-1985

OBITUARY NOTICE—See index for *CA* sketch: Born April 11, 1896, in Millville, N.J.; died of cerebral hemorrhage suffered in a fall, February 16, 1985, in St. Petersburg, Fla. Clergyman, educator, and author. Corson, a much-honored Methodist bishop, served as the president of the World Methodist Council from 1961 to 1966 and as a delegate-observer at the Second Vatican Council from 1962 to 1965. He became president of Dickinson College in 1934 and served in that capacity until he was named bishop in 1944. His numerous publications include *The Pattern of a Church, Your Church and You, Pattern for Successful Living, The Christian Imprint, Steps to Christian Unity,* and *Documents of the Vatican Two.*

OBITUARIES AND OTHER SOURCES:

BOOKS

Current Biography, Wilson, 1961, April, 1985.
The International Who's Who, 47th edition, Europa, 1983.

PERIODICALS

Chicago Tribune, February 20, 1985.

New York Times, February 19, 1985.

*   *   *

CORTAZZI, (Henry Arthur) Hugh 1924-

PERSONAL: Surname is pronounced Cor-*tat*-si; born May 2, 1924, in Senbergh, Yorkshire, England; son of Frederick E. Mervyn (a teacher) and Madge (a housewife; maiden name, Miller) Cortazzi; married Elizabeth Esther Montague (a housewife), April 3, 1956; children: William, Rosemary, Charlotte. *Education:* University of London, B.A., 1949; University of St. Andrews, M.A., 1944.

ADDRESSES: Home and office—British Embassy, Tokyo, Japan.

CAREER: Foreign Office, London, England, third secretary, 1949, third secretary in Singapore, 1950-51, second secretary in Tokyo, Japan, 1951-54, and at Foreign Office, 1954-58, first secretary in Bonn, West Germany, 1958-60, Tokyo, 1961-65, and at Foreign Office, 1965-66, commercial counselor in Tokyo, 1966-70, counselor at Royal College of Defense Studies, 1971, commercial minister in Washington, D.C., 1972-75, deputy undersecretary of state at Foreign and Commonwealth Office, 1975-84, ambassador in Tokyo, 1984—. *Military service:* Royal Air Force, 1943-47; became flight lieutenant.

MEMBER: Royal Air Force Club.

AWARDS, HONORS: Companion, Order of St. Michael and St. George, 1969; Knight Commander, Order of St. Michael and St. George, 1980.

WRITINGS:

IN ENGLISH

(Translator) Keita Genji, *The Ogre and Other Stories of the Japanese Salaryman,* Japan Times, 1972 (also see below).
(Translator) Genji, *The Guardian God of Golf and Other Humorous Stories,* Japan Times, 1972 (also see below).
(Translator) Genji, *The Lucky One and Other Humorous Stories* (contains *The Ogre and Other Stories of the Japanese Salaryman* [see above] and *The Guardian God of Golf and Other Humorous Stories* [see above]), Japan Times, 1980.
(Editor) Mary Crawford Fraser, *A Diplomat's Wife in Japan: Sketches at the Turn of the Century,* Weatherhill, 1982.
Isles of Gold: Antique Maps of Japan, Weatherhill, 1983.
Dr. Willis in Japan (monograph), Athlone, 1985.

IN JAPANESE

(Editor) *Nigashi no Shimaguni, Nishi no Shimaguni* (title means "Eastern Inland Country, Western Inland Country"), Chuokoron, 1984.

Contributor to Japanese journals and newspapers, including *Transactions of the Asiatic Society of Japan.*

WORK IN PROGRESS: Editing *Mitford's Japan,* a selection of writings by nineteenth-century British lord A.B. Mitford, for Athlone; a collection of essays for Japanese high school students studying English titled "Thoughts From a Sussex Garden."

SIDELIGHTS: In his 1983 book, *Isles of Gold: Antique Maps of Japan,* Hugh Cortazzi, a literary translator and connoisseur of Japanese culture, argues that old maps of Japan, by Japanese and European cartographers, were created not merely to perform a function but also as works of art. As Edward Seidensticker wrote in the *New York Times Book Review,* Cortazzi supports his claim by showing "admirable plates" and by comments that are "a model of conciseness." Furthermore, Seidensticker praised the "sound scholarship" underlying Cortazzi's thesis that Japanese and European cartography influenced each other, and summed up his work as appealing to "both the eye and the intellect."

The author's interest in Japan resulted in another literary effort; he edited the correspondence of an American expatriate, Mary Crawford Fraser, who a century ago was posted with her husband at the British embassy in Tokyo. According to Susan Mary Alsop of *Washington Post Book World,* readers of *A Diplomat's Wife in Japan: Sketches at the Turn of the Century* are indebted to Cortazzi for rescuing the correspondence from "dusty oblivion." The book, a collection of letters, describes social and political events during the dramatic Meiji era (1867-1912), when Japan, breaking with its ancient feudal tradition, developed into a modern industrial state. Alsop noted that Cortazzi "illustrated the book with eight superb wood-block prints in color which depict everyday life in Tokyo" at the end of the nineteenth century. Impressed by the "enthusiastic" author's vivid discriptions of Tokyo when it was still a "city of gardens," Alsop lauded Cortazzi "for having given us this beautifully produced book."

Cortazzi told *CA:* "My writings arise out of my interest in Japan, its culture and history."

BIOGRAPHICAL/CRITICAL SOURCES:

PERIODICALS

New York Times Book Review, October 3, 1982, December 11, 1983.
Washington Post Book World, December 26, 1982.

*   *   *

COSSLETT, Tess 1947-

PERSONAL: Born April 8, 1947, in Cambridge, England; daughter of Vernon Ellis (a physicist) and Anna (a physicist; maiden name, Wischin) Cosslett. *Education:* St. Hilda's College, Oxford, B.A. (English), 1969, B.Phil., 1971, D.Phil., 1977.

ADDRESSES: Home—27A Queen St., Lancaster LA1 1RX, England. *Office*—Department of English, University of Lancaster, Bailrigg, Lancaster, England.

CAREER: University of Lancaster, Lancaster, England, lecturer in English literature, 1973—.

WRITINGS:

(Contributor) William Brock and others, editors, *John Tyndall,* Royal Dublin Society, 1980.
The "Scientific Movement" and Victorian Literature, St. Martin's, 1982.
(Editor and author of introduction) *Science and Religion in the Nineteenth Century,* Cambridge University Press, 1983.

Contributor to *Prose Studies.*

WORK IN PROGRESS: Researching feminist criticism, especially of women writers of the nineteenth century; planning a study of female friendships in nineteenth-century women's writing.

SIDELIGHTS: In *The "Scientific Movement" and Victorian Literature* Tess Cosslett explores the influence of science on Victorian literature. Selecting writings from George Eliot, Thomas Hardy, George Meredith, and Alfred, Lord Tennyson, the author demonstrates how the nineteenth century's atmosphere of scientific ferment permeated the works of that era's poets and novelists. Peter Kemp wrote in the *Times Literary Supplement* that Cosslett's "arguments are gradual, patient, cumulative.... She is closely observant, and scrupulous in formulating her conclusions." He added: "Dr. Cosslett's is a stimulating and important book. At its best when looking through a close-focus lens, it sifts expertly through lines, paragraphs, passages, bringing to light revealing data. And, while it covers only a quite confined area of a fascinating field, it provides invaluable information and guide-lines for further profitable exploration."

BIOGRAPHICAL/CRITICAL SOURCES:

PERIODICALS

Times Literary Supplement, March 25, 1983.

*   *   *

COSTELLO, Joseph P(atrick) 1924-

PERSONAL: Born April 25, 1924, in St. Louis, Mo.; son of Joseph Patrick (a physician) and Elsa (a housewife; maiden name, Rapp) Costello; married Ellen Denvir (a housewife), February 15, 1947; children: Marianne, Christine, Joseph, John. *Education:* Attended University of Notre Dame; St. Louis University, M.D., 1946. *Religion:* Roman Catholic.

ADDRESSES: Home—P.O. Box 37, Chesterfield, Mo. 63017. *Office*—950 Francis Pl., Suite 310, St. Louis, Mo. 63105.

CAREER: Worked at Jefferson Barracks Veterans Administration Hospital, 1949-52; private practice of medicine, 1952—. Medical director of St. Louis Chronic Hospital, 1955-68; medical director and member of board of directors of Charter Mutual Life Insurance Co., 1963-77. *Military service:* U.S. Army, 1943-46. U.S. Public Health Service, served at National Cancer Institute, 1947-49.

MEMBER: St. Louis Metropolitan Medical Society.

WRITINGS:

Can Modern Man Survive Modern Government?, Green Hill, 1983.

SIDELIGHTS: Joseph Costello told *CA* that his book is "based upon thirteen years of municipal and seven years of federal governmental experience. The municipal service was politically tumultuous, due to active confrontation with the political system in an effort to improve care of the aged. My experience with private enterprise included fourteen years of service as medical director and member of the board of directors of an insurance subsidiary of a floundering New York Stock Exchange finance corporation. Additional private enterprise experience included personal promotion, development, and disposal of a large and successful health care facility for the aged. In these sideline hobbies I was exceptionally fortunate to have been present to observe the decision-making process.

"Because all of these were conducted against the economic security of a private medical practice, I was permitted an unusually dispassionate view of both the public and private sectors. In addition, trained professional skills permitted even deeper confidence and discussion from all levels of command.

The kindly questioning of the bland family physician provided intimate details no other writer could ever enjoy.

"At the time, my motivations were simply a scientific awe, an insatiable curiosity, and an endless wonderment at the patterns of human behavior in varied situations. The Kennedy-Johnson-Nixon era's revelations resulted in my gradual realization that my political exposures and experiences were the rule and not the exception. Written in the context of my long-standing interest in history, *Can Modern Man Survive Modern Government?* resulted from my shocking comprehension of the extent of the worldwide inadequacy of mankind's present governmental process.

"There is a peaceful solution! History and personal observations convinced me the root cause of our problem lies in the ancient political principle of the King protecting his obedient subjects. It is a primitive compact in which the ruler is granted unlimited force but any resistance by the subject is considered to be insurrection.

"Problems arose with the accumulation of knowledge by the common man which resulted in incredible intellectual achievement and gave the ruler the technical capacity to destroy the species. I believe the genius of the individual has totally fractured the primitive political compact.

"The solution is found in Jefferson's immortal Declaration of Independence: 'Governments derive their just powers through consent of the governed.' Mankind must turn to the individual through a 'Consent of the People' mechanism if the species is to survive. With a 'Consent of the People' referendum the citizen may peacefully veto and ultimately guide the conduct of the ruler.

"The innate talent of the individual citizen will assure mankind's growth and prosperity."

*   *   *

COTICH, Felicia   1926-

PERSONAL: Born January 24, 1926, in Malmsbury, Australia; came to the United States in 1945, naturalized citizen, 1969; daughter of James W. (a timber mill worker) and Elsie (a housewife; maiden name, Rea) Taylor; married Peter J. Cotich (a service manager), September 30, 1943; children: Lynne K. Cotich Cote, Patricia Cotich Consolo, Kenneth. *Education:* Attended high school in Melbourne, Australia. *Politics:* Independent. *Religion:* Roman Catholic.

ADDRESSES: Home—101 Vly Rd., Albany, N.Y. 12205. *Agent*—Carol Mann Literary Agency, 168 Pacific St., Brooklyn, N.Y. 11201.

CAREER: Myers Emporium, Melbourne, Australia, apprentice tailor, 1941-44; employed in clothing trade, 1945-51; writer, 1955—. Also worked as hospital receptionist and switchboard operator. Creative writing teacher in adult education programs, 1974-76; public speaker. *Member:* Society of Children's Book Writers, Literary Advocacy Pals, Society of Albany.

WRITINGS:

Valda (juvenile novel), Coward, 1983.

Work represented in anthologies, including *Look for Tomorrow and Other Stories for Today*, Scholastic Book Services. Contributor of stories to magazines, including *Colorado Quarterly, Raconteur, Antioch Review, Ingenue, Co-Ed*, and *Ante*.

WORK IN PROGRESS: Season of Scarlet Flowers, a young adult novel; *The Rooms That Maggie Lived In*, an adult novel.

SIDELIGHTS: "We lived a lonely life at timber mills," Felicia Cotich told *CA*. "An early introduction to classic literature through my well-educated English mother, coupled with the Australian bush stories told by my loquacious father, gave me a deep love of words, a sense of story, and a desire to write.

"Although I did not set out to be a children's writer, my first published story was for young adults. Subsequent stories were written and accepted for that market. Later, a group of short stories set in Australia and designed to depict several facets of the Australian character were published in several quarterlies.

"I write about men and women caught in the dilemma of their own personalities, as well as the small private wars fought by each individual, wars for survival. *Valda*, for instance, is the story of personal growth for a fourteen-year-old girl growing up in Australia during the Depression.

"My personal view is that human beings are born with an innate personality which more than anything will determine the outcome of their lives. In my work I very often depict characters who are the victims of their personalities or temperaments, but who triumph in spite of them."

*   *   *

COTTRELL, Leonard S(later), Jr.   1899-1985

OBITUARY NOTICE—See index for *CA* sketch: Born December 12, 1899, in Hampton Roads, Va.; died March 20, 1985, in Chapel Hill, N.C. Social psychologist, educator, and author. A specialist in the field of marriage and the family, Cottrell taught at Cornell University from 1935 to 1951 and at the University of North Carolina from 1968 to 1972. During the intervening years, he served as secretary and research director of the Russell Sage Foundation. His publications include *Delinquency Areas, Predicting Success or Failure in Marriage, Public Reaction to the Atomic Bomb and World Affairs, The American Soldier, Further Explorations in Social Psychiatry*, and *Sociological Traditions From Generation to Generation*.

OBITUARIES AND OTHER SOURCES:

PERIODICALS

New York Times, March 22, 1985.

*   *   *

COUGHLAN, William C(arlisle), Jr.   1946-

PERSONAL: Born February 2, 1946, in Portland, Maine; son of William Carlisle (an oil company executive) and Nancey Rose Coughlan. *Education:* Boston University, B.A., 1968, M.Ed. and M.A., both 1978. *Politics:* "Radical left." *Religion:* None.

ADDRESSES: Home and office—14 Homer St., Brookline, Mass. 02146.

CAREER: Boston Center for the Blind, Boston, Mass., child care worker, 1971; Kingsley School, Boston, teacher of learning-disabled children, 1971-73; Boston Food Co-op, Inc., Allston, Mass., chairperson of the board, 1973-74; Ancros Human Development Foundation, Jamaica Plain, Mass., youth counselor, 1974; New England Food Co-op, Cambridge, Mass., founding member and administrative coordinator, 1974-75; coordinator, author, and distributor of *The Food Co-op Handbook,* 1974-76; Jamaica Plain Neighborhood House, Jamaica Plain, administrator, teacher, and resource person of after-school teaching program, 1976. New England Co-op Network, Cambridge, founding volunteer organizer, 1978—; Tri-Community Action Program, Malden, Mass., 1979-80, began as nutritional research assistant, became acting food and nutrition coordinator; U.S. Government, Community Services Administration, Boston, Community Action Program field representative, 1980; New England Co-op Network, Cambridge, supervisor of VISTA (Volunteers in Service to America) workers in five states, 1980-81; Co-operative Publishing Ltd., Boston, president, 1982—. *Military service:* Served in U.S. Air Force.

MEMBER: Disabled American Veterans.

WRITINGS:

The Organizer's Manual, Bantam, 1970.
The Food Co-op Handbook, Houghton, 1975.
(With Monte Francke) *Going Co-op: The Complete Guide to Buying and Owning Your Own Apartment,* Harper, 1983.

WORK IN PROGRESS: Research on theory of co-ops and medical co-ops.

*   *   *

COUPERUS, Louis (Marie Anne)   1863-1923

BRIEF ENTRY: Born June 10, 1863, at The Hague, Netherlands; died of blood poisoning, July 16, 1923, in De Steeg, Netherlands. Dutch educator and author of works in several genres. Couperus wrote numerous novels in the style of Emile Zola's social realism. He turned to writing fiction after first dabbling in poetry. His first novel, *Eline Vere* (1889; translated in 1892), is the story of a woman convinced of her own inability to overcome the handicaps of her heredity. In this and subsequent works Couperus established himself as a master chronicler of the Dutch bourgeoisie. His most celebrated work is probably *De Boeken der Kleine Zielen* (1901-03; translated as *The Books of the Small Souls,* 1914-1918), a four-volume epic of a Dutch family's decline in the wake of an inability to love. Among Couperus's other works is *Van Oude Menschen de Dingen die Voorbijgaan* (1906; translated as *Old People and the Things That Pass,* 1918), which tells the story of people whose lives are affected by a murder committed before they were born, and *De Komedianten* (1917; translated as *The Comedians,* 1926). Couperus also wrote several novels about ancient Rome and Greece, including *Iskander* (1920), an account of Alexander the Great. His autobiography is entitled *Van en Over Mijzelf en Anderen* (1910-17; title means "Of and Concerning Myself and Others").

BIOGRAPHICAL/CRITICAL SOURCES:

BOOKS

Cyclopedia of World Authors, Harper, 1958.
Longman Companion to Twentieth Century Literature, Longman, 1970.
The Reader's Encyclopedia, 2nd edition, Crowell, 1965.
Twentieth-Century Literary Criticism, Volume 15, Gale, 1985.

*   *   *

COUSENS, Frances Reissman   1913-1985

OBITUARY NOTICE: Born March 13, 1913, in Kosow, Po-

land; died of pancreatic cancer, April 6, 1985, in Dearborn, Mich. Educator and author. Cousens taught sociology at the University of Michigan—Dearborn for twenty years, beginning her tenure as an associate professor and becoming a full professor in 1970. Previously she had served for several years as the first research director of the Michigan Fair Employment Practices Commission and had then spent two years as a research associate for Detroit Public Schools' Great Cities Project. In 1965 she received a $200,000 grant from the U.S. Equal Opportunity Commission to study the relationship between the civil rights movement and employment opportunities for blacks. From this research came the book *Promise Us Performance.* Cousens's other writings include the 1969 book *Public Civil Rights Agencies and Fair Employment.*

OBITUARIES AND OTHER SOURCES:

BOOKS

Who's Who in America, 41st edition, Marquis, 1980.

PERIODICALS

Detroit Free Press, April 9, 1985.

*   *   *

COWAN, Ruth Schwartz   1941-

PERSONAL: Born April 9, 1941, in Brooklyn, N.Y.; daughter of Louis E. (a business executive) and Betty (a housewife; maiden name, Adickman) Schwartz; married Neil M. Cowan (a public information officer), January 21, 1968; children: Jennifer Rose, May Deborah, Sarah Kiva. *Education:* Barnard College, A.B., 1961; University of California, Berkeley, M.A., 1964; Johns Hopkins University, Ph.D., 1969.

ADDRESSES: Home—Glen Cove, N.Y. *Office*—Department of History, State University of New York at Stony Brook, Stony Brook, N.Y. 11794.

CAREER: State University of New York at Stony Brook, instructor, 1967-69, assistant professor, 1969-74, associate professor of history, 1974—. Visiting assistant professor at Princeton University, 1972-73.

MEMBER: American Association for the Advancement of Science, Society for the History of Technology, History of Science Society.

AWARDS, HONORS: National Science Foundation grants, 1975-77, 1979-80; Phi Beta Kappa Lecturer, 1981-82; Dexter Prize from Society for the History of Technology, 1984, for *More Work for Mother.*

WRITINGS:

More Work for Mother: The Ironies of Household Technology From the Open Hearth to the Microwave, Basic Books, 1983.
Technology in American History (tentative title), Oxford University Press, in press.

Contributor to history journals and scientific periodicals.

SIDELIGHTS: Ruth Schwartz Cowan told *CA:* "I was trained as a scholar in the field called 'the history of science and technology.' I have always believed that scholarship and life should be and are inseparable from each other, so that, several years ago, when I was casting about for an interesting research topic, I decided to explore the history of household technology; at that time I was spending just as many hours of the day being a housewife as being a scholar. The book resulting from this effort, *More Work for Mother,* is as much a personal testament to the point of view that I developed over the years of doing research as it is a report of that research itself. I was at first interested in finding out how the development of household technology in the twentieth century had lightened labor for housewives and made it possible for them to expend their energies doing other things. As the research progressed I discovered that my original hypothesis was false. Washing machines and vacuum cleaners had, in some very important ways, created more work for mothers. I also discovered the extent to which I myself had been victimized.

"I am pleased that other historians of technology regard my book as a significant scholarly contribution to our field, but I am even more pleased when people tell me that the book has helped them to see themselves more clearly. If scholarship doesn't illuminate life, why bother with it?"

*   *   *

COX, George W(yatt)   1935-

PERSONAL: Born February 10, 1935, in Williamson, W. Va.; son of Ira F. and Edna D. Cox; married Carolyn C. Kay, December 21, 1957 (divorced, 1969); married Darla G. Bell (a school administrator), June 6, 1969; children: Daniel R., David W. *Education:* Ohio Wesleyan University, A.B. (with honors), 1956; University of Illinois at Urbana-Champaign, M.S., 1958, Ph.D., 1960.

ADDRESSES: Office—Department of Biology, San Diego State University, 5300 Campanile Dr., San Diego, Calif. 92182.

CAREER: University of Alaska, College, assistant professor of biology, 1960-61; California Western University (now United States International University), San Diego, assistant professor of biology, 1961-62; San Diego State University, San Diego, assistant professor, 1962-66, associate professor, 1966-69, professor of biology, 1969—. Director of Ecology Program for National Science Foundation, 1978-79.

MEMBER: American Association for the Advancement of Science, Ecological Society of America, Sigma Xi.

WRITINGS:

Laboratory Manual of General Ecology, W. C. Brown, 1967, 5th edition, 1984.
(Editor) *Readings in Conservation Ecology,* Appleton, 1969, 2nd edition, 1974.
(With B. D. Collier, A. W. Johnson, and P. H. Miller) *Dynamic Ecology,* Prentice-Hall, 1973.
(With Michael D. Atkins) *Agricultural Ecology: An Analysis of World Food Production Systems,* W. H. Freeman, 1979.

Author and narrator of "Biosphere and Biosurvival" series, broadcast by KPBS-TV, 1973-74. Contributor to scientific journals and popular science magazines. Member of board of editors of *Ecology.*

WORK IN PROGRESS: Research on the ecology of East and South Africa, interactions of mammals with the natural vegetation and physical landscape, evolution of migration in birds, agricultural ecology, and the ecology of Mediterranean-climate regions of the world.

SIDELIGHTS: George W. Cox told *CA:* "Entering the field of ecology in 1960, I found myself not only in a field that was growing in scientific capability, but also in one that was cap-

turing strong public concern. My interests in theoretical ecology have led me into field studies in Alaska, Central America and the Caribbean, all five of the world's areas of Mediterranean climate, and, most recently, East Africa. Regions of Mediterranean climate, like that of Southern California, have intrigued me because of the combination of striking similarities and subtle differences between California and the other regions: the European Mediterranean, central Chile, the South African Cape, and parts of Australia. East Africa has proved to be the most fascinating area in which I have carried out field work; in a real sense, this area presents a picture of the interrelations of man and nature over the whole of human evolution.

"My concern with the application of ecological principles to man, which also arose in the 1960's, has led me to examine the science of agriculture from an ecological perspective, and, most recently, to consider the important questions of conservation of wildlife and natural diversity. Ecology has been a field in constant change since I was first introduced to it in the 1950's, and I expect new and important focuses of this rapidly maturing branch of science to continue to emerge."

*   *   *

COX, John H(enry)   1907-1975

OBITUARY NOTICE: Born February 8, 1907, in Coburg, Ore.; died September 7, 1975, in Bethel, Conn. Historian, educator, and author. Cox joined the faculty of the City College of the City University of New York in 1941 and maintained this affiliation for thirty years, despite the interruption of his World War II military service. During his tenure with the school, Cox advanced from the rank of instructor to professor of history and became known as a leading scholar of the post-Civil War period of American history. With his fellow historian and wife, LaWanda Fenlason Cox, Cox researched and wrote articles for the *Journal of Southern History* and two books on the Reconstruction era, *Politics, Principles, and Prejudice, 1865-1866: The Dilemma of Reconstruction America* and *Reconstruction, the Negro, and the New South.* For the former the authors won the 1964 John H. Dunning Prize from the American Historical Association and the first book award from the Phi Alpha Theta history fraternity. Cox's other writings include a two-volume history of the Mediterranean-based Army Air Force Engineer Command, which Cox served as historian and director of research during the 1940's. He also collaborated on a project funded by the Social Science Research Council that resulted in *Imports and Exports of the English Colonies in America.*

OBITUARIES AND OTHER SOURCES:

BOOKS

The National Cyclopaedia of American Biography, Volume 60, James T. White, 1981.

PERIODICALS

American Historical Review, April, 1976.
Journal of Southern History, February, 1976.
New York Times, September 9, 1975.

*   *   *

CRAGG, D. J.
See CRAGG, Dan

CRAGG, Dan 1939-
(D. J. Cragg)

PERSONAL: Born September 6, 1939, in Rochester, N.Y.; son of James Wilson (a cavalryman) and Gertrude (Finucane) Cragg; married Sun Pok Yi (a homemaker), March 28, 1974; children: Tam Le (son). *Education:* University of Maryland at College Park, B.A. (summa cum laude), 1982; graduate study at George Mason University, 1983—. *Politics:* Conservative. *Religion:* "Deist."

ADDRESSES: Home and office—5607 Heming Ave., Springfield, Va. 22151.

CAREER: U.S. Army, career soldier, 1958-80, duty assignments include tours of duty in the Republic of Vietnam (South Vietnam; now Socialist Republic of Vietnam), 1962-63 and 1965-69, served with Military Advisory Assistance Group, Saigon, as U.S. adviser to the 5th Vietnamese Infantry Division, Bien Hoa, on the personal staff of Gen. William Westmoreland, commander, U.S. Military Assistance Command, Vietnam (MACV), Saigon, and as clerk of the U.S. liaison detachment to the headquarters elements of Free World Forces countries, retiring as sergeant major; *National Vietnam Veterans Review*, Washington, D.C., bureau chief, 1982—. Member of board of directors of Veterans Press Syndicate, 1983—.

MEMBER: Francis Grose Society (member of board of directors), Company Military Historians, Disabled American Veterans, Phi Kappa Phi.

AWARDS, HONORS—Military: Republic of Vietnam Honor Medal, Vietnam Service Medal (with eleven campaign stars).

WRITINGS:

The NCO Guide, Stackpole, 1982.
A Travel Guide to Military Installations, Stackpole, 1983.
(With John Elting and Ernest Deal) *A Dictionary of Soldier Talk*, Scribner's, 1984.

Contributor to magazines, including *Army Times*, *Verbatim*, and *Maledicta*, and to newspapers. Contributing editor of *Army* magazine.

UNDER NAME D. J. CRAGG

(Editor and author of introduction, notes, and biographical sketch of author) Francis Grose, *The Mirror's Image: Advice to the Officers of the British Army, With a Biographical Sketch of the Life and a Biography of the Works of Captain Francis Grose, F.S.A.*, Owlswick, 1978.

WORK IN PROGRESS: Researching material for a full-length biography of Francis Grose, the eighteenth-century British antiquary, humorist, satirist, and friend of the poet Robert Burns; research on themes of death in English literature, 1300-1800; collecting materials on military slang and jargon for a future revision of *A Dictionary of Soldier Talk;* "writing a novel of my Vietnam experiences."

SIDELIGHTS: "In view of my long military service," Dan Cragg informed *CA*, "most of my writing and research has a distinct military flavor. The highlight of my military career was my service in the Republic of South Vietnam. In the early years, 1962-1963, I served with the Military Advisory Assistance Group, first at the headquarters in Saigon and later as the clerk to the senior U.S. adviser to the 5th Vietnamese Infantry Division at Bien Hoa. During the latter months of this assignment the division commander was none other than Col.

Nguyen Van Thieu, whom we all respected in his role as the division's commander. Later I served two years on Gen. William C. Westmoreland's personal staff at the Military Assistance Command headquarters in Saigon and two more years as the chief clerk of the U.S. liaison detachment to the headquarters elements of the various Free World Forces—Australian, New Zealand, Korean, Thai, Philippine, Chinese (Republic of China), and Spanish—serving and fighting alongside us in South Vietnam. During this assignment I visited New Zealand for a month as an unofficial guest of the New Zealand Army.

"I believe that our effort in Vietnam represents one of the more noble and altruistic gestures our country has made in this century; paradoxically, our subsequent abandonment of the South Vietnamese constitutes one of the most despicable acts of collective cowardice by any nation in this century. I believe the Vietnam War was lost at home by an incompetent government whose inept decisions fueled a dissent among the people which gave a clear signal to our Communist enemies that time was ultimately on their side in the war.

"I am proud of my own service in Vietnam and I think every American who served there in any capacity deserves the thanks and respect of his countrymen. I think the course America has taken toward Vietnam since 1975—refusal to recognize its Communist government—is entirely appropriate. While I think we should do more to help resettle the thousands of homeless people from Indochina, I am satisfied that our admission of so many Indochinese refugees into this country since 1975 is an act of humanity that goes far toward cleansing our national escutcheon of the stain it acquired when our pusillanimous Congress voted to abandon them to their fate in 1975.

"I wrote *The NCO Guide* as a sort of 'farewell' gesture to the Army. In it I attempted to distill the knowledge acquired over twenty-two years into a book I hope has been of some help to the soldiers who are now filling the noncommissioned officer grades.

"I think the strength and uniqueness of the *Guide* derives from the fact that it goes far beyond telling soldiers how to fill out forms, how to get promoted, how the system works—the traditional focus of books like this, although my version has all that in it too. But where I parted with tradition was by including frank discussions of ethics and morality buttressed by practical and real-life experience, so *The NCO Guide* not only gives soldiers points on how to do their jobs but direction toward how to discharge responsibly the trust placed in noncommissioned officers for the welfare and safety of their soldiers.

"Likewise, my contribution to *A Dictionary of Soldier Talk*, originally undertaken as a hobby, developed into an obligation to preserve the language of soldiers and hopefully endow it with a degree of scholarly respectability. I was fortunate in this work to find two like-minded partners in John R. Elting and Ernest LaFayette Deal.

"I undertook to compile *The Mirror's Image*, a labor of love, while still on active duty. The book was 'published privately.' I became interested in Francis Grose when I first read extracts from his *Advice to the Officers of the British Army*, one of the finest satires of the military life ever written. Although first published in 1782, this little book is still very contemporary in many ways; and as a professional soldier, I was enormously impressed by its insight and incisive Juvenalian wit (I wish all my colleagues had been similarly impressed). A desire to know more about Grose led to research into his life and ultimately the biographical sketch which accompanies the Owlswick reprint of *Advice*. This research in turn led to an interest in the eighteenth century in general and studies in eighteenth-century English literature in particular, which has been the focus of my academic efforts since.

"As a soldier, I had to consider the possibility of my own death and this led me to become interested in how others face the same prospect. Reading Middle English death lyrics in college inspired me to trace the theme further, and this has taught me that we moderns have forgotten that the closer we are to death, the sweeter is life and that studiously not thinking about death—the practice these days—stultifies the spirit and dulls the vision to the achievements and enjoyments possible in life.

"The earliest and most profound literary influences in my life were the writings of the historians William H. Prescott and Francis Parkman and the horror fiction of Howard Phillips Lovecraft, all of which I was consuming with avidity by the time I was fifteen years old. Subsequently, the poetry of Emily Dickinson struck a chord in me and although I never appreciated Shakespeare until I was about thirty-five, when the recognition finally came I was overwhelmed by how much I'd missed because I hadn't read him long before.

"For me, writing is mostly sheer drudgery enlivened by flashes of pure ecstasy on those rare occasions when what I am trying to express happens to come out just the way I want it to. I've never been able to understand how that happens or how to make it happen when I most want it to, but the joy of those moments when the creative process works for me is enough to make me keep on trying. And I must confess that the thrill of seeing my stuff published, whether done for money or free, whether rewrites or serious attempts at creative writing, goes a long way toward making up for all the hard work involved in producing it. I guess writing is my 'letter to the World that never wrote to Me' and that at heart I will always be an amateur in this business.

"I believe that while some people may be born with the native talent to be good writers, becoming one is an acquired process during which talent and desire are developed and refined through practice and experience, the harder the better. My advice to aspiring writers is to read widely and write constantly; never allow yourself to become discouraged by criticism and rejection; write about what you know (or write convincingly about what you don't); and never give up faith in your own ability to write.

"The financial rewards of writing are few for most people and those who make their living from it are not always the best writers, a fact many tyros miss. But that first commercial success, no matter how small, is sufficiently charged with delirium to keep most writers' feet a couple of inches off the ground for the rest of their lives."

BIOGRAPHICAL/CRITICAL SOURCES:

PERIODICALS

Army, December, 1979.
Military Review, October, 1979.
Royal United Services Institute Journal, March, 1979.
Verbatim, summer, 1984.

CRAMPTON, Helen
See CHESNEY, Marion

*   *   *

CREEL, George   1876-1953

BRIEF ENTRY: Born December 1, 1876, in Lafayette County, Mo.; died October 3 (one source says October 2), 1953, in San Francisco, Calif.; buried in Mt. Washington Cemetery, Kansas City, Mo. American civil servant, journalist, and author. Best known as chairman of the Committee on Public Information during the Woodrow Wilson administration, Creel was responsible for directing the flow of government propaganda concerning World War I. He began his journalism career at the age of twenty as a reporter for the *Kansas City World,* and from 1899 until 1913 he served consecutive editorships with the *Kansas City Independent,* the *Denver Post,* and the *Rocky Mountain News.* During these years Creel established himself as an exuberant crusader against corruption and dishonesty. He moved to New York City in 1915, where he worked as a free-lance writer for such periodicals as *Harper's Weekly* and *Everybody's* and devoted time to the woman's suffrage movement.

Active in President Wilson's 1916 reelection campaign, Creel wrote publicity for the Democratic National Committee and published a book, *Wilson and the Issues* (1916). By appointment of President Wilson, Creel became chairman of the Committee on Public Information in 1917. In that capacity he established a system of voluntary press censorship and enlisted the help of writers, advertising men, artists, photographers, and public speakers to promote the national cause and avert wartime hysteria. Creel also published the *Official Bulletin,* a daily newspaper with a circulation of one hundred thousand. Initially, Creel's appointment to the committee stirred controversy with the press, but his performance as chairman eventually won the praise of some of his most severe critics, as well as commendations from President Wilson.

Following his chairmanship Creel remained active in both magazine work and politics, and during the 1930's he worked on political campaigns, including that of Franklin Delano Roosevelt. Creel later served President Roosevelt as a regional administrator for the U.S. Recovery Act, and in 1934 he unsuccessfully ran for governor of California. In 1938 President Roosevelt appointed Creel as head of the Golden Gate International Exposition held in San Francisco. Creel was the author of numerous books, including *How We Advertised America* (1920), *The War, the World, and Wilson* (1920), *The People Next Door* (1926), *Tom Paine—Liberty Bell* (1931), *War Criminals* (1944), and *Russia's Race for Asia* (1949). He also published an autobiography, *Rebel at Large: Recollections of Fifty Crowded Years* (1947).

BIOGRAPHICAL/CRITICAL SOURCES:

BOOKS

Chenery, William L., *So It Seemed,* Harcourt, 1952.
Dictionary of Literary Biography, Volume 25, *American Newspaper Journalists, 1901-1925,* Gale, 1984.
Lansing, Robert, *War Memoirs of Robert Lansing,* Bobbs-Merrill, 1935.
McGraw-Hill Encyclopedia of World Biography, McGraw, 1973.
Mock, James R., *Censorship 1917,* Princeton University Press, 1941, DaCapo Press, 1972.

Perkin, Robert L., *The First Hundred Years*, Doubleday, 1959.
Sullivan, Mark, *Our Times, 1900-1925*, Volume 5: *Over Here: 1914-1918*, Scribners, 1936.

*   *   *

CROFTS, Freeman Wills   1879-1957

BRIEF ENTRY: Born in June, 1879, in Dublin, Ireland; died April 11, 1957. Irish railway engineer and author. Crofts was a civil engineer for an Irish railway until 1929; in that year he became a full-time writer. His best known work is the crime novel *The Cask* (1920). Like most of Crofts's popular mysteries, it features a criminal investigation in which the guilty character has an airtight alibi that must be exposed by the detective. Some of Crofts's books reflect the author's railway experience. He invented the famous Inspector French, whose adventures have been recounted in *Inspector French's Greatest Case* (1925), *Inspector French and the Cheyne Mystery* (1926), *The 12:30 From Croydon* (1934), and *French Strikes Oil* (1952).

BIOGRAPHICAL/CRITICAL SOURCES:

BOOKS

Encyclopedia of Mystery and Detection, McGraw, 1976.
Longman Companion to Twentieth Century Literature, Longman, 1970.

*   *   *

CROOK, Beverly Courtney

PERSONAL: Born in Baltimore, Md.; daughter of Robert A. (a stockbroker) and Edith (a store owner; maiden name, Lamberth) Courtney; married Compton N. Crook (a professor; died, 1981); children: Judy, Stephen, Leslie. *Education:* Received B.S. from Towson State University; received M.L.A. from Johns Hopkins University. *Politics:* Independent. *Religion:* Protestant.

ADDRESSES: Home—2829 Merryman's Mill Rd., Phoenix, Md. 21131. *Agent*—McIntosh & Otis, Inc., 475 Fifth Ave., New York, N.Y. 10017.

CAREER: Worked as an elementary schoolteacher in Baltimore, Md.; free-lance writer. Teaches typing and creative writing classes.

MEMBER: Authors Guild, Society of Children's Book Writers, Nature Conservancy, Save Our Streams, Towson State University Alumni Association (past executive director).

WRITINGS:

ALL FOR YOUNG READERS

April's Witches (fiction), Steck, 1971.
Invite a Bird to Dinner: Simple Feeders You Can Make, Lothrop, 1978.
Fair Annie of Old Mule Hollow (fiction), McGraw, 1978.

Contributor of short stories to children's magazines. Past editor of Towson State University Alumni Association magazine.

SIDELIGHTS: Beverly Courtney Crook told *CA:* "I am a native Marylander who has traveled widely, but all roads have led back to Maryland. I now live in the middle of a woods that is a wildlife refuge. Although it is a lovely setting, there are drawbacks: Wild critters of various sorts have been encouraged to take up residence here, and when raccoons turn over the trash cans, groundhogs burrow in the bean patch, and

deer nibble the lettuce, I am tempted to pull in the welcome mat. Still, that is a small price to pay for living so close to nature. Actually the local politicians are a much bigger problem. They persist in believing that 'progress' means a shopping mall on every corner.

"In my travels, I like to get away from cities and into remote areas. I especially like to visit Africa, where I can observe the wildlife in its natural habitat—before it vanishes.

"When I was first married, my husband, an underpaid biology teacher at the time, worked for the National Park Service during summer vacations. From June until September, we lived high in the Rockies in a tiny one-room cabin with a big stove, one cold-water faucet—and an outhouse over the hill. (A trip there at night, with the possibility of meeting a bear along the way, was not undertaken lightly.) But the magnificent surroundings more than compensated for lack of any creature comforts and awakened in me a deep interest in conservation. It is not surprising that this interest colors my writings, and I hope that some of it rubs off on my readers.

"I have always liked to write, but most of my writing was job-related nonfiction. Then my husband, who wrote fiction under a pen name, urged me to try writing for children. I finally took his advice and discovered, rather belatedly, that this was the type of writing that I really wanted to do. Since his illness and subsequent death, I have been unable to write. However, ideas are now beginning to stir.

"My primary goal in writing is to entertain, but with the hope that perhaps a new awareness or understanding will come about through the entertainment."

*   *   *

CROSS, Gary Scott   1946-

PERSONAL: Born September 25, 1946, in Spokane, Wash.; son of Clarence (a scientist) and Shirley (an administrator; maiden name, Weigle) Cross; married first wife, Nola, 1969 (divorced); married Maru Miller (a teacher), March, 1984; children: Benjamin. *Education:* Washington State University, B.A., 1968; Harvard University, M.Div., 1972; University of Wisconsin—Madison, M.A., 1973, Ph.D., 1977.

ADDRESSES: Office—Department of History, Pennsylvania State University, University Park, Pa. 16802.

CAREER: Lake Forest College, Lake Forest, Ill., lecturer in history, 1978-79; University of Wisconsin—Parkside, assistant professor of history, 1979-80; University of Wisconsin—Milwaukee, assistant professor of history, 1980-83; Pennsylvania State University, University Park, assistant professor of history, 1983—.

WRITINGS:

(Contributor) *Labor Insurgence and Workers' Control, 1900-1925*, Temple University Press, 1982.
Immigrant Workers in Industrial France: The Making of a New Laboring Class, Temple University Press, 1983.

Also contributor to *The Politics of Immigration: France and Non-Citizen Labor, 1900-1940*, published by Temple University Press. Contributor of articles to history journals.

WORK IN PROGRESS: Origins of the Eight-Hour Day in France and Britain, 1880-1930.

SIDELIGHTS: Gary Scott Cross told *CA:* "I focus on the origins of the contemporary industrial relations order in Europe. In particular, I am interested in the relationship between the state and social change in the twentieth century; for example, ways in which the state has shaped the labor market (as in the case of immigrant labor) and in which the government, through hours legislation, has re-allocated social time available for work, leisure, and family life.''

*   *   *

CROWE, Cecily (Teague)

BRIEF ENTRY: Born in New York, N.Y. American author of romance and Gothic novels. Crowe's writings include *Miss Spring* (Random House, 1953), *The Tower of Kilraven* (Holt, 1965), *Northwater* (Holt, 1968), *The Twice-Born* (Random House, 1972), *Abbeygate* (Coward, 1977), and *The Talisman* (St. Martin's, 1979). *Address:* Brick House, Mirror Lake, N.H. 03853.

BIOGRAPHICAL/CRITICAL SOURCES:

BOOKS

The Writers Directory: 1984-1986, St. James Press, 1983.

*   *   *

CULPEPPER, R(ichard) Alan   1946-

PERSONAL: Born March 2, 1946, in Little Rock, Ark.; son of Hugo H. (a professor) and Ruth (a librarian; maiden name, Cochrane) Culpepper; married Jacquelyn McClain (a teacher), June 24, 1967; children: Erin Lynn, Rodney Alan. *Education:* Baylor University, B.A. (cum laude), 1967; Southern Baptist Theological Seminary, M.Div., 1970; attended Goethe Institute, Brannenburg, West Germany, 1970; Duke University, Ph.D., 1974.

ADDRESSES: Office—Box 1762, Southern Baptist Theological Seminary, 2825 Lexington Rd., Louisville, Ky. 40280.

CAREER: Ordained Southern Baptist minister, 1968; pastor of Baptist church in Madison, Ind., 1968-70; Duke University, Durham, N.C., instructor in religion, 1971; Southern Baptist Theological Seminary, Louisville, Ky., assistant professor, 1974-80, associate professor of New Testament interpretation, 1980—. Visiting professor at Vanderbilt University, autumn, 1983.

MEMBER: National Association of Baptist Professors of Religion, Society of Biblical Literature, Studiorum Novi Testamenti Societas.

AWARDS, HONORS: Grant from Association of Theological Schools for research at Cambridge University, 1980-81.

WRITINGS:

The Johannine School, Scholars Press, 1975.
Anatomy of the Fourth Gospel: A Study in Literary Design, Fortress, 1983.
1, 2, 3 John, John Knox, in press.
Pentecost: Proclamation Three, Fortress, in press.

Contributor to *International Standard Bible Encyclopedia.* Contributor of more than fifty articles and reviews to magazines, including *Biblical Illustrator, Catholic Biblical Quarterly, Journal of Biblical Literature,* and *Interpretation.* Editor of *Review and Expositor,* 1982—.

SIDELIGHTS: R. Alan Culpepper told *CA:* "I am committed to pursuing the study of the Gospels in the context of theo-

logical education. William Stafford's statement rings true with my own experience: 'A writer is not so much someone who has something to say as he is someone who has found a process that will bring about new things he would not have thought of if he had not started to say them.'

"This is an exciting time for students of the New Testament because so many new directions for study are opening up and most of the 'assured results' from the work of earlier generations are now open to debate again. The intriguing mix of history, theology, and story in each of the Gospels is now becoming more apparent. I think that one of the significant discussions for the next few years will be how to relate recent studies of the Gospels as narrative literature to more traditional historical-critical concerns.

"My dissertation, *The Johannie School,* identified characteristics the Johannine community shared with other ancient philosophical and religious schools. And *Anatomy of the Fourth Gospel* shows that John is a coherent narrative, which makes skillful use of the narrator, point of view, characterization, irony, and symbolism.

"I grew up in Chile and Argentina, the son of Southern Baptist foreign missionaries. My wife and I spent the summer of 1970 studying German and traveling on the continent. Professional meetings have given me the opportunity for short trips to Europe, England, and Scandinavia; and I have led four tours to Egypt, Turkey, Israel, Jordan, and Greece.''

AVOCATIONAL INTERESTS: Travel, boating, fishing, racquetball, woodworking, personal computers.

*   *   *

CUNNINGHAM, J(ames) V(incent)   1911-1985

OBITUARY NOTICE—See index for *CA* sketch: Born August 23, 1911, in Cumberland, Md.; died of heart failure, March 30, 1985, in Waltham (one source says Marlboro), Mass. Educator, translator, poet, and editor and author of literary criticism. The founding chairman of the Brandeis University Department of English, Cunningham taught at Stanford University and at the universities of Hawaii, Chicago, and Virginia before beginning his association with Brandeis in 1952. He became professor emeritus in 1980. Cunningham was also a well-known poet, whose terse and witty style was praised by many critics. Nine collections of his verse have been published: they include *The Helmsman, Doctor Drink,* and *To What Strangers, What Welcome.* He also wrote such prose works as *In Quest of the Opal,* which is a commentary on the author's own poetry, and *Woe or Wonder,* a book-length essay that deals with Shakespeare's tragedies. In addition, Cunningham translated P. Nicole's *Essay on True and Apparent Beauty* . . . and edited several volumes of criticism.

OBITUARIES AND OTHER SOURCES:

BOOKS

Contemporary Literary Criticism, Gale, Volume 3, 1975, Volume 31, 1985.

PERIODICALS

Chicago Tribune, April 4, 1985.
Detroit Free Press, April 3, 1985.
New York Times, April 3, 1985.
Washington Post, April 5, 1985.

CUTT, W(illiam) Towrie   1898-1981

OBITUARY NOTICE—See index for *CA* sketch: Born January 26, 1898, in Orkney, Scotland; died August 25, 1981. Educator and author. Cutt, who was a teacher in Alberta, Canada, from 1928 to 1963, did not begin to write stories for children until he was in his seventies. His publications include *On the Trail of Long Tom, Message From Arkmae, Seven for the Sea, Carry My Bones Northwest,* the autobiography *Faraway World,* and with his wife, Margaret Nancy Cutt, *The Hogboon of Hell and Other Strange Orkney Tales.*

OBITUARIES AND OTHER SOURCES:

BOOKS

Twentieth-Century Children's Writers, 2nd edition, St. Martin's, 1983.
The Writers Directory: 1982-1984, Gale, 1981.

D

DABRINGHAUS, Erhard   1917-

PERSONAL: Surname is pronounced *Dob*-bring-house; born April 18, 1917, in Essen, Germany (now West Germany); immigrated to United States, 1930, naturalized citizen, 1933; son of Gustav (a self-employed engineer) and Bertha (a housewife; maiden name, Schulz) Dabringhaus; married Jeanne Marie Laber (a housewife), June 2, 1945; children: Shirley Dabringhaus Kjos, Denise Dabringhaus La Milza, Greta Dabringhaus Fleischer. *Education:* Miami University, Oxford, Ohio, B.A., 1939; Wayne (now Wayne State) University, M.A., 1953; University of Michigan, Ph.D., 1957.

ADDRESSES: Home—1280 South Renaud, Grosse Pointe Woods, Mich. 48236.

CAREER: Wayne State University, Detroit, Mich., instructor, 1954-63, assistant professor, 1963-78, associate professor of German language and cultural history, 1978-83, associate professor emeritus, 1983—. Commercial real estate salesman, 1957—. Civilian employee of U.S. Army, 1948. *Military service:* U.S. Army, 1942-46, in Military Intelligence, 1948-50; served in Germany and at Normandy; became major; received Bronze Star, five battle stars.

WRITINGS:

Klaus Barbie: The Shocking Story of How the U.S. Used This Nazi War Criminal as an Intelligence Agent, Acropolis Books, 1984.

Creator of record album and instruction manual "Let's Learn German," released by RCA Custom Records in 1963. Contributor to *University of Michigan Alumni* (magazine) and *Penthouse.*

WORK IN PROGRESS: War Bride (tentative title), for Acropolis Books, completion expected in 1985; *Argus* (tentative title), about a well-trained German shepherd, for Acropolis Books, completion expected in 1986.

SIDELIGHTS: Erhard Dabringhaus told *CA:* "I decided that the world should know that a well-known Nazi war criminal once worked as an informant for the American Army's Counter Intelligence Corps. I believe that a man who has committed murder should defend himself in a court of law. The circumstances surrounding Klaus Barbie are documented in my book as well as supported by the Ryan Report of the Justice De-

partment in August, 1983. In the year of the fortieth anniversary of V-E Day, I believe it is time to tell the truth.

"*War Bride* is an action-filled novel based on my own World War II courtship and ultimate marriage to my Belgian wife. It includes my experiences during the postwar period as a Counter Intelligence agent and a previously untold spy story during the Battle of the Bulge."

Dabringhaus conducts his research in Belgium, France, and Germany nearly every year.

BIOGRAPHICAL/CRITICAL SOURCES:

BOOKS

Bower, Tom, *Klaus Barbie: The Butcher of Lyon,* Pantheon, 1984.
Murphy, Brendan, *The Butcher of Lyon,* Empire Books, 1983.
Terkel, Studs, *The Good War,* Pantheon, 1984.

PERIODICALS

Detroit News, November 4, 1984.
Jewish News, November 9, 1984.

*   *   *

DALGLEISH, Oakley Hedley   1910-1963

OBITUARY NOTICE: Born in 1910 in New Liskeard, Ontario, Canada; died following a heart attack, August 16, 1963. Publishing executive and journalist. Editor and publisher of the Toronto *Globe and Mail* from 1957 until his death, Dalgleish began his affiliation with the newspaper in 1935. Prior to becoming its editor and publisher, he served the *Globe and Mail* as political writer, editorial writer, and editor in chief and assistant publisher. As head of the *Globe and Mail,* Dalgleish introduced a weekly world-wide edition of the paper, which is edited in Toronto but distributed by the London *Times,* and instituted the paper's "Report on Business" section.

OBITUARIES AND OTHER SOURCES:

BOOKS

Who Was Who in America, With World Notables, Volume IV: *1961-1968,* Marquis, 1968.

PERIODICALS

New York Times, August 18, 1963.

*   *   *

DALRYMPLE, Ian (Murray) 1903-

PERSONAL: Born August 26, 1903, in Johannesburg, South Africa; son of William (a mining company director) and Isabel (Rayner) Dalrymple; married Muriel Connochie, 1927 (marriage ended, 1937); married Joan Margaret Craig (an antique shop manager), June 3, 1939; children: (first marriage) Janet (Mrs. Michael John Eldon Swiney), Ian Sebastian William; (second marriage) Douglas Hugh Murray, Robert Gordon. *Education:* Trinity College, Cambridge, B.A., 1925. *Politics:* Conservative. *Religion:* Church of England.

ADDRESSES: Home—3 Beaulieu Close, Cambridge Park, East Twickenham, Middlesex TW1 2JR, England.

CAREER: Gainsborough Pictures and Gaumont-British Picture Corp., London, England, film editor, 1928-35; London Film Productions Ltd., London, screenwriter, 1936-38; Metro-Goldwyn-Mayer (MGM), London, screenwriter, 1938-39; Crown Film Unit of British Ministry of Information, London, executive producer, 1940-43; MGM, London, associate executive producer, 1943-46; Wessex Film Productions Ltd., London, founder, producer, and managing director, 1946-64. Producer of motion pictures, including "Fires Were Started," "Western Approaches," "Coastal Command," "Ferry Pilot," "Close Quarters," "Wavell's 30,000," "Target for Tonight," and "London Can Take It," all for the Crown Film Unit, 1940-43; producer of feature films and documentaries for Wessex, both for independent release and on commission from other companies, including "Esther Waters," "Family Portrait," "Chaucer's Tale," "What Is a Computer," "The Changing Face of Europe" (a series of six short films on European recovery), "The Bank of England at Work," "The Boy and the Pelican," "The Woman in the Hall," "Three Cases of Murder," "The Admirable Crichton," "A Cry From the Streets," "Raising a Riot," and "A Hill in Korea," 1946-64. Advisory producer to British Lion Film Corp. Ltd., 1952-54; films adviser to Argo Record Co., 1967-69. *Military service:* Civil Defense and Home Guard during World War II.

MEMBER: Royal Society of Arts (fellow), British Film Academy (chairman, 1957-58), British Film Producers Association (past member of executive council), Children's Film Foundation Ltd. (past director).

AWARDS, HONORS: Academy Award for best screenplay adapted from another medium from the Academy of Motion Picture Arts and Sciences for "Pygmalion" and Academy Award nomination for best screenplay adapted from another medium for "The Citadel," both 1938; "Pygmalion" and "The Citadel" named to the *New York Times*'s "Ten Best Films of the Year" list and "The Citadel" named the best motion picture of the year by the New York Film Critics, all 1938.

WRITINGS:

SCREENPLAYS

(With Frank Wead and Elizabeth Hill) "The Citadel" (based on the novel of the same title by Archibald Joseph Cronin), Metro-Goldwyn-Mayer (MGM), 1938.
"South Riding" (based on the novel of the same title by Winifred Holtby), London Film Productions, 1938.

(And director) "Storm in a Teacup" (based on the play "Storm Over Patsy" by Bruno Frank, as adapted from the German by James Bridle), United Artists, 1938.
(With Cecil Lewis and W. B. Lipscomb) "Pygmalion" (based on the play of the same title by George Bernard Shaw), MGM, 1938.
"Clouds Over Europe" (originally released as "Q Planes"), Columbia, 1939.
(With A. de Grunwald) "French Without Tears" (based on the play of the same title by Terence Rattigan), Paramount, 1939.
(With Jack Lee) "The Woman in the Hall" (based on the novel of the same title by Gladys Bronwyn Stern), Eagle Lion, 1948.
"The Wooden Horse," Wessex Film Productions, 1950.
(With Donald Bull) "Dear Mr. Prohack" (based on the novel *Mr. Prohack* by Arnold Bennett), Pentagon Pictures Corp., 1950.
"The Heart of the Matter" (based on the novel of the same title by Graham Greene), Associated Artists Productions, 1952.
(With Donald Wilson and Sidney Carroll) "Three Cases of Murder," Associated Artists Productions, 1955.
(With Hugh Perceval and James Matthews) "Raising a Riot" (based on the novel of the same title by Alfred Toombs), Continental Distributing, 1958.

Also author of screenplays "The Lion Has Wings," 1939, "Once a Jolly Swagman," 1946, "The Admirable Crichton" (based on the play of the same title by James Matthew Barrie), 1957, "A Cry From the Streets," 1958, "Lady in Distress" (originally released as "A Window in London"), Times Film Corp., "Action for Slander," "The Divorce of Lady X," and "A Hill in Korea."

SIDELIGHTS: In 1938 Ian Dalrymple earned two Academy Award nominations for screenplay adaptations. Although he was already an experienced film editor, this year marked his debut as a scriptwriter. Dalrymple and his co-authors won the Oscar for adapting George Bernard Shaw's play "Pygmalion" for the screen. The second nomination recognized the adaptation of A. J. Cronin's novel *The Citadel.* Frank S. Nugent of the *New York Times* credited the scriptwriters of the latter film with having "tightened and heightened [Cronin's] dramatic story" and with giving its characters "the necessary shadings and gradations lacking in the novel." He named both "The Citadel" and "Pygmalion" to the *Times*'s list of the ten best films of the year.

Nugent also commended Dalrymple's screenplay for another 1938 release, "South Riding." "The greatest tribute one can give any film edition of a book is to say that it has been faithful to its characters and their actions," he maintained. Characterizing the source for this script, Winifred Holtby's novel of the same title, as "essentially not screen material," the critic noted that Dalrymple "had to sacrifice a great deal" of the broad cross-section of Yorkshire life that it presents. Nevertheless, he felt that the film "still clings to the warm, human, vital frame of the novel."

Dalrymple debuted as a director in the same year with "Storm in a Teacup." According to Nugent, "the comedy has been delightfully played, scampers along like a pup under the joint direction of Victor Saville and Ian Dalrymple and has as flavorsome [a] dialogue . . . as we have heard this season."

Throughout his career Dalrymple continued to write and produce a wide variety of motion pictures. He formed Wessex

Film Productions in 1946 and made both documentaries and feature films for the company. For several of his screenplays he drew on novels and plays by Terence Rattigan, G. B. Stern, Arnold Bennett, J. M. Barrie, and Alfred Tombs, among others. One such film, the 1954 release "The Heart of the Matter," which Dalrymple wrote and produced, dramatized Graham Greene's best-selling tale of a devoted husband's anguish over his adulterous affair. Finding the film "provocative and disturbing," the reviewer for the *New York Times* noted: "The producers have given their story added color in filming most of it in Freetown, Sierra Leone. The sights, sound and natives make an exciting background to somber drama."

Often, however, Dalrymple's films kept closer to home in location and tone. *New York Times* critic Bosley Crowther on more than one occasion pointed out the distinctly British flavor of a Dalrymple film. He called "Dear Mr. Prohack," a 1950 release, "an unmistakably British film" and feared that "the humors of this effort were almost exclusively designed to capture the Britishers' fancy and will mainly be appreciated by them." "Three Cases of Murder," 1955, was a compendium of suspense tales which the same critic found "interesting in their virtuosity and cozily British in style." Frank S. Nugent had similarly noted that "The Citadel" has "the honest characterization typical of England's best films."

Reflecting on his long career, Dalrymple told *CA:* "My love of music helped me become a competent film cutter and editor. My literary interests aided my writing of screenplays. A general appreciation of art was a help in film production. I consider my education to have been a boon not merely for vocational ends but for understanding human beings and enjoying life from my early years to my present retirement—and senility!"

AVOCATIONAL INTERESTS: Reading history and biography, weeding.

BIOGRAPHICAL/CRITICAL SOURCES:

PERIODICALS

New York Times, March 22, 1938, August 2, 1938, November 4, 1938, January 1, 1939, January 24, 1949, July 15, 1950, November 19, 1954, March 16, 1955, May 8, 1957.

*   *   *

DALTON, Dennis (Gilmore) 1938-

PERSONAL: Born March 12, 1938, in Morristown, N.J.; son of Andrew J. and Emily (Snow) Dalton; married Sharron Louise Scheline (a professor), May 22, 1961; children: Kevin Andrew, Shaun Michael. *Education:* Rutgers University, B.A., 1960; University of Chicago, M.A., 1962; University of London, Ph.D., 1965.

ADDRESSES: Home—105 Thompson St., Apt. 12, New York, N.Y. 10012. *Office*—Department of Political Science, Barnard College, Columbia University, 606 West 120th St., New York, N.Y. 10027.

CAREER: Columbia University, Barnard College, New York, N.Y., assistant professor, 1969-71, associate professor, 1971-78, professor of political science, 1978—. Lecturer at London School of Oriental and African Studies, London, England, 1965-69.

AWARDS, HONORS: Senior fellow of American Institute of Indian Studies, 1975.

WRITINGS:

The Indian Idea of Freedom, Academic Press (Delhi, India), 1982.
(Editor with A. Jeyaratnam Wilson) *The States of South Asia: A Problem of National Integration,* University Press of Hawaii, 1983.

Contributor of articles on Indian political thought to journals.

WORK IN PROGRESS: A book on the thought and leadership of Mahatma Gandhi, focusing on his "Salt March" of 1930, publication expected in 1986.

SIDELIGHTS: Dennis Dalton told *CA:* "For the last twenty-five years, my research has focused on the political thought and leadership of Mohandas K. Gandhi. The research has convinced me of the profound significance of nonviolent action. I have visited India on four occasions since 1960 to research Gandhi's life and ideas, interview scores of his associates, and examine written materials relating to his civil disobedience campaigns and other activities. His theory and practice of nonviolence, I believe, have both current and universal implications."

*   *   *

DALY, Kathleen N(orah)

BRIEF ENTRY: Born in London, England. Editor and author. Daly received a master's degree from the University of Glasgow in 1951 and became a children's book editor for the London publishing firm of Blackie & Son the following year. In 1953 she accepted a post editing children's books for Artists & Writers Press in New York City. Daly is also the author of numerous books for children, including *Animal Stamps* (Simon & Schuster, 1955), *Ladybug, Ladybug* (American Heritage Press, 1969), *A Child's Book of Animals* (Doubleday, 1975), *Hide and Defend* (Golden Press, 1977), and *Body Words: A Dictionary of the Human Body, How It Works, and Some of the Things That Affect It* (Doubleday, 1980). In addition, she has adapted children's stories, including those based on the Raggedy Ann and Andy and the Strawberry Shortcake characters.

BIOGRAPHICAL/CRITICAL SOURCES:

BOOKS

Authors of Books for Young People, 2nd edition supplement, Scarecrow, 1979.
Who's Who of American Women, Marquis, 1958.

*   *   *

d'AMBOISE, Christopher 1960-

PERSONAL: Born February 4, 1960, in New York, N.Y.; son of Jacques J. d'Amboise (a dancer) and Carolyn George (a dancer). *Education:* Attended School of American Ballet, 1967-78.

ADDRESSES: Home—244 West 71st St., New York, N.Y. 10023. *Office*—c/o Jacques d'Amboise, National Dance Institute, 244 West 71st St., New York, N.Y. 10023. *Agent*—Richard Boehm Agency, 737 Park Ave., New York, N.Y. 10021.

CAREER: New York City Ballet, New York, N.Y., dancer, appearances include principal roles in "Stars and Stripes," "Four Temperaments," "Mozartiana," "Tango," "Interplay,'' ''Fancy Free,'' ''Dancers at a Gathering,'' ''Piano Pieces,'' and ''The Gershwin Concerto,'' 1978-83; stage dancer appearing in ''On Your Toes,'' 1983—.

WRITINGS:

Leap Year: A Year in the Life of a Dancer, photographs by mother, Carolyn George, Doubleday, 1982.

WORK IN PROGRESS: Shifting Respects, a novel.

SIDELIGHTS: In his journal *Leap Year* Christopher d'Amboise recounts his first year with the New York City Ballet. Just eighteen years old and newly graduated from high school when he joined the ballet company, the young dancer shares anecdotes about his family (his father is Jacques d'Amboise, thirty-year veteran of the New York City Ballet), the company, and his life as a performer. Richard Christiansen, writing in the *Chicago Tribune Book World*, called *Leap Year* ''an engrossing memoir.'' D'Amboise ''is forthright and outgoing, an approach especially salubrious when compared with the often pretentious, reserved and genteel style of so much writing about the dance world,'' the critic continued. ''This is a refreshing human document, as well as a revealing look at a talented dancer working into the complexities of a major dance company.''

Not so enthusiastic was dance expert Dale Harris, who noted in the *New York Times Book Review* that—because of d'Amboise's great youth—his journal, for the most part, ''consists of the stray thoughts of a very young man on subjects like life, death, adolescence, friendship, sex, love, alienation, loneliness and, of course, sincerity—in other words, all the large and overfamiliar questions about which the immature believe they have such interesting things to say.'' Jennifer Dunning agreed in a *New York Times* critique, remarking that while ''lively and touching at it best,'' the book frequently takes a ''premature leap into print.'' ''But despite its adolescent bromides,'' the critic acknowledged, '''Leap Year' does create a striking picture of the loneliness and anguish dancers seem so easily to fall into early in their careers in the exacting, competitive world of the big ballet company.''

D'Amboise told *CA:* ''I was born into the life of the New York City Ballet; George Balanchine seemed almost a grandfather. Yet I found that the strict and limited world of the ballet dancer was not enough. I still wanted to read, to write, to see theatre, to appreciate women. So in 1983 I chose to leave behind a bright career in the New York City Ballet and have since turned to the Broadway stage, where one can still be a dancer but have enough free time to engage in many other interests.''

MEDIA ADAPTATIONS: Leap Year is being considered for adaptation as a feature film.

BIOGRAPHICAL/CRITICAL SOURCES:

PERIODICALS

Chicago Tribune Book World, December 5, 1982.
New York Times, March 3, 1983.
New York Times Book Review, January 2, 1983.

*   *   *

DANZIGER, Paula 1944-

PERSONAL: Born August 18, 1944, in Washington, D.C.

ADDRESSES: Home—New York, N.Y., and Woodstock, N.Y.

CAREER: Writer. Worked as junior high school teacher.

AWARDS, HONORS: Award from New Jersey Institute of Technology and nomination for California Young Reader Medal, both 1976, both for *The Cat Ate My Gymsuit;* book-of-the-year award from Child Study Association, 1978, and nominations for California Young Reader Medal, 1981, and Arizona Young Reader Award, 1983, all for *The Pistachio Prescription;* award from New Jersey Institute of Technology, 1980, and Land of Enchantment Book Award from New Mexico Library Association, 1982, both for *Can You Sue Your Parents for Malpractice?;* Read-A-Thon Author of the Year Award from Multiple Sclerosis Society, and Parents Choice Award, both 1982, both for *The Divorce Express.*

WRITINGS:

YOUNG ADULT NOVELS

The Cat Ate My Gymsuit, Delacorte, 1974.
The Pistachio Prescription, Delacorte, 1978.
Can You Sue Your Parents for Malpractice?, Delacorte, 1979.
There's a Bat in Bunk Five, Delacorte, 1980.
The Divorce Express, Delacorte, 1982.
It's an Aardvark Eat Turtle World, Delacorte, 1985.

SIDELIGHTS: Paula Danziger commented: ''I began to write during graduate school. I felt very out of control because of an accident (the car I was in was hit head-on by a drunk driver). The last time I felt that way was when I was a kid. When you're a kid, everyone seems to be in charge, to have the right to tell you what to do, how to feel. In hospitals and in schools it seemed to be the same way. So I wanted to confront all of that.

''I had taken a course in creative writing. I had also taken a course in literature for adolescents—an excellent course that taught me there was more to the field than 'Barbie gets acne, triumphs over it to become homecoming queen and the girlfriend of the captain of the football team.' Since I really missed teaching my eighth graders (I was permanent sub. Full time. German classes. Boys' health. Everything.) I decided to write a book to talk to them about survival—learning to like oneself, dealing with school systems, and being able to celebrate one's own uniqueness. The result was *The Cat Ate My Gymsuit.*

''Next came the desire to deal with families that can't make it as a unit, hypochondria, addiction to pistachio nuts, and being able to accept yourself as a winner: *The Pistachio Prescription*. My third book, *Can You Sue Your Parents for Malpractice?*, is about not doing malpractice on oneself, trying to see parents as separate human beings, and the need to do what is right for you.

''So here I am a full-time writer, a 'grown-up' who chooses to write about kids. I've made this choice because I think that kids and adults share a lot of the same feelings and thoughts, that we have to go through a lot of similar situations.''

BIOGRAPHICAL/CRITICAL SOURCES:

BOOKS

Contemporary Literary Criticism, Volume 21, Gale, 1982.

PERIODICALS

New Yorker, December 3, 1979.
New York Times Book Review, March 18, 1979, June 17, 1979, December 23, 1980.
Washington Post Book World, May 12, 1985.

DAPPING, William Osborne   1880-1969

OBITUARY NOTICE: Born June 12, 1880, in New York, N.Y.; died August 1, 1969; buried in Fort Hill Cemetery, Auburn, N.Y. Radio and newspaper executive and journalist. After graduating from Harvard University, where he had worked as a reporter for the *Harvard Crimson* student paper under the editorship of Franklin D. Roosevelt, Dapping went on to become an award-winning reporter for the *Auburn Citizen-Advertiser* in New York. He won both the Pulitzer Prize and an award from the Associated Press in 1930 for his coverage of an Auburn State Prison riot that left nine people dead. Dapping remained with the *Citizen-Advertiser* until his retirement in 1960, serving variously as editorial writer, editor, managing editor, secretary, and treasurer of the newspaper. In 1938 he assumed additional responsibilities as president of WMBO, a radio station affiliated with the *Citizen-Advertiser*. He also headed various professional and conservationist organizations during his lifetime, including the New York State Group of the Associated Press, the Associated Dailies of New York, and the Conservation Committee of the Finger Lakes Association.

OBITUARIES AND OTHER SOURCES:

BOOKS

Who Was Who in America, With World Notables, Volume V: *1969-1973,* Marquis, 1973.
Who Was Who in Journalism, 1925-1928, Gale, 1978.

PERIODICALS

New York Times, August 2, 1969.

*   *   *

DARACK, Arthur J.   1918-

PERSONAL: Born January 1, 1918, in Royal Oak, Mich.; son of Edward Charles and Sonia (Resnikov) Darack; married Jean Claire Puttmyer, May 28, 1942; children: Glenn Arthur, Brenda Lee. *Education:* Cincinnati Conservatory, Mus.M., 1949; Indiana University—Bloomington, Ph.D., 1951.

ADDRESSES: Home and office—9018 Sleeping Bear Rd., Skokie, Ill. 60076. *Agent*—Saul Cohen, 11 Mabro Drive, Denville, N.J. 07834.

CAREER: Cincinnati Enquirer, Cincinnati, Ohio, music editor, 1951-61, feature writer and author of column "Offbeat," 1961-62, book and art editor, 1962-67; *Encyclopaedia Britannica,* Chicago, Ill., associate editor, 1967-70; senior editor of *Actual Specifying Engineering,* 1971—. Adjunct associate professor at University of Cincinnati. President of Consumer Group, Inc., 1978—. *Military service:* U.S. Army, 1941-45.

MEMBER: Pi Kappa Lambda.

WRITINGS:

Repair Your Own Car for Pennies: It's Easy, Consumers Digest, 1973, 3rd edition, 1976.
Buying Guide to 1974 Cars, Consumers Digest, 1974.
The Eat Right and Live Longer Cookbook, Consumers Digest, 1975.
Which Foods Are Best for You?: Your Food Nutrition Guide, Consumers Digest, 1974.
Outdoor Power Equipment: How It Works, How to Fix It, Stein & Day, 1977.

The Consumers Digest Automobile Repair Book, McGraw, 1978.
(With wife, Jean P. Darack, and Sander Goodman) *The Great Eating, Great Dieting Cookbook,* Crowell, 1978.
The Guide to Home Appliance Repair, McGraw, 1979.
Playboy's Book of Sports Car Repair, Playboy Press, 1980.
Used Cars: How to Avoid Highway Robbery, Prentice-Hall, 1983.
How to Repair and Care for Small Home Appliances, Prentice-Hall, 1983.

Author of "Buy Right," a column for the Des Moines *Register* and the Des Moines *Tribune,* 1977-81, and "The Darack Column" for *Money Letter,* 1979-84. Contributor to *Saturday Review.* Co-founder and editor of *Dimension* magazine, 1963-65; editor of *Consumers Digest,* 1972-78; contributing editor of *Money Letter,* 1979—.

WORK IN PROGRESS: Two novels about Chicago; a book on car repair for women; a book on investments.

SIDELIGHTS: Arthur J. Darack told *CA:* "My review on consumer-oriented subjects is that the average person finds the cards stacked against informed buying decisions—not because the marketplace is deceptive but because it is difficult. Yet buying decisions control the quality of life, as do investment decisions. Investments ultimately require as much art as science. My consumer writing has been based on digging out the facts and presenting them in a readable, easily understood fashion.

"Journalism became my field and remains so, but I find today's journalism vastly different from what it was when I began in 1951. Investigative journalism, as it applies to consumer subjects, can be very helpful if it goes to the basics of the subject. If investigative journalism is used to support an existing point of view, as too often is the case, it becomes propaganda. In the old days, the propaganda came from the right. Today it comes from the left, but I do not see this as an advance."

AVOCATIONAL INTERESTS: The fine arts; "tinkering" with automobiles.

*   *   *

DARGO, George   1935-

PERSONAL: Born July 22, 1935, in New York, N.Y.; son of Nathan and Dora (Benowitz) Dargo; married Lois Chasin, 1968; children: Jessica Lynn and Stephen Nathan. *Education:* Columbia University, B.A., 1957, M.A., 1958, Ph.D., 1970; Northeastern University, J.D., 1981.

ADDRESSES: Office—New England School of Law, 154 Stuart St., Boston, Mass. 02116.

CAREER: High school social studies teacher in New York City, 1958-69; Hunter College of the City University of New York, New York City, adjunct assistant professor of U.S. history, 1969-71; City College of the City University of New York, New York City, assistant professor of history, 1971-76; University of Massachusetts at Boston, visiting lecturer in history, 1977-78; College of the Holy Cross, Worcester, Mass., visiting assistant professor of history, 1978-79; U.S. District Court, Boston, Mass., law clerk, 1981-82; attorney in private practice, 1982-83; New England School of Law, Boston, Mass., associate professor of law, 1983—. Fellow at Harvard University, 1976-77. Representative at Brookline Town Meeting, 1981—. *Military service:* U.S. Army Reserve, 1959-65.

MEMBER: American Bar Association, Law and Society Association, Massachusetts Bar Association.

AWARDS, HONORS: Fellow of American Council of Learned Societies and Social Science Research Council, 1976-77; grant from American Bar Foundation, 1977-78.

WRITINGS:

Roots of the Republic: A New Perspective on Early American Constitutionalism, Praeger, 1974.
Jefferson's Louisiana: Politics and the Clash of Legal Traditions, Harvard University Press, 1975.
Law in the New Republic, Knopf, 1983.

WORK IN PROGRESS: Research in constitutional history.

*   *   *

DASSAULT, Marcel (Bloch)   1892-

BRIEF ENTRY: Name originally Marcel Bloch; born January 22, 1892, in Paris, France. French aircraft designer, industrialist, banker, editor, and author. Dassault, who is best known as the designer of the Mystere and Mirage series of jet airplanes, worked on military aircraft as early as World War I. He spent the World War II-years alternately in hiding and in the concentration camp at Buchenwald, then emerged after the war to rebuild old factories and establish new aircraft plants throughout France. By the early 1950's the designer's own aeronautics firm was producing Europe's first supersonic planes, the French Mysteres. The first of his Mirage planes followed in 1956.

Although regarded as the most important, aeronautics is only one of Dassault's many business activities. In 1957 he created the weekly magazine *Jours de France,* and he has also served as the editor of other periodicals, including *Oise Liberee.* In addition, Dassault has been involved in real estate and banking enterprises and served his government as both a senator and a deputy. Among his numerous awards are the Grand Croix of the French Legion of Honor, the Croix de guerre, and the Medaille de l'aeronautique. He wrote *The Talisman: The Autobiography of Marcel Dassault, Creator of the Mirage Jet* (Arlington House, 1971). *Address:* 4 place de la Porte-de-Passy, 75016 Paris, France; and Assemblee Nationale, 75355 Paris, France.

BIOGRAPHICAL/CRITICAL SOURCES:

BOOKS

Current Biography, Wilson, 1970.

*   *   *

DAVID, Stephen M(ark)   1934-1985

OBITUARY NOTICE: See index for *CA* sketch: Born June 18, 1934, in Brooklyn, N.Y.; died of cancer, April 9, 1985, in New York, N.Y. Political scientist, educator, and author. David, a specialist on urban politics, began teaching at Fordham University in 1965. Included among his publications are *Race and Politics in New York City; Urban Riots: Violence and Social Change; Alienation: Plight of Modern Man; History of the Narcotic Addiction Political Arena in New York: An Initial Exploration; Urban Politics and Policy: The City in Crisis;* and *Urban Problems and Public Policy.* He also wrote numerous articles and book reviews and contributed chapters to several books on urban politics.

OBITUARIES AND OTHER SOURCES:

BOOKS

Who's Who in the East, 19th edition, Marquis, 1983.

PERIODICALS

New York Times, April 10, 1985.

*   *   *

DAVIDS, Bob
   See DAVIDS, L(eonard) Robert

*   *   *

DAVIDS, L(eonard) Robert   1926-
   (Bob Davids)

PERSONAL: Born March 19, 1926, in Kanawha, Iowa; son of James and Katie (Bakker) Davids; married Yvonne Revier (a homemaker), June 13, 1953; children: Roberta Davids Hefner. *Education:* University of Missouri—Columbia, B.J., 1949, M.A., 1951; Georgetown University, Ph.D., 1961. *Religion:* Christian Reformed.

ADDRESSES: Home—4424 Chesapeake St. N.W., Washington, D.C. 20016.

CAREER: Department of Defense, Public Information Office, Washington, D.C., assistant night chief for press branch, 1951-52; Department of the Navy, Washington, D.C., associated with *Navy Civil Engineer Corps Bulletin* as assistant editor, 1952-54, editor, 1954-58; Atomic Energy Commission (AEC), Washington, D.C., technical reports officer, 1958-62, program plans analyst, 1962-65, management reports officer and editor of AEC *Activity Digest,* 1965-68, special assignments officer, 1969-72, speechwriter for office of information services, 1972-75; Energy Research and Development Administration, Washington, D.C., chief of special projects branch, 1975-77; Department of Energy, Washington, D.C., special events coordinator, 1977-81; free-lance writer-historian, 1981—.

Congressional Fellow to U.S. Congress, 1968-69. Society for American Baseball Research (SABR), founder, 1971, administrative worker, 1971-84, publisher and editor, under name Bob Davids, of *Baseball Briefs* (newsletter), 1971-74, editor of SABR publications, including the annual *Baseball Research Journal,* 1972-83. Commissioner of Church Fellowship Softball League, 1961-84. *Military service:* U.S. Army Air Forces, 1944-46; served on Okinawa and in the Philippines.

MEMBER: Society for American Baseball Research (founder; member of board of directors; president, 1971-72, 1975-76, 1982-84), Phi Alpha Theta.

AWARDS, HONORS: U.S. Congressional fellow, 1968-69; award from Society for American Baseball Research, 1981.

WRITINGS:

EDITOR

This Date in Baseball History, Society for American Baseball Research, 1976.
Minor League Baseball Stars, Society for American Baseball Research, 1978.
Great Hitting Pitchers, Society for American Baseball Research, 1979.
Baseball Historical Review, Society for American Baseball Research, 1981.

Insider's Baseball, Scribner, 1983.

Contributor to magazines, including *Sporting News* and *Roll Call.*

WORK IN PROGRESS: Celebrated Centenarians, about well-known men and women who attained the age of one hundred; a book tentatively titled *They Played the Game*, publication expected in 1987; research on prominent U.S. military men who did not attend service academies.

SIDELIGHTS: L. Robert Davids told *CA:* "In the 1960's I wrote some thirty byline articles on congressional history for *Roll Call* magazine, and they have become the primary basis for a book on Congress. To be published during the one-hundredth Congress, which begins in 1987, *They Played the Game* (working title) is not a book on legislative history but deals with the individuals who 'played the game' over the last two hundred years. It concerns members of Congress who served from more than one state (one senator served from three states); members with military backgrounds (one senator/colonel was killed on active duty during the Civil War); members who changed parties; members who fought duels; members who served the longest; the youngest and the oldest members; the first women members, black members, and foreign-born members; brothers and fathers and sons who served at the same time; presidential succession as it pertains to Congress; and many other unusual aspects not published before.

"I would like to do a biography of General Frederick Funston, a soldier who had not attended a military academy, who always seemed to show up where things happened. He was a volunteer in the Spanish-American war who was invaluable in Cuba because of previous experience there. He went to the Philippines where he captured Aguinaldo, the revolutionary leader. He was promoted to brigadier general in 1901, when he was thirty-six years old and had only three years' experience. As a local military leader he took charge of affairs at the time of the San Francisco earthquake in 1906. He was commanding in Texas when the United States went into Mexico in 1914-15. And he was a leading candidate to head the U.S. expeditionary force in Europe when he died suddenly in 1917. Funston is an example of the forgotten person I would like to publicize—someone who made a contribution, an interesting one in his case, but who has been overlooked."

*   *   *

DAVIDSON, Alice Joyce   1932-

PERSONAL: Born September 2, 1932, in Cincinnati, Ohio; daughter of David (a merchant) and Yetta (a merchant; maiden name, Hymon) Citron; married Marvin Davidson (in sales), September 6, 1953; children: Edward Lewis, Carol Sue Davidson Kessler. *Education:* Attended University of Cincinnati, 1951-53.

ADDRESSES: Home—6315 Elbrook Ave., Cincinnati, Ohio 45237. *Agent*—Mary Jane Ross, 85 Sunset Lane, Tenafly, N.J. 07670.

CAREER: Gibson Greeting Cards, Cincinnati, Ohio, editor, 1963-65; free-lance writer for advertising agencies and greeting card companies, 1965-67; WXIX-TV, Cincinnati, continuity director, 1967-69; WCPO-TV, Cincinnati, promotion manager, 1969-72; Gibson Greeting Cards, 1972-81, began as editorial director, became inspirational manager.

WRITINGS:

BOOKS OF POEMS

A Cat Called Cindy (for children), Whitman Publishing, 1981.
Because I Love You, Fleming Revell, 1982.
Reflections of Love, Fleming Revell, 1983.
Loving One Another, Fleming Revell, 1984.

"ALICE IN BIBLELAND" SERIES; FOR CHILDREN

The Story of Creation, C. R. Gibson, 1984.
Noah and the Ark, C. R. Gibson, 1984.
The Story of Jonah, C. R. Gibson, 1984.
Psalms and Proverbs for You, C. R. Gibson, 1984.
David and Goliath, C. R. Gibson, 1985.
The Baby Moses, C. R. Gibson, 1985.
Daniel in the Lion's Den, C. R. Gibson, 1985.
The Story of the Loaves and Fishes, C. R. Gibson, 1985.
The Story of the Baby Jesus, C. R. Gibson, 1985.
Monkeys Never Say Please, Beware When Elephants Sneeze, C. R. Gibson, in press.
Daniel in the Lion's Den, C. R. Gibson, in press.
The Prodigal Son, C. R. Gibson, in press.
Prayers and Graces, C. R. Gibson, in press.
The Teachings of Jesus, C. R. Gibson, in press.

OTHER

Author of television stories for children. Creator of greeting cards, calendars, and gift books.

WORK IN PROGRESS: Additional books in the "Alice in Bibleland" series, for C. R. Gibson.

SIDELIGHTS: Alice Joyce Davidson told *CA:* "I feel writers have a responsibility to their readers. Our words can influence and help shape lives—and shape the world. In my poet's mind I visualize a world of peace, where the common denominator is love. With my 'Alice in Bibleland' series I wanted to reach the unaffiliated, as well as the affiliated, of all denominations. By teaching our children moral values—the values taught in the Bible—perhaps the time will come when greed, fear, and hate are replaced by hope, love, and brotherhood."

BIOGRAPHICAL/CRITICAL SOURCES:

PERIODICALS

Bookstore Journal, September, 1984.

*   *   *

DAVIES, Stanley Powell   1892-1985

OBITUARY NOTICE: Born June 22, 1892, in Philadelphia, Pa.; died following a brief illness, April 5, 1985, in Tarrytown, N.Y. Welfare advocate, social worker, and author. Davies devoted his career to improving the social welfare and mental health programs for New York City's poor, mentally ill, and mentally handicapped residents. He was perhaps best known as the director of the influential New York Community Service Society. He served in that capacity from 1939 until his 1958 retirement, at which time then President of the United States Dwight D. Eisenhower commented: "His devotion to the healthy concept of family life will have an enduring effect on social workers throughout the land."

Prior to directing the Community Service Society Davies wrote the book *Social Control of the Mentally Deficient* and served as head of the New York State Committee on Mental Hygiene for four years, as associate secretary of the State Charities Aid

Association for nearly ten years, and as general director of New York City's Charity Organization Society from 1933 until 1939. He later served as deputy planning director for the New York State Department of Mental Hygiene. Among his other writings are *The Mentally Retarded in Society,* with Katharine G. Ecob, and *Toward Community Mental Health.*

OBITUARIES AND OTHER SOURCES:

BOOKS

Who's Who in America, 39th edition, Marquis, 1976.

PERIODICALS

New York Times, April 14, 1985.

*   *   *

DAVIES, Thomas   1941-
(Tom Davies)

PERSONAL: Born April 10, 1941, in Pontypridd, Wales; son of Jack (a steelworker) and Phyllis (a homemaker; maiden name, Ford) Davies; married Liz Evans (a journalist), March 4, 1967; children: Julian, Steffan, Nathan. *Education:* University College, Cardiff, B.A. (with honors), 1963.

ADDRESSES: Home—Middlesex, England. *Agent*—Elaine Greene, 16 Newington Green, London N16 9PU, England.

CAREER: Worked at odd jobs, including sailing as a merchant seaman on ships to Australia and Africa; drove a bus through Europe and India; served as a social worker on the lower east side of New York; associated with the British Voluntary Services Overseas as a teacher in Indonesia; owner of a coal yard in Penarth, Wales; host of talk show on Harlech Television, Wales; journalist with *Western Mail* in Cardiff, Wales; reporter for British newspapers, including *Sunday Telegraph* and *Sunday Times,* and served for two years as diarist/Pendennis for *The Observer;* full-time writer.

WRITINGS:

UNDER NAME TOM DAVIES

Merlyn the Magician and the Pacific Coast Highway, New English Library, 1982.
Electric Harvest, New English Library, 1984.
Stained Glass Hours: A Modern Pilgrimage, New English Library, 1985.
One Winter of the Holy Spirit, Macdonalds, 1985.

WORK IN PROGRESS: Pick, Rock, Bolt, and Nut, a novel, set during the miner's strike of 1948, which also attempts to tell the story of modern Wales.

SIDELIGHTS: In *Merlyn the Magician and the Pacific Coast Highway,* Tom Davies recounts his bicycle adventures in Europe, the Far East, and North America, sharing his spiritual insights as well as his travel observations. Reviewer Alastair Sutherland noted in the *Listener* that "the bicycle gives a distinctive approach to Davies's experience of cities" and that neither illustrations nor photographs could add to "what the writer has seen. . . . He is inside his travel, and not only writing from outside." The critic also observed that while Davies's frequent condemnations of the corrupt, motorized modern world are not "endearing," his descriptions and comments on bicycling "are so good that the book cannot be ignored by anyone interested in the literature of bikes. . . . Every time he returns to bikes, Tom Davies is enjoyable, and imparts the *joie de vivre* of his travels."

Davies, who was the subject of a 1984 television documentary, "Visions of a Media Man," told *CA:* "All my work is of a religious nature—I want to explore the mind of God and his relevance to the modern world. My work is committed to attacking the modern writer who, I believe, with his persistent search for violence, viciousness, perversion, and cruelty has abandoned the God of his forefathers and is actively attacking and destroying our world."

BIOGRAPHICAL/CRITICAL SOURCES:

PERIODICALS

Listener, February 3, 1983.
Times (London), January 13, 1982, September 13, 1984.

*   *   *

DAVIES, Tom
See DAVIES, Thomas

*   *   *

DAVIS, Frederick C(lyde)   1902-1977
(Murdo Coombs, Stephen Ransome, Curtis Steele)

OBITUARY NOTICE: Born June 2, 1902, in St. Joseph, Mo.; died in 1977. Author of novels and short stories involving murder, mystery, and suspense. During the 1930's, 1940's, and 1950's Davis contributed hundreds of stories to such pulp magazines as *Dime Detective, Black Mask, Detective Tales,* and *Dime Mystery.* Some of the best known of these stories are those comprising a detective casebook series for *Dime Detective* featuring Doctor Carter Cole as their main character. Among Davis's longer works are sixteen novels under his own name, including a series of books concerning Professor Cyrus Hatch and his adventures, several books featuring detective partners Schyler Cole and Luke Speare, and two non-serial novels titled *Deep Lay the Dead* and *High Heel Homicide.* Davis also wrote one novel, *A Moment of Need,* under the pseudonym Murdo Coombs and more than twenty thrillers for the detective series "Secret Operator No. Five" under the name Curtis Steele. Davis's most successful pseudonym was Stephen Ransome, a name he used for nearly forty years and under which he wrote more than twenty mystery novels, including *The Shroud Off Her Back, The Unspeakable,* and *One-Man Jury.*

OBITUARIES AND OTHER SOURCES:

BOOKS

American Authors and Books: 1640 to the Present Day, 3rd revised edition, Crown, 1962.
Twentieth-Century Crime and Mystery Writers, St. Martin's, 1982.

*   *   *

DAVIS, Kenneth Culp   1908-

BRIEF ENTRY: December 19, 1908, in Leeton, Mo. American attorney, educator, and author. Davis became a professor of law at the University of San Diego in 1976. His previous posts were at West Virginia University, the University of Texas at Austin, the University of Minnesota—Twin Cities, and the University of Chicago, where he served as John P. Wilson Professor of Law from 1961 to 1976. His book *Discretionary Justice: A Preliminary Inquiry* (Louisiana State University Press, 1969) argues for increasing administrative controls at all levels of the judicial process to prevent selective enforcement of the law. This book was followed by *Police Discretion* (West, 1975) and *Discretionary Justice in Europe and America* (University of Illinois Press, 1976). *Address:* 2480 Rue Denise, La Jolla, Calif. 92037; and Department of Law, University of San Diego, Alcala Park, San Diego, Calif. 92110.

BIOGRAPHICAL/CRITICAL SOURCES:

BOOKS

Directory of American Scholars, Volume IV: *Philosophy, Religion, and Law,* 8th edition, Bowker, 1982.

PERIODICALS

Virginia Quarterly Review, summer, 1969, winter, 1977.

*   *   *

DAVIS, Rupert (Charles) Hart
    See HART-DAVIS, Rupert (Charles)

*   *   *

de ARAGON, Ray John   1946-

PERSONAL: Born January 19, 1946, in Las Vegas, N.M.; son of Maximo (in business) and Cloefas (a homemaker; maiden name, Sanchez) de Aragon; married Rose Maria Calles (an editor and artist), December 1, 1972; children: Rosalia, Lucia, Ramon, Linda. *Religion:* Roman Catholic. *Education:* University of Albuquerque, B.S. (secondary education), 1972, B.S. (elementary education; cum laude), 1973.

ADDRESSES: Home—2213 Hot Springs Blvd., Las Vegas, N.M. 87701. *Office*—West Las Vegas Schools, Las Vegas, N.M. 87701. *Agent*—Scott Meredith Literary Agency, 845 Third Ave., New York, N.Y. 10022.

CAREER: Patio Market Enterprises, Albuquerque, N.M., plant supervisor, 1966-67; Washington Junior High, Albuquerque, Spanish teacher, 1972-73; West Las Vegas Schools, Las Vegas, N.M., media specialist, 1973-74, reading specialist, 1974-80, art coordinator, 1980—. University of Albuquerque, chairman of programming committee for student affairs and activities director, 1971-72, and cultural consultant to the Multicultural Enrichment Program, 1973-73; artist-in-schools coordinator for New Mexico Arts Division, 1981—; literary chairman of Albuquerque Feria Artesana Arts Council, 1983—. Lecturer and public speaker. Summer lecturer, Millicent Rogers and Harwood Foundation, Taos, New Mexico; lecturer and consultant for New Mexico Humanities Council. Member of board of directors of the Very Special Arts Festival for the Handicapped. President of Rio Grande Community Credit Union, 1972-73. *Military service:* Air National Guard of the United States, 1966-68. U.S. Air Force, 1968-70; became staff sergeant.

MEMBER: National Education Association, Associacion de Lenguas y Culturas Hispanicas (president, 1972-73), Western Writers of America, Rio Grande Writers Association, P.E.N., Las Vegas Associated Galleries.

AWARDS, HONORS: Blue Feather Press Award for history, 1978, for *Padre Martinez and Bishop Lamy;* International Literary Award from Pan-American Publishing, 1980, for *The Legend of La Llorona;* New Mexico Governor's Award nominee for "Excellence in the Arts—Literature," 1984.

WRITINGS:

(Translator) *Memorias de Padre Martinez* (title means "Recollections of Father Martinez"), Lightening Tree, 1978.
Padre Martinez and Bishop Lamy, Pan-American Publishing, 1978, revised edition published as *Grey Eminence of Taos,* 1984.
City of Candy and Streets of Ice Cream (juvenile), illustrations by wife, Rose Maria Calles de Aragon, Pan-American Publishing, 1979.
The Legend of La Llorona, Pan-American Publishing, 1980.
The Great Lovers, Pan-American Publishing, 1983.
Hymns of Passion, Pan-American Publishing, 1983.
Santeros and Curanderas, Pan-American Publishing, 1983.
Fright on Halloween Night (juvenile fantasy), Pan-American Publishing, 1984.
The Way of the Witch (folklore), Pan-American Publishing, 1985.
Dodo the Bird (juvenile fantasy), Pan-American Publishing, 1985.
Messalina (historical romance), Pan-American Publishing, in press.
The Seance (historical novel), Pan-American Publishing, in press.

Contributor to periodicals, including *New Mexico Magazine* and *La Luz* (magazine). Columnist for *El Sol de Nuevo Mexico;* El Hispano and historical features writer for *Mora County Star.*

WORK IN PROGRESS: Two books of short stories, *Beyond Man's Powers,* publication by Pan-American Publishing expected in 1987, and *Tales of the Undead,* publication by Pan-American Publishing expected in 1987.

SIDELIGHTS: A Las Vegas, New Mexico, native who writes frequently on northern New Mexico history and traditions, Ray John de Aragon first captured the attention of the reading public with his book *Padre Martinez and Bishop Lamy.* A historical account of the religious controversy between a priest and his bishop, the book challenges Willa Cather's account of the classic struggle—favoring Lamy—in her novel *Death Comes for the Archbishop. Padre Martinez and Bishop Lamy* was written, according to the author, in order to set the record straight.

As a youth, de Aragon heard legends of Padre Martinez from Taos that proclaimed him "El Conciliador" (the Unifier) and lauded his good works—which included establishing a coeducational school, a seminary, and the first newspaper in New Mexico. Later, reading Cather's book as a university student, de Aragon found himself distressed by her portrayal of Martinez as an immoral rebel and began doing research on the padre. Although he discovered that the facts refuted Cather's assessment, his vindication of the priest in *Padre Martinez and Bishop Lamy* has been controversial, making de Aragon, declared a reviewer in the *Las Vegas Optic,* "one of the most frequently reviewed Hispanic authors." Despite the media attention his book has received, de Aragon has not yet managed to get Martinez's excommunication ban of 1857 rescinded. But neither has he found his efforts unrewarded. Since the release of his book the Catholic church has produced a documentary film that includes information on Father Martinez as an early, noteworthy leader of the church, and the Public Broadcasting Service [PBS] aired a children's television program depicting Martinez's accomplishments.

With *Padre Martinez and Bishop Lamy* de Aragon also hoped to help change the stereotype of Spanish Americans, telling

CA: "I became so upset with the bandido image of Hispanic men and the portrayal of the women as ignorant childbearers on television and in motion pictures, as well as on the written page, that I knew something had to be done. I am proud that my book has taken the form of a social protest. Many reviewers have either praised me or criticized me for it, but if I had it to do over again, I would not change a thing. I also feel that depicting our history in the framework of actual personalities and events has very definitely enhanced Americans' understanding of the contributions from all Hispanics who have helped make the United States the great nation it is."

More recently, de Aragon has gained acclaim for *The Legend of La Llorona,* an account of the famous Hispanic legend of the wailing woman. Though many story variations exist, the basic legend tells of a beautiful woman who murders her two illegitimate children when their father doesn't marry her; since then, she has wandered in the night, a tormented spirit seeking her children. The book, noted for its mystical and philosophical qualities, was a regional bestseller and won the 1980 Pan-American International Literary Award.

De Aragon told *CA:* "I entered the world of imagination as a very young boy. In dreamlike thoughts I envisioned fair damsels heroically rescued by knights in shining armor. Don Quixote became a true-to-life personification of romantic idealism. He sought to change a world caught up in the struggle of material competitiveness and return in a mist to the carefree days of the sweet Dulcineas and roving minstrels. Cervantes, with pen in hand, taught the world to live life for its own wondrous sake. With the beauty of words, he made men think. He made them weep. He made them laugh.

"This one guiding influence inspired me to create with words, to paint scenes of bygone eras and recreate images we often envision in fantasies. The written word is indeed powerful. It is the one Time Machine that can take us into the past or propel us into the future. It can serve to advance civilization or, if abused, destroy society. Writers are endowed with a special gift. They have the ability to gaze into a crystal ball and lead the world into any vision.

"I have a special attachment to my own Hispanic culture. It is a vision of an enduring oral history and I feel the endless urge to document it before it vanishes. The Hispanic Southwest is, indeed, overwhelmingly rich with folk traditions and mystical legends. The old storytellers breathe life into tales that were ancient when Columbus discovered the New World. The legend of La Llorona, which has been described as a 'frightening ghost story yet a powerful love story at the same time,' was known at the time of Christ, but in New Mexico it is a living legend.

"In writing, my interests run the gamut of the literary scene. In *Padre Martinez and Bishop Lamy,* I sought to research the life of a folk-hero priest. I have tried my hand at children's stories, short stories, and novels and hope to do a play some day. Whenever possible, I do try to write in both Spanish and English. I also believe that my interest in the creative arts and my avocational interest in anthropology and archaeology has influenced my passion for the literary arts immensely.

"Writing per se is not an easy business. It requires an extensive amount of hard work, perseverance, and dedication. Unfortunately, this alone does not guarantee success. But it does insure a great deal of self-satisfaction. Writing is truly a wonderfully fulfilling and rewarding experience."

MEDIA ADAPTATIONS: Under the title "The Grey Eminence of Taos," *Padre Martinez and Bishop Lamy* has been optioned as either a major motion picture or a television miniseries.

BIOGRAPHICAL/CRITICAL SOURCES:

PERIODICALS

Albuquerque Tribune, November 20, 1980.
El Visitante Dominical, August, 1980.
Feria Artesana, August, 1982.
Highland's University Alumni Magazine (New Mexico), November, 1979.
La Luz, April, 1977.
Las Vegas Optic, November 24, 1982.
New Mexico School Review, December, 1979.
The New Mexican, October 30, 1980.
University of Albuquerque Alumni Magazine, June, 1977.

*   *   *

DeBOLT, Margaret Wayt 1930-

PERSONAL: Born August 5, 1930, in Moundsville, W.Va.; daughter of William Blaine (a teacher) and Margaret (a teacher; maiden name, Allen) Wayt; married Frank Crutcher DeBolt (a pilot), May 4, 1953; children: Frank, Brian, Jennifer. *Education:* West Virginia University, B.J., 1952. *Politics:* Independent. *Religion:* Unitarian-Universalist.

ADDRESSES: Home—10 Kingsridge Court, Savannah, Ga. 31419.

CAREER: Savannah News-Press, Savannah, Ga., staff writer, 1974-76; free-lance writer.

AWARDS, HONORS: Nutritional writing award from Carnation Milk, 1976; best bicentennial editorial award from *Savannah News-Press,* 1976.

WRITINGS:

Savannah: A Historical Portrait, Donning, 1976, revised edition, 1984.
Savannah Sampler Cookbook, Donning, 1978.
Georgia Sampler Cookbook, Donning, 1983.
Savannah Spectres (nonfiction), Donning, 1984.

Author of "Wayts of Millsboro" and "Kitchen in the Hills" columns in *Hillbilly.*

WORK IN PROGRESS: A country cookbook; a Civil War novel.

SIDELIGHTS: Margaret DeBolt told *CA* that her writing reflects her interests in southern and Civil War history, the psychic, regional cooking, hill country and mountain life, folklore, and women's history.

*   *   *

DECKER, William 1926-

BRIEF ENTRY: Born in 1926 in Richmond, Va. American cowboy, horse trainer, professional polo player, editor, and author. Decker's western novels are based on the author's ranching experience in California, Oregon, and Nevada. *To Be a Man* (Little, Brown, 1967) deals with change and the western cowboy from the 1880's through the 1940's. *The Holdouts* (Little, Brown, 1979) has a more contemporary setting—Arizona during the 1960's—but Decker's theme is still the conflict between changing times and the western way of life. Decker received the Spur Award of the Western Writers of America in 1980.

BIOGRAPHICAL/CRITICAL SOURCES:

PERIODICALS

New York Times, November 13, 1967.
Washington Post Book World, December 20, 1979.

* * *

DECKERS, Jeanine 1933(?)-1985
(Sister Luc-Gabrielle; Sister Smile, Soeur Sourire, The Singing Nun, pseudonyms)

OBITUARY NOTICE: Name in religion, Sister Luc-Gabrielle; born c. 1933; committed suicide, c. March 31 in 1985, in Wavre, Belgium. Nun, singer, administrator, and songwriter. Deckers gained international fame in 1963 with her hit recording "Dominique." She was a novice in the Dominican convent of Fichermont in Belgium when she was asked to record her song, which became a number-one hit on the U.S. pop music charts, sold millions of copies world-wide, and earned Decker a 1963 National Academy of Recording Arts and Sciences Award for best gospel or other religious recording. Following the success of "Dominique," Deckers—noted for her high, pure voice—recorded several other songs using such names as The Singing Nun, Soeur Sourire, and Sister Smile. She left the convent in 1966 to pursue her singing career and to "be closer to the people." Her success, however, did not continue, and she began giving private lessons in painting and guitar. Deckers later operated an institute for autistic children, but this project met with financial difficulties. Depressed, in part by the fate of her children's home, she committed suicide with a friend by taking an overdose of sedatives.

OBITUARIES AND OTHER SOURCES:

PERIODICALS

Chicago Tribune, April 3, 1985.
Los Angeles Times, April 2, 1985.
Newsweek, November 4, 1974, April 15, 1985.
New York Times, April 2, 1985.

* * *

DELANEY, John Joseph 1910-1985

OBITUARY NOTICE—See index for *CA* sketch: Born August 28, 1910, in New York, N.Y.; died April 10, 1985, in Jamaica, Queens, N.Y. Editor, translator, and author. Delaney worked for the Macmillan & McMullen publishing firms before accepting a post with Doubleday in 1954 as director of Image Books, a Roman Catholic paperback line. The following year he also became editor of the Catholic Family Book Club, the Catholic Youth Book Club, and Echo Books. In 1970 Delaney was named editorial director of Doubleday's department of Catholic books. His publications include *A Woman Clothed With the Sun, Dictionary of Catholic Biography, The Best in Modern Catholic Reading, A Guide to Catholic Reading,* and *Saints Are Now.* He also served as translator for Brother Lawrence of the Resurrection's *The Practice of the Presence of God.*

OBITUARIES AND OTHER SOURCES:

PERIODICALS

New York Times, April 12, 1985.

de la PENA, Augustin (Mateo) 1942-

PERSONAL: Born December 28, 1942, in Brownsville, Tex.; son of Augustin Mateo (a grocery store owner) and Hortencia (a housewife; maiden name, Munoz) de la Pena. *Education:* University of Texas at Austin, B.A. (cum laude), 1964; Stanford University, Ph.D., 1970; University of California, Los Angeles, Postdoctoral Certificate in Developmental Psychophysiology, 1972.

ADDRESSES: Office—Psychiatry and Psychology Service, Audie L. Murphy Memorial Veterans Administration Hospital, San Antonio, Tex. 78284; and Behavioral Medicine Section, Department of Psychiatry, University of Texas Health Science Center at San Antonio, 7703 Floyd Curl Dr., San Antonio, Tex. 78284.

CAREER: University of California, Los Angeles, assistant research psychologist at Medical School, 1972-73; Audie L. Murphy Memorial Veterans Administration Hospital, San Antonio, Tex., staff psychologist, 1974—, associate chief of Clinical Psychophysiology Laboratory and Sleep Clinic, 1976-78, chief of laboratory and clinic, 1978—. University of Texas Health Science Center at San Antonio, assistant professor, 1974-80, research assistant professor, 1980-83, research associate professor, 1983—; chairman of symposia; presents workshops on sleep and arousal disorders.

MEMBER: American Association for the Advancement of Science, American Psychological Association, Sleep Research Society, Association for the Psychophysiological Study of Sleep, Society for Psychophysiological Research.

AWARDS, HONORS: Fellow of National Institutes of Health, 1971-72; grants from Veterans Administration, 1975, 1975-76, 1976-78, 1978-80, 1979-80, 1984-86, Hogg Foundation of Texas, 1978-79, and National Heart, Lung, and Blood Institute, 1981-84.

WRITINGS:

The Psychobiology of Cancer: Automatization and Boredom in Health and Disease, Praeger, 1983.
(Contributor) R. L. Williams and Ismet Karacan, editors, *Sleep Disorders: Diagnosis and Treatment,* Wiley, 1978.
(Contributor) William Gray, Jay Fidler, and John Battista, editors, *General Systems Theory and the Psychological Sciences,* Volume II, Intersystems Publishers, 1983.
(Contributor) Bessel van der Kolk, editor, *New Perspectives on Post-Traumatic Stress,* American Psychiatric Press, 1984.

Contributor of more than twenty articles and reviews to journals in the behavioral sciences.

WORK IN PROGRESS: Toward a Psychobiology of Health and Disease: Implications for New Directions in Medicine and Health Science.

SIDELIGHTS: Augustin de la Pena told *CA:* "Much of my work argues that orthodox and holistic medicine approaches to the conceptualization and empirical study of stress-health interrelations are of limited utility and validity because both employ a set of premises that have been borrowed from an obsolete, seventeenth-century physical science and philosophy of science. Consequences of the obsolete paradigm are (a) a body of literature containing findings that are not only difficult to replicate, but are so confusing and paradoxical that an uncomfortable aura of randomness exists when considered in toto, (b) embarrassingly imprecise, confused, and inconsistent definitions of health and disease, and (c) ontologically flawed conceptualizations of health and disease, as well as misdirected goals of health science and medicine—that is, the conquest of disease, personal immortality.

"My approach builds upon recent developments in cognitive psychology, neuroscience, developmental psychophysiology, information and control theory, and philosophy of science. I suggest that the chief threat to the health of man and his environment is *not* the array of ills traditionally cited by health care providers, such as individual and collective violence, cancer, heart disease, alcoholism and drug abuse, depression, and paranoia. Rather, most varieties of these phenomena are suggested to be secondary, compensatory, information-augmenting sequelae of a more fundamental problem—man's knowledge system, or more precisely, man's current relationship with his knowledge system and his environment, the transactional nature of which almost always generates for most adult individuals the experience of boredom and a feeling of alienation from the cosmos.

"My developmental-structural approach points out that as any structure gains experience with its environment it develops increasingly different information-reduction strategies for processing the information in its respective environment. The result is an attenuation of information flow in ordinary environments, since most of the information is already encoded in structural or memory processes. The result is a relative informational isolation from the environment, the phenomenologic correlate of which is the experience of boredom. Relatively isolated-bored structures have a variety of information flow control mechanisms for rectifying sub-optimal information flow to higher levels which are associated with organized function and the experience of interest. One type of information-flow control mechanism is disease expression. Most forms of disease in mature, developed individuals are posited to an interest-generating role. That is, they provide challenge and entertainment that help to rectify the boredom-isolation experienced by excessively isolated-bored structures in nature."

*   *   *

DELMAN, David   1924-

BRIEF ENTRY: Born December 12, 1924, in Scranton, Pa. American advertising executive and author of several mystery novels. Delman's books include *The Hard Sell* (Jarrolds, 1959), *Sudden Death* (Doubleday, 1972), *A Week to Kill* (Doubleday, 1972), *He Who Digs a Grave* (Doubleday, 1973), *One Man's Murder* (McKay, 1975), and *The Nice Murderers* (Morrow, 1977).

BIOGRAPHICAL/CRITICAL SOURCES:

PERIODICALS

New York Times Book Review, September 2, 1973, May 11, 1975, October 9, 1977.
Observer, November 20, 1977.
Times Literary Supplement, January 9, 1976.

*   *   *

De MILLE, Cecil B(lount)   1881-1959

BRIEF ENTRY: Born August 12, 1881, in Ashfield, Mass.; died of a heart ailment, January 21, 1959, in Hollywood, Calif.; buried at Hollywood Memorial Park, Hollywood, Calif. American actor, film director and producer, and playwright.

Considered the quintessential Hollywood director, De Mille was best known for his lavish motion picture extravaganzas, including "The Ten Commandments," "Cleopatra," and "The Greatest Show on Earth." During his career De Mille produced approximately seventy feature films, most of which were characterized by opulent sets, spectacular effects, and extravagant budgets. The films generally won praise for their narrative skill, and they scored huge box-office successes, but they were often criticized for their lack of artistic subtlety. Regarded as an innovator in lighting effects and the use of technicolor, De Mille was honored by the Academy of Motion Picture Arts and Sciences in 1949 with a special award for thirty-five years of pioneering in the film industry.

De Mille studied at the American Academy of Dramatic Arts, and in 1900 he made his stage debut. He spent the next twelve years as an actor and as manager of a theatrical company owned by his mother. During this time he also wrote several moderately successful plays with his brother William, such as "The Genius" (1904), "The Royal Mounted" (1908), and "After Five" (1913); with David Belasco he collaborated on the play "The Return of Peter Grimm" (1911). In partnership with Jesse L. Lasky and Samuel Goldwyn, De Mille formed Jesse L. Lasky Features in 1913, and in 1914 the trio went to Hollywood to produce their first film, "The Squaw Man." De Mille served as director of the film, which was a critical and commercial success and was among the first motion pictures to be produced in Hollywood. With De Mille as its acknowledged creative force, the Lasky company soon expanded to become Paramount Pictures. De Mille served as overseer for the company's entire output, as well as director and producer of many of its motion pictures. He has been credited with influencing the switch from two- or three-reelers to feature-length commercial films and with helping to make Hollywood the motion picture center of the world. In 1953, forty years after producing his first film, De Mille won his first Oscar for "The Greatest Story Ever Told."

BIOGRAPHICAL/CRITICAL SOURCES:

BOOKS

Brownlow, Kevin, *Parade's Gone By,* University of California Press, 1976.
Current Biography, Wilson, 1942, March, 1959.
Essoe, Gabe and Raymond Lee, *DeMille: The Man and His Pictures,* Barnes, 1970.
Higham, Charles, *Cecil B. DeMille,* Scribner, 1973.

PERIODICALS

Life, February 2, 1959.
Newsweek, February 2, 1959.
New York Times, January 22, 1959, January 24, 1959.
Time, February 2, 1959.

*   *   *

DENNING, A. T.
See DENNING, Alfred Thompson

*   *   *

DENNING, Alfred Thompson   1899-
(A. T. Denning, Lord Denning, Right Honourable Lord Denning)

BRIEF ENTRY: Born January 23, 1899, in Whitchurch, Hampshire, England. British lawyer, judge, and author. Denning is most widely known as the official investigator of the Profumo Case—the 1963 political sex scandal that eventually toppled the Conservative government of British Prime Minister Harold Macmillan. The case centered on the affair between John D. Profumo, then secretary of state for war, and a party girl, Christine Keeler, who was at the same time involved with a Russian intelligence officer assigned to the Soviet Embassy in London. Questions of possible security leaks were resolved in Denning's report, which concluded that although British security had not been breeched by the affair, confidence in British security had been greatly diminished. Within one month of the report, Harold Macmillan resigned as prime minister, claiming ill health.

Denning's legal career began when he was called to the Bar in 1923. He was appointed king's counsel in 1938 and served as a judge of England's High Court of Justice from 1944 to 1948, as a lord justice of Appeal from 1948 to 1957, and as a lord of Appeal in Ordinary from 1957 to 1962. He then became master of the Rolls, a position he held until 1982. He was knighted in 1944 and created Baron Denning of Whitchurch in 1957. His writings include *The Profumo-Christine Keeler Affair* (Popular Library, 1963), *The Discipline of Law* (Butterworth, 1979), *The Due Process of Law* (Butterworth, 1980), *The Family Story* (Butterworth, 1981), *Misuse of Power* (BBC Publications, 1981), and *The Closing Chapter* (Butterworth, 1983). *Address:* The Lawn, Whitchurch, Hampshire, England; and 11 Old Sq., Lincoln's Inn, London W.C. 2, England.

BIOGRAPHICAL/CRITICAL SOURCES:

BOOKS

Current Biography, Wilson, 1965.
Who's Who, 136th edition, St. Martin's, 1984.

PERIODICALS

Times (London), May 28, 1981, January 7, 1984.

*   *   *

DENNIS, Rutledge M(elvin)   1939-

PERSONAL: Born August 16, 1939, in Charleston, S.C.; son of David Dennis (a ship's mechanic) and Ora Jane (a housewife; maiden name, Porcher) Dennis; married Sarah Helen Bankhead, August 16, 1967; children: Tchaka Lateef, Imaro Aki, Kimya Nuru, Zuri Sanyika. *Education:* South Carolina State College, B.A. (with honors), 1965; Washington State University, M.A., 1969, Ph.D., 1975.

ADDRESSES: Home—Richmond, Va. *Office*—Department of Sociology and Anthropology, 312 North Schafer St., Richmond, Va. 23284.

CAREER: Virginia Commonwealth University, Richmond, assistant professor of sociology, 1971—, coordinator of Afro-American studies, 1971-78, associate professor of sociology and anthropology, 1978—. Member of Eastern Virginia International Consortium, 1972-77; co-coordinator of Southeastern Regional African Seminar, 1973-76; commissioner of Richmond Redevelopment and Housing Authority and Housing Opportunities Made Equal, both 1976—; trustee and member of executive council of National Assault on Illiteracy Program, 1982—.

MEMBER: African Heritage Association, American Association for the Advancement of Science, Association for the Study

of Afro-American Life and Culture, Association of Black Sociologists (president, 1981-83), American Sociological Association, National Association for the Advancement of Colored People, Southern Sociological Association, Virginia Sociological Association (member of executive committee, 1974-75), New York Academy of Science, Sigma Xi, Alpha Mu, Alpha Phi Alpha.

AWARDS, HONORS: Grants from Ford Foundation, 1970-71, National Endowment for the Humanities, 1978, and National Institute of Mental Health, 1980-82; Reise-Melton Award, 1980; Boys Club of America Award, 1980; Merit Award, 1985, for the National Assault of Illiteracy Program.

WRITINGS:

(Editor with Charles Jarmon) *Afro-Americans: Social Science Perspectives*, University Press of America, 1977.
(With John V. Moeser) *The Politics of Annexation: Oligarchic Power in a Southern City*, Schenkman, 1982.

Contributor of articles and poems to sociology, education, and ethnic studies journals. Author of unpublished short stories.

WORK IN PROGRESS: Books on leadership, religion, and families of Black Middletown; a book on W.E.B. DuBois and Charles Johnson.

SIDELIGHTS: Rutledge M. Dennis told *CA*: "Writers such as W.E.B. DuBois (*The Souls of Black Folks*), Langston Hughes (poetry and short stories), and Percy Bysshe Shelley served as intellectual models during my formative years. Race and racial inequality provided a focus for my interest in the social sciences, and the idea of elites in social change became a special interest. Consequently, during the past sixteen years, my academic, intellectual, and social interests have revolved around inequality and community aand social change as these relate to minority-majority relations. The Middletown books will be a continuation of these interests.

"In 1980 Dr. Vivian V. Gordon—then an associate professor of sociology at the University of Virginia—and I were awarded a grant to conduct research in Muncie, Indiana, the site of the famous Middletown studies by Robert and Helen Lynd. In their studies, *Middletown* (1929) and *Middletown in Transition* (1937), the Lynds intentionally avoided an analysis of a small black community in Muncie. Our 1980 study was designed to fill the gap, and thus we were interested in historical as well as contemporary data. The historical data was collected via interviews with senior citizens and through census reports and organizational records. The contemporary data was collected via a community survey, which consisted of questions relating to family life, religion, occupation, leisure, and racial attitudes. Two sub-surveys were also conducted, which consisted of data on black women and on black leadership. One of the key questions concerned the strategies used by blacks in medium-sized midwestern cities and the degree to which these strategies might differ from those of blacks in cities of the South and Northeast. In addition to the variables above, we also analyzed the community via the variables of stratification, modernization, and alienation."

*   *   *

DENVIR, Bernard   1917-

PERSONAL: Born January 26, 1917, in Whitehaven, England. *Education:* St. Benet's Hall, Oxford, B.A., 1937, M.A., 1962.

ADDRESSES: Home—85 Knatchbull Rd., London SE5 9QU, England. *Office*—*Art and Artists,* 43 B Gloucester Rd., Croydon CR0 2DH, England.

CAREER: Ravensbourne College of Art, Chislehurst, Kent, England, head of department of art history, 1956-80; *Art and Artists,* Croydon, England, editor, 1980—. Member of Council for National Academic Awards, 1972-78. *Military service:* British Army, 1940-45.

MEMBER: International Association of Art Critics (president of British section, 1973-76, 1982—), Art Historians' Association, Arts Club (London; member of board of directors; chairman of picture committee).

WRITINGS:

Impressionism, Thames & Hudson, 1974.
Fauvism and Expressionism, Thames & Hudson, 1974.
Art Treasures of Italy, Orbis, 1980.
Van Gogh, Octopus, 1981.
A Documentary History of Taste in England, four volumes, Longman, 1982-85.

Contributor to art journals.

*   *   *

de VALOIS, Ninette 1898-

BRIEF ENTRY: Born June 6, 1898, in Baltiboys, Blessington, County Wicklow, Ireland. British dancer, choreographer, and author. De Valois was a prima ballerina at Covent Garden in 1919. She worked as a member of the Diaghilev Russian Ballet and as a choreographer at the Old Vic Festival Theatre. She founded the Royal Ballet and the Royal Ballet School in 1931 and directed both until 1963; she is now governor of the Royal Ballet. De Valois was named a chevalier of the French Legion of Honor and a companion of honour in England; she received the Erasmus Prize in 1974. Her books include *Invitation to the Ballet* (Oxford University Press, 1938), *Come Dance With Me: A Memoir, 1898-1956* (Hamish Hamilton, 1957), and *Step by Step: The Formation of an Establishment* (W. H. Allen, 1977). *Address:* c/o Royal Ballet School, 153 Talgarth Rd., London W.14, England.

BIOGRAPHICAL/CRITICAL SOURCES:

BOOKS

The International Who's Who, 46th edition, Europa, 1982.
1000 Makers of the Twentieth Century, David & Charles, 1971.

*   *   *

DEVERELL, William H(erbert) 1937-

PERSONAL: Born March 4, 1937, in Regina, Saskatchewan, Canada; son of Robert J. (a journalist) and Grace Amy (Barber) Deverell; married Tekla Melnyk (a Jungian psychologist); children: Daniel Mark, Tamara Lise. *Education:* University of Saskatchewan, B.A., LL.B., 1962.

ADDRESSES: Home—North Pender Island, British Columbia, Canada V0N 2M0. *Office*—2 Gaolers Mews, Vancouver, British Columbia, Canada.

CAREER: Saskatoon Star-Phoenix, Saskatoon, Saskatchewan, 1956-60, began as reporter, became night editor; associated with Canadian Press, Montreal, Quebec, 1960-62; *Vancouver Sun,* Vancouver, British Columbia, transportation editor, 1963;

partner and trial attorney with firm in Vancouver, 1964-79; writer, 1979—.

MEMBER: Writers Union of Canada, British Crime Writers Association, Crime Writers of Canada, British Columbia Civil Liberties Association (founding member; past president).

AWARDS, HONORS: McClelland & Stewart/Seal First Novel Award, 1979, and book of the year award from Periodical Distributors Association of Canada, 1980, both for *Needles.*

WRITINGS:

NOVELS

Needles, McClelland & Stewart, 1979, Little, Brown, 1980.
High Crimes, McClelland & Stewart, 1979, St. Martin's, 1981.
Mecca, McClelland & Stewart, 1983, Bantam, 1985.

WORK IN PROGRESS: "The Button Man," a pilot film and series for the Canadian Broadcasting Corporation (CBC-TV).

SIDELIGHTS: In the late 1970's William H. Deverell fulfilled a lifelong ambition by taking a sabbatical from his successful criminal law practice in order to write a novel. "I'd read lots of thrillers, and lawyers being naturally competitive, thought I could do better," he told Eleanor Wachtel of *Western Living.* Tackling the project with determination, Deverell often spent up to fifteen hours a day at his manual typewriter. His efforts ultimately paid off when his psychological thriller *Needles* won a $50,000 McClelland & Stewart/Seal First Novel Award.

Upon returning to his law partnership after one year, Deverell became the target of office banter. Colleagues greeted him exclaiming, "What a scam you pulled off," said Wachtel. It was "as if there were some sort of trickery" involved in Deverell's success. For a short time Deverell attempted to juggle a writing career with his practice of law, but he eventually decided to write full time. "I'm over forty, I started late. With the first [book] I was determined to attract a publisher, produce a good read that would sell, but also be dramatic, say something. There are a lot of things I want to say about the world that I haven't yet."

Deverell and his family live on British Columbia's Gulf Islands in what he describes as a "white man's tee-pee." Wachtel describes the home as "a cedar, mandala-shaped tree-house" with "eight supporting beams [rising] to meet at the centre of a three-story octagon."

BIOGRAPHICAL/CRITICAL SOURCES:

PERIODICALS

Western Living, November, 1979.

*   *   *

DIAMOND, Donna 1950-

PERSONAL: Born October 19, 1950, in New York, N.Y. *Education:* Boston University, B.F.A.; attended School of Visual Arts.

ADDRESSES: Home—62 Phillips St., Boston, Mass. 02114.

CAREER: Writer and illustrator.

WRITINGS:

ADAPTER OF BOOKS FOR CHILDREN:

(And illustrator) *The Seven Ravens: A Grimm's Fairy Tale,* Viking, 1979.

(With Clive Barnes; and illustrator) *Swan Lake,* Holiday House, 1980.

(And illustrator) *The Bremen Town Musicians: A Grimm's Fairy Tale,* Delacorte, 1981.

(And illustrator) *The Pied Piper of Hamelin,* Holiday House, 1981.

(And illustrator) *Rumpelstiltskin: A Grimm's Fairy Tale,* Holiday House, 1983.

ILLUSTRATOR OF BOOKS FOR CHILDREN:

Jane H. Yolen, *The Transfigured Heart,* Crowell, 1975.
Constance C. Greene, *Beat the Turtle Drum,* Viking, 1976.
John Weston, *The Boy Who Sang the Birds,* Scribner, 1976.
Andre Norton, *Red Hart Magic,* Crowell, 1976.
Daniel Curley, *Ann's Spring,* Crowell, 1977.
Katherine Paterson, *Bridge to Terabithia,* Crowell, 1977.
Olga Litowinsky and Bebe Willoughby, *The Dream Book,* Coward, 1978.
Richard Kennedy, *The Dark Princess,* Holiday House, 1978.
Elizabeth Winthrop, *Are You Sad, Mama?,* Harper, 1979.
Steven J. Myers, *The Enchanted Sticks,* Coward, 1979.
Esther R. Hautzig, *A Gift for Mama,* Viking, 1981.
Charlotte Graeber, *Mustard,* Macmillan, 1982.
Barbara Wersba, *The Crystal Child,* Harper, 1982.
Penny Pollock, *Keeping it Secret,* Putnam, 1982.

SIDELIGHTS: Donna Diamond commented: "I was always very attracted to children's books and I like to draw. But, at Boston University you couldn't major in drawing. It was painting or sculpture; I chose sculpture. When I graduated, I went back to New York and I thought a lot about my career and making a living. People suggested that I draw, so I took courses in illustration at the School of Visual Arts. I met some amazing people, who were very encouraging. I started trying to do editorial illustration. Many people said, 'You should try and do children's books.' And so I went to a children's book editor, Selma Lanes. She recommended that I go to Anne Beneduce, and I did my first book with her. That's how sculpture turned into illustration.

"In a manuscript I look for excuses to do pictures I would like to do. I'm happy that the things that I've been offered seem to relate to the things that I'm interested in. Until very recently I didn't know how to draw teeth so none of the characters in my books smiled. So I think I got the reputation of being an illustrator of moody books. And so I got a lot of manuscripts about people who die and I think that was less about who I am and more about the fact that I didn't know how to draw teeth, so nobody ever smiled.

"I don't understand how people are writers. For me, situations appear in my brain as pictures. I remember incidents visually, and the emotional implications of an incident suggest visual motifs—for me, all the triggers are visual. For writers, stories occur to them. Things put themselves together in terms of words. I don't know how that happens in their brains. And it also seems so lonely. If I'm drawing a character, I'm trying to keep that character looking consistent. There has to be a real person in front of me in order for me to get enough information. I'm not sure a writer needs that."

BIOGRAPHICAL/CRITICAL SOURCES:

PERIODICALS

New York Times Book Review, January 29, 1984.

DILL, Clarence C(leveland) 1884-1978

OBITUARY NOTICE: Born September 21, 1884, near Fredericktown, Ohio; died January 14, 1978, in Spokane, Wash. Politician, lawyer, educator, and author. A U.S. senator from the state of Washington from 1923 until 1935, Dill worked on drafting the Federal Communications Act and promoted the construction of the Grand Coulee Dam on the Columbia River. Prior to his two terms in the Senate, Dill taught at high schools in Iowa and Washington, worked as deputy prosecuting attorney of Spokane County, Washington, and served two terms in the U.S. House of Representatives. He later practiced law in Washington, D.C., and Spokane, Washington, and served as special assistant to the U.S. attorney general. His writings include *How Congress Makes Laws, Our Government,* and *Where the Water Falls,* which concerns the Grand Coulee Dam.

OBITUARIES AND OTHER SOURCES:

BOOKS

Biographical Directory of the American Congress: 1774-1971, U.S. Government Printing Office, 1971.
Obituaries On File, Facts on File, 1979.
Who's Who in American Politics, 4th edition, Bowker, 1973.
Who Was Who in America, With World Notables, Volume VII: *1977-1981,* Marquis, 1981.

*   *   *

DIOR, Christian 1905-1957

BRIEF ENTRY: Born January 21, 1905, in Normandy, France; died of a heart attack, October 24, 1957, in Montecatini, Italy. French fashion designer, business executive, and author. Dior, who established his own haute couture salon on the avenue Montaigne in Paris in 1946, has been credited with enabling postwar France to maintain its position as leader of the fashion world. His intention as a fashion designer, he said, was "to make elegant women more beautiful; to make beautiful more elegant." Dior is perhaps best remembered for his 1947 innovation of the "New Look" in fashion, which emphasized femininity with fitted bodices, narrow waists, and long skirts. The "New Look" immediately won popularity all over the Western world, and, because the design required multiple yards of fabric, it provided a much-needed boost to France's failing textile industry. In later years Dior introduced such styles as the "Umbrella," the "Scissor," the "Horseshoe," and the "A-Line," all of which were commercially successful.

Prior to his involvement with the fashion industry, Dior opened a Paris art gallery, one of the first to exhibit surrealist paintings by such artists as Salvador Dali and Jean Cocteau. Illness forced him to give up the business in 1934, and after convalescing for one year Dior accepted a position with *Figaro Illustrated* as an illustrator for the haute couture page. Following that, he designed hats for Paris milliner Agnes and dresses for couturier Robert Piguet. In 1941 Dior began working for leading fashion designer Lucien Lelong. When the French Ministry of Production lifted cloth rationing regulations in 1946, Dior opened his own salon. A phenomenal success from the outset, Dior interests included enterprises in twenty-four countries at the time of the designer's death. Gross earnings for that year reportedly reached $15 million. Dior was the author, with Elie Rabourdin and Alice Chavane, of *Talking About Fashion* (1954). He also wrote *Christian Dior's Little Dictionary of Fashion* (1954) and *Christian Dior and I* (1957), translated by Antonia Fraser.

BIOGRAPHICAL/CRITICAL SOURCES:

BOOKS

Beaton, Cecil Walter Hardy and Kenneth Tynan, *Persona Grata*,
    Putnam, 1954.
Current Biography, Wilson, 1948, January, 1958.
Latour, Anny, *Kings of Fashion*, Coward-McCann, 1958.

PERIODICALS

Life, November 11, 1957.
Newsweek, November 4, 1957.
New York Times, October 24, 1957, October 30, 1957.
Publishers Weekly, November 25, 1957.
Time, November 4, 1957.
Vogue, March 1, 1957, March 15, 1957.

* * *

DOCHERTY, James L.
    See RAYMOND, Rene (Brabazon)

* * *

DODDS, Edward Charles   1899-1973

OBITUARY NOTICE: Born October 13, 1899, in Liverpool,
England; died December 16, 1973, in London, England.
Biochemist, educator, and author. From the age of twenty-six
Dodds was professor of biochemistry at the University of London's University College, where he conducted endocrinolog-
ical research and promoted treating medical problems through
biochemical methods. Among his important discoveries was
that stilboestrol, a synthetic chemical, simulates properties of
the female hormone oestrone. This finding led to the use of
stilboestrol in the treatment of female hormone disorders. Dodds
was knighted in 1954 and served as president of the Royal
College of Surgeons from 1962 until 1966. He co-authored
the books *Recent Advances in Medicine* and *The Chemical and
Physiological Properties of Internal Secretions*.

OBITUARIES AND OTHER SOURCES:

BOOKS

Twentieth-Century Culture: A Biographical Companion, Har-
    per, 1983.

* * *

DONOVAN, Hedley (Williams)   1914-

PERSONAL: Born May 24, 1914, in Brainerd, Minn.; son of
Percy Williams (a mining engineer) and Alice (Dougan) Donovan; married Dorothy Hannon, October 18, 1941 (died, 1978);
children: Peter Williams, Helen Welles, Mark Vicars. *Education:* University of Minnesota, B.A. (history; magna cum
laude), 1934; Hertford College, Oxford, B.A. (history), 1936.
Politics: "Card-carrying independent." *Religion:* Congrega-
tionalist.

ADDRESSES: Home—Harbor Rd., Sands Point, N.Y. 11050;
190 East 72nd St., New York, N.Y. 10021.

CAREER: Journalist. *Washington Post*, Washington, D.C., reporter, 1937-42; Time Inc., New York, N.Y., writer for *Fortune* magazine, 1945-51, associate managing editor of *Fortune*, 1951-53, managing editor of *Fortune*, 1953-59, editorial
director of Time Inc., 1959-64, editor in chief of all Time Inc.
publications, 1964-79, consultant to Time Inc., 1979-84,

member of board of directors, 1962-79, director of Time-Life
Books, 1976-83, director of Washington Star Co., 1978-81;
Harvard University, Cambridge, Mass., fellow on the John F.
Kennedy School of Government's faculty, 1981—. Member
of U.S. State Department chosen to observe electoral process
in Soviet Union, 1958; member of President Lyndon B. Johnson's Task Force on Education, 1964; director of Council on
Foreign Relations, 1969-79; member of Trilateral Commission, 1971-79; senior adviser to President Jimmy Carter, 1979-
80. Member of advisory council of Woodrow Wilson Center,
1969—. Trustee of New York University, 1964-82, Mount
Holyoke College, 1972-82, Ford Foundation, 1975-84, and
the Carnegie Endowment for International Peace. Member of
board of directors of National Humanities Center, 1980—,
Aerospace Corporation, 1981—, and Asia Society, 1981—.
Military service: U.S. Naval Reserve, Intelligence, 1942-45;
became lieutenant commander.

MEMBER: American Academy of Arts and Sciences (fellow,
1972—), Pilgrims of the United States, Century Association,
Phi Beta Kappa, Delta Upsilon, St. Botolph Club (Boston),
University Club of New York, Manhasset Bay Yacht Club,
Sands Point Golf Club, Metropolitan Club, 1925 F St. Club
(Washington, D.C.).

AWARDS, HONORS: Rhodes scholar, 1934-36; Loeb Journalism Award, 1978; Gallatin Medal from New York University, 1979; Litt.D. from Pomona College, Boston University,
and Mount Holyoke College; L.H.D. from Southwestern at
Memphis, University of Rochester, and Transylvania University; LL.D. from Carnegie-Mellon University, Lehigh University, and Allegheny College; named honorary fellow of
Hertford College, Oxford.

WRITINGS:

*Roosevelt to Reagan: A Reporter's Encounters With Nine
    Presidents*, Harper, 1985.

Contributor of articles to periodicals.

WORK IN PROGRESS: "Might do a book on the press."

SIDELIGHTS: Hedley Donovan was affiliated with Time Inc.—
the firm that publishes Time-Life Books and *Time, Life, Fortune, Money, Sports Illustrated, Discover*, and *People* magazines—for nearly forty years, serving as editor in chief of the
company from 1964 until his retirement in 1979. After his
resignation from Time Inc., Donovan spent a year as a senior
adviser to former President Jimmy Carter. He has since pursued various projects, among them a book on his encounters
with nine U.S. presidents, articles for *Time* and *Fortune* magazines, and a seminar on the press and society, which he conducts at Harvard University's John F. Kennedy School of Government.

A Rhodes scholar in history, Donovan came to Time Inc. after
working for five years as a *Washington Post* reporter and
spending four years in U.S. Naval intelligence during
World War II. Time Inc. hired Donovan in 1945 as a *Fortune*
staff writer, and beginning in the 1950's Donovan assumed
increasing editorial responsiblity at Time Inc. He became an
associate managing editor of *Fortune* in 1951, *Fortune*'s managing editor in 1953, and editorial director of Time Inc. in
1959. As editorial director Donovan was second in command
to Henry R. Luce, co-founder and then-editor in chief of Time
Inc. He also served as managing editor of *Time, Life*, and
Sports Illustrated, organized a research and development di-

vision for the corporation, and worked to expand the scope of Time Inc.'s other non-periodical activities.

Donovan was given Time Inc.'s top editorial post in 1964 when Luce, who had decided to step down as editor in chief, assumed the title of editorial chairman and designated Donovan as his successor. As reported in *Time* magazine, Luce explained his retirement and the appointment of Donovan in a memo to his staff: "There are many good reasons for this change of command. . . . The best and sufficient reason is that Hedley Donovan is highly qualified to be editor in chief." But Luce need not have justified his selection. As Bernard M. Auer, Time Inc.'s publisher, noted in *Time:* "To his colleagues . . . the choice of Donovan as editor-in-chief came as no surprise." Donovan's proven competence in prior positions made the selection "obvious" and "inevitable."

During the fifteen years that Donovan served as editor in chief, Time Inc. continued to be the viable, growing company it had been under Luce, adding the magazines *Money, People,* and the monthly *Life* to its list of publications and increasing *Fortune*'s publication from once a month to once every two weeks. Under Donovan's leadership Time Inc. also dropped the publication of *Architectural Forum* (which was absorbed by *Fortune*), *House and Home,* and the weekly *Life.* Donovan continued, while head of Time Inc., to impress colleagues such as William S. Rukeyser, managing editor of *Fortune,* who recalled Donovan's tenure as editor in chief: "In his fifteen years in that job he gave me and 18 other Time Inc. managing editors a fringe benefit impossible to negotiate: the chance to work for a boss of awesome intelligence, competence, and character." Time Inc.'s chairman of the board Andrew Heiskell similarly commented in *Time* on the occasion of Donovan's retirement: "He helped transform Time Inc. from the largely personal domain of its brilliant founder into a publicly held, diverse company, while preserving, we feel, its essential spirit and broadening its range. With great strength of character and a formidable intellect, he guided our publications through the bitterly divisive years of Viet Nam and Watergate, reaffirming or changing editorial policy. . . . The legacy of the Donovan years is a rich one, most obviously in staff and resources, but, most important, in thoughtfulness, courage, and excellence."

Donovan continued to contribute articles to Time Inc. publications while editor in chief, giving public voice to the insights and guidance he provided through his editorial policy. He wrote, for example, on the Viet Nam War and the questions arising from it concerning the motives, justifications, and value of the United States' participation in the war. His views of the war, as Don Oberdorfer explained in his book *Tet!,* changed from support of the United States' intervention in the war to the belief that victory in Viet Nam was either unattainable or not worth the price that would have to be paid to achieve it. But even after what John Franklin Campbell, in his *New York Times Book Review* critique of *Tet!,* termed a "slow evolution from hawk to dove," Donovan made an effort to assure his fellow Americans that we "do not need to flagellate ourselves" for our mistakes in Viet Nam. Rather, Donovan asserted in a 1971 issue of *Time,* Americans, including politicians, must be able to admit their misjudgments and focus on learning from the Viet Nam experience by making choices "regarding how Americans think about what they have been through in Viet Nam."

Concerning the initial decision to intervene on behalf of non-Communist South Viet Nam in 1965, Donovan commented:

"Surely nobody then in the White House, the Pentagon or Congress could have imagined that the commitment would grow to more than half a million men and the cost, at its peak, to nearly \$30 billion a year [and] that more than six years later there would still be a quarter of a million Americans there. . . . For my own part, I happen still to think that the U.S. was right to try in 1965 to prevent the forcible takeover of South Viet Nam by Communism." But, Donovan continued in the 1971 article, "I would say now, though I did not see it then, that we went on in 1966 and 1967 to expand the U.S. effort far out of proportion to our original purposes, and that this enlarged commitment then began to take on a life of its own and even to work against our original purposes. . . . We first became involved in Viet Nam to contain China [and its Communism]. . . . If it is now safe for us to trade with China . . . , it should be safe, at last, to bring our soldiers home from Viet Nam."

Donovan admitted in the *Time* essay that it "took . . . the better part" of 1966 and 1967 for him to realize that the United States' intervention in Viet Nam had gone too far and that he wished he "had been wiser sooner." He also explained his motives in publicly admitting his errors in judgment, writing in *Time:* "I mention my own record not because it is important in itself but to suggest a kind of Viet Nam autobiography that many of us carry around, whether we like it or not. . . . Some will conclude that they were right all along, and perhaps some were. But if the country is to come to terms with the Viet Nam experience, the process must begin with a good many individuals studying and acknowledging their own errors."

After retiring from Time Inc. in 1979 Donovan received a call from the White House—President Jimmy Carter wished Donovan to serve as one of his senior advisers who would, in the words of press secretary Jody Powell, quoted in *New Republic,* "provide substantive advice on the full range of matters before the President." Donovan joined the White House staff for a year, stipulating two conditions: that he would not be required to campaign or politick for Carter and that he would not be asked to influence the media's treatment of Carter and his administration. Donovan, who chose not to be compensated by the government for his advisory position, was given direct and frequent access to Carter.

In a 1980 article for *Fortune,* Donovan revealed observations of press-government relations that he formulated while serving as a presidential adviser. He noted, for instance, the accuracy and timeliness of the press in its reporting of government affairs: "On the inside, you knew some things sooner than the press did—for only a day or two in most cases—but the fact that the press lacked some momentarily secret items of information seldom led to egregiously misleading coverage." One reason cited by Donovan for the timeliness of the press's reporting was that "the use of leaks . . . is pervasive" among government officials. And, according to Donovan, in addition to the large amount of bureaucratic warfare "conducted via the leak," any "sudden piece of good news will be broken by the government itself as soon as it happens, if not a little before."

With regard to the Carter administration's view of journalists, Donovan observed that the "President and his inner circle had a basically low opinion of the quality of the press, a considerable mistrust of its motives, and an incomplete understanding of its role." White House officials, according to Donovan, pictured "an enormous press corps ready to pounce" on and expose their mistakes and problems but content to overlook their successes and strong points. Donovan attributed this perception of the Carter administration in part to the general antagonism between press and government officials that had developed from differences in their respective functions. And, Donovan remarked, the "profound difference between the White House—not just the Carter White House, anybody's—and the press is the difference between a story and a problem. And usually the tougher the problem, the better the story." Moreover, given the government's tendency to reveal any items of good news concerning its functioning, Donovan explained, "anything broken by the press, almost by definition, will be negative," adding to the impression that journalists look only for bad news.

The definition of "news" itself contributed to Donovan's analysis of press-government relations. As Donovan noted, "news" is synonymous with "novelty" and so focuses on the new and exceptional in society, and in "a reasonably orderly, honest, effective society, the exceptions will mainly be bad news." Donovan pointed out, however, that not all news is bad and that the problems and insecurity of the Carter administration may have inspired both negative news reports and a penchant among administration officials for dwelling on their bad press rather than on overall news coverage. Donovan stated: "Trends and movements are also news, and sometimes the change is for the better; personalities are news, sometimes attractive, even inspiring; 'situations' are news, sometimes encouraging. The press carries more of a good news-bad news mix about America than the [Carter] White House noticed. The White House naturally focused on coverage of the Carter Administration, and the net of that coverage in 1979-80 was probably unfavorable."

In *Fortune,* Donovan warned against officials becoming overly sensitive to negative press coverage, stating: "I dislike the notion of an 'adversary relationship' between the press and the executive branch." He further commented that "the tense view is dangerous. It can easily lead to the conviction that the press is a greater problem than the problems it reports, or indeed that there are few problems except as the press creates them." Donovan acknowledged that the "press does, of course, have different purposes and perspectives from those of the White House." But, he asserted, "the free press was seen from the earliest days of the Republic as charged with an indispensable role in our political system." Moreover, through the "impact of TV and the emergence of a 'national press,'" Donovan continued, the "press has truly become one of the 'powers' in the 'separation of powers,' one of the 'checks' in our system of checks and balances. Congress and the executive, and the courts and the executive, may often find themselves adversaries, but they are not locked into an 'adversary relationship.' The press and the White House need not be." Rather, concluded Donovan, executive officials could take a "somewhat relaxed view of the Washington press corps" and "use the press the way most readers and viewers do—to enlarge their understanding of what's going on."

CA INTERVIEW

CA interviewed Hedley Donovan by telephone July 20, 1984, at his home in Sands Point, New York.

CA: At the beginning of your career, you decided to join the Washington Post *as a reporter rather than become a history professor. What's your opinion of that decision, in retrospect?*

DONOVAN: I never had any regrets about it. I had originally thought of doing newspaper work as a way of earning a little money for a couple of years and then going back to college to get a Ph.D. But as soon as I started reporting I discovered I liked it a lot.

CA: When you worked for the Post, *there was a great deal of newspaper competition in Washington, as opposed to today, when the* Post's *only competition is the* Washington Times. *Did the competition provide a lot of excitement for you as a reporter?*

DONOVAN: There were five papers, all very competitive nationally and locally. They all paid low wages, even taking inflation since that time into account. But the *Post* was a great paper to start out on, because the better people were constantly being hired away by government agencies, or better-paying publications, and a young reporter on the *Post* who could put up with the wages could get extremely attractive assignments within a short time. At the age of twenty-seven, having been there only four years, I was covering the White House and the State Department.

CA: Is there any one period during your time at the Post *that stands out in your memory?*

DONOVAN: Yes, when I was covering the White House and the State Department immediately before and after Pearl Harbor.

CA: Yes, that must have been quite exciting. By the way, speaking of the war, is it still too early to talk about your wartime work with Naval Intelligence?

DONOVAN: No. I was mainly editing a confidential bulletin for fleet officers dealing with enemy equipment and deployments and the general progress of the war.

CA: As editor in chief of Time Inc., you worked directly for the legendary Henry Luce. What was working for Mr. Luce like?

DONOVAN: It was very stimulating. He had a lively and brilliant mind.

CA: Did you two ever have any disagreements?

DONOVAN: Yes, we had a lot of them, the friendly kind. He loved to argue, and so did I.

CA: I was reading in David Halberstam's book, The Powers That Be, *that you were troubled at one point by what Halberstam called* Time *magazine's "overt partisanship" under Luce. Do you think that's a fair description of some of the things the magazine was doing then?*

DONOVAN: Well, I think during one period, roughly from the end of World War II through the late 1950's, *Time* magazine's partisanship at times was troubling. Luce was concerned that the magazine had that reputation, and asked me to help correct the situation, although we both agreed that *Time* should have a point of view.

CA: Halberstam gives you credit for removing some of the partisanship from the magazine. How did you go about doing that?

DONOVAN: You don't just do this sort of thing with one stroke, or by issuing one memo. It builds up by the way you handle particular stories and particular issues.

CA: Halberstam also wrote, in reference to Time *magazine's reporting of the Vietnam War, that you changed your mind about the war and led* Time *to change its mind on that subject. Is that true?*

DONOVAN: There's a somewhat better account of my part in that change in a book Don Oberdorfer of the *Washington Post* wrote called *Tet!*.

CA: In previous interviews, you have said that the most significant changes you made while editor in chief of Time Inc. were starting People, Money, *and the reborn (monthly)* Life *magazine. Do you still consider those your most significant acts at the company?*

DONOVAN: Yes, along with improvements in our existing magazines. But many other people at the company were involved in those decisions.

CA: Has the reborn Life *been successful?*

DONOVAN: Yes, but of course not on the scale of the weekly *Life* in its heyday. Of course, the monthly *Life* is a much smaller operation.

CA: When Time Inc. decided to start these new magazines, were its decisions based mostly on research or on hunches about what the public was interested in?

DONOVAN: Some hunch, some research.

CA: Time *magazine certainly has been criticized over the years, but* People *also has come in for a lot of criticism. Critics say it's a lightweight gossipy magazine aimed mainly at heavy TV watchers. What's your response?*

DONOVAN: There's room in the publishing spectrum for different sorts of magazines.

CA: Do many people read both Time *and* People*?*

DONOVAN: I'm not familiar with the recent figures, but as of a few years ago the answer would be no. *People* was distributed mostly in supermarkets and other such outlets whereas *Time* was sold mostly by mail subscription, which means somewhat different audiences for each.

CA: In 1953, the publisher of Fortune *became a special assistant to President Eisenhower. Then, in 1979, you became a senior adviser to President Carter. Is that just a coincidence, or is there some tendency to give those jobs to Time Inc. people?*

DONOVAN: The publisher of *Fortune* took a leave of absence to become one of a number of special assistants to President Eisenhower. We've had people take leaves to work in presidential campaigns. And one of the *Time* editors, Jim Keogh, left *Time* and went to work for the Nixon Administration. But I was appointed by Carter, as senior adviser, immediately after my retirement. So I don't think the jobs were reserved for Time Inc. people.

CA: Was it a wrench for you to go from being a publishing executive to being a presidential adviser?

DONOVAN: Well, it's something of a wrench to retire. And I only worked for President Carter for a year. But it was somewhat frustrating.

CA: How was it frustrating?

DONOVAN: I'm writing a book about that now. You'll just have to take my word for it.

CA: Oh, I see. Well, without being coy, let me ask you about your work at the White House. According to contemporary news accounts, you insisted on three major conditions before taking the job. One was direct access to the president . . .

DONOVAN: I didn't insist on that. He made the point very strongly that I would have direct access, although I might not have taken the job if I didn't have it. The conditions I made were that I didn't want to be involved in press relations, and I didn't want to be involved in working on the president's campaign. The idea of direct access was his, one of the first things he brought up; he was trying to build up the importance of the job. Just a couple of days before, he had given Hamilton Jordan the title of chief of staff, although Jordan pretty much performed that function already. And Carter made it official that everyone on the White House staff except [Zbigniew] Brzezinski would report to the president through Jordan. Carter was making it clear that I would also be an exception to that rule.

CA: Did the president honor those agreements during the year you were there?

DONOVAN: Yes, he did.

CA: You handled several projects during that year. You were involved with a presidential commission to define national goals, you apparently gave some advice to Carter on the alleged Soviet combat brigade in Cuba, and you were involved with other projects. How well did those projects go?

DONOVAN: Well, I'm writing about all of this, and I don't know that I want to get into the details of my White House work before the book comes out.

CA: This will be your first book, won't it?

DONOVAN: Yes.

CA: Do you find the sort of writing that goes into a book different than the writing you used to do at Time Inc.?

DONOVAN: Well, it's a lot of work.

BIOGRAPHICAL/CRITICAL SOURCES:

BOOKS

Halberstam, David, *The Powers That Be*, Knopf, 1979.
Oberdorfer, Don, *Tet!*, Doubleday, 1971.

PERIODICALS

Fortune, December 29, 1980, September 21, 1981.
New Republic, January 26, 1980.
Newsweek, April 27, 1964, August 6, 1979.
New York Times, April 17, 1964.

New York Times Book Review, October 17, 1971.
Time, April 24, 1964, June 14, 1971, June 11, 1979, August 6, 1979.
Times Literary Supplement, January 11, 1980.

—*Sketch by Lori R. Clemens*

—*Interview by Peter Benjaminson*

*   *   *

DORSEY, David Frederick, Jr. 1934-

PERSONAL: Born June 30, 1934, in Philadelphia, Pa.; son of David Frederick and Isabel Barbara (Miller) Dorsey. *Education:* Haverford College, A.B., 1956; University of Michigan, A.M., 1957; Princeton University, A.M., 1965, Ph.D., 1967.

ADDRESSES: Office—Department of English, Atlanta University, 223 Chestnut St., Box 263, Atlanta, Ga. 30314.

CAREER: Howard University, Washington, D.C., instructor, 1960-63 and 1966-67, assistant professor of classics and director of introductory humanities, 1967-79; New York University, Washington Square College, New York, N.Y., assistant professor of classics, 1969-72; Atlanta University, Atlanta, Ga., associate professor of English and American studies, 1972—, associate dean of School of Arts and Sciences, 1983—.

MEMBER: African Studies Association, College Language Association, African Literature Association, American Dialect Society, Linguistic Society of America, Phi Beta Kappa.

AWARDS, HONORS: Woodrow Wilson fellow, 1957; Danforth fellow, 1963-66; Ford Foundation fellow, 1970-71.

WRITINGS:

(Contributor) Vernon J. Dixon and Badi G. Foster, editors, *Black or White: An Alternate America,* Little, Brown, 1971.
Formal Elements of the Black Aesthetic, Center for African and Afro-American Studies, Atlanta University, 1972.
(Contributor) Pio Zirimu and Andrew A. Gurr, editors, *Black Aesthetics,* East African Literature Bureau, 1973.
(Editor with Phanuel Egejuru and Stephen H. Arnold) *Design and Intent in African Literature,* Three Continents Press, 1982.
(Contributor) Lemuel A. Johnson, Bernadette Cailler, and others, editors, *Toward Defining the African Aesthetic,* Three Continents Press, 1982.
(Contributor) Mari Evans, editor, *Black Women Writers: A Critical Evaluation,* Anchor/Doubleday, 1984.

WORK IN PROGRESS: Humanistic Inquiry, "an attempt to outline the general concepts, principles of validity, and the like in human disciplines"; a study of issues critical to the analysis of African fiction.

SIDELIGHTS: David Frederick Dorsey, Jr., told *CA:* "All my work has sought to demonstrate what wealth lies in the diversity of mankind's cultural traditions—conscious and unconscious, philosophical and aesthetic—and what prodigal folly there is in any reductive search for sameness."

*   *   *

DOUGHTY, Charles M(ontagu) 1843-1926

BRIEF ENTRY: Born August 19, 1843, in Suffolk, England; died January 20, 1926, in Sissinghurst, Kent, England; cremated, and ashes buried in the cloister at Golder's Green, England. British author. Doughty is best remembered as a writer of Victorian prose, though he considered himself to be primarily a poet. He once stated that his life's goal had always been "to help towards a better common knowledge and use of the Mother Tongue," and to this end he traveled extensively to study various elements of the English language. In 1875 Doughty embarked on a twenty-one-month trip to Arabia, and in 1888 he published the nonfiction work *Travels in Arabia Deserta,* which is generally regarded as his masterpiece. Written in an austere and powerful style that incorporates elements of Arabic and Old English, the book was well-received by scholars but won little public attention until a revised edition appeared in 1921.

Doughty described his next major work, the six-volume series titled *The Dawn in Britain,* as a poem "written in the Homeric tradition." With a few exceptions, its reviews were highly unfavorable. Similarly, none of Doughty's later poems met with widespread critical acclaim. They did, however, win the respect of playwright George Bernard Shaw and such poets as W. H. Auden, William Butler Yeats, Ezra Pound, Hugh MacDiarmid, and John Heath-Stubbs. Among Doughty's more successful poems were *Adam Cast Forth* (1908), in which Adam and Eve are reunited after banishment from Eden, and his last work, *Mansoul,* which Doughty felt was his finest. He was working on a second revision of *Mansoul* at the time of death. Additional writings include *The Cliffs* (1909), *The Clouds* (1912), and *The Titans* (1916).

BIOGRAPHICAL/CRITICAL SOURCES:

BOOKS

Davenport, Guy, *The Geography of the Imagination,* North Point Press, 1980.
Davis, Herbert, *Charles Doughty, 1843-1926,* Wells College Press, 1945.
Dictionary of Literary Biography, Volume 19: *British Poets, 1880-1914,* Gale, 1983.
Fairley, Barker, *Charles M. Doughty: A Critical Study,* Cape, 1927.
Heath-Stubbs, John, *The Darkling Plain,* Eyre & Spottiswoode, 1950.
MacDiarmid, Hugh, *Selected Essays,* edited by Duncan Glen, Cape, 1969.
Tabachnick, Stephen, *Charles Doughty,* Twayne, 1980.
Treneer, Anne, *Charles M. Doughty: A Study of His Prose and Verse,* Cape, 1935.

*   *   *

DOUGLAS, Ellen
See HAXTON, Josephine Ayres

*   *   *

DOVLATOV, Sergei 1941-

PERSONAL: Born September 3, 1941, in Ufa, Bashkiria, U.S.S.R.; immigrated to United States, 1979; son of Donat Mechik (a theatre director) and Nora (a proofreader) Dovlatov; married Elena Ritman (a typesetter), October, 1963; children: Katherine, Nicholas. *Education:* Attended Leningrad A.A. Zhdanov State University, 1959-62.

ADDRESSES: Home—105-38 63rd Dr., Apt. 6S, Forest Hills, N.Y. 11375. *Agent*—Andrew Wylie Agency, 48 West 75th St., New York, N.Y. 10023.

CAREER: Worked as journalist in the U.S.S.R., 1963-78; free-lance writer in Europe and the United States, 1979—. Freelance writer for Radio Liberty in New York, N.Y., 1979—. *Military service:* Soviet Army, 1962-65; conscripted as prison guard.

MEMBER: International P.E.N.

WRITINGS:

IN RUSSIAN, EXCEPT AS NOTED

Nevidimaia kniga, Ardis, 1977-78, translation by Katherine O'Connor and Diana L. Burgin published as *The Invisible Book: Epilogue,* Ardis, 1979 (also see below).
Solo na undervude (satirical anecdote; title means "Solo on Underwood"), Tret'ia Volna (Paris), 1980.
Kompromiss, Serebrianyi vek, 1981, translation by Anne Frydman published as *The Comprise,* Knopf, 1983.
Zona, Ermitazh, 1982, translation by Anne Frydman published as *The Zone,* Knopf, 1985.
Nashi (title means "The Clan"), Ardis, 1983.
Zapovedrik (title means "Reservation"), Ermitazh, 1983.
Remeslo (title means "Craft"; contains rewritten version of *Nevidimaia kniga* [also see above] and *Nevidimaia gazeta* [title means "The Invisible Newspaper"]), Ardis, 1985.

SHORT STORIES

"The Jubilee Boy," published in *New Yorker,* June, 1980.
"Somebody's Death," published in *New Yorker,* October, 1981.
"Straight Ahead," published in *New Yorker,* January, 1982.
"My First Cousin," published in *New Yorker,* December, 1982.

Editor in chief of a Russian weekly, *New American,* 1980-82. Contributor to periodicals, including *New Yorker, Partisan Review, Saturday Review,* and *Village Voice.*

SIDELIGHTS: In 1978 author Sergei Dovlatov was forced to emigrate from his homeland, thus becoming one among the twentieth century's "third wave" of emigrants from the Soviet Union. Although he had been a journalist in good standing in his native land, Dovlatov was virtually unknown to the Soviets as a writer of fiction, having tried, but failing, to publish his work through official means. The aspiring author was undeterred by official circumvention, however, and began publishing fiction in unauthorized publications, including the Russian-language edition of *Kontinent,* and smuggling his manuscripts to the West. As a result, he found himself dismissed from the journalists' union, and then arrested. In Dovlatov's case, however, publicity from the West prompted officials to release him, and shortly thereafter they offered him the opportunity to emigrate. Persuaded to leave, Dovlatov immigrated to the United States, where he has lived since 1979. With his newfound freedom, the former journalist has earned recognition both as a founding editor of *New American,* a newspaper for Russian emigres, and as a writer of short stories and novels.

The Invisible Book, Dovlatov's first manuscript to see publication in the United States, was hailed as "an important literary event" by reviewer Walter F. Kolonosky in *World Literature Today.* Written as an epilogue to a long novel for which Dovlatov was unable to secure a Soviet publisher, the book, according to Kolonosky, constitutes a "literary autobiography." Beginning by recounting his boyhood, Dovlatov goes on to detail his jobs as a journalist and journal editor, and finally, to recount his experience as an unemployed person. In the process, Dovlatov—frustrated by his inability to get an honest book published—manages not only to discourse on his colleagues, but to air his views on publishing and cen-

sorship. His use of anecdotes, puns, and digressions, together with his inclusion of correspondence from literary bureaucrats and reprints of rejection slips, make this account of his book's thwarted publication, in Kolonosky's words, a "satire in the tradition of Arkanov, Gorin, Kamov, and Uspensky."

Although still concerned with censorship issues, since immigrating to the United States Dovlatov has found himself free to write on subjects of his choice and to speak openly about the Soviet system. In an article for the *New York Times,* Walter Goodman quoted him as saying that in the U.S.S.R. "you can't write about crime or slums or drunkenness or the emptiness, boredom, dullness of big-city youth today. You can criticize some aspects of the system, like the failure of a grain plan—but you can't criticize the system." Consequently, Dovlatov added, writers in the Soviet Union "must master the art of knowing what you can write and what you can't write. They know the line where you have to stop." Some Russian emigres, however, believe that the artistic freedom they sought is not to be found in the West. Writing for *Saturday Review,* Susan Schiefelbein explained that Russian artists who come to the United States often get angry at the paucity of support for new American artists and believe that they have simply traded "censorship by the state for censorship by the marketplace." Dovlatov, however—like other of his compatriots—prefers commercial censorship to Soviet censorship. Dovlatov asserted, as Schiefelbein quoted in *Saturday Review:* "Maybe only three out of a thousand intellectual books are marketable in the United States. In the Soviet Union, zero of a thousand reaches the public. The American figure is small but at least it's measurable."

Dovlatov's *The Compromise* is part of that measurable figure. Based on the author's experience as journalist—and narrated by a journalist also named Dovlatov—the novel, declared reviewer Adam Gussow in the *Village Voice,* is one of "inspired madness, pathos, and frontier low humor . . . an unexpectedly compassionate vision of contemporary Soviet life." Each of the book's eleven chapters opens with one of the reporter's news stories and then is followed by his account of what actually happened. In the process, wrote Frank Williams in a *Times Literary Supplement* review, Dovlatov reveals the "absurdity of Soviet life, the fudging, the smudging and the bureaucratic ineptitude that bring some relief to the dreary existence of *homo sovieticus,* whose life is blighted by personal inadequacy, alcoholism and bad sex." At the heart of the book, Williams concluded, is the "axiomatic assumption" that "the truth will always be compromised."

Living in the United States, Dovlatov, no longer forced into the compromises of Soviet life, is able to work freely as a fiction writer and has recently completed another novel, *Nevidimaia gazeta* ("The Invisible Newspaper"). Participating in a March, 1983, public forum sponsored by the Center for Russian and East European Study at the University of Michigan, Dovlatov lamented that he would "never be able to speak Russian to [his] young son, soul to soul." But a few such grievances aside, he and other emigres have found, the *Detroit Free Press* quoted Dovlatov, that "our dreams turned out to be very real."

Dovlatov told *CA:* "In his diaries Dostoevsky wrote that he was always surprised when the adjective 'brave' was added to the word 'general.' After all, the very title general implies bravery. A cowardly general is an absurdity, nonsense. The same thing can be said about a writer's honesty. An honest writer sounds absurd, because a dishonest writer isn't a writer at all.

"The dilemma of the contemporary Soviet writer consists of the following choice: your native land or freedom. Your native land without freedom or freedom without your native land. I chose freedom without my native land, and I don't regret it. Because one way or another I can live in freedom without my native land, but I'm physically incapable of living without freedom."

BIOGRAPHICAL/CRITICAL SOURCES:

PERIODICALS

America, November 7, 1981.
Atlantic, November, 1983.
Commentary, February, 1980.
Detroit Free Press, March 30, 1984.
Harper's, September, 1983.
Los Angeles Times, November 15, 1982, November 24, 1983.
LSA (University of Michigan), Volume 8, number 1, fall, 1984.
Nation, November 5, 1983.
New Statesman, November 25, 1983.
Newsweek, April 27, 1981.
New York Times, December 10, 1981, April 21, 1983, August 30, 1983, October 2, 1983, March 13, 1984.
Observer, February 5, 1984.
Partisan Review, Volume 4, 1983, Volume I, 1984.
Saturday Review, September, 1980.
Time, March 12, 1984.
Times (London), November 24, 1983.
Times Literary Supplement, December 16, 1983.
U.S. News & World Report, March 2, 1981, January 9, 1984.
Village Voice, February 21, 1984.
World Literature Today, winter, 1980.

—*Sketch by Nancy H. Evans*

* * *

DOYLE, Donovan
See BOEGEHOLD, Betty (Doyle)

* * *

DOYLE, Edward Park   1907-1985

OBITUARY NOTICE: Born September 26, 1907, in Rochester, N.Y.; died after a fall, February 19, 1985, in Chicago, Ill. Journalist, editor, and public relations specialist. Doyle was known as the executive director of the now-defunct *Chicago Today* newspaper. A Phi Beta Kappa graduate of the University of Rochester, Doyle served in the U.S. Navy from 1942 to 1946, attaining the rank of lieutenant commander. After World War II he embarked on a journalistic career, working for various newspapers. In 1955 Doyle became executive editor of the *Chicago American,* which later became *Chicago's American,* and, finally, *Chicago Today.* In 1961, when he left *Chicago Today,* Doyle was appointed associate editor at Encyclopedia Britannica Incorporated, where he remained until 1965. He joined the Infoplan division of Interpublic as an executive and three years later became vice-president for public relations at the Alberto-Culver Company. Doyle edited *As We Knew Adlai,* a 1967 book of reminiscences about the prominent American statesman Adlai Stevenson, Jr. In ill health for a few years prior to his death, Doyle is thought to have committed suicide.

OBITUARIES AND OTHER SOURCES:

BOOKS

Dun and Bradstreet Reference Book of Corporate Managements, 1979-1980, Dun & Bradstreet, 1979.
Who's Who in Public Relations (International), 5th edition, PR Publishing, 1976.

PERIODICALS

Chicago Tribune, February 21, 1985, February 22, 1985.

* * *

DRAYNE, George
See McCULLEY, Johnston

* * *

DREGER, Georgia   1918-

PERSONAL: Surname rhymes with "beggar"; born October 16, 1918, in Lamar, Mo.; daughter of George W. (a mail carrier) and Grace (Wilson) Poff; married Ralph M. Dreger (a university professor), August 1, 1959 (divorced); children: David; stepchildren: Philip, Patricia. *Education:* Vanderbilt University, B.S., 1947; Columbia University, M.A., 1955, Ed.D., 1962. *Politics:* Democrat. *Religion:* Society of Friends (Quaker).

ADDRESSES: Home and office—1501 Clairmont Rd., Apt. 2013, Decatur, Ga. 30033.

CAREER: Free-lance writer and editor. Baptist Sunday School Board, Nashville, Tenn., editorial assistant, 1945-48; Friendship Press, New York City, assistant to sales manager, 1948-49; American Baptist Publication Society, Philadelphia, Pa., junior high editor, 1949-52; *Journal of Consulting Psychology,* New York City, editorial secretary, 1952-55; The Marriage Council, Philadelphia, intern in marriage counseling, 1956-57; marriage counselor at Palm Beach County Guidance Center, 1958; Behavioral Classification Project, Jacksonville University, Jacksonville, Fla., research associate, 1962-63; Psychological Research and Services, Baton Rouge, La., associate director, 1965-73; Center for Research in Social Change, Emory University, Atlanta, Ga., research specialist, 1974.

Salvation Army Southern Headquarters, Atlanta, staff member of men's social service department, 1975-76; Emory University, Atlanta, assistant for education programs in School of Medicine's department of rehabilitation medicine, 1976-78, assistant to the editors of *Endocrinology,* 1978-79, assistant to the Woodruff Medical Center information officer, 1979-81; *Words on Paper,* Decatur, Ga., writer and editor, 1982. Acting executive director of Florida Council on Human Relations, 1961; state president of Family Relations Council of Louisiana, 1968-70. Consultant in research and education to Baton Rouge Consumer Protection Center, 1972.

AWARDS, HONORS: A Different Dream was selected by the Association of Christian Schools International as one of the ten best youth books of 1982.

WRITINGS:

A Different Dream (novel for young people), Broadman, 1983.

Also author of *Year of Promise* (novel for young people), 1984, and *Heirloom Stitchery: You Can Do It!,* 1984.

WORK IN PROGRESS: Vows Shall Stand, a novel for adults.

DRYSDALE, Vera Louise 1923-

PERSONAL: Born May 4, 1923, in Peking, China; American citizen born abroad; daughter of Charles Lewis (a Presbyterian minister) and Vera (a church organist and teacher; maiden name, McCormick) Irwin; married Alexander T. Drysdale (in plumbing and heating), July 14, 1951; children: Linda Ann Drysdale Ackerman, Charles Alexander. *Education:* College of Wooster, B.A., 1944.

ADDRESSES: Home—705 Rio Grande Ave., Santa Fe, N.M. 87501. *Office*—Hunka Studio Gallery, 705 Rio Grande Ave., Santa Fe, N.M. 87501.

CAREER: Hallmark (greeting card publisher), Kansas City, Mo., stylist, 1945-46; free-lance artist and illustrator, 1968—. Creator of card and print series "Original Americans," 1968. Judge at American Indian arts and crafts annual exhibitions in Arizona and New Mexico. Paintings and drawings included in exhibitions of galleries, including Fenn, Jamison, Kachina & Dewey-Kofron Galleries, Santa Fe, N.M., Northland Gallery, Flagstaff, Ariz., Trailside Galleries, Jackson Hole and Scottsdale, Ariz., American Indian Collection, Beverly Hills, Calif., and Institute of American Indian Arts, Santa Fe. Lecturer for California art associations.

AWARDS, HONORS: Southwest Book Award from Southern Books Competition, 1972, for *Kee's Home.*

WRITINGS:

(Illustrator) Geraldine Hall and Irvy Goossen, *Kee's Home: A Beginning Navajo-English Reader,* Northland Press, 1972.
(Editor and illustrator) *The Gift of the Sacred Pipe* (new edition of *The Sacred Pipe* by Joseph Epes Brown), University of Oklahoma Press, 1982.

ILLUSTRATOR; "GOD'S HAND IN HISTORY" SERIES

Mary Wilson, *Pioneers,* Blandford, 1960.
Wilson, *Son of God,* Blandford, 1969.
Wilson, *A Rushing Mighty Wind,* Blandford, 1963.
Wilson, *Builders and Destroyers,* Blandford, 1968.

WORK IN PROGRESS: Illustrations of early Plains Indian life and ceremony.

SIDELIGHTS: Vera Louise Drysdale told *CA:* "I have been interested in Plains Indian mysticism for some time, and I have wanted to use my artistic gift to illustrate some of their greater concepts. I was able to accomplish this fully in *The Gift of the Sacred Pipe.* The paintings and drawings in this book are my own dream perceptions pictorialized. They all emerged from an inner visionary knowledge and seemed almost to paint themselves. The American Indian philosophies, so uniquely suited to this continent and hemisphere, have long fascinated discerning people all over the world. They are coming around again, and in fresh dimensions to inspire mankind.

"*The Gift of the Sacred Pipe* was based on Black Elk's original account of the seven sacred rites of the Oglala Sioux, as recorded by Joseph Epes Brown in 1947 for *The Sacred Pipe.* I spent four-and-one-half years creating eight major paintings and twenty-eight drawings—inspired by reading Black Elk's original book. At Joseph Epes Brown's request, I edited and condensed the earlier edition in order to make room for the many illustrations featured in the new larger format edition."

DUKE, Robin (Antony Hare) 1916-1984

OBITUARY NOTICE: Born March 21, 1916; died November 27, 1984. Public servant and author. Educated at Oxford University, Duke was a British Council official for three decades. Serving with Britain's Royal Artillery from 1939 to 1946, Duke was on staff in the Middle East and the Mediterranean between 1942 and 1945, then worked for one year for Britain's political adviser's office in Athens, Greece. Duke joined the British Council in 1947, serving in various countries before becoming the council's representative in Japan, where he stayed from 1967 to 1977. A recipient of the Japanese Order of the Sacred Treasure, 3rd Class, Duke was made an officer of the Order of the British Empire in 1961, advancing to the rank of commander in 1970; in 1975 he was named commander of the Royal Victorian Order. Duke was a connoisseur of Japanese culture and in 1979 published *The Pillow Book of Sei Shonagon,* considered a masterpiece of Japanese medieval literature. His other writings include *The English Governess at the Court of Siam.*

OBITUARIES AND OTHER SOURCES:

BOOKS

Who's Who, 134th edition, St. Martin's, 1982.

PERIODICALS

Times (London), December 11, 1984.

* * *

DULLES, John Foster 1888-1959

BRIEF ENTRY: Born February 25, 1888, in Washington, D.C.; died of cancer, May 24, 1959, in Washington, D.C.; buried at Arlington National Cemetery, Arlington, Va. American attorney, diplomat, statesman, and author. The architect of American foreign policy in the 1950's, Dulles served as President Dwight D. Eisenhower's secretary of state from 1953 to 1959. Dulles, who has been described as one of the most powerful secretaries of state in U.S. history, advocated a firm military and diplomatic policy toward the Communist bloc. This policy became known as "brinkmanship" because of the implication that the nation was prepared to go to the brink of nuclear war to prevent the expansion of communism and Soviet hegemony.

Early in his career Dulles acted as legal counsel for the American delegation at the 1919 Versailles Peace Conference, and in 1944 he participated in the Dumbarton Oaks Conference that laid the foundation for the United Nations. As a consultant to the Department of State, Dulles successfully negotiated a peace treaty with Japan in 1951 that restored the Asian nation's sovereignty. The following year he was named secretary of state by President Eisenhower. Dulles played an important role in several international crises; during the dispute between China and Taiwan, for example, Dulles's diplomatic efforts defused a crisis that threatened to turn into war. Dulles failed, however, to prevent Soviet military intervention following the 1956 uprising in Hungary. In addition, he alienated Great Britain, France, and Israel by refusing to support them in their attempt to wrest the Suez Canal from Egypt, then a Soviet ally. Dulles represented Western interests in the 1958 Berlin crisis—precipitated by Soviet leader Nikita S. Khrushchev's demand that West Berlin become an autonomous city—but his illness prevented him from completing his mission.

Dulles's writings include two books, *War, Peace, and Change* (1939), in which the statesman argues that nations resort to war because of the lack of international mechanisms whereby disagreements can be settled, and *War or Peace* (1950), an analysis of international relations in the aftermath of World War II.

BIOGRAPHICAL/CRITICAL SOURCES:

BOOKS

Current Biography, Wilson, 1953.
Guhin, Michael, *John Foster Dulles: A Statesman and His Times,* Columbia University Press, 1972.
Hoopes, Townsend, *The Devil and John Foster Dulles,* Little, Brown, 1973.

PERIODICALS

New York Times, May 25, 1959.
Times (London), May 25, 1959.

* * *

DUNCAN, Carl P(orter) 1921-

BRIEF ENTRY: Born December 27, 1921, in Presque Isle, Me. American psychologist, educator, and author. After four years at Brown University, Duncan began teaching at Northwestern University in 1947. He became a professor of psychology there in 1960. Duncan edited *Thinking: Current Experimental Studies* (Lippincott, 1967) and co-edited *Human Memory: A Festschrift in Honor of Benton J. Underwood* (Appleton, 1972). *Address:* Department of Psychology, Northwestern University, Evanston, Ill. 60201.

BIOGRAPHICAL/CRITICAL SOURCES:

BOOKS

Who's Who in America, 42nd edition, Marquis, 1982.

* * *

DUNCAN, William (Robert) 1944-

PERSONAL: Born August 12, 1944, in Watford, England; son of Andrew Alan (an engineer) and Dora (an artist; maiden name, Young) Duncan; married Ikuko Hiroe (a book designer), March 14, 1970; children: Catherine Atsuko. *Education:* Attended Middlesex Business School. *Politics:* Liberal.

ADDRESSES: Office—Duncan Publishing, 3 Colin Gardens, Hendon, London NW9 6EL, England.

CAREER: Northorpe Hall Trust (charity for delinquent children), Mirfield, Yorkshire, England, assistant to director, 1964-66; associated with Japan National Tourist Organisation and Japanese National Railways in London, England, and Tokyo, Japan, 1966-70; free-lance leader of luxury tours through India, Southeast Asia, and Japan, 1970-71; Egon Ronay Organisation, London, editor and inspector of oriental restaurants, 1971-75; Kluwer Publishing, London, editorial manager, 1975-79; Oyez Publishing, London, managing editor, 1979-80; Duncan Publishing, London, managing partner, 1980—.

WRITINGS:

A Guide to Japan, Ward, Lock, 1970.
Japanese Markets Review, Gower Press, 1974.
Doing Business With Japan: A Guide to Setting-Up Operations, Trading, Travel, and Leisure, Gower Press, 1976.

Thailand: A Complete Guide, Tuttle, 1976, 2nd edition, Roger Lascelles, in press.
Business With Japan (tentative title), Penguin, in press.

Contributor to magazines. Editor in chief for Japan for monthly newspaper *Export Times.*

SIDELIGHTS: William Duncan told *CA:* "My aim is to produce books of high quality which are both useful and entertaining. They may also make some contribution towards a better understanding between peoples of different nations.

"A favorite part of my work is traveling to the Far East and exploring lesser-known, relatively inaccessible places, staying in villages. I believe that people living in the modern cities of the West have much to learn and benefit from the people who live close to nature in the East.

"I am impressed by the Eastern people's stronger commitment to care for others in their family and in their community, particularly in the provincial towns and villages. Their smiling faces are a constant reminder that human happiness does not come from an abundance of material possessions but rather from within oneself and by maintaining warm relationships with others. By contrast, city life in the West creates many lonely people and can easily become self-destructive if we allow ourselves to succumb to the pressures of the modern competitive, commercial world."

* * *

DUNKELL, Samuel (V.) 1919-

BRIEF ENTRY: Born August 7, 1919, in Paterson, N.J. American psychiatrist, educator, and author. After medical training at the University of Zurich, Dunkell became an instructor at New York City's Postgraduate Center for Mental Health in 1962. He was appointed medical director of the center in 1974. In addition, Dunkell has maintained a private practice of psychiatry and has taught at Cornell University. He wrote *Sleep Positions: The Night Language of the Body* (Morrow, 1977) and *Lovelives: How We Make Love* (Morrow, 1978). *Address:* 124 East 28th St., New York, N.Y. 10016; and 1065 Lexington Ave., New York, N.Y.

BIOGRAPHICAL/CRITICAL SOURCES:

PERIODICALS

New York Times, February 22, 1977.
Washington Post Book World, April 17, 1977.

* * *

DWYER, Thomas A. 1923-

PERSONAL: Born November 18, 1923, in New York, N.Y. *Education:* University of Dayton, B.S., 1945; Case Institute of Technology (now Case Western Reserve University), M.S., 1951, Ph.D., 1960.

ADDRESSES: Office—Department of Computer Science, University of Pittsburgh, 4200 Fifth Ave., Pittsburgh, Pa. 15260.

CAREER: Mathematics teacher and department chairman at high school in Cleveland, Ohio, 1947-57; University of Dayton, Dayton, Ohio, associate professor of computer science,

1960-67; University of Pittsburgh, Pittsburgh, Pa., associate professor, 1968-76, professor of computer science, 1976—. Research associate at Argonne National Laboratory, 1963-64.

MEMBER: American Mathematical Society, Society for Industrial and Applied Mathematics, Association of Computing Machinery.

AWARDS, HONORS: National Science Foundation fellow, 1960.

WRITINGS:

(With Michael Kaufman) *A Guided Tour for Computer Programming in BASIC,* Houghton, 1973.
(With Margot Critchfield) *Computer Resource Book: Algebra,* Houghton, 1976.
(With Critchfield) *BASIC and the Personal Computer,* Addison-Wesley, 1978.
(With Critchfield) *A Bit of BASIC,* Addison-Wesley, 1980.
(With Critchfield) *You Just Bought a Personal What?,* McGraw, 1980.
(With Critchfield) *CP-M and the Personal Computer,* Addison-Wesley, 1983.

(With Critchfield) *Structured Program Design With the TRS-80 BASIC,* McGraw, 1983.
(With Critchfield) *Pocket Guide to Microsoft BASIC,* Addison-Wesley, 1983.
(With Critchfield) *Pocket Guide to CP-M,* Addison-Wesley, 1983.
(With Kaufman) *A Guided Tour of Computer Programming in BASIC,* Entelek, 1984.
(With Critchfield) *A Bit of IBM BASIC,* Addison-Wesley, 1984.
(With Critchfield) *BASIC: A Guide to Structured Programming,* Houghton, 1985.
A Bit of Applesoft BASIC, Addison-Wesley, 1985.
(With Critchfield) *C and the Personal Computer,* Addison-Wesley, 1985.
(With Critchfield) *MS-DOS and the Personal Computer,* Addison-Wesley, in press.

AVOCATIONAL INTERESTS: Flying (commercial pilot's license, instrument land/seaplane/multi-engine flight instructor's license).

E

EAST, Bob 1920(?)-1985

OBITUARY NOTICE: Born c. 1920; died following cancer surgery, c. March 6 in 1985, in Miami, Fla. Photojournalist. East, a prize-winning newspaper photographer, had a thirty-three-year career with the *Miami Herald*. East's death was determined to be the result of medical malpractice that occurred when he underwent surgery for the removal of a cancerous eye. A formaldehyde-like solution intended to preserve the diseased eye for analysis was accidentally injected into East's spinal column, causing irreversible brain damage. Five days after the operation, when mechanical life support systems were withdrawn, East was declared dead.

OBITUARIES AND OTHER SOURCES:

PERIODICALS

New York Times, March 10, 1985.

* * *

EBERSTADT, Lindley E. 1910(?)-1985

OBITUARY NOTICE: Born c. 1910 in Little Silver, N.J.; died in 1985. Bookseller, collector, and bibliographer. Eberstadt was president of Edward Eberstadt & Sons, an antiquarian book firm founded by his father in 1907. Eberstadt's principal interest was Americana, including books, manuscripts, and art, and he helped build important collections at institutions such as the Yale University Library, the Harvard University Library, and the Library of Congress. Eberstadt's extensive collection contained manuscripts, maps, and diaries dating from the Spanish conquest of the American Southwest. He wrote many bibliographical monographs, some of which were published in 1965 as a four-volume collection titled *Eberstadt Catalogues of Americana.*

OBITUARIES AND OTHER SOURCES:

PERIODICALS

AB Bookman's Weekly, April 8, 1985.

* * *

EDHOLM, O(tto) G(ustav) 1909-1985

OBITUARY NOTICE: Born in 1909; died January 18, 1985.

Physician, educator, and author. Edholm, who was a known authority on human survival in harsh environments and an expert on blood circulation, developed research projects for the British Antarctic Survey. During World War II Edholm studied the effect of hemorrhage on the human circulatory system for the shock committee of Britain's Medical Research Council, which in 1949 appointed him first head of its division of human physiology. In 1944 Edholm was a professor of physiology at the Royal Veterinary College in London, and shortly after the war he taught physiology in London, Ontario, Canada. He also served on various British defense committees.

Edholm served as visiting professor of physiology in Jerusalem, Israel, in 1962, and in 1973 he went to Antarctica as a guest of the British Antarctic Survey. The 1970 Bellingausen Medalist of the antarctic research committee of the Soviet Academy of Science, the educator was elected a fellow of the Royal College of Physicians in 1975 in recognition of his scientific publications. Edholm was also awarded an honorary doctorate by the University of Surrey in 1979. Edholm's 1954 work, *Man in a Cold Environment,* was written with Alan C. Burton. His other books include *Exploration Medicine, Physiology of Human Survival, The Biology of Work, Polar Human Biology,* and *Principles and Practice of Human Physiology.*

OBITUARIES AND OTHER SOURCES:

PERIODICALS

Times (London), February 16, 1985.

* * *

EHRLICH, Max 1909-1983

OBITUARY NOTICE—See index for *CA* sketch: Born October 10, 1909, in Springfield, Mass.; died in 1983. Journalist, screenwriter, and author. Ehrlich worked for the *Knickerbocker Press and Evening News* in Albany, New York, and the *Daily News* in Springfield, Massachusetts, before becoming a full-time writer in 1949. He was the author of numerous novels, including *First Train to Babylon, The Takers,* and *The Reincarnation of Peter Proud.* Ehrlich also wrote screenplays, including "Z.P.G.," "The Edict," and "The Savage Is Loose," and scripts for television series, including "Star Trek," "The Defenders," and "Wild Wild West." (Date of death provided by wife, Margaret Druckman Ehrlich.)

OBITUARIES AND OTHER SOURCES:

BOOKS

International Authors and Writers Who's Who, 9th edition,
  [and] *International Who's Who in Poetry,* 6th edition,
  Melrose, 1982.
The Writers Directory: 1984-1986, St. James Press, 1983.

* * *

EIGEN, Michael 1936-

PERSONAL: Born January 11, 1936, in Passaic, N.J.; son of
Sol (a lawyer) and Jeanette (a teacher; maiden name; Brody)
Eigen. *Education:* University of Pennsylvania, A.B. (with
honors), 1957; New School for Social Research, Ph.D., 1974.

ADDRESSES: Office—225 Central Park W., New York, N.Y.
10024.

CAREER: Psychologist and psychoanalyst. Senior member,
faculty and training analyst at National Psychological Association for Psychoanalysis; former director of training at Institute for Expressive Analysis; faculty member and supervisor
at New Hope Guild. Professional musician.

MEMBER: American Academy of Psychotherapists, Phi Beta
Kappa.

WRITINGS:

(Editor with Marie Coleman Nelson, and contributor) *Evil:
  Self and Culture,* Human Sciences Press, 1984.

Also author of poems and short stories. Contributor of more
than forty articles and reviews to journals and books in the
behavioral sciences, including *International Journal of Psychoanalytic Psychotherapy, Psychoanalytic Review,* and *International Review of Psychoanalysis.*

WORK IN PROGRESS: Madness (tentative title), a book on
psychosis, for Chiron.

SIDELIGHTS: Michael Eigen told *CA:* "Personal crises at the
age of twenty-one precipitated an extended inner search that
evolved into a twenty-year career as a psychotherapist. The
psychotherapeutic session has afforded me an excellent microcosm within which to trace and participate in the moment-to-
moment offering and refusal/acceptance of grace. In my paper
'On Working With "Unwanted Patients"' (*International Journal
of Psychoanalytic Psychotherapy,* 1977), I tried to portray work
with aspects of the self that will not budge, a sort of hardening
of the psychic arteries that often appears revolting and mad-
dening. I tried to tie in the structure of this process with broader
aspects of our age in 'Demonic Aspects of the Self' (*Evil: Self
and Culture*).

"In 'On the Significance of the Face' (*Psychoanalytic Review,*
1980), I explored the centrality of the 'face of the other' in
the rebirth process and the constitution of the self. Perhaps my
fullest statements to date on what I take to be the basic structures of the self may be found in the 'Area of Faith in Win-
nicott, Lacan and Bion' (*International Journal of Psychoanalytic Psychotherapy,* 1981) and 'Dual Union or
Indifferentiation?: A Critique of the Sense of Psychic Crea-
tiveness in Marion Miller' (*International Review of Psychoanalysis,* 1983).

"Today madness and evil are felt to be profoundly intertwined, in spite of rationalistic beliefs of criminal justice to
the contrary. Deep therapeutic work always involves an en-

counter with madness-evil. If someone is a therapist or patient
in more than name this seems obvious. We are very much
entangled in evil and grace in ways that run through the whole
social fabric. In therapy, at least, two people do make a difference to each other. How does therapy differ from any other
encounter in that respect? For certain people, like myself, it
does—although we are still finding out how."

* * *

ELICKER, Charles W. 1951-1978

OBITUARY NOTICE: Born in 1951; died in 1978. Author.
Elicker's writings include *Journeys Without Maps . . . Stories
of How Youth Are Finding Their Ways in the Church,* written
with Sara Ashby Sawtell and Robert W. Carlson. (Year of
death provided by publisher, Robert L. Burt.)

* * *

ELLERBEE, Linda 1944-

PERSONAL: Born August 15, 1944, in Bryan, Tex.; married
third husband, John David Klein (a television reporter); children: Vanessa, Joshua. *Education:* Attended Vanderbilt University.

ADDRESSES: Office—NBC-News, 30 Rockefeller Plaza, New
York, N.Y. 10020.

CAREER/WRITINGS: WVON-Radio, Chicago, Ill., news-
caster and disc jockey, 1964-67; KSJO-Radio, San Francisco,
Calif., program director, 1967-68; associated with KJNO-Radio,
Juneau, Alaska, beginning in 1969; worked as a reporter for
Associated Press (AP), Dallas, Tex.; KHOU-TV, Houston,
Tex., reporter, 1972-73; WCBS-TV, New York City, re-
porter, 1973-76; National Broadcasting Co. (NBC-TV), New
York City, "NBC Nightly News" correspondent in Washing-
ton, D.C., 1975-78, co-anchor of weekly television program
"NBC News Weekend," 1978-82, co-anchor and general ed-
itor of nightly television program "NBC News Overnight,"
1982-83, co-anchor of weekly television program "Summer
Sunday U.S.A.," beginning in 1984.

SIDELIGHTS: Linda Ellerbee gained prominence in the field
of broadcast journalism as co-anchor of "NBC News Overnight," the late-night television news program that aired five
times weekly from July of 1982 to December of 1983. Described by *People*'s Kristin McMurran as "a bright light in
the murky realm of night-owl newscasting," Ellerbee brought
to the critically acclaimed show what McMurran called a "refreshing blend of stylish prose and wry delivery."

Ellerbee first joined the National Broadcasting Company (NBC)
in 1975 as a news correspondent in Washington, D.C. Assigned to cover the U.S. House of Representatives, she soon
developed a dislike for Washington politicians.

She explained in an interview with McMurran: "I don't like
the idea that the way to get a story is to cozy up to them. . . .
It's a very bad practice to be socializing with those people.
Besides," Ellerbee chided, "they probably have diseases."
After three years in the nation's capital, she moved to New
York City, where she and Lloyd Dobyns anchored "NBC News
Weekend," a weekly program with a magazine format. In
1982, the network launched "NBC News Overnight," naming
Ellerbee and Dobyns (who was later replaced by Bill Schech-
ner) as the show's anchors.

Critics attributed the success of "Overnight" to its mixture of a straight-forward, no-nonsense approach with what Christopher Connelly defined in *Rolling Stone* as "bracing wit and a dash of hard-won cynicism." Reviewing "Overnight" when it was first broadcast, Martin Kitman noted in *New Leader* that "After the most important stories, which take up only the first 10 minutes of the show, the last 50 minutes of Dobyns and Ellerbee gives you a feeling of what is actually going on in the country." Connelly praised the program for "news that emphasized the reporting and interpreting skills of its anchors and correspondents instead of flashy graphics or stagy, on-camera confrontations."

Despite the show's popularity, NBC announced the cancellation of "Overnight" in the fall of 1983. The announcement prompted more than fifteen hundred letters from viewers protesting the show's demise, and many sympathetic "Overnight" fans sent money in hopes that their contributions would offset NBC's reported loss of $6 million in advertising revenues. "The loss of 'Overnight' is a tough one," Connelly lamented, "for it deprives the airwaves of the only news show that embodied two of mankind's most appealing qualities: intelligence and a sense of humor."

CA INTERVIEW

CA interviewed Linda Ellerbee by phone on October 31 and November 15, 1983, at her office in New York City.

CA: What did you study at Vanderbilt?

ELLERBEE: I studied history, but I quit when I was nineteen.

CA: Why did you quit?

ELLERBEE: Because at age nineteen I really couldn't find my bottom side with both hands. No particularly good reason.

CA: Do you recommend the study of history for people who want to go into broadcasting?

ELLERBEE: It makes a lot more sense than communications schools. People who want to be reporters should study all of the history, political science, languages, literature, and so forth that they can. We have too many people right now who go to communications schools and when they come out they know everything about holding a microphone, but they don't know what to ask.

CA: How did you move from a job as a reporter for Associated Press (AP) to a job as a TV reporter?

ELLERBEE: I wrote a letter at work, at my computer terminal. In the letter, I maligned a couple of Texas newspapers and the Vietnam War and said that when a friend of mine left the AP Bureau the bureau chief probably would hire a half-black Chicano lesbian. Then I hit the wrong button by mistake. The letter went out over the AP wire in four states and I was fired.

CA: Did you have regrets about moving to TV?

ELLERBEE: Well, I certainly did at the time. But at first I was comforted by the fact that they were paying me twice what I had been making at the AP. That soothes a lot of regrets. And over the ten years that I have been in the business I have really come to like television and working with pictures.

CA: Do you like it better than working with print?

ELLERBEE: I couldn't answer that because there are certain stories that are better for television, and there are other stories that are better for writing. Sometimes when the story is one that would be easily written you feel that having the camera crew with you gets in the way. And that's true of a lot of political coverage, where TV people end up relying on pictures of parades and speeches, which is not what real political coverage is about. For covering politics, writing for print is a lot easier. But when something happens such as the Marines being bombed in Lebanon, print cannot begin to show you or tell you what a picture does.

CA: What do you think of the job TV does in Washington, where most of the stories are political?

ELLERBEE: Not much. But in Washington you're working with a lot of restrictions on picture taking. All the TV pictures that come from the House of Representatives, for instance, are controlled by the House itself and not by television. The TV people can't turn the camera; they can't point at one thing or another. No cameras are allowed in the Senate, and in the White House you're locked in a little press room. It's very difficult to do television stories under those circumstances. Also, a lot of what happens in Washington is more easily understood and reported in print. It's just not picturesque.

CA: How did you move from being a reporter on "NBC Nightly News" to being a co-anchor on "Weekend"?

ELLERBEE: "Weekend" had been on the air once a month for three years. They decided to make it once a week and put it in prime time. In order to handle the work load of turning a once-a-month show into a once-a-week show, they had to have a second reporter. And Reuven Frank, who was executive producer of the show [now president of NBC-News], asked me to do the job.

CA: Did you prefer "Weekend" to your next show, "NBC News Overnight"?

ELLERBEE: That's a hard question to answer. They are the two favorite shows I've ever done. The only advantage one has over the other is that I got to go to bed at night when I was doing "Weekend."

CA: What about in terms of their news content?

ELLERBEE: "Weekend" was a magazine and that's a very different thing than a five-night-a-week news show, so they're very hard to compare.

CA: Why was "Weekend" taken off the air?

ELLERBEE: Fred Silverman [president and chief executive of NBC] didn't like it, and it kept moving around. You can imagine what happened to its ratings when first it was on Friday nights, then it was on Saturday nights, and then for a short time it was on Thursday nights, which is hard when you're calling the show "Weekend." Finally, Fred Silverman simply canceled it.

CA: Do you think "NBC News Overnight" was given enough time to succeed? ["NBC News Overnight" was canceled in

November, 1983, along with the competing overnight news shows on the other two networks.]

ELLERBEE: Yes, I do. The show did succeed. There's no question about the show succeeding. Even NBC, when it canceled it, said, "The show is wonderful. The show is a success." The problem was that their studies showed that there never would be enough people awake at 1:30 A.M. for them to make a profit on the show. It didn't matter how much of the audience we had. Had we had it all it wouldn't have been enough.

CA: Then there weren't any changes you could have made?

ELLERBEE: No. That's what they said. In fact, at one point they said, "You know, if the show wasn't so good, you'd probably still be on the air, because we'd still be trying to fix it."

CA: And that makes sense?

ELLERBEE: In the terrible world of television, it does make sense, which ought to worry you.

CA: Who do you think comprised "Overnight"'s audience?

ELLERBEE: The network never found out who the audience was or never really tried. I think our audience was split between those pepole for whom we were their only newscast because they worked second or third shift, and those people for whom we were not their only newscast but simply their newscast of choice.

CA: What will that audience do now?

ELLERBEE: I don't know. According to the network, that audience doesn't exist, despite all the letters and phone calls we've been getting.

CA: You're well known for using a lot of quotations and odd little facts in your lead-ins. Why do you do that?

ELLERBEE: You try to put a story in context. A lead-in ought to add something to a story, not repeat something that's in the story. A lead-in ought to give you something you're not getting in the story, and sometimes that's the odd fact. Sometimes it's a thought that someone else said better than you could.

CA: If you were to be transferred to a daytime or evening news show now, would you write the news differently than you were writing it for "Overnight"?

ELLERBEE: No. Not in style. But if I were doing a half-hour news show, obviously my copy would have to be shorter than it would be for an hour news show.

CA: But you wouldn't change your writing style in any other way?

ELLERBEE: Would I harness myself in some way? No. Unless of course they offered me enough money.

CA: You're not really a mercenary, are you?

ELLERBEE: Oh God, who knows? It's easy to say you're not a mercenary when nobody has offered you enough money. Offer me $15 million and find out whether or not I'm a mercenary.

CA: You have been quoted as saying you "make more money than God." [Ellerbee earned more than $300,000 in 1983.]

ELLERBEE: That was really out of context. A friend was on the phone saying, "Can you pay me the five dollars you owe me?" and I said, "Of course, don't I make more money than God?"

CA: What do you think of the apparent inclination of the networks to hire people for their looks rather than for their ability?

ELLERBEE: I think it sucks. But I don't know if that's really true of the networks. I think you find more of that at local stations.

CA: You don't sound too enthusiastic about television as a whole.

ELLERBEE: No, I'm not; but I've watched it, haven't you? It's hard to be too enthusiastic about television as a whole if you've watched it.

CA: Is there anything that you'd do to improve it other than improve the newswriting?

ELLERBEE: My God, if you improved the writing that would be a 90 percent improvement all across the board.

CA: You keep one or two broken TV sets around. Is that some kind of subconscious hatred of TV?

ELLERBEE: There's nothing subconscious about it. One of them was an empty, broken RCA set from 1949 with a round screen that I found on the street with two bullet holes in it, and I kept it. The other was a perfectly workable television I threw out of a second-story window one night, but it still works even though it's cracked.

CA: Why do you keep them around?

ELLERBEE: The one that works I keep around because you can see television on it. The one that doesn't work I keep around because you can't.

CA: Let's say you were put in charge of the news at all three networks right now and you could do anything you wanted with them. What would you do?

ELLERBEE: Right away? Nuke 'em.

CA: You don't think TV should be in the news business at all?

ELLERBEE: TV should be in the news business, but we're only marginally in the news business. Some of us are in the news business, but the people who run it are in the profit business.

It's an imperfect medium. It's better than most people think it is in some ways, and it's worse in ways they never stop to consider. It's nothing to be satisfied about, but no, I wouldn't do away with it.

CA: What are the ways television news is better than most people think it is?

ELLERBEE: There is no conspiracy to distort the news we do. There really isn't. Most reporters are pretty damn fair and they try. The problem is a lot of them aren't good writers, so they're dull, or they get fooled. But it's better than most people think it is. It's not a villain at its worst, and at its best, it's sort of a reflection of our worst and our best. It's not anything at all by itself.

CA: How is it worse than people think it is?

ELLERBEE: People like to believe that a camera can't lie, but it's easy to lie with a camera. And people like to think that people on television know what they're talking about, but that's not always true either.

CA: Do you ever feel when doing a story that you don't know what you're talking about?

ELLERBEE: Of course I do. Everybody does.

CA: On any particular kind of story?

ELLERBEE: Every story! Particularly when you're depending on wire service reports and third- or fourth-hand news, which is what you depend on when you're doing a news program.

CA: You don't know where it came from, is that what you mean?

ELLERBEE: Just because it says "AP" on the top does not give you the greatest feeling of security.

CA: Is your long-run ambition to be the sole anchor of one show or another?

ELLERBEE: No. My ambition in the long run is to be out of this business and living happily on the beach somewhere. If I have to work, I'd like to direct movies.

CA: What kind of movies?

ELLERBEE: Good ones. Movies with a story and nice pictures.

CA: Have you made any moves in that direction?

ELLERBEE: Yes, I have. I've spent ten years in a network learning how to produce and edit.

BIOGRAPHICAL/CRITICAL SOURCES:

PERIODICALS

Film Comment, February, 1984.
Los Angeles Times, November 11, 1983, November 23, 1983, December 5, 1983, June 14, 1984.
New Leader, September 6, 1982.
Newsweek, July 2, 1984.
New York, May 30, 1983.
New York Times, November 26, 1983.
People, June 27, 1983.
Rolling Stone, January 19, 1984.
Washington Post, October 18, 1983.

—*Interview by Peter Benjaminson*

ELLIS, Charles D(aniel)   1937-

BRIEF ENTRY: Born October 22, 1937, in Boston, Mass. American executive, consultant, and author. In 1972 Ellis became president of Greenwich Research Associates. He is a chartered financial analyst who has worked for Rockefeller Brothers, Incorporated, and Donaldson, Lofkins & Jewette. He wrote *Institutional Investing* (Dow Jones-Irwin, 1971), *The Repurchase of Common Stock* (Ronald, 1971), and *The Second Crash* (Simon & Schuster, 1973). *Address:* 135 East Putnam Ave., Greenwich, Conn. 06830.

BIOGRAPHICAL/CRITICAL SOURCES:

PERIODICALS

Newsweek, May 28, 1973.
New York Times Book Review, July 1, 1973.

*   *   *

ELLIS, Peter F(rancis)   1921-

PERSONAL: Born April 27, 1921 in New York, N.Y.; son of Thomas William (an electrical engineer) and Margaret (a homemaker; maiden name, McGuire) Ellis; married Judith Monahan (a homemaker), October 18, 1975; children: Marc, Eric. *Education:* Mount St. Alphonsus Seminary, M.S., 1948; Angelicum, Rome, Italy, S.T.L., 1949; Pontifical Gregorian University, S.S.L., 1951. *Politics:* Democrat. *Religion:* Roman Catholic.

ADDRESSES: Home—Clapp Hill Rd., No. 218A, Lagrangeville, N.Y. 12540. *Office*—Graduate School of Religion and Religious Education, Fordham University, Bronx, N.Y. 10458.

CAREER: Mount St. Alphonsus Seminary, Esopus, N.Y., professor of sacred scripture, 1951-68; Fordham University, Bronx, N.Y., assistant professor, 1968-72, associate professor, 1972-78, professor of biblical theology, 1978—.

MEMBER: Catholic Biblical Association of America, Society of Biblical Literature.

WRITINGS:

The Men and the Message of the Old Testament, Liturgical Press, 1963.
The Yahwist: The Bible's First Theologian, Liturgical Press, 1967.
I and II Kings, Liturgical Press, 1969.
Matthew: His Mind and His Message, Liturgical Press, 1973.
The Christian Scriptures, Sadlier, 1981.
Seven Pauline Letters, Liturgical Press, 1982.
An Access Guide to John, Sadlier, 1983.
The Genius of John, Liturgical Press, 1984.
Jeremiah and Baruch, Liturgical Press, 1984.

WORK IN PROGRESS: The Spiritualities of the Four Gospels, publication expected in 1988.

SIDELIGHTS: Peter F. Ellis told *CA:* "*The Spiritualities of the Four Gospels* best describes where my interests lie now. The men who wrote the Gospels had their own visions of what following Jesus entailed. I call these visions their spirituality and feel it is extremely important in this period of great change in Christendom."

ELMHIRST, Leonard Knight 1893-1974

OBITUARY NOTICE: Born June 6, 1893, in Howden, Yorkshire, England; died April 16, 1974, in Beverly Hills, Calif. Agricultural economist and author. During World War I, Elmhirst, then a student at Cambridge University, volunteered for the Young Men's Christian Association (YMCA) overseas service in India. It was at that time that he first became aware of the Asian nation's rural poverty and need for agricultural reform. Following the war, Elmhirst earned a degree in agriculture from Cornell University and returned to India in the early 1920's to found the Institute of Rural Reconstruction at Sriniketan. He later served as consultant to the Indian Government on such projects as the Damodar Valley Corporation and the Committee on Higher Education for Rural Areas.

In 1925 Elmhirst and his wife purchased the 820-acre, fourteenth-century Dartington Hall estate in Devon, England. Together they restored the manor and established a planned community, whose activities included farming, forestry, sawmilling, textile work, and several innovative educational and cultural programs. Eventually, the estate's commercial enterprises subsidized all of its educational programs. In addition to his activities at Dartington, Elmhirst served as founding president of the International Conference of Agricultural Economists and the Dartmouth Cattle Breeding Centre, as president of the Royal Forestry Society of England and Wales, and as chairman of Political and Economic Planning. His writings include *Robbery of the Soil, Rural Reconstruction, Trip to Russia, Social Trends in Rural Areas, Collected Notes on Agricultural Problems in Bengal,* and *Rabindranath Tagore, Pioneer in Education.*

OBITUARIES AND OTHER SOURCES:

BOOKS

The International Who's Who, 37th edition, Europa, 1973.
Who Was Who in America, With World Notables, Volume VI: *1974-1976,* Marquis, 1976.

PERIODICALS

New York Times, April 18, 1974.
Times (London), April 18, 1974.

*   *   *

ELVIN, Harold 1909-1985

OBITUARY NOTICE—See index for *CA* sketch: Born June 12, 1909, in London (one source says Buckhurst Hill, Essex), England; died January 20, 1985. Artist, designer, bicyclist, and author. Elvin worked at a variety of art-related occupations, including those of set designer, motion picture art director, ceramic artist, painter, and interior designer. He was the author of numerous novels, such as *Song of Siberia,* but is best known for his travelogues and memoirs based on his many bicycle journeys throughout the world, including *A Cockney in Moscow, The Ride to Hell: Thirty Countries on a Bicycle,* and *Elvin's Rides.* He also wrote the prize-winning books *The Gentle Russian* and *The Incredible Mile.*

OBITUARIES AND OTHER SOURCES:

BOOKS

International Authors and Writers Who's Who, 9th edition, [and] *International Who's Who in Poetry,* 6th edition, Melrose, 1982.
The Writers Directory: 1984-1986, St. James Press, 1983.

PERIODICALS

Times (London), January 31, 1985.

*   *   *

ENCEL, Sol
See ENCEL, Solomon

*   *   *

ENCEL, Solomon 1925-
(Sol Encel)

PERSONAL: Born in 1925, in Warsaw, Poland; son of G. and Ethel (Kutner) Encel; married Diana Helen Hovev (a research assistant), June 23, 1949; children: Vivien, Deborah, Daniel, Sarah. *Education:* University of Melbourne, B.A., 1949, M.A., 1952, Ph.D., 1960.

ADDRESSES: Office—Department of Sociology, University of New South Wales, P.O. Box 1, Kensington, New South Wales 2033, Australia.

CAREER: University of Melbourne, Parkville, Australia, lecturer in political science, 1952-55; Australian National University, Canberra, senior lecturer, 1956-62, reader in political science, 1962-66; University of New South Wales, Kensington, Australia, professor of sociology, 1966—. Visiting fellow at Harvard University, 1960, and University of Sussex, 1968, 1973, and 1978. Radio broadcaster. Member of administrative research committee of New South Wales Public Service Board, 1975-78; member of Australian Science and Technology Council, 1975; member of New South Wales Education Commission, 1980-83, and Higher Education Board, 1981-83; consultant to Telecom Australia and Royal Commission on Australian Government Administration. *Military service:* Royal Australian Air Force, 1944-45.

MEMBER: Sociological Association of Australia and New Zealand (chairman, 1969-70).

WRITINGS:

Cabinet Government in Australia, Melbourne University Press, 1962, revised edition, 1974.
(Editor with A. F. Davis, M. Berry, and L. Bryson, and contributor) *Australian Society: Introductory Essays,* Longman Cheshire, 1965, 4th edition, 1980.
Equality and Authority, Tavistock Press, 1970.
(With M. Cass and C. Bullard) *Librarians: A Survey,* New South Wales University Press, 1972.
(With B. S. Buckley) *The New South Wales Jewish Community,* New South Wales University Press, 1972, revised edition, 1978.
(With N. MacKenzie and M. Tebbutt) *Women and Society,* Longman Cheshire, 1974, revised edition, 1986.
(With P. Marstrand and W. Page) *The Art of Anticipation,* Martin Robertson, 1975.
(Editor with D. Horne and E. Thompson, and contributor; under name Sol Encel) *Change the Rules!,* Penguin, 1977.
(Editor with Colin Bell, and contributor) *Inside the Whale,* Pergamon, 1978.
(With C. Johnston) *Compensation and Rehabilitation,* New South Wales University Press, 1978.
(Editor with J. R. Ronayne) *Science, Technology, and Public Policy,* Pergamon, 1979.
(Editor with P. S. Wilenski and B. B. Schaffer, and contributor) *Decisions,* Longman Cheshire, 1981.

(Editor) *The Ethnic Dimension,* Allen & Unwin, 1981.
Technological Change: Some Case Histories (monograph), University of New South Wales, 1982.

CONTRIBUTOR

J. M. Bennett and others, editors, *Automation and Unemployment,* Australian and New Zealand Association for the Advancement of Science, 1979.
T. G. Whiston, editor, *The Uses and Abuses of Forecasting,* Macmillan, 1979.
R. J. Birrell and others, editors, *Quarry Australia?,* Oxford University Press (Australia), 1982.
John McLaren, editor, *A Nation Apart,* Longman Cheshire, 1983.
Russel Lansbury and Ed Davis, editors, *Technology, Work, and Industrial Relations,* Longman Cheshire, 1983.

Contributor to sociology journals.

WORK IN PROGRESS: Research for a book on the problems of working life, completion expected in 1988.

SIDELIGHTS: Solomon Encel told *CA:* "In the last six or seven years my main research interest has been the role of work in the life of the individual and the related problems of organizing work in contemporary industrial society. This links up with my interest in the status of women in technological change and in the problems of the future."

BIOGRAPHICAL/CRITICAL SOURCES:

Times Literary Supplement, April 9, 1976.

* * *

EPSTEIN, Ellen Robinson 1947-

PERSONAL: Born February 9, 1947, in Washington, D.C.; daughter of Stanley J. (in business) and Karlyn D. Robinson; married David Epstein (an attorney), August 15, 1971; children: Jeremy, Asher, Barak, Dina, Kira. *Education:* Connecticut College for Women (now Connecticut College), B.A., 1969; attended University of London, 1969-70.

ADDRESSES: Home and office—7507 Wyndale Rd., Chevy Chase, Md. 20815.

CAREER: Architectural historian with General Services Administration, 1970-73; Center for Oral History, Chevy Chase, Md., director, 1973—. Director of Jewish Historical Oral History Project and Oral History Project of the Jewish Community Council; project director for oral histories collected at American Gathering of Jewish Holocaust Survivors, 1983.

MEMBER: American Jewish Historical Society, Oral History Association, Oral History in the Middle Atlantic States (life member), Columbia Historical Society.

WRITINGS:

The East and West Wings of the White House, Columbia Historical Society, 1972.
Record and Remember: Tracing Your Roots Through Oral History, Simon & Schuster, 1978.
The Bar/Bat Mitzvah Planbook, Stein & Day, 1982.

WORK IN PROGRESS: "A book to put symbolism and tradition back into the Fourth of July and Thanksgiving as American holidays."

SIDELIGHTS: Ellen Robinson Epstein told *CA:* "I suppose my main achievement is that I have produced my books and carried on the business of the Center for Oral History for the past ten years, from nine o'clock at night until two o'clock in the morning, while spending my days raising five children full time. It proves that if one has a lot of energy and a good attitude, one can be extremely productive in one's career, even if one does not have a nine-to-five job outside the home."

* * *

EPSTEIN, Samuel S(tanley) 1926-

PERSONAL: Born April 13, 1926, in Middlesborough, England; came to United States, c. 1961, naturalized citizen; son of Isidore and Gertrude (Joseph) Epstein; married wife, Catherine; children: Mark, Julian, Emily. *Education:* University of London, B.Sc., 1947, M.B., B.S., 1950, Diploma of Tropical Medicine and Hygiene, 1952, Diploma of Pathology, 1954, M.D., 1958; graduate study at Royal Army Medical College, 1952.

ADDRESSES: Home—860 North Lake Shore Dr., Apt. 25M, Chicago, Ill. 60611. *Office*—School of Public Health, University of Illinois at the Medical Center, P.O. Box 6998, Chicago, Ill. 60680.

CAREER: Guy's Hospital, London, England, demonstrator in morbid anatomy, 1950; St. John's Hospital, London, house physician, 1951; University of London, Institute of Laryngology and Otology, London, lecturer in pathology and bacteriology, 1955-58; Hospital for Sick Children, London, tumor pathologist, 1958-60; Children's Cancer Research Foundation, Inc., Boston, Mass., research associate in pathology and microbiology and chief of Laboratories of Carcinogenesis and Toxicology, Applied Microbiology and Histology, all 1961-71, senior research associate in pathology, 1962-71; certified in public health and medical laboratory microbiology by the American Board of Microbiology, 1963; Case Western Reserve University, Cleveland, Ohio, Swetland Professor of Environmental Health and Human Ecology, professor of pharmacology, and director of environmental health programs, 1971-76; University of Illinois at the Medical Center, Chicago, professor of occupational and environmental medicine, 1976—, professor of preventive medicine at Abraham Lincoln School of Medicine, 1980—.

British Empire Cancer Campaign research fellow at Chester Beatty Cancer Research Institute, 1958-60; research associate at Children's Hospital Medical Center, Boston, 1961-71, and Harvard Medical School, Boston, 1962-71; director of State of Illinois Environmental Health Resource Center, 1978-79; director of occupational toxicology programs at Great Lakes Center for Occupational Safety and Health, 1980-81. Henry J. Kaiser Lecturer at Yale University, 1981; Harold Levine Memorial Lecturer at Chicago Lung Association, 1983. Member of Air Pollution Control Board and American Board of Microbiology; chairman of U.S. Department of Health, Education, and Welfare panels on pesticides and drug abuse, 1969; member of Environmental Protection Agency's National Air Quality Criteria Advisory Committee, 1972-75, and Environmental Health Advisory Committee, 1975-79. President of Rachel Carson Trust, 1974—; chairperson of Commission for the Advancement of Public Interest Organizations, 1974—; member of advisory council of Center for Science in the Public Interest; member of board of directors of Consumers Union of the United States; consultant to U.S. Senate Committee on Public Works, National Institute of Mental Health, and Oil,

Chemical, and Atomic Workers Union. *Military Service:* British Army, Royal Army Medical Corps, specialist in pathology, 1952-55; received Montefiore Gold Medal in Tropical Medicine, Montefiore Prize in Tropical Medicine, and Ranald Martin Prize in Military Surgery.

MEMBER: Society for Pathology and Bacteriology, Society of Clinical Pathologists, Society for General Micobiology, Society of Protozoologists, American Society for Experimental Biology, American Society for Experimental Pathology, American Association for Cancer Research, Environmental Mutagen Society (executive secretary, 1969-72), American Association for the Advancement of Science, Society for Occupational and Environmental Health (president, 1974-76), Air Pollution Control Association (chairman of committee on biological effects of air pollution, 1963-73; member of technical council, 1963-73), Society of Toxicology, Royal Society of Health (fellow), New York Academy of Sciences (fellow).

AWARDS, HONORS: Achievement award from Society of Toxicology, 1969; D.H.L. from Northeastern Illinois University, 1983.

WRITINGS:

(Editor with M. Legator) *The Mutagenity of Pesticides,* MIT Press, 1971.

(Editor) *Drugs of Abuse: Genetic and Other Chronic Non-Psychiatric Hazards,* MIT Press, 1971.

(Editor with D. Grundy) *The Legislation of Product Safety: Consumer Health and Product Hazards,* MIT Press, Volume I: *Chemicals, Electronic Products, Radiation,* 1974, Volume II: *Cosmetics and Drugs, Pesticides, Food Additives,* 1974.

The Politics of Cancer, Sierra Books, 1978, revised edition, Doubleday, 1979.

(With C. Pope and L. Brown) *Hazardous Wastes in America: Our Number One Environmental Crisis,* Sierra Books, 1982.

(With L. Doyal) *Cancer in Britain: The Politics of Prevention,* Pluto Press, 1983.

CONTRIBUTOR

Advance in Chemotherapy, Volume I, Academic Press, 1964.

W. Nakahara, editor, *Chemical Tumor Problems,* Japanese Society for the Promotion of Science, 1970.

F. Vogel and G. Rohrborn, editors, *Chemical Mutagens,* Springer-Verlag, 1970.

A. Hollaender, editor, *Environmental Chemical Mutagens,* Plenum, 1971.

Environment and Cancer, Williams & Wilkins, 1972.

E. S. Barrekette, editor, *Pollution: Engineering and Scientific Solutions,* Plenum, 1972.

E. V. Perrin and M. J. Finegold, editors, *Pathobiology of Development,* Williams & Wilkins, 1973.

H. Moghissi, editor, *Birth Defects and Fetal Development,* C. C Thomas, 1974.

W. McKee, editor, *Environmental Problems in Medicine,* C. C Thomas, 1974.

W. N. Murdoch, editor, *Environment: Resources, Pollution, and Society,* 2nd edition, Sinauer Associates, 1975.

H. H. Hiatt, J. D. Watson, and J. A. Winsten, editors, *Origins of Human Cancer,* Cold Spring Harbor Laboratory, 1977.

Contributor of more than two hundred articles to medical journals, including *Cancer Research, Nature, Environment, Experientia,* and *Preventive Medicines,* and to popular magazines, including *Newsday.*

ERVIN, Sam(uel) J(ames), Jr. 1896-1985

OBITUARY NOTICE: Born September 27, 1896, in Morganton, N.C.; died of respiratory and kidney failure, April 23, 1985, in Winston-Salem, N.C. Attorney, politician, and author. Ervin, a former U.S. senator and a constitutional scholar, is remembered for his key role in the 1973 Watergate investigation that eventually led to the resignation of thirty-seventh U.S. President Richard M. Nixon. In the early 1920's, following graduation from Harvard University, Ervin established himself as an attorney in his hometown. He worked as a judge in North Carolina during the 1930's, eventually serving as a state supreme court justice. Ervin became a U.S. senator in 1954 and soon gained national attention for his work on the Senate Select Committee to Investigate Censure Charges Against Senator Joseph McCarthy. McCarthy, a senator from Wisconsin, had been waging a massive campaign against numerous American public figures, whom he denounced as Communists; Ervin's unequivocal condemnation of McCarthy's practices significantly contributed to the Senate's decision to censure McCarthy. The McCarthy investigation brought Ervin the respect of his colleagues, and he remained one of the most prominent members of the Senate throughout his tenure. Known as a non-partisan Democrat, Ervin often baffled political analysts who could not always classify Ervin's policies. For example, he defended civil liberties and decried government encroachment on individual freedom, but adamantly opposed civil rights legislation, maintaining that civil rights for blacks meant stealing "freedom from one man to confer it on another." Ervin himself saw nothing paradoxical in his political opinions, explaining that his foremost concerns were individual freedom and the U.S. Constitution.

Ervin won considerable national acclaim in 1973, when his colleagues in the Senate chose him to chair the Senate Select Committee on Presidential Campaign Activities. Popularly known as the Watergate Committee, this body was entrusted with the investigation of criminal activities surrounding the illegal entry into the Democratic headquarters in Washington's Watergate apartment complex during the 1972 presidential election campaign. At the outset of the televised hearings Ervin declared that the Watergate affair possibly constituted a conspiracy to deny Americans "the right to vote in a free election." Observers noted that he conducted the investigation with characteristic verve, charming the nation with a folksy wit and eloquent rhetoric laced with pungent quotes from Shakespeare and the Bible. Determined in his efforts to expose the Watergate cover-up, Ervin challenged White House claims that Nixon's aides were protected by executive privilege, dismissing this reasoning as "executive poppycock" and threatening to arrest any presidential aide who would not testify. He retired from the Senate in 1974, shortly after the end of the Watergate investigation and Nixon's resulting resignation. Ervin's account of the Watergate probe was published in 1981 as *The Whole Truth: The Watergate Conspiracy.* His other writings include *Preserving the Constitution, Role of the Supreme Court: Policymaker or Adjudicator?,* written with Ramsey Clark, and *Humor of a Country Lawyer,* as well as numerous contributions to periodicals.

OBITUARIES AND OTHER SOURCES:

BOOKS

Clancy, Paul R., *Just a Country Lawyer: A Biography of Senator Sam Ervin,* Indiana University Press, 1974.

Dabney, Dick, *A Good Man: The Life of Sam J. Ervin,* Houghton, 1976.

Dash, Samuel, *Chief Counsel: Inside the Ervin Committee—The Untold Story of Watergate*, Random House, 1976.

PERIODICALS

Chicago Tribune, April 25, 1985.
Detroit Free Press, April 24, 1985.
Los Angeles Times, April 24, 1985.
New York Times, April 24, 1985.
Time, May 6, 1985.
Washington Post, April 24, 1985.

* * *

ESPRIU, Salvador 1913-1985

OBITUARY NOTICE: Born in 1913 in Santa Coloma de Farners, Catalonia, Spain; died of heart failure, February 22, 1985, in Barcelona, Spain. Poet, playwright, novelist, and author of short stories. Regarded as one of the foremost Catalan writers of the twentieth century, Espriu was nominated for the Nobel Prize in 1970 and 1980. Except for Espriu's first book, a volume of Biblical sketches titled *Israel* that was written in Spanish, all of the author's work was written in Catalan, a Romance language with a literary tradition originating in the Middle Ages. Espriu is said to have deliberately cultivated a clear and austere writing style to present the two themes, death and Spanish Jewishness, that dominate his writings.

Espriu published several volumes of prose in the 1930's, including *Petites Proses blanques,* a book of prose poems. His work was considerably affected by the Spanish Civil War, which he condemned from a moral, rather than an ideological, point of view, and the moral tone evident in his later work seems to betray Espriu's preoccupation with Spain's unresolved conflicts. In 1939 the forces of rightist dictator Francisco Franco invaded Catalonia, imposing both political repression and the Spanish language on Espriu's native land. This action prompted Espriu to write his acclaimed drama ''Antigona,'' inspired by Sophocles's ancient Greek tragedy about the individual's solitary struggle against tyranny; the play was not published until 1955. After World War II, when it was once again possible to print books in Catalan, Espriu began to publish poetry in which he developed the myth of Sinera, an imaginary land within a larger realm called Sepherad. Espriu's poetic vision of these two mythological regions—which correspond, respectively, to Catalonia and Spain—contains a hope for the reconciliation between the peoples living in Spain. Espriu's writings in English translation include *Lord of the Shadow: Poems,* published in 1975. His awards include the Premio del la Critica, for his 1971 work *Setmana Santa,* the 1971 Montaigne Prize, and the 1978 Ignasi Iglisias award.

OBITUARIES AND OTHER SOURCES:

BOOKS

Cassell's Encyclopedia of World Literature, revised edition, Morrow, 1973.
Castellet, Jose Maria, *Iniciacion a la poesia de Salvador Espriu,* Taurus (Madrid), 1971.
Columbia Dictionary of Modern European Literature, Columbia University Press, 2nd revised edition, 1980.
Contemporary Literary Criticism, Volume 9, Gale, 1978.
The Oxford Companion to Spanish Literature, Clarendon Press, 1978.

PERIODICALS

Los Angeles Times, February 27, 1985.
Times (London), February 25, 1985.
Washington Post, February 25, 1985.

* * *

ETCHISON, Dennis (William) 1943-
(Jack Martin)

BRIEF ENTRY: Born March 30, 1943, in Stockton, Calif. American educator and author. Known for his best-selling horror and fantasy fiction, Etchison won his first writing award at age twelve, and at age seventeen he published his first short story. His work, which is written in a spare and unemotional style that a *Fantasy Newsletter* critic described as ''clean and precise as a surgeon's scalpel,'' often focuses on characters who are societal outcasts and examines such themes as the horror of isolation and loneliness in everyday life. And the settings are often commonplace, such as all-night convenience stores, laundromats, and highway rest areas. Etchison's short story collection, *The Dark Country* (Scream Press, 1983), won both the World Fantasy Award and the British Fantasy Award for short fiction. He is also the author of *Red Dreams* (Scream Press, 1985), and his stories are represented in numerous science fiction and fantasy anthologies. In addition, Etchison is a frequent contributor to magazines, including *Fantasy and Science Fiction, Cavalier, Whispers, Mystery Monthly,* and *Fantastic.* In 1980 he published *The Fog* (Bantam), a novelization of the motion picture of the same title. Other novelizations of films by Etchison include *Halloween II* (Zebra, 1981), *Halloween III: The Season of the Witch* (Jove, 1982), and *Videodrome* (Zebra, 1984). Etchison, who teaches creative writing at the University of California, Los Angeles, is working on a motion picture adaptation of his short story ''The Late Shift.'' *Address:* Los Angeles, Calif.

BIOGRAPHICAL/CRITICAL SOURCES:

BOOKS

Who's Who in Horror and Fantasy Fiction, Elm Tree Books, 1977.

PERIODICALS

Fantasy Newsletter, March, 1981, February, 1983.
Fantasy Review, June, 1984.
Washington Post Book World, October 30, 1983.

* * *

ETHRIDGE, Mark Foster, Jr. 1924-1985

OBITUARY NOTICE: Born July 29, 1924, in New York, N.Y.; died of cancer, March 1, 1985, in Chapel Hill, N.C. Educator and journalist. Ethridge, who worked as editor of the *Detroit Free Press,* is remembered as an opponent of the American involvement in the Vietnam war and an advocate of black political power. A graduate of Princeton University, Ethridge began his career as a journalist with the *Washington Post* in 1947, but later joined the staff of *Newsday,* serving there as editorial page editor when the newspaper won the 1954 Pulitzer Prize for meritorious public service. In 1960 Ethridge became an editorial writer for the *Detroit Free Press,* rising to the post of editor six years later. During Ethridge's tenure as editor the newspaper received the 1968 Pulitzer Prize for general reporting for its coverage of the 1967 race riots in Detroit, as well as the 1971 William Allen White Award for excellence in editorial writing. Ethridge left the *Detroit Free Press* in 1973 to join the *Akron Beacon Journal,* where he worked as editor and vice-president until 1976. The following year he began teaching journalism at the University of South Carolina. In the early 1980's Ethridge was publisher of the *Lexington Dispatch News* in North Carolina. His honors include awards from the American Bar Association and the Freedoms Foundation as well as two citations from the Overseas Press Club of America. At the time of his death Ethridge was collecting material for a book on his late father, publisher and journalist Mark Foster Ethridge, Sr.

OBITUARIES AND OTHER SOURCES:

BOOKS

Who's Who in America, 39th edition, Marquis, 1976.

PERIODICALS

Los Angeles Times, March 4, 1985.
New York Times, March 4, 1985.
Washington Post, March 3, 1985.

* * *

EVANS, Gareth Lloyd   1923-1984

OBITUARY NOTICE: Born in 1923 in Rhosymedre, Wales; died in October, 1984, in Stratford-Upon-Avon, Warwickshire, England. Educator and author. Evans, who was senior lecturer at Britain's Birmingham University, wrote on English drama. His writings include *J. B. Priestley, the Dramatist, Shakespeare in the Limelight, Shakespeare One, Shakespeare Two, Shakespeare Three, Shakespeare Four,* and contributions to periodicals. (Death information provided by wife, Barbara Lloyd Evans.)

* * *

EVANS, Susan H(ope)   1951-

PERSONAL: Born October 20, 1951, in Berlin, N.H.; daughter of Jack (in retail business) and Arline (Silverman) Evans. *Education:* University of Michigan, A.B., 1973, Ph.D., 1981. *Religion:* Jewish.

ADDRESSES: Office—Annenberg School of Communications, University of Southern California, 3502 South Hoover St., Los Angeles, Calif. 90089-0281.

CAREER: Market Opinion Research, Detroit, Mich., study director, 1973-76; Sage Publications, Inc., Beverly Hills, Calif., production and sales analyst, 1978; University of Michigan, Ann Arbor, assistant research scientist, 1981; University of Southern California, Los Angeles, director of academic development, 1982—.

MEMBER: International Communication Association, American Political Science Association, Association for Education in Journalism, American Association for Public Opinion Research.

WRITINGS:

(Contributor) James Ettema and D. C. Whitney, editors, *Communications in Context: Current Research on Mass Communications,* Sage Publications, 1982.
Covering Campaigns: Journalism in Congressional Elections, Stanford University Press, 1983.

Associate editor of series "CommText," Sage Publications, 1979—. Contributor to communication journals.

WORK IN PROGRESS: Exploring how communication can improve the experience of cancer patients and close friends; examining the social impacts of the 1984 Summer Olympic broadcasts.

SIDELIGHTS: Susan H. Evans told *CA:* "My research and writing originate with a concern for the social issues that they address—whether limitations in electoral competition or frustrations experienced by cancer patients. My hobbies are finding the communication processes that affect an issue and trying to illuminate how the improved uses of the media will be helpful. I enjoy collaborating with others on projects, which is fortunate since most of my work requires collecting and analyzing a staggering variety of information about communication content, audience effects, and the contexts in which human behavior takes place.

"*Covering Campaigns* illustrates my affection for reaching a wide audience with the implications of research on media. That study identified way in which journalists, sometimes unwittingly, limit the opportunities of challengers to unseat members of Congress through selective omissions of campaign themes, preferential attention to incumbents, editorial endorsement policies, and other means. Study results are presented so that the general reader can understand them or, if working in the press, can apply them to practical situations."

F

FAIRFAX, Ann
See CHESNEY, Marion

* * *

FAIZ, Faiz Ahmad   1912(?)-1984

OBITUARY NOTICE: Some sources list middle name as Ahmed; born in 1912 (one source says 1911) in Sialkot, British India (now Pakistan); died following an asthma attack, November 20, 1984, in Lahore, Pakistan. Educator, journalist, and poet. Highly esteemed for his Urdu writings, Faiz was generally regarded as Pakistan's unofficial poet laureate. He was particularly praised for both his lyric poetry and his mastery of the traditional verse form known as *ghazal*, but he was also admired for his political poetry, which was written in a contemporary vein. Some of his poems have been translated into English by V. G. Kiernan and published in the collection *Poems by Faiz.*

Faiz, who was involved with the Marxist Progressive Movement during the 1930's, was known for his leftist views. Following service in the Indian Army during World War II, the poet helped establish labor unions in his homeland and served as editor of the *Pakistan Times,* an English-language daily newspaper founded by opposition leader Mian Iftikharuddin. Faiz became editor of the leftist publication following the end of British rule in India and Pakistan's subsequent establishment as an independent republic in 1947. Four years later, Faiz was found guilty of taking part in an attempt to overthrow the government of Pakistan. Sentenced to death for his part in the abortive coup, Faiz instead was imprisoned for several years. His collection of narrative poems, *Zindan namah,* details the poet's experiences in prison. After his release in 1955, Faiz returned to his post at the *Pakistan Times,* but he—like other known leftists—was removed from his post following a military coup in 1958. When civilian rule returned to Pakistan, Faiz was restored to prominence and was given the responsibility of establishing a National Council for the Arts. In 1962 he was awarded the Lenin Peace Prize by the Soviet Union.

OBITUARIES AND OTHER SOURCES:

BOOKS

Cassell's Encyclopedia of World Literature, revised edition, Morrow, 1973.

Dictionary of Oriental Literatures, Volume II: *South and Southeast Asia,* Basic Books, 1974.
Encyclopedia of World Literature in the Twentieth Century, revised edition, Ungar, 1981.

PERIODICALS

Chicago Tribune, November 22, 1984.
Times (London), November 22, 1984.

* * *

FARIS, Wendy B(ush)   1945-

PERSONAL: Born November 3, 1945, in Palo Alto, Calif.; daughter of Robert Nelson (a professor) and Nancy (a psychologist; maiden name, Burton) Bush; married David E. Faris (a psychologist), August 5, 1971. *Education:* Stanford University, B.A., 1967; Harvard University, M.A., 1970, Ph.D., 1975.

ADDRESSES: Home—1701 North Waterview Dr., Richardson, Tex. 75080.

CAREER: University of Texas at Dallas, assistant professor of comparative literature, 1975-82; Colgate University, Hamilton, N.Y., assistant professor of Romance languages, 1982-84, Crawshaw Professor of Literature, 1982-83; writer. Guest lecturer at Rutgers University, 1982; visiting assistant professor at University of Texas at Arlington, spring, 1984.

MEMBER: International Comparative Literature Association, Instituto Internacional de Literatura Iberoamericana, American Comparative Literature Association, Modern Language Association of America, South Central Modern Language Association (president of Comparative Literature Division, 1981), Philological Association of the Pacific Coast (president of Comparative Literature Division, 1982), Phi Beta Kappa.

AWARDS, HONORS: Fulbright fellowship for University of Toulouse, 1967-68, and University of Paris-X, 1971-72; grants from National Endowment for the Humanities, 1979, 1981, and 1984.

WRITINGS:

Carlos Fuentes, Ungar, 1983.
(Contributor) Elaine Ginsberg and Laura Gottlieb, editors, *Virginia Woolf: Centenary Essays,* Whitston Publishing, 1983.

Contributor of articles and reviews to literature journals, including *Comparative Literature Studies, Georgia Review, Kentucky Romance Quarterly,* and *World Literature Today.*

WORK IN PROGRESS: The Labyrinth: Symbolic Landscape and Narrative Design in Modern Fiction; a book on Elizabeth Bowen, for Ungar; a study of the influence of James Joyce's *Ulysses* on recent Latin American fiction.

*　　*　　*

FARRELL, William E.　1936(?)-1985

OBITUARY NOTICE: Born c. 1936; died of cancer, March 17, 1985, in New York, N.Y. Journalist. Farrell, who worked for the *New York Times* for twenty-three years, witnessed the 1981 assassination of Egyptian president Anwar el-Sadat and covered the peace treaty between Israel and Egypt. He began his career in the early 1960's as a news clerk and eventually became a reporter, deputy metropolitan editor, and bureau chief in Albany, New York, in Jerusalem, Israel, and in Cairo, Egypt. Farrell also wrote the columns "About New York" and, later, "Briefing." He was known for his spontaneity and his affinity for puns.

OBITUARIES AND OTHER SOURCES:

PERIODICALS

Chicago Tribune, March 19, 1985, March 20, 1985.
New York Times, March 18, 1985.

*　　*　　*

FAUNCE-BROWN, Daphne (Bridget)　1938-

PERSONAL: Born July 9, 1938, in Launceston, England; daughter of Thomas Holman (in leather business) and Vera Margaret (a nurse; maiden name, Thomas) Hender; married Michael Raoul Faunce-Brown (in business), July 24, 1965; children: Timothy, Caroline, Christopher. *Education:* Attended secondary school in Weston-super-Mare, England. *Religion:* Church of England.

ADDRESSES: Home—Oakley Bungalow, 145 Bletchingley Rd., Merstham, Surrey RH1 3QN, England. *Agent*—Shelley Power, 48 King's Rd., Long Ditton, Surrey, England.

CAREER: Writer. Bookkeeper and receptionist for a number of hotels in England, 1954-65; held a variety of jobs, including curtain salesperson and assistant matron at a school for boys, 1965-84.

WRITINGS:

Snuffle's House (for children), Terrapin Books, 1980.

"COBWEB" SERIES FOR CHILDREN

Cobweb Helps a Friend, Studio Publications, 1983.
. . . Takes a Holiday, Studio Publications, 1983.
. . . At the End of the Rainbow, Studio Publications, 1983.
. . . Saves the Day, Studio Publications, 1983.
. . . To the Rescue, Studio Publications, 1983.
. . . Sets a Trap, Studio Publications, 1985.
Cobweb's Sixth Birthday, Studio Publications, 1985.

WORK IN PROGRESS: Shadow Out of Harness, about the adventures of a lost dog; additional books for the "Cobweb" series.

SIDELIGHTS: Daphne Faunce-Brown told *CA:* "Having my own children and reading to them daily inspired me to write.

Among my favorite children's books are *Where the Wild Things Are,* by Maurice Sendak, and stories by Roald Dahl. There are so many children's books published that it is not difficult to find some to read and enjoy. But I'm not interested in books that encourage children to use bad language or in ones that promote bad moral attitudes. I think there are far too many books like that. I would like to think that my own books will influence children for the good and will help them to learn.

"I am fond of animals and when I was a child there always seemed to be several hedgehogs about. Hence the characters Snuffles and Cobweb came about. They both are mischievous hedgehogs who often play tricks on others. But the tricks are always good-natured, never spiteful or untruthful in the real sense; and the characters always help their friends out of trouble. The books also teach colors and numbers, directions, left and right, days of the week, monetary units, time, and shapes."

*　　*　　*

FAVA, Sylvia Fleis　1927-

PERSONAL: Born June 1, 1927, in New York, N.Y.; daughter of Joseph and Anna (Karner) Fleis; married John L. Fava (a municipal budget officer), August 12, 1951. *Education:* Queens College (now of the City University of New York), B.A., 1948; Northwestern University, M.A., 1950, Ph.D., 1956.

ADDRESSES: Office—Department of Sociology, Brooklyn College of the City University of New York, Bedford Ave. and Avenue H, Brooklyn, N.Y. 11210.

CAREER: Brooklyn College of the City University of New York, Brooklyn, N.Y., lecturer, 1951-58, assistant professor, 1958-64, associate professor, 1964-72, professor of sociology, 1972—.

MEMBER: American Sociological Association, Society for the Study of Social Problems, Eastern Sociological Society.

WRITINGS:

(Editor with Jerome Himelhoch) *Sexual Behavior in American Society: The First Two Kinsey Reports,* Norton, 1955.
(With Noel P. Gist) *Urban Society,* 5th edition, Crowell, 1963, 6th edition, Harper, 1974.
Urbanism in World Perspective, Crowell, 1968.
(Editor with Gerald Handel and Vernon Boggs) *The Apple Sliced: Sociological Studies of New York City,* J. F. Bergin, 1983.

WORK IN PROGRESS: Research on life cycle and career patterns of men and women physicists.

*　　*　　*

FAY, Erica
See STOPES, Marie (Charlotte) Carmichael

*　　*　　*

FEDERBUSCH, Simon
See FEDERBUSH, Simon

*　　*　　*

FEDERBUSH, Simon　1892(?)-1969
(Simon Federbusch)

OBITUARY NOTICE: Born February 15, 1892 (one source

says 1890) in Narol, Austria-Hungary; died August 20 (one source says August 21), 1969, in New York, N.Y. Jewish religious and political leader, scholar, editor, and author. Federbush, who served as chief rabbi of Finland in the 1930's was the author of a well-known Hebrew textbook and a long-time chairman of the World Union for Hebrew Language and Culture. Educated in Poland and Austria, Federbush was ordained a rabbi in 1923 at the Vienna Rabbinical Seminary. In the 1920's Federbush was a member of the Polish parliament and became involved in the Zionist movement; he was president of Mizrachi, a Zionist organization in Polish Galicia, and he also co-founded Tora Va'Avod—Torah and Labor, a Zionist labor movement. At that time he also became an influential member of the World Jewish Congress and the World Zionist Council. In 1930 Federbush went to Finland, where he worked as chief rabbi until 1940. During that period he saved numerous Jewish refugees from Nazi Germany by persuading the Finnish authorities to issue them visas.

In 1940 Federbush immigrated to the United States, establishing himself as a respected scholar and Jewish leader. Involved in many Jewish organizations, Federbush was a long-time chairman of the World Union of Hebrew Language and Culture. His scholarly writings, which deal with a variety of Jewish topics, include *Hikre Talmud*, a 1937 collection of essays on Talmud literature, *ha-Musar veha mishpat be-Yisrael*, a 1947 study of ethics and law in Israel, and *ha-Lashon ha-'ivrit be-Yisrael uva-'amim*, a 1967 discussion of the Hebrew language in Israel and elsewhere. Federbush's writings in English include *The Jewish Concept of Labor* and *World Jewry Today*. He was associated with several Jewish publications, including the New York quarterly *Judaism*, for which he served as member of the editorial board.

OBITUARIES AND OTHER SOURCES:

BOOKS

Who's Who in World Jewry: A Biographical Dictionary of Outstanding Jews, Pitman, 1972.
Who Was Who in America, With World Notables, Volume V: 1969-1973, Marquis, 1973.

PERIODICALS

New York Times, August 21, 1969.

*   *   *

FEIN, Albert 1930-

PERSONAL: Born August 27, 1930, in New York, N.Y.; son of Samuel W. Fein (in sales) and Gertrude (a homemaker; maiden name, Fleischman); married Sandra Friedman (a teacher), August 24, 1958; children: Seth W., Laura G. *Education:* Brooklyn College (now Brooklyn College of the City University of New York), B.A. (magna cum laude), 1952; Columbia University, M.A., 1954, Ph.D., 1969.

ADDRESSES: Home—2107 Avenue O, Brooklyn, N.Y. 11210. *Office*—Department of History-Urban Studies, Long Island University, Brooklyn, N.Y. 11201.

CAREER: University of Maryland, Overseas Program, Bamberg, West Germany, instructor in American history, 1955; high school teacher of social studies in Brooklyn, N.Y., 1956-57; Long Island University (now Brooklyn Center of Long Island University), Brooklyn, N.Y., instructor, 1958-62, assistant professor, 1962-69, associate professor of history, 1969-76, professor of history and urban studies, 1976—, director

of urban studies, 1968-70, director of master of arts program in urban studies, 1970-76, chairperson of graduate department of urban studies, 1976—, member of graduate council of Connolly College, 1975—, chairperson, 1976-78 and 1980—. Adjunct professor at City University of New York Graduate Center, 1972; visiting lecturer or professor at Harvard University, 1966—, Columbia University, 1969-70, and University of Pennsylvania, 1975; moderator of annual Frederick Law Olmsted Lecture at Harvard, 1974-75 and 1977; lecturer at Pennsbury Manor Farm, 1967.

Harvard junior fellow in landscape architecture history, Dumbarton Oaks Library, 1964-65, senior fellow, 1965. Director of annual urban affairs conferences at Long Island University, 1963-64 and 1967-70; co-chairperson of "Seminar on the City" at Columbia University, 1971-74. Director of a study on the profession of landscape architecture for the Ford Foundation and the American Society of Landscape Architecture Foundation, 1969-72; director of a study of the history of the Fort Greene neighborhood, Brooklyn, 1972-74, and of the Prospect Heights neighborhood, Brooklyn, 1976-78. Consultant to museum exhibitions, historical sites, parks, academic programs, and the public television series "Architecture and Design." U.S. representative to UNESCO International Symposium on Preservation of the Historic Landscape, 1977. Member of Prospect Park Advisory Board, 1969, historical committee of the New York City Bicentennial Corporation, 1972-76, and Brooklyn borough president's advisory committees on history and on Prospect Park, 1980-81. *Military service:* U.S. Army, 1953-55, served in West Germany.

MEMBER: International Federation of Landscape Architects, Alliance for Landscape Preservation (steering committee, 1978-80), American Society of Landscape Architects (honorary member), Long Island Historical Society (councilor, 1972-74), Phi Beta Kappa, Kappa Delta Pi.

AWARDS, HONORS: Erb fellow in American history, Columbia University, 1957-58; Fulbright fellow in urban history, Birkbeck College, University of London, 1961-62; American Council of Learned Societies fellow, 1971-72; *Frederick Law Olmsted and the American Environmental Tradition* named one of the outstanding academic books of the year by *Choice*, 1972; Bradford Williams Award for outstanding paper from the American Society of Landscape Architects, 1973, for "Summary Report of the Study of the Profession of Landscape Architecture"; award for special achievement from the Victorian Society in America, 1973, for co-authorship of proposal to designate Fort Greene a historical district; honor award from the American Society of Landscape Architects, 1983, for co-authorship of historic landscape report on the ravine district of Prospect Park.

WRITINGS:

(With Henry Hope Reed) *Guide to Central Park* (pamphlet), Municipal Arts Society, 1961.
(Editor and author of introductory essay and notes) *Landscape Into Cityscape: Frederick Law Olmsted's Plans for a Greater New York City*, Cornell University Press, 1967, reissued with new introduction, Van Nostrand, 1981.
(Contributor) Edgar Kaufmann, Jr., editor, *The Rise of an American Architecture*, Metropolitan Museum of Art, 1970.
(Editor with Elliott Gatner) *University and Community: The New Partnership* (proceedings of the Seventh Long Island University International Conference on Urban Affairs), Long Island University Press, 1971.

A Study of the Profession of Landscape Architecture: Technical Report, American Society of Landscape Architects Foundation, 1972.

Frederick Law Olmsted and the American Environmental Tradition, Braziller, 1972.

(With Lois Gilman and Donald Simon) *A Proposal for the Designation of Fort Greene as an Historical District,* Fort Greene Landmarks Preservation Committee, 1973.

(Author of introduction) Ben Whitaker and Kenneth Browne, *Parks for People,* Schocken, 1973.

(Contributor) Milton M. Klein, editor, *New York City: The Centennial Years, 1676-1976,* Kennikat, 1976.

(Author of introduction) Alan Emmet and others, *Cambridge, Massachusetts: The Changing of a Landscape,* Harvard University Printing Office, 1978.

(Author of foreword) Dana F. White and Victor Kramer, editors, *Olmsted South,* Greenwood, 1979.

Wave Hill, Riverdale and New York City: Legacy of a Hudson River Estate (booklet), Wave Hill Center for Environmental Studies, 1979.

(Contributor) Bruce Kelley and others, *The Art of the Olmsted Landscape,* New York City Landmarks Preservation Committee, 1981.

(With others) *The Great East River Bridge, 1883-1983,* Brooklyn Museum, 1983.

Contributor to scholarly journals, including *The American Historical Review, Journal of the Society of Architectural Historians, Landscape Architecture,* and *New York History.* Consulting editor on environmental planning and design for Praeger, 1971-75; consulting editor on landscape and landscape architecture for McGraw, 1976-79. Contributing editor to *Landscape Architecture,* 1977. Member of advisory board of *Journal on Utopian Studies,* 1977, and member of editorial board of *Land Planning,* 1976—.

WORK IN PROGRESS: Editing *A Guide to the Professional Papers of Robert C. Weinberg,* with Elliott S.M. Gatner; a history of Brooklyn's park system, for the Architectural History Foundation; lectures on the history of landscape architecture, for Harvard University.

SIDELIGHTS: Albert Fein, a historian of landscape architecture and urban studies specialist, has devoted much of his career to the study of Frederick Law Olmsted, the eminent nineteenth-century landscape designer. Perhaps best known as the creator of New York's Central Park, Olmsted designed more than a dozen other major urban parks, the community of Riverside, Illinois, and other planned suburbs, the campus of Stanford University, and the estates of such millionaires as George Vanderbilt. Fein has researched and analyzed Olmsted's many projects and their lasting impact.

In *Landscape Into Cityscape: Frederick Law Olmsted's Plans for a Greater New York City* Fein compiled and annotated nine of the designer's reports relating to various parks and other civic projects. A few other plans and autobiographical fragments round out the book, providing researchers with documentation of Olmsted's theories and principles.

Fein examined the designer's contributions in an area of modern concern for *Frederick Law Olmsted and the American Environmental Tradition.* In that work, reported Charles C. McLaughlin in the *American Historical Review,* Fein suggests that Olmsted was "as wide-ranging and important in his accomplishments as Benjamin Franklin, Thomas Jefferson, and William Penn and that he was one of the first to insist that we must do the planning of our living environment in harmony with natural ecology." The book presents the designer's career in two distinct phases—the early years devoted to public works and founded in ideals of social justice, and the later years characterized by a wealthy clientele and a greater emphasis on aesthetic principles. In a letter to *CA,* Fein further explained that the two phases of the designer's career responded in aesthetic terms to large-scale changes within American society. Fein wrote: "Although Olmsted's social and environmental objectives did not change, he was compelled to shift in certain large projects from a small-scaled picturesque aesthetic to one embodying principles of neoclassical formal design. The nation had changed and Olmsted remained influential in part by adjusting to this movement."

Reviewing *Frederick Law Olmsted and the American Environmental Tradition* for the *Journal of American History,* Neil Harris opined: "Fein has provided an interesting and important argument, an axis on which to pivot future observations and discussions." McLaughlin, however, while agreeing that Olmsted in some respects set examples for the modern ecology movement, asserted that the designer was not preservationist and that "however admiring we can be of Olmsted, we must understand that he deliberately manipulated nature to produce aesthetic effects refreshing to the harried city dweller of his day rather than to the passing migratory bird." In the same critique, McLaughlin praised an essay that Fein contributed to *The Rise of an American Architecture,* calling it "one of the best appraisals of Olmsted in print because it makes a persuasive synthesis of Olmsted's social thought and his design accomplishment."

Fein told *CA:* "All scholarship—no less that related to history—is a personal and social statement. For the historian, as for scholars of other disciplines, the selection of a topic and the way it is defined, researched, and presented is as individual as a fingerprint; at the same time, historical research is a social process, for each work is time-bound to a brief span of years within which events and ideas influence the historian as they do everyone else. In the most elemental matters—sustenance, shelter, sex, travel, recreation (books and newspapers read, television and films viewed)—we are all children of our age.

"If ever there was a question that the recording of history reflects the contours of a given time, this doubt should have been dispelled by the development since the 1960's of substantial bodies of literature and of college courses constituting such specializations as ethnicity, race, women, the city, and the environment. In addition, a profound change has taken place in the ways in which some historians gather data and document and communicate their analysis—for example, computer systems have become important tools of research, millions are being educated through images on television, and visual materials of all types are more than ever before used as historical evidence.

"Notwithstanding such new approaches, the profession of the historian still depends on at least two long-established practices. First, the voice of the historian, to be valid, must, as ever, be a verifiable distillation of the period studied; thus, letters, diaries, newspapers, official documents, photographs and such are basic sources. Second, previous scholarship must be considered because any issue significant in a given era will have been discussed, however differently, by one's contemporaries as well as by prior generations of historians. Awareness of the interplay of continuity and change facilitates the creation of a synthesis of the past that describes, if it cannot fully explain, the pathways to the present.

"Within the specialization of urban and environmental history, I remain interested in several interrelated themes: the American city as part of the national experience; the mosaic of public and private interventions that have given us an urban, suburban, and rural landscape; the contributions of city planning and landscape architecture to that mosaic; and the use of history in public education and in historic preservation and restoration."

BIOGRAPHICAL/CRITICAL SOURCES:

PERIODICALS

American Historical Review, June, 1973.
The Journal of American History, June, 1973.
Nation, December 11, 1972.
New York Times, September 2, 1972.

*   *   *

FENN, Elizabeth A.   1959-

PERSONAL: Born September 22, 1959, in Arlington, Calif.; daughter of Robert S. and Ann (Heim) Fenn. *Education:* Duke University, B.A., 1981; graduate study at Yale University, 1982—.

ADDRESSES: Home—107 North Wake St., Hillsborough, N.C. 27278. *Office*—Department of History, Yale University, New Haven, Conn. 06520.

CAREER: Historian.

WRITINGS:

Natives and Newcomers, University of North Carolina Press, 1983.

WORK IN PROGRESS: Research on Native American millenarian movements, 1680-1814.

*   *   *

FERMI, Enrico   1901-1954

BRIEF ENTRY: Born September 29, 1901, in Rome, Italy; immigrated to United States in 1939, naturalized citizen in 1944; died of stomach cancer, November 28, 1954, in Chicago, Ill. American physicist, educator, and author. Known as one of the creators of the atomic bomb, Fermi made significant theoretical and practical contributions to various areas of physics. Fermi became a leading theoretical physicist while still in his twenties with several major discoveries to his credit, including the Fermi-Dirac statistics, which explain the behavior of atomic particles. In the late 1920's Fermi began working in experimental physics; in 1934, during his tenure as professor of physics at the University of Rome, the scientist inadvertently achieved nuclear fission—previously thought impossible—by bombarding uranium with neutrons. Fermi received the 1938 Nobel Prize for his experimental work on nuclear bombardment.

In 1939 Fermi, an opponent of the Fascist regime in Italy, came to the United States, where he became professor of physics at Columbia University. While at Columbia he conducted additional experiments involving uranium fission that revealed the possibility of a controlled chain reaction. Believing his discoveries could be used for the construction of a powerful weapon, Fermi attempted to convince the U.S. Government of the necessity of building an atomic bomb, especially in view of Nazi efforts in that direction. However, it was not until

Fermi and other concerned scientists persuaded the eminent physicist Albert Einstein to send a letter of warning to President Franklin D. Roosevelt that the Manhattan Project, the enterprise that eventually led to the development of the atomic bomb, was initiated. Fermi, working under the aegis of the Manhattan Project, effected the first controlled chain reaction in 1942 at the University of Chicago. Shortly thereafter the scientist went to Los Alamos, New Mexico, where he became directly involved in the construction of the atomic bomb, which was completed in 1945. The following year Fermi returned to the University of Chicago, where his research shifted to high-energy nuclear physics, concentrating on mesons—the elementary particles that hold the atomic nucleus together.

Fermi's writings available in English include *Thermodynamics* (1937), *Elementary Particles* (1951), *Notes on Quantum Mechanics: A Course Given at the University of Chicago* (1961), *Molecules, Crystals, and Quantum Statistics* (1966), *Notes on Thermodynamics and Statistics* (1966), and *Nuclear Physics* (1974).

BIOGRAPHICAL/CRITICAL SOURCES:

BOOKS

Asimov's Biographical Encyclopedia of Science and Technology, 2nd revised edition, Avon, 1982.
Current Biography, Wilson, 1945.
Fermi, Laura, *Atoms in the Family: My Life With Enrico Fermi,* University of Chicago Press, 1954.

PERIODICALS

New York Times, November 29, 1954.
Times (London), November 29, 1954.

*   *   *

FERNALD, John (Bailey)   1905-1985

OBITUARY NOTICE—See index for *CA* sketch: Born November 21, 1905, in Mill Valley, Calif.; died April 2, 1985, in London, England. Educator, director, and author. A native Californian, Fernald spent most of his adult life in England. He directed dozens of plays in London during the 1930's and was a member of the teaching staff of London's Royal Academy of Dramatic Art from 1934 to 1940, also serving as a principal there for ten years beginning in 1955. His publications include *The Play Produced: An Introduction to the Technique of Producing Plays, Destroyer From America, Sense of Direction,* and a play written with his wife, Jenny Laird, *And No Birds Sing.*

OBITUARIES AND OTHER SOURCES:

BOOKS

Who's Who, 136th edition, St. Martin's, 1984.
Who's Who in the Theatre: A Biographical Record of the Contemporary Stage, 17th edition, Gale, 1981.

PERIODICALS

Daily Variety, April 8, 1985.

*   *   *

FEULNER, Edwin J(ohn), Jr.   1941-

PERSONAL: Surname is pronounced *Full*-ner; born August 12, 1941, in Chicago, Ill.; son of Edwin John and Helen J. (Franzen) Feulner; married Linda C. Leventhal, March 8, 1969;

children: Edwin John III, Emily V. *Education:* Regis College, B.Sc., 1963; attended London School of Economics and Political Science, London, 1965; University of Pennsylvania, M.B.A., 1974; University of Edinburgh, Ph.D., 1981. *Politics:* Republican. *Religion:* Roman Catholic.

ADDRESSES: Home—6216 Berkeley Rd., Alexandria, Va. 22307. *Office*—Heritage Foundation, 214 Massachusetts Ave. N.E., Washington, D.C. 20002.

CAREER: U.S. Department of Defense, Washington, D.C., confidential assistant to U.S. Secretary of Defense, 1969-70; U.S. House of Representatives, Washington, D.C., administrative assistant to U.S. Representative Philip M. Crane, 1970-74, executive director of Republican Study Committee, 1974-77; Heritage Foundation, Washington, D.C., president, 1977—. Public affairs fellow at Hoover Institution on War, Revolution, and Peace, 1965-67; guest lecturer at colleges and universities. Publisher of *Policy Review.* Chairman of national advisory board of Center for Research and Education in Free Enterprise at Texas A & M University; chairman of Institute for European Defense and Strategic Studies, London, England, 1979—, and of U.S. Advisory Commission on Public Diplomacy; member of scientific committee of Centre for Applied Economic Research, Rome, Italy; member of advisory council of Institut Economique de Paris; member of board of trustees of the Manhattan Institute, 1977—, Rockford Institute, Lehrman Institute, Roe Foundation, Foundation Francisco Marroquin, and Intercollegiate Studies Institute; member of President's Commission on White House Fellows, 1981-83, and Commission on Security and Economic Assistance, 1983.

MEMBER: International Institute for Strategic Studies, American Economic Association, American Political Science Association, U.S. Strategic Institute, Transportation Research Forum, Mont Pelerin Society, Union League Club, University Club (Washington, D.C.), Reform Club (London, England), Philadelphia Society.

AWARDS, HONORS: Honorary doctorates from Nichols College, 1981, Universidad Francisco Marroquin, 1982, and Hanyang University, 1982.

WRITINGS:

Congress and the New International Economic Order, Heritage Foundation, 1976.
(Editor) *China: The Turning Point,* Council on American Affairs, 1976.
Looking Back, Heritage Foundation, 1981.
(Editor) *U.S.-Japan Mutual Security,* Heritage Foundation and Japan Center for the Study of Security Issues, 1981.
Conservatives Stalk the House: The Republican Study Committee, 1970-1982, Green Hill, 1982.

Contributor to professional journals.

*   *   *

FEYDY, Anne Lindbergh
   See SAPIEYEVSKI, Anne Lindbergh

*   *   *

FIFO, Ray
   See GLAZAR, Bob

FILAS, Francis L(ad)   1915-1985

OBITUARY NOTICE—See index for *CA* sketch: Born June 4, 1915, in Cicero, Ill.; died following a heart attack, February 15, 1985, in Chicago, Ill. Clergyman, educator, and author. Filas, a Jesuit priest and professor of theology at Loyola University since 1950, was one of the leading experts researching the Shroud of Turin, a burial cloth believed by some to have been used in Christ's burial and to have been imprinted with his image. Filas's publications include *The Man Nearest to Christ, His Heart in Our Work, Joseph Most Just, The Parables of Jesus, Sex Education in the Family,* and *How to Read Your Bible.*

OBITUARIES AND OTHER SOURCES:

BOOKS

Directory of American Scholars, Volume IV: *Philosophy, Religion, and Law,* 8th edition, Bowker, 1982.
Who's Who in America, 43rd edition, Marquis, 1984.

PERIODICALS

Washington Post, February 18, 1985.

*   *   *

FINCHER, Ernest B(arksdale)   1910-1985

OBITUARY NOTICE—See index for *CA* sketch: Born March 21, 1910, in Mescalero, N.M.; died February 12, 1985, in Easton, Pa. Educator and author. Fincher, who taught political science at New Jersey State College in Montclair (now Montclair State College) from 1946 until his retirement in 1973, wrote numerous books on political science and foreign affairs for juveniles and adults. His publications include *Democracy at Work, The President of the United States, The Government of the United States, The War in Korea, The Vietnam War,* and *American-Mexican Relations.*

OBITUARIES AND OTHER SOURCES:

PERIODICALS

New York Times, February 18, 1985.

*   *   *

FINDLATER, Richard
   See BAIN, Kenneth Bruce Findlater

*   *   *

FINN, Edward E(rnest)   1908-

PERSONAL: Born September 26, 1908, in Omaha, Neb.; son of John Maurice (a musician) and Mary (a housewife; maiden name, Stevens) Finn. *Education:* Attended Creighton University, 1927; St. Louis University, A.B., 1932, M.A., 1935, Ph.L., 1937, S.T.L., 1943. *Politics:* Independent.

ADDRESSES: Home and office—Jesuit Residence, Marquette University, 1404 West Wisconsin St., Milwaukee, Wis. 53233.

CAREER: Entered Society of Jesus (Jesuits), 1928, ordained Roman Catholic priest, 1941; high school English teacher in Prairie du Chien, Wis., 1935-38; St. Louis University, St. Louis, Mo., instructor, 1943-48, assistant professor, 1949-56, associate professor of religion, 1956; Creighton University, Omaha, Neb., associate professor of theology, 1956-58; Marquette University, Milwaukee, Wis., associate professor of theology, 1958-76, associate professor emeritus, 1976—, director of Scripture Conference for Priests and Institute for the Re-Union of Christians, both 1962, assistant librarian at Jesuit Residence, 1980—.

Chairman of Wisconsin Province Commission for the Revision of Ministries of the Society of Jesus, 1968-71; member of Catholic Commission on Intellectual and Cultural Affairs, National Catholic Liturgical Conference, and Milwaukee Archdiocesan Catholic/Orthodox Churches Dialogue Commission.

MEMBER: Catholic Biblical Association of America, Catholic Theological Society of America, College Theology Society (founder and director of St. Louis region, 1956).

WRITINGS:

Brothers East and West, Liturgical Press, 1975.
These Are My Rites, Liturgical Press, 1983.

Contributor to *New Catholic Encyclopedia.* Contributor to magazines, including *Worship* and *Religious Education.*

WORK IN PROGRESS: Research on ecumenism.

SIDELIGHTS: Edward E. Finn told *CA:* "I am retired from classroom duties. For over forty years I have been a sort of one-man ecumenical movement in St. Louis, Omaha, and Milwaukee. I first became attracted to the Eastern Rite churches through the beautiful singing I heard in them. At the same time I became dissatisfied by the lack of communication between them that I discovered. I began a steady program of personal visits to the homes of the pastors of these churches as well as taught one course in each of the universities where I was stationed: St. Louis University, Creighton University, and Marquette University. My first writing on the subject was in the St. Louis archdiocesan newspaper.

"My writings have been greatly influenced by the writings of Fr. Frantisek Dvornik, a professor of Byzantine history at the Dumbarton Oaks Research Center at Harvard University. My students in the university courses became my first audience. I was appalled at the absence of knowledge of the Eastern Rite churches that I found in general among Western Rite Catholics. I set out to reduce that ignorance. My aim has been to promote oneness among Catholics and Orthodox. My approach has been historical and liturgical rather than theological."

*   *   *

FIORENZA, Francis S(chuessler)   1941-

PERSONAL: Born February 27, 1941, in Brooklyn, N.Y.; son of Nicholas and Josephine (Buonadonna) Fiorenza; married Elisabeth Schuessler (a professor), 1967; children: Christina. *Education:* St. Mary's Seminary (now Seminary and University), Baltimore, Md., A.B., 1961, S.T.B., 1963; University of Muenster, D.Th., 1972. *Religion:* Roman Catholic.

ADDRESSES: Office—Department of Theology, Catholic University of America, Washington, D.C. 20064.

CAREER: University of Notre Dame, Notre Dame, Ind., assistant professor of theology, 1971-77; Villanova University, Villanova, Pa., assistant professor of theology, 1977-79; Catholic University of America, Washington, D.C., associate professor of theology, 1979—. Visiting scholar at Union Theological Seminary, New York, N.Y., 1974-75; fellow at University of Chicago, 1978-79.

MEMBER: American Academy of Religion, Catholic Theological Society of America (president-elect), Society for Val-

ues in Higher Education, College Theology Society, Hegel Society.

AWARDS, HONORS: Kent fellow of Danforth Foundation, 1966-70; German Academic Exchange fellow, 1964-66; fellow of Association of Theological Schools, 1982-83.

WRITINGS:

L'assenza di Dio come probleme teologica, Queriniana, 1970.
(Editor and translator) Friedrich Ernst Daniel Schleiermacher, *Open Letters on the Glaubenslehre,* American Academy of Religion, 1981.
Religion und Politik, Volume 27, Herder, 1982.
Foundation Theology: Jesus and the Church, Crossroad/Continuum, 1984.
Mission of Church: From Political to Public Theology, Winston Press, in press.

Contributor to theology journals.

WORK IN PROGRESS: Introduction to Theology.

SIDELIGHTS: Francis S. Fiorenza told *CA:* "My writings focus on the nature of theology—its sources and criteria—and on the mission of the church. These two interests merge in political theology that shows the interrelation between religious beliefs and political practice. I argue, however, for a conception of political theology as public theology in order to stress the importance of public discourse and rational consensus as prerequisites for a political theology in a democratic and pluralistic society."

*   *   *

FISHER, Shelton   1911-1985

OBITUARY NOTICE: Born May 7, 1911, in Memphis, Tenn.; died of respiratory failure, March 15, 1985, in Stamford, Conn. Publisher. Fisher was a key executive with McGraw-Hill, having begun his career with the publishing company in 1940 as promotion manager of *Business Week.* In 1947, after serving in World War II, he returned to the company as assistant publisher of *Science Illustrated.* Fisher eventually published other periodicals, including *Fleet Owner* and *Electrical Merchandising,* before becoming senior vice-president and president of the publications division. Fisher was named president of McGraw-Hill in 1966, chief executive officer in 1968, and chairman of the board in 1974. He held all three positions until his retirement in 1976. Fisher also held other corporate posts, including directorships for such companies as Borden, Sperry Rand, Rockwell, and Kroger.

OBITUARIES AND OTHER SOURCES:

BOOKS

Who's Who in America, 42nd edition, Marquis, 1982.

PERIODICALS

Chicago Tribune, March 17, 1985, March 19, 1985.
New York Times, March 16, 1985.
Washington Post, March 18, 1985.

*   *   *

FISHOF, David   1956-

PERSONAL: Born June 18, 1956, in New York, N.Y.; son of Mark (a cantor) and Edith (a teacher; maiden name, Lieberman) Fishof; married Monica Schoenberg (a teacher), February 20, 1977; children: Shira Rachel, Joshua Benjimen. *Education:* Bernard M. Baruch College of the City University of New York, B.A., 1977.

ADDRESSES: Office—David Fishof Productions, Inc., 1775 Broadway, New York, N.Y. 10019. *Agent*—Mel Berger, William Morris Agency, 1350 Avenue of the Americas, New York, N.Y. 10019.

CAREER: David Fishof Productions, Inc., New York, N.Y., president, 1974—.

WRITINGS:

Putting It on the Line, Morrow, 1983.

*   *   *

FLAHERTY, Robert J(oseph)   1884-1951

BRIEF ENTRY: Born February 16, 1884, in Iron Mountain, Mich.; died July 23, 1951, in New York, N.Y. American explorer, filmmaker, and author. Considered a leading figure in the field of documentary cinema, Flaherty was known for his immensely successful ''Nanook of the North,'' a 1922 film about Eskimo life. Flaherty's documentaries, which critics praised for their powerful realism, are said to have exerted a great influence on a number of film pioneers. ''Tabu,'' a feature film that Flaherty directed with German filmmaker Friedrich Walter Murnau, received an Academy Award for best photography in 1932. The director's widely acclaimed ''Man of Aran,'' a 1934 documentary film about a fisherman's life on a desolate island off the coast of Ireland, won several awards, including first prize at the 1934 Venice Exposition. Flaherty's writings include *Samoa* (1932) and *The Captain's Chair: A Story of the North* (1938).

BIOGRAPHICAL/CRITICAL SOURCES:

BOOKS

A Biographical Dictionary of Film, 2nd revised edition, Morrow, 1981.
Calder-Marshall, Arthur, *The Innocent Eye: The Life of Robert J. Flaherty,* W. H. Allen, 1963.
Current Biography, Wilson, 1949, September, 1951.
Dictionary of Film Makers, University of California Press, 1972.
Film Encyclopedia, Crowell, 1979.

*   *   *

FLASTER, Donald J(ohn)   1932-

PERSONAL: Born August 29, 1932, in New York, N.Y.; son of Murray J. and Theresa (Brenner) Flaster; divorced; children: Elisabeth Ann, Andrew Paul. *Education:* Johns Hopkins University, A.B., 1953; University of Naples, M.D., 1959; Blackstone School of Law, LL.B., 1970.

ADDRESSES: Home—Morris Plains, N.J. *Office*—Scientific & Regulatory Services Consulting, Inc., 10 Park Pl., Morristown, N.J. 07960.

CAREER: Meyer Memorial Hospital, Buffalo, N.Y., intern, 1959-60; Millard Fillmore Hospital, Buffalo, Mead Johnson Residency fellow, 1960; private practice of medicine in Valley Cottage, N.Y., 1961-67; Pfizer, Inc., New York, N.Y., medical officer in charge of clinical research, 1967-69; U.S.V. Pharmaceutical Co., Tuckahoe, N.Y., director of clinical research, 1969-71; Sandoz Pharmaceutical Co., East Hanover, N.J., medical officer in charge of clinical research, 1971-74; Scientific & Regulatory Services Consulting, Inc., Morristown, N.J., president and medical-legal consultant in Morristown, 1974—. Member of administrative staff of Nyack Hospital; adviser to Nyack Ambulance Corps; fire surgeon for Valley Cottage Fire Department; consultant to law firms and health products manufacturers. Volunteer reader for Recordings for the Blind, Inc.

MEMBER: American Academy of Family Physicians (charter fellow), American Diabetes Association, American Heart Association, American Society of Law and Medicine, American Society for the Advancement of Medical Instrumentation, New Jersey Medical Society, Morris County Medical Society, Rockland County Medical Society, Rockland County Academy of Family Practice (past president).

AWARDS, HONORS: Special recognition award from New York Academy of Family Physicians, 1970.

WRITINGS:

Malpractice: A Guide to the Legal Rights of Patients and Doctors, Scribner, 1983.

Contributor to medical and law journals.

WORK IN PROGRESS: A novel—a psychological study of a malpractice case.

SIDELIGHTS: Donald J. Flaster told *CA:* ''I have not treated the sick since 1967, and I do not litigate cases. I function primarily in the area of government regulatory compliance. My specialties are medical malpractice and the concerns of health products manufacturers.

''I wrote my book, *Malpractice,* to clarify and inject sense into the absurd malpractice crisis. It is the first book on the subject that was written for the patient, rather than the physician or attorney. The average patient is quite ignorant of his or her legal rights, to say nothing of what *is* malpractice (failure to practice a profession up to the accepted standards of the day) as contrasted with the assorted dissatisfactions and angers a patient feels toward a physician. Conversely, the average *physician* is equally ignorant about those 'irritation factors' that lead a patient, already conditioned to our litigious society, to think lawsuit when dissatisfied with the results of a doctor-patient relationship. Sometimes this is because of treatment failure, though the best known treatment may well have been rendered. There is no guarantee of cure in medicine, for it remains still too inexact a science, and most treatment failures do *not* involve negligence or incompetence on the part of the physician. Envy of the physician's earnings (usually perceived to be far in excess of reality) further primes a dissatisfied patient to think of litigation, hoping to effect a Robin Hood-like redistribution of wealth. The sad part is that it works to destroy the mutual trust that used to be the quintessential foundation of that close relationship between a doctor and his or her patient, significantly reduces the quality of care, and destroys the pleasure the physician once received from the practice of his or her profession, leaving only the financial reward as a motivation. Finally, the cost of health care increases through the practice of 'defensive medicine.'

''I believe the world should operate on a 'fair play' basis, rather than pursue constantly conflicting self-interests. I care *what*'s right, not *who*'s right.''

FLEETWOOD-HESKETH, (Charles) Peter (Fleetwood) 1905-1985

OBITUARY NOTICE: Born February 5, 1905; died February 10, 1985. Architect, illustrator, and author. Highly regarded in English architectural circles for his expertise and versatility, Fleetwood-Hesketh was known as a supporter of conservation and of other important causes. Following his studies in London, Fleetwood-Hesketh worked for several well-known architectural firms. He served in World War II as a liaison officer with the resistance in Nazi-occupied France. Later involved in various aspects of public life, he served as a lay member of the General Synod of the Church of England from 1975 to 1980. Fleetwood-Hesketh illustrated several books, including poet John Betjeman's 1933 book on architecture, *Ghastly Good Taste.* His writings include *Murray's Architectural Guide to Lancashire* (1955), as well as contributions on a variety of architectural topics to books and periodicals. Fleetwood-Hesketh was also architectural correspondent to the London *Daily Telegraph* from 1964 to 1967.

OBITUARIES AND OTHER SOURCES:

BOOKS

Blue Book: Leaders of the English-Speaking World, St. Martin's, 1976.
Who's Who, 135th edition, St. Martin's, 1983.

PERIODICALS

Times (London), February 12, 1985.

* * *

FLEISCHMANN, Raoul H(erbert) 1885-1969

OBITUARY NOTICE: Born August 17, 1885, in Ischl, Austria-Hungary (now Austria); died after a long illness, May 11, 1969, in New York, N.Y. Bread manufacturer and publisher. A scion of the family of Fleischmann's Yeast fame, Fleischmann is remembered as a co-founder and longtime publisher of *New Yorker* magazine. He joined the family business in 1907, but Fleischmann, whose circle of friends included known literary figures, eventually became bored by the baking industry. Consequently, he readily accepted editor Harold Ross's suggestion that they found a magazine. In 1924 Fleischmann and Ross agreed that the publication should center around New York City, and in February of the following year *New Yorker* magazine was launched. Although *New Yorker* initially enjoyed success, serious financial difficulties almost caused Fleischmann to abandon the entire enterprise. He persevered, however, and between 1925 and 1927 more than $700,000 of Fleischmann's capital was invested in the publication. In 1928 *New Yorker* recorded a profit, eventually becoming a consistently successful publication, reputed for its literary excellence. At *New Yorker* Fleischmann generally gave free rein to the editors, limiting himself to the business aspects of publishing. Fleischmann remained publisher of *New Yorker* until his death.

OBITUARIES AND OTHER SOURCES:

BOOKS

American Authors and Books: 1640 to the Present Day, 3rd revised edition, Crown, 1962.
Obituaries on File, Facts on File, 1979.
Who Was Who in America, With World Notables, Volume V: *1969-1973,* Marquis, 1973.

PERIODICALS

New York Times, May 12, 1969.

* * *

FLEMING, Ray(mond) 1945-

PERSONAL: Born February 27, 1945, in Cleveland, Ohio; son of Theodore Robert and Ethel (Dorsey) Fleming; married Nancy Lu Runge, November 15, 1969; children: John Kenneth, Peter Carlton, Stephen Robert. *Education:* University of Notre Dame, B.A., 1967; attended University of Florence, 1967-68; Harvard University, Ph.D., 1976.

ADDRESSES: Home—710 South Oak, Oxford, Ohio 45056. *Office*—102 Roudebush Hall, Miami University, Oxford, Ohio 45056.

CAREER: U.S. Department of State, Washington, D.C., assistant officer at political desk, summer, 1966; University of Notre Dame, Notre Dame, Ind., instructor in Italian, 1969-72; University of California, San Diego, La Jolla, assistant professor of comparative literature, 1973-80; Miami University, Oxford, Ohio, associate professor of Italian and assistant dean of Graduate School, 1980—. Consultant to U.S. Foreign Service. Visiting professor of literary theory at Centre Universitaire (Luxembourg), spring, 1984.

MEMBER: Dante Society of America.

AWARDS, HONORS: Fulbright scholar in Italy, 1967-68; Woodrow Wilson fellow, 1968-69; poetry award from Ingram-Merrill Foundation, 1971; Ford Foundation fellowship for black Americans, 1972-73; American Council of Learned Studies fellowship, spring/summer, 1978; Alexander von Humboldt fellow in Germany, 1978-79; fellowship from Northwestern University's School of Criticism and Theory, 1981.

WRITINGS:

Ice and Honey (poems), Dorrance, 1979.
Diplomatic Relations (poems), Lotus Press, 1982.

(Contributor) Spiro Peterson, editor, *International Bibliography of Daniel Defoe Scholarship,* G. K. Hall, in press.

WORK IN PROGRESS: Talking Back to the Moon, poems, publication expected in 1986.

SIDELIGHTS: Ray Fleming told *CA:* "Much like Tennyson's Ulysses I would like to think that I am part of all that I have met. My travels to other countries gave me a necessary and liberating exposure that I could never have received in America. The opportunity to live with people in different cultures has made my poetry more global in its settings (thereby revealing the communality of human experience) and more aware of the many voices that a poet must hear if that poetry is to speak to a wide audience.

"My training as a comparatist has enabled me to be at home within the contexts of both European and Afro-American poetry, and my reference seeks to combine those traditions when possible and to point out the contradictory assumptions of these cultures with humor and compassion."

* * *

FLEURE, H. J.
See FLEURE, Herbert John

FLEURE, Herbert John   1877-1969
(H. J. Fleure)

OBITUARY NOTICE: Born June 6, 1877, in Guernsey, Channel Islands, United Kingdom; died July 1, 1969, in Cheam, Surrey, England. Educator, scientist, editor, and author. Fleure taught zoology, geology, and anthropology at the University of Aberystwyth in the 1910's and served as honorary secretary of the Geographical Association. He was also professor of geography at Manchester University from 1930 to 1944. Among his writings are the ten-volume *Corridors of Time,* which he wrote with H. J. E. Peake, and *A Natural History of Man in Britain.* Under the name H. J. Fleure he also edited *South Carpathian Studies* with E. Estyn Evans.

OBITUARIES AND OTHER SOURCES:

BOOKS

Twentieth-Century Culture: A Biographical Companion, Harper, 1983.

*   *   *

FLINT, Lucy   1954-

PERSONAL: Born March 4, 1954, in Madrid, Spain; U.S. citizen born abroad; daughter of Weston (a professor) and Nora (a teacher; maiden name, Clayton) Flint. *Education:* Attended University of Madrid, 1974-75; Wesleyan University, Middletown, Conn., B.A., 1976; Columbia University, M.A., 1979.

ADDRESSES: Home—250 West 99th St., No. 8B, New York, N.Y. 10025.

CAREER: Solomon R. Guggenheim Museum, New York, N.Y., research assistant, 1978-79, curatorial assistant, 1980-81, curatorial coordinator, 1981-83; free-lance art historian, 1983—.

AWARDS, HONORS: Award of Merit from American Association of Museums, 1984, for *Handbook.*

WRITINGS: (Translator) Margit Rowell, *New Images From Spain,* Guggenheim Foundation, 1980.

Handbook: The Peggy Guggenheim Collection, Abrams, 1983.

Contributor to *Beaux-Arts.*

WORK IN PROGRESS: Walker Art Center Permanent Collection: Paintings, Sculpture, and Drawings, publication expected in 1987.

SIDELIGHTS: Lucy Flint told *CA:* "In my work I intend to provide information that will be useful and illuminating for the scholar, and yet accessible enough not to dismay the interested lay person."

*   *   *

FLOOD, Curt(is Charles)   1938-

BRIEF ENTRY: Born January 18, 1938, in Houston, Tex. American professional baseball player and author. Flood was an outfielder for the St. Louis Cardinals from 1958 until 1969, when he became involved in a legal battle against baseball's reserve clause, a contractual means by which a player could be traded to another team without the athlete's consent. In 1971 the suit came before the U.S. Supreme Court, which determined that the reserve system was legal. Four years later, however, the reserve system was overturned when an arbitration panel ruled in favor of pitchers Dave McNally and Andy

Messersmith when they filed a grievance similar to that of Flood. He told his side of the controversial story in *The Way It Is* (Trident, 1971). After a brief stint with the Washington Senators, Flood retired from baseball in 1971. *Address:* Alameda, Calif.

BIOGRAPHICAL/CRITICAL SOURCES:

PERIODICALS

Ebony, July, 1968.
Newsweek, April 2, 1979.
New York Times, May 26, 1981.
Sports Illustrated, August 19, 1968.

*   *   *

FLOOD, John M(ichael)   1947-

PERSONAL: Born September, 1947, in Hearst, Ontario, Canada. *Education:* St. Dunstan's University (now University of Prince Edward Island), B.A., 1969; University of Calgary, M.A., 1973.

ADDRESSES: Office—Department of English, College Universitaire de Hearst, Laurentian University of Sudbury, Hearst, Ontario, Canada.

CAREER: High school English teacher in Hearst, Ontario, 1971-72; Laurentian University of Sudbury, College Universitaire de Hearst, Hearst, Ontario, professor of English, 1972—. Founding editor and publisher of Penumbra Press, 1979—. Part-time member of faculty at College Universitaire de Hearst, 1971-72. Member of Canadian Book Information Centre and Literary Press Group; member of Canadian Conference of the Arts, 1981-84; member of board of directors of Moonbeam Public Library. Program director, producer, and host of "Thursday North," a weekly program on CKAP-Radio, 1975-77; gives readings from his works; presents seminars; judge of writing contests.

MEMBER: Canadian Booksellers Association, Canadian Periodical Publishers' Association (member of board of directors, 1980-82), Association for the Advancement of Scandinavian Studies in Canada, Northeastern Modern Language Association, Ontario Library Association, Toronto Arts and Letters Club.

WRITINGS:

The Land They Occupied (poems), Porcupine's Quill, 1976.
Author of one-act plays "Donald Kelly: Killer!," "Berth Shaw: Pioneer," and "Reesor Siding Incident," all produced as part of radio program "Northern Delights," first produced in Timmons, Ontario, 1978.

EDITOR

Mooskek, Black Moss Press, 1978.
J.E.H. Macdonald, *Sketchbook,* Penumbra Press, 1979.
Thoreau Macdonald, *Notebooks,* Penumbra Press, 1980.

OTHER

Work represented in anthologies, including *Northern Ontario Anthology.* Contributor of poems to magazines, including *Antigonish Review, Fiddlehead, Poetry Canada Review, CV II, Squatchberry Journal,* and *Poetry Toronto.* Editor of *Boreal,* 1974-79; editor and publisher of *Northward Journal,* 1979—.

WORK IN PROGRESS: "To maintain and reinforce the cultural significance of a *northern* publishing firm."

SIDELIGHTS: John M. Flood's *The Land They Occupied* concerns the harsh treatment of Indians by the white Canadian government during the signing of the James Bay Treaty, negotiated by Duncan Campbell Scott between 1905 and 1906. According to Flood: "Today it is evident that what the Indians were giving away was their birthright as well as their right to live according to the design of their own culture. What they were getting in return in no way compensated them for what they forfeited."

Flood told *CA:* "I am interested in Northern subjects and themes, whether the Far North, the Boreal Forest, or the Scandanavian North." He further stated that humanism is an important element in his writing.

*   *   *

FLOYD, Samuel A(lexander), Jr. 1937-

PERSONAL: Born February 1, 1937, in Tallahassee, Fla.; son of Samuel A. and Theora (Combs) Floyd; married Barbara Jean Nealy (a retail manager), 1956; children: Wanda, Cecilia, Samuel A. III. *Education:* Florida Agricultural and Mechanical University, B.S., 1957; Southern Illinois University at Carbondale, M.M.E., 1964, Ph.D., 1969.

ADDRESSES: Home—115 South Plymouth Ct., No. 607, Chicago, Ill. 60605. *Office*—Center for Black Music Research, Columbia College, 600 South Michigan Ave., Chicago, Ill. 60605.

CAREER: Teacher of instrumental music at high school in Arcadia, Fla., 1957-62; Florida Agricultural and Mechanical University, Tallahassee, instructor in music and assistant director of bands, 1962-64; Southern Illinois University at Carbondale, 1964-78, began as instructor, became associate professor of music; Fisk University, Nashville, Tenn., professor of music, 1978-83; Columbia College, Chicago, Ill., director of Center for Black Music Research, 1983—.

Member of advisory panel on the performing arts for Illinois Arts Council, 1977; consultant and panelist for the Southern Regional Conference on the Funding of Research in the Humanities, 1980. Proposal reviewer for the National Endowment for the Humanities, 1977—; and for the Fund for the Improvement of Post Secondary Education, 1977. Consultant to the Office for the Advancement of Public Negro Colleges, 1976-77; general consultant to the Fisk University Learning Library Program, 1981-83. Member of board of directors of Southern Illinois University Employees Credit Union, 1975-77, Nashville Institute for the Arts, 1979-82, and John W. Work Foundation, 1979-83.

MEMBER: College Music Society (member of national council, 1979-80), Sonneck Society, Pi Kappa Lambda.

AWARDS, HONORS: Five research grants from Southern Illinois University, 1970-77; grants from Newberry Library, 1972 and 1979, National Endowment for the Humanities, 1976 and 1980, National Endowment for the Arts, 1976, Illinois Arts Council, 1976, Carbondale Bicentennial Committee, 1976, and the Justin and Valere Potter Foundation, 1979.

WRITINGS:

Ninety-nine Street Beats, Cadences, and Exercises for Percussion, Hansen Publishing, 1961.
One Hundred One Street Beats, Cadences, and Exercises for Percussion, Hansen Publishing, 1965.

Contemporary Exercises and Cadences for Marching Percussion, University of Miami Music Publications, 1975.
The Great Lakes Experience: An Oral History, Southern Illinois University, 1977.
(With Marsha J. Reisser) *Black Music in the United States: An Annotated Bibliography of Selected Reference and Research Sources*, Kraus International, 1983.
Black Music Biography: An Annotated Bibliography, Kraus International, in press.

Editor of *Black Music Research Newsletter*, 1977, and *Black Music Research Journal*, 1980; member of editorial board of *Black Perspective in Music*, 1979—, and *American Music*, 1984—. Contributor to journals, including *Illinois Music Education, Music and Man, School Musician, Chronicle of Higher Education*, and *Music Educator's Journal*.

WORK IN PROGRESS: The Continuity of Black American Music.

SIDELIGHTS: Samuel A. Floyd, Jr., told *CA:* "My concerns are with stimulating research activity in the field of black music and the encouragement of their eventual inclusion in mainstream writing. The academic writers who have had the most influence on my work are philosopher and scholar John Dewey—especially through his *Art and Experience*—and Harvard professor Eileen Southern, author of *The Music of Black Americans* and other works. Dewey's concepts of history, continuity, and art guide my aesthetic, historical, and literary thinking; Southern's works stand as exemplars of impeccable scholarship and stimulate my scholarly activity."

*   *   *

FLYNN, David H(oughton) 1953-

PERSONAL: Born October 15, 1953, in Hartford, Conn.; son of Benedict D., Jr. (an insurance broker) and Priscilla H. (an artist) Flynn; married Elizabeth T. Palmer (a teacher). *Education:* University of North Carolina at Chapel Hill, A.B., 1976; University of Connecticut, J.D., 1979.

ADDRESSES: Office—Gross, Hyde & Williams, One Financial Plaza, Hartford, Conn. 06103. *Agent*—Dominick Abel Literary Agency, Inc., 498 West Ave., No. 12C, New York, N.Y. 10024.

CAREER: Tyler, Cooper & Alcorn, New Haven, Conn., attorney, 1979-81; Gross, Hyde & Williams, Hartford, Conn., attorney, 1981—.

WRITINGS:

(With Michael P. Pancheri) *The IRA Handbook,* New Century, 1983, 3rd edition, 1985.

Contributor to law periodicals.

SIDELIGHTS: David H. Flynn told *CA:* "I embarked on *The IRA Handbook* project for two primary reasons—there is a need for a plain language explanation for this area of tax law, and I enjoy expository writing. The book definitely espouses the IRA concept, which will, in one form or another, eventually replace social security as the central core of our pension system. The rules are very complicated in some instances. My co-author, Michael P. Pancheri, brought extensive experience in this area from the point of view of a tax lawyer; my background was banking law, and I have also done some articles for legal periodicals. I believe there is a need for more 'simple English' words on some of the laws which affect most Americans. But, as stated in the book, such guides should only be used in conjunction with a professional's advice (not necessarily a tax attorney—an accountant or competent retirement planner will do just fine).''

*   *   *

FORD, Henry   1863-1947

BRIEF ENTRY: Born July 30, 1863, near Dearborn, Mich.; died April 7, 1947, in Dearborn, Mich. American engineer, industrialist, philanthropist, publisher, and author. One of the founders of the automobile industry in America, Ford revolutionized production and is said to have single-handedly launched the automobile as a mass market commodity. Having founded the Ford Motor Company in 1903, Ford translated his technical inventiveness into the world famous Model T, an affordable and efficient car that destroyed the myth of the automobile as a luxury object. Ford's 1913 introduction of the assembly line considerably increased productivity but also, as critics charged, made worker's jobs more monotonous than usual. The following year Ford instituted the five-dollars-a-day minimum wage, by far the highest in the industry. He was, however, a staunch opponent of the labor movement and forcibly resisted attempts to unionize his factories. An unwillingness to adapt his product to consumers' demands is said to have ultimately cost the industrialist his leading position in the automobile industry.

Ford's numerous activities included philanthropy, politics, and publishing. A professed pacifist, Ford chartered a ship in 1915 and sailed to Europe in a futile attempt to end World War I. In 1919 Ford became publisher of the Dearborn *Independent,* which subsequently began printing vicious attacks on Jews. Although Ford later apologized for this involvement in anti-Jewish propaganda, he accepted the Grand Cross of the German Eagle that the Nazis conferred on him on his seventy-fifth birthday. The industrialist's wide-ranging philanthropic activity resulted in several important institutions, including Henry Ford Hospital in Detroit, Henry Ford Museum and Greenfield Village in Dearborn, and the Ford Foundation. Ford's books, written with Samuel Crowther, include *My Life and Work* (1922), *Today and Tomorrow* (1926), *Moving Forward* (1930), and *Edison as I Know Him* (1930). *Address:* Dearborn, Mich.

BIOGRAPHICAL/CRITICAL SOURCES:

BOOKS

Current Biography, Wilson, 1944, May, 1947.
McGraw-Hill Encyclopedia of World Biography, McGraw, 1973.
The Oxford Companion to American History, Oxford University Press, 1966.
Sward, Keith Theodore, *The Legend of Henry Ford,* Rinehart, 1948. ·
Webster's American Biographies, Merriam, 1979.

*   *   *

FORD, Philip J(ohn)   1949-

PERSONAL: Born March 28, 1949, in Ilford, England; son of Peter James (a postal worker) and Leah (Alvarez) Ford; married Lenore Muskett, July 17, 1982. *Education:* King's College, Cambridge, B.A., 1971, M.A., 1975, Ph.D., 1977; University of Bordeaux III, Maitre es Lettres, 1977.

ADDRESSES: Home—18 Greville Rd., Cambridge CB1 3QL, England. *Office*—Clare College, Cambridge University, Cambridge CB2 1TL, England.

CAREER: Cambridge University, Cambridge, England, research fellow at Girton College, 1977-78; University of Aberdeen, Aberdeen, Scotland, lecturer in French, 1978-81; Cambridge University, lecturer in French, 1982—, fellow at Clare College and director of studies in modern languages, 1982—, praelector and fellows' steward, 1984—.

MEMBER: International Association for Neo-Latin Studies, Society for French Studies, Modern Humanities Research Association, Society for Seventeenth-Century French Studies.

WRITINGS:

George Buchanan, Prince of Poets: With an Edition of the Miscellaneorum Liber (the latter edited by Ford and W. S. Watt), Aberdeen University Press, 1982.
(Editor) Alexandre Hardy, *Panthee* (critical edition), University of Exeter, 1984.

Contributor to language journals.

WORK IN PROGRESS: The Poetry of Pierre de Ronsard and the Visual Arts, publication expected in 1986; *Homeric Allegory in the Renaissance.*

SIDELIGHTS: Philip J. Ford told *CA:* "I first became interested in George Buchanan when I was an undergraduate at King's College, Cambridge, where I benefited from the teaching of Robert Bolgar. His impressively wide knowledge of Renaissance Europe opened up areas of interest that were not often to be found on university syllabuses at that time. Subsequently, I was very fortunate to have as my Ph.D. supervisor Ian McFarlane of Wadham College, Oxford. He was one of the founding fathers of neo-Latin studies and the author of an impressive biography of George Buchanan.

"My particular interest in the Scottish poet and humanist has centered upon his political writings. And in my book I set out to establish the theory of neo-Latin versification and poetics (based on a study of the various manuals written in the first half of the sixteenth century), and to see how Buchanan fits into this context. I am also interested in the interaction between neo-Latin and vernacular poetry and the ways in which the latter often had considerable debts to the former in the early part of the century.

"My attention has since turned to France's greatest vernacular poet of the sixteenth century, Pierre de Ronsard. He is undoubtedly one of the most pictorial poets of the century, and this has important implications for our approach to reading his poetry. Frequently his imagery requires interpretation in an iconographical as well as in a literary sense. And in my present study of Ronsard I intend to establish the links between his methods and the methods of the artists of the School of Fontainbleau, for example.

"My interest in Homeric allegory grew as a result of my study of Ronsard. Just as the painters of the period frequently use Homeric myths in an allegorical manner, so too does Ronsard in his poetry. He was in any case taught by Jean Dorat, who was himself an exponent of the allegorical approach to Homer. In my study of Homeric allegory I intend to make available to a wider audience works that are at present only found (in Latin) in Renaissance books or manuscripts. I also intend to assess their influence on sixteenth-century French authors.''

FORMISANO, Ronald P. 1939-

BRIEF ENTRY: Born March 31, 1939, in Providence, R.I. American historian, educator, and author. Formisano, who taught American history at Wayne State University, the University of Pittsburgh, and the University of Rochester, joined the faculty of Clark University in 1973. He wrote *The Birth of Mass Political Parties: Michigan, 1827-1861* (Princeton University Press, 1971) and *The Transformation of Political Culture: Massachusetts Parties, 1790's-1840's* (Oxford University Press, 1983). *Address:* Department of History, Clark University, 950 Main St., Worcester, Mass. 01610.

BIOGRAPHICAL/CRITICAL SOURCES:

PERIODICALS

American Historical Review, February, 1975.

*   *   *

FORREST, James Taylor 1921-

PERSONAL: Born September 22, 1921, in New Castle, Ind.; son of Jesse E. (a businessman) and Katie M. (a housewife; maiden name, Lee) Forrest; married Suzanne de Borhegyi (a historian and writer), 1979; children: Mary Christine, Barbara Lee. *Education:* Attended Hanover College, 1938-39, and Indiana University—Bloomington, 1941; University of Wisconsin—Madison, B.S. (with honors), 1948, M.S., 1949, further graduate study, 1949-50.

ADDRESSES: Home—2035 Spring Creek Dr., Laramie, Wyo. 82070. *Office*—P.O. Box 3138, Laramie, Wyo. 82070.

CAREER: Civilian research associate with U.S. Air Force Strategic Air Command, 1950-53; Colorado State Museum, Denver, curator, 1953-55; Gilcrease Institute of American History and Art, Tulsa, Okla., director, 1955-61; Museum of New Mexico, Santa Fe, director of fine arts, 1961-62, director of museum, 1962-64; Bradford Brinton Memorial Ranch, Big Horn, Wyo., director, beginning in 1964; University of Wyoming, Laramie, director of art museum, 1968—. Instructor at Sheridan College. Wyoming Council on the Arts, member of council, 1967-82, member of board of directors, 1967, chairman, 1971-82; project director at Civic Responsibility Center, Sheridan, Wyo., 1966-67; consultant to National Cowboy Hall of Fame. *Military service:* U.S. Army Air Forces, 1942-45; served in China-Burma-India theater.

MEMBER: American Association of Museums (member of council), American Association for State and Local History, Mountain-Plains Museum Association, Western Association of Art Museums, Colorado-Wyoming Association of Museums (chairman, 1980-81), Omaha Historians Council (president), Santa Fe Westerners (acting president, 1962-63).

WRITINGS:

History of New Mexico, Teachers College Press, 1971.
Bill Gollings: The Man and His Art, Northland Press, 1978.

Contributor to museum journals. Editor of *American Scene,* 1968-71.

WORK IN PROGRESS: American Landscape Painters of the Nineteenth Century and the Environmental Movement; a photographic survey and commentary on English parish churches.

SIDELIGHTS: James Forrest told *CA:* "Reading has led to writing, and seeing to better understanding of the need for clarity of thinking and writing. Many authors have had their influence on me, beginning with Thomas Wolfe and Ray Bradbury. But, as an artist and photographer, my research and writing are tied directly to my abilities to see and be a witness to the world I find of interest and of my particular focus."

*   *   *

FRANK, Roberta 1941-

PERSONAL: Born November 9, 1941, in New York, N.Y.; daughter of Norman and Doris (Birnbaum) Frank; married Walter Goffart (a professor), December 31, 1976. *Education:* New York University, B.A., 1962; Harvard University, M.A., 1964, Ph.D., 1968.

ADDRESSES: Home—171 Lowther Ave., Toronto, Ontario, Canada M5R 1T6. *Office*—Center for Medieval Studies, University of Toronto, Toronto, Ontario, Canada M5S 1V4.

CAREER: University of Toronto, Toronto, Ontario, assistant professor, 1968-73, associate professor, 1973-78, professor of English and medieval studies, 1978—.

MEMBER: International Saga Society, International Society of Anglo-Saxonists (first vice-president, 1982-85; president, 1985-87), Society for the Advancement of Scandinavian Studies in Canada, Mediaeval Academy of America (member of council, 1981-84), Modern Language Association of America (chairman of executive committee of Old English Group, 1978).

AWARDS, HONORS: Elliott Prize from Mediaeval Academy of America, 1972, for "Onomastic Play in Kormakr's Verse: The Name Steingerdr"; fellow of American Council of Learned Societies, 1973-74, 1979-80.

WRITINGS:

(Editor with Angus Cameron and John Leyerle) *Computers and Old English Concordances,* University of Toronto Press, 1970.
(Editor with Cameron) *A Plan for the Dictionary of Old English,* University of Toronto Press, 1973.
Old Norse Poetry: The "Drottkvaett" Stanza, Cornell University Press, 1978.
Old Norse-Icelandic Literature: A Critical Guide, edited by Carol Clover and John Lindow, Cornell University Press, 1985.

CONTRIBUTOR

H. Bekker-Nielson, U. Dronke, G. Helgadottir, and G. W. Weber, editors, *Speculum Norrocnum: Norse Studies in Memory of Gabriel Turville-Petre,* Odense, 1981.
Colin Chase, editor, *The Dating of Beowulf,* University of Toronto Press, 1981.
L. D. Benson and S. Wenzel, editors, *The Wisdom of Poetry: Essays in Early English Literature in Honor of M. W. Bloomfield,* Medieval Institute, 1982.

OTHER

General editor of "Toronto Old English Series," University of Toronto Press, 1976—, and "Publications of the Dictionary of Old English," University of Toronto Press. Contributor to literature journals.

WORK IN PROGRESS: The Politics of Germanic Heroic Legend in England; articles on Old English and Norse poetic style.

SIDELIGHTS: Roberta Frank told *CA:* "Scholarly writing, too, is both craft and art; and I hope that one who works hard enough at the craft may in time bring forth something artistic."

FRANKLIN, Benjamin V 1939-
(Nathanael Charles)

PERSONAL: Born September 10, 1939, in Gallipolis, Ohio; son of Benjamin IV (a teacher) and Virginia (a teacher; maiden name, Hoover) Franklin; married Jo Taft, August 25, 1962; children: Abigail, Rebecca Jane. *Education:* Ohio State University, B.A. and B.S., both 1965; Ohio University, M.A., 1966, Ph.D., 1969.

ADDRESSES: Office—Department of English, University of South Carolina at Columbia, Columbia, S.C. 29208.

CAREER: University of Michigan, Ann Arbor, assistant professor of English, 1969-76; University of South Carolina at Columbia, associate professor, 1976-81, professor of English, 1981—. Host of "Jazz in Retrospect," a radio program syndicated by Southern Educational Communication Association, 1976—; editor of Camden House, Inc. Fulbright professor at University of Athens, 1982-84; member of board of education of American Community Schools of Athens, 1983-84. *Military service:* U.S. Army Reserve, 1960-66.

AWARDS, HONORS: Louis I. Bredvold Award from University of Michigan, 1975, for outstanding publication.

WRITINGS:

(Author of introduction) Samuel Clemens, *Short Stories by Mark Twain,* Airmont, 1968.
(Author of introduction) Frank Norris, *The Octopus,* Airmont, 1969.
Anais Nin: A Bibliography, Kent State University Press, 1973.
Anais Nin (1903-1977): An Exhibition of Her Books, Library, University of South Carolina at Columbia, 1977.
(With Duane Schneider) *Anais Nin: An Introduction,* Ohio University Press, 1979.

EDITOR

The Poetry of the Minor Connecticut Wits, Scholars' Facsimiles and Reprints, 1970.
The Prose of the Minor Connecticut Wits, three volumes, Scholars' Facsimiles and Reprints, 1974.
(With Matthew J. Bruccoli, C. E. Frazer Clark, Jr., and Richard Layman) *First Printings of American Authors,* four volumes, Gale, 1977-79.
Mather Byles: Works, Scholars' Facsimiles and Reprints, 1978.
The Plays and Poems of Mercy Otis Warren, Scholars' Facsimiles and Reprints, 1980.
Boston Printers, Publishers, and Booksellers, 1640-1800, G. K. Hall, 1980.
David Everett: Works, Scholars' Facsimiles and Reprints, 1983.

Also editor of *The Life and Death of That Reverend Man of God, Mr. Richard Mather,* 1966.

OTHER

Contributor to literature journals; contributor to jazz magazines, sometimes under pseudonym Nathanael Charles.

WORK IN PROGRESS: Editing "La Vie de boheme," a column by Wambly Bald that appeared in the *Paris Tribune* from 1929 until 1933; a study of Philadelphia publishing through 1800; a book on novelist Gayle Jones.

SIDELIGHTS: Benjamin Franklin V told *CA:* "Soon after reading Anais Nin for the first time in 1966 I discovered that no one—not even Nin—knew precisely what she had written. I therefore set out to complete her bibliography. Concurrent with that project, Duane Schneider and I discussed Nin's literary creations and finally wrote a book about them. Still, Nin remains one of this century's most misunderstood authors.

"If Nin is open to serious, fresh interpretation, so too is early American literature in general. It was our first literature; it is also our least read and least appreciated literature. This belief inspired me to edit books by the Connecticut wits Byles, Warren, and Everett, and about Boston publishers.

"My interest in jazz began around 1956. It struck me immediately as attractively anti-establishment and possibly archaic music that offered welcome respite from my more traditional and legitimate interests (including baseball). Jazz invigorates me. It must be heard live to be appreciated fully."

* * *

FRANKLIN, Olga 1912-1985

OBITUARY NOTICE—See index for *CA* sketch: Born July 29, 1912, in Birmingham, England; died February 11, 1985, in Birmingham, England. Broadcaster, translator, journalist, and author. Franklin worked as a German-English translator for Austin Motors during the 1930's. She became a sub-editor with the Reuters News Agency in 1941 and later worked for the *Oxford Mail* and the *Daily Sketch and Graphic* as a reporter before becoming a columnist for the *London Daily Mail.* Her "Frankly Yours" column appeared in the *Daily Mail* from 1956 until 1971, when she became a broadcaster and translator for the British Broadcasting Corporation (BBC-Radio). Franklin's publications include *Born Twice, Oh That Spike!, Making Money at Home, Biography of Dr. Anna Aslan, Only Uncle,* and an autobiography, *Steppes to Fleet Street.*

OBITUARIES AND OTHER SOURCES:

BOOKS

The Writers Directory: 1984-1986, St. James Press, 1983.

PERIODICALS

Times (London), February 16, 1985.

* * *

FREBURGER, William J. 1940-

PERSONAL: Born October 6, 1940, in Baltimore, Md.; son of William (an accountant) and Nellie (Bagdonas) Freburger; married Mary Elizabeth Algeo (a teacher of mathematics), February 23, 1979; children: William Daniel. *Education:* Attended St. Charles's College, 1960; St. Mary's Seminary, Baltimore, Md., B.A., 1962; Gregorian University of Rome, S.T.L., 1966. *Politics:* Independent. *Religion:* Roman Catholic.

ADDRESSES: Home—8805 Custer Trail, Kansas City, Mo. 64131. *Office*—NCR Publishing Co., P.O. Box 281, Kansas City, Mo. 64141-0281.

CAREER: Ordained Roman Catholic priest, 1965, legally released from obligations of the priesthood; associate pastor of Roman Catholic churches in Jessup, Md., 1966-68, and Baltimore, Md., 1968-70; Archdiocese of Baltimore, Baltimore, director of Division of Liturgy, 1970-76; Time Consultants, Severna Park, Md., vice-chairperson, 1975, program coordinator, 1976-78; NCR Publishing Co., Kansas City, Mo., editor of *Celebration: A Creative Worship Service,* 1978—. Assistant executive secretary of Liturgical Commission of Archdiocese of Baltimore, 1968-70; member of board of directors of Federation of Diocesan Liturgical Commissions, 1970-76, vice-chairman, 1974; adviser to U.S. Bishops' Committee on the Liturgy, 1973-75.

MEMBER: North American Academy of Liturgy.

WRITINGS:

Baptism for Parents, Alba House, 1970.
Repent and Believe, Ave Maria Press, 1972.
This Is the Word of the Lord, Ave Maria Press, 1974, revised edition, 1984.
(With James Haas) *Eucharistic Prayers for Children,* Ave Maria Press, 1976.
(With Haas) *The Forgiving Christ,* Ave Maria Press, 1977.
Liturgy: The People's Work, Twenty-Third Publications, 1984.

Author of "Liturgy With Life," a column in *Today's Parish,* 1976-78, cartoonist, 1983—.

WORK IN PROGRESS: Songs of the New Israel: The Responsorial Psalm in the Sunday Liturgy; The Dance of Time: The Meaning of the Liturgical Year Today; Liturgical Values for Teenagers.

SIDELIGHTS: William J. Freburger told *CA:* "My writing has been confined to the religious field: popular explanations of the liturgical reform in the Roman Catholic church over the last twenty years. I have a novel in my desk drawer, but other activities have prevented me from giving it the full attention I would like."

*   *   *

FREEMAN, Jean Kenny 1929-
(Jean Kenny)

PERSONAL: Born August 23, 1929, in Havre, Mont.; daughter of Fredrich Walker (a carpenter) and Hazel Etta (a teacher; maiden name, Sauer) Kenny; married James T. Pancak, September, 1948 (divorced August, 1967); married Bill G. Freeman (a minister), November 24, 1972; children: Jeni Pancak Foster, Jamie, K. C., Mark. *Education:* Attended high school in Malta, Mont. *Religion:* Society of Friends (Quakers).

ADDRESSES: Home—P.O. Box 695, Highway 200, Hope, Idaho, 83836.

CAREER: Public speaker and counselor; writer.

WRITINGS:

(Under name Jean Kenny) *This Angry Loving Land* (novel), Bethany House, 1981.

WORK IN PROGRESS: Lullaby the Found Mama, a novel about creative parenting and women's status in the Church.

SIDELIGHTS: "As an evangelical pastor's wife," Jean Kenny Freeman told *CA,* "I am committed to the organized church. I am also dismayed by the average Christian's position that godliness produces material comforts to use while one awaits permanent rescue in 'the day of the Lord.' I use fiction to inspire the reader to the present reality of Christ's kingdom, into which we, through servanthood and justice, seek to draw a suffering world.

"I grew up in my grandmother's hotel in Dodson, Montana, a prairie town, and I still regard the prairie as one of the last

frontiers of free and individual expression. It is here we see the ideals of self-sufficiency and the willingness to battle severe natural elements with raw courage. In my contemporary novel, *This Angry Loving Land,* I treat the pioneer spirit with respect and sympathy while at the same time I reveal the pride and selfishness of that spirit through land baron Dow Garstin. When the young people in a prairie commune are exposed in their brokeness and powerlessness through the indifference and scorn of the Garstin-led establishment, we confront the self-protecting violence of a church-inclusive society.

"I feel that we Christians largely adopt the spirit of Dow Garstin, in our attitude toward our own society and the world at large, protecting what we have for ourselves instead of taking on the servanthood of Christ in order to build the Kingdom of God. God in Christ in us wants to redeem all creation and he can only get the job done if we understand what he's after and commit ourselves to his will.

"In *Lullaby the Found Mama* I address my own conviction for the equality of women in vocational and religious work. But through this fiction tale I play up the maternal God-like psyche of woman who finds her first responsibility to her children and to the whole of creation. She is eternal mother, and when set upon and claimed by the Holy Spirit she becomes the creative and self-effacing love that draws all humanity into Christly purpose."

BIOGRAPHICAL/CRITICAL SOURCES:

PERIODICALS

Christian Herald, September, 1981.
Religious Book Review, August, 1981.

*   *   *

FREUD, Sigmund 1856-1939

BRIEF ENTRY: Name originally Sigismund Solomon Freud; born May 6, 1856, in Freiberg, Moravia (now Pribor, Czechoslovakia); died of cancer, September 23, 1939, in London, England. Austrian physician, psychoanalyst, educator, and author. Known as the founder of psychoanalysis and considered one of the greatest minds in Western intellectual history, Freud began his career in the field of medicine at the University of Vienna, making some significant contributions to neurology while still a young man. As a neurologist, Freud searched for physiological explanations for psychological phenomena; however, under the influence of Jean Martin Charcot's studies on hysteria and Josef Breuer's application of hypnosis as a therapy for hysteria, Freud gradually shifted from a physiological to a purely psychological approach to the mind. Realizing the limitations of hypnosis, he developed the method of free association, which, given its analytic power, became the cornerstone of psychoanalysis.

In the late 1890's Freud applied his analytical method on himself, publishing some of his findings in 1900 in his seminal work, *The Interpretation of Dreams,* in which he effectively utilized dreams as a means of grasping the unconscious. Freud not only uncovered the awesome power of the unconscious over man's conscious mind, but also identified the unconscious as the locus of such fundamental conflicts as the Oedipus complex—the child's sexual desire toward the parent of the oppsite sex combined with jealousy toward the other parent.

In the early 1900's Freud's teachings began attracting a small number of supporters, who regularly discussed psychoanalysis at Freud's home. They formed the nucleus of a growing group that in 1910 became the International Psychoanalytic Association. Freud and his followers all realized the relevance of psychoanalysis for the study of human culture, and Freud's writings reflected increasingly philosophic preoccupations. Freud published *Beyond the Pleasure Principle* (1922), in which he postulates the existence of a death instinct, and in *Civilization and Its Discontents* (1930), he discusses his perception of the fundamental flaws of civilization. Freud's last great work, *Moses and Monotheism* (1939), traces the origin of Jewish monotheism to the solar religion of Egyptian Pharaoh Ikhnaton. The volume was completed and published in England, where Freud, gravely ill with cancer, sought refuge after the 1938 Nazi invasion of his native Austria. Freud's other writings available in English include *Psychopathology of Everyday Life* (1914) and *Totem and Taboo* (1918). *Address:* Berggasse 19, Vienna, Austria.

BIOGRAPHICAL/CRITICAL SOURCES:

BOOKS

Bettelheim, Bruno, *Freud and Man's Soul,* Knopf, 1983.
Encyclopedia of World Literature in the Twentieth Century, revised edition, Ungar, 1981.
McGraw-Hill Encyclopedia of World Biography, McGraw, 1973.
The Oxford Companion to German Literature, Clarendon Press, 1976.
Twentieth-Century Authors: A Biographical Dictionary of Modern Literature, H. W. Wilson, 1942.

* * *

FRIEDLAENDER, Walter (Ferdinand) 1873-1966

OBITUARY NOTICE: Born March 10, 1873, in Berlin, Germany; died September 6, 1966, in New York, N.Y. Art historian, educator, and author. One of the world's leading art historians, Friedlaender was an authority on mannerism and an expert on the work of seventeenth-century artist Nicolas Poussin. Friedlaender taught art history at the University of Freiburg in Germany from 1914 until 1933, when the Nazis ousted him from the university for being Jewish. In 1935 Friedlaender, who had been planning to retire before his dismissal, immigrated to the United States and began a new career with the Institute of Fine Arts in New York. He became a popular, respected instructor at the institute and in 1963 was honored with two *festschrift* volumes, one comprised of tributary essays by his former colleagues in Germany, the other of essays by his American associates. Friedlaender's books include *A Monograph on the Casino of Pius IV in Rome, Carvaggio Studies, David to Delacroix, Mannerism and Anti-Mannerism in Italian Painting,* and a book on Titian completed shortly before Friedlaender's death. He also edited and provided the text for several volumes of drawings by Nicolas Poussin.

OBITUARIES AND OTHER SOURCES:

BOOKS

Who Was Who in America, With World Notables, Volume IV: *1961-1968,* Marquis, 1968.

PERIODICALS

New York Times, September 8, 1966.
Time, September 16, 1966.

FRISCH, Karl (Ritter) von 1886-1982

OBITUARY NOTICE—See index for *CA* sketch: Born November 20, 1886, in Vienna, Austria; died June 12, 1982, in Munich, West Germany. Educator, zoologist, and author. Frisch was named a co-recipient of the Nobel Prize for medicine in 1973 for his research on sense perception and communication in bees. After becoming known for his zoological experiments proving that fish have color vision and auditory acuity, Frisch turned to the study of insects. He learned how bees communicate the location of food supplies to other members of their colonies and how they use the sun as a compass and remember landmarks to avoid getting lost. Frisch was professor of zoology and director of the zoological institute at the University of Munich and held posts at zoological institutes at the Universities of Rostock, Breslau, and Graz. His publications include *The Dancing Bees* and *Animal Architecture.*

OBITUARIES AND OTHER SOURCES:

BOOKS

Current Biography, Wilson, 1974.

PERIODICALS

Times (London), June 21, 1982.
Washington Post, June 19, 1982.

* * *

FRISCH, Ragnar Anton Kittil 1895-1973

OBITUARY NOTICE: Born March 3, 1895, in Oslo, Norway; died January 31, 1973, in Oslo. Econometrician, educator, editor, and author. A professor of economics at the University of Oslo from 1931 to 1965, Frisch was co-recipient of the first Nobel Prize in economics in 1969. His field was econometrics, a science that applies mathematical and statistical analysis to economic problems. In 1931 Frisch, who originated the term econometrics, founded the Econometric Society; he edited its journal, *Econometrica,* for more than twenty years.

Frisch's writings include *Planning for India: Selected Explorations in Methodology* and, with A. Nataf, *Maxima et minima: Theorie et applications economiques.* His few scholarly papers were collected in *Economic Planning Studies.*

OBITUARIES AND OTHER SOURCES:

BOOKS

Twentieth-Century Culture: A Biographical Companion, Harper, 1983.
Who's Who, 126th edition, St. Martin's, 1974.

PERIODICALS

New York Times, February 1, 1973.

* * *

FROEHLICH, Margaret W(alden) 1930-

PERSONAL: Born June 17, 1930, in New Kensington, Pa.; daughter of Lloyd Leighton (a hardware wholesaler) and Hazel (a housewife; maiden name, Mays) Walden; married John A. Froehlich (a mechanical engineer), April 12, 1955; children: Catherine Froehlich Ednie, Andrea Froehlich Carlson, Gregory, Carl, Kristin, Rosemary, David, Margaret. *Education:*

College of Notre Dame of Maryland, B.A., 1951; Johns Hopkins University, M.Ed., 1955.

ADDRESSES: Home—283 Redding Rd., West Redding, Conn. 06896.

CAREER: Second-grade teacher at elementary schools in Baltimore, Md., 1951-55; mother and homemaker, 1955—. Presenter of preschool story hours at Mark Twain Library.

AWARDS, HONORS: Hide Crawford Quick was named a notable children's book by American Library Association, 1984.

WRITINGS:

Hide Crawford Quick (juvenile), Houghton, 1983.

WORK IN PROGRESS: A novel, for ages twelve through fourteen, set in western Pennsylvania during the 1890's.

SIDELIGHTS: Margaret W. Froehlich told *CA:* "I think I write for children in order to make sense of my own childhood. My childhood impressions from an early age seem to lie within me, whole, waiting to be milled."

*   *   *

FRY, Roger (Eliot) 1866-1934

BRIEF ENTRY: Born December 14, 1866, in London, England; died of injuries sustained in a fall, September 9, 1934, in London, England. British artist, aesthetician, art critic, art historian, translator, and author. A member of the Bloomsbury circle, which included the eminent English novelists Virginia Woolf and E. M. Forster, Fry gained renown as an influential theorist and an advocate of modern art. Inspired by the work of such artists as Paul Cezanne, Vincent van Gogh, and Paul Gaugin, whom he named "postimpressionists," Fry stressed the paramount importance of color and form in art, defining art itself as "meaningful form." Although associated with postimpressionist art, which he presented to an initially unreceptive British public in a controversial exhibit in 1910, Fry was a versatile scholar whose expertise also included Renaissance art. In addition, the art critic, who had close links with the *Burlington Magazine,* served as director of the New York Metropolitan Museum of Art from 1905 to 1910. In 1933 he was named Slade Professor of Fine Art at Cambridge University. Fry's writings include *Giovanni Bellini* (1899), *Vision and Design* (1920), *Transformations: Critical and Speculative Essays on Art* (1926), *Flemish Art: A Critical Survey* (1927), and *The Arts of Painting and Sculpture* (1932).

BIOGRAPHICAL/CRITICAL SOURCES:

BOOKS

Longman Companion to Twentieth Century Literature, Longman, 1970.
McGraw-Hill Dictionary of Art, McGraw, 1969.
New Century Handbook of English Literature, revised edition, Appleton-Century-Crofts, 1967.
Twentieth-Century Authors: A Biographical Dictionary of Modern Literature, H. W. Wilson, 1942.
Woolf, Virginia, *Roger Fry: A Biography,* Harcourt, 1940.

*   *   *

FURMAN, Bess 1894-1969

OBITUARY NOTICE: Born December 2, 1894, in Danbury, Neb.; died May 12, 1969, in Woodacres, Md.; buried in Rock Creek Cemetery, Washington, D.C. Administrator, journalist, and author. Furman was best known for her *New York Times* coverage of Washington, D.C. She joined the paper in 1943 after working for Omaha publications and the Associated Press. While with the *Times* Furman became established as an authority on White House history and presidential families. In 1961 she left journalism for a position with the U.S. Department of Health, Education, and Welfare, where she remained until 1963. Furman wrote of her Washington, D.C., experiences in *Washington By-Line* and *White House Profile.*

OBITUARIES AND OTHER SOURCES:

BOOKS

American Authors and Books: 1640 to the Present Day, 3rd revised edition, Crown, 1962.
Ross, Ishbel, *Ladies of the Press,* Arno Press, 1974.

PERIODICALS

Independent Woman, October, 1953.
Newsweek, February 7, 1949.
New York Times, May 13, 1969.

*   *   *

FURNEAUX, Robin
See SMITH, Frederick William Robin

G

GABRE-TSADICK, Marta 1932-

PERSONAL: Surname is pronounced Gab-re-Sa-dick; born April 10, 1932, in Nekempti, Ethiopia; daughter of Gabre-Tsadick Ali (a missionary helper and coffee grower) and Wolete Maskal (a missionary helper); married Peter Myhre, October, 1949 (died July, 1958); married Demeke Tekla-Wold (in business), January 31, 1959; children: (first marriage) Samuel, Michael, Priscilla Myhre Sims-Yemisrach; (second marriage) Bete Demeke, Lalibela Demeke. *Education:* Attended New Mexico Highlands University, 1953-55; Adams State College, B.A., 1958. *Politics:* Independent. *Religion:* Christian.

ADDRESSES: Home—7237 Leo Rd., Fort Wayne, Ind. 46825. *Office*—Project Mercy, P.O. Box 5515, Fort Wayne, Ind. 46805.

CAREER: Project Mercy (refugee aid organization), Fort Wayne, Ind., founding member, 1977—; In Trust of God (I.T.G.; commercial trade organization), Fort Wayne, president, 1977—; Hel-Mar, Inc. (parachute manufacturers), Fort Wayne, vice-president, 1978—. Served as president of the Young Women's Christian Association in Ethiopia, chairman of the Tensaiberhan Orphanage in Ethiopia, and as the first woman senator in the Ethiopian Parliament.

MEMBER: Philanthropic Educational Organization.

AWARDS, HONORS: Medallion from Pope, 1971; two awards from Ethiopian ruler Haile Selassie I, for service to Ethiopia.

WRITINGS:

(With Sandra Aldrich) *Sheltered by the King* (nonfiction), Chosen Books, 1983.

WORK IN PROGRESS: Another book.

SIDELIGHTS: Marta Gabre-Tsadick told *CA:* "*Sheltered by the King* is the story of our escape from our beloved Ethiopia in 1975. It was written to illustrate God's protection of his own, even today.

"People are a vital concern of mine, specifically the well-being of the human race, spiritually most of all, then physically and financially. This concern is the basis of Project Mercy. My wish is to make life easier for others. I don't always succeed, but I try."

She added a comment about names in her family: "In Ethiopia the woman's name does not change when she marries. When the children are born, their father's first name becomes their last name."

*   *   *

GACKENBACH, Dick 1927-

PERSONAL: Born February 9, 1927, in Allentown, Pa.; son of William and Gertrude (Riechenbach) Gackenbach. *Education:* Attended Jameson Franklin School of Art, N.Y., and Abbott School of Art, Washington, D.C.

ADDRESSES: Home—Washington Depot, Conn. *Agent*—McIntosh & Otis, Inc., 475 Fifth Ave., New York, N.Y. 10017.

CAREER: J. C. Penney Co., New York, N.Y., 1950-72, became creative director; free-lance author and illustrator, 1972—.

AWARDS, HONORS: Garden State Children's Book Award from New Jersey Library Association, 1979, for *Hattie Rabbit*.

WRITINGS:

FOR CHILDREN; SELF-ILLUSTRATED

Claude the Dog: A Christmas Story (Junior Literary Guild selection), Seabury, 1974.
Do You Love Me?, Seabury, 1975.
Claude and Pepper, Seabury, 1976.
Hattie Rabbit, Harper, 1976.
Hound and Bear, Seabury, 1976.
Harry and the Terrible Whatzit (Junior Literary Guild selection), Seabury, 1977.
Hattie Be Quiet, Hattie Be Good, Harper, 1977.
The Leatherman, Seabury, 1977.
Mother Rabbit's Son Tom, Harper, 1977.
Ida Fanfanny, Harper, 1978.
Pepper and All the Legs, Seabury, 1978.
The Pig Who Saw Everything, Seabury, 1978.
Crackle Gluck and the Sleeping Toad, Seabury, 1979.
More From Hound and Bear, Clarion Books, 1979.
Hattie, Tom, and the Chicken Witch: A Play and a Story, Harper, 1980.
A Bag Full of Pups, Clarion Books, 1981.
Little Bug, Clarion Books, 1981.

McGoogan Moves the Mighty Rock, Harper, 1981.
Annie and the Mud Monster, Lothrop, 1982.
(Adapter) *Arabella and Mr. Crack: An Old English Tale*, Macmillan, 1982.
Binky Gets a Car, Clarion Books, 1983.
Mr. Wink and His Shadow Ned, Harper, 1983.
(Adapter) *The Princess and the Pea*, Macmillan, 1983.
What's Claude Doing?, Clarion Books, 1984.
Poppy the Panda, Clarion Books, 1984.
The Dog and the Deep Dark Woods, Harper, 1984.
King Wacky, Crown, 1984.
The Perfect Mouse, Macmillan, 1984.

ILLUSTRATOR

Gertrude Norman, *The First Book of Music*, F. Watts, 1954.
Steven Kroll, *Is Milton Missing?*, Holiday House, 1975.
Sally Cartwright, *What's in a Map?*, Coward, 1977.
Miriam Anne Bourne, *What Is Papa Up to Now?*, Coward, 1977.
Jim Murphy, *Rat's Christmas Party*, Prentice-Hall, 1979.
Kroll, *Amanda and the Giggling Ghost*, Holiday House, 1980.
Marjorie N. Allen, *One, Two, Three—Ah-Choo!*, Coward, 1980.
Kroll, *Friday the Thirteenth*, Holiday House, 1981.
Janice L. Smith, *The Monster in the Third Dresser Drawer and Other Stories About Adam Joshua*, Harper, 1981.
Barbara Isenberg and Susan Wolf, *The Adventures of Albert, the Running Bear*, Clarion Books, 1982.
Crescent Dragonwagon, *I Hate My Brother Barry*, Harper, 1983.

SIDELIGHTS: Dick Gackenbach told *CA:* "In 1972, I decided to enter the field of children's literature for several reasons. One was that over the years I collected many children's books; as a child I never had any because I grew up during the Great Depression and my family was poor. I later developed a great love for children's books, especially picture books. Also, I like children and as a writer and illustrator I have become somewhat like a grandfather to many, many children: I get a chance to tell them stories and draw pictures for them. The best way I can explain is just to say that my writing is a lot of fun.

"At first I planned only to illustrate children's books. After trying to get illustration assignments with no success, I decided to try to write my own books. I was very lucky and my first book was accepted by Seabury in 1974. Whenever I get letters from people who tell me they want to illustrate children's books, I advise them to try to write their own."

AVOCATIONAL INTERESTS: Classical music, gourmet cooking, dogs.

BIOGRAPHICAL/CRITICAL SOURCES:

PERIODICALS

New York Times Book Review, December 9, 1979, February 22, 1981.

*   *   *

GALLAGER, Gale
See OURSLER, Will(iam Charles)

*   *   *

GALLAGHER, Vera   1917-

PERSONAL: Born August 1, 1917, in Calgary, Alberta, Canada; daughter of Dominic (a teacher) and Teresa (a teacher; maiden name, Price) Gallagher. *Education:* Received B.A. from the College of St. Thomas, St. Paul, Minn.; received M.A. from Seattle University; received D.Min. from the Jesuit School of Theology, Berkeley, Calif.

ADDRESSES: Home—11544 Phinney Ave. N., Seattle, Wash. 98133.

CAREER: Roman Catholic nun. Principal of Good Shepherd schools in several states, 1939-70; St. Patrick's Church, Seattle, Wash., pastoral minister, 1972-83; affiliated with Christ the King Convent, Seattle, 1983—. Founder and coordinator of services for the poor.

WRITINGS:

Hearing the Cry of the Poor, Liguori Publications, 1983.

Also author of *Little Nellie of Holy God*, Bruce Publishing, and *Shepherdess for Christ*, Catechetical Guild. Contributor of numerous articles to religious and secular magazines.

WORK IN PROGRESS: An autobiography; a book for divorced and "single-again" persons; another book.

SIDELIGHTS: Sister Vera Gallagher told *CA:* "I have always hoped to become a writer, and I am now devoting 75 percent of my time to it. I have traveled widely. My particular interest lies in religious writing."

*   *   *

GANCI, Dave   1937-

PERSONAL: Born March 8, 1937, in Poughkeepsie, N.Y.; son of Joseph D. and Gwen Ganci. *Education:* Arizona State University, B.Sc., 1972, M.S., 1984. *Politics:* "Just right of Genghis Khan." *Religion:* "My own."

ADDRESSES: Home and office—6737 North 18th Pl., Phoenix, Ariz. 85016.

CAREER: Blue-collar worker, part-time writer and photographer, 1958-69; retail manager of Wilderness sporting goods stores, 1969-79; Arizona State University, Tempe, faculty associate, 1979-82. Director of Arizona Outdoor Institute, a school for outdoor recreation and education. *Military service:* U.S. Army Reserve, 1960-64; became first lieutenant.

WRITINGS:

Hiking the Southwest: Arizona, New Mexico, and West Texas, Sierra Club Books, 1983.
Desert Hiking, Wilderness Press (Berkeley, Calif.), 1984.

Contributor to magazines, newspapers, and trade journals.

WORK IN PROGRESS: Research on the four seasons of the Grand Canyon for "an odyssey through a full year in the Seventh Wonder of the World."

SIDELIGHTS: Dave Ganci told *CA:* "I am motivated to help educate recreationists in the wise stewardship of the outdoor environment with a minimum need for governmental interference. My writings come from personal experience both as a civilian and as a soldier. I have an academic research and experimentation background in physiology and geography. I believe in experimental education, that is, learning by doing. My survival school is oriented toward real-life situations of environmental stress—how to cope with 'worst case' situations. Some poet said, 'Education is the process of separating the bull from the bullshit.' That's what we do at Arizona Outdoor Institute, and that's what I try to do in my writings.''

*   *   *

GANZ, Yaffa 1938-

PERSONAL: Born March 26, 1938, in Chicago, Ill.; daughter of George and Dorothy Siegel; married Abraham Ganz (a teacher of Bible and Talmud), 1960; children: four sons, one daughter. *Education:* University of Chicago, B.A., 1962.

ADDRESSES: Home—Jerusalem, Israel. *Office*—Feldheim Publishers, P.O. Box 6525, Jerusalem, Israel.

CAREER: Homemaker and mother, 1964-79; Feldheim Publishers, Jerusalem, Israel, editor of Young Reader's Division, 1979—.

WRITINGS:

FOR CHILDREN

Savta Simcha and the Incredible Shabbos Bag, Feldheim, 1980.
Yedidya and the Esrog Tree, Feldheim, 1980.
The Riddle Rhyme Book, Feldheim, 1981.
The Adventures of Jeremy Levi, Feldheim, 1981.
Who Knows One: A Book of Jewish Numbers, Feldheim, 1983.
Follow the Moon: A Journey Through the Jewish Year, Feldheim, 1984.
Savta Simcha and the Cinnamon Tree, Feldheim, 1984.

OTHER

Contributor of articles on Judaism and Israel to magazines and newspapers in the United States, Canada, England, and Israel.

WORK IN PROGRESS: A third volume of the Savta Simcha books.

SIDELIGHTS: Yaffa Ganz told *CA:* "The world of the Jew and his Torah is the unending story of Man, the Divine, and the wondrous world we live in. Bringing even a tiny bit of this vast wealth, wisdom, or beauty to light, especially to a Jewish child . . . this is my task; from this do I derive my pleasure; in this do I delight. And, may I add, I work very hard at getting it all down on paper!''

*   *   *

GARBER, Emil 1901(?)-1985

OBITUARY NOTICE: Born c. 1901; died April 25, 1985, in St. Petersburg, Fla.; buried in Woodlawn Memory Gardens, St. Petersburg, Fla. Promotion manager and journalist. Garber was a reporter for such newspapers as the *Chicago Herald and Examiner,* the *Chicago Daily News,* and the *Chicago Sun-Times.* Among his notable assignments was coverage of a steel mill strike in Gary, Indiana, in 1919. Garber left reporting in 1949 to become a promotion manager for the *Pittsburgh Sun Telly.*

OBITUARIES AND OTHER SOURCES:

PERIODICALS

Chicago Tribune, April 28, 1985.

*   *   *

GARDINER, Muriel
See BUTTINGER, Muriel Gardiner

GARE, Fran
See MANDELL, Fran Gare

*   *   *

GARLAND, George
See ROARK, Garland

*   *   *

GATLEY, Jimmy 1931(?)-1985

OBITUARY NOTICE: Born c. 1931; died of a heart ailment, March 17, 1985, in Nashville, Tenn.; buried in Springfield, Mo. Singer, musician, and songwriter. Gatley was fiddler for country-music performer Bill Anderson. He also performed gospel music and wrote songs such as "Alla My Love," with Harold Donny, "The Minute You're Gone," and "Bright Lights and Country Music."

OBITUARIES AND OTHER SOURCES:

PERIODICALS

Chicago Tribune, March 21, 1985.

*   *   *

GENTILE, Gennaro L. 1946-

PERSONAL: Born November 14, 1946, in New York, N.Y.; son of Saverio R. (a transporter) and Filomena (a bookkeeper; maiden name, Quatrano) Gentile. *Education:* Cathedral College, B.A., 1967; St. Joseph's Seminary, M.A., 1970; Iona College, M.S.Ed., 1978.

ADDRESSES: Home and office—33 Massitoa Rd., Yonkers, N.Y. 10710.

CAREER: Roman Catholic priest. Pastor of Roman Catholic churches in Wappingers Falls, N.Y., 1970-71, Poughkeepsie, N.Y., 1971-76, Hopewell Junction, N.Y., 1976-82, and Marlboro, N.Y., 1982-83; St. Eugene's Church, Yonkers, N.Y., priest, 1983—.

WRITINGS:

The Mouse in the Manger, Ave Maria Press, 1978.

Contributor to magazines.

WORK IN PROGRESS: A book on the nature of evil, for children or junior high school students.

*   *   *

GERASIMOV, Innokentii Petrovich 1905-1985

OBITUARY NOTICE: Given name also transliterated as Innokentiy and Innokenti; born December 22 (one source says December 9), 1905, in Kostroma, Russia (now U.S.S.R.); died after a long illness, March 30, 1985, in Moscow, U.S.S.R. Geographer, scientist, and author. Gerasimov, who was internationally known, served as director of the Soviet Institute of Geography from 1951 until his death. As such he was in charge of all scientific research conducted for the purpose of Soviet land development and construction. In addition, Gerasimov was known for his work in soil science and geomorphology. A recipient of the Order of Lenin, the scientist served as vice-president of the Soviet Geographical Society, the International

Geographical Union, and the International Society of Soil Scientists. Gerasimov's publications in English translation include *Man, Society, and the Environment, Geography and Ecology,* and *Fundamentals of Soil Science and Soil Geography.*

OBITUARIES AND OTHER SOURCES:

BOOKS

The International Who's Who, 47th edition, Europa, 1983.
Who's Who in Socialist Countries, K. G. Saur, 1978.

PERIODICALS

New York Times, April 4, 1985.

* * *

GERRARD, Jean 1933-

PERSONAL: Born July 23, 1933, in Blackpool, Lancashire, England; daughter of John (an electrical contractor) and Dorothy (a teacher) Thatcher; married Roy Gerrard (an artist and author), March 28, 1958; children: Sally Gerrard Turpie, Paul. *Education:* Avery Hill College, Teaching Diploma, 1953.

ADDRESSES: Home—117 Moorend Rd., Mellor, Stockport, England.

CAREER: Secondary school art teacher, 1953-60; secondary school remedial education teacher, 1966-68; Marple Ridge High School, Stockport, Cheshire, England, head of remedial department, 1968-81, head of lower school, 1981—.

WRITINGS:

Matilda Jane (juvenile), Farrar, Straus, 1983.

* * *

GERSHATOR, David 1937-
(Jack Alchemy)

PERSONAL: Born December 2, 1937, on Mount Carmel, Palestine (now Israel); immigrated to United States, 1945; son of Abraham (a teacher) and Miriam (a secretary; maiden name, Fisher) Gershator; married Phillis Manuela Dimondstein (a librarian and writer), October 19, 1962; children: Yonah, Daniel. *Education:* City College (now of the City University of New York), B.A., 1958; Columbia University, M.A., 1960; New York University, Ph.D., 1967.

ADDRESSES: Home—Charlotte Amalie, St. Thomas, U.S. Virgin Islands. *Agent*—Greater Shelter, 69 MacDougal St., New York, N.Y. 10012.

CAREER: Rutgers University, New Brunswick, N.J., instructor in romance languages, 1963-67; Adelphi University, Garden City, N.Y., assistant professor of Spanish, 1967-68; City University of New York, New York City, assistant professor of foreign languages, 1968-69; College of the Virgin Islands, St. Thomas, U.S. Virgin Islands, associate professor of English and modern languages, 1969-72; Brooklyn College of the City University of New York, Brooklyn, N.Y., associate professor of humanities, 1973-75; part-time teacher, writer, and editor of a small press in New York City, 1975-79; Long Island University, Brooklyn Center, Brooklyn, adjunct professor of English, 1979-82; writer and painter, 1982—. Lecturer on world cruise of SS *Rotterdam,* 1980; gives readings from his works.

MEMBER: Poetry Society of America, Association for Poetry Therapy, Downtown Poets Co-Op (co-founder), New York Poets Co-op (co-founder).

AWARDS, HONORS: Grant from National Endowment for the Humanities, 1971; poetry award from New York State Creative Arts Public Service, 1977-78.

WRITINGS:

Elegy for Val (poetry), X Press Press, 1975.
(Under pseudonym Jack Alchemy) *For Sex and Free Road Maps* (poetry), Downtown Poets Co-Op, 1976.
Kanji: Poems of Japan, Downtown Poets Co-Op, 1977.
Play Mas (poetry), Downtown Poets Co-Op, 1981.
(Editor and translator) Federico Garcia Lorca, *Selected Letters,* New Directions Publishing, 1983.
Sabra (poems), Cross-Cultural Communications, 1985.

Contributor to magazines, including *Roots, Antaeus, Occident, Confrontation,* and *Revista Interamericana.* Contributing editor of *Poets,* 1978; associate editor of *Home Planet News,* 1979.

SIDELIGHTS: Of European and American heritage, David Gershator was born on Mount Carmel and raised in Haifa and in a kibbutz in Israel. He came to New York from Egypt on the first civilian ship to cross the Atlantic after World War II. Gershator was then brought up in Brooklyn, where he attended Boys High School and became a fan of the Brooklyn Dodgers.

* * *

GERTZ, Theodore G(erson) 1936-

PERSONAL: Born September 8, 1936, in Chicago, Ill.; son of Elmer (an attorney) and Ceretta (Samuels) Gertz; married Suzanne Feldman (an artist), June 19, 1960; children: Craig, Candace, Scott. *Education:* University of Chicago, B.A., 1958; Northwestern University, J.D., 1962. *Politics:* Independent. *Religion:* Jewish.

ADDRESSES: Home—680 Thornmeadow Rd., Riverwoods, Ill. 60015. *Office*—Pretzel & Stouffer, 1 South Wacker Dr., Chicago, Ill.

CAREER: Marks, Marks & Kaplan (law firm), Chicago, Ill., associate attorney, 1962-67; Lowitz, Vihon, Kipnis, Stone & Gertz (law firm), partner, 1967-71; Pretzel & Stouffer (law firm), Chicago, Ill., director and treasurer, 1971—. General counsel and director of Hull House Associates; general counsel to American Student Dental Association; member of Chicago Estate Planning Council; fellow of Chicago Bar Foundation and Illinois Bar Foundation. Lecturer at Purdue University, 1983; speaker on tax planning. *Military service:* U.S. Army, 1962.

MEMBER: Illinois Bar Association, Chicago Bar Association, Executives Club.

WRITINGS:

A Guide to Estate Planning, Southern Illinois University Press, 1983.
Illinois Advanced Estate Planning, Professional Educational Systems, 1984.

SIDELIGHTS: Theodore G. Gertz told *CA:* "I want to make the process of estate planning understandable, and in the process I enjoy writing and speaking. I also render legal services to artists and writers at greatly reduced fees.

"There is a great deal of misinformation about the entire area of probate, estate planning, tax reduction techniques, and the like. Far too many people feel that it is unethical and terribly expensive to take steps to reduce one's taxable estate through tax avoidance techniques. I feel that it is important to educate the populace on this subject and to dispel many of the negative assumptions associated with tax planning."

*   *   *

GIAP Vo Nguyen
See VO NGUYEN Giap

*   *   *

GIDEONSE, Harry David   1901-1985

OBITUARY NOTICE: Born May 17, 1901, in Rotterdam, Netherlands; died March 12, 1985, in Port Jefferson, N.Y. Economist, academic administrator, radio broadcaster, editor, and author. The president of Brooklyn College from 1939 to 1966, Gideonse is often credited with bringing about the school's rise to prominence in the 1950's. He had previously held positions with several other educational institutions. From 1924 to 1926 Gideonse lectured in economics at Columbia University, where he subsequently served as professor of economics and chairman of the department of economics and sociology. Following a two-year tenure as assistant professor of economics at Rutgers University, the educator became, in 1930, associate professor of economics at the University of Chicago; while there he was also a popular speaker on the university's radio program "Round Table." During his eight years with the University of Chicago, Gideonse established his reputation in economics.

Gideonse was affiliated with numerous organizations, including the Chicago and New York councils on foreign relations, the Woodrow Wilson Foundation, and Freedom House—an organization that supported research and publications on democratic ideals. Gideonse wrote extensively on international economics, political economy, and foreign affairs. His publications included *The Commodity Dollar, The Higher Learning in Democracy, Organized Scarcity and Public Policy, Against the Running Tide,* and *United States Foreign Policy: Its Organization and Control.* He was editor of *Public Policy Pamphlets.*

OBITUARIES AND OTHER SOURCES:

BOOKS

Current Biography, Wilson, 1940.
The International Yearbook and Statesmen's Who's Who, Thomas Skinner Directories, 1982.

PERIODICALS

Chicago Tribune, March 16, 1985.
New York Times, March 14, 1985.

*   *   *

GILBERT, Celia   1932-

PERSONAL: Born September 9, 1932, in Philadelphia, Pa.; daughter of I. F. (a writer) and Esther (Roisman) Stone; married Walter Gilbert (a scientist), December 29, 1953; children: John, Kate. *Education:* Smith College, B.A., 1954; Boston University, M.A., 1973.

ADDRESSES: Home—107 Upland Rd., Cambridge, Mass. 02140.

CAREER: Poet and editor.

MEMBER: International P.E.N., Authors Guild, Poetry Society of America.

AWARDS, HONORS: Discovery Award from Young Men's-Young Women's Hebrew Association, New York, N.Y., 1974, for a selection of ten poems; Borestone Mountain Prize, 1976, for "Room 635, Wing B"; Emily Dickinson Award from Poetry Society of America, 1981, for "The Silence"; Pushcart Prize, 1984-85, for "Lot's Wife," a poem from her collection *Bonfire.*

WRITINGS:

Queen of Darkness (poems), Viking, 1977.
Bonfire (poems), Alice James Books, 1983.

Contributor to magazines, including *Atlantic, Ms., Paris Review, Partisan Review,* and *Kayak.* Poetry and fiction editor of *Boston Phoenix,* 1973-75.

WORK IN PROGRESS: The Founders of Honey, a book of poems; a play about Florence Nightingale.

BIOGRAPHICAL/CRITICAL SOURCES:

BOOKS

Daniels, Pamela, and Sara Ruddick, editors, *Working It Out,* Pantheon, 1977.

PERIODICALS

Boston Globe, August 21, 1983.

*   *   *

GILBERT, Russell Wieder   1905-1985

OBITUARY NOTICE—See index for *CA* sketch: Born September 3, 1905, in Emmaus, Pa.; died in 1985. Educator, editor, poet, and author of nonfiction works. Gilbert taught German and speech at Susquehanna University from 1930 until 1970, when he became professor emeritus. His publications include *Walk the Long Years, A Picture of the Pennsylvania Germans, Pennsylvania German Wills, The Saga of the Pennsylvania Germans in Wisconsin,* and *The Story of Susquehanna University.*

OBITUARIES AND OTHER SOURCES:

BOOKS

Directory of American Scholars, Volume III: *Foreign Languages, Linguistics, and Philology,* 8th edition, Bowker, 1982.

PERIODICALS

Allentown Morning Call, March 4, 1985.

*   *   *

GILLEN, Lucy
See STRATTON, Rebecca

*   *   *

GILLESPIE, A(braham) Lincoln, Jr.   1895-1950
(Link Gillespie)

BRIEF ENTRY: Born June 11, 1895, in Philadelphia, Pa.; died

September 10, 1950, in Philadelphia, Pa. American writer. Gillespie, a high school mathematics teacher, traveled to Paris during the 1920's while on a trip to recuperate from injuries suffered in an automobile accident. He then met and began associating with a group of American writers living in Paris that included Gertrude Stein and Ernest Hemingway. Gillespie reportedly decided to become a writer after being told that he looked like James Joyce. In 1927 he presented some samples of his new craft to Elliot Paul, an editor at *transition* magazine.

Paul had no illusions about the literary merits of Gillespie's work, but, in what has been described as "an act of bravado," he published pieces that author Dougald McMillan noted "were generally considered a joke." In a supreme act of self-delusion Gillespie began to think of himself as an important writer and is even said to have left his wife because he no longer considered her his intellectual equal. Gillespie contributed a number of articles to *transition* from 1927 until 1932, when he returned to the United States, and also contributed two pieces to *Readies for Bob Brown's Machine* (1931).

BIOGRAPHICAL/CRITICAL SOURCES:

BOOKS

Dictionary of Literary Biography, Volume 4, *American Writers in Paris, 1920-1939*, Gale, 1980.
McMillan, Dougald, *"transition": The History of a Literary Era, 1927-1938*, Braziller, 1976.

*   *   *

GILLESPIE, Link
    See GILLESPIE, A(braham) Lincoln, Jr.

*   *   *

GILMER, Wesley, Jr.   1928-

PERSONAL: Born September 24, 1928, in Cincinnati, Ohio; son of Wesley (a farmer) and Esther (a housewife; maiden name, Chandler) Gilmer; married Mary Elizabeth Minor (a housewife), September 4, 1954; children: John Wesley III, Louise Gilmer Magee, Betsy. *Education:* University of Cincinnati, B.A., 1949, J.D., 1950; University of Kentucky, M.S.L.S., 1972.

ADDRESSES: Home—404 Meadow Lane, Danville, Ky. 40422. *Office*—Kentucky State Law Library, State Capitol, Room 200, Frankfort, Ky. 40601.

CAREER: Private practice of law in Danville, Ky., 1952-67; University of Cincinnati, Cincinnati, Ohio, assistant law librarian and faculty member of the College of Law, 1967-76; Kentucky State Law Library, Frankfort, Kentucky State law librarian, 1976—. Part-time member of faculty at Midway College, 1977-80, Eastern Kentucky University, 1980-81, and Sullivan Centre, 1981. *Military serivce:* U.S. Army, 1950-52; became sergeant.

MEMBER: American Association of Law Libraries, Kentucky Library Association, Kentucky Bar Association.

WRITINGS:

Cochran's Law Lexicon, 5th edition, Anderson Publishing, 1973, 6th edition, in press, paperback editions published as *The Law Dictionary*.
Kentucky Legal Forms, Volume I, 2nd edition, Banks-Baldwin, 1975, supplement, 1977.

Anderson's Manual for Notaries Public, 5th edition, Anderson Publishing, 1976, supplements, 1977, 1979.
Legal Research, Writing, and Advocacy: A Sourcebook, Anderson Publishing, 1978, 2nd edition, in press.
Legal Research, Writing, and Advocacy: Paralegal Instructor's Manual, Anderson Publishing, 1979.
Guide to Kentucky Legal Research: A State Bibliography, Administrative Office of the Courts, Commonwealth of Kentucky, 1979.

SIDELIGHTS: Wesley Gilmer, Jr., told *CA:* "As a small-town Kentucky lawyer with fifteen years experience in 1967, I believed that I had useful knowledge and insights that I could share with law students that would help them to become competent lawyers more quickly, and that had not been taught to me in law school. My law-teaching employment was as assistant law librarian, the duties of which included, among other things, teaching legal research and writing and appellate advocacy. I found that many persons who taught in law schools had advance degrees past the J.D., and that some law librarians had masters' degrees in library science. I elected to pursue the library science course part-time when I was in my forties.

"When a constitutional amendment called for a new court system for Kentucky in 1976, I was fortunate to receive an invitation to set up statewide law-library support for Kentucky judges. I accepted the invitation and have not regretted it. I was allowed to offer innovative law-library services for 235 judges in 120 counties; it has been a challenging and pleasant experience.

"My books have been related to my teaching and law-library employment; most of them were written in my off-duty hours. They tend to offer selected practical information that has been chosen because of various questions that have been asked of me over the years."

*   *   *

GLAZAR, Bob   1954-
    (Ray Fifo)

PERSONAL: Born March 4, 1954, in Wilkensburg, Pa.; son of Chester S. (a motel co-owner) and Eleanor H. (a housewife and bookkeeper; maiden name, Zych) Glazar; married Julie A. Adolphson (a speech therapist), June 18, 1977. *Education:* Northern Arizona University, B.S., 1977.

ADDRESSES: Home—2102 West Earll Dr., Phoenix, Ariz. 85015. *Office*—c/o Chucklynn, Inc., 2102 West Earll Dr., Phoenix, Ariz. 85015.

CAREER: Imperial 400 Motel, Flagstaff, Ariz., relief manager, 1970-74; KAFF/KFLG-Radio, Flagstaff, news reporter, disc jockey, and sales representative, 1974-77; KMCR-FM Radio, Phoenix, Ariz., development director, 1977—.

WRITINGS:

(Under pseudonym Ray Fifo) *The Official Silicon Valley Guy Handbook*, Avon, 1983.

RECORDINGS

"Silicon Valley Guy," released by Birdzerk Productions, 1982.

WORK IN PROGRESS: "Silicon Valley Guy," a screenplay; a pilot script for a television situation comedy; a script for a stand-up comedy act.

SIDELIGHTS: Bob Glazar's phonograph record, "Silicon Valley Guy," sold out of 3,200 copies within the first six months of release (primary distribution of the record was through mail orders and local record shops). And the record climbed to number seven on the "Demented Top Ten" of the nationally syndicated radio program "Dr. Demento."

*   *   *

GLENN, Christine Genevieve 1947-

PERSONAL: Born February 22, 1947, in New York, N.Y.; daughter of Edmund Stanislaus (a professor of communications) and Marjorie (a housewife; maiden name, Rugg) Glenn; married Milton Tepper Cohen (a physician), January 6, 1980; children: Sophie Amanda Glenn Cohen. *Education:* Tufts University, B.S., 1969; Washington University, St. Louis, Mo., Ph.D., 1976.

ADDRESSES: Home—5623 Northeast Cleveland, Portland, Ore. 97211.

CAREER: Carnegie-Mellon University, Pittsburgh, Pa., instructor in psychology, 1976-78; Good Samaritan Hospital, Portland, Ore., psychologist, 1978-83; in private practice, 1983—.

MEMBER: American Psychological Association.

WRITINGS:

(With father, Edmund Stanislaus Glenn) *Man and Mankind: Conflict and Communication Between Cultures,* Ablex Publishing, 1981.

Member of board of advisory editors of *Journal of Educational Psychology.*

*   *   *

GLUYAS, Constance 1920-

BRIEF ENTRY: Born in 1920, in England. American author. Gluyas is the author of more than a dozen romance and gothic novels, noted for the romantic and often ferocious coupling of strong heroines and even stronger heroes. Her writings include *Savage Eden* (New American Library, 1976), *Rogue's Mistress* (New American Library, 1977), *Flame of the South* (New American Library, 1979), *Lord Sin* (New American Library, 1980), *The Passionate Savage* (New American Library, 1980), and *The Bridge to Yesterday* (New American Library, 1981).

BIOGRAPHICAL/CRITICAL SOURCES:

BOOKS

The Writers Directory: 1984-1986, St. James Press, 1983.

*   *   *

GOEBBELS, Josef
See GOEBBELS, (Paul) Joseph

*   *   *

GOEBBELS, (Paul) Joseph 1897-1945
(Joseph Paul Goebbels, Josef Goebbels)

BRIEF ENTRY: Born October 29, 1897, in Rheydt, Germany (now West Germany); committed suicide, May 1, 1945, in Berlin, Germany. German politician, propagandist, editor, playwright, and author. Considered the only intellectual among Nazi leader Adolf Hitler's inner circle, Goebbels earned a doctorate in literature at the University of Heidelberg in 1921.

His inability to secure a publisher for his novel, *Michael* (1921), or producers for his two plays, "Blutsaat" and "Der Wanderer," embittered Goebbels, who later admitted to feelings of failure and humiliation. These feelings apparently were assuaged once he found his niche in the National Socialist (Nazi) Party in 1924.

In 1927 Hitler made Goebbels the political boss of Nazi operations in Berlin. Through Goebbels's editorship of the party newspaper *Der Angriff* (title means "The Attack") popular support for the Nazis grew. He became Hitler's campaign manager, and when Hitler became Germany's chancellor in 1933 he named Goebbels to the post of minister of propaganda and public enlightenment. As Nazi Germany's propagandist he assumed control of the country's mass media and developed many of the techniques of state-directed mind control. Using these techniques he crushed opposition to Hitler's rule and encouraged the entire nation to believe the myth of racial superiority that fueled the hate campaign that ultimately resulted in the deaths of more than six million Jews. On May 1, 1945, hours after Hitler took his own life, Goebbels and his wife committed suicide after killing their children. Goebbels published numerous books and pamphlets, including *My Part in Germany's Fight* (1935); several of his diaries have also been published.

BIOGRAPHICAL/CRITICAL SOURCES:

BOOKS

Current Biography, Wilson, 1941.
McGraw-Hill Encyclopedia of World Biography, McGraw, 1973.
1000 Makers of the Twentieth Century, David & Charles, 1971.

PERIODICALS

Los Angeles Times Book Review, April 17, 1983.

*   *   *

GOEBBELS, Joseph Paul
See GOEBBELS, (Paul) Joseph

*   *   *

GOITEIN, S(helomo) D(ov) 1900-1985
(Solomon Dob Fritz Goitein)

OBITUARY NOTICE—See index for *CA* sketch: Born April 3, 1900, in Burgkunstadt, Germany; died of a heart attack, February 6, 1985, in Princeton, N.J. Educator and author. Goitein, a Hebraic and Arabic scholar and a leading authority on Islamic culture, immigrated to Palestine (now Israel) in 1923 to become head of the Department of Education of the Palestine Mandate. In 1949 he accepted the post of director of the School of Oriental Studies at the Hebrew University in Jerusalem.

Goitein came to the United States in 1957 and was professor of Arabic at the University of Pennsylvania until 1971, when he became associated with the Institute for Advanced Study in Princeton, New Jersey. In 1983 he received a lifetime annual stipend from the John D. and Catherine T. MacArthur Foundation. Goitein, who sometimes published under the name Solomon Dob Fritz Goitein, wrote numerous books on the Middle East, including *From the Land of Sheba: Tales of the Jews of Yemen, Jews and Arabs: Their Contacts Through the Ages, Letters of Medieval Jewish Traders, Palestinian Jewry in Early Islamic and Crusader Times, The Yemenites: History, Communal Organization, Spiritual Life,* and *The Geniza Collection at the University Museum of the University of Pennsylvania.*

OBITUARIES AND OTHER SOURCES:

PERIODICALS

Chicago Tribune, February 12, 1985.
New York Times, February 10, 1985.
Times (London), February 15, 1985.

*   *   *

GOITEIN, Solomon Dob Fritz
   See GOITEIN, S(helomo) D(ov)

*   *   *

GOLDIN, Grace   1916-

PERSONAL: Born September 13, 1916, in Tulsa, Okla.; daughter of Alfred E. (a businessman) and Millicent (a housewife; maiden name, Lubetkin) Aaronson; married Judah Goldin (a professor of Hebrew literature), June 21, 1938; children: Robin (daughter; deceased), David. *Education:* Barnard College, B.A., 1937. *Politics:* Democrat. *Religion:* Jewish.

ADDRESSES: Home—405 Thayer Rd., Swarthmore, Pa. 19081.

CAREER: Hospital historian and photographer. Writer and researcher, 1938-60; Yale University, New Haven, Conn., research assistant, 1960-70; writer and researcher, 1970—. Interlocutor with husband, Judah Goldin, of summer radio series "The Eternal Light," 1978; presents slide lectures on the history of hospitals at hospitals and universities.

One-woman exhibits of photography on hospitals at Yale Medical Library, New Haven, Conn., February-April, 1969, University of British Columbia, Vancouver, May-July, 1969, University of Minnesota, Minneapolis, December, 1982-May, 1983, and National Library of Medicine, Washington, D.C., October, 1984-April, 1985. Work represented in Smithsonian Institution files.

MEMBER: International Association of the History of Medicine, American Association of the History of Medicine, American Association of Architectural Historians, Societe francaise d'histoire des hopitaux, College of Physicians of Philadelphia (Section on Medical History).

AWARDS, HONORS: Harry and Florence Kovner Memorial Poetry Award for best poem of the year on a Jewish theme from Jewish Book Council of National Jewish Welfare Board, 1958, for *Come Under the Wings;* grants from American Philosophical Society, summer, 1966, and Wellcome Foundation (for England), summer, 1967.

WRITINGS:

(Contributor) Elliot E. Cohen, editor, *Commentary on the Jewish Scene,* Knopf, 1953.
Come Under the Wings: A Midrash on Ruth (poem), Jewish Publication Society, 1958, 2nd edition, 1980.
(With John D. Thompson) *The Hospital: A Social and Architectural History,* Yale University Press, 1975.
Winter Rise (poems), Patten Press (Richmond, England), 1981.
To Love That Well (poems), Patten Press, 1984.

Contributor to *Encyclopaedia Britannica Medical and Health Annual.* Contributor to periodicals, including *Midstream,*

Commentary, Menorah Journal, Yale Review, Journal of the History of Medicine and Allied Sciences, and *Bulletin of the History of Medicine.*

SIDELIGHTS: Grace Goldin described herself as a "research scholar in the history of hospitals." She began her research in England in 1963; since then the author has conducted meticulous studies in Belgium, Denmark, Norway, Germany, Austria, France, Italy, the Netherlands, Spain, Malta, Greece, and Israel. In 1978 she turned her attention to modern British hospices.

Goldin's photographs were exhibited in "Some Photogenic Hospitals of the Fourteenth to Eighteenth Centuries" at Yale University in 1969, and "Historic Hospitals of Europe, 1200-1981" at the University of Minnesota—Twin Cities in 1982. The latter exhibit moved to the National Library of Medicine in Washington, D.C., in 1984. Her photographs also illustrate the slide lectures the author presents at universities and hospitals; fifteen of these photographs are included in her book *The Hospital: A Social and Architectural History.*

Goldin told *CA:* "I'd consider myself a poet if I were able to write poetry consistently, however slowly, but I write in bursts, fast. In between I can't imagine how poetry is written; the ability to do so is sealed off without a scar. I had one such burst some thirty-five years ago, and another recent run produced two volumes of 'poems of aging' for my sixty-fifth birthday. I can't afford another thirty-five-year hiatus, but one can't force poetry nor, being supersensitive to alcohol and the possessor of particularly bad feet, can I try A. E. Housman's suggestion of beer for lunch and a long walk in the fields.

"In the considerable stretches between writing verse, I take photographs, which can be done well in any mood, season, or weather, and I have made a real business of hospital history, a fascinating and maverick field that has to do with many disciplines: history of medicine, nursing, pharmacy, architecture, technology, and the history of art—this last to interpret contemporary pictorial records—and history of religion almost above all. It is a sparsely populated field, very refreshing English literature, where every line belongs to somebody, and some authors' lines present a real battlefield. They welcome you in the old hospitals, they are so pleased that you want to know about them, that you don't shun them. The trick is to find old hospitals not completely gutted, removed, updated, modernized, or otherwise unfit to study. Somebody with young feet should go out to the undeveloped areas of the world (South America especially) and photograph and record old hospitals there. I never got across the Iron Curtain, either. I know no foreign languages, and I did not need political complications. Even so, I was swamped with work."

*   *   *

GOLDSMITH, Raymond W(illiam)   1904-

PERSONAL: Born December 23, 1904, in Brussels, Belgium; immigrated to United States, 1930, naturalized citizen, 1939; son of Alfred and Camilla (Marcus) Goldschmidt; married Selma Fine, May 17, 1939 (died April 15, 1962); children: Jane, Donald, Paul. *Education:* University of Berlin, Ph.D., 1927; attended London School of Economics and Political Science, London, 1933.

ADDRESSES: Home—111 Park St., New Haven, Conn. 06519. *Office*—37 Hillhouse Ave., New Haven, Conn. 06520.

CAREER: Worked in German Central Statistical Office, Berlin, Germany, 1927-29; worked for U.S. Security and Exchange Commission, Washington, D.C., 1934-41, served as chief of research, 1938-41; War Production Board, Washington, D.C., economist, 1942-44, director of Planning Division, 1944-46; New York University, New York, N.Y., professor of economics, 1956-61; Yale University, New Haven, Conn., professor of economics, 1962-73, professor emeritus, 1974—. Member of U.S. Government mission on German currency reform, 1946; U.S. economic adviser to Austrian Treaty Negotiations, 1947; member of research staff of National Bureau of Economic Research, 1952-69; vice-president of Organization for Economic Cooperation and Development's Development Center, Paris, France, 1963-65.

MEMBER: International Association for Research in Income and Wealth (past chairman), American Economic Association, Economic History Association.

WRITINGS:

Kapitalpolitik (title means "Capital Policy"), Juncker & Duennhaupt, 1933.
The Changing Structure of American Banking, G. Routledge & Sons, 1933.
A Study of Saving in the United States, three volumes, Princeton University Press, 1955-56.
Financial Intermediaries in the American Economy Since 1900, Princeton University Press, 1958.
The National Wealth of the United States in the Postwar Period, Princeton University Press, 1962.
(With Robert Lipsey and Morris Mendelson) *Studies in the National Balance Sheet of the United States*, Princeton University Press, 1963.
Financial Structure and Development, Yale University Press, 1969.
The National Balance Sheet of the United States, 1953-1980, Columbia University Press, 1981.
The Financial Development of Japan, 1868-1977, Yale University Press, 1983.
The Financial Development of India, 1860-1977, Yale University Press, 1983.
The Financial Development of India, Japan, and the United States: A Trilateral Institutional, Statistical, and Analytic Comparison, Yale University Press, 1983.
Comparative National Balance Sheets, Chicago University Press, 1985.

Also author of *Flow of Capital Funds in the Postwar Economy*, 1965.

WORK IN PROGRESS: *The Financial Development of Brazil, 1850-1984*, publication expected in 1985; *Pre-Modern Financial Systems*.

SIDELIGHTS: "During my service in the federal government," Raymond W. Goldsmith reported, "I was concerned mainly with the securities market, war finance, and the German currency reform of 1946. Since 1948 I have concentrated on statistical and institutional aspects of financial institutions, saving, capital stock and national balance sheets, first for the United States, then, beginning in the 1960's, on an international comparative basis. In these fields I regard as my main innovations the estimation of saving by forms; the development of the perpetual inventory method of estimating capital stocks as the cumulated price adjusted net investment, first applied to the United States, but then to many other countries; and the introduction of the financial interrelations ratio (financial assets to tangible assets) and the financial intermediation ratio (assets of financial institutions to total financial assets), along with the development of formulas that identify the main determinants of the financial interrelations ratio.''

*   *   *

GOODALL, Norman   1896-1985

OBITUARY NOTICE: Born August 30, 1896, in Birmingham, England; died January 1, 1985. Clergyman and author. Goodall, a minister of the United Reformed church, is remembered for his service to the ecumenical movement. Most notable was his role in effecting the integration of the International Missionary Council and the World Council of Churches at the third assembly of the World Council of Churches in 1961. Goodall was the author of several books, including *With All Thy Mind, Pacific Pilgrimage, One Man's Testimony, The Ecumenical Movement, Christian Missions and Social Ferment,* and *Second Fiddle: Recollections and Reflections.*

OBITUARIES AND OTHER SOURCES:

BOOKS

Who's Who, 136th edition, St. Martin's, 1984.

PERIODICALS

Times (London), January 3, 1985.

*   *   *

GOODFELLOW, Peter   1935-

PERSONAL: Born October 18, 1935, in Rochester, England; son of Frank (an inspector of naval ordnance) and Hilda (a housewife; maiden name, Cranfield) Goodfellow; married June Christie (a pharmacist and housewife), April 9, 1960; children: David, Andrew. *Education:* University of Exeter, B.A. (with honors), 1957. *Politics:* "Liberal, with a small 'l'."

ADDRESSES: *Home*—6 Dunraven Dr., Plymouth PL6 6AR, England.

CAREER: Schoolmaster in Plymouth, England, 1958-76; Coombe Dean School (comprehensive school), Plymouth, teacher and head of faculty of English and drama, 1976—. Methodist local preacher in Plymouth area, 1964—.

MEMBER: Profesional Association of Teachers (chairman, 1979—), Devon Birdwatching Society (member of council), Plymouth Shakespeare Society (member of council, 1980—).

AWARDS, HONORS: *Birds as Builders* voted best bird book of the year by British Broadcasting Corporation's radio program "The Living World."

WRITINGS:

Projects With Birds, David & Charles, 1973.
Birds as Builders, Arco, 1977.
Shakespeare's Birds, Overlook Press, 1983.

WORK IN PROGRESS: *Birds of the Bible; Prehistoric Birds; Famous Birdwatchers*.

SIDELIGHTS: Peter Goodfellow told *CA:* "Writing is a pleasure, not a career or a compulsion. *Projects With Birds* describes eighty birdwatching projects for beginners. I wrote *Birds as Builders* as a detailed study of birds' nests throughout the world when I couldn't find such a book in the library! *Shakespeare's Birds* is my only book so far written by me as an

English teacher. Shakespeare knew English birds very well— he cited over forty species, and always named a species in a striking image that helped describe well a character or situation. I haven't firmly settled on the next book. The idea of famous birdwatchers particularly interests me since I discovered recently that in Taiwan lives a bird called Goodfellow's firecrest. It has nothing to do with me, so who was this Goodfellow? Perhaps compulsion is creeping into my writing after all.''

*   *   *

GORDON, Andrew (Mark) 1945-

PERSONAL: Born January 23, 1945, in Miami Beach, Fla.; son of Harry (a stockbroker) and Adele (a teacher; maiden name, Reisner) Gordon; married Judy Taylor (a nurse), August 8, 1973; children: Daniel Taylor. *Education:* Rutgers University, B.A. (with high honors), 1965; University of California, Berkeley, M.A., 1967, Ph.D., 1973.

ADDRESSES: Office—Department of English, University of Florida, Gainesville, Fla. 32611.

CAREER: University of Florida, Gainesville, assistant professor, 1975-80, associate professor of English, 1980—. Fulbright junior lecturer in American literature at University of Valencia, Valencia, Spain, 1973-74, University of Barcelona, Barcelona, Spain, 1973-75, and University of Oporto, Oporto, Portugal, 1979; Fulbright senior lecturer at University of Nis, Nis, Yugoslavia, 1984-85.

MEMBER: International Association for the Fantastic in the Arts, Modern Language Association of America, American Film Society, National Association for Psychoanalytic Criticism, Science Fiction Research Association, South Atlantic Modern Language Association (chairman of Psychology and Literature Discussion Circle, 1984), Fulbright Alumni Association, Phi Beta Kappa.

AWARDS, HONORS: University of Florida Humanities Faculty Research Award, 1980.

WRITINGS:

An American Dreamer: A Psychoanalytic Study of the Fiction of Norman Mailer, Fairleigh Dickinson University Press, 1980.

CONTRIBUTOR

Thomas J. Remington, editor, *Selected Proceedings of the Science Fiction Research Association 1978 National Conference,* University of Northern Iowa, 1979.
Thom Dunn and Richard Erlich, editors, *The Mechanical God: Machines in Science Fiction,* Greenwood Press, 1982.
Dictionary of Literary Biography, Volume 28: *Twentieth-Century American-Jewish Fiction Writers,* Gale, 1984.
Bernard J. Paris, editor, *Third Force Psychology and the Study of Literature,* Fairleigh Dickinson University Press, 1985.
Donald Palumbo, editor, *Eros in the Mind's Eye: Sexuality and the Fantastic in Art and Film,* Greenwood Press, 1985.

OTHER

Contributor of articles and reviews to scholarly journals, including *Literature and Psychology, Literature/Film Quarterly, Science-Fiction Studies,* and to popular magazines, including *Rolling Stone* and *New Republic.* Editorial consultant to *Science-Fiction Studies.*

WORK IN PROGRESS: An entry on Ursula Le Guin for a *Dictionary of Literary Biography* volume on twentieth-century American writers for children, publication by Gale expected in 1985; *Myths for Our Time: The Science Fiction and Fantasy Films of George Lucas and Steven Spielberg,* completion expected in 1985; a study of the fiction of Saul Bellow.

*   *   *

GORELICK, Bryna Siegel
See SIEGEL-GORELICK, Bryna

*   *   *

GORKIN, Jess 1913-1985

OBITUARY NOTICE: Born October 23, 1913, in Rochester, N.Y.; died of a heart attack, February 19, 1985, in Longboat Key, Fla. Editor. Gorkin was editor of the Sunday magazine *Parade* from 1949 to 1978. Under his editorial direction, the periodical became the country's most widely circulated Sunday supplement. Gorkin began his career in Iowa as editor in chief of the *Daily Iowan* in 1936. After moving to New York the following year, he joined *Look* as associate editor. During World War II Gorkin served the U.S. Office of War Information, creating and editing an overseas picture magazine. He then spent two years as managing editor of *Parade* before he was appointed editor. When he retired from that publication, Gorkin became editor of the periodical *Fifty Plus* and later acted as consulting editor to *Parade* as well. He was credited with proposing a hot line between Washington D.C., and Moscow in an open letter in *Parade* in 1960.

OBITUARIES AND OTHER SOURCES:

BOOKS

Who's Who in America, 43rd edition, Marquis, 1984.

PERIODICALS

Newsweek, March 4, 1985.
New York Times, February 23, 1985.

*   *   *

GRAD, Eli 1928-

PERSONAL: Born November 4, 1928, in Vilno, Poland (now Vilnius, U.S.S.R.); immigrated to United States, 1947, naturalized citizen, 1957; son of Shraga (a merchant) and Miriam (a teacher; maiden name, Lewin) Grad; married Geraldine Pescov (a social worker), June 22, 1952; children: Roni, Oren, Jonathan. *Education:* Jewish Theological Seminary, B.R.E. (with distinction), 1950, M.R.E. and B.D., both 1955; New York University, M.A., 1951; Wayne State University, Ph.D., 1965.

ADDRESSES: Home—25 Hobart Rd., Newton Centre, Mass. 02159. *Office*—Hebrew College, 43 Hawes St., Brookline, Mass. 02146.

CAREER: Principal at Jewish school in Washington, D.C., 1950-56; director of education at Jewish schools in Detroit, Mich., 1956-66, and Toronto, Ontario, 1965-70; Hebrew College, Brookline, Mass., professor of education, dean of faculty, and president of college, all 1970—. Visiting professor at New York University Graduate School of Education, 1972-83.

MEMBER: National Council for Jewish Education (president, 1973-75), American Association for Jewish Education (member of governing council), Association for Higher Education.

AWARDS, HONORS: D.J.Ped. from Jewish Theological Seminary, 1976.

WRITINGS:

(Editor) *The Recruitment and Training of Educational Personnel*, Educators Assembly, 1966.
(Editor) *The Teenager and Jewish Education*, Educators Assembly, 1967.
(With Bette Roth) *Congregation Shaarey Zedek, 5622-5742, 1861-1981*, Wayne State University Press, 1982.

Editor of *Judaica Post: Journal of Philatelic Judaica*, 1960-77.

WORK IN PROGRESS: The Small College: Beyond Survival, completion expected in 1987; *The Uses and Abuses of Time,* completion expected in 1988.

SIDELIGHTS: Eli Grad told *CA:* ''My thirty-three years in Jewish education have been the most agonizing and exhilarating career available—agonizing because there are always hopes unfulfilled and dreams unrealized, but also exhilarating because I am dealing with the soul of a people.

''I have watched American Judaism 'go public.' The resurgence of ethnic pride in our society has brought Judaism from the home 'into the streets.' Jews have no hesitation about public demonstrations for Soviet Jewry, for Israel, for Ethiopian Jewry, and the like. In the process of going public, Jews gave up the private domain. In other words, Judaism has not expanded beyond the home and into the street—it *left the home* and went into the street, which is far more superficial. More and more Jews are proudly ready to stand up and identify themselves publicly as Jews, but fewer and fewer understand the Jewish tradition—what it means and what it teaches.

''General education has moved the Jew to the superficial periphery of Jewish life; only Jewish learning can begin moving American Jews toward the center again. The need to make my small contribution toward the creation of a learning community is a fire burning in my bones that I cannot contain.''

AVOCATIONAL INTERESTS: Philately, numismatics, photography, music, reading.

*   *   *

GRADY, Don(ald Wyndham)   1929-

PERSONAL: Born January 25, 1929, in Wellington, New Zealand; son of Wyndham (in sales) and Freda (a dental nurse assistant; maiden name, Topp) Grady; married Patricia Snowden Smith, March 20, 1961 (died March 4, 1963); married Marilyn Grogan (a registered nurse), December 27, 1967; children: Kim Michelle Grady Hooper, Richard Leonard, Simon John, Benjamin James. *Education:* Attended secondary school in Nelson, New Zealand. *Politics:* Labour. *Religion:* Church of England.

ADDRESSES: Home—Omaio, 33 Crofton Rd., Christchurch 5, New Zealand. *Office*—The Star, 99 Kilmore St., Christchurch, New Zealand.

CAREER: Seaman on cargo ships to Central America and Europe, 1945-47; *Otago Daily Times*, Dunedin, New Zealand, cadet, 1947; *Rotorua Post*, Rotorua, New Zealand, reporter,

1948-49; *Southern Cross*, Wellington, New Zealand, reporter and Hutt Valley correspondent, 1950-51; Australian Broadcasting Commission, Darwin, Australia, reporter, 1951-52; *Christchurch Star*, Christchurch, New Zealand, reporter, 1952-54; *Sunday Telegraph*, Sydney, Australia, senior journalist, 1954-63; *Press*, Christchurch, industrial reporter, 1963-68; Clifford Associates, Christchurch, public relations consultant, 1968-72; *Weekend Star*, Christchurch, reporter, 1973—.

MEMBER: P.E.N. New Zealand Centre, New Zealand Journalists Union, Papanui Working Men's Club.

AWARDS, HONORS: A.W. Reed Memorial Book Award from A.H. & A.W. Reed Ltd., 1980, and J.M. Sherrard Award for regional history from the New Zealand Historical Society (Canterbury branch), 1984, both for *The Perano Whalers of Cook Strait, 1911-1964.*

WRITINGS:

Guards of the Sea, Whitcoulls, 1978.
The Perano Whalers of Cook Strait, 1911-1964, A.H. & A.W. Reed, 1982.
Sealers and Whalers in New Zealand Waters, Reed-Methuen Publishers, 1985.

WORK IN PROGRESS: A book on the Cobham Outward Bound School at Anakiwa, New Zealand, publication by the Hutchinson Group expected in 1987.

SIDELIGHTS: Don Grady told *CA:* ''The ten years that I spent as a writer on the *Sunday Telegraph* newspaper in Sydney, Australia, had a big bearing on my attitude toward life and people. On this newspaper in a city of 3.5 million people I covered almost every subject known to mankind. Coming to live in the quieter, lower-profile, less populated atmosphere of New Zealand and away from the hurly-burly of life I found myself becoming more and more involved with historical adventure, present-day adventurers, and colorful people. In New Zealand I have had more time to dig deeper and longer.

''I write largely about adventurous underdogs who have lived challenging lives. My speciality to date has been sealers and whalers, but I am now expanding to write about New Zealand youth in challenging situations, including those from prison institutions, from the probation service, the physically handicapped, mentally handicapped, the blind, deaf, and little people. I've found that the early sealers and whalers who came to New Zealand waters, beginning in 1791, were the most exciting pioneers and adventurers in this part of the Pacific. Now I find plenty of excitement in the challenges young people are finding in the Outward Bound movement.

''The sealers and whalers of many nations, including large numbers of Americans, who once abounded on the New Zealand coast, were special because of their hardiness, adventurousness, resilience, self-sufficiency, independence, guts, exceptional seamanship, and ability to meet and overcome any exigency that the sea, elements, their hazardous industry, or indigenous local populations might throw up. In the late 1700's and early 1800's the Maoris in New Zealand were, of course, cannibals and extremely warlike. And many of the local early shore-whalers in New Zealand were escaped convicts from penal settlements in Australia, or criminals from elsewhere in the world, or runaway sailors.

''In my work on New Zealand whalers and sealers, I have studied the detailed logbooks of ninety different American whaleships that once whaled in New Zealand waters. In many cases the early whaling logbooks are matched up with illustrations of the respective nineteenth-century American whale-ships, telling graphically of the fortunes, dangers, lives, and experiences of the whalers. A few of the early American sealers in New Zealand were a particularly tough lot. As well as drawing on logbooks, *Sealers and Whalers in New Zealand* uses a wide range of contemporary accounts to retell the stories of hardship and brutality, courage, disaster, and comradeship that characterized the early days of the industry. Hundreds of photographs and other illustrations have been assembled to present one of the richest and most fascinating aspects of New Zealand history.

"The Outward Bound movement originated in the United Kingdom during the early days of World War II as a survival course for merchant seamen cadets. In view of its success, and because survival and growth are continuing challenges, the course was adapted for a peacetime role in the United Kingdom following the war to ensure the development and continuance of the education program. Since then similar trusts have been set up in about thirty-five different countries, including New Zealand, where one has been in operation since 1962. So far there has been an intake of 18,500 students (of both sexes) in New Zealand and a current annual intake of 1,300 students at the Outward Bound School at Anakiwa, New Zealand.

"I have known of the Outward Bound School for many years through newspaper articles and magazine feature stories, but my real awareness of its ideals, objectives, activities, and achievements with New Zealand youth was greatly accentuated and developed through my buying a small hillside holiday property amid indigenous native bush overlooking the Queen Charlotte Sounds at Anakiwa, three hundred meters from the Outward Bound School. Each morning from my eagle-top aerie I can see (and hear) the students pounding along the road below my section and then leaping off a jetty into the sea about daybreak. Using binoculars or a camera-telephoto lense I can see the students abseiling on a sheer cliff-face behind the Outward Bound School, as well as a wide range of their other activities. As Anakiwa is a small community, I soon came to know many of the school's instructors and maintenance staff, which also stimulated my interest in the school, its activities, and what it was trying to do. To me the Outward Bound School holds out great hope for the future of youth in a challenging and fast-changing world."

BIOGRAPHICAL/CRITICAL SOURCES:

PERIODICALS

Star (Christchurch, New Zealand), April 13, 1981.

* * *

GRAF, Oskar Maria   1894-1967

OBITUARY NOTICE: Born July 22, 1894, in Berg am Starnberger See, Bavaria, Germany (now West Germany); died June 28 (one source says April 28), 1967, in New York, N.Y.; buried in Bogenhausen Cemetery, Munich, West Germany. Author. Graf was known as an outspoken opponent of Germany's Nazi regime, which rose to power following World War I, and is remembered for his autobiographical novels. He began writing as a teenager while supporting himself with various odd jobs in Munich. His works—which then consisted of poems, essays, and short stories—addressed themes of social revolution and protest. After World War I Graf turned to autobiographical writing and wrote about his Bavarian heritage.

When Graf's stories attracted public attention, the Nazi regime, which claimed a basis in German nationalism, also became interested in the author. Recognizing Graf's literature for its distinctly German qualities and hoping to capitalize on its national appeal, the Nazis recommended Graf's books and tried to make the author their spokesman. Graf resisted and accused the regime of trying to replace Germanism with nationalism. He subsequently published a formal protest during a mass book-burning in 1933 and demanded that his books be burned along with those of other German authors. As a result of his opposition, Graf was deprived of his citizenship, and his books were banned. The author immigrated to the United States in 1938, following a self-imposed exile in Czechoslovakia. His publications include *Prisoners All, The Life of My Mother, The Stationmaster,* and *The Wolf.*

OBITUARIES AND OTHER SOURCES:

BOOKS

Encyclopedia of World Literature in the Twentieth Century, updated edition, Ungar, 1967.
Twentieth-Century Authors: A Biographical Dictionary of Modern Literature, H. W. Wilson, 1942.
Who Was Who in America, With World Notables, Volume V: *1969-1973,* Marquis, 1973.

PERIODICALS

New York Times, June 29, 1967.

* * *

GRANT, Ambrose
See RAYMOND, Rene (Brabazon)

* * *

GRATTAN, Virginia L(ee)   1932-

PERSONAL: Born December 16, 1932, in San Jose, Calif.; daughter of Worthin F. and Eva May (Horn) Grattan. *Education:* San Jose State College (now University), B.A., 1954; University of Califonia, Berkeley, General Secondary Credential, 1959; San Francisco State University, M.A., 1977.

ADDRESSES: Home—P.O. Box 6547, Albany, Calif. 94706-0547.

CAREER: Worked as high school English teacher, in Pittsburg, Santa Clara, and San Bruno, California, 1959-65; San Mateo High School, San Mateo, Calif., English teacher, 1965-78; writer, 1978—.

WRITINGS:

Mary Colter: Builder Upon the Red Earth, Northland Press, 1980.

WORK IN PROGRESS: Research.

SIDELIGHTS: Virginia L. Grattan told *CA:* "I'm interested in the lives of women who have made contributions to our culture and yet haven't been included in the history books. I'm interested in preserving their stories.

"Mary Colter's story was very nearly lost. She died nearly twenty years before I knew of her, and the company for which she worked had moved and dispersed the old records. So it was often by chance that I found people who knew her and clippings in old boxes that told her story.

"She was an architect and decorator for Fred Harvey and the Santa Fe Railway in the Southwest shortly after the turn of the century. I learned of her on a vacation at the Grand Canyon when I remarked about the strange concave ceiling at Hermit's Rest. I was told that the building had been designed by Mary Colter, who had designed many of the Grand Canyon buildings. I had never heard of her and could find nothing about her even in the library at the University of California. So I began my search.

"I am pleased that Mary Colter has now been included in the Arizona Women's Hall of Fame and that her story was not lost."

* * *

GRAVES, Phillip E(arl) 1945-

PERSONAL: Born December 20, 1945, in Hammond, Ind.; son of Earl Edwin (a teacher) and Ruth Marie (a homemaker; maiden name, Carmichael) Graves; married Patricia Neal, June 10, 1967 (divorced May, 1973); children: Wendy Marie, Jessica Joanne. *Education:* Indiana University—Bloomington, A.B. (with honors and distinction), 1968; Northwestern University, M.A., 1971, Ph.D., 1973.

ADDRESSES: Home—889 14th St., Boulder, Colo. 80302. *Office*—Department of Economics, Econ 223, University of Colorado at Boulder, Boulder, Colo. 80309.

CAREER: Arizona State University, Tempe, assistant professor of economics, 1971-74; University of Chicago, Chicago, Ill., postdoctoral research fellow, 1974-78; University of Colorado at Boulder, associate professor of economics, 1978—.

MEMBER: American Economic Association, Regional Science Association, Association of Environmental and Resource Economists, Air Pollution Control Association, Western Economic Association, Phi Beta Kappa.

WRITINGS:

(With G. S. Tolley and J. L. Gardner) *Urban Growth Policy in a Market Economy,* Academic Press, 1979.
(With Tolley and G. C. Blomquist) *Environmental Policy: Elements of Environmental Analysis,* Ballinger, 1981.
(With Tolley and A. S. Cohen) *Environmental Policy: Air Quality,* Ballinger, 1982.
(With Ronald J. Krumm) *Health and Air Quality: Evaluating the Effects of Policy,* American Enterprise Institute for Public Policy Research, 1983.
(With E. S. Mills) *The Economics of Environmental Quality,* Norton, 1985.
Urban Economics: Problems and Policies, Prentice-Hall, in press.
Economic Behavior, Harcourt, in press.
Intermediate Microeconomics, Harcourt, in press.

Member of editorial board of *American Economic Review* and *Journal of Regional Science.*

SIDELIGHTS: Phillip E. Graves told *CA:* "I view as very positive trends toward economic incentives, as opposed to detailed direct control requirements, in environmental policy. I am much more pessimistic, however, about the future of the Northeast and Midwest than are most of my colleagues in economics."

AVOCATIONAL INTERESTS: Dance, painting, skiing, teaching wine courses, European travel, "hot-tubbing," basketball, racquetball, aerobics.

GRAY, Ellington
See JACOB, Naomi Ellington

* * *

GREEN, Ben K. 1911(?)-1974

OBITUARY NOTICE: Born c. 1911; died of a heart attack in 1974. Author. Green is remembered for his contribution to Texas literature, which won him a special award from the Texas Institute of Letters. His books include *Horse Tradin'*, *Some More Horse Tradin'*, *Wild Cow Tales*, *The Village Horse Doctor: West of the Pecos*, *The Last Trail Drive Through Downtown Dallas*, and *A Thousand Miles of Mustangin'*.

OBITUARIES AND OTHER SOURCES:

BOOKS

Authors in the News, Volume I, Gale, 1976.

PERIODICALS

Houston Post, November 3, 1974.

* * *

GREEN, Harvey 1946-

PERSONAL: Born September 15, 1946, in Buffalo, N.Y.; son of Herman (a laboratory technician) and Bessie (a homemaker; maiden name, Krassen) Green; married Susan Williams (a curator), June 21, 1980. *Education:* University of Rochester, B.A., 1946; Rutgers University, M.A., 1970, Ph.D., 1976.

ADDRESSES: Home—Rochester, N.Y. *Office*—Margaret Woodbury Strong Museum, 1 Manhattan Sq., Rochester, N.Y. 14607.

CAREER: Margaret Woodbury Strong Museum, Rochester, N.Y., historian and deputy director for interpretation, 1976—. Consultant to various historical organizations. Adjunct associate professor of history at University of Rochester, 1984—.

MEMBER: American Association for State and Local History, American Studies Association, Organization of American Historians, Gallery Association of New York State (member of board of directors).

WRITINGS:

(With Mary-Ellen Perry) *The Light of the Home: An Intimate View of the Lives of Women in Victorian America,* Pantheon, 1983.

WORK IN PROGRESS: Physical Fitness and Sport in America: 1830-1940, publication expected in 1986; editing and contributing to a visitor's guide to historic American homes, publication expected in 1986.

SIDELIGHTS: Gathering material for his book *The Light of the Home: An Intimate View of the Lives of Women in Victorian America,* historian Harvey Green analyzed thousands of advertisements, diaries, advice columns and manuals, labor-saving gadgets, kitchen tools, and furniture. The result, according to Elizabeth Crow of *Washington Post Book World,* is a "fascinating, lavishly illustrated, and very disturbing inventory of the means by which 'woman's place' was defined in the years between 1870 and 1940 and by which it has been maintained for the past century." The book, said Snow, "is most grimly compelling'' when Green ''catalogues the dark side of Victorian housewifery.'' The critic further mentioned that ''Green's examination of 19th-century kitchen middens is as interesting as the humor and persistence with which he links his Victorian subjects with women of our day. In explaining our past, he has provided insight into our present, especially in his analysis of the economics of a sexually stratified society.''

A book reviewer for *Time* similarly praised *The Light of the Home*: ''Delightfully illustrated with pictures of artifacts from the Margaret Woodbury Strong Museum,'' the book ''illuminates the deadening burden that male supremacy imposed during the 19th century.'' The reviewer concluded that ''Green's hindsight is an education.''

BIOGRAPHICAL/CRITICAL SOURCES:

PERIODICALS

New York Review of Books, April 12, 1984.
Time, July 4, 1983.
Washington Post Book World, August 12, 1983.

*   *   *

GREEN, Joann   1938-

PERSONAL: Born January 16, 1938; children: Shoshanna, Jonas Shaw.

ADDRESSES: Home—Cambridge, Mass. *Office*—American National Theatre, Kennedy Center, Washington, D.C. 20566.

CAREER: The Cambridge Ensemble, Cambridge, Mass., artistic director, 1973-79; Harvard University, Cambridge, lecturer in dramatic arts, 1979-83; Boston Shakespeare Company, Boston, Mass., associate director, 1983-84; American National Theatre, Washington, D.C., artistic associate, 1984—.

WRITINGS:

(Contributor) Pamela Daniels and Sara Ruddick, editors, *Working It Out,* Pantheon, 1977.
The Small Theatre Handbook, Harvard Common, 1981.

PLAYS

''Tales of Chelm'' (two-act adaptation of folk tales), first produced in Cambridge, Mass., by the Cambridge Ensemble, April, 1973.
''The Southern Route'' (one-act adaptation of story by Julio Cortazar), first produced in Cambridge by the Cambridge Ensemble, April, 1974.
''Oresteia'' (two-act adaptation of trilogy by Aeschylus), first produced in Cambridge by the Cambridge Ensemble, April, 1975.
''Gulliver's Travels'' (two-act adaptation of novel by Jonathan Swift), first produced in Cambridge by the Cambridge Ensemble, April, 1976.
''The Scarlet Letter'' (two-act adaptation of novel by Nathaniel Hawthorne), first produced in Cambridge by the Cambridge Ensemble, April, 1977.
''Brer Rabbit and Friend'' (one-act adaptation of tales of Joel Chandler Harris), first produced in Cambridge by the Cambridge Ensemble, April, 1978.

*   *   *

GREENMAN, Robert   1939-

PERSONAL: Born December 11, 1939, in Brooklyn, N.Y.;

son of Bert B. (a frozen foods broker) and Martha (Ehrlich) Greenman; married Carol Sokolov (a medical secretary), May 28, 1960; children: Lisa, Sara, Rachel. *Education:* Emerson College, B.S., 1961. *Religion:* Jewish.

ADDRESSES: Home—4272 Bedford Ave., Brooklyn, N.Y. 11229.

CAREER: High school teacher of English and journalism, 1962—. Adjunct member of faculty at Kingsborough Community College of the City University of New York, 1980.

AWARDS, HONORS: Gold Key Award from Columbia Scholastic Press Association, 1984.

WRITINGS:

The Rap Book, Price, Stern, 1979.
The New York Times Captive Vocabulary, New York Times, 1980, revised edition, 1982.
Words in Action, Times Books, 1983.

Author of ''Watch Your Language,'' a column in *New York Times School Weekly,* 1974-82. Contributor to newspapers.

WORK IN PROGRESS: The Adviser's Companion, a handbook for high school journalism advisers.

SIDELIGHTS: Robert Greenman told *CA:* ''*Captive Vocabulary* is a promotional book I produced for the *New York Times.* For it I collected one thousand sentences from the *Times,* each of which featured a 'vocabulary' word that high school students are likely to encounter while reading the *Times.* A brief definition and a pronunciation accompany each word. The book's title derives from the fact that, despite its reputation as a newspaper for the well educated, the *Times* uses a core of less than two thousand 'educated' words again and again to such an extent that mastery of them means, virtually, mastery of the *Times* (in terms of its word usage). In fact, almost every word in the book can be found on high school vocabulary lists. The book is given free to students and teachers with in-school subscriptions to the *Times.*

''*Captive Vocabulary* led me to *Words in Action,* which is composed of fifteen thousand passages from the *Times,* each featuring a word that should be a part of everyone's writing and speaking vocabularies. Unlike *Captive Vocabulary, Words in Action* was written for a general audience and contains not only the usual type of enrichment word, such as *obfuscate* and *punctilious,* but also Yiddish words and slang. The common theme among all the book's entries is that they make one's communication more precise, alive, and colorful. I begin the book with a series of short chapters on different aspects of today's language, such as slang, allusions, and questions of good usage.

''*The Rap Book* is a place for adults to record memories of their childhood and youth—everything from their favorite toys, to their first crush, to their greatest disappointment. It is not an attempt to get people to uncover repressed or suppressed thoughts (it's far too direct for that), but simply to recall things they might not have thought about for a long time. Although writing down one's responses can be self-enlightening and even therapeutic, my intention was simply to encourage people who devote almost all their time and thought to the present and future to give a little thought to their past, and hopefully to receive some pleasure from it.

''My handbook for high school journalism advisers, *The Adviser's Companion,* is being published serially in seven issues of the *School Press Review.* Publication as a book will follow. *The Adviser's Companion* is the result of what I learned during my thirteen years advising a student newspaper. It deals with hundreds of major and minor problems, questions, and situations encountered by every high school newspaper adviser. Subjects range from reporting to layouts, and from advertising to libel—with an emphasis on the need for advisers and staffs to professionalize their attitudes and practices.

"A school newspaper should exist not to enhance the school's image or promote the administration's goals, but to report truthfully the way things are in school and to help students better cope with the problems they encounter in and out of school. I urge advisers to think of their newspapers as adversaries of the administration, which is much the same role professional papers play with respect to government. I also show advisers how to live with this kind of relationship."

* * *

GREEVES, Frederic   1903-1985

OBITUARY NOTICE: Born June 1, 1903; died in 1985. Clergyman, educator, and author. Greeves, a Methodist minister and teacher, pioneered the study of the theology of pastoral training. For twenty-one years he held the tutorial Randles Chair of Religion at Britain's Didsbury College. After retiring from Didsbury, the clergyman continued teaching at Bristol University. Greeves also served as chairman of the British Broadcasting Corporation's West Regional Religious Advisory Council for five years and as president of the Methodist Conference in 1963 and 1964. He wrote *Jesus, the Son of God, Talking About God, The Meaning of Sin, Theology and the Cure of Souls: An Introduction to Pastoral Theology,* and *The Christian Way.*

OBITUARIES AND OTHER SOURCES:

BOOKS

Who's Who, 136th edition, St. Martin's, 1984.
The Writers Directory: 1984-1986, St. James Press, 1983.

PERIODICALS

Times (London), March 5, 1985.

* * *

GREGORY, Sinda   1947-

PERSONAL: Born December 9, 1947, in Clovis, N.M.; daughter of John V. (a professor) and Adelaide (a teacher; maiden name, Self) Gregory; married Larry F. McCaffery (a professor and writer), May 21, 1977; children: Mark Urton. *Education:* University of Illinois at Urbana-Champaign, B.A., 1971, M.A., 1974, Ph.D., 1980.

ADDRESSES: Home—3133 Gregory St., San Diego, Calif. 92104.

CAREER: San Diego State University, San Diego, Calif., lecturer in English, 1977—. Part-time member of faculty at University of California, San Diego.

WRITINGS:

Private Investigations: The Novels of Dashiell Hammett, Southern Illinois University Press, 1984.
(Editor with husband, Larry McCaffery) *No Real Center: Interviews With Contemporary American Writers,* University of Illinois Press, 1985.

Also contributor to *Dictionary of Literary Biography,* Gale.

Contributor of essays, interviews, poems, and stories to magazines, including *Mississippi Review, Fiction International, Conjunctions, Indiana Review, Black American Literature Forum,* and *Pacific Poetry Review.*

SIDELIGHTS: Sinda Gregory told *CA: "No Real Center* is a collection of interviews with authors Raymond Carver, Edmund White, Russell Hoban, Ursula LeGuin, Samuel Delany, William Kennedy, Barry Hannah, Max Apple, Tom Robbins, Thomas McGuane, Ron Silliman, Ann Beattie, and Walter Abish. The primary focus of these talks was on the writing process itself—what we wanted the authors to discuss in particular were their methods of composition. How does their fiction get started in the first place? Does the idea come by way of an interesting plot situation? By a character? Has a specific sentence popped into existence that leads to another? Is there a metaphor they're trying to explore? The answers vary widely, of course, because each writer has different methods of mining the imagination and different notions of what fiction should be, but all these interviews provide a unique look into the solitary and intuitive act of writing."

* * *

GRIM, Patrick   1950-

PERSONAL: Born October 29, 1950, in Pasadena, Calif.; son of Elgas Shull (an artist) and Dorathy Mae (a potter; maiden name, O'Neal) Grim; married Ellen Louise Forde, May 30, 1970 (divorced, 1974); married Kriste Taylor (a philosopher), 1977. *Education:* University of California, Santa Cruz, A.B. (philosophy) and A.B. (anthropology), both 1971; University of St. Andrews, B.Phil., 1975; Boston University, M.A., 1975, Ph.D., 1976.

ADDRESSES: Home—Port Jefferson, N.Y. *Office*—Department of Philosophy, State University of New York at Stony Brook, Stony Brook, N.Y. 11794.

CAREER: State University of New York at Stony Brook, visiting assistant professor, 1976-77, assistant professor, 1978-84, associate professor of philosophy, 1984—. Member of Center for Scientific Anomalies Research.

MEMBER: American Philosophical Association, Society for the Philosophical Study of the Paranormal.

AWARDS, HONORS: Fulbright fellow, 1971-72; Mellon Foundation fellow at Washington University, St. Louis, Mo., 1977-78.

WRITINGS:

(Contributor) Frederick Elliston, Jane English, and Mary Vetterling-Braggin, editors, *Feminism and Philosophy,* Littlefield, 1977.
(Editor with John T. Sanders and David Boyer) *The Philosopher's Annual,* Volumes I-V, Rowman & Littlefield, 1979-81.
(Editor) *Philosophy of Science and the Occult,* State University of New York Press, 1982.

Contributor to philosophy journals.

WORK IN PROGRESS: Editing volume VI of *The Philosopher's Annual* for Ridgeview Publishing; philosophical research on paradox and the limits of truth and knowledge.

SIDELIGHTS: Patrick Grim told *CA:* "I consider my work in various fields to be simply disciplined imagination. Both parts are crucial: discipline without imagination is pedantry, but imagination without discipline is sterile. I have a great respect for craft and for careful sketching in advance and have very little tolerance for the myth of genius.

"In my opinion philosophy is presently enjoying a golden age comparable only to that of Athens in the fifth century before Christ. Contemporary analytic philosophy profits immensely from close ties with mathematical logic—though those ties are complicated and far from one-sided—and it is this, I think, that gives it its current vigor. Logic offers a possibility of clear codification and at the same time facilitates a subtlety and sophistication of argument that characterizes philosophical thought at its best. Logic also offers, I think, a freedom for creative imagination with regard to interpretation, and that freedom has paid off in the last ten to twenty years with new logics and new metaphysical, epistemological, and—perhaps eventually—ethical views based on them.

"*Philosophy of Science and the Occult* was an attempt to 'up the ante' in discussions of parapsychology in particular but also of astrology, UFOs, and the like, by introducing some of the deep and perennial questions in standard scholastic philosophy of science. At the same time, however, I thought that treatment of such topics would make an enjoyable and accessible pedagogical aid in the teaching of standard issues in the philosophy of science. Therefore consideration in detail of various aspects of 'the occult' seemed a natural. Certainly it is a source of constant fascination and general skepticism. On the other hand, I have a healthy respect for new areas of investigation, however checkered their history."

BIOGRAPHICAL/CRITICAL SOURCES:

BOOKS

Vetterling-Braggin, Mary, editor, *Sexist Language: A Modern Philosophical Approach,* Littlefield, 1981.

*   *   *

GRIMSTEAD, Hettie   1903-
(Marsha Manning)

BRIEF ENTRY: Born in 1903, in Manchester, England. British journalist and novelist. Associated wth United Press International for twenty-five years, Grimstead has also been a novelist for more than fifty years. She has written more than seventy romances, many under the pseudonym Marsha Manning. Among her most recent titles are *The Tender Vine* (Mills & Boon, 1974), *Wedding of the Year* (Mills & Boon, 1974), *Sister Rose's Holiday* (Mills & Boon, 1975), *Chance Encounter* (Mills & Boon, 1975), *Day of Roses* (Mills & Boon, 1976), and *The Passionate Rivals* (R. Hale, 1978). *Address:* c/o Curtis Brown Ltd., 1 Craven Hill, London W2 3EP, England.

BIOGRAPHICAL/CRITICAL SOURCES:

BOOKS

The Writers Directory: 1984-1986, St. James Press, 1983.

*   *   *

GROESCHEL, Benedict J(oseph)   1933-

PERSONAL: Born July 23, 1933, in Jersey City, N.J.; son of Edward Joseph (a civil engineer) and Marjulea (a housewife; maiden name, Smith) Groeschel. *Education:* Capuchin Theological Seminary, B.A., 1955; Iona Pastoral Counselors Institute, M.S., 1965; Columbia University, Ed.D., 1972.

ADDRESSES: Home and office—Trinity Retreat, 1 Pryer Manor Rd., Larchmont, N.Y. 10538.

CAREER: Entered Order of Friars Minor Capuchin (Capuchin Franciscan Friars), 1951, ordained Roman Catholic priest, 1959; Children's Village, Dobbs Ferry, N.Y., chaplain, 1960-73; Roman Catholic Archdiocese of New York, New York, N.Y., director of spiritual development, 1974—. Associate professor at Iona Pastoral Counselors Institute, 1971—, St. Joseph's Seminary, Dunwoodie, N.Y., 1973—, and Maryknoll School of Theology, 1973—. Director of St. Francis House for Homeless Boys, Brooklyn, N.Y. Postulator of Cause of Beatification of Terence Cardinal Cooke.

MEMBER: American Psychological Association, National Chaplains Association for Youth Rehabilitation (past president), National Association of Catholic Chaplains.

WRITINGS:

God and Us, St. Paul Editions, 1981.
St. Catherine of Genoa, Paulist Press, 1981.
Spiritual Passages: The Psychology of Spiritual Development, Crossroad/Continuum, 1983.
Listening at Prayer, Paulist Press, 1984.

Author of adult education tape series for Paulist Press, Credence Cassettes, and Argus Communications.

WORK IN PROGRESS: "*Thy Will Be Done,*" an official biography of Terence Cardinal Cooke, Archbishop of New York, publication by Paulist Press expected in 1987; *The Psychology of Religious Experience,* Crossroad/Continuum, 1987.

SIDELIGHTS: Benedict J. Groeschel told *CA:* "My principal interest is relating contemporary psychological theory and research to religious experience and spiritual growth. I am also deeply involved in social conerns as the director of a small agency for homeless boys. I usually spend my summer vacation overseas, teaching foreign missionaries, and I have done this on every continent. Another interest is ecumenical relations of various religious denominations, particularly Catholic-Jewish relations.

"I am writing a biography of Cardinal Cooke because I was a close personal adviser and because I am postulator of his cause for sainthood."

*   *   *

GRONBJERG, Kirsten A(ndersen)   1946-

BRIEF ENTRY: Born March 8, 1946, in Sonderborg, Denmark. Sociologist, educator, and author. Gronbjerg began teaching sociology at Loyola University in 1976 and also spent three years on the faculty of State University of New York at Stony Brook. Gronbjerg wrote *Mass Society and the Extension of Welfare, 1960-1970* (University of Chicago Press, 1977) and *Poverty and Social Change* (University of Chicago Press, 1978). *Address:* Department of Sociology, Loyola University, 6525 North Sheridan Rd., Chicago, Ill. 60626.

*   *   *

GRONEWOLD, Sue Ellen
See GRONEWOLD, Susan Ellen

GRONEWOLD, Susan Ellen 1947-
(Sue Ellen Gronewold)

PERSONAL: Born April 18, 1947, in Peoria, Ill.; daughter of Herman Job (a farmer) and Eleanor Jean (in management; maiden name, Canden) Gronewold; married Peter Winn (a Latin American history professor, writer, and film adviser), May, 1976; children: Ethan. *Education:* Attended University of Aix-Marseille, 1967-68; University of Wisconsin—Madison, B.A., 1969, M.A., 1973; Columbia University, Certificate from East Asian Institute, 1980, M.Phil., 1983, doctoral study, 1983—.

ADDRESSES: Home—31 Grozier Rd., Cambridge, Mass. 02138.

CAREER: High school social studies teacher in Madison, Wis., 1972-75, and Princeton Junction, N.J., 1975-77; American Museum of Natural History, New York, N.Y., part-time lecturer on Asia, 1980—; Smith College, Northampton, Mass., professor of Chinese history, 1984-85. Instructor for "China: Imagery of Nature and the Nature of Imagery," a joint project of China Trade Museum and public schools of Hingham, Mass., 1984-86; presents workshops; public speaker. Research director for proposed television miniseries "Women in China," for Carter-Grant Productions.

WRITINGS:

Beautiful Merchandise: Prostitution in China, 1860-1936, Haworth Press, 1982.

Contributor of articles and reviews to history and Asian studies journals.

WORK IN PROGRESS: Women in China; China Trade; an article on state-of-the-art research on women in China for *Trends in History;* an article on Chinese architecture, under name Sue Ellen Gronewold, for *Natural History.*

* * *

GROSSMANN, Reinhardt 1931-

PERSONAL: Born January 10, 1931, in Berlin, Germany; came to the United States in 1955, naturalized citizen, 1963; son of Willy and Margarete Grossmann; married Anne Marcy; children: Marcy, Martin. *Education:* Attended Paedagogische Hochschule, Berlin, West Germany, 1950-54; University of Iowa, Ph.D., 1958.

ADDRESSES: Home—4910 East Ridgewood Dr., Bloomington, Ind. 47401. *Office*—Department of Philosophy, Indiana University—Bloomington, Bloomington, Ind. 47405.

CAREER: University of Illinois at Urbana-Champaign, Urbana, instructor, 1958-61, assistant professor of philosophy, 1961-62; Indiana University—Bloomington, assistant professor, 1962-65, associate professor, 1965-70, professor of philosophy, 1970—.

WRITINGS:

(With E. B. Allaire, May Brodbeck, Herbert Hochberg, and Robert G. Turnbull) *Essays in Ontology,* Nijhoff, 1963.
The Structure of Mind, University of Wisconsin Press, 1965.
Reflections on Frege's Philosophy, Northwestern University Press, 1969.
Ontological Reduction, Indiana University Press, 1973.
Meinong, Routledge & Kegan Paul, 1974.
The Categorical Structure of the World, Indiana University Press, 1983.

Phenomenology and Existentialism: An Introduction, Routledge & Kegan Paul, 1984.

WORK IN PROGRESS: A book, *Perception, Introspection, and Mathematical Knowledge: Three Essays on Knowledge.*

* * *

GROTEN, Dallas 1951-

PERSONAL: Born April 10, 1951, in Albert Lea, Minn.; son of John H. (a contractor) and Viola (a housewife; maiden name, Backlund) Groten; married Caroline Griebel (a registered nurse), December 25, 1981. *Education:* Augsburg College, B.A., 1973.

ADDRESSES: Home—815 Fourth Ave. S.E., Stewartsville, Minn. 55976.

CAREER: Lay minister and youth counselor at Lutheran church in Fort Wayne, Ind., 1974-76; Good Earth Village (American Lutheran Church camp), Spring Valley, Minn., program director, 1977-79; Wykoff Public Schools, Wykoff, Minn., Title I instructor, counselor, and head track coach, 1978—. Writer.

WRITINGS:

Winning Isn't Always First Place (stories for young people), Bethany House, 1983.
What's So Great About Losing? (tentative title), Bethany House, 1985.

SIDELIGHTS: Dallas Groten told *CA:* "For the last fourteen years I have been involved in professional youth work and lay ministry. I have been employed by churches, camps, and schools, wherever I have felt needed, but it is important to note that I have always enjoyed participating in the creative process. This interest became a decision in 1975 when I decided to become a professional writer.

"The road to publication was never easy. In my struggle to be a writer, I read as many of the world's great books as I could, in hope that some of the 'greatness' would rub off on me. I wrote thousands of pages of prose, poetry, and song, relying strongly upon my excellent literary background at Augsburg College. At last, after eight years of work and study, with only a poem and brief magazine article in print, Bethany House released *Winning Isn't Always First Place.*

"Though in the past I had written about many different subjects in both fiction and nonfiction, I could not get a book published until I wrote about my own practical experiences as a track coach. *Winning Isn't Always First Place* is a book of short stories, based upon true events, that string together in a novelistic and thematic unity. Each story sets the stage for a Christian devotional lesson and Bible verse. Questions are included at the end of each chapter for personal dissection. I trust that the vast majority of my future work will be within this format of writing nonfiction in a novelistic manner.

"I am not ashamed to state that I am a Christian. Therefore I look at my writing as a means by which I can share the love of Jesus Christ, but I always attempt to keep the balance between theology and art, sermonizing and telling a story."

* * *

GRUELLE, John (Barton) 1880-1938
(Johnny Gruelle)

BRIEF ENTRY: Professionally known as Johnny Gruelle; born December 24, 1880, in Arcola, Ill.; died of heart disease,

January 9, 1938, in Miami Springs, Fla. American cartoonist, illustrator, and author. Gruelle, who created the popular "Raggedy Ann and Raggedy Andy" children's book series, began his career as a newspaper cartoonist. During the early 1900's he worked on the *Indianapolis Star,* drawing sports cartoons, political cartoons, front-page cartoons, and comics. In 1910 he entered and won first prize in the *New York Herald*'s comic strip contest with his entry "Mr. Twee Deeddle." The prize entitled him to publish a "Mr. Twee Deeddle" comic strip in the *New York Herald* until 1921 and led to syndication of the strip.

While executing his "Mr. Twee Deeddle" cartoons, Gruelle wrote a number of stories based on an old rag doll that his daughter Marcella found in the family attic. The rag doll became the character Raggedy Ann, a doll with a secret life, and the tales, published in 1918 as *Raggedy Ann Stories,* were set in Marcella's nursery. Then, in 1920, Gruelle provided Raggedy Ann with a little brother, Raggedy Andy, in the book *Raggedy Andy Stories: Introducing the Little Rag Brother of Raggedy Ann.* These first books inaugurated the series of more than forty Raggedy Ann and Andy books, including *Raggedy Ann and Andy and the Camel With the Wrinkled Knees* (1924) and *Raggedy Ann's Wishing Pebble* (1925), that Gruell wrote and illustrated himself, as well as numerous works based on the characters but written by others after Gruelle's death. In addition to the Raggedy Ann and Andy series, Gruelle wrote and illustrated fifteen more children's books, including *Beloved Belindy* (1926) and *The Paper Dragon* (1926). He also wrote and illustrated stories for periodicals, such as *Judge, Life, College Humor, Woman's World,* and *Good Housekeeping.*

BIOGRAPHICAL/CRITICAL SOURCES:

BOOKS

American Authors and Books: 1640 to the Present Day, 3rd revised edition, Crown, 1962.
The ASCAP Biographical Dictionary of Composers, Authors, and Publishers, 3rd edition, American Society of Composers, Authors, and Publishers, 1966.
Banta, Ricahrd E., *Indiana Authors and Their Books, 1816-1916,* Wabash College Press, 1949.
Dictionary of Literary Biography, Volume 22: *American Writers for Children, 1900-1960,* Gale, 1983.

* * *

GRUELLE, Johnny
See GRUELLE, John (Barton)

* * *

GRUNDLEHNER, Philip 1945-

PERSONAL: Born July 24, 1945, in New York, N.Y.; married Nora Winay (an attorney), June 3, 1972; children: Eric Paul. *Education:* University of Pennsylvania, B.A., 1967; Tufts University, M.A., 1968; Ohio State University, Ph.D., 1972.

ADDRESSES: Office—Department of German, Johns Hopkins University, Baltimore, Md. 21218.

CAREER: Middlebury College, Middlebury, Vt., assistant professor of German, 1971-72; University of Illinois at Urbana-Champaign, Urbana, assistant professor of German, 1972-78; Johns Hopkins University, Baltimore, Md., assistant professor of German, 1978—.

MEMBER: Modern Language Association of America, American Association of Teachers of German.

WRITINGS:

The Lyrical Bridge: Essays From Holderlin to Benn, Fairleigh Dickinson University Press, 1978.
Sprich Deutsch (title means "Speak German"), Holt, 1979, 2nd edition, 1983.
Points de Vue, Holt, 1981.
Que Pasa (title means "What's Happening?"), Holt, 1984.
The Poetry of Friedrich Nietzsche, Oxford University Press, 1985.

Contributor to language journals.

WORK IN PROGRESS: Nietzsche's "Zarathustra": A Commentary.

SIDELIGHTS: Philip Grundlehner told *CA:* "My principal innovation has been the integration of modern culture into foreign language texts. I have accomplished this by the use of my own photographs of everyday situations and scenes from the respective cultures. Otherwise, I use the 'realia' from newspapers, phone books, train schedules, magazines, etc.

"The book on the poetry of Friedrich Nietzsche was prompted by a desire to examine a part of Nietzsche's production that was unique yet had never been evaluated before. His poems are part of every German poetry anthology, yet surprisingly little has been done to elucidate his poems."

* * *

GRUNWALD, Joseph 1920-

PERSONAL: Born June 25, 1920, in Vienna, Austria; immigrated to United States, 1938, naturalized citizen, 1943; son of Arthur and Marie (Laub) Grunwald; married June 2, 1949; children: Peter, Kenneth, Timothy. *Education:* Johns Hopkins University, B.S., 1943; Columbia University, Ph.D., 1950.

ADDRESSES: Office—Institute of the Americas, 10111 North Torrey Pines Rd., La Jolla, Calif. 92037.

CAREER: Factory worker, 1938-40; Comfy Manufacturing Co., Baltimore, Md., personnel manager, 1940-43; Rutgers University, New Brunswick, N.J., lecturer in economics, 1946-47; Adelphi College (now University), Garden City, N.Y., assistant professor of economics, 1947-50; Puerto Rico Planning Board, San Juan, acting director of Economic Division and economic adviser to governor, 1950-52; City College (now of the City University of New York), New York, N.Y., assistant professor of economics, 1952-54; University of Chile, Santiago, professor of economics and organizer and director of Institute of Economic Research and Graduate School of Economics, 1954-61; Yale University, New Haven, Conn., professor of economics, 1961-63; Brookings Institution, Washington, D.C., senior fellow in foreign policy studies and general coordinator of Program on Joint Studies on Latin American Economic Integration (ECIEL), 1963—, member of board of directors of Brazil program in Rio de Janeiro, 1979—. Lecturer at Columbia University, 1946-47, and Johns Hopkins School of Advanced International Studies, 1963-73; professorial lecturer at Georgetown University, 1974-76; adjunct professor at George Washington University, 1972—. Deputy assistant secretary for economic policy of U.S. Department of State's Bureau of Inter-American Affairs, 1976-77. Member of board of directors of Chilean-North American Cultural Institute, Santiago, 1956-61; Social Science Research Council and American Council of Learned Societies, chairman of Joint Committee on Latin American Studies, 1962-73, chairman of Subcommittee on Economic History, 1968-81; member of advisory board of Library of Congress Hispanic Foundation Studies, 1965-78; coordinator and member of committees of experts of Alliance for Progress, 1963-68; chairman of National Academy of Sciences Brazil-U.S. Study Group on Transportation Research, 1970; Council on the International Exchange of Scholars, chairman of Latin American Advisory Committee, 1971-74, member of executive committee, 1971-73; member of international editorial committee of "Latin American International Affairs Series," Center for Inter-American Relations, 1975-81; member of international advisory committee of Corporacion de Investigaciones para el Desarrollo, Santiago, 1976—; consultant to Twentieth Century Fund, Ford Foundation, and Carnegie Endowment for International Peace. *Military service:* U.S. Army, with Combat Engineers, Psychological Warfare Division, and Military Government, 1943-45; served in Europe.

MEMBER: Latin American Studies Association (member of executive council, 1967-69; vice-president, 1975; president, 1976).

AWARDS, HONORS: Senior fellow of Rockefeller Foundation, 1960-61; named academic member of University of Chile, 1964; commander of Chile's Order of Bernardo O'Higgins, 1969.

WRITINGS:

National Economic Budgeting in Norway, Columbia University Press, 1950.
(With Britton Harris, Alexander Ganz, and Harvey Perloff) *Economic Development of Puerto Rico, 1940-1950, 1951-1960,* Puerto Rican Government Printing Office, 1951.
(With Kenneth Flamm) *The Global Factor,* Brookings Institution, 1955.
(With others) *Desarrollo economico de Chile, 1940-1956* (title means "The Economic Development of Chile, 1940-1956"), University of Chile, 1956.
(With Donald Baerresen and Martin Carnoy) *Latin American Trade Patterns,* Brookings Institution, 1965.
(With Philip Musgrove) *Natural Resources and the Economic Development of Latin America,* Johns Hopkins University Press, 1970.
(With Carnoy and Miguel Wionczek) *Latin American Economic Integration and U.S. Policy,* Brookings Institution, 1972.
(Editor and contributor) *Latin America and World Economy: A Changing International Order,* Sage Publications, 1978.
(With Howard J. Wiarda and Mark Falcoff) *The Crisis in Latin America and in U.S.-Latin American Relations,* American Enterprise Institute for Public Policy Research, 1984.

CONTRIBUTOR

Albert O. Hirschman, editor, *Latin American Issues: Essays and Comments,* Twentieth Century Fund, 1961.
Changing Roles and Patterns in Higher Education, University of Arizona Press, 1962.
Marion Clawson, editor, *Natural Resources and International Development,* Johns Hopkins University Press, 1964.
Werner Baer and Isaac Kerstenetzsky, editors, *Inflation and Growth in Latin America,* Irwin, 1964.
Training and Research in Development, Organization for Economic Cooperation and Development, 1966.

Alberto Martinez Piedra, editor, *Socio-Economic Change in Latin America,* Catholic University of America Press, 1970.
D. J. Daly, editor, *International Comparisons of Prices and Output,* Columbia University Press, 1972.
Stephen E. Guisinger, editor, *Trade and Investment Policies in the Americas,* Southern Methodist University Press, 1973.
D. T. Geitham, editor, *Fiscal Policy for Industrialization and Development in Latin America,* University of Florida Press, 1975.
Roger W. Fontaine and James D. Theberge, editors, *Latin America's New Internationalism: The End of the Hemispheric Isolation,* Praeger, 1976.
Robert Ferber, editor, *Consumption and Income Distribution in Latin America,* Organization of American States, 1980.
Charles Foster and Albert Valdman, editors, *Haitian Dilemmas,* Duke University Press, 1984.
Jose Nunez del Arco, Eduardo Margain, and Rochelle Cherol, editors, *Current Issues in Latin American Economic Integration,* Inter-American Development Bank, 1984.
Lay James Gibson, editor, *Regional Impacts of United States-Mexico Economic Relations,* University of Arizona Press, 1985.

OTHER

Contributor to *Dictionary of American History.* Contributor of about a dozen articles to political science and international studies journals in English and Spanish. Regional editor of *Columbia Journal of World Business,* 1965; member of editorial board of *Latin American Research Review,* 1976-80.

SIDELIGHTS: Joseph Grunwald told *CA:* "Lack of understanding, if not misunderstanding, is at the root of poor relations among peoples. I write in a modest attempt to improve communications between the North and South in this hemisphere.

*   *   *

GUCHES, Richard (Clement) 1938-

PERSONAL: Surname rhymes with "duchess"; born July 2, 1938, in Medford, Ore.; son of Chester Walter (a county treasurer) and Janet (a community health care activist; maiden name, Clement) Guches; married Judith Lobdell, July 6, 1961 (divorced October 1, 1980); married Candace Denise Cave (a writer), December 21, 1983; children: Patti Lynn Slattery, Jennifer Christie, Sean Richard. *Education:* University of Oregon, B.S., 1961, M.S., 1964; Nova University, Ed.D., 1977. *Religion:* None.

ADDRESSES: Home—4548 Auburn Blvd., No. 104, Sacramento, Calif. 95841. *Office*—Department of English, American River College, 4700 College Oak Dr., Sacramento, Calif. 95841.

CAREER: High school English teacher and department chairman in Rio Linda, Calif., 1964-70; American River College, Sacramento, Calif., professor of English, 1970—. *Military service:* U.S. Army, 1961-63.

MEMBER: California Writers Club, Point San Pablo Yacht Club.

WRITINGS:

(With Robert Frew and Robert E. Mehaffy) *Writer's Workshop,* Peek Publications, 1972, 3rd edition, 1984.

(With Frew and Mehaffy) *Survival,* Peek Publications, 1975, 2nd edition, 1985.
Sequel, Peek Publications, 1979.
(With Frew and Mehaffy) *A Writer's Guidebook,* Peek Publications, 1982.

WORK IN PROGRESS: Revising *Sequel;* studying South Pacific culture; right brain research.

SIDELIGHTS: Richard Guches told *CA:* "My books are concerned with the craft of academic writing, literary study, and critical thinking. My magazine writing consists of nonfiction pieces about sailing—how to, cruising, and exotic destinations. Somewhere between these two writing interests rest my future efforts.

"I spent a five month's sabbatical visiting schools in the South Pacific during 1978 and I cruised my own boat through French Polynesia for nearly a year in 1983. These experiences have led to a fascination with island culture, especially that of the Marquesas group, and an interest in the cultural and mythic origin of these people. While in this group, we (the crew consisted of my wife and son) explored the island of Fatu Hiva, where Thor Heyerdahl spent a year living and about which he wrote in his book *Fatu Hiva.* Later, on the island of Nuka Hiva, we anchored in the bay and explored the Tai Pi valley, which was the setting of Herman Melville's first novel, *Typee.*

"From these experiences and interest, I hope to publish more nonfiction and photography. Also, I plan to attempt some fiction, related to this and to my interest in right brain thinking. This latter may well be a collaborative effort with my wife, Candace Cave."

AVOCATIONAL INTERESTS: Sailing (especially to the South Pacific), photography, scuba diving.

* * *

GUDENIAN, Haig (Krikor) 1918-1985(?)

OBITUARY NOTICE: Born April 16, 1918, in Kensington, London, England; died c. 1985. Publisher, association executive, and journalist. Gudenian, who began his career as a journalist, worked first for Odhams Press and then for a number of British periodicals; he served *John Bull* as chief subeditor and assistant editor from 1946 to 1952, *Illustrated* as assistant editor and associate editor from 1952 to 1955, and *Ideal Home* as editor from 1957 to 1964. In 1966 Gudenian became co-founder of the publishing company Gudenian, Rockall & Mayer. He subsequently joined Stonehart Publications and was founding edtior of "Tax and Insurance Letter" and the successful *Running* magazine. In addition, Gudenian was noted for creating and designing various other British publications. He also officiated as chairman of the Muscular Dystrophy Group of Great Britian and Ireland for twenty-four years and in 1980 was appointed officer of the British Empire in honor of his contributions to public life and the Muscular Dystrophy Group.

OBITUARIES AND OTHER SOURCES:

BOOKS

International Authors and Writers Who's Who, 7th edition, Melrose, 1976.
Who's Who, 136th edition, St. Martin's, 1984.

PERIODICALS

Times (London), February 22, 1985.

* * *

GUNN, Mrs. Aneas 1870-1961

OBITUARY NOTICE: Author. Gunn is known for *Little Black Princess* and *We of the Never-Never,* works which depict life in the Australian outback in the early 1900's.

OBITUARIES AND OTHER SOURCES:

BOOKS

Twentieth-Century Writing: A Reader's Guide to Contemporary Literature, Transatlantic, 1971.

PERIODICALS

Washington Post Book World, August 26, 1984.

H

HADLEY CHASE, James
See RAYMOND, Rene (Brabazon)

* * *

HALLGREN, Chris 1947-

PERSONAL: Born July 17, 1947, in DeKalb, Ill.; son of Kenneth (a lumber dealer) and Carol Hallgren; married Linda Morris, June 31, 1967 (divorced); married Patricia Graw, November 31, 1978; children: Max, Casey, Janine. *Education:* University of Illinois, B.A., 1969.

ADDRESSES: Home—7 George St. S., Toronto, Ontario, Canada M5A 4B1. *Office*—Honeywell, Inc., 515 Consumers Road, Willowdale, Ontario, Canada.

CAREER: Hall Community Centre, Toronto, Ontario, social worker, 1969-74; Construction Workers Union, Vancouver, British Columbia, laborer, 1974-76; full-time playwright in Toronto, 1976-80; Sears, Toronto, technical writer, 1980-84; Honeywell, Inc., Willowdale, Ontario, technical writer, 1984—. Director of Woodsworth Co-operative, 1978-79.

AWARDS, HONORS: Grant from Canada Council, 1978, for "The Assassination of D'Arcy McGee"; grant from Ontario Arts Council, 1978, for "Yellow House at Arles"; second place award from Theatre Ontario, 1979, for "Tomte of Hurds Lake."

WRITINGS:

Tangled Passage (poems), Coach House Press, 1973.

PLAYS

"So Inside, No Closer" (five-act), first produced in Toronto, 1976.
Westroy Hotel (two-act; first produced in Toronto at Open Circle Theatre, 1976), Playwrights Canada, 1978.
"Tomte of Hurds Lake" (two-act), first produced in Toronto at Theatre Ontario Showcase, 1979.
(With Dennis Hayes and Richard Payne) "Yellow House at Arles" (two-act), first produced in Toronto at Tarragon Theatre, 1983.

Editor of *The Forum,* 1973—, and *Mayday Arts Magazine,* 1975-76. Contributor of theatre criticism to periodicals, including *Scene Changes, Toronto Theatre Review,* and *Toronto Clarion.*

WORK IN PROGRESS: "Another Irish Martyr: The Tragedy of D'Arcy McGee," a play about terrorism and democracy; "Labyrinth Monrings, Prison Afternoons," a "retelling of a portion of the tragedy of the house of Atreus"; "Looser Take All," a play about "male burnout on women and success"; "Dr. Lenin Debates Jack Kautsky on the Decay of the Capitalist State," a play about "the absurd debate between capitalism and socialism"; preparing stage directions for "So Inside, No Closer"; "Last Trick," a play about "women in the vortex of self-destructive narcissism."

SIDELIGHTS: Chris Hallgren told *CA:* "I have always loved language. The word defines culture. It solidifies all other images in a context, and yet remains fluid. English especially spits out its verbs and drapes its adjectives over a brittle and passionate world view. Its coldness conceals a fire.

"My motivation for writing plays and poems is to affect ordinary perception by revealing its extraordinary dimensions. We are a house of fragments that carry on a conversation all the time, and yet we hear only the unidimensional voice that tells us the time of day and other banalities. The quotidian needs a recharge.

"I began writing plays at eight. I started acting at age twelve. People said I was a very good actor. I loved doing it. But I left it because of the heady political atmosphere of the late 1960's. From the United States antiwar movement I immigrated to the Canadian draft evasion network, even though my local board gave me conscientious objector status. My disrespect for the United States had grown to a sort of loathing, and I had to get away.

"In Canada I helped to found a very offbeat community centre. We had life drawing, ballet, job counseling, drug counseling. We did some amazing things. One year we built a tent city for transients on the University of Toronto campus. The cops cleared us out at three o'clock one morning. I didn't feel much like writing plays at the time, but only because too much was happening too fast.

"My play 'So Inside, No Closer' was an attempt to create a sound/dance poetic allegory of the communal living experience I went through for three years during that period. Everything was subliminal and ambiguous. Everyone was willing to be intimate, but minds do not overlap so neatly. 'So Inside, No Closer' was stunning. The audience could not speak for five minutes after it ended. It drove the three actresses in it crazy.

"'Westroy Hotel' came about as a practical joke. Open Circle Theatre advertised for a topical play on Quebec after the election of a separatist government. I wanted to do a play in a men's lavatory in a Montreal bar, using the graffiti to show the political transition. To this I added the idea that I would use Comedia Delle Arte Quebec stereotypes (sagacious cleaning lady; mouthy Italian bartender; corrupt official; innocent, idealistic niece; dissatisfied Quebecois taxi driver; antiseparatist political hotshot; and a Montreal English banker), make it into a farce with all the usual absurd subplots (niece of corrupt official falls in love with the radical youth, hotshot politician ends up giving a separatist speech, bathroom antics loosen the banker's financial backing), and make it into a musical as well.

"Every audience I sat in laughed their heads off. The reviewers hated it. Montreal people asked me if I had lived in Montreal (I hadn't) and told me not to use such cliched stereotypes (they've never appeared in any literature to my knowledge). I guess the moral is that English people cannot write French comedies that are liked by either group.

"'Tomte of Hurds Lake' is a personal play. The title refers to a Norwegian folk character who is sort of like an elf. Tomte governs domestic environments, determines their level of tranquility or chaos, establishes whether socks are in surplus or do not match, etc. The lead character is a combination of my Swedish grandfather, Thure, and a man named Klute who lived on Hurd's Lake near Renfrew, Ontario, during a summer that I lived in the country. It is the closest to a traditional, Ibsen-like drama I have ever written.

"I have been on a hiatus from the theatre for three years. The amount of neurotic trivia had grown too large for one mind. Projects were started and abandoned half finished. The need to make money and get productions overcame the need to be clear and excellent. Also, I love my family dearly. It was time to establish myself in a career to sustain me and them over the long term (an amateur writer can afford to be very picky). So I have learned the world of computers well enough to be a systems analyst/technical writer for a large data-processing shop. The side of the brain I lived from switched to the linear dimension for the shock period, but images are coming back to the creative half. Learning about systems and clear, economical writing have contributed a great deal to my skills, as well."

*   *   *

HALPERN, Ben(jamin)   1912-

BRIEF ENTRY: Born April 10, 1912, in Boston, Mass. American sociologist, historian, and author. Halpern, who became managing editor of *Jewish Frontier* in 1943, left that position in 1949 to serve as director of the education and culture program of New York City's Jewish Agency. He later became a professor of Near Eastern studies at Brandeis University, where he taught from 1961 until his retirement in 1980. Halpern was a Guggenheim fellow in 1961 and a senior fellow of the National Endowment for the Humanities in 1970. Known as a historical sociologist, Halpern wrote *The American Jew: A Zionist Analysis* (Theodor Herzl Foundation, 1956), *The Idea*

of the Jewish State (Harvard University Press, 1961), *The Jewish National Home in Palestine* (Ktav, 1970), and *Jews and Blacks: The Classic American Minorities* Herder, 1971). He also co-edited *The Responsible Attitude: Life and Opinions of Giora Josephthal* (Schocken, 1967). *Address:* 187 Mason Ter., Brookline, Mass. 02146.

BIOGRAPHICAL/CRITICAL SOURCES:

PERIODICALS

Time, October 24, 1969.

*   *   *

HAMBLIN, Douglas H.   1923-

PERSONAL: Born September 23, 1923, in Wincanton, England; son of Daniel and Elizabeth Ann (Stone) Hamblin.

ADDRESSES: Home—29 Waterloo Pl., Brymill, Swansea SA2 0DE, Wales.

CAREER: Worked as senior lecturer in education at the University of Wales, University College of Swansea; became an independent lecturer and consultant.

WRITINGS:

The Teacher and Counselling, Basil Blackwell, 1974.
The Teacher and Pastoral Care, Basil Blackwell, 1978.
Teaching Study Skills, Basil Blackwell, 1981.
(Editor and contributor) *Problems and Practice of Pastoral Care,* Basil Blackwell, 1981.
Guidance: Sixteen to Nineteen, Basil Blackwell, 1983.
Pastoral Care: A Training Manual, Basil Blackwell, 1984.
Problems and Practice of Pastoral Care, Basil Blackwell, 1981.
The Pastoral Curriculum, Basil Blackwell, 1985.

Contributor to journals. Co-editor of *British Journal of Guidance and Counselling,* 1973-82.

*   *   *

HAMILTON, (John) Alan   1943-

PERSONAL: Born April 22, 1943, in Edinburgh, Scotland. *Education:* Attended University of Edinburgh, 1961-66.

ADDRESSES: Office—*Times,* 200 Gray's Inn Rd., London WC1X 8E2, England.

CAREER: Reporter and correspondent for the London *Times* newspaper. Radio broadcaster for British Broadcasting Corp.

WRITINGS:

Essential Edinburgh, Deutsch, 1978.
Queen Elizabeth II, Hamish Hamilton, 1982.
Paul McCartney, Hamish Hamilton, 1982.
The Queen Mother, Hamish Hamilton, 1983.
(With W. S. Lacey) *Britain's National Parks,* Windward, 1984.
The First One Hundred People in Line of Succession to the Throne of Britain, M. Joseph, 1985.

*   *   *

HAMILTON, Nancy   1908-1985

OBITUARY NOTICE: Born July 27, 1908, in Sewickley, Pa.; died following a long illness, February 18, 1985, in New York, N.Y. Actress, lyricist, radio and film scriptwriter, and playwright. Known as one of the first women to succeed as a lyricist, Hamilton was also author of an award-winning documentary on the life of Helen Keller, and she wrote the sketches and lyrics for several successful Broadway revues. She made her Broadway acting debut in the 1934 show "New Faces," which she also co-authored. As a songwriter Hamilton wrote the lyrics for the Broadway hits "One for the Money," "Two for the Show," and "Three to Make Ready" as well as the songs "I Hate Spring," "The Old Soft Shoe," and "How High the Moon." In 1956 the writer received an Academy Award for her documentary film "Helen Keller in Her Story." In addition, Hamilton wrote the scripts for several of the Columbia Broadcasting System's radio programs, including Billie Burke's "Fashions in Rations."

OBITUARIES AND OTHER SOURCES:

BOOKS

The Biographical Encyclopaedia and Who's Who of the American Theatre, James Heineman, 1966.
Encyclopaedia of the Musical Theatre, Dodd, 1976.
Notable Names in the American Theatre, James T. White, 1976.

PERIODICALS

New York Times, February 19, 1985.

*   *   *

HAMM, Edward Frederick, Jr.   1908-1985

OBITUARY NOTICE: Born March 27, 1908, in Chicago, Ill.; died of cancer March 19, 1985, in Washington, D. C. Business executive, government official, and publisher. Hamm, who specialized in various aspects of traffic management and control, was founder of American Society of Traffic and Transportation and an officer of the Associated Traffic Clubs Foundations. In addition, he served as director of the Interstate Commerce Commission and council member of the U.S. Department of Commerce. Hamm was president of the Washington, D. C., publishing firm Traffic Service Corporation for fifty-two years. As such he published the journals *Traffic World, Traffic Bulletin,* and *Daily Traffic World.* During World War II, he acted as consultant to the printing and publishing division of the War Production Board.

OBITUARIES AND OTHER SOURCES:

BOOKS

Who's Who in America, 43rd edition, Marquis, 1984.

PERIODICALS

Washington Post, March 22, 1985.

*   *   *

HAMMACK, David C(onrad)   1941-

PERSONAL: Born May 22, 1941, in Coulee Dam, Wash.; son of Charles W. (a civil engineer) and Dorothy (a children's librarian; maiden name, Morgan) Hammack; married Loraine Shils, May 6, 1966; children: Peter Samuel, Elizabeth Rose. *Education:* Harvard University, B.A., 1963; Reed College, M.A.T., 1964; Columbia University, Ph.D., 1973.

ADDRESSES: Office—Department of History, Case Western Reserve University, Cleveland, Ohio 44106.

CAREER: High school social studies teacher in Newton, Mass., 1964-67; Herbert H. Lehman College of the City University

of New York, Bronx, N.Y., instructor, 1972-73, assistant professor of history, 1973-74; Princeton University, Princeton, N.J., assistant professor of U.S. history, 1974-81; University of Houston, Houston, Tex., associate professor of history, 1982-84; Case Western Reserve University, Cleveland, Ohio associate professor of history, 1984—. Associate member of National Humanities Faculty, 1976—; resident scholar at Russell Sage Foundation, 1980-82.

MEMBER: American Historical Association, Organization of American Historians, Social Science Historical Association.

WRITINGS:

(Contributor) Stuart Bruchey, editor, *Small Business in American Life,* Columbia University Press, 1980.
Power and Society: Greater New York at the Turn of the Century, Russell Sage Foundation, 1982.

Contributor to history journals.

WORK IN PROGRESS: The Fiscal Crises of New York City: 1914, 1933, 1975; a contribution to *Social Research in New York City: The Russell Sage Foundation.*

SIDELIGHTS: David C. Hammack told *CA:* "My Oregon family encouraged me to explore the world. An extraordinary high school teacher stimulated my interest in New York City when he told me to read *The Autobiography of Lincoln Steffens,* a book that describes another westerner's encounter with New York. Years later, I wrote *Power and Society.*

"For the future I am torn between the fascinating but unexplored world of the Germans in nineteenth-century U.S. cities and the challenge of sorting out the relationship between society and power in nineteenth-century London and Berlin. Perhaps, however, my next work will leave aside the writing of history for its intrinsic interest and seek instead to find whether history can be made useful in the solution of present problems."

*   *   *

HAMRICK, Samuel J., Jr.   1929-
(W. T. Tyler)

BRIEF ENTRY: Born October 19, 1929, in Texas. American diplomat and author. Hamrick, whose novels are published under the pseudonym of W. T. Tyler, is a twenty-year veteran of the U.S. Foreign Service. After retiring from the State Department in 1980, he moved to a farm in Facquier County, Virginia, to devote himself to writing. The Tyler pseudonym, he said, was taken from Wat Tyler, the leader of a fourteenth-century peasant revolt in England. Tyler's four critically and commercially successful novels of foreign intrigue recall the author's diplomatic experience and his knowledge of such countries as Lebanon, Ethiopia, Zaire, and Somalia.

Widely praised for its authenticity, detailed characterizations, and skillful handling of dialogue, Tyler's first novel, *The Man Who Lost the War* (Dial, 1980), is a spy story set in Germany at the height of the Berlin Wall crisis. It chronicles the friendship between a disillusioned ex-CIA agent and a Soviet agent. A later book, *The Shadow Cabinet* (Harper, 1984), is a fictionalized account set in the first year of President Ronald Reagan's administration. According to a *Washington Post Book World* reviewer, Tyler's depiction is "deadly accurate," written as if a rock has been "lifted to reveal the whole crawling nether world of Washington." Additional works by Tyler include *The Ants of God* (Dial, 1981) and *Rogue's March* (Harper, 1982). *Address:* Facquier County, Va.

BIOGRAPHICAL/CRITICAL SOURCES:

PERIODICALS

Los Angeles Times Book Review, March 26, 1981, February 5, 1984.
Newsweek, March 3, 1980.
New York Times Book Review, March 15, 1981, March 11, 1984.
Times Literary Supplement, March 6, 1981.
Virginia Quarterly Review, spring, 1983, summer, 1984.
Washington Post Book World, March 6, 1981, October 6, 1982, January 29, 1984.

* * *

HANNUM, Alberta Pierson 1906-1985

OBITUARY NOTICE—See index for *CA* sketch: Born August 3, 1906, in Condit, Ohio; died in February, 1985. Author. Hannum wrote a number of books, including *The Hills Step Lightly, The Mountain People, Paint the Wind,* and *Look Back With Love: A Recollection of the Blue Ridge.* She also adapted two of her books for other media, writing the radio play for *Spin a Silver Dollar: The Story of a Desert Trading Post* and the screenplay for *Roseanna McCoy.*

OBITUARIES AND OTHER SOURCES:

PERIODICALS

Wheeling News-Register, March 3, 1985.

* * *

HANSEL, C(harles) E(dward) M(ark) 1917-

BRIEF ENTRY: Born October 11, 1917, in Bedford, England. British psychologist, educator, and author. Hansel has been a lecturer in psychology at Victoria University of Manchester since 1949. His research has led him into the area of parapsychology, particularly extra-sensory perception. He is the author of *ESP: A Scientific Evaluation* (Scribner, 1966). A new edition of the volume was published in 1980 under the title *ESP and Parapsychology: A Critical Reevaluation* (Prometheus). *Address:* Department of Psychology, Victoria University of Manchester, Manchester, England.

BIOGRAPHICAL/CRITICAL SOURCES:

BOOKS

Biographical Dictionary of Parapsychology, With Directory and Glossary: 1964-1966, Garret Publications, 1964.
Encyclopedia of Occultism and Parapsychology, 2nd edition, Gale, 1984.

* * *

HARFORD, Henry
See HUDSON, W(illiam) H(enry)

* * *

HARRAH, Michael 1940-

PERSONAL: Born February 19, 1940, in Marion, Ind.; son of Walter S. (a carpenter) and Mary (Bailey) Harrah; married Wendy Watson (a book illustrator), December 19, 1970 (di-

vorced, 1981); children: Mary Cameron, James. *Education:* University of Toledo, B.A., 1958, M.A., 1977.

ADDRESSES: Home—3157 Glanzman, Toledo, Ohio 43614. *Agent*—Marilyn Marlow, Curtis Brown Ltd., 575 Madison Ave., New York, N.Y. 10022.

CAREER: Worked as high school writing teacher, 1962-64; professional actor and singer, including ensemble work with New York City Opera and principal roles with regional companies, 1967-72; Lucas County Juvenile Court, Toledo, Ohio, counselor, 1977-83; WGTE-Radio, Toledo, producer-host, programmer, and announcer for classical music, 1984—.

WRITINGS:

First Offender (young adult novel), Collins, 1980.

WORK IN PROGRESS: Dreamspinner, a novel; a detective novel; a novel about a nineteenth-century rogue; a contemporary novel.

SIDELIGHTS: Michael Harrah told *CA:* "*First Offender* is a young adult novel about a boy who is wrongly accused of a crime, his reaction to a detention center, and how the mess is resolved. Motivation for writing the book came from my experience in juvenile court and from the desire to tell a story that would appeal to the sense of isolation many adolescents experience. Other ideas came from various experiences I have either had or witnessed, or just from an interesting supposition.

"I have traveled mostly in the southwest United States, where my parents lived before their deaths, and I lived for several years in New York City. I see a unity in writing, acting, and singing in that all share the purpose of telling a story."

* * *

HARRIS, Barbara J. 1942-

PERSONAL: Born August 12, 1942, in Newark, N.J.; daughter of Samuel M. and Sadie Z. Rous; married Joel B. Harris, 1965 (divorced, 1985); children: Clifford S. *Education:* Vassar College, A.B. (summa cum laude), 1963; Harvard University, A.M., 1964, Ph.D., 1968.

ADDRESSES: Home—19 Grace Court, Apt. 6B, Brooklyn, N.Y. 11201. *Office*—Department of History, Pace University—New York, Pace Plaza, New York, N.Y. 10038.

CAREER: Pace University—New York, Brooklyn, N.Y., assistant professor, 1968-74, associate professor, 1974-78, professor of history, 1978—. Visiting professor at Vassar College, 1979-81; member of executive committee of Columbia University Seminar on Women and Society, 1984—; member of Family History Research Group of Institute for Research for History, New York, N.Y.

MEMBER: North American Conference on British Studies, American Historical Association, Berkshire Conference of Women Historians, Coordinating Committee of Women in the Historical Profession, Middle Atlantic Conference on British Studies, Phi Beta Kappa.

AWARDS, HONORS: Woodrow Wilson fellow, 1963-64, 1966-67; junior fellow of National Endowment for the Humanities, 1976.

WRITINGS:

(Contributor) R. H. Hilton, editor, *Peasants, Knights, and Heretics,* Cambridge University Press, 1977.

Beyond Her Sphere: Women and the Professions in American History, Greenwood Press, 1978.
(Editor with Alan Roland) *Career and Motherhood: Struggles for a New Identity,* Human Sciences, 1978.
(Editor with Jo Ann McNamara) *Women and the Social Order: Selected Research From the Fifth Berkshire Conference on the History of Women,* Duke University Press, 1984.
(Contributor) Miriam Lewin, editor, *In the Shadow of the Past: Psychology Portrays the Sexes,* Columbia University Press, 1984.

Contributor of articles and reviews to historical journals. Member of editorial board of *Journal of Social History,* 1984—.

WORK IN PROGRESS: A monograph on Edward Stafford, Third Duke of Buckingham, 1477-1521, publication by Stanford University Press expected in 1986; research for a book on upper-class women in Yorkist and early Tudor England.

* * *

HARRIS, Joseph Pratt   1896-1985

OBITUARY NOTICE—See index for *CA* sketch: Born February 18, 1896, in Candor (one source says Sulphur Springs), N.C.; died February 13, 1985, in Berkeley, Calif. Political scientist, educator, inventor, and author. A professor of political science for more than twenty-five years, Harris is best remembered as inventor of the automatic voting machine that bears his name, the Harris Votamatic. The device, one of the first to be used in the United States, uses a punch-card system of balloting that allows votes to be tallied by computers rather than by hand. The machine was patented in 1962, first used in 1968, and, in a modified form, is still in use in the 1980's. Harris was also a consulting editor of the McGraw-Hill political science series from 1940 to 1964 and wrote several books, including *Registration of Voters in the United States, Election Administration in the United States, County Finances in the State of Washington, Advice and Consent: A Study of Confirmation of Appointment, Public Administration in Modern Society,* and *Congressional Control of Administration.*

OBITUARIES AND OTHER SOURCES:

BOOKS

Who's Who in America, 39th edition, Marquis, 1976.

PERIODICALS

Los Angeles Times, February 17, 1985.

* * *

HARRIS, Richard J(ohn)   1948-

PERSONAL: Born April 5, 1948, in Belgrade, Minn.; son of Johnny Lee (a laborer) and Marjorie (a housewife; maiden name, Meyers) Harris; married Carolyn Besser (an instructor in accounting), June 26, 1970; children: Karl, Mark. *Education:* Macalester College, B.A., 1971; Cornell University, M.A., 1974, Ph.D., 1976.

ADDRESSES: Home—6819 Forest Haven, San Antonio, Tex. 78240. *Office*—Division of Social and Policy Sciences, University of Texas at San Antonio, San Antonio, Tex. 78285.

CAREER: University of Texas at San Antonio, assistant professor, 1976-84, associate professor of social and policy sciences, 1984—. Conducted field research in La Paz, Bolivia, summer, 1969; member of Southern Regional Demographic

Group, 1977—; member of economic analysis panel of Greater San Antonio Chamber of Commerce, 1979-80. *Military service:* U.S. Air Force Reserve, 1969-73; became staff sergeant.

MEMBER: American Sociological Association, Population Association of America, American Academy of Political and Social Science, Southwestern Social Science Association, Southern Sociology Association.

AWARDS, HONORS: Dewitt Wallace Grant from Minnesota Student Project for Amity Among Nations (S.P.A.N.) Association, for research in Bolivia, 1969; fellow of Population Research Laboratory and Ethel Percy Andrus Gerontology Center at University of Southern California, 1980-82; grant from Trull Foundation, 1982.

WRITINGS:

(Editor with J. A. Booth and D. R. Johnson, and contributor) *The Politics of San Antonio: Community Progress and Power,* University of Nebraska Press, 1983.
(Contributor) Glen Elder, Jr., editor, *Life Course Dynamics: From 1968 to the 1980's,* Cornell University Press, 1984.
(Contributor) R. C. Jones, editor, *Graphic Perspectives on Undocumented Migration: Mexico and the U.S.,* Rowman & Allanheld, 1984.

Contributor of articles and reviews to professional journals. Member of editorial board of *Sociology and Social Research,* 1981-82.

WORK IN PROGRESS: Research on the demographic aspects of aging in the United States; research on income distribution and inequality.

* * *

HARRIS, Trudier   1948-

PERSONAL: Born February 27, 1948, in Mantua, Alabama; daughter of Terrell and Unareed (Burton) Harris. *Education:* Stillman College, A.B., 1969; Ohio State University, M.A., 1972, Ph.D., 1973.

ADDRESSES: Home—716 Tinkerbell Rd., Chapel Hill, N.C. 27514. *Office*—534 Greenlaw 066A, University of North Carolina, Chapel Hill, N.C. 27514.

CAREER: College of William and Mary, Williamsburg, Va., assistant professor of English, 1973-79; University of North Carolina, Chapel Hill, associate professor of English and black American literature, 1979—.

MEMBER: Modern Language Association of America, College Language Association (vice-president, 1980-81), American Folklore Society, Association of African and African American Folklorists, Zeta Phi Beta.

AWARDS, HONORS: Grants from National Endowment for the Humanities, 1977-78, the Bunting Institute, 1981-82, and Ford Foundation, 1982-83.

WRITINGS:

NONFICTION

(Contributor) R. Baxter Miller, editor, *Black American Literature and Humanism,* University Press of Kentucky, 1981.
From Mammies to Militants: Domestics in Black American Literature, Temple University Press, 1982.
(Contributor) Chester J. Fontenot and Joe Weixlmann, editors, *Studies in Black American Literature,* Penkevill, 1983.

(Editor with Thadious Davis) *Afro-American Novelists After 1955*, Gale, 1984.
Exorcising Blackness: Historical and Literary Lynching and Burning Rituals, Indiana University Press, 1984.
Black Women in the Fiction of James Baldwin, University of Tennessee Press, 1985.

Contributor to periodicals, including *Melus* and *Southern Humanities Review*.

WORK IN PROGRESS: *Moms Mabley and American Humor*, completion expected in 1986; *How I Got Off the Mourners' Bench: Folk, Popular, and Literary Tales of Religious Conversion*, completion expected in 1987.

SIDELIGHTS: In *From Mammies to Militants* Trudier Harris analyzes the rendering of black domestics in black fiction. She discusses twenty-four works, including Toni Morrison's "The Bluest Eye" and Richard Wright's story "Man of All Work." Fran R. Schumer, reviewing *From Mammies to Militants* in *New York Times Book Review*, wrote that "this book sheds light on a subject that has gotten far less attention than it deserves."

Harris told *CA:* "The topics I have written about have frequently embarrassed people or made them cringe; nonetheless, because these subjects are intrinsic to the history of Afro-Americans, I am continually inspired to write about them. I am motivated, particularly, by being a member of a new generation of Afro-American scholars, especially women, who have the unique opportunity to shape the future course of scholarship by and about black people."

BIOGRAPHICAL/CRITICAL SOURCES:

PERIODICALS

New York Times Book Review, March 6, 1983.

*   *   *

HART-DAVIS, Rupert (Charles)   1907-

BRIEF ENTRY: Born August 28, 1907, in England. British actor, publisher, editor, and author. Hart-Davis left Oxford University in 1927 to study acting at London's Old Vic Theatre. During the following year he worked as an actor with Lyric Theatre, but he gave up the profession in 1929 to join the publishing firm of William Heinemann. He was director of Jonathan Cape from 1933 until 1940 and, following his service in World War II, established his own publishing house, Rupert Hart-Davis Limited, in 1942. Hart-Davis's first important book, according to critics, was *Hugh Walpole: A Biography* (Macmillan, 1952), which met with widespread praise. In later years he edited several volumes of correspondence from famous persons, including *The Letters of Oscar Wilde* (Hart-Davis, 1962).

Hart-Davis began corresponding with his former Eaton schoolmaster George Lyttelton in 1955, after the teacher complained of never hearing from his students by letter. Hart-Davis subsequently edited *The Lyttelton Hart-Davis Letters* (J. Murray). Published in six volumes between 1978 and 1984, the collection received critical acclaim for its range of humor and literary reference. Hart-Davis also won commendations for editing the three-volume series *Siegfried Sassoon Diaries* (Faber, 1981-84). Equally well-received was Hart-Davis's tribute to his mother, *The Arms of Time: A Memoir* (David & Charles, 1979). Descibed as "part elegy, part love-letter," the book was lauded by reviewers for its candor, grace, and compassion. Additional

works by Hart-Davis include *The Autobiography of Arthur Ransom* (Cape, 1976) and *A Beggar in Purple* (David & Charles, 1983). Hart-Davis was knighted in 1967. *Address:* Old Rectory, Marske-in-Swaledale, Richmond, North Yorkshire, England.

BIOGRAPHICAL/CRITICAL SOURCES:

BOOKS

World Authors, 1950-1970, H. W. Wilson, 1975.

PERIODICALS

Economist, March 19, 1983.
New Statesman, April 29, 1983.
Times (London), May 26, 1981, May 13, 1982.
Times Literary Supplement, February 22, 1980, April 17, 1981, July 9, 1982, September 24, 1982, April 22, 1983, May 13, 1983, May 24, 1984.
Washington Post Book World, September 9, 1984.

*   *   *

HARTLEY, Keith   1940-

PERSONAL: Born July 14, 1940, in Leeds, England; son of Walter and Ivy (Stead) Hartley; married Winifred Kealy (a teacher), April 12, 1966; children: Adam, Lucy, Cecilia. *Education:* University of Hull, B.Sc. in Econ., 1962, Ph.D. 1974. *Religion:* Roman Catholic.

ADDRESSES: *Office*—Institute for Research in the Social Sciences, University of York, Heslington, York YO1 5DD, England.

CAREER: University of York, Heslington, York, England, lecturer, 1964-72, senior lecturer, 1972-77, reader in economics, 1977—, director of Institute for Research in the Social Sciences, 1982—. Visiting associate professor at University of Illinois, 1974; visiting professor at National University of Malaysia, 1984. Specialist adviser to the House of Commons Select Committee on Defense, 1984-85.

MEMBER: Royal Economic Society.

AWARDS, HONORS: NATO research fellowship, 1977-79.

WRITINGS:

Expert Performance and Pressure of Demand, Allen & Unwin, 1970.
Problems of Economic Policy, Allen & Unwin, 1977.
(With Clem Tisdell) *Micro-Economic Policy*, Wiley, 1981.
(With Douglas Dosser and David Gowland) *Collaboration of Nations*, Martin Robertson, 1982.
NATO Arms Co-operation: A Study in Economics and Politics, Allen & Unwin, 1983.
(Contributor) G. Repo, editor, *Future British Defense Policy*, Chatham House, 1985.

Contributor to *Brasseys/Rusi Yearbook*, 1985.

WORK IN PROGRESS: Work on defense policy, public choice, and training policy.

SIDELIGHTS: In *NATO Arms Co-operation: A Study in Economics and Politics* Keith Hartley investigates how arms procurement could be better facilitated between the participating countries of the North Atlantic Treaty Organization (NATO). Examining the complex military, economic, and political factors that affect arms cooperation and development, the author gives economics priority, advocating a laissez-faire, open market where competition will foster reduced costs and improved product capabilities. While *Times Literary Supplement* reviewer Michael Carver perceived some real problems in Hartley's "relentless quest for the best buy," such as inequity between nations and technical disparity with the Soviets, he commended the author for debunking "many of the facile platitudes which echo round the marble halls of Nato when questions of arms procurement are discussed."

Hartley told *CA:* "My NATO book analyzes, evaluates, and quantifies the costs and benefits of alternative weapons procurement policies. It provides evidence on the costs of nationalism, of collaboration and co-production. Recognition is given to the role of political factors in public choices."

AVOCATIONAL INTERESTS: Music, sports, angling.

BIOGRAPHICAL/CRITICAL SOURCES:

PERIODICALS

Times Literary Supplement, July 29, 1983.

*   *   *

HARTMANN, Franz   1838-1912

BRIEF ENTRY: Born November 22, 1838, in Bavaria (now West Germany); died August 7, 1912, in Kempten, Bavaria, (now West Germay). German physician, mystic, and author. Hartmann traveled to the United States and India in search of religious and philosophical truths, and at various times he was associated with spiritualism, theosophy, and the Rosicrucians. His publications include *Magic, White and Black* (1886; reissued, 1970), *An Adventure Among the Rosicrucians* (1897), *Life and Doctrines of Paracelsus* (1891), *Occult Science in Medicine* (1893), and *The Life and Doctrines of Jacob Boehme* (1891).

BIOGRAPHICAL/CRITICAL SOURCES:

BOOKS

Encyclopedia of Occultism and Parapsychology, 2nd printing with revisions, Gale, 1979.

*   *   *

HARVEY, Mose Lofley   1910-1985

OBITUARY NOTICE: Born November 25, 1910, in Friendship, Ga.; died of arteriosclerosis, February 25, 1985, in Fort Wayne, Ind. Diplomat, educator, editor, and author. Known as an authority on Soviet affairs and East European trade, Harvey is remembered as director of the Advanced International Studies Institute in Bethesda, Maryland. His career included many U.S. diplomatic and educational posts. Upon joining the State Department in 1947, Harvey became consultant on Soviet affairs. In 1948 he was made chief of the department's division of research and intelligence for the U.S.S.R. and Eastern Europe, and by 1955 Harvey was director of the State Department's political affairs division. He also served during the 1960's as U.S. representative to the International Atomic Energy Agency and as member of the State Department's Policy Planning Council.

In addition to his diplomatic service, Harvey held various teaching positions. He was professor of history at Emory University from 1933 to 1941 and lecturer on Soviet history at Johns Hopkins University from 1947 to 1948. From 1964 until his death, Harvey served as professor of history at Florida's

University of Miami. While there the educator organized the Center for Advanced International Studies, and when the institute moved to Bethesda, Maryland, Harvey continued as the school's director. He was the author of *Focus on the Soviet Challenge, Crisis in Central America, East-West Trade and United States Policy, Science and Technology as an Instrument of Soviet Policy,* and *Soviet Strategy for the Seventies.* Harvey was also the editor of *Soviet World Outlook.*

OBITUARIES AND OTHER SOURCES:

BOOKS

American Men and Women of Science: The Social and Behavioral Sciences, 13th edition, Bowker, 1978.
Who's Who in America, 40th edition, Marquis, 1978.

PERIODICALS

Washington Post, March 2, 1985.

*   *   *

HAWKINS, Gary J(ames)   1937-

PERSONAL: Born September 4, 1937, in Youngstown, Ohio; son of Ralph and Margaret (Fair) Hawkins; married Annick Luneau (divorced December, 1978); married Karen Leslie Granberg (a teacher), May 21, 1979; children: Benjamin R. *Education:* Ohio University, B.S., 1959, M.A., 1960, Ph.D., 1964. *Religion:* Atheist.

ADDRESSES: Home—Sacramento, Calif.

CAREER: University of Washington, Seattle, instructor in speech, 1962-65; San Francisco State University, San Francisco, Calif., assistant professor, 1965-68, associate professor of speech communications, 1968-76; "house parent" and writer, 1976—.

WRITINGS:

(With wife, Karen Hawkins) *Bicycle Touring in Europe,* Pantheon, 1973, revised edition, 1980.
(With K. Hawkins) *Bicycle Touring in the Western United States,* Pantheon, 1982.
U.S.A. by Bus and Train, Pantheon, 1985.

Contributor to speech journals.

WORK IN PROGRESS: Bicycle Touring in Europe: Interconnecting Routes.

SIDELIGHTS: Gary J. Hawkins told *CA:* "The first edition of *Bicycle Touring in Europe* was the result of a four-month trip that Karen and I took. We'd had difficulty finding information on the subject before we left, and as we rode we kept saying to one another, 'We ought to write a book about this.' We did. We collaborated on both the riding and the writing for the revised edition and also covered the seventy-five hundred miles together it took to research *Bicycle Touring in the Western United States.* I pulled our (then) four-year-old son in a special bicycle trailer. All of our books are the result of covering the routes on bicycles.

"*U.S.A. by Bus and Train* is a departure in several ways from the other books. First, I did all the traveling (twenty-five thousand miles) by myself or with my son, Ben. Obviously, it doesn't deal with bicycling, and that imposed great difficulties on me personally. Mostly it differs in that interspersed with practical data are small sections or chapters called 'Comments.' These reflect my personal experiences while on the road, mostly dealing with the people I met. My editor at Pantheon, Wendy Wolf, played a critical role in encouraging me to write as freely as I did, then giving those sections a great deal of critical attention. I couldn't have done it without her. At one point she said, 'Try to make it as unlike a typical travel book as you can.' It turned out differently from anything I'd written, and I expect a bit different from most travel books as well.''

* * *

HAXTON, Josephine Ayres 1921-
(Ellen Douglas)

PERSONAL: Born July 12, 1921, in Natchez, Miss.; daughter of Richardsen (an engineer) Laura (a homemaker; maiden name, Davis) Ayres; married R. K. Haxton, Jr.; children: Richard, Ayres, Brooks. *Education:* University of Mississippi, B.A., 1942.

ADDRESSES: Home—1600 Pine St., Jackson, Miss. 39202. *Agent*—Robert L. Rosen, 7 West 51st St., New York, N.Y. 10019.

CAREER: Writer. Northeast Louisiana University, Monroe, writer-in-residence, 1976-79; University of Mississippi, Oxford, writer-in-residence, 1979-83; University of Virginia, Charlottesville, writer-in-residence, spring, 1984. Faculty member of Faulkner Symposium, University of Mississippi, 1980. Guest reader and lecturer.

AWARDS, HONORS: Short story ''On the Lake'' included in O. Henry collection, 1961; *A Family's Affairs* was awarded the Houghton Mifflin fellowship, 1961, and named one of the five best novels of the year by the *New York Times; Black Cloud, White Cloud* was named one of the five best works of fiction of 1963 by the *New York Times;* National Book Award nomination from National Book Committee, 1973, for *Apostles of Light;* National Endowment for the Humanities fellowship, 1976; Mississippi Institute of Arts and Letters awards for literature, 1979 and 1983.

WRITINGS:

UNDER PSEUDONYM ELLEN DOUGLAS

A Family's Affairs (novel), Houghton, 1962.
Black Cloud, White Cloud: Two Novellas and Two Stories, Houghton, 1963.
Where the Dreams Cross (novel), Houghton, 1968.
Apostles of Light (novel), Houghton, 1973.
The Rock Cried Out (novel), Harcourt, 1979.
A Lifetime Burning (novel), Random House, 1982.

Contributor to periodicals, including *Harper's, New York Times Book Review, Esquire, New Yorker,* and *New Republic.*

SIDELIGHTS: Like William Faulkner, Ellen Douglas has created a fictional Mississippi county in which many of her novels and stories take place. Called Homochito County, it is the setting for Douglas's fourth novel, *The Rock Cried Out*—a tale that explores the southern staples of ''secret love, unrevealed parentage, miscegenation, hatred, revenge and murder,'' reported Doris Grumbach in the *Washington Post Book World.* ''Some of the elements are gothic,'' she continued, ''but in Ellen Douglas's talented hands the story unfolds slowly, believably, without the piled-up, exclamatory haste of the gothic novel.''

The narrator of *The Rock Cried Out* is an ex-hippie who returns to his native Chickasaw Ridge to reconnect with the land and

his past. His serenity is shattered, however, when another native son returns and stirs up buried information about a gory car accident that took place several years ago, at the height of the town's civil rights and Ku Klux Klan activities. Jonathan Yardley wrote in the *New York Times Book Review* that it is Douglas's ''admirably sensitive treatment'' of ''the corrosive effect upon whites and their families of massive, violent reaction to the civil-rights movement . . . that gives 'The Rock Cried Out' its true distinction.'' Yardley further explained that ''the author does not present this as an apology; it's an attempt, to me a persuasive one, at explanation.''

A *New Yorker* critic noted that in *The Rock Cried Out* ''Miss Douglas achieves . . . an illuminating portrait of an exceptionally troubled region and era.'' Grumbach concurred, calling the book ''a valuable and impressive fictional portrait. Here we are brought to know, poignantly, a time, a young man's loss of innocence, a civilization's endurance despite the menace of outside forces and, most of all, a place,'' she added. And Yardley concluded: ''Miss Douglas knows her fellow Mississippians well, and her exploration of their hearts and lives is at once passionate and clinical. She will have nothing of evasions and deceptions; she forces all of her characters to confront the legacy of their past head-on. She writes very well and thinks very clearly. 'The Rock Cried Out' is powerful and disturbing. It should secure Ellen Douglas's place in the literature of the South.''

In *A Lifetime Burning* Douglas takes a departure from her southern narratives, presenting her fifth novel in the form of a diary of a sixty-two year old Southern woman—a literature professor named Corinne—who bitterly tries to make sense of her life. Corinne's discovery of her husband's love affair has forced a lifetime of past hurts and confusions to resurface; she professes to write the diary for the illumination of her grown children but her real need is to piece together an existence that holds meaning for her. Susan Isaacs, writing in the *New York Times Book Review,* observed that ''Corinne is engaging and credibly drawn. Because she is so intelligent and literate, Corinne can express her hurt eloquently. . . . It is fascinating to watch Corinne expose herself as she peels off layers of lies and facile explanation.''

Because the diary shifts back and forth between dream and reality, invention and confession, the reader can never be sure of the ''truth'' of Corinne's revelations. ''Lies, distortions, deceptions, evasions—these are essential to the maintenance of the delicate fabric of which family and society are made,'' explained Yardley in a second *Washington Post Book World* review. He continued: ''This, as I interpret it, is the central theme of *A Lifetime Burning:* we are separate beings and cannot be otherwise, we are mysteries to each other and will always be. In order to keep the structure of our lives intact, it is necessary to withhold the full truth; we invent ourselves for others—and, perhaps, for ourselves.'' The critic deemed the book ''a splendid piece of writing . . . [Douglas's] finest novel.'' Expressing similar praise, Isaacs stated that, while the book has ''too literary'' moments when ''technique overpower[s] characterization,'' it ''is for the most part a beautifully constructed work of fiction.'' She added that ''Ellen Douglas has all the qualities a reader could ask of a novelist: depth, emotional range, wit, sensitivity and the gift of language. 'A Lifetime Burning' is a fine showcase for her talents.''

BIOGRAPHICAL/CRITICAL SOURCES:

PERIODICALS

Esquire, May, 1973.

Observer (London), June 13, 1983.
New York Times Book Review, February 18, 1973, September 23, 1979, November 25, 1979, October 31, 1982.
New Yorker, March 3, 1973, October 8, 1979.
Newsweek, March 5, 1973.
Time, April 15, 1974.
Washington Post Book World, September 9, 1979, December 9, 1979, October 31, 1982.

*   *   *

HAYANO, David M(amoru)   1942-

PERSONAL: Born November 29, 1942, in Poston, Ariz.; son of Mieki and Lillian Koh (a housewife; maiden name, Watanabe) Hayano; married Ruth Margolis (a teacher), July, 1981. *Education:* University of Illinois, B.A., 1963, M.A., 1965; University of California, Los Angeles, Ph.D., 1972.

ADDRESSES: Office—Department of Anthropology, California State University, Northridge, Calif. 91330.

CAREER: California State University, Northridge, assistant professor, 1972-75, associate professor, 1975-79, professor of anthropology, 1979—.

MEMBER: American Anthropological Association, American Ethnological Society, Society for Applied Anthropology, Society for the Study of Symbolic Interaction, Southwestern Anthropological Association.

WRITINGS:

Poker Faces: The Life and Work of Professional Card Players, University of California Press, 1982.

Contributor of articles to professional journals, including *American Ethnologist, Human Organization, Oceania, Urban Life,* and *Social Problems.*

WORK IN PROGRESS: Ethnographic studies of the peoples of Papua New Guinea; further studies of professional gamblers; an examination of sex and gender in contemporary America; a book on the life history of a Papua New Guinea tribesman.

SIDELIGHTS: In *Poker Faces: The Life and Work of Professional Card Players* David M. Hayano presents an ethnographic study of professional cardplayers, analyzing "the social organization of the cardroom, the psychology, beliefs, and jargon of the winners and losers, the nature of their community," described Michael Dirda in the *Washington Post Book World.* Determined to conduct his study as a full-fledged member of the group he sought to examine, the author also tells of his total seduction into the world of high-stake poker in the legalized cardrooms of Gardena, California. Christopher Lehmann-Haupt noted in the *New York Times* that "this background—and the appendix in which Professor Hayano recounts it—is a good deal more instructive and entertaining than the book that resulted"; the critic called the author's academic study of cardplayers "a complex way to describe the obvious." *Times Literary Supplement* reviewer Anthony Holden agreed, observing that in *Poker Faces* "all Hayano has done is to codify a somewhat unusual and colourful area of human activity into the jargon of his trade." Yet Dirda was not so put off by Hayano's academic language. "None of the ethnography is difficult to understand and most of it is fascinating," he wrote. "For drama one can turn to Hayano's long appendix defending his methodology. . . . [*Poker Faces*] will

undoubtedly become the classic ethnographical study of the players and their game."

Hayano told *CA:* "Writing as an anthropologist, I am devoted to studying other people—whether in contemporary American culture or elsewhere—as closely as possible from an *insider's* point of view. This means, essentially, participating in their lives and lifestyles as much as possible to understand how human realities are experienced, defined, and talked about. My writings are intended to make the reader enter lives which he may not have time or energy to explore himself, and will open his eyes to a substantially different experience."

BIOGRAPHICAL/CRITICAL SOURCES:

PERIODICALS

New York Times, April 26, 1982.
Times Literary Supplement, August 27, 1982.
Washington Post Book World, May 9, 1982.

*   *   *

HAYDN, Richard   1905-1985

OBITUARY NOTICE: Born in 1905 in London, England; was found dead April 25, 1985, in Pacific Palisades, Calif. Actor, director, and author. Haydn, a British actor who went to Hollywood, was known for his prissy, eccentric roles. As an actor he appeared in more than a dozen movies, including "Please Don't Eat the Daisies," "Forever Amber," "Mutiny On the Bounty," "The Sound of Music," and "Young Frankenstein." Haydn directed the films "Mrs. Tatlock's Millions" and "Dear Wife." Adopting the persona of the fictional character Edwin Carp, Haydn wrote *The Journal of Edwin Carp,* which was published in 1954.

OBITUARIES AND OTHER SOURCES:

BOOKS

International Motion Picture Almanac, Quigley, 1985.
Who's Who in America, 39th edition, Marquis, 1976.
The World Encyclopedia of Film, A. & W. Visual Library, 1972.

PERIODICALS

Chicago Tribune, April 27, 1985.

*   *   *

HAYES, Zachary (Jerome)   1932-

PERSONAL: Born September 21, 1932, in Chicago, Ill.; son of Robert Joseph (a police officer) and Elizabeth Clare (Lehman) Hayes. *Education:* Quincy College and Seminary (now Quincy College), B.A., 1956; University of Bonn, Th.D., 1964. *Religion:* Roman Catholic.

ADDRESSES: Home and office— Catholic Theological Union, 5401 South Cornell, Chicago, Ill. 60615.

CAREER: Entered Franciscan Order, 1952, ordained Roman Catholic priest, 1959; St. Joseph Seminary, Teutopolis, Ill., lecturer in systematic theology, 1964-68; Catholic Theological Union, Chicago, Ill., associate professor, 1968-74, professor of history of theology, 1974—. Professor at St. Bonaventure University, summer, 1966; visiting lecturer at St. John's Seminary, Brighton, Mass., 1969-70; guest lecturer at University of Chicago, 1979. Member of advisory board of Franciscan Herald Press, 1980—, and board of trustees of Quincy College, 1984—.

MEMBER: Catholic Theological Society of America, Society for the Scientific Study of Religion.

AWARDS, HONORS: Litt.D. from St. Bonaventure University, 1974; Association of Theological Schools grant, 1977, scholarship, 1978.

WRITINGS:

The General Doctrine of Creation in the Thirteenth Century, Schoeningh, 1964.
What Manner of Man?: Sermons on Christ by St. Bonaventure, Franciscan Herald, 1964.
(Translator) J. Ratzinger, *The Theology of History in St. Bonaventure,* Franciscan Herald, 1971.
To Whom Shall We Go: Christ and the Mystery of Man, Franciscan Herald, 1975.
(Contributor) Romano Almagno and Conrad Harkins, editors, *Studies Honoring Ignatius Brady,* Franciscan Institute Publications, 1976.
Disputed Questions on the Trinity, Franciscan Institute Publications, 1979.
The Hidden Center: Spirituality and Speculative Christology in St. Bonaventure, Paulist Press, 1981.
What Are They Saying About Creation?: Christ, the Bible, and Science, Paulist Press, 1980.
What Are They Saying About the End of the World?, Paulist Press, 1983.
Christology in Roman Catholic Thought of the Modern Era, Paulist Press, 1985.

Contributor to theology journals.

SIDELIGHTS: Zachary Hayes told *CA:* "Since my college days my approach to philosophy and theology has been strongly influenced by several outstanding North American Franciscan scholars: Philotheus Boehner, Allan Wolter, and Ignatius Brady. They opened me to the plurality of viewpoints in the medieval period of Western Christian history. This in turn opened the way for what has been my primary concern over many years, namely, the relationship of present Christian experience to the rich resources of Christian tradition.

"During the years of my doctoral work in Germany, the thought of Johann Auer and Joseph Ratzinger was particularly influential. This academic stimulation was supplemented by extensive travel throughout all the countries of Western Europe during a four-year period. This provided a first-hand experience of the culture and the church life of both Catholics and Protestants in the early 1960's, the years immediately prior to the Vatican II Council.

"In the years following completion of my doctoral studies, the direction of my research, teaching, and writing has been strongly influenced by the secularist and humanist movements that swept the United States during the late sixties and the seventies. It has been my concern to find a way of maintaining a healthy dialectical relation between the legitimate concerns and values of the modern search for the meaning of the human and the positive contribution implied on the fundamental Christian claims and values. It has been the concern for this sort of dialectical relation between the sacred and the secular dimensions of human experience that has led to the shift in my research from the medieval period to the modern period, particularly the nineteenth century.

"This period of history, which is virtually unknown to large segments of the Catholic scholarly world, is a fascinating and significant time when various attempts were made to relate Christian thought and experience to the values, questions, and concerns which have left their impact on the human psyche from the time of Descartes up to the present. My research has included an extended stay in Tuebingen, West Germany, during the summer of 1984, since the University of Tuebingen was an important center in the development of Catholic thought during that important period.

"At this point, I would describe my work as an ongoing search for a healthy Christian humanism which is deeply immersed in the experience of contemporary humanity on the one hand, and yet is firmly rooted in the rich resources of Christian spiritual and theological tradition on the other hand. I am convinced that this sort of orientation will allow culture and religion to interact in a mutually constructive manner."

*   *   *

HEARN, M(illard) F(illmore, Jr.)   1938-

PERSONAL: Born August 18, 1938, in Lincoln, Ala.; son of Millard Fillmore and Olivia (Richey) Hearn; married Jana Srba (a historian), June 18, 1966; children: John, Susannah. *Education:* Auburn University, B.A., 1960; Indiana University—Bloomington, M.A. (history), 1964, M.A. (art history), 1966, Ph.D., 1969; attended University of California, Berkeley, 1965-66, and Courtauld Institute of Art, 1966-67.

ADDRESSES: Office—104 Frick Fine Arts Bldg., University of Pittsburgh, Pittsburgh, Pa. 15260.

CAREER: University of Pittsburgh, Pittsburgh, Pa., instructor, 1967-69, assistant professor, 1969-72, associate professor, 1972-80, professor of medieval art and architecture, 1980—, chairman of department of fine arts, 1974-78, director of architectural studies program, 1981—. Visiting professor at Carnegie-Mellon University, fall, 1979. *Military service:* U.S. Navy, 1960-62; became lieutenant junior grade; named poet laureate of the Atlantic Fleet, 1961.

MEMBER: International Center of Medieval Art (member of board of directors, 1985—), Society of Architectural Historians.

AWARDS, HONORS: Kress fellow, 1965-66; Carnegie fellow, 1966-67; grants from American Philosophical Society, 1977, and American Council of Learned Societies, 1977.

WRITINGS:

Romanesque Sculpture: The Revival of Monumental Stone Sculpture in the Eleventh and Twelfth Centuries, Cornell University Press, 1981.
Ripon Minster: The Beginning of the Gothic Style in Northern England, American Philosophical Society, 1983.

Contributor to art and archaeology journals, including *Gesta, Speculum, Journal of the Society of Architectural Historians,* and *Journal of the British Archaeological Association.* Contributing editor, *Pittsburgh,* 1982-84.

WORK IN PROGRESS: Researching twentieth-century American architecture.

SIDELIGHTS: In *Romanesque Sculpture: The Revival of Monumental Stone Sculpture in the Eleventh and Twelfth Centuries* M. F. Hearn constructs a systematic theory to explain the development of Romanesque sculpture, with its reclaimed features of classical antiquity. Alan Borg noted in the *Times Literary Supplement* that because the author attempts to do more than present a general style survey "what we have here is a personal account of the development of Romanesque sculpture, and one which does not, in fact, give us a balanced picture.'' The critic found some disconcerting simplifications and exclusions in Hearn's traditional theory of the Romanesque movement; still he concluded that ''Hearn's observations are always revealing and if this book does not provide us with a definitive introduction to Romanesque sculpture it will find an honourable place in the historiography of the style.''

In response to the critiques of his book *Romanesque Sculpture,* Hearn told *CA:* ''There is no evidence in Borg's review to indicate that he read any of the book other than the first thirty pages and pages 41, 68, 119, and 169. On a broader consideration, the biggest surprise to me was that none of the fifteen or so people who produced a written account of the book agreed on any point. Moreover, one reviewer did not read the book, and most of the others only listed details that they disagreed with. The point is that virtually no one reads the book that the author writes, if they read it at all. In the final analysis one writes a book for oneself. But it is worth the effort anyway.''

BIOGRAPHICAL/CRITICAL SOURCES:

PERIODICALS

Times Literary Supplement, August 28, 1981.

*   *   *

HEATH, Mary Ellen 1928-

PERSONAL: Born January 13, 1928, in Cheyenne, Wyo.; daughter of F. Waldo (a teacher) and Mary Ruth (a teacher; maiden name, Smith) Inman; married Gaylord T. Heath, August 28, 1950 (died March 24, 1976); married C. W. Spink (a county public works department supervisor), January 1, 1981; children: (first marriage) Gay Ellen, Fred Edward. *Education:* Southwest Baptist College (now University), A.A., 1949; attended University of Oregon, 1966-71. *Religion:* Baptist.

ADDRESSES: Home—1580 Acacia Ave., Eugene, Ore. 97401.

CAREER: Kansas City Star, Kansas City, Mo., linotype operator, 1949-50; *St. Louis Globe-Democrat,* St. Louis, Mo., linotype operator, 1950; *Honolulu Star-Bulletin,* Honolulu, Hawaii, linotype operator, 1950-51; *Vallejo Times-Herald,* Vallejo, Calif., linotype operator, 1951-52; *Kansas City Star,* linotype operator, 1954-60; *Albany Democrat-Herald,* Albany, Ore., linotype operator, 1960-61; *Eugene Register-Guard,* Eugene, Ore., linotype operator, 1961-62; Briggs Printing, Eugene, linotype operator, 1962-71.

MEMBER: Oregon Association of Christian Writers.

WRITINGS:

Benjamin and Jon (novel), Jeremy Books and Bethany Fellowship, 1979.

Editor of *Label Facts,* for Woman's International Auxiliary of International Typographical Union, 1977-79.

WORK IN PROGRESS: A novel entitled *Not Meant for a Burden;* a third novel.

SIDELIGHTS: Mary Ellen Heath told *CA:* ''*Benjamin and Jon* is the story of two runaways, an old man and a boy, who join forces and become inseparable in their fight for survival. Benjamin, unable to bear the confines of a nursing home, walks out determined never to return. Jon is a strange and vulnerable child who nurses a painful secret of child abuse, which he

eventually shares with his elderly friend. The adventures of the two take them to a campsite deep in a wooded park and then on a long journey through the countryside to the refuge of a cave on Benjamin's farm. The coming winter brings crisis and a difficult decision for Benjamin.''

*   *   *

HEAT MOON, William Least
See TROGDON, William (Lewis)

*   *   *

HEGRE, Theodore A. 1908-1984

OBITUARY NOTICE: Born March 17, 1908, in Woodville, Wis.; died October 28, 1984, in Singapore. Clergyman and author. Hegre was pastor of Bethany Missionary Church in Minneapolis, Minnesota, from 1943 to 1984. He wrote numerous journal articles and such books as *The Cross and Sanctification, How to Find Freedom From the Power of Sin,* and *Creative Faith.* (Date of death provided by wife, Lucile Hegre.)

*   *   *

HELGESEN, Sally 1948-

PERSONAL: Born July 1, 1948, in St. Cloud, Minn. *Education:* Received B.A. from Hunter College of the City University of New York.

ADDRESSES: Home—271 West 11th St., New York, N.Y. 10014. *Agent*—Georges Borchardt, Inc., 136 East 57th St., New York, N.Y. 10022.

CAREER: Journalist.

MEMBER: Authors Guild.

WRITINGS:

Wildcatters: A Story of Texans, Oil, and Money, Doubleday, 1981

Contributor to magazines, including *Vogue* and *Glamour,* and newspapers. Contributing editor of *Harper's.*

WORK IN PROGRESS: A novel, for Doubleday.

*   *   *

HELLER, Trudy (Marie) 1944-

PERSONAL: Born March 18, 1944, in New York, N.Y.; daughter of Sidney (an administrator) and Ida (a secretary; maiden name, Rosenbloom) Heller; married Theodore J. Century, August 28, 1963 (divorced, 1972); married Jon Van Til (a professor), January 2, 1976; children: (second marriage) Ross Heller, Claire Heller. *Education:* Attended Shimer College, 1961-64; Temple University, B.A., 1966, Ph.D., 1979; University of Pennsylvania, M.S., 1973; National Training Laboratories, graduate of Graduate Student Professional Development Program, 1978.

ADDRESSES: Home and office—437 South 46th St., Philadelphia, Pa. 19143.

CAREER: Rutgers University, Camden Campus, Camden, N.J., counselor, 1973-75; Pennsylvania State University, Ogontz Campus, Abington, Pa., adjunct professor of management, 1980, 1981; Temple University, Philadelphia, Pa., adjunct professor of organizational behavior, 1981-83; researcher, consultant, and writer, 1983—.

MEMBER: Certified Consultants International, Academy of Management, American Association for Counseling and Development, Organization Development Network.

WRITINGS:

Women and Men as Leaders: In Business, Educational, and Social Service Organizations, Praeger, 1982.
(Contributor) Mel S. Moyer, editor, *Managing Voluntary Organizations: Proceedings of a Conference,* York University, 1983.
(Contributor) John D. Adams, editor, *Transforming Work,* Educational Challenges, 1984.
(Senior editor, with husband, John Van Til, and Louis A. Zurcher) *Leaders and Followers: Challenges for the Future,* Jai Press, 1985.
Changing Authority Patterns: A Cultural Perspective, Academy of Management Review, 1985.

Senior contributing editor of *Journal of Applied Behavioral Sciences,* Volume XVIII, number 3, 1982.

WORK IN PROGRESS: Research on the professional worker under stress; evaluating the establishment of a worker-owned market in a poverty community; a long-term study of leadership aspirations of business school students.

SIDELIGHTS: Trudy Heller told *CA:* "An important impetus to my writing has been the constraints of childbearing and childrearing. Writing has provided me with a way of keeping alive intellectually and professionally during years of heavy family responsibilities.

"My personal dedication to exploring the issues of women and men as leaders dates from a traumatic experience with my first boss, a woman. My work in this area has led me to fear that women in management may be on a collision course with the future; that they are emulating a male leadership model at a time when that model is changing rapidly. I believe that, in the future, we may see a 'feminization' of the workplace in such ways as: democratization and flattening of hierarchies, serial careers becoming the norm for both men and women, and greater legitimization for both sexes of work done at home and of volunteer or nonpaid work."

*   *   *

HEMPHILL, Betty
 See HEMPHILL, Elizabeth Anne

*   *   *

HEMPHILL, Elizabeth Anne   1920-
 (Betty Hemphill)

PERSONAL: Born March 30, 1920, in Fort Collins, Colo.; daughter of David James and Katherine (Higgins) Roach; married Robert Frederick Hemphill (a colonel in the U.S. Air Force), May 21, 1942; children: Robert Fredrick, Jr., Virginia Anne Hemphill Adams, David F. *Education:* University of Nebraska—Lincoln, B.F.A., 1941; George Washington University, M.A., 1962; Sanz School of Foreign Languages, Intermediate Certificate in Japanese, 1964; attended St. Louis-Chaminade Education Center (now Chaminade College of Honolulu), 1975-76, and Hawaii Loa College, 1980-81. *Politics:* Liberal Democrat. *Religion:* "All-purpose Protestant."

ADDRESSES: Home—122 Lanipo Dr., Kailua, Hawaii 96734.

CAREER: Testro Brothers, Tokyo, Japan, editor, 1968-73; Marsh Consulting Services, Honolulu, Hawaii, instructor, 1973—. Member of council and board of directors of Japan International Christian University, 1970-73.

MEMBER: American Association of University Women (state president, 1978-82), Friends of the Calimari.

AWARDS, HONORS: Leadership award from Young Women's Christian Association, 1982.

WRITINGS:

A Treasure to Share, Judson, 1964.
The Road to Keep: The Story of Paul Rusch in Japan, Walker & Co., 1969.
(Under name Betty Hemphill) *Third Testament Women,* Lydian Press, 1979.
The Least of These, Weatherhill, 1980.

Contributor of articles, poems, and reviews to magazines, including *Contemporary Japan, Japan Christian Quarterly, Pacific, Imperial, Woman Alive,* and *Ferity,* and newspapers.

WORK IN PROGRESS: The Crossroads Witness, "a history of the Honolulu Church of the Crossroads, a liberal, interracial church which sponsored a coffee house for young people during the 1960's and offered sanctuary to deserting servicemen during the Vietnam War," publication expected in 1985; *Show and Tell,* poems about children, "not necessarily *for* children," publication expected in 1985.

SIDELIGHTS: Elizabeth Anne Hemphill told *CA:* "I come from a letter-writing family. My mother, my sister, and I all exchanged daily letters. Nothing develops skill in expression so well as writing something—anything—every day. By a lucky coincidence, as I was planning my first serious work—a biography—I met Dr. Clifton E. Olmstead of George Washington University and learned from him about historical methods and research. I like telling the stories of people's lives, particularly of those who have made some significant contributions to their times. I like telling these stories so that other people can share them and be inspired by them.

"Poetry is a change of pace from historical and journalistic writing. It has such a variety of subjects and forms—limited only by the imagination of the poet. Children are wonderful subjects for poetry because of the funny, touching, and unexpected incidents in their lives. I have been inspired in particular by my own four grandchildren and their friends."

BIOGRAPHICAL/CRITICAL SOURCES:

PERIODICALS

American Historical Review, winter, 1970-71.

*   *   *

HENDERSON, Eva Pendleton   1890-

PERSONAL: Born January 9, 1890, in Lakey, Tex.; daughter of William Edwin (a rancher) and Susan Iona (a rancher's wife; maiden name, Chishum) Bass; married Thomas Manor Pendleton (a rancher), September 4, 1912 (died, 1937); married Lee Henderson (a rancher), September 12, 1941 (deceased); children: (first marriage) Hazel Marie Harvey, George Edwin. *Education:* Attended Western New Mexico Teachers College, 1919, Instituto Allende San Miguel, 1954-55, and

New Mexico State University, 1960. *Religion:* Christian Science.

ADDRESSES: Home and office—1101 Boutz Rd., Apt. 5, Las Cruces, N.M. 88001.

CAREER: Teacher at rural schools in Eddy County, N.M., 1906, Grant and Hidalgo Counties, N.M., 1912-24; rancher, 1924-46; owner and manager of apartments in Donna County, N.M., 1946-70. Founder of Welcome Stranger Club, Las Cruces, N.M.; member of New Mexico Cattle Growers; charter member of Hidalgo Library Board.

MEMBER: Order of the Eastern Star.

AWARDS, HONORS: Inducted into Donna Ana County Historical Society's Hall of Fame, 1981.

WRITINGS:

Wild Horses, Sunstone Press, 1983.

Contributor to *New Mexico.*

WORK IN PROGRESS: A book tentatively titled *The Love of My Family.*

SIDELIGHTS: Eva Henderson was three years old when her family traveled from Texas to New Mexico in a covered wagon. Regarding *Wild Horses* she told *CA:* "This narrative is set in the territorial days of New Mexico, beginning in the year 1895. I know it is authentic because I lived it. We lived on the ragged edge of life. My father was clean and fine, poor and proud. We rode wagons or saddle horses. Our schooling was scarce, but our lives were rich with experience."

*   *   *

HENNESSY, Thomas C(hristopher)   1916-

PERSONAL: Born November 3, 1916, in New York, N.Y.; son of Thomas C. and Anna E. (Regan) Hennessy. *Education:* Georgetown University, B.A., 1940; Fordham University, M.A., 1947, M.S.Ed., 1957, Ph.D., 1962.

ADDRESSES: Home—1404 West Wisconsin Ave., Milwaukee, Wis. 53233. *Office*—School of Education, 176 Schroeder Complex, Marquette University, Milwaukee, Wis. 53233.

CAREER: Entered Society of Jesus (Jesuits), 1934, ordained Roman Catholic priest, 1947; Fordham Preparatory School, New York City, instructor in Latin and French, 1941-44 and 1949-52, student counselor at Preparatory School, 1952-61; Fordham University, New York City, assistant professor, 1962-68, associate professor, 1968-78, professor of counseling education, 1978-81; director of W.A. Kelly Counseling Laboratory, 1969-81; Marquette University, Milwaukee, Wis., professor of education and dean of School of Education, 1981—. Member of board of directors of Alfred Adler Mental Hygiene Clinic, 1978-81.

MEMBER: American Psychological Association, Association for Counseling and Development.

WRITINGS:

EDITOR AND CONTRIBUTOR

The Inner Crusade: The Closed Retreat in the U.S., Loyola University Press, 1965.
The High School Counselor Today, Daughters of St. Paul, 1966.
The Interdisciplinary Roots of Guidance, Fordham University Press, 1966.

Values and Moral Development, Paulist Press, 1976.
Values/Moral Education: The Schools and the Teachers, Paulist Press, 1979.

Contributor to education, counseling, and psychology journals.

WORK IN PROGRESS: Counselor Role and Function: A Value-Ethical Perspective, an introductory counseling text.

SIDELIGHTS: Thomas C. Hennessy told *CA:* "The role of the high school counselor has changed since publication of *The High School Counselor Today* in 1966 because we now know more about the dynamics of counseling, thanks to researchers who began as followers of C. Rogers, including Carkhuff, Ivery, and Gazda, and to researchers in career counseling, especially Super and Crites.

"I try to keep both public and parochial schools in mind in my work, which involves preparation for professional personnel in both public and private education. It seems to me that some of the newer approaches enable the interested school functionary to work in an open climate for positive value growth. What we have learned about values applies equally to public and private education."

*   *   *

HERMAN, Victor   1916(?)-1985

OBITUARY NOTICE: Born c. 1916 in Detroit, Mich.; died following a heart attack, March 25, 1985, at Providence Hospital in Southfield, Mich. Athlete, pilot, parachutist, and author. Herman, an American who left the United States in 1931, was held prisoner by the Soviet Union for eighteen years. He moved with his family to the U.S.S.R. so that his father, a Ford Motor Company employee, could work in an auto plant there. During his first seven years in the U.S.S.R., Herman became an adept athlete and pilot. In 1934 he set a world record in parachute jumping and attracted Soviet interest. The pilot was pressured to renounce his U.S. citizenship, thereby giving the U.S.S.R. claim to his parachuting record. When Herman refused, he was arrested for counter-revolutionary activities and sent into Siberian exile. Although the American regained his freedom for brief periods, he was not permitted to return to the United States until 1976. Two years after returning to his native country, Herman filed a law suit against Ford Motor Company blaming the automaker for his ordeal in the U.S.S.R. His book *Coming Out of the Ice: An Unexpected Life,* which recounts the former pilot's incarceration, was adapted as a television movie that aired in 1982. Herman also wrote *Realities.*

OBITUARIES AND OTHER SOURCES:

PERIODICALS

Chicago Tribune, March 31, 1985.
Los Angeles Times, March 29, 1985.
New York Times, March 29, 1985.
Washington Post, April 1, 1985.

*   *   *

HERN, Nicholas   1944-

PERSONAL: Born February 15, 1944, in London, England; son of George Anthony (a journalist) and Frances (a journalist; maiden name, Starr) Hern; married Patricia Andrews (a teacher), August 6, 1966; children: Abigail, Nicola. *Education:* University of Bristol, B.A. (with first class honors), 1965.

ADDRESSES: Home—London, England. *Office*—Methuen London Ltd., 11 New Fetter Lane, London EC4P 4EE, England.

CAREER: Lintas Ltd. (advertising agency), London, England, account executive, 1965-67; University of Hull, Hull, England, lecturer in drama, 1967-72; University of Glasgow, Glasgow, Scotland, lecturer in drama, 1972-74; Methuen London Ltd., London, senior editor, 1974—.

WRITINGS:

Peter Handke, Oswald Wolff, 1971, Ungar, 1972.

Contributor to *Theatre Quarterly.*

SIDELIGHTS: Nicholas Hern informed *CA:* "Theatre has been important to me for most of my life, both vocationally and recreationally. Having taken a first degree in drama (jointly with German), I then taught the subject for some years before becoming drama editor of Methuen, the largest publisher of plays and theatre books in Britain. My published work has all been on aspects of the theatre, often German theatre. The chief reward of my present job is the opportunity to work closely with playwrights, both established and tyronic, as they prepare their work for publication, often alongside the stage premiere."

*   *   *

HERON, Alasdair I(ain) C(ampbell) 1942-

PERSONAL: Born July 24, 1942, in Murree, Pakistan; son of John (a minister) and May (a teacher; maiden name, Campbell) Heron; married Helen S. Thomson (a teacher), September 6, 1968; children: Jeanette, Patricia. *Education:* Sidney Sussex College, Cambridge, B.A., 1965, M.A., 1968; University of Edinburgh, B.D., 1968; University of Tuebingen, D.Th., 1973. *Politics:* Liberal. *Religion:* Presbyterian.

ADDRESSES: Home—Schenkstrasse 69, D-8520 Erlangen, West Germany. *Office*—Faculty of Theology, University of Erlangen, Kochstrasse 6, D-8520 Erlangen, West Germany.

CAREER: Ordained minister of the Church of Scotland, 1975; Irish School of Ecumenics, Dublin, research lecturer in systematic theology, 1973-74; University of Edinburgh, Edinburgh, Scotland, lecturer in Christian dogmatics, 1974-81; University of Erlangen, Erlangen, West Germany, professor of reformed theology, 1981—. Kerr Lecturer at Trinity College, Glasgow, 1976-79. Director of Handsel Press.

MEMBER: Academie Internationale des Sciences Religieuses, Wissenschaftliche Gesellschaft fuer Theologie, Society for the Study of Theology.

WRITINGS:

Two Churches, One Love, A.P.C.K., 1977.
A Century of Protestant Theology, Westminster, 1980.
The Holy Spirit, Westminster, 1983.
(Editor) *The Westminster Confession in the Church Today,* St. Andrew, 1982.
Table and Tradition, Westminster, 1984.
(Editor with Joachim Staedtke and others) *Heinrich Bullinger Werke, Dritte Abteilung: Theologische Werke* (title means "The Works of Heinrich Bullinger, Section Three: Theological Works"), Volume II: *Unveroeffentlichte Werk der kappeler Zeit: Theologica* (title means "Unpublished Works of the Kappel Period: Theological"), Theologischer Verlag, in press.

(With Gillian Evans and Allan Galloway) *History of Christian Theology,* Volume 4: *History of Philosophical Theology,* Marshall, Morgan & Scott, in press.
(With George Stroup) *A Handbook of Reformed Theology,* Westminster, in press.

Contributor of about twenty articles to theology journals. Editor of *Scottish Journal of Theology.*

WORK IN PROGRESS: Editing further volumes of Heinrich Bullinger's works.

SIDELIGHTS: Alasdair I.C. Heron told *CA:* "My books so far have all been written out of my work teaching ecumenical, historical, and systematic theology over the last decade. So far, too, they have all been written because someone asked me to write them. *A Century of Protestant Theology* surveys the main lines of thinking in the nineteenth and twentieth centuries and is intended primarily as an introductory work for students, though I try to avoid the style of a dull academic textbook. The same applies to *The Holy Spirit* and to *Table and Tradition* (a study of the meaning of the Eucharist with special concentration on the Roman Catholic and Reformed traditions, ranging from the New Testament evidence to contemporary ecumenical considerations). One also hopes that books of this kind can be of interest to nonspecialists in theology and make a contribution to theological thinking outside the faculties and seminaries. My more technical work has up till now generally appeared in the form of articles in specialist theological journals or collections of essays.

"The theological position I represent would probably be labelled neo-orthodox—especially by those who do not share it. I would prefer to describe it as catholic and reformed, as owing a particular debt, among twentieth-century theologians, to Karl Barth and Thomas Torrance, as concerned for dialogue with the past history of Christian thinking on major themes, with other Christian traditions, and with other disciplines. One area I would be keen to explore more fully in the future is the relation between Christian theology and natural science, with a view both to the history of their interaction in past and present and to the possible integration of theological and scientific thinking. This is certainly not the only major intellectual challenge facing theology today, but it is one of them."

*   *   *

HERRING, Jack W(illiam) 1925-

PERSONAL: Born August 28, 1925, in Waco, Tex.; son of Ben O. (a college professor) and Bertha (Shiplet) Herring; married Daphne Norred (a college administrator), June 10, 1944; children: Penny Elizabeth Herring Flood, Paul William. *Education:* Baylor University, B.A., 1947, M.A., 1948; University of Pennsylvania, Ph.D., 1958. *Religion:* Baptist.

ADDRESSES: Home—200 Guittard, Waco, Tex. 76706. *Office*—Armstrong Browning Library, Baylor University, Box 6336, Waco, Tex. 76706.

CAREER: Howard College (now Samford University), Birmingham, Ala., instructor in English, 1948-50; Grand Canyon College, Phoenix, Ariz., associate professor of English and acting chairman of department, 1951-55; Arizona State University, Tempe, assistant professor of English, 1955-59; Baylor University, Waco, Tex., professor of English and director of Armstrong Browning Library, 1959—, Margaret Root Brown Chair of Robert Browning Studies, 1973—. *Military service:* U.S. Army, Infantry Signal Corps, 1944-46.

MEMBER: Modern Language Association of America, American Association of University Professors, Conference on Christianity and Literature, South Central Modern Language Association, Downtown Waco Kiwanis Club (vice-president, 1974-75; lieutenant governor, 1983-84).

AWARDS, HONORS: American Institute of Graphic Arts named The Old Schoolfellow one of fifty best books of the year in 1972.

WRITINGS:

The Old Schoolfellow: The Artistic Relationship of Two Robert Brownings, Beta Phi Mu, 1972.
(Editor with Robert G. Collmer) American Bypaths: Essays in Honor of E. Hudson Long, Baylor University Press, 1980.

Also author of The Armstrong Browning Library, 1968. Contributor to literature journals.

WORK IN PROGRESS: Editing Baylor-Ohio edition of Robert Browning's complete works.

*　　*　　*

HERTZLER, Daniel 1925-

PERSONAL: Born October 19, 1925, in Elverson, Pa.; son of Melvin L. (a farmer) and Susan (a homemaker; maiden name, Shenk) Hertzler; married Mary Yoder (a homemaker), July 12, 1952; children: Dennis, Ronald, Gerald, Daniel. Education: Eastern Mennonite College, B.A., 1951; Goshen Biblical Seminary, Goshen, Ind. (now Elkhart, Ind.), B.D., 1955; University of Pittsburgh, Ph.D., 1966. Religion: Mennonite.

ADDRESSES: Home—Route 1, Box 257-A, Scottdale, Pa. 15683. Office—Mennonite Publishing House, Scottdale, Pa. 15683.

CAREER: Mennonite Publishing House, Scottdale, Pa., editor, 1952—, editor of Gospel Herald, 1973—. Moderator of Allegheny Mennonite Conference.

MEMBER: Religious Education Association, Associated Church Press.

WRITINGS:

NONFICTION

From Germantown to Steinbach, Herald Press, 1981.
Not by Night, Herald Press, 1983.

SIDELIGHTS: Daniel Hertzler commented: "My first book is a series of profiles of Mennonite congregations around the border of the United States. It is based on personal visits to each congregation. The second book is a compilation of writings from the Gospel Herald in honor of its seventy-fifth anniversary as a publication.

"Both of my books grew out of my work as editor of Gospel Herald, a weekly publication for Mennonites in the United States and Canada. Mennonite churches have had a strong traditional concern for Christian discipleship and peace. My research in From Germantown to Steinbach was to document the current support for these traditions, particularly in some of the younger congregations. Not by Night illustrates the ebb and flow of discussion in the pages of the Gospel Herald throughout its seventy-five-year history. Readers of Not by Night, for example, have been interested to see that the issue of better relationships between blacks and whites which came to focus in the 1960's was already promoted in the Gospel Herald in 1909."

HESKETH, (Charles) Peter (Fleetwood) Fleetwood
See FLEETWOOD-HESKETH, (Charles) Peter (Fleetwood)

*　　*　　*

HEST, Amy 1950-

PERSONAL: Born April 28, 1950, in New York, N.Y.; daughter of Seymour Cye and Thelma (Goldberg) Levine; married Lionel Hest (a lawyer), May 19, 1977; children: Sam, Kate. Education: Hunter College of the City University of New York, B.A., 1971; C. W. Post College of Long Island University, M.L.S., 1972.

ADDRESSES: Home—20 West 64th, New York, N.Y. 10023.

CAREER: New York Public Library, New York City, children's librarian, 1972-75; Viking Press, Inc., New York City, assistant editor, 1977; writer, 1977—.

MEMBER: Society of Children's Book Writers.

WRITINGS:

Maybe Next Year (juvenile novel), Houghton, 1982.
The Crack-of-Dawn Walkers, Macmillan, 1984.

BIOGRAPHICAL/CRITICAL SOURCES:

PERIODICALS

New York Times Book Review, May 13, 1984.

*　　*　　*

HETHERINGTON, Eileen Mavis (Plenderleith) 1926-

PERSONAL: Born November 27, 1926; children: three. Education: University of British Columbia, B.A., 1947, M.A., 1948; University of California, Berkeley, Ph.D., 1958.

ADDRESSES: Office—Department of Psychology, University of Virginia, Charlottesville, Va. 22901.

CAREER: Clinical psychologist at British Columbia Child Guidance Clinic, 1948-51, senior psychologist, 1951-52; clinical intern at Langley Porter Clinic, 1956-57; San Jose State College (now University), San Jose, Calif., instructor in psychology, 1957-58; Rutgers University, New Brunswick, N.J., assistant professor of psychology, 1958-60; assistant professor at University of Wisconsin, 1960-63, associate professor, 1963-66, professor of psychology, 1966-70; University of Virginia, Charlottesville, professor of psychology, 1970-80, James Page Professor of Psychology, 1980—, chairman of department, 1980-83. Visiting professor at Stanford University, 1975-76; fellow at Center for Advanced Studies in the Behavioral Sciences, Palo Alto, Calif., 1978-79. Member of board of directors of Child Trends, 1979—, chairman of board, 1982—; member of advisory council of National Institute for Child Health and Human Development, 1980-83, chairman of planning committee, 1980—; member of President's Commission on Mental Health.

MEMBER: American Psychological Association (fellow; chairman of publication board, 1976-77; division president, 1978), Society for Research in Child Development (president-elect, 1983—), Midwestern Psychological Association, Virginia Psychological Association.

WRITINGS:

(Editor) *Review of Child Development Research,* Volume V, University of Chicago Press, 1974.
(With R. D. Parke) *Child Psychology: A Contemporary Viewpoint,* McGraw, 1975, 2nd edition, 1979.
(Editor with Parke, and contributor) *Contemporary Readings in Child Psychology,* McGraw, 1977, 2nd edition, 1981.
(Editor) *Personality and Social Development,* Volume IV: *Handbook of Child Psychology,* Wiley, 1983.
(With D. L. Featherman and K. A. Camara) *Cognitive and Academic Functioning of Children From One-Parent Families,* National Institute of Education, 1982.

CONTRIBUTOR

Spencer and Kass, editors, *Perspectives in Child Psychology: Research and Review,* McGraw, 1969.
Quay and Wherry, editors, *Psychological Disorders of Childhood,* Wiley, 1972.
F. Horowitz, editor, *Review of Child Development Research,* Volume IV, University of Chicago Press, 1974.
J. S. Sherman and F. L. Denmark, editors, *The Psychology of Women: Future Directions in Research,* Psychological Dimensions, 1977.
J. H. Stevens, Jr., and M. Matthews, editors, *Mother-Child, Father-Child Relationships,* National Association for the Education of Young Children, 1978.
H. Hoffman and D. Reiss, editors, *The American Family: Dying or Developing,* Plenum, 1978.
J. Gullahorn, editor, *Psychology and Transition,* V. H. Winston, 1978.
V. Vaughn and T. Brazelton, editors, *The Family: Setting Priorities,* Science and Medicine, 1979.
R. Henderson, editor, *Parent-Child Interaction: Theory, Research, and Prospect,* Academic Press, 1981.
M. Lamb, editor, *Nontraditional Families,* Lawrence Erlbaum Associates, 1982.
J. Spence, editor, *Assessing Achievement,* W. H. Freeman, 1982.

Also contributor to *Introductory Psychology in Depth: Developmental Topics,* Harper. Contributor to *American Encyclopedia of Education.* Contributor of about forty articles and reviews to journals in the behavioral sciences. Editor of *Child Development,* 1977— (member of editorial board, 1966-69); associate editor of *Developmental Psychology,* 1973-77 (member of editorial board, 1968-73), and *Abnormal Child Psychology,* 1973—; member of editorial board of *Contemporary Psychology,* 1973-76, and *Sex Roles,* 1973-76.

*   *   *

HEWETT, John H(arris) 1952-

PERSONAL: Born September 3, 1952, in St. Augustine, Fla.; son of Warren D. (a supervisor) and Evelyn June (a teacher) Hewett; married June L. Martin, June 22, 1974; children: Martin Allen. *Education:* Stetson University, B.A., 1974; Southern Baptist Theological Seminary, M.Div., 1977, Ph.D., 1981.

ADDRESSES: Home—1010 Anduin Court, St. Louis, Mo. 63131. *Office*—Kirkwood Baptist Church, 211 North Woodlawn Ave., Kirkwood, Mo. 63122.

CAREER: Ordained Southern Baptist minister, 1971; associate pastor of Baptist church in Bunnell, Fla., 1970-72; youth minister at Baptist church in Holly Hill, Fla., 1973-75; pastor of Baptist churches in Elmsburg, Ky., 1975-79, and Graefen-

burg, Ky., 1979-81; Kirkwood Baptist Church, Kirkwood, Mo., pastor, 1982—. Theological resident in medical ethics at Norton Psychiatric Clinic, Louisville, Ky., 1978; member of board of trustees of Missouri Baptist College, 1982-86; Midwestern Baptist Theological Seminary, Kansas City, Mo., adjunct professor, 1982—.

MEMBER: Society of Christian Ethics, Americans United for Separation of Church and State, Charles Haddon Spurgeon Society, Missouri Baptist Hospital Association, St. Louis Metro Baptist Association, Omicron Delta Kappa, Pi Kappa Phi, Chi Alpha, Honorable Order of Kentucky Colonels.

AWARDS, HONORS: Clyde T. Francisco Preaching Award from Southern Baptist Theological Seminary, 1976; Walter Pope Binns fellow at William Jewell College, 1983.

WRITINGS:

After Suicide, Westminster, 1980.
Niemand Is Ohne Hoffnung (title means "Nothing Is Without Hope"), Verlag Styria, 1983.
Rational Suicide: Issues and Answers, Westminster, in press.

Contributor to *Dictionary of Pastoral Care and Counseling.*

WORK IN PROGRESS: A manual for ministers under thirty-five years of age, publication by Westminster expected in 1986.

SIDELIGHTS: John H. Hewett told *CA:* "*After Suicide* grew out of an increasing awareness that there existed in print nothing to give to families and friends grieving in the aftermath of suicide. I have been pleased by the widespread acceptance with which the book has been reviewed, both in this country and in Europe.

"People who've had a family member or close friend who killed himself/herself are in an absolute crisis of shock and despair. We wanted *After Suicide* to speak to them at their point of deepest need, to answer their questions about what suicide is and what it isn't, and to begin to help bind up their wounds and point them in the direction of recovery and return to wholeness. There's nothing else like this book to give to a person who has had a suicide in his or her immediate circle of friends or family. We have heard regularly from people whose lives have been touched and have said that it punctured the silence and helped them cope when nothing else could. It seems to me that that kind of writing is a ministry. I guess that's why I spend so much time trying to write and write well. This book has touched seventeen thousand families, more people than I'll preach to in a long, long time.

"My writing style is very much different from my speaking style, and I have to work hard to make them be the same. *Rational Suicide* is a scholarly text which is a revision of my dissertation. It deals with suicides that are done for 'good reasons.' By that I mean sacrificial suicides, euthanatic suicides, and what the literature calls 'balance-sheet' suicides, or suicides that are completed on the basis of logical, reasoned deductions. That book has been written for pastors and professionals in the fields of mental health.

"The book directed to ministers under thirty-five is a whimsical approach to a serious problem. Many of us charge out of the seminary equipped for the task of ministry and are hit head-on by the conceptions and misconceptions of the people with whom we will minister. I'm trying to write out of my experience as a minister who began service at the age of eighteen and who has worked on church staffs continuously since that time. I want my colleagues to know some of what I've been through, and I hope this book will share some of the things they've been through and be of better service to us all.''

* * *

HEWITT, Foster (William)   1903(?)-1985

OBITUARY NOTICE: Born November 21, 1903 (some sources say 1902), in Toronto, Ontario, Canada; died April 21, 1985, in Toronto, Ontario, Canada. Broadcaster and author. Known as Canada's voice of hockey, Hewitt broadcast approximately three thousand hockey games during his fifty-year career. He began broadcasting on radio in 1923 and eventually moved to television. Hewitt, who received numerous broadcasting awards, became a member of the Hockey Hall of Fame in 1965. He was the author of *Down the Ice: Hockey Contacts and Reflections, He Shoots . . . He Scores, Hello Canada, Along Olympia Road,* and *Hockey Night in Canada: The Maple Leafs' Story.*

OBITUARIES AND OTHER SOURCES:

BOOKS

The Canadian Who's Who, Volume 19, University of Toronto Press, 1984.

PERIODICALS

Chicago Tribune, April 24, 1985.

* * *

HEYRMAN, Christine Leigh   1950-

PERSONAL: Born January 9, 1950, in Boston, Mass.; daughter of Robert Charles (a management consultant) and Verona (a housewife; maiden name, Monfils) Heyrman. *Education:* Macalester College, B.A., 1971; Yale University, Ph.D., 1977.

ADDRESSES: Home—26255 Via California, Capistrano Beach, Calif. 92624. *Office*—Department of History, University of California, Irvine, Calif. 92717.

CAREER: University of California, Irvine, acting assistant professor, 1976-77, assistant professor, 1977-82, associate professor of American colonial history, 1982—.

MEMBER: Organization of American Historians, American Historical Association, League of Women Voters.

WRITINGS:

Commerce and Culture: The Maritime Communities of Colonial Massachusetts, 1690-1750, Norton, 1984.
(Contributor) David Hall, John Murnin, and Thad Tate, editors, *Saints and Revolutionaries: Essays on Early American History,* Norton, 1984.

WORK IN PROGRESS: Research on religion and society in the lower South in the eighteenth century.

* * *

HIGGINBOTHAM, Virginia   1935-

PERSONAL: Born November 6, 1935, in Dallas, Tex. *Education:* Southern Methodist University, B.A., 1957, M.A., 1962; Tulane University, Ph.D., 1966.

ADDRESSES: Office—Department of Spanish and Portuguese, University of Texas, Austin, Tex. 78712.

CAREER: University of Texas, Austin, assistant professor, 1966-73, associate professor of Spanish and Portuguese, 1973—.

MEMBER: American Association of Teachers of Spanish and Portuguese, Modern Language Association of America, Philological Association of the Pacific Coast.

WRITINGS:

The Comic Spirit of Federico Garcia Lorca, University of Texas Press, 1976.
Luis Bunuel, Twayne, 1979.
(Contributor) F. Colecchia, editor, *Garcia Lorca: Annotated Bibliography of Criticism,* Garland Publishing, 1979.

Contributor to literature journals. Member of editorial board of *Garcia Lorca Review.*

WORK IN PROGRESS: Spanish Film Under Franco.

SIDELIGHTS: Virginia Higginbotham commented: ''I cannot force myself to work. I work when I feel like it. Luckily, I feel like working most of the time.''

BIOGRAPHICAL/CRITICAL SOURCES:

PERIODICALS

Times Literary Supplement, September 10, 1976.

* * *

HIGGS, Robert J(ackson)   1932-

PERSONAL: Born February 23, 1932, in Lewisburg, Tenn.; son of Robert Lee (a farmer) and Mary Lee (a housewife; maiden name, Cummings) Higgs; married Irene Loy (a secretary), August 18, 1958; children: Julia, Laura. *Education:* United States Naval Academy, B.S., 1955; University of Tennessee, Knoxville, M.A., 1964, Ph.D., 1967.

ADDRESSES: Office—Department of English, East Tennessee State University, Box 24 374, Johnson City, Tenn. 37601.

CAREER: Eastern Kentucky University, Richmond, assistant professor of English, 1966-67; East Tennessee State University, Johnson City, associate professor, 1967-74, professor of English, 1974—. *Military service:* U.S. Air Force, 1958-63; became captain.

MEMBER: National Council of Teachers of English, North American Society of Sports History, Popular Culture Association, Sports Literature Association, Appalachian Studies Conference, South Atlantic Modern Language Association.

WRITINGS:

(Editor) Anne W. Armstrong, *This Day and Time,* East Tennessee State University, 1970.
(Editor with Ambrose N. Manning) *Voices From the Hills: Selected Readings From Southern Appalachia,* Ungar, 1975.
(Contributor) Jerry W. Williamson, editor, *Essays in Honor of Cratis Williams,* Appalachian Journal Press, 1977.
The Sporting Spirit: Athletes in Literature and Life, Harcourt, 1977.
Laurel and Thorn: The Athlete in American Literature, University Press of Kentucky, 1981.
Sports: A Reference Guide, Greenwood Press, 1982.

WORK IN PROGRESS: A Jungian Approach to the Art of Thinking and *God in the Stadium and Muscle in the Church (and State): The Heresy of Sports and Play in the Modern World.*

SIDELIGHTS: Robert J. Higgs told *CA:* ''Most of my writing has dealt with the subjects of Appalachian culture and sports, partly, I suspect, because of my background and experience. A native Tennessean, I expended considerble time and effort as a youth in sports, including varsity baseball and football at the Naval Academy. My interest in these areas is not, however, solely autobiographical. I feel that both Appalachian culture and sports can tell us a great deal about the American experience. Through a study of Appalachian folklore we can gain a clearer understanding of our frontier heritage and perhaps our national character—our self-reliance and ingenuity on the one hand and our conspicuous waste and consumption on the other.

"Through the study of sports we can gain some understanding of our masslore. Unlike folklore, which was transmitted orally for a particular group, masslore is mass produced, usually instantaneously, for a mass audience. Though some of the principles of psychology can be seen in both genres as in the creation of legends, for example, those of Davy Crockett and Muhammad Ali, masslore presents specific problems in the easy and relentless affirmation of the presumed values of sports, for example, the belief that sports are good for the soul, as espoused in one way or another by practically every modern evangelist from Billy Sunday to Billy Graham to Oral Roberts and Jerry Falwell.

"In Mary Gordon's novel *A Company of Women* the priest calls sports 'a protestant heresy,' but at present I'm pursuing the thesis that it is a Catholic heresy as well, indeed a worldwide one at odds with the law, prophets, saints, and even Karl Marx. (My chapter on communist sport in this regard is called: 'Get One for Karl and Vladimir: Jock Missionaries of the Atheist State.')

"Modern sports indeed may be regarded, as Thorstein Veblen argued at the turn of the century in *Theory of the Leisure Class,* as one of the four occupations of predatory cultures, the others being government, warfare, and religion. Sports have become a means of proselytism and symbols of national or ethnic pride, reflecting the prophetic principle of all religions but certainly not the mystical which requires stillness, physical and otherwise, and meditation. Looking at sports and the problems they reflect, one is tempted to conclude with Pascal in *Pensees* that all man's problems stem from his inability to sit still in a room. The nuclear arms race is of course the most pressing example at present of the sporting mentality and conspicuous waste, a subject I've entitled 'Practicing for Armageddon: Holy War Games and ICBM's' in my proposed book on the heresy of sports."

*   *   *

HILLEL, Yehoshua Bar
See BAR-HILLEL, Yehoshua

*   *   *

HILLMAN, Arthur   1909-1985

OBITUARY NOTICE: Born June 26, 1909, in Nevada City, Calif.; died April 10, 1985, in Chicago, Ill. Sociologist, educator, and author. In 1974 Hillman became professor emeritus at Roosevelt University, where he had taught for nearly thirty years. A noted sociologist and Fulbright scholar, the educator is remembered for his service as director of the Hull House center from 1960 to 1969 and for his studies on the city of Chicago. Hillman was the author of *The Unemployed Citizens' League of Seattle; Community Organization and Planning; Tomorrow's Chicago,* with Robert J. Casey; *Sociology*

and Social Work; Urban Church Planning: The Church Discovers Its Community, with Walter Kloetzli; and *Norway's Families: Trends, Problems, Programs,* with Thomas Dawes Eliot.

OBITUARIES AND OTHER SOURCES

BOOKS

American Men and Women of Science: The Social and Behavioral Sciences, 13th edition, Bowker, 1978.
Who's Who in America, 40th edition, Marquis, 1978.

PERIODICALS

Chicago Tribune, April 13, 1985.

*   *   *

HINDS, Dudley S.   1926-

PERSONAL: Born February 26, 1926, in Memphis, Tenn.; son of Milford Everett (a chemist) and Pattie Lee (a musician; maiden name, Sims) Hinds; married Jane Augusta Lindsay (a teacher), June 13, 1952; children: Sims, John, Arthur, Lindsay, Helen, Frederick. *Education:* Attended Southwestern at Memphis, 1943-44; University of Wisconsin—Madison, B.S., 1946; University of North Carolina, M.R.P., 1952.

ADDRESSES: Home—710 Gladstone Rd. N.W., Atlanta, Ga. 30318. *Office*—Department of Real Estate, Georgia State University, Atlanta, Ga. 30303.

CAREER: County of Charleston, S.C., director of planning, 1957-62; City of Miami, Fla., director of planning, 1962-68; Georgia State University, Atlanta, 1968—, began as assistant professor, became associate professor of real estate and urban affairs. Worked as staff city planner in Little Rock, Ark., Providence, R.I., and Jackson, Tenn. *Military service:* U.S. Army Air Forces, 1944-45.

MEMBER: International Real Estate Federation, American Real Estate and Urban Economics Association, American Planning Association, American Institute of Certified Planners, National Association of Corporate Real Estate Executives.

WRITINGS:

(Editor with Edwin Gorsuch, and contributor) *The Future of Atlanta's Central City,* Publishing Services Division, Georgia State University, 1977.
(With Neil Carn and Nicholas Ordway) *Winning at Zoning,* McGraw, 1979.
(With Ordway) *International Real Estate Investment,* Real Estate Education, 1983.

Contributor to real estate, law, and economic journals.

WORK IN PROGRESS: Assessing Risk in Rezoning of Property.

*   *   *

HODGKIN, Thomas Lionel   1910-1982

OBITUARY NOTICE: Born April 3, 1910, in Oxford, England; died March 25, 1982. Historian, educator, and author. An authority on African affairs, Hodgkin served with universities in several different countries. He held numerous positions with Oxford University including serving as a member of the tutorial staff from 1939 to 1945 and as a fellow of Oxford's Balliol College from 1945 to 1952 and again from 1965 to 1970. Hodgkin was also a visiting lecturer at Northwestern University in Illinois, a research associate at the Institute of Islamic Studies at McGill University in Montreal, and director of the Institute of African Studies at the University of Ghana. In 1971 the educator became professor emeritus at Oxford University. Hodgkin wrote *African Political Parties: An Introductory Guide*, *The Colonial Empire: A Students' Guide*, *Nationalism in Colonial Africa*, *Nigerian Perspectives: An Historical Anthology*, *Three Early African Empires*, and *Vietnam: The Revolutionary Path*.

OBITUARIES AND OTHER SOURCES:

BOOKS

International Authors and Writers Who's Who, 9th edition [and] *International Who's Who in Poetry*, 6th edition, Melrose, 1982.
The International Who's Who, 47th edition, Europa, 1983.
Who's Who, 134th edition, St. Martin's, 1982.

PERIODICALS

Times (London), September 3, 1981.

*   *   *

HODGKINSON, Christopher 1928-

PERSONAL: Born March 10, 1928, in England; son of Albert and Hilda (Lesse) Hodgkinson; married Madge Smith, May 2, 1952. *Education:* University of London, B.Sc. (with honors), 1959; University of British Columbia, M.Ed., 1964; University of California, Berkeley, Ph.D., 1968. *Politics:* "Uncommitted organizationally." *Religion:* "Uncommitted organizationally."

ADDRESSES: Home—1159 Beach Dr., No. 403, Victoria, British Columbia, Canada V8S 2N2. *Office*—Department of Communication and Social Foundations, University of Victoria, P.O. Box 1700, Victoria, British Columbia, Canada V8W 2Y2.

CAREER: Held various posts in government and the private sector, 1962-67; teacher of economics and history at high schools in West Vancouver and North Vancouver, British Columbia, 1967; University of Victoria, Victoria, British Columbia, professor of public and educational administration, 1971—. Instructor of administration at University of British Columbia, Vancouver, 1978; visiting professor of educational administration at McGill University, Montreal, Quebec, 1982; visiting fellow and senior research scholar in public and educational administration at Cambridge University, Cambridge, England, 1983.

MEMBER: Canadian Education Association, Canadian Society for the Study of Education, Commonwealth Council for Educational Administration, American Educational Research Association, Phi Delta Kappa.

AWARDS, HONORS: Canada Council fellow, 1975-76; fellow of Social Science and Humanities Research Council of Canada, 1982-83; senior research scholar at Corpus Christi College, Cambridge, 1982-83.

WRITINGS:

Towards a Philosophy of Administration, Basil Blackwell, 1978.
The Philosophy of Leadership, Basil Blackwell, 1983.
Leadership in Educational Administration, State University of New York, in press.

Contributor to professional journals.

WORK IN PROGRESS: The Executive Passions.

SIDELIGHTS: Christopher Hodgkinson wrote: "Throughout my academic career I have been preoccupied with the problem of values. This is reflected in my work, which is now tending in the direction of speculative analyses of the emotions and the will. I have always maintained that philosophy and administration are inseparable. Moreover, the essential human problems of our time are administrative problems. Leaders will have to become better philosophers than they are now, generally speaking. I attempt to help.

"Our society is increasingly technological, organizational, and bureaucratic. In a word: *administrative*. The quality of our lives depends on administrators and, protestations to the contrary, the bulk of the evidence goes to show that they are *not* very honorable men. If anything, villainy is directly proportional to altitude in the hierarchy of leadership. In appointing executives the moral qualities of the candidate are almost never examined while great pains are taken to examine the *technical* qualifications. I seek some redress. I seek to expound a theory of value and a philosophy of honor and make them available to men and women in leadership positions."

BIOGRAPHICAL/CRITICAL SOURCES:

PERIODICALS

Die Verwaltung, Volume XIV, number 1, 1981.
Journal of Educational Administration, October, 1979.
Political Quarterly, March, 1980.
Political Studies, March, 1980.
Public Administration, summer, 1979.
Social Policy and Administration, spring, 1980.

*   *   *

HOFFMAN, David Herbert 1932(?)-1985

OBITUARY NOTICE: Born c. 1932 in Coral Gables, Fla.; died of cardiorespiratory arrest, February 15, 1985, in Alexandria, Va. Pilot, editor, and journalist. Hoffman, who wrote for numerous periodicals, is remembered as Saigon bureau chief for the *Washington Post*. He joined the newspaper in 1967 following a period of employment as a pilot for Trans World Airlines and as an aviation editor of the *New York Herald Tribune*. During Hoffman's career with the *Washington Post*, the journalist became known for submitting one of the newspaper's most notorious expense accounts. The $100 expenditure—incurred when the journalist hired a military escort for protection while on assignment in Vietnam—was initially disputed by the paper's management. Later the problem was resolved, but Hoffman's name became permanently linked with the incident. After the journalist left his position with the *Washington Post* in 1971, he served a brief period working for the *Miami Herald*. Hoffman then went back to Washington, D.C., and began to write on a free-lance basis.

OBITUARIES AND OTHER SOURCES:

PERIODICALS

Washington Post, February 19, 1985.

*   *   *

HOGARTH, Charles
See BOWEN, (Ivor) Ian

HOLLAND, Patricia G.   1940-

PERSONAL: Born June 24, 1940, in Oakland, Calif.; daughter of William Lancelot (an Asian studies scholar) and Doreen (McGarry) Holland; married G. Putnam Barber, September 23, 1961 (divorced, 1971); children: Jonathan H., Lucy G. *Education:* Bryn Mawr College, A.B., 1961; University of Massachusetts, Ph.D., 1975.

ADDRESSES: Home—105 Blackberry Lane, Amherst, Mass. 01002. *Office*—University of Massachusetts, 303 New Africa, Amherst, Mass. 01003.

CAREER: University of Massachusetts, Amherst, editor of "The Correspondence of Lydia Maria Child," 1976-80, historical editor of "The Papers of Elizabeth Cady Stanton and Susan B. Anthony," 1980—. Representative of Amherst Town Meeting, 1981—.

MEMBER: Association for Documentary Editing.

WRITINGS:

(Editor with Milton Meltzer) *The Collected Correspondence of Lydia Maria Child, 1817-1880,* KTO Microform, 1980.
(Editor with Meltzer) *Lydia Maria Child: Selected Letters, 1817-1880,* University of Massachusetts Press, 1982.

WORK IN PROGRESS: Editing *The Papers of Elizabeth Cady Stanton and Susan B. Anthony,* with Ann D. Gordon, publication expected in 1993.

*   *   *

HOLLINRAKE, Roger (Barker)   1929-

PERSONAL: Born June 2, 1929, in Auckland, New Zealand; son of Horace (a professor) and Phyllis (Hoyle) Hollinrake. *Education:* Peterhouse, Cambridge, B.A., 1951, M.A., 1954, Mus.B., 1970; Merton College, Oxford, M.A., 1960, D.Phil., 1971.

ADDRESSES: Home—16 St. John St., Oxford OX1 2LQ, England.

CAREER: University of Auckland, Auckland, New Zealand, lecturer in history of music, 1955-61; recital organist in Australia and New Zealand, 1961-63; Oxford University, Oxford, England, assistant university organist, 1963-65. Resident fellow at Harvard University, 1951-52; lecturer at Oxford University, 1969, 1983.

MEMBER: International Musicological Society, Royal Musical Association, Schopenhauer Gesellschaft.

AWARDS, HONORS: Donald Tovey Memorial Prize from Oxford University, 1960; Michael Foster Memorial Scholar at University of Heidelberg, 1961-62.

WRITINGS:

Nietzsche and Wagner, Allen & Unwin, 1982.

Contributor to music periodicals, including *Music Letters,* and German studies journals.

WORK IN PROGRESS: Translating and annotating Nietzsche's *Also sprach Zarathustra.*

SIDELIGHTS: Roger Hollinrake studied musical composition with Herbert Howells at the Royal College of Music and Aaron Copland at the Berkshire Music Center at Tanglewood. He studied organ with Melville Smith at Longy School of Music,

Cambridge, Massachusetts, and with Fernando Germani in Italy.

Hollinrake told *CA:* "My theory, advanced in 1960, that much of Nietzsche's writing—specifically the theory of recurrence in *Zarathustra,* part three,—was polemically pitted against Wagner the artist, speculative thinker, and messianic leader, had no precedent and conflicted with scholarly opinion."

*   *   *

HOLMES, John (Albert)   1904-1962

OBITUARY NOTICE: Born January 6, 1904, in Somerville, Mass.; died June 22, 1962. Educator, poet, and author. A graduate of Tufts College (now Tufts University), Holmes taught English at his alma mater from 1934 until his death, starting as an instructor and advancing to the rank of professor in 1961. Named Phi Beta Kappa poet at Tufts in 1935 and 1960, at Brown University in 1950, at William and Mary College in 1955, and at Harvard in 1956, Holmes published several volumes of poetry, including *Address to the Living, The Double Root, The Fortune Teller,* and *The Symbols.* His *Selected Poems* appeared posthumously in 1965. He also published a nonfiction work titled *Writing Poetry.* In 1958 he received the William Rose Benet Poetry Prize.

OBITUARIES AND OTHER SOURCES:

BOOKS

American Authors and Books: 1640 to the Present Day, 3rd revised edition, Crown, 1962.
World Authors: 1950-1970, H. W. Wilson, 1975.

*   *   *

HOLMES, John L.   1925-

PERSONAL: Born January 18, 1925, in Sydney, Australia; son of Leonard and Doris Holmes; married Elise Mayer, August 30, 1965; children: Lucie, Andrew. *Education:* University of Sydney, B.Econ., 1949.

ADDRESSES: Home—31 Mawson Dr., Canberra, Australian Capital Territory 2607.

CAREER: Worked for Commonwealth Public Service in Australia, 1948-54; began in 1956 with Australian Department of Trade, became trade commissioner at embassies in Kuala Lumpur, Malaysia, 1962-63, Singapore, 1963, Djakarta, Indonesia, 1963-64, London, England, 1964-66, Lagos, Nigeria, 1966-67, Los Angeles, Calif., 1969-71, Bangkok, Thailand, 1972-74, Tel Aviv, Israel, 1975-77, Berlin, Germany, 1978-81, and Vienna, Austria, 1981-84. *Military service:* Royal Australian Air Force, 1943-46.

WRITINGS:

Conductors on Record, Greenwood Press, 1982.

Contributor to *Fanfare.*

SIDELIGHTS: John L. Holmes told *CA:* "*Conductors on Record* is a biographical dictionary of conductors who have made gramophone records, from Nikisch to the present day, or at least until the end of 1977. For the major artists there are extensive essays discussing their personalities, styles, and influence, and every entry includes a discography."

Conductors on Record has been well received by critics in England and the United States. It has been described as a comprehensive, insightful, and lively compilation.

BIOGRAPHICAL/CRITICAL SOURCES:

PERIODICALS

Punch, September 15, 1982.

* * *

HOLMES, Olive 1911-
(Oliver Wyman, a joint pseudonym)

PERSONAL: Born February 28, 1911, in Massachusetts; daughter of Nicholas (a physician) and Emma (a nurse; maiden name, Anderson) Cousens; married Wyman Holmes (a writer and editor), June 25, 1939; children: Anne. *Education:* Wellesley College, B.A., 1931; attended Columbia University, 1932-33, and Sorbonne, University of Paris, summer, 1933. *Politics:* Democrat. *Religion:* Humanist.

ADDRESSES: Home and office—321 Park St., North Reading, Mass. 01864.

CAREER: Denishawn dancer during 1930's; Harvard University, Cambridge, Mass., chief editor at Fairbank Center for East Asian Research, 1963-76; affiliated with Edindex (editors), North Reading, Mass.

AWARDS, HONORS: Honorable mention from De La Torre Bueno Prize from *Dance Perspectives* and Wesleyan University Press, 1980.

WRITINGS:

The Thesis and the Book, Toronto University Press, 1976.
(Editor) *Motion Arrested: Dance Reviews of H. T. Parker,* Wesleyan University Press, 1982.

Contributor of articles to *Gourmet, Down East, Sea,* and *Horticulture,* and of short stories to *Cosmopolitan, Saturday Evening Post, Ladies' Home Journal,* and *Redbook.* Also author of short stories with husband, Wyman Holmes, under joint pseudonym Oliver Wyman.

WORK IN PROGRESS: With husband, Wyman Holmes, a book about an island off the coast of Maine.

SIDELIGHTS: Motion Arrested: Dance Reviews of H. T. Parker is a collection of texts of dance criticisms written by H. T. Parker, drama critic of the *Boston Evening Transcript* from 1905 until 1934. Olive Holmes's edition serves to establish Parker as a pioneer in American dance criticism. As noted by Anna Kisselgoff in the *New York Times Book Review,* Parker's prowess as a dance critic may have remained forever neglected had it not been for Holmes's book.

Holmes told *CA:* "My husband (Wyman Holmes) and I are at present involved in a home editing business (Edindex) with an emphasis on computerized indexing. We are also working together on a book about our island off the coast of Maine, the subject of articles in *Gourmet, Down East, Sea,* and *Horticulture.*"

BIOGRAPHICAL/CRITICAL SOURCES:

PERIODICALS

New York Times Book Review, May 15, 1983.

* * *

HOPKINS, Robert S(ydney)
(Robert Rostand)

PERSONAL: Born in Los Angeles, Calif. *Education:* Educated in Los Angeles, Calif.

ADDRESSES: P.O. Box 15911, Honolulu, Hawaii, 96815.

CAREER: Writer. Worked as lecturer in geography and with U.S. State Department in Washington, D.C.

WRITINGS:

(With Albert B. Carr) *Islands of the Deep Sea* (juvenile nonfiction), John Day, 1967.
Darwin's South America (nonfiction), John Day, 1969.
I've Had It: A Practical Guide to Moving Abroad, Holt, 1972.
Riviera: A Novel About the Cannes Film Festival, Morrow, 1980.

NOVELS UNDER PSEUDONYM ROBERT ROSTRAND

The Killer Elite, Delacorte, 1973.
The Raid on Villa Joyosa, Putnam, 1973.
Viper's Game, Delacorte, 1974.
The D'Artagnan Signature, Putnam, 1976.
A Killing in Rome, Delacorte, 1977.

MEDIA ADAPTATIONS: "The Killer Elite," a feature film based on Hopkins's novel of the same name and starring James Caan and Robert Duvall, was released by United Artists in 1975.

* * *

HOPPER, Nancy J. 1937-

PERSONAL: Born July 25, 1937, in Lewistown, Pa.; daughter of David L. (a school superintendent) and Joyce (Beaver) Swartz; married James A. Hopper (a professor and artist), August 20, 1960; children: Christopher J., Jennifer A. *Education:* Juniata College, B.A., 1959.

ADDRESSES: Home—2341 Ridgewood, Alliance, Ohio 44601.

CAREER: High school English teacher at public schools in Tyrone, Pa., 1959-60; Freeport Public Schools, Freeport, N.Y., high school English teacher, 1960-62; housewife and writer.

MEMBER: Authors Guild.

WRITINGS:

JUVENILE NOVELS

Secrets, Elsevier/Nelson, 1979.
The Seven-and-One-Half Sins of Stacey Kendall, Dutton, 1982.
Just Vernon, Lodestar, 1982.
Hang On, Harvey!, Dutton, 1983.
Lies (young adult), Lodestar, 1984.
Ape Ears and Beaky, Dutton, 1984.

SIDELIGHTS: Nancy Hopper commented: "I like to work from character, the character coming first, the story happening at least partially as a result of that character. The largest part of my writing is both for and about people between the ages of nine and sixteen. I find individuals in this age group to be fascinating. They have a fresh, critical eye on life and are quite often endowed with a great sense of humor. They are engaged in the all-encompassing battle to grow up, to mature, to understand; and I think that is, to a great extent, what life is about, at either age one month or age eighty years. It seems to me that between the ages of nine and sixteen, individuals make a frontal attack on this issue, acting with determination, courage, and a willingness to take their bumps and to write off their losses. This enables them as real people, and as people in books, to move in and out of situations that offer much in the way of opportunity for excitement, and, best of all, to regard life as what it really is: an adventure."

AVOCATIONAL INTERESTS: Reading, bird-watching, walking, bicycling, attending concerts and the movies, making Ukrainian eggs.

* * *

HORNE, Kenneth 1900-1975

OBITUARY NOTICE: Born April 28, 1900, in Westminster, England; died June 5, 1975, in London, England. Screenwriter and playwright. Horne wrote numerous plays from 1933 to 1970, including "A Lass and a Lackey," "Fools Rush In," "Trial and Error," "Public Mischief," and "The Coming-Out Party." He also worked on many film adaptations.

OBITUARIES AND OTHER SOURCES:

BOOKS

Obituaries on File, Facts on File, 1979.
Who's Who in the Theatre: A Biographical Record of the Contemporary Stage, 15th edition, Pitman, 1972.

* * *

HOUSER, Caroline

PERSONAL: Born in Walla Walla, Wash.; daughter of Alton and Elizabeth (Patterson) Houser. *Education:* Mills College, B.A.; Harvard University, A.M., Ph.D.; attended American School of Classical Studies in Athens.

ADDRESSES: Office—Department of Art, Smith College, Northampton, Mass. 01063.

CAREER: University of Texas at Austin, assistant professor of art, 1975-78; Smith College, Northampton, Mass., associate professor of art, 1979—. Member of managing committee of American School of Classical Studies in Athens.

MEMBER: College Art Association of America, Archaeological Institute of America.

AWARDS, HONORS: Andrew W. Mellon fellow at Harvard University, 1978-79.

WRITINGS:

Dionysos and His Circle: Ancient Through Modern, Fogg Art Museum, Harvard University, 1979.
Greek Monumental Bronze Sculpture From the Fifth to the Second Century, B.C., Vendome, 1983.

Contributor to art history, architecture, and archaeology journals.

WORK IN PROGRESS: Research on art and politics in Hellenistic Greece, Greek and Roman sculpture in bronze, Praxiteles, and plaster casts of classical sculpture.

* * *

HOUSTON, Jean

BRIEF ENTRY: American actress, psychologist, and author. In 1965 Houston and her husband, Robert E. L. Masters, established the Foundation for Mind Research to conduct research on mental and psychic experiences. Her books include *The Varieties of Psychedelic Experience* (Holt, 1966), *Mind Games* (Viking, 1972), *Listening to the Body* (Dell, 1979), *Lifeforce: The Psycho-Historical Recovery of Self* (Delacorte, 1980), and *The Possible Human: A Course in Extending Your Physical, Mental, and Creative Abilities* (J. P. Tarcher, 1982).

Houston is also an award-winning playwright. *Address:* Foundation for Mind Research, P.O. Box 600, Pomona, N.Y. 10970.

BIOGRAPHICAL/CRITICAL SOURCES:

PERIODICALS

Los Angeles Times Book Review, December 5, 1982.
New Age, February, 1983.

* * *

HOWARD, Kenneth I(rwin) 1932-

PERSONAL: Born October 19, 1932, in Chicago, Ill.; son of Simon and Florence (Bergman) Howard; married April R. Zweig (a lawyer), December 15, 1979; children: Deborah, Peter, Lisa, David, Rebecca. *Education:* University of California, Berkeley, A.B., 1954; University of Chicago, Ph.D., 1959. *Religion:* Jewish.

ADDRESSES: Home—2626 Sheridan Rd., Evanston, Ill. 60201. *Office*—Department of Psychology, Northwestern University, 633 Clark St., Evanston, Ill. 60201.

CAREER: Northwestern University, Evanston, Ill., visiting associate professor, 1966-67, associate professor, 1967-70, professor of psychology, 1970—. *Military service:* U.S. Army, 1954-56; became first lieutenant.

MEMBER: American Psychological Association (fellow), Society for Psychotherapy Research (president), Society for Multivariate Experimental Psychology.

WRITINGS:

(With David Orlinsky) *Varieties of Psychotherapeutic Experience,* Teachers College Press, Columbia University, 1975.
(With Eric Ostrov and Daniel Offer) *The Adolescent: A Psychological Self-Portrait,* Basic Books, 1981.
(With Ostrov and Offer) *The Teenage World,* Plenum, in press.

* * *

HOWES, Frank Stewart 1891-1974

OBITUARY NOTICE: Born April 2, 1891, in Oxford, England; died September 28, 1974; buried in Combe, England. Educator, music critic, and author. Howes was chief music critic for the London *Times* for seventeen years. He began as the periodical's assistant music critic in 1925 and became chief music critic in 1943. In addition, Howes was a professor of music at the Royal College of Music in London from 1938 to 1970, and he was active in numerous organizations benefiting musical concerns. Howes's publications include *A Key to the Art of Music, The Music of Ralph Vaughan Williams, Full Orchestra, Man, Mind, and Music, The English Musical Renaissance,* and *Folk Music of Britain—and Beyond.*

OBITUARIES AND OTHER SOURCES:

BOOKS

The Oxford Companion to Music, 10th edition, Oxford University Press, 1974.
Who Was Who in America, With World Notables, Volume VI, 1974-1976, Marquis, 1976.
Who's Who in Music and Musician's International Directory, 6th edition, Hafner, 1972.

HUDSON, W(illiam) H(enry) 1841-1922
(Henry Harford)

BRIEF ENTRY: Born August 4, 1841, in Quilmes, Argentina; died of heart disease, August 18, 1922, in London, England. English naturalist and author. The son of transplanted Americans, Hudson was born on the Pampas of Argentina, where he developed an almost mystical love of nature. He spent his early childhood collecting bird skins and studying bird migration for the Smithsonian Institution. In his mid-thirties Hudson moved to England, where he and his wife, fifteen years his senior, were to spend nearly the rest of their lives in poverty.

Despite his financial hardships Hudson managed to make at least one trip to the English countryside each year, resulting in such studies as *Hampshire Days* (1903) and *Afoot in England* (1909). Hudson also wrote novels, including *The Purple Land That England Lost* (1885) and the book for which he is best remembered, *Green Mansions: A Romance of the Tropical Forest* (1904). He wrote the novel *Fan: The Story of a Young Girl's Life* under the pseudonym Henry Harford. In addition to these works, he also published several collections of short stories and an autobiography, *Far Away and Long Ago: A History of My Early Life* (1918).

BIOGRAPHICAL/CRITICAL SOURCES:

BOOKS

Twentieth-Century Authors: A Biographical Dictionary of Modern Literture, H. W. Wilson, 1942.

PERIODICALS

Saturday Review of Literature, April 12, 1974.
Times (London), September 11, 1982.

*   *   *

HUGGINS, Charles B(renton) 1901-

BRIEF ENTRY: Born September 22, 1901, in Halifax, Nova Scotia, Canada; naturalized U.S. citizen, 1933. American surgeon, educator, and author. Huggins joined the faculty of the University of Chicago in 1927; he became a professor of surgery there in 1936 and was named William B. Ogden Disntinguished Service Professor in 1962. A specialist in the surgical and therapeutic treatment of prostate and breast cancer, he directed the Ben May Laboratory for Cancer Research from 1951 to 1969 and served as chancellor of Acadia University from 1972 to 1979. Among the oncologist's numerous awards are the prestigious Lasker Clinical Research Award, received in 1963 for his advancement of cancer research, and the Nobel Prize for medicine and physics, presented in 1966 for his research on the use of hormones in the treatment of cancer. Huggins has written nearly three hundred medical articles and scientific books, including *Experimental Leukemia and Mammary Cancer: Induction, Prevention, and Cure* (University of Chicago Press, 1979). *Address:* 5807 Dorchester Ave., Chicago, Ill. 60637; and Ben May Laboratory for Cancer Research, University of Chicago, 950 East 59th St., Chicago, Ill. 60637.

BIOGRAPHICAL/CRITICAL SOURCES:

BOOKS

Current Biography, Wilson, 1965.
Who's Who in America, 42nd edition, Marquis, 1982.

HULBERT, Jack 1892-1978

OBITUARY NOTICE: Born April 24, 1892, in Ely, Cambridgeshire, England; died March 25, 1978, in London, England. Actor, producer, director, singer, dancer, choreographer, and librettist. Considered one of the most prominent English comedians, Hulbert formed an internationally acclaimed partnership with his wife Cicely Courtneidge, appearing in numerous musicals and motion pictures. Following their first success, the musical "By the Way," Hulbert and Courtneidge appeared in many stage productions, including "Clowns in Clover," "Under Your Hat" and "Full Swing" (Hulbert choreographed and was co-librettist for the latter two). Hulbert's and Courtneidge's films include "Jack Ahoy" and "The Camels Are Coming." Hulbert also wrote the autobiographical stage production of "Once More With Music."

OBITUARIES AND OTHER SOURCES:

BOOKS

Encyclopedia of the Musical Theatre, Dodd, 1976.
Who's Who, 126th edition, St. Martin's, 1974.

PERIODICALS

New York Times, March 26, 1978.

*   *   *

HUNGRY WOLF, Adolf 1944-

PERSONAL: Name originally Adolf Gutohrlein; born February 16, 1944, Germany; married Beverly Little Bear (a writer), October, 1971; children: Adolf, Jr., Okan, Iniskim, Star. *Education:* Long Beach State College (now University of California, Long Beach), B.A., 1966.

ADDRESSES: Home—P.O. Box 844, Skookumchuck, British Columbia, Canada V0B 2E0. *Agent*—Theron Raines, Raines & Raines, 475 Fifth Ave., New York, N.Y. 10017.

CAREER: Writer, 1962—. Locomotive fireman for Union Pacific Railroad, Los Angeles, Calif., 1962-65; high school history teacher in Long Beach, Calif., 1967.

MEMBER: Crazy Dogs Society.

AWARDS, HONORS: Preis der Leseratten from German Scholastic Association, 1983, for Der Rabe weiss wo die Sonne wohnt.

WRITINGS:

The Good Medicine Book, Warner Paperback Library, 1973.
The Blood People, Harper, 1977.
Rails in the Canadian Rockies, Good Medicine Books, 1980.
A Good Medicine Collection, Good Medicine Books, 1983.
(With wife, Beverly Hungry Wolf) *Shadows of the Buffalo,* Morrow, 1983.

WORK IN PROGRESS: A novel; research on Native American culture, western history, railways, and photographic history.

SIDELIGHTS: Adolf Hungry Wolf is raising his family in the wilderness. Without telephones, electricity, and formal educational institutions, he practices "life in harmony with nature." He and his family have adopted traditions passed on by Native American forebears, and they participate in Blackfeet tribal events. Hungry Wolf writes from an office he made in one of his railroad cars. He owns four cabooses, a hand car, and some track.

HUNT, Garry Edward 1942-

PERSONAL: Born May 23, 1942, in London, England; son of Edward and Amy Louisa Hunt; married Wendy Thomas, April 9, 1966; children: Sarah-Jane Clare, Susannah Helen Wendy. *Education:* University of London, B.Sc. (with first class honors), 1964, Ph.D., 1966, D.Sc., 1981. *Politics:* Conservative. *Religion:* Church of England.

ADDRESSES: Home—Elbury, 37 Blenheim Rd., Raynes Park, London S.W.20, England. *Office*—Centre for Remote Sensing, Imperial College of Science and Technology, University of London, London SW7 2AZ, England. *Agent*—Belinda Harley Associates, 17 Norland Sq., London W11 4PX, England.

CAREER: Research fellow at Atlas Computer Laboratory, 1966-67; University of Reading, Reading, England, lecturer in applied mathematics, 1967-69; senior research fellow at Atlas Computer Laboratory, 1969-70; Jet Propulsion Laboratory, Pasadena, Calif., senior scientist in space sciences division, 1970-72; Meteorological Office, Bracknell, England, senior scientific officer, 1972-73, principal scientific officer, 1973-77, group leader of Global Atmospheric Research Program (GARP) and climate studies, 1974-76, group leader of atmospheric radiation transfer, 1976-77; University College, London, England, senior fellow in department of physics and astronomy and head of Laboratory for Planetary Atmospheres, 1977-82; Imperial College of Science and Technology, London, head of atmospheric physics department, 1982—, director of Centre for Remote Sensing, 1983—.

Chairman of European Space Agency (ESA) science applications panel, 1976-77; chairman of Science Research Council planetary sciences review panel, 1977-78; chairman of Planetary Sciences Studies Commission planetary atmospheres working group, 1982. Visiting professor in department of physics at University of Missouri, 1984; visiting associate professor on planetary science division at Kitt Peak National Observatory, Tucson, Ariz., 1971; visiting associate professor in division of applied mathematics in Argonne, Ill., 1971 and 1972; distinguished visiting scientist in division of atmospheric research of Commonwealth Scientific and Industrial Research Organization (CSIRO), 1984; visiting scientist at National Center for Atmospheric Research, Boulder, Colo., 1972 and 1984; research associate in department of atmospheric physics at Oxford University, 1968-71. Member of National Academy of Sciences space sciences board, 1970, American Meteorological Society atmospheric radiation working group, 1970-72, and atmospheric radiation committee for GARP Atlantic Tropical Experiment, 1971-72, Science Research Council geophysics working group, 1973-74, International Committee on Dynamical Meteorology, 1973-75, International Radiation Commission, 1973-77, National Aeronautics and Space Administration (NASA) and European Space Research Organization (ERSO) Pioneer Jupiter Orbiting Committee, 1974, British National Committee for Space Research, 1974—, ESA Solar System Committee, 1975-77, International Union of Geodesy and Geophysics International Radiation Commission, 1975-83, Committee on Space Research (COSPAR), 1977-79, and National Academy of Sciences space science board committee on data management and computation, 1982—.

Principal investigator on NASA space missions Voyager (including flybys of Jupiter, 1979, Saturn, 1980-81, Uranus, 1986, and Neptune, 1989) and Viking (including Mars orbit), 1977-82; co-investigator of imaging team for ESA flyby of Halley's Comet.

MEMBER: International Astronomical Union (secretary of Commission 16: The Planets, 1979-82; vice president of commission, 1982—); International Commission on Planetary Atmospheres and Their Evolution (secretary, 1978-83; president, 1983—); Royal Institution of Great Britain, British Computer Society, American Meteorological Society, American Astronomical Society (fellow of division of planetary sciences), American Geophysical Union, Royal Astronomical Society (fellow and councillor), Royal Meteorological Society (fellow), Institute of Mathematics and Its Applications (fellow).

AWARDS, HONORS: Exceptional Achievement Awards from NASA, 1981, for work on Voyager project and Voyager imaging team; Gaskell Medal from Royal Meteorological Society, 1983, for distinguished planetary and satellite meteorology research.

WRITINGS:

(With Patrick Moore) *Jupiter*, Rand McNally, 1981.
(Editor) Moore, *The Moon*, Rand McNally, 1981.
(With Moore) *The Planet Venus*, Faber, 1982.
(Editor) *Uranus and the Other Planets*, Cambridge University Press, 1982.
(With K. Y. Kondratyev) *Weather and Climate of the Planets*, Pergamon, 1982.
Saturn, Rand McNally, 1982.
(With Moore) *Atlas of the Solar System*, Mitchell Beazley, 1983.

Contributor to magazines and newspapers. Associate editor of *Climate Change*, 1976-81, *Journal of Quantitative Spectroscopy and Radiative Transfer*, 1977—, *Vistas in Astronomy*, 1982—, *Earth, Moon, and Planets*, 1984—, and *Earth Oriented Applications of Space Technology*.

WORK IN PROGRESS: Books on space technology and planetary exploration.

SIDELIGHTS: Garry Edward Hunt told *CA:* "I intend to convey to the general reader details of current scientific knowledge in a readable manner."

AVOCATIONAL INTERESTS: Travel.

BIOGRAPHICAL/CRITICAL SOURCES:

PERIODICALS

Times Literary Supplement, February 17, 1984.

*   *   *

HUSE, Dennis P(aul) 1944-

PERSONAL: Born January 30, 1944, in Wichita, Kan.; son of Leo C. (a farmer) and Dorothy J. (Jarmer) Huse. *Education:* Attended Creighton University, 1962-65; Cardinal Glennon College, B.A., 1967; St. Louis University, M.Div., 1971.

ADDRESSES: Home—211 East Fifth, Hutchinson, Kan. 67501. *Office*—1400 East 17th St., Hutchinson, Kan. 67501.

CAREER: Ordained Roman Catholic priest, 1971; high school teacher in Pittsburg, Kan., 1971-72, Wichita, Kan., 1972-76, and Hutchinson, Kan.

WRITINGS:

Speak, Lord, I'm Listening, Ave Maria Press, 1980.

SIDELIGHTS: Dennis P. Huse told *CA:* "My concern for children in church prompted me to write *Speak, Lord, I'm Listen-*

ing. The book contains thirty-nine liturgical celebrations on a variety of themes which can be used throughout the school year. Though they were written specifically for junior high students, they can easily be adapted to any age.''

*   *   *

HUSSMAN, Lawrence Eugene, Jr.   1932-

PERSONAL: Born March 20, 1932, in Dayton, Ohio; son of Lawrence Eugene and Genevieve Hussman; married, 1959 (divorced, 1984); children: Stephen, Sarah. *Education:* University of Dayton, B.A., 1954; University of Michigan, M.A., 1957, Ph.D., 1964.

ADDRESSES: Home—440 Green St., Yellow Springs, Ohio 45387. *Office*—Department of English, Wright State University, Colonel Glenn Highway, Dayton, Ohio 45435.

CAREER: University of Portland, Portland, Ore., instructor, 1961-63, assistant professor of English, 1963-65; Wright State University, Dayton, Ohio, assistant professor, 1965-67, associate professor, 1968-79, professor of English and chairman of department, 1980—. *Military service:* U.S. Army, 1954-56.

MEMBER: Modern Language Association of America.

WRITINGS:

Dreiser and His Fiction: A Twentieth-Century Quest, University of Pennsylvania Press, 1983.

Contributor to literature journals.

WORK IN PROGRESS: Free Lancer: The Story of a Volunteer Counter-Terrorist, with Sam Hall and Felicia Lewis, publication expected in 1985; *The Fiction of Frank Norris*, publication expected in 1986.

SIDELIGHTS: Lawrence Eugene Hussman, Jr., told *CA:* "*Free Lancer* is the biography of a middle-aged volunteer counter-terrorist who has fought in Lebanon, Angola, Zimbabwe, and El Salvador. *The Fiction of Frank Norris* is about Norris's development from naturalist to mystic and from Darwinian to love-ethic advocate."

*   *   *

HY, Ronald John   1942-

PERSONAL: Born November 8, 1942, in Bay City, Mich.; son of John (a construction worker) and Adeline (a housewife) Hy; married Star Williams (a housewife), August, 1974; children: Star, Adelphine. *Education:* Central Michigan University, B.S., 1965, M.A., 1967; Miami University, Oxford, Ohio, Ph.D., 1972.

ADDRESSES: Home—3430 Southwest Mission, Topeka, Kan. 66614. *Office*—Department of Political Science, Washburn University of Topeka, Topeka, Kan. 66621.

CAREER: West Liberty State College, West Liberty, W.Va., instructor in political science, 1969-71; University of Mississippi, University, assistant professor of political science, 1972-83; Washburn University of Topeka, Topeka, Kan., professor of political science and chairman of department, 1983—. Chairman of Task Force to Reorganize City Government, Topeka.

MEMBER: International Personnel Management Association, American Society for Public Administration (member of ex-

ecutive committee of section on public administration education), Policy Studies Organization, Southern Political Science Association.

AWARDS, HONORS: Fellowships from U.S. State Department, Miami University, and University of Michigan, 1971-74; grants from University of Mississippi, 1976-77.

WRITINGS:

(Contributor) Joseph Parker and Thomas Landry, editors, *Mississippi Government and Politics in Transition*, Kendall/Hunt, 1976.
(Contributor) Donald S. Vaughan, editor, *A Manual of Mississippi Municipal Government*, Bureau of Governmental Research, University of Mississippi, 1977.
Using the Computer in the Social Sciences: A Nontechnical Approach, Elsevier-North Holland, 1977.
(Contributor) William Coplin, editor, *Teaching Policy Studies*, Lexington Books, 1978.
(With Douglas Feig and Robert Regoli) *Research Methods and Statistics*, Anderson Publishing, 1983.

Contributor of about twenty-five articles to professional journals. Member of editorial board of *Public Administration Quarterly.*

WORK IN PROGRESS: Local and State Government, an urban administration text, with William Waugh, publication expected in 1986.

SIDELIGHTS: Ronald John Hy told *CA:* "My primary reason for writing is to explain to readers unfamiliar with government, statistics, and computers the way these entities operate and in terms that readers can understand. I see my writing as an extension of teaching. I concentrate on informing readers."

*   *   *

HYATT, I. Ralph   1927-

PERSONAL: Born December 17, 1927, in Philadelphia, Pa.; married Susan Dunner (an executive assistant), 1952; children: Glenn A., Sherry J. *Education:* Yeshiva University, B.A., 1948; Temple University, M.A., 1949; Ed.D., 1958; doctoral study at Bryn Mawr College, 1949-50, and University of Pennsylvania, 1950-51. *Religion:* Jewish.

ADDRESSES: Home—245 Wiltshire Rd., Philadelphia, Pa. 19151. *Office*—Department of Psychology, St. Joseph's University, 5600 City Ave., Philadelphia, Pa. 19131.

CAREER: Cedars Nursing Home, Philadelphia, Pa., counseling psychologist, 1953-55; Municipal Court of Philadelphia, Philadelphia, clinical psychologist at Family Court, 1955-58; State Correctional Institution, Philadelphia, chief clinical psychologist, 1958-61; St. Joseph's University, Philadelphia, professor of psychology, 1961—, chairperson of department, 1965—. Private practice of psychology, 1951—. Member of advisory board of Philadelphia Psychiatric Center's Community Mental Health Center; guest on radio and television programs; chief consultant with Educational and Vocational Guidance Consultants, Inc. *Military service:* U.S. Army, clinical psychologist with Medical Service Corps, 1951-53; became first lieutenant.

MEMBER: International Society of Hypnosis, American Psychological Association, American Association of University Professors, National Rehabilitation Association, Council for Exceptional Children, Society for Clinical and Experimental

Hypnosis, National Association of Rehabilitation Professionals, American Psychology-Law Society, American Orthopsychiatric Association, Eastern Psychological Association, New Jersey Academy of Psychology (founding member), Pennsylvania Psychological Association (fellow), Philadelphia Society of Clinical Psychologists, Sigma Xi.

AWARDS, HONORS: Grants from National Science Foundation, 1967, 1968, and U.S. Office of Education, 1972.

WRITINGS:

(With Norma Rolnick) *Teaching the Mentally Handicapped Child,* Behavioral Publications, 1974.
Before You Marry . . . Again, Random House, 1977.
Before You Love Again, McGraw, 1980.

Contributor of articles and reviews to magazines, including *Cosmopolitan, New Woman, Journal of Divorce,* and *Family Circle,* and newspapers. Senior editor of *USA Today;* editor of newsletter of Philadelphia Society of Clinical Psychologists and of Pennsylvania Psychological Association.

*   *   *

HYSOM, John L(eland, Jr.)   1934-

PERSONAL: Born June 27, 1934, in Parsons, Kan.; son of John Leland and Alice (Hunt) Hysom; married Julia Stanford, October 23, 1960 (divorced July, 1974); married Savitri Ahuja (a teacher and writer), June 27, 1981. *Education:* University of Kansas, B.S.B.A., 1957; University of Missouri—Kansas City, M.B.A., 1964; American University, Ph.D., 1973. *Politics:* Republican. *Religion:* Methodist.

ADDRESSES: Home—5180 34th St. N.W., Washington, D.C. 20008. *Office*—Department of Finance, George Mason University, 4400 University Dr., Fairfax, Va. 22030.

CAREER: American Telephone & Telegraph, Kansas City, Mo., engineer, 1957-63; Midwest Research Institute, Kansas City, economist, 1963-66; J. L. Hysom & Associates (consultants), Washington, D.C., president, 1967-77; George Mason University, Fairfax, Va., assistant professor, 1977-80, associate professor of business, 1980—. Chairman of board of directors of Crossfield Investment Corp.; consultant in land planning and development. *Military service:* U.S. Army, Quartermaster Corps, 1957-58; became captain.

MEMBER: Urban Land Institute, National Association of Home Builders, American Planning Association, Academy of Management, Urban Regional Information Systems Association, Lambda Alpha (vice-president; member of board of directors), Cosmopolitan Club (president).

AWARDS, HONORS: Award from American Institute of Planners, 1976, for directing development of the Urban Development Information System of Fairfax County, Va.

WRITINGS:

(With William J. Bolce) *Business and Its Environment* (textbook), West Publishing, 1983.

Contributor to business and land management journals.

WORK IN PROGRESS: Modern Real Estate, a textbook, publication by West Publishing expected in 1987; with wife, Savitri, *The Arthritis Exercise and Diet Book,* completion expected in 1987; research on business management, environment of business, land development, public and private land use planning, and real estate finance and investment.

I

INGERSOLL, Ralph (McAllister) 1900-1985

OBITUARY NOTICE—See index for *CA* sketch: Born December 8, 1900, in New Haven, Conn.; died following a stroke, March 8, 1985, in Miami Beach, Fla. Journalist, editor, publisher, and author. Although educated as an engineer, Ingersoll dedicated the greater part of his life to publishing, first gaining recognition as managing editor of the *New Yorker,* where he organized the publication's original "Talk of the Town" section during the late 1920's. He continued his success as associate and then managing editor of *Fortune* during the early 1930's, as vice-president and general manager of Time, Incorporated—under whose auspices he helped found *Life* magazine—from 1935 to 1938, and as publisher of *Time* magazine from 1937 to 1939. During the 1940's the editor made journalism history by creating *PM,* a New York City daily tabloid newspaper. Designed to run without advertisements or comics and to feature well-known writers, the paper was launched amid much fanfare but failed to live up to expectations, eventually folding in the late forties. Ingersoll subsequently founded Ingersoll Publications and for the twenty or so years prior to his 1975 retirement owned and operated a string of small-town Northeastern newspapers. He also wrote a number of books, including an autobiography and two best-sellers based on his experiences serving in World War II, *The Battle Is the Payoff* and *Top Secret.*

OBITUARIES AND OTHER SOURCES:

BOOKS

Hoopes, Roy, *Ralph Ingersoll: A Biography,* Atheneum, 1985.

PERIODICALS

Chicago Tribune, March 10, 1985.
Los Angeles Times, March 9, 1985.
Newsweek, March 18, 1985.
New York Times, March 9, 1985.
Time, March 18, 1985.

*   *   *

INNAURATO, Albert 1948(?)-

BRIEF ENTRY: Born June 2, 1948 (some sources say 1947), in Philadelphia, Pa. American theatrical director, screenwriter, and playwright. Known for his black comedies, Innaurato is considered by many critics to be one of the most talented and original playwrights in the theatre today. His plays, which combine personal experience with imaginings, are noted for portraying the foibles of the human condition while satirizing contemporary society. Among Innaurato's most popular plays are *The Transfiguration of Benno Blimpie* (Dramatists Play Service, 1977; first produced in 1973), which the playwright also directed, and *Gemini: A Play in Two Acts* (Dramatists Play Serivce, 1977; first produced in 1976), a long-running Broadway hit. Both plays received Obie awards in 1977, and "Gemini" was also later adapted as the 1980 film "Happy Birthday, Gemini." Innaurato's other works include *Ulysses in Traction* (Dramatists Play Serivce, 1978; first produced in 1977); a musical play, with Christopher Durang, *The Idiots Karamazov* (Dramatists Play Service, 1981; first produced in 1974); *Passione* (Dramatists Play Service, 1981; first produced in 1980), also directed by Innaurato; and *Bizarre Behavior: Six Plays* (Avon, 1980), a collection that contains an introduction by the playwright. In addition to his plays, Innaurato has written for television and film. *Address:* c/o Helen Merrill, 337 West 22nd St., New York, N.Y. 10011.

BIOGRAPHICAL/CRITICAL SOURCES:

BOOKS

Contemporary Dramatists, 3rd edition, St. Martin's, 1982.
Contemporary Literary Criticism, Volume 21, Gale, 1982.
McGraw-Hill Encyclopedia of World Drama, 2nd edition, McGraw, 1984.

PERIODICALS

Chicago Tribune, April 11, 1985.
Los Angeles Times, March 2, 1984.
New York Times, September 22, 1980, February 4, 1985.
New York Times Magazine, December 17, 1978.

*   *   *

IRONSIDE, Henry Allan 1876-1951

BRIEF ENTRY: Born October 14, 1876, in Toronto, Ontario, Canada; came to United States, 1886; died of a heart ailment,

January 15, 1951, at Rotu Rua, New Zealand; buried in Auckland, New Zealand. Clergyman, educator, publisher, and author. Former pastor of the historic Moody Memorial Church in Chicago, Ironside has been called the "archbishop of fundamentalism." During his more than fifty years as home missionary, itinerant preacher, Bible teacher, and pastor, he gained a place of national prominence. From 1925 to 1943 he served as visiting professor of biblical literature at the Evangelical Theological Seminary in Dallas, Texas. He was also chairman of the board of directors of the Southern Bible Training School in Dallas and founder and director of the Western Book & Tract Company, which distributed, on a nonprofit basis, thousands of biblical treatises.

Known for his good memory and powerful voice, Ironside was considered remarkably adept at the brief expository sermon, and he consistently drew large audiences to his sanctuary at Moody Memorial and to his popular radio broadcasts. In addition to his preaching activities, the clergyman wrote numerous books and tracts on religion. His publications include *Notes on Jeremiah* (1900), *Addresses on First Corinthians* (1938), *Random Reminiscences from Fifty Years of Minsitry* (1939), *A Historical Sketch of the Brethren Movement* (1942), and *Except Ye Repent,* which won the American Tract Society's one-thousand-dollar prize in 1936. *Address:* 221 East Union Ave., Wheaton, Ill.

BIOGRAPHICAL/CRITICAL SOURCES:

BOOKS

Current Biography, Wilson, 1945, February, 1951.
Dictionary of American Biography, Supplement Five: 1951-1955, Scribner, 1977.
English, E. Schuyler, *H. A. Ironside: Ordained of the Lord,* Zondervan, 1946.
Who Was Who Among North American Authors, 1921-1939, Gale, 1976.

PERIODICALS

New York Times, January 17, 1951.

*   *   *   **

ISAAC, Joseph Ezra 1922-

PERSONAL: Born in 1922; married Golda Taft (a botanist), May 29, 1947. *Education:* Received B.A. from University of Melbourne, B.Com., 1945; London School of Economics and Political Science, London, Ph.D., 1949.

ADDRESSES: Home—5 Vista Ave., Kew, Victoria 3101, Australia.

CAREER: University of Melbourne, Parkville, Australia, lecturer beginning in 1950, became senior lecturer and reader, professor of economics, 1962-64, fellow of Queen's College, 1963; Monash University, Clayton, Australia, professor of economics, 1964-73; deputy president of Australian Conciliation and Arbitration Commission, 1974—. Deputy chancellor of Monash University, 1979—. Member of Flight Crew Officers Industrial Tribunal, 1968-71, and Royal Commission on Australian Government Administration, 1974-76; adviser to government of Ghana, 1962.

MEMBER: Economic Society of Australia and New Zealand (president, 1969), Industrial Relations Society of Victoria (president, 1964-65).

AWARDS, HONORS: Honorary fellow of London School of Economics and Political Science, London, 1977—.

WRITINGS:

(Editor with G. W. Ford) *Australian Labor Economics Readings,* Verry, 1967, 2nd edition (with John R. Niland), 1974, 3rd edition (with Niland and B. Chapman), 1984.
Wages and Productivity, Cheshire, 1967.
(Editor with Ford) *Australian Labor Relations Readings,* Sun Books, 1968.

Also author of *Compulsory Arbitration in Australia,* 1970, and *The Structure of Unskilled Wages in Papua New Guinea,* 1970.

*   *   *   **

IVIE, Robert L(ynn) 1945-

PERSONAL: Born July 29, 1945, in Medford, Ore.; son of Robert Grant (a sales supervisor) and Jean (a homemaker; maiden name, Poling) Ivie; married Nancy Lee Haagensen (a homemaker), December 11, 1965; children: Eric Robert, Sara Louise. *Education:* California State College (now University) at Hayward, B.A., 1967; Washington State University, M.A., 1968, Ph.D., 1972.

ADDRESSES: Home—Northwest 2010 Turner Dr., Pullman, Wash. 99163. *Office*—Department of Communications, Washington State University, Pullman, Wash. 99164-2520.

CAREER: Gonzaga University, Spokane, Wash., assistant professor of speech, 1972-74; Idaho State University, Pocatello, assistant professor of speech, 1974-75; Washington State University, Pullman, assistant professor, 1975-80, associate professor, 1980-85, professor of communications, 1985—. *Military service:* U.S. Naval Air Reserve, active duty, 1968-70.

MEMBER: International Society for the History of Rhetoric, Speech Communication Association, Rhetoric Society of America, Western Speech Communication Association (second vice-president, 1982-83).

WRITINGS:

(With Ronald Hatzenbuehler) *Congress Declares War: Rhetoric, Leadership, and Partisanship in the Early Republic,* Kent State University Press, 1983.

Contributor to communication and history journals. Editor of *Western Journal of Speech Communication,* 1984-88.

WORK IN PROGRESS: The Savage Enemy: Presidential War Rhetoric in the Nuclear Age, an examination of "the literalization of the metaphor of savagery during the Truman era, its deliteralization during the Johnson presidency, and its revitalization by Ronald Reagan," publication expected in 1986.

SIDELIGHTS: Robert L. Ivie told *CA:* "My principal motive for scholarship is to understand better how we talk ourselves into war. Symbols, not material conditions, are the immediate cause of war, for conflict among human beings is ultimately an intentional act, a matter of choice rather than fate. We know relatively little about the impact of symbols upon the body politic, even in this age of cold war when the next holocaust will be the last. Paranoid visions of a diabolical enemy are institutionalized in our political rhetoric, transforming mere metaphors of an adversary's savagery into 'literal' threats against freedom and civilization. From the presidency of Harry Truman to that of Ronald Reagan, America's rivals have been decivilized routinely as beasts of prey, primitives, machines of destruction, criminals, fanatics, ideologues, and instruments of Satan. We must learn more about how the signs of rationality, embedded as they are in conventions of political discourse, become intertwined with the language of insanity. Only then will we be free of the lethal choice between life and civilization.''

J

JACK, Daniel Thomson 1901-1984

OBITUARY NOTICE: Born August 18, 1901, in Glasgow, Scotland; died December 15, 1984. Political economist, arbitrator, educator, and author. A David Dale Professor of Economics, Jack was known as one of Scotland's most experienced industrial arbitrators. His conciliatory skills—many acquired while serving with the Ministry of Labor during World War II—were utilized in various positions in Scotland and later in East Africa. The arbitrator spent a long period as member of his homeland's Industrial Disputes Tribunal acting as mediator between employers and union members. Later he became involved in organizing a system of collective bargaining in East Africa. Jack also lectured in political economics at Scotland's University of St. Andrews and the University of Glasgow and became a David Dale Professor of Economics at King's College, Newcastle upon Tyne (now University of Newcastle upon Tyne). Jack resigned from the school in 1961 to serve as chairman of the Air Transport Licensing Board, a post he held for ten years. He was author of several books on international monetary affairs, including *The Economics of the Gold Standard, The Restoration of European Currencies, International Trade, Currency and Banking, Studies in Economic Warfare,* and *Economic Relations Within the Empire.*

OBITUARIES AND OTHER SOURCES:

BOOKS

Who Was Who in Literature: 1906-1934, Gale, 1979.
Who's Who, 136th edition, St. Martin's, 1984.

PERIODICALS

Times (London), January 15, 1985.

*　　*　　*

JACKSON, Diane 1938-

PERSONAL: Born June 10, 1938, in Tulsa, Okla.; daughter of Lewis Burk (in oil business) and Louise (Houston) Jackson; divorced; children: Edward Burk. *Education:* Attended Finch College; Parsons School of Design, Certificate in Graphics, 1962.

ADDRESSES: Office—L. B. Jackson Co., 4609 East 31st St., Tulsa, Okla. 74135.

CAREER: Associated with L. B. Jackson Co., Tulsa, Okla. Artist, with commissions and exhibitions of her paintings.

WRITINGS:

August in Abiquin, Sunstone Press, 1980.

WORK IN PROGRESS: Windows, Gates, and Doors.

*　　*　　*

JACKSON, Margaret Weymouth 1895-1974

OBITUARY NOTICE: Born February 11, 1895, in Eureka Springs, Ark.; died April 5, 1974. Editor, educator, and author. A two-time recipient of the O. Henry Prize and the winner of both the O'Brien Prize in literature and the Literary Digest Award, Jackson began her writing career when she was twenty years old as a contributor of short stories to *Farm Life* in Spencer, Indiana. She later served as woman's editor and assistant editor of *Farm Life* and associate editor of *Better Farming.* Much later she became a lecturer in English at Indiana University, a position she held until her retirement. Jackson's writings include *Elizabeth's Tower, Beggars Can Choose, Jenny Fowler, First Fiddle, Sarah Thornton,* and *Kindy's Crossing.* More than three hundred of her short stories were published in magazines, including *McCall's, Saturday Evening Post,* and *Ladies' Home Journal.*

OBITUARIES AND OTHER SOURCES:

BOOKS

Authors in the News, Volume I, Gale, 1976.
Indiana Authors and Their Books: 1917-1966, Wabash College, 1974.
Who Was Who in America, With World Notables, Volume VI: *1974-1976,* Marquis, 1976.

*　　*　　*

JACOB, Naomi Ellington 1884(?)-1964
(Ellington Gray)

OBITUARY NOTICE: Born July 1, 1884 (some sources say 1889), in Ripon, Yorkshire, England; died August 27 (one source says August 26), 1964, in Sirmione, Italy. Actress, educator, and author. A prolific writer, Jacob began writing in the mid-1920's after ill health forced her to give up a successful acting career. Her well-received first book, *Jacob Ussher*, published in 1926, was followed by as many as two books a year for more than thirty years. Among her most popular stories were those that formed the Gollantz Saga, including *The Founder of the House, Gollantz: London, Paris, Milan,* and *Gollantz and Partners.* Jacob also wrote a series of autobiographical volumes consisting of such titles as *Me and the Mediterranean, Me—Over There, Me and Mine, Me Looking Back,* and *Me—Likes and Dislikes.* Her other books include *Young Emmanuel, Fade Out, This Porcelain Clay, A Passage Perilous, Antonia, Great Black Oxen, Flavia,* and *Saffron Bridesails* (written under the pseudonym Ellington Gray).

OBITUARIES AND OTHER SOURCES:

BOOKS

Catholic Authors: Contemporary Biographical Sketches, Volume I: *1930-1947,* St. Mary's Abbey, 1948.
Obituaries on File, Facts on File, 1979.
The Penguin Companion to English Literature, McGraw, 1971.
Twentieth Century Authors: A Bibliographical Dictionary of Modern Literature, H. W. Wilson, 1942.
Twentieth-Century Romance and Gothic Writers, Gale, 1982.

PERIODICALS

New York Times, August 28, 1964.

*   *   *

JACOBS, Al(bert T.)   1903-1985

OBITUARY NOTICE: Born January 22, 1903, in San Francisco, Calif.; died following a stroke, February 13, 1985, in Laurel, Md. Performer, publisher, composer, and lyricist. A songwriter in the 1930's and 1940's, Jacobs wrote approximately three thousand songs. Among his most popular compositions were "This Is My Country," "There'll Never Be Another You," and "If I Give My Heart to You." In addition, Jacobs composed the music for films "Dancing Daughters," "Seven Wonders of the World," and "Kon Tiki." During his varied music career, Jacobs managed a number of music publishing companies, including Sherman & Clay Company, Miller Music Company, and Melrose Music. He also worked as a pianist and singer for radio stations KGO and KJBS and was assistant musical director of Al Pearce's radio program.

OBITUARIES AND OTHER SOURCES:

BOOKS

The ASCAP Biographical Dictionary of Composers, Authors, and Publishers, 3rd edition, American Society of Composers, Authors, and Publishers, 1966.
The Complete Encyclopedia of Popular Music and Jazz, 1900-1950, Arlington House, 1974.

PERIODICALS

Washington Post, February 15, 1985.

*   *   *

JACOBSON, Marcia   1941-

PERSONAL: Born October 12, 1941, in Berkeley, Calif.; daughter of Louis (a professor) and Selma (a homemaker; maiden name, Cooperman) Jacobson. *Education:* University of California, Berkeley, B.A. (with distinction), 1963, M.A., 1965, Ph.D., 1972.

ADDRESSES: Home—Auburn, Ala. *Office*—Department of English, Auburn University, Auburn, Ala. 36849.

CAREER: Pennsylvania State University, University Park, instructor in English, 1968-71; University of Wisconsin—Madison, instructor, 1971-72, assistant professor of English, 1972-77; Auburn University, Auburn, Ala., associate professor, 1978-84, Hargis Professor of American Literature, 1984—. Humanist administrator of National Endowment for the Humanities, 1984-85.

MEMBER: Modern Language Association of America, Phi Beta Kappa.

AWARDS, HONORS: Fellow at the Institute for Research in the Humanities of the University of Wisconsin—Madison, 1977-78; fellow of National Endowment for the Humanities, 1980, 1983, 1984.

WRITINGS:

Henry James and the Mass Market, University of Alabama Press, 1983.

Contributor to magazines, including *Biography, American Literary Realism, Western American Literature, Modern Philology, Philological Quaterly,* and *Journal of English and Germanic Philology.*

WORK IN PROGRESS: Being a Boy Again: The Nineteenth-Century American Boy Book, a study of "boy books" such as *Huckleberry Finn* and *Tom Sawyer.*

SIDELIGHTS: Marcia Jacobson told *CA:* "Both my work on Henry James and my study of the 'boy books' reflect my interest in the relationship between the work of major authors and their popular literary context. The James book, in arguing that James turned to the themes and forms of popular fiction as a means of commenting on the values of his society and as an attempt to attract a popular following, counters the too pervasive myth that James was an ivory tower artist. The study of the 'boy books' will focus on the way in which an autobiographical impulse was translated into a popular fictional genre and will examine the reasons for the transformation and the literary consequences of it."

*   *   *

JAFFE, Sam(uel Adason)   1929(?)-1985

OBITUARY NOTICE: Born c. 1929 in San Francisco, Calif.; died of lung cancer, February 8, 1985, in Bethesda, Md. Journalist. Jaffe was a television correspondent for CBS News from 1955 to 1961 and for ABC News from 1961 to 1969. During his career he covered many major news events, including the 1959 visit of Soviet Premier Nikita Khrushchev to the United States, the 1960 Moscow spy trial of U-2 pilot Francis Gary Powers, and the 1962 Cuban missile crisis, and he was among the first to report Khrushchev's fall from power in 1964. After resigning from ABC amid rumors that he was a foreign agent, Jaffe had difficulty finding suitable assignments. He spent the last fifteen years of his life engaged in an ultimately successful legal struggle to clear his name after the CIA and FBI alleged that he had spied for the Soviet Union. In 1972 and 1974 he travelled to China as a free-lance correspondent for United Press International and the *Chicago Tribune,* and in the late 1970's he hosted a weekly radio show. For his coverage of the Vietnam War Jaffe received an Overseas Press Club prize.

OBITUARIES AND OTHER SOURCES:

PERIODICALS

Chicago Tribune, February 10, 1985.
Los Angeles Times, February 12, 1985.
New York Times, February 9, 1985.
Washington Post, February 9, 1985.

*   *   *

JAMES, Edward (Frank Willis) 1907-1984

OBITUARY NOTICE: Born in 1907; died December 2 (one source says December 3), 1984, in San Remo, Italy. Philanthropist, art collector, publisher, and author. As a patron of the arts James benefitted a variety of artists and performers, including choreographer George Balanchine, composer Kurt Weill, writer Bertolt Brecht, and surrealist painter Salvador Dali. He also established the James Press, which printed several of his own volumes of poetry and his novel, *The Gardener Who Saw God.* The firm also issued the first collection of verse to be published by John Betjeman, who later became Britain's poet laureate. James sponsored the surrealist magazine *Minotaure* in the 1930's and accumulated one of the finest private collections of surrealist art in the world.

OBITUARIES AND OTHER SOURCES:

PERIODICALS

Chicago Tribune, December 5, 1984.
Times (London), December 4, 1984.
Washington Post, December 7, 1984.

*   *   *

JEPHCOTT, E(dmund) F(rancis) N(eville) 1938-

BRIEF ENTRY: Born November 22, 1938, in Enfield, Middlesex, England. British educator and author. Jephcott was appointed lecturer in German and European studies at the University of Sussex in 1965. He wrote *Proust and Rilke: The Literature of Expanded Consciousness* (Chatto & Windus, 1972). Jephcott translated Theodor Adorno's *Minima Moralia: Reflections From Damaged Life* (New Left Books, 1974) and Norbert Elias's *Power and Civility: The Civilizing Process,* Volume II (Pantheon, 1982).

BIOGRAPHICAL/CRITICAL SOURCES:

PERIODICALS

Times Literary Supplement, November 9, 1973.

*   *   *

JOHNSON, Jack
See JOHNSON, John Arthur

*   *   *

JOHNSON, John Arthur 1878-1946
(Jack Johnson)

BRIEF ENTRY: Professionally known as Jack Johnson; born March 31, 1878, in Galveston, Tex.; died of injuries sustained in an automobile accident, June 10, 1946, in Raleigh, N.C.; buried at Graceland Cemetery, Chicago, Ill. American laborer, lecturer, performer, actor, boxer, and author. Johnson, who was professional boxing's heavyweight champion from 1908 to 1915, began boxing while working as a longshoreman in Galveston, Texas. In 1899 he toured America with other black fighters, and by 1902 he had established himself as a fearsome contender for the heavyweight title. But the racism then prevalent in the boxing business prevented him from realizing quick success with his skills, and Johnson was compelled to devise a vaudeville act to maintain an increasingly flamboyant lifestyle.

By 1908 Johnson had fought fifty-seven matches—winning all but three—and had beaten all contenders for the title, thus finally earning a match with champion Tommy Burns. They fought in Sydney, Australia, and Johnson won in fourteen rounds. His victory, however, was unfavorably received by racists, and many began clamoring for a "great white hope" to take the title from Johnson. Former champion Jim Jeffries, who had retired as undefeated champion in 1905, was prompted to fight Johnson. Their fight ended in fifteen rounds when Johnson knocked out the challenger. In the years immediately following his title defense, Johnson was involved in several scandals; one resulted in a trial in which the boxer was convicted of transporting a woman across state lines for immoral purposes, a violation of the Mann Act. Protesting the decision, he fled to Europe and worked there as an entertainer. In 1915 he agreed to fight another "white hope," Jess Willard.

Held in Havana, Cuba, the match lasted twenty-six rounds before Johnson was knocked out. After losing the title to Willard, Johnson returned to Europe and resumed working as a performer. In 1920 he came back to the United States to serve his sentence. Upon release from prison, Johnson supported himself by boxing, lecturing, and selling stocks. Among his writings are the French *Mes Combats* (1914) and the autobiographical *Jack Johnson: In the Ring and Out* (1927); reprinted under Johnson's real name, John Arthur Johnson, as *Jack Johnson Is a Dandy,* 1969).

BIOGRAPHICAL/CRITICAL SOURCES:

BOOKS

Farr, Finis, *Black Champion: The Life and Times of Jack Johnson,* Scribner, 1964.
Gilmore, Al-Tony, *Bad Nigger!: The National Impact of Jack Johnson,* Kennikat, 1975.

*   *   *

JOHNSON, M. L.
See ABERCROMBIE, M(innie) L(ouie) J(ohnson)

*   *   *

JOHNSON, Mark 1949-

PERSONAL: Born May 24, 1949, in Kansas City, Mo.; son of Milton L. (an auditor) and Mary (a secretary; maiden name, Petri) Johnson; married Sandra McMorris (an artist), September 16, 1971; children: Paul Michael. *Education:* University of Kansas, B.A. (with honors), 1971; University of Chicago, M.A., 1972, Ph.D., 1977.

ADDRESSES: Home—209 Pine Lane, Carbondale, Ill. 62901. *Office*—Department of Philosophy, Southern Illinois University, Carbondale, Ill. 62901.

CAREER: Southern Illinois University, Carbondale, assistant professor, 1977-83, associate professor of philosophy, 1983—.

MEMBER: American Society for Aesthetics, American Philosophical Association, Illinois Philosophical Association, Phi Beta Kappa.

WRITINGS:

(With George Lakoff) *Metaphors We Live By,* University of Chicago Press, 1980.
Philosophical Perspectives on Metaphor, University of Minnesota Press, 1981.
The Body in the Mind, University of Chicago Press, in press.

Member of editorial board of *Metaphor and Symbolic Activity.*

SIDELIGHTS: Mark Johnson told *CA:* "My interest in metaphoric processes is motivated by the belief that metaphor is not merely a rhetorical device or an artistic ornament; instead, I am convinced that it is a basic, pervasive process of human understanding and even of the structure of our experience. In the last decade philosophers, psychologists, and linguists have just begun to take seriously the view that there are metaphoric structures of cognition by which we can have meaningful, coherent experiences that we are able to comprehend. In *Metaphors We Live By* Lakoff and I argue that such metaphoric processes are not reducible to literal language and that much of our conceptual system is organized by means of metaphorical projections. If this is true, then there is no single correct or absolute way to comprehend our experience—there are many possible metaphorical structures that can make sense of our experience. Taking metaphor seriously as an irreducible cognitive process thus leads one to deny absolute knowledge. Still, this doe not lead to relativism, for our metaphorical processes are constrained by our bodies, by our conceptual system, by our culture, and by physical structures of objects we encounter.

"My current research grew out of my earlier collaborative work on metaphor. Since I claimed that metaphorical structure was experientially grounded, I needed to show how that is possible in some detail. This led me to realize that I needed an account of imagination, since metaphoric processes are structures of imagination. Thus I am now exploring the way in which meaning structures emerge preconceptually in our bodily experience. I also am concerned with the way such structures of imagination get extended to connect up our entire network of meanings."

*   *   *

JOHNSON, Raynor C(arey)   1901-

BRIEF ENTRY: Born April 5, 1901, in Leeds, England. Physicist, educator, and author. Johnson has taught physics at Queen's University in Belfast and the University of London's King's College. He became the master of Queen's College at the University of Melbourne in 1934. In addition to writing on physics, Johnson has produced several books on parapsychology, including *Nurslings of Immortality* (Harper, 1957), *Watcher on the Hills: A Study of Some Mystical Experiences of Ordinary People* (Hodder & Stoughton, 1959), *A Religious Outlook for Modern Man* (Hodder & Stoughton, 1963), *The Light and the Gate* (Hodder & Stoughton, 1964), *The Spiritual Path* (Harper, 1971), and *A Pool of Reflections: For the Refreshment of Travellers on the Spiritual Path* (Hodder & Stoughton, 1975). *Address:* Queen's College, University of Melbourne, Parkville, Victoria 3052, Australia.

BIOGRAPHICAL/CRITICAL SOURCES:

BOOKS

Biographical Dictionary of Parapsychology, With Directory and Glossary: 1964-1966, Garret Publications, 1964.
Encyclopedia of Occultism and Parapsychology, 2nd printing with revisions, Gale, 1979.

*   *   *

JOHNSON ABERCROMBIE, M. L.
See ABERCROMBIE, M(innie) L(ouie) J(ohnson)

*   *   *

JONES, Guy Salisbury
See SALISBURY-JONES, Guy

*   *   *

JONES, Jack   1884-1970

OBITUARY NOTICE: Born November 24, 1884, in Merthyr Tydfil, Glamorganshire, Wales; died May 7, 1970, in Rhiwbina, near Cardiff, Wales. Journalist, playwright, and novelist. Jones won acclaim for his novels depicting life in industrial Wales. A miner at the age of twelve, Jones later worked as a trade union official, book salesman, and lecturer—among other things—before embarking on a literary career. Additionally, Jones fought in World War I and participated in the war effort during World War II as a propagandist. Jones's novels, the first of which, *Rhondda Roundabout,* was published when he was fifty, include *Black Parade, Bidded to the Feast, Off to Philadelphia in the Morning,* and *Some Trust in Chariots.* His other writings include autobiographical volumes, plays, and a biography of British statesman David Lloyd George. He was created a commander of the Order of the British Empire in 1948.

OBITUARIES AND OTHER SOURCES:

BOOKS

Cassell's Encyclopedia of World Literature, revised edition, Morrow, 1973.
Longman Companion to Twentieth Century Literature, Longman, 1970.
World Authors: 1950-1970, H. W. Wilson, 1975.

PERIODICALS

Times (London), May 9, 1970.

*   *   *

JONES, Kenneth Glyn   1915-

PERSONAL: Born November 13, 1915, in New Tredegar, Wales; son of John Henry (a business executive) and Beatrice Alice (a housewife; maiden name, Russell) Jones; married Gwyneth Brown-Morgan, January 1, 1944 (died April 3, 1968); married Brenda Margaret Keefe (a secretary), June 8, 1969. *Education:* Attended grammar school in Penarth County, Wales. *Politics:* Liberal. *Religion:* "Anti-religion."

ADDRESSES: Home and office—Wild Rose, Church Rd., Winkfield, Windsor, Berkshire SL4 4SF, England.

CAREER: Joseph Rank Ltd. (millers), Cardiff, Wales, bookkeeper, 1933-38; British Airways, London, England, air navigator and training officer, 1945-74. *Military service:* Royal Air Force, navigator, 1938-45; became flight lieutenant; received Pacific Star, Burma Star, and Coronation Medal.

MEMBER: British Astronomical Association, Royal Astronomical Society (fellow), Webb Society (president).

WRITINGS:

Messier's Nebulae and Star Clusters, Elsevier-North Holland, 1968.
The Search for the Nebulae, Neale Watson, 1975.
(Editor) *The Webb Society Deep-Sky Observer's Handbook,* Ridley Enslow, Volumes I-II, 1979, Volume III, 1980, Volume IV, 1981, Volume V, 1982.

Contributor to astronomy journals. Editor of *Quarterly Journal of the Webb Society.*

WORK IN PROGRESS: In Search of Mme. Putbus' Maid, a psychoanalytical study of Proust's novel; "The Englishman's Comet," a dramatic reconstruction for television of the events of the 1759 appearance of Halley's Comet.

SIDELIGHTS: Kenneth Glyn Jones told *CA* that *In Search of Mme. Putbus' Maid,* his work in progress, "attempts to show that from a psychoanalytical point of view, the most important character in *A la recherche du temps perdu* is one who never actually appears in the novel, namely the continually pursued but never encountered Mme. Putbus' maid. From this 'clue,' in conjunction with many other revealing episodes in the novel (and also in Proust's own life), it seems very likely that Proust's complex character—including his peculiar brand of homosexuality (actually a deviation from an original form of heterosexual timidity)—had its origins in a precocious and traumatic sexual encounter with a servant girl at Illiers (Combray). The evidence seems compelling.

"To me the world is full of fascinating puzzles awaiting solution—the Song the Sirens sang, Achilles' name when he masqueraded as a girl—all are worth at least conjecture. The greatest and most fascinating puzzle of all is, of course, that of the existence—or nonexistence—of God. After a brief adolescent flirtation with 'belief,' I took an easy refuge in agnosticism but this soon appeared to be much too equivocal an attitude. Reason then compelled me to uphold a strongly atheistic view for most of my life. In recent years, however, following a lifetime's interest in astronomy, I am inclined to accept the so-called 'anthropic principle,' in which observation seems to demonstrate that many of the cosmological parameters have been 'selected' to lead to 'habitable planets'—life on at least one planet—and the existence of man. The universe, then, seems to have a 'purpose' and Purpose in this context is only a synonym of God.

"At present I think it very probable that God, in an essential form, does in fact, exist, and that Liebniz's 'cosmological argument' and the 'argument from design' are valid. Having said that, however, it seems to me that one can say nothing more. As to what God's ultimate purpose may be, we have no inkling whatever, and those who pretend they can interpret 'God's will' for the rest of us are—to put the best construction upon it—misguided.

"The philosopher Hans Vaihinger wrote a book, *The Philosophy of 'As If,'* in which he claimed to be an atheist but thought it expedient to behave 'as if' God did exist. This seems to me to be absurd, and my own stance is entirely opposite. God exists but it would be wiser to behave 'as if' he did not.

"As for all other puzzles, having dealt with the 'mystery without,' one naturally turns to the 'mystery within'—who am I? And does it matter? Life is a progression from the cradle to the grave; that progress is very interesting and I hope it will always continue to be so."

* * *

JULESBERG, Elizabeth Rider Montgomery 1902-1985
(Elizabeth Montgomery, Elizabeth Rider Montgomery)

OBITUARY NOTICE—See index for *CA* sketch: Born July 12, 1902, in Huaras, Peru; American citizen born abroad; died after a long illness, February 19, 1985, in Seattle, Wash. Author of books for children, most under the name Elizabeth Montgomery. Julesberg was best known as author of the elementary-school reading primers featuring Dick, Jane, Sally, and Spot. As a first grade teacher in Los Angeles, California, during the 1940's, Julesberg wrote *We Look and See,* the first book of the series, in response to what she saw as a dearth of interesting reading books for children. It was soon followed by such titles as *We Work and Play, We Come and Go, Good Times With Our Friends,* and *Three Friends,* with the author eventually signing a writing contract with Scott, Foresman & Company, a publisher of educational books. In all, Julesberg wrote more than seventy books for children, including fiction, nonfiction, and plays, with many of the latter being produced on radio and television.

OBITUARIES AND OTHER SOURCES:

BOOKS

Who's Who of American Women, 12th edition, Marquis, 1981.

PERIODICALS

Chicago Sun Times, February 21, 1985.
Detroit Free Press, February 22, 1985.
Washington Post, February 22, 1985.

K

KAEUPER, Richard W(illiam) 1941-

BRIEF ENTRY: Born June 20, 1941, in Richmond, Ind. American historian, educator, and author. Kaeuper began teaching medieval history at the University of Rochester in 1969. A Guggenheim fellow in 1978, the educator was R. T. French Visiting Professor at Oxford University's Worcester College from 1979 to 1980. He wrote *Bankers to the Crown: The Riccardi of Lucca and Edward I* (Princeton University Press, 1973). *Address:* Department of History, University of Rochester, Wilson Blvd., Rochester, N.Y. 14627.

BIOGRAPHICAL/CRITICAL SOURCES:

PERIODICALS

American Historical Review, December, 1973.
Times Literary Supplement, September 21, 1973.

*   *   *

KAJENCKI, Francis C(asimir) 1918-

PERSONAL: Surname is pronounced Ka-*yent*-ski; born November 15, 1918, in Erie, Pa.; son of Antoni A. (a laborer) and Antonina (a homemaker; maiden name, Staszewska) Kajencki; married Virginia T. Bierasinski (deceased); children: Francis C., Jr., Anthony A. II, Miriam Kajencki Orton, AnnMarie. *Education:* U.S. Military Academy, B.S., 1943; University of Southern California, M.S., 1949; University of Wisconsin—Madison, M.S. (journalism), 1967; George Mason University, M.A., 1976. *Politics:* Independent. *Religion:* Roman Catholic.

ADDRESSES: Home—3308 Nairn St., El Paso, Tex. 79925.

CAREER: U.S. Army, career officer, 1943-73; served in the Pacific theater during World War II; instructor in guided missiles at Air Defense School, Ft. Bliss, Tex., 1949-53; commanded U.S. Nuclear Warhead Support Group, Turkey, 1961-62; on general staff, Department of Army, 1963-66; chief of public information division, Allied Land Forces Southeast Europe, Ismir, Turkey, 1967-69; assistant chief of information, Department of Army, 1972-73, retiring as colonel, 1973. Writer. Member of advisory board of trustees of El Paso Community Foundation.

MEMBER: National Press Club, Polish National Alliance, Polish American Congress of Texas (president, 1984), U.S. Military Academy Alumni Association.

AWARDS, HONORS—Military: Two Meritorious Service Medals; Legion of Merit.

WRITINGS:

Star on Many a Battlefield: Brevet Brigadier General Joseph Karge in the American Civil War, Fairleigh Dickinson University Press, 1980.

Contributor of articles and reviews to journals, including *Louisiana History, Arizona and the West,* and *Polish American Studies,* and newspapers.

WORK IN PROGRESS: Research on the contribution of early Polish settlers to the history of New Mexico Territory.

SIDELIGHTS: Francis C. Kajencki told *CA:* "I enjoyed my military career of thirty-six years. Nevertheless, I had found it somewhat technical and restrictive, and felt an urge to be more expansive and creative. Writing seemed to be the vehicle for releasing my suppressed energy.

"I turned to the field in which I had some knowledge and experience—military history. While a student at the U.S. Army Command and General Staff College, Ft. Leavenworth, Kansas (1957-58), I found an unusual amount of data on Polish-born Brevet Brigadier General Joseph Karge, a cavalry commander in the Civil War. As an American of Polish descent, I took a keen interest in Karge and wondered why no historian had rescued him from obscurity. I wanted to tell about Karge's contribution to the Northern victory—among other things, General Karge was the first Union commander to beat Confederate General ('That Devil') Nathan Bedford Forrest—and the result was *Star on Many a Battlefield: Brevet Brigadier General Joseph Karge in the American Civil War.*

"After relocating to El Paso, Texas, in 1975, following my active military service, I 'discovered' a number of Poles who made significant contributions to the history of New Mexico Territory. Among them, two were prominent and successful merchants. A third ran a hostelry on the famous Santa Fe Trail, and his ranch, during the Civil War, served as the field headquarters for the Union forces. And yet another Pole was a high-ranking member of the joint U.S.-Mexican Boundary

Commission that set the new boundary between the two countries following the war with Mexico, 1846-48. My purpose is to document their contributions in historical journals and to establish their places in New Mexico history. To date, no other historian has written about them. Therefore, I believe I'm doing pioneer historical research and satisfying my creative instincts.''

* * *

KAMERMAN, Jack B. 1940-

PERSONAL: Born December 15, 1940, in Brooklyn, N.Y.; son of Jacob (an insurance salesman) and Fanny (a bookkeeper; maiden name, Goldman) Kamerman; married Constance Lynn Munro (a magazine copy editor), June 3, 1979. *Education:* Brooklyn College of the City University of New York, B.A., 1962; graduate study at University of Minnesota—Twin Cities, 1962-65; New York University, Ph.D., 1979.

ADDRESSES: Home—Douglaston, N.Y. *Office*—Department of Sociology and Social Work, Kean College of New Jersey, Union, N.J. 07083.

CAREER: University of Minnesota—Twin Cities, Minneapolis, instructor in social science, 1965-68; Adelphi University, Garden City, N.Y., instructor in sociology, 1968-73, lecturer in social work, 1968-72; William Paterson College of New Jersey, Wayne, instructor in sociology, 1974-77; Kean College of New Jersey, Union, assistant professor of sociology, 1978—. Part-time instructor at St. Barnabas Hospital, Methodist Hospital, and Abbott Hospital, all in Minneapolis, and Mound-Midway Hospital, St. Paul, Minn., spring, 1968; instructor for lecture series ''Man in Society,'' on KTCI-TV, 1973—; chairman of symposia.

MEMBER: American Sociological Association, Society for the Study of Symbolic Interaction, Society for the Study of Social Problems, Eastern Sociological Society.

WRITINGS:

(Contributor) Nicholas Kittrie and Jackwell Susman, editors, *Legality, Morality, and Ethics in Criminal Justice,* Praeger, 1979.
(Editor with Rosanne Martorella, and contributor) *Performers and Performances: The Social Organization of Artistic Work,* Praeger, 1983.
(Contributor) John Stimson and Ardyth Stimson, editors, *Sociology: A Contemporary Reader,* F. E. Peacock, 1983.

Author of liner notes for phonograph albums. Contributor of articles and reviews to sociology journals and newspapers.

WORK IN PROGRESS: A book tentatively titled *The Playing Holidays,* with John Podracky; research on life changes, stress, and death.

SIDELIGHTS: Jack Kamerman told *CA:* ''I've been interested in music for most of my life. I began collecting records at the age of ten. The beauty of the sociological approach is that you can use it to study almost anything. It seemed only natural to apply my professional viewpoint to my major avocational interest. My doctoral dissertation, for example, was an explanation, in terms of social, economic, and artistic forces, of the development of symphony conducting as an occupation. My wife encouraged me to do it. She pointed out that I had done all the reading on conductors anyway and that I might as well get double mileage out of it.

''Unfortunately, too much of the work in the sociology of the arts isn't very true to the arts and isn't very good sociology. *Performers and Performances* was our attempt to bring together solid work that would make sense to sociologists *and* to performing artists. That's one reason we included, in addition to sociological studies, interviews with performers, something often missing from sociological work *about* performers.

''I've always considered myself a great 'good' writer. I have written mediocre poetry and fiction, but great professional articles and reviews. While my friends have had novels perpetually in progress, I've had scholarly articles and reviews in print. Since I began doing work on the sociology of death, I have had to give up one of my ambitions: to use my writing to make people laugh.''

* * *

KAMINSKAYA, Dina 1920-

PERSONAL: Born January 13, 1920, in Dnepropetrovsk, Ukrainian S.S.R., U.S.S.R.; came to United States, April 5, 1978; daughter of Issaak (a lawyer) and Olga (a dentist; maiden name, Elinson) Kaminsky; married Konstantin Simis (a writer and journalist), April 14, 1942; children: Dimitry. *Education:* Attended Moscow University, 1937-43.

ADDRESSES: Home—119 West Annandale Rd., Falls Church, Va., 22046. *Agent*—John Brockman, 2307 Broadway, New York, N.Y. 10024.

CAREER: Worked as defense attorney in Moscow, U.S.S.R., 1940-77; writer. Free-lance commentator for Radio Liberty.

WRITINGS:

Final Judgment: My Life as a Soviet Defense Attorney, Simon & Schuster, 1983.

SIDELIGHTS: Dina Kaminskaya's *Final Judgment* describes her experiences as a defense attorney in the Soviet Union's legal system. She details a case in which she learned of verdicts and sentences before the trial began, and exposes the jury-less Soviet courts as tools of a repressive state. Dennis Drabelle, reviewing *Final Judgment* in the *Washington Post,* wrote: ''In the course of recounting her greatest cases, Kaminskaya sketches the outline of Soviet criminal practice. The function of defense attorney is anomalous in the Soviet Union, where the state makes no errors, but is tolerated for the sake of the regime's image abroad.'' Drabelle called *Final Judgment* ''absorbing and instructive.''

Kaminskaya told *CA:* ''For thirty-seven years I was a member of the Moscow Bar Association. I represented some dissidents in the courts (Bukovsky, Litvinov, Galansky, and others). In 1977 I was disbarred for my activities in political trials and was forced to emigrate.''

BIOGRAPHICAL/CRITICAL SOURCES:

PERIODICALS

Washington Post, May 16, 1983.

* * *

KAMINSKY, Susan Stanwood 1937-
(Brooks Stanwood, a joint pseudonym)

PERSONAL: Born May 3, 1937, in Wellesley, Mass.; daughter of William Reid (in sales) and Elisabeth (a housewife; maiden name, Mitchell) Stanwood; married Howard Kaminsky (a publishing executive and author), January 31, 1970; children: Jessica May. *Education:* Vassar College, B.S., 1958.

ADDRESSES: Home—390 West End Ave., New York, N.Y. 10024.

CAREER: Clerk in publishing house in London, England, 1958-59; Macmillan Publishing Co., Inc., New York City, copywriter, 1960-62; St. Martin's Press, Inc., New York City, copywriter and assistant editor, 1962-63; *Saturday Evening Post,* New York City, senior fiction editor, 1963-69; E. P. Dutton, New York City, senior editor, 1969-77; writer.

AWARDS, HONORS: The Glow was named to *Publishers Weekly* best-seller list in 1980.

WRITINGS:

NOVELS

(With husband, Howard Kaminsky, under joint pseudonym Brooks Stanwood) *The Glow* (Literary Guild selection), McGraw, 1979.
(With H. Kaminsky, under Stanwood pseudonym) *The Seventh Child,* Linden Press, 1982.
(With H. Kaminsky) *Talent,* Bantam, in press.

SIDELIGHTS: The Glow, Susan Stanwood Kaminsky's first collaboration with her husband, Howard Kaminsky, is a psychological thriller written under the joint pseudonym Brooks Stanwood. The book's plot centers on a sadistic group of elderly joggers who derive their characteristic youthful "glow" from consuming the blood of the unsuspecting young runners who become their victims. The elderly joggers—four married couples—share an attractive townhouse in a neighborhood on New York's East Side and befriend a young, enterprising couple, Pete and Jackie Lawrence, soon inviting them to fill a vacancy in the desirable building. Gradually, as they witness the building's other young tenants mysteriously disappearing, the Lawrences realize that they have been carefully selected as donors in an experiment in long life. A runaway best-seller, *The Glow* sold more than one million paperback copies and commanded $150,000 from Producer's Circle for movie rights.

In a *New York Times* interview with Judy Klemesrud the Kaminskys recalled how the idea for *The Glow* originated during a drive home from the Berkshires one summer Sunday. The sight of attractive young couples jogging along the West Side Highway started them thinking about the national obsession with fitness and the possibility of a "dark side" to this seemingly worthy activity. Once the couple agreed to expand this speculation into a book, Howard drew up a detailed outline of the plot, divided in the fashion of a screenplay into fifty-six "scenes." For the next year and a half the Kaminskys took turns writing the "scenes," each one rewriting what the other had written before continuing the story. The result was, according to critic Jack Sullivan of the *New York Times Book Review,* "an ingeniously topical horror novel" marked by "too many names of 'lit-biz luminaries,' fashionable restaurants and trendy clothing stores," but nevertheless "an intriguing and suspenseful tale."

The pseudonymous Brooks Stanwood went on to produce a second novel, *The Seventh Child,* a horror story set in the Berkshires. Like *The Glow,* it is the tale of a seemingly idyllic life eventually exposed for what it really is—in this case, a grisly plot to recruit children whose physical appearances suit them for roles in the reenactment of a bizarre seventeenth-

century tragedy, in which enraged townspeople eradicated a children's coven.

BIOGRAPHICAL/CRITICAL SOURCES:

PERIODICALS

New York Times, October 6, 1979.
New York Times Book Review, November 4, 1979.
People, November 26, 1979.
Times Literary Supplement, February 1, 1980.

*   *   *

KARBO, Joe   1925(?)-1980

OBITUARY NOTICE: Born c. 1925 in Los Angeles, Calif.; died of an apparent heart attack, November 12, 1980, in Huntington Harbour, Calif. Television personality and author. Karbo became a millionaire by writing *The Lazy Man's Way to Riches.* Also a television actor, Karbo appeared in early 1950's shows, including "This is Your FBI" and "Halls of Ivy." His other books include *The Power of Money Management.*

OBITUARIES AND OTHER SOURCES:

BOOKS

Los Angeles Times, November 13, 1980.

*   *   *

KASHDAN, Isaac   1905-1985

OBITUARY NOTICE: Born November 19, 1905, in New York, N.Y.; died February 20, 1985, in Los Angeles, Calif. Chess player, editor, and columnist. An international grandmaster, Kashdan figured prominently in the world of chess for more than fifty years. During his peak playing years in the 1930's Kashdan was considered one of the ten best players in the world. Seven times captain of the U.S. Chess Olympics team, he led the Americans to four world championships. As chess editor of the *Los Angeles Times* Kashdan wrote a column that appeared regularly in the Sunday edition of the newspaper for nearly thirty years. A leading organizer and judge of chess competitions, Kashdan directed several tournaments in Lone Pine, California that annually attracted large numbers of first-class players from around the world. He also organized the 1963 and 1966 Piatigorsky Cup tournaments and later edited books about the two events. In addition, Kashdan was editor of *Chess Correspondent* and *Chess Review,* which he founded, and a contributor to other chess periodicals.

OBITUARIES AND OTHER SOURCES:

BOOKS

Golombek's Encyclopedia of Chess, Crown, 1977.
Who's Who in America, 43rd edition, Marquis, 1984.
Who's Who in American Jewry, Standard Who's Who, 1980.

PERIODICALS

Los Angeles Times, February 22, 1985.
New York Times, February 23, 1985.

*   *   *

KATES, Carol A.   1943-

PERSONAL: Born November 5, 1943, in Coral Gables, Fla.; daughter of Bruce L. (an aircraft company manager) and Betty (a housewife; maiden name, Caldwell) Kates. *Education:* University of California, Berkeley, B.A., 1965; Tulane University, M.A., 1967, Ph.D., 1968; further graduate study at Cornell University.

ADDRESSES: Office—Department of Philosophy, Ithaca College, Ithaca, N.Y. 14850.

CAREER: Ithaca College, Ithaca, N.Y., assistant professor, 1968-71, associate professor, 1971-82, professor of philosophy, 1982—. Research associate in linguistics at Cornell University, 1973.

MEMBER: Linguistic Association of Canada and the United States, American Philosophical Association, Society of Women Philosophers, Southern Society of Philosophy and Psychology.

AWARDS, HONORS: Grants from National Endowment for the Humanities, 1973, and American Council of Learned Societies, 1976-77.

WRITINGS:

Pragmatics and Semantics: An Empiricist Theory, Cornell University Press, 1980.
(Contributor) John Sallis, editor, *Philosophy and Archaic Experience,* Duquesne University Press, 1982.

Contributor to philosophy and linguistic journals.

SIDELIGHTS: Carol A. Kates told *CA:* "In previous years I have been caught up in 'pure' academic theory and research in linguistics and phenomenology, especially research on topics of explaining how children acquire language and describing language through a new, phenomenological form of empiricism. I have basically accomplished my goals in that area.

"My focus now is research in economics and labor history, which can be used to bring about political changes, to help overcome class divisions and facilitate economic independence for women. I am currently pursuing a master's degree in industrial labor relations. I would like to contribute, as a researcher, to groups like the Service Employees International Union, which support the idea of comparable worth as a means of improving women's economic status."

AVOCATIONAL INTERESTS: Travel (Europe and Asia.)

* * *

KATKOV, George   1903-1985

OBITUARY NOTICE: Born November 27, 1903, in Moscow, Russia (now U.S.S.R.); died January 20, 1985. Historian, educator, and author. Raised in Kiev and educated at the Russian University in Prague, Katkov was one of the rare experts in modern Russian history to have experienced life in Russia under both the Tsarist and Soviet regimes. After moving to England during the 1930's, he taught philosophy and Russian studies at Oxford University. A popular teacher for many years, he became known for his ability to spark student interest in his subjects. Katkov's publications include *Russia: February 1917, The Trial of Bukharin, The Kornilov Affair,* and several articles on Russian history.

OBITUARIES AND OTHER SOURCES:

PERIODICALS

Times (London), January 26, 1985.

KATO, Hidetoshi   1930-

PERSONAL: Born April 26, 1930, in Tokyo, Japan; son of Yoshihide (in the military) and Yasue (Ukita) Kato; married Takae Murayama (a corporate president), October 22, 1955; children: Mari, Fumitoshi. *Education:* Hitotsubashi University, B.A. and M.A., both 1953, Ph.D., 1976.

ADDRESSES: Home—5-13-39 Shiroganedai Minato-ku, Tokyo, Japan 108. *Office*—University of the Air, Wakaba 2 chome, Chiba City, Japan; and, East-West Center, Honolulu, Hawaii 96822. *Agent*—Kato and Associates, Inc., 5-13-39 Shiroganedai, Minato-Ku, Tokyo, Japan 108.

CAREER: Research Institute for Humanistic Studies, Kyoto, Japan, research associate and assistant professor of sociology, 1953-70; Gakushuin University, Tokyo, Japan, professor of sociology, 1974-84, director of Research Institute for Oriental Cultures, 1977-79; University of the Air, Chiba City, Japan, professor, 1984—. Part-time researcher at East-West Center, East-West Communication Institute, Honolulu, Hawaii, 1972—. Executive director of Japanese Association for Future Research. Vice-president of Futuribles, Paris. Consultant for National Language Research Institute. Member of advisory committee of Japan Foundation; member of central education board of Ministry of Japan; member of UNESCO national committee, Japan. Visiting professor at universities in Japan and the United States.

MEMBER: International Sociological Association, International P.E.N., Japanese Association for Sociology.

AWARDS, HONORS: Ford Foundation fellow, 1959-60; Rockefeller Foundation fellow, 1963-64; International House fellow, 1970.

WRITINGS:

ALL NONFICTION; IN ENGLISH

(Editor and translator) *Japanese Popular Culture: Studies in Mass Communication and Cultural Exchange Made at the Institute of Science of Thought, Japan* (originally titled "Shiso no kagaku kenkyukai"), Tuttle, 1959.
(Editor) *Some Interview Records in an English Community,* Research Institute for Humanistic Studies, Kyoto University (Japan), 1968.
(Author of text "The Fantast of the Monster"; and in Japanese) Yasuhiro Ishimoto, *Tokyo,* translated by Tsutomu Kano and Patricia Murray, Chou-Koran-Sha, 1971.
Japanese Research on Mass Communication: Selected Abstracts, foreword by Wilbur Schramm, University Press of Hawaii, 1974.
(Editor) *Popular Images of America,* East-West Center, East-West Communication Institute (Honolulu, Hawaii), 1977.
(Editor with William H. Whyte and others) *A Comparative Study of Street Life: Tokyo, Manila, New York,* Research Institute for Oriental Cultures, Gakushuin University (Tokyo), 1977.
Education and Youth Employment in Japan, Carnegie Council on Policy Studies in Higher Education (Berkeley, Calif.), 1978.
Communication Policies in Japan, UNESCO (Paris), 1978.
(Editor) *Japan and Western Civilization,* Tokyo University Press, 1984.

IN JAPANESE

Chukan bunka (title means "Middle Brow Culture"), Heibonsha, 1957.

Me to mimi no sekai (title means "The World of Eyes and Ears"), Asahishimbun, 1962.

Atarashi Amerika (title means "New America"), Shogako-Kan, 1963.

(With Toshinao Yoneyama) *Kitahami no bunka* (title means "The Culture of Kitahami"), Shakai Shisosha, 1963.

Amerika no chiisana machi kara (title means "From a Small Town in Midwest America"), Asahi Shimbun, 1965.

Amerika no shisho (title means "American Philosophy"), N.H.K. Books, 1965.

Misemono kara terebi e (title means "From Vaudeville to Television"), Iwanami, 1965.

Ningen kankei (title means "Human Relations"), Chuokoron Sha, c. 1966.

Yogensura nihonjin (title means "Japanese Prophets"), Takeushi, 1966.

Meiji Taisho Showa seso shi (title means "Everyday Life History of Meiji Taisha Era"), Shakai Shisosha, 1967.

(With Tamito Yoshida) *Shakaiteki komyunikeshon* (title means "Social Communication"), Baifu kan, 1967.

Amerikajin (title means "Americans"), Kodansha, 1967.

Shaso kara mita nihon (title means "Japan as Seen From a Train Window"), Kotsukosha, 1967.

Teshigoto hyakutai (title means "The World of Handcrafts"), Tankosha, 1967.

(Editor with Takeo Ota) *Gendai josei no kikkonkan rikonkan* (title means "Marriage and Divorce: An Attitude Survey of Contemporary Japanese Women; The Case of Osaka and Matsue Area"), Yuhikaku, 1968.

(Editor) "Nihon bunka no tembo" (essays; title means "Perspectives of Japanese Culture"), published in *Hoso Asahi*, January-December, 1967, published under same title, Japan Productivity Center, 1968.

Hikaku bunka e no shikaku (title means "Comparative Cultures"), Chuokoron Sha, 1968.

Igirisu no chiisana machi kara (title means "From a Small Town of England"), Asahi Shimbunsha, 1969.

Ningen kaihatsu (title means "Human Development"), Chuokoron Sha, 1969.

Nisen-ichinen no nihon (title means "Japan-Year 2000"), Asahi Shimbunsha, 1969.

Toshi to Goraku (title means "City and Entertainment"), Kashima Shuppan, 1969.

"Ikigai no shuhen" (title means "Values of Life"), published in *Rikuruto*, January, 1969-June, 1970, published under same title, Bungei Shunjusha, 1970.

Jiko hyogen (title means "Expression of Self"), Chuokoron Sha, 1970.

Sogai to kan'yo (title means "Alienation and Generosity"), Tankosha, 1970.

Tayo no naka no toitsu (title means "Convergence in Divergence"), Nanundo, 1970.

(With Todashi Inoue and Ota) *Kazoku mondai bunken shusei* (title means "Bibliographics on Family Problems"), Yuhikaku, 1970.

(Compiler with Jiro Iwasaki) *Showa seso shi* (title means "History of Everyday Life in Showa Era"), Shakai Shisosha, 1971.

(Editor with Soichi Iijima) *Ningen to wa nani ka* (essays; title means "Being Human"), Diamond Sha, 1971.

Bunka to komyuneishon (title means "Culture and Communication"), Shisakusha, 1971.

Joho kankyo kara no chosen (title means "A Challenge From New Information Environment"), Jitsugyouo Nihonsha, 1971.

Kurashi no shiso (title means "Thoughts on Everyday Life"), two volumes, Chuokoron Sha, 1971-73.

Nihon no shichokaka bunka (title means "Japan's Audio-Visual Media"), Toshiba Audio-Visual Center, 1971.

Seikatsuko (essays; title means "On Everyday Life"), Bunka Shoppan, 1971.

(With Sakyo Komatsu and Tadao Umesao) *Hyakka jiten soju ho* (title means "The Uses of Encyclopedia"), Heibonsha, 1973.

Honoruru no machikado kara (title means "From a Street Corner of Honolulu"), Chuokoron Sha, 1973.

Nichijosei no shakaigaku (title means "Sociology of Everyday Life"), Bunka Shuppan, 1974.

(With Takeo Kuwabara) *Nijisseiki no yoshiki* (essays; title means "The Styles of the Twentieth Century"), Kodansha, 1975.

Dokugaku no susume (title means "Encouragement of Self Learning"), Bungeishunju, 1975.

Shuzaigaku (title means "Gathering of Materials"), Chuokoron Sha, 1975.

(With Kuwabara and Chie Nakane) *Rekishi to bummei no tankyu* (title means "Explorations of History and Civilization"), two volumes, Chuokoron Sha, 1976.

Kukan no shakaigaku (title means "Sociology of Space"), Chuo Koronsha, 1976.

Media no shushen (essays; title means "On the Problems of Media"), Bungeishunjusha, 1976.

(With Shunsuke Kamei) *Nihon to Amerika* (title means "Mutual Images: Japanese"), Gakujutsu Shinkokai, 1977.

Amerika no chiisana machi kara (title means "From a Small Town of America"), Asahai Shimbunsha, 1977.

Meiji Taisho Showa shokuseikatsu seso shi (title means "Chronology of Food Habits in Modern Japan"), Shibata Shoten, 1977.

CM Nijugonenshi (title means "Twenty Five Years of History of Commericals"), Japan Ad Center, 1978.

Shimbun shuroku Taisho shi (title means "Abstracts of Newspaper Articles of Taisho Era"), Volume I: *1912-1913*, Volume II: *1914*, Volume III: *1915*, Volume IV: *1916*, Volume V: *1917*, Volume VI: *1918*, Volume VII: *1919*, Volume VIII: *1920*, Volume IX: *1921*, Volume X: *1922*, Volume XI: *1923*, Volume XII: *1924*, Volume XIII: *1925*, Volume XIV: *1926*, Volume XV: *Index*, Taisha Shuppasha, 1978.

Shoku no shakaigaku (title means "Sociology of Food"), Bungeishunjusha, 1978.

Shuzoku no shakaigaku (title means "Sociology of Folklore"), PHP Kenkyujo, 1978.

Bungei no shakaigaku (title means "Sociology of Literature"), PHP Kenkyujo, 1979.

"Yuki no keifu" (title means "Chronicles of Challengers"), published in *Mainichi shimbun*, October, 1978-January, 1979, published under same title, Diamond Sha, 1979.

Funso no kenkyu (title means "A Study of Social Conflicts"), Nogyoson Sinko Shuppan, 1979.

I no shakaigaku (essays; title means "Sociology of clothing"), Bungeishunjusha, 1980.

Kikaku no giho (title means "Planning"), Chuokoron Sha, 1980.

(With Ai Maeda) *Meiji media ko* (title means "Media in Meiji Era"), Chuokoron Sha, 1980.

Nippon yuranki (title means "Traveling Around Japan"), Bungei Shunju, 1982.

Shoshiki to joho no bunmeiron (title means "Organization and Information"), PHP Kenkyujo, 1982.

"Tokyo" no shakaigaku (title means "Sociology of Tokyo"), PHP Kenkyujo, 1982.

"KODANSHA GENDAI SHINSHO" SERIES

(With Tatsusaburo Hayashiya) *Kyowarabe kara machishu e* (title means "History of Kyoto: Part 1"), Kodansha, 1974.
(With Hayashiya) *Kyoto shomin seikatsu shi* (title means "History of Kyoto: Part 2"), Kodansha, 1974.
(With Hayashiya) *Chonin kara shimin e* (title means "History of Kyoto: Part 3"), Kodansha, 1975.
(With Hayashiya) *Koto no kindai hyakunen* (title means "History of Kyoto: Part 4"), Kodansha, 1975.
"*Nihonjin no shuhen*" (title means "Some Observations on Japanese"), published in *Mitshubishi*, January, 1972-December, 1974, published under same title, Kodansha, 1975.
Gakumon no sekai (title means "The World of Academia"), Kodansha, 1978.
Seikatsu rizumu no bunkashi (title means "A History of the Rhythm of Life"), Kodansha, 1982.
Kiko o tabisuru (title means "A Study of Travelogues"), Chuokoron Sha, 1984.
Pachinko to Nihonjin (title means "Pachinko to Japanese"), Kodansha, 1984.

OTHER

Also author of a column in *Yomiuri* newspaper.

WORK IN PROGRESS: Editing *Handbook of Japanese Popular Culture*, with Gid Powers, for Greenwood Press.

SIDELIGHTS: Hidetoshi Kato told *CA:* "I find myself an interdisciplinary person whose interests vary from history to education, from travel to computer science."

*   *   *

KATZ, Benjamin   1904-1985

OBITUARY NOTICE: Born in 1904 in Lithuania (now U.S.S.R.); died of cancer, February 24, 1985, in northern Virginia. Naval officer, business executive, and author. Katz, whose career with the U.S. Navy spanned more than thirty years, graduated from the U.S. Naval Academy in 1926 and retired as a rear admiral in 1957. At the beginning of World War II the naval officer served in the North Atlantic as the commander of a destroyer assigned to convoy duty. He was transferred to the South Pacific in the 1942 as a captain, and he later participated in the Solomon Islands campaign and commanded the flagship of the Seventh Fleet. Katz was awarded the Navy Cross, the Silver Star, the Bronze Star, and the Legion of Merit for his wartime service.

Before retiring in 1957, the admiral served as communications officer at the Pacific Fleet Headquarters in Pearl Harbor and as a deputy director of the Office of Communications-Electronics of the Joint Chiefs of Staff. In the 1960s he held an executive position with ICM Systems and worked as a consultant. Katz wrote *Now Is the Time!: To Prepare a Guide for Your Survivor.* His other writings include books on small businesses.

OBITUARIES AND OTHER SOURCES:

PERIODICALS

Washington Post, February 26, 1985.

KATZ, Carol   1939-
(Penny Allison, Rosalynn Carroll)

PERSONAL: Born February 13, 1939, in Detroit, Mich.; daughter of Hyman (a chemist) and Celia (a storyteller) Goodman; married Eugene Martin Katz (a builder), June 25, 1961; children: David Alan, Paul Benjamin. *Education:* Wayne State University, B.A., 1961; University of Michigan, M.S.L.S., 1973.

ADDRESSES: Home—2760 Lakehurst Lane, Ann Arbor, Mich. 48105. *Agent*—Irene Goodman Literary Agency, 521 Fifth Ave., 17th Floor, New York, N.Y. 10017.

CAREER: English teacher at public schools in Detroit, Mich., 1961-68; *Observer*, Livonia, Mich., reporter, 1970-72; *Eagle*, Wayne-Westland, Mich., reporter, 1972-74; full-time writer, 1980—.

MEMBERS: Authors Guild of America, Romance Writers of America, Detroit Women Writers.

WRITINGS:

The Berry Cookbook, Butterick, 1980.
(Under pseudonym Rosalynn Carroll) *Enchanted Encore* (romance novel), New American Library, 1984.
Then Came Laughter (romance novel), Harlequin, 1985.

Contributor to *Horn Book*.

ROMANCE NOVELS UNDER PSEUDONYM PENNY ALLISON

King of Diamonds, Silhouette, 1982.
Reckless Venture, Silhouette, 1983.
Night Train to Paradise, Silhouette, 1984.
North Country Nights, Silhouette, 1984.

WORK IN PROGRESS: In the Arms of Lady Luck, a romance novel.

SIDELIGHTS: Carol Katz told *CA:* "I write about love as a vital force in human relationships, probably because of my experience with love in a marriage of almost twenty-three years. I'm especially interested in the subject of romantic love as it affects contemporary life. Love and laughter as a healing force is the theme of my novel, *Then Came Laughter*. Unemployment in a marriage is the subject of *North Country Nights*. In *Night Train to Paradise* I deal with a conflict of values: upward mobility and 'yuppie' style success versus personal satisfaction.

"I'm mindful, of course, that the subject of romantic love is not a trendy one in many current circles, that it is seen as a foolish hangover of the 1950's or simply as an illusion for immature minds, but the most profound experiences of my life have taught me otherwise. Although I'm a staunch believer in women's rights and independence, I also believe that lasting love between men and women can be a reality in modern life and a very necessary one, at that. When viewed from a long-range perspective, in fact, romantic love is the force that not only brings men and women together, but is ultimately responsible for the creation of children and primary family bonds. The very future of human life is vitally linked both to the successes and the failures of romantic love, a subject that is as delightful to me as it is profoundly serious."

Katz's books have been translated into French, German, Italian, and Japanese.

KAUFMAN, Herbert 1922-

BRIEF ENTRY: Born September 21, 1922, in New York, N.Y. American political scientist, educator, and author. Kaufman taught political science at Yale University for more than fifteen years before he became a senior fellow of the Brookings Institution in 1969. He has been a fellow at the Center for Advanced Study in the Behavioral Sciences and a visiting scholar at the Russell Sage Foundation. A past chairman of the New Haven Housing Authority, Kaufman is a consultant to the U.S. Bureau of the Budget. His books include *Governing New York City* (Norton, 1965), *The Limits of Organizational Change* (University of Alabama Press, 1971), *Are Government Organizations Immortal* (Brookings Institution, 1976), *Red Tape: Its Origins, Uses, and Abuses* (Brookings Institution, 1977), and *The Administrative Behavior of Federal Bureau Chiefs* (Brookings Institution, 1981). *Address:* Brookings Institution, 1775 Massachusetts Ave. N.W., Washington, D.C. 20036.

BIOGRAPHICAL/CRITICAL SOURCES:

BOOKS

Who's Who in American Jewry, Standard Who's Who, 1980.

* * *

KAVANAUGH, John F(rancis) 1941-

PERSONAL: Born March 14, 1941, in St. Louis, Mo.; son of John (a laborer) and Julia (a laborer; maiden name, Connally) Kavanaugh. *Education:* St. Louis University, B.A. (magna cum laude), 1965, M.A. (philosophy), 1967, M.A. (dogmatic theology), 1971; Washington University, St. Louis, Mo., Ph.D., 1973.

ADDRESSES: Office—Department of Philosophy, St. Louis University, 221 North Grand Blvd., St. Louis, Mo. 63103.

CAREER: Entered Society of Jesus (Jesuits), 1959, ordained Roman Catholic priest, 1971; St. Louis University, St. Louis, Mo., assistant professor, 1974-78, associate professor of philosophy, 1978; writer. Worked at Tin Wan Social Center, Hong Kong, and House for the Dying, Calcutta, India; member of Jesuit National Board of Social Ministries, 1976-84; gives lectures and workshops on religious vows and justice. Past member of St. Louis Jesuit Musicians Group.

AWARDS, HONORS: First place award from National Catholic Press Association, 1978, and second place award, 1983, both for column "Viewpoint."

WRITINGS:

Human Realization: A Philosophy of Human Nature, Corpus-World, 1970.
Following Christ in a Consumer Society: Spirituality as Cultural Resistance, Orbis, 1981.

St. Louis Review, film critic, 1966-71, author of column "Viewpoint," 1977—. Contributor to magazines and newspapers.

WORK IN PROGRESS: Articles on political economy and Christian faith and religious vows as political resistance; *The Multiple Faces of Poverty,* a collection of his articles and lectures previously published in periodicals.

SIDELIGHTS: John F. Kavanaugh told *CA:* "A major expenditure of my time is for lectures and workshops on the relationship between faith and culture. A slide presentation, 'Advertising, Consumerism, and the Formation of Con-

science,' has been given in South America and Europe, and throughout Canada and the United States.

"Advanced industrial society and nationalistic capitalism serve as the cultural ambient from which many of our religious, mythic, spiritual, and moral 'reality criteria' emerge. These criteria, providing the standards whereby we evaluate ourselves and legitimate our standing in community, are for the most part unquestioned and for that very reason immensely powerful in their influence upon our consciousness. Cultural critique is deconstruction of idolatry."

* * *

KEEL, John A.
See Kiehle, John Alva

* * *

KEIDEL, Levi (Jr.) 1927-

PERSONAL: Surname is pronounced *Kigh*-del; born January 18, 1927, in Goodfield, Ill.; son of Levi O. (a farmer) and Anne (a housewife; maiden name, Holliger) Keidel; married Eudene King (a housewife and writer), September 24, 1948; children: Paul, Priscilla Keidel Miller, Perry, Ruth. *Education:* Attended Illinois State University, 1944-45 and 1978; Bob Jones University, B.A., 1950; Northwestern University, M.S. (journalism), 1962; Trinity Evangelical Divinity School, M.A. (cum laude), 1984. *Religion:* Mennonite.

ADDRESSES: Home—2348 Alder St., Clearbrook, British Columbia, Canada V2T 2N7.

CAREER: Africa Inter-Mennonite Mission, Elkhart, Ind., missionary to Zaire, evangelist, teacher, and creator of literature in the Tshiluba language, 1950-81; Faith and Life Bookstore, Newton, Kan., manager, 1968-70; Columbia Bible Institute, Clearbrook, British Columbia, instructor and director of Center for Mission, 1984—. *Military service:* U.S. Navy, 1945-46.

AWARDS, HONORS: Award from Evangelical Literature Overseas, 1966, for outstanding achievement in overseas Christian literature distribution; Ken Anderson Films award, 1966, for best eight-millimeter missionary movie; Order of the Leopold medal from Government of Zaire, 1973, for distinguished service to social development; second place award from World Vision, 1975, for sermon/essay contest; Gold Medallion from Evangelical Publishers Association, 1979, for novel *Caught in the Crossfire.*

WRITINGS:

Footsteps to Freedom (biography), Moody, 1969.
Stop Treating Me Like God (autobiography), Creation House, 1971.
Black Samson (biography), Creation House, 1975.
War to Be One (historical biography), Zondervan, 1977.
Caught in the Crossfire (novel), Herald Press, 1979.

Author of books and brochures in the Tshiluba language of Zaire. Contributor of articles to more than fifty periodicals in North America. Founder and editor of *Tuyaya Kunyi.*

WORK IN PROGRESS: Research on religious phenomenology, with a book expected to result.

SIDELIGHTS: Levi Keidel told *CA:* "While in the Navy I had a personal faith encounter with Christ that totally reoriented my life. The joy and gratitude springing from that experience made me want to spend my one life helping others make this discovery in order to enjoy the fulfilling kind of life it affords. I felt that best use would be made of my life if I invested it in helping those in a foreign land whose opportunities are limited and few. The girl I was then dating (now my wife) had specific plans for missionary service in Zaire. Missionaries from there showed me how my personal gifts and experience matched existing needs there. Why seek further?

"Our career led us through three eras: the era of colonialism, when the white man created the game plan and called the plays; the era of interdependency, when political independence and maturing African leadership mandated a transfer of authority from the white man to the national; and the era of African autonomy, when the white missionary came upon invitation of the African church and took a servanthood posture under its leadership.

"During our time in Zaire my wife and I and our four children survived two violent revolutions. In 1960, with the advent of political independence, a mutinying army vented longstanding grievances against whites and anarchy spread like darkness over the land; we fled as refugees. In 1964 a Communist-supported insurrection swept across most of the country and was stopped just north of the city in which we lived. How the mounting tension affected us emotionally is related in a part of *Stop Treating Me Like God*. (How it affected Zairian Christians who bore the full brunt of it is related in *Caught in the Crossfire*.) The Zairian people demonstrated two remarkable qualities: the resilience to absorb wave after wave of devastating loss and still retain the will to rise up and build again, and the fearless courage to stick to what they believe in the face of harassment and mortal danger.

"*Footsteps* relates the life story of a Zairian pastor—the happiness of his childhood steeped in Zaire's cultural milieu, his confusion in defining the role of the newly-arrived white missionary (as opposed to the roles of other white men he has encountered), his education and eventual conversion on the mission station, and his struggle with aspects of his culture (witchcraft, barrenness, tribalism, war) that are incompatible with his newfound faith.

"*Stop Treating Me Like God* stresses that Christian missionaries do not sit on pedestals with halos around their heads. They are ordinary people with temptations, struggles, and foibles common to all human beings.

"*Black Samson* is a true account of an African of commanding strength who compensated for a personal sense of unworth inherited from a slave tribe ancestry by demonstrating his contempt for any restraints of normal decorum. While drunk he kills a white civil authority and begins his term of life imprisonment. His learning by surreptitious reading of Scripture that Old Testament beliefs and rituals parallel those of his ancestors is a key to his rediscovery of self-worth. A conversion experience changes his lifestyle from terrorizing to servitude, which in turn leads to his eventual release. Outside of prison his commitment to service and love is as radical and unorthodox as his previous commitment to license and hate.

"*War to Be One* is about an unpretentious veteran missionary and his Zairian pastor-colleague of many years who find themselves caught in the wanton violence and demographic upheaval that followed in the wake of political independence. Together they battle the ravages of famine and war to rescue an African tribe from oblivion and to heal the wounds of strife.

"*Caught in the Crossfire* is a novel about three Zairian men, caught in the 1964 pro-Communist insurrection, who try to integrate their Christian faith with the exigencies of their new situation, choose three different courses (resistance, compromise, collaboration), and endure the consequences."

Commenting on the contemporary African scene, Keidel continued: "The motives of African heads of state range from self-serving to altruistic. The interwoven nature of the world's economic structure, efforts of great powers to extend their influence, the unavailability of resources, and varying degrees of corruption in government greatly handicap prospects for normal social development. They have little interest in the East-West power struggle. They will take help toward solving their crushing social problems from whatever quarter it is offered, with little regard for ideology.

"It is an opinion common among perceptive Africans that the Industrial Revolution was initiated and has been sustained by natural resources taken from their countries. Those same resources were of strategic importance to our winning World War II. Our standard of living, which consumes 45 percent of the world's natural resources to sustain, and which comprises a per capita income of twelve to fifteen times theirs, is already beyond the range of achievability for them. Our refusal to much more generously provide financial and technical assistance that foster programs for education and social development, and to alleviate human suffering, can only further nurture grievances and ultimately foster enmity.

"The Church's decline of vitality and influence in the West is more than compensated for by its spiritual dynamism and growth in Third World countries. Numerically, its center of gravity has now shifted to Africa."

AVOCATIONAL INTERESTS: Jogging, photography, music (violin).

* * *

KELLEHER, Catherine McArdle 1939-
(Catherine McArdle)

BRIEF ENTRY: Born January 19, 1939, in Boston, Mass. American political scientist, educator, and author. Kelleher has been a member of the faculty at Barnard College and the University of Illinois at Chicago Circle. In 1973 she was appointed associate professor of political science at the University of Michigan. She has also been a fellow at Columbia University's Institute for War and Peace Studies and at Harvard University's Center for West European Studies, as well as a member of the Inter-University Seminar on the Armed Forces and Society.

Kelleher's books include *Political-Military Systems: Comparative Perspectives* (Sage Publications, 1974) and *Germany and the Politics of Nuclear Weapons* (Columbia University Press, 1975). Under the name Catherine McArdle, she also published *The Role of Military Assistance in the Problem of Arms Control: The Middle East, Latin America, and Africa* (Center for International Studies, Massachusetts Insitute of Technology, 1964). *Address:* Department of Political Science, University of Michigan, Ann Arbor, Mich. 48104.

* * *

KELLEY, Arleon L(eigh) 1935-

PERSONAL: Born May 5, 1935, in Cass City, Mich.; son of

Harley L. and L. Elna (Aurand) Kelley; married Jacqueline Ann Wisel, August 29, 1959 (divorced); children: Erin Marie, Timothy Leigh. *Education:* Taylor University, A.B., 1956; Christian Theological Seminary, Indianapolis, Ind., B.D., 1960; Boston University, Th.D., 1971. *Politics:* Independent.

ADDRESSES: Home—New York, N.Y. *Office*—National Council of Churches, Room 625, 474 Riverside Dr., New York, N.Y. 10115.

CAREER: Ordained United Methodist minister, 1960; pastor of United Methodist churches in Ft. Wayne, Auburn, and Bluffton, Ind., 1956-61, and Pawtucket, R.I., 1961-63; Indiana Council of Churches, Indianapolis, Ind., executive director of planning and research, 1963-69; Ohio Council of Churches, Columbus, Ohio, associate executive director, 1969-72; National Council of Churches, New York, N.Y., associate executive director of Commission on Regional and Local Ecumenism, 1972—. Affiliate professor at Christian Theological Seminary, 1963-69; instructor at Methodist Theological School in Ohio, 1969-72. Vice-president of Religious Research Association, Inc., 1968-69; director of Resource Recovery Systems, Inc., 1977—.

MEMBER: North American Academy of Ecumenists, American Sociological Association, Society for the Scientific Study of Religion, Religious Research Association, Council on Christian Unity.

WRITINGS:

(Editor) *Ecumenical Designs,* Committee on Church and Community Life, 1966.
Your Church: A Dynamic Community, Westminster, 1982.

WORK IN PROGRESS: The Transformation of Work, publication expected in 1985.

SIDELIGHTS: Arleon L. Kelley told *CA:* "I was prompted to write *Your Church: A Dynamic Community* to challenge the local church to better understand itself and fulfill its calling. Theologically, it develops the perspective that the Church is called to be the prototype of the struggle for wholeness and fulfillment—pointing to the wholeness and fulfillment I believe God intends for the whole creation. Sociologically, the book explores the organizational dynamics that both impede and enhance this possibility in the community. The concluding chapters deal with the nature of leadership and how the prototype people make their contribution in the community.

"I believe the book has several uniquenesses: first, it is an argument for an authentic universal expression of the Church in the community; second, it is a theological and sociological description of the dynamics of the Church; and third, it views the role of the Church in the community in process theology terms. The book is designed to be used by the lay reader with little experience in theology or sociology."

Regarding his work in progress, *The Transformation of Work,* Kelley commented: "We are at the end of the industrial-cultural era. Our culture is undergoing a significant transformation. Much of the work (jobs) we do at the end of this era has become meaningless because the worker does not feel a connection between what she or he is doing and the central purpose of life.

"The Church has worked hand in hand with the industrial culture—just as it did before with the agricultural and trading cultures—to help people feel that particular meaning came to their life by what they *did*—their work. Without meaningful

work for people in the new cultural era, what will give meaning to life?

"Theologically, work is more often dealt with in terms of vocation. And vocation has much more to do with how humankind uses its energy to participate in the creation than it has to do with the production of the industrial society. Thus the first thesis of the book is that we need to begin building new values about what gives meaning to life. Authentic work is really vocation. Vocation has only marginal relationship to production, marketing, and profit. Rather, it has to do with quality of life—participating in it—an appropriate idea for a society that can do most of its work with cybernetic systems.

"This raises the related questions: How do you organize vocation in such a world so quality of life is a possibility? And even more important, how do you distribute the wealth of the society when you no longer do it by hourly paid jobs or annual salaries? These issues are linked to the individual models of production, marketing, investments, and profits. We need new economic values and new economic models that are more creative than capitalism *or* communism *or* socialism.

"Although the book does not propose solutions, it does probe some possible visions or models for the future. If the church fails to give leadership in the transformation and ties its future to the past, it will, like many other social systems tied to the industrial order, find itself obsolete. I am optimistic the third world church can make the transition. I am pessimistic about the church in the first world. We like the glories of our past greatness! But there is hope!"

*   *   *

KELSEN, Hans   1881-1973

OBITUARY NOTICE: Born October 11, 1881, in Prague, Austria-Hungary (now Czechoslovakia); died April 19, 1973. Legal philosopher, educator, and author. An authority on international and constitutional law, Kelsen is best known for his doctrine of pure law. The doctrine, first formulated in Kelsen's 1911 work *Hauptprobleme der Staatsrechtslehre,* views systems of legal norms as immanent—independent of political, social, or metaphysical theories. According to Kelsen, the validity of a system of law is derived from a basic norm which is universally accepted.

A professor of public law and jurisprudence at the University of Vienna from 1911 to 1930, Kelsen advised the Austrian Government and wrote a draft of the Austrian constitution. He taught at the University of Cologne from 1930 to 1933, transferring to the University of Geneva, Switzerland, not long after the Nazis came to power in Germany. In 1940 Kelsen immigrated to the United States to teach at Harvard University. Two years later he became professor of international law and jurisprudence at the University of California, Berkeley, where he remained until his retirement in 1952. Kelsen's numerous awards include the Certificate of Merit of the American Society of International Law and the Karl Preis der Stadt Wien. A recipient of honorary degrees from many universities, Kelsen was also a member of many learned societies, American and foreign. Among his writings are *General Theory of Law and State, The Pure Theory of Law, Principles of International Law, What is Justice?,* and *Society and Nature: A Sociological Inquiry.*

OBITUARIES AND OTHER SOURCES:

BOOKS

Current Biography, Wilson, 1957, November, 1973.
The Oxford Companion to Law, Clarendon Press, 1980.
Webster's American Biographies, Merriam, 1979.
Who Was Who in America, With World Notables, Volume V: 1969-1973, Marquis, 1973.

PERIODICALS

New York Times, April 20, 1973.

*　　*　　*

KENNEDY, Roger G(eorge) 1926-

PERSONAL: Born August 3, 1926, in St. Paul, Minn.; son of Walter J. and Elisabeth (Dean) Kennedy; married Frances Hefren (an educational consultant), August 23, 1958; children: Ruth. *Education:* Yale University, B.A., 1949; University of Minnesota, LL.B., 1952.

ADDRESSES: Home—208 North Quaker Lane, Alexandria, Va. 22304. *Office*—National Museum of American History, 14th St. and Constitution Ave. N.W., Washington, D.C. 20560.

CAREER: Admitted to Minnesota Bar, 1952, District of Columbia Bar, 1953; Justice Department, Washington, D.C., attorney, 1953; National Broadcasting Company (NBC), New York City, Washington correspondent, 1954-57; Dallas Council of World Affairs, Dallas, Tex., director, 1958; Department of Labor, Washington, D.C., special assistant to secretary, 1959; Northwestern National Bank, St. Paul, Minn., assistant vice-president, 1959-66, chairman of executive committee and director, 1967-69, served as vice-president; University of Minnesota, Minneapolis, vice-president of investments and executive director, 1969-70; Ford Foundation, New York City, vice-president for financial affairs, 1970-80, vice-president for the arts, 1978-79; Smithsonian Institution, Washington, D.C., director of National Museum of American History, 1979—. Department of Health, Education, and Welfare, special assistant to secretary, 1957, counselor to secretary, 1969. Trustee of Bowery Savings Bank and of C. G. Jung Foundation. *Military service:* U.S. Naval Reserve, active duty, 1944-46.

WRITINGS:

Minnesota Houses, Dillon, 1966.
Men on a Moving Frontier, American West, 1968.
American Churches, Stewart, Tabori, 1982.
Architecture and Money, Random House, 1985.

Contributor to twenty-six Public Broadcasting Service (PBS-TV) documentaries and NBC radio and television programs, including "Outlook" and "Today." Contributor to periodicals, including *Harper's, Atlantic Monthly, Smithsonian, Reader's Digest, Harvard Business Review,* and *Law and Contemporary Problems.*

SIDELIGHTS: In *American Churches* Roger G. Kennedy examines more than one hundred churches and temples that represent different currents in American religious architecture. Discussing all sizes, styles, and periods—from the Spanish mission churches of the Southwest to New England's clapboard meetinghouses—the author also considers the psychology of religious buildings. Architecture critic Paul Goldberger observed in the *New York Time Book Review* that "the thesis of Roger G. Kennedy's 'American Churches' is that the greatest religious buildings have been those which have tried, in some way, to convey a sense of the mystery that virtually all religion involves."

Writing in the *Chicago Tribune Book World,* architecture critic Paul Gapp called *American Churches* "a pictorial showpiece . . . of unqualified distinction." "While it does not try to be encyclopedic," he added, "it helps fill what has been a rather large gap in U.S. ecclesiastical design literature." *Washington Post Book World* reviewer Edgar Tafel noted that, while Kennedy may overglorify the process of designing a religious building, "his selection of churches and synagogues is exemplary" and America's religious architectural history is "compellingly told and beautifully portrayed." And Goldberger deemed *American Churches* "an unusual and impressive book" that goes beyond its coffee table dazzle with a text that is "thoughtful and even profound."

BIOGRAPHICAL/CRITICAL SOURCES:

PERIODICALS

Chicago Tribune Book World, December 5, 1982.
New York Times Book Review, December 26, 1982.
Washington Post Book World, April 3, 1983.

*　　*　　*

KENNEY, Alice P(atricia) 1937-1985

OBITUARY NOTICE—See index for *CA* sketch: Born May 1, 1937, in Schenectady, N.Y.; died February 4, 1985, in Delmar, N.Y. Historian, educator, and author. An authority on Dutch colonial history, Kenney taught at Cedar Crest College for nearly twenty years and had been a research associate with the Albany Institute of History and Art beginning in 1979. The educator, herself confined to a wheelchair, directed the National Endowment for the Humanities-funded Museum Access Project, which sought to make museums and historical sites accessible for the handicapped. The *Hospital Heritage* handbook resulted from this project. Kenney was named one of the fifty outstanding young women of America by the Outstanding Americans Foundation in 1968 and an outstanding educator of America in 1971. Her writings include *History of the American Family, The Gansevoorts of Albany: Dutch Patricians in the Upper Hudson Valley, Stubborn for Liberty: The Dutch in New York, Albany: Crossroads of Liberty,* and *Access to the Past.*

OBITUARIES AND OTHER SOURCES:

PERIODICALS

Allentown Morning Call, March 1, 1985.

*　　*　　*

KENNEY, Lona B(ronberg) 1921-

PERSONAL: Born December 15, 1921, in Luck, Poland; came to United States in the early 1940's; naturalized U.S. citizen in the late 1940's; daughter of Elias (a physician) and Natalie (Devinpierre) Bronberg; married Michael Kenney (a physician, professor, author, and artist), 1937 (died April 29, 1982). *Education:* Educated in England, France, Germany, and Italy. *Politics:* "I vote for the best candidate, Democrat or Republican." *Religion:* "I do not practice any."

ADDRESSES: Home—3 Peter Cooper Rd., 3-F, New York, N.Y. 10010.

CAREER: Writer. Worked as opera and concert singer during the 1930's. Accredited volunteer at Veterans' Administration

Hospital in New York, N.Y., 1953-56. *Wartime service:* American Theatre Wing War Service, 1944-45.

MEMBER: Authors Guild, Writers Guild of America, National Academy of Television Arts and Sciences.

AWARDS, HONORS: Certificate of Merit from Veterans' Hospital in New York, N.Y., 1955, for steadfast volunteer service; Boston University Mugar Memorial Library's establishment of a Lona B. Kenney special collection, 1966; National Paraplegia Foundation Award for special contribution, 1968, for *A Caste of Heroes.*

WRITINGS:

A Caste of Heroes (novel), Dodd, 1966.
Mboka: The Way of Life in a Congo Village (memoir), Crown, 1973.
The One Thing Worth Having (novel), Allen, Bennington, 1982.

TELEVISION SCRIPTS

"Tales of Tomorrow," released by the American Broadcasting Company (ABC-TV) during the early 1950's.
"Trapped," broadcast by WOR-TV of Seacaucus, N.J., during the early 1950's.
"True Story," released by the National Broadcasting Company (NBC-TV) during the early 1960's.

Contributor of articles and short stories to *This Month.*

WORK IN PROGRESS: "A rough outline of a novel set in Poland before World War II, dealing in part with its ingrained anti-Semitism, which had tragically played into the hands of the Nazi invaders and their murder of innocent millions."

SIDELIGHTS: Lona B. Kenney's first book, the novel *A Caste of Heroes,* portrays the lives of paraplegics in a veterans' hospital and is based on knowledge and insights gained by the author as an accredited volunteer at a Veterans Administration hospital. According to James Smittkamp in the *Paraplegia News,* though *A Caste of Heroes* is fictionalized, the struggles, pains, and problems it depicts are real. Moreover, in Smittkamp's assessment, the "author's insight into these problems indicates a fine sensitivity and sympathetic understanding rare among non-paraplegics." And Charles Purvis of the *Chicago Tribune* noted that the reader "is likely to be drawn into these lives [of paraplegic patients] more than he expects. And there is even a moral—that what counts is what you make of what you have."

Kenney's second book, *Mboka: The Way of Life in a Congo Village,* recounts her experiences in the Belgian Congo when she accompanied her husband—a Belgian medical officer who specialized in tropical diseases—to Africa, where he treated and healed many afflicted people. A reviewer for the *New York Times Book Review* briefly noted that "Kenney recalls her adventures in this other time and place with charm and feeling." And K. N. Maxwell, in his review of *Mboka* for the *Cleveland Press,* remarked that "Lona Kenney had a kinship with the Congo natives which somehow shines through and makes her book a classic."

Kenney told *CA:* "I think that behind each of my decisions to write on a certain theme, there's a conviction that the subject is valid and the story is worth telling. For example, *A Caste of Heroes* was inspired by my indelible experience in the paraplegic wards of a VA hospital. *Mboka* is the account of my life in an equatorial back country, European outpost, and in a neighboring isolated hamlet among its Africans, who enriched my mind by allowing me to share their communal life and learn about their ancient culture; *Mboka* also recounts my special relationship with the villagers, many of whom I learned to respect, and my friendship with their children, most of whom I grew to love.

"*The One Thing Worth Having* is a psychological novel about our society's obsession with youth and the drama of aging in such a society, which, in the end, victimizes us all. *A Caste of Heroes* deals with physical disability and mental suffering. *The Only Thing Worth Having* concerns itself with psychological pain only. But, in the words of George Bernard Shaw (which I'm here apologetically paraphrasing), however earnest the theme, it is the author's obligation to the reading public to write on it entertainingly."

Kenney also told *CA* this anecdote about her work with paraplegics: "While a volunteer in the paraplegic wards at the Bronx VA hospital, I had arranged with the CBS-TV producers of 'Youth Wants to Know,' a 1954 quiz show, to have four young vet paraplegics as guest panelists on the program. As you know, of course, in the 1950's and 1960's any reference to disability, or other such topics, was taboo on the air. Since there was no studio audience the television people in charge decided—just in case—to have the front of the makeshift table, behind which the four wheelchairs were placed, draped with a full-length cloth to conceal them from the eye of the camera and, hence, from the home viewers. (The boys, including a quadriplegic, were such a hit, incidentally, that they were booked on the program again.)"

A trained linguist, Kenney is fluent in many languages.

BIOGRAPHICAL/CRITICAL SOURCES:

PERIODICALS

Chicago Tribune, May 29, 1966.
Cleveland Press, February 23, 1973.
New York Times Book Review, April 15, 1973.
Paraplegia News, February, 1967.

*   *   *

KENNEY, Susan (McIlvaine) 1941-

PERSONAL: Born April 28, 1941, in Summit, N. J.; daughter of James Morrow (a lawyer and executive) and Virginia (a housewife; maiden name, Tucker) McIlvaine; married Edwin James Kenney, Jr. (a college professor), November 28, 1964; children: one son, one daughter. *Education:* Northwestern University, B.A. (with honors), 1963; Cornell University, M.A., 1964, Ph.D., 1968. *Politics:* Liberal. *Religion:* Protestant.

ADDRESSES: Office—Department of English, Colby College, Waterville, Maine 04901. *Agent*—Maxine Groffsky Literary Agency, 2 Fifth Ave., New York, N.Y. 10011.

CAREER: Colby College, Waterville, Maine, assistant professor, 1968-82, associate professor of English, 1982—. Member of board of trustees of Albert Church Brown Memorial Library, China, Maine.

MEMBER: Authors Guild, Phi Beta Kappa.

AWARDS, HONORS: First prize from O. Henry Awards, 1982, for story "Facing Front"; fellow of National Endowment for the Arts, 1983-84.

WRITINGS:

Garden of Malice (novel), Scribner, 1983.

In Another Country (novel), Viking, 1984.

Contributor of stories and articles to magazines, including *Massachusetts Review, Hudson Review, McCall's,* and *Ladies' Home Journal.*

WORK IN PROGRESS: Graves in Academe, a mystery novel; another novel.

SIDELIGHTS: The recipient of a 1982 O. Henry Award for her story "Facing Front," Susan Kenney has also written two novels. *In Another Country* was warmly received by critics such as Anne Tyler, who wrote in the *New York Times Book Review:* "'In Another Country' could have been maudlin, or sententious, or slickly 'inspirational.' It's none of these. By maintaining exactly the right balance of tone—level and blessedly cool—Susan Kenney has created a distinguished novel. She writes unerringly. She possesses the kind of certainty that leaves readers feeling lucky." Writing in the *Philadelphia Inquirer,* Avery Rome opined: "Susan Kenney's quiet debut as a novelist may signal the most breathtaking achievement of the literary year." Rome also noted the "startling resonance and emotional impact" of *In Another Country,* adding: "Through her unswerving control, her steadfast resistance to sentimentality and her direct handling of the most complex feelings, Kenney creates a compelling inner life for her character, and the richness here depends every bit as much on how details are conveyed as on what those details are."

Susan Kenney told *CA:* "I always wanted to be a writer. I was spurred on by my mother, who is a great reader and also a writer (unpublished). In grade school I tried to turn other assignments into creative writing and sometimes got into trouble for it, but I also got a lot of encouragement. When I see my own children and students in school now, I'm convinced that they don't get to do enough writing, creative or otherwise; when they get to freshman English they can diagram the blazes out of any sentence you give them, but they can't write one. They know more technical terms than I do—quick! what's a progressive verb?—but are very unsure of their own style. After two months of weekly writing assignments, it is as though they've had a revelation. I love teaching composition and creative writing; the results are so concrete. If you and the student keep at it, you both get better."

Commenting on *In Another Country,* Kenney continued: "The book is composed of six connected stories, narrated by a young woman, Sara, who teaches English at a small college in Vermont. Her husband, Phil, also teaches English, and they are the parents of a son and daughter three years apart. People who know that I and my husband, Ed, teach English at Colby College and that our son and daughter are three years apart often ask whether *In Another Country* is autobiographical. The only story that is what I would call directly autobiographical is 'The Death of the Dog and Other Rescues.' And even with that one, when my son read it, his comment was, 'Hey, Mom, that's not the way it happened.' The other stories are more or less fabrications, although based on incidents in my own life. For example, in the story 'Hallways,' Sara's eight-year-old daughter gets lost in the hospital where Phil lies gravely ill. Sara finds Linnie huddled in the angle of the floor and wall in a corridor just off the one Phil's room is on. My daughter has never been lost in a hospital, but she once missed her way in a large motel, and after considerable searching, was found similarly huddled in one of the motel corridors.

"About the process that leads me to choose and arrange incidents, it's my sense of what makes a good story. Most of the time life doesn't provide very good stories, or art, period. Art makes stories—or pictures or music or sculpture—out of what life has to offer. Realism is realism; whether something really happened or not is irrelevant. If you can make a story seem real, then it seems autobiographical, as though it really happened to the person telling or experiencing the story. That's realism as Joseph Conrad defined it: 'My task which I am trying to achieve is by the power of the written word to make you hear, to make you feel—it is above all, to make you see.'

"I have worked on the stories that make up *In Another Country* since 1971, seriously committing my time in 1978, when my daughter went to school full time. For me, writing full time is writing two or three hours a day, in the morning, sitting at the typewriter, or more recently, the word processor. But, of course, the time I spend thinking over and making up and arranging and rearranging is incalculable; when I'm writing a first draft I think about it all day long and sometimes dream about it at night, and the same is true when I'm doing heavy revision, which I do a fair amount of.

"While *In Another Country* was in progress, I completed a mystery novel, *Garden of Malice.* I've recently completed a second mystery novel (that's what I do for fun), and am fairly well into a second novel about Phil and Sara. I want the characters in my fiction to be representative of ordinary people who are beset by extraordinary problems, but who somehow manage not to give in or go under. In a way this is what the mysteries are about as well: people confronted by an evil or an injustice who don't give in until the mystery is solved and justice is done."

BIOGRAPHICAL/CRITICAL SOURCES:

PERIODICALS

New York Times Book Review, August 5, 1984.
Philadelphia Inquirer, July 1, 1984.
Times Literary Supplement, November 2, 1984.
Washington Post Book World, June 13, 1984.

* * *

KENNY, Jean
See FREEMAN, Jean Kenny

* * *

KERBER, Linda K(aufman) 1940-

BRIEF ENTRY: Born January 23, 1940, in New York, N.Y. American historian, educator, and author. Kerber joined the history faculty of the University of Iowa in 1971 and became a full professor in 1975. Her previous teaching experience was acquired at Stern College for Women, San Jose State College (now University), and Stanford University. The educator's research has been funded by the American Philosophical Society, the American Bar Foundation, the American Council of Learned Societies, and the National Endowment for the Humanities. From 1977 to 1978 she served on the biography jury for the Pulitzer Prize. Kerber is the author of *Federalists in Dissent: Imagery and Ideology in Jeffersonian America* (Cornell University Press, 1970) and *Women of the Republic: Intellect and Ideology in Revolutionary America* (University of North Carolina Press, 1980). She co-edited *Women's America: Refocusing the Past* (Oxford University Press, 1982). *Address:* Department of History, University of Iowa, Iowa City, Iowa 52242.

BIOGRAPHICAL/CRITICAL SOURCES:

PERIODICALS

American Historical Review, April, 1971.
New York Times Book Review, December 28, 1980.

* * *

KESSLER, Ethel 1922-

BRIEF ENTRY: Born January 7, 1922, in Pittsburgh, Pa. American author. Kessler, who has considerable experience working with children in summer camps, and her husband, Leonard Kessler, have collaborated on more than twenty books for children. Their titles include *What's Inside the Box* (Dodd, 1976), *Two, Four, Six, Eight: A Book About Legs* (Dodd, 1980), *Pig's New Hat* (Garrard, 1981), *Pig's Orange House* (Garrard, 1981), and *Night Story* (Macmillan, 1981).

BIOGRAPHICAL/CRITICAL SOURCES:

BOOKS

Fifth Book of Junior Authors and Illustrators, Wilson, 1983.

* * *

KEYS, Donald (Fraser) 1924-

PERSONAL: Born June 9, 1924, in Sierra Madre, Calif.; son of Gilbert S. (a civil engineer) and Margaret (Snell) Keys; married Betty Jane Pedersen, September, 1950 (divorced, 1963); married Martha McDougle (an educator), June 9, 1974; children: Fraser Theusen, Christopher Webster. *Education:* Attended Pasadena Junior College (now Pasadena City College) and University of Southern California.

ADDRESSES: Home—Palo Alto, Calif. *Office*—Planetary Citizens, P.O. Box 426, Menlo Park, Calif. 94026.

CAREER: KWSD-Radio, Mount Shasta, Calif., chief engineer, 1948-52; U.S. Forest Service, Santa Barbara, Calif., FM communication engineer, 1952-55; United World Federalists, Los Angeles, Calif., California field representative, 1955-56; Lucis Trust-World Goodwill, New York City, member of staff, 1956-58; National Committee for a Sane Nuclear Policy (SANE), New York City, executive secretary, program director, and executive director, 1958-67; International League for Human Rights, New York City, director, 1968-69; World Association of World Federalists, New York City, United Nations representative, 1969-82; Planetary Citizens, Menlo Park, Calif., president, 1974—. President of International Center for Integrative Studies, New York, N.Y., 1969-72. Consultant to the chairman of United Nations Experts Group on the Interrelationship Between Disarmament and Security; member of board of directors of World Federalist Association and Lamaist Buddhist Monastery of America; member of advisory council of Kentucky Institute of Psychosynthesis, London Institute of Psychosynthesis, and Interface, Boston, Mass.; speechwriter for United Nations Secretary General U Thant; annual lecturer at Findhorn Foundation. *Military service:* U.S. Army Air Force, member of bomber crew, 1943-45; served in Italy; became technical sergeant; received Air Medal with three oak leaf clusters.

AWARDS, HONORS: Ira D. and Miriam G. Wallach Award from Institute for World Order, 1982, for monograph "Abolition of War: Neglected Aspects."

WRITINGS:

(Editor with Steve Allen) *God and the H-Bomb,* Random House, 1961.
(Contributor) Elton B. McNeil, editor, *The Nature of Human Conflict,* Prentice-Hall, 1965.
(Contributor) Ervin Laszlo, editor, *Goals for Mankind,* Dutton, 1977.
The United Nations and Planetary Consciousness, Agni Press, 1977.
(Editor with Laszlo) *Disarmament: The Human Factor,* Pergamon, 1981.
Earth at Omega: Passage to Planetization, Branden Press, 1983, second revised edition, 1985.

Author of "World Progress Report," a column in *Saturday Review,* 1973, and "Planetarium," a column in *Onearth,* 1981-82. Contributor to magazines, including *Fellowship, American Theosophist, Friends Journal, Journal of Humanistic Psychology, World Order,* and *Transnational Perspectives.*

WORK IN PROGRESS: Birth of a Sacred Planet (tentative title), on the prophecies, myths, and experiences of planetary change and transformation, including commentary on various alternative future scenarios, especially problems dealing with global security and peace.

SIDELIGHTS: Donald Keys told *CA:* "My life has been given to awakening humanity to its new estate: in charge of a planet, and too interdependent and powerful to have another major war. My effort proceeded on parallel tracks until recently, when they became publicly convergent: the campaign for a humane world order, the illumination of the individual search for meaning, and the effort to accelerate spiritual growth in a saving, 'critical mass' of humanity. My range of activity and writing has run from consulting and speech writing for United Nations ambassadors to presenting annual workshops at Findhorn Foundation on training world warriors for peace.

"Many young people have gone on a search for meaning and have found higher values in the intentional communities which now dot the entire Western world. Rather than taking refuge in monasteries or Himalayan caves, they want to apply their new values in social change and building a better world. This takes a particular kind of training and the inner discipline similar to the warriorhood of old. Agents of change are not usually welcomed.

"We can all play a part in the next goal for humanity—that of its becoming aware of itself as a single, global species in charge of a planet, with grown-up responsibilities for all inhabitants and for the planet itself. We can all acknowledge and act on behalf of the new, global community of which we are a part. There are no other, 'quick fix' solutions to humanity's problems."

* * *

KHODASEVICH, Vladislav (Felitsianovich) 1886-1939

BRIEF ENTRY: Born May 29, 1886, in Moscow, Russia (now U.S.S.R.); died June 14, 1939, in Paris, France. Russian critic, essayist, translator, and poet. Khodasevich, who was described by fellow ex-patriate Vladimir Nabokov as the "greatest Russian poet of our time," completed his first volume of poetry, *Molodost* (title means "Youth"), in 1908. This work reveals the considerable influence of Russian symbolists such as Andrei Bely and Valeri Bryusov. After the revolution of

1917, however, Khodasevich adapted a neo-classical style derived from the verse of Alexander Pushkin. *Putem zerna* (1920; title means "The Grain's Way") and *Tyazhelaya lira* (1922; title means "The Heavy Lyre"), Khodasevich's first works following the successful uprising, are considered the poet's finest accomplishments. In both volumes he presents the metaphysical world in a manner both ironic and tragic. Among his greatest poems from these works is "Ballada" (title means "Ballad"), in which the speaker ponders his bleak existence.

In 1922 Khodasevich left his homeland and immigrated to Europe. He settled in Paris, where he devoted most of his subsequent literary endeavors to criticism and to the study of Pushkin. Khodasevich completed only a few poems in these years, most of which appeared in the modest collection *Evropeyskaya noch* (1927; title means "European Night"). A frail man, he fell ill in Paris in 1939 and died after an operation—possibly to remove a malignant tumor—failed. His poems are included in several English-language anthologies, including *The Penguin Book of Russian Verse* (1962).

BIOGRAPHICAL/CRITICAL SOURCES:

BOOKS

Cassell's Encyclopaedia of World Literature, revised edition, Morrow, 1973.
Columbia Dictionary of Modern European Literature, Columbia University Press, 1947.
The Reader's Encyclopedia, 2nd edition, Crowell, 1965.
Twentieth-Century Literary Criticism, Volume 15, Gale, 1985.

* * *

KIEHLE, John Alva 1930-
(John A. Keel)

BRIEF ENTRY: Professionally known as John A. Keel; born March 25, 1930, in Hornell, N.Y. American magician and author. During the 1950's, while stationed in Germany with the Armed Forces Network, Kiehle produced a Halloween radio broadcast that created a furor similar to that which followed Orson Welles's famous program about Martian invaders. Two years later he presented a similar Halloween broadcast from the Great Pyramid at Giza in Egypt. After resigning from the Armed Forces Network, Kiehle traveled to India and Tibet, where he investigated such mysteries as the Indian rope trick, snake charming, and the legend of the Abominable Snowman. The book *Jadoo* (Gilbert Press, 1957) is based upon the author's experiences in the East.

Kiehle is particularly interested in the phenomenon of unidentified flying objects—often called UFOs—which he claims have appeared on earth for many centuries. These UFOs, according to Kiehle, are actually "ultraterrestrial" beings who interfere with human civilization. In earlier, less technologically advanced eras these creatures assumed such disguises as fairies and angels, depending on the culture or sophistication level of the societies with which they chose to interact. Kiehle's books include *Why UFOs?* (Manor Books, 1970), *UFOs: Operation Trojan Horse* (Putnam, 1970), *Strange Creatures From Time and Space* (Gold Medal, 1970), *The Eighth Tower* (Saturday Review Press, 1975), and *The Mothman Prophecies* (Saturday Review Press, 1975).

BIOGRAPHICAL/CRITICAL SOURCES:

BOOKS

Encyclopedia of Occultism and Parapsychology, Supplement, Gale, 1982.

PERIODICALS

Newsweek, March 24, 1975.
Washington Post Book World, July 6, 1975.

* * *

KIERNAN, Robert F(rancis) 1940-

PERSONAL: Born October 21, 1940, in Rahway, N.J.; son of Daniel F. (a lawyer) and Beatrice M. (an actuary; maiden name, Velten) Kiernan. *Education:* Catholic University of America, B.A. (cum laude), 1963; Manhattan College, M.A., 1968; New York University, Ph.D. (with distinction), 1971. *Politics:* Democrat. *Religion:* Roman Catholic.

ADDRESSES: Home—5050 Fieldston Rd., Bronx, N.Y. 10471. *Office*—Department of English, Manhattan College, Riverdale, N.Y. 10471.

CAREER: English teacher at private boys' high school in West New York, N.J., 1963-71; Manhattan College, Riverdale, N.Y., instructor, 1971-73, assistant professor, 1973-81, associate professor of English, 1981—.

MEMBER: Modern Language Association of America, College English Association, Phi Beta Kappa.

WRITINGS:

Katherine Anne Porter and Carson McCullers: A Reference Guide, G. K. Hall, 1976.
Gore Vidal, Ungar, 1982.
American Writing Since 1945: A Critical Survey, Ungar, 1983.
Noel Coward, Ungar, 1985.

Contributor to journals, including *Studies in Short Fiction* and *Journal of Modern Literature*. Associate editor of *Literary Research Newsletter*, 1976-84.

SIDELIGHTS: Robert F. Kiernan told *CA:* "As a professional reader, I find writing a vital experience. The struggle to organize words on paper sensitizes me to the small miracles of expression that are almost commonplace in great writing—the lively pacing of a sentence, for instance, or the inescapably right positioning of an adjective, or the delicate, difficult balance between density and clarity. I try in my teaching and critical writing to attune people to these grace notes of literature as well as to the major chords.

"As a consequence, I tend to be interested in writers like Porter, Coward, and Vidal, who are essentially stylists, and the whole range of 'camp' writers. The wit and taste of such writers are a constant education of my own sensibility. What I would give to turn a sentence as elegantly as Porter or Vidal, or to possess the adjectival insouciance of Coward!"

* * *

KILLY, Jean-Claude 1943-

BRIEF ENTRY: Born August 30, 1943, in St. Cloud, France. French skier and author. Killy, who became a member of the Special Brigade of Chamonix Skiers in 1965, was the French slalom, giant slalom, and downhill skiing champion during the middle 1960's. Known as one of the great ski racers of all time, the athlete went on to win three Olympic gold medals at Grenoble, France, in 1968. He subsequently gave up his amateur status and began skiing professionally, in addition to working as a consultant, model, and syndicated columnist. He also embarked on a career as an auto racer. His passport, according to some sources, lists Killy as a customs official. Killy wrote *One Hundred Thirty-three Skiing Lessons* (DBI Books, 1975) and *Jean-Claude Killy's Guide to Skiing* (Barron's, 1981). *Address:* 13 Chemin Bellefontaine, 1223 Cologny, Geneva, Switzerland.

BIOGRAPHICAL/CRITICAL SOURCES:

BOOKS

Celebrity Register, 3rd edition, Simon & Schuster, 1973.
Current Biography, Wilson, 1968.
1000 Makers of the Twentieth Century, David & Charles, 1971.

*   *   *

KILODNEY, Crad [a pseudonym]   1948-

PERSONAL: Born February 13, 1948, in Jamaica, N.Y. *Education:* University of Michigan, B.S., 1968.

ADDRESSES: Home—134 Haddington Ave., Toronto, Ontario, Canada M5M 2P6. *Office*—Charnel House, P.O. Box 281, Station S, Toronto, Ontario, Canada M5M 4L7.

CAREER: Burke Baker Planetarium, Houston, Tex., lecturer in astronomy, 1968; Exposition Press, Smithtown, N.Y., copywriter, 1970-73; employed as warehouse laborer, salesman, and office worker by Toronto area publishers, 1973-78; writer, 1978—. Creator and owner of publishing imprint, Charnel House, 1979—.

WRITINGS:

SATIRE

Mental Cases, privately printed, 1978.
World Anaesthesia, Charnel House, 1979.
Gainfully Employed in Limbo, Charnel House, 1980.
Lightning Struck My Dick, Virgo Press, 1980.
Human Secrets, Charnel House, Book I, 1981, Book II, 1982, Book III: *Terminal Ward*, 1983.
Sex Slaves of the Astro-Mutants, Charnel House, 1982.
Pork College, Coach House Press, 1984.
Bang Heads Here, Suffering Bastards, Charnel House, 1984.
The Orange Book, Charnel House, 1984.

Author of advice column in Canadian magazine *Rustler*, 1978-81. Contributor to magazines in the United States, Canada, and England.

WORK IN PROGRESS: Collections of stories, for Charnel House.

SIDELIGHTS: Crad Kilodney told *CA:* "To the best of my knowledge I am the only writer in the world who publishes his own books and sells them on the street as a full-time occupation. I began this practice in 1978 with my first collection of satirical fiction, *Mental Cases*, which was published as a special issue of the New Orleans literary magazine, *Lowlands Review*. The following year I established my own imprint, Charnel House, under which I have published eight short books of satirical fiction. All these books were produced with my own money, and all of them turned a profit.

"I have no formal training in literature and creative writing and consider myself self-taught. Almost all my writing is satirical, ranging from farce to black humor. Because I sell my books on the streets of Toronto, my readership is mostly local. I have lived well below the poverty line since 1978, the year that I became a full-time writer. I decided to publish my own books and sell them on the street because I had no confidence

in the publishing industry and because I wanted to restore some integrity to the book as an art form and a product of human endeavor. I write in a variety of styles, both conventional and experimental, and I'm also an ardent devotee of bad writing, ever since my job with a vanity press in the early seventies."

BIOGRAPHICAL/CRITICAL SOURCES:

PERIODICALS

Gargoyle, April, 1985.

*   *   *

KING, Martin Luther, Sr.   1899-1985

OBITUARY NOTICE: Born December 19, 1899, in Stockbridge, Ga.; died of heart disease, November 11, 1985, in Atlanta, Ga. Clergyman, civil rights activist, civic leader, and author of autobiography. King, who was the father of prominent civil rights leader Martin Luther King, Jr., worked for more than fifty years to eliminate racism in the United States. He began preaching in the early 1930's after graduating from Morehouse College. He assumed the pastorate of the Ebenezer Baptist Church in Atlanta and soon began campaigning for black rights. After joining the National Association for the Advancement of Colored People (NAACP), King worked to eliminate discrimination in teachers' salaries and protested racist voting practices in Georgia. He was also active in the Atlanta business community as a member of governing boards for institutions such as Atlanta University and the National Baptist Convention.

But King's struggle for equality and success was marred by personal tragedy. His son Martin Luther King, Jr., was assassinated in 1968; the next year another son drowned; and in 1974 King's wife, Alberta, was murdered in church by a gunman who later claimed that his real target had been King. Even after his wife's death the clergyman preached universal love and religious faith. "I do not hate the man who took the life of my dead son," he said. "I am not going to hate the young man who came and killed my wife. I am every man's brother. I'm going on with my job." With Clayton Riley, King wrote of his life in *Daddy King*.

OBITUARIES AND OTHER SOURCES:

BOOKS

Who's Who Among Black Americans, 3rd edition, Who's Who Among Black Americans, 1981.

PERIODICALS

Los Angeles Times Book Review, January 4, 1981.
Newsweek, November 26, 1984.
New York Times, November 12, 1984.
Time, November 26, 1984.

*   *   *

KINSEY, Alfred C(harles)   1894-1956

BRIEF ENTRY: Born June 23, 1894, in Hoboken, N.J:.; died of a heart ailment and pneumonia, August 25, 1956, in Bloomington, Ind. American zoologist, educator, sex researcher, and author. Kinsey is probably best known for his seminal studies *Sexual Behavior in the Human Male* (1948) and *Sexual Behavior in the Human Female* (1953), both written with Wardell B. Pomeroy and Clyde E. Martin. Kinsey became interested in sex research in the late 1930's while working as a professor of zoology at Indiana University. Prompted by earlier research in insect taxonomy, he began interviewing peers on their sexual behavior and established a statistical base for evaluating his findings.

With the aid of grants, Kinsey and colleagues Pomeroy and Martin interviewed thousands of men, representing all ages, racial, and social groups. When the results of the study were published as the eight hundred-page *Sexual Behavior in the Human Male,* the clinical volume became popular with the lay reader. Kinsey's findings—especially differences in sex habits according to social status—were contested by many but hailed as revolutionary by others. The subsequent work, *Sexual Behavior in the Human Female,* also proved controversial, especially in contending that female sexuality was less influenced by social groups than was that of males.

Prior to working in sex research Kinsey distinguished himself as a zoologist with special expertise on the gall wasp. Among his many scientific writings are *An Introduction to Biology* (1926), *The Origin of Higher Categories in Cynips* (1936), and *Methods in Biology* (1938). He spent most of his academic career at Indiana University, where he established the Institute for Sex Research in 1942.

BIOGRAPHICAL/CRITICAL SOURCES:

BOOKS

Christenson, Cornelia V., *Kinsey: A Biography,* Indiana University Press, 1971.
Pomeroy, Wardell Baxter, *Dr. Kinsey and the Institute for Sex Research,* Harper, 1972.
Robinson, Donald, *Miracle Finders,* McKay, 1976.

* * *

KISHTAINY, Khalid 1929-

PERSONAL: Born October 10, 1929, in Baghdad, Iraq; son of Shakir (a teacher) and Sabria (Mustafa) Kishtainy; married Margaret Hitchcock, September 20, 1972; children: Niall Alexander, Adam Charles. *Education:* Academy of Fine Arts, Baghdad, diploma, 1952; Baghdad University, license in law, 1953. *Politics:* Pacificist. *Religion:* Muslim.

ADDRESSES: Home—63 Compton Rd., London SW19 7QA, England.

CAREER: Academy of Fine Arts, Baghdad, Iraq, teacher of arts and theatre design, 1958-59; British Broadcasting Corporation, London, England, translator and program assistant, 1959-64; free-lance writer and translator, 1964-81; Iraqi Cultural Centre, London, adviser and editor, 1981-83; free-lance writer, 1983—.

WRITINGS:

Verdict in Absentia, Palestine Research Centre, 1965.
Palestine in Perspective, Palestine Research Centre, 1971.
The New Statesman and the Middle East, Palestine Research Centre, 1972.
The Barrel (plays), Iraqi Cultural Centre (London), 1979.
The Prostitute in Progressive Literature, Allison & Busby, 1982.
Arab Political Humour, Quartet, 1985.

Editor of *Iraq Monthly,* 1981-82.

WORK IN PROGRESS: A collection of short stories.

SIDELIGHTS: In *The Prostitute in Progressive Literature* Khalid Kishtainy examines the literary view of prostitution over the past century, analyzing such fictional characters as Zola's Nana, Tolstoy's Maslova, Brecht's Pirate Jenny, and Galsworthy's Chloe. According to *Times Literary Supplement* reviewer Fiona MacCarthy, the author maintains that literary attitudes towards the prostitute have changed markedly over the years—going from a perception of the whore as a tragic individual to one symbolizing capitalist evil and Marxist alienation. While James Kaufman, writing in the *Los Angeles Times Book Review,* found Kishtainy's "knee-jerk Marxist criticism . . . unceasing although not particularly penetrating," MacCarthy judged "the point of this book . . . an arresting one, well-argued, with a sharp choice of quotation."

Kishtainy told *CA:* "My main interest is the relationship between art and politics and the use of art and literature in the service of political ideals. For me, these include the establishment of just democracy, human brotherhood and peace, and the replacement of violence by nonviolent means."

BIOGRAPHICAL/CRITICAL SOURCES:

PERIODICALS

Los Angeles Times Book Review, March 27, 1983.
Times Literary Supplement, December 9, 1982.

* * *

KLAASSEN, Walter 1926-

PERSONAL: Born May 27, 1926, in Laird, Saskatchewan, Canada; son of Henry T. (a farmer) and Judith (a housewife; maiden name, Epp) Klaassen; married Ruth Strange (a peace researcher), 1952; children: Frank, Michael, Philip. *Education:* McMaster University, B.A., 1954, B.D., 1957; Oxford University, D.Phil., 1960.

ADDRESSES: Home—Site 12A, C23, R.R. 7, Vernon, British Columbia, Canada V1T 7Z3. *Office*—Conrad Grebel College, University of Waterloo, Waterloo, Ontario, Canada N2L 3G6.

CAREER: Bethel College, North Newton, Kan., assistant professor, 1960-61, associate professor of Bible and chairman of department, 1962-64; University of Waterloo, Waterloo, Ontario, associate professor, 1964-73, professor of history, 1973—.

MEMBER: North American Committee for Documenting Free Church Origins, Canadian Society of Church History, Canadian Peace Research and Education Association, American Society of Church History, Mennonitischer Geschichtsverein, Commissie tot de Uitgave von Documenta Anabaptistica Neerlandica.

AWARDS, HONORS: Canada Council grants, 1970-74, 1978-79.

WRITINGS:

What Have You to Do With Peace?, Mennonite Central Committee, 1969.
Anabaptism: Neither Catholic Nor Protestant, Conrad, 1973.
Michael Gaismair: Revolutionary and Reformer, E. J. Brill, 1978.
(Editor with William Klassen) *The Writings of Pilgram Marpeck,* Herald Press, 1978.
Anabaptism in Outline: Selected Primary Documents, Herald Press, 1981.

CONTRIBUTOR

Hans-Juergen Goertz, editor, *Die Mennoniten,* Evangelisches Verlags-Werk, 1971.
Goertz, editor, *Umstrittenes Taeufertum* (title means "Controversial Anabaptism"), Vandenhoeck & Ruprecht, 1975.
I. B. Horst, A. F. de Jong, and D. Vissar, editors, *De Geest in Het Geding* (title means "The Spirit in the Form"), Tjeenk Willinck, 1978.
A. Raddatz and K. Luethi, editors, *Evangelischer Glaube und Geschichte* (title means "Evangelical Faith and History"), Vienna, 1984.

OTHER

Author of "Between World and Faith," a column in *Mennonite Reporter.* Contributor to magazines, including *Peace Research Reviews, Mennonite Quarterly Review,* and *Church History.* Editor of *Conrad Grebel Review.*

WORK IN PROGRESS: Research on apocalyptic views in the Radical Reformation.

SIDELIGHTS: Walter Klaassen told *CA:* "My languages include Low German, Dutch, Latin, and German. I have traveled and studied in England and Europe, including Switzerland, Austria, the Germanys, the Netherlands, and Italy.

"I write on history and contemporary subjects in the light of history because I believe that historical perspective is essential to our self-understanding. It helps us understand our religious and cultural and national traditions. It helps to overcome ethno- and aeto-centrism and makes us more charitable towards those who move in thoughtworlds other than our own, past and present. All of this is essential to the gradual establishment of world peace and the living together of the kaleidoscope of languages, peoples, and nations.

"I write also because I enjoy the creative process, for writing history is very close to writing novels. The role of the imagination is very high in writing history, always constrained, of course, by historical evidence. But even evidence, as it is presented, is sifted through the creative imagination. I am a necromancer; I have received and developed some skills by which I am able to call up, coax back into our field of vision, persons long dead, but who still have something to say to us. I get them to say it and pass it along to my contemporaries. I enjoy the writings of historians who are not afraid to make moral judgments about the events which they describe, for the person most intimately acquainted with an event is in the best position to make judgments about it.

"With my wife and sons I recently built a home on a hill overlooking a lake where I now spend most of my time studying and writing. The absence of the sounds of 'getting and spending,' the immediacy of natural sounds and smells, and the unhurried pace make for a perpetual holiday."

BIOGRAPHICAL/CRITICAL SOURCES:

PERIODICALS

American Historical Review, June, 1979.

*   *   *

KLARSFELD, Serge   1935-

PERSONAL: Born September 17, 1935, in Bucharest, Hungary; son of Arno and Raissa (a pharmacist; maiden name, Strimban) Klarsfeld; married Beate Kuenzel (an anti-Nazi activist), November 7, 1963; children: Arno David, Lida Myriam. *Education:* Sorbonne, University of Paris, Maitrise, 1959, Diploma; Institute of Political Science (Paris), Diploma, 1960; attended Paris University law school, 1974.

ADDRESSES: Home—8 Place de la Porte de St. Cloud, 75016 Paris, France. *Agent*—Raines Theron, 475 Fifth Ave., New York, N.Y. 10012.

CAREER: Lawyer, anti-Nazi activist, and writer. *Military service:* French Army, 1960-62; named Chevalier de l'Ordre du Merite.

MEMBER: Sons and Daughters of the Jewish Deportees From France (president).

AWARDS, HONORS: Named Chevalier of the French Legion of Honor, 1984; received Le Prix des arts des lettres et des sciences, 1984, from Foundation of French Judaism; received HAIS Liberty Award for "outstanding contributions to the furtherance of peace and freedom," 1984.

WRITINGS:

IN ENGLISH

(Editor) *The Holocaust and the Neo-Nazi Mythomania,* translated by Barbara Rucci, Beate Klarsfeld Foundation, 1978.
Les Enfants d'Iziev, [Paris], 1984, translation published as *The Children of Iziev: A Jewish Tragedy,* Abrams, 1985.

OTHER

(Editor) *Die Endloesung der Judenfrage in Frankreich: Deutsche Dokumente, 1941-1944* (title means "The Final Solution in France: German Document, 1941-1944"), Beate Klarsfeld Foundation, 1977.
Le Memorial de la deportation des juifs de France (title means "The Memorial of the Deportation of French Jews"), Beate Klarsfeld Foundation, 1978.
Le Livre des otages: La Politique des otages menee par les autorites allemandes d'occupation en France de 1941-1943 (title means "The Book of Hostages: Hostage Policy of the German Authorities Occupying France, 1941-1943"), Editeurs Francais Reunis, 1979.
L'Album d'Auschwitz (title means "The Album of Auschwitz"), Beate Klarsfeld Foundation, 1981.
Vichy-Auschwitz: Le Role de Vichy dans la solution finale de la question juifs de France (title means "Vichy-Auschwitz: The Role of Vichy in the Final Solution to the Question of French Jews"), Fayard, Volume 1: *1942,* 1983, Volume 2: *1943-1944,* 1985.
Le Memorial de la deportation de 25124 juifs de Belgique: (title means "The Memorial of the Deportation of 25,124 Belgian Jews"), Beate Klarsfeld Foundation, 1981.

WORK IN PROGRESS: The Memorial for the Jews Deported From the Protectorate of Bohemia and Moravia, for the Beate Klarsfeld Foundation.

SIDELIGHTS: Serge Klarsfeld and his wife, Beate, are known for their relentless pursuit of former Nazis. The Klarsfelds met in 1960 while Serge was studying political science in Paris; three years later they married. For Beate, who confessed to relative ignorance regarding Germany's Nazi years, marriage to the Jewish Serge proved enlightening and disturbing; for Serge, whose own family had suffered from Nazi persecution, marriage to the inquisitive Beate prompted him to delve deeper into his own background.

The Klarsfelds began their political activity in 1967 after former Nazi Kurt Georg Kiesinger was elected chancellor of West Germany. They were outraged that someone like Kiesinger—who had served in the Nazi party and dispensed anti-Jew propaganda during World War II—had been chosen to fill such an important position. Working to thwart Kiesinger's chancellorship, Beate began publishing articles in Paris about Kiesinger's Nazi past and his questionable exoneration—he was declared "denazified"—after the war by a dubious review board whose members included his own father-in-law; Serge, meanwhile, researched Jewish archives for documentation of Kiesinger's Nazi activities.

After Beate was fired from her French foreign relations position because of her inflammatory articles, the Klarsfelds decided to dedicate themselves to opposing former Nazis. "We made up our minds then and there to fight," Beate later told the *New York Times Magazine*. "It was a decision reached in a moment with scarcely a word spoken. But it was a total commitment."

While Serge continued his work in the archives, Beate began traveling into West Germany to oppose Kiesinger. She spoke at rallies and presented extensive documentation, compiled by Serge, of Kiesinger's Nazi background. The campaign reached its most dramatic moment in November, 1968, when Beate actually slapped Kiesinger in public. The incident was greatly publicized and thus provided the Klarsfelds with additional opportunities to denounce Kiesinger. And when Beate was taken to court for slapping the chancellor, she continually referred to his past activities. The case was finally dismissed when Kiesinger failed to appear on his own behalf.

Within months of the court case West Germany held another election, and Kiesinger lost the chancellorship to anti-Nazi candidate Willy Brandt. The Klarsfelds counted Kiesinger's defeat as a personal triumph and saw in it proof that people and events could be influenced by the truth. "Now we had shown ourselves . . . that truth is stronger," Serge told the *New York Times Magazine*.

In 1971 Chancellor Brandt signed a pact with France allowing West Germany to try former Nazis already convicted of war crimes in France. Prior to this time, both East and West Germany were forbidden to prosecute their own war criminals, and France had shown little interest in punishing Nazis who had been prosecuted *in absentia* by French tribunals. Consequently, hundreds of convicted Nazis enjoyed complete freedom in their German lands.

Encouraged by West Germany's apparent willingness to prosecute its war criminals, the Klarsfelds selected several former Nazis for indictment. Among their most notorious targets were Herbert Hagen, a former S.S. official who supervised the capture of all Jews in the Bordeaux region of France, and Ernest Heinrichsohn, a member of the Gestapo's anti-Jew unit who had shown special delight in designating Jews for deportation to the concentration camps.

The Klarsfelds' most notorious case, however, has probably been Klaus Barbie, the infamous "Butcher of Lyons" who reportedly participated in countless tortures and authorized thousands of murders and deportations. Barbie escaped capture after the war by bargaining with American intelligence, and though he disclosed mostly meaningless information, he remained under American protection. "There were 20 [French requests] urging the U.S. authorities in Munich to surrender him to the French authorities," Serge told *Newsweek* in 1983. "They remained unanswered."

Barbie supposedly escaped American custody in 1951 and fled to South America. He settled in Bolivia, where he lived under the name Klaus Altmann. He was discovered in 1971 after the Klarsfelds began sending his photograph to newspapers everywhere. After a reformist government arrested Barbie in 1983, he was returned to France to await trial. The case against Barbie will reportedly center on his alleged deportation of Jews from a children's home. Among the evidence against him is a telegram—found by Serge in Jewish archives—ordering the deportation.

Other Nazis still hunted by the Klarsfelds include Walter Rauff, inventor of the mobile gas vans that experts believe claimed more than 250,000 lives. According to Beate, Rauff has lived in Chile for many years under government protection. She is pessimistic about Rauff's possible deportation during the rule of Chilean president Augusto Pinochet, but she expressed hope that the next government in Chile will be less tolerant of Rauff's Nazi past. "I met with [Pinochet's] opposition," she told the *Detroit Free Press* in 1984. "They said that should they come to power, they immediately would expel Rauff."

While Beate, with her numerous media appearances and controversial stunts, is the more publicized of the Klarsfelds, Serge is known as a meticulous researcher and a leading authority on the Holocaust. Among his most notable works is *Le Memorial de la deportation des juifs de France*, an extensive cataloging of Jews deported from France during the period from 1942 to 1944. Henry H. Weinberg, who reviewed the volume for the *Jerusalem Post Magazine*, wrote that "Klarsfeld provides an explanatory note for each list, as well as occasional eye-witness accounts and documents."

Weinberg was particularly moved by the testimony accompanying a list for the first transport comprised exclusively of children. He wrote: "The eye-witness account that accompanies the list describes the suffering of the children at Drancy, prior to the departure of the trains. Hungry, unwashed, and suffering from diarrhoea, they cried incessantly, calling for their parents."

Serge Klarsfeld's other literary works include *Le Memorial de la deportation de 25124 juifs de Belgique*, which documents the deportation of Belgian Jews, and *The Holocaust and Neo-Nazi Mythomania*—edited by Serge—which contains two essays responding to propaganda that rejects evidence of the Holocaust.

BIOGRAPHICAL/CRITICAL SOURCES:

PERIODICALS

Jerusalem Post, June 24, 1982, January 19, 1985.
Jerusalem Post Magazine, June 8, 1979, March 18, 1983.
Newsweek, July 22, 1974, February 21, 1983.
New York Times, December 18, 1984.
New York Times Magazine, November 4, 1979.
Philadelphia Jewish Exponent, November 23, 1973, February 28, 1975, November 24, 1975, November 22, 1979.

—*Sketch by Les Stone*

*   *   *

KLASSEN, Walter
See KLAASSEN, Walter

KLEIN, Fred 1932-

BRIEF ENTRY: Born December 27, 1932, in Vienna, Austria. Psychiatrist and author. Klein has worked as a staff psychiatrist at a New York prison and as a clinician at Long Island Community Mental Center. He began a private practice of psychiatry in 1974 and one year later became director of the Institute of Sexual Behavior. Klein wrote *The Bisexual Option: A Concept of One Hundred Percent Intimacy* (Arbor House, 1978). He is a co-author of *The Male: His Body, His Sex* (Anchor Press, 1978).

*   *   *

KNIGHT, G(eorge) Wilson 1897-1985

OBITUARY NOTICE—See index for *CA* sketch: Born September 18, 1897, in Sutton, Surrey, England; died March 20, 1985. Literary critic, educator, actor, author. Knight, who taught English for more than forty years, became known both as a Shakespearean scholar and actor. At the University of Toronto prior to World War II and at the University of Leeds after the war, the educator produced Shakespearen plays memorable for their color and symbolism. Knight also acted in the productions and subsequently developed a one-man show, "Shakespeare's Dramatic Challenge," which he performed in England and the United States. His writings include works for the British stage and television, but Knight's books of literary criticism constitute the bulk of his publications. Among the latter are *Myth and Miracle: An Essay on the Mystic Symbolism of Shakespeare, The Burning Oracle: Studies in the Poetry of Action, The Crown of Life: Essays in Interpretation of Shakespeare's Final Plays, The Golden Labyrinth: A Study of British Drama,* and *Neglected Powers: Essays on Nineteenth-and Twentieth-Century Literature.* Knight was also the author of *Principles of Shakespearian Production, With Special Reference to the Tragedies.*

OBITUARIES AND OTHER SOURCES:

PERIODICALS

New York Times, March 27, 1985.
Times (London), March 23, 1985.

*   *   *

KNIGHT, Richard S. 1936-

PERSONAL: Born June 19, 1936, in Salt Lake City, Utah; son of Richard (in business) and Gale (a teacher; maiden name, Stewart) Knight; married Ruth Hughes (a homemaker); children: Jane, Jeffrey, Thomas. *Education:* University of Utah, B.S., 1961; University of Michigan, M.A., 1968, Ph.D., 1971.

ADDRESSES: *Home*—4283 South Hollow Rd., Logan, Utah 84321. *Office*—Department of Secondary Education, Utah State University, Logan, Utah 84322.

CAREER: High school teacher and department head in Salt Lake City, Utah, 1962-65; social worker for the Bureau of Public Assistance, 1965-66; Utah State University, Logan, 1968—, began as assistant professor, became associate professor of education. Member of Nibley Planning and Zoning Commission; consultant to U.S. Air Force Reserve. *Military service:* Army National Guard, 1954-61. U.S. Army, 1961-62; became sergeant.

MEMBER: National Council of Social Studies, Association for Supervision and Curriculum Development, National Institute for the Study of Education, World Future Society.

WRITINGS:

Students' Rights: Issues in Constitutional Freedoms, Houghton, 1974.
(With Larry Cyril Jensen) *Moral Education: Historical Perspectives,* University Press of America, 1981.

Contributor to *Social Education.*

WORK IN PROGRESS: *Active Teaching in the Social Studies; Advanced Teaching Methods,* with James Cangelosi; *Traditional Values Education: Rediscovering the American Heritage.*

*   *   *

KOHN, Richard H(enry) 1940-

PERSONAL: Born December 29, 1940, in Chicago, Ill.; son of Henry L. (an attorney) and Kate H. (a physician; maiden name, Hirschberg) Kohn; married Lynne Holtan (a teacher and registered nurse), August 15, 1964; children: Abigail, Samuel. *Education:* Harvard University, A.B., 1962; University of Wisconsin—Madison, M.S., 1964, Ph.D., 1968.

ADDRESSES: *Office*—Building 5681, Hg U.S. Air Force/CHO Bolling Air Force Base, Washington, D.C. 20332.

CAREER: City College of the City University of New York, New York, N.Y., assistant professor of history, 1968-71; Rutgers University, New Brunswick, N.J., assistant professor, 1971-75, associate professor, 1975-83, professor of history, 1983-84. Harold Keith Johnson Visiting Professor of Military History at U.S. Army Military History Institute, U.S. Army War College, 1980-81; Department of the Air Force, Washington, D.C., chief of Office of Air Force History, 1981—. Member of Inter-University Seminar on Armed Forces and Society.

MEMBER: Organization of American Historians, American Historical Association, American Military Institute, Air Force Historical Foundation.

AWARDS, HONORS: National Endowment for the Humanities bicentennial grant, 1970-71; American Philosophical Society research grant, 1970-71; Binkley-Stephenson Prize for best article from Organization of American Historians, 1973, for an article in the *Journal of American History;* American Council of Learned Societies fellow, 1977-78; Department of the Army certificate of appreciation for patriotic civilian service, 1982.

WRITINGS:

Eagle and Sword: The Federalists and the Creation of the Military Establishment in America, 1783-1802, Free Press, 1975.
(Contributor) Don Higginbotham, editor, *Reconsiderations on the Revolutionary War,* Greenwood Press, 1978.
(Co-editor) *Air Superiority in World War II,* Office of Air Force History, 1983.

"THE AMERICAN MILITARY EXPERIENCE" SERIES

Military Laws of the United States From the Civil War Through the War Powers Act of 1973: An Original Anthology, Arno, 1979.
Anglo-American Anti-Military Tracts, 1697-1830: An Original Anthology, Arno, 1979.

Also editor of series volumes 1-32, Arno, 1979.

Contributor to periodicals, including *William and Mary Quarterly, Journal of American History,* and *American Historical Review.*

WORK IN PROGRESS: Conducting and editing oral history interviews with senior retired U.S. Air Force officers to be published by the Office of Air Force History.

SIDELIGHTS: In *Eagle and Sword* Richard H. Kohn examines the development of the U.S. national army during the last two decades of the eighteenth century. The author discusses the standing army's most active advocates—particularly Alexander Hamilton—and explores the existing domestic conditions that, in many ways, justified the establishment of a national army at that time. One critic, writing in the *New York Review of Books,* commended Kohn's comprehensive scholarship and the "valuable information" he presents on the period. "Kohn's thesis will provoke controversy," the reviewer added; "his research commands attention."

Kohn told *CA:* "In the years since *Eagle and Sword* was finished, my interests have broadened to include virtually all of American military history. I continue to be fascinated and puzzled by the contradictions in our military past. Our security absorbs an immense amount of our wealth and energy; keys to understanding our predicament, I continue to believe, lie in unraveling our past. We neglect it at our peril. Historical understanding can, indeed, help us to live with the present and meet the future.

"My long-term projects include studies on how the United States makes and experiences war, and how the nation came to possess a large military establishment after World War II."

BIOGRAPHICAL/CRITICAL SOURCES:

PERIODICALS

New York Review of Books, October 16, 1975.
New York Times Book Review, November 30, 1975.
Times Literary Supplement, November 26, 1976.

*   *   *

KOLBENSCHLAG, Madonna (Claire)   1935-

BRIEF ENTRY: Born November 2, 1935, in Cleveland, Ohio. American educator and author. Kolbenschlag was appointed assistant professor of American studies at the University of Notre Dame in 1973. Her book, *Kiss Sleeping Beauty Goodbye: Breaking the Spell of Feminine Myths and Models* (Doubleday), was published in 1979.

BIOGRAPHICAL/CRITICAL SOURCES:

PERIODICALS

America, August 23, 1980.

*   *   *

KONTOS, Peter G(eorge)   1935-1977

OBITUARY NOTICE—See index for CA sketch: Born April 21, 1935, in Cleveland, Ohio; died after a long illness, April 3, 1977, in Atlanta, Ga. Educator, business executive, editor, and author. Kontos began his career teaching in the Cleveland, Ohio, public schools and then went on to become president and chairman of the board of EDR, a corporation involved in designing textbook programs, adult education tapes, and consulting services for both public and private educational institutions. He was also president of the Protestant Radio and

Television Center in Atlanta from 1974 to 1976 and was serving as executive director of the Institute for Contemporary Curriculum Development at the time of his death. Kontos wrote a number of books, including *The United States: Past and Present* and *The City: Promise and Problem,* and he collaborated with his wife, Cecille P. Kontos, on the six-volume "Readings in the Humanities" series. In addition, he was a co-author of *Patterns of Civilization: Europe* and *Patterns of Civilization: Africa* as well as a co-editor of *Teaching Urban Youth: A Source Book for Urban Education.*

OBITUARIES AND OTHER SOURCES:

PERIODICALS

New York Times, April 7, 1977.

*   *   *

KOOPMANS, Tjalling (Charles)   1910-1985

OBITUARY NOTICE: Born August 28, 1910, in 's Graveland, Netherlands; died after a short illness, February 26, 1985, in New Haven, Conn. Educator, economist, editor, and author. Koopmans was co-winner of the 1975 Nobel Prize in economics. He began his career as a lecturer at the University of Rotterdam in the mid-1930's. After coming to the United States in 1940 Koopmans worked as a research associate at Princeton University. He held subsequent posts as a researcher and statistician before joining the University of Chicago's faculty in 1944 as a research associate of the Cowles Commission for Research in Economics. In 1946 he became associate professor at the university and two years later he was named professor of economics. When the Cowles Commission moved to Yale University—and became the Cowles Foundation—in 1955, Koopmans moved too, retaining the rank of professor of economics. At Yale he worked at developing econometrics, a branch of economics devised to mathematically analyze problems involving productivity and efficiency. For his work Koopmans received the Nobel Prize with Leonid Kantorovich, an economist conducting similar research in the Soviet Union. He wrote *Three Essays on the State of Economic Science* and edited works such as *Statistical Inference in Dynamic Economic Models, Activity Analysis of Production and Allocation.* Koopmans collaborated with William C. Hood on editing *Studies in Econometric Method.* He also contributed to other volumes and journals.

OBITUARIES AND OTHER SOURCES:

BOOKS

The International Who's Who, 48th edition, Europa, 1984.
Who's Who in America, 43rd edition, Marquis, 1984.

PERIODICALS

New Haven Journal-Courier, March 1, 1985.
New York Times, March 2, 1985.
Washington Post, March 2, 1985.

*   *   *

KORN, Frank J(ames)   1935-

PERSONAL: Born February 20, 1935, in Elizabeth, N.J.; son of George F. and Ann Korn; married Camille Gatto (a secretary), December 27, 1958; children: Frank J., Jr., Ronald, John. *Education:* Seton Hall University, B.A., 1958; attended American Academy in Rome, 1970; Montclair State College,

M.A., 1972; also attended Institute of Dante, Rome, Italy. *Politics:* "Extreme moderate." *Religion:* Roman Catholic.

ADDRESSES: Home—620 Clinton Ave., Kenilworth, N.J. 07033. *Office*—Department of English, County College of Morris, Randolph, N.J. 07869.

CAREER: County College of Morris, Randolph, N.J., associate professor of English, 1974—. Caldwell College, Caldwell, N.J., associate professor of Italian, 1979—. Chairman of foreign language studies at public schools in Irvington, N.J., 1982—. Has taught on-site courses in Roman civilization and early Christianity at the Instituto Romano in Rome, Italy.

AWARDS, HONORS: Fulbright scholar in Rome, Italy, 1969; Princeton Prize for Distinguished Teaching from Princeton University, 1982.

WRITINGS:

Rome: The Enchanted City, Our Sunday Visitor, 1976.
From Peter to John Paul II, Alba House, 1980.
Vatican City: Country of the Spirit, St. Paul Editions, 1982.
The Story of St. Patrick's, Celtis Press, 1983.

Contributor to magazines, including *Visitor* and *Catholic Digest*, newspapers and professional journals.

WORK IN PROGRESS: Rome . . . A Poem in a Word, poems about Italy, publication expected in 1985; *Clouds Over the White House*, on the U.S. presidency, publication expected in 1986.

SIDELIGHTS: Frank J. Korn told *CA:* "I have taught, and studied intimately, the life and times and works of Marcus Tullius Cicero. The first-century Roman statesman sparked and fueled my love for the beauty of the spoken and written word. He has influenced my style enormously. I consider 'Tully' my mentor.

"I have lectured on Rome at such places as Yale University and the Instituto Romano. I have been a tour guide to Rome and central Italy.

"My first impression of Rome was that the novelist Thomas Wolfe was dead wrong, that you *can* go home again! For in Rome I found that in some respects time had charmingly stood still. Many of the simple joys and values I knew as a boy growing up in the predominantly Catholic Port section of Elizabeth, New Jersey, I rediscovered along the banks of the venerable Tiber.

"In Rome, I noticed, church bells still ring, priests still walk the streets in long black cassocks, nuns in full length habits. On balmy summer nights neighbors still sit in clusters on the front steps and gab the hours away. Neighbors there still actually know one another, help one another, prefer one another's company to the telly. My first few days in Rome I learned that one can still get an ice-cream cone, ride a bus, have dinner at a sidewalk table, take in a new film, go to the opera or to the beach without taking out a second mortgage; that one can still go off to the neighborhood outdoor market each day for fresh fruit, fresh vegetables, fresh eggs, fresh meat; that a stroll in the evening and on Sunday afternoon is still a popular institution; that one's worth is measured not by wealth, not by position, not by the size of one's home or car, but by one's love for life. Early on, I learned that everything the Roman does, he or she does with a concentrated passion—this includes conversation, perhaps the real national pastime there. The Roman people taught me and my family—by word and

by example—that life is indeed meant to be lived. If I could use one word to describe Rome and the Romans I would say: *'Vivace!* Alive!'

"My bride and my brood and I soon realized too that the advice of Ambrose to Augustine is still valid sixteen centuries later, i.e.: *'Quum Romae, Romano vivite more.'* So when in Rome we do as the Romans do and get along just fine. We have observed some Americans ignoring Ambrose's wisdom and then being frustrated, irritated, maddened by some of the idiosyncrasies of the Roman life style.

"I love Rome—her warm people, her magnificent art, her lyrical language. Her fountains, her piazzas, her churches, her cafes are all in my blood. Never blasé about the city's wonders, I love to go back again and again to the splendor of St. Peter's, to the glory of the Sistine Chapel, to the brooding ruins of the Colosseum, to the majestic rubble of the Forum. I love Rome unabashedly and it is precisely this love that I seek to impart and to propagate through my writings on the city. The two decades that have passed since my first visit to *Urbs Aeterna* have not dimmed in the least but rather have intensified my feelings for the place. On a recent trip to the Italian capital, my thirty-seventh, I tried to while away the final hour of the long flight by trying my hand at some verse. Just after breakfast over the Alps, and with the plane already in its descent toward Leonardo da Vinci Airport, I managed these few lines:

I am always at home in enchanting old Rome,
The city that Romulus founded;
Where the green Tiber flows and the tall cypress grows,
And history and art are unbounded.

How I long to be there in the soft summer air,
In the long golden days of late June;
Where the church bells still ring and the people still sing,
And the fountains all play a sweet tune.'

"Come to think of it, those two stanzas are a kind of summation of my attraction to Rome Eternal."

AVOCATIONAL INTERESTS: Collecting books and records (mostly opera and the great composers); running (thirty to forty miles per week); good food, good wine, and good company; his summer apartment in the Monteverde section of Rome; golf with sons Frank, Jr., and Ronald; tennis with wife Camille and son John.

*　　*　　*

KOTCHEFF, Ted
See KOTCHEFF, William Theodore

*　　*　　*

KOTCHEFF, William Theodore   1931-
(Ted Kotcheff)

PERSONAL: Professionally known as Ted Kotcheff; born April 7, 1931, in Toronto, Ontario, Canada.

ADDRESSES: Agent—Stan Kamen, William Morris Agency, 151 El Camino, Beverly Hills, Calif. 90212.

CAREER: Associated with Canadian Broadcasting Corp. (CBC), 1952-57, and with American Broadcasting Companies, Inc. (ABC-TV) in London, England, 1957; director, screenwriter, and producer of motion pictures, 1962—. Director of plays, including "Of Mice and Men," "Desperate Hours," "Prog-

ress to the Park,""Lub,""Maggie May,""The Au Pair Man."
Director of motion pictures, including "Tiara Tahita," 1962,
"Life at the Top," 1965, "Two Gentlemen Sharing," 1970,
"Wake in Fright," 1970, "Outback," 1971, "Billy Two Hats,"
1973, "The Apprenticeship of Duddy Kravitz," 1974, "Fun
With Dick and Jane," 1977, "Who Is Killing the Great Chefs
of Europe?," 1978, "North Dallas Forty," 1979, "Cap-
tured," 1981, "Split Image," 1982, "First Blood," 1982,
"Uncommon Valor," 1984. Producer of motion picture
"Captured," 1981.

WRITINGS:

SCREENPLAYS

(With Peter Gent and Frank Yablans; and director) "North
Dallas Forty" (based on the novel of the same title by
Gent), Paramount, 1979.

SIDELIGHTS: Ted Kotcheff returned to his native Canada to
direct "The Apprenticeship of Duddy Kravitz" after spending
over a decade directing motion pictures in Britain. In a review
of the 1974 film *Newsweek*'s Paul D. Zimmerman predicted,
"[It] threatens to become the first big movie hit to come out
of Canada in living memory." The film earned director Ted
Kotcheff greater recognition in Hollywood and won an Oscar
nomination from the Academy of Motion Picture Arts and
Sciences for Mordecai Richler's screenplay adaptation.

With antic and sometimes poignant humor, "Duddy Kravitz"
depicts a young Jewish man's schemes to hustle his way out
of Montreal's lower class in the late 1940's. Although the title
character, portrayed by Richard Dreyfuss, realizes his goal of
owning property, he does so at the cost of his family's respect
and his girlfriend's love. One of the other characters describes
Duddy as "a cretinous little money-grubber who causes anti-
Semitism," and this frank portrayal sparked some fears that
the film might perpetuate negative stereotypes. Jay Cocks of
Time, however, averred, *The Apprenticeship of Duddy Kravitz* is fierce and clear-eyed, and shows toward its hero much
the same attitude displayed by his grandfather—knowing but
still affectionate." According to *Newsweek*'s Zimmerman,
Kotcheff "describes Duddy's hyperthyroidal thrust toward the
top with affectionate amusement and a clear unpretentious
style." He concluded that "the film explains and embraces its
hustler hero—not merely as the charming victim of an immigrant subculture but as the flamboyant expression of everybody's dream to stake out his own acre."

Kotcheff explored material success from another perspective
in his next comedy, "Fun With Dick and Jane." The protagonists of this 1977 release, a contemporary California couple
played by George Segal and Jane Fonda, suffer downward
mobility when the husband loses his job. As their credit rating
collapses, even the lawn around their upper-middle-class dream
house is rolled up and trucked away. Dick and Jane eventually
turn to robbery, finding that it solves their economic problems
and revitalizes their marriage. A *Saturday Review* critic expressed appreciation for Kotcheff's "deft hand with a social
probe" but was disappointed with the movie's midway switch
from realistic social comedy to caper plotting.

Troubled by what she termed the film's "sour message," Pauline Kael of the *New Yorker* objected: "It starts by saying that
America makes everybody corrupt, and then, having ration-
alized crookedness, makes the biggest crooks the heroes."
Newsweek's Janet Maslin, however, felt that Kotcheff "clearly
intends this as a movie with a message," and she assessed,
"What emerges is a delightfully comic fusion of innocence

and intelligence, broad yet carefully detailed, without a hint
of condescension that might have soured the whole thing."

Kotcheff continued in the comic vein with the 1978 farce "Who
Is Killing the Great Chefs of Europe?" According to the *New
Yorker,* the screenplay offered "the kind of irresistable gim-
mick plot that several of the most memorable English comedies of the fifties had." An American fast-food king's romantic pursuit of his pastry-chef ex-wife is complicated by the
mysterious murders of several of her famous colleagues. The
killer polishes off his victims in the style of their masterpieces.
One chef, for example, is baked like a pigeon in pastry.

Saturday Review noted Kotcheff's "poetic eye for food," and
the *New Yorker*'s critic observed that the "airy pastel cine-
matography gives the images a soft, innocently decadent pastry-
shop sensuousness." Kotcheff's direction was deemed "a little too broad for so subtle a screenplay," by *Saturday Review.*
But David Ansen of *Newsweek* remarked that "when a film
supplies as much civilized laughter as this, one hates to complain." He found the film on the whole "a wonderfully frivolous concoction."

For his next motion picture, "North Dallas Forty," director
Kotcheff joined producer Frank Yablans and former Dallas
Cowboys football player Peter Gent in writing the screenplay
based on Gent's 1973 novel. Although handled with humor,
the film is serious in its depiction of professional football as
"big business with the cleats showing," David Ansen remarked. "North Dallas Forty" centers on Phil Elliott, a veteran pass catcher for the North Dallas Bulls. Elliot is provoked
to wisecracking rebellion by his growing awareness that the
Bulls' tycoon owner, their zealous manager, and their front-
office computer comprise the real team, while the players merely
serve as the equipment. Yet, despite his "bad attitude" and
constant physical pain from injuries suffered on the field, Elliott desperately wants to continue playing football.

Actor Nick Nolte explained his conception of the role to Geraldine Fabrikant of the *New York Times:* "Elliott is a man
caught in his bubble-gum card days. He operates from childhood desire. It's not the money and it's not the glory—he's
hooked on football because it's the only thing he knows how
to do and he does it well." Although critics applauded Nolte's
performance, Veronica Geng in the *New Yorker* contended that
the writers seem "to have counted on Nolte to fill in the character." David Ansen, on the other hand, praised the writers
of "North Dallas Forty" for allowing their story to live through
its characters.

The film's inside look at the world of professional football
prompted *Time*'s Richard Schickel to comment that it "retains
enough of the original novel's authenticity to deliver strong,
if brutish entertainment." Ansen praised Kotcheff because he
"captures the vulgar, born-again spirit of noveau riche Dallas
society, but he never condescends," and he concluded that
"'North Dallas Forty' isn't subtle or finely tuned, but like a
crunching downfield tackle, it leaves its mark."

Kotcheff's 1982 release "First Blood," like "North Dallas
Forty," is action-oriented. Actor Sylvester Stallone portrays
a Vietnam veteran driven to gory revenge by police harassment
in the rural Northwest. "'First Blood' may prove to be [Kot-
cheff's] most crowd-pleasing film, disturbingly so," said Ansen. But the critic questioned the film's attempt to "appeal to
all political stances by making the hero both a maligned patriotic warrior and a countercultural loner," and by intellectually condemning his reprisal while emotionally endorsing it.

The moderate conclusion of the story, according to Ansen, gave the audience "a right to feel powerfully misused." However, *Time*'s Richard Schickel saw the movie's real business as "the celebration of primitive masculine competence in a succession of well-made action sequences." He observed "a kind of purity in its pursuit of these primary movie colors." Ansen, too, allowed that "as a macho fantasy 'First Blood' is successful."

"Split Image," also released in 1982, depicted yet another kind of extreme action. In this film an upper-middle-class college student, with aspirations as an Olympic gymnast, rejects what he regards as his parents' materialistic values. He joins a religious cult, but the parents hire a "deprogrammer" to break him away from the group. "Kotcheff makes the deprogrammer a fascinatingly ambiguous figure" with ferocious methods and questionable motives, remarked Ansen. The critic analyzed the film as "part satire, part love story, and, in its lurid deprogramming scenes, pure horror story. Not everything jells." He found, however, that Kotcheff "has again delivered a compelling entertainment and one savvy enough to raise more questions than it answers."

Kotcheff's 1984 film, "Uncommon Valor," again involved Vietnam-era soldiers. A military officer leads five young veterans on a mission to search a Laotian labor camp for one of their comrades—his son—who was declared missing-in-action ten years earlier. Lawrence O'Toole of *Maclean's Magazine* commented that "the characters of 'Uncommon Valor' represent a cross-section of gung-ho virility: one is a model of quiet bravado while another is a noisy braggart." He faulted the script because "each member of the team is limited to a single character trait," but, judging it a "1950's style war movie," the critic remarked, "Director Ted Kotcheff . . . displays the action in the film with considerable skill."

Summarizing the director's career to date, Ansen observed: "Ted Kotcheff is not a director to whom academies give awards. Yet over the years he has consistently delivered the goods, providing rough-edged entertainments laced with social satire."

BIOGRAPHICAL/CRITICAL SOURCES:

PERIODICALS

Maclean's Magazine, January 2, 1984.
Newsweek, July 29, 1974, February 21, 1977, October 9, 1978, August 6, 1979, October 5, 1982.
New Yorker, February 28, 1977, November 13, 1978, August 13, 1979.
New York Times, July 29, 1979.
Saturday Review, February 19, 1977, November 25, 1978.
Time, September 2, 1974, September 3, 1979, November 8, 1982.*

—*Sketch by Linda S. Hubbard*

*   *   *

KOURDAKOV, Sergei   1951-1973

OBITUARY NOTICE: Born in 1951; died of gunshot wound to the head, January 1, 1973, in Running Springs, Calif. Evangelist and author. Kourdakov was a Soviet defector who jumped from a Russian trawler off the west coast of Canada and swam to freedom. Kourdakov eventually moved to the United States, where he gained notoriety for his work on behalf of the Underground Evangelism sect. His death by gunshot on New Year's Eve, 1972, prompted speculation of suicide and murder. Among his writings are *The Persecutor* and *Sergei.*

OBITUARIES AND OTHER SOURCES:

PERIODICALS

New Yorker, May 5, 1973.

*   *   *

KREISLER, Fritz   1875-1962

OBITUARY NOTICE: Born February 2, 1875, in Vienna, Austria-Hungary (now Austria); died of a heart condition, January 29, 1962, in New York, N.Y. Violinist, composer, and author. Considered one of this century's greatest violinists, Kreisler was a popular concert artist in Europe and America for almost five decades. A child prodigy, Kreisler was admitted to the Vienna Conservatory at the age of seven and won the gold medal for first prize in violin when he was ten. He then studied at the Paris Conservatory, graduating with a premier prix in 1887. Following a brief American tour Kreisler abandoned the violin after the 1890 concert season to study medicine and complete his military service.

In 1899 Kreisler returned to music and after only eight weeks of practice gave a recital with the Berlin Philharmonic. He was recalled to military service with the outbreak of World War I and was severely wounded. He managed to recover from his wounds and returned to the U.S. concert stage, where he received great critical acclaim until America entered the war. Then, in the wake of strong anti-German and anti-Austrian feelings in the United States, Kreisler was regarded as an undesirable alien. Following the First World War however, his popularity in the United States returned. In 1935 he surprised the music world with his admission that some of the pieces he performed in concert and that had been attributed to such old masters as Martini, Porpora, and Vivaldi were actually his own compositions.

In 1939 Kreisler returned to the United States permanently and continued his concert career with great success, remaining active until 1947, despite serious injury in a 1941 traffic accident. He continued performing on the radio until 1950. Among Kreisler's approximately two-hundred musical compositions are the operettas *Apple Blossoms* and *Sissy;* he also wrote two books, *Valuable and Important Incunabula and Other Rare Early Printed Books and Illustrated Manuscripts, Together With Notable Specimens of Later Periods,* a compilation, and *Four Weeks in the Trenches: The War Story of a Violinist.*

OBITUARIES AND OTHER SOURCES:

BOOKS

Current Biography, Wilson, 1944, March, 1962.
The New Grove Dictionary of Music and Musicians, Macmillan, 1980.
The Oxford Companion to Music, 10th edition, Oxford University Press, 1974.
Webster's American Biographies, Merriam, 1979.
Who Was Who in America, With World Notables, Volume IV: *1961-1968,* Marquis, 1968.

PERIODICALS

New York Times, January 30, 1962.

*   *   *

KROEBER, Donald W(alter)   1934-

PERSONAL: Born December 28, 1934, in Arlington Heights,

Ill.; son of Walter (an architect) and Adele (Taege) Kroeber; married Jamie S. White (a librarian), October 11, 1961; children: David A., Eric W. *Education:* Park College, B.A. (summa cum laude), 1968; Boston University, M.S.B.A. (with high honors), 1970; University of Georgia, Ph.D., 1976.

ADDRESSES: Home—463 Eagle Lane, Harrisonburg, Va. 22801. *Office*—Department of Information and Decision Sciences, James Madison University, Harrisonburg, Va. 22807.

CAREER: U.S. Army, career officer, 1956-76, officer's candidate and artillery battery commander, 1956-63, member of faculty at U.S. Army Artillery School, 1963-65, district adviser in Can Gio District, South Vietnam, 1965-66, member of faculty at U.S. Army Artillery School, 1966-67, student at U.S. Army Command and General Staff College, 1967-68, plans and operations officer at Management Information Systems Directorate for Europe, 1968-71, executive officer of missile command in South Korea, 1971-72, instructor in military science at University of Georgia, Athens, 1972-75, member of faculty at U.S. Army Command and General Staff College, 1975-76, retiring as lieutenant colonel; James Madison University, Harrisonburg, Va., assistant professor, 1976-80, associate professor of information and decision sciences and chairman of department, 1983—, assistant vice-president for academic affairs, 1978-80. Lecturer at University of Maryland, Far East Division, 1971-72; public speaker.

MEMBER: American Society for Quality Control, American Institute for Decision Sciences, Southern Management Association, Beta Gamma Sigma, Sigma Iota Epsilon.

AWARDS, HONORS—Military: Bronze Star; Purple Heart; two Meritorious Service Medals.

WRITINGS:

(With R. L. LaForge) *Study Guide for Business Statistics,* Macmillan, 1978.
Test Manual for Business Statistics, Macmillan, 1980.
(With LaForge) *The Manager's Guide to Statistics and Quantitative Methods,* McGraw, 1980.
(Contributor) M. J. Riley, editor, *Computers for Business: A Book of Readings,* BPI, 1980.
Management Information Systems, Free Press, 1982.
(Contributor) Jerry Banks, editor, *Tables, Graphs, and Nomographs for the Industrial Engineer and Manager,* Reston, 1983.
(With Hugh J. Watson) *Computer-Based Information Systems: A Management Approach,* Macmillan, 1984.

Contributor to *Encyclopedia of Professional Management, World Book Encyclopedia,* and *Handbook of Business Administration.* Contributor to computer and information science journals.

WORK IN PROGRESS: A second edition of *Computer-Based Information Systems: A Management Approach.*

AVOCATIONAL INTERESTS: Golf, tennis, sailing, camping.

*   *   *

KRONK, Gary (Wayne)   1956-

PERSONAL: Born March 23, 1956, in Granite City, Ill.; son of Richard, Jr., and Jacqueline Joy (a librarian; maiden name, Bobo) Kronk; married Karen Jo Longhi, August 21, 1981. *Education:* Southern Illinois University at Edwardsville, B.S., 1981.

ADDRESSES: R.R.1, Box 168 A, Collinsville, Ill. 62234.

CAREER: Edwardsville Journal, Edwardsville, Ill., reporter and photographer, 1978-80; Wal-Mart (discount store), Glen Carbon, Ill., department manager, 1981—.

MEMBER: Association of Lunar and Planetary Observers.

WRITINGS:

Comets: A Descriptive Catalog, Ridley Enslow, 1984.
Meteor Showers: A Descriptive Catalog, Ridley Enslow, 1985.

WORK IN PROGRESS: A companion to *Comets,* covering observations of about four hundred comets that were not observed accurately enough to determine their orbits, publication by Ridley Enslow expected in 1986.

SIDELIGHTS: Gary Kronk told *CA:* "My major hobby is astronomy. I enjoy research in areas where I can contribute my observations, especially of comets and meteor showers. It is from this research that I hope to produce three books before my thirtieth birthday. I am such a stickler for detail that I hope each of my books will be considered definitive works on their respective subjects. Thereafter, I want to return to newspaper or magazine writing.

"Although my books and articles have all been factual, I have several short stories and a partially written novel which I may try to publish someday.

"My other major hobby is photography. I use my camera for astronomy, when I travel (which I love), and I have photographed weddings and anniversary parties on a free-lance basis."

*   *   *

KUCZKIR, Mary   1933-
(Fern Michaels, a joint pseudonym)

PERSONAL: Born April 9, 1933, in Hastings, Pa.; daughter of Albert and Lucy Kovac; married Michael Kuczkir (an engineer), October 3, 1952; children: Cynthia, Susy, Patty, Mike, Dave.

ADDRESSES: Home—9 David Ct., Edison, N.J. 08820.

CAREER: Writer. Worked as market researcher.

WRITINGS:

My Dish Towel Flies at Half Mast (collected columns), Ballantine, 1979.

Also author of "Merry Mary," a column in *Barnesboro Star.*

WITH ROBERTA ANDERSON UNDER JOINT PSEUDONYM FERN MICHAELS

Vixen in Velvet (romance), Ballantine, 1976.
Captive Passions (romance), Ballantine, 1977.
Valentina (romance), Ballantine, 1978.
Captive Embraces (romance), Ballantine, 1979.
Captive Splendors (romance), Ballantine, 1980.
The Delta Ladies (romance), Pocket Books, 1980.
Captive Innocence (romance), Ballantine, 1981.
Without Warning (thriller), Pocket Books, 1981.
Sea Gypsy (romance), Silhouette, 1981.
Golden Lasso (romance), Silhouette, 1981.
Whisper My Name (romance), Silhouette, 1981.
Beyond Tomorrow (romance), Silhouette, 1981.
Wild Honey (romance), Pocket Books, 1982.

Night Star (romance), Silhouette, 1982.
Panda Bear Is Critical (thriller), Macmillan, 1982.
Paint Me Rainbows (romance), G. K. Hall, 1982.
All She Can Be (romance), Ballantine, 1983.
Free Spirit (romance), Ballantine, 1983.
Nightstar (romance), G. K. Hall, 1983.
Tender Warrior (romance), Ballantine, 1983.
Cinders to Satin (romance), Ballantine, 1984.
Texas Rich (romance), Ballantine, 1985.

WORK IN PROGRESS: With Anderson under pseudonym Fern Michaels, *Ever the Empire,* for Ballantine.

SIDELIGHTS: Under the joint pseudonym Fern Michaels, Mary Kuczkir and collaborator Roberta Anderson have written some of the romance genre's best-selling novels. Among their many popular works are *Captive Passions,* about a noblewoman who disguises herself as a pirate and plunders her husband's trading vessels, and *Valentina,* which concerns the experiences of a handmaiden in the court of Richard the Lionheart. *Valentina,* the handmaiden, is imprisoned, raped, and sold at auction to a wealthy Emir before coming to Richard's aid and sparking further violence.

CA INTERVIEW

CA interviewed Mary Kuczkir by telephone on July 5, 1984, at her home in Edison, New Jersey.

CA: By all accounts, you met your writing partner, Roberta Anderson, on your first job as a market researcher, during which the two of you tested a drain-unclogging device and blew up somebody's bathroom. Was it friendship at first sight?

KUCZKIR: Yes, it was. We got along very well. There was an instant camaraderie.

CA: Neither of you had ever thought about writing before you tried it together?

KUCZKIR: No, I don't think so—other than the way people always say they'd like to write a book.

CA: You must have had a feeling pretty quickly after meeting that you could work together.

KUCZKIR: Oh, yes, because we did so well on the market research!

CA: How did you celebrate the first book sale?

KUCZKIR: We didn't really. We were so shocked that we didn't quite know what to do. As far as the money went, Roberta bought powder blue carpeting—she calls it her "pride and passion carpeting." I have five children, and I blew all of mine on one tremendous, glorious grocery order.

CA: How did your families react initially?

KUCZKIR: They were not impressed, I can tell you that. They were definitely not impressed, neither my family nor Roberta's. They thought it was sort of a joke. I don't think they were impressed until *Captive Passions* made the best-seller list. Then it wasn't funny anymore, it wasn't a fluke. It was serious business, because the amount of money changed at that time too.

CA: William J. Slattery, who wrote an early article on your work for Writer's Digest *(December 1978), said the two of you had "the shakiest grasp of grammar, none of syntax, and not the veriest notion of what an English sentence is." Did that kind of criticism bother you?*

KUCZKIR: Bill Slattery is a friend of mine. Before he let that go to the magazine, he let me see it, and I said it was OK. That article didn't bother us at all. We had one bad review that bothered us, the one *Publishers Weekly* did on *Captive Passions.* They quoted us as saying that we read all the historical romances and we thought we could do better. They commented, "They were wrong." But we've never gotten a really bad one from them since. *Kirkus Review* gave us a bad review for *Panda Bear Is Critical.* But I think they give everybody a bad review, so that didn't bother me. After a while you have to develop a thick hide. It's the same as rejection; you can't let it bother you, because if you did, you'd never write another book. And it's only one person's opinion.

CA: Originally you and Roberta talked on the phone a lot to work out your plots, then each of you wrote the parts you wanted to write, leaving out the sex scenes, which you collaborated on when everything else was done. Has the process changed at all?

KUCZKIR: No. We stick to what works for us. Sometimes we write the end of the book and then start at the beginning. That can be much easier, because you know what the characters are doing; you can go back and flesh it all out. It depends on what book we're working on. We just did a contemporary saga that was a thousand pages long when we turned it in. Now that's one hell of a big book, and it took us a long time to write it. I think it's probably one of the best things we've done. I think the best thing we've done to date was *Cinders to Satin,* which came out in January 1984. The fan mail on that book was so fantastic I wanted to cry over some of the letters—they were that good.

CA: What kind of readers do you hear from mostly? Can you tell much about them?

KUCZKIR: The mail comes from all over, mostly from married women in, I would say, the thirty-to-fifty age group. Ballantine holds our mail until they get a whole batch, so we don't always answer everything right away, but we do answer it all. We take turns answering it. The heaviest mail we got was on the "Captive" series. That came by the bagful. And what happens is that a lot of these people become your pen pals. There's a little girl who lives in Detroit who has been writing to me for over a year.

CA: Doesn't it take a lot of time to keep up with the mail?

KUCZKIR: It takes a lot of time, but they're really nice people. If they're going to take the time to go out and buy the books and then sit down and write us a letter, we owe them something.

CA: How much help have you gotten from editors along the way? Have they been good?

KUCZKIR: Oh, sure. We've had good editors all the way down the line; no complaints. They pretty much let us do what we want to do. We don't get much back for rewrites; mostly they ask us to expand. Very rarely are we asked to take anything out because it doesn't fit. We do a pretty tight outline and write a pretty tight book. Usually they just want a little more on this or a little more on that, and whatever it is, we can do it in a week's time. We've never had a major rewrite.

CA: How much research do you do for the books with historical settings?

KUCZKIR: Tons!

CA: Do you enjoy that part of the work?

KUCZKIR: I hate it. We don't do it ourselves anymore. We pay a researcher. She comes up with tons of stuff, and out of it all, we use a very small amount. We always say we start out with twenty-five pounds and use two pounds. But you never know what you're going to need.

CA: Where do you get the wonderfully exotic names like Regan van der Rhys and Royall Banner?

KUCZKIR: We work very hard at that. It's not easy. We sometimes will spend more time picking just the right names than we do on the book outline itself. We've anguished over names that you wouldn't believe. I must have two dozen books of babies' names—the kind you get when you're going to have a new baby—in every language. That's what we go by. And we always watch the credits on television—who does the photography and everything. Once in a while an odd name will jump out at you. Like in *Wild Honey*, the name Sloane MacAlister struck me as absolutely perfect. That came from television credits. The book that we just turned in is set in Australia. It took us a long time to come up with the guy's name, and believe me, we were sorry we did, but it was just perfect. *Quaid.* You know, that's a bitch to type on the typewriter. Your little finger has to go to the shift key for the *Q*. Our typist was not amused.

CA: Do you go to the romance writers' conventions?

KUCZKIR: I went to the one in California this past February. We didn't go to the Romance Writers of America one in Detroit. The reason I went to the one in California was because my daughter lives in San Diego and the convention was in LA, so it was on the way. There's one in England next year that we're going to. The plan is to go over on the QE2, stay for the convention, then tour Europe and fly back on the Concorde. Roberta and I decided we'd go to that one. I'm going to take my two sisters and Roberta is going to take her sister. The five of us will tour Europe together.

CA: Do you ever compare your novels with those being done by other romance writers?

KUCZKIR: No. And for the most part, we really don't read them, because we don't want to get confused, you know? We skim over them to see their stories and plot lines to make sure we don't duplicate them, because everything has been done. There's been such a glut on the market. And now we don't have time to read like we used to. There was a time, right after the first couple of years we'd been writing, when Roberta would read half of a book and I'd read the other half. Then we'd talk about it. Just for the pure enjoyment of reading, I like the occult and mystery stories, or espionage, and Roberta likes pretty much the same things. You can shift into neutral and enjoy reading those just for the sake of reading, because

we don't write them. But to pick up a historical and read it—we would pick it apart, and there's no enjoyment in reading them.

CA: Do you think Fern Michaels is a better writer now than in the beginning?

KUCZKIR: Oh, yes! Sometimes we go back and read some of the things we did and say, "I don't believe we wrote that. I don't believe they *bought* that!" We've grown a lot. I think people who've kept up with our writing from the beginning can see that. *Cinders to Satin* really shows the growth in our writing. It shows even in *Panda Bear*. You know, they say you can't be a great chef unless you can cook everything, so how can you be a good writer if you limit yourself to, let's say, category romance? Don't you want to spread your wings, do something besides change the dates and characters' names in the same story? That's what they are, and I know, because we did six of them. They were the hardest things that we've ever written, because you have to write to a formula. We couldn't discipline ourselves to do that indefinitely. We have free license to write what we want in historical romance—within the boundaries of the time period, of course.

CA: Is it still as much fun as it was?

KUCZKIR: No. Well, yes, it's fun, but a different kind of fun. We take it very seriously now. It's a job. In the beginning it was a lark, in a way. We didn't need the money to survive, because we had husbands to support us. And we belong to a time period that says you have to have a man and he has to support you, and no matter how much money you make, he's still the breadwinner. Now we have a profession. Now if somebody says, "What do you do?" I don't slip up and say "Housewife" anymore. I say, "I'm a writer." I never did that in the beginning, and neither did Roberta. We were mothers and housewives. Now we're writers, mothers, and housewives!

CA: You ventured off on your own to do the newspaper humor column for a while, which resulted in the book My Dish Towel Flies at Half-Mast. *Would either of you like to do more writing separately?*

KUCZKIR: I suppose, if we had the time. I do write short stories for foreign markets and I'm doing a novel now for IPC in England. Not a lot; just when I have time. I like to write; I don't think I'm really happy unless I'm creating something.

CA: What's the nicest thing about the success?

KUCZKIR: Probably the respect I get from the children. And another nice thing is the feeling of independence that I have. I think it's the same for Roberta; we've discussed that. Although I'm still a housewife and mother, I'm my own person. My kids respect that in me now. Before, I guess they didn't—or if they did, I wasn't aware of it. But now I see it in everyday things. And I'm really pleased about that.

CA: Is there anything you'd like to change?

KUCZKIR: Well, there are times when I get very aggravated with the nonsense with those organizations pushing the category books that are all alike. They're all like Barbara Cartland's. I frown on that. I don't consider that kind of thing a real book. I can say that because we wrote them. If you're going to take the time to write, for God's sake write something worthwhile, something with some guts to it. Give the reader her money's worth. Formula writing drives me up the wall.

When I went to the convention in California, there were all these authors there, but very few who write the bigger books like we write. I sort of felt like an outsider, like I didn't really belong there, because I have nothing to contribute to what they do. Those books are hard as hell to write, and they pay so poorly that by the time you're through, I don't think you've made minimum wage. They've been done thirty-seven different ways, up one side and down the other and across the middle, and still those writers are pumping them out and the publishers are publishing them. Money is the name of the game. It's the authors who suffer in the end.

Everybody says, though, that the reader has become more selective, that she searches for books by the author's name. It must be true. A year and a half ago I'd go into the Dalton and Walden chains—they're the biggest bookstores around where I live—and I swear to you half the store was devoted to romances. Now that's gone. All those special displays are gone and the books are on the rack on the wall—and not much space is given to them, either. There are a lot of big authors out there, and the backlist isn't there for all of them. The stores just aren't carrying that much romance anymore.

We're pleased, though, that our books, like the Captive series, are in their twelfth, thirteenth, fourteenth printings. I think we've made inroads in a lot of different directions. We've come a long way, and I hope we're around for a long time to come and that we will be capable of writing whatever is in demand in the marketplace. I hope it lasts.

BIOGRAPHICAL/CRITICAL SOURCES:

BOOKS

Falk, Kathryn, *Love's Leading Ladies*, Pinnacle Books, 1982.

PERIODICALS

New York Times Book Review, July 8, 1979.
Us, June 27, 1978.
Writer's Digest, December, 1978.

—*Interview by Jean W. Ross*

*   *   *

KUH, Charlotte 1892(?)-1985

OBITUARY NOTICE: Born c. 1892; died March 4, 1985, in Cambridge, Mass. Educator and author. Kuh taught at Chicago's Francis Parker School from 1914 to 1919 and served as a trustee of the private school from 1945 to 1957. Her teaching experiences prompted a concern for the welfare of children and adolescents that led her eventually into the fields of social work and social reform. Kuh's early concerns were for the rights of small children who worked at menial jobs. She served as president of the Juvenile Protection Association in the early 1950's and campaigned in Illinois for laws to regulate safety, working conditions, and working hours for children.

Later the educator turned her attention to adolescents with social and behavioral problems and young people in trouble with the law. She reorganized the Juvenile Court Committe in her community and succeeded in her attempt to provide professional guidance for troubled youth. Kuh also found time to write children's books such as the preschool story *A School, a Train, and a Ship*.

OBITUARIES AND OTHER SOURCES:

PERIODICALS

Chicago Tribune, March 8, 1985.

*   *   *

KUO, Shirley W. Y. 1930-

PERSONAL: Born January 25, 1930, in Tainan, Taiwan. *Education:* National Taiwan University, B.A., 1952; Massachusetts Institute of Technology, M.S., 1972.

ADDRESSES: Home—539 11F-1 Tun-hwa South Rd., Taipei, Taiwan 106. *Office*—2 Roosevelt Rd., Section I, Taipei, Taiwan 107.

CAREER: Economic Planning Council, Executive Yuan, Taipei, Taiwan, vice-chairman, 1973-77; Council for Economic Planning and Development, Executive Yuan, Taipei, vice-chairman, 1977-79; National Taiwan University, Taipei, professor, 1966—. Fulbright professor at Massachusetts Institute of Technology, 1972. Deputy governor of Central Bank of China, 1979—.

MEMBER: Chinese Economic Association.

AWARDS, HONORS: Sun Yat-sen Academic Award, 1966; Sun Yat-sen Cultural Award, 1966; award from China Committee for Publication, 1967.

WRITINGS:

(With Gustav Ranis and John C.H. Fei) *Growth With Equity: The Taiwan Case*, Oxford University Press, 1979.
(With Ranis and Fei) *The Taiwan Success Story: Rapid Growth With Improved Distribution in the Republic of China, 1952-1979*, Westview, 1981.
The Taiwan Economy in Transition, Westview, 1983.

L

LAFFONT, Jean-Pierre 1935-

PERSONAL: Born January 29, 1935, in Alger, Algeria. *Education:* Attended photography school in Vevey, Switzerland.

ADDRESSES: Office—Sygma Photo News, 225 West 72nd St., New York, N.Y. 10023.

CAREER: U.S. correspondent for *Reporters Associes,* 1966-68; U.S. correspondent for *Gamma,* 1968-73; *Sygma Photo News,* New York, N.Y., permanent correspondent, 1973—.

WRITINGS:

C. B. Bible, Doubleday, 1976.
Women of Iron, Wideview, 1981.

BIOGRAPHICAL/CRITICAL SOURCES:

PERIODICALS

Photo, July, 1979, November, 1981.

*   *   *

LaFLEUR, William R. 1936-

PERSONAL: Born July 23, 1936, in Paterson, N.J.; married Mariko Nishi. *Education:* Calvin College, A.B., 1957; University of Michigan, M.A., 1963; University of Chicago, M.A., 1971, Ph.D. (with distinction), 1973.

*ADDRESSES: Home—*1748 Glendon Ave., Los Angeles, Calif. 90024. *Office—*Department of East Asian Languages and Cultures, University of California, Los Angeles, Calif. 90024.

CAREER: Princeton University, Princeton, N.J., assistant professor of Japanese, 1973-80; University of California, Los Angeles, associate professor of Japanese language, 1981—.

MEMBER: International Society for Asian and Comparative Philosophy, Association of Asian Studies, American Academy of Religion.

AWARDS, HONORS: Named distinguished lecturer by Northeast Asia Council, 1983.

WRITINGS:

(Translator) *Mirror for the Moon: A Selection of Poems by Saigyo, 1118-1190,* New Directions, 1978.

The Karma of Words: Buddhism and the Literary Arts in Medieval Japan, University of California Press, 1983.
(Editor) *Zen and Western Thought: The Essays of Masao Abe,* Macmillan, 1984.
(Editor) *Dogen Studies,* University Press of Hawaii, 1984.

Contributor to *Encyclopedia of Japan.*

WORK IN PROGRESS: An Intellectual Biography of Watsuji Tetsuro; editing *Buddhism in Japanese Literature and Arts,* with James Sanford; *Brushes With Sages,* poems;

SIDELIGHTS: William R. LaFleur told CA: "My focus is on understanding traditional patterns of Japanese thought and literary modes—as important tools for understanding contemporary Japanese society. I am concerned with the lives and values of the medieval Japanese and Japanese poetry, especially as it reflects thought patterns and cross-cultural comparisons. Why do the Japanese repeatedly surprise the West?"

*   *   *

LAFOURCADE, Bernard 1934-

PERSONAL: Born August 10, 1934, in Grenoble, France; son of Georges (a professor) and Madeleine (Charlet) Lafourcade; married Pierrette Seguy (a professor), July 27, 1961; children: Mathieu. *Education:* University of Grenoble, Licence es lettres, Diplome d'Etudes Superieures, 1955; attended Worcester College, Oxford, 1958; Sorbonne, University of Paris, Agregation, 1959.

*ADDRESSES: Home—*11 boulevard Marechal-Leclerc, 38000 Grenoble, France. *Office—*Department of English, Universite de Savoie (Chambery), Domaine Universitaire de Jacob-Bellecombette, B.P. 143, 73011 Chambery, France.

CAREER: University of St. Andrews, St. Andrews, Scotland, assistant in French, 1955-57; University of Tunis, Tunis, Tunisia, lecturer in French, 1962-77; Universite de Savoie (Chambery), Chambery, France, lecturer in English, 1977—. Associated with Centre National de la Recherche Scientifique, 1971-73. *Military service:* French Army, 1959-62.

MEMBER: Centre de Recherches Imagination et Creation (CRIC), Centre de Recherches sur les Pays de Langue Anglaise, Wyndham Lewis Society (England).

WRITINGS:

(With Bradford Morrow) *A Bibliography of the Writings of Wyndham Lewis,* Black Sparrow Press, 1978.
(Editor) Wyndham Lewis, *The Complete Wild Body,* Black Sparrow Press, 1982.
(Editor) Lewis, *Snooty Baronet,* Black Sparrow Press, 1984.
(Editor) Lewis, *Tarr,* Black Sparrow Press, 1984.

TRANSLATOR FROM THE ENGLISH

Wyndham Lewis, *Cantleman's Spring-Mate,* Minard, 1968.
Lewis, *Tarr,* Christian Bourgois, 1970.
Lewis, *La Rancon de L'amour,* L'Age d'homme, 1980.
Lewis, *Le Corps sauvage,* L'Age d'homme, 1983.

WORK IN PROGRESS: Translating Wyndham Lewis's *Maudite soit la France,* for publication by L'Age d'homme.

SIDELIGHTS: Bernard Lafourcade told *CA:* "My goal is to introduce Wyndham Lewis to France and to promote his works in Anglo-Saxon countries. My conviction is that Lewis, who is still generally underrated, is possibly the most comprehensive Anglo-Saxon creative artist and analyst of the first half of the century and a man for our times. His energy, idiosyncratic perception of ideology, and hard-edged perception of the human body suggest he might be a missing 'vortex' for our age."

BIOGRAPHICAL/CRITICAL SOURCES:

PERIODICALS

Times Literary Supplement, July 6, 1984.

*   *   *

LaGATTUTA, Margo   1942-

PERSONAL: Born September 18, 1942, in Detroit, Mich.; daughter of Edwin Olaf (a designer) and Elizabeth (a painter; maiden name, True) Grahn; married Steven LaGattuta (a creative director at an advertising agency), November 14, 1964; children: Mark, Erik, Adam. *Education:* Attended Western Michigan University, 1960-62, and Pratt Institute, 1962-64; Oakland University, B.A. (with honors), 1980; attended Warren Wilson College, 1981-82; Vermont College, M.F.A., 1984.

ADDRESSES: Home and office—2134 West Gunn Rd., Rochester, Mich. 48064.

CAREER: Paint Creek Center for the Arts, Rochester, Mich., writing teacher, 1983—. Creator and director of Deetroit Poets reading series, 1979-80; writing teacher at Upland Hills Awareness Center, 1983—, and Oakland Writers Conference, 1984; assistant director and member of board of trustees of Cranbrook Writers Conference; gives poetry readings at libraries, museums, colleges, and universities, and on WDET-Radio.

MEMBER: Poets and Writers, Poetry Society of America, Detroit Women Writers, Metro-Detroit Book and Author Society, Cranbrook Writers Guild (member of board of trustees, 1981—).

WRITINGS:

Diversion Road (poems), State Street Press, 1983.

Work represented in anthologies, including *1984 Anthology of Magazine Verse.* Contributor of poems to literary magazines, including *Woman Poet, Green River Review, New Laurel Review, Calliope, Cincinnati Poetry Review,* and *Passages North.*

WORK IN PROGRESS: The Blue Fox, poems.

SIDELIGHTS: Margo LaGattuta told *CA:* "I am motivated by the energy of active imagination. My recently completed manuscript, *The Blue Fox,* was created over a period of three years in graduate school (at Warren Wilson College and Vermont College), during which my study was directed toward the understanding of the creative process in myself and others. I have sought the balance of the intuitive and logical modes of thinking and have learned the importance of leading with the intuitive energy in my own poetry. I find I must begin with an overall pattern of wholeness, then work with the critical mind to fill in the parts. My work is also inspired by the music and suggestibility of language and might be called lyrical surrealism.

"I write for the joy of seeing, for the sense of connecting my inner and outer landscapes, for that moment of awareness in which I feel most truly alive. I write so that I may connect to you."

BIOGRAPHICAL/CRITICAL SOURCES:

PERIODICALS

Detroit Free Press, October 10, 1979.
Detroit News, October 21, 1979.

*   *   *

LAGUERRE, Michel S(aturnin)   1945-

PERSONAL: Born August 18, 1945, in Lascahobas, Haiti; came to the United States in 1971; son of Magloire and Anilia (Roseau) Laguerre. *Education:* University of Quebec, B.A., 1971; Roosevelt University, M.A., 1973; University of Illinois at Urbana-Champaign, Ph.D., 1976.

ADDRESSES: Office—Department of Afro-American Studies, 3335 Dwinelle Hall, University of California, Berkeley, Calif. 94720.

CAREER: Fordham University, Bronx, N.Y., assistant professor of sociology, 1977-78; University of California, Berkeley, assistant professor, 1978-82, associate professor of anthropology and Caribbean studies, 1982—. Member of board of trustees of Refugee Policy Group, Washington, D.C., 1983—; consultant to Inter-American Institute of Agricultural Sciences of the Organization of American States, 1974-76.

MEMBER: American Anthropological Association (fellow), Caribbean Studies Association.

AWARDS, HONORS: Humanities fellow of University of California, Berkeley, 1982-83.

WRITINGS:

Etudes sur le vodou haitien (title means "Studies on Haitian Voodoo"), University of Montreal Press, 1979.
School in Haiti, Teachers College Press, 1979.
Voodoo Heritage, Sage Publications, 1980.
The Complete Haitiana: A Bibliographic Guide to the Scholarly Literature, two volumes, Kraus International Publications, 1982.
Urban Life in the Caribbean, Schenkman, 1982.
American Odyssey: Haitians in New York City, Cornell University Press, 1984.

Member of editorial board of *Migration Today,* 1978—.

WORK IN PROGRESS: Ethno-Medicine in Afro-America: Toward a Sociology of a Rejected Knowledge; The Toussaint Louverture Papers.

LAHEY, Edwin A(loysius) 1902-1969

OBITUARY NOTICE: Born January 11, 1902, in Chicago, Ill.; died of complications of emphysema, July 17, 1969, in Washington, D.C.; buried in Gate of Heaven Cemetery, Silver Spring (one source says Wheaton), Md. Journalist. A long-time chief correspondent and chief of the Washington, D.C., bureau for Knight newspapers, Lahey started his career as a journalist in 1927, and joined the Chicago *Daily News* in 1929. He gained acclaim as a crime reporter, later becoming famous for his coverage of social and political events, including labor issues, while retaining as his personal trademark his mordant and often irreverent wit. During World War II Lahey was a correspondent from the Asian theater of operations; he also reported from Europe, Africa, and Latin America. He was named chief of the *Daily News* Washington bureau in 1956, and remained with Knight newspapers after the *Daily News* was sold in 1959. Lahey retired as bureau chief in 1967, but continued as chief correspondent until his death. Among his best-known journalistic accomplishments are his coverage of the resignation of Martin Durkin, U.S. President Eisenhower's first secretary of labor, and his interview with U.S. Senator Robert A. Taft, Eisenhower's unsuccessful opponent in the race for the 1952 Republican presidential nomination.

OBITUARIES AND OTHER SOURCES:

BOOKS

Obituaries on File, Facts on File, 1979.
Who Was Who in America, With World Notables, Volume V: *1969-1973,* Marquis, 1973.

PERIODICALS

Newsweek, July 28, 1969.
New York Times, July 18, 1969.

*   *   *

LaMARRE, Virgil E. 1910(?)-1985

OBITUARY NOTICE: Born c. 1910; died February 19, 1985, in Farmington, Mich. Business executive and author. Former vice-president of the D'Arcy-MacManus-Masius advertising agency in Bloomfield Hills, Michigan, LaMarre also wrote more than three hundred detective stories, publishing under his own name and four pseudonyms. In pursuit of his lifelong hobby of flying, the writer logged more than four thousand hours as an airplane pilot and was one of the first glider pilots to be licensed by the state of Michigan.

OBITUARIES AND OTHER SOURCES:

BOOKS

Who's Who in Public Relations, 5th edition, PR Publishing, 1976.

PERIODICALS

Detroit News, February 22, 1985.

*   *   *

LANCE, H(ubert) Darrell 1935-

PERSONAL: Born June 8, 1935, in Indianapolis, Ind.; son of Hubert Herman (a radio engineer) and Anna (a housewife; maiden name, Price) Lance. *Education:* Wabash College, B.A.,

1957; Colgate Rochester Divinity School, B.D., 1961; Harvard University, M.A., 1965, Ph.D., 1971. *Politics:* Democrat. *Religion:* American Baptist.

ADDRESSES: Home—Rochester, N.Y. *Office*—Colgate Rochester/Bexley Hall/Crozer Theological Seminary, 1100 South Goodman St., Rochester, N.Y. 14620.

CAREER: Ordained Baptist minister, 1961; Colgate Rochester/Bexley Hall/Crozer Theological Seminary, Rochester, N.Y., assistant professor, 1965-69, associate professor, 1969-75, professor of Old Testament, 1975—. Member of archaeological excavations at Shechem, Jordan, 1962, 1964; associate director of Hebrew Union College excavations at Gezer, Israel, 1964-71; W. F. Albright Institute of Archaeological Research, member of board of trustees, 1970-77, annual professor, 1973-74.

MEMBER: Archaeological Institute of America, Society of Biblical Literature, American Schools of Oriental Research (president of alumni association, 1975; associate trustee, 1979-81).

AWARDS, HONORS: Guggenheim fellow, 1973-74.

WRITINGS:

(With William G. Dever and G. Ernest Wright) *Gezer I: Preliminary Report of 1964-1966 Excavations,* Hebrew Union College Press, 1970.
(With Dever, R. G. Bullard, D. P. Cole, and J. D. Seger) *Gezer II: Report of the 1967-1970 Seasons in Fields I and II,* Hebrew Union College Press, 1974.
(Contributor) F. M. Cross, W. E. Lemke, and P. D. Miller, Jr., editors, *Magnalia Dei: The Mighty Acts of God,* Doubleday, 1976.
(Editor with Dever) *A Manual of Field Excavation,* Hebrew Union College Press, 1978.
The Old Testament and the Archaeologist, Fortress, 1981.
(Associate editor) *Gezer V: Caves I.3A and I.10,* Hebrew Union College Press, in press.

Contributor to theology and archaeology journals. Co-editor of *Biblical Archaeologist,* 1971-75.

WORK IN PROGRESS: The Excavations at Shechem, for Thomas Nelson.

SIDELIGHTS: H. Darrell Lance told *CA:* "When professor G. Ernest Wright of Harvard University accepted a sabbatical appointment for 1964-65 at the Hebrew Union College Biblical and Archaeological School (HUCBAS) in Jerusalem (now the Nelson Glueck School of Biblical Archaeology), he suggested that I accompany him and mount a small excavation at Gezer as the basis for my doctoral dissertation. The project began as such in the fall of 1964, but Wright soon conceived of the idea of enlarging the undertaking and making it a long-range research project of HUCBAS.

"Ultimately, the dig endured for ten years. Our primary goal was to reconstruct the archaeological history of the site—in which we succeeded—but we also made major contributions in archaeological method (published in *A Manual of Field Excavation*) and introduced the academic field school for archaeological projects in Israel, setting the pattern for many subsequent digs in both Israel and Jordan. Our major finds include an important Late Bronze age tomb along with the re-excavation (Gezer was first excavated in the early 1900's) of the city walls, a city gate of the period of Solomon, and a 'high place' of monumental standing stones."

LANG, H. Jack 1904-

PERSONAL: Born June 24, 1904, in Cleveland, Ohio; son of Hascal Charles and Rosetta (Stettiner) Lang; married Frances Wise, August 10, 1935; children: Wendy, John. *Education:* Antioch College (now University), B.A., 1928.

ADDRESSES: Home—1737 Andrews Rd., Cleveland Heights, Ohio 44118. *Office*—Lang, Fisher, Stashower, Inc., 1010 Euclid Ave., Cleveland, Ohio 44115.

CAREER: Lang, Fisher, Stashower, Inc. (advertising agency), Cleveland, Ohio, founder and president, 1932-69, chairman of executive committee, 1969-72, member without portfolio, 1972—. Mount Sinai Hospital, Cleveland, trustee, 1947-72, honorary trustee, 1973—; past member of board of trustees of Planned Parenthood of Cleveland, Antioch College (now University), and Cleveland Better Business Bureau; past member of executive committee of American Red Cross of Cleveland. *Military service:* U.S. Army Air Forces, 1942-46; became lieutenant colonel.

MEMBER: Manuscript Society, Western Reserve Historical Society, Rowfant Club, Communicators Club, Oakwood Club, Midday Club.

AWARDS, HONORS: George Washington Medal from Freedoms Foundation, 1964, for *Letters of the Presidents,* and 1965, for *Lincoln's Log Cabin Library;* inducted into Cleveland Advertising Club Hall of Fame, 1977; *The Rowfant Manuscripts* was named one of the best books of the year by American Institute of Graphic Arts, 1979.

WRITINGS:

The Wit and Wisdom of Abraham Lincoln, Greenberg, 1941.
Letters of the Presidents, Times-Mirror Press, 1964.
Lincoln's Fireside Reading, World Publishing, 1965.
Two Kinds of Christmases, World Publishing, 1965.
Lincoln's Log Cabin Library, World Publishing, 1965.
The Rowfant Manuscripts, Rowfant Club, 1977.
(Editor) *Letters in American History: Words to Remember, 1770 to the Present,* Harmony Books, 1982.

Also author of ''Letters of the Presidents,'' a syndicated newspaper feature. Editor of *Wolf Magazine of Letters,* 1934—.

WORK IN PROGRESS: A work tentatively titled *The Fine Art of Epistolary Wit.*

SIDELIGHTS: H. Jack Lang told *CA:* ''My interest in letter writing began with my editing of the *Wolf Magazine of Letters,* a house magazine for the Wolf Envelope Company of Cleveland and Detroit. The magazine contains letters of every type: literary, historical, humorous, sales, and collection. Together, the fifty bound volumes constitute a vast epistolary source unmatched anywhere for cleverness, wit, and uniqueness. Each letter must pass what I call the 'I'll be damned test.' Unless it brings this reaction from the reader, it does not deserve to be in the magazine.

''Continuing interest in letters led to my editing and writing six books, mostly anthologies of letters. It also led to my adventures in acquiring a collection of original autograph letters—important not for their quantity but for the excellence of their content. The theme of the collection, the only one of its kind, is 'The Best Practitioners of the Art of Letter Writing,' with examples from Madame de Sevigne, Voltaire, and Sam-

uel Johnson to Oscar Wilde, John Steinbeck, George Bernard Shaw, and Winston Churchill, who number among my favorites.''

* * *

LANG, Martin A(ndrew) 1930-

PERSONAL: Born May 2, 1930, in Brooklyn, N.Y.; son of Robert (a railroad inspector) and Ruth (a homemaker; maiden name, Sweeting) Lang; married Carol Anne Johnson (a teacher), August 1, 1969; children: Jay, Martin, Carol Anne, Nardia, Sonia. *Education:* Marist College, B.A., 1951; Catholic University of America, M.A., 1960, Ph.D., 1964. *Religion:* Roman Catholic.

ADDRESSES: Office—Graduate Division of Religious Education, Fairfield University, North Benson Rd., Fairfield, Conn. 06430.

CAREER: Marist College, Poughkeepsie, N.Y., assistant professor of theology, 1964-68; St. Norbert College, De Pere, Wis., associate professor of theology, 1968-70; Fairfield University, Fairfield, Conn., associate professor, 1970-77, professor of religious studies, 1977—, director of pastoral ministry and Graduate Division of Religious Education, 1970—.

MEMBER: American Academy of Religion, Catholic Biblical Association of America, Religious Education Association, Directors of Graduate Programs in Religious Education (vice-president, 1974-75).

AWARDS, HONORS: Fellow of Union Theological Seminary, New York, N.Y., at Columbia University, 1966-67.

WRITINGS:

The Inheritance: What Catholics Believe, Pflaum/Standard, 1970.
(Contributor) John Van Bemmel, editor, *Continuing Christian Development,* Twenty-Third, 1973.
(Contributor) Gloria Durka and Joanmarie Smith, editors, *Emerging Issues in Religious Education,* Paulist Press, 1976.
Acquiring Our Image of God: The Emotional Basis for Religious Education, Paulist Press, 1983.
Sexual Development (juvenile), Twenty-Third, 1985.

Contributor to theology and education journals.

WORK IN PROGRESS: Religion and Psychology.

SIDELIGHTS: Martin A. Lang told *CA:* ''I am in full agreement with a line from theologian Paul Tillich: 'I do not think it is possible today to elaborate a Christian doctrine of man . . . without using the immense material brought forth by depth psychology.' Psychology sheds light on religious experience, and religious insights can be of benefit to the field of psychology. Religion and psychology are combined most effectively in literature and in theatre.

''My work in religion and psychology is sympathetic to Carl Gustav Jung but relinquishes some Jungian categories for categories long established within the tradition of Christian mysticism. At the center of the self is the God imprint, the basic human need to give and receive love. Love is threatened only by fear. Fear is diminished and love enhanced by pursuing a regimen of thoughts and acts that correlate with the divine within. This leads to a reduction in conflict and ultimately to a fullness and wholeness of the self which is beyond simple psychological adjustment.

''*Sexual Development*, a work for young readers ages nine to twelve, is an effort to link total development with the developments of puberty. Without being moralistic the book shows how bodily sexual development is an important part of God's plan and should be approved and welcomed. Cartoons create a light atmosphere.''

*　　*　　*

LANGSTAFF, J(ohn) Brett   1889-1985

OBITUARY NOTICE—See index for *CA* sketch: Born March 22, 1889, in New York, N.Y.; died February 12, 1985, in Morristown, N.J. Clergyman, editor, and author. Ordained a deacon and priest of the Protestant Episcopal church, Langstaff was associated with churches in the Philippines, England, and the United States, where he served as rector of New York City's St. Edmund's Church for more than twenty-five years. The clergyman took a special interest in children, establishing a nondenominational cathedral for young people in New York in 1926 and the David Copperfield Library for children in London prior to World War II. Langstaff was the editor of *Not So Bad As We Seem* and the author of a number of books, including *Harvard of Today, The Holy Communion Service in Great Britain and America, David Copperfield's Library, From Now to Adam,* and *Oxford 1914*. He also contributed to children's books on nursery rhymes and wrote poetry which he had privately printed.

OBITUARIES AND OTHER SOURCES:

PERIODICALS

New York Times, February 14, 1985.

*　　*　　*

LANTZ, Fran
See LANTZ, Francess L(in)

*　　*　　*

LANTZ, Francess L(in)   1952-
(Fran Lantz)

PERSONAL: Born August 27, 1952, in Trenton, N.J.; daughter of Frederick W. (an architect) and Dorothea (a secretary and housewife; maiden name, Lingrell) Lantz; married Craig Shaw Gardner (a science fiction author), January, 1981 (divorced, 1983); married John M. Landsberg (a physician), April 30, 1984. *Education:* Dickinson College, B.A., 1974; Simmons College, M.L.S., 1975. *Politics:* Democrat.

ADDRESSES: Home and office—15 Perry St., Brookline, Mass. 02146. *Agent*—Merrilee Heifetz, Writers House, Inc., 21 West 26th St., New York, N.Y. 10010.

CAREER: Dedham Public Library, Dedham, Mass., children's librarian, 1976-79; writer, 1979—. Semi-professional musician in Boston, Mass., 1974-79; ''nanny'' for babies in Boston, 1979-83. Interviewer for American Field Service's exchange student program, 1974—.

WRITINGS:

NOVELS FOR YOUNG ADULTS

Good Rockin' Tonight, Addison-Wesley, 1982.
A Love Song for Becky, Berkley Publishing, 1983.
Surfer Girl, Berkley Publishing, 1983.
Rock 'n' Roll Romance, Berkley Publishing, 1984.

Senior Blues, Berkley Publishing, 1984.
Birds of a Feather, Dell, 1985.

Contributor of articles and reviews to *Kliatt* and *Rockingchair*.

WORK IN PROGRESS: Rock 'n' Roll Love; Softball Sweetheart; Birds of a Feather, a series of two or three books under the name Fran Lantz, publication expected in 1985.

SIDELIGHTS: Francess Lantz told *CA:* ''I was an only child with loving parents who encouraged my creative impulses. When I was ten, I wanted to be a writer, an artist, and a boy. At thirteen I discovered the guitar, decided it was okay to be female, and spent the next years making music.

''My novels are about contemporary teenagers trying to discover who they are and what they believe in. My protagonists often feel pressured by their parents and their peers to behave in certain ways. In the course of the novel, the main character struggles to do what she or he thinks is right, despite outside influences.

''All my novels are set in the present and contain references to current clothes, movies, music, etc. The reasons are three-fold: (1) I find it natural to write about what I know. I was a consumer of popular culture (rock 'n' roll, fashion, movies, etc.) as a teenager and I still enjoy it (especially rock 'n' roll) so I include it in my books. (2) Kids like to read about their world and their problems, especially if the author is close enough to their world to write realistically about it. I think I can do that. (3) Protagonists of teen romances must be modern middle class teens. Consequently, I write about current issues and fads out of necessity as well as out of love.

''When I worked as a children's librarian I used to put on a graveyard story-hour every year (yes, I took the kids to a nearby graveyard and scared the pants off them). After a couple of years I was having trouble finding new stories that were short, easy to read aloud, and really scary. In desperation, I wrote some myself. They were a big hit with the kids and that was when I first thought, hey, maybe I could write children's books. My first attempts were picture book texts. After a few of those I wrote a scary fantasy novel, followed by two mysteries. None of those sold and my next try was a young adult novel, *Good Rockin' Tonight*. Like many early novels, it was loosely based on my own life.

''For some reason I find it very easy to remember my teenage years. I can vividly recall my feelings when I first heard the Sergeant Pepper album, when my mother caught me rolling around on the sofa with my boyfriend, when I learned that my father had died. At the same time, I can now view these events from an adult perspective.

''Both these views, I feel, are required to write young adult novels. If the author can see the world through a teenager's eyes and nothing more, his book will be one-dimensional and claustrophobic. If he can only view teenagers from an adult perspective, his story will be manipulative and didactic. So far I think I've been able to integrate both perspectives. If I ever lose that ability, it will be time to stop writing young adult novels and move on to something else.

''I plan to write more novels for young adults, but I definitely won't write any more straight romance novels. They're too confining. So far my books have been rather light and humorous. In the future I'd like to deal with some more serious subjects—suicide, runaways, fans who become obsessed with their idols, to name a few. I want to write books that are realistic, with endings that are hopeful, although not necessarily happy. Eventually I'd like to try an adult novel and some essays.''

*   *   *

LAPINSKI, Susan   1948-

PERSONAL: Born May 27, 1948, in Baltimore, Md.; daughter of Jerome G. (a guidance counselor) and Eleanore (a teacher; maiden name, Althoff) Lapinski; married Micheal deCourcy Hinds (a reporter), December 31, 1973; children: Jessica, Susannah. *Education:* College of Notre Dame of Maryland, B.A., 1970; University of North Carolina at Chapel Hill, M.A.C., 1972.

ADDRESSES: Home and office—120 Boerum Pl., 3G, Brooklyn, N.Y. 11201. *Agent*—Molly Friedrich, Aaron Priest Agency, 344 East 51st St., New York, N.Y. 10022.

CAREER: Lady's Circle, New York City, staff writer, 1977-78, editor in chief, 1978-79; *Family Weekly,* New York City, senior editor, 1979; free-lance writer.

MEMBER: Writers' Network.

AWARDS, HONORS: Poetry award from *Atlantic,* 1970, for ''At the Coffeehouse.''

WRITINGS:

(With husband, Michael deCourcy Hinds) *In a Family Way: A Husband and Wife's Diary of Pregnancy, Birth, and the First Year of Parenthood,* Little, Brown, 1982.

Contributor to periodicals, including *McCall's, Glamour, Redbook, Bride's, American Baby,* and *Parents.*

SIDELIGHTS: In a Family Way, written by Susan Lapinski with her husband, Michael deCourcy Hinds, is a joint diary documenting Lapinski's pregnancy and the birth and first year of their child. Jane Freundel Levey, in her review for *Washington Post Book World,* cited the book's ''good prose'' and the co-authors' insights and observations.

Lapinski told *CA:* ''Before becoming a mother I specialized in profiles and travel pieces and general features. Now, with two young children to inspire me, I concentrate on family topics. I cherish the opportunity to write at home and spend time with my daughters.''

BIOGRAPHICAL/CRITICAL SOURCES:

PERIODICALS

Los Angeles Times, December 20, 1982.
Newsday, October 17, 1982.
Pasadena Star News, June 12, 1983.
Saskatoon Star Phoenix, April 2, 1983.
Washington Post Book World, December 18, 1982.

*   *   *

LARNER, Christina (Ross)   ?-1983

OBITUARY NOTICE: Educator and author. Larner taught in the history, sociology, and politics departments of the University of Glasgow. She wrote the book *Enemies of God: The Witch-hunt in Scotland* and articles on the modern British Foreign Service. (Date of death provided by Diane Infante of publicity department, Chatto & Windus.)

LARSON, Gary O(tto)   1949-

PERSONAL: Born July 11, 1949, in Hayward, Calif.; son of Clay Albion (a printer) and Louise (a housewife; maiden name, Bedford) Larson. *Education:* University of California, Berkeley, A.B., 1973; University of Minnesota—Twin Cities, M.A., 1975, Ph.D., 1981

ADDRESSES: Home—2514 K St. N.W., No. 11, Washington, D.C. 20037. *Office*—National Endowment for the Arts, Washington, D.C. 20506.

CAREER: Minneapolis/St. Paul (magazine), Minneapolis, Minn., contributing editor, 1979-80; National Endowment for the Arts, Washington, D.C., national council coordinator, 1980—.

MEMBER: Phi Beta Kappa.

AWARDS, HONORS: Fellow of National Endowment for the Arts, 1977; grant from National Endowment for the Humanities, 1984.

WRITINGS:

The Reluctant Patron: The United States Government and the Arts, 1943-1965, University of Pennsylvania Press, 1983.
(Contributor) Judith Balfe and Margaret Wyszomirski, editors, *Art, Ideology, and Politics,* Praeger, 1985.

WORK IN PROGRESS: Research on cultural diplomacy, ''specifically the U.S. government's use of art in foreign relations since 1938.''

SIDELIGHTS: Gary Larson told *CA:* ''I have always been fascinated by the collision that invariably takes place between art—often unpredictable, recalcitrant, even 'subversive'—and those institutions that attempt to present and promote art. When that institution is the federal government, moreover, presenting art abroad for its public relations value, for example, or promoting art at home in an alleged concern for the soul and spirit of the body politic, the collision reveals much about American culture. My work has attempted to illuminate the two worlds of art and politics: the danger, of course, is that in unraveling all of the complications of the latter, one loses sight of the magic of the former. In my case, a study of electronic music, and a passionate interest in other forms of music, serve as an excellent reminder.''

*   *   *

LARSON, Glen A.   1937(?)-

BRIEF ENTRY: American television producer and writer, screenwriter, and author. Remembered as one of the original members of the Four Preps singing group during the late 1950's, Larson has since become a prolific Hollywood producer and writer. His numerous television credits as a producer include the shows ''It Takes a Thief,'' ''Alias Smith and Jones,'' ''Quincy,'' and ''Magnum P.I.'' In addition, Larson wrote movie adaptations of his novels *Battlestar Galactica* (Berkley, 1978), written with Robert Thurston, and *Buck Rogers in the Twenty-Fifth Century* (Fotonovel, 1979), written with Leslie Stevens. Larson has also written two novelizations based on the ''Hardy Boys/Nancy Drew'' television series. *Address:* c/o Twentieth Century-Fox Television, P.O. Box 900, Beverly Hills, Calif. 90213.

BIOGRAPHICAL/CRITICAL SOURCES:

BOOKS

Who's Who in America, 42nd edition, Marquis, 1982.

PERIODICALS

People, October 23, 1978.

* * *

LARSON, James F(rederick)   1947-

PERSONAL: Born September 23, 1947, in Watertown, S.D.; son of George Phillip (a clergyman) and Dorothy Mae (a registered nurse; maiden name, Huseth) Larson; married Leone Marie Jordahl (a social worker), February 14, 1970; children: Grete Anne, Katie Rebecca. *Education:* St. Olaf College, B.A., 1969; attended Luther-Northwestern Theological Seminary, 1969-70; Stanford University, A.M., 1976, Ph.D., 1978. *Religion:* Lutheran.

ADDRESSES: Home—14204 Southeast 52nd Pl., Bellevue, Wash. 98006. *Office*—School of Communications, DS-40, University of Washington, Seattle, Wash. 98195.

CAREER: U.S. Peace Corps, Washington D.C., instructor in English at Kangwon National University in Chun Chon, Korea, 1971-72; University of Texas at Austin, assistant professor of communication, 1979-84; University of Washington, Seattle, assistant professor of communications, 1984—. Editor and writer for Worldwide English Division of Voice of America; broadcaster on WCAL-Radio and WCAL-FM Radio. Consultant to National Academy of Sciences.

MEMBER: International Communication Association, Association for Education in Journalism and Mass Communication.

AWARDS, HONORS: Research grant from George Washington University's Television and Politics Study Program, 1980-83.

WRITINGS:

Television's Window on the World: International Affairs Coverage on the U.S. Networks, Ablex Publishing, 1984.

Contributor to *Journal of Communication* and *Gazette.*

WORK IN PROGRESS: A book or monograph on international marketing communications (principally advertising).

SIDELIGHTS: James F. Larson told *CA:* "I began working for a public radio station while a student at St. Olaf College. That work provided me with my first experience in such areas as announcing, news editing, and studio engineering. It also led to a 1968 summer internship with the Voice of America in Washington, D.C., where I subsequently worked for a longer period of time as a writer and editor in the Worldwide English Division. My two years of Peace Corps service in the Republic of Korea, as a teacher of English to speakers of other languages, helped me in many ways. That brief experience living in a small, rapidly developing nation strengthened my resolve to later study international communication—in particular how U.S. television covers international affairs.

"In the United States television has become the principal medium through which the public learns of events in other parts of the world. In other words, the American public receives much more visual news from overseas than it did during the pre-television years. Yet despite the technological breakthroughs of communication satellites and lightweight cameras and editing equipment, the major U.S. television networks continue to provide a sharply circumscribed view of the world, with far too little coverage of developing nations and some smaller developed countries. They are still too often preoccupied with coverage of crises and news-breaking events, sometimes to the exclusion of social processes and the struggle of many nations toward change and development. Ultimately, the solution to this problem will involve the allocation of more air time for coverage of international affairs and a broadened definition of what constitutes news."

* * *

LARSSON, Carl (Olof)   1853-1919

BRIEF ENTRY: Born May 28, 1853, in Gamla Stan, Stockholm, Sweden; died following a stroke, January 22, 1919, in Falun, Sweden. Swedish educator, artist, illustrator, and author. Larsson produced paintings and murals for institutions, including theatres, in Stockholm and Paris. He also wrote and illustrated many volumes of nonfiction, including *Ett hem: or, Ett hem i dalarna* (1899; translated as *A Home,* 1974, and as *Our Home,* 1976), *Spadarvet* (1906; translated as *A Farm,* 1976, and as *Our Farm,* 1977), *Aat solsidan* (1910; title means "A House in the Sun"), *Andras barn* (1913; title means "Other People's Children"), and the autobiography *Jag* (1931; title means "Me").

BIOGRAPHICAL/CRITICAL SOURCES:

BOOKS

Cavalli-Bjoerkman, Goerel, Bo Lindwall, and Hans-Curt Koester, *The World of Carl Larsson,* translated by Allan Lake Rice, Green Tiger Press, 1982.
Hard, Ulf, *Carl Larsson's Home,* Addison-Wesley, 1978.
Larkin, David, editor, *The Paintings of Carl Larsson,* Scribner, 1976.

PERIODICALS

New York Times, August 17, 1980.

* * *

La TOUR du PIN, Patrice de   1911-1975

OBITUARY NOTICE: Born March 16, 1911, in Paris, France; died October 28, 1975, in Paris, France. Poet. A scion of an old aristocratic French family, La Tour du Pin was known as a traditionalist whose main preoccupations were metaphysical and religious. In 1933 he published *La Quete de joie* (title means "The Quest of Joy"), a critically acclaimed volume of predominantly religious poems that was originally conceived as part of a long-term project investigating the spirituality of man. La Tour du Pin's work was interrupted when he was drafted into the army at the beginning of World War II. The poet was seriously wounded and held as a prisoner in Germany for three years; he was repatriated in 1942. Four years later, in 1946, La Tour du Pin published *Une Somme de poesie* (title means "A Sum of Poetry"), the first volume of a massive poetic work attempting to encompass the totality of man's spiritual life. His writings in English translation include *The Dedicated Life in Poetry* and *The Correspondence of Laurent de Cayeux.*

OBITUARIES AND OTHER SOURCES:

BOOKS

Columbia Dictionary of Modern European Literature, Columbia University Press, 2nd revised edition, 1980.
Encyclopedia of World Literature in the Twentieth Century, revised edition, Ungar, 1981.

The Penguin Companion to European Literature, McGraw, 1969.

* * *

LATTA, William (Charlton, Jr.)   1929-

PERSONAL: Born September 24, 1929, in East Liverpool, Ohio; son of William Charlton (a Presbyterian minister) and Marjorie (Clippard) Latta; married Nancy Carnahan (a weaver), July 22, 1952; children: William Charlton III, Linda Jean, Leslie Jan, Thomas Hugh. *Education:* Sterling College, B.A., 1952; Kansas State University, M.A., 1960; University of Nebraska, Ph.D., 1961.

ADDRESSES: Home—Lethbridge, Alberta, Canada. *Office*—Department of English, University of Lethbridge, Lethbridge, Alberta, Canada T1K 3M4.

CAREER: High school English teacher in Plevna, Kan., 1956-58; University of Nebraska—Lincoln, instructor in English, 1961-62, 1964-65, visiting professor, summer, 1969; University of Saskatchewan, Regina Campus (now University of Regina), Regina, assistant professor of English, 1965-67; University of Lethbridge, Lethbridge, Alberta, assistant professor, 1967-71, associate professor, 1971-78, professor of English, 1978—. *Military service:* U.S. Air Force, Russian language specialist, 1952-56.

MEMBER: League of Canadian Poets, Association of Canadian University Teachers of English, Writers' Guild of Alberta (member of executive committee, 1980-82, 1983-84).

AWARDS, HONORS: Fiction award from *Prairie Schooner,* 1961, for "But the Old Men Know"; Fulbright scholar at University of Nottingham, 1963-64; Vreeland Award from University of Nebraska, 1963, for creative writing projects.

WRITINGS:

Summer's Bright Blood (poems), Thistledown Press, 1976.
Drifting Into Grey (poems), Four Humours Press, 1977.
Number Facts (poems), League of Canadian Poets, 1980.

Work represented in anthologies, including *Best Poems of 1966,* 1967; *Aurora: New Writing in Canada,* 1978; *Alberta Diamond Jubilee Anthology,* 1979; *Ride Off Any Horizon,* 1983.

Contributor to magazines. Editor of *Contemporary Verse II,* April, 1983; past member of editorial board of *Prairie Forum* and *Wascana Review.*

WORK IN PROGRESS: Correction Line, poems, publication expected in 1985; *To Be an Eagle* (tentative title), a novel, 1986.

SIDELIGHTS: William Latta told *CA:* "My life has been a series of fortunate accidents which have all moved me toward words and love, and I have decided that the two are essentially the same. I try to say very old things for the first time."

* * *

LAURIE, Bruce   1943-

PERSONAL: Born in 1943 in New Jersey; son of Philip and Lillian (Siminoff) Laurie; married Leslie Tarr (a health planner), June 1, 1969. *Education:* Rutgers University, B.A. (with honors), 1965; University of Pittsburgh, received M.A., received Ph.D., 1971.

ADDRESSES: Office—Department of History and Labor Studies, University of Massachusetts at Amherst, Amherst, Mass. 01003.

CAREER: University of Pennsylvania, Philadelphia, research associate of Philadelphia Social History Project, 1977-78; associated with department of history and labor studies at University of Massachussetts at Amherst. Visiting senior lecturer at Centre for the Study of Social History, University of Warwick, 1983-84.

WRITINGS:

(Editor with Milton Cantor) *Class, Sex, and the Woman Worker,* Greenwood Press, 977.
Working People of Philadelphia, 1800-1850, Temple University Press, 1980.

WORK IN PROGRESS: A study of the decline of artisans and artisanship in nineteenth-century America, for Arthur Wang.

SIDELIGHTS: Bruce Laurie told *CA:* "I am motivated by my love for history and hope for the future."

* * *

LAWRENCE, T(homas) E(dward)   1888-1935
(Lawrence of Arabia, J. H. Ross, T. E. Shaw)

BRIEF ENTRY: Born August 15, (some sources say August 1 or August 16), 1888, in Tremadoc, Caernarvonshire, Wales; died from injuries sustained in a motorcycle accident, May 19, 1934, in Bovington Camp Military Hospital, England. British archaeologist, soldier, and author. Lawrence, who became known as Lawrence of Arabia while serving with the British Army during World War I, was also an archaeologist and traveled on expeditions in southwest Asia between 1910 and 1914. During those years of archaeological study and exploration, Lawrence lived among the Arab people and gained an understanding of their culture and geography. The knowledge he acquired established Lawrence as an expert in Arab affairs. Later, after the outbreak of World War I, he became attached to the British Intelligence Service in Egypt. Lawrence was then assigned as liaison officer between the British and the Arabs, who were in revolt against their Turkish rulers. In support of the Arab's opposition to Turkish domination, the officer organized Arab tribes with British troops and launched a guerrilla resistance that eventually defeated the Turks. Lawrence's daring exploits in the Arab defense earned the soldier his reputation as a hero.

Following World War I, Lawrence attended the Versailles Peace Conference and worked to achieve independence for the Arab states. With his efforts proving unsuccessful, however, Lawrence renounced the peace conference and tagged it a betrayal of Arab interests. He later served the British Government as adviser on Middle Eastern affairs. When he resigned from that post, Lawrence sought a life of obscurity and enlisted in the Royal Air Force under the assumed name T. E. Shaw, which he legally adopted in 1927.

Lawrence's publications include *Seven Pillars of Wisdom: A Triumph,* written in 1919 while the author was attending the Versailles Peace Conference; it first appeared in a limited edition in 1926 and was later published in 1927 in an abridged version entitled *Revolt in the Desert.* Winston Churchill, one of Lawrence's greatest admirers, compared the book to *Robinson Crusoe* and *Gulliver's Travels.* In addition, Lawrence wrote a thesis on mediaeval military architecture that was published in two volumes as *Crusader Castles* (1936) as well as a translation of Homer's epic poem *The Odyssey*. Lawrence's book *The Mint: Notes Made in the Royal Air Force Depot Between August and December 1922, and at Cadet College in 1925*, which was written under the pseudonym J. H. Ross, was posthumously published by Doubleday, Doran in 1936.

BIOGRAPHICAL/CRITICAL SOURCES:

BOOKS

Longman Companion to Twentieth-Century Literature, Longman, 1970.
McGraw-Hill Encyclopedia of World Biography, McGraw, 1973.
Twentieth-Century Authors: A Biographical Dictionary of Modern Literature, H. W. Wilson, 1942.
Who's Who in Military History: From 1453 to the Present Day, Morrow, 1976.

*   *   *

LAWRENCE of ARABIA
See LAWRENCE, T(homas) E(dward)

*   *   *

LEA, Tom 1907-

BRIEF ENTRY: Born July 11, 1907, in El Paso, Tex. American artist, journalist, and author. Known for his paintings and books depicting Mexico and the American Southwest, Lea became familiar with the life and history of those regions while growing up in a culturally mixed area of Texas. His first full-scale novel, *The Brave Bulls* (Little, Brown, 1949), is set in Mexico and provides detailed information about the art and business of bullfighting. According to some critics, the widely acclaimed work successfully blends romanticism and realism in chronicling the life of the bullfighter Luis Bello, the central character of the novel. *The Brave Bulls* was adapted as a motion picture starring Mel Ferrar. In 1952 Lea's popular novel *The Wonderful Country* was published by Little, Brown. It sold more than one million copies, and it too appeared in a film version.

Lea's early books, *A Grizzly From the Coral Sea* (Hertzog, 1944) and *Peleliu Landing* (Hertzog, 1945), were based upon the author's experiences in the Pacific theater as a correspondent for *Life* magazine during World War II. Other novels by Lea include *The Primal Yoke* (Little, Brown, 1960) and *The Hands of Cantu* (Little, Brown, 1964). *The King Ranch* (Little, Brown, 1957) and *In the Crucible of the Sun* (King Ranch, 1974) are among Lea's nonfiction volumes. *Address:* 2401 Savannah St., El Paso, Tex. 79930.

BIOGRAPHICAL/CRITICAL SOURCES:

BOOKS

Dictionary of Literary Biography, Volume 6: *American Novelists Since World War II, Second Series*, Gale, 1980.
West, John O., *Tom Lea: An Artist in Two Mediums*, Steck, 1967.

*   *   *

LEAMAN, David R(ay) 1947-

PERSONAL: Born July 27, 1947, in York, Pa.; son of J. Eby (a pastor) and Elva (Eshleman) Leaman; married Joyce Schwartz (an elementary school teacher and counselor) in 1970; children: Shonelle, Roshana. *Education:* Wheaton College, B.S., 1969; Shippensburg State College, M.S., 1973; Ball State University, Ed.D., 1975.

ADDRESSES: Home—724 Lesher Ave., Waynesboro, Pa. 17268. *Office*—131 West Fifth St., Waynesboro, Pa. 17268.

CAREER: High school biology and life science teacher and head wrestling coach in Dillsburg, Pa., 1969-72; Bedford-Somerset Mental Health/Mental Retardation Center, Bedford, Pa., staff psychologist, 1975-79; Brook Lane Psychiatric Clinic, Hagerstown, Md., clinical psychologist, 1979-82; private practice of psychology in Waynesboro, Pa., 1982—. Adjunct professor at Shippensburg State College, 1981—; conducts weekend family, marriage enrichment, and stress management seminars. Member of board of directors of Young Life International Ministries; teacher of counseling courses for ministers.

MEMBER: American Personnel and Guidance Association, American Psychological Association, Christian Association for Psychological Studies, Society for Experimental and Clinical Hypnosis, Pennsylvania Psychological Association.

WRITINGS:

Making Decisions: A Guide for Couples, Herald Press, 1979.

Contributor to psychology journals.

WORK IN PROGRESS: At Ease in an Uptight World, completion expected in 1986.

SIDELIGHTS: David R. Leaman told *CA:* "My writing springs from both personal experiences and the motivation to help others become whole persons. I believe that what I communicate is useful for developing emotional and spiritual maturity. I have been impressed with the unity of spiritual principles and psychological insights. My religious belief in a transcendent personal God permeates all of my life activities, whether recreational or for serious growth. Although writing can be entertaining, my primary purpose as an author is to challenge personal growth and provide helpful guidelines toward that end. For example, my book on making decisions includes not only personal sharing but also systematic steps for making difficult choices within the context of an intimate relationship."

*   *   *

LEASHER, Evelyn M(arie) 1941-

PERSONAL: Born March 10, 1941, in Rosebush, Mich.; daughter of George Francis (a farmer) and Olive (a homemaker; maiden name, Owens) Leasher. *Education:* Central Michigan University, B.A., 1956; Pratt Institute, M.L.S., 1967.

ADDRESSES: Home—913 Northwest 28th St., Corvallis, Ore. 97330. *Office*—Oregon State University Library, Corvallis, Ore. 97331.

CAREER: Peace Corps, Washington, D.C., volunteer librarian in Bangkok, Thailand, 1967-69; New York City Planning Department, New York City, librarian, 1970-72; New York Public Library, New York City, librarian, 1973-75; Oregon State University Library, Corvallis, Ore., librarian, 1976—. Laubach Literary Action tutor, 1978-80.

MEMBER: American Library Association, American Association of University Women, Oregon Historical Society.

WRITINGS:

(With Robert Millward) *Cemeteries and Urban Land Use,* Council of Planning Librarians, 1975.
(Compiler) *Oregon Women: A Bio-Bibliography,* Oregon State University Press, 1981.
(Compiler) *Oregon State University Theses and Dissertations, 1978-1982,* Oregon State University Press, 1984.
(Editor with Robert Frank) Margaret Jewett Bailey, *The Grains; or, Passages in the Life of Ruth Rover,* Oregon State University Press, 1985.

SIDELIGHTS: Evelyn M. Leasher told *CA:* "*Oregon Women: A Bio-Bibliography* was compiled to fill a research need at the Oregon State University Library. There is little published information available about many of the women who were important in the development of Oregon. In an attempt to pull together the information available in collective biographies and Oregon periodicals a file was started. This file was then published as *Oregon Women* to enable others to have access to the information. In compiling the bibliography I discovered Margaret Jewett Bailey and her book *The Grains,* which has been out of print and forgotten for a hundred years. The book, an autobiographical novel, provides a look at life in Oregon between 1837 and 1854, told from the perspective of an intelligent woman. Margaret Bailey was a teacher at the Oregon Mission, the first white woman settler in Oregon, the first poet to be published in Oregon, the first woman editor of a newspaper column in Oregon, and the first woman writer to have a book published in Oregon. Researching the life of Margaret Bailey and editing *The Grains* for re-publication has been interesting."

*   *   *

LEAST HEAT MOON, William
See TROGDON, William (Lewis)

*   *   *

LEBOVICH, William Louis   1948-

PERSONAL: Born February 10, 1948, in Boston, Mass.; son of Harry and Florence (a housewife; maiden name, Goldfarb) Lebovich; married Karen Sloan (in public relations), June 9, 1974; children: Jennifer. *Education:* Brandeis University, B.A. (with honors), 1970; attended New York University School of Law, 1970-71; Boston University, M.A., 1974. *Religion:* Jewish.

ADDRESSES: Home—7302 Summit Ave., Chevy Chase, Md. 20815. *Office*—National Park Service, Washington, D.C. 20240.

CAREER: National Park Service, Washington, D.C., architectural historian, 1974—. Architectural and commercial photographer, 1981—.

MEMBER: Society of Architectural Historians, Society for Industrial Archeology, Society for History and Technology.

WRITINGS:

(Contributor) Richard Guy Wilson, editor, *AIA Gold Medal,* McGraw, 1983.
America's City Halls, Preservation Press (Washington, D.C.), 1984.
(Contributor) *Built in USA* (tentative title), Preservation Press (Washington, D.C.), 1985.

Contributor to magazines, including *Inland Architect, Commonwealth, Nineteenth Century,* and *Art and Australia.*

WORK IN PROGRESS: Research on synagogue architecture.

SIDELIGHTS: "The goal of my writing and research," William Louis Lebovich told *CA,* "is to provide an integrated view of architecture, showing through a particular building or type of building how architecture reflects and influences economic, political, cultural, as well as artistic factors. No building is independent of the time and society that built it and no building should be written about without discussing the larger context of time and society.

"My current job is with the Historic American Buildings Survey/Historic American Engineering Record, which is concerned with documenting, through photos, measured drawings, and reports, important American architecture and industrial and engineering structures. All of our documentation is deposited in the Library of Congress, where it is available to scholars and the public alike.

"The *America's City Halls* book is the catalogue for my exhibition with the Smithsonian Institution Traveling Exhibitions (SITES) Program. Jim Gossen (a former employee of the U.S. Conference of Mayors) and I came up with the idea of having an exhibit on my office at the annual meeting of the Conference of Mayors. We were going to mount an exhibit on city halls we had documented. When we found that my office had documented only a few city halls, we undertook a joint project—National Park Service, U.S. Conference of Mayors, and the American Institute of Architects—to document city halls. I served as project director and wrote the catalog based on information and photos supplied by city historians and local chapters of the American Institute of Architects. Several very prominent architectural photographers, such as Balthazar Korab, Julius Shulman, and Hedrich-Blessing, participated; and I photographed two of the city halls. The book illustrates my approach because the buildings are examined in terms of political, social, and economic factors as well as architectural history."

*   *   *

LEE, Patricia   1941-

PERSONAL: Born June 1, 1941, in New York, N.Y.; daughter of James Dudley and Mary Josephine (Kelly) Bullock; married David A. Lee, December, 1967 (divorced, 1969). *Education:* Attended Hunter College of the City University of New York, 1966-69, and New York University, 1978, 1984.

ADDRESSES: Home and office—311 East 50th St., New York, N.Y. 10022.

CAREER: Champion International, New York City, manager of administrative services, 1965-75; Norlin Corp., New York City, office manager and assistant to chairman of the board, 1976-77; Patricia Lee Associates, New York City, consultant, 1978—. President of Workshare, Inc., 1980—. Member of Creative Women's Exchange; consultant to Labor Zionist Letters, Inc.

MEMBER: Authors Guild.

WRITINGS:

The Complete Guide to Job Sharing, Walker & Co., 1983.

Contributor to magazines.

WORK IN PROGRESS: Taking Control of Your Work Life.

SIDELIGHTS: Patricia Lee told *CA:* "I wrote *The Complete Guide to Job Sharing* as a result of several years of intensive research and consulting. My purpose was to provide a practical, step-by-step guide that anyone could utilize in creating a job-sharing program.

"Job sharing is a voluntary work arrangement in which two people hold responsibility for what was formerly one full-time position. Salary and fringe benefits are pro-rated according to time worked. For employers, job sharing provides greater flexibility in work scheduling, retention of valued employees, reduced turnover, a wider range of skills in one job title, new options for older employees, and a reduction of absenteeism. For individuals, job sharing provides an opportunity to reduce their work schedule while maintaining their position in their chosen profession. Often individuals may choose to job share while raising a family, pursuing a second career, or furthering education. In other cases, the individual may be facing retirement or interested in spending more time on a volunteer activity. Job sharing gives people an opportunity to have greater control over their work schedules and enhances their quality of life.

"My current concerns include quality of life issues, alternative work patterns, entrepreneurship, and time management."

BIOGRAPHICAL/CRITICAL SOURCES:

PERIODICALS

Journal of College Placement, summer, 1984

*   *   *

LeFLORE, Ron(ald)   1948(?)-

BRIEF ENTRY: Born June 16, 1948 (some sources say 1952), in Detroit, Mich. American professional athlete and author. A convicted felon, LeFlore learn to play baseball while interned at Jackson (Michigan) state prison. His athletic skills were brought to the attention of Billy Martin, then manager of the American League's Detroit Tigers baseball team, who gave the ballplayer an opportunity to try out for the team. LeFlore played as an outfielder for the Tigers from 1974 until 1979. He then joined the Montreal Expos as a free agent. During his years with the Tigers, LeFlore played on the American League All-Star Team in 1976, and he set league records for stolen bases in 1978. The story of LeFlore's life, beginning with his childhood in a Detroit ghetto, is related in his autobiography, *Breakout: From Prison to the Big Leagues* (Harper, 1978). The book was adapted as a film for television, "One in a Million."

BIOGRAPHICAL/CRITICAL SOURCES:

BOOKS

Buchard, Marshall, *Sports Hero: Ron LeFlore,* Putnam, 1979.

PERIODICALS

Ebony, October, 1975.
New York Times, April 17, 1980.
New York Times Book Review, March 12, 1978.
Sports Illustrated, February 6, 1978.
Time, July 30, 1973.

*   *   *

LEHMAN, Peter   1944-

PERSONAL: Born December 25, 1944, in Janesville, Wis.;

son of Ernest and Anne (Heinemann) Lehman; married second wife, Melanie Magisos, June 16, 1983; children: (first marriage) Eleanor. *Education:* University of Wisconsin—Madison, B.S. (with honors), 1967, graduate study, 1967-68, M.A., 1973, Ph.D., 1978; graduate study at Queens College of the City University of New York, 1968-69.

ADDRESSES: Home—1525 South Moonlight Dr., Tucson, Ariz. 85748. *Office*—Department of Drama, University of Arizona, Tucson, Ariz. 85721.

CAREER: English teacher at public junior high schools in New York, N.Y., 1968-71; Ohio University, Athens, visiting professor of film, 1975-77, assistant professor of film and director of annual Film Conference, 1977-83, co-director of conference, 1984; University of Arizona, Tucson, associate professor of film, 1983—. Visiting lecturer at University of California, Santa Barbara, summer, 1982.

MEMBER: Society for Cinema Studies.

WRITINGS:

(Co-author) *Authorship and Narrative in the Cinema: Issues in Contemporary Aesthetics and Criticism,* Putnam, 1977.
(With William Luhr) *Blake Edwards,* Ohio University Press, 1981.
(Contributor) Patricia Mellencamp and Philip Rosen, editors, *Cinema Histories, Cinema Practices,* American Film Institute, 1984.
(Contributor) Randall Clark, editor, *American Film Directors Since World War II,* Gale, 1985.

Contributor of about thirty articles and reviews to magazines, including *Velvet Light Trap, Film Reader,* and *Cineaste.* Editor of *Wide Angle: A Film Quarterly of Theory, Criticism, and Practice;* member of editorial advisory board of *Ca Cinema.*

WORK IN PROGRESS: Blake Edwards, Volume II, with William Luhr, publication by Ohio University Press expected in 1987.

SIDELIGHTS: Peter Lehman told *CA:* "When I was a freshman in college, I saw the film 'The Pink Panther' and enjoyed it so much that I went back to see it over and over. I memorized the scenes which I thought were funny and in the process I discovered how much of the humor had to do with composition, use of space, and cutting patterns. I had had no film education of any kind, and this was my real discovery of some of the significant elements of the medium. Years later, when I became a film graduate student, I wanted to write my master's thesis or doctoral dissertation on Blake Edwards. I could not find an adviser who would agree that it was a worthwhile project (one professor sarcastically referred to Edwards as 'that party-going director'), so I chose John Ford instead. I resolved, however, that, at the first opportunity, I would do on my own what I could not do in academia at that time."

*   *   *

LeMAY, Alan   1899-1964

OBITUARY NOTICE: Born June 3, 1899, in Indianapolis, Ind.; died April 27, 1964, in Pacific Palisades, Calif. Motion picture director and producer, screenwriter, journalist, and author. Internationally known for his western stories and screenplays, LeMay was educated at the University of Chicago and worked as a journalist before beginning his career as a novelist in 1927. *Painted Ponies* was the first of more than a dozen novels he wrote in the western genre, including such well-known titles as *The Searchers* and *The Unforgiven,* which were both adapted into successful motion pictures. In 1940 LeMay wrote "North West Mounted Police," launching his career as a screenwriter. Among the many screenplays that followed were "The Story of Mark Twain," "Reap the Wild Wind," "Gunfighters," and "San Antonio." LeMay also produced and directed two of his own screenplays, "The Sundowners" and "High Lonesome." A prolific contributor of western stories and serials to magazines, LeMay wrote some works outside the western genre as well, including the novel *One of Us Is a Murderer* and such screenplays as "I Dream of Jeannie" and "Blackbeard the Pirate."

OBITUARIES AND OTHER SOURCES:

BOOKS

Twentieth-Century Western Writers, Gale, 1982.

*   *   *

LENGYEL, Emil 1895-1985

OBITUARY NOTICE—See index for *CA* sketch: Born April 26, 1895, in Budapest, Hungary; died after a heart attack, February 12, 1985, in New York, N.Y. Journalist, historian, educator, and author. An authority on World War II and the rise of Nazism, Lengyel had a first-hand view of war and its consequences as a soldier during World War I. He was drafted into the Austro-Hungarian army as a young man and fought in the trenches on the eastern front before being captured by the Russians and sent to Siberia. While imprisoned, the soldier managed to learn a number of languages, including English, and after his release immigrated to the United States, where he worked as a journalist for the *New York Times* and other publications. He subsequently became a professor of social sciences and was associated with New York University for nearly twenty years and with Fairleigh Dickinson University for fifteen years. Lengyel's best-known book, *Siberia,* is a fictionalized account of the author's years of imprisonment. His other works include *Hitler, Millions of Dictators: A Study of Public Opinion, Dakar: Outpost of Two Hemispheres,* and *The Changing Middle East.* Lengyel was also associated with the Foreign Policy Association's "Headline Series" publications and the Oxford Book Company's social studies pamphlets.

OBITUARIES AND OTHER SOURCES:

BOOKS

Current Biography, Wilson, 1942, April, 1985.

PERIODICALS

New York Times, February 15, 1985.

*   *   *

LEON, Henry Cecil 1902-1976
(Henry Cecil)

OBITUARY NOTICE: Born September 19, 1902, in Middlesex, England; died May 23, 1976. Attorney and author. Leon, a prolific writer of crime novels published under the name Henry Cecil, was educated at Cambridge University and began practicing law in 1923. He published his first book in 1948, after serving in World War II. Entitled *Full Circle,* it was a collection of stories that the author had invented to entertain his battalion during the war. Leon became a county court judge

in 1949 and served in that capacity until 1967, while continuing to write a stream of suspense novels, romantic comedies, radio and television scripts, plays, and nonfiction books on the law. Among his publications are *A Child Divided, Ways and Means, Brothers in Law,* and *Sober as a Judge.* Many of Leon's plays have been produced on London's West End, including a stage adaptation of his book *Settled Out of Court,* on which the author collaborated with popular author William Saroyan in 1960.

OBITUARIES AND OTHER SOURCES:

BOOKS

Twentieth-Century Crime and Mystery Writers, St. Martin's, 1980.
Who's Who in the Theatre: A Biographical Record of the Contemporary Stage, Marquis, 1977.
World Authors, 1950-1970, H. W. Wilson, 1975.

*   *   *

LEONE, Leonard 1914-

PERSONAL: Born September 13, 1914, in Highland Park, Mich.; son of Leonard (an importer) and Maria (a homemaker; maiden name, Catino) Leone; married Bertha Lishka (an artist), July 11, 1938; children: Leslie, Paula Leone Benedict. *Education:* Wayne (now Wayne State) University, B.A., 1936, M.A., 1937; also attended University of Florence, 1938, and University of Wisconsin—Madison, 1939.

ADDRESSES: Home—2111 Edgewood Blvd., Berkley, Mich. 48072. *Office*—University Theatres, Wayne State University, 95 Hancock, Detroit, Mich. 48202.

CAREER: Wayne State University, Detroit, Mich., instructor, 1941-45, assistant professor, 1945-51, associate professor, 1951-57, professor of speech, 1957-62, Distinguished Professor of Theatre Arts, 1962—, director of University Theatres, 1946—, established Bonstelle Theatre, 1952, Hilberry Theatre, 1963, Children's Theatre, 1945, Black Theatre Curriculum, 1970, director of Globe Playhouse Reconstruction Project, 1979—, director of theatre's tours to India, 1958, and Europe, 1962, director and producer of more than 250 plays and operas. Member of central committee of American College Festival, 1966-74; member of board of directors of Michigan Council of the Arts; member of National Theatre Conference.

MEMBER: International Federation for Theatre Research, American Theatre Association (fellow; president, 1985-86), American Society for Theatre Research, National Collegiate Players, American Educational Theatre Association (chairman of overseas touring committee, 1963-66), University Resident Theatre Association (co-founder, 1969; member of executive committe, 1969-74), British Society for Theatre Research.

AWARDS, HONORS: Recognition Award from Italian-American Society, 1956; certificate of esteem from U.S. Department of Defense, 1962; Gold Medal from Michigan Academy of Arts and Sciences, 1972; grant from Federal Republic of West Germany, 1974; named Theatre Man of the Year by Michigan Theatre Association, 1977; Gold Medal from American Oil Co. (AMOCO), 1979; Award of Merit from American Theatre Association, 1982; Silver Medal from American College Theatre Festival, 1984.

WRITINGS:

(With N. Joseph Calarco) *A State-University Resident Theatre,* American Theatre Association, 1973.

(Editor with C. Walter Hodges and Samuel Schoenbaum) *The Third Globe: Symposium for the Reconstruction of the Globe Playhouse,* Wayne State University Press, 1979.

WORK IN PROGRESS: Bernardo Buontalenti and the Medici Theatre, publication expected in 1987; *Scene Designers of the Italian Renaissance,* publication expected in 1988.

SIDELIGHTS: At work on a book titled *Bernardo Buontalenti and the Medici Theatre,* Leonard Leone told *CA:* "Bernardo Buontalenti (1536-1608) was an Italian theatre architect and scene designer who spent all his life in the service of the Medici family in Florence. He was the architect for the theatre in the Uffizi Palace in 1585. Some historians credit him with the development of the wing set and raised auditorium floor and with being one of the foremost scenic designers of the sixteenth century. At present there is no comprehensive study in English on his contributions and life's work.

"I began to promote the Globe reconstruction project in Detroit in 1979, when an international symposium of Elizabethan scholars was held at Wayne State University. The chairman of the symposium and designer for the project is C. Walter Hodges, distinguished scholar and author of *The Globe Restored* and *Shakespeare's Second Globe: The Missing Monument.* Research and development has continued since 1979 and projected plans call for construction on the Detroit riverfront in 1988. The research for the project was funded by public contributions in cooperation with Wayne State University. Construction of the playhouse is to be by private developers who are redeveloping sections of the waterfront."

AVOCATIONAL INTERESTS: Photography.

BIOGRAPHICAL/CRITICAL SOURCES:

PERIODICALS

Times Literary Supplement, April 23, 1982.

*   *   *

LeROY, Gen

BRIEF ENTRY: Born in Highland Park, N.J. American author. LeRoy's stories for children and young adults have received critical attention for their strong characterization and for their treatment of serious subject matter with humor. The former model and working artist received New Jersey Authors awards for two of her books, *Emma's Dilemma* (Harper, 1975) and *Hotheads* (Harper, 1977). Her other books include *Bridget* (Harper, 1973), *Cold Feet* (Harper, 1979), *Lucky Stiff!* (McGraw, 1981) and *Billy's Shoes* (McGraw, 1981), *Address:* New York, N.Y.

*   *   *

LESTER, Helen 1936-

PERSONAL: Born June 12, 1936, in Evanston, Ill.; daughter of William Howard (a businessman) and Elizabeth (Sargent) Doughty; married Robin Lester (a headmaster of a private school), August 26, 1967; children: Robin Debevoise, James Robinson. *Education:* Bennett Junior College, A.A.S., 1956; Wheelock College, B.S., 1959. *Religion:* Protestant.

ADDRESSES: Home—147 West 91st St., New York, N.Y. 10024.

CAREER: Elementary school teacher in Lexington, Mass., 1959-62; Francis W. Parker School, Chicago, Ill., second grade

teacher, 1962-69; writer. Volunteer worker in New York City soup kitchen.

WRITINGS:

Cora Copycat (self-illustrated juvenile), Dutton, 1979.
The Wizard, the Fairy, and the Magic Chicken (juvenile), Houghton, 1983.
It Wasn't My Fault (juvenile), Houghton, 1985.
The Revenge of the Magic Chicken (juvenile), Houghton, in press.

WORK IN PROGRESS: A Porcupine Named Fluffy.

SIDELIGHTS: Helen Lester commented: "My books are written for the three-to-six-year-old age group. As a mother of young children I felt a need for more short but satisfying bedtime stories, and that need spurred me into writing. My stories are humorous approaches to a message (*The Wizard* involves cooperation; *It Wasn't My Fault* is about guilt and is written for the clumsy of the world). Life's pretty serious sometimes, and I feel the heavier concepts are better received if given a lighter touch.

"Although I illustrated my own first book, I now have a superb illustrator in Lynn Munsinger, who draws what I would if I could. Though we never need to confer, each of us is delighted with the other's work."

AVOCATIONAL INTERESTS: Cooking, running, tennis, writing country and western songs.

*   *   *

LEVIN, Kenneth 1944-

BRIEF ENTRY: Born April 19, 1944, in Philadelphia, Pa. American psychiatrist, educator, and author. In 1976 Levin became an assistant psychiatrist at Boston's McLean Hospital and a clinical instructor at Harvard University. He wrote *Freud's Early Psychology of the Neuroses: A Historical Perspective* (University of Pittsburgh Press, 1978).

*   *   *

LEVINE, Lawrence W(illiam) 1933-

BRIEF ENTRY: Born February 27, 1933, in New York, N.Y. American historian, educator, and author. Levine joined the faculty of the University of California, Berkeley, in 1962; he became a professor of American history in 1970. He has also taught at the University of East Anglia and the Free University of Berlin. Levine was awarded the Chicago Folklore Prize in 1977.

His books include *Defender of the Faith: William Jennings Bryan; The Last Decade, 1915-1925* (Oxford University Press, 1965), *The Shaping of Twentieth-Century America: Interpretive Essays* (Little, Brown, 1965), *The National Temper: Readings in American Culture and Society* (Harcourt, 1968), and *Black Culture and Black Consciousness: Afro-American Folk Thought From Slavery to Freedom* (Oxford University Press, 1978). *Address:* Department of History, University of California, Berkeley, Calif. 94720.

BIOGRAPHICAL/CRITICAL SOURCES:

PERIODICALS

American Historical Review, February, 1978.
Christian Science Monitor, March 15, 1977.
New Republic, December 3, 1977.

South Atlantic Quarterly, autumn, 1978.

*   *   *

LEVY, Jack Steven   1948-

PERSONAL: Born April 15, 1948, in Los Angeles, Calif.; son of Kenneth L. (an engineer) and Sophia (Cornbleth) Jonas. *Education:* Harvey Mudd College, B.S., 1970; University of Wisconsin—Madison, M.A., 1972, Ph.D., 1976.

ADDRESSES: Home—330 Beverly Rd., Austin, Tex. 78703. *Office*—Department of Government, University of Texas at Austin, Austin, Tex. 78712.

CAREER: Tulane University, New Orleans, La., visiting assistant professor of political science, 1977-78; University of Texas at Austin, assistant professor, 1978-84, associate professor of government, 1984—.

MEMBER: International Studies Association, American Political Science Association.

AWARDS, HONORS: Helen Dwight Reed Award from American Political Science Association, 1977, for dissertation "Military Power Alliances and Technology: An Analysis of Some Structural Determinants of International Wars Among the Great Powers, 1495-1975."

WRITINGS:

War in the Modern Great Power System, 1495-1975, University Press of Kentucky, 1983.

Contributor to political science and international studies journals.

WORK IN PROGRESS: Research on the causes of war.

*   *   *

LEWIS, Dorothy Roe   1904-1985
(Dorothy Roe)

OBITUARY NOTICE: Professionally known as Dorothy Roe; born May 18, 1904, in Alba, Mo.; died March 24, 1985, in Columbia, Mo. Educator, publisher, journalist, and author. Roe was women's editor for the Associated Press from 1960 to 1970 and a columnist for the Chicago Tribune-New York News Syndicate during the following decade. Before holding these positions she was a reporter for the *El Dorado Daily News* in Arkansas, a feature writer for the *Los Angeles Examiner* and the *Chicago Herald-Examiner,* a national assignment reporter for Universal Service in New York, and an assistant women's editor for King Features. She also briefly owned and published the *Burlington Daily Enterprise* with her husband, John B. Lewis. In her later years Roe edited the *Missouri Republican,* a publication of the Missouri Republican State Committee, and she taught at the University of Missouri, which presented her with an award for distinguished performance and services in the field of journalism. Roe wrote *The Trouble With Women Is Men* and collaborated with Lilly Dache on *Talking Through My Hats* and *Lilly Dache's Glamour Book.*

OBITUARIES AND OTHER SOURCES:

BOOKS

Foremost Women in Communications, Bowker, 1970.
Who's Who of American Women, 14th edition, Marquis, 1984.

PERIODICALS

Chicago Tribune, March 27, 1985.

Detroit Free Press, March 26, 1985.
New York Times, March 26, 1985.

*   *   *

LEWIS, Jan (Ellen)   1949-

PERSONAL: Born July 10, 1949, in St. Louis, Mo.; daughter of Edward W. (in business) and Suzanne (a bookkeeper; maiden name, Greensfelder) Lewis; divorced; children: James. *Education:* Bryn Mawr College, B.A., 1971; University of Michigan, M.A. (American studies), 1972, M.A. (history), 1974, Ph.D., 1977.

ADDRESSES: Office—Department of History, Rutgers University, Newark Campus, Newark, N.J. 07102.

CAREER: Rutgers University, Newark Campus, Newark, N.J., assistant professor, 1977-83, associate professor of history, 1983—.

MEMBER: American Historical Association, Organization of American Historians, American Studies Association, Society of Historians of the Early American Republic, Southern Historical Association.

WRITINGS:

The Pursuit of Happiness: Family and Values in Jefferson's Virginia, Cambridge University Press, 1983.

Contributor to history journals.

WORK IN PROGRESS: A history of motherhood in America.

SIDELIGHTS: Jan Lewis commented: "Although I have written primarily about the history of the southern family, I am interested in all expressions of what is sometimes called 'American character.' I'm fascinated by the connections between our beliefs and our behavior and the intersection between our private lives and public views. I read a great deal of fiction and follow politics with interest and enthusiasm.

"My book, *The Pursuit of Happiness,* was, in many ways, a traditional history book, using standard sources—manuscript letters and diaries, and speaking to issues of interest to historians—the origins of the modern family, the distinctiveness of the Southern family. It was also addressed to the general reader, for whom I tried to recreate the emotional world of Thomas Jefferson's Virginia and to show why men and women came to believe that their earthly happiness would be found in love.

"My current project is a cultural and intellectual history of motherhood in America. I chose this topic because of my interest in women's history and my discovery that most women's historians have overlooked it or considered it an aspect of women's work, akin to housecleaning. Yet views of motherhood—what it means to be a good mother, whether women are mothers by nature or training, whether motherhood is good for mothers themselves—have changed greatly, and it is these changes I intend to explore. My sources will include sermons, advice literature, medical and psychiatric literature, and fiction.

"I don't yet know what I'll find. I am not a polemicist, and I have no conclusion or program in mind beyond showing the complexity and richness of history and the ways that a myriad of factors could affect the ways in which Americans could define something they like to think of as changeless: motherhood.

"Most of my research is about the sense people have made out of their lives. I also love the aesthetic and ethical dimensions of writing history. Writing history can be, in a strange way, un-American, for we Americans are a peculiarly ahistorical people. We believe in the fresh start, the new beginning. Yet history seeks to establish the patterns of causation, the connections, the link between cause and result, the because, and the why. It can be an aesthetic endeavor, when it establishes an order, and an ethical one, when it shows that actions have results."

*   *   *

LEWIS, Larry L(ynn) 1935-

PERSONAL: Born January 27, 1935, in Mexico, Mo.; son of Artie Francis (a farmer) and Mary (a teacher; maiden name, Whiteside) Lewis; married Betty Jo Cockerel (a homemaker), February 28, 1964; children: Janet Lynn, Christy Ann, Mark Ray. *Education:* Hannibal-LaGrange College, A.A., 1954; University of Missouri—Columbia, B.A., 1956; Southwestern Baptist Theological Seminary, B.D. and M.R.E., both 1960; Luther Rice Seminary, D.Min., 1978.

ADDRESSES: Home—3035 Muir, Hannibal, Mo. 63401. *Office*—Hannibal-LaGrange College, Hannibal, Mo. 63401.

CAREER: Ordained Southern Baptist minister, 1954; associate pastor of Baptist church in Springfield, Mo., 1960-61; pastor of Baptist churches in Columbus, Ohio, 1960-66, and Willingboro, N.J., 1966-71; Baptist Convention of Pennsylvania/South Jersey, Harrisburg, Pa., director of religious education, 1971-73; pastor of Baptist church in St. Louis, Mo., 1974-81; Hannibal-LaGrange College, Hannibal, Mo., president of college and part-time instructor in personal evangelism and church administration, 1981—. President of Missouri Baptist Convention Pastor's Conference; vice-president of Southern Baptist Convention Pastor's Conference; member of executive committee and executive board of Christian Civic Fund. Hannibal Chamber of Commerce, member of board of directors, 1982-84, president, 1985; member of board of trustees of Hannibal-LaGrange College, 1975-78, and Hannibal Young Men's Christian Association, 1984.

MEMBER: Missouri School Administrators Association, Historic Hannibal Association, Rotary International.

WRITINGS:

The Bus Ministry, Baptist Convention of Pennsylvania/South Jersey, 1971.
(Contributor) Reginald M. McDonough, editor, *Outreach With Church Buses,* Convention Press, 1972.
Organize to Evangelize, Victor Books, 1980.

Contributor of more than fifty articles to magazines, including *Sunday School Builder, Training Union, Outreach,* and *Church Adminsitration.* Contributing editor of *Bring Them In,* 1971-74, and *Builder.*

SIDELIGHTS: Larry L. Lewis told *CA:* "Most of my writing has been related to church growth, Sunday school growth, and church bus outreach.

"*The Bus Ministry* is, to my knowledge, the first book that was written by a Southern Baptist as a manual on church bus outreach. It tells how to organize a bus ministry with a bus captain, co-captain, and teen-age Crusaders who spend at least three hours every Saturday enlisting riders, ride the bus on Sunday, conducting a program of singing, Bible games, and various activities. It tells how to conduct a Saturday morning bus workers meeting and how to organize and conduct a children's worship service.

"*Organize to Evangelize* is basically a manual on church growth. It develops a formula for growth, first outlined in the 1920's by Dr. Arthur Falke, general secretary of the Baptist Sunday School Board. It emphasizes how to discover prospects, set up a visitation program, train and motivate workers, and unique ways of providing space to house new Sunday School classes and increase attendance. It also tells how to plan, promote, and conduct an effective revival or Bible school. It also explains how to have an effective follow-up on those who are enlisted and have reached for Christ.

"After twenty-five years in the pastoral ministry, I felt led of God to resign the large five-thousand-member Tower Grove Baptist Church to become president of Hannibal-LaGrange College. I was challenged by the prospect of helping train and develop young people for effective service, especially those who are called to the ministry. My three-year tenure as president of Hannibal-LaGrange has been at times frustrating, but also very rewarding. I expect to continue this ministry as a Christian educator until I retire."

*   *   *

LEWIS, Warren 1940-

PERSONAL: Born January 22, 1940, in Corpus Christi, Tex.; son of C. Wayne (a rancher) and Laura (Robinson) Lewis; married Lynne Yadon, May 20, 1962 (divorced); married Judee Reel (a writer and editor), September 18, 1975; children: Phoebe Yadon-Lewis, Austin. *Education:* Abilene Christian College (now University), B.A., M.A., 1962; Harvard University, S.T.B., 1965; University of Toronto, M.S.L., 1968; University of Tuebingen, D.Th., 1972.

ADDRESSES: Home—Freeland, Wash. *Agent*—Alice Volpe, Northwest Literary Agency, 2815 Boylston Ave., No. 304, Seattle, Wash. 98102.

CAREER: New York Theological Seminary, New York, N.Y., lecturer, 1973-75; Unification Theological Seminary, Barrytown, N.Y., professor of church history, 1975-80; Western Washington University, Bellingham, currently adjunct lecturer in history. Member of Global Congress of the World's Religions, 1976-80, and World Congress of Faiths.

MEMBER: North American Religious Liberties Association (co-founder), American Academy of Religion, Shaker Historical Society.

AWARDS, HONORS: Grant from World Council of Churches, 1968-70.

WRITINGS:

The Lord's Supper, Sweet Publishing, 1964.
(Contributor) J. Hopkins and H. Richardson, editors, *Trinity, Incarnation, and Redemption,* Harper, 1971.
Witnesses to the Holy Spirit: An Anthology, Judson, 1975.
Towards a Global Congress of the World's Religions, Rose of Sharon, 1978, Supplement I, 1979, Supplement II, 1980.
(Contributor) D. Dayton and A. D. Bryant, editors, *American Millenial Traditions,* Rose of Sharon, 1983.
Moon, Beacon Press, 1984.

WORK IN PROGRESS: The Gospel According to Mother Ann Lee: The Life and Searching of the Foundress of the Shakers;

Hitler's Religion: A Study in the Theology of Power; A History of Christianity in Black Africa; Risen Indeed, "a four-letter-word Anglo-Saxon theology of Jesus's resurrection"; *Grandpa,* a novel; *Mamma,* a novel; "Northwest Edda," a narrative poem.

SIDELIGHTS: Warren Lewis told *CA:* "Most writing about religion is uninteresting as literature. In my 'Gospel of True Father' in *Moon,* I've written a spiritual biography, to humanize Moon and to break the barrier between 'good literature' and historical research. In *Risen Indeed,* I am writing serious theology, but only in those words that are 'true' English; that is, no Greek, Latin, or French derivatives. To write lyrically, persuasively, humanely about someone else's religion (which one does not believe in oneself) is an essentially ecumenical act of polyconsciousness."

* * *

LEYTON, Sophie
See WALSH, Sheila

* * *

LIDOFF, Joan (Ilene) 1944-

PERSONAL: Born June 14, 1944, in Washington, D.C.; daughter of Herbert James (a patent examiner) and Evelyn (Hillerson) Lidoff. *Education:* George Washington University, B.A. (with honors), 1966; Harvard University, M.A., 1967, Ph.D., 1976. *Politics:* Democrat. *Religion:* Jewish.

ADDRESSES: Home—Austin, Tex. *Office*—Department of English, University of Texas at Austin, Austin, Tex. 78712.

CAREER: Middlesex Community College, Bedford, Mass., instructor in English, 1972-74; University of Massachusetts at Boston, instructor in English, 1974-78; University of Texas at Austin, assistant professor, 1978-84, associate professor of English, 1984—. Research assistant at Massachusetts Office of State Planning and Management, 1970-72; instructor at Boston College, 1976.

MEMBER: Modern Language Association of America, Phi Beta Kappa.

AWARDS, HONORS: Woodrow Wilson fellow, 1966-67; Dexter fellow of Harvard University in England, 1973; grant from National Endowment for the Humanities, 1979.

WRITINGS:

Christina Stead, Ungar, 1982.
(Contributor) Eric Sundquist, editor, *American Realism: New Essays,* Johns Hopkins University Press, 1982.
(Contributor) Juliann Fleenor, editor, *The Female Gothic,* Eden Press, 1983.

Contributor to *Ungar Encyclopedia of World Literature.* Contributor of articles and reviews to journals, including *Southerly, New Boston Review, American Quarterly, Shenandoah, Aphra,* and *Women's Studies Quarterly.*

WORK IN PROGRESS: Fluid Boundaries: The Origins of a Distinctive Women's Voice in Literature, for University of Chicago Press; "Virginia Woolf's Feminine Sentence: The Mother-Daughter World of *To the Lighthouse*"; "Her Mother's Voice: Reading Towards a Feminist Poetics, Tillie Olsen and Grace Paley."

SIDELIGHTS: Joan Lidoff reported: "The concerns of the women's movement of the sixties led me to refocus my inter-

ests in literature and psychology and close textual analysis with a continuing study of women writers, their themes and styles—their distinctive ways of shaping experience."

* * *

LIE, Jonas (Lauritz Idemil) 1833-1908(?)

BRIEF ENTRY: Born November 6, 1833, in Drammen (some sources say Hokksund), Norway; died near Oslo, Norway, July 5, 1908 (some sources say 1909). Norwegian lawyer, journalist, poet, playwright, and novelist. Lie is one of nineteenth-century Norway's most prolific and important authors. He began writing in the late 1860's after abandoning his career as a lawyer. His first novel, *Den fremsynte* (1870; translated as *The Visionary,* 1874), concerns a clairvoyant's experiences in northern Norway. The novel proved sufficiently successful to enable Lie to leave Norway, and he lived abroad for much of his life. In subsequent works Lie focused on the Norwegian middle class. Novels such as *Lodsen og hans hustru* (1874; translated as *The Pilot and His Wife,* 1877), *Familjen paa Gilje* (1883; translated as *The Family at Gilje,* 1920), and *Komamndorens dotre* (1886; translated as *The Commodore's Daughters,* 1892) established his reputation as an unflinching portrayer of the bourgeoisie. These works, with their impressionistic renderings, secured Lie's reputation as an accomplished stylist. In later writings, notably *Trold* (1891) and *Trold II* (1892; translated with *Trold* as *Weird Tales From the Northern Seas,* 1893), he returned to the mysticism of *Den fremsynte,* but he merged it with more overtly supernatural elements. In addition to his novels, Lie wrote plays and poems, though they are regarded as much less important. His death followed that of his wife, Thomasine—also the author's editor-collaborator—who died in 1907.

BIOGRAPHICAL/CRITICAL SOURCES:

BOOKS

Everyman's Dictionary of European Writers, Dutton, 1968.
Jorgenson, Theodore, *History of Norwegian Literature,* Macmillan, 1933.
Twentieth-Century Literary Criticism, Volume 5, Gale, 1981.

* * *

LIMB, Sue 1946-
(Sue Porter)

PERSONAL: Born September 12, 1946, in Hitchin, Hertfordshire, England; daughter of Lewis Wilfred (a civil servant) and Margaret Winifred (a teacher) Limb; married Roy Sydney Porter (a historian), August 15, 1970 (divorced September, 1982); married Johannes Nickolaas Maria Vriend (a composer and conductor), March 21, 1984. *Education:* Newnham College, Cambridge, B.A. (with honors), 1968, graduate study, 1968-72.

ADDRESSES: Agent—Tessa Sayle, 11 Jubilee Pl., London SW3 3TE, England.

CAREER: St. Ivo School, St. Ives, England, teacher of English and drama, 1974-77; writer, 1977—.

MEMBER: Royal Horticultural Society, Migraine Association, Campaign for Nuclear Disarmament.

AWARDS, HONORS: Best children's radio program award from Sony Corp., 1983, for "Big and Little" comedy series.

WRITINGS:

(With Patrick Cordingley) *Captain Oates: Soldier and Explorer* (biography), Batsford, 1982.
Up the Garden Path (comic novel), Bodley Head, 1984.

Under name Sue Porter: *Action Pack: Situations for Drama*, Edward Arnold, 1977.
Problem Page, Edward Arnold, 1980.
"Monkey" (play; adapted from a Chinese myth), first produced in London in 1981.
Play It Again, Edward Arnold, 1984.
She Was Awful (novel), Bodley Head, in press.

Author of comedy series for British Broadcasting Corp. (BBC), including "Big and Little" (for children), 1983, and "The Wordsmiths at Gorsemere: An Everyday Story of Towering Genius," 1985. Contributor to the *Observer*.

SIDELIGHTS: Sue Limb told *CA:* "We must laugh to stay healthy. Most of my writing is comedy. I'm extremely happy to try to make people laugh. Comedy can contain profound truths about human life, and it can be a political and moral weapon. It demands enormous discipline. Like many comedians, I am rather a solitary creature and, if not exactly misanthropic, I am quite hermit-like.

"My first book, the biography of Captain Oates, grew out of a childhood fascination with Scott's 1913 expedition to the Antarctic and the light it throws on English social history. Assisted by Oates's octogenarian sister, I wrote the book in 1964, when I was eighteen. The manuscript remained unpublished, however, until Major Patrick Cordingley, an officer in Oates's regiment, appeared and proposed he help me with a rewrite. Cordingley provided much invaluable military research, and we rewrote the book together in 1980.

"The comic novel *Up the Garden Path* and my comic series 'The Wordsmiths of Gorsemere' much more closely represent the type of work I am doing now. I find it impossible to resist cracking jokes, however bad they may be. I am also aware that the harder I try to write great literature the more abysmally I fail. My modest aim now is to amuse and perhaps comment sardonically *en passant* upon the more outrageous absurdities of life.

"It is interesting that some people are surprised to find that there are funny women, but it is no surprise to the women. Male publishers, editors, and the male-dominated literary establishment are now eagerly promoting any woman with pretensions toward comedy, in an attempt to make up for centuries of conditioning which only a few brave geniuses (such as Jane Austen) have been defiant enough to ignore. Even Jane Austen apologized for her own incisive intelligence and malicious wit—a sure sign of the depth and pervasiveness of the male prejudice against female satire. At last, things seem to be changing."

*   *   *

LIND, Millard C.   1918-

PERSONAL: Born October 10, 1918, in Bakersfield, Calif.; son of Norman A. (a minister) and Sarah (a home builder; maiden name, Flohr) Lind; married Miriam Sieber (a writer), 1943; children: seven. *Education:* Goshen College, Goshen, Ind., B.A., 1942; Goshen Biblical Seminary, Goshen, Ind. (now in Elkhart, Ind.), B.D., 1947; Xenia Theological Seminary, Th.M., 1955; Pittsburgh Theological Seminary, Th.D., 1963.

ADDRESSES: Home—1123 South Eighth St., Goshen, Ind. 46526. *Office*—Associated Mennonite Biblical Seminaries, 3003 Benham Ave., Elkhart, Ind. 46514.

CAREER: Ordained Mennonite minister, 1943; pastor of Mennonite congregation in Kouts, Ind., 1943-47; Mennonite Publishing House, Scottdale, Pa., staff writer, 1947-60, editor of magazine, 1955-60; Associated Mennonite Biblical Seminaries, Elkhart, Ind., assistant professor, 1960-65, professor of Old Testament, 1965—.

MEMBER: American Schools of Oriental Research (associate trustee, 1982-85), Society of Biblical Literature.

AWARDS, HONORS: Fellow of American Association of Theological Schools, 1968-69.

WRITINGS:

Biblical Foundations for Christian Worship, Herald Press, 1973.
(Contributor) J. R. Burkholder and C. Redekop, editors, *Kingdom, Cross, and Community*, Herald Press, 1976.
Yahweh Is a Warrior, Herald Press, 1980.
The New Way of Jesus, edited by William Klassen, Faith and Life, 1980.

Contributor to theology journals.

WORK IN PROGRESS: Law and the Bible; "The Politics of the Prophets."

SIDELIGHTS: Millard C. Lind wrote: "I am interested primarily in the Bible and the church as a new, nonviolent way to achieve a measure of the good community and justice in the world.

"*Yahweh Is a Warrior* is a title taken from the ancient poetry of the book of Exodus (15:3, *Jerusalem Bible*). In this book I challenge the conventional wisdom regarding holy war in the Bible, which is that because Yahweh fought, the troops fought all the harder. As used in this ancient poem, Yahweh fights while Israel looks on. This ancient deliverance at the Sea was a paradigmatic experience for Israel ever since, often linking a prophetic-like figure with the resolution of conflict rather than a human warrior figure.

"This experience also affected Israel's government, in that Yahweh as only warrior became early Israel's only king. Because of this, early Israel saw Yahweh's relation to kingship as Yahweh *versus* kingship rather than Yahweh *and* kingship, the latter being characteristic of the Near East. This development is the religious foundation of separation of church and state, as known in the West.

"The 'new way' of Jesus fits in precisely with this thesis in that Jesus established a new type of leadership: 'You know that those who are supposed to rule over the nations lord it over them, and their great men exercise authority over them. But it shall not be so among you; but whoever would be great among you must be your servant, and whoever would be first among you must be slave of all. For the Son of man also came not to be served but to serve, and to give his life . . . for many.'

"Related to this is the politics of the prophets. Their strange foreign policy has been discussed by German scholars since 1903 when a Semitic scholar, H. Winckler, wrote an essay with the provoking thesis that all the great prophets were collaborators with the enemy, Isaiah collaborating with the Assyrians, Jeremiah with the Babylonians, etc. No modern scholar agrees with this thesis, but many opinions have been offered why the great prophets prohibited Israel's alliances with the

West (Egypt) or the East (Assyria), or to put its trust in armaments. My thesis is that Isaiah, *et al.*, was against integration with Near Eastern imperialism with its oppressive structures, because he favored a new kind of internationalism where nations mutually agreed to use Yahwistic judicial structures for settling differences. This new internationalism was based on the example of early Israel's inter-tribal relationships in which the tribes mutually agreed to negotiate differences rather than resorting to war. In any case it is obvious that the prophets are interested not only in inter-personal relations, but also in international relations, and address the problems of war and peace. I am interested in this from the modern perspective and address my writings to the present religious community.''

*　　*　　*

LINDBERGH, Anne
See SAPIEYEVSKI, Anne Lindbergh

*　　*　　*

LINDSAY, Merrill K(irk)　1915-1985

OBITUARY NOTICE—See index for *CA* sketch: Born September 10, 1915, in Topeka, Kan.; died of viral pneumonia, April 6, 1985, in New Haven, Conn. Publisher, editor, and author. Although he had been associated with both the Winchester and Arma presses as publisher and with October House as an editor, Lindsay was best known as an expert on antique arms and armor. He founded the Eli Whitney Museum and Armory in Hamden, Connecticut, in 1979 and wrote a variety of arms-related books, including *Gunpowder; or, How It All Didn't Start, One Hundred Great Guns, Miniature Arms, Master French Gunsmiths' Designs From the Seventeenth to the Nineteenth Centuries, Twenty Great American Guns,* and *The Lure of Antique Arms.*

OBITUARIES AND OTHER SOURCES:

PERIODICALS

New York Times, April 10, 1985.

*　　*　　*

LINKLETTER, John A(ustin)　1923-1985

OBITUARY NOTICE—See index for *CA* sketch: Born February 11, 1923, in Winnipeg, Manitoba, Canada; died after a brief illness, April 18, 1985, in Greenwich, Conn. Journalist. Linkletter began his career working as a reporter for the *Newton Daily News* (Iowa) and later served as a managing editor of *Better Homes and Gardens.* He is best remembered, however, as editor of *Popular Mechanics* magazine. He joined the publication as an associate editor in 1959, became managing editor in 1962, and editor in chief in 1974.

OBITUARIES AND OTHER SOURCES:

BOOKS

Who's Who in America, 42nd edition, Marquis, 1982.

PERIODICALS

Chicago Tribune, April 20, 1985.
Washington Post, April 22, 1985.

*　　*　　*

LIPPINCOTT, Bertram　1898(?)-1985

OBITUARY NOTICE: Born c. 1898; died April 28, 1985, in Philadelphia, Pa. Publishing executive, yachtsman, and author. A graduate of Princeton University, Lippincott joined his grandfather's publishing firm, J. B. Lippincott & Company, after serving in World War I. During more than thirty years as an editor, he was responsible for the publication of such popular titles as *The Story of the Trapp Family Singers* and *My Friend Flicka.* One of the editor's hobbies was yacht racing, and he served as the commodore of the Conanicut Yacht Club in Rhode Island. Lippincott also wrote two books of Rhode Island history, *Indians, Privateers, and High Society: A Rhode Island Sampler* and *Jamestown Sampler.*

OBITUARIES AND OTHER SOURCES:

PERIODICALS

Chicago Tribune, May 3, 1985.
Detroit Free Press, May 2, 1985.
Los Angeles Times, May 5, 1985.
New York Times, May 2, 1985.
Philadelphia Daily News, May 1, 1985.

*　　*　　*

LIPSCOMB, Elizabeth J(ohnston)　1938-

PERSONAL: Born December 5, 1938, in Tuscaloosa, Ala.; daughter of G. Burke (a professor) and Mary Tabb (a homemaker and writer; maiden name, Lancaster) Johnston; married C. Lloyd Lipscomb (an Episcopal clergyman), August 22, 1964; children: William, George, Thomas. *Education:* Sweet Briar College, B.A. (summa cum laude), 1959; attended University of Birmingham, 1959-60; Harvard University, Ph.D., 1964. *Religion:* Episcopalian.

ADDRESSES: Home—1460 Northwood Circle, Lynchburg, Va. 24503. *Office*—Department of English, Randolph-Macon Woman's College, Box 408, Lynchburg, Va. 24503.

CAREER: Mary Baldwin College, Staunton, Va., instructor in English, 1963-64; Winston-Salem State University, Winston-Salem, N.C., instructor, 1966-67; Virginia Highlands Community College, Abingdon, lecturer in English, 1969-71; Randolph-Macon Woman's College, Lynchburg, Va., assistant professor, 1973-80, associate professor of English, 1980—. Chairman of Friends of the Sweet Briar College Library, 1975-77; regional panelist on Virginia Commission for the Arts, 1984-85.

MEMBER: National Council of Teachers of English, Conference on College Composition and Communication, American Association of University Women, Virginia Association of Teachers of English, Writing Program Administrators of Virginia, Phi Beta Kappa.

AWARDS, HONORS: Fulbright scholar in England, 1959-60; Woodrow Wilson fellow, 1960-61; American Association of University Women fellow, 1962-63.

WRITINGS:

(With mother, Mary Tabb Johnston) *Amelia Gayle Gorgas: A Biography,* University of Alabama Press, 1978.

Contributor to *Magill's Literary Annual.*

SIDELIGHTS: Elizabeth J. Lipscomb told *CA:* "What particularly interested me about the life of Amelia Gayle Gorgas was what it revealed about the strengths of nineteenth-century southern women and the demands made upon them. Through her father, a governor of Alabama and a U.S. representative, her husband, head of ordnance for the Confederate Army, and her son, well known for his work in eradicating yellow fever in the Panama Canal Zone, Gorgas was a part of significant historical events. Family papers show her responding to these events with warmth, intelligence, and resiliency—accepting new roles as circumstances required her to do so. She was primarily supporter and partner to her husband in the relatively comfortable pre-war years when he was building a career in the U.S. Army, during the conflict itself, and in the difficult times of the Reconstruction when they struggled to build a new life. After his death in 1883 she established her own career as librarian of the University of Alabama, where she served until she was eighty. The university's library bears her name.''

*   *   *

LIPSKY, Eleazar   1911-

BRIEF ENTRY: Born September 6, 1911, in New York, N.Y. American attorney and author. Lipsky began his practice of law in 1934 and later became assistant district attorney for New York County. His experience provided him with the material for his novel *The People Against O'Hara* (Doubleday, 1950). The book was a Mystery Guild selection and was made into a feature film starring Spencer Tracy and Pat O'Brien. Lipsky's subsequent novels have covered a wide range of subjects, but all rely on his understanding of courtroom practice and judicial procedure. *Lincoln McKeever* (Appleton, 1953) deals with a murder case in the Southwest, *The Scientists* (Appleton, 1959) considers the problems associated with pharmaceutical research and discovery, and *Malpractice* (Morrow, 1972) examines a fictional medical malpractice suit from the perspective of both the prosecuting and defending attorneys. Lipsky is also the author of an original screenplay, ''The Kiss of Death'' (Twentieth Century-Fox, 1947), which was later published as a novel.

BIOGRAPHICAL/CRITICAL SOURCES:

BOOKS

Current Biography, Wilson, 1959.

*   *   *

LISS, Robert E.   1945(?)-1979

OBITUARY NOTICE: Born c. 1945; died of leukemia in June, 1979. Journalist and author. Liss worked as a general assignment feature writer for the *Miami Herald.* His book, *Fading Rainbow: A Reporter's Last Story,* is an account of his battle with cancer.

OBITUARIES AND OTHER SOURCES:

PERIODICALS

Washington Post, July 15, 1980.

*   *   *

LITTAUER, Florence   1928-

PERSONAL: Born April 27, 1928, in Newton, Mass.; daughter of Walter (a shopkeeper) and Katie (a violinist; maiden name, MacDougall) Chapman; married Fred Littauer (a business executive), April 11, 1953; children: Lauren Littauer Briggs, Marita Littauer Noon, Frederick. *Education:* University of Massachusetts at Amherst, B.A. (with honors), 1949.

ADDRESSES: Home—Redlands, Calif. *Office*—1666 East Highland Ave., San Bernardino, Calif. 92404.

CAREER: Worked as a high school teacher in Houerhill, Mass., 1949-53, New Haven, Conn., 1954-55, and North Haven, Conn., 1956-58; public speaker and writer, 1974—. Also worked as theatrical director and fashion commentator for R. H. Macy's; member of founding staff of Long Wharf Theatre, New Haven, Conn.; guest on television and radio programs.

MEMBER: National Speakers Association, Women's Club of San Bernardino.

AWARDS, HONORS: Award from National Speakers Association, 1983.

WRITINGS:

The Pursuit of Happiness (autobiography), Harvest House, 1978.
Blow Away the Black Clouds, Harvest House, 1979.
After Every Wedding Comes a Marriage, Harvest House, 1981.
(With daughter, Marita Noon) *Shades of Beauty,* Harvest House, 1982.
Say it With Class, Harvest House, 1983.
Personality Plus, Revell, 1983.
It Takes So Little to Be Above Average, Harvest House, 1983.
How to Get Along With Difficult People, Harvest House, 1984.
Out of the Cabbage Patch, Harvest House, 1984.

SIDELIGHTS: Florence Littauer told *CA:* ''From the time I was a child I have had a love for the English language. My British father made vocabulary lessons fun and taught my two brothers and me tongue-twisters and complicated sayings such as: 'People who live in transparent domiciles should refrain form hurling geological specimens promiscuously.' The three of us could each recite this sentence and many more from the time we were four years old and we practiced on the customers who patronized our little variety store. My two brothers took singing, piano, and trumpet lessons but my musical mother would explain to her friends, 'Florence takes elocution lessons because she has no talent.'

''I memorized poetry, skits, and scripture, was in the senior class play and won the poetry reading contest in high school. I majored in English and speech and went on to teach these subjects on both the high school and college level. During my early married years I did some teaching, professionally directed musical comedies, and was a fashion commentator for R. H. Macy's. Everything seemed to be going my way until I gave birth, one after another, to two brain-damaged sons who had ten to twelve convulsions a day, screamed round the clock, and were both hopeless. I learned that you can be sitting in a twelve-room home, be driving a Lincoln Continental, and have a maid in uniform, but when you're holding a dying child none of that seems to matter. How I pulled through this time of depression is the subject of my best-selling book, *Blow Away the Black Clouds.* From that time on, I dedicated my life to the service of the Lord Jesus and to those people who needed my help and encouragement. As I began to speak of my life, my troubles, and my victories, I found that the audience received hope for their own lives. Because they asked for my messages in writing, I composed my first book *The Pursuit of Happiness,* a cinderella story of my life.

''We adopted a son, Frederick, when he was three months old, and my latest book, *Out of the Cabbage Patch,* includes the story of his adoption.

''When my life was easy and prosperous, I didn't spend time looking around me for people with problems, but by the time

I'd been through two traumas, both ending in death, I became sensitive to the emotional and spiritual needs of others and now dedicate my life to comforting those who hurt.

"All of my books stem from my own experiences. They are written with humor and—most important of all—they give hope to others."

*   *   *

LIU, Sarah   1943-

PERSONAL: Born December 14, 1943, in Shanghai, China; came to the United States in 1960, naturalized citizen, 1973; daughter of David (a missionary) and Mary (Feng) Lamb; married Kenneth Liu (a clergyman), August 14, 1965; children: Sharene Janelle. *Education:* Wheaton College, Wheaton, Ill., B.S., 1964; University of Dayton, M.S., 1979.

ADDRESSES: Home—1454 Roamont Dr., Centerville, Ohio 45459.

CAREER: Centerville City Schools, Centerville, Ohio, teacher, 1966—.

WRITINGS:

(With Mary Lou Vittitow) *Games Without Losers,* Incentive Publications, 1975.
(With Vittitow) *Creative Bible Activities for Children,* Victor Books, 1977.
(With Vittitow) *Every Day Is a Special Day,* Incentive Publications, 1978.
(With Vittitow) *Christians Celebrate,* Christian Publications, 1981.

SIDELIGHTS: Sarah Liu told *CA:* "All of my books include games and activities for school children to make learning more fun."

*   *   *

LIU E   1857-1909

BRIEF ENTRY: Born in 1857 in Kiangsu Province, China; died in 1909 abroad. Chinese physician, business reformer, and novelist. Liu E is probably best known in the West for his serialized novel *Lao-Ts'an yu chi* (1904-07; translated as *The Travels of Lao Ts'an,* 1952), which concerns a philanthropic scholar's adventures while opposing tyranny in the Chinese countryside. The novel has been praised for its poignant insights and eloquent descriptions of nature. Prior to writing *Lao Ts'an* Liu E practiced medicine and made several unsuccessful attempts to establish modern business firms in China. In 1900, with Peking under Russian control, Liu E acquired imperial grain for distribution to his countrymen. For this deed he was eventually exiled.

BIOGRAPHICAL/CRITICAL SOURCES:

BOOKS

The Penguin Companion to Classical, Oriental, and African Literature, McGraw, 1969.
Twentieth-Century Literary Criticism, Volume 15, Gale, 1985.

PERIODICALS

Choice, December, 1967.

LIVINGSTON, Martha   1945-

PERSONAL: Born November 21, 1945, in New York, N.Y.; daughter of David (an accountant) and Sara (a teacher; maiden name, Chaleff) Livingston; married David Bellin (a teacher, computer scientist, and writer), May 1, 1975; children: Roger. *Education:* Brooklyn College of the City University of New York, B.A., 1972; University of Regina, M.A., 1975; State University of New York at Stony Brook, Ph.D., 1985.

ADDRESSES: Home—Flushing, N.Y. *Office*—Department of Psychology, State University of New York at Stony Brook, Stony Brook, N.Y. 11794.

CAREER: National Union of Hospital and Health Care Employees, New York, N.Y., union organizer, 1974-77; mother, 1977—.

MEMBER: American Psychological Association, American Public Health Association, American Orthopedic Association, International Childbirth Education Association, American Association for Psychoprophylaxis in Obstetrics, National Women's Health Network, Cesarean Prevention Movement, Psi Chi.

WRITINGS:

(With Paul Lowinger) *The Minds of the Chinese People: Mental Health in New China,* Prentice-Hall, 1983.

SIDELIGHTS: Martha Livingston told *CA:* "I wrote *The Minds of the Chinese People* (not my title, by the way, but the publisher's) because I was most interested in how a developing, socialist nation handled people's everyday personal problems, as well as their more severe mental health problems.

"Although the Chinese are poor by our standards, unable to afford many of the material goods we take for granted, their social organization makes it possible for them to be involved in a rich network of social relationships at home, in the community, and on the job. Most everyday problems that people face in China are solved with the help of co-workers, neighbors, relatives, and friends, who are expected to look after one another and be involved in each other's lives. In this way, routine problems are solved in the community, and only people with severe, persistent mental health problems come into contact with mental health professionals and institutions.

"The information for the book was gleaned from a number of sources: several trips to China, visits with Chinese mental health professionals in the United States as well as in China, interviews with westerners who had visited Chinese facilities, and, of course, background library research using both Chinese and Western sources. Until very recently, not very much has been known about mental health in China, and we used every available source.

"Briefly, what can we learn from the Chinese experience? That material wealth is not as important to mental health as relationships among people. The Chinese, poor though they may be in some respects, are rich in knowing that their work contributes to the building of their country as a whole, and rich also in a sense of community and participation.

"My current research area is childbirth and, in particular, the psychological effects on birthing women of current medical practices. In this age of 'high-tech' medicine, birth has been redefined as a high-risk medical procedure rather than a normal physiological event. As a result of this philosophy, and also because of a need to pay for complicated medical machinery by using it as much as possible, equipment which is appropriate in only high-risk situations is being used on almost all pregnant and birthing women. The needs of normal birthing women—for support, comfort, the ability to move about and change position freely, the need for sustenance during what is truly an enormous physical effort—are not being met. We are transforming birth into a risky medical procedure, using fetal monitors, ultrasound, and other such machinery, and ignoring simple common-sense techniques like walking around during labor. Complications soar, and the psychological as well as physical consequences to birthing women are enormous: a rate of cesarean sections which has *more than doubled* in this country in the last ten years is but one dramatic example. There is a growing movement of parents and professionals to help return birth to the family, where it belongs, and my research will be, I hope, a small contribution to this movement.''

*   *   *

LOCHHEAD, Marion Cleland   1902-1985

OBITUARY NOTICE—See index for *CA* sketch: Born April 19, 1902, in Wishaw, Lanarkshire, Scotland; died January 19, 1985, in Edinburgh, Scotland. Journalist, editor, and author. Lochhead contributed to Scottish letters as a poet, biographer, and fiction writer, taking a special interest in Scottish history and traditional lore. Her writings include *The Scots Household in the Eighteenth Century: A Century of Scottish Domestic and Social Life; The Renaissance of Wonder in Children's Literature; John Gibson Lockhart,* a biography that some consider Lochhead's best work; *Elizabeth Rigby, Lady Eastlake,* a biography; and *The Episcopal Church in Nineteenth-Century Scotland.* In addition, Lochhead edited several works, including *Scottish Tales of Magic and Mystery,* and worked as a free-lance journalist. She became a member of the Order of the British Empire in 1963.

OBITUARIES AND OTHER SOURCES:

PERIODICALS

Times (London), January 26, 1985.

*   *   *

LOCKWOOD, Allison   1920-

PERSONAL: Born October 15, 1920, in Northampton, Mass.; daughter of William Lorenzo and Sarah Mary (Sharpe) McCrillis; married Paul Lockwood, June 4, 1946; children: Charles, John. *Education:* Smith College, B.A. (cum laude), 1943; University of Iowa, M.A., 1949. *Politics:* Independent. *Religion:* Episcopalian.

ADDRESSES: Home—3308 Rittenhouse St. N.W., Washington, D.C. 20015.

CAREER: John Wiley & Sons, Inc. (publisher), New York, N.Y., advertising copywriter, 1945-46; State University of New York at Buffalo, director of public information, 1958-60; American University, Washington, D.C., part-time instructor in English, 1960-66; Montgomery College, Rockville, Md., 1966-78, began as instructor, became associate professor of English; writer, 1978—. Member of board of directors of Buffalo Council on World Affairs, International Institute, and World Hospitality Association, all 1957-58. Member of Calvin Coolidge Memorial Foundation. *Military service:* U.S. Army, 1943-45.

MEMBER: Victorian Society of America, Nelson Society (England), Johnson Society of London, Smith College Alumnae Association, Friends of the Smith College Library.

WRITINGS:

Passionate Pilgrims: The American Traveler in Great Britain, 1800-1914, Fairleigh Dickinson University Press, 1981.

Contributor of articles to periodicals, including *New York Times, American History Illustrated, Washington Post, British Heritage, Wall Street Journal, Nineteenth Century, Christian Science Monitor, Hampshire Life,* and *Smithsonian.*

WORK IN PROGRESS: Two books.

SIDELIGHTS: Allison Lockwood commented: ''As a result of all the research for *Passionate Pilgrims* (more than five hundred nineteenth-century travel memoirs had to be studied), I found myself practically 'living' in that century. Much of my magazine writing since then seems to have spun off my book in one way or another. One day I hope to move up in time.''

BIOGRAPHICAL/CRITICAL SOURCES:

PERIODICALS

History Today, April, 1983.
New York Times, October 25, 1981.
Wall Street Journal, January 4, 1982.

*   *   *

LOCKYER, Herbert   1888(?)-1984

OBITUARY NOTICE: Born c. 1888; died November 30, 1984. Clergyman and author. Lockyear was a pastor in Scotland and England for a quarter of a century before coming to the United States to lecture at the Moody Bible Institute in Chicago. Known for his many Bible study and reference books, the clergyman wrote *Fairest of All, and Other Sermons, Give Us This Day: Daily Portions for Pilgrims, Satan the Anti-Christ,* and *''V'' for Victory: Sermons on the Christian's Victories.*

OBITUARIES AND OTHER SOURCES:

PERIODICALS

Christian Herald, February, 1985.

*   *   *

LODGE, Henry Cabot (Jr.)   1902-1985

OBITUARY NOTICE—See index for *CA* sketch: Born July 5, 1902, in Nahant, Mass.; died of congestive heart failure, February 27, 1985, in Beverly, Mass. Politician, diplomat, and author. Born into one of Boston's most prominent families, Lodge continued his forebears' tradition of public service when he entered politics. He first served as a Republican member of the Massachusetts legislature, then went on to serve three terms in the U.S. Senate, taking a special interest in American foreign policy. He interrupted his senatorial career to volunteer for active duty in the U.S. Army during World War II—the first senator to serve in the American armed forces since the Civil War.

Lodge returned to the senate in 1946 with a renewed interest in Republican party affairs. He persuaded Dwight D. Eisenhower to become the Republican Candidate for president in 1952 and became a major force in the war hero's successful campaign. Neglecting his own bid for reelection in his efforts on Eisenhower's behalf cost Lodge his senate seat to his Democratic opponent, John F. Kennedy. Eisenhower subsequently appointed Lodge to the United Nations, where his hard-line policy toward the Soviets influenced the temper of the cold war and made him a popular television personality. Lodge's celebrity prompted his selection as Richard Nixon's running mate in the latter's first, unsuccessful, bid for the presidency on the Republican party ticket. The politician was subsequently appointed U.S. ambassador to South Vietnam by then-President Kennedy, and he remained in that position during the escalation of the Vietnam War. Lodge later represented the United States at peace talks in Paris in 1969. The diplomat wrote several books, including *The Cult of Weakness, The United Nations: A Place to Promote Peace, You and the United Nations,* and an autobiography, *The Storm Has Many Eyes: A Personal Narrative.*

OBITUARIES AND OTHER SOURCES:

BOOKS

Current Biography, Wilson, 1954, April, 1985.

PERIODICALS

Chicago Tribune, March 1, 1985.
Esquire, October, 1983.
Los Angeles Times, February 28, 1985.
Newsweek, March 11, 1985.
New York Times, February 28, 1985.
Time, March 11, 1985.
Times (London), March 1, 1985.
Washington Post, February 28, 1985.

*   *   *

LOESCHKE, Maravene Sheppard 1947-

PERSONAL: Surname is pronounced *Lus*-ky; born January 28, 1947, in Baltimore, Md.; daughter of Joseph T. and Lila A. (a secretary; maiden name, Shriner) Sheppard; married G.R. Loeschke, August 16, 1969 (divorced, 1980); married C.R. Gillespie (a university professor), April 5, 1981; children: (stepchildren from second marriage) Joy Lynn, Douglas. *Education:* Towson State College (now University), B.S., 1969, M.Ed., 1972; Union Graduate School, Ph.D., 1975.

ADDRESSES: Home—2135 Chapel Valley Lane, Timonium, Md. 21093. *Office*—Department of Theatre Arts, Towson State University, Baltimore, Md, 21204.

CAREER: Worked as actress and production assistant for Maryland Center for Public Broadcasting, 1969-70; Towson State University, Baltimore, Md., assistant professor, 1975-82, associate professor of theatre arts, 1982—, chairperson of department. Professional actress on stage and film and in television commercials.

WRITINGS:

Mime: A Movement Program for the Visually Handicapped (monograph), American Foundation for the Blind, 1977.
All About Mime: Understanding and Performing the Expressive Silence, Prentice-Hall, 1982.

WORK IN PROGRESS: Ensemble for the Theatre, theory and exercise for creating artistic ensembles in the theatre; *The Path Between,* a novel covering the years following Emily Dickinson's death.

SIDELIGHTS: Maravene Loeschke commented: "I am interested in the use of Jungian psychology in the acting process.

Jung's concept of the introvert/extrovert and his concept of the thinking/feeling/sensation/intuitive types are helpful to actors in the development of emotional and physical rhythm changes.

"I am also concerned with the uses of ensemble building as part of the process of acting class and production preparation. I have a great interest in feminist theatre and all that it embodies in theory and production. Feminist theatre refers to plays about women, for women, by women. As a theatre movement, feminist theatre refers to plays written since roughly 1960. Because feminist plays are frequently written in an expressionistic style, the plays often require an acting style particular to that style. Actresses are required to develop plays without conflict, to reveal character through monologue and poetry and to use abstractions. Finally, I am deeply convinced of the importance of humanism in the theatre."

*   *   *

LOFTHUS, Myrna 1935-

PERSONAL: Born March 9, 1935, in Seattle, Wash.; daughter of John Oral (a machinist) and Iola Ida (a librarian; maiden name, Kleinschmidt) Berg; married Richard Arthur Lofthus (a sales representative), March 29, 1958; children: Michael Richard. *Education:* Pacific Lutheran University, B.A. (magna cum laude), 1956.

ADDRESSES: Home and office—1919 196th S.W., No. 32, Lynnwood, Wash. 98036.

CAREER: Northwest Orient Airlines, Seattle, Wash., administrative secretary, 1956-57; American Insurance Co., Seattle, executive secretary, 1958-59; teacher of astrology and self-awareness classes in Seattle and Lynnwood, Wash., 1974—.

MEMBER: Washington State Astrological Association.

WRITINGS:

A Spiritual Approach to Astrology, CRCS Publications, 1983.

WORK IN PROGRESS: Research on solar eclipses, lunar eclipses, and asteroids, and their effects on a natal chart and in world affairs.

SIDELIGHTS: Myrna Lofthus commented: "In 1953 I became interested in the answers to questions that the present-day religious concepts were, and are, unable to answer. My questioning began prior to this, but this was the turning point into metaphysical concepts. I could find no answer for the many injustices present in the world. In that year my Old Testament teacher in college tried to fob my question off with the statement, 'God wants us to learn compassion, so he makes other people suffer.' I could not justify that statement with his continual pronouncement of 'God is love.' Did God love me more? Did he love them less? As the years passed and I continued to study the Bible intensively for answers, I became more and more dissatisfied with my denomination's answers. I then turned to studying other religions to see if they had the answers. Unfortunately, they did not have the answers either.

"There is a saying that when a disciple sincerely tries to pursue answers to the meaning of life, the answers will finally be provided. Thus it was that in 1962 I read my first book concerning Edgar Cayce. He was a very religious man, but he found that in his trance state he talked about a soul incarnating over and over again in order to perfect itself so that it could return to God. He mentioned that the planets influence a soul's response to physical living and that they were specifically chosen for certain effects. That sparked an instinctive response within me and eventually led to my study of astrology. In the meantime I read every available book concerning metaphysical thoughts and Eastern philosophy. I was not particularly attracted to Eastern philosophy but responded to their teaching of reincarnation. However, I did adopt many of the meditative techniques from Zen and Tibetan Buddhism. The meditative techniques gave me greater insights into myself and the world in general. During my meditations it became clear to me that Master Jesus brought us the technique of opening our 'heart chakra.' 'Love' was the key.

"The basic message in Eastern religions was and is the control over the 'solar plexus chakra,' or our desire nature. If we could control our desire nature (solar plexus chakra), then we would be ready to develop the heart chakra of forgiveness, self-sacrifice, and love. Thus, my teachings and my book are based on the soul's spiritual quest to perfect its nature, through the control of the solar plexus chakra and the opening of the heart chakra. The soul makes many errors in its sojourns. Just as a baby must learn to crawl, walk, and talk, so, too, does a soul. It can be both painful and pleasurable. If we make a mistake, it must be rectified. The Bible refers to this as 'An eye for an eye, a tooth for a tooth.' We call it karma. Every thought, word, and deed is recorded in your record and must eventually be repaid. Thus, there is no injustice, although we must try as best we can to assist the suffering in the world, or a greater karma will befall us for our inhumanity.

"I have utilized the word 'spiritual' in the title of my book, because it denotes the quest to uplift the soul to a higher plane and ultimately to reside with God. The term 'religious' indicates one who has accepted a higher being as their creator. However, the person may or may not practice the principles that have come from God through the many earthly religious teachers.

"My teachings are only opposed to the traditional religious teachings in that I believe a soul incarnates over and over again, but in *human form only*. There are other minor points, similar to the differences in the various denominations, and, therefore, not of great consequence.

"After I began studying astrology, I was amazed at how many astrologers believed in reincarnation. Many of the books present at that time revealed this. During this time, I also studied many metaphysical books. One of my favorite authors was Gina Cerminara. She very aptly answered the question of how programming your life astrologically and God's gift of free will correlate. She utilized an analogy of a dog on a leash. The dog's freedom is limited by the length of his leash, but within that length, he has perfect freedom, both as to his movements, and as to how he chooses to react psychologically to this limitation. I see the 'length of the leash' as our programming, accomplished by planetary influences. We have free will to react in any manner we desire to this limitation.

"Astrology has the ability to answer many questions that the teachings of orthodox religions are unable to do. The most important answers are what you wish to accomplish this lifetime, in what areas of life you need the most work, and in what areas of life you will experience difficulties and the reasons for them. It reveals a just and kind God, who grants many, many lifetimes to change our negative ways. If one lifetime were a reality, all souls would have to accept a wrathful, unjust God, who had favorites.

"It was in the fall of 1974 that I began teaching an astrology class as a part of an adult continuing education program through the schools. I decided to air my personal theories on astrology to see how they were accepted. My class was enthusiastic and encouraged me to continue the class by teaching them advanced studies. At that point it became more convenient to teach from my home, which I am still doing, although it is now a self-awareness class based on a belief in reincarnation, rather than astrology only. It was during the next two years that I discovered I had many lecture notes. My papers grew. It wasn't long before my students were asking me for copies of the lecture notes. Finally, they asked me to put the material into a comprehensive book form. I devoted some of my time to writing and rewriting the material until the book was finished. I decided to call it *A Spiritual Approach to Astrology*, because that best described my emphasis: We are divine creatures with a divine mission to perfect ourselves, utilizing the myriad energies provided by our Divine Creator.

"The purpose of my book is to throw down the proverbial glove and challenge the reader to look deeply into the incredible ingeniousness of the challenges and karmic experiences that the soul has accepted as its programming for this incarnation. On a spiritual level, it will help you come to terms with your experiences and to learn from them. And on a personal level, you can learn how to utilize the planetary energies to build a creative, harmonious, happy life during your present sojourn."

*   *   *

LOGSDON, John M(ortimer III)   1937-

BRIEF ENTRY: Born October 17, 1937, in Cincinnati, Ohio. American political scientist, educator, and author. Logsdon began teaching political science at George Washington University in 1970, and in 1972 he was appointed director of the school's Graduate Program in Science, Technology, and Public Policy. He was a fellow at the Woodrow Wilson International Center for Scholars in 1974 and was named vice-president of Technoscience Associates in 1977. Logsdon is the author of *The Decision to Go to the Moon: Project Apollo and the National Interest* (MIT Press, 1970). He edited *The Research System in the 1980's: Public Policy Issues* (Franklin Institute Press, 1982). *Address:* Department of Political Science, George Washington University, 2121 I St. N.W., Washington, D.C. 20052.

BIOGRAPHICAL/CRITICAL SOURCES:

PERIODICALS

Commonweal, May 7, 1971.
Times Literary Supplement, April 2, 1971.

*   *   *

LONG, Huey P(ierce)   1893-1935

BRIEF ENTRY: Born August 30, 1893, in Winnfield, La.; died from an assassin's gunshot, September 10, 1935, in Baton Rouge, La.; buried on State Capitol grounds in Baton Rouge, La. American lawyer, politician, and author. Regarded as Louisiana's champion of the common people, Long is remembered both for his tyrannical political leadership and for improving the lot of the state's poor—first as governor of Louisiana and later as a U.S. senator. Long, who became known as the Kingfish, was admitted to the Bar of Louisiana in 1915, and he continued to practice law even while holding public office. As governor of his home state from 1928 to 1931, the politician established such wide-reaching political control over

Louisiana that his opponents described him as an American-style dictator. Though Long gained support for his agrarian social and economic reforms, critics condemned him for corruption within his administration, and his unorthodox tactics eventually precipitated an impeachment attempt.

The gubernatorial impeachment proceedings failed, and Long was subsequently elected to the U.S. Senate. After assuming his senatorial duties, however, Long refused to relinquish his gubernatorial post to the lieutenant governor—a staunch enemy—and instead appointed one of his trusted cohorts to the office, thereby preserving his dominance over the state. As a senator, Long instituted reform legislation that included a "Share-Our-Wealth" economic plan, but he opposed President Franklin D. Roosevelt's New Deal programs. He had announced plans to challenge Roosevelt in the next presidential election the month before he was shot by an assassin at the state capitol in Baton Rouge.

Long—the subject of many studies and novels, including Robert Penn Warren's Pulitzer Prize-winning *All the King's Men* (1946)—wrote *Every Man a King: The Autobiography of Huey P. Long* (1933) and the posthumously published *My First Days in the White House* (1935). *Address:* New Orleans, La.

BIOGRAPHICAL/CRITICAL SOURCES:

BOOKS

Harris, Thomas O., *The Kingfish: Huey P. Long, Dictator,* Pelican Publishing, 1938.
McGraw-Hill Encyclopedia of World Biography, McGraw, 1973.
Webster's American Biographies, Merriam, 1979.
Williams, T. Harry, *Huey Long,* Knopf, 1969.

*   *   *

LONGYEAR, Marie Marcia Bernstein   1928-

PERSONAL: Born April 26, 1928, in New York, N.Y.; daughter of Benno Alexander and Marcia Barbara (Trzecka) Bernstein; married Peter Rudston Longyear, July 2, 1949 (died, 1959); married Robert J. Dunphy (an editor at the *New York Times*); children: (first marriage) John R. *Education:* Radcliffe College, B.A. (cum laude), 1949. *Politics:* Republican. *Religion:* Episcopalian.

ADDRESSES: Home—300 Riverside Dr., New York, N.Y. 10025. *Office*—McGraw-Hill Book Co., 1221 Avenue of the Americas, New York, N.Y. 10020.

CAREER: McGraw-Hill Book Co., New York, N.Y., supervisor of editorial training, 1960-66, manager of editing services, 1966-74, director of publishing services, 1974—. Volunteer career counselor for Harvard University. Member of board of directors of Three Hundred Owners Corp., 1980-82.

MEMBER: Linnaean Society, Gilbert and Sullivan Society, National Audobon Society, Authors League, Radcliffe Club.

WRITINGS:

The McGraw-Hill Style Manual: A Concise Guide for Writers and Editors, McGraw, 1983.

WORK IN PROGRESS: Research on electronic publishing.

SIDELIGHTS: Regarding *The McGraw-Hill Style Manual,* Marie Marcia Bernstein Longyear told *CA:* "The recommendations in this book are based on McGraw-Hill Book Company in-house style manuals, with which I have long been associ-

ated. New material written expressly for this book includes a chapter on grammar and usage, procedures for copy editing, and helpful suggestions for achieving bias-free text and illustrations. Although it serves as a general style manual, covering rules for spelling, capitalization, hyphenation, tabular and bibliographic style, etc., this manual also contains more information on technical and scientific style (for mathematics, chemistry, life sciences, and electronics) than can be found in any other single source."

Longyear also told *CA* of her current work-in-progress on electronic publishing: "The increasing use of word processors and their impact on the process of editing and book production will be described in lay terms for writers planning to submit electronic manuscript for publication. Coding for typesetting will be discussed, as well as the need for structured typing in all aspects of electronic-manuscript preparation. The preparation of mathematical material and indexes on a word processor will also be explored."

*   *   *

LORD DENNING
See DENNING, Alfred Thompson

*   *   *

LORTIE, Dan C(lement)   1926-

PERSONAL: Born February 10, 1926, in Montreal, Quebec, Canada; married, 1956; children: four. *Education:* McGill University, B.A., 1947; University of Chicago, M.A., 1949, Ph.D., 1958.

ADDRESSES: Office—Department of Education, University of Chicago, 5801 Ellis Ave., Chicago, Ill. 60637.

CAREER: University of Chicago, Chicago, Ill., field director of National Opinion Research Center, 1951-54, assistant professor of human development and associate director of Kansas City study of adult life, 1955-57; Harvard University, Cambridge, Mass., lecturer and research associate at Graduate School of Education, 1958-63; University of Chicago, associate professor, 1963-74, professor of education, 1974—.

MEMBER: American Sociological Association, American Educational Research Association.

WRITINGS:

Schoolteacher: A Sociological Study, University of Chicago Press, 1975.

WORK IN PROGRESS: Researching the principalship role and school district organization.

SIDELIGHTS: In *Schoolteacher: A Sociological Study,* Dan C. Lortie examines the attitudes and guiding principles of America's two million schoolteachers. The empirical study finds teachers to be motivated by individualistic yet conservative concerns. Lortie also notes a great deal of insecurity to exist within the ranks of American teachers. Writing in *Commonweal,* George W. Shea praised Lortie's "clear" style, but also noted that many of the book's conclusions were "fairly obvious."

BIOGRAPHICAL/CRITICAL SOURCES:

PERIODICALS

Commonweal, April 15, 1977.

LOTZ, David W(alter) 1937-

BRIEF ENTRY: Born July 1, 1937, in Houston, Tex. American historian, educator, and author. Lotz taught religion at Concordia College from 1963 to 1964, then joined the faculty at Union Theological Seminary, where he later became Washburn Professor of Church History. He has also lectured at Woodstock College in New York and at General Theological Seminary. Lotz is the author of *Ritschl and Luther: A Fresh Perspective on Albrecht Ritschl's Theology in the Light of His Luther Study* (Abingdon, 1974). *Address:* Department of Church History, Union Theological Seminary, 3041 Broadway, New York, N.Y. 10027.

* * *

LOVEJOY, Paul E(llsworth) 1943-

PERSONAL: Born May 6, 1943, in Girard, Pa.; son of Warren B. and Gertrude (Ells) Lovejoy; married Elspech Cameron, 1977; children: Beatrix, Hugo, Henry. *Education:* Clarkson College of Technology, B.S., 1965; University of Wisconsin—Madison, M.S., 1967, Ph.D., 1973.

ADDRESSES: Office—Department of History, York University, Toronto, Ontario, Canada M3J 1P3.

CAREER: York University, Toronto, Ontario, associate professor, 1971-82, professor of history, 1983—, chairman of department, 1983—. Honorary lecturer at Ahmadu Bello University, 1975-76.

MEMBER: African Studies Association, Canadian Association for African Studies, Canadian Historical Association.

WRITINGS:

Caravans of Kola: The Hausa Kola Tribe, 1700-1900, Ahmadu Bello University Press, 1980.
(Editor) *The Ideology of Slavery in Africa,* Sage Publications, 1981.
Transformations in Slavery: A History of Slavery in Africa, Cambridge University Press, 1983.
Salt of the Desert Sun: A History of Salt Production and Trade in the Central Sudan, Cambridge University Press, 1985.
(Editor with Catherine Coquery-Vidrovitch) *The Labor of African Trade,* Sage Publications, 1985.
(Editor) *Africans in Bondage: Studies in Slavery and the Slave Trade,* African Studies Program, University of Wisconsin—Madison, in press.

Editor of "Sage Series on African Modernization and Development," Sage Publications. Contributor to history journals.

WORK IN PROGRESS: The End of Slavery in Northern Nigeria, with J. S. Hogendorn.

SIDELIGHTS: Paul E. Lovejoy told *CA:* "My interest in slavery and African history derives from my concern for the plight of Afro-Americans, and most especially because of my ancestry: I have two abolitionist forebearers, including a Lincoln Republican and Elijah P. Lovejoy, abolitionist and newspaper editor who was assassinated in Alton, Illinois.

"I have spent a total of almost four years in Africa, mainly in Nigeria, where I have taught and conducted research. In 1969-70, I was a Fulbright-Hays scholar. From 1974 to 1976, I taught at Ahmadu Bello University. Much of my research involved interviewing elderly people in Hausa, and as a result

of this work I collected several hundred hours of taped material on economic and social topics.

"My publications are meant to be a contribution to the discipline of history. The area of focus—Africa—is incidental. I would describe myself as a social and economic historian, not an Africanist historian as such. The difference is important. African history is not a sub-discipline but part of the mainstream of the field of history. The same methodology—the search for verifiable historical reconstruction—applies to specialists of African history as it does to other historians."

BIOGRAPHICAL/CRITICAL SOURCES:

PERIODICALS

American Historical Review, June, 1984.

* * *

LOW, Francis 1893-1972

OBITUARY NOTICE: Born November 19, 1893, in Finzean, Aberdeenshire, Scotland; died September 18, 1972. Journalist and author. Low began his journalism career as a staff reporter for the *Aberdeen Free Press* in 1910. In 1920, after serving in World War I, he returned to that newspaper as chief reporter. Low went to Bombay in 1922 to become sub-editor of the *Times of India,* and in 1923 he accepted the editorship of the *Evening News of India.* Two years later he returned to the *Times* as assistant editor and in 1932 became editor. Under Low's direction the circulation of the *Times* surpassed that of any other newspaper in India. The journalist was knighted in 1943, and in 1948 he retired his editorship and went back to England as the London representative for the *Times of India.* Low was the author of *Struggle for Asia* and a contributor to *The Annual Register of World Events.*

OBITUARIES AND OTHER SOURCES:

BOOKS

The Author's and Writer's Who's Who, 6th edition, Burke's Peerage, 1971.
The Writer's Directory: 1974-1976, St. Martin's, 1973.

PERIODICALS

Times (London), September 20, 1972.

* * *

LOWENTHAL, David 1923-

PERSONAL: Born April 26, 1923, in New York, N.Y.; son of Max (a lawyer) and Eleanor (Mack) Lowenthal; married Mary Alice Lamberty (an editor), 1970; children: Eleanor. *Education:* Harvard University, B.S., 1943; University of California, Berkeley, M.A., 1950; University of Wisconsin—Madison, Ph.D., 1953.

ADDRESSES: Home—Howard House, Harrow-on-the-Hill, Middlesex, England. *Office*—Department of Geography, University College, University of London, Gower St., London W.C.1, England.

CAREER: U.S. Department of State, Washington, D.C., research analyst, 1945; Vassar College, Poughkeepsie, N.Y., assistant professor of geography and chairman of department, 1952-56; American Geographical Society, New York, N.Y., research associate, 1956-72, secretary, 1967-72; University of London, London, England, professor of geography, 1972—.

Columbia University, seminars associate, 1957-72, chairman of Seminar on American Civilization, 1960-61; visiting professor at Massachusetts Institute of Technology, 1966, Clark University, 1966 and 1969, University of California, Berkeley, 1969 and 1977, University of Washington, Seattle, Syracuse University and City University of New York, both 1971, and University of Minnesota—Twin Cities, 1972; associate research professor at Harvard University, 1966-68; Regents' Lecturer at University of California, Davis, 1973. Maconochie Foundation, member, 1962—, president, 1973; Caribbean consultant to U.S. Peace Corps, 1958-67; consultant to Institute for Race Relations, London, England, and Resources for the Future. *Military service:* U.S. Army, 1943-45.

MEMBER: American Geographical Society (fellow), American Association for the Advancement of Science (member of council, 1964-71), Association of American Geographers (member of council, 1968-71), American Anthropological Association, American Historical Association, American Studies Association, Caribbean Studies Association (member of council, 1975-76), Society for Caribbean Studies (chairman, 1977-79).

AWARDS, HONORS: Fulbright fellow at University College of the West Indies (now University of the West Indies), 1956-57; Herfurth Award from University of Wisconsin—Madison, 1959, award from Geographical Society of Chicago, 1960, and meritorious contribution award from Association of American Geographers, 1960, all for biography *George Perkins Marsh: Versatile Vermonter;* Guggenheim fellow, 1965-66.

WRITINGS:

George Perkins Marsh: Versatile Vermonter (biography), Columbia University Press, 1958.
(Translator and author of introduction and notes) Charles Louis de Secondat Montesquieu, *Considerations on the Causes of the Greatness of the Romans and Their Decline,* Free Press, 1965.
West Indian Societies, Oxford University Press, 1972.
Publications in Environmental Perception, Volume I (with Marquita Riel): *Environmental Assessment: A Case Study of New York City,* Volume II: *Environmental Assessment: A Case Study of Boston,* Volume III: *Environmental Assessment: A Case Study of Cambridge, Massachusetts,* Volume IV: *Environmental Assessment: A Case Study of Columbus, Ohio,* Volume V: *Environmental Assessment: A Comparative Analysis of Four Cities,* Volume VI (with Riel): *Structures of Environmental Associations,* Volume VII (with Riel): *Milieu and Observer Differences in Environmental Associations,* Volume VIII (with Riel): *Environmental Structures: Semantic and Experiential Components,* American Geographical Society, 1972.
The Past Is a Foreign Country, Cambridge University Press, 1985.

EDITOR

The West Indies Federation: Perspectives on a New Nation, Columbia University Press, 1961.
George P. Marsh, *Man and Nature,* Harvard University Press, 1965.
Environmental Perception and Behavior, Department of Geography, University of Chicago, 1967.
(With Lambros Comitas; also co-author of introduction) *Consequences of Class and Color: West Indian Perspectives,* Anchor Press, 1973.

(With Comitas; also co-author of introduction) *The Aftermath of Sovereignty: West Indian Perspectives,* Anchor Press, 1973.
(With Comitas; also co-author of introduction) *Work and Family Life: West Indian Perspectives,* Anchor Press, 1973.
(With Comitas; also co-author of introduction) *Slaves, Free Men, Citizens: West Indian Perspectives,* Anchor Press, 1973.
(With wife, Mary Alice Lamberty, and Martyn J. Bowden; and contributor) *Geographies of the Mind: Essays in Historical Geography in Honor of John Kirtland Wright,* Oxford University Press, 1976.
(With Marcus Binney) *Our Past Before Us: Why Do We Save It?,* M. T. Smith, 1981.

Contributor to geography journals. Co-editor of *Progress in Human Geography* and *London Journal.*

WORK IN PROGRESS: Editing *The Uses and Misuses of the Past,* with Victor Konrad, publication expected in 1985.

SIDELIGHTS: The author of a biography on George Perkins Marsh, David Lowenthal told *CA:* "George Perkins Marsh was the pioneer conservationist in America. As a nineteenth-century Vermont congressman and later U.S. ambassador to Turkey and to Italy, he was the first to see the consequences of human impact on the face of the earth and the need for restoration of a harmonious balance. I became interested in Marsh for that reason and also because he early advocated an understanding of history, from the ground up, through the analysis of everyday artifacts and the life stories of ordinary people."

Also the author of works on the West Indies, Lowenthal added: "The West Indies seemed a remarkable laboratory for understanding how life takes different social and cultural forms among people in islands quite similar in their terrain, resources, and histories and differentiated mainly by accidents of European settlement and language. I still believe that islands provide unique chances for understanding of this and other kinds.

"*Geographies of the Mind* reflects the awareness that we all inhabit a world not to be understood in terms of its physical characteristics alone, but of the perceptions and attitudes we form about environments, places, and peoples."

*   *   *

LOYD, Marianne   1955-

PERSONAL: Born July 10, 1955, in Denton, Tex. *Education:* Wells College, B.A. (magna cum laude), 1976; Syracuse University, M.A., 1980, doctoral study, 1980-83.

ADDRESSES: Home—324 Vreeland Ave., Boonton, N.J. 07005. *Office*—Department of English, Lamar University, Beaumont, Tex. 77710.

CAREER: Title examiner for Morris County Abstract Co., Inc., 1977-78; Lamar University, Beaumont, Tex., instructor in English, 1983—.

MEMBER: Poets and Writers, Phi Beta Kappa.

AWARDS, HONORS: Alan Birk Memorial Award for poetry, 1980.

WRITINGS:

Journey to a Western Island, Tamarack Press, 1981.

WORK IN PROGRESS: The Angels and the Hills, poems; *Here Today,* a novel.

AVOCATIONAL INTERESTS: Running, squash, karate, travel (especially England and Ireland), playing recorder and Irish tin whistle.

* * *

LUBIN, Leonard B.

BRIEF ENTRY: Born in Detroit, Mich. American illustrator and author. Lubin is the author and illustrator of *The Elegant Beast* (Viking, 1981), which won an American Book Award for its illustrations. Described in the *New York Times Book Review* as "delightfully amusing," the book is a history of costume in which various animals model clothes from past centuries. Lubin made his debut as an illustrator in a new edition of Lewis Carroll's book *The Pig-Tale* (Little, Brown, 1975), which appeared on the *New York Times* list of best illustrated children's books for 1975 and was selected for the Children's Book Showcase in 1976. Lubin also illustrated Sheila Fox's collection *The Little Swineherd and Other Tales* (Dutton, 1978), a National Book Award finalist. In addition, Lubin has adapted and illustrated such children's books as Marie d'Aulnoy's tale *The White Cat* (Little, Brown, 1978) and *Aladdin and His Wonderful Lamp* (Delacorte, 1982), as well as a collection of libretti by William Schwenck Gilbert entitled *Gilbert Without Sullivan* (Viking, 1981).

BIOGRAPHICAL/CRITICAL SOURCES:

BOOKS

Illustrators of Children's Books: 1967-1976, Horn Book, 1978.

PERIODICALS

New York Times Book Review, April 26, 1981.

* * *

LUDWIG, Lyndell 1923-

PERSONAL: Born December 6, 1923, in Berkeley, Calif.; daughter of Albert Philip (a college professor) and Gladys (a child development teacher; maiden name, Newman) Ludwig. *Education:* University of Washington, Seattle, B.A. 1945; attended University of California, Berkeley, 1945-46, and California College of Arts and Crafts, 1948-56.

ADDRESSES: Home—Berkeley, Calif.

CAREER: University of California, Berkeley, secretary at Associated Students Store, 1947-64; researcher and writer, 1964—. Free-lance lettering and poster work, 1958-64.

WRITINGS:

JUVENILE; SELF-ILLUSTRATED

Ts'ao Chung Weighs an Elephant, Creative Arts Book Co., 1983.
The Shoemaker's Gift, Creative Arts Book Co., 1983.

WORK IN PROGRESS—Children's books, based on Chinese stories: *Ring a Bell to Catch a Thief; The Little White Dragon; How the Rabbit Got His Long Ears; The Country Goose; One Can Always Find a Way to Do Anything; Why the Cock Crows When the Sun Comes Up;* "*Kerplunk*"; *The Tree, and the Foolish King.*

SIDELIGHTS: Lyndell Ludwig told *CA:* "My father taught at Nan Kai School in Tientsin, China, from 1916 to 1918, and

returned with a love for the Chinese people and their culture. Exposed to things Chinese from my earliest years I, too, developed similar interests, which led to majoring in Far Eastern studies at the University of Washington and study for a year at the University of California in Berkeley. In my introduction to the Chinese language, I came across many intriguing stories for children, fascinating tales with basic human values. Over the years, while reading through Chinese books, I have found many more. When children know about the cultures of those in other lands, we all become the richer for it.

"In addition, I subscribe to several magazines and periodicals from mainland China which help me to understand present conditions there. Also, for the past several years I have been studying T'ang poems and ancient Chinese essays with a Chinese friend. Character by character, line by line, the ideas unfold, and I am continually impressed by the richness and beauty of the Chinese language."

* * *

LUNCH, Lydia [a pseudonym] 1959-

PERSONAL: Born June 2, 1959, in Rochester, N.Y.; daughter of Leonard L. and Lucy (Vicarri) Koch.

ADDRESSES: Office—c/o S. Martin, No. 1203, 161 West 54th St., New York, N.Y. 10019.

CAREER: Actress, guitarist, songwriter, storyteller, and poet.

WRITINGS:

(With Exene Cervenka) *Adulterers Anonymous* (poetry collection), Grove, 1982.

WORK IN PROGRESS: Garbage Hearts, a compilation of works, publication expected in 1985; *Unknown Artists,* another volume of compiled works.

SIDELIGHTS: Writing in the *Village Voice Literary Supplement,* Jessica Hagedorn described the poetry in *Adulterers Anonymous* as "pure rock 'n' roll, moving from page to page with a certain shallow urgency." Hagadorn praised Lydia Lunch's "sustained rage" and concluded that Lunch and co-author Exene Cervenka "work well together." The critic also noted that "these ladies obviously had some fun with this book, in spite of their deliberate, black-on-black flirtation with a doomed and bankrupt landscape."

Lunch told *CA:* "I am besieged. Mediocrity, complacency, apathy, and rot refuse to leave me alone and force me to strike out artistically. Terrorist drama is what I refer to 'this' as."

BIOGRAPHICAL/CRITICAL SOURCES:

PERIODICALS

Village Voice Literary Supplement, December, 1982.

* * *

LUSINCHI, Victor 1912-1985

OBITUARY NOTICE: Born January 7, 1912, in San Francisco, Calif.; died of complications of emphysema, April 3, 1985, near Grenoble, France. Journalist. Resident contributor in Geneva, Switzerland, for the *New York Times* beginning in 1958, Lusinchi worked for fifty years as a foreign correspondent for several publications. As a journalist for the British news agency *Exchange Telegraph* he covered the dramatic session in 1935 of the now-defunct League of Nations at which Emperor Haile

Selassie of Abyssinia (now Ethiopia) appealed in vain for help against the invasion of his homeland by the troops of Italian dictator Benito Mussolini.

OBITUARIES AND OTHER SOURCES:

PERIODICALS

Chicago Tribune, April 4, 1985.
New York Times, April 4, 1985.

*　　*　　*

LUTZ, Charles P(aul) 1931-

PERSONAL: Born August 10, 1931, in New Prague, Minn.; son of Paul Carl (a clergyman) and Olga (a homemaker; maiden name, Cornelius) Lutz; married Hertha E. Bieber (an accountant), September 4, 1955; children: Timothy Karl, Gretchen Kay, Nathan Kent. *Education:* Wartburg College, B.A., 1953; Capital University, Theological School, Columbus, Ohio (now Trinity Lutheran Seminary), M.Div., 1957; graduate study at University of Minnesota—Twin Cities. *Religion:* Lutheran.

ADDRESSES: Home—4937 Aldrich Ave. S., Minneapolis, Minn. 55409. *Office*—American Lutheran Church, 422 South Fifth St., Minneapolis, Minn. 55415.

CAREER: One (magazine for Lutheran youth), Minneapolis, Minn., editor, 1956-66; Center for Urban Encounter, Minneapolis, director, 1966-69; World Council of Churches, U.S. Conference, New York City, associate executive secretary, 1969-71; Lutheran Council of the United States of America, New York City, director of Office of Selective Service Information, 1971-73; American Lutheran Church, Minneapolis, director of Church in Community, Life, and Mission in Congregation, 1974-80, director of Office of Church in Society, 1981—.

AWARDS, HONORS: Merit award for editorial courage from Associated Church Press, 1963, for *One* magazine; citation from Anti-Defamation League of Minnesota and the Dakotas, 1969; Archbishop Ireland Distinguished Service Award in Urban Ministries from Roman Catholic Archdiocese of St. Paul/Minneapolis, 1970; named among the most influential Lutherans of 1982 by *Lutheran Perspective,* 1983.

WRITINGS:

(With James Stolee Kerr) *A Christians's Dictionary: 1,600 Names, Words, and Phrases,* Fortress, 1969.
You Mean I Have a Choice?, Augsburg, 1971.
(With Richard Killmer) *The Draft and the Rest of Your Life,* Augsburg, 1972.
(Editor and contributor) *Farming the Lord's Land,* Augsburg, 1980.
(Editor with Jerry L. Folk, and contributor) *Peaceways: Sixteen Christian Perspectives on Security in a Nuclear Age,* Augsburg, 1983.
Church Roots: Stories From the Nineteenth-Century Origins of the American Lutheran Church, Augsburg, 1985.

Contributor to magazines.

SIDELIGHTS: Charles P. Lutz told *CA:* "I have a particular interest in relating biblical faith to issues of contemporary society. *Farming the Lord's Land* is a collection of essays on ethical issues in American agriculture from the perspective of biblical stewardship of the earth—which sees the land as God's, with the role of God's people being to manage it responsibly."

*　　*　　*

LUTZ, Cora Elizabeth 1906-1985

OBITUARY NOTICE—See index for *CA* sketch: Born October 23, 1906, in Rockville, Conn.; died after a long illness, March 28, 1985, in Mount Carmel (one source says Hamden), Conn.; buried in Grove Hill Cemetery, Rockville, Conn. Educator, editor, and author. An educator for more than fifty years, Lutz taught classics at Wilson College, beginning as an associate professor in 1935 and becoming professor emeritus in 1969. She was noted as a specialist in medieval history and in that capacity cataloged medieval manuscripts at Yale University's Beinecke Library. Lutz also wrote a number of commentaries on scholarship and education in the ninth century, and she received two Guggenheim fellowships for researching schoolmasters of the Middle Ages. Her publications include *Dunchad: Glossae in Martianum; Musonius Rufus: The Roman Socrates; Remigius Autissiodorensis: Commentum in Martianum Capellam; Essays on Manuscripts and Rare Books; Schoolmasters of the Tenth Century;* and *The Oldest Library Motto and Other Library Essays.*

OBITUARIES AND OTHER SOURCES:

PERIODICALS

Hartford Courant, March 29, 1985.

*　　*　　*

LYTTON, Noel (Anthony Scawen) 1900-1985

OBITUARY NOTICE—See index for *CA* sketch: Born April 7, 1900, in London, England; died January 18, 1985. Military officer, farmer, and author. Lytton served in the British Army from 1919 to 1946, beginning with a commission in the Rifle Brigade. He went to Kenya as part of the King's African Rifles in the early 1920's, saw action in North Africa, Italy, and Greece during World War II, and eventually retired as a lieutenant colonel. In 1951 Lutz succeeded his father as Earl of Lytton, and in 1959 he took up farming. He was the author of the novels *Mickla Bendore* and *Lucia in Taormina: A Sicilian Romance.* The autobiographical *Desert and the Green, The Stolen Desert: A Study of the Uhuru in North East Africa,* and *Wilfrid Scawen Blunt: A Memoir by His Grandson* are among Lytton's works of nonfiction.

OBITUARIES AND OTHER SOURCES:

PERIODICALS

Times (London), January 23, 1985.

M

MacDONALD, Edgar E(dgeworth) 1919-

PERSONAL: Born March 5, 1919, in Richmond, Va.; son of John Edgar (a trainman) and Marie (a teacher; maiden name, Edgeworth) MacDonald. *Education:* Attended University of Virginia, 1936-38, and Sorbonne, University of Paris, 1947-48; Richmond Professional Institute (now Virginia Commonwealth University), B.S., 1952; University of Richmond, M.A., 1953; University of Paris, D. de l'Univ., 1957. *Religion:* "Agnostic Episcopalian."

ADDRESSES: Home—P.O. Box 565, Ashland, Va. 23005. *Office*—Department of English, Randolph-Macon College, Ashland, Va. 23005.

CAREER: U.S. Army, chief of civilian personnel in Paris, France, 1945-47; Randolph-Macon College, Ashland, Va., instructor, 1953-55, professor of English, 1957—. Visiting lecturer at Virginia Commonwealth University; Fulbright lecturer in Leningrad, U.S.S.R., spring, 1984; public speaker; guest on radio and television programs. *Military service:* U.S. Army, Infantry, 1942-45; served in Europe; received Purple Heart, Bronze Star, and three battle stars.

MEMBER: Association Internationale des Docteurs de l'Universite de Paris, Modern Language Association of America, College English Association, Ellen Glasgow Society, Virginia Writers Club.

WRITINGS:

The American Edgeworths, privately printed, 1970.
(Editor) *The Education of the Heart: The Correspondence of Rachel Mordecai Lazarus and Maria Edgeworth,* University of North Carolina Press, 1977.
(Editor with Tonnette Bond Inge) *Ellen Glasgow: A Reference Guide,* G. K. Hall, 1984.
(Editor with M. Thomas Inge, and contributor) *James Branch Cabell: Centennial Essays,* Louisiana State University Press, 1983.

CONTRIBUTOR

M. T. Inge, editor, *Ellen Glasgow: Centennial Essays,* University Press of Virginia, 1976.
F. Elaine Penninger, editor, *A Festschrift for Margurite Roberts,* University of Richmond, 1976.

Louis D. Rubin, Jr., editor, *A History of Southern Literature,* Louisiana University Press, 1984.

OTHER

Contributor of more than fifty articles to history, genealogy, and literature journals and to literary magazines, including *Stylus, Southern Literary Journal, American Literature, Mississippi Quarterly, Resources for American Literary Study,* and *Cabellian.* Editor of *Ellen Glasgow Newsletter* and *Magazine of Virginia Genealogy,* 1984—.

WORK IN PROGRESS: " 'Absalom, Absalom' as an Extended Poem," for *Mississippi Quarterly,* publication expected in 1985; *Memoirs of Pocahontas,* publication expected in 1986.

SIDELIGHTS: Edgar E. MacDonald told *CA:* "I feel that a critical analysis of a work of literature should combine several approaches. Even when one is using the work to develop a specific thesis or has to limit his approach owing to time and space requirements, he should not restrict his overall consideration to a narrow vision. A succinct summation of a work should be based on a comprehensive viewing from a wide number of critical viewpoints.

"Some forty years ago many students in the United States were influenced by what was termed the 'New Criticism,' the title of a work by John Crowe Ransom and a phrase still associated with the name of the venerable American critic Cleanth Brooks. Basically, the New Criticism was a conscientious attempt to refocus critical attention on the work, rather than the writer. There was a feeling that biography and literary history had replaced careful textual analysis. On the other end of the critical spectrum, the comparatist approach with its historical emphasis was still honored, and many reputable critics continued to feel that no work is created in a pure vacuum and to ignore the matrix from which a work grows is to limit perception to a laboratory concept unrelated to actual experience.

"The most pervasive form of criticism is, of course, the subjective response to a work. On an elementary level, the reader reads the work and then gives his emotional reaction; most frequently the work evokes a 'feeling' of like or dislike, depending in large part on the reader's background, his ability to 'relate' to the work dependent on a number of sociological factors. Such 'criticism' tells us much about the reader, but little about the work read. On a higher level, this subjective response composes the bulk of the literary reviews appearing in the mass-appeal publications. Some of the critics associated with these journals have highly respected names. One calls to mind H. L. Mencken and Edmund Wilson from the past and John Updike of today. One might add with some justification that criticism in the United States is currently dominated by the writers themselves—Warren, Barth, Baldwin—many of whom are also teachers.

"One finds the criticism of these writers interesting from a number of viewpoints: they write well, they are practitioners of the art, and their reviews appear in prestigious publications. At the same time, part of our interest is predicated on what Updike has to say about Saul Bellow, who Norman Mailer is feuding with, and the asperity with which John Aldridge assesses William Styron. These reviews are usually footnoted by a naming of the reviewer's latest novel, giving us to understand that these are not nameless critics, incompetent to write anything except criticism. A thoughtful reader realizes that these critics can indulge in *ex cathedra* pronouncements, that they evince little compulsion to support their opinions with objective criteria. The sheer bulk of criticism produced by John Updike, gathered into large tomes every few years, assures us that he *has* to write *ex cathedra,* that there is little time for meditative critical analysis—and deadlines have to be met. Today, we read the criticism of Mencken and Wilson for the charm of the writing itself, not so much for the critical opinions they expressed.

"The most informative criticism comes from the scholar who reads widely, meditates, and re-reads. He experiences a work from a broad perspective. If he reads a new novel by a writer he is familiar with, he is conditioned to look for certain characteristics associated with that writer. When, on the other hand, the analytical critic reads the work of a writer unknown to him, he depends more directly on the work itself to reveal itself, very much in the manner advocated by the New Critics of the forties.

"As a teacher, I have little interest in the subjective effusions of students, interpretations of a 'message' largely imagined. Leaving that area of appreciation to educationists and religious psychologists, I try instead to instill in a student a respect for an objective appraisal of a work, one based on a preliminary consideration of forms. If one is going to be made to feel, he ought to understand the techniques and processes by which he is made to feel. Form and function are interdependent, and a mathematical appraisal of the form of a poem or novel seems to me a necessary preliminary to comprehension as opposed to mere reading. Such preliminary analysis makes for a heightened enjoyment in the reading or experiencing of work: we observe where we are going and how we get there. Our subjective enjoyment is augmented by the cerebral pleasure of understanding how a poem or novel works. Every work of art is a commentary on life. For the unanalytical reader, the message is filtered through his neuroses; for the analytical, through his intellectual rationale.

"Such a structural approach, however, should not be a counterpart of biological morphology, simply an analysis of form for its own ends. Rather, such an approach should lead to a cleared concept of function. Just as William Faulkner affirms that the tale and the teller are indivisible, we see that the form, static in appearance, functions. It makes its commentary as surely as do the characters, if more subtly, and it constitutes, in a sense, the author's 'rules of the game.' The student unob-

servant of forms will let his imagination range beyond the limiting 'rules' to unsupported guessing; the observer of structure will be guided to accurate assessment. Seeing clearly is the goal of every serious critic, for without clear vision any message is distorted.

"The clear conception of what the structure of a work 'is saying' allows us then to test the relevance of biography and history. Certainly our appreciation of *Absalom, Absalom* as an extended 'poem,' an epic, is enhanced by our knowledge of Faulkner's preoccupation with poetry in his formative years. That knowledge reinforces our perception of Rosa Coldfield as the primary exemplar of the 'failed poet,' echoing that quality in all the other characters. The proofs, however, are not in Faulkner's biography; they are in the novel itself, in its forms, its imagery, and in its subtle allusions to John Keats and Edgar Allan Poe, and above all in the poetic structures inherent in the work. Not to see the poetic structures is to miss the poetic message. While the plethora of criticism directed to the work's sociology, psychology, philosophy, and political viewpoint may all by admirably relevant, none of it carries the poignant message directly from Faulkner's heart to ours—that we are all failed poets.

"I am personally grateful to those critics who help me comprehend that my understanding of a work has been deficient because I did not see for myself what is there to be seen. The best critics help us to see more clearly, thereby sharpening our perspectives, aiding us to be the observant readers we aspire to be. The unobservant reader has little to offer us. He rarely appreciates the best, for his structural blindness limits his comprehension to those facile writers who provide the readily obvious. John Irving's joke books with their cliched pretensions to literature are accepted enthusiastically, his sorry circus of freaks being accorded the same admiration merited by the vital creations of the artist. Carson McCullers and Flannery O'Connor looked with compassion at the freak, but they wrote out of an inner vision of order which gave structure and meaning to their works.

"The analytical reader comes to understand that he re-reads the best literature to measure his own critical growth. The timeless creations are mirrors in which we see ourselves. I measure what I saw yesterday with what I see today. If what I see is more illuminating, I know it is not the work that has changed, but rather my perceptions. Seeing oneself distinctly is the first step in self-determination, in stepping from the confines of ego into the liberation of comprehension. Paradoxically, from the complexity of self I move into the simplicity of universal being."

*   *   *

MacDONALD, Ruby (DeAngelo Norton) 1930-

PERSONAL: Born June 27, 1930, in Ontario, Calif.; daughter of Frank (a rancher) and Frances (a homemaker; maiden name, Marabella) De Angelo; married Thomas Wayne MacDonald (a commercial developer and builder), April 5, 1975; children: Tim Norton, Tobi Norton Petersen; (stepchildren) Shannon, Debbie, Mike. *Education:* Attended Clark College, Vancouver, Wash., Everett Community College, Edmonds Community College, Marylhurst College for Life-Long Learning, California Western University (now United States International University), and Eastern Oregon State College. *Politics:* Republican. *Religion:* Presbyterian.

ADDRESSES: Home—P.O. Box 2997, Vancouver, Wash. 98668. *Office*—Speakers and Writers, Ink, P.O. Box 1925, Lake Oswego, Ore. 97034. *Agent*—Sherry Robb, P.O. Box 727, Hollywood, Calif. 90028.

CAREER: Chaffey College, Alta Loma, Calif., secretary, 1949-51; Pacific Airmotive, Chino, Calif., secretary, 1951-54; homemaker and part-time stenographer, 1960-66; General Telephone Co., Everett, Wash., in public relations, 1969-75, administrative assistant, 1970-75; associated with Clark College, Vancouver, Wash., 1976-84; Speakers and Writers, Ink, Lake Oswego, Ore., founder and president, 1984—. Instructor at Warner Pacific College; member of Pacific Northwest Writers Conference; presents seminars and workshops; guest on television and radio programs; Yokefellow group leader and coordinator of Vancouver-Portland area, manager of first Southern California office.

MEMBER: Authors Guild, National Speakers Association, Oregon Association of Christian Writers, Pacific Northwest Writers, Willamette Writers Association.

AWARDS, HONORS: Writer of the Year award from Inspirational Division of Warner Pacific Writer's Conference, 1983, for *Rita McDonald's Forty Plus and Feeling Fabulous Book;* Angel Award for Excellence in Religion and Media from Religion in Media, 1983, for *Ruby MacDonald's Forty Plus and Feeling Fabulous Book.*

WRITINGS:

Ruby MacDonald's Forty Plus and Feeling Fabulous Book, Fleming Revell, 1982.

Contributor to magazines, including *Virtue, Woman, Today's Christian Woman, Moody Monthly, Aglow, Grit,* and *Catholic Digest.* Founder and publisher of newsletter *SWI NEWS.*

WORK IN PROGRESS: Work on a variety of subjects, including marriage, self-improvement through positive thinking, and women at midlife; a book of devotionals; a book on how to write nonfiction.

SIDELIGHTS: Ruby MacDonald told *CA:* "The greatest motivation in my career is the encouragement of my husband, children, critique group, and friends. Without those, I might have gone on to do other things when those rejection slips arrived. This is one business where a writer truly knows 'no person is an island.'

"I've always wanted to write and knew that I someday would. But it wasn't until I attended college as a midlife student that I found the encouragement I needed. Fortunately for me, my English 101 instructor was also a journalist/novelist and recognized my talent and desire to write. From there, I enrolled in one class after another, gathering all the information I needed to become a professional writer. It was two years before I presented my first book proposal to an editor at the Warner Pacific Christian Writer's Conference in Portland, Oregon.

"Mine is a Cinderella story. An editor from Fleming H. Revell liked my book idea, then titled 'Ageless Woman,' and felt sure his publishing house would go for it. Within a couple of weeks, my husband twirled me around as we celebrated the phone call which told me the contract was on the way. After six months of intense learning and writing to meet my deadline, I was off to New York City, where the red carpet was rolled out for me. Dinner at Sardi's, Broadway shows, and shopping was part of that exciting, never-to-be-forgotten trip.

"That was an unexpected plus. The reason I wrote *Ruby MacDonald's Forty Plus and Feeling Fabulous Book* was to share with women how to have a more positive self-image, to defeat the age barriers, and to know that all things are possible to those who believe, because we can be transformed by the renewing of our minds as we are told in Romans 12:2.

"I have published only nonfiction so far. However, I do have a romance novel started. Writing romances has helped to improve my writing skills because I've been forced to play with words. It's challenging to see what you can do with words to create a feeling or mood. And I like to use fiction techniques when writing nonfiction; it makes it more interesting for the reader. Someday I may write a complete novel, but right now, I have too many nonfiction books buzzing around inside my head.

"One of the things I enjoy about being a writer is the opportunity to help and inspire other writers. It's like giving back what people have given to me. Speakers and Writers, Ink, is an organization that was established to help both the aspiring and advanced writer and speaker to go forward. Remembering how difficult it was to learn what we needed as new writers, four of us writers-speakers (Sally Stuart, Patricia Rushford, Lauraine Snelling, and I) decided to form this group. After a year of step-by-step preparation, we incorporated in July, 1984. We hold conferences four times a year in Portland, Oregon, and are available to bring those conferences to any part of the United States."

*   *   *

MacLENNAN, Toby   1939-

PERSONAL: Born March 20, 1939, in Detroit, Mich.; daughter of Wiley (a designer) and Virginia Chapman. *Education:* University of Michigan, B.A., 1961; Wayne State University, B.F.A., 1965; School of the Art Institute of Chicago, M.F.A., 1969.

ADDRESSES: Home—185 Rushton Rd., Toronto, Ontario, Canada M6G 3J2. *Office*—Department of Fine Arts, York University, 4700 Keele St., Downsview, Ontario, Canada M3J 1P3.

CAREER: Faculty member with the department of fine arts at Wayne State University, Detroit, Mich., 1968, and at University of British Columbia, Vancouver, 1973-76; York University, Downsview, Ontario, professor of fine arts, 1976—. Member of faculty at Rutgers University, 1983-84.

AWARDS, HONORS: Canada Council grants, 1967-84.

WRITINGS:

One Walked Out of Two and Forgot It (novel), Something Else Press, 1971.
Singing the Stars, Coach House Press, 1982.

Also author of *The Shape of the Stone Was Stone-Shaped,* 1976.

SIDELIGHTS: Toby MacLennan told *CA:* "I am a multi-media performance artist. My writings are most often used in connection with live visual art performance pieces."

*   *   *

MacMASTER, Richard Kerwin   1935-

PERSONAL: Born February 4, 1935, in Flushing, N.Y.; son

of Frank Jarvis (a writer) and Josephine H.R. (Kerwin) MacMaster; married Eve Ruth Bowers (a writer of children's books), February 3, 1968; children: Samuel Albro, Thomas Jarvis, Sarah Rees. *Education:* Fordham University, A.B., 1958, M.A., 1962; Georgetown University, Ph.D., 1968.

ADDRESSES: Home—105 West College St., Bridgewater, Va. 22812. *Office*—Shendoah Valley Historical Institute, James Madison University, Harrisonburg, Va. 22807.

CAREER: Western Carolina University, Cullowhee, N.C., assistant professor of history, 1969-72; Montgomery County Bicentennial History Project, Rockville, Md., director, 1973-76; James Madison University, Harrisonburg, Va., associate professor of history, 1976—, director of Shenandoah Valley Historical Institute, 1981—.

MEMBER: Conference on Faith and History (vice-president, 1984—), American Society of Church History.

AWARDS, HONORS: Grant from National Endowment for the Humanities, 1984-85.

WRITINGS:

(With Pamela C. Copeland) *The Five George Masons: Patriots and Planters of Virginia and Maryland,* University Press of Virginia, 1975.
Christian Obedience in Revolutionary Times, Mennonite Central Committee, 1976.
A Grateful Remembrance: The Story of Montgomery County, Maryland, Mongomery County, 1976.
Conscience in Crisis: Peace Churches in America, 1739-1789, Herald Press, 1979.
Land, Piety, Peoplehood: The Establishment of Mennonite Communities in America, 1683-1790, Herald Press, 1984.
Augusta County, Virginia: 1865-1960, Augusta County Historical Society, 1985.
Hardy County, West Virginia: A Bicentennial History, Hardy County Bicentennial Commission, in press.

WORK IN PROGRESS: Cultural Pluralism in the Shenandoah Valley of Virginia, 1730-1819, publication expected in 1986; a book on Emily Hobhouse in South Africa, for Herald Press.

SIDELIGHTS: Richard Kerwin MacMaster told *CA:* "I have always been interested in the influence of ordinary people on the events of history. I've focused more and more in recent years on social history and community studies as a way of understanding this influence.

"*The Five George Masons* was the story of a typical Virginia planter family over five generations, more social history than biography. It attempted to show how the stage was set for the influential George Mason of Gunston Hall to argue successfully for individual liberty in the Virginia Declaration of Rights and the U.S. Bill of Rights. This book grew out of my study of eighteenth-century Virginia tobacco traders that also resulted in a number of articles in historical journals.

"The Montgomery County, Maryland, history and two more recent studies—of Augusta County, Virginia, and Hardy County, West Virginia—provided an apprenticeship in the new social history, as did an opportunity to study with Dr. Jack P. Greene at the Johns Hopkins University in 1982.

"Religious history has strongly appealed to me in part because the churches frequently reflected the concerns of ordinary people. I've published articles on black abolitionists, such as the Presbyterian leader Henry Highland Garnet, and on conscientious objectors to war. *Christian Obedience in Revolutionary Times* and *Conscience in Crisis* both deal with Mennonites, Quakers, Methodists, and others—those who were out of step when their neighbors took up arms without hesitation.

"*Land, Piety, and Peoplehood* is a study of Mennonite communities in Pennsylvania, Maryland, and the Shenandoah Valley of Virginia and their context in the rural townships where they lived and developed their churches and schools. My current study of the Shenandoah Valley study grew out of this effort to understand one religious community in its relation to its neighbors. I'm trying to see how many different groups interacted with one another in the context of a major channel for westward migration, our Shenandoah Valley."

MacMaster's other work-in-progress concerns Emily Hobhouse. He commented: "Emily Hobhouse described herself in a letter as a mere woman, middle-aged and somewhat dowdy. She succeeded in calling attention to the results of the first total war when the British devastated farms and herded women and children into deadly concentration camps during the South African War of 1899-1901. She went to South Africa on a self-appointed mission of reconciliation, bringing relief funds raised in England for war refugees. By her persistence and the searchlight of publicity she fixed on the appalling conditions in the camps, this very unimportant person forced the goverment to reverse its policy.

"Emily Hobhouse, George Mason of Gunston Hall, and the nearly nameless Quakers and Mennonites of eighteenth-century America are the sort of people who did extraordinary things. They were reluctant actors on the stage of history, who sought not personal power, but the power of truth.

"It may seem rather silly for someone who has written academic books of marginal interest to say that my major purpose in writing and in teaching is to encourage people to think for themselves. Like the old Roman rhetoricians I was exposed to as a schoolboy, I continue to find history a fertile source of examples to emulate."

*   *   *

MacNAMARA, Brinsley
See WELDON, John

*   *   *

MacNEICE, Jill   1956-

PERSONAL: Born January 14, 1956, in Bermuda. *Education:* Brown University, A.B., 1978.

ADDRESSES: Home—2153 California St. N.W., No. 309, Washington, D.C. 20008. *Office*—1333 H St. N.W., Suite 570, Washington, D.C. 20005.

CAREER: Associated with States News Service; Washington correspondent for Illinois newspapers, 1981-82; Washington telecommunications correspondent at Fairchild Publications, 1982—.

MEMBER: Washington Independent Writers, Phi Beta Kappa.

WRITINGS:

The Group House Handbook, Acropolis Books, 1982.

Washington correspondent for *Video Age,* 1983—.

MACRIDIS, Roy C(onstantine) 1918-

PERSONAL: Born December 25, 1918, in Constantinople, Ottoman Empire (now Istanbul, Turkey); came to the United States in 1941, naturalized citizen, 1943; married Jacklyn Williams, 1946. *Education:* Licentiate of University of Paris, 1940; Harvard University, M.A., 1943, Ph.D., 1947.

ADDRESSES: Home—653 Concord Ave., Belmont, Mass. 02178 *Office*—Department of Politics, Brandeis University, Waltham, Mass. 02254.

CAREER: Employed by U.S. Office of Strategic Services, Washington, D.C., 1943-45; Harvard University, Cambridge, Mass., instructor in government, 1946-49; Northwestern University, Evanston, Ill., assistant professor, 1949-52, associate professor of political science, 1952-56; Washington University, St. Louis, Mo., associate professor, 1958-59, professor of political science, 1961-62; Brandeis University, Waltham, Mass., 1970—, began as professor of politics, became Wien Professor of International Cooperation. University of Nanterre, Nanterre, France, Fulbright Professor of History, 1972-73; visiting lecturer in political science at the University of Paris; distinguished visiting professor at the University of Athens, Greece, 1979.

MEMBER: International Political Science Association, American Political Science Association, French Political Science Association.

AWARDS, HONORS: Rockefeller fellow, 1956, 1958, 1962; Rockefeller travel and research grants, 1958, 1961, and 1963; Fulbright fellow, 1958; L.H.D. from University of Clermont-Ferrand.

WRITINGS:

The Study of Comparative Government, Doubleday, 1955.
(Editor) *Foreign Policy in World Politics,* Prentice-Hall, 1958, 5th edition, 1976.
(With Bernard E. Brown) *The De Gaulle Republic: Quest for Unity,* Dorsey Press, 1960.
(Editor with Brown) *Comparative Politics: Notes and Readings,* Dorsey, 1961, 5th edition, 1977.
Modern Political Systems, Prentice-Hall, 1963, 5th edition published as *Modern Political Systems: Europe,* 1983.
(Editor) *De Gaulle: Implacable Ally,* Harper, 1966.
(Editor) *Political Parties: Contemporary Trends and Ideas,* Harper, 1967.
(Editor) *Modern European Governments: Cases in Comparative Policy Ranking,* Prentice-Hall, 1968.
(Editor, with James A. Bough) *Virgin Island, America's Caribbean Outpost: The Evolution of Self-Government,* W. F. Williams, 1970.
French Politics in Transition: The Years After De Gaulle, Winthrop Publishers, 1975.
Contemporary Political Ideologies: Movements and Regimes, Winthrop Publishers, 1980, 2nd edition, Little, Brown, 1982.
Whither Greek Socialism, Hoover Institution Press, 1984.
Modern Political Institutions, Little, Brown, 1984.
Greek Politics at a Crossroads: What Kind of Socialism, Hoover Institution Press, 1984.

Contributor of articles to periodicals, including *American Political Science Review, World Politics, Journal of Politics, Yale Review, Virginia Quarterly, Government and Opposition* (London), and *Revue francaise de science politique* (Paris).

SIDELIGHTS: Roy C. Macridis told *CA* that he strives "to explain political action and behavior through the analysis of conflict and leadership and the uses, and especially misuses, of political power. The constant search for freedom and justice brings recurrent disappointments for those who seek them, i.e., all of us!"

*   *   *

MADDEN, Myron C(rowson) 1918-

PERSONAL: Born February 19, 1918, in Fryeburg, La.; son of James A. (a farmer) and Anna (a homemaker; maiden name, Crowson) Madden; married Mary Ben Grey, June 3, 1942 (died June 13, 1981); married Ann Elizabeth Thomason (a housewife), May 21, 1983; children: Myron C., Jr., Julie Madden David, John, Benjamin, Merritt. *Education:* Louisiana State University, A.B., 1939; Southern Baptist Theological Seminary, Th.M., 1942, Ph.D., 1950. *Religion:* Baptist.

ADDRESSES: Home—823 Pine St., New Orleans, La. 70118.

CAREER: Ordained Southern Baptist minister, 1939; Friendship Baptist Church, Jonesville, Va., pastor, 1942-43; Kentucky State Hospital, Danville, chaplain, 1947-51; First Baptist Church, Richmond, Va., associate pastor, 1951-54; St. Charles Avenue Baptist Church, New Orleans, La., pastor, 1954-59; Baptist Hospital, New Orleans, director of pastoral care, 1960-83; Louisiana State University Medical Center, New Orleans, clinical professor of psychiatry, 1983—. *Military service:* U.S. Army, chaplain, 1943-46; received Bronze Star.

MEMBER: American Association of Pastoral Counselors (diplomate), College of Chaplains (fellow).

WRITINGS:

The Power to Bless, Abingdon, 1970.
Raise the Dead, Word, Inc., 1976.
(With wife, Mary Ben Madden) *The Time of Your Life,* Broadman, 1977.
(With M. B. Madden) *For Grandparents: Wonders and Worries,* Westminster, 1980.
Claim Your Heritage, Westminster, 1984.

Author of "Questions and Answers," a monthly column in *Home Life.*

WORK IN PROGRESS: "I am pondering the theme 'How to find out who I am.'"

SIDELIGHTS: Myron C. Madden told *CA:* "My first book, *The Power to Bless,* is my most unique contribution. It deals with family patterns of blessing or affirming or loving (empowering) children. The customary picture: Fathers tend to bless first daughters and second sons; mothers reverse this, blessing first sons and second daughters. If this pattern is altered or reversed, there is a big story or history behind the shift. In counseling families, the patterns of 'favoring' or blessing need to be dealt with. The place of the church is one of blessing the 'unblessed' children from the past. Usually the church is blind to what the needs are on this score.

"My pilgrimage has been to get beyond pretenses, beyond role and expectation. It has also been an attempt to challenge others on the same pilgrimage to be themselves, to come to self-awareness and self-acceptance. I have dealt chiefly with clergy, and now I'm involved with medical students. Many students are in medical school under the drive to 'do it for mother' (or father). So many believe they will earn a secure place in the affection of parents if they succeed. Blessing and genuine affirmation are never earned with either in family or otherwise. To be sure, there is an affirmation upon the successful person from parents and society. But most of us yearn for an acceptance based on our *being* rather than our *performing*.

"My last book, *Claim Your Heritage*, is a sort of sequel to *The Power to Bless*. In it I deal with the need to get beyond proving one's worth. As long as I am trying to prove, I am in some sense short of accepting who I am. The reason we need to prove ourselves tends to originate from our childhood need to overcome threat, disapproval, etc. These things cling to us like beggar lice until we defuse them by claiming all of our history, good and bad."

* * *

MADDEN, Peter 1939-

PERSONAL: Born October 14, 1939, in Toronto, Ontario, Canada; son of Gerald (a janitor) and Mary Alice (a homemaker; maiden name, Uequart) Madden; children: Sean, Ryan. *Education:* "I spent most years from age eleven through thirty-one in training schools, reformatories, and prisons." *Politics:* None. *Religion:* None.

ADDRESSES: Home—3125 A Brighton Ave., Montreal, Quebec, Canada H3S 1V1.

CAREER: Playwright and screenwriter.

MEMBER: Playwrights Canada, Playwrights' Workshop, Montreal Playreaders.

AWARDS, HONORS: Best screenplay awards from Canadian Film Awards and from Association of Canadian Television and Radio Artists (ACTRA), both 1976, both for "One Man."

WRITINGS:

PLAYS

"Criminal Record" (one-act), first produced at Collin's Bay Penitentiary, March, 1971.
"Takes Two to Make a Pair" (three-act), first produced at Centaur Theatre, Montreal, Quebec, June, 1975.
The Night No One Yelled (one-act; first produced at Playwrights' Workshop, Montreal, in 1975), Playwrights Co-Op, 1975.
"The Trial of the Rosenbergs" (three-act), first produced at Saidye Bronfman Centre, Montreal, March, 1978.

OTHER

"One Man" (screenplay; released for theatrical distribution, April 27, 1977).

Author of radio dramas, including "Not Even a Mouse" (first broadcast on Canadian Broadcasting Corp. [CBC]), December 5, 1981. Contributor of short stories and poetry to periodicals, including *Quarry, Fiddlehead,* and *Mainline.*

WORK IN PROGRESS: "Moravagine," a three-act play; "The Day the Fairy Princess Died," a three-act play; "When I Told Her That She Started to Laugh," an adaptation of "Quand j'y ai dit ca' a partie a rire," a Quebecois play by Leo Levesque.

SIDELIGHTS: Peter Madden told *CA:* "Part of the joy of writing—though it is not always joyous—is bringing characters to life, to public attention, that might otherwise live, if at all, only in obscurity. Writing offers the opportunity to ask

and sometimes answer questions that might not otherwise be either asked or answered, to free characters from their earthly bonds, refute absolutes, expose injustices, and ridicule the myth that all men are created equal."

* * *

MAILLET, Antonine 1929-

BRIEF ENTRY: Born May 10, 1929, in Bouctouche, New Brunswick, Canada. French-Canadian playwright, short story writer, and novelist. Maillet has earned wide critical acclaim for her works expressing the character, spirit, culture, and philosophy of the people of New Brunswick (Acadians). Writing in the Acadian vernacular, Maillet has also received praise for preserving the rich oral traditions of her ancestry. The play *La Sagouine* (Lemeac, 1973; first produced in 1971), originally a sixteen-part radio series, was Maillet's first major success; it was adapted for television in the late 1970's. Maillet's novel *Don l'Orignal* (Lemeac, 1972; translation published as *The Tale of Don L'Orignal,* Clarke, Irwin, 1978) won a Governor General's Award, and her novel *Pelagie-la-Charrette* (Lemeac, 1979; translation published as *Pelagie: The Return to a Homeland,* Doubleday, 1982) gained Maillet recognition in 1979 as the first non-European to win France's coveted Prix Goncourt. Her novels *Mariaagelas* (Lemeac, 1973) and *Les Cordes-de-Bois* (Lemeac, 1977) have also been Prix Goncourt contenders. *Address:* 735 Antonine Maillet Ave., Montreal, Quebec, Canada H2V 2Y4; and c/o Mercedes Palomino, 355 Gilford St., Montreal, Quebec, Canada H2T 1M6.

BIOGRAPHICAL/CRITICAL SOURCES:

BOOKS

Canada's Playwrights: A Biographical Guide, CTR Press, 1980.
Supplement to the Oxford Companion to Canadian History and Literature, Oxford University Press, 1973.

PERIODICALS

Times Literary Supplement, December 3, 1982.
Washington Post Book World, March 28, 1982.

* * *

MALINO, Frances 1940-

PERSONAL: Born March 6, 1940, in Danbury, Conn.; daughter of Jerome R. (a rabbi) and Rhoda (a teacher; maiden name, Simon) Malino; married Robert J. Hoffman, August 28, 1960 (divorced, 1971); married Eugene Charlton Black (a professor and author) March 26, 1983; children: Daniel, Elizabeth. *Education:* Skidmore College, B.A., 1961; Brandeis University, M.A., 1963; Ph.D., 1971. *Religion:* Jewish.

ADDRESSES: Home—63 Nehoiden Rd., Waban, Mass. 02168. *Office*—Department of History, University of Massachusetts, Harbor Campus, Boston, Mass. 02125.

CAREER: University of Massachusetts, Harbor Campus, Boston, assistant professor, 1970-76, associate professor, 1976-83, professor of Near Eastern, French, and Jewish history, 1983—. Brandeis University, visiting professor, 1971, fellow at Tauber Institute and director of Conference on the Jews of Modern France, 1983; visiting professor at Yale University, 1974; fellow at Mary Ingraham Bunting Institute, Radcliffe College, 1979-80. Member of Commission Francaise des Archives Juives; member of history prize committee for Jewish Book Awards, 1982-84.

MEMBER: American Historical Association, Association for Jewish Studies, Society for French Historical Studies, Middle East Studies Association.

AWARDS, HONORS: Fellow of National Foundation for Jewish Culture, 1967-68; Fullbright fellow, 1968-69; Lown fellow of Brandeis University, 1970-71; Fellow of American Council of Learned Societies 1979-80; grants from American Philosophical Society, 1978; and American Council of Learned Societies, 1979-80.

WRITINGS:

The Sephardic Jews of Bordeaux: Assimilation and Emancipation in Revolutionary and Napoleonic France, University of Alabama Press, 1978.
(Editor with Phyllis Cohen Albert, and contributor) *Essays in Modern Jewish History: A Tribute to Ben Halpern,* Fairleigh Dickinson University Press, 1983.
(Editor with Bernard Wasserstein) *The Jews in Modern France,* University Press of New England, 1984.
The Jews and the Parlement of Metz, Privat, 1985.

CONTRIBUTOR

Michael IV, Diaspora Research Institute (Tel Aviv, Israel), 1976.
Jehuda Reinharz and Daniel Swetschinski, editors, *Essays in Jewish Intellectual History in Honor of Alexander Altmann,* Duke University Press, 1982.
Michael A. Meyer, editor, *World History of the Jewish People,* Jewish History Publications of Israel, 1984.
Gilbert Dahan, editor, *Les Juifs devant l'histoire: Melanges en l'honneur de Bernhard Blumenkranz,* Privat, 1985.

Contributor to *Dictionary of Napoleonic France.* Contributor to history journals.

WORK IN PROGRESS: Women, Autonomy, and Authority in Eighteenth-Century Metz, publication expected in 1986; *Autonomy and Citizenship in Eighteenth-Century France,* publication by State University Press of New York expected in 1987; a biography of Zalkind Hourwitz.

BIOGRAPHICAL/CRITICAL SOURCES:

PERIODICALS

American Historical Review, February, 1979.

*   *   *

MALLONE, George 1944-

PERSONAL: Born November 28, 1944, in Dallas, Tex.; son of George H., Jr., and Lexie (Ray) Mallone; married Bonnie Burns (a Christian Fellowship worker), July 28, 1968; children: Eryn Faye, Scott, Meredyth Lynn. *Education:* East Texas State University, B.Sc., 1968; Regent College, Diploma in Christian Studies, 1973, M.C.S., 1974.

ADDRESSES: Home—7325 MacPherson Ave., Burnaby, British Columbia, Canada V5J 4N8.

CAREER: InterVarsity Christian Fellowship, Houston, Tex., campus chaplain, 1968-71; teaching elder at Christian chapel in Vancouver, British Columbia, 1972-82; Burnaby Christian Fellowship, Vancouver, pastor, 1983—. Sessional lecturer at Regent College, Vancouver, 1981—.

WRITINGS:

Furnace of Renewal: A Vision for the Church, Inter-Varsity Press, 1982.

Those Controversial Gifts, Inter-Varsity Press, 1983.
Canadian Revival: It's Our Turn!, G. R. Welch, 1984.

Contributor to journals.

WORK IN PROGRESS: Division: The Great Scandal of the Church, for Multnomah Press.

SIDELIGHTS: George Mallone told *CA:* "The perspective that most North Americans have on the church is weak and tarnished compared to the picture given in the New Testament. I was motivated to begin writing out of a great concern for the renewal of the established church, and thus far all my books have dealt with the central theme of renewal.

"*Those Controversial Gifts* speaks on such subjects as dreams, visions, prophetic words, and healing. Many churches believe that these gifts, which were recognized in the New Testament, are no longer to be practiced in the church. I have attempted some sane and sensible solutions, with certain safeguards, for the re-emergence of those gifts into the church.

"My most recent publication is *Canadian Revival: It's Our Turn.* Canada has never had a coast-to-coast religious awakening as in the United States and concern about it led me to write a specific word to the Canadian church regarding its own culture, history, and religious hinderances.

"*Division: The Great Scandal of the Church,* my work in progress, addresses the fact that the church is divided (there are more than three thousand denominations) and needs to be united in order to have an impact on the society in which we live."

*   *   *

MALTZ, Albert 1908-1985

OBITUARY NOTICE—See index for *CA* sketch: Born October 28, 1908, in Brooklyn, N.Y.; died April 26, 1985, in Los Angeles, Calif. Novelist, playwright, short story writer, and screenwriter. Maltz is best remembered as one of the Hollywood Ten—the group of Hollywood writers who refused to respond to House Un-American Activities Committee queries about whether they were Communists. Prior to his indictment and subsequent blacklisting, which curtailed his writing for approximately twenty years, Maltz had written a number of memorable works in a variety of genres. He earned a name for himself as a protest writer during the 1930's with his short stories "The Way Things Are," "Season of Celebration," and "Man on a Road," which some critics believe exemplify his best work. In addition, his tale "The Happiest Man on Earth" won an O. Henry Memorial Award as the best short story in 1938. Most notable, perhaps, were his popular screenplays produced during the 1940's. His credits include "This Gun for Hire," "Destination Tokyo," and "The House I Live In," which earned him a special Academy Award in 1945. Maltz also wrote Broadway plays, radio plays, and novels. Many of the latter are political in nature, and they include *The Underground Stream,* the best-seller *The Cross and the Arrow,* and his last work, *Bel Canto,* which is set in France during World War II.

OBITUARIES AND OTHER SOURCES:

BOOKS

Contemporary Dramatists, 3rd edition, St. Martin's, 1982.
Contemporary Novelists, 3rd edition, St. Martin's, 1982.
Current Biography, Wilson, 1940.

The Oxford Companion to American Literature, 4th edition, Oxford University Press, 1966.

PERIODICALS

Chicago Tribune, April 30, 1985.
Detroit Free Press, April 29, 1985.
Los Angeles Times, April 28, 1985.
Newsweek, May 13, 1985.
New York Times, April 29, 1985.
Time, May 13, 1985.
Washington Post, April 29, 1985.

*   *   *

MALVERN, Corinne   1905-1956

BRIEF ENTRY: Born in 1905; died November 9, 1956, in Weston, Conn. Artist, illustrator, and author. An artist who held one-woman shows of her work, Corinne Malvern was also known for collaborating with her sister, Gladys Malvern, on a number of children's books. The sisters, children of stage-performing parents, grew up in the milieu of hotels, boarding houses, and trains on the theatre circuit, eventually becoming actresses themselves. Corinne was first to leave the theatre and subsequently began studying at the Art Students League in New York City. Later, after moving to Los Angeles, she worked as an artist in fashion advertising by day while continuing to study art at night. When Gladys gave up the theatre and began to write, the two sisters pooled their talents and as a team published numerous books for children. Their co-authored books, which were illustrated by Corinne, include *Land of Surprise* (1939) and *The Story Book of Brownie and Rusty* (1940). Corinne also illustrated books written solely by Gladys, including *Valiant Minstrel: The Story of Sir Harry Lauder* (a 1943 Julia Ellsworth Ford Prize winner) and *Foreigner: The Story of a Girl Named Ruth* (a 1954 Junior Literary Guild selection). Among the many other books Corinne illustrated are Johanna Spyri's *Heidi: A Story for Children* (1954) and Clement Clark Moore's *Night Before Christmas* (1960).

BIOGRAPHICAL/CRITICAL SOURCES:

BOOKS

Illustrators of Books for Young People, 2nd edition, Scarecrow, 1975.
Junior Book of Authors, 2nd revised edition, Wilson, 1951.

PERIODICALS

New York Times, November 10, 1956.

*   *   *

MAN, Felix H.
See BAUMANN, Hans Felix S(iegismund)

*   *   *

MANDELL, Fran Gare   1939-
(Fran Gare)

PERSONAL: Born December 5, 1939, in Jersey City, N.J.; daughter of David A. and Henrietta (Rich) Rhein; married Ivan D. Gare, January 19, 1963 (divorced April, 1972); married Marshall Mandell (a physician and writer), October 21, 1979; children: (first marriage) David, Marc. *Education:* Fairleigh Dickinson University, B.A., 1963, M.A., 1965; New York School of Interior Design, Certificate, 1966; Braintridge

Forest School, Naturopathic Dr., 1977; University of Bridgeport, M.S., 1980. *Religion:* Jewish.

ADDRESSES: *Home*—180 Steephill Rd., Weston, Conn. 06883. *Agent*—Connie Clausen Associates, 250 East 87th St., New York, N.Y. 10028. *Office*—3A Brush St., Norwalk, Conn. 06850.

CAREER: Writer. Formerly associated with Fran Gare Interiors, Tenafly, N.J.; Wynken, Blynken & Nod, Englewood, N.J., owner, 1967-70; Nutri-Plan, Inc., New York, N.Y., president, 1975-80; Basket Magic, Inc., Westport, Conn., president, 1980-84; past president of MarFran Publications, Inc. (now Gare, Inc.).

MEMBER: Association of Food Technologists, American Society of Journalists and Authors, New York Academy of Sciences, Atrium Club.

WRITINGS:

UNDER NAME FRAN GARE

(With Robert Atkins and Helen Monica) *Dr. Atkins Diet Revolution: The High Calorie Way to Stay Thin Forever*, McKay, 1972.
(With Atkins), *Dr. Atkins Diet Cook Book*, Crown, 1974.
(With Monica; introduction by Atkins), *The Super Energy Diet Cook Book*, New American Library, 1978.

OTHER

(With husband, Marshall Mandell and Jill Bomser) *Dr. Mandell's Allergy Cookbook*, Pocket Books, 1980.
(With Marshall Mandell) *The Nutrition Cookbook*, Morrow, 1982.
(With Marshall Mandell) *The Mandells' It's Not Your Fault You're Fat Diet*, Harper, 1983.

Also author, with Alan Pressman, of *A Complete Guide to Chiropractic*, 1981. Contributor to magazines.

WORK IN PROGRESS: A book with Patricia Hayes titled *Sex on Saturday Night; Health Signs*, with Frederick Daves.

*   *   *

MANHEIM, Ralph   1907(?)-

BRIEF ENTRY: Born c. 1907 in New York, N.Y. Translator. Regarded as the doyen of professional translators, Manheim has more than one hundred books to his credit. His highly praised translations, which are said to constitute a veritable library of European classics, include works by such renowned thinkers as Johann Jakob Bachofen, Sigmund Freud, Carl Gustav Jung, Wilhelm Reich, Karl Jaspers, Ernst Cassirer, Martin Heidegger, and Erich Auerbach. He also translated fiction by E.T.A. Hoffmann, Hermann Hesse, Hermann Broch, Bertolt Brecht, Erich Maria Remarque, Marcel Proust, Michel Tournier, Emile Ajar, Slawomir Mrozek, and other celebrated writers. Although he is best known for his translations of German and French works, Manheim has also published translations from other languages, including Dutch and Polish.

In 1983 Manheim received the coveted MacArthur Foundation Award—$60,000 a year for life—in recognition of his outstanding contribution to literature. He is also the laureate of several other important prizes, including the 1964 P.E.N. Translation Prize for his translation of Guenter Grass's book *The Tin Drum* (Secker & Warburg, 1962), the 1966 Schlegel-Tieck Translation Prize for his translation of Grass's *Dog Years*

(Harcourt, 1965), the National Book Award for his translation of Louis-Ferdinand Celine's *Castle to Castle* (Blond, 1969), and the 1976 Goethe House-P.E.N. Translation Prize for his translation of Peter Handke's work *A Sorrow Beyond Dreams: A Life Story* (Farrar, Straus, 1975). Manheim also translated *The Neverending Story* (Doubleday, 1983), Michael Ende's best-selling fantasy epic that was adapted for the screen. *Address:* Paris, France.

BIOGRAPHICAL/CRITICAL SOURCES:

PERIODICALS

Chicago Tribune Book World, February 2, 1984.
New York Times, July 12, 1984.
New York Times Book Review, March 14, 1982.
Time, November 19, 1984.
Times Literary Supplement, February 17, 1984.

* * *

MANNING, Marsha
   See GRIMSTEAD, Hettie

* * *

MARCOVICH, Miroslav   1919-
   (Miroslav Markovic)

PERSONAL: Birth-given name, Miroslav Markovic; born March 18, 1919, in Belgrade, Yugoslavia; immigrated to United States, 1969, naturalized citizen, 1979; son of Svetozar and Mila (Sakic) Markovic; married Verica Tosic, May 30, 1948; children: Dragoslav. *Education:* University of Belgrade, B.A., 1942.

ADDRESSES: Home—2509 Cottage Grove St., Urbana, Ill. 61801. *Office*—Department of Classics, 4072 F.L.B., University of Illinois at Urbana-Champaign, Urbana, Ill. 61801.

CAREER: University of Belgrade, Belgrade, Yugoslavia, lecturer in classics and Byzantine studies, 1946-54; Universidad de los Andes, Merida, Venezuela, professor of classics, 1955-69; University of Illinois at Urbana-Champaign, Urbana, George A. Miller Visiting Professor of classics and philosophy, 1969-70, chairman of department, 1973-77, associate member of Center for Advanced Study, 1978. Visiting scholar at Visva-Barati University, 1954-55, and at University of Bonn, 1962-63. Paddison Visiting Professor at University of North Carolina at Chapel Hill, 1975; visiting professor at University of Michigan, 1979-80, and at Trinity College, Dublin, Ireland, 1984. Member of advisory committee for *Thesaurus Linguae Graecae,* 1973-81.

MEMBER: American Philological Association, Phi Kappa Phi.

AWARDS, HONORS: Premio Sesquicentenario Gold Medals from government of Venezuela, 1962 and 1964; Silver Cross from Mount Athos, Greece, 1963, for work on Greek manuscripts; distinguished scholarship award from University of Illinois, 1973; John Simon Guggenheim fellowship, 1981 and 1984.

WRITINGS:

Byzantinische Urkunden im Staatsarchiv Ragusa (title means "Byzantine Documents in the State Archives of Dubrovnik"), Serbian Academy of Sciences, 1952.
(Editor and author of introduction) Marcus Marulus, *M. Maruli Davidiadis libri XIV* (title means "The Davidiad in Fourteen Books by Marcus Marulus"), Universidad de los Andes, 1957.

(Editor, commentator, and author of introduction) Franjo Bozicevic-Natalis, *Carmina* (title means "Songs"), Serbian Academy of Sciences, 1958.
(Editor and translator from Sanskrit into Spanish) *El Canto del Senor,* Universidad de los Andes, 1958 (original language edition published as *Mahabharata: Bhagavadgita*).
Estudios de filosofia griega (title means "Studies in Greek Philosophy"), Universidad de los Andes, 1965.
(Editor, translator, and author of introduction) *Heraclitus: Greek Text With a Short Commentary,* Universidad de los Andes, 1967.
Filozofija Heraklita mracnog (title means "The Philosophy of Heraclitus the Obscure"), Nolit (Belgrade), 1983.
Three-Word Trimeter in Greek Tragedy, Anton Hain, 1984.
(Editor) Hippolytus, *Refutatio omnium haeresium* (title means "A Refutation of All Heresies"), Walter de Gruyter, 1984.
(Editor) Diogenes Laertius, *Vitae philosophorum* (title means "Lives of Philosophers"), Teubner, 1985.
Athenagoras, Walter de Gruyter, 1985.
Theophilus of Antioch, Walter de Gruyter, 1985.

Founder and editor of *Illinois Classical Studies,* 1975—. Contributor to *Paulys Realencyklopaedie der Classischen Altertumswissenschaft.* Contributor to numerous scholarly journals, including *Gnomon, Classical World, Classical Philology, American Journal of Philology, Journal of Theological Studies, Hermes,* and *Mnemosyne.*

SIDELIGHTS: Known as an authority on the pre-Socratic philosopher Heraclitus, Miroslav Marcovich has contributed to various fields of Greek and Latin scholarship, including Greek, Roman, and Byzantine literature and philosophy, Renaissance literature, palaeography—the study of ancient texts and inscriptions, and patristics—the study of the writings of the church fathers. Prominent among Marcovich's early accomplishments is an edition, based on a manuscript found in the National Library of Turin, Italy, of *The Davidiad,* a Latin epic poem by the Croatian poet Marko Marulic, also known by his Latin name Marcus Marulus, who lived from 1450 to 1524. Marulic's intention, Marcovich explains in his introduction to the poem, was to present the ancient Hebrew king David as an example of an ideal Christian. Identifying the profound religiosity evinced by *The Davidiad* as Marulic's most important characteristic, Marcovich described the poem as an original work, and not an imitation of the great Latin classics. Marcovich also edited a volume of Latin *Songs* by Marulic's biographer Franjo Bozicevic-Natalis, who wrote in the first half of the sixteenth century. In 1958, during his tenure as professor of classics at Universidad de los Andes, Marcovich published a Spanish translation of *Bhagavad-Gita,* the classical religious poem from the Sanskrit epic *Mahabharata.* Wishing to make *Bhagavad-Gita* accessible to readers in his native Yugoslavia, Marcovich also published a Serbo-Croatian version of the poem.

In 1967 Marcovich published *Heraclitus: Greek Text With a Short Commentary,* which was immediately hailed as a major work of Heraclitus scholarship. Heraclitus identified fire as the fundamental cosmic element and taught that the world is a flux controlled by logos, or reason. The philosopher's writings, which many scholars have considered enigmatic, survive in fragments and are subject to numerous interpretations, sometimes contradictory. Marcovich, affirmed H. von Staden in the *American Journal of Philology,* succeeds in establishing "that Heraclitus' doctrines were reported, misinterpreted, and, especially, vaguely echoed by more authors from classical antiquity to the early Renaissance than most scholars knew."According to von Staden, "Marcovich's discerning knowledge of a mob of more than two hundred modern interpreters is astounding and admirable." The scholar, von Staden declared, "has left few Heraclitean stones untouched; even duplicate and triplicate pebbles washed on to Byzantine and Renaissance shores were raked together assiduously." In addition, remarked G. B. Kerferd in the *Classical Review,* "Marcovich has much to say that is important and novel." For example, when discussing "the actual process of transformation," during which, according to Heraclitus, all things change into fire and vice versa, Marcovich focuses on processes "described to be those that occur regularly every day, such as the daily ignition of the heavenly bodies, the ebb and tide of the sea in relation to the earth . . . and so on." Kerferd revealed that "the special feature" of Marcovich's analysis is his insight that Heraclitus's "basic divine fire is extra-cosmic, and that within the cosmos we have a movement between three actors only, earth, sea," and sky-fire.

"The publication of this volume," wrote Kerferd about *Heraclitus: Greek Text With a Short Commentary,* "is an important contribution to the study of Heraclitus, and it will be valuable to all future students from at least three points of view, as a tool of research and a collection of materials facilitating further investigations, as a presentation of texts revised at a number of important points, and for its record of discussions of the interpretation of individual fragments and of Heraclitus as a whole." Kerferd opined that Marovich's edition of Heraclitus "is the most important since G. S. Kirk's *Heraclitus, the Cosmic Fragments* published in 1954 and should undoubtedly find its place in all classical libraries."

In his *Knjizevna rec* review of Marcovich's 1983 book on Heraclitus, Nikolaj Timcenko praised the author for revealing the Greek philosopher as a poet and the founder of the tradition of philosophical poetry in European literary history. In Timcenko's view, the author opposed earlier commentators by demonstrating that Heraclitus's teaching is not a rigid philosophical system. Emphasizing the importance of this particular insight, Timcenko summed up Marcovich's book as a significant contribution to readers' understanding of Heraclitus.

BIOGRAPHICAL/CRITICAL SOURCES:

PERIODICALS

American Journal of Philology, October, 1972.
Classical Review, December, 1970.
Gnomon, Volume 42, 1970.
Knjizevna rec (Belgrade), May 10, 1984.
Library Journal, March 15, 1976.
Phronesis, Volume XI, number 1, 1966.

*   *   *

MARINE, Nick
   See OURSLER, Will(iam Charles)

*   *   *

MARKOVIC, Miroslav
   See MARCOVICH, Miroslav

*   *   *

MARKS, Bayly Ellen   1943-

PERSONAL: Born July 31, 1943, in Baltimore, Md.; daughter of J. Sinclair (a certified public accountant) and Lillian Bayly

(a genealogist; maiden name, Johnson) Marks. *Education:* Randolph-Macon Woman's College, A.B., 1965; University of Virginia, M.A., 1967; University of Maryland at College Park, Ph.D., 1979.

ADDRESSES: Office—Department of History, Catonsville Community College, 800 South Rolling Rd., Catonsville, Md. 21228.

CAREER: Maryland Historical Society, Baltimore, curator of manuscripts, 1967-69; Catonsville Community College, Catonsville, Md., instructor, 1969-83, professor of American history, 1983—. Past vice-chairman of Baltimore County Landmarks Preservation Commission.

WRITINGS:

(Editor with Mark Norton Schatz) *Between North and South: A Maryland Journalist Views the Civil War; The Narrative of William Wilkins Glenn, 1861-1869,* Fairleigh Dickinson University Press, 1976.

Contributor to history journals.

SIDELIGHTS: Bayly Ellen Marks told *CA:* "William Wilkins Glenn's family owned the estate on which Catonsville Community College is located. As I was researching the history of the estate, Mark Schatz was also researching Glenn and had uncovered Glenn's journal at the Maryland Historical Society. We naturally joined forces. Schatz did the transcription and provided detailed knowledge of the Civil War, while I researched the footnotes and the glossary.

"Glenn, a Maryland editor and publisher from an influential family, was in a rare position as border state observer of the inner workings of the Confederacy and of Confederate sympathizers. More importantly, he was a link between the British and the South, smuggling Englishmen into the South.

"My current research centers on the study of an antebellum staple crop system, specifically the one in St. Mary's County, Maryland, between 1790 and 1864. I am interested in what happens when a community attempts to diversify agriculturally, in urban domination of rural areas, migration in and out of these areas, and attempts at occupational diversification. Also, the past fascinates me—how people lived, their values, what they accomplished with their lives. My research is with the 'little' people—not the great or famous—but the friends, neighbors, and even outcasts of communities one hundred or more years in the past."

*   *   *

MARSHALL, George C(atlett), Jr.   1880-1959

BRIEF ENTRY: Born December 31, 1880, in Uniontown, Pa.; died from complications following two strokes, October 16, 1959, at Walter Reed Hospital in Washington, D.C.; buried in Arlington National Cemetery. American military leader, statesman, and author of *Selected Speeches and Statements of General of the Army George C. Marshall* (1945). Marshall is best remembered as principal designer of the post-World War II European recovery program known as the Marshall Plan, which he devised while serving as secretary of state under President Harry S. Truman. Before entering the diplomatic service, however, Marshall was a military career man, serving the U.S. Armed Forces both at home and abroad for nearly fifty years. His most notable wartime post was his command as U.S. Army chief of staff during World War II. In that capacity he directed American military strategy and became instrumental in determining victory for the Allied forces; he was considered a military genius for his ability to organize and direct military operations.

Resigning as chief of staff in 1945, Marshall became secretary of state in 1947 and secretary of defense in 1950. In addition to the Marshall Plan, the soldier was associated with establishing the North Atlantic Treaty Organization (NATO) and the Western Hemisphere Defense Pact. In addition, he helped secure U.S. membership in the World Health Organization as well as amicable diplomatic relations between the United States and several other countries. In 1953 Marshall was honored with a Nobel Peace Prize for devising the Marshall Plan.

BIOGRAPHICAL/CRITICAL SOURCES:

BOOKS

Current Biography, Wilson, 1940, December, 1959.
McGraw-Hill Encyclopedia of World Biography, McGraw, 1973.
National Cyclopaedia of American Biography, Volume 45, James T. White, 1962.
Pogue, Forrest C., *George C. Marshall*, Viking, Volume I: *Education of a General, 1880-1939*, 1963, Volume II: *Ordeal and Hope, 1939-1942*, 1966, Volume III: *Organizer of Victory, 1943-1945*, 1973.

PERIODICALS

New York Times, October 17, 1959.

*   *   *

MARSHALL, Raymond
See RAYMOND, Rene (Brabazon)

*   *   *

MARSHALL, Thomas R.   1949-

PERSONAL: Born September 2, 1949, in La Crosse, Wis. *Education:* Miami University, Oxford, Ohio, B.A., 1971; University of Minnesota, Ph.D., 1976.

ADDRESSES: Office—Department of Political Science, University of Texas at Arlington, Arlington, Tex. 76019.

CAREER: University of Texas at Arlington, assistant professor, 1976-81, associate professor of political science, 1981—. Legal consultant.

MEMBER: American Political Science Association, Midwest Political Science Association.

WRITINGS:

Presidential Nominations in a Reform Age, Praeger, 1981.

WORK IN PROGRESS: Research on public opinion and presidential elections.

*   *   *

MARTIN, Andrew   1906-1985
(Notarius)

OBITUARY NOTICE: Born April 21, 1906, in Budapest, Austria-Hungary (now Hungary); died February 27, 1985. Attorney, educator, broadcaster, and author. In 1937 Martin left an established international law practice in his native Hungary to read for the British Bar, becoming a barrister in 1940 and a judge in 1976. An expert in international commercial arbi-

tration, he taught for six years at Oxford University before joining, in 1954, the faculty of law at the University of Southampton, where from 1963 until retiring in 1977 Martin held a part-time chair in international and comparative law. He was a member of Amnesty International, of the Executive Committee of the United Nations Association, and of the British branch of the International Commission of Jurists.

During World War II Martin interrupted his legal career to work for the British Broadcasting Corporation, serving variously as editor, scriptwriter, and, under the pseudonym "Notarius," broadcaster of a weekly Hungarian-language political commentary. For two decades following the war Martin continued the commentary as "Andrew Martin's Column." He contributed articles to journals and co-edited the 1963 book *Law Reform Now* and its 1983 successor, *More Law Reform Now*.

OBITUARIES AND OTHER SOURCES:

BOOKS

Who's Who, 136th edition, St. Martin's, 1984.

PERIODICALS

Times (London), March 2, 1985.

*   *   *

MARTIN, Frederick M(orris)   1923-1985

OBITUARY NOTICE: Born October 2, 1923, in London, England; died February 1, 1985. Social scientist, educator, and author. Professionally concerned with social policy questions, Martin began teaching at the London School of Economics and Political Science in 1949, then in 1952 joined the research staff of the London School of Hygiene and Tropical Medicine. For ten years, beginning in 1956, he served on the faculty of the University of Edinburgh's department of social medicine, then spent five years working in various capacities on the Greater London Council. Returning to Scotland in 1972, Martin joined the faculty of the University of Glasgow, where he served as professor of social administration and social work, and, from 1976 to 1978, as dean of the newly created faculty of social sciences. Acting on his convictions about the importance of the social sciences to the practice of medicine and to the evaluation of social policy, Martin investigated Britain's 1959 Mental Health Act and subsequently co-authored both the 1968 book *Patterns of Performance in Community Care* and the 1972 work *Plans and Provisions for the Mentally Handicapped*. Another volume co-authored by Martin, the 1956 study *Social Class and Educational Opportunity*, is considered to be a requisite text for students of the social sciences. *Between the Acts*, Martin's analysis of recent trends in caring for the mentally ill, was published in 1984.

OBITUARIES AND OTHER SOURCES:

BOOKS

Who's Who, 136th edition, St. Martin's, 1984.

PERIODICALS

Times (London), February 12, 1985.

*   *   *

MARTIN, Jack
See ETCHISON, Dennis (William)

MARTIN, Maurice 1946-

PERSONAL: Given name is pronounced *Mor*-ris; born January 9, 1946, in Waterloo, Ontario, Canada; son of Abraham Sauder (a farmer) and Ellen (a homemaker; maiden name, Bauman) Martin; married Phyllis Audrey Mae Shantz (a laboratory technician and homemaker), August 27, 1968; children: Benjamin Luke, Joelle Amy. *Education:* University of Waterloo, B.A., 1968; Goshen Biblical Seminary, M.Div., 1974.

ADDRESSES: Home and office—125 Second Ave. S.W., Box 218, Chesley, Ontario, Canada N0G 1L0.

CAREER: Ordained Mennonite minister, 1982; Hill Park Secondary School, Hamilton, Ontario, teacher of English, 1968-71; pastor of Mennonite churches in Elmira, Ontario, 1974-76, and Markham, Ontario, 1976-82; Hanover-Chesley Mennonite Fellowship, Chesley, Ontario, pastor, 1982—.

MEMBER: Canadian Association for Pastoral Education.

WRITINGS:

Identity and Faith: Youth in a Believers' Church, Herald Press, 1981.
(With Helen E. Reusser) *In the Midst of the Congregation: Nurture for Christian Commitment,* Mennonite Publishing House, 1983.

Author of church school curriculum material and contributor to *Conrad Grebel Review.*

WORK IN PROGRESS: Editing *Ontario Portrait,* a pictorial essay of two hundred years of Mennonite presence in Ontario, publication expected in 1986.

SIDELIGHTS: Maurice Martin told *CA:* "*Identity and Faith,* though written in a fairly technical manner, really grew out of my personal experience of faith and life, my growth to maturity, and theological reflections based on my experience and studies. From my clinical pastoral education studies I had come to terms with the psychological and emotional foundations of who I am. Subsequently in my seminary studies I attempted to integrate the 'language of feelings' with the language of belief and faith. This resulted ultimately in *Identity and Faith.*

"*In the Midst of the Congregation* is in many respects a sequel, an attempt to write in a more popular and practical style. It is a type of handbook for congregational educators and others interested in the faith development of children and youth.

"I find the analogy of the family useful in describing the place of youth in the Mennonite church. Children born into families feel very much that they belong. They are nurtured to maturity and learn to take a place of increasing responsibility and autonomy in family and society. They learn to make decisions about life and faith. Mennonite youth are encouraged to make commitments concerning the Lordship of Christ in their lives. As they do this, they are invited to receive baptism and become church members. As Vernard Eller stated so well: 'Children of the church are in a camel caravan. They are part of the caravan, going in the same direction. And some day they will choose to steer their own camels.'

"Congregational educators need to be aware of the ages and stages of development of children and youth and then nurture accordingly. The faith expressions and understanding of a five-year-old, a fifteen-year-old, and a twenty-five-year-old are quite distinct from one another. And individual needs vary from person to person. Only as you recognize these individual stages of change and growth can you help youth develop 'real faith for a real world.'

"It is true of faith—as in many other areas of development—that much more is 'caught' than 'taught.' If our faith is real and relevant, near and dear to us, it will become so to our youth as well. And above all, one should not be afraid of the hard questions youth often ask. These are not signs of doubt; they are stepping-stones to mature faith."

*   *   *

MARTINEZ SIERRA, Gregorio 1881-1947

BRIEF ENTRY: Born May 6, 1881, in Madrid, Spain; died of cancer, October 1, 1947, in Madrid. Spanish theatrical producer, editor, translator, poet, critic, and playwright. Martinez Sierra is among the contemporary Spanish theatre's most important figures. His first writings were in poetry and criticism, but he turned to playwriting in the 1900's and subsequently collaborated on numerous works with his wife, Maria. Although Gregorio is listed as sole author of their plays—at his wife's request—critics now believe that his primary service was as editor and that Maria was responsible for most of the actual writing. Several of their plays feature proto-feminists—bright, independent women who champion equality—and advocate basic Christian values while confirming the virtues of piety. Their collaborations include *Cancion de cuna* (1910; translated as *The Cradle Song,* 1917)—probably their most popular work—about a foundling left at a Catholic orphanage, *El reino de Dios* (1915; translated as *The Kingdom of God,* 1922), and *Don Juan de Espana* (1921).

Martinez Sierra also founded and directed the Compania Lirico Dramatica, once Spain's most important and innovative theatrical company. For this company he translated more than fifty works, including Henrik Ibsen's *A Doll's House.* Martinez Sierra's other writings include the verse collection *Flores de escarcha* (1900), the novel *Tu eres la paz* (1907; translated as *Ana Maria,* 1921), and the autobiographical *Un teatro de arteen Espana* (1926), which recounts the author's experiences in the theatre.

BIOGRAPHICAL/CRITICAL SOURCES:

BOOKS

McGraw-Hill Encyclopedia of World Drama, McGraw, 1972.
Modern World Drama: An Encyclopedia, Dutton, 1972.
The Oxford Companion to Spanish Literature, Clarendon Press, 1978.

*   *   *

MARTINEZ SIERRA, Maria (de la O'LeJarraga) 1874-1974

OBITUARY NOTICE: Born December 28, 1874, in San Millan de la Cogolla, Spain; died June 28, 1974, in Buenos Aires, Argentina. Political activist, translator, poet, and dramatist. Maria Martinez Sierra began writing poems and short stories with her husband, Gregorio Martinez Sierra, three years before their marriage in 1900; they eventually collaborated on more than fifty plays. Critics now believe that Maria was the principal writer in the Martinez Sierra partnership, with Gregorio serving mainly as editor. The extent of individual contribution is difficult to determine, however, because Maria had insisted that all her writings—even her solo efforts—be published under her husband's name only.

During the early 1930's Maria served as Socialist deputy to the Spanish Parliament while her husband was away working as a screenwriter in Hollywood, California. At the outbreak of the Spanish Civil War, Gregorio abandoned his wife permanently, eloping to Buenos Aires, Argentina, with actress Catalina Barcena. Maria Martinez Sierra subsequently lived for a time in both France and Switzerland before settling in Buenos Aires, where she died in 1974.

Though the Martinez Sierra dramas support traditional values, they often focus on intelligent female characters and espouse equal rights as well as equal responsibilities for women. The pair's best-known and most popular play is perhaps *Cancion de cuna* (translated as *The Cradle Song*), which remains a standard in international repertory. Additional works by the Martinez Sierras include *Lirio entre espinas* (translated as *A Lily Among Thorns*) and *Primavera en otono* (translated as *Spring in Autumn*). Several of their plays were translated and published in the two-volume collection *The Plays of Gregorio Martinez Sierra*.

OBITUARIES AND OTHER SOURCES:

BOOKS

Encyclopedia of World Literature in the Twentieth Century, revised edition, Ungar, 1983.
O'Connor, Patricia Walker, *Gregorio and Maria Martinez Sierra,* Twayne, 1977.
Twentieth-Century Literary Criticism, Volume 6, Gale, 1982.

* * *

MASTERS, Anthony 1948(?)-1985

OBITUARY NOTICE: Born c. 1948; died January 3, 1985, in London, England. Journalist and drama critic. Masters, who became deputy theatre critic of the London *Times* in 1983, was regarded as an insightful and concise reviewer. Before joining the *Times* Masters had worked on Ernest Benn's "Blue Guides" and with the Egon Ronay organization.

OBITUARIES AND OTHER SOURCES:

PERIODICALS

Times (London), January 1, 1985.

* * *

MATHER, Bob
See MATHER, Robert E(dward)

* * *

MATHER, Jean 1946-

PERSONAL: Born October 23, 1946, in Bay City, Mich.; daughter of Jean Milford (in sales) and LaDonna (a housewife; maiden name, Foucault) Bleicher; married Robert E. Mather (a business consultant and writer), June 29, 1968; children: Julie Kirsten, Michael Robert. *Education:* Central Michigan University, B.A., 1968; California State University, Fullerton, M.A., 1981.

ADDRESSES: Home—24572 Aguirre, Mission Viejo, Calif. 92692.

CAREER: Substitute teacher at public schools in Dearborn, Mich., 1968-69; junior high school English teacher in Livonia, Mich., 1969-70; substitute teacher at Roman Catholic school in Encino, Calif., 1970-71; high school English teacher in La Puente, Calif., 1971; junior high school teacher at Roman Catholic school in Stanton, Calif., 1971-72; substitute teacher at public schools in Anaheim, Calif., 1972-73; high school English teacher in Livonia, 1973-74; substitute teacher at public schools in Woodhaven, Mich., 1974-76; adult education teacher at public schools in Flat Rock, Mich., 1976, and Irvine, Calif., 1977-81; California State University, Fullerton, part-time instructor in writing, 1981; Saddleback Community College, Mission Viejo, Calif., instructor in literature and grammar, 1981—.

MEMBER: National Council of Teachers of English; California State University, Fullerton, Alumni Association; Central Michigan University Alumni Association.

WRITINGS:

CHILDREN'S BOOKS

(With Ruth Radlauer, Ed Radlauer, and husband, Bob Mather) *Computer Tech Talk,* Childrens Press, 1984.
(With R. Radlauer, E. Radlauer, and B. Mather) *Satellite Tech Talk,* Childrens Press, 1984.
(With R. Radlauer, E. Radlauer, and B. Mather) *Robot Tech Talk,* Childrens Press, 1985.

Contributor to *Business Week.*

SIDELIGHTS: Jean Mather told *CA:* "In my composition classes we always read 'An Author to Her Book,' by Anne Bradstreet, and we discuss the analogy of the book and a baby. I'm very proud of my 'babies' and always remind my students to make sure their 'babies' look their best. Proofreading saves a lot of embarrassment. A lot of work goes into producing an appealing product.

"The concept of *Computer Tech Talk* is to explain technical 'computerese' in 'kidspeak.' The dictionary format explains computer terms in an easy-to-understand vocabulary that is supplemented with cartoons and photos of actual computer hardware. *Satellite Tech Talk* and *Robot Tech Talk* use the same format to simply explain satellite and robot technology and history. The books are all written at a sixth-grade level for the eight- to eighteen-year-old market, but are readily welcomed by adults. Reading what satellites, computers, and robots do without being bogged down by complicated explanations of how they function technically relieves adults' comprehension anxiety.

"*Computer Tech Talk* and *Robot Tech Talk* are both being used in classroom sets in school computer labs as well as for handy reference guides. *Satellite Tech Talk* is used as a reference in school space history units. All three are all-around informative, yet enjoyable, books."

AVOCATIONAL INTERESTS: Camping, water skiing, community activities.

* * *

MATHER, Robert E(dward) 1945-
(Bob Mather)

PERSONAL: Born November 20, 1945, in Detroit, Mich.; son of James Frank (a typesetter) and Kathryn (a housewife; maiden name, Graham) Mather; married Jean Bleicher (an instructor and writer), June 29, 1968; children: Julie Kirsten, Michael Robert. *Education:* Northern Michigan University, B.S., 1968; Wayne State University, M.B.A., 1970.

ADDRESSES: Home—24572 Aguirre, Mission Viejo, Calif. 92692. *Office*—Integrated Commercial Applications, Tustin, Calif.

CAREER: Worked as systems manager for Ford Motor Co. at various locations in Michigan and California, 1971-79; Fluor Corp., Irvine, Calif., senior systems analyst, 1979-80; Integrated Commercial Applications, Tustin, Calif., principal and business consultant, 1981—. Instructor at Saddleback Community College, 1976—, and University of California, Irvine, 1980-83. *Military service:* U.S. Army Reserve, 1968-74.

WRITINGS:

CHILDREN'S BOOKS

(Under name Bob Mather; with Ruth Radlauer, Ed Radlauer, and wife, Jean Mather) *Computer Tech Talk,* Childrens Press, 1984.
(Under name Bob Mather; with R. Radlauer, E. Radlauer, and J. Mather) *Satellite Tech Talk,* Childrens Press, 1984.
(Under name Bob Mather; with R. Radlauer, E. Radlauer, and J. Mather) *Robot Tech Talk,* Childrens Press, 1985.

SIDELIGHTS: Robert E. Mather told *CA:* "I have participated in numerous seminars to introduce people to computer technology, so I felt a real sense of purpose as a co-author of *Computer Tech Talk.* So many people have fragmented knowledge concerning computers, but are confused about the computer field as a whole. As with sex education, a child is better off learning the exact definitions of computer terms, rather than relying on hearsay. The book also gave me an opportunity to work with my wife."

BIOGRAPHICAL/CRITICAL SOURCES:

PERIODICALS

Saddleback Valley News, March, 1983.

*　　*　　*

MATHEWS, Janet　1914-

PERSONAL: Born January 18, 1914, in Wollongong, New South Wales, Australia; daughter of James Wilson (a solicitor) and Mary Irene (a pianist; maiden name, McLelland) Russell; married Frank Mathews (an engineer), December 3, 1936 (died, 1982); children: Susan (Mrs. Angus Kennedy), Jane (Mrs. J. H. Wooten), Robert. *Education:* Attended Conservatorium of Music, Sydney, Australia, 1930-35. *Politics:* Liberal. *Religion:* Presbyterian.

ADDRESSES: Home—29/37 Barry St., New South Wales 2089, Australia. *Agent*—Curtis Brown Proprietary Ltd., P.O. Box 19, Paddington, Sydney, New South Wales 2021, Australia.

CAREER: Concert pianist, 1935-53; piano teacher, 1953-66; writer, 1972—. Original council member of concert series for Australian Broadcasting Corp. in Wollongong, New South Wales, Australia; field researcher for Australian Institute of Aboriginal Studies, Canberra, 1977-84; speaker at schools for groups interested in aboriginal studies.

MEMBER: Australian Society of Authors, Children's Book Council of Australia, National Book Council of Australia.

WRITINGS:

Wurley and Wommera: Aboriginal Life and Craft (juvenile), Collins (Sydney), 1977, Collins (New York), 1979.
Totem and Taboo: Aboriginal Life and Craft (juvenile), Collins (Sydney), 1979.
Fossils and Families (juvenile), Collins (Sydney), 1981.
The Aboriginal Spirit of Life. This Does Not Die, Australian Institute of Aboriginal Studies, 1985.

Contributor to newsletter of Australian Institute of Aboriginal Studies.

WORK IN PROGRESS: Contributing a biography of aboriginal woman Lorna Dixon, to anthology *Fighters and Singers,* edited by I. M. White, Betty Meehan, and Diane Barwick, for Allen & Unwin.

SIDELIGHTS: Janet Mathews told *CA:* "I was about to receive the Diploma of Music in 1935 when I was offered piano work in Paris, France, where I lived with a French family for one year. I decided exams could wait until my return, although I had passed all but the final one. I married soon after coming back to Australia and decided there was not much point in taking that exam as I had rather progressed past it.

"In about 1960, I received my Braille Writers Certificate. I had always had some sympathy for the blind and felt that I might become involved in the new system of writing music in Braille. However, as I was teaching so much, I decided there was almost too much music in my life. I confined myself to putting numerous books into Braille. When I started work as an author, there was no time for Braille, and I reluctantly retired.

"In 1963, due to my musical training, I was asked to do research in the field with aborigines. New South Wales was my area, but the music was almost too easy. I became intensely interested in the many languages and customs and was asked to clarify tribal boundaries and many other aspects of tribal life.

"This field research involved moving through very remote areas with tape recorders, finding aborigines who still had linguistic or other important knowledge. Within about three months in the field, I was classified as a linguist, and as time progressed I came to be fairly knowledgeable in most aspects of aborigines' past. When asked to 'tidy up' a tremendous number of tapes recorded with one aborigine in 1972, I did so. This request came from the Australian Institute of Aboriginal Studies in Canberra, for whom I had been doing the research. The 'tidying up' took two years and was then sent to someone at the Institute who, to my surprise, said: 'This is a book—we are going to publish it.' That was the beginning of my career as an author. Field research with aborigines continued until 1977, and I still become involved in rather unexpected ways.

"Added to my own aboriginal research for *The Aboriginal Spirit of Life. This Does Not Die* is work done by my husband's grandfather, R. H. Mathews, who did early and major research when he was a surveyor about one hundred years ago. His information has been possibly the main foundation of aboriginal knowledge in Australia. Masses of his study have been published in the form of monographs and are in my possession because I am the only interested member of the family. My book of myths contains many of his that I have re-written, as his style was somewhat Victorian. There are explanatory comments throughout—on languages, customs, and many aspects of the tribal life. When I was in the field, I kept trying to add to his research. When writing, I delve into his material frequently because this collection is very valuable. Eventually, it will go to the National Library in Canberra.

"The three books in the Collins series, *Wurley and Womera, Totem and Taboo,* and *Fossils and Families* are completely factual and I do not feel they are actually 'for children.' When people ask me, I say they are for young readers. Numerous adults have read them with interest when their knowledge about aborigines is limited."

*   *   *

MATHEWS, Mitford M(cLeod)   1891-1985

OBITUARY NOTICE: Born in 1891 in Jackson, Ala.; died February 14, 1985, in Chicago, Ill. Linguist, educator, lexicographer, editor, and author. Considered a preeminent expert on Americanisms in the English language, Mathews spent six years producing his masterwork, the fifty-thousand-word *Dictionary of Americanisms,* originally published in 1951 and the first dictionary of its kind. The dictionary lists words and phrases—such as *poppycock, flunk, electrocute, ivory tower, sideburns, Bible Belt,* and *vamoose*—which were either invented or given new meaning in America. In the 1930's Mathews assisted Sir William Craigie in the compilation of *A Dictionary of American English on Historical Principles.* He lectured in linguistics at the University of Chicago and, from 1944 to 1956, served as chief of the dictionary department at the University of Chicago Press. An editorial consultant for *Webster's New World Dictionary* from 1957 to 1981, Mathews wrote the *Dictionary*'s "Americanisms" section. His other publications include *The Beginnings of American English, Some Sources of Southernisms,* and *Words: How to Know Them.*

OBITUARIES AND OTHER SOURCES:

BOOKS

American Authors and Books: 1640 to the Present Day, 3rd revised edition, Crown, 1962.

PERIODICALS

New York Times, February 16, 1985.
Washington Post, February 18, 1985.

*   *   *

MATTHEWS, Geoffrey M.   1920-1984

OBITUARY NOTICE: Born in 1920; died December 9, 1984. Educator, editor, and author. Matthews, who taught English at such institutions as Leeds and Reading universities, was a prominent authority on the English romantic poet Percy Bysshe Shelley. The educator published many articles on Shelley, as well as a selection of his poetry and prose and an introductory text for the British Council entitled *Shelley.* Matthews died before completing a revised and enlarged edition of Shelley's writings for the Longman "Annotated English Poet's" series.

OBITUARIES AND OTHER SOURCES:

PERIODICALS

Times (London), December 18, 1984.

*   *   *

MATTHEWS, Stanley   1915-

BRIEF ENTRY: Born February 1, 1915, in Hanley, Stoke-on-

Trent, England. British professional soccer player and author. Matthews, who began playing soccer as early as 1931, was a member of the Blackpool Football Club from 1947 to 1961. An award-winning player, he earned a reputation for fair play that, according to some sources, endeared him to his fans. Matthews's books include *Feet First* (Evans & Dale, 1948), *Feet First Again* (Transworld, 1955), *The Stanley Matthews Story* (1960), and *Back in Touch* (Arthur Barker, 1981). *Address:* Idle House, Marsaxlokk, Malta.

BIOGRAPHICAL/CRITICAL SOURCES:

BOOKS

1000 Makers of the Twentieth Century, David & Charles, 1971.
Who's Who, 134th edition, St. Martin's, 1982.

*   *   *

MATTICK, Paul   1904-1981

OBITUARY NOTICE: Born March 13, 1904, in Pomerania; died February 7, 1981. Craftsman, educator, editor, and author. Employed as a tool and die maker for various firms, Mattick was a guest professor at Roskilde University in Denmark in 1974. Among his writings are *Marx and Keynes: The Limits of the Mixed Economy; Critique of Marcuse; Anti-Bolshevik Communism; Economics, Politics, and the Age of Inflation; Economic Crisis and Crisis Theory;* and *Marxism, Last Refuge of the Bourgeoisie?* Mattick also edited *Chicagoer Arbeiterzeitung, International Council Correspondence, Living Marxism,* and *New Essays.* (Date of death provided by son, Paul Mattick, Jr.)

*   *   *

MAVROGORDATOS, George T(hemistocles)   1945-

PERSONAL: Born March 27, 1945, in Athens, Greece; son of Themistocles J. (a dental surgeon) and Stavroula (a housewife; maiden name, Paraskevopoulou) Mavrogordatos. *Education:* University of Athens, B.A., 1967; Purdue University, M.A., 1972; University of California, Berkeley, Ph.D., 1979.

ADDRESSES: Home—3 Neophytou Douca St., Athens GR-10674, Greece. *Office*—Department of Political Science, University of Athens, 19 Omirou St., Athens GR-10672, Greece.

CAREER: University of Athens, Athens, Greece, assistant professor of political science and history, 1982—. *Military service:* Greek Coast Guard and Army, 1966-68.

MEMBER: American Political Science Association, Greek Political Science Association.

AWARDS, HONORS: Grants from Fulbright Foundation, 1970 and 1983; dean's fellowship from University of California, Berkeley, 1973-75; Woodrow Wilson Foundation Book Award from American Political Science Association, 1984, for *Stillborn Republic.*

WRITINGS:

Stillborn Republic: Social Coalitions and Party Strategies in Greece, 1922-1936, University of California Press, 1983.
Rise of the Green Sun: The Greek Election of 1981, University of London, King's College, 1983.

Contributor to periodicals.

WORK IN PROGRESS: "Research on the Left-Right dimension in Greece and cross-nationally."

SIDELIGHTS: In *Stillborn Republic: Social Conditions and Party Strategies in Greece, 1922-1936,* George T. Mavrogordatos analyzes party politics during the first Greek Republic (1924-1936), focusing on the rift between royalists and anti-royalists. As Richard Clogg wrote in the *Times Literary Supplement,* the author "seeks to explain the establishment and downfall of the Republic not in terms of elite politics or military praetorianism but rather of cleavages which manifested themselves in mass politics." Mavrogordatos, Clogg continued, provides many "illuminating insights into the nature and evolution of party politics in Greece" and should be highly commended "for his skill in unravelling the truly Byzantine complexities of electoral law during the inter-war period." Mavrogordatos's book, concluded Clogg, "constitutes a quantum leap forward in our understanding of the nature of the Greek political process and is worthy to stand alongside John Petropulos's splendid *Politics and Statecraft in the Kingdom of Greece 1833-1843.*"

Mavrogordatos told *CA:* "I entered political science from politics out of an early commitment to my country and its people. Accordingly, my principal book and all other writings essentially represent a continuous effort to reconstruct and understand their tortuous and tortured recent history."

BIOGRAPHICAL/CRITICAL SOURCES:

PERIODICALS

Times Literary Supplement, June 15, 1984.

*   *   *

MAYBURY, Anne
See BUXTON, Anne (Arundel)

*   *   *

MAYER, Robert   1879-1985

OBITUARY NOTICE: Born June 5, 1879, in Mannheim, Germany (now West Germany); died January 9, 1985. Industrialist, philanthropist, and author. As founder of the Robert Mayer Children's Concerts in 1923 and Youth and Music in 1954, Mayer is remembered for his lifelong contributions to the musical education of British children and adolescents. Mayer used the fortune he accumulated from the industrial metals business both in Great Britain and abroad during the first quarter of the twentieth century to fund his many philanthropic interests. He also founded the London Symphony Orchestra in 1932 with Sir Thomas Beecham and served as its co-chairman. Knighted in 1939, Mayer received several other honors when he celebrated his centenary year in 1979, among them knight commander of the Royal Victorian Order, presented by Queen Elizabeth II, and the Albert Medal of the Royal Society of Arts. He wrote a book on juvenile delinquency entitled *Young People in Trouble* and an autobiography, *My First Hundred Years.*

OBITUARIES AND OTHER SOURCES:

BOOKS

International Who's Who in Music and Musicians Directory, 9th edition, Melrose Press, 1980.
Who's Who, 136th edition, St. Martin's 1984.

PERIODICALS

New Yorker, April 21, 1980.

New York Times, September 22, 1979.
Times (London), January 15, 1985.

*   *   *

MAYNARD, Robert C(lyve)   1937-

PERSONAL: Born June 17, 1937, in Brooklyn, N.Y.; son of Samuel Christopher and Robertine Isola (Greaves) Maynard; married second wife, Nancy Hicks, January 1, 1975; children: Dori J., David H., Alex Caldwell. *Education:* Attended Harvard University, 1966.

ADDRESSES: Office—The Tribune Tower, P.O. Box 24424, Oakland, Calif. 94623.

CAREER/WRITINGS: Afro-American News, Baltimore, Md., reporter, 1956; *Gazette and Daily,* York, Pa., reporter, 1961-67; *Washington Post,* Washington, D.C., reporter, 1967-72, associate editor and ombudsman, 1972-74, editorial writer, 1974-77; Institute for Journalism Education, Berkeley, Calif., founder and chairman, 1977-79; *Oakland Tribune,* Oakland, Calif., editor, publisher, and president, 1979—. Contributor of articles and criticism to periodicals. Co-director of Summer Program for Minority Group Members at Columbia University Graduate School of Journalism, 1972.

Member of board of directors of American Society of Newspaper Editors, American Bar Association Commission on Public Understanding About the Law, Western Regional Advisory Board of the American Press Institute, National News Council, Council on Foreign Relations, Inc., College Preparatory School, American Newspaper Publishers Association government affairs committee, Marcus A. Foster Educational Institute, Oakland Chamber of Commerce, Bay Area Council. Affirmative-action consultant to Gannett newspapers; member of United States-Japan Policy Studies Forum; chairman of YMCA capital development committee.

MEMBER: Society of Professional Journalists, Sigma Delta Chi.

AWARDS, HONORS: Nieman fellow at Harvard University, 1966.

SIDELIGHTS: After spending six years as a reporter for the *Gazette and Daily* in York, Pennsylvania, Robert C. Maynard joined the *Washington Post* in 1967. As the *Post*'s first black, full-time national correspondent Maynard "gave us eyes and ears that we lacked somewhat in black affairs in this country," commented the newspaper's managing editor, Howard Simons, in *Newsweek.* Maynard remained at the *Post* for ten years, serving as reporter, ombudsman, and editorial writer. He left in 1977 to found the Institute for Journalism Education in Berkeley, California, and to serve as affirmative-action consultant to Gannett newspapers. And in 1979 he became the first black editor, publisher, and president of a major metropolitan newspaper—the *Oakland Tribune* of Oakland, California.

When Maynard took over the leadership of the *Oakland Tribune,* the paper was in poor financial condition due to low circulation. According to Arlie Schardt and Michael Reese in *Newsweek,* the *Tribune,* which had for many years promoted the conservative views of its owner Republican Senator William F. Knowland, suffered because "the paper's audience [was] vastly different from the halcyon days of the Knowlands." Schardt and Reese concluded that if Maynard were to "vitalize the Tribune," he would have to "turn it from the voice of the Establishment to an outlet for the everyday needs of the city's 333,000 people." Maynard also recognized the paper's need to address issues pertinent to Oakland's 54 percent nonwhite population and attributed the *Tribune*'s circulation problems to a lack of local reporting and investigative articles. He told *Newsweek:* "Oakland is a city that has put its problems of social adjustment behind it. Now the job is to get the Trib's pages to reflect that."

AVOCATIONAL INTERESTS: Hiking, photography, woodcarving.

CA INTERVIEW

CA interviewed Robert C. Maynard by telephone at his *Oakland Tribune* office on June 23, 1983.

CA: You were a Nieman fellow at Harvard. Yet prior to that you dropped out of high school to write for newspapers. What's your opinion of the value of formal education?

MAYNARD: My father was big on the notion that there was a phenomenon called the educated fool: someone who went to college for four years, got a degree, and then assumed he knew everything. My father's idea was that education really was a lifelong process, in that we were born ignorant and died only slightly less ignorant. What we needed to do, he thought, and I agree, was to display a certain amount of humility about whatever acquired knowledge we might have. We also should work very hard, he said, to keep from assuming that education is over or that education comes in only one form. We were always encouraged to read and think critically, and to rely primarily on our own wit and wisdom as opposed to that imparted by way of lecturing. He was extremely Socratic in his approach and spent a lot of his time not pontificating but asking us pointed questions about life and learning.

CA: You and [Washington Post *executive editor*] *Ben Bradlee got into an argument at Harvard. What was it about?*

MAYNARD: I told him I didn't think the *Post* was as good as he thought it was. He replied, "The trouble is that smart-asses like you spend all their time telling me how bad the paper is but don't come and help me make it better." This went on for a while and led to my going to the *Post.*

CA: As Post *ombudsman, was there any single major problem you found yourself dealing with?*

MAYNARD: That was during Watergate, so the biggest problem was explaining to then-President Richard M. Nixon's supporters why we were running all those stories about him.

CA: Would you call the Post *editorials you wrote liberal or conservative?*

MAYNARD: You could call them liberal to moderate. I'm just terrible at those labels, though. I don't like them and I don't know what they mean. On one issue, I might take what some would regard as a conservative stand, and on another I might take what would be regarded as a liberal position. I really believe in independent thought. I think people ought to respond to issues on the merits of those issues rather than with pre-formed notions.

CA: What was wrong with the publishing approach that the Knowlands and Combined Communications Company [owners *of the* Tribune *before Gannett newspapers and Maynard*] *were taking with the* Tribune?

MAYNARD: It's not a matter of what was wrong with it. It probably was right for an earlier time. But the East Bay has been evolving over the years. A recent study of ethnic diversity in American cities concluded that Oakland is the single most ethnically diverse city in the United States. What that means is that less than 2 percent of the blacks in Oakland live in exclusively black neighborhoods and less than 20 percent of the whites live in exclusively white neighborhoods. That means that for all intents and purposes there are virtually no all-white or all-black communities in this city. Beyond that, this city has a population of other minorities, including Latin Americans and Asians. Many blacks came to this city during World War II and then stayed on and became educated in what was at the time an outstanding public educational system. What that led to was a large, urban, ethnically-mixed population that was educated and middle-class as well as working-class and that looked to the newspaper to reflect the whole community and not just certain segments of the community.

CA: Was the Tribune, *under its previous owners, reflecting the entire community?*

MAYNARD: No. And what we have tried to do here is broaden the perspective of our coverage so that it goes to every corner of the East Bay and gives representative coverage to the whole of the ethnic and geographic community. It's partly a matter of making certain that those parts of the community with concerns different from middle-class white concerns don't get ignored.

CA: What was your aim and that of Gannett's in starting Eastbay Today?

MAYNARD: For 108 years we had been an afternoon newspaper, but we recognized that the long-term survival of the newspaper was in the morning. We began our foray into the morning by publishing the morning *Eastbay Today,* to get people focusing on us as a morning product, while continuing to publish the *Tribune* in the afternoon. We produced *Eastbay Today* strictly for street sales, thinking that we would get the most market recognition for our morning operation that way, and developed *Eastbay Today* to the point where it had more than 100,000 readers. We felt that we could comfortably make the conversion of the whole newspaper from afternoon to morning by moving the *Tribune* from the afternoon and combining it with *Eastbay Today* in the morning. We have completed that process. We sustained some losses from the large circulation base we had created artificially by selling *Eastbay Today* for ten cents per copy, and so when we converted we contracted to a number that was near the number of readers we had before we converted—about 160,000—but now we are firmly in the morning, which will make a big difference for our future.

CA: Are you saying that you and Gannett planned all along to move the whole operation to the morning?

MAYNARD: We didn't know when we would go into the morning field, but we certainly knew that it would be very difficult to maintain this paper as an afternoon paper over the next fifteen to twenty years, because the readers of the afternoon *Tribune* were predominantly in the forty-nine to sixty-nine age group. If you have that kind of age group situation, you recognize that you're going to be in trouble in a few years.

CA: Is the paper you're now putting out merely Eastbay Today *retitled ''The Tribune'' or is it a whole new paper?*

MAYNARD: Gannett had some pretty fixed ideas on what it wanted *Eastbay Today* to look like: peach-colored newsprint and so forth. The paper's slogan was ''Reach for the Peach.'' Now that we are no longer owned by Gannett, we have a new designer redoing our paper to make it look more like the intelligent alternative to the competing papers we think it ought to be. I'm not sure that the sort of bastardized half-*Eastbay Today*, half-old *Tribune* approach that we now have solves any of those problems. So we're going to redo it and make it a hell of a lot better.

CA: Better in terms of graphics, or of content as well?

MAYNARD: Both. We also are doing a lot of reorganizing of the way we cover the news to try to be much more effective in local reporting. *Eastbay Today* was supposed to be a quick read. It leaned toward wire copy, briefs packages, and the like, and fewer stories of substance. We're trying to bring back a balance. Some short stories in the newspaper are a good idea; we all can use editing. But at the same time, we shouldn't be so busy being a commuter paper that we forget that the *Tribune*'s base is really in home delivery, not in commuters. It's fine to have a street sales version, and we will have one, but we're going to edit our paper on the presumption that 75 to 90 percent of all of our readers are going to be reading it at home and not on the street.

CA: You're including neighborhood and suburban sections in the new Tribune, *aren't you? Didn't some of the paper's previous owners try that?*

MAYNARD: What they had were called regional editions, one for southern Alameda, one for Contra Costa. They had a little bit of news and a little bit of local advertising, but not a hell of a lot of either one. All they ever had localized was a calendar of events: the VFW is going to meet, so-and-so is going to speak at the Lions, and that was about it. But last year we started the Neighbors sections. We turned them into tabloids and made them sort of colorful. We included a lot more of what I call micro-news: divorces, weddings, property transfers, police calls, fire calls, zoning permits, liquor permits, births, bus schedules, school lunch menus. We've broken them for the moment into four zones. Eventually, I suppose there could be as many as ten.

They serve a much more important function than the old regionals did, have proven extremely popular, and are producing revenue. Each one of them has an advisory committee for its neighborhood, made up of elected officials, school teachers, principals, Lions Club people, etc. I have breakfast with each zone advisory committee once a month, along with a few of our department heads, some news people, a circulator, a marketing representative, and the general manager of the section. We talk about our paper, about their communities, and about what's going on in their communities that we should be doing a better job of covering, and how we can do better the things we did during the previous month. It's an extended and continuous dialogue with our readers on how to make each Neighbors section better and how to make the newspaper better.

CA: One of your staffers criticized you for spending too much of your time as publisher involving yourself in community activities. Do you think that's a fair criticism?

MAYNARD: I don't spend as much time on community activities as I used to, but I certainly regard it as valid that I spent a lot of time during my first three or so years here learning about this community, meeting with the people throughout these two counties and in San Francisco, letting them meet me and see me and interact with me as a new person in the community. After all, I was a new person with an unusual profile: this was the first time there ever was a black editor of a major metropolitan newspaper. I wanted to let them see who this fellow is and what sort of person he is. I think it's good for the editor of an institution like this to be visible in the community anyway, but in this case there was a particular need to make certain that we got over any notions of what it means that the editor is black.

I remember once, years ago, watching Ben Bradlee spend a little bit of time interacting with the Washington, D.C., community. One of his critics said, ''If I were Ben Bradlee, I'd never leave this building and go out and meet with the citizens. I'd spend my time sitting in my office with the door closed editing the *Washington Post*.'' Well, I think we're in an era where the public needs to know who edits our newspapers and what they stand for. I don't think it's a good idea for editors to be isolated from the communities they seek to serve.

CA: Is that one of the reasons you write your ''Letter From the Editor'' column?

MAYNARD: It sure is. Regular communications between the editor and the readers are important. This notion that we can somehow edit a newspaper by osmosis, relying on our reporters to keep us informed of what's going on in the community, is a mistake. And I think it has something to do with the low status the press has in the eyes of so many citizens. Part of the problem is because they don't know who we are. They think we're some arrogant, remote people who don't care what the people we seek to serve think. And that's a bad profile for us, a bad posture to be in.

CA: Soon after you became editor you banned salacious pinups in the newsroom. Is that kind of feeling reflected in your coverage as well? Do you cover women's issues more thoroughly than they used to be covered?

MAYNARD: Yes. First of all, we have more women decision-makers on the staff than ever before in the history of this newspaper. And we cover concerns of women to a greater degree than we used to. I hope everybody does. It just seemed to me that as we brought more women into the news organization, as reporters or decision makers or whatever, that it was inappropriate to have pictures of naked women hanging on the walls of this news organization. It was in bad taste, and it was wrong to treat our colleagues in that fashion.

CA: You mentioned putting women in decision-making positions. You also hired more black and Hispanic reporters. Was that with the specific intent of adding ethnicity to the staff?

MAYNARD: I wanted the newspaper to more accurately reflect the community it seeks to serve. Oakland is more than one-half minority, and the Bay Area is 20 to 25 percent minority, yet when I arrived here our news staff was something like 6 percent minority. It was just imbalanced.

CA: Has adding minority reporters to the staff caused any problems with the older, white staffers?

MAYNARD: The degree to which we have differences within our staff is more related to differences in perception because of age and sex. I'd put race third. It's true everywhere. At first everybody's uptight as to what to expect from the other guy, but as they get to know each other some of that begins to peel away.

CA: Why do you think American newspapers in general still seem to shy away from hiring minority staffers?

MAYNARD: There's a perception problem. The perception is, without necessarily having any evil intent, "Gee, we hear that blacks get the worst possible education, they tend to go to college in smaller numbers than whites, and they tend to go to graduate school in smaller numbers still. Therefore, there probably aren't any qualified minorities out there." It's a presumption based on social perceptions that need to be revised. As the perceptions are revised, we'll see changes in practice.

CA: You have been quoted as saying that transforming the Tribune *into an intelligent alternative to the two San Francisco papers has been a harder job than you expected. What in particular were you referring to?*

MAYNARD: I was referring to the fact that I look at the *San Francisco Chronicle* [the morning San Francisco paper and the largest paper in the area] and see a news product that shows no creativity, no feeling for the community, no sensitivity, no reflection of what San Francisco is as a community, except as it may relate to bizarre sex and drug stories, which is not San Francisco either. It's a portion of San Francisco, but it's by no means the whole San Francisco or Bay Area community. If you look at it from that viewpoint, you say, "Gee, if you produce a really first-rate newspaper, you'll be able to compete with these guys easily."

What I did not take fully into account was the effect of the *San Francisco Chronicle* and *Examiner* being a protected monopoly in the marketplace. They are exempt under the Newspaper Preservation Act from having to compete with each other and as a consequence they have an ability to affect the marketplace to a far greater degree than one would expect them to be able to given the mediocrity of their performance. For instance, they can blanket the area with reduced-price offers: take the *Chronicle* for one month, get the second month free; take the *Chronicle*, get the *Examiner* free, that sort of thing.

CA: Have they improved their editorial product at all?

MAYNARD: Not a hell of a lot.

CA: Has your new role as majority stockholder in the Tribune Company caused any changes in the way the paper and the company are going to operate?

MAYNARD: Yes, since we're no longer part of a big group. We're now an independent company, a small independent company. You do a lot of things differently when you're on your own. You watch costs more carefully, and you work harder on making your company reflect the aims of this particular management as opposed to the bifurcation into which you easily fall when you're operating a paper on behalf of someone else, when some of the objectives are yours and some are theirs. You can sit down with your employees, and as they present problems you can say, "I can tell you how we'll solve that. We'll solve it by doing A, B, and C." And you do not

have to leave that meeting and call Rochester, New York [Gannett Headquarters], and say, "Is it all right if I do A, B, and C?" If that's what we decide is important to do, we do it.

BIOGRAPHICAL/CRITICAL SOURCES:

PERIODICALS

Newsweek, September 24, 1979.
Sepia, August, 1973.

—Interview by Peter Benjaminson

*   *   *

MAYNES, J. O. Rocky, Jr.
See MAYNES, J. Oscar, Jr.

*   *   *

MAYNES, J. Oscar, Jr. 1929-
(J. O. Rocky Maynes, Jr.)

PERSONAL: Born May 7, 1929, in El Paso, Tex.; son of J. Oscar (a pharmacist) and Rae (a homemaker; maiden name, Visconti) Maynes; married Mary Rebecca Sigworth (a homemaker), January 19, 1952; children: Jay, Robin, Christopher, Gina, Bridget, Fritz, Vito, Ingrid, Claudia, Kristin. *Education:* Arizona State University, B.A., 1952, M.A. (Spanish), 1955, M.A. (education), 1964, Ph.D., 1973; University of Colorado, Certificate, 1959; Universidad de los Andes, Diploma, 1960.

ADDRESSES: Home—5725 West Belmont Ave., Glendale, Ariz. 85301. *Office*—Division of Migrant Child Education, Arizona Department of Education, 1535 West Jefferson, Phoenix, Ariz. 85007.

CAREER: State of Arizona, Maricopa County public schools, high school teacher of Spanish, 1952-57; Glendale High School, Glendale, Ariz., teacher of Spanish and chairman of department, 1957-66; Arizona Department of Education, Migrant Child Education and Foreign Languages Divisions, Phoenix, director, 1966—. Instructor in Spanish, University of Nevada, summer, 1961-62, Phoenix College, 1962-66, San Jose State College (now University), summer, 1963-65; participant in Foreign Language Supervisor's Institute at Indiana University, summer, 1966.

MEMBER: American Council of Teachers of Foreign Languages, American Association of Teachers of Spanish and Portugese (president, 1960-61), National Association of State Directors of Migrant Education (president, 1983-84), National Education Association, Arizona Foreign Language Association (president, 1957-58), Arizona School Administrators' Association.

AWARDS, HONORS: Fulbright fellowship from Universidad de los Andes, 1960, for teaching Spanish linguistics, culture, literature, history, and language; named National Migrant Educator of the Month, February, 1975.

WRITINGS:

Use and Misuse of Foreign Language Laboratories, Arizona State University, 1964.
Cancionero alegre (title means "The Happy Songbook"), Arizona Department of Education, 1968.

The Development of Guidelines for Model Child Care, Pre-school, and Kindergarten Programs for Migrant Children, Arizona Department of Education, 1971.

(With Guillermina M. Supervia and Richard H. Sweet) *Actualidad hispanica* (title means "Hispanic World Nowa-days"), Allyn & Bacon, 1972.

(With Nicholas J. Silvaroli and Jann T. Skinner, under name J. O. Rocky Maynes, Jr.) *Oral Language Evaluation*, EMC Corp., 1977.

(With son, Jay Maynes, under name J. O. Rocky Maynes, Jr.) *Cancionero lindo* (title means "Beautiful Songbook"), Media Marketing, 1979.

UNDER NAME J. O. ROCKY MAYNES, JR.; WITH WARREN WHEE-LOCK; "HISPANIC HEROES OF THE U.S.A." JUVENILE BI-OGRAPHY SERIES

Paul H. Castro: Adversity Is My Angel, EMC Corp., 1976.
Tommy Nunez: NBA Ref., EMC Corp., 1976.
Presenting Vikki Carr!, EMC Corp., 1976.
Henry B. Gonzales: Greater Justice For All, EMC Corp., 1976.
Trini Lopez: The Latin Sound, EMC Corp., 1976.
Edward Roybal: Awaken the Sleeping Giant, EMC Corp., 1976.
Carmen Rosa Maymi: To Serve American Women, EMC Corp., 1976.
Roberto Clemente: Death of a Proud Man, EMC Corp., 1976.
Jose Feliciano: One Voice, One Guitar, EMC Corp., 1976.
Tony Perez: The Silent Superstar [and] *Lee Trevino: Supermex* [and] *Jim Plunkett: He Didn't Drop Out*, EMC Corp., 1976.

OTHER

Co-editor of *Forum*, 1966-68.

WORK IN PROGRESS: Translations of stories, brochures, speeches, and documents from English into Spanish.

SIDELIGHTS: J. Oscar Maynes, Jr., told *CA:* "I was motivated to write for young people by the thousands of students I taught during my fourteen years of high school teaching, by eighteen years thus far of meeting the needs of agricultural migrant children, and by raising ten children of my own.

"During the past thirty-two years I realized that young people need models to emulate, thus the series 'Hispanic Heroes of the U.S.A.' Also, thousands of young people lack reading skills due to what I feel is the lack of oral communicative skills—listening and speaking—thus *Oral Language Evaluation*. And the best vehicle in overcoming cross-cultural barriers and better understanding diverse cultures in America is music, thus *Cancionero alegre* ('The Happy Songbook').

"My own children deserve credit for making me better understand some of the needs and expectations of today's youth."

*   *   *

McARDLE, Catherine
See KELLEHER, Catherine McArdle

*   *   *

McCAFFERY, Larry   1946-

PERSONAL: Born May 13, 1946, in Dallas, Tex.; son of L.F. (in U.S. Air Force) and Othene (a bookkeeper; maiden name, Maulden) McCaffery; married Sinda J. Gregory (a professor of English and writer of fiction), May 21, 1977. *Education:*

University of Notre Dame, B.A., 1969, Ph.D., 1975. *Politics:* Democrat.

ADDRESSES: Home—3133 Gregory St., San Diego, Calif. 92104. *Office*—School of Literature, San Diego State University, San Diego, Calif. 92104.

CAREER: University of Illinois at Urbana-Champaign, Urbana, lecturer in American literature, 1975-76; San Diego State University, San Diego Calif., assistant professor, 1976-78, associate professor, 1978-81, professor of literature, 1981—.

WRITINGS:

The Metafictional Muse: The Work of Robert Coover, Donald Barthelme, and William H. Gass, University of Pittsburgh Press, 1982.
(Editor with Tom LeClair) *Anything Can Happen: Interviews With Contemporary American Novelists*, University of Illinois Press, 1983.
(Editor) *Postmodern Fiction: A Bio-Bibliographical Guide*, Greenwood Press, 1985.
(Editor with wife, Sinda Gregory) *Interviews With Writers of the Eighties*, University of Illinois Press, 1985.

Contributor of articles and reviews to magazines. Co-editor of *Fiction International*, 1983—.

WORK IN PROGRESS: Researching a study of the interaction between postmodern fiction in Europe, North America, and Latin America.

SIDELIGHTS: Larry McCaffery told *CA:* "My professional life began amidst the disruptive but liberating energies of the late 1960's, a period which produced in me (and in many of the authors I admire) a healthy distrust for authority figures (be they literary or political) and for conventional modes of discourse. Much of my professional life has been involved with analyzing and teaching—and, in a sense, promoting—nontraditional fiction. My interest is not in experimentalism per se, but in fiction which challenges our assumptions, makes us feel uncomfortable, encourages us to re-examine our lives. I admire artists who take risks—Coover, Barthelme, Pynchon, Gaddis, Calvino, and Kennedy in fiction; Coppola, Woody Allen, Godard, Roeg, and Kubrick in film; and David Byrne, Bruce Springsteen, Lou Reed, and David Bowie in popular music.

"The postmodern intersection of highbrow and popular culture seems to me a welcome phenomenon. I'm as passionately involved in baseball and rock music as I am in literature, and I'm interested in exploring these interconnections in my writings and in my personal life. As a self-professed 'groupie' whose biggest thrill was once shaking Mickey Mantle's hand, I have sought out writers, tried to talk with them, have drinks with them, and get to know them as people whenever possible. The result has been *Anything Can Happen* and *Interviews With Writers of the Eighties*. These have been easily the most rewarding work I've done, other than earning the daily reward of being able to go into a classroom and talk about literature and ideas with my students."

BIOGRAPHICAL/CRITICAL SOURCES:

PERIODICALS

American Book Review, November, 1983.
American Literary Scholarship, June, 1984.
American Literature, October, 1983.
Studies in the Humanities, September, 1983.

McCANN, Dennis P(atrick)   1945-

PERSONAL: Born June 1, 1945, in Newark, Ohio. *Education:* St. Charles Borromeo Seminary, A.B., 1967; Pontifical Gregorian University, S.T.L. (cum laude), 1971; University of Chicago, Ph.D. (with distinction), 1976; graduate study at De Paul University, 1982—. *Religion:* Roman Catholic.

ADDRESSES: Office—Department of Religious Studies, De Paul University, 2323 North Seminary, Chicago, Ill. 60614.

CAREER: Reed College, Portland, Ore., assistant professor of religion, 1976-80; Lewis and Clark College, Portland, visiting assistant professor of religious studies, 1980-81; De Paul University, Chicago, Ill., assistant professor, 1981-84, associate professor of religious studies, 1984—. Adjunct lecturer at University of South Florida, spring, 1976; adjunct assistant professor at University of Portland, summer, 1980. Member of Theologians and Executives in Dialogue and University of Chicago's Seminar on Religion and Public Life, both 1981—; public speaker.

MEMBER: American Academy of Religion (chairman of Oregon area group, 1978-81), Society of Christian Ethics, Society for Business Ethics.

WRITINGS:

Christian Realism and Liberation Theology: Practical Theologies in Creative Conflict, Orbis, 1981.
(Contributor) Don Browning, editor, *Practical Theology: The Emerging Field in Theology, Church, and World,* Harper, 1983.
(Contributor) James T. Johnson, editor, *The Bible in American Law, Politics, and Rhetoric,* Fortress, 1984.
(Contributor) John Houck and Oliver Williams, editors, *Catholic Social Teaching and the American Economy,* University of Notre Dame Press, 1984.
(With Charles R. Strain) *Polity and Praxis: A Program for American Practical Theology,* Seabury, 1985.

Editor of "Notes on Recent Publications," in *Religious Studies Review,* 1981—. Contributor of more than thirty articles and reviews to theology journals. Member of editorial board of *Journal of Religious Ethics,* 1981—.

WORK IN PROGRESS: Translating the political writings of Ernst Troeltsch; research for a book on the pastoral letter of the National Conference of Catholic Bishops, the process involved in composing the letter, and an assessment of the economic and social teaching generated by it; research on the culture of nuclear deterrence and alternative forms of international order; research on international trade, multinational corporations, and international economic justice.

SIDELIGHTS: Dennis P. McCann told *CA:* "During the mid-1960's I was marginally involved in the civil rights movement and the protests against the war in Vietnam. The questions raised by these youthful experiences have helped shape the focus of my work as a teacher and writer ever since. In particular I am interested in trying to understand the role of religion in politics, specifically, the role of organized religious social activists in the processes of public policy formation in a pluralistic society. I seek not just to document what this role has been, but also to develop recommendations concerning what it ought to be.

"The work of Protestant theologian Reinhold Niebuhr has served as a model for me. He managed to achieve a balance of political realism and religious faithfulness that I would also hope to realize. Unlike Niebuhr, who was more of an activist than I have turned out to be, I am trying to institutionalize this balance in an explicitly academic discipline, what Charles Strain and I have called an American Practical Theology.

"My current research projects—in the short term, an investigation of the pastoral letter process by which the American Catholic bishops are evaluating the structure and performance of the American economy in light of modern Catholic social teaching, and in the long term, an exploration of the ways in which American business instituions might contribute to the development of alternatives to the culture of nuclear deterrence—are designed to show how Practical Theology can open up new perspectives for public policy discussion."

BIOGRAPHICAL/CRITICAL SOURCES:

PERIODICALS

Commonweal, November 6, 1981.

*   *   *

McCANN, Sean   1929-

BRIEF ENTRY: Born in 1929 in Dublin, Ireland. Irish journalist and author. McCann has been a journalist in England and Ireland, as well as a television and radio writer. He is the author of such books as *The Fighting Irish* (Frewin, 1972), *Hot Shot!* (Hodder & Stoughton, 1979), and *Shoot on Sight* (Hodder & Stoughton, 1981). He edited *The Wit of Brendan Behan* (Frewin, 1968), *The Wit of the Irish* (Frewin, 1968), and *The Wit of Love* (Frewin, 1972).

*   *   *

McCARTEN, John (Bernard Francis James)   1916(?)-1974

OBITUARY NOTICE: Born September 10, 1916 (some sources say 1911), in Philadelphia, Pa.; died of cancer, September 26, 1974, in New York, N.Y. Journalist. McCarten, whose career with the *New Yorker* magazine spanned more than forty years, is remembered for his humorous short stories, his caustic profiles of many celebrities, and his terse film and drama reviews. McCarten was also a contributor to *Fortune, American Mercury, Time,* and other magazines. He spent the last six years of his life in Ireland, continuing to write articles, which appeared in the *New Yorker's* "Irish Sketches" column.

OBITUARIES AND OTHER SOURCES:

BOOKS

The Biographical Encyclopaedia and Who's Who of the American Theatre, James Heineman, 1966.
Who Was Who, Volume VI: *1961-1970,* A. & C. Black, 1972.
Who's Who in America, 38th edition, Marquis, 1974.

PERIODICALS

New Yorker, October 7, 1974.
New York Times, September 26, 1974.

*   *   *

McCARTHY, David Seymour   1935-

PERSONAL: Born June 11, 1935, in Portsmouth, N.H.; son of Justin Seymour and Jeanne (Doucette) McCarthy; married Marlene Moxley, June 7, 1957; children: Deborah McCarthy Bonnette, Denise McCarthy Kea, Darla Joy. *Education:*

Northwestern College, Roseville, Minn., B.A., 1957; Gordon-Conwell Theological Seminary, B.D., 1960; Southern Baptist Theological Seminary, M.R.E., 1964.

ADDRESSES: Home—11100 Arlington Church Rd., Charlotte, N.C. 28212. *Office*—Dulin's Grove Advent Christian Church, 11200 Arlington Church Rd., Charlotte, N.C. 28212.

CAREER: Ordained Advent Christian minister, 1959; pastor of Advent Christian churches in Old Orchard Beach, Me., 1957-58, New Bedford, Mass., 1959-61, New Albany, Ind., 1961-65, Penfield, N.Y., 1968-71, Somerville, Mass, 1971-75, and Augusta, Ga., 1975-81; Dulin's Grove Advent Christian Church, Charlotte, N.C., pastor, 1981—. Advent Christian Church, national director of youth work, 1965-68, national director of Christian education, 1967-68.

AWARDS, HONORS: Dwight L. Moody Award for *Decision*, 1971.

WRITINGS:

Youth Fellowship Guidebook, Advent Christian Publications, 1967.
Memo to a Weary Sunday School Teacher, Judson, 1978.
Gifts That Never Wear Out, Judson, 1980.
Invitation to Discipleship, Advent Christian Publications, 1980.
Practical Guide for the Christian Writer, Judson, 1983.
That Unforgettable Encounter, Nazarene Publishing, 1983.
Devotions From a Stamp Album, Baker Book, 1983.
Our Constant Companion, Judson, 1984.

Contributor to magazines, including *Christianity Today, Moody Monthly, Christian Herald, Voice, Eternity*, and *Decision*. Editor of *Insight*, 1970—.

SIDELIGHTS: David Seymour McCarthy was a regular speaker on the Advent Christian national radio broadcast from 1977 to 1980. He has also served as chaplain to major league baseball teams.

*   *   *

McCHESNEY, Kathryn 1936-

PERSONAL: Born January 14, 1936, in Curwensville, Pa.; daughter of Orland William and Lillian (Morrison) Spencer; married Thomas David McChesney; children: Eric Spencer. *Education:* University of Akron, B.A. (cum laude), 1962; Kent State University, M.L.S., 1965, further graduate study, 1971—.

ADDRESSES: Home—3611 Edison St. N.W., P.O. Box 57, Uniontown, Ohio 44685. *Office*—School of Library Science, Kent State University, Kent, Ohio 44242.

CAREER: Head librarian at public high school in Akron, Ohio, 1965-68; Kent State University, Kent, Ohio, assistant professor of library science, 1969—, assistant dean of School of Library Science, 1969-77.

MEMBER: American Library Association, American Association of School Librarians, Association of American Library Schools, Ohio Library Association (chairperson of Library Education Roundtable, 1971-72), Ohio Association of School/Media Librarians.

WRITINGS:

(With A. R. Rogers) *The Library in Society: An Overview of the Social, Philosophical, Historical, Political, Economic, and Educational Foundations of the Library*, With

a *Sampling of Current Issues Facing Librarianship*, Libraries Unlimited, 1983.

WORK IN PROGRESS: "A book developed from frustrations of students needing sources that were widely scattered and not readily accessible. We also wanted to include international aspects."

*   *   *

McCLELLAN, Edwin 1925-

BRIEF ENTRY: Born October 24, 1925, in Kobe, Japan. Educator and author. McClellan taught Japanese language and literature at the University of Chicago from 1957 to 1972. In 1972 he joined the faculty of Yale University, and in 1979 he was named Sumitomo Professor of Japanese Studies. McClellan wrote *Two Japanese Novelists: Soseki and Toson* (University of Chicago Press, 1969). He has translated into English the work of Natsume Soseki and Naoya Shiga. *Address:* 641 Ridge Rd., Hamden, Conn. 06517; and Department of East Asian Languages and Literatures, 307 Hgs, Yale University, New Haven, Conn. 06520.

BIOGRAPHICAL/CRITICAL SOURCES:

BOOKS

Director of American Scholars, Volume III: *Foreign Languages, Linguistics, and Philology*, 8th edition, Bowker, 1982.

PERIODICALS

Virginia Quarterly Review, spring, 1970.

*   *   *

McCLOSKEY, Patrick 1948-

PERSONAL: Born May 23, 1948, in Howell, Mich.; son of Gerald Richard (a dentist) and Gertrude (a teacher; maiden name, Devereaux) McCloskey. *Education:* Duns Scotus College, B.A. (magna cum laude), 1971; University of Dayton, M.A. (theology), 1974; St. Leonard College, M.Div., 1975; St. Bonaventure University, M.A. (Franciscan studies), 1981.

ADDRESSES: Home—42 Calhoun St., Cincinnati, Ohio 45219.

CAREER: Entered Order of Friars Minor (Franciscans), 1967, ordained Roman Catholic priest, 1975; Roger Bacon High School, Cincinnati, Ohio, teacher of religion and English, 1975-84, academic dean, 1978-84; St. Anthony Messenger Press, Cincinnati, assistant promotion director, 1984—. Member of Cushwa Center for the Study of American Catholicism.

MEMBER: Cincinnati Historical Society.

WRITINGS:

(Contributor) Leonard Foley, editor, *Saint of the Day*, St. Anthony Messenger Press, Volume I, 1974, Volume II, 1975.
St. Anthony of Padua: Wisdom for Today, St. Anthony Messenger Press, 1977.
Franciscan Saint of the Day, St. Anthony Messenger Press, 1981.

Author of "Thanksgivings," a column in *St. Anthony Messenger*, 1972-80. Contributor to magazines, including *Queen City Heritage*.

WORK IN PROGRESS: Freedom and the Following of Jesus: Recognizing Genuine and Counterfeit Freedom.

SIDELIGHTS: Since the late 1970's, Patrick McCloskey has been involved in a massive research project on the origins of the Franciscan province of St. John the Baptist in Cincinnati, Ohio. He began by editing and translating the letters of Father William Unterthiner, founder of the province. He then proceeded to work with others on translating materials for a history of the province, beginning in 1840. This ongoing project, which McCloskey has edited and footnoted, has so far resulted in more than fifteen hundred pages of manuscript.

In 1982 McCloskey spent the summer in Italy and Austria. He conducted research for his history project and participated in a Franciscan renewal program. He was able to see the originals of some letters he had worked on only from transcripts.

McCloskey told *CA:* "History of all kinds is one of my lifelong interests. Human beings are mixed bags of noble and ignoble motives, but history leaves me optimistic.

"*St. Anthony of Padua: Wisdom for Today* includes fifty magazine columns of contemporary reflections on some sections of St. Anthony's sermon notes; he was one of the most well known preachers of the early thirteenth century. The book includes chapters on the historical setting, the life of St. Anthony, and prayers to him. Anthony is one of the best-known Roman Catholic saints.

"*Freedom and the Following of Jesus* grows from the idea that the ways of sin always promise us more freedom and yet take away freedom. The ways of Jesus, as shown in the beatitudes, represent real freedom. Finding one's way through genuine and counterfeit freedoms is no easy task. Courage is a key virtue in a truly human life. Discipleship—the following of Jesus—is based on living in authentic freedom."

*　　*　　*

McCOMBS, Don 1948-

PERSONAL: Born June 10, 1948, in Vancouver, Wash.; son of Arlie Alvin (a line operator) and Viola May (a housewife; maiden name, Moeller) McCombs; married Mavis Lee Northcutt (a tutor and teacher), August 8, 1970; children: Kelli Anne, Shannon Lee. *Education:* California State University, Chico, B.A., 1970, M.A. (with highest honors), 1974. *Politics:* Democrat. *Religion:* Roman Catholic.

ADDRESSES: Home—1446 Chelsea Way, Livermore, Calif. 94550. *Office*—A T & T Communications, 5918 Stoneridge Mall Rd., Pleasanton, Calif. 94566. *Agent*—Peri Winkler, 8541 Charl Lane, Los Angeles, Calif. 90046.

CAREER: Federal Aviation Administration, Fremont, Calif., air traffic controller, 1974-81; Bailey's Nursery, Lodi, Calif., salesman, 1981-84; A T & T Communications, Pleasanton, Calif., account executive, 1984—. College history teacher. *Military service:* U.S. Army, 1970-73.

MEMBER: Veterans of Foreign Wars (historian).

AWARDS, HONORS: Special Achievement Award from Federal Aviation Administration, 1979.

WRITINGS:

(With Fred L. Worth) *World War II Superfacts,* Warner Books, Volume I, 1983, Volume II, in press.
(With Worth) *World War II Strange and Fascinating Facts,* Greenwich House, 1984.
Contributor to *Trivia Unlimited* and to newspapers.

WORK IN PROGRESS: Quiz Book on Military History; James Bond Encyclopedia; D. B. Cooper: American Folk Hero, on the hijacker, D. B. Cooper.

SIDELIGHTS: Don McCombs told *CA:* "Education is the cornerstone of man's getting along in the world. The more we understand each other the easier it becomes to tolerate and accept others. Tantamount to this is a knowledge of history. Mankind should learn from the mistakes of the past so it will not be condemned to the same mistakes in the future. To understand the past we must realize that history is made by people. That personal level provides its real driving force.

"My interest in World War II began with the stories of my father, who served with the Army Air Force in Italy. I enjoyed listening as he and his friends talked about their experiences and realized that that was only an isolated part of the whole. I also decided that as the media continued to encroach on Americans' ability to learn about history, many valuable first-hand accounts would be lost to future generations.

"America prior to television and our hectic life-style cherished the stories and traditions of the elder, more worldly members of society. Now many children and grandchildren have no knowledge of what their immediate relatives did in World War II or the Depression. And as the older generation dies the knowledge will be lost.

"I once interviewed an eighty-six-year-old retired general who took nearly all day to tell me about his military career. Afterwards, when I was ready to leave, he stopped me and said that as a boy growing up in Kansas, his Sunday afternoon entertainment was to sit in the town square and listen to Civil War veterans swap stories. He felt the greatest adulation was to have the youth ask the old to describe their lives. When he retired he looked forward to that. I was the first person to ask him about his experiences. I thought it a shame that this person who had given forty years of his life to his country had not had someone show some interest in him.

"There are vast worlds locked in the minds of the elderly that are left untapped. Many were involved intimately in the immediate historic events that are shaping our world today, yet this tremendous human resource is virtually being ignored.

"I have been asked what lessons we can learn from World War II. I would like to think that humanity learns from its mistakes; unfortunately, we don't. In reality, while the memory is fresh we usually avoid the same pitfall for twenty or thirty years. Then, as the events fade into the past, we begin to forget the impact on a personal level. Psychologists say we have no memory of pain. Maybe if we did we would be more inclined to pay attention to the past."

*　　*　　*

McCONKIE, Bruce R(edd) 1915-1985

OBITUARY NOTICE: Born July 29, 1915, in Ann Arbor, Mich.; died of cancer, April 19, 1985, in Salt Lake City, Utah. Attorney, civil servant, clergyman, church official, editor, and author. McConkie, who was ordained to the ministry of the Church of Jesus Christ of Latter-day Saints in 1946, became a member of the Quorum of the Twelve Apostles, the Mormon church's highest advisory body, in 1972. He had previously served on another of the church's governing bodies, the First Council of the Seventy, for twenty-six years. Before becoming a church official, McConkie had practiced law in Salt Lake City and served as assistant Salt Lake County attorney and

Salt Lake City prosecutor. He also worked on the editorial staff of the Mormon newspaper, the *Deseret News*. McConkie edited a three-volume collection of the writings of Joseph Fielding Smith, sixth president of the Mormon Church and nephew of its founder, Joseph Smith. He wrote *Mormon Doctrine*, the three-volume *Doctrinal New Testament Commentary*, *The Promised Messiah—The First Coming of Christ*, a four-volume study titled *The Mortal Messiah—From Bethlehem to Calvary*, and *The Millennial Messiah—The Second Coming of the Son of Man*.

OBITUARIES AND OTHER SOURCES:

BOOKS

Who's Who in the West, 20th edition, Marquis, 1984.

PERIODICALS

Chicago Tribune, April 21, 1985.

*   *   *

McCONNELL, William T(ate)   1941-

PERSONAL: Born April 29, 1941, in San Antonio, Tex.; son of William James (an army officer and university professor) and Natalie Pearl (Tate) McConnell; married Lu Beth McLeran (a teacher), June 13, 1964; children: William Scott, Elizabeth Jane, Debora Natalia. *Education:* University of Colorado, B.A. (cum laude), 1963; Conservative Baptist Theological Seminary (now Denver Conservative Baptist Seminary), B.D. (summa cum laude), 1966; Luther Rice Theological Seminary, D.Min., 1982. *Religion:* Christian (evangelical).

ADDRESSES: Home—Rua Aramis Dalla Torre, 375 Sao Paulo, SP 04826 Brazil. *Office*—Alianca Biblica Universitaria, R. Embau 235, Sao Paulo, SP 04039 Brazil.

CAREER: Inter-Varsity Christian Fellowship, Madison, Wis., area director, 1966-72; International Fellowship of Evangelical Students, London, England, serving in Sao Paulo, Brazil, as director of ABU Press, publishing house of Alianca Biblica Universitaria, 1972—. Visiting professor at Sao Paulo Baptist Seminary, 1977. Member of Conference on Faith and History, 1970—.

MEMBER: Associacao Brasileira de Editores Evangelicos.

AWARDS, HONORS: Award for academic excellence from Conservative Baptist Theological Seminary, 1966.

WRITINGS:

The Gift of Time, Inter-Varsity Press, 1983.
(Editor) *Tive fome: Um desafio a servir a Deus no mundo* (title means "I Was Hungry: A Challenge to Serve God in the World"), Alianca Biblica Universitaria Press, 1983.

Contributor of articles to *HIS*, *Fisherman's Net*, *Comunidad*, and *In Touch*.

SIDELIGHTS: William T. McConnell told *CA:* "Before writing can perform a service, it must first grow from some form of service. The first thing I had published was a letter I wrote to a student persuading her to attend a summer training project at Estes Park, Colorado. But when *HIS* magazine got a hold of that letter and published it in the form of an article, I was annoyed. I realized that what I wrote sprang from what I was and from what I was committed to, and I didn't want future psychologists—amateur or otherwise—to dissect and discard me as I had seen my professors do with all else historical.

Later, as I became more free to share myself with others, writing ceased to be such an embarrassment. Nevertheless, through the years it has been helpful to anchor my writing in my service or ministry, as a way of putting in a more precise and orderly form what I've already been saying and doing in another context.

"*The Gift of Time* grew out of the personal struggle to adapt to unfamiliar patterns of time usage, and the most enthusiastic reception to the book has come from others going through the same struggle, mostly in the third world countries."

BIOGRAPHICAL/CRITICAL SOURCES:

BOOKS

Lowman, Pete, *The Day of His Power*, Inter-Varsity Press, 1983.

PERIODICALS

HIS, February, 1979.

*   *   *

McCORMICK, Robert   1911-

PERSONAL: Born August 11, 1911, in Danville, Kentucky; son of William W. (a railroad executive) and Maud (a teacher; maiden name, Burman) McCormick; married Margaret Hall, August 18, 1934 (died December, 1976); children: Karen McCormick Skilling, Nora McCormick Pepper. *Education:* Attended George Washington University, 1929-32.

ADDRESSES: Home—521 Lakeside Ave., Tarpon Springs, Fla. 33589.

CAREER: Washington Daily News, Washington, D.C., editor and columnist, 1930-36; *Collier's Weekly*, New York City, staff writer, 1936-42; National Broadcasting Company (NBC), New York City, news broadcaster in Washington, D.C., Europe, and the Pacific, 1942-76.

MEMBER: Cosmos Club (Washington, D.C.).

AWARDS, HONORS: Robert E. Sherwood Award from Fund for the Republic for "The American Stranger."

WRITINGS:

Facing Alcoholism, Oak Tree, 1982.

Also author of "The American Stranger."

SIDELIGHTS: A self-described "recovering alcoholic," Robert McCormick offers advice for other alcoholics and their families in his book *Facing Alcoholism*. Also included are descriptions of various physical maladies caused by alcoholism and discussions of both traditional and newer approaches for rehabilitation. Hope is the underlying theme of the book, and McCormick warns in his final paragraph that "neither the alcoholic nor those who want to give him a hand should give up hope until far after the point of hopelessness is reached." According to a *Los Angeles Times Book Review* article by Bill Stout, *Facing Alcoholism* is "a useful book for those who want both ammunition and advice for dealing with the problem, whether one's own or someone else's."

McCormick told *CA:* "I never had the slightest desire to write a book, and after my bitter experience with Oak Tree, I now know I was right the first time. I realize some publishers do better, but I still have the deepest sympathy for those people who turn out books for a living and who have compulsions to write, which includes many of my friends."

BIOGRAPHICAL/CRITICAL SOURCES:

PERIODICALS

Los Angeles Times Book Review, July 11, 1982.

*   *   *

McCULLEY, Johnston   1883-1958
(Raley Brien, George Drayne, Frederic Phelps, Rowena Raley, Harrington Strong)

BRIEF ENTRY: Born February 2, 1883, in Ottawa, Ill.; died November 23, 1958; buried in Forest Lawn Cemetery, Glendale, Calif. American journalist, screenwriter, and author. Regarded by many critics as a hack writer, McCulley was best known as the author of the "Zorro" novels, an adventure series about a fictional hero of the American West. The series, which contains more than thirty volumes, includes such titles as *The Mark of Zorro* (1924), *Zorro Rides Again* (1931), *Holsters in Jeopardy* (1939), *Gold of Smoky Mesa* (1942), *South of the Pass* (1949), *The Cougar Kid* (1950), and *The Tenderfoot* (1957). During his career, McCulley worked for newspapers as a special correspondent in the United States and abroad and contributed more than one hundred short stories to western-genre magazines, including *Argosy, Adventure, All-Story, Western Story, Thrilling Ranch Stories, Texas Rangers,* and *Exciting Western.* Among the screenplays he co-authored are "Ride for Your Life" (1924), "The Trusted Outlaw" (1937), "Rose of the Rio Grande" (1938), and "Mark of the Renegade" (1951), and from 1957 to 1959 he wrote scripts for the "Zorro" television series. Also a writer of crime thrillers, McCulley published nearly twenty mystery novels, including *The Black Star* (1921), *The Demon* (1925), *Alias the Thunderbolt* (1927), *The Avenging Twins* (1927), *The Rollicking Rogue* (1939), and *The Devil's Dubloons* (1955).

BIOGRAPHICAL/CRITICAL SOURCES:

BOOKS

American Authors and Books: 1640 to the Present Day, 3rd revised edition, Crown, 1962.
The Men Behind Boys' Fiction, Howard Baker, 1970.
Reader's Encyclopedia of American Literature, Crowell, 1962.
Who Was Who Among English and European Authors, 1931-1949, Gale, 1978.

*   *   *

McDONALD, Robert   1943-

PERSONAL: Born October 25, 1943, in Vancouver, British Columbia, Canada; son of F.W. and Violet McDonald; married wife, Donna, 1965. *Education:* University of British Columbia, B.A. (with honors), 1964.

ADDRESSES: Home—London, England.

CAREER: Free-lance writer and broadcaster, 1966—.

WRITINGS:

Pillar and Tinderbox: The Greek Press and the Dictatorship, Marion Boyars, 1983.

WORK IN PROGRESS: History of the Greek Dictatorship, 1967-1974.

McDOWELL, David   1918(?)-1985

OBITUARY NOTICE: Born c. 1918 in Minneapolis, Minn.; died April 8, 1985, in Monteagle, Tenn. Publishing executive and author. McDowell began his career as a sales manager and publicity director at New Directions, and he worked as an editor at Random House for eight years, beginning in 1949. In 1957 he and Ivan Obolensky established the publishing company McDowell, Obolensky. One of the first books released by the firm was James Agee's Pulitzer Prize-winning novel *A Death in the Family.* After resigning from the company in 1960, McDowell joined the staff of Crown Publishers. At the time of his death, McDowell was writing a biography of Agee.

OBITUARIES AND OTHER SOURCES:

PERIODICALS

New York Times, April 14, 1985.

*   *   *

McELENEY, Neil Joseph   1927-

PERSONAL: Born August 8, 1927, in Charlestown, Mass.; son of Neil Patrick and Mary (McDevitt) McEleney. *Education:* St. Paul's College, Washington, D.C., A.B., 1950, M.A., 1953; Catholic University of America, S.T.L., 1954; Pontifical Biblical Institute, Rome, Italy, S.S.B., 1955, S.S.L., 1956.

ADDRESSES: Home—St. Paul's College, Washington, D.C. 20017. *Office*—Department of Theology, Catholic University of America, Washington, D.C. 20017.

CAREER: Entered Congregatio Sancti Pauli (Paulists; C.S.P.), 1946, ordained Roman Catholic priest, 1953; St. Paul's College, Washington, D.C., professor of Sacred Scripture, 1956-73; William Foxwell Albright Institute for Archaeological Research, Jerusalem, Israel, research associate, 1973-74; St. Patrick's Seminary, Menlo Park, Calif., professor of New Testament studies and Greek, 1975-78; Catholic University of America, Washington, D.C., adjunct associate professor of theology, 1979—. Catholic Biblical Association Annual Professor at Pontifical Biblical Institute, Rome, Italy, 1982; visiting professor at Catholic University of America, 1961, Marist College, 1964, University of Dayton, 1965, 1966, and St. Louis University, 1969.

MEMBER: American Academy of Religion, Catholic Theological Society of America, Catholic Biblical Association of America (president, 1980), Studiorum Novi Testamenti Societas, Society for Biblical Literature, Society for Old Testament Study (England), Catholic Biblical Association (England).

WRITINGS:

(Contributor) R. E. Brown, J. A. Fitzmyer, and R. E. Murphy, editors, *Jerome Biblical Commentary,* Prentice-Hall, 1968.
The Growth of the Gospels: An Introduction to Their Formation and Theology, Paulist Press, 1979.

General editor of "Pamphlet Bible Series," Paulist Press, 1960-73. Contributor to theology journals. *Catholic Biblical Quarterly,* associate editor, 1968-75, book review editor, 1969-71.

WORK IN PROGRESS: Research on New Testament ethics and the Gospels, specifically the Sermon on the Mount, with publications expected to result.

SIDELIGHTS: Neil Joseph McEleney told CA: "Nothing is so important as knowing, loving, and serving God in this world, so as to be happy with him in the next. My work is directed to bringing myself and others to appreciate this and to act accordingly.

"I have traveled extensively in Europe, Egypt, and the Middle East," McEleney added, "and have various degrees of competency in Italian, French, German, Spanish, modern Hebrew, Greek, and Latin. I have also studied several other ancient languages."

*　　*　　*

McFADDEN, Maggie
See McFADDEN, Margaret

*　　*　　*

McFADDEN, Margaret   1941-
(Maggie McFadden)

PERSONAL: Born August 1, 1941, in Lafayette, Ind.; daughter of William A. (a Methodist minister) and Glenora (a home economics teacher and homemaker; maiden name, English) McFadden; married Leslie E. Gerber (a college professor and writer), September 2, 1967; children: Leslie Noel. Education: University of Denver, B.A. (summa cum laude), 1963; Boston University, A.M., 1964; Emory University, Ph.D., 1973.

ADDRESSES: Home—201 Junaluska Rd., Boone, N.C. 28607. Office—Office of Women's Studies, General College, Appalachian State University, Boone, N.C. 28608.

CAREER: Northern Michigan University, Marquette, instructor in English, 1964-66; Clark College, Atlanta, Ga., instructor in English, 1966-67; Spelman College, Atlanta, assistant professor of English, 1969-71; University of Maryland, European Division, Wiesbaden and Ramstein, West Germany, lecturer in English, 1971-74; Metropolitan State College, Denver, Colo., assistant professor of English, 1974-75; University of Colorado at Colorado Springs, lecturer in English, 1974-75; Appalachian State University, Boone, N.C., 1975—, became associate professor of interdisciplinary studies and coordinator of women's studies in 1978.

MEMBER: American Association of University Women, Modern Language Association of America, National Women's Studies Association (regional representative), Association for Women Students, National Organization for Women, Organization on the Status of Women, Phi Beta Kappa.

AWARDS, HONORS: Whiting Foundation fellow, 1982; fellow at Women's Studies Research Center, University of Wisconsin—Madison, 1982; postdoctoral grants from Appalachian State University.

WRITINGS:

(With husband, Leslie E. Gerber) Loren Eiseley, Ungar, 1983.

Contributor of articles (some under name Maggie McFadden) and reviews to literature and women's studies journals and anthologies.

WORK IN PROGRESS: Thinking Woman, an anthology of early documents on feminist theory, both European and American, with full biographical and critical introductions; research on nineteenth-century feminist theory.

SIDELIGHTS: Margaret McFadden told CA: "I have been working in the area of women's studies for the past ten years,

developing new courses, writing grants, coordinating efforts, and doing research in feminist theory. A sabbatical in 1982 took me to Europe to study current European feminist theory, then allowed me to work on nineteenth-century documents at Wisconsin and, in 1984, at Harvard. I am also interested in feminist film theory and women's history.

"European feminist theory has become an important influence in the United States, especially in areas that wish to maximize differences between women and men (and celebrate these differences), areas such as psychoanalysis, attitudes toward war and the military, and women's culture. The lines of influence go both ways, of course, but American feminists are becoming more open to various European models."

*　　*　　*

McFARLAND, Marvin W(ilks)   1919-1985

OBITUARY NOTICE: Born November 15, 1919, in Philadelphia, Pa.; died of a heart attack, February 25, 1985, in Silver Spring, Md. Librarian, historian, and editor. McFarland was associated with the Library of Congress for more than thirty years, the last twelve as chief of its science and technology division. For his service during World War II as an Army Air Force historian in Europe, McFarland earned a Bronze Star. Following his retirement from the Library of Congress in 1980 he became curator of the Stephen Giraud Collection in Philadelphia. McFarland also edited the two-volume Papers of Wilbur and Orville Wright, contributed to American Heritage's History of Flight, served as technical adviser for the television film "The Winds of Kitty Hawk," and published articles in professional journals.

OBITUARIES AND OTHER SOURCES:

BOOKS

Directory of American Scholars, Volume I: History, 8th edition, Bowker, 1982.
Who's Who in America, 42nd edition, Marquis, 1982.

PERIODICALS

Washington Post, March 2, 1985.

*　　*　　*

McGILL, Leonard J(ames)   1956-

PERSONAL: Born October 21, 1956, in Melbourne, Fla.; son of Robert William (an electrical engineer) and Jacqueline (Battaglia) McGill; married Doreen Elizabeth Garcia (a financial planner), August 31, 1981. Education: University of Florida, B.S., 1977.

ADDRESSES: Home and office—270 Riverside Dr., No. 6E, New York, N.Y. 10025. Agent—Connie Clausen Associates, 250 East 87th St., New York, N.Y. 10028.

CAREER: Gentleman's Quarterly, New York, N.Y., contributing editor, 1982-84; free-lance writer and publicist, 1984—. Public relations representative for Fibers Division of Celanese, Inc.

MEMBER: American Society of Journalists and Authors.

WRITINGS:

Disco Dressing, Prentice-Hall, 1981.
Stylewise: A Man's Guide to Looking Good for Less, Putnam, 1983.

More Dash Than Cash, Fawcett, 1984.
Men's Hair, Rawson Associates, 1984.

Contributor to magazines, including *Men's Wear* and *Where,* and newspapers.

WORK IN PROGRESS: Love and the Upwardly Mobile Man; Fila's Guide to the Ultimate Tennis Lifestyle.

SIDELIGHTS: Leonard J. McGill told *CA:* "I decided to become a journalist while flipping through the University of Florida college catalog. My father had told me, 'You'll be successful at anything you do,' and, since my father is an honest guy, I believed him.

"I thought the writing life attractive. After all, you can write at any time of the day, live anywhere you want, and the only limit to your income is how hard you're willing to work, right? (Though experience has done its best to vaporize these daydreams of a young man, I still—amazingly—believe in them.)

"Graduating from college I found my journalism degree worth about as much as one of these electric metal detectors people use to find 'treasure' on the beach: it might help you find gold, but you're more likely to pick up small change. I decided I needed a specialty, and settled on men's clothing. For a shy young man with a great need to express himself, an interest in clothing came as naturally as an interest in writing. Which is not to say that I want to spend the rest of my life pondering the importance of double-breasted suits versus single-breasted versions. It's time to add other specialties and I'm working on it.

"I think of myself as trying to be a clever writer. In the everyday world cleverness eludes me. I'm not quick enough. Writing gives me time to construct interesting (to me, anyway) thoughts. The best part of writing, however, is creating a sentence that makes me laugh.

"Writing not only allows me to reach, but to enjoy the stretch as well. In life, illusions come and go, but for me the writing life is an illusion holding eternal promise."

*　　　*　　　*

McGOLDSTEIN, Paddy
　　See PAGE, William

*　　　*　　　*

McKAY, John H(arvey)　1923-

BRIEF ENTRY: Born July 5, 1923, in Everettsville, W.Va. American football coach and author. McKay coached college football teams at the University of Oregon from 1949 to 1959 and at the University of Southern California from 1959 to 1976. He then became the coach of the National Football League team Tampa Bay Buccaneers. McKay wrote *Football Coaching* (Ronald, 1966), and *McKay: A Coach's Story* (Atheneum, 1974). *Address:* c/o Tampa Bay Buccaneers, 1 Buccaneer Pl., Tampa, Fla. 33607.

BIOGRAPHICAL/CRITICAL SOURCES:

BOOKS

Libby, Bill, *The Coaches,* Regnery, 1972.
Who's Who in America, 42nd edition, Marquis, 1982.

PERIODICALS

Newsweek, October 29, 1962, January 13, 1975.

McKENDRICK, (Hector) Fergus　1933-

PERSONAL: Born July 1, 1933, in Motherwell, Scotland; son of James (a dentist) and Jessie (a housewife; maiden name, Ferguson) McKendrick; married Jean Lansbury (a housewife), August 8, 1958; children: Iain, Jane. *Education:* Wadham College, Oxford, M.A., 1954.

ADDRESSES: Home—37A De Parys Ave., Bedford MK40 2TR, England. *Office*—Bedford School, Burnaby Rd., Bedford, England.

CAREER: Teacher at Sutton County Grammar School, Surrey, England, 1956-57; Bedford School, Bedford, England, biology master, 1957—.

WRITINGS:

Pulpit Cricket and Other Stories, Collins, 1983.
The Season at Nether Pothole (humorous stories about the game of cricket), Collins, in press.

SIDELIGHTS: Fergus McKendrick told *CA:* "Cricket is the major summer sport of England, Australia, New Zealand, South Africa, India, Pakistan, and Sri Lanka. It is the main legacy the English left behind in places they colonized or conquered in their Imperialist era, and most thinking Englishmen would argue that it has a greater civilizing influence than the other, more celebrated remnants of their rule—namely the parliamentary system of government, the rule of law, and the Christian religion. All these former colonies prove this by sending national teams across regularly to beat the English side thoroughly; they never send religious, political, or legal teams to do anything equivalent.

"No foreigner who has fully grasped the character of the English does not realize that the really top level cricket matches take five days, and in the majority of cases they end in a draw. I think that one of the great differences between English and American attitudes to sport—and by extrapolation, to life—is that to a true cricketer, a good draw can be exciting, enjoyable, satisfactory, and much to be preferred to a win gained by play tainted with the ungentlemanly, the underhanded, or (horror of horrors!) the professional.

"I played the game to a moderate, but not high, level, but I limit myself these days to coaching young boys and umpiring adult matches, both of which occupations give a gratifying sensation of power without the danger of exposing to test an always doubtful and now aging competence in the actual playing of the game.

"My stories are fictional, though based, of course, on experience. I am very fond of the game of cricket, but far from obsessed with it. It is a fringe activity in my life. I wrote about cricket, rather than something else, because that was what I was asked to write about and it was the first time anyone had asked me to write about anything. Most of the not-very-great number of people who have read the books seem to enjoy them. I am engaged in another set of cricket stories but am also trying to move out into wider fields; this could well come to nothing, for wide fields are easy places to get lost in."

*　　　*　　　*

McKENZIE, Doug
　　See THOMAS, Dave

McKEON, Richard P(eter)   1900-1985

OBITUARY NOTICE: Born April 26, 1900, in Union Hill, N.J.; died March 31, 1985, in Hyde Park, Ill. McKeon, who was highly regarded in academic circles as a philosophical scholar, began teaching at Columbia University in 1925 and earned his doctorate there three years later. He went to the University of Chicago in 1935 as dean of the humanities division, and he served as the Charles F. Grey Distinguished Service Professor of Greek and Philosophy from 1947 until his retirement in 1974. McKeon had also been a member of the U.S. delegation to UNESCO, attending the first three general conferences, which were held in Paris, Mexico City, and Beirut. In addition, he served as an adviser on political philosophy and on educational matters to the governments of India, France, Norway, and Puerto Rico. McKeon's many honors included being named Carus Lecturer of the American Philosophical Society in 1963 and receiving the 1971 Quantrelle Award for excellence in undergraduate teaching from University of Chicago. Among his publications are *The Philosophy of Spinoza: The Unity of His Thought, Freedom and History: The Semantics of Philosophical Controversies and Ideological Conflicts, The Basic Works of Aristotle,* and *Thought, Action, and Passion.* He was also a contributor of articles to professional journals.

OBITUARIES AND OTHER SOURCES:

BOOKS

Finkelstein, Louis, editor, *Thirteen Americans,* Institute for Religious and Social Studies, 1953.
Twentieth-Century Authors: A Biographical Dictionary of Modern Literature, 1st supplement, Wilson, 1955.

PERIODICALS

Chicago Tribune, April 4, 1985.
New York Times, April 3, 1985.

* * *

McLELLAN, Robert   1907-1985

OBITUARY NOTICE—See index for *CA* sketch: Born January 28, 1907, in Lanark, Scotland; died January 27, 1985. Poet, playwright, and author of short stories. McLellan is best remembered for championing the revival of the Scots dialect as a medium of expression suitable for dramatic works. He used the idiom to advantage in his own plays, among which are "Jeddart Justice," "Toom Byres," "Young Auchinleck," and "Jamie the Saxt: A Historical Comedy," which some critics consider his best play. McLellan also wrote verse, earning the Scottish Arts Council Poetry Prize in 1956 for his dramatic poem "Sweet Largie Bay," and he was the author of various works for radio and television. His short stories are included in such anthologies as *Scottish Short Stories* and *Best Broadcast Stories.*

OBITUARIES AND OTHER SOURCES:

PERIODICALS

Times (London), February 2, 1985.

McNALLY, Gertrude Bancroft   1908(?)-1985

OBITUARY NOTICE: Born c. 1908; died of Alzheimer's disease, January 28, 1985, in Washington, D.C. Economist, stat-

istician, and author. Considered an authority on measurements of employment, McNally participated in the development of the Current Population Survey. She began her career in the mid-1930's as a coordinator for manpower statistics in the population division of the U.S. Census Bureau. From there McNally joined the U.S. Bureau of Labor Statistics, where she rose to assistant to the commissioner; she served in that capacity until her retirement in the late 1960's. McNally held a master's degree in economics from the University of Pennsylvania and studied at the London School of Economics and Political Science. She was a fellow of the American Statistical Association and author of a 1957 book, *The American Labor Force.*

OBITUARIES AND OTHER SOURCES:

PERIODICALS

Washington Post, January 31, 1985.

* * *

McNEELY, Jerry Clark   1928-

BRIEF ENTRY: Born June 20, 1928, in Cape Girardeau, Mo. American educator and author. McNeely taught communication arts at the University of Wisconsin—Madison from 1956 to 1975. Then he turned his attention to writing for television. He created, wrote, and directed the series "Owen Marshall, Counselor at Law," which was based on his own 1970 screenplay. McNeely also wrote and directed "Lucas Tanner," and he was the writer and producer of "Something for Joey" and "The Critical List." In addition, he has worked as a scriptwriter for such television series as "Dr. Kildare," "The Man From U.N.C.L.E.," "The Virginian," "Marcus Welby, M.D.," and "The Streets of San Francisco." *Address:* c/o CBS Studio Center, 4024 Radford Ave., Studio City, Calif. 91604.

BIOGRAPHICAL/CRITICAL SOURCES:

BOOKS

Directory of American Scholars, Volume II: *English, Speech, and Drama,* 7th edition, 1978.

* * *

McOWAN, Rennie   1933-

PERSONAL: Surname is pronounced Mak-*oh*-an; born January 12, 1933, in Stirling, Scotland; son of Robert (a teacher) and Janet (a teacher; maiden name, Ross) McOwan; married Agnes Mooney (a teacher), August 1, 1959; children: Lesley Clare, Michael, Thomas, Niall. *Politics:* Scottish Nationalist. *Religion:* Roman Catholic.

ADDRESSES: Home and office—7 Williamfield Ave., Stirling FK7 9AH, Scotland.

CAREER: Journalist and feature writer associated with the *Stirling Journal,* Kemsley Newspapers, Scotsman Publications, and the *Evening Dispatch,* 1950-60; in public relations and publicity with National Trust for Scotland, 1961-79; *Evening News,* Edinburgh, Scotland, senior feature writer, 1979-84; free-lance writer, 1984—.

MEMBER: International P.E.N., National Union of Journalists, Dollar Civic Trust (honorary member).

WRITINGS:

The Man Who Bought Mountains, National Trust for Scotland, 1976.
Tales of Stirling Castle and the Battle of Bannockburn (history book), Lang Syne Publishing, 1978.
Tales of Ben and Glen (Ben Nevis), Lang Syne Publishing, 1979.
(Contributor) *Walking in Scotland,* Spur Publications, 1981.
(Contributor) Hamish Brown, editor, *Poetry of the Scottish Hills,* Aberdeen University Press, 1982.
Light on Dumyat (juvenile novel), St. Andrew Press, 1982.
Walks in the Trossachs and the Rob Roy Country, St. Andrew Press, 1983.
The Scottish Clans (history book), Lang Syne Publishing, 1985.

Contributor of poems and articles to magazines, including *Scots Magazine* and *Leopard,* and to newspapers, including the *Glasgow Herald.*

WORK IN PROGRESS: A sequel to *Light on Dumyat; The Green Hills; Tales of the Scottish Clans.*

SIDELIGHTS: Rennie McOwan told *CA:* "I am intensely interested in Scottish politics, history, and conservation issues. I am a mountaineer, and I guide American walking groups in Scotland each summer.

"My walking groups want to be taken on pass or glen walks of about ten miles—longer and rugged or shorter and easier, depending on age and fitness of the party—and like being told about the area's history, flora, and fauna. I try to tell them of today's 'face' and then link it to past centuries. They are keen to know how the area functions—jobs, housing, family patterns, and so on. I try to link Scots history with their own. They are nearly all delightful people and I enjoy it very much. I also take some of them to stately homes or historic site on specific days.

"I also write en route commentaries covering the countryside we drive through and deliver the material over a microphone (I do this for Scottish groups too). Sometimes we include visits to islands, which are always very popular.

"I have camped, climbed, and walked in Scotland for thirty years and am a member of outdoor clubs and was—until business pressure made it impossible—a member of a rescue team. I have done some hill walking in England, Wales, Ireland, Kenya, and Tanzania (the last two walking experiences were snatched while on journalistic visits).

"I write for the pleasure of self-expression, of trying to pass on to others, however inadequately, the pleasure that areas of activity give me. My love of Scotland and the great need for urgent and sensible conservation policies to be implemented by the government, the spiritual quality of wilderness, and the 'feel' of Scottish history are, I think, shown in my writing. My adventure novel for children, *Light on Dumyat* (pronounced Dum-eye-at, a peak in the Ochil Hills in central Scotland) was chosen by the Central Region in 1983 as the theme of the primary, or junior, schools conference at Stirling University because it covers adventure, nature lore, history, and conservation.''

*   *   *

McSHINE, Kynaston (Leigh)   1935-

BRIEF ENTRY: Born February 20, 1935, in Port of Spain, Trinidad. Art historian, educator, and author. McShine taught at Hunter College of the City University of New York and at the School of Visual Arts. He also served as curator of painting and sculpture at New York City's Jewish Museum. In 1968 he accepted a position at the Museum of Modern Art, where he was appointed senior curator of painting and sculpture in 1980. McShine's books include *Information* (Museum of Modern Art, 1970), *Marcel Duchamp* (Museum of Modern Art, 1973), *The Natural Paradise: Painting in America, 1800-1950* (Museum of Modern Art, 1976), and *Joseph Cornell (Museum of Modern Art, 1980). Address:* Museum of Modern Art, 11 West 53rd St., New York, N.Y. 10019.

BIOGRAPHICAL/CRITICAL SOURCES:

BOOKS

Who's Who in American Art, 15th edition, Bowker, 1982.

PERIODICALS

New York Times Book Review, December 5, 1976.

*   *   *

MECKSTROTH, Jacob A.   1887(?)-1985
(Jake Meckstroth)

OBITUARY NOTICE: Born c. 1887 in New Knoxville, Ohio; died February 9, 1985; buried in New Knoxville, Ohio. American journalist. Meckstroth's career in journalism began when he left Ohio State University in 1912 as a member of the school's first journalism graduating class. After working briefly for the *Dayton Journal,* the *Dayton Herald,* and *Canton Repository,* he was hired by the *Ohio State Journal* in 1913. He became a political writer for the publication in 1920 and edited the newspaper from 1921 to 1959. In addition, Meckstroth wrote campaign speeches for Warren G. Harding when he ran for the U.S. Senate. Later, however, he served as a publicity representative for James Cox, Harding's opponent for the 1920 Democratic Presidential nomination.

OBITUARIES AND OTHER SOURCES:

PERIODICALS

Chicago Tribune, February 12, 1985.

*   *   *

MECKSTROTH, Jake
See MECKSTROTH, Jacob A.

*   *   *

MEGGENDORFER, Lothar   1847-1925

BRIEF ENTRY: Born November 6, 1847, in Munich, Bavaria (now West Germany); died in 1925 in Munich, Germany. German cartoonist, illustrator, and author. Meggendorfer is probably best remembered for an invention called "toy" books that he created during the 1880's. These books, which he also wrote and illustrated, gave life-like motion and expression to pictures through a system of tabs, wheels, wires, and slats activated with certain movements by the reader. Meggendorfer's work earned him recognition as a master of the art of moveable books and was considered a high point of creative inventiveness in nineteenth-century book publishing. Before creating his toy books, Meggendorfer was a cartoonist and illustrator for such German magazines as *Fliegende Blaetter* (comparable to Britain's *Punch*) and *Muenchener Bilderbogen.*

In 1889 he began publishing *Meggendorfer's Blaetter*, a humorous magazine that remained in publication until 1928.

Including his famous toy books, Meggendorfer wrote and illustrated more than sixty children's books, which sold over a million copies. When interest in moveable books declined around 1910, Meggendorfer turned to making puppets and producing puppet shows. A recent revival of interest, however, has resulted in the reissue of several of his most popular works. Among them are *The Doll's House* (1979), *The International Circus* (1980), *The City Park* (1981), and *Surprise! Surprise!* (1982). Original works by Meggendorfer are highly prized and sought after by collectors world-wide.

BIOGRAPHICAL/CRITICAL SOURCES:

BOOKS

Catalogue of the Meggendorfer Archive, Sotheby Parke Bernet, 1982.
World Encyclopedia of Cartoons, Chelsea House, 1976.

*   *   *

MELFORD, Austin (Alfred) 1884-1971

OBITUARY NOTICE: Born August 24, 1884, in Alverstoke, England; died August 19, 1971. Actor, director, producer, playwright, and screenwriter. Melford, whose acting career spanned more than fifty years, made his London stage debut in 1904. He served as producer for various London theatres, such as the Gaiety and the Drury Lane, and he acted in motion pictures, including "A Warm Corner," "Night of the Garter," and "Chicken Every Sunday." Beginning in 1934 Melford devoted his time mainly to writing and directing films. Among his screenwriting credits were "Ships With Wings," "Three Cockeyed Sailors," and "Let George Do It." In addition, Melford was the author or co-author of such plays as "The Daredevils," "It's a Girl," "Battling Butler," and "Patricia."

OBITUARIES AND OTHER SOURCES:

BOOKS

International Motion Picture Almanac, Quigley, 1985.
Who Was Who in the Theatre, 1912-1976, Gale, 1978.
Who's Who in the Theatre: A Biographical Record of the Contemporary Stage, 16th edition, Pitman, 1977.

*   *   *

MELL, Donald C(harles), Jr. 1931-

PERSONAL: Born May 20, 1931, in Akron, Ohio; son of Donald Charles and Josephine (Seiberling) Mell; married Katherine Lyon (a realtor), December 21, 1957; children: Donald Charles III, Elizabeth Louise. *Education:* Yale University, B.A., 1953, M.A., 1959; University of Pennsylvania, Ph.D., 1961.

ADDRESSES: Home—19 Harlech Dr., Wilmington, Del. 19807. *Office*—Department of English, University of Delaware, Newark, Del. 19716.

CAREER: Rutgers University, New Brunswick, N.J., instructor in English, 1961-65; Middlebury College, Middlebury, Vt., assistant professor of English, 1965-68; University of Delaware, Newark, assistant professor, 1968-73, associate professor, 1973-82, professor of English, 1983—. Field bibliographer for *The Eighteenth-Century: A Current Bibliography*, AMS Press, 1980—.

MEMBER: Modern Language Association of America, American Society for Eighteenth-Century Studies, English Institute.

WRITINGS:

A Poetics of Augustan Elegy: Studies of Poems by Dryden, Pope, Prior, Swift, Gray, and Johnson, Rodopi, 1974.
(Editor with John Irwin Fischer) *Contemporary Studies of Swift's Poetry*, University of Delaware Press, 1982.
English Poetry, 1660-1800: A Guide to Information Sources, Gale, 1982.
(Editor with Fischer and James Woolley) *The Poems of Jonathan Swift*, University of Delaware Press, in press.

Contributor to literature journals.

BIOGRAPHICAL/CRITICAL SOURCES:

PERIODICALS

Times Literary Supplement, October 23, 1981.

*   *   *

MENASHE, Samuel 1925-

PERSONAL: Born September 16, 1925, in New York, N.Y.; son of Berish Weisberg and Brantzia Barak. *Education:* Attended Queens College of the City of New York (now Queens College of the City University of New York), 1942-43, and 1946-47; Sorbonne, University of Paris, *doctorat d'universite*, 1950.

ADDRESSES: Home—New York, N.Y.

CAREER: Writer. *Military service:* U.S. Army, Infantry, 1943-46; served in Europe.

WRITINGS:

POETRY

The Many Named Beloved, Gollancz, 1961.
No Jerusalem But This, October House, 1971.
Fringe of Fire, Gollancz, 1973.
To Open, Viking, 1974.
Collected Poems, National Poetry Foundation, 1985.

Work represented in anthologies, including *A Green Place: Modern Poems*, Delacorte, 1982, and in textbooks. Contributor of poems to numerous periodicals, including *New York Review of Books*, *Times Literary Supplement*, *Antioch Review*, *Proteus*, *Poetry Nation Review*, *Midstream*, *Commonweal*, *Yale Review*, and *Harper's*.

WORK IN PROGRESS: Poems.

SIDELIGHTS: Samuel Menashe has earned acclaim as the creator of numerous compact and precise poems. His first American volume, *No Jerusalem But This*, was praised by Stephen Spender for "language intense and clear as diamonds." Spender declared that Menashe "can compress an attitude to life that has an immense history into three lines."

To Open, Menashe's 1974 collection, impressed *Christian Science Monitor* critic Victor Howes with its concentrated works. "The art of Samuel Menashe is a jeweler's art," Howes claimed. He noted that Menashe's "inner rhymes, his assonances, his occasional plays upon words make even the simplest-seeming statement a construct to read again with heightened attention."

Although Menashe has published only a few volumes, he is nonetheless prized by critics such as Donald Davie and Hugh Kenner as a unique and worthwhile poet. In *National Review*

Kenner praised Menashe's "taut energies," and in an *Inquiry* review of Davie's *The Poet in the Imaginary Museum*, Kenner focused almost entirely on Davie's elucidation of Menashe's art. In "The Poetry of Samuel Menashe," Davie linked Menashe to William Blake and wrote, "If we continue to ignore Menashe, or allow him only the abstracted nod that we give to an unclassifiable oddity, we are in effect saying that he doesn't deserve to profit by the promise that Blake made."

CA INTERVIEW

CA interviewed Samuel Menashe in January, 1984, in New York City.

CA: You are a real New Yorker—born in New York, continuing to live there most of the time, and, if I am not mistaken, immersing yourself in its currents every day. How much has the psychology of big-city living got to do with your poetry, either directly or through the isolation it imposes?

MENASHE: One morning, years ago, when I was returning from Europe, I did not rush up to the deck to see the Statue of Liberty. Later, when I looked out of the porthole, the ship was being nosed toward the West Houston Street pier—there was the Archives Building like Babylonia itself. I was amazed by the words that burst out of me, "My native city!" I had just come from France—the *ne* was very strong in *native*. But my patriotism is local. Had the ship docked uptown, I might not have been so exultant. When I came down the gangplank, I walked home in a few minutes, as if I lived in a small seaport—Old New York. I live here, yes, but I am not a social realist. My ivory tower is in a tenement on Thompson Street.

In my youth and as a young man, starting with the war, I was away for several years, but as I get older I find it hard to leave, to travel—except to escape the heat:

> Who would eat
> an egg you fry
> on the sidewalk
> in July?

About fifteen years ago I said that I would like to travel as far as I could walk in a day. A friend, now dead, told me that Plato said that the size of the ideal republic would be the distance a man could walk in a day. However, because I want to get out of the streets quickly, I commute—by subway—to Central Park almost every afternoon. I remember being taken to a concert in the park fifty-five years ago:

> One of those hours
> in early afternoon
> when nothing happens
> but time makes room.

Yes, I've lived a lifetime here. Of course, life in the city is not what it was. It is dangerous now—increasingly so as one gets older.

It is not the city which imposes isolation. I am isolated because I am not in the network of poet-editors or poet-professors—a very exclusive club.

CA: There are only rare specific references to the city in your poems. Would you comment?

MENASHE: I am not a descriptive poet, but there are poems like "Sheep Meadow" or "Sunset, Central Park":

> A wall of windows
> Ignited by the sun
> Burns in one column
> Of fire on the lake
> Night follows day
> As embers break.

Or "Autumn":

> I walk outside the stone wall
> Looking into the park at night
> As armed trees frisk a windfall
> Down paths which lampposts light.

CA: How would you describe the landscape, if any, of your poems?

MENASHE: The landscape of my poems is Central Park. It is a miniature landscape, but as you step into it you are in another world of trees, slopes, boulders, the lake, the reservoir. A friend wrote to me from England after a first, brief visit here. He said that when he was asked about New York he told his friends about the trees. We spent three October days walking in Central Park. It is usually assumed that the following lines come from the coast of Maine:

> A flock of little boats
> Tethered to the shore
> Drifts in still water
> Prows dip, nibbling.

I saw that "flock" on the lake in the park. Yet, there are unmistakable city poems. "In Stride":

> Streets at night like decks
> With spars overhead
> Whose rigging ropes
> Stars into scope.

Or "Tenement Spring":

> Blue month of May, make us
> Light as laundry on lines
> Wind we do not see, mind us
> Early in the morning.

CA: It is interesting that, though you write in a city where everything is on so large a scale, your poems are on so small a scale. How did you happen on what might be called the miniature mode?

MENASHE: I wonder what Plato said about the ideal length of a poem—after all, the Greeks had Sappho as well as Homer. And Goliath was felled by a pebble—well aimed. I have always experienced the penetrating thrust of a few words.

I have also been called a minimalist. I did not decide to make this kind of a poem anymore than I decided to be a poet. What I do must be my way—natural to me. The struggle is against words, words, words. Dante says that the word should be a crystal through which you see the thing itself. Stephen Crane says you should not tell how you feel—you should give the facts of feeling. Simone Weil says that the duty of the writer is like that of the translator—to stick to the text of reality without adding or subtracting a syllable. I am paraphrasing authors I read a long time ago. Whenever I came across such passages there was immediate, joyous assent to what they said. A lot of words do not necessarily create what is called reality. A few words—*les mots justes*—may put us in touch with it, a light touch. One critic said that my poems were like line drawings—think what a few lines of Matisse do. If words are being counted, and—of course—I resist that way of appraising a poem, one must say that in a short poem every word counts. Didn't Poe tell us that in a long poem not all the lines are poetry?

CA: Are there any poets ancient or modern who have influenced you in this way?

MENASHE: When I was about fourteen years old, I read the following passage posted in front of an old Quaker meeting-house: "... But the Lord was not in the wind: and after the wind an earthquake; but the Lord was not in the earthquake: and after the earthquake a fire; but the Lord was not in the fire: and after the fire a still small voice." Those words of the prophet Elijah made a tremendous impression on me as did some of the psalms and short poems of William Blake. I was possessed by them at sight—they were a revelation—but such influences are not literary. I was not a young poet finding models to emulate.

After the war the word "zen" entered the fashionable jargon, and sometimes "haiku" is ignorantly applied to my poems. Before he reviewed my first book, one critic wanted to know if I had read Landor. I liked the sound of the name, but it was unknown to me—I thought it was Greek. I am not trying to make a claim for originality—that is not my concern—but I did not become a poet by conventional, literary descent. Before the war I was a biochemistry major.

In my twenty-fourth year—without forseeing it the day before—with no thought of being a poet, I woke up one winter night under the bare windows of my room in Paris. Thrust among the stars by this sudden awakening, I began my first poem, which tells this experience. In my day, one did not decide to be a poet or take courses to become one. One never expected to meet a poet.

CA: What about your critics and readers? How have they responded to the brevity of most of your poems?

MENASHE: Those who like my work call it concise or economical. Those who dislike it call it slight. I find that people do tend to dwell on the shortest poems—on the quatrains or those of two or three lines. In fact, most of my poems are of six, eight, and ten lines. Some of them are longer. By what right can one claim that one has a poem in a few words? By a dive deep enough below the surface of experience to come up with a depth charge, sometimes.

CA: There are some of fewer than a dozen words, such as "The Niche":

> The niche narrows
> Hones one thin
> Until his bones
> Disclose him.

Would you explicate this one, or in some way comment on it?

MENASHE: If I have succeeded, the impact of the last verb is physical—it makes the poem happen. One morning, instantly, after a month of knocking my head against the wall, *disclose* came through the ceiling like a bolt of lightning. I think the poem itself is a disclosure. Once I was asked, "What does one do with a poem of four lines with a word on each line?" I said, "One reads it again." None of my poems is

that short, but the question did indicate the general tendency to see my poems briefer than they are. As for the work, it should never show, but because I am working in such a small space—at close quarters with each word—the concentration, the pressure I am under until the breakthrough, is very strong. John Thornton, an old friend and my first critic, once said, "You do not merely thread the needle—you try to go through the needle yourself."

CA: I believe your first book was published not in New York, but in London. How did that come about?

MENASHE: My first book was published in London because I could not get a publisher here—despite the fact that I had accumulated some good magazine credits: the *Yale Review,* the *Antioch Review, Commonweal, Harper's,* etc. Most editors do not read poetry. The poetry editor is almost invariably the house poet or a person who is working with the interlocking directorate of establishment poets. Government censorship could not be more effective, but here you can't be sent to Siberia—you are just kept out of print.

A friend gave me an introduction to someone in London. He told me at once that I would never find a publisher there. However, after a few months in England, I sent my poems to Kathleen Raine, an English poet at Cambridge University. She did not know me from Adam, but I thought of her because she was a Blake scholar. Raine sent the manuscript to Victor Gollancz, who published it with a foreword by her. She wanted to call me a young poet. I pleaded with her to drop that adjective. I was thirty-six years old.

CA: How much have you published altogether?

MENASHE: Four books—two in London and two in New York. The "latest" book, *To Open* (Viking Press), came out in 1974. It is out of print. Of course, I have more than enough poems for another book, but I have no publisher—either in London, where Victor Gollancz Ltd. is no longer publishing poetry, or in New York. I am now back where I was in 1960 when I went to London for the first time, but now I am almost an old man. Mine is hardly a successful "career."

Yet, Hugh Kenner now has joined the critics who have written favorably about my work. Support like this—in three essays that I know about—strengthens my wrists, but I am still a cliff-hanger and those on the top of the cliff trample your fingers to make you let go. If it were up to the poets in power here, not a poem of mine would have been published—let alone a book. In 1971, when I last submitted an application to a famous foundation, I could tell that the book they returned to me had never been opened, cracked. As I started to open it myself, I stopped—the binding was absolutely stiff. When I pointed this out to the executive secretary of the foundation, he was unperturbed. "Undoubtedly, our judges were familiar with your work," he said. Backing my application was a recent review by Stephen Spender in the *New York Review of Books* (July 22, 1971). I never applied again. You can be defeated.

CA: You still publish frequently in the Times Literary Supplement, *don't you? Are there other editors partial to the short poem?*

MENASHE: At this point I ask to be spared the adjective *short*. Admittedly, I don't write narrative or epic poetry, but I would like to point out that many of the most celebrated poems in

English are no longer than eight or ten lines. Even a sonnet is only fourteen lines long. Donald Davie and Kathleen Raine publish my poems. P. N. Furbank published them when he was an editor. He said about them: "Samuel Menashe is a strange and remarkable poet, whose tiny poems—perfect little mechanisms, minute cathedrals—are not only very elaborate structures but are, as it were, all structure: acoustic structures, counterchanging assonance and internal rhyme; syntactical structures concentrating great charges of energy; etymological structures, reenacting the life history of words. . . . His is as fine a talent as any working in English today."

CA: That must have been very welcome acclaim. In general how important to you are the responses of critics?

MENASHE: Very important. Unless they write about you, few people will know that your work exists—even if it has been published. Moreover, as Thoreau said, "It takes two people to say a truth—one to say it and one to say yes to it." It is encouraging indeed to think that Davie and Furbank and Kenner and Bedient are right about my work.

CA: There is a politics of poetry, as you suggested, especially in a center like New York, which radiates from an establishment and to a certain extent determines who is in and who is out. How do you feel about this?

MENASHE: Awful. A critic in the *Saturday Review* called me a maverick who has antagonized everyone in the world of poetry in New York. He said that my "enemies would gnash their teeth" when they saw that I was doing my own "thing"— which he approved. I antagonized them by succeeding in England after I had been dismissed here. I was not meant to be seen again, but I came back from England with a success which any of the politicos here would have been glad to have: a well-known British publisher, the lead review by Donald Davie in the *New Statesman* when that journal was read like holy writ by the New York intelligentsia. P. N. Furbank in the *Listener*, Austin Clarke in the *Irish Times* praised the poems, but to no avail here. Not only was the door not opened for me in New York, but it was slammed even harder in my face. Instead of accepting my failure here, I had stepped out of line by going to England and obtained that which I had no right to. It was not until 1971—ten years later—that a small publisher brought my first book out here. Professionally, I had an excellent British passport but I could not get an American visa for it. I was not to be allowed in. I live a kind of domestic exile in my native city. William Blake says, "For now the sneaking serpent walks in mild humility and the just man rages in the wilds where lions roar." Once an old friend invited me to a small, quiet party—not even vaguely literary. I never get to those. A poet, professor, editor—one of the most venal and powerful politicians in the business—asked me, "What are you doing here?"

CA: What about the poet-professors?

MENASHE: Poet-professors should mold students in their own image in poetry workshops, extending the network of power. If you are a good disciple, publication begins for you and you in turn become a poet-professor or editor or both. You also become astute at getting grants from national or local agencies for the arts. These poets also read at each other's colleges. Their coteries cover the country.

CA: Is it your notion that a "following" would put more or less strain on a poet's productivity?

MENASHE: Less. Just to have a publisher, not to have to struggle to find one, would make life much easier. I don't make poems for my drawer or a few friends. I do have some readers—particularly in Great Britain, where I am published in textbooks and anthologies as well as in journals. I am sure that there is a literate public, estranged from most contemporary poetry, which would respond to my poems if they were published here.

CA: How did you become a poet? Was it inevitable from childhood?

MENASHE: Who knows what is inevitable? By a hair the balance tips from one side to the other. Thirty years ago when I moved into this flat—no longer cold-water but with the bathtub still in the kitchen—I could not imagine myself as I am here now, older than my parents were then. Looking back at a lifetime it seems that what is called fate hinges on chance. Is it inevitable for some young men to die in wars while others survive without knowing why they did? The youth I was before the war might have led a more conventional life. Not that I was making poems when I was in the infantry, but the war defined—intensified—me. We lived only in the moment encircled by death. The following poem, "Warrior Wisdom," was made ten years after the war:

> *Do not scrutinize*
> *A secret wound—*
> *Avert your eyes—*
> *Nothing's to be done*
> *Where darkness lies*
> *No light can come.*

A few years later I saw that the wound *secretes* darkness.

CA: What is the whole range of your experience outside New York?

MENASHE: I was in Europe in the war (1944-1945) and then— under the G. I. Bill—for about three and a half years after the war. I was awarded a *doctorat d'universite* at the Sorbonne for a thesis called "Un Essai sur l'experience poetique (etude introspective)." What I meant by the poetic experience is that awareness which is the source of poetry.

I also lived in California for a year, spent almost two years in London, at various times during long visits. I was in Spain for over a year—nine months of it in Ibiza while it was still a pastoral island. I have spent many months during various visits in Israel, Italy, Ireland, Holland, and Norway.

CA: Which languages besides English do you know, and do you ever write poetry in them?

MENASHE: I know French and Spanish and Yiddish well. I understand Italian—from the Spanish—and I can make myself understood in it. As a child I was bilingual. Yiddish, a German dialect, connected me to the German root of English. I was not aware of this for many years. Without my intending it, the diction of my poetry is of Anglo-Saxon origin—the one-syllable words which are closest to physical experience.

CA: I know you are a music lover. Does this have any influence on your poetic composition?

MENASHE: I hope so. Isn't poetry a music made with words— one way of defining it? Moreover, I rhyme. For me poetry without rhyme is like music without melody.

CA: Do you ever expect to undertake larger forms?

MENASHE: I don't think that I will ever write an epic. I can spend months devising a poem that has been published already. The new version is always more concise than the original.

CA: You should have the last word in this interview. What is it?

MENASHE: When my mother was my age she was dying of cancer. A few weeks before her death she had a stroke and lost her speech. By an heroic struggle she regained it. One day—speaking slowly but clearly—she said, "I love language. Language should not be used freely—I mean loosely. Language commands respect."

A few years earlier, looking up from one of my "shortest" poems, she said, "When one sees the trees in leaf one thinks the beauty of the tree is in its leaves and then one sees the bare tree."

If the very last word is to be mine, it seems appropriate to conclude this interview with the following poem, "At a Standstill":

> That statue, that cast
> Of my solitude
> Has found its niche
> In this kitchen
> Where I do not eat
> Where the bathtub stands
> Upon cat feet—
> I did not advance
> I cannot retreat.

BIOGRAPHICAL/CRITICAL SOURCES:

BOOKS

Davie, Donald, *The Poet in the Imaginary Museum*, Persea Press, 1978.

PERIODICALS

Christian Science Monitor, August 28, 1974.
Commonweal, August 15, 1975.
Inquiry, May 29, 1978.
Listener, October 25, 1973.
Nation, March 6, 1972.
National Review, November 27, 1981.
New Statesman, January 4, 1974.
New York Review of Books, July 22, 1971.
Times Literary Supplement, January 25, 1974.

—*Interview by Fred Bornhauser*

* * *

MENDENHALL, Thomas C(orwin II)   1910-

PERSONAL: Born June 14, 1910, in Chicago, Ill.; married, 1938; children: three. *Education:* Yale University, B.A., 1932, Ph.D., 1938; Oxford University, B.A., 1935, B.Litt., 1936.

ADDRESSES: Home—R.F.D. 501, Vineyard Haven, Mass. 02568.

CAREER: Yale University, New Haven, Conn., 1937-59, began as instructor, became associate professor of history, director of foreign area studies, 1944-46; master of Berkeley College, 1950-59; Smith College, Northampton, Mass., professor of history and president of college, 1959-75, professor and president emeritus, 1975—.

AWARDS, HONORS: Fellow of Huntington Library, 1956; LL.D. from Amherst College, 1960; L.H.D. from University of Massachusetts, 1961, Medical College of Pennsylvania, 1971, and Smith College, 1978.

WRITINGS:

A Short History of American Rowing, Charles River, 1981.
(With James Howard) *Making History Come Alive*, Council on Basic Education, 1983.

Contributor to journals.

* * *

MERLIN, Samuel   1910-

PERSONAL: Born January 17, 1910, in Kishinev, Russia (now U.S.S.R.); came to the United States in 1940; son of Abraham (in business) and Miriam (Rabin) Merlin; married Winona Weber, October, 1950. *Education:* Attended Sorbonne, University of Paris, 1931-33, and L'Ecole des Hautes Etudes Sociales, Paris, France, 1931-33; received baccalaureate.

ADDRESSES: Home—27 East 62nd St., New York, N.Y. 10021. *Office*—Institute for Mediterranean Affairs, 428 East 83rd St., New York, N.Y. 10028.

CAREER: Secretary-general of world executive of Zionist Revisionist Organization, 1934-38; *Di Tat* (title means "The Deed"), Warsaw, Poland, editor in chief, 1938-39; secretary-general of Hebrew Committee for National Liberation, 1944-48; member of first Knesset, Israel's national legislative body, 1948-51; president of Israel Press Ltd., 1950-57; Institute for Mediterranean Affairs, New York, N.Y., began as director of political studies, became director of institute. Special emissary of French Ministry of Blockage and Boycott Against Germany to the United States, 1940. Part-time faculty member at Fairleigh Dickinson University, 1967—; lecturer at colleges and universities; guest on television programs in the United States and England.

AWARDS, HONORS: Elected honorary member of the Arab municipality of Abu Ghosh, Israel.

WRITINGS:

The Palestine Refugee Problem: A New Approach and a Plan for a Solution, Institute for Mediterranean Affairs, 1957.
(With Alex Wilf) *Ascent of Man*, Yoseloff, 1963.
(Editor) *The Cypress Dilemma: Options for Peace*, Institute for Mediterranean Affairs, 1967.
(Editor and contributor) *The Big Powers and the Present Crisis in the Middle East: A Colloquium*, Fairleigh Dickinson University Press, 1968.
The Search for Peace in the Middle East: The Story of President Bourguiba's Campaign for a Negotiated Peace Between Israel and the Arab States, Yoseloff, 1969.
Guerre et paix au Moyen Orient (title means "War and Peace in the Middle East"), Denoel, 1970.

Also author, with Ben Heicht, of *Shylock, My Brother*. Contributor of several hundred articles to periodicals in the United States and abroad. Past member of editorial staffs of newspapers in Romania, France, and Israel; editor of *Answer*, 1943-46; past chairman of editorial board of *Herut*.

WORK IN PROGRESS: Without a Mandate, three volumes; *From Solution to Problem: The Origins of Israel's Predicament*.

SIDELIGHTS: Samuel Merlin told *CA:* "From 1934 until 1938 I was secretary-general of the Zionist Revisionist Organization's world executive and a close collaborator and friend of Vladimir Jabotinsky, president of the movement. But I left the Revisionist party in 1938 and joined the Hebrew Underground (Irgun Z'vai Leumi). *Di Tat* ('The Deed'), of which I was editor in chief from 1938 until 1939, was a daily newspaper that promoted the ideas and activities of the Irgun.

"With the proclamation of the State of Israel, the Irgun surfaced from the underground and became a political party under the name of Herut. I was, together with Menachem Begin, a co-founder of that party in 1948. I also arranged for the publication of a daily newspaper equally named *Herut*, and I was chairman of the paper's editorial board.

"My three-volume documentary, *Without a Mandate*, is the history of the Committee for a Jewish Army, the Emergency Committee to Save the Jewish People of Europe, the Hebrew Committee of National Liberation, and the American League for a Free Palestine. These organizations came into being and were inspired and, to a considerable extent, oriented by a group of Palestinians. All were members of the Irgun, the United States group of which was headed by Peter H. Bergson (also known as Hillel Kook). The Hebrew Committee of National Liberation was established in 1944 and was dissolved with the creation of the State of Israel in 1948. I was executive director of both the Committee for a Jewish Army and the Committee to Save the Jewish People of Europe, and I served as secretary-general of the Hebrew Committee for National Liberation.

"The motivations of my writings on Jewish and Zionist affairs were the abnormal conditions of the Jewish people in Eastern Europe, that vast zone of distress, and the vision of a free Palestine in the sense that it is not administered or ruled by a foreign power. The actual establishment of Israel, which is a unique and almost incomprehensible achievement in the history of mankind, was nonetheless anticlimactic. It did not exactly fit into the vision I had during the years of our struggle to create the state. My study on the history of Zionism, *From Solution to Problem: The Origins of Israel's Predicament*, deals with this. As its title implies and as my manuscript explains, a Jewish state was supposed to be the solution to the Jewish problem, mainly in Eastern Europe. Instead, Israel became a problem to the Jews of the world.

"Though all my adult life I was dedicated to the idea of a Hebrew renaissance in a sovereign state in Palestine, and during the war years I concentrated on the rescue of the European Jews, my intellectual curiosities, activities, and writings transcend that specific dedication. I am interested in philosophy, literature, and the arts. *The Ascent of Man* and my brochure, 'Towards a Property-Owning Society,' do not deal with Jewish or Palestinian problems. And I have written, with the late Ben Hecht, a work on William Shakespeare titled *Shylock, My Brother*. It deals not only with Shakespeare's play *The Merchant of Venice*, but with the life and ethnic origins of Shakespeare as well.

"I should say that my personal philosophical ideal is a free society that permits the autonomy of the individual. I cherish this not only as an ideal. I judge government policies and behavior only as they affect the rights of the individual. I do not consider collective rights, not even when they are applied to class or to special groups. To me, a stretched arm with a closed fist belonging to a man who is yelling 'all power to the people' or all power to whomever, is both absurd and evil.

"My favorite philosophers are Hans Vaihinger, author of *The Philosophy of 'As If,'* and Jose Ortega y Gasset, Soeren Kierkegaard, Friedrich Nietzsche, and Ecclesiastes."

BIOGRAPHICAL/CRITICAL SOURCES:

PERIODICALS

National Review, July 1, 1969.

*   *   *

MEYERSON, Martin   1922-

BRIEF ENTRY: Born November 14, 1922, in New York, N.Y. American educator, administrator, and author. Meyerson began his teaching career in 1948 and was the Frank Backus Williams Professor of City Planning and Urban Research at Harvard University from 1957 to 1963. During the same years he directed the Joint Center for Urban Studies of Harvard and the Massachusetts Institute of Technology. Meyerson has also served as executive director of the American Council to Improve Our Neighborhoods and as an adviser to the United Nations in Yugoslavia, Indonesia, and Japan. He was appointed president of the State University of New York at Buffalo in 1966 and president of the University of Pennsylvania in 1970.

The educator's books include *Housing, People, and Cities* (McGraw, 1962), *Face of the Metropolis* (Random House, 1963), *Boston: The Job Ahead* (Harvard University Press, 1966), *The City and the University* (Macmillan of Canada, 1969), and *Gladly Learn and Gladly Teach: Franklin and His Heirs at the University of Pennsylvania, 1740-1976* (University of Pennsylvania Press, 1978). Meyerson edited *The Conscience of the City* (Braziller, 1970). *Address:* 2016 Spruce St., Philadelphia, Pa. 19174; and 100 College Hall, University of Pennsylvania, Philadelphia, Pa. 19174.

BIOGRAPHICAL/CRITICAL SOURCES:

BOOKS

The International Who's Who, 46th edition, Europa, 1982.

PERIODICALS

American Historical Review, October, 1979.
Christian Century, June 16, 1971.

*   *   *

MICHAELS, Fern
See ANDERSON, Roberta
and KUCZKIR, Mary

*   *   *

MILES, Ian (Douglas)   1948-

PERSONAL: Born February 21, 1948, in Gloucester, England; son of Albert Edward (an aviator and publican) and Marie Elsie (a publican, shopkeeper, and nursing auxiliary; maiden name, Atkinson) Miles; married Valerie Kay Francis, December, 1969 (separated); children: Lera Jane. *Education:* Victoria

University of Manchester, B.Sc., 1969. *Politics:* "Leftward." *Religion:* "Agnostic/atheistic."

ADDRESSES: Home—57 Upper Lewes Rd., Brighton, East Sussex BN2 3FG, England. *Office*—Science Policy Research Unit, Mantell Building, University of Sussex, Brighton, Sussex, England.

CAREER: University of Sussex, Brighton, England, research fellow at Science Policy Unit, 1972—. Consultant to United Nations.

MEMBER: Campaign for Nuclear Disarmament (member of national council, 1983), British Society for Social Responsibility in Science, World Futures Studies Federation, Society for International Development, Conference of Socialist Economists, Radical Statistics Group.

WRITINGS:

(Contributor) Solomon Encel, Pauline Marstrand, and William Page, editors, *The Art of Anticipation,* Martin Robertson, 1975.
The Poverty of Prediction, Lexington Books, 1975.
(Contributor) Christopher Freeman and Marie Jahoda, editors, *World Futures: The Great Debate,* Martin Robertson, 1978.
(Contributor) Thomas Whiston, editor, *Uses and Abuses of Forecasting,* Macmillan (England), 1979.
(Editor with John Irvine and Jeff Evans) *Demystifying Social Statistics,* Pluto Press, 1979.
(Editor with Irvine) *The Poverty of Progress,* Pergamon, 1982.
(With others) *The Nuclear Numbers Games,* Radical Statistics Group, 1982.
(With J. I. Gershuny) *The New Service Economy,* Frances Pinter, 1983.
(With Samuel Cole) *Worlds Apart,* Wheatsheaf, 1984.
(With others) *War Plan: Brighton,* Brighton Campaign for Nuclear Disarmament, 1984.
Social Indicators for Human Development, Frances Pinter, 1985.

Contributor to journals, including *Futures.*

WORK IN PROGRESS: A work tentatively titled *What Lies Beyond Work?* on the social impact of unemployment and its implications for the future of work; research on information technologies and services and possible long-term developments.

SIDELIGHTS: Ian Miles told *CA:* "Employment is only one of the ways in which people contribute to society and in which they work in the broadest sense. Yet employment is often identified with work and remains a major means of distributing incomes—and a whole range of important social and psychological benefits, such as social contacts, status, and time structure. Technological and economic change are reshaping employment, and new forms of association are demonstrating that there is 'life after employment.' But social attitudes and institutional regulations have yet to catch up with the need to rethink the boundaries drawn between work and nonwork, gainful employment and unemployment. At the end of the twentieth century, this is one of the most important challenges facing us, both as individuals planning our daily lives and careers and as social beings to create humane and just societies.

"I have been extremely fortunate to find the colleagues and institutes that enable me to bring together my lifelong interests in the future and in what makes people tick. I have been able to get out of the compartments of academic disciplines while not losing the discipline to do and present research. After a couple of months of completing major reports I can testify that this takes hard work, and it brings rewards along with the exhaustion! I have been working for many years on fairly short-term research contracts, in a unit that measures itself against scholarly rather than consulting standards. This has meant that I've had to change intellectual direction a number of times. It has been important in keeping my mind open, leading me to confront new challenges, and stopping me from becoming a narrow expert.

"The trouble with research into social and technological change, and studies of the future in particular, is that it is often hard to see the consequences of your work. For me, it is important *not* to become a 'free-floating intellectual,' but instead to be related to, and working with, social movements. The dialogue here has been important both to my intellectual development and my social action.

"I like novels, the good 5 percent of science fiction, films, performance art, creating performance art, painting, microcomputing, personal growth, love. I am exceptionally bad at dancing and have never been able to play any musical instrument. I like children and childcare, cooking, hunting wild mushrooms. I speak other languages worse than English, but have a nodding relationship with French and Spanish. I have visited most parts of the world, but had short stays in all of them except Western Europe. Much of my insight into life here has come from overseas visitors.

"I don't like traditional constructions of masculinity and their manifestation in the nitpicking careerism of academia and the status-symbol consumerism of business. I don't like blind optimism or blanket pessimism. The future is being made here and now, and the important thing is to see how this is happening and where it's coming from: thinking about the future is always only a way of helping decisions to be made about creating the future.''

BIOGRAPHICAL/CRITICAL SOURCES:

BOOKS

Calder, Nigel, *1984 and After,* Century Publishing, 1983.

*   *   *

MILLARD, Charles W(arren III)   1932-

BRIEF ENTRY: Born December 20, 1932, in Elizabeth, N.J. American museum curator and author. In 1974 Millard was named chief curator of the Hirshhorn Museum and Sculpture Garden at the Smithsonian Institution. He began his career at Harvard University in 1963, at the William Hayes Fogg Art Museum, and he has also been associated with Dumbarton Oaks, the Washington Gallery of Modern Art, and the Los Angeles County Museum of Art. Millard was appointed art editor of *Hudson Review* in 1972. His specialty, nineteenth-century French sculpture, is reflected in his well-received *The Sculpture of Edgar Degas* (Princeton University Press, 1976). Millard also wrote *Miro: Selected Paintings* (Smithsonian Institution Press, 1980). *Address:* 2853 Ontario Rd. N.W., Washington, D.C. 20009; and Hirshhorn Museum and Sculpture Garden, Eighth St. and Independence Ave. S.W., Washington, D.C. 20560.

BIOGRAPHICAL/CRITICAL SOURCES:

New York Times Book Review, February 27, 1977.
Times Literary Supplement, March 18, 1977.

MILLER, Gabriel 1948-

PERSONAL: Born August 3, 1948, in Bronx, N.Y.; son of Harold Louis and Leah (Pauker) Miller; married Katharine Fraser, May 18, 1974; children: Lisabeth Jane, Lauren Jessica. *Education:* Queens College of the City University of New York, B.A., 1970; Brown University, Ph.D., 1975.

ADDRESSES: Office—Department of English, Rutgers University, Newark Campus, Newark, N.J. 07102.

CAREER: Arizona State University, Tempe, assistant professor of English and film, 1975-76; Illinois State University, Normal, assistant professor of English, 1977-80; Rutgers University, Newark Campus, Newark, N.J., assistant professor of English, 1980—.

MEMBER: Modern Language Association of America, American Film Institute, National Film Society.

WRITINGS:

Daniel Fuchs, Twayne, 1979.
Screening the Novel: Rediscovered American Fiction in Film, Ungar, 1980.
(Author of introduction) Alvah Bessie, *Alvah Bessie's Short Fictions,* Chandler & Sharp, 1982.
John Irving, Ungar, 1982.
Clifford Odets, Ungar, in press.

Contributor to film and literature journals.

WORK IN PROGRESS: Four of the Ten: A Study of the Literary Careers of Alvah Bessie, Albert Maltz, Samuel Ornitz, and Trumbo.

SIDELIGHTS: Gabriel Miller told *CA:* "My interest has always been to expose readers to the neglected figures of American literature. It is necessary that we broaden our understanding of our literary heritage. This should include writers and artists normally not studied in university literature courses.

"The purpose of my study on *Four of the Ten* is to provide a detailed analysis of the literary careers and achievements of four American novelist-screenwriters who have received little or no critical attention. The writers—Alvah Bessie, Albert Maltz, Samuel Ornitz, and Dalton Trumbo—are known primarily as four of the 'Hollywood Ten,' the group of film artists who were imprisoned during the blacklist years of the forties and fifties for refusing to answer certain questions put to them by the House Un-American Activities Committee. But these four men, in addition to the notoriety of their Hollywood careers, also produced significant works of fiction that deserve notice as statements of the embattled liberal consciousness.

"While the subject of the blacklist, especially as it applied to the entertainment industry, has received much attention in the past fifteen years, there has been no serious study of the 'victims' themselves. And despite the fact that film scholarship has recently turned its attention to the screenwriter (Tom Dardis's book *Sometime in the Sun* considers the screenwriting careers of five major novelists, neglected chapters in their famous lives), no one has yet analyzed the screenwriter's career outside of Hollywood. Bessie, Ornitz, and Maltz, in fact, are interesting figures more for their accomplishments in fiction than for their careers in films. Dalton Trumbo, one of the motion picture industry's most successful writers, also pursued a literary career as a counterpart to his time in Hollywood.

Most important, however, is that these men's lives and art provide valuable insights to why they chose prison rather than compromise their principles and direct manifestations of what those principles were.

"Beyond this significance in literary history, the novels of these four are worthy of study in themselves. This is not to say that the work of any of them stands in the forefront of American letters—there are no undiscovered geniuses here—yet many of the books display both vigorous energy and considerable talent. Why these talents didn't develop even more fully is an aesthetic question that requires some investigation, especially into the relationship between radical politics and art. Can the radical novelist merge art with ideology and achieve a creative peace? This is perhaps the most central problem to be confronted in this study of four representative careers.

"It is important to recognize, of course, that despite the fact that these men were singled out for being Communists, their work is actually—except in one or two cases—not Communist in focus. Their fiction is more truly 'humanitarian' than narrowly ideological. Albert Maltz's novels demonstrate more concern for a clear achievement of the democratic ideal than for preaching the party line. Ornitz concerned himself most deeply with themes of religious tolerance, the pure life (in a strangely religious sense), and Jewish history. Alvah Bessie could evoke the terrors of loneliness and the frustrations of failure as effectively as any writer, and Dalton Trumbo concentrated on exploring the ethos of the small American town. Such broadly human concerns were common to them all, and their work represents what is best in the American spirit. It is one of the ironies and shames of our history that we sent them to prison for defending these ideals."

*   *   *

MILLER, Jonathan (Wolfe) 1934-

PERSONAL: Born July 21, 1934, in London, England; son of Emanuel (a psychiatrist) and Betty Bergson (a writer; maiden name, Spiro) Miller; married Helen Rachel Collet (a physician), July 27, 1956; children: Tom, William, Kate. *Education:* St. John's College, Cambridge, M.B., 1959, B.Ch., 1959; attended University College Hospital Medical School.

CAREER: National Theatre, London, England, associate director, 1973-75; Greenwich Theatre, London, associate director, beginning in 1975; physician, actor, and producer and director of stage, opera, radio, and television productions. Actor in stage productions, including "Out of the Blue," 1954, "Between the Lines," 1955, and "Beyond the Fringe," 1960-63; actor in films, including "One Way Pendulum," 1965; appeared on television programs, including "The Tonight Show," British Broadcasting Corp. (BBC-TV), "Tempo," Associated Television Ltd. (ATV), October, 1961, "The Jack Parr Show," National Broadcasting Co. (NBC-TV), December, 1962, "A Trip to the Moon," Columbia Broadcasting System (CBS-TV), February 12, 1964, telecast of "Beyond the Fringe," BBC-TV, first broadcast December 19, 1964, "Books for Our Times," 1964, "Intimations," BBC-TV, 1965-66, "Sunday Night," BBC-TV, February 6, 1966, and "Review," BBC-TV, January 8, 1974. Guest on talk shows, including "The Johnny Carson Show" and "The David Susskind Show."

Director of stage productions, including "Under Plain Cover," 1962, "The Old Glory," 1964, "Come Live With Me," 1967, "Benito Cereno," 1967, "Prometheus Bound," 1967 and 1971,

"The School for Scandal," 1968, 1972, and 1983, "The Seagull," 1968, 1973, and 1974, "Twelfth Night," 1969, "King Lear," 1969 and 1970, "Merchant of Venice," 1970, "The Tempest," 1970, "Hamlet," 1970, 1971, and 1974, "Danton's Death," 1971, "Richard II," 1972, "Julius Caesar," 1972, "The Taming of the Shrew," 1972, "The Devil Is an Ass," 1973, "The Malcontent," 1973, "Measure for Measure," 1973 and 1975, "Ghosts," 1974, "The Freeway," 1974, "Family Romances," 1974, "The Importance of Being Earnest," 1975, "All's Well That Ends Well," 1975, "Three Sisters," 1976, and "She Would If She Could," 1979.

Director of operas, including "Arden Must Die," 1974, "Cosi fan Tutte," 1974 and 1982, "The Cunning Little Vixen," 1975, "Rigoletto," 1975, "Orfeo," 1976, "Eugene Onegin," 1977, "The Marriage of Figaro," 1978, "La Traviata," 1979, "The Turn of the Screw," 1979, "Arabella," 1980, "Falstaff," 1980 and 1981, "Fidelio," 1982 and 1983, "The Magic Flute," and "Don Giovanni."

Director of television productions, including "What's Going On Here?" (revue), WNEW-TV, April, 1963, "Plato's Dialogues" (film series), BBC-TV, July 3, 1966, NET-TV, 1971, "Alice in Wonderland," BBC-TV, December 28, 1966, "From Chekhov With Love," BBC-TV, "Whistle and I'll Come to You," BBC-TV, and "The Body in Question" (thirteen-part series), BBC-TV, 1978, Public Broadcasting Service (PBS), 1979; director of radio programs, including "Saturday Night on the Light" and "Monday Night at Home," both broadcast by BBC-Radio; director of motion pictures, including "Take a Girl Like You," Columbia, 1970.

Executive producer of BBC-TV Shakespeare series, 1979-81. Editor of television program "Monitor," BBC-TV, 1964-65. Resident fellow in history of medicine at University College, London, 1970-73; visiting professor of drama at Westfield College, London, beginning in 1977; teacher of drama at Yale Drama School; researcher in neuropsychology at Sussex University.

MEMBER: Arts Council of Great Britain, 1975-76, British Actors' Equity Association, British Medical Association.

AWARDS, HONORS: London Evening Standard award for best revue or musical, 1961, special citation from New York Drama Critics Circle, 1962, and special Antoinette Perry (Tony) Award from League of New York Theatres and Producers, 1963, all for "Beyond the Fringe"; named Director of the Year by Society of West End Theatre, 1976; Silver Medal from Royal Television Society, 1981; D.Litt. from University of Leicester, honorary fellow of St. John's College, Cambridge, 1982; named Commander of the Order of the British Empire, 1983.

WRITINGS:

(Author with Peter Cook, Alan Bennett, and Dudley Moore) *Beyond the Fringe* (satirical revue; first produced in Edinburgh at the Royal Lyceum Theatre, August, 1960; produced on the West End at the Fortune Theatre, May 10, 1961; produced on Broadway at the John Golden Theatre, October 17, 1962), Samuel French, 1963.
Harvey and the Circulation of the Blood (nonfiction), Grossman, 1968.
McLuhan (biography), Fontana, 1971, published in the United States as *Marshall McLuhan,* Viking, 1971.
(Editor) *Freud: The Man, His World, His Influence,* Little, Brown, 1972.

The Body in Question (nonfiction; based on thirteen-part television documentary series of the same name), Random House, 1978.
(With Borin Van Loon) *Darwin for Beginners,* Norton, 1982.
States of Mind: Conversations With Psychological Investigators, Pantheon, 1983.
The Human Body (picture book), Viking, 1983.
(With Pelham) *The Facts of Life* (picture book), Viking, 1984.

TELEVISION SCRIPTS

"The Anne Hutchinson Story" for NBC-TV series "Profiles in Courage," first broadcast January 10, 1965.
"Alice in Wonderland," first broadcast by BBC-TV, December 28, 1966.
"The Body in Question" (thirteen-part documentary series), broadcast by BBC-TV, 1978, and by PBS, 1979.

OTHER

Contributor of articles and reviews to periodicals, including *New Yorker, New York Herald Tribune, Partisan Review, Commentary, Spectator,* and *New Statesman.*

WORK IN PROGRESS: A picture book on the human eye.

SIDELIGHTS: Jonathan Miller was a physician specializing in neurology at a London hospital in 1961 when he left the medical profession for a career in the performing arts. A veteran of student revues at Cambridge, Miller had been approached in 1959 by John Bassett, assistant director of the Edinburgh Festival, with the idea of putting together a satirical comedy revue called "Beyond the Fringe." Miller agreed to the suggested collaboration with Peter Cook, Alan Bennett, and Dudley Moore, and the resulting revue proved an immense success in London and was equally well received when it opened on Broadway in 1962. For Miller, "Beyond the Fringe" marked the beginning of a new career in which he went from performing to producing and directing numerous productions for stage, opera, and television.

Dubbed a "Renaissance man" in his native England, Miller has become well known for his unique interpretations of Shakespeare and opera classics, as well as for his controversial dramatization of "Alice in Wonderland," which he adapted for television for the British Broadcasting Company (BBC-TV) in 1966. In "Alice" Miller attempted to portray eccentric Victorian society through the eyes of a young child and, instead of representing the characters as animals—as in Lewis Carroll's book—he chose to present them as humans, complete with their own Victorian psychoses. Prior to its telecast, "Alice in Wonderland" was deemed unsuitable for children by the BBC and even led to a motion in Parliament that deplored tampering with childhood classics.

Similarly, Miller gave his much acclaimed version of Shakespeare's "Merchant of Venice" a Victorian context. In an interview appearing in the *Chicago Tribune,* he remarked to Richard Christiansen: "I imagined the relationship between [characters] Antonio and Bassanio as something like that between Oscar Wilde and Lord Alfred Douglas. You know, the older man always giving money to and doing favors for the younger man. With all that in mind, I abandoned the usual pre-Raphaelite vision of the play and placed it in a framework of the Victorian period." Miller's production, which featured Sir Laurence Olivier as the principal character of Shylock, garnered mixed reviews; *New Statesman*'s Benedict Nightingale acknowledged his "sneaking preference" for Miller's version, while other critics bemoaned the director's elimination of Shakespearean magic.

In addition to his theatrical pursuits, Miller has written several books reflecting his fascination with medicine and science. One of these, *The Body in Question,* evolved from a thirteen-part television documentary that Miller created for the BBC. The book explores the history of healing, including some classic medical frauds of the past, and examines, in a chapter entitled "Self-Help," the body's defense mechanisms and reflexes, with particular focus on respiration, the circulatory and nervous systems, reproduction, and genetics. "The book is something of a hybrid," remarked *New York Times* critic Glenn Collins. "It is a historical investigation, a beginner's medical textbook, a pop-science primer and a grand, eccentric Jonathan Miller indulgence."

Throughout *The Body in Question* Miller uses metaphors to describe various medical concepts. For example, the author compares a coma patient to an astronaut in orbit, who is traveling in an automatically piloted craft. The patient's "safety is monitored and managed for him; he is carefully steered through all the natural risks until he is ready to link up again with his own command module and assume these responsibilities for himself." Miller also employs metaphor to demonstrate the clotting process of blood: "It is rather like a series of orders, locked safes and sealed levers which prevent the accidental launching of a nuclear missle." "What distinguishes 'The Body in Question,'" wrote Lawrence K. Altman in the *New York Times,* "is Jonathan Miller's deftness and originality in using metaphors to clarify so accurately much of the biological basis of medicine." Altman added: "Rarely have metaphors been used so well to communicate complex medical concepts and pay tribute to the magnificence of the human body."

In his next book, *Darwin for Beginners,* Miller and co-author Borin Van Loon present, in laymen's terms, a general explanation of Charles Darwin's theory of evolution. Illustrated throughout with what a *New Yorker* reviewer called "fanciful and relevant drawings," the book drew praise from *New York Review of Books* critic R. C. Lewontin, who wrote that *Darwin for Beginners* is "a superb introduction to a very tricky subject. It puts all the emphasis in the right place, is historically correct, scientifically impeccable, and contains as a postscript the best 250-word piece on reductionist social explanation yet written." Lewontin further commented, "Anyone who reads and understands Jonathan Miller's text will know a good deal more about Darwinism than most biologists and historians, while the pictures will be a constant reminder not to take the life of the mind more seriously than it deserves."

Miller followed *Darwin for Beginners* with *States of Mind: Conversations With Psychological Investigators.* Like *The Body in Question, States of Mind* is also based on a BBC television series in which Miller interviewed psychologists, philosophers, sociobiologists, and other such "psychological investigators." The book contains fifteen interviews with people who, according to *Los Angeles Times Book Review* critic Elaine Kendall, "vary widely in their ability to communicate their research to the public." Faulting many of the interview subjects for lapsing into "technical jargon of their specialties," Kendall noted that *States of Mind* is "an unevenly fascinating book, dense with information elicited by Miller's informed and sensitive questions. . . . Without Miller's intervention, much of the provocative material here would remain in academic cold storage for years to come." Similarly, *New York Review*

of Books critic Rosemary Dinnage found that the "level of dialogue is often quite abstruse yet always lucid, and greatly helped by the polymath interviewer [Miller], who wraps up the topics in happy analogies and crisp turns of phrase of his own."

For his next project, Miller collaborated with designer David Pelham to produce two three-dimensional "pop-up" picture books, *The Human Body* and *The Facts of Life.* The first of these, originally intended for children as an illustrated primer on human anatomy—not including the sexual organs—"crept into a lot of doctors' offices and an awful lot of adults got it for themselves," Miller told *Washington Post* interviewer Sandy Rovner. Also designed for children, *The Facts of Life* takes the concept of *The Human Body* a step further to include six movable illustrations of the male and female sex organs, sperm fertilizing a mature egg cell, and the development of the human fetus depicted at forty days, twenty-four weeks, and at nine months, just prior to birth.

In the interview with Rovner, Miller described *The Facts of Life* as "straightforward and all mechanical . . . [it is] sensible and explanatory and decent, and you really can't ask for anything more." Responding to speculation that his graphic approach to reproduction might spark controversy, Miller was quoted in the *New York Times* as saying that his book is "so matter-of-fact that even to anticipate trouble you'd have to be very, very neurotic. Look around the room. Everyone you see is here because of what is shown in the book. Surely it's not rude to ask how." Reviewing *The Facts of Life* in the *Times Literary Supplement,* Eric Korn noted that accompanying the six pop-up illustrations is "a lucid, sophisticated text [and] an impressive number of words that none the less do not muffle the [book's] visual impact."

BIOGRAPHICAL/CRITICAL SOURCES:

PERIODICALS

Chicago Tribune Book World, March 18, 1979.
Commonweal, April 11, 1980.
Detroit News, October 25, 1984.
Esquire, February 27, 1979.
Guardian, July 16, 1969, February 27, 1983.
Harper's Magazine, May, 1979.
History Today, June, 1982.
Horizon, June, 1983.
Life, August 16, 1963.
Los Angeles Times Book Review, October 3, 1982, July 3, 1983.
New Statesman, October 20, 1978, January 28, 1983.
Newsweek, April 9, 1979, April 27, 1981.
New Yorker, September 8, 1962, May 7, 1979, November 8, 1982.
New York Review of Books, April 9, 1979, June 16, 1983, August 18, 1983.
New York Times, March 6, 1979, August 25, 1979, October 8, 1984.
New York Times Book Review, April 15, 1979, November 25, 1979, October 30, 1983.
New York Times Magazine, January 22, 1967, August 1, 1982.
Observer, November 19, 1978.
Psychology Today, September, 1973, March, 1979, December, 1979.
Punch, November 1, 1978.
Saturday Review, September, 1980, June, 1982.
Spectator, November 11, 1978, May 15, 1982.
Time, June 6, 1983.

Times Literary Supplement, March 23, 1973, November 24, 1978, February 11, 1983, June 17, 1983, January 4, 1985.
Village Voice, August 27, 1979, December 3, 1980.
Wall Street Journal, October 22, 1979.
Washington Post, March 23, 1979, October 31, 1984.
Washington Post Book World, July 10, 1983.*

—Sketch by Louise Mooney

*   *   *

MILLER, Margery
See WELLES, Margery Miller

*   *   *

MILLER, R(onald) Baxter   1948-

PERSONAL: Born October 11, 1948, in Rocky Mount, N.C.; son of Marcellus C. (a chemistry teacher) and Elsie (an elementary school teacher; maiden name, Bryant) Miller; married Jessica Garris (an educational and public administrator), June 6, 1971; children: Akin Dasan (son). *Education:* Yale University, Certificate, 1969; North Carolina Central University, B.A. (magna cum laude), 1970; Brown University, A.M., 1972, Ph.D., 1974.

ADDRESSES: Home—1433 Pine Springs Rd., Knoxville, Tenn. 37922. *Office*—Department of English, University of Tennessee, Knoxville, Tenn. 37996-0430.

CAREER: Roger Williams College, Bristol, R.I., instructor in English, 1973; Haverford College, Haverford, Pa., assistant professor of English, 1974-76; University of Tennessee, associate professor, 1977-82, professor of English, 1982—, director of black literature program, 1977—. Special lecturer at State University of New York College at Oneonta, spring, 1974.

MEMBER: Modern Language Association of America (member of executive committee of Afro-American Literature Discussion Group, 1980-84, chairman of group, 1982, 1983; founder of division on Black American Literature and Culture, 1983, and first chair, 1984; member of delegate assembly, 1984-86), College Language Association, Langston Hughes Society (founding member), South Atlantic Modern Language Association, Committee for Black South Literature and Art (vice-president, 1981-82).

AWARDS, HONORS: Grant from American Council of Learned Societies, 1978.

WRITINGS:

(Contributor) Chester J. Fontenot, Jr., editor, *Writing About Black Literature,* Nebraska Curriculum Development Center, University of Nebraska, 1976.
Langston Hughes and Gwendolyn Brooks: A Reference Guide, G. K. Hall, 1978.
(Editor and contributor) *Black American Literature and Humanism,* University Press of Kentucky, 1981.
(Editor and contributor) *Black Poets Between Worlds, 1940-1960,* University of Tennessee Press, 1986.
The Literary Imagination of Langston Hughes, Louisiana State University Press, 1986.

Contributor of about fifty articles and reviews to literature and black studies journals, including *Phylon, Melus, Modern Fiction Studies, Southern Literary Journal,* and *New York History.* Guest editor of *Black American Literature Forum,* au-

tumn, 1981, member of editorial board, 1982—; member of editorial board of *WATU: A Cornell Journal of Black Writing,* 1978-79, *Obsidian: Black Literature in Review,* 1979—, *Callaloo,* 1981—, *Langston Hughes Review,* 1982—, and *Middle Atlantic Writers Association Review,* 1982—.

WORK IN PROGRESS: Intertextuality and Tradition: From Wright to Fair, publication expected in 1989; *The Legacy of Black American Literary Criticism, 1937-1982,* publication expected in 1993.

SIDELIGHTS: R. Baxter Miller told *CA:* "From the age of fourteen I have been inexplicably compelled to write. In junior high and high school, I was the juvenile poet; then I experimented with colloquial verse during my undergraduate years in Durham, North Carolina. Finally, I became a professional critic and scholar.

"What unifying patterns underlie it all? The boy wrote passionately to envision social justice, and the adolescent did so in order to externalize the emotional self in verbal form. The young man loved to communicate the joy of reading and interpretation as regards literature or life, the complementary angles. The great concern has naturally emerged as freedom—freedom from social limitation, temporality, or even elite discourse. I have invited others to share the aesthetic experience that literary craft creates while artfully concealing its own method. When the opportunity came to extend personal experience beyond North Carolina to as far as Rhode Island, I seized the day, or accepted the grants, yet still sensed a debt to the southern past and black folk.

"Writing becomes a medium to preserve communion with and to rekindle selfhood; it becomes a double identification in which the artistic self relives aesthetic experience yet the theoretical self stands as well aside, examining carefully the critical principles involved. While the scholar may be discursively brilliant, the critic-scholar must be completely human, for the former thinks in only one way, though the latter thinks in two dimensions.

"Regarding my interest in and work on Langston Hughes and Gwendolyn Brooks, as well as Blyden Jackson and George Kent, I intend to reveal and practice the process of double identification. The posture is at once inside and outside black American literature. Indeed, the tendency completes the pattern across some twenty years. It began when the late Randolph Worsely, my seventh-grade teacher, introduced me to 'I, Too, Sing America,' a poem by Langston Hughes. And when, as a college freshman, I finally read the *Selected Poems,* the pattern continued six years later. What intrigued me then was Hughes's talent for illuminating the discrepancy between the experiential world and the historically formulaic one, perhaps less charitably known as blind tradition. I could not express it so then any more than I could recognize Hughes's literary limitations. Still, fifteen years later *Black American Literature and Humanism* reconfirmed a common belief. Humanity still superseded and supersedes the forms and standards it imperfectly animates. I merely transpose the personal preoccupations of a lifetime to black American and Euro-American literary traditions: What honest and critical theories would free them?"

BIOGRAPHICAL/CRITICAL SOURCES:

PERIODICALS

American Literary Scholarship, 1983.
Callaloo, October, 1982.

Georgia Historical Quarterly, December, 1982.
Mississippi Quarterly, spring, 1982.
Modern Fiction Studies, winter, 1982-83.
South Atlantic Review, May, 1983.
Tennessee Studies in Literature, 1980.

* * *

MILLER, Sandra (Peden) 1948-
(Sandy Miller)

PERSONAL: Born December 25, 1948, in Horton, Kan.; daughter of Norman Leslie and Beckie (Wagoner) Peden; married Brian Miller (a writer and vice-president of a boys' ranch), May 18, 1968; children: Benjamin, Jeffery, Philip, Matthew, Elizabeth, Rebecca. *Education:* Attended Washburn University. *Religion:* Protestant.

ADDRESSES: Home and office—Bethesda Boys Ranch, P.O. Box 311, Mounds, Okla. 74047. *Agent*—Merrilee Heifetz, Writers House Inc., 21 West 26th St., New York, N.Y. 10010.

CAREER: Bethesda Missionary Society, missionary in Jamaica, 1969-71; Bethesda Boys Ranch, Mounds, Okla., household coordinator, 1971—. Free-lance writer.

MEMBER: Oklahoma Writers Federation, Tulsa Tuesday Writers (president, 1982), Tulsa Christian Writers (vice-president, 1981).

WRITINGS:

UNDER NAME SANDY MILLER; FOR YOUNG ADULTS; PUBLISHED BY NEW AMERICAN LIBRARY, EXCEPT AS NOTED

Two Loves for Jenny, 1982.
Smart Girl, 1982.
Chase the Sun, 1983.
Lynn's Challenge, 1984.
This Song Is for You, Warner Books, 1984.
Freddie the Thirteenth, 1985.
A Tale of Two Turkeys, 1985.

WORK IN PROGRESS: Changing Charlie, a young adult novel for New American Library.

SIDELIGHTS: Sandy Miller told *CA:* "My earliest memories are of sitting on one of my parents' laps while they read Little Golden Books to me, or lying between them in bed as my father read aloud from a novel. As soon as I learned to read for myself at the age of five, that was all I wanted to do. During my early teenage years, I stayed up many nights hiding in my closet with a good book. I always stuck a towel under the crack of the door so my parents wouldn't see the light and tell me to go to bed. I still like to read children's and young adult books. Perhaps that's why I like to write them so much.

"I was an only child for ten years before my parents had four more children. Consequently, I entertained myself. We lived in the country and there were always wonderful things to do, such as climb the windmill, silo, or apple tree. One of my favorite places was a ditch that curved through the length of our pasture. It became all kinds of magical things: a trench for soldiers, a creek for a wagon train crossing the prairie, the yellow brick road leading to Oz. That must be where my imagination got such a productive start, and it's never stopped. I will always love to daydream. When I was eleven, we moved to town. I missed the country, but I built a desk in an elm tree and spent many hours there thinking and writing.

"I began writing poems at the age of seven, and sold the first one, 'My Country,' to *Grit* when I was thirteen. I sold several more poems and two articles when I was a teenager. When I was twenty-seven, I took a correspondence course that started me writing seriously. With six young children, it was hard for me to find time to write, so my first book was written from 4:30 to 6:30 every morning.

"When I write my books, I can remember exactly how I felt when I was a teenager. Though times and situations may change, people's feelings will always be the same. I like to write happy books with uplifting endings because I think it's good for people to read positive, wholesome books."

MEDIA ADAPTATIONS: Two Loves for Jenny was adapted for television and broadcast as "Between Two Loves" by ABC-TV, October 27, 1982.

* * *

MILLER, Sandy
See MILLER, Sandra (Peden)

* * *

MILLS, Hilary (Paterson) 1950-

PERSONAL: Born February 7, 1950, in Chicago, Ill.; daughter of Edwin S. Mills (a broadcasting executive) and Joan Paterson Kerr (an art editor and author); married Robert D. Loomis (an executive editor and vice-president of Random House), September 18, 1983. *Education:* Sarah Lawrence College, B.A., 1972.

ADDRESSES: Agent—Sterling Lord, 660 Madison Ave., New York, N.Y. 10021.

CAREER: Writer.

WRITINGS:

Mailer: A Biography, Empire Books, 1982.

Author of a weekly publishing column for the *Washington Star,* 1978-81, and for syndication, 1981-82. Fiction editor for *Book Digest,* 1975-80.

WORK IN PROGRESS: A biography of Lillian Hellman, publication by Putnam expected in 1987.

SIDELIGHTS: Hilary Mills's *Mailer* is a biography of Norman Mailer, the controversial author of prize-winning works such as *The Armies of the Night* and *The Executioner's Song.* Mark Harris, who reviewed *Mailer* for the *New York Times Book Review,* was impressed by Mills's ability to synthesize Mailer's often chaotic life and work. Harris declared that the book provides "for the first time a coherent sense of this saintly and dastardly writer" and praised Mills for having "clarified Mailer without celebrating him." Lis Schwarzbaum, writing in the *Detroit News,* echoed Harris's comments. Schwarzbaum wrote, "It's admirable that Hilary Mills has ordered such a disorderly life into a comprehensive chronicle."

Elaine Kendall, assessing *Mailer* in the *Los Angeles Times Book Review,* wrote: "There is a minimum of speculation here: just the facts—substantiated, attributed, credited, quoted, dated, sorted and indexed; facts protectively insulated in prose designed to hold them in place without calling any particular attention to itself. But what flashy facts they are: six wives, eight children, literary and intellectual feuds, brilliant successes and abysmal failures, intervening doldrums; scandals, accolades, outrages and atonements; public spectacles and private miseries, violence and gentleness; acclaim and anathema—a life and career at the extremes of experience.'' And Jonathan Yardley concluded, in his *Washington Post* critique of *Mailer:* ''Hilary Mills has done an extraordinary job of interviewing and digging, has tied it all together with deft but unobtrusive commentary on the impulses that underlie Mailer's behavior and writing, and has brought off a feat that I had thought quite beyond possibility: she has made Norman Mailer almost—if not quite—a sympathetic figure.''

Concerning her motivation for writing a biography on Mailer, Mills told *CA:* ''I first met Mailer in the fall of 1979 when I was interviewing him for the *Saturday Review.* I was struck during the course of the interview by the discrepancy between Mailer's public image as a macho, provocative *enfant terrible* and the rather sweet, gentle, courtly man across from me. I began to think his life story would make an incredible saga of what early fame had done to this nice Jewish boy from Brooklyn and how he coped by creating a body of work and a public image that revolutionized literature.''

BIOGRAPHICAL/CRITICAL SOURCES:

PERIODICALS

Chicago Tribune, December 20, 1982.
Chicago Tribune Book World, March 6, 1983.
Detroit News, January 16, 1983.
Houston Post, January 4, 1983.
Los Angeles Times Book Review, November 28, 1982.
Newsweek, January 24, 1983.
New York Times Book Review, December 19, 1982.
Philadelphia Inquirer, December 15, 1982.
Times Literary Supplement, December 9,1983.
Village Voice Literary Supplement, February 19, 1983.
Washington Post, November 15, 1982.
Washington Post Book World, February 12, 1983.

*   *   *

MILLS, Irving   1894-1985

OBITUARY NOTICE: Born January 16, 1894, in New York, N.Y. (one source says Russia; now U.S.S.R.); died of heart failure, April 21, 1985, in Palm Springs, Calif. Musician, talent manager, publisher, composer, and lyricist. Mills, who was best known for his musical collaborations with Duke Ellington, is credited with having discovered Ellington and other popular jazz musicians such as the Mills Brothers and Cab Calloway. In 1919 he founded Mills Music Publishing Company with his brother Jack. The firm was originally started to print sheet music, but it soon expanded to include record production. In the 1920's Mills formed a jazz band called Irving Mills and His Hotsy Totsy Gang, and around the same time he began scouting dance halls and nightclubs for talent; he spotted Ellington playing in a New York club in 1926. The Hotsy Totsy Gang had become dissatisfied with their pianist/bandleader, so Mills hired Ellington as a replacement. The two began writing songs together, producing such hits as ''Mood Indigo,'' ''Sophisticated Lady,'' and ''Solitude.''

During this time, Mills also obtained radio air time for Ellington's own band, despite the obstacles that black musicians faced in broadcasting during the 1920's. Mills continued to manage the Duke Ellington Band until 1939, scheduling concerts for them in music halls that were previously restricted to white musicians. By the early 1940's Mills had firmly established himself as a talent manager and impresario, counting

among his clients comedian Milton Berle. He was reportedly also instrumental in launching the careers of songwriter Hoagy Carmichael and singer Rudy Vallee, among others. He sold Mills Music in 1965 but continued to publish songs through his new mail-order house, Irving Mills' Around the World in Music. Additional songs that Mills wrote alone or with others include ''It Don't Mean a Thing if It Ain't Got That Swing,'' ''When My Sugar Walks Down the Street,'' and ''Minnie the Moocher.''

OBITUARIES AND OTHER SOURCES:

BOOKS

The Complete Encyclopedia of Popular Music and Jazz, 1900-1950, Arlington House, 1974.
Feather, Leonard, *Passion for Jazz,* Horizon, 1980.

PERIODICALS

Chicago Tribune, April 24, 1985.
Daily Variety, April 23, 1985.

*   *   *

MINDT, Heinz R.   1940-
(Felix R. Paturi)

BRIEF ENTRY: Born November 3, 1940, in Breslau, Germany (now Wroclaw, Poland). German publicist and author. Using the pseudonym Felix R. Paturi, Mindt wrote *The Escalator Effect: How to Get to the Top Without Effort* (Peter Wyden, 1973), *Nature, Mother of Invention: The Engineering of Plant Life* (Harper, 1976), and *Prehistoric Heritage* (Scribner, 1979). *Address:* c/o Sanford J. Greenburger Associates, Inc., 825 Third Ave., New York, N.Y. 10022.

BIOGRAPHICAL/CRITICAL SOURCES:

PERIODICALS

Virginia Quarterly Review, spring, 1977.

*   *   *

MIRABEHN
See SLADE, Madeleine

*   *   *

MIRANDE, Alfredo M(anuel)   1940-

PERSONAL: Born October 7, 1940, in Mexico City, Mexico; came to the United States in 1950, naturalized citizen, 1963; son of Xavier Mirande Zalazar and Rosa Maria (Gonzalez) Mirande; children: Michele, Lucia, Alejandro. *Education:* Illinois State Normal University (now State University), B.A., 1963; University of Nebraska—Lincoln, M.A., 1965, Ph.D., 1967.

ADDRESSES: Office—Department of Sociology, University of California, Riverside, Calif. 92521.

CAREER: University of Nebraska—Lincoln, instructor in sociology, summers, 1965-66; University of Kentucky, Lexington, assistant professor of sociology, 1967-70; Virginia Polytechnic Institute and State University, Blacksburg, associate professor of sociology, 1970-71; University of North Dakota, Grand Forks, associate professor of sociology, 1971-74; University of California, Riverside, lecturer, 1974-75, assistant professor, 1975-78, associate professor, 1978-81, professor of sociology and Chicano studies, 1981—, chairman of Chicano studies, 1980-83.

MEMBER: American Sociological Association, Society for the Study of Social Problems, National Association for Chicano Studies, Midwest Sociological Society.

AWARDS, HONORS: Grant from U.S. Department of Labor, 1977-78; National Research Council postdoctoral fellowship, 1984.

WRITINGS:

The Age of Crisis: Deviance, Disorganization, and Societal Problems, Harper, 1975.
(With Evangelina Enriquez) *La Chicana: The Mexican American Woman,* University of Chicago Press, 1979.
Alma Abierta: Pinto Poetry (monograph), University of California, Riverside, 1980.
The Chicano Experience: A Critical Perspective, University of Notre Dame Press, 1984.
Chicano Inequality: An Emergent Paradigm for the Social Sciences, University of Notre Dame Press, 1985.

CONTRIBUTOR

John N. Edwards, editor, *The Family and Change,* Knopf, 1969.
Arthur S. Wilke, editor, *The Hidden Professoriate,* Greenwood Press, 1979.
J. J. McWhirter, editor, *Sourcebook for Problem Solving With Families,* Arizona State Department of Economic Security, 1980.
Arlene Skolnick and Jerome H. Skolnick, editors, *Family in Transition: Rethinking Marriage, Sexuality, Child Rearing, and Family Organization,* 3rd edition, Little, Brown, 1980.
David Baptiste and Leanor Johnson, editors, *Diversity: Studies and Essays About Minority Families in America,* International Library, 1984.
Geoffrey K. Leigh and Gary W. Peterson, editors, *Adolescence in a Family Context,* South-Western, 1984.
Livie I. Duran and H. Russell Bernard, editors, *Introduction to Chicano Studies,* Macmillan, 1982.

Contributor of about twenty-five articles and reviews to sociology and Chicano studies journals, including *Journal of Marriage and the Family, Sociological Quarterly, Pacific Sociology,* and *Hispanic Journal of Behavioral Sciences.*

OTHER

Editor of special issue of *De Colores,* 1982; advisory editor of *Sociological Quarterly.*

WORK IN PROGRESS: Analyzing attitudes of members of the Riverside barrio, Casa Blanca, toward the police and the law; a comparative analysis of patterns of domestic violence and abuse among Anglo, black, and Chicano respondents; research on elderly hispanics in government work-training programs.

SIDELIGHTS: Alfredo M. Mirande told *CA:* "My intent in writing is to convey the Chicano experience to a larger audience. Much of what is written about Chicanos is negative and does not reflect a Chicano point of view. My goal is to develop a Chicano perspective on sociology and social science and to apply it to Chicano experience."

MITCHELL, James (Alexander Hugh) 1939-1985

OBITUARY NOTICE: Born July 20, 1939; died after a long illness, March 12, 1985, in Hampshire, England. Publisher and editor. Mitchell is best remembered as the co-founder of the publishing house Mitchell Beazley, which, according to the London *Times,* "revolutionised the publishing in Britain of superbly designed, illustrated books of information." One of their successful endeavors was the ten-volume *Joy of Knowledge Encyclopaedia,* edited by Mitchell himself. Criticized at first for its arrangement, which is thematic instead of alphabetical, the encyclopedia has appeared since in twenty-eight editions in twenty-three languages.

Mitchell began his publishing career in 1961 as an editor for Constable & Company, before becoming editorial director of Thomas Nelson & Sons in 1967. It was at Nelson that Mitchell became acquainted with design and production director John Beazley, and in 1969 the two formed their own company. Business began to falter for the first time in the late 1970's, and in 1980 a controlling interest was sold to American Express. Mitchell remained as chairman; in 1983 he and the board of directors bought out the American Express holdings. Among the company's best-known publications are Alex Comfort's *The Joy of Sex* and Hugh Johnson's *Wine Atlas of the World.*

OBITUARIES AND OTHER SOURCES:

BOOKS

Who's Who, 136th edition, St. Martin's, 1984.

PERIODICALS

Publisher's Weekly, April 15, 1985.
Times (London), March 15, 1985.

*   *   *

MOFFETT, Hugh (Oliver) 1910-1985

OBITUARY NOTICE—See index for *CA* sketch: Born August 17, 1910, in Cherryvale, Kan.; died April 7, 1985. Congressman, journalist, and editor. Beginning his career as a journalist, Moffett worked as an assistant city editor for the *Des Moines Tribune* during the 1930's and early 1940's and then as a bureau head for *Time* magazine from 1944 to 1951. In addition, he served as news editor and then as assistant managing editor of *Life,* and during his tenure there had the opportunity to interview Soviet leader Nikita S. Khrushchev and Dr. Albert Schweitzer. During the mid-1970's Moffett became a member of the Vermont House of Representatives, where he earned a reputation for the sense of humor and balance he brought to the legislature.

OBITUARIES AND OTHER SOURCES:

PERIODICALS

Chicago Tribune, April 13, 1985.
New York Times, April 10, 1985.

*   *   *

MOKGATLE, (Monyadio Moreleba) Naboth 1911-1985

OBITUARY NOTICE—See index for *CA* sketch: Some sources list name as Naboth Nyadioe Mokgatle or Nyadioe Naboth Mokgatle; born April 1, 1911, in Phokeng, Transvaal, South Africa; died February 12, 1985. Labor leader and author. An expert on the history, philosophy, and institutions of the Bafokeng tribe of Basotho, South Africa—from which he was descended—Mokgatle was a political activist who opposed apartheid in South Africa. He was associated for a time with a Communist group in Pretoria and Johannesburg and was the founder of the Pretoria non-European Distributive Workers Union. Arrested a number of times, Mokgatle left South Africa in 1954, spending the rest of his life in exile in London. He wrote an autobiography, published in Britain in 1970 as *Naboth Mokgatle of Phokeng: An Autobiography* and in the United States the following year as *The Autobiography of an Unknown South African.*

OBITUARIES AND OTHER SOURCES:

BOOKS

African Authors: A Companion to Black African Writing, Volume I: *1300-1973,* Black Orpheus Press, 1973.
Who's Who in America, 40th edition, Marquis, 1978.

PERIODICALS

Times (London), February 23, 1985.

*   *   *

MOKGATLE, Naboth Nyadioe
     See MOKGATLE, (Monyadio Moreleba) Naboth

*   *   *

MOKGATLE, Nyadioe Naboth
     See MOKGATLE, (Monyadio Moreleba) Naboth

*   *   *

MONAGHAN, E(dith) Jennifer   1933-

PERSONAL: Surname is pronounced *Mahn-a-han;* born January 19, 1933, in Cambridge, England; came to the United States in 1957, naturalized citizen, 1981; daughter of Clement Willoughby (a physician) and Margery Alys Eveline (Elton) Walker; married Charles Monaghan (a free-lance writer), December 13, 1958; children: Leila Frances, Anthony Andrew, Claire Margery. *Education:* Lady Margaret Hall, Oxford, B.A., 1955, M.A., 1976; University of Illinois at Urbana-Champaign, M.A., 1958; Yeshiva University, Ed.D., 1980. *Politics:* Democrat.

ADDRESSES: Home—Brooklyn, N.Y. *Office*—Department of Educational Services, Brooklyn College of the City University of New York, Brooklyn, N.Y. 11210.

CAREER: War Office, London, England, 1955-57, began as file clerk, became junior assistant officer; Barnard High School for Girls, New York, N.Y., teacher of French and Latin, 1959-60; homemaker and mother, 1960-72; Adult Remand Shelter, Rikers Island Prison, N.Y., tutor in reading, 1972-73; tutor at Queensborough Community College, Queens, N.Y., 1972-73, and at Medgar Evers Community College, Brooklyn, N.Y., 1973; New York City Board of Education, Brooklyn, corrective reading teacher for Title I nonpublic school programs, 1973-75; private tutor in reading, writing, and spelling disabilities, 1976-78; New York City Community College, Brooklyn, adjunct assistant teaching reading, 1977-78; Brooklyn College of the City University of New York, Brooklyn, instructor in reading, 1978-81, assistant professor, 1981—.

MEMBER: International Reading Association (founder of Special Interest Group in the History of Reading), History of Ed-

ucation Society, American Educational Research Association, Society for Historians of the Early American Republic, Society for the Study of Curriculum History, William and Mary Society.

AWARDS, HONORS: Fulbright travel grant, 1957-58; co-recipient of the Outstanding Dissertation Award from the Society for the Study of Curriculum History, 1983.

WRITINGS:

(Translator from French) Lucien Bodard, *Green Hell,* Outerbridge & Dienstfrey, 1974.
A Common Heritage: Noah Webster's Blue-Back Speller, Shoe String, 1983.

Editor of *History of Reading News.*

WORK IN PROGRESS: The Three R's in Colonial America.

SIDELIGHTS: E. Jennifer Monaghan told *CA:* "I happened into a teaching and researching career that has brought me much pleasure almost by luck: when my children were still small, I volunteered to help a child learn to read, for a couple of hours a week, at our local public school in Brooklyn. This triggered an interest that started me off on my doctorate in reading. So I bring an understanding of linguistic theory, as well as my own classroom experience, to my historical research.

"Just as this background in reading has helped me as an educational historian, so, I believe, can today's teachers of reading be enriched by a knowledge of the history of reading and of literacy. Noah Webster's spelling books, to give just one small example, give the prospective teacher more information about letter-sound correspondences than does many a modern teacher's manual.

"I am currently studying the acquisition of literacy by the Indians of New England in the seventeenth century as part of a larger study on learning to read and write in colonial America."

*   *   *

MONCREIFFE, (Rupert) Iain (Kay)   1919-1985

OBITUARY NOTICE: Born April 9, 1919; died February 27, 1985, in London, England. Diplomat, geneologist, publishing executive, and author. Moncreiffe, who earned an international reputation as an expert in heraldry and Scottish lore, spent more than forty years tracing his own ancestry back to 326 B.C. He held a law degree and a doctorate from the University of Edinburgh and was considered knowledgeable in Georgian and Byzantine geneologies. Following his World War II service as a captain in the Scots Guards, Moncreiffe was the military liaison officer for Norway to Admiral William Wentworth and in 1949 became an attache to the British Embassy in Moscow and private secretary to the British ambassador to the Soviet Union. He was subsequently associated with Lloyds of London, Debrett's Peerage, and, finally, Burke's Peerage, serving as president of that firm from 1983 until his death. Moncreiffe's books include *Simple Heraldry, Simple Custom, Blood Royal, Map of Scotland of Old, The Highland Clans,* and *Royal Highness.*

OBITUARIES AND OTHER SOURCES:

PERIODICALS

Detroit Free Press, February 28, 1985.

Times (London), July 16, 1982, February 28, 1985.
Times Literary Supplement, September 3, 1982, October 23, 1983.
Washington Post, March 1, 1985.
Washington Post Book World, November 28, 1982.
Washington Times, February 28, 1985.

* * *

MONEGAL, Emir Rodriguez
See RODRIGUEZ MONEGAL, Emir

* * *

MONTESSORI, Maria 1870-1952

BRIEF ENTRY: Born August 31, 1870, in Chiaravalle, Ancona, Italy; died May 6, 1952, in Noordwijk, Holland, Netherlands. Italian physician, psychiatrist, educationist, and author. Montessori is best remembered for developing the Montessori teaching method, by which preschool children are encouraged to learn in an unstructured environment. The first woman to receive a medical degree in Italy, Montessori worked as a psychiatrist at the University of Rome. In 1898 she became director of Italy's Orthophrenic School, where she explored methods of teaching retarded children. In 1907 she opened her first *casa dei bambini* (children's house) and implemented her educational methods—which had been successful with learning-disabled children—in a curriculum for normal preschoolers. Thereafter, Montessori schools were established throughout Europe and the United States.

Enthusiasm for the Montessori system waned in the 1930's, however, primarily because of opposition by those who felt the educationist's method failed to promote discipline in young children. During the 1950's Montessori's program enjoyed a revival, and by 1960 followers of the method created the American Montessori Society. The pioneering educationist, who is also credited with the invention of child-scale furniture for classroom use, wrote several books. English translations of her writings include *The Montessori Method* (1912), *The Advanced Montessori Method* (two volumes; 1917), *The Secret of Childhood* (1936), *Education for a New World* (1946), *What You Should Know About Your Child* (1948), *To Educate the Human Potential* (1948), and *The Absorbent Mind* (1949).

BIOGRAPHICAL/CRITICAL SOURCES:

BOOKS

Kramer, Rita, *Maria Montessori: A Biography,* Putnam, 1976.
1000 Makers of the Twentieth Century, David & Charles, 1971.
Standing, E. M., *Maria Montessori: Her Life and Work,* Academy Guild Press, 1959.

PERIODICALS

New York Times Book Review, November 12, 1967.
Times (London), May 7, 1952.

* * *

MONTGOMERY, Elizabeth
See JULESBERG, Elizabeth Rider Montgomery

* * *

MONTGOMERY, Elizabeth Rider
See JULESBERG, Elizabeth Rider Montgomery

MONTHAN, Doris Born 1924-

PERSONAL: Surname is pronounced *Mon*-tan; born May 26, 1924, in Manitowoc, Wis.; daughter of Edgar Jacob (a banker) and Linda Sophia (Vogt) Born; married Guy Monthan (a teacher and photographer), September 20, 1952; children: William Edgar. *Education:* Attended University of Arizona, 1943-44, New York University, 1948-49, Columbia University, 1950-51, and Northern Arizona University, 1976, 1982. *Politics:* Democrat. *Religion:* Episcopalian.

ADDRESSES: Home—P.O. Box 1698, Flagstaff, Ariz. 86002. *Office*—Writing Lab, United Bank Plaza, 22 West Birch, Flagstaff, Ariz. 86001.

CAREER: Tucson Daily Citizen, Tucson, Ariz., women's editor, 1944-45; *Women's Wear Daily,* New York City, section editor, 1945-46; University of Arizona, Tuscon, writer for Press Bureau and publicist for Artists and Lecture Series, 1946-47; free-lance writer and tutor in Mexico City, Mexico, 1947-48; Bretanno's, New York City, clerk-typist, 1948; Gunther-Jaeckel (women's clothing store), New York City, in publicity and public relations, 1948; *Simplicity Fashion,* New York City, associate editor, 1949-51; Stamps-Conhaim Newspaper Mat Service, Los Angeles, Calif., copywriter, 1952; Rexall Drug Co., Los Angeles, copywriter, 1952-53; Crown Sleep Shops, Pasadena, Calif., advertising manager, 1953-67; free-lance writer in Pasadena, 1967-68; May Co., Los Angeles, copywriter, 1968; Northland Press, Flagstaff, Ariz., editor in chief, 1970-72; Museum of Northern Arizona, Flagstaff, editor of museum notes, 1972-75; free-lance writer and editor, 1975—. Owner of Writing Lab; member of board of directors of Flagstaff Festival of the Arts, 1971-82; panelist for Arizona Commission on the Arts and Assistance League of Flagstaff, 1983—.

MEMBER: Kappa Kappa Gamma.

AWARDS, HONORS: Best Western Book Award from Rounce and Coffin Club and nonfiction award from Border Regional Library Association, both 1975, for *Art and Indian Individualists;* national alumnae achievement award from Kappa Kappa Gamma, 1984.

WRITINGS:

The Thief (novel), Putnam, 1961.
(Editor) *Harmsen's Western Americana,* Northland Press, 1971.
(Editor) *Scholder/Indians,* Northland Press, 1972.
(With husband, Guy Monthan) *Art and Indian Individualists,* Northland Press, 1975.
R.C. Gorman: The Lithographs, Northland Press, 1978.
Nacimientos: Nativity Scenes by Southwest Indians, Northland Press, 1979.
(With G. Monthan and Barbara Babcock) *The Pueblo Storyteller* (art book), University of Arizona Press, 1985.

Contributor to *American Indian Art.*

WORK IN PROGRESS: Gerald Nailor, Navajo Artist, with Clay Lockett, publication expected in 1985.

SIDELIGHTS: Doris Born Monthan told *CA:* "Fiction and poetry are my first loves, but the need to make a living has led me into the marketplace. I have done almost every type of writing in my checkered career—news stories and features for newspapers and magazines, advertising and publicity copy on every subject from pharmaceuticals to fashion. I have enjoyed most of the jobs and felt they kept me limber, like the daily practice of a pianist does. I have also had many jobs unrelated to writing, which never appear on my resumes, but for a writer, they are all grist for the mill. I have sat on both sides of the desk, as editor and author. They are very compatible positions and each career can supply helpful insight for the other.

"What later became a chapter in my novel, *The Thief*, began as a short story in the Writing Workshop at Columbia University. The people I met at a guest ranch while working there as a waitress and maid formed the cast of characters (though much-changed and transformed) for the novel, and the guest ranch itself provided the setting. I also wrote a story based on some of the people I met while working at Brentanno's Out of Print Department. It was never published (or even sent out), but I have been thinking of it recently as a play, which I hope to get to soon.

"Regarding Indian art and artists in the Southwest: It is interesting to note that of the seventeen artists I wrote about in *Art and Indian Individualists* ten years ago, one has died, one is permanently disabled by an accident, one is very aged and no longer produces; but of the remaining fourteen at least half are now millionaires, and all of the others are very well off. This affluence could never have occurred, even among the most famous Indian artists, before the 1970's or mid-1970's. Many younger Indian artists in all media are returning to native crafts after careers in business or are selecting them immediately. There is a tremendous revival in pottery, the second oldest craft after basket making, particularly in figurative art.

"I am particularly aware of this having just finished *The Pueblo Storyteller* book, a survey of pueblo potters who make Storyteller figures and other figurative art. We have documented 233 potters, ranging in age from eight to eighty-five, who are now engaged in making clay figures and other more traditional pottery, and most of them are making their living from it. Almost all of them have been taught by their mothers or some other family member. There are also three times as many sculptors as there were ten years ago and many new painters and jewelry designers and craftsmen. I believe Southwest Indian art has not yet reached its peak, though many thought it had in the early 1970's. Many young artists are benefiting from art training at the college level—using new materials and techniques, and seeking a wider range of expression."

*   *   *

MOONEY, Patrick   1937-

PERSONAL: Born December 10, 1937, in County Leix, Ireland; came to the United States in 1956, naturalized citizen, 1968; son of Sean (in business) and Julia (Hennessy) Mooney. *Education:* Catholic University of America, B.A., 1965; Fairfield University, M.A., 1976.

ADDRESSES: Office—St. Mary Church, 178 Greenwich Ave., Greenwich, Conn. 06830.

CAREER: Ordained Roman Catholic priest, 1965; worked in Africa, 1966-68; associated with St. Mary Church, Greenwich, Conn., 1984—.

WRITINGS:

Contemplation for New Earth, Paulist Press, 1970.
Praise to the Lord of the Morning, Ave Maria Press, 1973.
Morning Is Your Other Name, Twenty-Third Publications, 1980.
A Gift of Love, Twenty-Third Publications, 1981.
Psalms, Twenty-Third Publications, 1984.

WORK IN PROGRESS: A slide program.

*   *   *

MORAN, George   1942-

PERSONAL: Born May 13, 1942, in Fall River, Mass.; son of Thomas S. (a contractor) and Mary (a housewife; maiden name, Wring) Moran. *Education:* College of the Holy Cross, A.B., 1964; attended Art Students' League, 1964-65.

ADDRESSES: Home—New York, N.Y. *Agent*—Betty Binns, Betty Binns Graphics, 31 East 28th St., New York, N.Y. 10016.

CAREER: Worked in Greece as cement carrier, road surveyor, and fishing boat worker, 1970-73; free-lance artist and illustrator, 1973—; writer. Part-time instructor at Bristol Community College in Fall River, Mass.

WRITINGS:

SELF-ILLUSTRATED

Eggs, Workman Publishing, 1975.
(With Jim Erskine) *Fold a Banana and One Hundred Forty-six Other Things to Do When You're Bored*, C. N. Potter, 1978.
(With Erskine) *Throw a Tomato*, C. N. Potter, 1979.
(With Erskine) *Hug a Teddy and One Hundred Seventy-two Other Ways to Stay Safe and Secure*, C. N. Potter, 1980.
(With Erskine) *Lie Down and Roll Over*, C. N. Potter, 1981.
(With Laurel Wright) *When Bad Dogs Happen to Good People*, Crown, 1983.

ILLUSTRATOR:

Susan Kelz Sperling, *Poplollies and Bellibones*, C. N. Potter, 1977.
Giles Brandreth, *Joy of Lex*, Morrow, 1980.
Michael Ryan, *Climbing*, Addison-Wesley, 1980.
Brandreth, *More Joy of Lex*, Morrow, 1982.

SIDELIGHTS: George Moran told *CA:* "In 1973, I took a trip to Montreal and ran out of funds. There exist in Montreal one or two spots where artists display and sell their work in the street. I bought paper and colored markers and made eight dollars the first day. Rooms were ten dollars a week at the time. I was rich. After a week or so, when I was drawing, an onlooker dropped her ice cream cone. There was a general sigh of pleasure prematurely terminated. I started drawing pictures on the tragedy of dropped cones. Another day, there was a splattered egg on the sidewalk, so I drew a series of egg funerals. A little procession of people, one carrying the yolk, another, the white, another, the shell. Thus, ironically enough, the egg was born. Later that year, I stopped teaching and traveled around the country to Key West and New Orleans, following the tourist crowd and drawing eggs. In the fall of 1974, I arrived in New York with hundreds of egg pictures. An old friend matched me up with the graphic designer Betty Binns who helped me make a mock-up Egg Book which Workman Publishers kindly agreed to publish.

"Jim Erskine and I were brought together by the late Jane West who was then in charge of Clarkson Potter Publishers. Jane called Betty and said that she had received an illustrator's book. Betty read me a list of 'things to do when you're bored' over the phone. The ideas were simple, whimsical, and delightfully outrageous. I agreed to take the job immediately. Jim and I had great fun doing these books.

"*When Bad Dogs Happen to Good People* was the brainchild of Laurel Wright, also known as Catherine Shaw. It was a take-off on the popular *When Bad Things Happen to Good People* by Rabbi Kushner. Having had an imaginative and cunning basset hound as a pal when a child, I immediately saw the possibilities. As for a theme or moral—in the words of Rabbi Ben Schnauzer, commentator of *Bad Dogs,* 'Bad dogs simply are.'

"A high school English teacher once observed that a deeply felt theme I had written (a green cathedral motif about finding spirituality and peace in the woods) was trite. She was right, and from that point on I have tried to find offbeat perspectives when approaching material. Another word of advice came from a college teacher of comparative religion who urged free association as a means of generating new ideas. A banana combined with a bicycle, for instance, might yield a wheeled banana or a peelable bike. A sense of irony has helped as well as outrage at life's vanities and hypocrisies. For inspiration along these lines, I often read the *Wall Street Journal.*"

* * *

MORGAN, Steven Michael 1942-

PERSONAL: Born June 15, 1942, in Bronx, N.Y.; son of Bernard Irwin (a manufacturer) and Sophie (a homemaker; maiden name, Golub) Morgan. *Education:* Goddard College, B.A., 1974; California School of Professional Psychology, M.A., 1976, Ph.D., 1979.

ADDRESSES: Office—Patton State Hospital, 3102 East Highland Ave., Patton, Calif. 92369.

CAREER: Patton State Hospital, Patton, Calif., staff psychologist, 1979—. Clinical director of family violence program for U.S. Marine Corps, Twenty-nine Palms, Calif. 1983-84.

MEMBER: American Psychological Association, California Psychological Association, Psi Chi, Lake Arrowhead Country Club.

WRITINGS:

Conjugal Terrorism: A Psychological and Community Treatment Model of Wife Abuse, R & E Research Associates, 1982.

SIDELIGHTS: Steven Michael Morgan reported: "Male violence toward the feminine in themselves and consequently toward females in society is, very likely, the progenitor of social disintegration. It attacks the level of trust in relationships and, without this safety, people find it difficult to survive and grow. While social development requires separation and individuation, it is a fallacy that violence in any of its forms promotes individuation. Competency is built on mastery, not dominance. Violence is the cry of the weak under pressure."

* * *

MORRISON, Bill 1935-

BRIEF ENTRY: Educator, illustrator, and author of children's books. Winner of several awards in national exhibitions held by the Society of Illustrators, Morrison is best known as an illustrator whose work has appeared on the pages of more than thirty books for children. Among them are Mae Freeman's *Where's Izzy?* (Follett, 1972), Sid Fleischman's *The Bloodhound Gang in the Case of Princess Tomorrow* (Random House, 1981), and a series of "Oz" books adapted by C. J. Naden.

Morrison has also written and illustrated three books for children. The works—*Squeeze a Sneeze* (Houghton, 1977), *Louis James Hates School* (Houghton, 1978), and *Simon Says* (Little, Brown, 1983)—have been praised for their exuberance and lightheartedness. *Address:* Massachusetts.

* * *

MORRISSEY, Stephen 1950-

PERSONAL: Born April 27, 1950, in Montreal, Quebec, Canada; married Pat Walsh; children: Jake. *Education:* Sir George Williams University (now Sir George Williams Campus, Concordia University), B.A. (with honors), 1973; McGill University, M.A., 1976.

ADDRESSES: Home—4359 Route 138, R.R.2, Huntingdon, Quebec, Canada J0S 1H0. *Office*—Champlain Regional College, St. Lambert, Quebec, Canada.

CAREER: Teacher at Champlain Regional College, St. Lambert, Quebec, 1976—. Guest on television and radio programs.

MEMBER: American Society of Dowsers.

AWARDS, HONORS: Canada Council grants, 1982, 1983-85.

WRITINGS:

The Trees of Unknowing, Vehicle Press, 1978.
Divisions, Coach House Press, 1983.

Work also represented in anthologies. Editor of *Montreal Journal of Poetics.*

WORK IN PROGRESS: By the Water.

* * *

MORSCHER, Betsy 1939-

PERSONAL: Born August 9, 1939, in Somonauk, Ill.; daughter of E. H. (a general contractor) and Frances (a housewife) Montgomery; married second husband, Gordon Eddolls (an executive), June 16, 1984; children: (from first marriage) Monica, Maria, Vincent. *Education:* Marquette University, B.S., 1961; attended University of Denver, 1962-63, and University of Colorado at Boulder; Columbia Pacific University, Ph.D., 1985.

ADDRESSES: Office—787 Elizabeth, Denver, Colo. 80206.

CAREER: Public speaker, consultant, and writer. Conducts stress and personal energy seminars; leads tours of spas in Europe and North America.

MEMBER: International Platform Speakers Association, National Speakers Association, National Writers Club, National Press Women, American Society for Training and Development, American Association of Professional Consultants, Colorado Speakers Association.

WRITINGS:

Heal Yourself the European Way, Prentice-Hall, 1980.
Risk-Taking for Women, Everest House, 1982.

Contributor to magazines, including *Cosmopolitan, Harper's Bazaar, Denver,* and *Club Ties.*

WORK IN PROGRESS: Research on health into the twenty-first century.

SIDELIGHTS: Betsy Morscher told *CA:* "Health problems in my family precipitated my interest in the research that led to *Heal Yourself the European Way.* Twelve family members had died of cancer. My research included travel to the major spas, *bads,* and clinics of Europe, then to more than thirty spas in North America for additional information."

*   *   *

MOSS, Bernard H(aym)   1943-

BRIEF ENTRY: Born April 17, 1943, in New York, N.Y. American historian, educator, and author. Moss taught modern French and European labor history at the University of Southern California from 1969 to 1980. He has studied in Belgium and edited the newsletter of the Study Group on European Labor and Working Class History. Moss wrote *The Origins of the French Labor Movement, 1830-1914: The Socialism of Skilled Workers* (University of California Press, 1976). *Address:* 3835 West 59th, Los Angeles, Calif. 90043.

BIOGRAPHICAL/CRITICAL SOURCES:

PERIODICALS

American Historical Review, April, 1977.
Times Literary Supplement, April 1, 1977.

*   *   *

MOULTON, Gary E(van)   1942-

PERSONAL: Born February 21, 1942, in Tulsa, Okla.; son of William Virgil (a salesman) and Cleo (a nursery supervisor; maiden name, Collins) Moulton; married Faye Whitaker Doss (an ombudsman), June 2, 1969; children: Kim Moulton Reynolds, Russell, Luanne. *Education:* Northeastern Oklahoma State College (now University), B.A., 1968; Oklahoma State University, M.A., 1970, Ph.D., 1973.

ADDRESSES: Home—420 Jeffery Dr., Lincoln, Neb. 68505. *Office*—Department of History, University of Nebraska—Lincoln, Lincoln, Neb. 68588.

CAREER: Southwestern Oklahoma State University, Weatherford, instructor, 1973-74, assistant professor of American history, 1974-79, editor of "Papers of Chief John Ross," 1975-79; University of Nebraska—Lincoln, associate professor of American history and editor of "Journals of the Lewis and Clark Expedition" at Center for Great Plains Studies, 1979—. Member of board of directors of Lewis and Clark Trail Heritage Foundation, 1980—; public speaker. *Military service:* U.S. Army Security Agency, 1961-64; served in Vietnam and Thailand.

MEMBER: Association for Documentary Editing, Western History Association, Westerners International (organizer and first sheriff of Lincoln Corral), Nebraska State Historical Society, Phi Alpha Theta.

AWARDS, HONORS: Grants from National Historical Publications and Records Commission, 1975-79, National Endowment for the Humanities, 1980-85, American Philosophical Society, 1982-85, Nebraska Committee for the Humanities, 1982 and 1983, and Lewis and Clark Trail Heritage Foundation, 1983; Wrangler Award from National Cowboy Hall of Fame, 1984, for *Atlas of the Lewis and Clark Expedition.*

WRITINGS:

John Ross, Cherokee Chief, University of Georgia Press, 1978.

(Editor) *Journals of the Lewis and Clark Expedition,* Volume I: *Atlas of the Lewis and Clark Expedition,* University of Nebraska Press, 1983.
(Editor) *The Papers of Chief John Ross,* University of Oklahoma Press, 1985.

CONTRIBUTOR

H. Glenn Jordan and Thomas H. Holm, editors, *Indian Leaders: Oklahoma's First Statesmen,* Oklahoma Historical Society, 1979.
R. David Edmunds, editor, *American Indian Leaders: Studies in Diversity,* University of Nebraska Press, 1980.

Contributor to *Encyclopedia of Southern History.* Contributor of nearly fifty articles and reviews to history journals.

SIDELIGHTS: Gary E. Moulton told *CA:* "I entered American Indian and western history, and finally historical editing, by the back door. In a graduate seminar in Oklahoma history I was assigned the topic 'Chief John Ross During the Civil War' and discovered that there was no biography of the man from which to 'glean' the necessary information. From that effort, I went on to develop a full-scale biography of Ross. In another seminar I did some work editing Will Rogers's daily telegrams and discovered the field of historical editing, flourishing in the 1960's. Having found a trove of Ross's letters and personal papers, I merged my two new interests and was able to persuade the National Historical Publications and Records Commission to fund a project to edit Ross's papers. With that work completed, I found that I could continue my editing endeavors and study of western history in a project just begun at the University of Nebraska to publish the journals of the Lewis and Clark expedition.

"The discipline of historical editing is as old as or older than the craft of history itself, but only in recent times has it taken a separate and individual identity. Previously viewed as a stepchild of the larger profession, historical editing has emerged since the 1950's as an important endeavor and field of study in its own right. Its 'renaissance' can be attributed partly to the large inflow of public and private funds and to the professionalization of its practitioners. In recent years this emerging profession has endeavored to give more attention to the training of editors, who were up to that time largely self-taught with a particular expertise in the person or institution whose papers were being edited. Historical editors, now more than ever, have much to teach documentary users about their sources, especially in terms of searching for, organizing, selecting, and transcribing those items. Moreover, editors' annotation and explication of documents has pointed writers toward new areas of research. The publication in recent years of great numbers of documents under rigorous standards of editing has enabled users to have a wider diversity of sources at their disposal and the completeness and accuracy of these works has been a boon to research. It has been my pleasure during the last decade to work as a historical editor, and I have found it to be an exciting field of research and a rewarding intellectual endeavor."

BIOGRAPHICAL/CRITICAL SOURCES:

PERIODICALS

American Historical Review, April, 1979.
Washington Post Book World, March 3, 1984.

*   *   *

MOUNTFIELD, Stuart   1903(?)-1984

OBITUARY NOTICE: Born c. 1903; died December 1, 1984.

Port administrator and author. Mountfield joined Liverpool's Mersey Docks and Harbour Board in 1918. He rose through the administrative hierarchy to become the general manager and secretary of the board in 1957, and he retired in 1962. During a career that lasted more than forty years, Mountfield became an expert on the port of Liverpool and its history. He recorded this knowledge in his book *Western Gateway*.

OBITUARIES AND OTHER SOURCES:

PERIODICALS

Times (London), December 14, 1984.

* * *

MOYNAHAN, John F. 1912-1985

OBITUARY NOTICE: Born April 11, 1912, in Boston, Mass.; died of cancer, March 26, 1985, in Stamford, Conn.; buried at Arlington National Cemetery, Arlington, Va. Military officer, business executive, journalist, and author. As a U.S. Army officer during World War II, Moynahan served as assistant to General Leslie Groves, director of the Manhattan Project, which produced the first atomic bomb. Moynahan also witnessed the testing of the A-bomb in New Mexico and in the Pacific, and he was aboard the airplane accompanying aircraft that bombed the Japanese city of Nagasaki. Retiring from the Army as lieutenant colonel in 1946, Moynahan received a Bronze Star for his contributions to the Manhattan Project. Two years later he founded an international public relations consulting firm, John Moynahan & Company. Later in his life Moynahan developed several types of cancer, which he suspected were the result of his close association with the atomic testing, although this was not conclusively proven. He was the author of *Atomic Diary, 1946*. Prior to his military service, Moynahan had worked for two years as a reporter for the *Boston Herald* and for seven years as a reporter for the *Newark News*.

OBITUARIES AND OTHER SOURCES:

BOOKS

Who's Who in Public Relations (International), 4th edition, P R Publishing, 1972.

PERIODICALS

Chicago Tribune, March 31, 1985.

* * *

MUNSON, Henry (Lee), Jr. 1946-

PERSONAL: Born November 1, 1946, in New York, N.Y.; son of Henry Lee and Monique (Ruzette) Munson; married Fatima Bernikho, June 26, 1971; children: Leila, John, Michael. *Education:* Columbia University, B.A., 1970; University of Chicago, M.A., 1973, Ph.D., 1980. *Religion:* None.

ADDRESSES: Home—20A University Park, Orono, Me. 04473. *Office*—Department of Anthropology, University of Maine at Orono, Orono, Me. 04469.

CAREER: University of Maine at Orono, assistant professor of anthropology, 1982—.

MEMBER: American Anthropological Association, Middle East Studies Association.

AWARDS, HONORS: Fulbright fellow, 1976-77; fellow of Social Science Research Council, 1976-77, and National Endowment for the Humanities, 1984.

WRITINGS:

(Recorder, translator, and editor) *The House of Si Abd Allah: The Oral History of a Moroccan Family*, Yale University Press, 1984.

Contributor to anthropology and Middle East studies journals.

WORK IN PROGRESS: Islam and Revolution in Egypt, Iran, and Morocco, a book on Islamic fundamentalism in the Middle East, primarily in Iran, Egypt, and Morocco.

SIDELIGHTS: Henry Munson, Jr., told *CA:* "*The House of Si Abd Allah: The Oral History of a Moroccan Family* is based upon a year and a half's 'field work' in Morocco. In the book I try to contrast how the history of Morocco over the past century is perceived by a middle-aged Muslim 'fundamentalist,' who is a peddler in Tangier, with how it is perceived by a westernized young Muslim woman who has lived for many years in the United States."

Reviewing *The House of Si Abd Allah* in the *New York Times Book Review*, Amal Rassam commented that this "juxtaposition of the two different perspectives makes for a rich account of life in a Muslim society today." Each chapter describes two accounts of the same events and the same people, from the point of view first of the middle-aged, streetwise al-Hajj Muhammad and then of the young, college-educated Fatima Zohra. The book, wrote Edmund Leach in the *London Review of Books*, has "really three authors. The two principal narrators, both born in Tangier, are first cousins" who "have made extensive tape-recordings for Munson in which they discuss their past lives, their general views of religion and society, and their kinsfolk. The third author is of course Munson himself, who provides an edited translation and a long and lucid Introduction." Leach also suggested that Munson's greater attention in that introduction to the conservative orthodoxy of al-Hajj Muhammad than to the liberal modernism of Fatima Zohra was intended to enlighten the American audience as to "how the Iranian masses could have preferred the fundamentalist tyranny of the Ayatollah Khomeini to the corrupt but Westernised (and therefore comprehensible) tyranny of the Shah." Although al-Hajj Muhammad never read the works of the Ayatollah or of other fundamentalists, his perspective, according to *Worldview* writer Sterret Pope, "epitomizes the Zealotism of Khomeini and his 'Party of God'."

Additionally, Leach commended Munson for his demonstration that the apparently dissimilar ideologies of the two cousins mask their common heritage and shared values: they both come from the same impoverished background and, according to Leach, "clearly share many family affections as well as a deeply felt conviction that all the misfortunes of Morocco as they know it derive from the colonial experience and from the Moroccan elite." Similarly, Pope commented: "One of the virtues of *The House of Si Abd Allah* is that it shows, particularly through Fatima Zohra's narrative, that Westernized Muslims still prize their Islamic heritage as a vital component of their political and cultural identity, even as they criticize it."

Critics praised *The House of Si Abd Allah*. Rassam assessed it "a valuable book for those interested in Moroccan culture." Pope concurred, adding that Munson's "book has much to say about the travails of rural indigence and urban migration, the problems and the joys of marriage and childbearing, and the trauma of modernization and cultural dependence in modern Morocco,'' and Leach lauded the work's ''original manner,'' its ''clear, uncluttered style,'' and its appeal even to ''people who have no professional interest in anthropology.''

BIOGRAPHICAL/CRITICAL SOURCES:

PERIODICALS

London Review of Books, August 2, 1984.
New York Times Book Review, April 15, 1984.
Times Literary Supplement, September 7, 1984.
Worldview, July, 1984.

*   *   *

MURPHY, Karen A(lee)   1945-

PERSONAL: Born March 16, 1945, in Brooklyn, N.Y.; daughter of Harold Arthur Adams and Marguerite Ellen Anderson; married Terence C. Murphy (owner and president of Curtis Archives), October 16, 1965; children: Sean Adam, Brianna Siobhan. *Education:* Attended Sorbonne, University of Paris, 1964; University of Washington, Seattle, B.A., 1967. *Politics:* Independent. *Religion:* None.

ADDRESSES: Home—3920 Sunnyside Ave. N., Seattle, Wash. 98103. *Agent*—Sandra Dijkstra, P.O. Box 2287, Del Mar, Calif. 92014.

CAREER: State of Washington, Seattle, caseworker, 1968-71; Holly Park Community Council Day Care Center, Seattle, social worker, 1971-75; owner and operator of day care home in Seattle, 1976-82, and editorial, typing, and writing service in Seattle, 1976—. Social worker at public schools in Glastonbury, Conn., 1973-74. Member of Park Street Potters, 1973-75.

WRITINGS:

A House Full of Kids (nonfiction), Beacon Press, 1984.

WORK IN PROGRESS: Research on the issues of licensing versus self-registration and alternative education.

SIDELIGHTS: Karen A. Murphy told *CA:* ''As a day care home operator I quickly learned that the public at large has little understanding of the lifestyle or the demands upon one in that position. I also learned that the mythology surrounding day care was thick and difficult to penetrate. After five years I decided it was important for me to somehow legitimize this activity and thus my own involvement and, even more important, for me to chip away at the mythology surrounding the child care field. Having been told hundreds of times by parents that I 'should write a book,' I finally sat down to the typewriter two months before retiring from the day care business.

''Knowing that to write of one's personal experience while it is happening gives a more accurate picture of the situation, I felt it was particularly important in this case to tell the truth about the child care home environment and the differences between child care homes and centers in general. This issue—homes and how they differ from centers—is of continuing interest to me, and I am now teaching seminars for the purpose of assisting parents in clarifying their own expectations and values in this area. I am submitting articles for publication to various magazines and hope that these discussions will be of help to parents facing the problems of choosing child care for their children.

''Currently, I am involved in alternative elementary education in Seattle (i.e. active as a parent in the classroom and curriculum planning) and will eventually write again on the subject of 'parenting' focused on the late adolescent years.''

AVOCATIONAL INTERESTS: International travel, pottery.

*   *   *

MUSES, C. A.
See MUSES, Charles Arthur

*   *   *

MUSES, Charles Arthur   1919-
(C. A. Muses)

BRIEF ENTRY: Born April 28, 1919, in New Jersey. American mathematician, physicist, philosopher, parapsychologist, and author. Muses, who coined the word ''noetics'' to define his parapsychological theory of nature and the alterations and potentials of consciousness, began his career as a chemist for Gar-Baker Laboratories in 1941. He went on to become the editor in chief of Falcon's Wing Press (publishers of books on philosophy and the occult), research director of the Barth Foundation, editor of the *Journal for the Study of Consciousness,* and, beginning in 1969, the director of research at the Center for Research on Mathematics and Morphology in California. In addition, the scientist has conducted cybernetic research with Norbert Wiener and anthropological studies involving Mexico and India.

Muses wrote *East-West Fire: Schopenhauer's Optimism and the Lankavatara Sutra; An Excursion Toward the Common Ground Between Oriental and Western Religion* (Falcon's Wing Press, 1955). He edited *Prismatic Voices: An International Anthology of Distinctive New Poets* (Falcon's Wing Press, 1958), *Esoteric Teachings of the Tibetan Tantra* (Falcon's Wing Press, 1961), and *Consciousness and Reality: The Human Pivot Point* (Outerbridge & Lazard, 1972). *Address:* Center for Research on Mathematics and Morphology, Santa Barbara, Calif. 93108.

BIOGRAPHICAL/CRITICAL SOURCES:

BOOKS

American Men and Women of Science, 13th edition, Bowker, 1976.
Encyclopedia of Occultism and Parapsychology, Supplement, Gale, 1982.

*   *   *

MYERS, Rollo Hugh   1892-1984(?)

OBITUARY NOTICE—See index for *CA* sketch: Born January 23, 1892, in Chislehurst, Kent, England; died c. 1984. Journalist, editor, translator, and author. Music was Myers's lifelong interest, particularly the French composers. As a result, he spent much of his life living alternately in Paris and London, establishing himself in the musical worlds of both cities. He began his career working as music correspondent in Paris for the London *Times* and *Daily Telegraph,* then served on the staff of the British Broadcasting Corporation's music department from 1935 to 1944 and subsequently became music officer for the British Council in Paris in 1945. From 1949 to 1956 he served as secretariat for the Organization for European Economic Cooperation in Paris. His books include *Modern Music,* a guide for the average music lover; *Erik Satie,* which gained him widespread acclaim; *Ravel: Life and Works;* and *Debussy.* Myers also translated books, including *An Illustrated History of Music,* and edited a number of works, among which was *Richard Strauss and Romain Rolland.*

OBITUARIES AND OTHER SOURCES:

BOOKS

Baker's Biographical Dictionary of Musicians, 6th edition, Schirmer, 1978.

PERIODICALS

Times (London), February 23, 1985.

N

NAGAI BERTHRONG, Evelyn   1946-

PERSONAL: Born May 1, 1946, in Ashcroft, British Columbia, Canada; daughter of Toshio and Frances Nagai; married John H. Berthrong; children: one son. *Education:* Attended University of California, Los Angeles, University of Poona, and University of Munich; University of British Columbia, B.A., 1968; University of Wisconsin—Madison, M.A., 1971; University of California, Berkeley, Ph.D., 1977.

ADDRESSES: Home—Toronto, Ontario, Canada. *Office*—Department of East Asian Studies, University of Toronto, Toronto, Ontario, Canada M5S 1A1.

CAREER: Los Angeles County Museum of Art, Los Angeles, Calif., curatorial assistant in Far Eastern art, 1972-73; University of Toronto, Toronto, Ontario, assistant professor of Oriental art, 1982—. Royal Ontario Museum, assistant curator of Far Eastern art, 1979-81, curatorial coordinator of "Silk Roads/China Ships," 1981-83. Instructor at San Francisco City College, 1978; lecturer for Archaeological Institute of America, 1984; public speaker.

MEMBER: College Art Association of America, Archaeological Institute of America, Canadian Asian Studies Association.

AWARDS, HONORS: Commonwealth fellow to India, 1969; research fellow of Canada Council, 1974.

WRITINGS:

(Contributor) *Treasures of the Orient*, Society for Asian Art, 1979.
Adventures of the Magic Monkey Along the Silk Routes, Royal Ontario Museum, 1983.
(With Anker Odum) *Silk Roads/China Ships: An Exhibition of East-West Trade*, Royal Ontario Museum, 1983.

Contributor to magazines, including *Rotunda, Orientations,* and *Archeology.*

WORK IN PROGRESS: Research on Buddhist art and the history of international contact between East and West.

SIDELIGHTS: Evelyn Nagai Berthrong told *CA:* "The most unique bit of writing and research I have ever done was the *Magic Monkey.* Since first hearing of the *Journey to the East* when I was a child, I had always wanted to do something with the story. When the opportunity arose, I proposed that an il-

lustrated version of some of the episodes from the ancient Chinese tale be published, using many of the objects in an exhibition in the drawings. For once, everything seemed to come together—a fine and willing artist, a superb printing house, an outlet, and a new and accurate translation of the original text. It's a book which is for children only on the surface, for although the drawings seem to be intended for the young, in fact very little of the philosophy has been left out. *Magic Monkey* is about everyone's dream of achieving success by one definition or another; and that means it's about me, too."

*   *   *

NAKADATE, Neil Edward   1943-

PERSONAL: Born September 1, 1943, in East Chicago, Ind.; son of Katsumi J. (an anesthesiologist) and Mary (a homemaker and teacher; maiden name, Marumoto) Nakadate; divorced; children: Nathaniel, Nicholas, Laurel. *Education:* Stanford University, A.B., 1965; Indiana University—Bloomington, M.A., 1968, Ph.D., 1972.

ADDRESSES: Home—903 Burnett Ave., Ames, Iowa 50010. *Office*—Department of English, Iowa State University, Ames, Iowa 50011.

CAREER: University of Texas at Austin, assistant professor of English, 1970-77; Iowa State University, Ames, assistant professor, 1977-80, associate professor of English, 1980—.

MEMBER: Conference on College Composition and Communication, Society for the Study of Southern Literature, Modern Language Association of America.

WRITINGS:

(Editor) *Robert Penn Warren: A Reference Guide*, G. K. Hall, 1977.
(Editor and contributor) *Robert Penn Warren: Critical Perspectives*, University Press of Kentucky, 1981.
(With James L. Kinneavy and William J. McCleary) *Writing in the Liberal Arts Tradition*, Harper, 1985.

Contributor to literature journals and little magazines.

WORK IN PROGRESS: A book-length commentary on aspects of the Japanese-American experience.

SIDELIGHTS: Neil Edward Nakadate told *CA:* "My interest in Robert Penn Warren was provoked in a graduate seminar and nourished by a generous mentor. It is an interest in a writer engaged in a lifelong process of definition and exploration—of self, family, history, and ideas—in an impressive range of literary forms.

"Behind my work in rhetoric and composition is a belief that writing must be learned and can be taught, and that writing and reading are the enabling skills of the learning process. The common denominators of my own best work: a struggle to solve the writing problems peculiar to a given project and anticipation of a clearly defined audience."

*   *   *

NANUS, Burt   1936-

PERSONAL: Born March 21, 1936, in New York, N.Y.; son of Max (a merchant) and Mollie (a bookkeeper; maiden name, Rothstein) Nanus; married Marlene Guttman (a youth services director), June 29, 1969; children: Leora. *Education:* Stevens Institute of Technology, M.E., 1957; Massachusetts Institute of Technology, M.S., 1959; University of Southern California, D.B.A., 1967.

ADDRESSES: Office—Department of Management, University of Southern California, University Park, Los Angeles, Calif. 90089.

CAREER: System Development Corp., Santa Monica, Calif., senior technical adviser to management, 1962-67; Management Technology, Inc., Los Angeles, Calif., president, 1967-69; University of Southern California, Los Angeles, lecturer, 1969-74, assistant professor, 1974-79, professor of management, 1979—, director of Center for Futures Research, 1971—. Strategic planning consultant to corporations and government agencies.

MEMBER: World Future Society, Academy of Management.

WRITINGS:

(With Joel M. Kibbee and Clifford J. Craft) *Management Games*, Reinhold Publishing, 1961.
(With Michael Wooton and Harold Borko) *Social Implications of the Use of Computers Across National Boundries*, AFIPS Press, 1973.
(With Herbert S. Dordick and Helen G. Bradley) *The Emerging Network Marketplace*, Ablex Publishing, 1981.
(With Warren Bennis) *Taking Charge*, Harper, 1985.

Member of board of editors of *New Management*.

WORK IN PROGRESS: Leadership and Future Analysis; Managing Change in State Government.

SIDELIGHTS: Burt Nanus told *CA:* "I have been developing methodologies for thinking about the future in a more systematic fashion, in order to help organizations and institutions learn how to manage change in their environments. I am convinced that if we do not learn how to do this, and learn it fast, we will be overwhelmed by the forces now building up in our society—hair-trigger nuclear diplomacy, technological meddling with brain (artificial intelligence) and body (genetic engineering), instability of economic and social systems, etc. We need a new kind of leader with a new set of leadership skills. This leader must be anticipative, nurturing, and capable of developing new visions, inspiring learning, and helping people find meaning in their social order."

NASS, Stanley   1940-

PERSONAL: Born April 15, 1940, in Poland; naturalized U.S. citizen; son of Levi and Maria (Sorgen) Nass. *Education:* City College of the City University of New York, B.A., 1962; New York University, M.A. (history), 1965; Columbia University, M.A. (counseling), 1970, Ed.D., 1976.

ADDRESSES: Home—225 East 73rd St., New York, N.Y. 10021. *Office*—Department of Guidance and Counseling, Brooklyn Center, Long Island University, University Plaza, Brooklyn, N.Y. 11201.

CAREER: High school social studies teacher in New York, N.Y., 1964-70; Long Island University, Brooklyn Center, instructor, 1971-73, assistant professor, 1973-77, associate professor, 1977-81, professor of guidance and counseling, 1981—, chairman of graduate department, 1974—, director of Evening and Weekend Degree Programs for Adults, 1980-82. Educational and cultural adviser to Jewish Philanthropies; consultant to National School of Savings Banking.

MEMBER: American Psychological Association, American Personnel and Guidance Association, American Association of Marriage and Family Counselors.

WRITINGS:

(Contributor) Gary S. Belkin, editor, *Counseling Theory and Practice*, Kendall/Hunt, 1977.
(Editor) *Crisis Intervention*, Kendall/Hunt, 1977.
(With Manfred Weidhorn) *Turn Your Life Around: Self-Knowledge for Self-Improvement*, Prentice-Hall, 1978.
(With Belkin) *Psychology of Adjustment*, Allyn & Bacon, 1983.

Contributor to education and psychology texts.

WORK IN PROGRESS: A critique of current approaches to treatment of the mentally ill, publication expected in 1986; a novel titled *The Traver Complex*.

SIDELIGHTS: Stanley Nass told *CA:* "My novel in progress, *The Traver Complex*, is about a psychiatrist who becomes involved in the solution of a murder. Dr. Traver believes that he has surpassed Freud and is waiting for the profession to adapt itself to his new theories—'the psychology of sadness.'"

*   *   *

NATHAN, Joe   1948-

PERSONAL: Born September 2, 1948, in Chicago, Ill.; son of C. Henry (a public information officer and college lecturer) and Ruth (a public school director of early childhood programs; maiden name, Kositchek) Nathan; married JoAnn Lukesh (a public school teacher of the handicapped), September 28, 1974; children: Elizabeth Mary and David Connor (twins). *Education:* Carleton College, B.A., 1970; University of Minnesota—Twin Cities, M.A., 1974, Ph.D., 1981. *Politics:* Progressive. *Religion:* Unitarian-Universalist.

ADDRESSES: Home—1852 Pinehurst, St. Paul, Minn. 55116. *Office*—Public School Incentives, 1885 University, St. Paul, Minn. 55104.

CAREER: St. Paul Public Schools, St. Paul, Minn., elementary school teacher, 1971-75, program coordinator and assistant director of public alternative program, 1975-77; assistant principal of public junior-senior high school in St. Paul, 1977-79; St. Paul Public Schools, assistant principal of junior high school in St. Paul, 1979-81, assistant principal on special assignment, 1981-83; Public School Incentives, St. Paul, research and program developer, 1984—. Speaker at more than eighty-five colleges and universities throughout North America; guest on radio and television programs. Member of Minnesota Governor's Council on Youth and Minnesota Education Council; member of board of directors of local community agencies.

AWARDS, HONORS: Columbia University's Teachers College Book Award, 1970; outstanding young educator award from Phi Delta Kappa, 1980.

WRITINGS:

Free to Teach: Achieving Equity and Excellence in Schools, Pilgrim Press, 1983, revised edition, Winston Press, 1984.

Contributor to magazines, including *Family Computing, Infoworld, Learning, Teacher, Kappan,* and *Corporate Report.*

WORK IN PROGRESS: The Coming Computer Fraud: Sense and Nonsense in Home and School Computer Use, publication expected in 1985.

SIDELIGHTS: Joe Nathan told *CA:* "I worked in public schools for more than a decade. One of my favorite classes involved helping students learn how to understand and help solve consumer problems. Over a period of several years the thirteen-to-eighteen-year-old students had more than three hundred cases and successfully resolved 75 percent of them. This class was described in *Reader's Digest, McCall's,* and *Parade,* as well as in many educational magazines. Another class involved six-to-nine-year-old students who developed the ideas and plans for a playground, gathered the materials, and built it for less than ten dollars.

"*Free to Teach* was written because I felt there were many creative ways to improve education, most of which would not cost more money per pupil, which were not being discussed. These ideas included shared facilities, where social service agencies and businesses share space in schools; youth participation projects, where students combine classroom work and community service; competence-based graduation requirements, where students are tested both with paper and pencil and with real world measures before graduation, much like people are tested before they get a driver's license; alternative routes into teaching, which do not require a degree in education; new career patterns for teachers to reward and encourage master teachers; and a 'G.I. Bill' for families, allowing them to select from a variety of schools.

"*Free to Teach* begins with a chapter called 'Day in the Life of an Assistant Principal.' It shows a typical day, with my own successes and failures. The book describes creative, effective educational programs and uses actual incidents to illustrate barriers faced by innovative educators. Fundamentally, my criticisms are of the public education system. There are no heroes or villains in my book, only people struggling to do the best they can. We must reverse the incentives, so there will be rewards for competence, not compliance; innovation, not inaction; creativity, not conformity; and results, not rationalizations.

"Because of the President's Commission, which appeared a month before my book was published, there was an enormous interest in education. The timing was lucky! Within a year more than seventy-five radio, television, and newspaper reporters interviewed me. Since the book appeared, I have been working closely with several Minnesota legislators, and I helped write several bills which passed the most recent legislative session. Winston Press allowed me to make substantial revisions of my book for the paperback edition.

"*Free to Teach* was written while I was an assistant principal in the St. Paul Public Schools. I used an Apple III computer, writing from four to six o'clock in the morning and ten to twelve o'clock at night on weekdays, as well as many hours on the weekends. My wife strongly supported the writing of this book, providing vital support, assistance, and encouragement. At present I'm on leave from the St. Paul Public Schools, and I am researching and advocating various structural improvements in education. I do not know whether or not I will return to public school work."

BIOGRAPHICAL/CRITICAL SOURCES:

PERIODICALS

Education Week, February 15, 1984.
Parade, August 7, 1977.
Scholastic Teacher, January, 1975.
St. Paul Pioneer Press/Dispatch, June 19, 1983.

*   *   *

NEFF, Miriam 1945-

PERSONAL: Born June 24, 1945, in Indiana; daughter of Immanuel Horace and Beulah MaDonna (McCoy) Hinds; married Robert Charles Neff (a broadcaster), January 31, 1965; children: Valerie, John, Charles, Robby. *Education:* Attended Indiana University—Bloomington; Northwestern University, B.A., 1967, M.A., 1968.

ADDRESSES: Home—1031 South Aldine, Park Ridge, Ill. 60068.

CAREER: High school guidance counselor in Park Ridge, Ill., 1969-72; Home Equity, Oakbrook, Ill., client counselor, 1984—.

MEMBER: Phi Beta Kappa.

WRITINGS:

Discover Your Worth, Victor Books, 1979.
Women and Their Emotions, Moody, 1983.

Contributor to magazines.

WORK IN PROGRESS: Research on women from the perspective of a "biblical feminist."

SIDELIGHTS: Miriam Neff told *CA:* "Writing is the overflow of what's happening in my life as a woman, mother, and worker. In order to write, I first have to live, work, and play. The quiet moments at the word processor are balanced by water skiing, noisy picnics, and the nonstop activity of a growing family."

BIOGRAPHICAL/CRITICAL SOURCES:

PERIODICALS

West Coast Review of Books, July, 1979.

*   *   *

NEIMARK, Paul G. 1934-

BRIEF ENTRY: Born October 13, 1934, in Chicago, Ill.

American author. A free-lance writer who has contributed more than four thousand articles to such publications as the *New York Times* and *Reader's Digest,* Neimark is also the author of books for both adults and children. He is perhaps best known for collaborating with various notable persons on their auto-biographies. These include *Blackthink: My Life as Black Man and White Man* (Morrow, 1970), written with Olympic gold medalist Jesse Owens; *Confessions of a Divorce Lawyer* (Regnery, 1975), the memoirs of Herbert A. Glieberman; and *Goodbye Loneliness* (Stein & Day, 1979), in collaboration with Jay H. Schmidt. *Cycle Cop: The True Story of Jack Muller, the Chicago Giant Killer Who Feared No Evil* (Putnam, 1976) and *Getting Along: How to Be Happy With Yourself and Others* (with Schmidt; Putnam, 1979) are among Neimark's books for children. In addition, he is the author of the "Wilderness World" children's series, published by Children's Press in 1981. Neimark received an M. K. Cooper Award in 1971 for best human relations book. *Address:* 920 Ridgewood Place, Highland Park, Ill. 60135.

BIOGRAPHICAL/CRITICAL SOURCES:

BOOKS

Authors of Books for Young People, 2nd edition supplement, Scarecrow, 1979.
International Authors and Writers Who's Who, 7th edition, Melrose, 1976.

*   *   *

NELSON, Janet   1930-

PERSONAL: Born November 29, 1930, in Detroit, Mich.; daughter of Robert R. (an engineer) and Isabell (Taylor) Wagner. *Education:* Michigan State College (now University), B.A., 1953.

ADDRESSES: Home and office—Finney Farm, P.O. Box 374, Croton-on-Hudson, N.Y. 10520. *Agent*—Phyllis Westberg, Harold Ober Associates, Inc., 40 East 49th St., New York, N.Y. 10017.

CAREER: Better Homes and Gardens, Des Moines, Iowa, writer, 1953-54; Michigan Bell Telephone Co., Detroit, Mich., editor, 1954-56; American Telephone and Telegraph, New York City, editor, 1956-60; *Good Housekeeping,* New York City, writer, 1960-63; *Parade,* New York City, articles editor, 1963-64; *Ski,* New York City, managing editor, 1964-68; free-lance writer, photographer, and radio broadcaster, 1968—. Part-time executive editor of *Ski Area Management.*

MEMBER: American Society of Magazine Photographers, Society of American Travel Writers, Canadian Ski Instructors' Alliance.

AWARDS, HONORS: School Bell Award from National Education Association, 1964, for articles in *Parade Magazine.*

WRITINGS:

How to Ski, Bruce-Royal, 1962.
Biking for Fun and Fitness, Award Books, 1970.
Skier's Guide to the East, Times-Mirror Press, 1974.
Skier's Guide to the West, Times-Mirror Press, 1974.
(With Peter Miller) *The Photographer's Almanac,* Little, Brown, 1983.

Contributor to magazines, including *Ski, Travel and Leisure, Diversion, Popular Photography,* and *American Health,* and to newspapers, including the *New York Times.*

WORK IN PROGRESS: 101 Successful Marketing Ideas.

SIDELIGHTS: Janet Nelson told *CA:* "I was a writer before becoming a skier and a skier before becoming a photographer. The three interests/careers have worked separately or in tandem, but they really come together in my position as an editor of *Ski Area Management,* a trade magazine. I have discovered over the years that the psychic reward of working at the things I love to do most—things other people do as hobbies—are gradually almost matched in monetary rewards. But it takes work, long and hard work. It is not a simple business."

*   *   *

NEUFELDER, Jerome M(ichael)   1929-

PERSONAL: Born March 14, 1929, in Haubstadt, Ind.; son of Lawrence O. (an accountant) and Pauline Marie (a housewife; maiden name, Hisker) Neufelder. *Education:* St. Meinrad College, B.A., 1969; St. Meinrad School of Theology, M.Div., 1970.

ADDRESSES: Home—4200 North Kentucky Ave., Evansville, Ind. 47711. *Office*—P.O. Box 4169, Evansville, Ind. 47711.

CAREER: Ordained Roman Catholic priest, 1955; associate pastor at churches in Washington, Ind., 1955-56, and Jasper, Ind., 1956-61; Sarto Retreat House, Evansville, Ind., director, 1961-68; St. Meinrad School of Theology, St. Meinrad, Ind., spiritual director, 1968-76; Roman Catholic Diocese of Evansville, Evansville, chancellor, 1976-84, director of continuing education, 1985. Member of board of directors of St. Meinrad School of Theology; member of clinical pastoral committee at Deaconess Hospital, Evansville.

WRITINGS:

(Editor with Marcy C. Coelho) *Writings on Spiritual Direction by Great Spiritual Masters,* Seabury, 1983.

WORK IN PROGRESS: The Sources of Spiritual Theology, a reference work on the richness of the Christian tradition and its contemporary relevance; a book on daily personal prayer, publication by Our Sunday Visitor expected in 1985.

SIDELIGHTS: Jerome M. Neufelder told *CA:* "*Writings on Spiritual Direction by Great Spiritual Masters* developed out of my workshops on this ministry over a period of seven years. The original manuscript was three times the size of the published volume. Mary C. Coelho joined me in the task of reducing it to one-third the original size. It is our hope that this volume will assist others in this ministry, especially women, and people outside the Roman Catholic church. That is why we tried to include Anglican, Protestant, and Orthodox authors.

"The book on prayer follows the liturgical year beginning with Advent. An essay on the spirit of the liturgical season introduces each section. There are six sections. Appropriate Scripture is chosen for each day in the season. Each day has a summary prayer given. Each day's prayer is also introduced by quotes from 365 writers on the meaning of prayer, beginning with Hippolytus, Origen, and Tertullian, and ending with a contemporary author."

*   *   *

NEVILLE, Joyce

PERSONAL: Married Edwin L. Neville (a professor of history). *Education:* B.A. *Politics:* Republican. *Religion:* Episcopal.

ADDRESSES: Home—175 Bryant St., Buffalo, N.Y. 14222.

CAREER: Writer. Member of faculty of Lay Ministry Training Program of Episcopal Diocese of Western New York and Cursillo/Koinonia Leadership Training Program; leader of workshops and seminars on lay ministry, small groups, prayer, and faith sharing all over the United States; coordinator of and speaker at renewal programs for Episcopal, Methodist, Lutheran, Roman Catholic, Swedish Reform, and Anglican churches in the United States and Canada.

MEMBER: Frontier Club of Republican Women (president).

WRITINGS:

How to Share Your Faith Without Being Offensive, Seabury, 1979, revised edition, 1983.

Contributor of articles and photographs to religious magazines.

WORK IN PROGRESS: A political book; a book on prayer.

SIDELIGHTS: Joyce Neville wrote that her teaching, workshops, and renewal programs cover the subjects of "personal relationship with Christ; faith; encountering Christ; Christian commitment; discerning God's presence; Christian community; how to let the Holy Spirit work through us; ways to witness in our lives; discovering our personal ministries; seeking, finding, and following God's guidance; performing lay ministries in church and community; how to live our faith better in home, business, and community; and Christian disciplines."

*   *   *

NEWMAN, Robert Chapman   1941-

PERSONAL: Born April 2, 1941, in Washington, D.C.; son of Allan L. C. (a lawyer) and Lois M. (a housewife; maiden name, Gardner) Newman. *Education:* Duke University, B.S. (summa cum laude), 1963; Cornell University, Ph.D., 1967; Faith Theological Seminary, M.Div., 1970; Biblical Theological Seminary, S.T.M., 1975; doctoral candidate at Westminster Theological Seminary. *Religion:* Evangelical Protestant.

ADDRESSES: Home—115 South Main St., Hatfield, Pa. 19440. *Office*—Biblical Theological Seminary, Hatfield, Pa. 19440.

CAREER: U.S. Weather Bureau, Washington, D.C., student trainee, summers, 1959-62, physicist, summer, 1963; Bartol Research Foundation, Swarthmore, Pa., postdoctoral research fellow, 1967-68; Shelton College, Cape May, N.J., associate professor of mathematics and physical science, 1968-71; Biblical Theological Seminary, Hatfield, Pa., associate professor, 1971-77, professor of New Testament, 1977—. Director of Interdisciplinary Biblical Research Institute, 1981—.

MEMBER: Evangelical Theological Society, American Scientific Affiliation, Phi Beta Kappa.

AWARDS, HONORS: Woodrow Wilson fellow, 1963.

WRITINGS:

(With Peter W. Stoner) *Science Speaks,* Moody, 3rd edition, 1969, 4th edition, 1976.
(With Herman J. Eckelmann, Jr.) *Genesis One and the Origin of the Earth,* Inter-Varsity Press, 1977, 2nd edition, Baker Book, 1981.

Contributor to religious and scientific journals.

WORK IN PROGRESS: The Bible and the Fourth Dimension; Then You Shall Know: Fulfilled Predictions of Scripture; research on apologetics and Christian evidences and on Christianity and science.

SIDELIGHTS: Robert Newman commented: "My conviction that the Bible is a communication from the most intelligent life in the universe (God!) and that the evidence for this is strong has led to my change in careers, and it motivates my research efforts. Biblical faith is no leap in the dark.

"One of the major reasons which led me to switch from a career in science to one in theology was the conviction that biblical Christianity is true. God exists just as certainly as our minds exist, and there is excellent evidence for this.

"The two books I have written so far deal with some of this evidence. *Science Speaks* suggests that the first chapter of Genesis and science are really in much better agreement than most people realize. This book also sketches some of the evidence for the existence of God from the fulfillment of predictions made in the Bible. *Genesis One and the Origin of the Earth* develops the former of these ideas further, with a more detailed treatment of the biblical text and modern discoveries in astrophysics and geophysics.

"My two works in progress will also continue along these general lines. *The Bible and the Fourth Dimension* will sketch some of the simple features of four-dimensional geometry, present evidence from modern physics for a fourth spatial dimension, and look at some biblical statements which are better understood in terms of a fourth dimension, especially those related to the location of heaven. *Then You Shall Know* will give more detail and historical documentation for a number of fulfilled prophecies.

"To those who wish to examine for themselves the evidence for Christianity, I would recommend the following authors or works. C. S. Lewis has been especially helpful to me, both fiction and essays; his *Mere Christianity* has an excellent argument for God from our own internal moral machinery. The best work on fulfilled prophecy still in print is John Urquhart's *Wonders of Prophecy.* The growing scientific evidence for God is especially well-treated in Alan Hayward's *God Is.* On the resurrection of Christ, I would suggest Frank Morison's *Who Moved the Stone?,* John Wenham's *Easter Enigma,* and any of several books that discuss the Shroud of Turin. I can personally testify that my own life and those of many I know have been transformed for the good by coming to know God in a personal way through his son Jesus of Nazareth."

BIOGRAPHICAL/CRITICAL SOURCES:

BOOKS

Barrett, Eric C., and David Fisher, *Scientists Who Believe,* Moody, 1984.

*   *   *

NEWSHAM, Ian (Alan)   1953-

PERSONAL: Born September 3, 1953, in Barrow-in-Furness, England; son of Geoffry Hornby (a clerk) and Margaret (a district nurse; maiden name, Bell) Newsham; married Wendy Dowson (a writer and housewife), August 16, 1980; children: Robert. *Education:* Manchester Polytechnic, B.A. (with honors), 1976; Royal College of Art, M.A., 1979. *Politics:* "None specific." *Religion:* "None specific."

ADDRESSES: Home—3 Princes Court, Leighton Buzzard, Bedfordshire LU7 7AY, England.

CAREER: Harrow College of Higher Education, Harrow, London, England, lecturer in illustration, 1979—; City of Leicester Polytechnic, Leicester, England, lecturer in illustration, 1982—, head of illustration, 1984—. Free-lance work for advertisers and television.

WRITINGS:

(With wife, Wendy Newsham) *The Monster Hunt* (juvenile), self-illustrated, Hamish Hamilton, 1983.
(With W. Newsham) *Lost in the Jungle* (juvenile), self-illustrated, Kaye & Ward, 1984.

ILLUSTRATOR

Clive King, *Ninny's Boat,* Kestrel, 1980.
Geoffery Ashe, *Arthurian Britain,* Longman, 1980.
S. H. Butron, *Eight Ghost Stories,* Longman, 1980.
Arthur Conan Doyle, *The Lost World,* Puffin, 1981.
W. H. Hudson, *A Shepherd's Life,* Macdonald & Co., 1981.
Angela Lock, *Mr. Mullett Owns A Cloud,* Chatto & Windus, 1982.
Polly Devlin, *The Far Side of the Lough,* Gollancz, 1983.
Brian Ball, *The Star-Buggy,* Heinemann, 1983.
Ann Pilling, *The Year of the Worm,* Kestrel, 1984.
Maggie Prince, *The Glory Hole,* Hodder & Stoughton, 1984.
Berlie Doherty, *Children of Winter,* Methuen, 1985.
Peter Dickinson, *The Box of Nothing,* Gollancz, 1985.

Also illustrator of *Le Club Noir,* Bayard, 1985. Contributor of illustrations to magazines, including *New Society, Miss London, Over 21,* and computer and publishing trade publications. Illustrator of textbooks, posters, and book covers.

SIDELIGHTS: Ian Newsham told *CA:* "My main interest is in illustration and, at the moment, I am particularly involved in the children's novel. From the point of view of the illustrator, the children's novel is a much underrated vehicle for the use of pictures. In fact, there has been no noticeable development since Tenniel's *Alice in Wonderland.* For a highly visually oriented world, we produce some very uninspiring children's books.

"I am trying to persuade publishers to show a greater interest in having more pictures in their juvenile novels and to produce a more cohesive and visually exciting package. The idea that every children's book should consist of five-by-eight-inch pages, full of grey type and the occasional picture, is something I quite frankly find dull and boring. I also believe a majority of children find this to be dull, and therefore they simply don't pick up the books and start to read all the wonderful stories authors produce. Two recent books, *A Box of Nothing,* by Peter Dickinson, and *The Far Side of the Lough,* by Polly Devlin, are perhaps steps in the direction of a more visually oriented and integrated book."

*   *   *

NEY, John 1923-

PERSONAL: Surname rhymes with "hay"; born May 3, 1923, in St. Paul, Minn.; son of John J. (in business) and Marie N. Ney; married Marian Wallace (a teacher), August 17, 1954; children: Sarah, Janet, Peter. *Education:* Attended University of California and London School of Economics and Political Science.

ADDRESSES: Office—Warfield Co., P.O. Box 537, Indiantown, Fla. 33456.

CAREER: Businessman and writer, 1950—; Warfield Co. (investment organization), Indiantown, Fla., president, 1978—.

AWARDS, HONORS: National Book Award finalist, 1977, for *Ox Under Pressure.*

WRITINGS:

Whitey McAlpine: A Tale of Ambition (adult novel), C. N. Potter, 1962.
Palm Beach: The Place, the People, Its Pleasures and Palaces (adult nonfiction), Little, Brown, 1966.
The European Surrender: A Descriptive Study of the American Social and Economic Conquest (adult nonfiction), Little, Brown, 1970.
Ox: The Story of a Kid at the Top (young adult novel), Little, Brown, 1970.
Ox Goes North: More Trouble for the Kid at the Top (young adult novel), Harper, 1973.
Ox Under Pressure (young adult novel), Lippincott, 1976.

WORK IN PROGRESS: For adults, *An Intelligent Woman's Guide to American Failure.*

SIDELIGHTS: John Ney told *CA:* "My connection with children's books, rather tenuous at best, has now come to a halt, and I haven't published one in seven years. The three that were published were about Ox Olmstead, a very large boy from a very rich family in Palm Beach. They formed a series of sorts, taking Ox from the age of twelve in the first book to seventeen in the last. I wrote the first book, *Ox: The Story of a Kid at the Top,* to amuse my children; it was the traditional start. It was published in 1970 and the next two, *Ox Goes North* and *Ox Under Pressure,* followed in 1973 and 1976. All three circulated to a certain critical acclaim and were published in paperback as well as hardback.

"These details are only interesting because I had been under the impression, from having written and published some adult books, that relatively successful books in any field lead publishers to want more from the same source, to say nothing of the same characters. I was evidently wrong. The problem seemed to be, as my last editor told me, that Ox 'grew out of his attractive weaknesses. He got stronger and more independent with each book until, in the last one, he doesn't need anybody. You have to understand that modern children's literature is all for the underdog—ethnically, emotionally, physically, whatever. You just can't make it with a kid who has nothing wrong with him.'

"Well, at least it was clear, and we understood each other. My choice was simple: write about underdogs or give up being published. I chose the latter. Actually, it was not a choice—I probably couldn't have written about underdogs well enough, anyhow.

"It isn't, I should make clear, that I have anything against underdogs. In fact, Ox himself is an underdog in that he is out of place because he is so truly independent. (Truly independent children always have more problems than the rest.) It's just that I am irresistibly (and fatally) drawn to a nonfashionable sort of underdog.

"I still write about those underdogs—or, more accurately, those outsiders—for my own amusement. I am also busy with business ventures, a number of grown children and grandchildren, and various sports. We live in the cattle country in Florida, far from the tourists, and usually go abroad in the summers.''

BIOGRAPHICAL/CRITICAL SOURCES:

PERIODICALS

New York Times Book Review, March 22, 1970.

* * *

NG, David 1934-

PERSONAL: Surname is pronounced Ing; born September 1, 1934, in San Francisco, Calif.; son of Hing (a cook) and Chin Shee (a housewife) Ng; married Irene Young (a women's program executive), June 15, 1958; children: Stephen Paul, Andrew Peter. Education: Westminster College, Salt Lake City, Utah, B.A. (summa cum laude), 1956; San Francisco Theological Seminary, M.Div., 1959. Politics: Democrat.

ADDRESSES: Home—160 Columbia Heights, No. 5E, Brooklyn, N.Y. 11201. Office—National Council of Churches of Christ in the U.S.A., 475 Riverside Ave., Room 704, New York, N.Y. 10115-0050.

CAREER: Ordained Presbyterian minister, 1959; pastor of Presbyterian churches in the Chinatown section of San Francisco, Calif., 1959-62, and Mendocino, Calif., 1962-66; United Presbyterian Church in the U.S.A., Board of Christian Education, Philadelphia, Pa., editor of youth resources, 1966-75; Austin Presbyterian Theological Seminary, Austin, Tex., associate professor of Christian education, 1975-81; National Council of Churches of Christ in the U.S.A., New York, N.Y., associate general secretary for education and ministry, 1981—. Past member of Mendocino County Grand Jury.

MEMBER: Association of Professors and Researchers in Religious Education, Religious Education Association.

WRITINGS:

See It! Do It!: Your Faith in Action (young adult), Friend Press, 1972.
(Editor) Context for Choice, Geneva Divinity School Press, 1973.
Youth Manual, Geneva Divinity School Press, 1977.
(With Virginia Thomas) Children in the Worshipping Community, John Knox, 1981.
Developing Leaders for Youth Ministry, Judson, 1984.
Youth in the Community of Disciples, Judson, 1984.
The Family in the Community of Faith, John Knox, in press.

Also author of religious curriculum material. Editor of Strategy.

WORK IN PROGRESS: Research on ethnic minority religious education; extending the concepts discussed in Youth in the Community of Disciples.

SIDELIGHTS: David Ng told CA: "In writing about the inclusion of children in worship and the place of youth in the community of faith, I am emphasizing the importance of the corporate aspect of the church. This will be continued and expanded in a future book on families in the community of faith (or family of God).

"Traditionally the church has dealt with youth ambiguously. It values them for their promise of the future but it relegates youth to second class membership and does not expect from them much in the way of discipleship, service, and sacrifice. I am convinced that more respect must be shown to youth.

They are capable of contributing vitality, curiosity, idealism, and openness to the community of faith. Through youth who are disciples in the New Testament sense, the church is constantly renewed. Church youth programs should not pander to youth in a futile attempt to maintain their interest; youth ministry should be exactly that—opportunities for young persons to be ministers to each other, to the church, and to society.''

* * *

NICKLE, Keith Fullerton 1933-

PERSONAL: Born June 10, 1933, in Keokuk, Iowa; son of George Herman (a teacher) and Vena Mignon (Keith) Nickle; married Marie Love (a picture framer), February 25, 1960; children: Neely, Stephen, John, Thomas. Education: Attended Texas A & M University, 1951-53; University of Texas at Austin, A.B., 1955; Austin Presbyterian Theological Seminary, B.D., 1958; University of Basel, D.Theol., 1966.

ADDRESSES: Office—First Presbyterian Church, 306 Church St., Jefferson City, Tenn. 37760.

CAREER: Ordained Presbyterian minister, 1958; minister of Presyterian churches in Navasota, Tex., 1958-60, and Port Arthur, Tex., 1963-67; St. Louis University, St. Louis, Mo., assistant professor, 1967-69, associate professor of biblical languages and literature, 1969-75, chairman of department, 1970-74, director of graduate studies at School of Divinity, 1974-75; Columbia Theological Seminary, Decatur, Ga., professor of New Testament language, literature, and exegesis, 1975-83; First Presbyterian Church, Jefferson City, Tenn., minister, 1983—.

MEMBER: American Association of University Professors, Society of Biblical Literature, Catholic Biblical Association of America, American Academy of Religion.

WRITINGS:

The Collection: A Study in the Strategy of Paul, S.C.M. Press, 1966.
The Synoptic Gospels: Conflict and Consensus, John Knox, 1980.
Paul for the Parish, Abingdon, in press.

Associate editor of Theology Digest, 1973-75.

* * *

NICOL, Charles (David) 1940-

PERSONAL: Born December 21, 1940, in St. Louis, Mo.; son of Erwin Martin (a sales representative) and Dorothea (a housewife; maiden name, Comfort) Nicol; married Susan Lawrence, June, 1962 (divorced, 1972); married Nancy Winegardner (a family counselor), November, 1972; children: David, John. Education: University of Kansas, B.A., 1962, M.A., 1966; Bowling Green State University, Ph.D., 1970. Politics: Libertarian. Religion; "Former Presbyterian."

ADDRESSES: Home—R.R.16, Box 429, Brazil, Ind. 47834. Office—Department of English, Indiana State University, Terre Haute, Ind. 47809.

CAREER: Indiana State University, Terre Haute, instructor, 1966-70, assistant professor, 1970-73, associate professor, 1973-80, professor of American literature and creative writing, 1980—. Fulbright senior lecturer at Tbilisi State University, 1984.

MEMBER: Modern Language Association of America, Popular Culture Association, Science Fiction Research Association, Melville Society, Vladimir Nabokov Society (former president; member of board).

WRITINGS:

(Contributor) L. S. Dembo, editor, *Nabokov: The Man and His Work,* University of Wisconsin Press, 1967.
(Editor with J. E. Rivers, and contributor) *Nabokov's Fifth Arc: Nabokov and Others on His Life's Work,* University of Texas Press, 1982.
(Contributor) Phyllis A. Roth, editor, *Critical Essays on Vladimir Nabokov,* G. K. Hall, 1984.

Work represented in anthologies, including *Fiction's Journey: Fifty Stories,* edited by Barbara McKenzie, Harcourt, 1978. Contributor to magazines, including *Atlantic, Harper's, Saturday Review,* and *National Review.* Associate editor of *Science-Fiction Studies,* 1974-78, and *Vladimir Nabokov Research Newsletter,* 1979—.

WORK IN PROGRESS: An Erotics of Nabokov's Novels; short stories.

SIDELIGHTS: Charles Nicol told *CA:* "My criticism, my research, my own fiction, the way I view life—all of these stem from three books: *Moby Dick, Alice in Wonderland,* and *Lolita.* Fiction must intersect with life in a way that throws 'normal' reality into question. All great literature is wildly original and totally subversive, a combination of devious autobiography and pure style.

"I hate team sports, enjoy tennis, chess, fishing, repairing my house, and acting. I recently spent four difficult months in the Soviet Union, but continue to study Russian. My politics are libertarian and antiwar. I play the piano frequently and poorly; the greatest composer is Beethoven."

*   *   *

NICOSIA, Gerald (Martin)   1949-

PERSONAL: Born November 18, 1949, in Berwyn, Ill.; son of Peter (a mailman) and Sylvia Anna (a secretary; maiden name, Fremer) Nicosia. *Education:* University of Illinois at Chicago Circle, B.A., 1971, M.A., 1973. *Religion:* Roman Catholic.

ADDRESSES: Home—San Francisco, Calif.

CAREER: Worked as substitute teacher at high schools in Chicago, Ill., 1973-77; writer.

AWARDS, HONORS: Distinguished Young Writer Award from National Society of Arts and Letters, 1978, for *Memory Babe,* a work in progress.

WRITINGS:

(With Richard Raff) *Bughouse Blues,* Vantage, 1977.
Memory Babe: A Critical Biography of Jack Kerouac, Grove, 1983.

Author of "North Beach Beat," a column in *Appeal to Reason.* Also author of unpublished novel *Failure* and script of documentary video "West Coast: Beat and Beyond," 1983. Contributor to *Dictionary of Literary Biography.* Contributor to periodicals, including *Review of Contemporary Fiction* and *American Book Review.*

WORK IN PROGRESS: Bowl Away the Stone, a film script about "a working-class boy from Chicago who is inspired by

visions of the Virgin Mary to become the world's bowling champion," completion expected in 1985; *Spiritual Athletes,* a novel examining "the qualifications necessary to become a holy man in current American society," completion expected in 1986.

SIDELIGHTS: Gerald Nicosia's *Memory Babe: A Critical Biography of Jack Kerouac* was described by John Rechy, who reviewed the work in the *Los Angeles Times Book Review,* as "a grand book about a haunting, haunted writer who may yet overcome the burden of his largely imposed legend." Peter Ross, who reviewed the biography in the *Detroit News,* declared that "one cannot read it and be unaffected by Kerouac the man."

Most reviewers of *Memory Babe* agreed that Nicosia's biography of Kerouac was the most exhaustive work on the Beat writer. Bruce Cook wrote in the *Washington Post Book World* that the biography was "easily the most comprehensive and detailed" book on Kerouac, and Peter Collier contended in the *Chicago Tribune Book World* that *Memory Babe* was "a study of the life and work so mammoth that it may well contain more than most people want to know about Kerouac." Collier claimed that previous works on Kerouac "pale beside Gerald Nicosia's" volume.

Nicosia told *CA:* "My interest in art generally is in its healing aspects, both for the individual and society. In *Memory Babe* I focused on the selfless gift of Kerouac's art and his attempt to bridge the many value splits of his generation and the fact that the public's (and especially critical) response was a vicious attack on his person as well as his art. In other words, I explore the paradox of the vital importance of the artist in modern American society vis-a-vis the general lack of appreciation and often overt hostility toward his or her work."

BIOGRAPHICAL/CRITICAL SOURCES:

PERIODICALS

Chicago Reader, April 6, 1979, September 9, 1983.
Chicago Tribune Book World, July 3, 1983.
Detroit News, October 9, 1983.
Los Angeles Times Book Review, August 7, 1983.
New York Times Book Review, July 3, 1983.
Washington Post Book World, July 24, 1983.

*   *   *

NIJINSKY, Vaslav (Fomitch)   1890-1950

BRIEF ENTRY: Given name transliterated as Waslaw in some sources; born February 28, 1890, in Kiev, Russia (now U.S.S.R.); died of nephritis, April 8, 1950, in London, England. Russian ballet dancer, choreographer, and author. Nijinsky received his first training as a dancer at the age of nine when he entered the Imperial School in St. Petersburg, Russia (now Leningrad, U.S.S.R.). He made his debut in Mozart's "Don Juan" at St. Petersburg's Maryinski Theatre in 1907. Nijinsky subsequently joined the Russian Imperial Ballet, where he met ballet director and producer Serge Diaghilev, who became the dancer's close friend and supporter. After two years with the Imperial company, Nijinsky was dismissed for appearing in improper costume before the dowager empress. He then joined the newly-established Diaghilev Ballet, a move that brought the dancer to the attention of Western audiences.

Memorable performances with Diaghilev's company include "Le Spectre de la rose" and "Petrouchka," as well as Debussy's "L'Apres-Midi d'un faune" and Stravinsky's "Le Sacre du printemps," for which he not only danced the principle roles but also served as choreographer. Nijinsky's career was interrupted at the beginning of World War I, when the dancer was detained in an Austrian prison camp. After his release in 1916 he rejoined the Diaghilev company and made his first U.S. appearance at the Metropolitan Opera House. Plagued by mental illness, Nijinsky retired from ballet in 1917 (one source says 1919) and spent many years in a Swiss sanitorium, where he produced a number of paintings and drawings. He wrote *The Diary of Vaslav Nijinsky,* which was edited by his wife, Romola Nijinsky, and published in 1968.

BIOGRAPHICAL/CRITICAL SOURCES:

BOOKS

Current Biography, Wilson, 1940, May, 1950.
Obituaries on File, Facts on File, 1979.
1000 Makers of the Twentieth Century, David & Charles, 1971.

PERIODICALS

New York Times, April 9, 1950.

*   *   *

NODDINGS, Nel 1929-

PERSONAL: Born January 19, 1929, in Irvington, N.J.; daughter of Edward and Nellie (Connors) Rieth; married James A. Noddings (an engineer and director of marketing at high technology facilities), August 20, 1949; children: Laura Langer, James, Nancy Noddings Bunch, William, Victoria, Chris, Wallace, Howard, Edward, Timothy, Sharon Miller. *Education:* Montclair State Teachers College (now Montclair State College), B.A., 1949; Rutgers University, M.A., 1964; Stanford University, Ph.D., 1973.

ADDRESSES: Home—Los Altos, Calif. *Office*—Department of Education, Educ 218, Stanford University, Stanford, Calif. 94305.

CAREER: Junior high school teacher in Woodbury, N.J., 1949-52; Matawan Regional High School, Matawan, N.J., mathematics teacher, department chair, and assistant principal, 1957-69; worked as curriculum supervisor in Montgomery Township, N.J., 1970-72; Pennsylvania State University, University Park, Pa., assistant professor of education, 1973; University of Chicago, Chicago, Ill., director of precollegiate education, 1975-76; Stanford University, Stanford, Calif., acting assistant professor, 1977-79, assistant professor, 1979-83, associate professor of education and director of teacher education, 1983—. Educational consultant. Member of board of directors of Sierra School, Berkeley, Calif.

MEMBER: Philosophy of Education Society (member of executive board, 1981-82), National Council of Teachers of Mathematics, American Educational Research Association.

WRITINGS:

Caring: A Feminine Approach to Ethics and Moral Education, University of California Press, 1984.
(With Paul J. Shore) *Awakening the Inner Eye,* Teachers College Press, Columbia University, 1984.
(Contributor) Edmund C. Short, editor, *Competence: Inquiries Into Its Meaning and Acquisition in Educational Settings,* University Press of America, 1984.

(Contributor) Edward A. Silver, editor, *Teaching and Learning Mathematical Problem Solving,* Franklin Institute Press, 1984.

Also contributor to *Learning the Ways of Knowing,* Part II, 84th Yearbook of the National Society for the Study of Education, edited by Elliot W. Eisner. Contributor to education and philosophy journals.

WORK IN PROGRESS: A New Look at Women and Evil.

SIDELIGHTS: Nel Noddings told *CA:* "My current work involves bringing my philosophical training to bear on the central interests of human (mainly feminine) experience: love, morality, caring, nurturance, family life, virtue, and peace."

BIOGRAPHICAL/CRITICAL SOURCES:

PERIODICALS

Ethics in Education, January, 1985.

*   *   *

NOESTLINGER, Christine 1936-

BRIEF ENTRY: Born in 1936 in Vienna, Austria. Austrian journalist and author. Although a working journalist for a Viennese daily newspaper, Noestlinger is best known as an award-winning author of books for young people. Earning praise for their realistic, direct handling of problems confronting youth, Noestlinger's young adult novels, translated from the German, include the autobiographical *Fly Away Home* (F. Watts, 1975) and the 1981 American Library Association Notable Book *Luke and Angela* (Harcourt, 1981). The author's books for children include *The Cucumber King: A Story With a Beginning, a Middle, and an End, in Which Wolfgang Hogelmann Tells the Whole Truth* (Abelard-Schuman, 1975), winner of the German Youth Literature Prize for the original German edition; *Konrad* (F. Watts, 1977), recipient of the 1977 Mildred L. Batchelder Award; *Achtung: Vranek sieht ganz harmlos aus* (title means "Careful: Vranek Seems to Be Totally Harmless"), which earned Noestlinger the Oesterreichischer Staatspreis fuer Kinder- und Jugendliteratur in 1975; and *Rosa Riedl, Schutzgespenst* (title means "Rosa Reidl, Guardian Ghost"), which earned the author the Oesterreichischer Staatspreis again in 1979. Among Noestlinger's other awards is the 1972 Friedrich-Boedecker Prize for contributions to children's literature. *Address:* Vienna, Austria.

BIOGRAPHICAL/CRITICAL SOURCES:

BOOKS

Fifth Book of Junior Authors and Illustrators, H. W. Wilson, 1983.
Twentieth-Century Children's Writers, St. Martin's, 1978.

*   *   *

NOLL, Mark A(llan) 1946-

PERSONAL: Born July 18, 1946, in Iowa City, Iowa; son of Francis Arthur (an engineer) and Evelyn Jean (Hummel) Noll; married Ruth Margaret Packer, 1969; children: Mary Constance, David Luther, Robert Francis. *Education:* Wheaton College, Wheaton, Ill., B.A., 1968; University of Iowa, M.A., 1970; Trinity Evangelical Divinity School, M.A., 1972; Vanderbilt University, M.A., 1974, Ph.D., 1975. *Religion:* Reformed Protestant.

ADDRESSES: *Office*—Department of History, Wheaton College, Wheaton, Ill. 60187.

CAREER: Trinity College, Deerfield, Ill., assistant professor of history, 1975-78; Wheaton College, Wheaton, Ill., associate professor, 1978-84, professor of history, 1984—. J. Omar Good Visiting Distinguished Professor at Juniata College, 1982-83.

MEMBER: American Historical Association, Organization of American Historians, American Society of Church History, American Catholic Historical Association, Conference on Faith and History.

WRITINGS:

Christians in the American Revolution, Eerdmans, 1977.
(With Nathan Hatch and John Woodbridge) *The Gospel in America: Themes in the Story of American Evangelicals*, Zondervan, 1979.
(Editor with Hatch, and contributor) *The Bible in America*, Oxford University Press, 1982.
(With Hatch and George Marsden) *The Search for Christian America*, Crossway, 1983.
(Editor) *The Princeton Theology: Scripture, Science, and Theological Method From Archibald Alexander to Benjamin Warfield*, Baker Book, 1983.
(Editor with Hatch, David Wells, and Marsden, and contributor) *Eerdmans Handbook to Christianity in America*, Eerdmans, 1983.

CONTRIBUTOR

James T. Johnson, editor, *The Bible in America: Law, Politics, and Rhetoric*, Fortress, 1984.
Marsden, editor, *Evangelicalism and Modern America, 1931-1980*, Eerdmans, 1984.
(Author of introduction) William Ringenberg, *The Christian College: A History of Protestant Higher Education in America*, Eerdmans, 1984.
Charles Kannengiesser, editor, *Bible de tous les temps* (title means "The Bible for the Ages"), Editions Beauchesne, 1985.

OTHER

Contributor to history and theology journals. Associate editor of *Christian Scholar's Review*, 1978-83; member of editorial committee of *Reformed Journal*, 1983—.

WORK IN PROGRESS: *Religion, Politics, and the Enlightenment in American Higher Education, 1776-1812;* research on evangelical scholarship on the Bible, 1880-1980.

SIDELIGHTS: Mark A. Noll told *CA:* "My writing arises out of my 'callings' as a historian and a Christian. Sometimes the vocations seem to get in the way of each other, but mostly it is a fruitful combination. The danger of moralizing in historical work, and relativizing religion, is always present. These are acceptable risks, given the intrinsic enjoyment in the task.

"Much of my writing has dealt with the history of conservative Protestants in America and with the effect of that life on the Protestantism which they inherited. *Christians in the American Revolution* was prompted largely by my curiosity about the ways in which Protestants supported the American Revolution. My personal views on violent revolution and my understanding of conditions in the second half of the eighteenth century made me dubious about the validity of Christian participation in the move for independence. Working on the book did not change my views about violent revolution, but it did suggest that

Americans then may not have seen the reality of their situation, at least in important particulars, as clearly as modern historians do. It was, in short, a far less desperate situation than our ancestors thought.

"*The Search for Christian America* was an attempt to show well-meaning evangelicals that the idea of a 'Christian America,' which has now vanished, is a bit of historical and theological wishful thinking. The Christian heritage has contributed a great deal to the American experience. But an objective weighing of the good (e.g., the pursuit of freedom for worship) versus the evil (e.g., the perpetuation of slavery) in the nation's past gives scant support to the idea of a uniquely Christian country. Neither does a reading of the Bible that perceives the universal implications of the gospel message support such a claim."

BIOGRAPHICAL/CRITICAL SOURCES:

PERIODICALS

Church History, December, 1984.
American Historical Review, December, 1978, June, 1983.

*   *   *

NORTHEDGE, Frederick Samuel   1918-1985

OBITUARY NOTICE—See index for *CA* sketch: Born October 16, 1918, in Derby, England; died March 3, 1985, in London, England. Political scientist, educator, editor, and author. A teacher at the London School of Economics and Political Science for more than thirty-five years, Northedge began as an assistant lecturer in 1949, advancing to full professor in 1968. He is best remembered for his contributions to the field of international relations. His books on that subject include *The Troubled Giant: Britain Among the Great Powers, 1916-1939*, *Order and the System of International Politics*, *A Hundred Years of International Relations*, with M. J. Grieve, and *International Disputes: The Political Aspects*, with Michael D. Donelan. Among the works Northedge edited are *The Foreign Policies of the Powers* and *The Use of Force in International Relations*. Northedge received the Carnegie Prize for research in international organization from the Carnegie Endowment for International Peace in 1955.

OBITUARIES AND OTHER SOURCES:

PERIODICALS

Times (London), March 8, 1985.

*   *   *

NOSTLINGER, Christine
See NOESTLINGER, Christine

*   *   *

NOTARIUS
See MARTIN, Andrew

*   *   *

NOYES, Joan   1935-

PERSONAL: Born February 19, 1935, in Toronto, Ontario, Canada; daughter of John A. (a certified public accountant) and Esther (Murray) Gair; married John W. Noyes (divorced); children: John W. Gair, Katherine Esther. *Education:* University of New Mexico, B.A., 1983.

ADDRESSES: Home—4 Kingsford Court, Islington, Ontario, Canada M9A 1X4. *Office*—Peel Board of Education, Mississauga, Ontario, Canada. *Agent*—Matie Molinaro, Canadian Speakers and Writers Service, 44 Douglas Cr., Toronto 5, Ontario, Canada.

CAREER: Association for Children With Learning Disabilities, Etobicoke, Mississauga, and Toronto, Ontario, developed and administrated remedial and recreational programs, 1965-75; Peel Board of Education, Mississauga, Ontario, early identification teacher, 1975-80, special education resource teacher, 1980—.

MEMBER: Council for Exceptional Children, Federation of Women Teachers.

WRITINGS:

(With Norma Macneill) *Your Child Can Win: Strategies, Activities, and Games for Parents of Children With Learning Disabilities,* Macmillan (Canada), 1982, Morrow, 1983.

WORK IN PROGRESS: Research on adolescents with learning disabilities.

SIDELIGHTS: Joan Noyes told *CA:* "I have learning disabilities. A learning disability is a hidden handicap. There is a need to educate the public so that fewer children grow up feeling inadequate and stupid.

"I developed programs to help learning disabled children on a volunteer basis. The remedial programs were set up specifically to work with children with perceptual problems. What we discovered was that as a result of interaction with the teenage volunteers, the learning disabled children's self-concept improved, and this became the prime focus of our programs.

"Children who have experienced repeated failures stop trying. If you can reverse this process and children feel they are 'winners,' they start to be 'winners.' The 'loser' complex in adolescents is compounded by the feelings of inadequacy common to that age group. It is therefore essential that we address these problems in school and in the home.

"Communication is essential, but especially communication among people of all ages who have learning disabilities—to make them aware they are not alone with their frustrations. Educators must look at changes in their total curriculum; the program should fit the child, not the child fit the program."

NUNN, John 1955-

PERSONAL: Born April 25, 1955, in London, England; son of James William (a civil servant) and Beryl (a housewife; maiden name, Payne) Nunn. *Education:* Oxford University, B.A., 1973, M.Sc., 1974, D.Phil., 1978. *Politics:* "Not interested in politics . . ." *Religion:* ". . . nor in religion."

ADDRESSES: Home—228 Dover House Rd., London SW15 5AH, England.

CAREER: Professional chess player, 1981—.

AWARDS, HONORS: Federation International des Echechs, named International Chess Master, 1975, and International Grandmaster, 1978.

WRITINGS:

The Pirc for the Tournament Player, Batsford, 1980.
Tactical Chess Endings, Allen & Unwin, 1981.
(With Michael Stean) *Sicilian Defence Najdorf Variation,* Batsford, 1982.
The Benoni for the Tournament Player, Batsford, 1982.
Beating the Sicilian, Batsford, 1984.
Solving in Style, Allen & Unwin, 1985.
(With Peter Griffiths) *Secrets of Grandmaster Play,* Allen & Unwin, in press.

SIDELIGHTS: John Nunn told *CA:* "My chess writing is just a sideline to my over-the-board tournament career. The main motivation for writing the books was to encourage me to do the necessary research on opening theory required to stay at the top in chess. On the 1985 world ranking I should be in the top ten, so perhaps the books have done me some good!"

* * *

NYKORUK, Barbara (Christine) 1949-

BRIEF ENTRY: Born February 1, 1949, in Detroit, Mich. American educator and editor. Barbara Nykoruk taught at Wayne State University from 1971 to 1972. She was an editor at Gale Research Company from 1973 to 1976 and a book editor for Prakken Publishers, beginning in 1977. Nykoruk edited *Biography News* (Gale, 1974-75), *Authors in the News* (Gale, 1975-76), and *Business People in the News: A Compilation of News Stories and Feature Articles From American Newspapers and Magazines Covering People in Industry, Finance, and Labor* (Gale, 1976). *Address:* 1408 Granger, Ann Arbor, Mich. 48104; and 416 Longshore Dr., Ann Arbor, Mich. 48107.

O

OCKENGA, Harold John 1905-1985

OBITUARY NOTICE—See index for *CA* sketch: Born July 6, 1905, in Chicago, Ill.; died of cancer, February 8, 1985, in Hamilton, Mass. Clergyman and author. An evangelist active in the conservative Protestant movement, Ockenga served Boston's historic Park Street Church as pastor from 1936 to 1969, becoming widely known for his preaching and his radio ministry. In addition, he led missionary journeys to such places as Asia and Africa, was co-founder of the Fuller Theological Seminary in Pasadena, California, and served as president of both the National Association of Evangelicals and the World Evangelical Fellowship. Ockenga was also chairman of the board of *Christianity Today* beginning in 1956, and he wrote a number of books on religious themes, including *These Religious Affections, Everyone That Believeth, Faithful in Jesus Christ, Women Who Made Bible History, A Christian Primer,* and *Faith in a Troubled World.*

OBITUARIES AND OTHER SOURCES:

PERIODICALS

Los Angeles Times, February 13, 1985.

*   *   *

OLD FAG
See BELL, Robert S(tanley) W(arren)

*   *   *

OLLIFF, Donathan C(arnes) 1933-

PERSONAL: Surname is pronounced *Aah*-liff; born January 11, 1933, in Ashford, Ala.; son of Otho Keland (a farmer) and Hettie (a housewife; maiden name, Carnes) Olliff; married Bobbie Deloise Johnson (a nurse), August 15, 1955; children: Keith, Karen. *Education:* Auburn University, B.A., 1957, M.A., 1966; University of Florida, Ph.D., 1974.

ADDRESSES: Office—Department of History, Auburn University, Auburn University, Ala. 36849.

CAREER: Columbus College, Columbus, Ga., instructor in social science, 1958-59; U.S. Department of State, Washington, D.C., foreign service officer in Tijuana, Mexico, 1960-62; U.S. Embassy, Karachi, Pakistan, consular section chief,

1963-64; University of Florida, Gainesville, instructor in social science, 1965-66; Auburn University, Auburn University, Ala., instructor in history, 1966-68; University of Florida, instructor in social science, 1968-69; Auburn University, instructor, 1970-74, assistant professor, 1974-81, associate professor of history, 1981—. *Military service:* U.S. Army, 1952-55; became sergeant.

MEMBER: Conference on Latin American History, Southeastern Council of Latin American Studies.

WRITINGS:

Reforma Mexico and the United States: A Search for Alternatives to Annexation, 1854-1861, University of Alabama Press, 1981.

WORK IN PROGRESS: Research on economic and entrepreneurial history in nineteenth- and twentieth-century Mexico.

SIDELIGHTS: Donathan C. Olliff told *CA:* "I am researching the activities of Gabor Naphegyi, a Hungarian who built the first gaslighting systems in Latin America, John Temple, a U.S. citizen who leased and operated the Mexican national mint, and William Spratling, an Alabamian whose artistic interests resulted in the revival of the silvercraft industry in Taxco. An interest shared by all three men is the transfer and adaptation of items from one culture to another.

"My primary interest is in the transfer of capital and technology from the more advanced Western Europe and the United States to Mexico and the adaptation of this technology to fit Mexico's needs. My research for *Reform Mexico and the United States: A Search for Alternatives to Annexation, 1854-1861* revealed several foreigners who sought their fortune by introducing new technology into Mexico during the mid-nineteenth century. Naphegyi and Temple are merely the most interesting and promising of these. Spratling, on the other hand, had close ties with the artists and intellectuals of the United States during the 1920's but decided to move to Taxco in 1929, where he served as an intermediary between artists and intellectuals of Mexico and the United States; he remained there until his death in 1967."

*   *   *

ORMOND, (Willard) Clyde 1906-1985

OBITUARY NOTICE—See index for *CA* sketch: Born March

342

19, 1906, in Rigby, Idaho; died of a heart attack, February 2, 1985, in Idaho Falls, Idaho; buried in Rigby Pioneer Cemetery, Rigby, Idaho. Journalist, educator, editor, and author. Ormond began his career teaching in the Idaho public schools in 1926 but became a free-lance writer in 1938. He contributed hundreds of articles to outdoor and gun magazines, wrote an outdoor column, ''Roamin' East Idaho,'' for the *Post-Register* beginning in 1943, and served as a contributing editor of *American Rifleman* from 1958 to 1965. Although Ormond was versatile—he was a musician in a professional dance band for nine years, a licensed boxer, and an inventor holding three patents—his lifelong fascination was with the outdoors. His books on the subject include *Hunting in the Northwest, Complete Book of Hunting, Complete Book of Outdoor Lore, Small Game Hunting, Outdoorsman's Handbook,* and *Bear!*

OBITUARIES AND OTHER SOURCES:

PERIODICALS

Idaho Falls Post, February 4, 1985.

* * *

OURSLER, Will(iam Charles)   1913-1985
(Gale Gallager, Nick Marine)

OBITUARY NOTICE—See index for *CA* sketch: Born July 12, 1913, in Baltimore, Md.; died after a long illness, January 7, 1985, in New York, N.Y. Radio commentator, journalist, editor, and author. Oursler began his career as a reporter for Hearst Papers during the late 1930's. He then worked as an assistant editor for a detective magazine and later was a Pacific war correspondent during World War II. The journalist turned to free-lance writing in 1945, taking a particular interest in inspirational subjects and often lecturing and writing on religion and narcotics. Oursler's more than forty books include *The Healing Power of Faith, Protestant Power and the Com-*

ing Revelation, and *Father Flanagan of Boys Town,* written with his father, Fulton Oursler. Oursler had also served as vice-president of the Mystery Writers of America and wrote mystery novels pseudonymously. As Nick Marine his book credits include *One Way Street,* and as Gale Gallager he was the co-author of *I Found Him Dead* and *Chord in Crimson.*

OBITUARIES AND OTHER SOURCES:

PERIODICALS

New York Times, February 28, 1985.

* * *

OWEN, Wyn F(oster)   1923-

BRIEF ENTRY: Born December 23, 1923, in Dorrigo, Australia; came to United States, 1952, naturalized citizen, 1969. American economist, educator, and author. Owen worked as an economic research officer for Australia's New South Wales Department of Agriculture from 1946 to 1953. He became a professor of economics at University of Colorado in 1962. Owen has also been director of the university's Economics Institute and International Economics Studies Center. He edited *American Agriculture: The Changing Structure* (Heath, 1969) and *Guide to Graduate Study in Economics, Agricultural Economics, and Related Fields: United States of America and Canada* (Economics Institute, University of Colorado, 1979). *Address:* Department of Economics, University of Colorado, 1200 University Ave., Boulder, Colo. 80309.

BIOGRAPHICAL/CRITICAL SOURCES:

BOOKS

American Men and Women of Science: The Social and Behavioral Sciences, 13th edition, Bowker, 1978.

P

P.Q.
    See QUENNELL, Peter (Courtney)

*   *   *

PAGE, William   1946-
    (Paddy McGoldstein)

PERSONAL: Born February 1, 1946, in London, England; son of Bill (a metallurgist) and Mary (an author; maiden name, Hacker) Page; married Gillian M. Struthers (an illustrator), December 12, 1976; children: Helen, Geoffrey. *Education:* University of Sussex, B.A., 1969.

ADDRESSES: Home and office—Beech Tree Publishing, 10 Watford Close, Guildford, Surrey GU1 2EP, England.

CAREER: Political and Economic Planning Ltd., London, England, researcher, 1970; Post Office Telecommunications, London, market researcher in Marketing Research and Forecasting Division, 1970-71; University of Sussex, Brighton, England, research fellow at Science Policy Unit, 1971-80; Butterworth Scientific Ltd., Journals Division, Guildford, England, managing editor of *Futures, Science and Public Policy,* and *Tourism Management,* 1980-83; Beech Tree Publishing, Guildford, journals publisher, 1983—.

MEMBER: World Futures Studies Federation, British Association for the Advancement of Science.

WRITINGS:

(With Charles de Hoghton and Guy Streatfield) *And Now, the Future,* Political and Economic Planning Ltd., 1971.
(With H.S.D. Cole and others) *Models of Doom,* Universe Books, 1974 (published in England as *Thinking About the Future: A Critique of "The Limits to Growth,"* Sussex University Press, 1974).
(Editor with Sol Encel and P. K. Marstrand) *The Art of Anticipation,* Martin Robertson, 1975.
(Contributor) Marie Jahoda and Christopher Freeman, editors, *World Futures: The Great Debate,* Martin Robertson, 1978.
(Editor) *The Future of Politics,* St. Martin's, 1983.

Contributor of about forty articles to journals, sometimes under pseudonym Paddy McGoldstein.

SIDELIGHTS: William Page commented: "It was an issue of

a now-extinct magazine, *Science Journal,* that got me interested in long-term issues. In the late 1960's, when I was job hunting, most work concerned with the future was in research. The main output of research can be publications, so like my mother, my sister, my wife, Gillian, and my brother, Martin, I ended up as a writer and publisher—publishing other people's work.

"I started off in the late 1960's being excited about the future, albeit with some concerns and qualms; now—when I stop to think about it—I can feel quite gloomy about the next few decades. This is not because I believe we are running out of physical resources or can only continue by destroying the planet, but because I see too little political will to tackle long-term problems if the remedies cannot be viewed in the usual short-term perspective. The most practical personal solution (at present) seems to be to ignore these problems and hope good fortune takes them away."

*   *   *

PALMER, Parker J.   1939-

PERSONAL: Born February 28, 1939, in Chicago, Ill.; son of Max J. (a business executive) and LaVerne (Hickman) Palmer; married Sarah Ann Hartley (a teacher), August 18, 1961; children: Brent, Todd, Carrie. *Education:* Carleton College, B.A., 1961; attended Union Theological Seminary, 1961-62; University of California, Berkeley, M.A., 1965, Ph.D., 1970. *Politics:* "Peace and justice." *Religion:* Quaker.

ADDRESSES: Home—Wallingford, Pa. *Office*—Pendle Hill Quaker Study Center, 338 Plush Mill Rd., Wallingford, Pa. 19086.

CAREER: Pacific School of Religion, Berkeley, Calif., director of Bureau of Community Research, 1963-65; Beloit College, Beloit, Wis., college examiner and instructor in sociology, 1965-67; Washington Center for Metropolitan Studies, Washington, D.C., senior research associate in urban sociology, 1969-74; Georgetown University, Washington, D.C., associate professor of sociology, 1972-74; Pendle Hill Quaker Study Center, Wallingford, Pa., dean of studies and instructor in religion, 1975—. Trustee of Carleton College, 1969-73; co-director of Institute for Public Life, Silver Spring, Md., 1971-74; faculty member of Auburn Theology Seminary, 1979—.

Consultant to Danforth Foundation, 1965-75, and Lilly Endowment, 1978—.

MEMBER: Phi Beta Kappa.

AWARDS, HONORS: Dana Award for personal achievement from Carleton College, 1961; graduate fellowship from Danforth Foundation, 1961; Uhrig Award for excellence in teaching from Beloit College, 1967; grants from Sloane Foundation, 1969-71, Irwin-Sweeny-Miller Foundation, 1971-72, Danforth Foundation, 1972-75, and Lilly Endowment, 1975—.

WRITINGS:

(Contributor) Kenneth Underwood, editor, *The Church, the University, and Social Policy,* Wesleyan University Press, 1969.
(Contributor) Robert Rankin, editor, *The Recovery of the Spirit in Higher Education,* Seabury, 1980.
The Promise of Paradox, Ave Maria Press, 1980.
The Company of Strangers: Christians and the Renewal of America's Public Life, Crossroad, 1981.
To Know as We Are Known, Harper, 1983.

Contributor of articles and poems to educational, theological, and social change journals, including *Christian Century, Liberal Education, NICM Journal, Friends Journal,* and *Warm Wind.* Also author of numerous monographs.

WORK IN PROGRESS: Researching the spiritual renewal of liberal Protestantism, the theory and practice of nonviolence, and the new monasticism.

SIDELIGHTS: In *The Company of Strangers: Christians and the Renewal of America's Public Life,* Parker J. Palmer argues that churches should eschew privacy and become more involved in the mainstream of American life. The author warns church leaders not to adopt the standard belief that individuals in American society are motivated primarily by self-interest, as he believes this assumption minimizes human potential.

After defining the essence of public life as the interdependence and interaction of strangers, Palmer notes that, in the biblical tradition, the stranger is a messenger from God. By encouraging interaction with "strangers," Palmer avers that a movement culminating in the rebuilding of America's public life can result.

Writing in *America,* James E. Hug lauded Palmer for a "stimulating" argument presented "clearly and provocatively." According to Max L. Stackhouse in *Commonweal,* Palmer's book represents "fresh efforts to articulate the core values of Christian piety in such a way that the transformed inner tissues of commitment become the source of wider public renewal."

Parker told *CA:* "I have long been concerned about three subjects: spirituality, education, and social change. These have been focused by ten years of living and working in a religious community—Pendle Hill—which is rooted in Quaker faith and practice. Here seventy people are deeply involved in alternative forms of education, in consensual decision-making and mutual support, and in the worldwide movement for justice and peace."

BIOGRAPHICAL/CRITICAL SOURCES:

PERIODICALS

America, March 13, 1982.
Commonweal, February 26, 1982.

PALUDAN, (Stig Henning) Jacob (Puggaard) 1896-1975

OBITUARY NOTICE: Born February 7, 1896, in Copenhagen, Denmark; died September 26, 1975, in Copenhagen, Denmark. Journalist and author of novels and essays. Paludan is best remembered for the popular two-volume novel *Joergen Stein,* published in English translation in 1966. Praised by critics as a true masterpiece, the book traces three generations of a European family in the aftermath of World War I. Paludan left Denmark at the age of twenty-four to live and work in New York and Ecuador for one year and upon his return worked for a variety of newspapers as a literary critic. His experiences in the United States were said to have left a deep impression on Paludan, and he began writing about the threat of "Americanization," which he feared would undermine all traditional values. His first novel, *De vestlige veje,* for example, satirized American civilization and helped establish Paludan as an astute critic of his age. In the mid-1930's Paludan began writing essays that often focused on feminism and the superficiality of modern society—especially in America. Some of the unifying themes of his later work were the relationship between the mind and nature, and man's relationship with time and space. Between 1973 and 1975 Paludan wrote three volumes of memoirs, *I hoestens maanefase, Sloeret sandhed,* and *Vink fra en fjern virkelighed.* A fourth volume, *Laasens klik,* was published posthumously. Paludan's essays have been collected in ten books.

OBITUARIES AND OTHER SOURCES:

BOOKS

Encyclopedia of World Literature in the Twentieth Century, updated edition, Ungar, 1967.

PERIODICALS

Times Literary Supplement, February 2, 1967.

* * *

PANGRAZZI, Arnaldo 1947-

PERSONAL: Born October 8, 1947, in Trento, Italy; son of Luciano (a farmer) and Gemma (a housewife; maiden name, Tolotti) Pangrazzi. *Education:* Weston School of Theology, M.Div., 1973; Boston College, M.Ed., 1976.

ADDRESSES: Home and office—Camilliani, Piazza della Maddalena 53, Rome 00186, Italy.

CAREER: Entered Order of St. Camillus (O.S. Cam.), 1964, ordained Roman Catholic priest, 1974; assistant pastor of Roman Catholic church in Somerville, Mass., 1973-77; St. Joseph's Hospital, Milwaukee, Wis., chaplain supervisor, 1977-83; Casa Genralizia, Rome, Italy, general consultor, 1983—. Clinical pastoral education supervisor; conducts seminars and support groups.

WRITINGS:

Your Words in Prayer: In Time of Illness, Alba House, 1982.
Grido a te, Signore (title means "I Cry to You, O Lord"), Editrice Elle Di Ci, 1983.

Contributor to magazines, including *Quarterly Linacre, Review for Religious, Sign, St. Anthony's Messenger,* and *Journal of Ministry and Supervision.*

WORK IN PROGRESS: Dinamismo pastorale per il mondo della salute (title means "Creative Ways of Doing Pastoral Ministry"), publication expected in 1986.

SIDELIGHTS: Father Arnaldo Pangrazzi commented: "I am a priest of the Order of St. Camillus, which specializes in the care of the sick. The articles I have written were the outgrowth of pastoral experiences. Major areas of interest are sickness, the humanization of hospitals, cancer, grief, suicide, and support groups."

*   *   *

PARISH, Helen Rand   1912-

BRIEF ENTRY: Born October 10, 1912, in Waterbury, Conn. American historian, consultant, and author. A newspaper reporter in New York and Georgia until 1930, Parish spent the World War II years with the Office of Censorship. From 1951 to 1955 she served as chief officer of Shelton Industrial Corporation. Parish wrote *At the Palace Gates* (Viking, 1949), *Our Lady of Guadalupe* (Viking, 1955), and *Estebanico* (Viking, 1974). She collaborated with Henry R. Wagner on *The Life and Writings of Bartolome de las Casas* (University of New Mexico Press, 1967).

BIOGRAPHICAL/CRITICAL SOURCES:

PERIODICALS

New York Times Book Review, January 26, 1975.

*   *   *

PARK, Sung-Bae   1933-

PERSONAL: Born September 21, 1933, in Chonnam, Korea; immigrated to the United States, 1969, naturalized citizen, 1974; son of Chang-ju (a farmer) and Yong-hyun (a housewife; maiden name, Hur) Park; married Chin-hoe Kim (a housewife), January 19, 1960; children: Hyun-A, Soon-A. *Education:* Dongguk University, B.A., 1958, M.A., 1960; University of California, Berkeley, Ph.D., 1979.

ADDRESSES: Home—37 Maple Rd., Setauket, N.Y. 11733. *Office*—Center for Religious Studies, State University of New York at Stony Brook, Stony Brook, N.Y. 11794.

CAREER: Dongguk University, Seoul, Korea, assistant professor, 1962-68, associate professor of Buddhist studies, 1968-69; State University of New York at Stony Brook, assistant professor, 1977-83, associate professor of religious studies, 1983—, executive director of studies in Korean religious thought and culture, 1981—.

MEMBER: American Academy of Religion, Association for Asian Studies, Association for Indian and Buddhist Studies.

WRITINGS:

(Associate editor; Lewis Lancaster, editor) *Descriptive Catalogue of the Korean Buddhist Canon,* University of California Press, 1980.
Buddhist Faith and Sudden Enlightenment, State University of New York Press, 1983.
Buddhist Syncretism in Korea, State University of New York Press, in press.

Contributor to scholarly journals.

SIDELIGHTS: "My goal is to introduce Americans to the spirit of total interpenetration in East Asian Buddhism," Sung-Bae

Park commented. "By total interpenetration I mean a holistic approach to the development of one's spirituality. Through an existential understanding of the concepts of nonduality, I hope that Westerners can come to grasp the unity of knowledge and action."

*   *   *

PARKER, Arthur C(aswell)   1881-1955

BRIEF ENTRY: Born April 5, 1881, in Iroquois, N.Y.; died January 1, 1955, in Naples, N.Y. American archaeologist, museum director, editor, and author. Parker studied archaeology under the distinguished educator Frederick Ward Putnam at Harvard University in the early 1900's. In 1905 he became archaeologist for the New York State Museum. He remained there until 1925, when he became director of the Rochester Museum of Arts and Sciences. Parker held that post for the next twenty years, becoming director emeritus of the museum in 1946. During his career Parker also served in executive capacities for such organizations as the American Association of Museums, of which he was history vice-president and counselor from 1928 to 1946, and the New York State History Association, of which he was president in the mid-1940's. He received several important awards for his work, including one from the Guggenheim Foundation in 1954. Among Parker's many writings are *The Life of General Ely S. Parker, Last Grand Sachem of the Iroquois and General Grant's Military Secretary* (1919), *The Archaeological History of New York* (1922), *An Analytical History of the Seneca Indians* (1926), *A Manual for History Museums* (1935), and the children's book *Red Streak of the Iroquois* (1950). Parker was also associate editor of *Builder* during the early 1920's. *Address:* Parrish Hill Rd., Naples, N.Y.

BIOGRAPHICAL/CRITICAL SOURCES:

BOOKS

Who Was Who in America, Volume III: *1951-1960,* Marquis, 1966.
Obituaries on File, Facts on File, 1979.

*   *   *

PARRISH, Anne   1888-1957

BRIEF ENTRY: Born November 12, 1888, in Colorado Springs, Colo.; died of a cerebral hemorrhage, September 5, 1957, in Danbury, Conn. American illustrator and author. Parrish, the daughter of illustrator Maxfield Parrish and portrait painter Anne Lodge Parrish, aspired to be an artist at an early age. She attended private schools in Colorado and Delaware and studied art at the Philadelphia School of Design for Women. Discouraged, however, by the demands of an artist's career, she chose instead to become a writer. Together with her brother Dillwyn, she wrote and illustrated a number of children's books, including *The Dream Coach* (1924), *Floating Island* (1930), and *The Story of Appleby Capple* (1950), all of which were nominated for Newbery Medals. Parrish was also sole author of more than a dozen novels, including *The Perennial Bachelor* (1925)—for which she won the Harper Prize—*Despondency's Daughter* (1938), *Pray for a Tomorrow* (1941), *Poor Child* (1945), *A Clouded Star* (1948), *And Have Not Love* (1954), and *The Lucky One* (1958). *Address:* Georgetown, Conn.

BIOGRAPHICAL/CRITICAL SOURCES:

BOOKS

American Authors and Books: 1640 to the Present Day, 3rd revised editon, Crown, 1962.
Illustrators of Children's Books, 1946-1956, Horn Book, 1958.
Twentieth-Century Authors: A Biographical Dictionary of Modern Literature, 1st supplement, H. W. Wilson, 1955.

PERIODICALS

Publishers Weekly, September 23, 1957.
Time, September 16, 1957.

* * *

PARTRIDGE, Elinore Hughes   1937-

PERSONAL: Born October 18, 1937, in Salt Lake City, Utah; daughter of Clifford N. (an engineer) and Helen (a teacher; maiden name, Stokes) Hughes; married Ernest D. Partridge (a professor and researcher), December 20, 1957. *Education:* University of Utah, B.A. (with high honors), 1958; New York University, M.A., 1963; University of California, Davis, Ph.D. (with high honors), 1970.

ADDRESSES: Home—P.O. Box 2244, Crestline, Calif. 92325. *Office*—Department of English, California State University, 5500 State College Parkway, San Bernardino, Calif. 92407.

CAREER: University of Wisconsin—Milwaukee, assistant professor of English, 1970-75; California State University, San Bernardino, instructor in English, 1981-84, assistant professor of English, 1984—. Visiting lecturer in the University of California system, 1980-81.

MEMBER: Phi Beta Kappa, Phi Kappa Phi.

WRITINGS:

American Prose and Criticism, Gale, 1982.
A Man for the Times: The Olpin Years, University of Utah Press, in press.

WORK IN PROGRESS: American Travel Literature; American Natural History Writing.

SIDELIGHTS: Elinore Hughes Partridge told *CA:* "My life-long interest in both experiencing and conserving wilderness areas in the United States led to my research in American literature. The discovery of nineteenth-century natural history writing and scientific reports (for example, those of Clarence Dutton, Thoreau, and Burroughs) contributed to my desire to explore nonfiction prose as literature.

"In both my introduction to the 1982 bibliography, *American Prose and Criticism,* and in my work in progress on travel and natural history writing, I argue that these works do fit into the category of 'literature' and some of them might be considered great literature by virtue of their images, descriptions, structure, and sensitivity to the power of prose."

* * *

PARTRIDGE, Ernest   1935-

PERSONAL: Born May 14, 1935, in New York, N.Y.; son of E. Dalton (a university professor) and Nell (Clark) Partridge; married Elinore Hughes (an assistant professor), August 20, 1971. *Education:* University of Utah, B.S. (with honors), 1957, M.S., 1961, Ph.D., 1976.

ADDRESSES: Home—1300 30th, B3-17, Boulder, Colo. 80303. *Office*—Cooperative Institute for Research in Environmental Sciences, Box 449, University of Colorado at Boulder, Boulder, Colo. 80309.

CAREER: High school mathematics teacher in Fair Lawn, N.J., 1958-59; ethics teacher in Bronx, N.Y., 1961-62; Paterson State College (now William Paterson College of New Jersey), Wayne, instructor in philosophy and education, 1962-64, director of outdoor education, 1963-64; Hunter College of the City University of New York, New York, N.Y., instructor in philosophy, 1965-67; Weber State College, Ogden, Utah, instructor in philosophy, 1968-70; University of Wisconsin—Milwaukee, instructor in cultural foundations of education, 1971-72; Environmental Education Council of Greater Milwaukee, Milwaukee, executive director, 1973-75; Weber State College, adjunct associate professor of philosophy, 1976-80; University of California, Santa Barbara, visiting associate professor of environmental studies, 1980-82; University of Colorado at Boulder, research associate at Cooperative Institute for Research in Environmental Studies and Center for the Study of Values and Social Policy, 1984—. Instructor at Rutgers University, 1963-65.

MEMBER: American Philosophical Association, Philosophy of Education Society (fellow), American Society for Political and Legal Philosophy, American Association for the Advancement of Science, American Society for Value Inquiry, Society for Philosophy and Public Affairs, Common Cause, Sierra Club, Wilderness Society, Friends of the Earth.

AWARDS, HONORS: Fellow of National Endowment for the Humanities, 1977, Rockefeller Foundation, 1978-79, and Liberty Fund, 1982; Interdisciplinary Incentive Award from National Science Foundation and National Endowment for the Humanities, 1984-86.

WRITINGS:

(Contributor) C. D. Linton and E. H. Litchfield, editors, *The Complete Reference Handbook,* Stravon, 1964.
(Editor and contributor) *Responsibilities to Future Generations: Environmental Ethics,* Prometheus Books, 1981.
(Contributor) Robert C. Schultz and J. Donald Hughes, editors, *Environmental Consciousness,* University Press of America, 1981.

Contributor of articles and reviews to scholarly journals and popular magazines, including *Alternative Future, Ethics,* and *Journal of Outdoor Education,* and newspapers. Guest editor of *Counseling and Values,* summer, 1974; member of editorial board of *Environmental Ethics* and *Journal of Environmental Education.*

WORK IN PROGRESS: Nature and the Future: Essays in Environmental Ethics and the Duty to Posterity, publication expected in 1986; *Ethical Issues in Earthquake Prediction and Seismic Safety Analysis,* publication expected in 1986; *What Good Is a Planet: Approaches to Environmental Ethics,* publication expected in 1987; *To Ourselves and Our Posterity,* a philosophical inquiry into the duty to future generations, publication expected in 1988.

SIDELIGHTS: Ernest Partridge told *CA:* "My current research and writing may be simply described: *applied ethics.* Within this field of applied ethics, I am particularly interested in the issue of the duty to posterity (an issue virtually ignored by contemporary philosophers until recently), environmental ethics ('Man's Responsibility for Nature'), public policy analysis, and peace studies. My motives for pursuing this work, and the content and objectives thereof, rest upon these premises: (a) Human civilization and perhaps even the entire human race face unprecedented dangers. The primary sources of these perils are environmental deterioration and nuclear annihilation. (b) These dangers are in turn due to the failure of moral perspective and will to keep pace with technological facility. We have, in a word, become far more clever than we are wise. (c) The most effective, and quite possibly the only, escape from these perils resides in a conscientious application of practical reason and moral perception. (d) ''Defense'' policies by the Great Powers are woefully lacking in reasonableness and moral perception and are locked into mutually reinforcing 'tracks' toward mutual, even species, annihilation. (e) Practical reason and moral responsibility are likewise inconspicuous in industrial practices and governmental policies regarding the natural environment. (f) The potentially useful role of the philosopher in clarifying and improving public policy decisions is radically misunderstood and generally ignored both by public policy-makers and by scholars outside of the philosopher's discipline.

''The primary purpose of my research and writing, therefore, is to enhance the role and effectiveness of practical reason and moral intelligence in public policy deliberations and implementations, and thus to put these philosopher's tools to work in the service of an acutely endangered civilization and species. I attempt to do this both by example and by force of reason. In this endeavor, I am joined by a significant number of contemporary philosophers who have also chosen to bring their discipline out of 'purely academic' seclusion, and to put it to practical, 'applied' work.

''Many of my more traditional colleagues look with disdain upon this 'applied turn' in their profession, dismissing it as a sort of 'philosophical engineering.' I reject this analogy, and instead regard applied ethics as the 'laboratory' of theoretical ethics. As any philosopher of science will affirm, while 'pure' empirical science (e.g. physics) might dispense with 'engineering' applications, it can not dispense with the 'laboratory' (i.e., with empirical validation). To paraphrase Immanuel Kant, in ethics, 'theory without application is empty; application without theory is blind.'

''In my study of environmental values in general and of the posterity question in particular, I have encountered an abundance of political and journalistic rhetoric and a scarcity of serious philosophical reflection and analysis. My scholarly and teaching endeavors are devoted to a remedy of this imbalance.

''My decision to devote my career to the study and teaching of environmental values has followed from some fundamental convictions about the human condition and about the teaching of environmental awareness. Among them:

''*First,* facts, practical intelligence, and objectivity bear significantly upon the resolution of issues of environmental morality and responsibility. Environmental ethics is not simply a matter of feeling, arbitrary choice, or social fashion, nor is environmental ethics usefully approached through as study of 'the history of ideas.'

''*Second,* the present time is best perceived, in the context of a vast human and natural history, as a 'passage' from the remote past to a far distant future. Thus I hope to encourage an appreciation and a respect for the products of long-term natural processes.

''*Third,* human beings are most appropriately perceived 'in the web of life'—as citizens in the community of life, not the center or even the purpose and justification of the life system.

''*Fourth,* an acknowledgement of human ignorance and frailty implies humility, caution, and conservatism in dealing with nature: 'micro-nature' in the genes, cells and organic compounds, and 'macro-nature' in organisms, ecosystems, and physical laws. As Aldo Leopold acutely observed, 'A wise tinkerer keeps all his parts.'

''*Fifth,* a human being is significantly, if not exclusively, a *natural* being. Involvement with and appreciation of the natural sources and sustenance of his being is essential to his welfare as an individual and as a species.

''*Finally,* ecological morality, like social morality, rests upon a paradox: It is in humanity's interest *not* to seek directly humanity's interest. Anthropocentric policies that transform natural values totally into 'use' values (utility) are destructive of *intrinsic* values associated with admiration and love. This principle leads directly to a respect for nature—an attitude of 'self-transcending' regard for nature as a realm to be admired, loved, even worshiped. Such an attitude enriches the life-quality of the human individual and of human society.

''In summary: If my education, teaching, and various professional activities can be said to have a unifying theme, it is a dedication to the application of critical, trained practical reason and moral intelligence toward the solution of such transcending human problems as environment deterioration, the threat of war and nuclear destruction, moral indifference and sophistry, educational sloth (often disguised as 'neoromanticism'), and the detachment of values from knowledge (the 'is ought problem') and from social and personal life ('alienation'). I expect that these issues will occupy my attention for the remainder of my productive life.''

*   *   *

PASCAL, Francine 1938-

BRIEF ENTRY: Born May 13, 1938, in New York, N.Y. American journalist, playwright, television scriptwriter, and author of nonfiction and fiction. Beginning her career writing articles for such magazines as *Ladies' Home Journal* and *Cosmopolitan,* Pascal went on to write for movie magazines and television soap operas, but recognition eluded her until she collaborated on the hit musical *George M!* (1969). The script, written with her husband, John Pascal, and Michael Stewart, highlights the career of George M. Cohan; Francine Pascal subsequently collaborated with her husband on the television adaptation.

Since that first success, Pascal has established herself as a writer for young adults with such novels as the popular *Hangin' Out With Cici* (Viking, 1977), televised as an American Broadcasting Companies ''After School Special,'' and *My First Love and Other Disasters* (Viking, 1979), which was named an American Library Association Best Book for Young Adults in 1980. Pascal has also created the twelve-book ''Sweet Valley High'' paperback series and written a nonfiction book, with John Pascal, titled *The Strange Case of Patty Hearst* (New American Library, 1973). She also wrote a novel for adults, *Save Johanna!* (Berkley Publishing), which was published in 1981. *Residence:* New York, N.Y.

BIOGRAPHICAL/CRITICAL SOURCES:

BOOKS

Fifth Book of Junior Authors and Illustrators, H. W. Wilson, 1983.

PERIODICALS

New York Times Book Review, April 29, 1979.
Variety, September 16, 1970.

* * *

PATTERSON, Jefferson   1891-1977

OBITUARY NOTICE: Born May 14, 1891, in Dayton, Ohio; died of a heart ailment, November 12, 1977, in Washington, D.C. Attorney, diplomat, and author. After working briefly as a lawyer Patterson joined the foreign services in 1921 as a secretary in the U.S. State Department. For the next twenty years he worked in American embassies throughout the world, including Asia and Scandinavia. In 1940 he worked in Berlin as a liaison for British, French, and Belgian prisoners, and after America entered World War II he spent five years in Lima as a deputy chief. Following the war Patterson served in Cairo for three years, then was stationed in Athens as U.S. representative to a special United Nations committee. He resigned from diplomatic duty in 1958 after two years as ambassador to Uruguay. Patterson wrote of his diplomatic experiences in *Capitals and Captives, Diplomatic Duty and Diversion,* and *Diplomatic Terminus.* He also wrote *Family Portraits,* which concerns his ancestors.

OBITUARIES AND OTHER SOURCES:

BOOKS

The National Cyclopaedia of American Biography, Volume 59, James T. White, 1980.
Who Was Who in America, With World Notables, Volume VII: *1977-1981,* Marquis, 1981.

PERIODICALS

Washington Post, November 14, 1977.

* * *

PATTULLO, George   1879-1967

OBITUARY NOTICE: Born October 9, 1879, in Woodstock, Ontario, Canada; died of a heart ailment, July 30, 1967, in New York, N.Y. Journalist and author. Pattullo, who was best known for his short stories and western adventure novels, worked on the staffs of various newspapers in Montreal, London, and Boston prior to 1908. During World War I he served the *Saturday Evening Post* as a special correspondent with the American Expeditionary Force. All of Pattullo's writings were at least partly autobiographical and were aimed at presenting a realistic picture of life in the American Southwest. His books include *The Untamed, All Our Yesterdays, The Sheriff of Badger,* and *Some Men in Their Time.* Pattullo was also the author of the screenplay for the 1922 motion picture "Minnie."

OBITUARIES AND OTHER SOURCES:

BOOKS

Twentieth-Century Western Writers, Gale, 1982.
Who Was Who in America, With World Notables, Volume VI: *1974-1976,* Marquis, 1976.

PERIODICALS

New York Times, July 30, 1967.

* * *

PATURI, Felix R.
See MINDT, Heinz R.

* * *

PAULY, Thomas H(arry)   1940-

PERSONAL: Born March 6, 1940, in Missoula, Mont.; son of Henry C. (an attorney) and Betty (a housewife; maiden name, Thomas) Pauly; married Rebecca Mehl (a college professor) in June, 1967 (divorced, 1980). *Education:* Harvard University, A.B., 1962; University of California, Berkeley, M.A., 1965, Ph.D., 1970.

ADDRESSES: Home—54 Cheswald Blvd., Apt. 509, Newark, Del. 19713. *Office*—Department of American Studies, 317 Ewing, University of Delaware, Newark, Del. 19711.

CAREER: University of Delaware, Newark, assistant professor, 1970-75, associate professor, 1975-83, professor of American literature, 1983—, director of American studies, 1983—.

MEMBER: Modern Language Association of America, Popular Culture Association. American Studies Association, Mid-Atlantic Studies Association (president, 1986).

AWARDS, HONORS: Fulbright fellow in Milan, Italy, 1975; Lillian Gish Prize for best article in *Journal of Popular Culture,* 1979; *Choice* award for best academic book of 1983.

WRITINGS:

An American Odyssey: Elia Kazan and American Culture, Temple University Press, 1983.

Contributor of articles on American literature and popular culture to journals, including *Western Humanities Review, American Literature, American Quarterly, New England Quarterly,* and *Texas Studies in Literature and Language.*

WORK IN PROGRESS: Articles and a book on the culture of post-World War II readjustment.

SIDELIGHTS: In *An American Odyssey: Elia Kazan and American Culture* Thomas H. Pauly traces the life and work of one of America's leading film and theatre directors. He discusses Kazan's staging of such productions as "Death of a Salesman," "Cat on a Hot Tin Roof," and "A Streetcar Named Desire" and examines his treatment of such films as "A Tree Grows in Brooklyn," "East of Eden," "Tea and Sympathy," and "On the Waterfront." *Times Literary Supplement* reviewer S. S. Prawer praised Pauly for emphasizing the reflection of contemporary social and political forces in Kazan's works and for demonstrating the pervasiveness of his artistic impulse for self-expression. "Pauly's narrative," assessed Prawer, "keeps us constantly alive to . . . [Kazan's] drive for approval and consequent need to work at all costs—even at the cost of naming names [in the House Un-American Activities Committee (HUAC) 1950's investigation of alleged communist sympathizers in the entertainment industry]." Prawer noted, however, that *An American Odyssey* fails to relate Kazan's work to "its place in the evolution of the cinema" and expressed disappointment at Pauly's disregard of the film "The Visitors." Examination of this film reputed to be Kazan's reaction to the Vietnam War is, in the critic's view, "essential in a book explicitly dedicated to a discussion of Kazan's involvement with American culture." Nevertheless, Prawer deemed Pauly a "fair-minded and justifiably sympathetic interpreter."

Pauly told *CA:* "I am interested in what the popular American novels, plays, and films since 1930 say about the times in which they appeared. Though I believe that these works cannot be understood apart from the individuals who created or shaped them, I am intrigued by the industrial and cultural conditions which profoundly influenced their commercial success."

BIOGRAPHICAL/CRITICAL SOURCES:

PERIODICALS

Times Literary Supplement, August 12, 1983.

* * *

PAVORD, Anna 1940-

PERSONAL: Born September 20, 1940, in Abergavenny, Wales; daughter of Arthur (a headmaster) and Christabel (a teacher; maiden name, Lewis) Pavord; married Trevor Ware (in marketing), June 18, 1966; children: Oenone, Vanessa, Tilly. *Education:* University of Leicester, B.A. (with honors), 1962. *Politics:* None. *Religion:* "Pantheist."

ADDRESSES: Home—Old Rectory, Puncknowle, Dorchester, Dorset, England. *Office—Observer,* 8 St. Andrews Hill, London EC4V 5JA, England. *Agent*—Caradoc King, A. P. Watt & Co., 26 Bedford Row, London WC1R 4HL, England.

CAREER: Lintas Ltd. (advertising agency), London, England, copywriter, 1962-63; BBC-TV, London, director, 1963-69; free-lance journalist, 1969—.

WRITINGS:

Growing Things (juvenile gardening book), Macmillan, 1982.

Contributor to newspapers.

WORK IN PROGRESS: Another gardening book.

SIDELIGHTS: Anna Pavord commented: "I write to keep our seventeenth-century house standing, a thirteenth-century dovecote in repair, my garden from becoming an impenetrable jungle, and my children educated. I have no pretensions to be anything but competent."

AVOCATIONAL INTERESTS: "I read Evelyn Waugh for pleasure, J. S. Mill for my soul. I walk with my husband and study landscape history and architecture."

* * *

PAYNE, Leanne 1932-

PERSONAL: Given name is pronounced Lee-*ann*; born June 26, 1932, in Omaha, Neb.; daughter of Robert Hugh (a pharmacist) and Forrest (Williamson) Mabrey; divorced, 1952; children: Deborah Payne Bostrom. *Education:* Wheaton College, Wheaton, Ill., B.A. (with honors), 1971, M.A. (with high honors), 1974; University of Arkansas, Fayetteville, M.Ed., 1973. *Religion:* Episcopalian.

ADDRESSES: Home—Milwaukee, Wis. *Office*—Pastoral Care Ministries, Inc., Milwaukee, Wis. 53217.

CAREER: Employed as a clerk and requirements analyst at Veterans Administration Hospital, Little Rock, Ark., 1957-

63; Wheaton College, Wheaton, Ill., member of student personnel staff, 1965-68, special instructor in English, 1973-76; pastoral counselor, 1976-78; lecturer and missioner, 1978—; Pastoral Care Ministries, Inc., Milwaukee, Wis., founder and president, 1982—. Member of faculty at Creighton University; research fellow at Yale University's Divinity School; mission leader at Episcopal, evangelical, and nondenominational churches; seminar speaker; lecturer at pastoral care retreats in the United States and abroad.

MEMBER: Lambda Iota Tau.

WRITINGS:

Real Presence: The Holy Spirit in the Works of C. S. Lewis, Crossway, 1979.
The Broken Image: Restoring Personal Wholeness Through Healing Prayer, Crossway, 1981.
The Healing of the Homosexual, Crossway, 1984.
Crisis in Masculinity, Crossway, 1985.

WORK IN PROGRESS: Gnosticism; Virtues and Vices; Christian Healing.

SIDELIGHTS: Leanne Payne wrote: "Like Agnes Sanford, Catherine Marshall, and most who have written and ministered in the area of prayer for healing, I found the healing presence of Christ when in drastic need of healing for myself. I came to understand and especially to emphasize the indwelling presence of Christ and the need to 'practice this presence' in the healing of persons. As I passed this understanding on to others, I saw them as dramatically healed as I had been. Later, taking up theological studies, I looked for theologians, philosophers, and Christian writers whose intellectual systems were large enough to contain the realities that I had experienced within the Christian faith. In C. S. Lewis I found such a mind and heart, and out of my study of him came *Real Presence.*

"*Real Presence* contains the theology that is present not only in the mind of C. S. Lewis, but in that of 'mere' Christians of all time; it is best expounded in the apostles Paul and John. This is the theology which explains my experience of healing, and is inherent in my books on prayer for healing. I have written specifically on prayer for the healing of sexual neuroses (rather than on healing of depression and so on) because the need for healing and understanding of how to pray for healing in this area is so very great. I hope to turn my attention to prayer for healing of other problems in future writing."

* * *

PAYNTER, Will(iam) 1903-1984

OBITUARY NOTICE: Born December 6, 1903, in Whitchurch, Wales; died December 11, 1984. Trade union official, miner, and author. Paynter, who served as general secretary to Great Britian's National Union of Mineworkers for nine years beginning in 1959, was considered largely responsible for establishing a uniform wage structure for miners. Also regarded as a leading British Communist, Paynter resigned from the party in 1969, the year after he retired from the union secretariat. He then served one year as a member of the Commission of Industrial Relations and from 1972 was an active member of the Arbitration Panel, now known as the Advisory, Arbitration, and Conciliation Service. Throughout his career, Paynter was concerned with reducing the occurrence of industrially-related diseases among miners. His autobiography, *My Generation,* was published in 1972.

OBITUARIES AND OTHER SOURCES:

BOOKS

International Who's Who, 48th edition, Europa, 1984.

PERIODICALS

Times (London), December 13, 1984.

*   *   *

PAYSON, Herb(ert III) 1927-

PERSONAL: Born May 14, 1927, in Cambridge, Mass.; son of Herbert, Jr. (in business) and Eileen (McHenry) Payson; married Pamela Deering, June 23, 1949 (divorced); married Nancy L. Crain (a photographer), January 17, 1970; children: (first marriage) Maharaj Kaur Khalsa, Philip D., Sarah K.; (second marriage; foster children) Connie L. Myers, Christopher S. Myers, Craig P. Myers. Education: Yale University, B.A., 1950, B.Mus., 1951; New England Conservatory of Music, M.Mus., 1954.

ADDRESSES: Home—Falmouth, Me.

CAREER: Professional entertainer and musician (jazz pianist) in Southern California, 1955-73; full-time writer, 1974—. Military service: U.S. Naval Reserve, active duty, 1945-47.

MEMBER: Authors Guild.

WRITINGS:

Blown Away (nonfiction), Sail Books, 1980.
You Can't Blow Home Again (nonfiction), Hearst Books, 1984.

Contributing editor of Sail.

SIDELIGHTS: Blown Away is the account of Herb Payson's experiences aboard the thirty-six-foot sailing yacht Sea Foam, which bore the author and his family to the South Seas in 1973. Payson told CA that he recently completed a fourteen-month sailing trip through Canada, the United States, and Baja California, which may result in another similar book.

Payson added: "The most commonly asked question regarding our South Seas cruise (beyond 'was it worth it?') is 'of all the places you went, where would you most like to go back to?' For its uniqueness, I would revisit the Galapagos, whose scenery and wilderness, plants and creatures were pure enchantment. For people—that's harder. In general, we found the Polynesians to be friendlier and therefore more attractive to revisit than some other cultures. But of all the people we met—Polynesian, Melanesian, Micronesian, Oriental, Indian, and Caucasian—each place and culture included individuals or groups we'd love to see again.

"It's more revealing, in my view, to consider the total experience. For example, our family, fragmented at the start, became closely knit, each person learning of his own value through his or her contribution to the whole—a contribution on which the rest of us depended.

"Mystical experiences, for those who have such hungers, occur more often at night, at sea, and in good weather than any other time. Although I never got through to the Lord, I did make contact with a guardian angel (GA), a Buchwaldian type who viewed whatever I thought or did with disapproval. 'Help,' I would pray, in extremis, to which (having shifted his unlit cigar—he was trying to quit—from one side of his mouth to the other) GA would always reply, 'Have you really done everything you can in your own behalf?' At that point an idea would occur to one of us, something we could do, which would indeed turn out successfully. After several such experiences I changed my prayer from 'Help!' to 'Got any suggestions?' ''

*   *   *

PEAKE, Lilian (Margaret) 1924-

BRIEF ENTRY: Born May 25, 1924, in London, England. British secretary, journalist, and author. Peake has written more than twenty romance novels. Virtually all of them are set in England's working world, and their heroines are from the ranks of ordinary people. The excitement in Peake's stories emerges from the romantic situations the author creates. Her recent novels are Promise at Midnight (Mills & Boon, 1980), A Ring for a Fortune (Mills & Boon, 1980), A Secret Affair (Mills & Boon, 1980), Strangers Into Lovers (Mills & Boon, 1981), Gregg Barratt's Woman (Mills & Boon, 1981), and Across a Crowded Room (Harlequin, 1981). Address: 48, Dungannon Chase, Thorpe Bay, Sound-on-Sea, Essex SS1 3NJ, England; and c/o Mills & Boon Ltd., 15-16 Brooks Mews, London W1A 1DR, England.

BIOGRAPHICAL/CRITICAL SOURCES:

BOOKS

International Authors and Writers Who's Who, 9th edition [and] International Who's Who in Poetry, 6th edition, Melrose, 1982.
The Writers Directory: 1984-1986, St. James Press, 1983.

*   *   *

PECK, George W(ilbur) 1840-1916

BRIEF ENTRY: Born September 28, 1840, in Henderson, N.Y.; died April 16, 1916. American editor, politician, and author. Peck learned the printing trade while in his teens and worked for several newspapers in Wisconsin before serving with the Union Army during the Civil War. Following the war a humorous article Peck had written caught the attention of Marcus M. "Brick" Pomeroy, who convinced Peck to join the staff of his New York Democrat. In 1871 a collection of articles Peck had written for the Democrat was published as Adventures of One Terence McGrant: A Brevet Irish Cousin of President Ulysses S. Grant. He returned to Wisconsin in 1871 and in 1878 started his own newspaper in Milwaukee, Peck's Sun.

In 1882 the first of the "Peck's Bad Boy" series appeared. Although the stories seem cruel and mean-spirited to modern readers, the dirty tricks played by Hennery, the Bad Boy, on his drunken father reflect the era's preoccupation with practical jokes. The articles, which appeared in published collections, including Peck's Bad Boy and His Pa (1883), Peck's Bad Boy Abroad (1904), Peck's Bad Boy with the Circus (1906), Peck's Bad Boy with the Cowboys (1907), Peck's Bad Boy in an Airship (1908), made Peck a household name and one of the most influential writers of his day.

Peck, who parlayed his popularity into a political career, was elected mayor of Milwaukee in 1890. He became the Democratic nominee for governor of Wisconsin that same year and waged a successful campaign based on his opposition to the unpopular Bennett Law, which had aroused the anger of Roman Catholics, Lutherans, and ethnic minorities by requiring English to be the only language taught in all schools in the state. The law was repealed in 1891. Peck was reelected to a second term in 1892 and used the power of his administration to fight corruption in the state treasury system.

BIOGRAPHICAL/CRITICAL SOURCES:

BOOKS

Dictionary of Literary Biography, Volume 23, *American Newspaper Journalists, 1873-1900*, Gale, 1983.
The National Cyclopaedia of American Biography, Volume 12, James T. White, 1904.
The Oxford Companion to American Literature, 4th edition, Oxford University Press, 1965.
Who Was Who in America, Volume I: *1897-1942*, Marquis, 1943.

*   *   *

PEDOLSKY, Andrea   1951-

PERSONAL: Born March 13, 1951, in New York, N.Y.; daughter of Milton and Beverly (Finger) Pedolsky. *Education:* Queens College of the City University of New York, B.A., 1975; Columbia University, M.S., 1978.

ADDRESSES: Office—Neal-Schuman Publishers, Inc., 23 Cornelia St., New York, N.Y. 10014.

CAREER: Association of the Bar of the City of New York, New York City, research assistant for Drug Law Evaluation Project, 1972-77; Neal-Schuman Publishers, Inc., New York City, managing editor, 1978—.

MEMBER: American Library Association, National Organization for Women (member of board of directors, 1981-83).

WRITINGS:

(Editor with Ellen Gay Detlefsen) *National Directory of Mental Health*, Wiley, 1980.
(Editor) *In-House Training and Development Programs*, Gale, 1981.
(Editor) *Continuing Education for Businesspeople*, Gale, 1981.
(Editor with John Ganly and Diane Sciattara) *Small Business Sourcebook*, Gale, 1983.
(Contributor) Betty-Carol Sellen, editor, *Librarian/Author: A Practical Guide on How to Get Published*, Neal-Schuman, 1985.

Editor of *New York Woman*, 1981-83.

*   *   *

PENNAR, Jaan   1924-

BRIEF ENTRY: Born June 12, 1924, in Tallinn, Estonia (now U.S.S.R.). American political scientist, educator, and author. From 1924 to 1970 Pennar was a counselor and representative of the Radio Liberty Committee in Munich, West Germany. His books include *The Politics of Soviet Education* (Praeger, 1960), *Modernization and Diversity in Soviet Education* (Praeger, 1971), *The U.S.S.R. and the Arabs: The Ideological Dimension* (Crane, Russak, 1973), and *The Estonians in America, 1627-1975: A Chronology and Fact Book* (Oceana, 1975). *Address:* c/o Estonian Learned Society, Estonian House, 243 East 34th St., New York, N.Y. 10016.

BIOGRAPHICAL/CRITICAL SOURCES:

PERIODICALS

Times Literary Supplement, January 11, 1974.

PENNINGTON, W(eldon) J(erry)   1919-1985

OBITUARY NOTICE: Born March 1, 1919, in Tacoma, Wash.; died in a boating accident, March 15, 1985, near Widbey Island, in Puget Sound, Wash. Accountant, federal agent, publisher, and journalist best known as the president and publisher of the *Seattle Times*. Pennington worked for one year as a staff accountant with a Seattle firm before becoming special agent with the Federal Bureau of Investigation (FBI) in 1942. Four years later Pennington joined the staff of Touche Ross & Company as a supervising accountant, leaving in 1951 to become chief financial officer of the *Seattle Times*. He served as the *Times*'s president and director from 1967 until being promoted to publisher, director, and chief executive officer in 1982. Beginning in 1971 Pennington also served as president and director of the *Walla Walla Union-Bulletin* and the Times Communication Company, and he served as president and director of Allied Daily Newspapers beginning in 1982.

OBITUARIES AND OTHER SOURCES:

BOOKS

Who's Who in the West, 20th edition, Marquis, 1984.

PERIODICALS

Chicago Tribune, March 17, 1985, March 19, 1985.
New York Times, March 17, 1985.
Washington Post, March 17, 1985.

*   *   *

PERRY, Richard   1944-

PERSONAL: Born January 13, 1944, in New York, N.Y.; son of Henry (a minister) and Bessie (a homemaker; maiden name, Draines) Perry; married Jeanne Gallo (a legal services administrator), September 14, 1968; children: Malcolm David, Alison Wright. *Education:* City College of the City University of New York, B.A., 1970; Columbia University, M.F.A., 1972.

ADDRESSES: Office—Department of English, Pratt Institute, 215 Ryerson St., Brooklyn, N.Y. 11205. *Agent*—Charlotte Sheedy Literary Agency, Inc., 145 West 86th St., New York, N.Y. 10024.

CAREER: Pratt Institute, Brooklyn, N.Y., associate professor of English, 1972—. *Military service:* U.S. Army, 1968-70.

MEMBER: P. E. N., Teachers and Writers Collaborative, National Writers Union, National Council of Teachers of English.

AWARDS, HONORS: New Jersey State Council on the Arts Award, 1980, for fiction; citation from New Jersey Writers Conference, 1985, for *Montgomery's Children*.

WRITINGS:

NOVELS

Changes, Bobbs-Merrill, 1974.
Montgomery's Children, Harcourt, 1984.

Contributor of articles and short stories to magazines, including *Essence*, *Black World*, *Southern Review*, *Black Creation*, and *Snakeroots*.

WORK IN PROGRESS: A novel, *Carla's Book*, completion expected in 1986.

SIDELIGHTS: Richard Perry's first novel, *Changes,* casts a black university teacher, Bill Taylor, as the protagonist. Recognizing that the circumstances of his own life have made him a part of the white man's world, Taylor still feels the need to be more involved in the fight for black rights. He does nothing, however, to act on those feelings, and his inaction "plays a crucial part in his growing dissatisfaction," suggested a *New York Times Book Review* critic. Taylor's ambivalent loyalties serve to compound his dilemma when he falls under the hypnotic spell of a mad scientist scheming to eliminate the white race by using a serum to turn white skin black. The novel examines one man's "admirably unpretentious struggle for self-definition," commented the reviewer in the *New York Times Book Review,* and raises the questions "about black men like Bill Taylor who try to resist apocalyptic solutions." "What is best about the book," the critic contended, "is its depiction of a conscientious man who fears he is doing less than he can."

In his second novel, *Montgomery's Children,* Perry focuses on several black families, mostly southern transplants seeking a share of World War II prosperity, and the changes that they undergo in the fictitious central New York town of Montgomery. As the story progresses from its 1948 beginnings through the next three decades towards its 1980 climax, the idyllic life these families have known is shattered as one after another of the evils of modern civilization—overcrowding, drugs, and crime—affects them and their offspring. Of the various characters in *Montgomery's Children,* representing two generations of black residents, three dominate the story—Norman Fillis, a middle-aged janitor who becomes both madman and prophet, foretelling the corruption and violence that will visit the townspeople; young Gerald Fletcher, so emotionally crippled by the brutal treatment he received as a child from his father that he eventually withdraws completely from life; and Gerald's girlfriend, Josephine Moore, also a victim of paternal abuse, both physical and sexual, who suffers first imprisonment for the murder of her father and, later, self-imposed exile.

Perry gained praise for *Montgomery's Children,* particularly for his delineation of character and his choice of language. Charles R. Larson, in his review for the *Detroit News,* lauded the novel for its "rich panorama of eccentric personalities." Critic Whitney Balliett of the *New Yorker* opined that Perry's narrative "has many voices, all of them original and patient and unflinching," complimented the author on "a good ear and a nice oral prose sense," and assessed *Montgomery's Children* as "a comic novel, a realistic novel, a light-handed fantasy, a vivid testament to what black people, kept low for so long, still suffer."

Additionally, critic John Kissell of the *Los Angeles Times Book Review* noted that "Perry draws his characters, even the less admirable, with compassion and insight," and Mel Watkins, reviewer for the *New York Times Book Review,* found the novel "studded with memorable characters . . . drawn in rich, evocative prose in which the comic and surreal are nicely balanced." Watkins capsulized *Montgomery's Children* as "an impressive novel about the evils of modernism and the redemptive powers of the spirit" and called Perry "an extremely talented writer whose work bears watching."

Perry told *CA:* "Writing is for me as necessary as loving; in fact, I would argue that writing *is* an act of love. Writing grew out of reading; as a child I decided that I wanted to be able to provide for myself the pleasure that books gave to me. Ulti-

mately, along with the strong urge to tell stories, the recognition that writing is a way of ordering experience is the primary reason that I write."

AVOCATIONAL INTERESTS: Tennis, golf.

BIOGRAPHICAL/CRITICAL SOURCES:

PERIODICALS

Bestsellers, April 1984.
Detroit News, February 5, 1984.
Los Angeles Times Book Review, February 19, 1984.
New Yorker, February 6, 1984.
New York Times Book Review, August 5, 1984.
Village Voice, April 17, 1984.

*   *   *

PETGEN, Dorothea   1903(?)-1985
(Dorothy Petgen)

OBITUARY NOTICE: Born c. 1903; died March 23, 1985, in New York, N.Y. Singer, actress, and author. Petgen began her singing career in Germany after World War I. In the United States she became an actress in road companies and on the New York stage. During the 1930's she appeared in such plays as "Plumes in the Dust" and "The School for Husbands." Under the name Dorothy Petgen, she collaborated with Herbert L. May on writing *Leisure and Its Use: Some International Observations.*

OBITUARIES AND OTHER SOURCES:

PERIODICALS

New York Times, March 25, 1985.

*   *   *

PETGEN, Dorothy
See PETGEN, Dorothea

*   *   *

PETTY, Anne C(otton)   1945-

PERSONAL: Born May 21, 1945, in Panama City, Fla.; daughter of William Albert (an accountant) and Clara Louise (a housewife; maiden name, Tucker) Cotton; married William Howard Petty (a computer systems software administrator), June 6, 1964; children: April Anne. *Education:* Florida State University, B.A., 1966, M.A., 1970, Ph.D., 1972. *Politics:* Liberal. *Religion:* Anglican.

ADDRESSES: Home—Route 3, Box 240-P, Crawfordville, Fla. 32327. *Office*—Center for Instructional Development, Florida State University, Tallahassee, Fla. 32306.

CAREER: High school teacher of English, journalism, and art history and director of art department in Panama City, Fla., 1966-67; Municipal Code Corp., Tallahassee, Fla., proofreader, 1971-72; Florida State University, Tallahassee, project editor at Center for Educational Technology, 1973-75, editorial assistant at Career Education Curriculum Laboratory, 1975; State of Florida, Tallahasee, publications consultant to Bureau of Comprehensive Planning, Division of State Planning, 1975-76; free-lance editorial consultant in Tallahassee, 1976-79; *Tennessee Street Rag,* Tallahassee, correspondent and feature writer, 1980; Florida State University, executive assistant in Office of the Regents Professor, 1980-84, administrative and technical assistant at Center for Color Graphics, 1982-84, research associate, writer, and editor at Center for Instructional Development and editor of *Lifeline* quarterly, 1984—. Piano tuner, 1974—. Promotional writer and member of board of directors of Tallahassee Symphony Association; ballet teacher; Tallahassee Civic Ballet, soloist, 1979-82, assistant artistic director, 1980, president of board of directors, 1983-84, vice-president, 1984-85; teacher at Senior Citizens Dance Therapy Workshops, 1980-82.

MEMBER: National Writers Club, Association for Educational Communications and Technology, State Dance Association of Florida, Florida Freelance Writers Association, Florida Folklore Society (past publicity chairman), Tallahassee Non-Fiction Writers Association, Tallahasse Young Men's Christian Association (YMCA; member of fitness board).

WRITINGS:

(Contributor) Russell Reaver, editor, *Emerson: Collected Essays,* Florida State University Press, 1971.
(With James F. Wilkey) *Principles of Learning: Programmed Text,* Center for Educational Technology, Florida State University, 1974.
One Ring to Bind Them: Tolkien's Mythology, University of Alabama Press, 1984.
(Contributor) *Selected Readings: Growing Up and Growing Old,* Florida Endowment for the Humanities, 1984.

Author of Microcomputer-Controlled Videodisc (MCIV) scripts for "Acids, Bases, and You" and other non-commercial television series.

Also author of copy for computer color graphics calendar series "Beauties of Mathematics," Center for Color Graphics, Florida State University, 1984. Contributor of articles, stories, and poems to magazines, including *North Florida Living,* and newspapers.

WORK IN PROGRESS: The Elfbook, children's fairy tales, for publication by Ferret Books; research for a book on Florida's lifestyles and folklore; research paper on computers in education and art; research paper on Microcomputer-Controlled Videodisc (MCIV) as an education medium.

SIDELIGHTS: Anne C. Petty told *CA:* "I seem to have a strong streak of whimsy that likes to grab an idea and let it create itself on paper that day, before it gets away. Not all of my work is like this, of course. My book on Tolkien, for example, took several years of careful deliberation, and other scholarly pieces were chewed at great length before they took shape in print. But I prefer light writing—children's material, jingles, riddles, puns, and writing for popular magazines.

"Lately I've become fascinated with writing for the educational medium of computers. Writing scripts for MCIV—where live tape sequences, slides, computer graphics, and the techniques for looping, branching, and multiple access are at the writer's disposal—is like constructing a maze of mythic proportions. I love puzzle solving and wordplay and find that this type of media technology appeals to those inclinations. Television scriptwriting, whether commercial or non-broadcast, requires a certain fatal attraction for self-abuse—one wonders why one does it, but one keeps on doing more!"

* * *

PFEFFER, Rose   1908-1985

OBITUARY NOTICE: Born September 9, 1908, near Chem-

nitz, Germany (now Karl-Marx-Stadt, East Germany); died following a heart attack, February 27, 1985, in New York, N.Y. Educator and author. Pfeffer, considered an authority on German philosopher Friedrich Nietzsche, had been a professor emeritus of philosophy at Long Island's Dowling University since 1977. After earning a doctorate from Columbia University in 1963, she taught at both Rutgers University and Brooklyn College; she joined the faculty of Dowling University in 1966. Pfeffer also became known as a leading advocate of the use of Socratic dialogue in teaching gifted children, and during the 1930's she was a proponent of the Planned Parenthood movement. In 1972 Pfeffer published a book, *Nietzsche: Disciple of Dionysus.* She also contributed articles to professional journals.

OBITUARIES AND OTHER SOURCES:

BOOKS

Directory of American Scholars, Volume IV, *Philosophy, Religion, and Law,* 7th edition, Bowker, 1978.

PERIODICALS

New York Times, February 28, 1985.

* * *

PFLAUM, Irving Peter   1906-1985

OBITUARY NOTICE—See index for *CA* sketch: Born April 9, 1906, in Chicago, Ill.; died April 24, 1985, in Alicante, Spain. Attorney, journalist, educator, and author. Best known as an expert on Latin America, Pflaum covered the Spanish Civil War for the United Press (now United Press International) during the late 1930's and subsequently served the *Chicago Times* (later *Chicago Sun-Times*) as foreign editor for nearly twenty-five years. His books on Cuba and Latin America include *Tragic Island: Communism in Cuba, Arena of Decision: Latin America in Crisis,* and, with Rufo Lopez-Fresquet, *My Fourteen Months With Castro.* Pflaum, who was admitted to the Illinois bar in 1930 and practiced law for several years, also worked variously as a syndicated newspaper columnist, a radio and television commentator, and a teacher at Inter-American University in Puerto Rico and at Northwestern University. He had been living in Spain, in retirement, since 1973.

OBITUARIES AND OTHER SOURCES:

PERIODICALS

Chicago Tribune, April 26, 1985.

* * *

PHELPS, Frederic
See McCULLEY, Johnston

* * *

PHILLIPS, E(ugene) Lee   1941-

PERSONAL: Born October 13, 1941, in St. Joseph, Mo.; son of Samuel Maxwell (a grocer) and Eulah (Sanders) Phillips. *Education:* Southwest Baptist College, A.A., 1961; Howard Payne College, B.A., 1963; Southwestern Baptist Theological Seminary, B.D. and M.R.E., both 1968; attended Institute of Religion at Texas Medical Center, 1968-69, and Southern Baptist Theological Seminary, 1974; Vanderbilt University, D.Min., 1976.

ADDRESSES: *Home*—792 Marstevan Dr. N.E., Atlanta, Ga. 30306.

CAREER: Ordained Baptist minister, June 9, 1968; Memorial Hospital, Houston, Tex., chaplain-intern, 1968-69; part-time nursing home chaplain and substitute schoolteacher in Louisville, Ky., 1970-73; Crescent Hill Baptist Church, Louisville, assistant to the pastor, 1973-74; First Presbyterian Church, Mt. Pleasant, Tenn., guest minister, 1975-76; supply preacher for churches in the Nashville, Tenn., area, 1976-77; writer, 1978—. Guest lecturer and preacher.

AWARDS, HONORS: Merit award from Dixie Council of Authors and Journalists, 1982, for *Prayers for Our Day.*

WRITINGS:

Prayers for Worship, Word Books, 1979.
Prayers for Our Day, John Knox, 1982.

Contributor of prayers to anthologies and annuals, including *Rejoice*, edited by Ronald E. Garman, Word Books, 1982; *The International Lessons Annual*, edited by Horace R. Weaver, Abingdon, 1983 and 1984; and *The Minister's Manual*, edited by James Cox, Harper, 1984 and 1985. Contributor of articles to periodicals, including *alive now!, Pulpit Digest, These Days,* and *Vista.*

WORK IN PROGRESS: *Ponderations: A Creative Form of Devotion; Breaking Silence Before the Lord*, a book of worship prayers; *Atlanta, How I Love You, How I Love You;* also writing short stories.

SIDELIGHTS: According to *Atlanta Journal and Constitution* writer Celestine Sibley, E. Lee Phillips's prayer collection *Prayers for Our Day* "is being highly praised by such diverse critics as Dr. Norman Vincent Peale and the former archbishop of Canterbury." Sibley added her own praise, noting that "there are some very moving passages in this little book."

Phillips told *CA:* "I have no idea what I will write until I sit down to write it. Of course, I try to stay within the subject area, but that has never prevented other kinds of totally unrelated writing from emerging. I may sit down to write religious poetry and come out with a dialogue from a fading English actress of the nineteenth century. It happens. Mine is the responsibility of releasing the voices that speak.

"I write a book until the book writes me. When that happens the lines often come unbidden—in the middle of the night, just when I wake up, quite often at intersections on my way to lunch when the traffic light turns from red to green!

"I am nocturnal and after supper until the wee hours there is no stopping me. I don't look at blank paper; I fill it up quickly by longhand. Then the writing is in the rewriting. It is a process of winnowing out the unnecessary until the lean crisp lines, alive with meaning, bring the page to life, gripping writer and reader. Great writing is not the use of extraordinary words in an ordinary way, but the extraordinary use of ordinary words.

"I've so many characters yet unborn, so many poems waiting to be birthed, so many truths looking for a plot to wrap around. The mind races onward and the heart overflows. I cannot not write.

"Poets have existed in my family for many generations, and I often think and write in pentameter. I study books on psychiatry."

AVOCATIONAL INTERESTS: Travel, floriculture.

BIOGRAPHICAL/CRITICAL SOURCES:

PERIODICALS

Atlanta Journal and Constitution, July 14, 1979, October 2, 1982, December 18, 1983.
Chronicle (Anderson, S.C.), November 16, 1983.

*   *   *

PHILLPOTTS, (Mary) Adelaide Eden 1896- (Mary Adelaide Eden Ross)

PERSONAL: Born 1896, in Ealing, England; daughter of Eden (an author) and Emily (Topham) Phillpotts; married Nicholas Ross (an artist; died July 28, 1967). *Education:* Attended Bedford College, London, 1921-22. *Politics:* Labour. *Religion:* "Humanism."

ADDRESSES: *Home*—Cobblestones, Kilkhampton, Bude, Cornwall EX23 9QW, England. *Agent*—Hughes Massie Ltd., 31 Southampton Row, London WC1B 4HL, England.

CAREER: Writer, 1916—. Secretary at Women's Service Bureau, London, England, 1917-18, and G. K. Ogden, Cambridge, England, 1918; worked in Red Cross hospitals, 1914-16.

WRITINGS:

Illyrion and Other Poems, Palmer & Hayward, 1916.
Man: A Fable, Constable, 1922.
A Song of Man, Linden Press, 1959.
Panorama of the World (travel book), R. Hale, 1969.
Reverie (autobiography), R. Hale, 1981.

Also author of works under name Mary Adelaide Eden Ross.

NOVELS

The Friend, Heinemann, 1923.
Lodgers in London, Butterworth & Co., 1925, Little, Brown, 1926.
Tomek the Sculptor, Little, Brown, 1927.
A Marriage, Butterworth & Co., 1928.
The Atoning Years, Butterworth & Co., 1929.
Yellow Sands (novelization of the play of the same name by Eden and Adelaide Eden Phillpotts [see below]), Chapman & Hall, 1930.
The Youth of Jacob Ackner, Benn, 1931.
The Founder of Shandon, Benn, 1932.
The Growing World, Hutchinson, 1934.
Onward Journey, Hutchinson, 1936.
Broken Allegiance, Hutchinson, 1937.
What's Happened to Rankin?, Rich & Cowan, 1939.
The Round of Life, Rich & Cowan, 1939.
Laugh With Me, Rich & Cowan, 1941.
Our Little Town, Rich & Cowan, 1942.
From Jane to John, Rich & Cowan, 1943.
The Adventurers, Rich & Cowan, 1944.
The Lodestar, Rich & Cowan, 1946.
The Fosterling, Rich & Cowan, 1949.
Stubborn Earth, Rich & Cowan, 1951.

PLAYS

Arachne (in verse), Palmer & Hayward, 1920.
Savitri the Faithful (in verse; one-act), Gowans & Gray, 1923.
Camillus and the Schoolmaster (in verse; one-act), Gowans & Gray, 1923.
Akhnaton (in prose and verse), Butterworth & Co., 1926.

(With father, Eden Phillpotts) *Yellow Sands* (three-act comedy [see above]; first produced in London, England, at Haymarket Theatre, 1926), Duckworth, 1926.
(With E. Phillpotts) *The Good Old Days* (three-act comedy), Duckworth, 1932.

EDITOR

Letters From John Cooper Powys to Nicholas Ross, Bertramrota, 1971.
A Wild Flower Wreath (autobiography), privately printed, 1974.

WORK IN PROGRESS: Two novels.

SIDELIGHTS: Adelaide Eden Phillpotts told *CA* that her father's encouragement was important to her career, and she advises all aspiring writers simply to write. Phillpotts added: "I have lived through three wars in which this land has engaged. I have worked for peace, with little hope for the future so long as arms trading goes on between nations."

AVOCATIONAL INTERESTS: Human relationships, art, nature, travel.

*   *   *

PIGGOTT, (Alan) Derek   1923-

PERSONAL: Born December 27, 1923, in Chadwell Heath, England. *Education:* Attended grammar school in Sutton County, England.

ADDRESSES: Office—Lasham Gliding Centre, near Alton, Hampshire, England. *Agent*—A.P. Watt Ltd., 26/28 Bedford Row, London WC1R 4HL, England.

CAREER: Lasham Gliding Centre, near Alton, England, chief flying instructor, 1954—. Lecturer on film flying, gliding, and soaring, with lecture tours in the United States, the Netherlands, and Australia. Stunt pilot for films, including "Those Magnificent Men and Their Flying Machines," "Blue Max," "Darling Lilli," "Red Baron," "Villa Rides," and "Skywards"; test pilot (gliders and light aircraft); instructor training specialist. *Military service:* Royal Air Force, pilot and instructor, 1942-45.

AWARDS, HONORS: Queen's Commendation.

WRITINGS:

Gliding: A Handbook on Soaring Flight, A. & C. Black, 1958.
Beginning Gliding, A. & C. Black, 1975.
Understanding Gliding, A. & C. Black, 1977.
Delta Papa: A Life of Flying (autobiography), Pelham, 1977.
Going Solo, A. & C. Black, 1978.

Author of scripts for a tape cassette series on gliding and soaring.

*   *   *

PIKE, William H.   1943-

PERSONAL: Born March 5, 1943, in Boston, Mass.; son of George M. (a physician) and Frances (a nurse; maiden name, Yarchin) Pike; married Karen Fischer (an art teacher), November 24, 1979; children: Benjamin David. *Education:* Massachusetts Institute of Technology, B.S., 1965; Columbia University, M.B.A., 1967.

ADDRESSES: Office—Fidelity Investments, 82 Devonshire St., Boston, Mass. 02109.

CAREER: Associated with Old Colony Trust, 1967-69, and Boston Co., 1969-71; Fidelity Investments, Boston, Mass., securities analyst, 1972-81, portfolio manager and vice-president of Fidelity High Income Fund, 1981—.

WRITINGS:

Why Stocks Go Up (and Down), Dow Jones-Irwin, 1983.

SIDELIGHTS: William H. Pike commented: "I am appalled by the quality of some investment books that have become best-sellers simply due to catchy titles and media hype. While there are no 'Ten Easy Steps to Millions,' I do believe that success in the stock market is attainable for almost anybody willing to devote sufficient time and energy.

"My book is the outgrowth of an introductory course I teach for the Boston Security Analyst Society. The course, like the book, is a primer for people interested in stock investing who have no prior knowledge of the subject but are willing to do some heavy reading.

"A future objective of mine is to write an analogous book to help novice readers/investors understand and interpret economic news without the ideological veneer imposed by the media."

*   *   *

PIKOULIS, John   1941-

PERSONAL: Surname is pronounced *Pick*-o-lis; born January 21, 1941, in Selukwe, Rhodesia (now Zimbabwe); son of Nicholas and Afrula (Petrakis) Pikoulis; married Lorraine Maxine Whiteman (an antiques dealer), June 9, 1969; children: Eliot, Zelda, Anna. *Education:* University of Cape Town, B.A., 1961, B.A. (with honors), 1962; Oxford University, Diploma in Education, 1964; University of Leicester, M.A., 1968; University of Wales, Ph.D., 1974.

ADDRESSES: Home—16 Station Rd., Dinas Powis, South Glamorgan, Wales. *Office*—Department of Extra-Mural Studies, University of Wales, University College, 38/40 Park Pl., Cardiff, Wales.

CAREER: University of Wales, University College, Cardiff, 1969—, became senior lecturer, 1984.

WRITINGS:

The Art of William Faulkner, Macmillan, 1982.
(Editor) *Alun Lewis: A Miscellany of His Writing,* Poetry Wales Press, 1982.
Alun Lewis: A Life, Poetry Wales Press, 1984.

Contributor to British and American journals.

WORK IN PROGRESS: Cartooning Auden, a critical study of W. H. Auden.

SIDELIGHTS: John Pikoulis told *CA:* "Americans may not realize this, but there is a remarkable resistancy in Britain as to some of America's greatest writers—in the twentieth century, Faulkner and Wallace Stevens are two of the worst blind spots. When I came to write my study of Faulkner, I reflected with some awe on the fact that mine would be only the second book to be published on him in England—a shameful and surprising fact. But then insularity is to be expected of an island, and fought against. Imagine a generation of students passing through not knowing Faulkner's rich, darkly imaginative works of the 1930's!

"Alun Lewis was another intriguing case of a potentially great writer smothered in obscurity (even more complete, I imagine, in America than in England). Most of his work is now out of print, and the circumstances of his life remained tantalizingly obscure when I began to write about him, so I decided to press ahead with his biography, the first to be written despite the fact that he died in 1944.

"I mentioned Lewis's obscurity in America, but I should say that John Berryman early recognized Lewis's gift and wrote a memorial poem to him which, I believe, contributed to Berryman's better known tribute to Ann Bradstreet, which followed shortly after. I ruefully record the fact that the poem remains uncollected and, apparently, unknown to the wider reading public.

"W. H. Auden, my next subject, is (by way of contrast) very well known to all and sundry. But why did he write the way he did? And how did the manner of his poetry reflect on its matter? How political really was he, and how playful? Not easy questions to answer, but I believe the clue lies in the similarity that exits between his work (especially the poems and dramas of the 1920's and '30's) and cartooning and caricaturing in general.

"Hence *Cartooning Auden,* which I am working on presently. The political cartoon as we know it today—and its near relation, the cinema cartoon—both came into their own in Auden's youth and early manhood, so it is not surprising that they should have influenced his work. How exactly they did so I hope to show in detail in the book.

"And then? To argue that the great war poet of 1914 to 1918 was not Wilfred Owen (Yeats was right about *him*) but Edward Thomas. And that Alun Lewis was his continuation by other means during the Second World War. And that Lewis tempered Auden's style and was the instrumental factor in effecting the transition of English poetry from the 1930's to the '50's.''

BIOGRAPHICAL/CRITICAL SOURCES:

PERIODICALS

Times Literary Suplement, September 28, 1984.

*   *   *

PIOWATY, Kim Kennelly   1957-

PERSONAL: Born September 7, 1957, in Spokane, Wash.; daughter of Thomas A. (a teacher) and Mikell Williams (a leasing agent; maiden name, O'Neil) Kennelly; married Timothy W. Piowaty (an insurance agent), September 6, 1975; children: Tara Marie, Katherine Deirdre. *Education:* University of Florida, B.A., 1977; also attended University of North Florida. *Religion:* Episcopalian.

ADDRESSES: Home—703 Milan Court, Altamonte Springs, Fla. 32714.

CAREER: W. C. Cherry Elementary School, Clay County, Fla., reading specialist, 1979-80; writer.

WRITINGS:

Don't Look in Her Eyes (juvenile novel), Atheneum, 1983.

Contributor to local newspapers.

WORK IN PROGRESS: Research on statistics and case histories dealing with runaway girls.

SIDELIGHTS: Kim Kennelly Piowaty told *CA:* "I began my novel as a short story in a creative writing class at the University of Florida when I was nineteen. At the same time my younger brother and sister and I were attempting to help our father, who had had a complete psychotic breakdown. I am the oldest of five children, and all of us had lived with only my father since I was fourteen. I think my drive to see my short story through to completion as a novel was in part due to my own need to understand and deal with my father's mental illness.''

*   *   *

PLANCK, Max (Karl Ernst Ludwig)   1858-1947

BRIEF ENTRY: Born April 23, 1858, in Kiel, Germany (now West Germany); died October 4 (one source says October 3), 1947, in Goettingen, West Germany. German physicist, philosopher, and author. Planck's development of quantum theory in 1900 became the dividing line between classical and modern physics. Quantum theory, based on Planck's observations of the thermodynamics of electromagnetic radiation, postulated that energy is not infinitely divisible but is comprised of "particles" or "bits" (which Planck termed quanta), the size of which is determined by the frequency of the electromagnetic radiation in question.

Quantum theory made possible the subsequent work of Niels Bohr, who in 1913 employed quantum theory in his work on the structure of the atom, and Albert Einstein. Planck was one of the first to recognize the genius of Einstein's special theory of relativity and was responsible for bringing Einstein to the University of Berlin in 1914. Planck received the Nobel Prize for his quantum theory in 1918. He retired ten years later and devoted his time to writing on general subjects, including philosophy and religion. During World War II Planck was distressed by the Nazi persecution of his Jewish friends and colleagues and unsuccessfully attempted to dissuade Hitler. Planck's writings in English translation include *Where Is Science Going?* (1932), *The Philosophy of Physics* (1936), and the five-volume *Introduction to Theoretical Physics* (1949).

BIOGRAPHICAL/CRITICAL SOURCES:

BOOKS

Asimov's Biographical Encyclopedia of Science and Technology, Avon, 1976.
Dictionary of Scientific Biography, Scribner, 1970.
McGraw-Hill Encyclopedia of World Biography, McGraw, 1973.
1000 Makers of the Twentieth Century, David & Charles, 1971.
Who Was Who in America, With World Notables, Volume IV: *1961-1968,* Marquis, 1968.

*   *   *

PLECK, Elizabeth Hafkin   1945-

BRIEF ENTRY: Born September 20, 1945. American historian, educator, and author. Pleck taught U.S. history at University of Michigan from 1973 to 1978. She then became a research associate at Wellesley College's Center for Research on Women. Pleck was also a visiting associate professor at Massachusetts Institute of Technology in 1982. She wrote *Black Migration and Poverty: Boston, 1865-1900* (Academic Press, 1979). Pleck co-edited *A Heritage of Her Own: Toward a New Social History of American Women* (Simon & Schuster, 1979) and *The American Man* (Prentice-Hall, 1980). *Address:* Center for Research on Women, Wellesley College, Wellesley, Mass. 02181.

BIOGRAPHICAL/CRITICAL SOURCES:

PERIODICALS

Washington Post Book World, January 27, 1980.

*   *   *

PLUNKET, Robert 1945-

PERSONAL: Born May 17, 1945, in Greenville, Tex.; son of John T. (in business) and Dolores (an art historian; maiden name, Nagoda) Plunket. *Education:* Williams College, B.A., 1967; Sarah Lawrence College, M.F.A., 1971; University of California, Los Angeles, M.B.A., 1976.

ADDRESSES: Home—Paseo Lomas Altas 368, Mexico City, Mexico 11950. *Agent*—Jay Julien, 1501 Broadway, New York, N.Y. 10036.

CAREER: Loft Film and Theatre Center, Bronxville, N.Y., teacher of film, 1968-71; New York State Council on the Arts, New York City, grants officer, 1975-81; Ruby Movies, New York City, story editor, 1981-83.

AWARDS, HONORS: Hutchinson fellowship from Williams College, 1967; Shubert fellowship from Sarah Lawrence College, 1971.

WRITINGS:

My Search for Warren Harding, Knopf, 1983.
Love Junkie (novel), Knopf, 1985.

PLAYS

"Mojave Confidential" (one-act), first produced in Los Angeles at La Mama Hollywood, 1976.
"Women at Work" (one-act), first produced in New York City at the New York Theatre Ensemble, 1972.

OTHER

Author of "The Sexual Elite" and "Devil With a Blue Dress." Also author of numerous video and audio productions.

SIDELIGHTS: My Search for Warren Harding is Robert Plunket's spoof on an aspiring academician's attempts at tracking down rare memorabilia which belonged to former President Warren Harding. Plunket's hero believes he has located the late president's former mistress. To gain access to her home and her rumored cache of presidential treasures, the hero rents an apartment from her and romances her portly granddaughter. Paul Gray, writing in *Time,* called the book's debut "riotous" and praised Plunket for establishing "the kind of moral guidelines essential to classical comedy."

Plunket told *CA:* "I'm not really a writer; I'm just a person with a lot of axes to grind. My idol is Paul Harvey, the radio commentator. How I wish I could get my own radio show! Then I could attract much more attention with much less effort. It would be a call-in format. I would give people advice and then force them to listen to records I like."

BIOGRAPHICAL/CRITICAL SOURCES:

PERIODICALS

Gentleman's Quarterly, August, 1983.
New Yorker, May 2, 1983.
Time, July 25, 1983.

Times Literary Supplement, July 27, 1984.

*   *   *

POLIVY, Janet 1951-

PERSONAL: Born February 9, 1951, in New York, N.Y.; daughter of Calvin (an attorney and judge) and Bernice (a real estate manager; maiden name, Malat) Polivy; married C. Peter Herman (a professor of psychology), August 3, 1975; children: Lisa Cesia, Eric Murray. *Education:* Tufts University, B.S. (magna cum laude), 1971; Northwestern University, M.A., 1973, Ph.D., 1974.

ADDRESSES: Home—Toronto, Ontario, Canada. *Office*—Department of Psychology, Erindale College, University of Toronto, Mississauga, Ontario, Canada L5L 1C6.

CAREER: Loyola University of Chicago, Chicago, Ill., assistant professor of psychology, 1974-76; University of Toronto, Toronto, Ontario, visiting assistant professor of psychology, 1976-77; Clarke Institute of Psychiatry, Toronto, research associate in psychosomatic medicine unit, 1976-83; University of Toronto, Erindale College, Mississauga, Ontario, associate professor of psychology and psychiatry, 1977—. Scientist with Addiction Research Foundation of Ontario; research associate in psychiatry at Toronto General Hospital, 1982—; member of obesity treatment advisory panel of Federal Ministry of Health, 1983—.

MEMBER: American Psychological Association, Association for the Advancement of Behavior Therapy, Society for Psychotherapy Research, Midwestern Psychological Association.

AWARDS, HONORS: U.S. Public Health Services fellowship, 1971-74; Grants from Ontario Mental Health Foundation, 1977-78, Social Sciences and Humanities Research Council of Canada, 1979-80, 1983-85, and Natural Sciences and Engineering Research Council of Canada, 1979-82, 1982-84.

WRITINGS:

(Editor with Kirk Blankstein and Patricia Pliner, and contributor) *Advances in the Study of Communication and Affect: Assessment and Modification of Emotional Behavior,* Plenum, Volume VI, 1980, Volume VII, 1982.
(With husband, C. Peter Herman) *Breaking the Diet Habit: The Natural Weight Alternative,* Basic Books, 1983.

CONTRIBUTOR

A. J. Stunkard, editor, *Obesity: Basic Mechanisms and Treatment,* Saunders, 1980.
Stunkard and Elliot Stellar, editors, *Eating and Its Disorders,* Raven Press, 1983.
P. L. Darby, P. E. Garfinkel, and D. M. Garner, editors, *Anorexia Nervosa: Recent Developments,* Alan R. Liss, 1983.
R. C. Hawkins, W. J. Fremoux, and P. F. Clement, editors, *Binge Eating: Theory, Research, and Treatment,* Springer, 1984.
H. B. Roback, editor, *Group Interventions With Medical-Surgical Patients and Their Families,* Jossey-Bass, 1984.
Herman, M. P. Zanna, and E. T. Higgins, editors, *Physical Appearance, Stigma, and Social Behavior,* L. S. Erlbaum Associates, in press.

Also contributor to *Advances in Behavioral Medicine,* edited by E. S. Katkin and S. B. Manuck, in press.

Contributor of articles and reviews to journals in the behavioral sciences. *Journal of Personality,* member of editorial board, 1979-81, associate editor, 1981—.

Consulting editor of *Journal of Abnormal Psychology,* 1981—.

WORK IN PROGRESS: Articles about the communication of emotion, to be published in scientific journals; research on "the effect of 'hot' versus 'cold' cognitions on amount eaten by restrained and unrestrained eaters"; research on changes in emotional responses over the course of psychotherapy.

SIDELIGHTS: Janet Polivy told *CA:* "My work began to focus on eating disorders because of the research I have been doing with my husband, C. Peter Herman, on dieting and eating. Since I am a clinical psychologist, I began receiving referrals of eating-disordered patients and soon found that my clinical practice was made up primarily of such patients. There seems to have been an upsurge of eating disorders of all types in the last decade or so, possibly contributed to by society's obsession with appearance and idealization of thinness for women. Cognitive-behavioral treatments that combine changes in thinking with increased awareness and acceptance of feelings seem to offer the most help for eating disorders—although there are no sure cures.

"My 1983 book, *Breaking the Diet Habit,* which I wrote with Herman, is an attempt to raise people's consciousness about the downside of dieting, the problems it causes, and the ones it as often as not fails to solve, so that people will be more aware of what they are doing and will make a more informed decision about whether or not to tamper with their weight and eating habits.

"My work on emotion is another area I have been pursuing for several years. I think awareness of emotions is critical both for interpersonal relationships and for one's own well-being. Many of my eating-disorder patients need to be trained to recognize and act on their own feelings. Often they find that their eating problems improve when they begin to accept their emotions and act on the basis of them."

*　　*　　*

POMEROY, John H(oward)   1918-1985

OBITUARY NOTICE: Born March 5, 1918, in St. Petersburg, Fla.; died of cardiac arrest, March 15, 1985, in Bethesda, Md. Scientist, editor, and author. Pomeroy, an organic chemist, participated in the development of the first commercially successful concentrated orange juice in 1938. In the following year Pomeroy researched the chemistry of uranium for the Manhattan Project, which developed the first atomic bomb. He received a doctorate in organic chemistry from Massachusetts Institute of Technology in 1949 and began working for the Argonne National Laboratory. Leaving that post in 1960, Pomeroy went to Washington, D.C., where he served for six years with the Atomic Energy Commission as program manager in chemistry. From 1967 to 1970 he was senior editor in physical sciences for *Encyclopaedia Britannica,* before joining the staff of the National Aeronautics and Space Administration (NASA). At NASA Pomeroy managed the international research programs on moon rocks gathered during Apollo space flights. He served on the staff of the National Academy of Sciences' Committee on Radioactive Waste Management from 1977 until his retirement in 1980. He was author of *Science,* an adult education textbook.

OBITUARIES AND OTHER SOURCES:

BOOKS

American Men and Women in Science: The Physical and Biological Sciences, 15th edition, Bowker, 1982.

PERIODICALS

Washington Post, March 20, 1985.

*　　*　　*

POOLE, Herbert Edmund   1912-1984

OBITUARY NOTICE: Born June 8, 1912, in Southgate, Middlesex, England; died December 22, 1984. Book designer, editor, journalist, and author. Poole worked as a journalist for several years before winning a scholarship to Cambridge University at the age of twenty-three, and he published his first book, an edition of lore by Andrew Boorde, while still a student. He also served as editor of the Cambridge *Democrat* from 1935 to 1938. After graduation Poole became chief education officer of the Worker's Education Association (WEA) and in that capacity developed an interest in typography and book production. He designed many publications for the association, and he also established one of the first extra-curricular courses at the University of London, titled "The Art of the Book." Leaving the WEA in 1960, Poole became production manager for the publishing firm Chatto & Windus. His writings include *Perspectives for Countrymen* and *The Teaching of English in the Worker's Education Association.* Poole also edited Charles Burney's *Music, Men and Manners in France and Italy, 1770.* A book on the history of music printing and publishing remained unfinished at the time of his death.

OBITUARIES AND OTHER SOURCES:

BOOKS

Who Was Who Among English and European Authors, 1931-1949, Gale, 1978.

PERIODICALS

Times (London), December 28, 1984.

*　　*　　*

POOLEY, Roger   1947-

PERSONAL: Born June 19, 1947, in Watford, England; son of Francis Richard and Daisy (Felstead) Pooley. *Education:* Jesus College, Cambridge, B.A., 1969, Ph.D., 1977.

ADDRESSES: Home—227 Church Plantation Flats, Keele, Staffordshire ST5 5AX, England. *Office*—Department of English, University of Keele, Keele, Staffordshire ST5 5BG, England.

CAREER: University of Wales, University College, Swansea, lecturer in English, 1972-73; University of Keele, Keele, England, lecturer in English, 1973—. Visiting professor at University of Tulsa, 1983.

WRITINGS:

(Editor) *George Gascoigne: The Green Knight; Selected Poetry and Prose,* Carcanet, 1982.
Spiritual Autobiography: A Do It Yourself Guide, Grove, 1983.
(Editor with David Barratt) *Reading Literature: Some Christian Approaches,* Universities and Colleges Christian Fellowship, 1984.

(With Philip Seddon) *A Reader in Christian Spirituality,* Collins, in press.

WORK IN PROGRESS: The Plain Style: Sixteenth Century to the Present.

SIDELIGHTS: Roger Pooley told *CA:* "My Christian writing is mostly the result of collective endeavor. Both the autobiography booklet and the spirituality reader arise from my membership in the Grove Spirituality group, based at St. John's College, Nottingham; and the *Reading Literature* collection from a group of research students and academics which I chair attached to UCCF (Universities and Colleges Christian Fellowship).

"My contributions to both chart some of my efforts to build a Christian mind in the context of teaching and writing about literature. Even the more explicitly academic work on the plain style arose partly out of my interest in Puritan stylistic standards. But I suspect I'm more of a synthesizer than my Puritan heroes."

*   *   *

PORTER, Alan L(eslie)   1945-

PERSONAL: Born June 22, 1945, in Jersey City, N.J.; son of Leslie Frank (an engineer) and Alice M. (a housewife; maiden name, Kaufman) Porter; married Claudia L. Ferrey (a speech therapist), June 14, 1968; children: Brett, Douglas, Lynn. *Education:* California Institute of Technology, B.S., 1967; University of California, Los Angeles, M.A., 1968, Ph.D., 1972.

ADDRESSES: Home—110 Lake Top Ct., Roswell, Ga. 30076. *Office*—School of Industrial and Systems Engineering, Georgia Institute of Technology, Atlanta, Ga. 30332. *Agent*—Heidi Lange, Sanford J. Greenburger Associates, 825 Third Ave., New York, N.Y. 10022.

CAREER: University of Washington, Seattle, research assistant professor of social management of technology, 1972-74; Georgia Institute of Technology, Atlanta, assistant professor, 1975-78, associate professor of industrial and systems engineering, 1978—, co-director of Technology Policy and Assessment Center, 1983—. Member of Transportation Research Board's Commission on Organization and Administration, 1974-76. *Military service:* U.S. Army Reserve, 1968-75; became first lieutenant.

MEMBER: International Association for Impact Assessment, American Psychological Association, American Association for the Advancement of Science, American Society for Engineering Education (chairman of Engineering and Public Policy Division, 1981-82), Institute of Electrical and Electronics Engineers, Systems, Man, and Cybernetics (chairman of Technical Forecasting Committee, 1981—).

AWARDS, HONORS: Grants from National Science Foundation, 1974-75, 1980-81, 1982-84, 1984-86, U.S. Department of Transportation, 1977-80, and Fund for the Improvement of Post Secondary Education, 1977-78.

WRITINGS:

(With Frederick A. Rossini, Stanley R. Carpenter, and A. Thomas Roper) *A Guidebook for Technology Assessment and Impact Analysis,* North-Holland, 1980.
(Editor with Thomas J. Kuehn) *Science, Technology, and National Policy,* Cornell University Press, 1981.
(Editor with Rossini) *Integrated Impact Assessment,* Westview, 1983.

(With Robert M. Mason, J. David Roessner, Frederick A. Rossini, and A. Perry Schwartz) *The Impact of Office Automation on Clerical Workers,* Greenwood Press, 1985.

Contributor to about fifty journals. Co-editor of *Impact Assessment Bulletin,* 1981-83.

WORK IN PROGRESS: Work Not, Want Not: The Coming Death of the Work Ethic.

SIDELIGHTS: Alan L. Porter informed *CA:* "My main professional interest lies in understanding the coming effects of technological change on society—technology assessment. A current concern involves the ways in which new information technology will alter the world of work.

"For the first time, society is automating more than one economic sector at a time. While robots and computers take over the factory, 'communications' automates the office and penetrates the service economy. German workers have dubbed these microelectronics job killers, and they are right. Tracking present policies and trends to just past the turn of the century leads to the conclusion of fifty million Americans (33 percent) unemployed.

"What can we do? Two approaches contrast with each other. One, a rear-guard action, fights to preserve every job. Failing that, it calls for government action to make work and to spread work (by restricting work hours and underground economic activity). In the end, it may call on the age-old cure for unemployment—war.

"The alternative approach gets rid of the work ethic. The Industrial Revolution created the notion that a man's worth resides in his job. Wealth came from labor, so man had to be convinced of the need to work for pay. The Information Age does not need this mass of workers, but how do we tell ourselves that?

"One vital step is to separate the means of production from the means of distributing wealth. Sharing a percentage of the industrial wealth could meet the basic human needs. Adding a free market for human services could provide economic incentive and remedy the horrors of welfare. Freed from the necessity of working to live, man and woman can develop their human potential in the directions they choose. Horizons dreamed of by the ancients open for us—if we can leave the work ethic behind."

*   *   *

PORTER, Sue
See LIMB, Sue

*   *   *

POSNER, Donald   1931-

BRIEF ENTRY: Born August 30, 1931, in New York, N.Y. American art historian, educator, and author. Posner began teaching at New York University in 1962; he was named Ailsa Mellon Bruce Professor of the History of Art in 1975. A fellow of the American Academy in Rome from 1959 to 1961, he also served as the academy's art historian in residence in 1968. Posner was awarded the Charles Rufus Morey Prize of the College Art Association of America in 1973. His books include *Seventeenth and Eighteenth Century Art: Baroque Painting, Sculpture, Architecture* (Abrams, 1971), *Annibale Carracci: A Study in the Reform of Italian Painting Around 1590*

(Phaidon, 1971), and *Watteau: "A Lady at Her Toilet"* (Viking, 1973). Posner edited the *Art Bulletin* from 1968 to 1971. *Address:* c/o Institute of Fine Arts, New York University, 1 East 78th St., New York, N.Y. 10021.

BIOGRAPHICAL/CRITICAL SOURCES:

BOOKS

Who's Who in America, 42nd edition, Marquis, 1982.

PERIODICALS

New York Times Book Review, December 2, 1973.
Times Literary Supplement, September 22, 1972, July 6, 1973.

*   *   *

POST, Jonathan F(rench) S(cott)   1947-

PERSONAL: Born May 11, 1947, in Rochester, N.Y.; son of Frederick W. (a lawyer) and Margaret S. (a teacher) Post; married Susan L. Gallick (a scholar), 1975; children: Jessica, Frederick. *Education:* Amherst College, A.B., 1970; University of Rochester, Ph.D., 1975.

ADDRESSES: Home—6906 Amestoy Ave., Van Nuys, Calif. 91406. *Office*—Department of English, 15 Rolfe, University of California, 405 Hilgard Ave., Los Angeles, Calif. 90024.

CAREER: Yale University, New Haven, Conn., assistant professor of English, 1975-80; University of California, Los Angeles, associate professor of English, 1980—.

AWARDS, HONORS: Fellow of Folger Shakespeare Library, 1974, and National Endowment for the Humanities, 1979-80; Guggenheim fellow, 1984-85.

WRITINGS:

Henry Vaughan: The Unfolding Vision, Princeton University Press, 1982.

Contributor to literature journals. Editor of *George Herbert Journal,* Volume VII, numbers 1 and 2, 1983.

WORK IN PROGRESS: Research on Sir Thomas Browne; research on Herbert, Milton, and Henry Vaughan.

SIDELIGHTS: Jonathan F.S. Post told *CA:* "I wrote a book on Henry Vaughan because I was moved by the combination of regional vision, religious belief, and political pressures, all of which come together to produce some extraordinary poetry, poetry different from that of his mentor, George Herbert, but very satisfying in its own right. Why does one put these thoughts on paper? First for sheer survival, to continue to be able to afford the luxury of reading and teaching poetry; then for less explicit but probably more important reasons: to try to understand what an author is doing, something that always escapes me in the lecture hall but, when I'm lucky, returns to me late at night or in the quiet moments during the day. It can, of course, never be finally captured, and probably for that reason, I keep up the quest of putting pen to paper."

BIOGRAPHICAL/CRITICAL SOURCES:

PERIODICALS

Virginia Quarterly Review, summer, 1983.

*   *   *

POVERMAN, C. E.   1944-

BRIEF ENTRY: American author. Poverman's novel *Solo-*

mon's Daughter (Viking, 1981) was well-received by critics, who described the book as a dramatic and powerful portrait of a family reunited by tragedy. The author's earlier writings include a collection of stories, *The Black Velvet Girl* (University of Iowa Press, 1976), and the novel *Susan* (Viking, 1977). *Address:* 67 Trumbull St., New Haven, Conn. 06510.

BIOGRAPHICAL/CRITICAL SOURCES:

PERIODICALS

New Republic, July 18, 1981.
New York Times Book Review, November 1, 1981.

*   *   *

POWERS, Lyall H(arris)   1924-

BRIEF ENTRY: Born July 13, 1924, in Winnipeg, Manitoba, Canada. Educator and author. Powers became a professor of English at the University of Michigan in 1967. He was a visiting professor at the University of Goettingen in 1973. Powers's books include *Henry James: An Introduction and Interpretation* (Holt, 1970), *Henry James and the Naturalist Movement* (Michigan State University Press, 1971), *Henry James's Major Novels: Essays in Criticism* (Michigan State University Press, 1973), and *Faulkner's Yoknapatawpha Comedy* (University of Michigan Press, 1980). *Address:* Department of English, 1635 Haven Hall, University of Michigan, Ann Arbor, Mich. 48104.

BIOGRAPHICAL/CRITICAL SOURCES:

PERIODICALS

New England Quarterly, December, 1971, September, 1973.
South Atlantic Quarterly, spring, 1972.

*   *   *

PREST, Alan Richmond   1919-1985

OBITUARY NOTICE—See index for *CA* sketch: Born March 1, 1919, in Yorkshire, England; died December 22, 1984, in London, England. Economist, educator, editor, and author. An internationally known expert on public finance, Prest taught economics at Cambridge University, at Victoria University of Manchester, and at the University of London's School of Economics and Political Science. He also devoted much of his time to research and writing, taking a particular interest in the policy problems of developing countries. The economist's publications include *A Fiscal Survey of the British Caribbean, Transport Economics in Developing Countries, Public Finance in Theory and Practice,* and the textbooks *Public Finance in Under-Developed Countries* and *The United Kingdom Economy.* He also wrote *Consumers Expenditure in the United Kingdom: 1900-1919,* the third volume in a series about national income and expenditure in the United Kingdom, and for a number of years he edited the *Three Banks Review.*

OBITUARIES AND OTHER SOURCES:

PERIODICALS

Times (London), January 2, 1985.

*   *   *

PREVIN, Andre (George)   1929-

PERSONAL: Name originally Andreas Ludwig Prewin; born April 6, 1929, in Berlin, Germany; immigrated to United States,

1939, naturalized citizen, 1943; son of Jacob (a lawyer, judge, and music teacher) and Charlotte (Epstein) Prewin; married Betty Bennett (a jazz singer; divorced); married Dory Langan (a jazz poet, composer, and singer), November 7, 1959 (divorced, 1970); married Mia Farrow (an actress), September 10, 1970 (divorced, 1979); married Heather Hales, 1982; children: (first marriage) Claudia, Alicia; (third marriage) Matthew Phineas and Sascha Villiers (twins), Fletcher, Daisy (adopted), Lark Song (adopted), Soon Yi (adopted), Kim, Summer, Tara. *Education:* Attended the Berlin Conservatory, 1935-38, the Paris Conservatory, 1938, and the University of California; studied conducting with Pierre Monteux and composition with Joseph Achron and Mario Castelnuovo-Tedesco.

ADDRESSES: Office—c/o Los Angeles Philharmonic Orchestra, 135 North Grand Ave., Los Angeles, Calif. 90012.

CAREER: Conductor, composer, pianist, and recording artist. Metro-Goldwyn-Mayer (MGM), Hollywood, Calif., held various positions in the music department, including posts as rehearsal conductor and orchestrator, 1945-50, film score composer and conductor, 1952-59; performed as a jazz pianist during the 1950's; worked as guest conductor and director of small orchestras during the 1960's; Houston Symphony, Houston, Tex., conductor in chief, 1967-69; London Symphony Orchestra, London, England, music director and principal conductor, 1968-79, conductor emeritus, 1979—; Pittsburgh Symphony Orchestra, Pittsburgh, Pa., music director, 1976-84; Royal Philharmonic Orchestra, London, director, 1985—; Los Angeles Philharmonic, Los Angeles, Calif., music director, 1986—.

Music director of the South Bank Summer Music Festival, London, 1972-74; guest conductor of Covent Garden Opera, of festivals in Salzburg, Edinburgh, Flanders, Vienna, Osaka, Prague, Berlin, Bergen, and of major symphony orchestras throughout the world. Conductor and host of several television programs, including the "Omnibus" and "Andre Previn's Music Night" series for the British Broadcasting Corporation (BBC-TV) and "Previn and the Pittsburgh," 1977-79, for the Public Broadcasting System (PBS-TV). Has taught twentieth-century music at Houston University and served as instructor at the Berkshire Music Center in Tanglewood, Mass.; faculty member of Guildhall School of Music and Drama in London and the Royal Academy of Music.

Piano soloist on recordings of the works of Paul Hindemith, Francis Poulenc, and Dimitri Shostakovich for Columbia Records. Pianist on popular and jazz LP recordings for Contemporary, including *Shelly Manne and His Friends*, 1956, *Andre Previn's Jazz Trio: King Size!*, 1959, *Andre Previn Plays Vernon Duke*, and (with Shelly Manne) *Bells Are Ringing;* for United Artists, including *Diahann Carroll* [and] *The Andre Previn Trio*, 1960; for Columbia, including *Piano Pieces for Children*, 1964, *A Touch of Elegance*, and (with Doris Day) *Duet;* for RCA Victor, including *Andre Previn Plays Music of the Young Hollywood Composers*, 1965, *Andre Previn All Alone*, 1967, *Right as Rain*, 1967, *Three Little Words, Andre Previn in Hollywood, Soundstage*, (with Shorty Rogers) *Collaboration*, and *Previn Plays Piano;* for Everest, including *The Early Years*, 1970; for Calliope, including *Sessions Live With Andre Previn, Shelly Manne, and Red Mitchell* [and] *Sessions Live With Count Basie and Joe Williams*, 1976; for Tops, including *Andre Previn Plays Fats Waller;* for MGM, including (with Leonard Feather's Stars) *West Coast vs. East Coast;* for Atlantic, including (with Betty Bennett) *Nobody Else But Me;* for Angel (with Itzhak Perlman), including *Joplin: The*

Easy Winners. Also pianist on recording (With Shelly Manne and Friends) of *My Fair Lady*, 1956.

Also pianist on popular and jazz single recordings for Sun, including "Take the 'A' Train" [and] "I Got It Bad," "Main Stem" [and] "Something to Live For," "Subtle Slough" [and] "Warm Valley," and "Blue Skies" [and] "Good Enough to Keep"; for RCA Victor, including "But Not for Me" [and] "Hallelujah" and "My Shining Hour" [and] "This Can't Be Love."

Conductor on classical music recordings with the London and Pittsburgh symphony orchestras for RCA, Angel, EMI, and Phillips, including the nine symphonies of Ralph Vaughan Williams, the nine symphonies of Anton Dvorak, Sergei Rachmaninoff's four piano concertos and "Fantasy for Orchestra, Op. 7," the symphonies of Sergei Prokofiev, and William Walton's "First Symphony" and "Belshazzar's Feast."

Military service: U.S. Army, 1950-52; became sergeant; performed with and composed for the Sixth Army Band in San Francisco, Calif.

MEMBER: American Composers League, National Composers and Conductors League, Composers Guild of Great Britian, Dramatists League, Garrick Club (London).

AWARDS, HONORS: Screen Composers Association Award for original music, 1955, for "Invitation to the Dance"; Academy Awards for best film score from the Academy of Motion Picture Arts and Sciences, 1958, for "Gigi," 1959, for "Porgy and Bess," 1963, for "Irma La Douce," and 1964, for "My Fair Lady"; more than a dozen Academy Award nominations for best film score from the Academy of Motion Picture Arts and Sciences; Television Critics Award, 1972; Grammy Award for best choral classical recording from the National Academy of Recording Arts and Sciences, 1973, for "Walton: Belshazzar's Feast"; Emmy Award nomination from the National Academy of Television Arts and Sciences, for the PBS-TV series "Previn and the Pittsburgh"; five awards from the National Grammophone Society; four awards from *downbeat* magazine; four Exhibitor Awards.

WRITINGS:

(With Antony Hopkins) *Music Face to Face*, Hamish Hamilton, 1971, Scribner's, 1971.

(Editor and author of introduction) *Orchestra*, interviews by Michael Foss, photographs by Richard Adeney, Doubleday, 1979.

Also author of *Andre Previn's Guide to the Orchestra*, Putnam, and *Matthew's Piano Book* (ten piano pieces).

Composer of ballets and musical plays, including: (With Gene Kelly) "Invitation to the Dance" (film ballet), 1957; (with lyricists Alan Jay Lerner and Dory Langan Previn) "Coco" (musical; includes the songs "Coco," "Fiasco," "Mademoiselle Cliche de Paris," "Gabrielle," "Always Mademoiselle," and "When Your Lover Says Goodbye"), first produced on Broadway, 1969; (with lyricist Johnny Mercer) *The Good Companions* (musical adapted from the novel of the same title by J. B. Priestly), stage book by Ronald Harwood, Chappell, 1974; (with Tom Stoppard) "Every Good Boy Deserves Favour" (musical), first produced by the Royal Shakespeare Company, England, at Her Majesty's Silver Jubilee.

Composer or arranger of film scores for MGM, including "The Sun Comes Up," 1949, "Tension," 1949, "Border Incident," 1949, "Scene of the Crime," 1949, "Shadow on the

Wall,'' 1950, "Three Little Words," 1950, "The Outriders," 1950, "Kim," 1951, "The Girl Who Had Everything," 1953, "Kiss Me, Kate," 1953, "Kismet" (ballet; music adapted from Aleksandr Porfirevich Borodin's opera "Prince Igor"), 1955, "Bad Day at Black Rock," 1955, "It's Always Fair Weather," 1955, "The Fastest Gun Alive," 1956, "The Catered Affair," 1956, "Designing Woman," 1957, "Silk Stockings," 1957, "House of Numbers," 1957, "Hot Summer Night," 1957, "Gigi," 1958, (with Ken Darby) "Porgy and Bess," 1959, "Bells Are Ringing," 1960, "The Subterraneans," 1960, "The Four Horsemen of the Apocalypse," 1962, and "Goodbye, Mr. Chips," 1969; for United Artists, including "Elmer Gantry," 1960, "One, Two, Three," 1961, "Two for the Seesaw," 1962, "Irma La Douce," 1963, "The Fortune Cookie," 1966, "The Way West," 1967, and "Rollerball," 1975; for Columbia, including "Who Was That Lady?" and "Pepe," both 1960; for Paramount, including "All in a Night's Work," 1961, "The Swinger," 1966, and "Catch 22," 1970; for Embassy, including "Long Day's Journey Into Night," 1962, and "The Graduate," 1967; for Twentieth Century-Fox, including "Goodbye, Charlie," 1964, and (with Johnny Williams) "Valley of the Dolls," 1967; for Lopert, including (with Betty Comden and Adolph Green) "Kiss Me, Stupid"; for Warner Bros., including "Dead Ringer," 1964, "My Fair Lady," 1964, "Harper," 1966, and "Inside Daisy Clover," 1966; for Universal, including "Thoroughly Modern Millie," 1967, and "Jesus Christ Superstar," 1973.

Composer of songs, including "You're Gonna Hear From Me," "Like Love," "The Faraway Part of Town," "Come Live With Me," "Give a Little More," "I'll Plant My Own Tree," "Music Is Better Than Words," "Second Chance," "Like Young," "Just for Now," "Change of Heart," "The Runaround," "You're Married," "Look Again," "Theme From the Valley of the Dolls," "One, Two, Three," "Irma La-Douce," and "Goodbye Charlie."

Composer of vocal and instrumental music, including: *Overture to a Comedy* (for orchestra), Leeds Music Corp., 1963; "Symphony for Strings," 1965; "Suite for Piano," 1967; "Cello Concerto," 1968; "Horn Concerto," 1968; "Four Songs for Soprano and Orchestra," 1968; "Two Serenades for Violin," 1969; "Violin Concerto," 1970; *Two Little Serenades for Violin and Piano* (contains "Noah" and "Naava"), Schirmer's, 1970; "Guitar Concerto," 1970; "Piano Preludes," 1972; "Woodwind Quintet," 1973; *Paraphrase* (adapted from "Pandarus's Theme" by William Walton from "Troilus and Cressida"), Novello, 1973; *Concerto for Guitar and Orchestra*, Shirmer's, 1974, Columbia, 1973; *The Invisible Drummer: Five Preludes for Piano*, Boosey & Hawkes, 1974; "Brass Quintet," 1975; *Four Outings for Brass Quintet*, Chester Music, c. 1975, recorded on the album *Divertimento*, Argo, 1977; *Five Pages From My Calendar* (for solo piano), Boosey & Hawkes, 1977; "Six Songs for Mezzo-Soprano," text by Philip Larkin, five published as *Five Songs for Mezzo-Soprano* (contains "Morning Has Spread Again," "Home Is So Sad," "Friday Night in the Royal Station Hotel," "Talking in Bed," and "The Trees"), Edition W. Hansen, c. 1978; *Peaches* (for flute and piano), Chester Music, c. 1978. Also composer of "Principals" (for orchestra), "Reflections" (for orchestra), "Five Songs for Soprano," "Portrait" (for strings), "Violin Sonata," "Concerto for Cello and Orchestra," "Five Soundings for Brass Quintet," "Summer Music for Orchestra," "Concerto for Trumpet and Orchestra," and "Impressions for Piano."

SIDELIGHTS: A world-renowned symphony orchestra conductor, Andre Previn has also distinguished himself as a composer, film scorer, and pianist. His musical training began while he was a child in Berlin, Germany, where his father—a skilled amateur pianist—instructed Previn at home. After showing an extraordinary aptitude for music and requesting music lessons, Previn entered the Berlin Conservatory of music when he was six years old. Three years later, in 1938, Previn was expelled from the conservatory because he was Jewish. Soon afterwards the Previn family fled Germany to escape Nazi persecution and stayed briefly in Paris, France, where Previn studied at the Paris Conservatory.

In 1939 Previn settled with his family in Los Angeles, California, and put his musical ability to use in high school musical productions, local radio shows, and the California Youth Symphony, both as a pianist and as a student conductor. By the age of sixteen, Previn had gained local notice as a jazz musician and was requested by Metro-Goldwyn-Mayer (MGM) movie studios to arrange a jazz number for the movie "Holiday in Mexico." Previn so impressed MGM that the studio continued to give musical assignments to the teenager, who worked variously at playing the piano for film rehearsals, synchronizing films with sound tracks, and arranging scores for motion pictures. Through his early experience, he learned to orchestrate and at age eighteen became composer-conductor for MGM. As such his energy and productivity quickly earned Previn the reputation as—in the words of *Newsweek's* Annalyn Swan—"M-G-M's boy-wonder composer and conductor."

According to Previn, as quoted in the *New Yorker*, his experience in Hollywood was significant in his development as a composer: "The best orchestra musicians in the world migrated there. And mixed in with the charlatans were . . . first-rate musicians, and I learned a lot—how to orchestrate better, more quickly. In a way, it beat any conservatory, because I was told to write something let's say on Monday, and I would hear it played impeccably four days later. . . . I learned what I was doing wrong. I don't care how many masters look at a score and say, 'Don't do that'—it doesn't have the same impact as hearing it."

While working at MGM Previn also pursued his interest in jazz and classical music. Between the 1940's and early 1960's he made more than sixty jazz recordings as a solo pianist with such musicians as violinist Itzhak Perlman, percussionist Shelly Manne, bass player Red Mitchell, guitarist Jim Hall, and jazz singer Betty Bennett, who became Previn's first wife. Among these recordings was the jazz rendition of *My Fair Lady*, one of the best-selling jazz recordings ever, which was recorded in 1956 by Shelly Manne and Friends with Previn as one of the Friends. During the 1950's Previn also played in jazz clubs with Mitchell and percussionist Frank Kapp, performed with chamber groups and symphonic orchestras, made recordings of Mozart's four-hand piano music with composer-pianist Lukas Foss, and played in his own group—The Andre Previn Trio. Previn also wrote songs during this period that were recorded by such popular singers as Judy Garland, Doris Day, and Sammy Davis, Jr.

During the late 1950's and 1960's Previn collaborated professionally with his second wife, poet and songwriter Dory Langan Previn. The two met while working for MGM on the music for the film "The Subterraneans," married in 1959, and soon afterwards left MGM. For the next ten years Dory provided many of the lyrics to Previn's songs for various studios, including the movie themes "One, Two, Three," "Irma

La Douce,'' ''Goodbye, Charlie,'' ''You're Gonna Hear From Me,'' and ''Theme From the Valley of the Dolls.'' The Previns were a successful musical team and won Academy Award nominations in 1960 for ''A Faraway Part of Town,'' from the movie ''Pepe,'' and in 1962 for ''Second Chance,'' from the film ''Two for the Seesaw.'' Previn himself won Academy Awards in 1958, 1959, 1963, and 1964 for the film scores to ''Gigi,'' ''Irma La Douce,'' ''Porgy and Bess,'' and ''My Fair Lady.'' But the Previns' marriage and professional partnership ended in 1969, when the highly publicized affair between Previn and actress Mia Farrow—whom he later married—resulted in the birth of twin sons.

Previn's involvement in jazz during the 1950's—when he was still working at MGM—proved a lasting influence on his musical taste. He explained in a 1983 *New Yorker* article: ''The period when I was active in jazz, the fifties—well, the jazz I admire most today is firmly rooted in that decade. I still have the same heroes [Oscar Peterson, Dizzy Gillespie, Charlie Parker, Lester Young]. Jazz is an enthusiasm of youth, and you get stuck with the particular era in which you first became interested.'' Despite his youthful interest in jazz, however, Previn eventually found it necessary to set it aside. As he told *New Yorker*'s Helen Drees Ruttencutter: ''When I played jazz, it consumed a fairly large part of my days, but I did it for fun. I knew it was not forever—certainly not to the exclusion of what I was after. With rare exceptions, I haven't played it in a long time, and not for reasons of misguided disdain. I admire good jazz musicians boundlessly, but I had to figure out which music activities in my life were expendable. I had to let *something* go.''

In addition to jazz, Previn decided to ''let go'' his Hollywood career. Though Previn continued to score films throughout the 1960's and 1970's, he had left MGM in 1959 to begin a career as a classical music conductor. He began this venture by recording piano and chamber music pieces—as a soloist—to fill out Columbia Records' classical music repertoire, so impressing Schuyler Chapin of Columbia that Chapin arranged a guest conductorship for Previn with the St. Louis Symphony. In addition to rehearsing the orchestra and conducting them in concerts, Previn recorded several pieces with the group. Among these was Benjamin Britten's ''Sinfonia da Requiem,'' which Britten himself, as reported the *New Yorker,* deemed ''the best performance [of the work] I've ever heard.'' Previn's success in St. Louis brought him to the attention of Ronald Wilford, then vice-president of Columbia Artists Management agency, who undertook to launch Previn's career as an orchestral conductor.

At first Wilford could only obtain assignments for Previn with obscure, second-rate orchestras, a situation that Previn attributes both to his inexperience as a conductor of classical music and to the distrust that many professional classical musicians have of their commercial or popular counterparts. As Previn commented in *Newsweek:* ''Musicians would have forgiven me for being the Boston Strangler, but they wouldn't forgive me for having worked in films.''

But Previn persisted, with the help and encouragement of Chapin and Wilford, and as he gained experience and proved his conducting skill through the performance of his orchestras, orchestral musicians took him more seriously. His reputation as a conductor also improved as a result of Previn's recording contract with RCA Victor, which he signed in 1964. Through RCA Previn was able to record at least four classical music albums per year, a circumstance that allowed him to gain na-

tional exposure and win the approval of significant musicians. After listening to the recordings on which Previn conducted, major orchestras more frequently invited him to serve as guest conductor, and in 1967 he was selected chief conductor of the Houston Symphony.

This first major post with the Houston Symphony led to others, notably those as music director and principal conductor of the London and Pittsburgh symphony orchestras. His selection as head of the London Symphony Orchestra (LSO), a post that Previn held from 1968 until 1979, was not only a great honor, but a vote of confidence from the orchestra members themselves because the players rather than a board of directors choose their conductor. Previn commented on the LSO's selection in *Newsweek:* ''It was a *phenomenal* gamble on their part. . . . That it worked out well was, obviously, the biggest thing that ever happened to me.'' According to former LSO clarinettist Gervase de Peyer, as quoted in the *New Yorker,* part of the reason that it worked—in addition to Previn's musical skill—was his ability to cut through tense situations: ''He's got a way with him, Andre. With all orchestras, there are difficult moments, and he's very good at using the moment for a witty, amusing remark that puts things in perspective.''

During the eleven-and-a-half years he spent with the LSO, Previn made numerous classical music recordings with the group, often serving as both conductor and piano soloist. He also worked to popularize classical music, making it readily available to television viewers in England by acting as host and conductor on British Broadcasting Corporation (BBC-TV) television broadcasts of the LSO in performance.

While conducting the LSO, Previn also collaborated with radio musicologist Antony Hopkins on the 1971 book *Music Face to Face* in which Previn and Hopkins discuss their careers and their views on the purpose, nature, and meaning of art in general and of music in particular. According to a *Times Literary Supplement* critic, the book ''was spoken, not written, but its consequent informality has not made it diffuse, nor has its colloquialism led to loose thinking on the various subjects discussed.'' Rather, the reviewer concluded, it is a ''modern example [of dialogue] at once vivid and engaging.''

Previn headed the Pittsburgh Symphony Orchestra from 1976 until 1984, when the orchestra released him from his contract so that he could prepare for two new directorships—one with the Royal Philharmonic Orchestra in London, the other with the Los Angeles Philharmonic. In his eight-year guidance of the Pittsburgh, Previn is credited by many critics and musicians with revitalizing the group, whose performance, according to some, had suffered during the last years of William Steinberg's term as conductor. Taking over Pittsburgh's direction from Steinberg, Previn drilled the orchestra with a relentless concentration both on technical precision and on style and achieved, according to Annalyn Swan of *Newsweek,* ''a rare clarity of sound, enviable teamwork and sharply focused detail.'' Previn had, Swan remarked, ''with his seemingly boundless energy and charm, as well as years of experience with the LSO in TV and recording studios, turned the orchestra around. Pittsburgh landed a recording contract with Angel Records. 'Previn and the Pittsburgh,' Previn's chatty TV series on PBS, was nominated for an Emmy—and made countless new Pittsburgh fans nationwide.'' And the *New Yorker* reported that Seymour Rosen, manager of the Pittsburgh Symphony Orchestra, remarked of Previn's joining the orchestra: ''They were the most exciting times Pittsburgh had known in many years. [Previn is] tremendously charismatic—he *ra-*

diates on that podium. . . . There are other conductors who play and compose, but they don't do as many things as brilliantly as Andre does. He's a true Renaissance man.''

In 1980, while Previn was still conducting the Pittsburgh Symphony Orchestra, the book *Orchestra* was published. Previn edited this volume and contributed to it an introductory discussion of his career and musical opinions. The body of the book consists of interviews—conducted by Michael Foss—with thirty-one members of symphony orchestras in the United States, Canada, England, Ireland, and Germany. In the *Los Angeles Times Book Review* Robert Riley deemed Previn's prefatory sketch ''the best part'' of the book, noting that many of the orchestra members' remarks amount to unimpressive ''chitchat.'' According to Joseph McLellan's review in the *Washington Post Book World,* however, the interviews are ''deep-probing'' and provide a ''unique, inside view of an art that is one of the most notable achievements of Western culture. . . . The comments are intelligent, pungent and revealing, and they give the book a depth and value far beyond what its cover promises. . . . Those who wonder what it is like backstage in a concert hall will find their questions answered in this volume.''

As a conductor of major symphony orchestras, Previn aims at providing his audiences with variety as well as quality in his concert programs. His orchestras play the well-known classical pieces of such composers as Ludwig van Beethoven, Johannes Brahms, and Wolfgang Amadeus Mozart, but their repertoire is balanced by works less traditional as concert fare. As Swan explained: ''Previn . . . tends to favor the Russian romantics and twentieth-century British composers, two of his favorites, over both classical and dissonant modern fare.'' He has made recordings of Benjamin Britten, William Walton, Ralph Vaughan Williams, Dimitri Shostakovich, and Sergei Rachmaninoff, and, as Richard Dyer of the *Boston Globe* commented, as quoted in the *New Yorker:* ''Previn is probably the best Rachmaninoff conductor before the public today.'' From time to time Previn also conducts some of his own pieces, such as ''Principals,'' a commissioned piece for the Pittsburgh orchestra that, Swan explained, shows off the first desk players. Said to be derivative of both Shostakovich and Sergei Prokofiev, ''Principals,'' according to Swan, mingles ''plaintive wind and string solos with a catchy Shostakovian march tune that [keeps] bursting forth.''

Previn, as quoted in the *New Yorker* by Ruttencutter, asserts that while he is not ''one of those people that are messianic'' about programming new music and while he does not program music just because it is new but ''because it *says* something'' to him, he does feel that playing new music is essential if new composition is to be encouraged and understood. With regard to objections on the part of public audiences, Previn, as quoted by Ruttencutter, told a group of students at the Berkshire Music Center in Tanglewood, Massachusetts: ''There's always been resistance to new music. But not as much as now. Because today the kind of event where a new work is played, and played around the world, is very rare—truly, truly rare. And it is because the vocabulary has got . . . so sophisticated—or, if you're on the other side of the fence, so needlessly complicated—that it alienates people at the first hearing. What I'm convinced of, though, is that familiarity breeds liking. That may sound like a paradox, but it's true, and if one heard a brand-new piece by a new composer with the *deadening* regularity that we hear Tchaikovsky Five a lot more people would love it. . . . Aaron Copland said that listening is a talent

that can be developed, like playing. And that's why the playing of new music is so necessary.''

Also, according to Previn, new musical approaches and interpretations evolve in order to express the changing times and ''I don't think that we have much choice about it.'' Previn explained to the students at Tanglewood: ''I don't think it's possible to be an artist, whether it's interpretive or creative, and live in a vacuum. I think everything affects us—absolutely everything. The unrest or ease of the world, the weather, our personal lives.'' Moreover, Previn remarked, ''I *like* the fact that music is so unpredictably quixotic—that it reflects the philosophy of everything that goes on in the whole world—and therefore I think that to worry about traditions of the past or possible solutions in the future is fine if you are writing a book, but if you're actually going to get up and do it you have to follow a purely personal conviction.''

Previn has written songs for musicals, themes for motion pictures, instrumental pieces for orchestras, chamber groups, and soloists—including ''The Invisible Drummer'' and ''Five Pages From a Calendar,'' which he wrote for the renowned pianist Vladimir Ashkenazy—and a music book for his son Matthew entitled *Matthew's Piano Book.* Nonetheless, as Previn told some students at the Berkshire Music Center, he considers himself ''a conductor who also composes, not a composer who also conducts.'' As such, Previn advises conducting students to take advantage of any opportunities to conduct that they might have, to continue playing musical instruments, and to sustain their love of music by constant involvement in its making.

Speaking to Tanglewood students, Previn remarked: ''Orchestral experience, to me, is not necessarily conducting [Richard Strauss's] 'Ein Heldenleben.' Orchestral experience is any situation, in any venue, where you are faced with living people playing instruments. If someone says to you, 'I'm sorry you can't conduct the New Jersey Symphony, but would you like to conduct The Ice Capades?'—*do* it!'' He continued: ''All of you come from certain instruments. It's a great mistake to let the instrument go, because, you see, as you work more and more there's a *huge yawning* trap in front of you if you stand on the rostrum day after week after month after year *telling* people how to play, without remembering how *bloody* hard it is. . . . For myself, I play endless chamber music and quite a few concerti with orchestras. I know from experience that the orchestras I've been most closely associated with *like* the fact that I will take the same specific gamble that they do. [If] you actually tell them in deed, not in word, that you realize how *damned* hard it is to play, and you gamble your reputation on a memory slip, on a finger slip, on lack of preparation, on the vagaries of the moment, it's a very good thing.''

Regarding the demands of a musical career and the lack of free time left him, Previn commented to Ruttencutter: ''You know, sometimes I'm very cynical about my profession, but no matter how grim it gets you *do* get the reward of the music. . . . A career in music, when you get to a certain point, a certain success—it takes all your effort just to *stay* there. . . . But the real point, the way I feel, is that I'm just *crazy* about music, and if a day goes by in which I don't have some involvement with it—be it practicing, studying a score, composing—it's a day lost forever, and I'm bereft.'' Carrying this point of view further, Previn advised his pupils at Tanglewood: ''If instead of making music you think about it, fantasize about it, that's a lost day . . . and you'll never recapture it. When you're involved with music, it makes you very happy, and when you lose that . . . you're in big trouble. . . . Sometimes the work grind dulls the edge of the voracious affair we all have with music. It's sad when that happens. The longer you can avoid that, the better. I think you have to be in love with music every day.''

BIOGRAPHICAL/CRITICAL SOURCES:

BOOKS

Bookspan, Martin and Ross Yockey, *Andre Previn: A Biography*, Doubleday, 1981.
Matheopoulos, Helena, *Maestro*, Harper, 1983.
Ruttencutter, Helen Drees, *Previn*, St. Martin's, 1985.

PERIODICALS

Detroit Free Press, September 17, 1974.
Detroit News, April 30, 1984, May 1, 1984.
Esquire, July, 1971.
High Fidelity, April, 1970, July, 1973, November, 1974, September, 1975, June, 1976, December, 1976.
Los Angeles Times Book Review, September 21, 1980.
New Statesman, December 28, 1973.
Newsweek, February 19, 1962, October 16, 1967, April 8, 1968, October 6, 1980.
New Yorker, February 12, 1972, January 10, 1983, January 17, 1983.
New York Times, March 10, 1968, April 4, 1968, March 14, 1976.
Saturday Evening Post, November 18, 1961, February 19, 1977.
Saturday Review, February 19, 1977.
Time, April 5, 1948, April 20, 1959, July 15, 1966, September 4, 1972.
Times Literary Supplement, January 14, 1972.
Washington Post Book World, May 5, 1980.*

—*Sketch by Lori R. Clemens*

* * *

PRICE, Charles P(hilip) 1920-

PERSONAL: Born October 4, 1920, in Pittsburgh, Pa.; son of Philip Wallis (an engineer) and Edith (Arensberg) Price; married Betty Haywood Farley, June 3, 1949; children: Edith Robbins. *Education:* Harvard University, A.B., 1941; Virginia Theological Seminary, B.D., 1949; Union Theological Seminary, New York, N.Y., Th.D., 1962.

ADDRESSES: Office—Department of Systematic Theology, Virginia Theological Seminary, Alexandria, Va. 22304.

CAREER: Ordained Episcopal minister, 1949; Episcopal rector in Ligonier, Pa., 1949-54; assistant minister at Episcopal church in New York, N.Y., 1954-56; Virginia Theological Seminary, Alexandria, assistant professor, 1956-59, associate professor of systematic theology, 1959-63; Harvard University, Cambridge, Mass., university preacher and Plummer Professor of Christian Morals, 1963-72; Virginia Theological Seminary, professor of systematic theology, 1972—. Member of Standing Liturgical Commission of the Episcopal Church, 1968—, and Anglican-Roman Catholic Dialogue, 1977—. *Military service:* U.S. Navy, 1941-46; became lieutenant, senior grade.

MEMBER: Society of Biblical Theologians, American Theological Society.

WRITINGS:

Introducing the Proposed Book of Common Prayer, Seabury, 1976.
Principles of Christian Faith and Practice, Islam and the Modern Age Society, 1977.
(Editor with Elizabeth Achtemeier and Gerhard Krodel) *Proclamation II*, Fortress, 1979-82.
A Matter of Faith, Morehouse, 1983.
(With Eugene Goetchius) *The Gifts of God*, Morehouse, 1985.

Contributor to theology journals.

SIDELIGHTS: Charles P. Price commented on his books: ''The volumes on liturgy were undertaken to interpret the 1979 Book of Common Prayer to the Episcopal Church. *Principles of Christian Faith and Practice* was written at the invitation of the Islam and the Modern Age Society, as part of a series to interpret the world's greatest religions to Indian society. *Proclamation II* is an eight-volume series of commentaries on the lessons in the lectionary now shared by a number of Christian churches, the successor to a previous similiar series.''

* * *

PRICE, Kenneth M(arsden) 1954-

PERSONAL: Born April 22, 1954, in Pomona, Calif.; son of Marsden (a teacher) and Barbara (Hill) Price; married Renee Hall, August 1, 1981; children: Ashley Marlene. *Education:* Whitman College, B.A. (magna cum laude), 1976; University of Chicago, M.A., 1977, Ph.D., 1981.

ADDRESSES: Home—1107 Edgewood, Bryan, Tex. 77802. *Office*—Department of English, Texas A&M University, College Station, Tex. 77843.

CAREER: Merritt Community College, Oakland, Calif., lecturer in English, summer, 1977; Rosary College, River Forest, Ill., lecturer in English, autumn, 1979; Texas A&M University, College Station, visiting assistant professor, 1981-82, assistant professor of English, 1982—. Guest on nationally syndicated radio program ''Conversations at Chicago.''

MEMBER: Modern Language Association of America, South Central Modern Language Association.

WRITINGS:

(Editor with Dennis Berthold) *Dear Brother Walt: The Letters of Thomas Jefferson Whitman*, Kent State University Press, 1984.

Contributor of articles and reviews to literature and library journals.

WORK IN PROGRESS: Whitman: ''Wellshaped Heir'' of Tradition.

* * *

PURVIS, Charles C. 1902(?)-1985

OBITUARY NOTICE: Born c. 1902 in Knapp, Wis.; died April 11, 1985, in Tubac, Ariz. Journalist. Purvis spent more than thirty years with the *Chicago Tribune* as a rewrite man at the telegraph desk. Until his retirement in 1967, the newsman's job was to review stories submitted to the *Tribune* from all over the world and to polish them to the newspaper's journalistic standards. Though his work usually appeared under the bylines of other journalists, it has been suggested that Purvis wrote more top news stories for the *Tribune* than any other reporter. Some of his stories, including Purvis's coverage of the riots that followed the 1956 enrollment of the first black student at the University of Alabama, also appeared in the *New York Times,* sometimes under his own byline.

OBITUARIES AND OTHER SOURCES:

PERIODICALS

Chicago Tribune, April 18, 1985.

* * *

PURYEAR, Alvin N(elson) 1937-

BRIEF ENTRY: Born April 6, 1937, in Fayetteville, N.C. American financial analyst, educator, and author. Puryear became a professor of management at Bernard M. Baruch College of the City University of New York in 1972. He has also worked as a financial analyst for Mobil Oil Corporation and as a computational systems specialist for the Allied Chemical Corporation. Puryear has edited the *Review of Black Political Economists* and has served as chairman of Inner City Merchandisers. He wrote *Black Enterprise, Inc.: Case Studies of a New Experiment in Black Business Development* (Anchor Press, 1973).

BIOGRAPHICAL/CRITICAL SOURCES:

BOOKS

Who's Who in America, 42nd edition, Marquis, 1982.

PERIODICALS

Washington Post Book World, May 20, 1973.

* * *

PURYEAR, Edgar F., Jr. 1930-

PERSONAL: Born February 24, 1930, in Washington, D.C.; son of Edgar F. (a lawyer) and Annie Frances (a homemaker; maiden name, Gooden) Puryear; married Agnes Braxton Green (a homemaker), January 26, 1957; children: B. S. P., Edgar F. III, S. Braxton, Alfred A. *Education:* University of Maryland at College Park, B.S., 1952; University of Denver, M.A., 1957; Princeton University, M.S., 1958, Ph.D., 1959; University of Virginia, LL.B., 1967.

ADDRESSES: Office—Puryear, Chandler & Early, P.O. Box 346, Madison, Va. 22727.

CAREER: U.S. Air Force, 1952-55, attached to U.S. Air Force Academy, Colorado Springs, Colo., as air training officer, coach of judo, boxing, and debate, navigation instructor, and teacher of political science, 1955-64, assistant dean of academy, 1962-64, leaving service as captain; Puryear, Chandler & Early (law firm), Madison, Va., partner, 1967—. Past member of faculty at University of Virginia; Cincinnati-Dance Lecturer at Virginia Military Institute; visiting professor at International School of Law (now George Mason University), 1977-78; lecturer at U.S. Army Command and General Staff School, Army War College, Air Force Command and Staff School, National War College, Industrial College of the Armed Forces, and U.S. Military Academy, West Point, N.Y. Civilian attorney adviser to Judge Advocate General's School for U.S. Army; substitute judge in general district courts and juvenile and domestic relations courts; consultant to chiefs of staff of U.S. Air Force and U.S. Army. Past member of board of directors of Culpeper Memorial Hospital.

MEMBER: American Bar Association, Virginia Bar Association, Madison County Lions Club (past president).

WRITINGS:

Nineteen Stars: A Study in Military Character and Leadership, Presidio Press, 1971.
Stars in Flight: A Study in Air Force Character and Leadership, Presidio Press, 1981.
General George S. Brown, U.S.A.F.: Destined for Stars, Presidio Press, 1983.

WORK IN PROGRESS: Profiles in Air Force Leadership.

SIDELIGHTS: Edgar F. Puryear, Jr., told *CA:* ''The books I have written have resulted in numerous requests for speaking engagements, all with the theme most important to me: the importance of character in successful American military leadership.

Character cannot really be defined, but must be described. My books proceed to describe the character, careers, and personalities of successful military personnel. It is my belief that much of the character development within the American military is based upon example, and I considered it imperative to capture the reasons for the success of these great men for the oncoming generations of military leaders. It would really be too expansive a response to do justice to the reasons. I had a very clearcut goal and purpose, however, and that was the hope that I could provide tomorrow's military leadership with some guidelines and examples worthy of emulation in the hopes that we would continue the truly superior, indeed brilliant, leadership our country has had since its inception.''

* * *

PYLE, Ernest Taylor 1900-1945
(Ernie Pyle)

BRIEF ENTRY: Born August 3, 1900, near Dana, Ind.; died of gunshot wounds to the head, April 18, 1945, in Ie Shima, Ryukyu Islands; buried at National Memorial Cemetery, Punchbowl Crater, Hawaii. American journalist and author. During World War II Pyle became nationally known for his columns depicting the everyday lives of American soldiers as he followed them in their maneuvers through England, Africa, Italy, France, and the Pacific theater. He began his career in journalism as a student at Indiana University at Bloomington, where he worked as a staff reporter, city editor, and, later, as editor in chief. He left the university during his senior year to work briefly as a reporter for the *La Porte Herald,* after which he joined the *Washington Daily News* in Washington, D.C. From 1926 to 1927 he worked at the copydesks of the *New York Evening World* and the *New York Evening Post,* returning to the *Washington Daily News* in late 1927 as a telegraphic editor. Pyle also wrote a column on aviation for the *Daily News* and in 1929 became the newspaper's full-time aviation reporter. Three years later he rose to the position of managing editor.

In the mid-1930's Pyle began a career as a syndicated columnist, traveling by automobile throughout the United States and producing daily columns that became popular for their chatty, informal style. In late 1940, with the start of World War II, Pyle traveled to England, where he covered the German bombing of London. A collection of his columns from that period were reprinted and published as *Ernie Pyle in England* (1941). He later joined the American and British troops in the North African campaign and compiled his stories for a second book, *Here Is Your War* (1943), which became a best-seller. His travels with the American forces took him to Italy and back to England before he returned to the United States, where he published a third book, *Brave Men,* in 1944. The same year he won a Pulitzer Prize for distinguished correspondence and accompanied the U.S. Navy and Marine Corps to the Ryukyu Islands in the Pacific. There he was killed by Japanese machine-gun fire and was buried on the Island of Ie Shima. His body was later moved to Hawaii. *Last Chapter* (1946), a book of Pyle's Pacific dispatches, and a collection of his prewar writings, *Home Country* (1947), were published posthumously.

BIOGRAPHICAL/CRITICAL SOURCES:

BOOKS

Current Biography, H. W. Wilson, 1941, May, 1945.
Dictionary of Literary Biography, Volume 29: *American Newspaper Journalists, 1926-1950,* Gale, 1984.
Miller, Lee Graham, *The Story of Ernie Pyle,* Viking, 1950.

PERIODICALS

American Heritage, February/March, 1981.
Newsweek, August 2, 1965.

*   *   *

PYLE, Ernie
   See PYLE, Ernest Taylor

Q

QUENNELL, Peter (Courtney) 1905- (P.Q.)

PERSONAL: Born March 9, 1905, in Bickley, Kent, England; son of Charles Henry Bourne (an architect and author) and Marjorie (an author and an illustrator of children's books; maiden name, Courtney) Quennell. *Education:* Attended Balliol College, Oxford, 1923-25.

ADDRESSES: Home—26 Cheyne Row, London S.W. 3, England.

CAREER: Free-lance writer for periodicals, including *New Statesman, Life and Letters, Times Literary Supplement,* and *Criterion,* 1925-30; Bunrika Daigaku, Tokyo, Japan, professor of English, 1930-31; worked as a copywriter for an advertising firm in London, England; *Daily Mail,* London, book critic, 1943-1956; *Cornhill Magazine,* London, editor, 1944-51; *History Today,* London, co-editor under name P.Q., 1951-79.

AWARDS, HONORS: Commander of the Order of the British Empire.

WRITINGS:

Masques and Poems, Golden Cockerel Press, 1922.
Poems, Chatto & Windus, 1926, J. Cape & H. Smith, 1930.
Baudelaire and the Symbolists: Five Essays, Chatto & Windus, 1929, revised edition, Weidenfeld & Nicholson, 1954.
The Phoenix-Kind (novel), Viking, 1931.
A Letter to Mrs. Virginia Woolf, L. & Virginia Woolf, 1932.
A Superficial Journey Through Tokyo and Peking, Faber, 1932.
Sympathy and Other Stories, Faber, 1933.
Byron, Duckworth, 1934, reprinted, Haskell House, 1974.
Byron: The Years of Fame, Viking, 1935, revised edition, Archon Books, 1967.
Victorian Panorama: A Survey of Life and Fashion From Contemporary Photographs, Scribner, 1937.
(With George Paston [pseudonym for Emily Morse Symonds]) *"To Lord Byron": Feminine Profiles, Based Upon Unpublished Letters, 1807-1824,* J. Murray, 1939.
Caroline of England: An Augustan Portrait, Collins, 1939, Viking, 1940.
Byron in Italy, Viking, 1941.
The Profane Virtues: Four Studies of the Eighteenth Century, Viking, 1945, reprinted, Greenwood Press, 1979 (published in England as *Four Portraits: Studies of the Eighteenth Century,* Collins, 1945, revised edition, Archon Books, 1965).
John Ruskin: The Portrait of a Prophet, Viking, 1949, reprinted, Greenwood Press, 1979.
The Singular Preference: Portraits and Essays, Collins, 1952, Viking, 1953.
Spring in Sicily, illustrations by Joan Rayner and others, Weidenfeld & Nicholson, 1952.
Hogarth's Progress, Viking, 1955.
The Sign of the Fish, Viking, 1960.
Shakespeare: A Biography, Collins & World, 1963 (published in England as *Shakespeare: The Poet and His Background,* Weidenfeld & Nicholson, 1963).
Alexander Pope: The Education of Genius, 1688-1728, Stein & Day, 1968.
Romantic England: Writing and Painting, 1717-1851, Macmillan, 1970.
Casanova in London and Other Essays, Stein & Day, 1971.
(With others) *The Colosseum,* Newsweek, 1971.
Samuel Johnson: His Friends and Enemies, Weidenfeld & Nicholson, 1972, American Heritage Press, 1973.
(With Hamish Johnson) *Who's Who in Shakespeare,* Morrow, 1973.
(With Johnson) *A History of English Literature,* Merriam, 1973.
The Marble Foot: An Autobiography, 1905-1938, Collins, 1976, Viking, 1977.
The Day Before Yesterday: A Photographic Album of Daily Life in Victorian and Edwardian England, Dent, 1978, Scribner, 1979.
Vladimir Nabokov: His Life, His Work, His World; A Tribute, Weidenfeld & Nicholson, 1979.
The Wanton Chase: An Autobiography From 1939, Collins, 1980.
Customs and Characters: Contemporary Portraits, Weidenfeld & Nicholson, 1982.

Also author of *Inscription on a Fountainhead* (poems), published as part of the "Ariel" series, 1929.

EDITOR

Aspects of Seventeenth Century Verse, J. Cape, 1933, revised edition, Home & Van Thal, 1947, reprinted, Folcroft Library Editions, 1970.

The Private Letters of Princess Lieven to Prince Metternich: 1820-1826, J. Murray, 1937.

Byron: Selections From Poetry, Letters, and Journals, Nonesuch, 1949.

Henry Mayhew, *Mayhew's London* (contains selections from *London Labour and the London Poor*), Pilot Press, 1949.

Alexander Pope, *The Pleasures of Pope,* Hamish Hamilton, 1949.

Byron, A Self-Portrait: Letters and Diaries, 1798 to 1824, Scribner, 1950.

H. Mayhew, *London's Underworld* (contains selections from *London Labour and the London Poor,* Volume 4: *Those That Will Not Work*), W. Kimber, 1951.

H. Mayhew, *Mayhew's Characters* (contains selections from *London Labour and the London Poor*), W. Kimber, 1951.

Selected Writings of John Ruskin, Falcon Press, 1952.

George Henry Borrow, *The Bible in Spain,* Macdonald, 1959.

Byronic Thoughts: Maxims, Reflections, and Portraits From the Prose and Verse of Lord Byron, J. Murray, 1960, Harcourt, 1961.

William Hickey, *Memoirs of William Hickey,* Hutchinson, 1960, new edition, Routledge & Kegan Paul, 1975, published as *The Prodigal Rake: Memoirs of William Hickey,* Dutton, 1962.

(With Alan Hodge) *The Past We Share,* Prometheus Press, 1960.

Henry Millon de Montherlant, *Selected Essays,* Weidenfeld & Nicholson, 1960.

Thomas Moore, *The Journal of Thomas Moore: 1818-1941,* revised edition, 1964.

Marjorie Quennell and Charles Henry Bourne Quennell, *A History of Everyday Things in England,* Volume 4: *1851-1914,* 6th edition, revised, Batsford, 1965.

Marcel Proust, 1871-1922: A Centenary Volume, Simon & Schuster, 1971.

Affairs of the Mind: The Salon in Europe and America From the Eighteenth to the Twentieth Century, New Republic, 1980 (published in England as *Genius in the Drawing-Room: The Literary Salon in the Nineteenth and Twentieth Centuries,* Weidenfeld & Nicholson, 1980).

A Lonely Business: A Self-Portrait of James Pope-Hennessy, Weidenfeld & Nicholson, 1981.

(With Cyril Connolly) *The Selected Essays of Cyril Connolly,* Stanley Moss/Persea, 1984.

TRANSLATOR

Al-Ram-Hurmuzi Buzurg Ibn Shahriyar, *The Book of the Marvels of India,* G. Routledge, 1928.

Anthony Hamilton, *Memoirs of the Comte de Gramont,* G. Routledge, 1930.

AUTHOR OF INTRODUCTION OR PREFATORY REMARKS

Jane Austen, *Sense and Sensibility,* J. Cape, 1933.

Cecil Beaton, *Time Exposure,* Batsford, 1941.

Novels by the Bronte Sisters, Pilot Press, 1947.

Charlotte Bronte, *Villette,* Pilot Press, 1947.

Diversions of History, Wingate, 1954.

John Cleland, *Memoirs of a Woman of Pleasure,* Putnam, 1963.

C. W. H. Beaton, *Royal Portraits,* Weidenfeld & Nicholson, 1963.

Henry Millon de Montherlant, *Chaos and Night,* translated by Terence Kilmartin, Weidenfeld & Nicolson, 1964.

De Montherlant, *The Girls: A Tetralogy of Novels,* translated by Kilmartin, Harper, 1968.

Contributor to periodicals, including *Atlantic Monthly, Horizon, Nation,* and *Saturday Review.*

SIDELIGHTS: "As a biographer, historian, editor, and critic, Peter Quennell has been one of England's radiant literary lights for more than half a century," declared critic Michael Demarest in *Time.* Esteemed for the civility of his writing and his graceful style, Quennell, assessed Michiko Kakutani in the *New York Times Book Review,* tends "to emphasize style over content." In contrast to the "vernacular revolutionaries," as author Cyril Connolly dubbed writers such as Ernest Hemingway and George Orwell in *Enemies of Promise,* Quennell is, he himself admitted in *The Marble Foot: An Autobiography, 1905-1938,* one of Connolly's "mandarins," continually preoccupied "with words and with their proper literary use." He explained: "It was only through evolving a style, I thought, that I could discover what I had to say, and give any discoveries I made the necessary shape and substance."

Quennell's preoccupation with words began early in life. He learned to read at age four or five, began writing rhymes at age seven or eight, and published his first book of poetry at age seventeen. Attributing much of his fascination with literature and history to his parents—who collaborated on writing and illustrating books for children, including the four-volume *A History of Everyday Things in England*—Quennell, in *The Marble Foot,* recalled growing up in what "some of our more philistine neighbors must have considered . . . an 'arty' household." He added: "Neither my sturdy brother nor my nervous and difficult sister was yet old enough to be particularly drawn towards my parents' occupations. But me they engrossed; my mind was full of hauberks and helms, capuchons and liripipes, and how the head-dress of a fifteenth-century gentleman had been evolved . . . to form a decorative coxcomb. I loved the Middle Ages and pored delightedly over the various medieval relics that my father had collected."

Quennell resolved to become an English poet while attending grammar school at Berkhamsted, where novelist Graham Greene's father was then headmaster. He explained his ambition to write poetry in *The Sign of the Fish* and reiterated his sentiments in *The Marble Foot:* "It was a genuine need that set me versifying as much as a youthful desire to make my mark; and the need was less to convey my sensations . . . than to release the tension that had been built up by the secret pressure of many different feelings, which might include both the pleasure I felt at the beauty of the world beneath my eyes and the emotions derived from a book first opened several days earlier. In combination they had engendered a state of excitement that could only be relieved if I attempted to write a poem; and during the attempt, I sought to produce a pattern of rhythmic and evocative words, through which the tension that excited and troubled me might be accounted for and exorcized."

Before he had left Oxford, however, Quennell was already beginning to feel that "the mood of high creative excitement" of his earlier days, as he described it, was on the wane. His only adult book of verse appeared in 1926, and his Oxford life was chiefly memorable for the friends he made. Instead of attending lectures, he kept company with such future luminaries as Graham Greene, Evelyn Waugh, Cyril Connolly, Anthony Powell, and Edward Sackville-West. He also began writing a biography of William Blake; and, after being rusticated, he lost his scholarship and decided to devote himself to writing prose.

Although Quennell's early novel, *The Phoenix-Kind,* failed to satisfy him, he fared well as a literary reviewer and contributor to periodicals, including the *New Statesman* and *Criterion,* and soon turned to writing books of biography and criticism. He was successful, becoming best known for his biographies. In the *Washington Post Book World,* critic Michael Dirda assessed his achievement in the genre thus: "Quennell is to biography what Auden was to occasional verse—a writer who can make an ordinary bit of writing into a little work of art." And if some of his works, reported Paul Fusell in the *New York Times Book Review,* were "disparaged by scholars and serious critics for their inaccuracy and superficiality," they nevertheless "delighted others for their humanity and charm."

In particular, Quennell is regarded as an expert on Byron and Pope. One of his first studies of George Gordon Byron, *Byron: The Years of Fame,* discusses the poet's career in England from 1811 until the failure of his marriage in 1816 and earned praise in both England and the United States. In the *New York Times* E. L. Buell called it "intelligent and deftly knit." Its sequel, *Byron in Italy,* covers the years 1816 to 1823 and was similarly well received, with a *New Yorker* reviewer commending it as "a superb narrative, charming, subtle, and intelligent." Quennell has always retained his interest in Byron and followed up these early books on the romantic poet with a number of edited works, including *Byron: Selections From Poetry, Letters, and Journals* in 1949, *Byron, a Self-Portrait: Letters and Diaries, 1789 to 1824* in 1950, and *Byronic Thoughts* in 1960.

If "Quennell's powers were triumphantly evident in his two-volume study of Byron," wrote a critic for *Time,* "in Alexander Pope, Quennell has found another genius for a subject." The first of two proposed volumes on the eighteenth-century poet and satirist, *Alexander Pope: The Education of Genius, 1688-1728* deals with Pope's life until the publication of the first version of his famous lampoon *The Dunciad.* According to Christopher Ricks in *Book World,* Quennell "writes without prurience or prudery on the delicate question of Pope's relations with women, and he writes with controlled indignation on the humiliations and disqualifications to which Pope, as a Roman Catholic, was continually liable. In short, a sensitive and economical biography." In like fashion, critic John Wain commented in the *Observer* that, while Quennell's account lacks urgency, it does evoke a sense of Pope's life "with an agreeable bustle of comings and goings and skilful portraits of the personalities who surrounded him." And as for the poems, reported Wain, Quennell both treats them "as events in the poet's life" and places them "in a reasonably full context of literary history." An *Economist* reviewer added: "Mr. Quennell's elegantly lucid style gives to the whole biography an air of easy inevitability."

Such elegant lucidity also characterizes the critic's autobiographies. According to Michiko Kakutani, it was Quennell's preoccupaion "with words and with their proper literary use" that "led to the lovely, ceremonious style" of *The Marble Foot* and *The Wanton Chase.* The former takes its title from the fragment of an ancient statue on the Via Pie di Marmo in Rome—an image Quennell invokes, informed Paul Fussell, "at the end of his book as an example of the odd but engaging images the poor irrational mind remembers"—and covers the years 1905 to 1935. The latter deals with the years from 1939, earning Quennell praise not only for "recounting the behavior of figures more outrageous and difficult than himself," which "contain the real substance of the book," according to Wil-

liam Pritchard in the *New York Times Book Review,* but also for what Michael Dirda described as his "exquisite prose."

Indeed, Quennell "still writes so purely that he winces at the thought of needlessly repeating a preposition," reported Dirda. And as a founder and co-editor of *History Today* for more than twenty-five years, Quennell, wrote A. L. Rowe in a *History Today* tribute to its editors, helped set the standard of "good scholarship and readability" for which the journal has become known. Rowe further explained that "the writing of specialist academic journals all too often sounds like the clinking of a hundred typewriters—no variation of rhythm, no sense of humour or irony, no colour or tone, in the end inhuman." But under the leadership of Peter Quennell and Alan Hodge—P.Q. and A.H., as they were known to the publication's readers—*History Today* managed "to bridge the gap between specialist journals, all too often unreadable by the general public, and the intelligent reader who wanted to read history." "Above all," concluded Rowe, the editors were "human and humane."

Quennell told *CA:* "I have often thought that critics attach rather too much importance to what, they believe, a writer 'has to say.' I prefer the view expressed by the French sage Joseph Joubert (1754-1824): 'When one composes,' he declared, 'one does not know what one wishes to say until one has said it. The word, in fact, is the agent that completes the idea and gives it existence. It is through the word that the idea achieves life.'"

BIOGRAPHICAL/CRITICAL SOURCES:

BOOKS

Quennell, Peter, *The Marble Foot: An Autobiography, 1905-1938,* Collins, 1976, Viking, 1977.
Quennell, Peter, *The Wanton Chase: An Autobiography From 1939,* Collins, 1980.

PERIODICALS

Atlantic, May, 1969.
Books and Bookmen, March, 1969.
Chicago Tribune, October 30, 1960.
Economist, December 28, 1968.
History Today, November, 1979.
Los Angeles Times, March 21, 1980.
Los Angeles Times Book Review, June 22, 1980.
New Republic, May 7, 1977.
New Statesman, July 16, 1960.
New Yorker, February 22, 1969.
New York Review of Books, February 27, 1969.
New York Times, June 4, 1980.
New York Times Book Review, October 23, 1960, December 22, 1968, April 10, 1977, March 16, 1980, October 24, 1980, December 21, 1980, January 30, 1983, December 21, 1983.
Observer, October 27, 1968.
Saturday Review, January 14, 1961, February 22, 1969.
Spectator, July 8, 1960.
Time, January 17, 1969, January 31, 1983.
Times (London), May 15, 1980.
Times Literary Supplement, July 29, 1960, January 27, 1961, December 19, 1968, June 13, 1980, July 4, 1980, June 19, 1981, November 11, 1982, November 26, 1982.
Washington Post Book World, January 18, 1981.

—*Sketch by Nancy H. Evans*

QUINN, John Francis   1925-

BRIEF ENTRY: Born May 7, 1925, in Dublin, Ireland. Philosopher, theologian, educator, and author. Quinn has served as professor of philosophy at the Pontifical Institute for Mediaeval Studies since 1966. In addition he was named professor of philosophy at the University of Toronto's School of Graduate Studies and at its University of St. Michael's College in 1976. Quinn wrote *The Historical Constitution of St. Bonaventure's Philosophy* (Pontifical Institute of Mediaeval Studies, 1973). *Address:* Pontifical Institute of Mediaeval Studies, 59 Queen's Park Cres. E., Toronto, Ontario, Canada M5S 2C4.

R

RADICE, Betty 1912-1985

OBITUARY NOTICE—See index for *CA* sketch: Born January 3, 1912, in Hessle, Yorkshire, England; died February 18, 1985. Educator, translator, editor, and author. A firm believer that the classics should be widely and inexpensively available in translation, Radice began her career as an educator and translator of the classics. The quality of her translations eventually earned her a place at Penguin Books, where she is best remembered for twenty years of service as co-editor of the Penguin Classics. In addition to her editorial responsibilities, Radice translated a variety of works for Penguin, including *The Letters of the Younger Pliny*, Terence's *The Comedies*, Erasmus's *Praise of Folly, The Letters of Abelard and Heloise*, and Livy's *Rome and Italy*. She also compiled and wrote the introduction to *Who's Who in the Ancient World* in 1971, a work that remains notable in its field.

OBITUARIES AND OTHER SOURCES:

PERIODICALS

Times (London), February 20, 1985.

* * *

RALEY, Rowena
See McCULLEY, Johnston

* * *

RANSOME, Stephen
See DAVIS, Frederick C(lyde)

* * *

RARICK, Carrie 1911-

PERSONAL: Surname rhymes with "barrack"; born December 16, 1911, in Somerset, Ohio; daughter of Frank Burrie (a farmer) and Mary (Hoover) Fisher; married Merrill Rarick (a teacher), February 4, 1932 (deceased); children: Mary Ann (Mrs. Richard O. Gibson). *Education:* Capital University, Two Year Normal Degree, 1931, B.A., 1975; Ohio Dominican College, Elder Hostel Certificate, 1980. *Religion:* Lutheran.

ADDRESSES: Home—723 Montrose Ave., Columbus, Ohio 43209.

CAREER: Teacher at public elementary schools in Hebron, Ohio, 1931-33, and Jersey, Ohio, 1939-56; Beechwood Elementary School, Whitehall, Ohio, teacher, 1957-79; writer, 1979—.

MEMBER: National Retired Teachers Association, Society of Children's Book Writers, Verse Writer's Guild of Ohio, Bexley Historical Society.

WRITINGS:

FOR CHILDREN

The Three Bears Visit Goldilocks, Rand McNally, 1950.
Little Penguin, Rand McNally, 1960.
Mom Says, North-Side Letter Shop, 1979.
Jeanie's Valentines, Follett, 1982.

Writer for Humane Society of the United States.

WORK IN PROGRESS: Dapper Dan and His Gold Motorcycle; a book based on Rarick's teaching career, for adults, expected in 1987; *Book of School Happenings,* true accounts of various school experiences.

SIDELIGHTS: Carrie Rarick told *CA:* "All my life I have been working with children. I grew up on a farm in a family of eight children. I taught young people for thirty-nine years and tutored three boys from Laos. I raised one child, had two grandchildren, and now I have great-grandchildren to inspire me. *Jeanie's Valentines* is named after my great-grandchild; it is an easy-to-read book at the second-grade level and is often used in schools as reading material for children who have to move or change schools."

BIOGRAPHICAL/CRITICAL SOURCES:

PERIODICALS

Columbus Dispatch News, June 8, 1980.

* * *

RAWCLIFFE, (John) Michael 1934-

PERSONAL: Born April 2, 1934, in Blackpool, England; son of John (a local government officer) and Gladys (a housewife and bookkeeper; maiden name, Foulkes) Rawcliffe; married Hilary Miles (a primary teacher), October 12, 1957; children: Frances, David, Peter. *Education:* University of Nottingham,

B.A. (with honors), 1955; Institute of Education, London, Postgraduate Certificate in Education, 1959, Diploma, 1961; University of Kent at Canterbury, M.A., 1976. *Religion:* Church of England.

ADDRESSES: Home—9 Copley Dene, Bromley, Kent BR1 2PW, England.

CAREER: Teacher at secondary modern school in Ilford, England, 1957-58, and grammar school in Walthamstow, England, 1959-62; Stockwell College of Education, Bromley, England, lecturer, 1962-65, senior lecturer, 1965-74, principal lecturer in history, 1974-80; St. Olaves School, Orpington, England, head of history department, 1980—. Exchange professor at Mankato State College (now University), 1972; lecturer at University of London; British Council lecturer. *Military service:* Royal Navy, 1955-57.

MEMBER: Victorian Society, British Association of Local History, Historical Association, Society for the Preservation of Ancient Buildings, National Trust for Historic Preservation, London Borough of Bromley Local History Society.

WRITINGS:

F. D. Roosevelt, Batsford, 1980.
Finding Out About Victorian Towns (juvenile), Batsford, 1984.
Victorian London, Batsford, 1985.
Nineteenth-Century Public Health and Housing, Batsford, in press.
Victorian Country Life, Batsford, in press.

CONTRIBUTOR

T. H. Corfe, editor, *History in the Field,* Blond, 1970.
W. H. Baerston and C. W. Green, editors, *Handbook for History Teachers,* Methuen, 1972.
W. A. Clareton, *The Use of Maps in Schools,* Blackwell, 1975.
F. L. M. Thompson, editors, *The Rise of Suburbia,* Leicester University Press, 1982.

Co-editor of series "Finding Out," Batsford.

WORK IN PROGRESS: Victorian Social Reforms.

SIDELIGHTS: Michael Rawcliffe told *CA:* "In 1980 Stockwell College of Education was closed because of the oversupply of teachers and the need to curtail training institutions. As posts in higher education were (and are) very few, I took up a school appointment, rather than my entitlement to a year of 'retraining.' I enjoy teaching, but would like to return to higher education in order to pursue my specialties and research.

"I very much enjoy field work and educational visits. In recent years I have led groups to the Soviet Union, Poland, Hungary, and Austria in connection with modern European history courses at degree and school level. In addition I regularly take a group of fourteen-year-olds to Belgium to study the battlefields of World War I.

"At home I have organized various courses to specific areas, such as Yorkshire and Sussex, and also ones based on museums or historic sites. So basically my interests are in modern history, especially Russian and American, both of which I have taught at degree level, allied with a very close academic interest in local history and the writing of history in schools."

*   *   *

RAWSON, Elizabeth (Donata) 1934-

BRIEF ENTRY: Born April 13, 1934, in London, England.

British historian, educator, and author. Rawson has taught ancient history at Cambridge University's New Hall, and, beginning in 1980, at Oxford University's Corpus Christi College. She has been a visiting professor at Pennsylvania State University and Princeton University. Rawson is the author of *The Spartan Tradition in European Thought* (Clarendon Press, 1969), *Life in Ancient Greece: Pictures From Poetry* (Longman Young Books, 1973), and *Cicero: A Portrait* (Allen Lane, 1975). *Address:* Corpus Christi College, Oxford University, Oxford, England.

BIOGRAPHICAL/CRITICAL SOURCES:

PERIODICALS

Times Literary Supplement, March 26, 1970, April 6, 1973, October 24, 1975.

*   *   *

RAYMOND, Rene (Brabazon) 1906-1985
(James Hadley Chase, James L. Docherty, Ambrose Grant, Raymond Marshall)

OBITUARY NOTICE: Born December 24, 1906, in London, England; died February 6, 1985, in Corseaux-sur-Vevey, Switzerland. Editor, playwright, and author of fiction. Raymond wrote approximately one hundred suspense novels under his pseudonyms James Hadley Chase, James L. Docherty, Ambrose Grant, and Raymond Marshall. He is perhaps best remembered for his first and most commercially successful book, *No Orchids for Miss Blandish,* a thriller that details the kidnapping of an heiress by gangsters. Like most of his later novels, *No Orchids* followed what critics have termed the "hardboiled" American fiction formula, which combines a fast pace, flashy characters, and complex plots with elements of sex and violence. Considered shocking—though highly popular—in their day, Raymond's books feature American settings and American protagonists—most often mobsters and private investigators. Raymond himself, however, was described by a London *Times* reporter as "a typical quiet Englishman," who gathered most of his background material from American slang dictionaries, police reports, and maps of U.S. cities.

Raymond's books enjoyed strong sales around the world and were especially popular in France and Italy, where many of the stories were adapted as motion pictures. His novels include *Twelve Chinks and a Woman, You're Lonely When You're Dead, You Find Him, I'll Fix Him,* and *Do Me a Favor—Drop Dead.* Raymond also wrote several plays, such as "Get a Load of This," which was adapted from his short story collection published under the same title in 1941, and "Last Page."

OBITUARIES AND OTHER SOURCES:

BOOKS

Twentieth-Century Writing: A Reader's Guide to Contemporary Literature, Transatlantic, 1969.

PERIODICALS

Los Angeles Times, February 7, 1985.
Time, February 18, 1985.
Times (London), February 7, 1985.
Washington Post, February 11, 1985.

REDGRAVE, Michael (Scudamore) 1908-1985

OBITUARY NOTICE: Born March 20, 1908, in Bristol, Gloucestershire, England; died of Parkinson's disease, March 21, 1985, in Denham, Buckinghamshire, England. Actor, playwright, and author. Redgrave, called one of the premier British actors of his generation, performed in thirty-five motion pictures, including "The Browning Version," "Goodbye Mr. Chips," "Nicholas and Alexandra," and Alfred Hitchcock's "The Lady Vanishes." Redgrave earned a reputation as an accomplished stage actor as well, winning great praise for what critics called his definitive interpretations of such roles as Hamlet, King Lear, Macbeth, and Marc Antony. Other dramatic successes included the leads in Chekov's "Uncle Vanya" and Ibsen's "The Master Builder." He has been described as a "cerebral" actor who excelled in brooding characterizations.

Redgrave, the father of actresses Vanessa and Lynn Redgrave, had been battling for years with a degenerative illness that made acting increasingly difficult for him. His last stage performance was in "The Close of the Play" in 1979, in which he played a stroke victim confined to a wheelchair. Late in his career, Redgrave became interested in producing and directing operas and writing plays. He was the author of books, including *The Actor's Ways and Means, Mask or Face,* and *In My Mind's I: An Actor's Autobiography.* Redgrave was knighted by Queen Elizabeth II in 1959.

OBITUARIES AND OTHER SOURCES:

BOOKS

Cole, Toby and H. K. Chinoy, editors, *Actors on Acting,* Crown, 1949.
Grebanier, Bernard, *Then Came Each Actor,* McKay, 1975.
Ross, Lillian and Helen Ross, *Player,* Simon & Schuster, 1962.

PERIODICALS

Chicago Tribune, March 28, 1985.
Detroit Free Press, March 22, 1985.
Los Angeles Times, March 22, 1985.
Newsweek, April 1, 1985.
New York Times, March 22, 1985.
Time, April 1, 1985.
Times (London), March 22, 1985.
Washington Post, March 22, 1985.

*   *   *

REID, Helen Rogers 1882-1970

OBITUARY NOTICE: Born November 23, 1882, in Appleton, Wis.; died July 27, 1970; buried in Sleepy Hollow Cemetery, Tarrytown, N.Y. Journalist. A former treasurer of the New York State Campaign for Women's Suffrage, Reid was associated with the *New York Tribune* (later the *New York Herald Tribune*) for almost forty years. After her graduation from Barnard College in 1903, Reid was employed as social secretary to the wife of *New York Tribune* publisher Whitelaw Reid and eight years later married his only son, Ogden Mills Reid. Her husband inherited the newspaper in 1912, and in 1918 Helen Rogers Reid joined the *Tribune* staff as advertising solicitor. Two months later she became advertising director, and in 1922 she was named vice-president. Under Reid's direction the *Tribune*'s advertising linage increased by 100 percent by 1923.

Reid, an ardent supporter of equal rights for women, advocated a women's draft during World War II and was appointed to the Advisory Committee on Women in the Services. While working at the *Tribune* she was responsible for the addition of women's columns, society pages, and recipes to the newspaper's format. Reid also encouraged typographical improvements and was influential in the hiring of new columnists. When her husband died in 1947, Reid took over the presidency of the *Tribune,* and in 1953 she became chairman of the publication's board of directors. She retired from that post at the age of seventy-two but continued to serve as a member of the board of directors.

OBITUARIES AND OTHER SOURCES:

BOOKS

Dictionary of Literary Biography, Volume 29: *American Newspaper Journalists, 1926-1950,* Gale, 1984.
Who Was Who in America, With World Notables, Volume V: *1969-1973,* Marquis, 1973.

*   *   *

REILLY, Patrick 1932-

PERSONAL: Born January 1, 1932, in Glasgow, Scotland; son of Edward (an insulator) and Catherine (Cassidy) Reilly; married Rose Fitzpatrick, March 3, 1957; children: Edward, Joseph, Patricia, James, Roseanne, Annemarie. *Education:* Glasgow University, M.A. (first-class honors), 1961; Pembroke College, Oxford, B.Litt., 1963. *Politics:* Labour. *Religion:* Roman Catholic.

ADDRESSES: Home—7 Arundel Dr., Bishopbriggs, Glasgow G64 3JF, Scotland. *Office*—Department of English, University of Glasgow, Glasgow G12 8QQ, Scotland.

CAREER: Writer. *Military service:* British Army, 1950-52; became sergeant.

MEMBER: Catholic Education Commission for Scotland, Newman Society.

WRITINGS:

Jonathan Swift: The Brave Desponder, Southern Illinois University Press, 1982.
George Orwell: The Age's Adversary, Macmillan, 1985.

Contributor to *Catholics and Scottish Literature, Innes Review, Critical Quarterly,* and *Was Tun.*

WORK IN PROGRESS: A book on Henry Fielding, with Ken Simpson, for Vision Press; *The Dark Epiphany: A Theme in Twentieth-Century Literature;* articles on Charles Dickens, James Joyce, George Eliot, Anthony Burgess, and Thomas More, and on education and religion.

SIDELIGHTS: According to *Times Literary Supplement* reviewer F. S. L. Lyons, Patrick Reilly presents an "informative and frequently illuminating" study in *Jonathan Swift: The Brave Desponder.* The critic observed that Reilly presents a picture of the English satirist with which some scholars would violently disagree; the author "places Swift firmly in a seventeenth-century rather than in an eighteenth-century context," Lyons wrote, "and sees him as essentially a backward-looking man." "One senses that in this brilliant and provocative book the stimulation of just such counter-currents is an important part of the author's aim," added the critic.

BIOGRAPHICAL/CRITICAL SOURCES:

PERIODICALS

Times Literary Supplement, October 15, 1982.

*   *   *

REIMERS, David   1931-

PERSONAL: Born September 16, 1931, in St. Louis, Mo.; married in 1959; children: two. *Education:* Princeton University, A.B., 1953; Washington University, St. Louis, Mo., M.A., 1954; University of Wisconsin—Madison, Ph.D., 1961.

ADDRESSES: Home—156 Gray St., Teaneck, N.J. 07666. *Office*—Department of History, Washington Square College, New York University, New York, N.Y. 10003.

CAREER: Hunter College of the City University of New York, New York City, instructor in history, 1960-62; Brooklyn College of the City University of New York, Brooklyn, N.Y., assistant professor of history, 1962-66; New York University, New York City, associate professor, 1966-71, professor of history, 1971—.

MEMBER: Organization of American Historians, American Studies Association, Immigration History Society (member of executive committee, 1982-85).

AWARDS, HONORS: Fellow of Rockefeller Foundation, 1983.

WRITINGS:

White Protestantism and the Negro, Oxford University Press, 1965.
(Editor) *The Black Man in America Since Reconstruction*, Crowell, 1970.
(Editor and contributor) *Essays in American Social History*, Holt, 1970.
(Editor and contributor) *The Slavery Experience*, Holt, 1970.
(With Len Dinnerstein) *Ethnic Americans: A History of Immigration and Assimilation*, New York University Press, 1975.
(With Dinnerstein and Roger Nichols) *Natives and Strangers*, Oxford University Press, 1979.

Contributor to history journals.

*   *   *

RENICH, Fred C.   1916-1979

PERSONAL: Surname is pronounced *Ren*-nick; born September 16, 1916, in Wilber, Wash.; died, 1979; son of Edward A. (in dairy business) and Ethel Emma (a homemaker; maiden name, Echel) Renich; married Jill Torrey (a writer and speaker), October 28, 1944; children: Jan Renich Barger, Rose Renich Oates, Fred C. II, Jacqueline Renich Newbrander. *Education:* Philadelphia School (now College) of the Bible, Diploma, 1940; Wheaton College, Wheaton, Ill., B.A. (with honors), 1957.

CAREER: Missionary, with posts in China and Australia, 1942-54; pastor of Christian church in Savanna, Ill., 1954-57; Missionary Internship, Farmington, Mich., director, 1957-72; Living Life Ministries, Montrose, Pa., founder and president, 1972-79. Member of board of directors of Child Evangelism Fellowship; public speaker and personal counselor.

WRITINGS:

What Happens When You Meet You, Living Life, 1975.
The Christian Husband, Living Life, 1976.

When the Chisel Hits the Rock, Victor Books, 1980.

Contributor to periodicals.

[Sketch verified by wife, Jill Renich]

*   *   *

RICHARDS, John F(olsom)   1938-

PERSONAL: Born November 3, 1938, in Exeter, N.H.; son of Frank F. and Ella O. (Higgins) Richards; married Ann Berry, 1961; children: Jennifer Ann, L. Benjamin. *Education:* University of New Hampshire, B.A. (summa cum laude), 1961; University of California, Berkeley, M.A., 1964, Ph.D., 1970.

ADDRESSES: Home—1012 Gloria Ave., Durham, N.C. 27701.

CAREER: University of Wisconsin—Madison, instructor, 1968-70, assistant professor, 1970-74, associate professor of history and South Asian studies, 1974-77; Duke University, Durham, N.C., associate professor, 1977-80, professor of history, 1981—. Member of Social Science Research Council-American Council of Learned Societies joint committee on South Asia, 1978-83; American Institute of Indian Studies, member of board of trustees, 1978—, member of executive committee, 1984—; member of board of trustees and executive committee of American Institute of Pakistan Studies, 1979-82; foreign adviser to Quaid-I-Azam University, 1982; organizer of conferences; consultant to Institute for Energy Analysis.

MEMBER: American Historical Association, Association for Asian Studies, Forest History Society, American Society for Environmental History, Phi Beta Kappa.

AWARDS, HONORS: Award from Foreign Area Fellowship Program for India, Iran, and Europe, 1965-68; grants from Social Science Research Council and American Council of Learned Societies for England and the Netherlands, 1971; awards from Comparative World History Fund for England, 1972, and American Institute of Indian Studies for India, 1973; American Philosophical Society grants, 1972-74; senior fellow of National Endowment for the Humanities, 1979-80; fellow at National Humanities Center, 1979-80; grants from Smithsonian Institution, 1984-85, Oak Ridge National Laboratories, 1985, and Ecosystems Center of Marine Biological Laboratory at Woods Hole, Mass., 1985.

WRITINGS:

Mughal Administration in Golconda, Clarendon Press, 1975.
(Editor and contributor) *Kingship and Authority in South Asia*, Center for South Asian Studies, University of Wisconsin—Madison, 1978.
(Editor and contributor) *Precious Metals in the Later Medieval and Early Modern World*, Carolina Academic Press, 1983.
(Editor with Richard Tucker, and contributor) *Global Deforestation and the Nineteenth-Century World Economy*, Duke University Pess, 1983.
(Editor and contributor) *The Imperial Monetary System of Mughal India*, Oxford University Press (New Delhi), in press.
The Mughal Empire, Cambridge University Press, 1986.

CONTRIBUTOR

P. M. Joshi, editor, *Studies in the Foreign Relations of India*, [Hyderabad], 1975.
Barbara Metcalf, editor, *Sources of Moral Authority in South Asian Islam*, University of California Press, 1984.

Kendall E. Bailes, editor, *Environmental History: Critical Issues in Comparative Perspective,* University Press of America, 1984.

Co-editor of series "The New Cambridge History of India," Cambridge University Press, 1979—. Contributor to *World Book Encyclopedia* and *Encyclopaedia Iranica.* Contributor of more than a dozen articles to scholarly journals. Assistant editor for South Asia, *Journal of Asian Studies,* 1972-77; member of editorial board of *Bulletin of Concerned Asian Scholars,* 1982—.

WORK IN PROGRESS: Banditry in Comparative Perspective, case studies of "historically visible" banditry in a global perspective; editing *World Deforestation in the Twentieth Century,* with Richard Tucker; "World Environmental History and Economic Development," to be included in *Sustainable Development of the Biosphere,* edited by W. C. Clark and R. E. Munn; text to accompany maps to be included in *Historical Atlas of Islamic Civilization,* edited by Herbert H. Bodman and Richard Kopec, for Westview.

* * *

RICHARDSON, Cecil Antonio   1928-
(Tony Richardson)

BRIEF ENTRY: Professionally known as Tony Richardson; born June 5, 1928, in Shipley, Yorkshire, England. British stage and film director, producer, and screenwriter. Richardson, who made theatrical history with his 1956 stage production of "Look Back in Anger," John Osborne's controversial indictment of British society, emerged as a leading filmmaker in the 1960's. His critically acclaimed motion pictures from that period include "Saturday Night and Sunday Morning" (Continental, 1960), the screen adaptation of Alan Sillitoe's novel about the working class, directed by Karl Reisz and produced by Richardson and Harry Saltzman. His film adaptation of Shelagh Delaney's play "A Taste of Honey" was also widely admired by critics. Richardson, who collaborated with Delaney on the screenplay, produced and directed the film. "Tom Jones," based on Osborne's adaptation of Henry Fielding's novel, brought Richardson the 1963 Academy Award for best director. Highly esteemed for his work, Richardson has directed numerous stars, including his former wife Vanessa Redgrave, Laurence Olivier, Lee Remick, Albert Finney, Richard Burton, Claire Bloom, Mick Jagger, Nastassia Kinski, Jodie Foster, and Wallace Shawn.

While a student at Oxford University, Richardson directed works from the classical theatre repertoire for the school's Dramatic Society. He later directed television plays for the British Broadcasting Corporation. In 1955 Richardson joined the progressive English Stage Company, for which he staged plays by classical, modern, and avant-garde authors, including Eugene Ionesco, Jean Giraudoux, William Faulkner, Tennessee Williams, Bertolt Brecht, and Anton Chekhov. The following year Richardson participated in the Free Cinema series with his 1955 short film "Momma Don't Allow," written and directed with Karl Reisz. Richardson was associated with the Free Cinema movement, which stressed realism and socially relevant themes, but he eventually became independent of film movements. Richardson co-authored scripts for his films "The Sailor From Gibraltar" (Lopert, 1967) and "Ned Kelly" (United Artists, 1970); he also directed and wrote "The Hotel New Hampshire" (Orion, 1984), the film version of John Irving's best-selling novel. Richardson's other writings include film

reviews for *Sight and Sound. Address:* 1478 North Kings Rd., Los Angeles, Calif. 90069.

BIOGRAPHICAL/CRITICAL SOURCES:

BOOKS

Current Biography, Wilson, 1963.
Film Encyclopedia, Crowell, 1979.
The Oxford Companion to Film, Oxford University Press, 1976.

PERIODICALS

New York, March 19, 1984.
New York Times, March 9, 1984.

* * *

RICHARDSON, Edgar Preston   1902-1985

OBITUARY NOTICE—See index for *CA* sketch: Born December 2, 1902, in Glens Falls, N.Y.; died after several strokes, March 27, 1985, in Philadelphia, Pa. Art historian, administrator, editor, and author. A well-known art historian, Richardson was associated with the Detroit Institute of Art for more than thirty years, serving as assistant director from 1933 to 1935 and as director from 1945 to 1962. He subsequently directed the Henri Francis du Pont Winterthur Museum, was affiliated with the Smithsonian Art Commission and the National Portrait Gallery Commission, and co-founded the Archives of American Art. Richardson took a particular interest in American painting, and his book *Painting in America: The Story of Four Hundred Fifty Years* is a classic in the field. Other books by Richardson include *Twentieth-Century Painting, The Way of Western Art: 1776-1914,* and *Washington Allston: A Study of the Romantic Artist in America.* He was also editorial consultant to *American Art Journal* beginning in 1969, edited *Art Quarterly* from 1938 to 1967, and at various times served as an editorial board member of *Magazine of Art, Art in America,* and *Pennsylvania Magazine of History and Art.*

OBITUARIES AND OTHER SOURCES:

PERIODICALS

New York Times, March 29, 1985.

* * *

RICHARDSON, Tony
See RICHARDSON, Cecil Antonio

* * *

RICO, Don(ato)   1917-1985

OBITUARY NOTICE—See index for *CA* sketch: Born September 26, 1917, in Rochester, N.Y.; died of cancer, March 27, 1985. Illustrator, artist, editor, and author. Rico was probably best known as the author and illustrator of Marvel Comics publications such as *Captain America* and *Daredevil.* In addition to his work on comic books, Rico wrote western novels and mysteries, including *Last of the Breed, Daisy Dilemma,* and *Bed of Lesbos,* and contributed scripts to the television series "Adam-12." He also produced wood engravings, many of which are on exhibit at the Metropolitan Museum of Art, and co-founded the Comic Arts Professional Society.

OBITUARIES AND OTHER SOURCES:

PERIODICALS

Chicago Tribune, April 20, 1985.

*   *   *

RIGGAN, (John) Rob(inson)   1943-

PERSONAL: Born December 11, 1943, in Essex, Conn.; son of George Arkel (a theologian) and Merle (a teacher; maiden name, Robinson) Riggan; married Margalee Oelrich (a computer specialist), June 5, 1971. *Education:* Haverford College, B.A., 1967; attended Vanderbilt University, 1971.

ADDRESSES: Leshure's Rd., Rowe, Mass. 01367.

CAREER: Morganton News-Herald, Morganton, N.C., reporter, 1971-73; *Raleigh News and Observer,* Raleigh, N.C., reporter, 1973; free-lance writer, 1973—. *Military service:* U.S. Army, Medical Corps, 1968-71.

WRITINGS:

Free Fire Zone (novel), Norton, 1984.

WORK IN PROGRESS: A novel for Norton.

SIDELIGHTS: Free Fire Zone, Rob Riggan's 1984 novel, relates the experiences of members of a medical unit stationed in Vietnam during the Vietnam War. According to Michiko Kakutani, reviewing *Free Fire Zone* in the *New York Times,* the book "deals . . . with the brutalizing effects of combat, with the pettiness of military bureaucrats, with the difficulties of going back to life in 'The World.'" Kakutani remarked, however, that *Free Fire Zone*'s distinguishing feature is that "Mr. Riggan has focused on the isolating effects of [wartime] experience." In reading Riggan's novel, concluded Kakutani, "we see how war can numb people's capacity for feeling, and in doing so, can also cripple their ability to connect with anyone or anything."

Rob Riggan told *CA:* "My second novel represents a continuation of themes explored in *Free Fire Zone,* but set in the United States rather than in Vietnam. Two of the main characters in the first novel appear in this second, but only in minor roles. The focus in the new work shifts from the personal devastation and disillusionment of men in Vietnam, to the difficulties of readjustment and further disillusionment in a peacetime world that in fact may not be as far removed from the war zone as these men so desperately need to believe. While I explored the nature of moral disintegration in *Free Fire Zone,* in the second book I am concentrating on the possibility of redemptive action.

"The nature of civilized behavior and civilized nations is of particular interest to me. I have a strong background in history and constitutional law, and I have always been fascinated by the need of humans to be governed by laws, whether imposed from without or submitted to voluntarily as in terms of a social contract. For instance, the underlying assumption that I perceive in the social contract seems to me to go to the heart of human behavior: the tacit recognition of the chaos that all of us are capable of producing, the human jungle (not the natural one).

"The conflicts that invariably occur when individuals, living under rules of law, encounter restraints on their behavior are both an affirmation of the human will, a source of hope, as I see it, and also the point of disintegration and despair. The exploration and, hopefully, understanding of these moments of conflict, and their consequences, is my prime interest in my writing. Viewed in this context, I find it easier to like and accept the people and events that I've known, and the people and worlds that I create."

BIOGRAPHICAL/CRITICAL SOURCES:

PERIODICALS

New York Times, February 13, 1984.
Writer, October, 1984.

*   *   *

RIGGS, John R(aymond)   1945-

PERSONAL: Born February 27, 1945, in Beech Grove, Ind.; son of Samuel H. (a chemical engineer) and Lucille (a bookkeeper; maiden name, Ruff) Riggs; married Cynthia Perkins, September 2, 1967 (divorced, 1976); children: Heidi Ann, Shawn Justin. *Education:* Indiana University—Bloomington, B.S., 1967, M.A., 1968; further graduate study at University of Michigan, 1970-71.

ADDRESSES: Home and office—506 Ohio, Greencastle, Ind. 46135.

CAREER: Teacher of English and athletic coach at schools in Greencastle, Ind., 1968-75; quality control night foreman at factory in Greencastle, Ind., 1975-78; DePauw University, Greencastle, crew chief for river research, 1979-84, archives researcher, 1983-85; high school football coach, 1983-85; writer. Member of board of directors of Oakala Lake Corp., 1975-76; member of Madison Township Volunteer Firemen.

WRITINGS:

MYSTERY NOVELS

The Last Laugh, Dembner, 1984.
Let Sleeping Dogs Lie, Dembner, 1985.
The Glory Hound, Dembner, in press.
A Dragon Lives Forever, Dembner, in press.

SIDELIGHTS: John R. Riggs commented: "I did not choose writing. It chose me. I started my first novel in the summer of 1972 while I was still teaching. Since then I've written at least fifteen unpublished novels, one unpublished musical, and lyrics for more than one hundred songs. At the same time I worked at anything, including carpentry, splitting wood, hunting, and trapping.

"I plan to continue writing as long as there is hope for publication (perhaps even if not). I did not know in the beginning how hard it would be to get a novel published. I might never have started, though I have since decided there is nothing else I want to do, no other way I would rather live.

"To write is to live free—free to fail, free to hope and dream, free to wander wherever my mind leads me. It's the freedom of childhood, with all its aches and pains, rejections and humiliations, and glorious possiblities that always seem to run one step ahead of me. It's the feeling that this day belongs to me and no one else. And no matter how tired or discouraged or frustrated I become, I have no one to blame except myself. There's something satisfying in that—and magical.

"My mysteries are set in the mythical town of Oakala, Wisconsin, which is based on my hometown of Mulberry, Indiana, and is (I hope) a good representative of small-town America. My protagonist is Garth Ryland, editor and publisher of the

Oakalla Reporter. Garth is a man of principle, but is also wryly aware of his own fallibility. He is a self-proclaimed 'duck' (a plodder rather than a prancer), a dogged seeker of truth, and while a romantic at heart, a realist in the face of life.

"Garth's search for the answers that puzzle him are in many ways my search for the answers that puzzle me. Why do we commit crimes against each other? What motivates each and every one of us to do good or to do evil or to fall somewhere in between? Why do some triumph where others fail? Is it luck, the cut of the cards, circumstance, or something born within us that drives us to both greatness and despair?

"More than anything else Garth finds that we are each unique, each with our own stories to tell, and that simple descriptions are usually inadequate for even the 'simplest' among us. And it is his interactions with the varied and colorful characters that live in Oakalla that are the heart of my mysteries."

*   *   *

RIGHT HONOURABLE LORD DENNING
See DENNING, Alfred Thompson

*   *   *

RILEY, Jocelyn (Carol) 1949-

PERSONAL: Born March 6, 1949, in Minneapolis, Minn.; daughter of G. D. (a sales engineer) and D. J. (a secretary; maiden name, Berg) Riley; married Jeffrey Allen Steele (a college professor), September 4, 1971; children: Doran Riley. *Education:* Attended Harvard University, summer, 1970; Carleton College, B.A., 1971.

ADDRESSES: Office—Box 5264—Hilldale, Madison, Wis. 53705. *Agent*—Jane Gelfman, John Farquharson Ltd., 250 West 57th St., New York, N.Y. 10107.

CAREER: Carleton Miscellany, Northfield, Minn., managing editor, 1971; Beacon Press (publisher), Boston, Mass., marketing assistant, 1971-73; free-lance writer and editor, 1973—. Media scriptwriter for American Family Insurance, Madison, Wis., 1983-85.

MEMBER: Women in Communications (vice-president of Madison chapter, 1983-84; president, 1984-85), Authors Guild, Society of Children's Book Writers, Association for Multi-Image, Council for Wisconsin Writers.

AWARDS, HONORS: Only My Mouth Is Smiling was named a "best book for young adults" by American Library Association, 1982; Arthur Tofte Memorial Award from Council for Wisconsin Writers, 1982, for *Only My Mouth Is Smiling.*

WRITINGS:

Only My Mouth Is Smiling (children's book), Morrow, 1982.
Crazy Quilt (children's book), Morrow, 1984.
Page Proof (essays) Windigo Press, in press.
Otherwise I Wouldn't Be Here (novel), Morrow, in press.

Author of "The Brass Ring" (television film based on *Only My Mouth Is Smiling*), first broadcast by Showtime-TV, February 2, 1985. Contributor of articles and reviews to magazines, including *Aspect, Boston, Publishers Weekly,* and *Writer,* and newspapers.

WORK IN PROGRESS: Sweet Talk, a novel, completion expected in 1987.

SIDELIGHTS: Jocelyn Riley commented: "A major concern of both my fiction and nonfiction is women's lives and women's work. My first two novels focused on very young women protagonists growing up in a predominantly female world that was nevertheless dominated by men in terms of actual (though unseen) power.

"A second major theme of my fiction has been the effect of a severely mentally disturbed person on a whole family, particularly the children involved. I chose to concentrate on children because they are stuck in a situation in a way that a spouse, for instance, is not."

BIOGRAPHICAL/CRITICAL SOURCES:

PERIODICALS

Boston Equal Times, August 22, 1982.
Cambridge Sojourner, October, 1982.
Houston Post, June 13, 1982.
Madison Sunshine, June 16, 1982.
Milwaukee Journal, April 11, 1982, February 1, 1985.
Minneapolis Star and Tribune, September 9, 1982, February 21, 1985.
San Diego Union, May 2, 1982.
Wisconsin Academy Review, December, 1983.
Wisconsin State Journal, February 28, 1982, December 2, 1984.

*   *   *

ROARK, Garland 1904-1985
(George Garland)

OBITUARY NOTICE—See index for *CA* sketch: Born July 26, 1904, in Groesbeck, Tex.; died following pneumonia, February 9, 1985, in Nacogdoches, Tex. Advertising sales manager and author. Roark held advertising posts with various stores in Texas from 1924 to 1946, when he quit to become a writer. Among his many novels are *Wake of the Red Witch,* which was adapted for film, *Fair Wind to Java, Slant of the Wild Wind, The Witch of Manga Reva,* and *Drill a Crooked Hole.* Roark also wrote several westerns under the pseudonym George Garland and was a feature writer and columnist for the *Houston Chronicle* in the early 1960's.

OBITUARIES AND OTHER SOURCES:

BOOKS

The Writers Directory: 1984-1986, St. James Press, 1983.

PERIODICALS

Houston Post, February 10, 1985.

*   *   *

ROBERT, Paul A.
See ROUBICZEK, Paul (Anton)

*   *   *

ROBERTS, Colette Jacqueline 1910-1971

OBITUARY NOTICE: Born September 16, 1910, in Paris, France; died August 9, 1971. Art critic, educator, and author. Roberts studied at Institut d'Art et Archeologie of the Sorbonne, the Ecole du Louvre, and the Academie Ranson, before coming to the United States in 1939. In New York City Roberts worked as a researcher for the French Press and Information Service and France Forever, and during the late 1940's served as gallery director for the National Association of Women Artists. She became gallery director for New York's Grand Central Moderns museum in 1952, where she specialized in modern American art. Leaving that position in 1968, Roberts went to the A. M. Sachs Gallery as associate director. She was also an organizer of cultural exchange programs sponsored by the American and French embassies. Beginning in 1953, Roberts served as an art critic for *France Amerique,* and from 1960 until 1968 she was an art critic for *Aujourd'hui* and *Art et Architecture.* She was the author of two monographs, *Mark Tobey* and *Louise Nevelson, Sculptor.* Roberts exhibited her own art work at the Salon d'Automne in Paris and, for fourteen years, was an adjunct professor of art history at New York University, where she organized and directed the "Meet the Artist" program.

OBITUARIES AND OTHER SOURCES:

BOOKS

Who Was Who in America, With World Notables, Volume V: *1969-1973,* Marquis, 1973.

*   *   *

ROBERTS, Michele (B.) 1949-

PERSONAL: Born May 20, 1949, in Bushey, Hertfordshire, England; daughter of Reginald George Roberts (a businessman) and Monique Pauline Joseph Caulle (a teacher). *Education:* Oxford University, B.A. (with honors), 1970; University of London Library Associate, 1972. *Politics:* "Socialist-feminist". *Religion:* "Unconventional."

ADDRESSES: Agent—Caroline Dawnay, A.D. Peters, 10 Buckingham St., London WC2, England.

CAREER: Has worked variously as a librarian, cook, teacher, cleaner, pregnancy counselor, and researcher; writer-in-residence in Lambeth Borough, London, England, 1981-82; writer-in-residence in Bromley Borough, London, 1983-84.

MEMBER: Writers Guild.

AWARDS, HONORS: Gay News Literary Award, 1978, for *A Piece of the Night.*

WRITINGS:

A Piece of the Night (novel), Women's Press, 1978.
(With Alison Fell and others) *Tales I Tell My Mother* (short stories), Journeyman Press, 1978.
(With Judith Karantris and Michelene Wandor) *Touch Papers* (poetry), Allison & Busby, 1982.
The Visitation (novel), Women's Press, 1983.
The Wild Girl (novel), Methuen, 1984.
The Mirror of the Mother (poetry), Methuen, 1985.
Mrs. Noah's Diary (novel), Methuen, in press.

Contributor of nonfiction to *City Limits* and of poems to periodicals.

WORK IN PROGRESS: A nonfiction work on women and writing, publication by Polity Press/Blackwell expected in 1986; two children's books.

SIDELIGHTS: Some of Michele Roberts's books have dealt with controversial subjects. In *A Piece of the Night* she writes of a woman's journey to self-realization—from convent schoolgirl to wife and mother to feminist and lesbian. In *The Wild Girl,* Roberts writes of biblical figure Mary Magdalene

and her life as a prostitute and as a follower of Christ. A reviewer for *Time Out* described this work as "a powerful attack on the law of the Father and a timely reminder that old myths do not just fade away."

Roberts told *CA:* "My writing generally is fueled by the fact that I am a woman. I *need* to write in order to break through the silence imposed on women in this culture. The love of friends is central to my life."

Roberts speaks French and Italian.

AVOCATIONAL INTERESTS: Cooking and eating, painting, mountain walking, dancing, swimming, traveling.

BIOGRAPHICAL/CRITICAL SOURCES:

PERIODICALS

London Review of Books, February 16, 1984.
New Statesman, November 3, 1978, April 22, 1983.
Spectator, November 4, 1978.
Time Out, December, 1984.
Times Literary Supplement, December 1, 1978.

*   *   *

ROBERTS, Rachel 1927-1980

OBITUARY NOTICE: Born September 20, 1927, in Llanelly, Wales; committed suicide, November 26, 1980, in Los Angeles, Calif. Actress and author. The former wife of British actor Rex Harrison, Roberts won international acclaim for her performances on stage, screen, and television. Her character portrayals in "Saturday Night and Sunday Morning" and "The Sporting Life" earned her British best film actress awards. In addition she won awards for her roles in the 1976 film "Picnic at Hanging Rock," John Schlesinger's 1980 film "Yanks," and in the British stage hit "Alpha Beta." She also gained widespread recognition for appearances on the television dramas "Great Expectations" and "A Circle of Children," for her regular part on television's "Tony Randall Show" series, and for her film roles in "Murder on the Orient Express" and "Foul Play." The diaries she kept during the last few years of her life, published posthumously as *No Bell on Sunday: The Journals of Rachel Roberts,* document the struggle with alcohol and drugs that led to her suicide.

OBITUARIES AND OTHER SOURCES:

BOOKS

Who's Who, 133rd edition, St. Martin's, 1981.

PERIODICALS

Los Angeles Times Book Review, September 9, 1984.
New York Times, November 28, 1980.

*   *   *

ROBINSON, Ray Charles 1932- (Ray Charles)

BRIEF ENTRY: Professionally known as Ray Charles; born September 23, 1932, in Albany, Ga. American singer, musician, bandleader, and author. The voice of Ray Charles can be heard in almost every genre of popular music. He started performing rhythm and jazz, playing the piano and saxophone, when he was a teenager in Georgia. Though blindness had struck him in childhood, he taught himself to compose and arrange music. By the time he began recording for Atlantic

Records in 1954, Charles had created his own style, which blended gospel and "soul" music with jazz and blues. Five years later he moved to ABC-Paramount Records, and his popularity spread quickly.

In 1962 Charles became the first black man to achieve success in the country music field following the release of his record album *Modern Sounds in Country and Western Music*. Single releases such as "Hard Times," "I Can't Stop Loving You," and "Let the Good Times Roll" contributed substantially to his fame. In 1973 Charles started his own company, Crossover Records, and he has become a popular concert and television performer. He was named honorary life chairman of the Rhythm and Blues Hall of Fame and the Songwriters Hall of Fame, and his dozens of awards include at least ten Grammy Awards and three Gold Records. Charles is the co-author of *Brother Ray: Ray Charles' Own Story* (Dial, 1978). *Address:* RPM International, 2107 West Washington Blvd., Los Angeles, Calif. 90018.

BIOGRAPHICAL/CRITICAL SOURCES:

BOOKS

Baker's Biographical Dictionary of Musicians, 6th edition, Schirmer, 1978.
Biography News, Volume I, Gale, 1974.
Current Biography, Wilson, 1965.
International Who's Who, 46th edition, Europa, 1982.

*   *   *

ROCCAPRIORE, Marie   1933-

PERSONAL: Born July 5, 1933, in Meriden, Conn.; daughter of Vitaliano and Josephine (Amato) Roccapriore. *Education:* Received A.A. from Villa Walsh Junior College, B.A. from Notre Dame College of Maryland, and M.A. from LaSalle College; graduate study at Temple University and Fordham University.

ADDRESSES: Home—112 Bellevue St., Meriden, Conn. 06450. *Office*—St. Bridget Church, 175 Main St., Cheshire, Conn. 06410.

CAREER: Name in religion, Sister Marie Roccapriore; entered order of Religious Teachers Filippini (M.P.F.), 1948, made final vows of Roman Catholic nun, 1952; teacher at elementary and junior high schools in New Jersey, Rhode Island, Connecticut, Maryland, and Pennsylvania, 1953-68; principal of Roman Catholic school in Philadelphia, Pa., 1966-78, and teacher, 1966-68; director of religious education at Roman Catholic parish in North Haven, Conn., 1978-84; St. Bridget Parish, Cheshire, Conn., director of religious education, 1985—. Adult education teacher for Roman Catholic Archdiocese of Hartford, Conn.

WRITINGS:

Anointing of the Sick and the Elderly: A Pastoral Guide for Home and Church, Alba House, 1980.

Also author of the pamphlet *The Sacrament of the Anointing of the Sick and the Elderly* and religious songs for children.

Work represented in anthologies, including *American Poetry Anthology*. Contributor to *Catholic School Teacher* and *Project Sharing*.

WORK IN PROGRESS: Religious poetry and reflections.

SIDELIGHTS: Marie Roccapriore told *CA:* "My work on the anointing of the sick and the elderly is the result of a personal interest and concern for continued pastoral care of the sick and the aged. Having experienced sickness and hospitalizations myself at different periods in my life, a sensitivity to ailing people through special prayer, compassionate concern, and communication remains a high priority of mine.

"The Anointing of the Sick is a sacrament of the Catholic church in which a sick or an elderly person is anointed by the priest with holy oil for spiritual and physical healing. For a long time, the Anointing was looked upon as an unwelcome rite. Under the name of Extreme Unction it was viewed as a sacrament for the terminally-ill, who received it as a preparation for death. Too often, people who were ill or who faced weakness due to old age, and who could have reaped the benefits of healing prayer, postponed the sacrament or delayed it entirely because of the attitude surrounding its reception.

"With the Second Vatican Council came revisions to the rites. The church fathers issued pastoral recommendations to restore the original meaning of the sacraments, among them—the Anointing. No longer was it to be viewed as the 'death-bed' sacrament. Rather, it was to be celebrated for healing, and the suffering participant would be the focal point of the celebration. The emphasis in the reception of the Anointing would shift from negative to positive, from private to public, from somber to faith-filled and joy-filled participation.

"I studied the pastoral documents issued by the bishops and engaged in extensive readings on this topic. The research brought me great excitement. I began to have a newer appreciation for this healing sacrament. As my interest and appreciation grew, my determination to implement the pastoral recommendations grew, and it wasn't long before I undertook the position of coordinating parish liturgical celebrations of anointing.

"I took slides of the parish celebrations and used them in my original presentations in sharing a catechesis on the new rite of anointing at workshops for catechists and at various parishes. It was extremely rewarding to see suffering people anticipate their participation in church for the liturgical celebrations—in wheelchairs, with walkers, canes, etc. . . . So many of them had seldom or never left their 'shut-in' environments. The response from medical personnel to join us was equally rewarding and inspirational.

"The effects of the sacramental anointing celebrations were so positive that I deeply desired to share them with others outside the parish communities. Being an amateur, I knew it would not be an easy task. Nonetheless, I followed the promptings within me and combined my research with personal experience and involvements with the sick into a 142-page paperback. The photos taken at various celebrations were included along with my original prayerful reflections. At the time of my writing, I was principal of a large inner-city school in Philadelphia. The parishioners of St. Nicholas of Tolentine Parish there were extremely helpful in providing me with honest expressions of their personal reactions after liturgical celebrations of anointing. Some of these were also included in my paperback."

AVOCATIONAL INTERESTS: "I enjoy creative poetry and reflections that come to me during quiet moments of prayer."

*   *   *

RODRIGUEZ MONEGAL, Emir   1921-

BRIEF ENTRY: Born July 28, 1921, in Uruguay. Uruguayan

educator and author. Rodriguez Monegal was a professor of English literature at Montevideo's Instituto de Profesores from 1952 to 1962. Since then he has been a visiting professor at institutions throughout the Western Hemisphere, including El Colegio de Mexico and Harvard University. In 1965 Rodriguez Monegal was appointed editor of the French literary magazine *Mundo Nuevo*. Though he has produced numerous books in his native language, only a few have appeared in English; these include *The Borzoi Anthology of Latin American Literature* (Knopf, 1977), which he edited, and *Jorge Luis Borges: A Literary Biography*, which was published by Dutton in 1978.

BIOGRAPHICAL/CRITICAL SOURCES:

PERIODICALS

Atlantic Monthly, December, 1978.
New Republic, February 3, 1979.
New Yorker, February 19, 1979.
World Literature Today, winter, 1978.

* * *

ROE, Dorothy
 See LEWIS, Dorothy Roe

* * *

ROE, F(rederic) Gordon 1894-1985
 (Uncle Gordon)

OBITUARY NOTICE—See index for *CA* sketch: Born September 24, 1894, in Chelsea, London, England; died January 6, 1985. Art expert, editor, and author. Roe was known for his many writings about art and artists, including *Henry Bright of the Norwich School, The Nude From Cranach to Etty and Beyond, Rowlandson: The Life and Art of a British Genius,* and *Victorian Corners: The Style and Taste of an Era.* Under the pseudonym Uncle Gordon he also wrote the children's book *Clarence Below the Basement*. Roe edited *Connoisseur* magazine from 1933 to 1935 and contributed to numerous periodicals.

OBITUARIES AND OTHER SOURCES:

BOOKS

International Authors and Writers Who's Who, 9th edition, [and] *International Who's Who in Poetry*, 6th edition, Melrose, 1982.
Who's Who, 136th edition, St. Martin's, 1984.

PERIODICALS

Times (London), January 10, 1985.

* * *

ROGERS, Jean 1919-

PERSONAL: Born October 1, 1919, in Wendell, Idaho; daughter of John Harvey and Maud (Powers) Clark; married George W. Rogers (a research economist), November 27, 1942; children: Shelley Rogers Eldridge, Geoffrey, Sidney Rogers Sisikin, Gavin (deceased), Sabrina, Garth. *Education:* University of California, Berkeley, B.A., 1943.

ADDRESSES: Home—1790 Evergreen Ave., Juneau, Alaska 99801.

CAREER: Writer. Member of Alaska Public Offices Commission, 1982-87; Capital Community Broadcasting, Inc., member of board of directors, 1975-83, past chairman of board.

MEMBER: American Library Association, Alaska Library Association.

AWARDS, HONORS: Honored Author Citation from Alaska State Reading Council, 1980; awards from International Reading Association and Juneau Reading Council, 1985, for service to libraries and promotion of reading.

WRITINGS:

FOR YOUNG PEOPLE

Goodbye, My Island, Greenwillow, 1983.
The Secret Moose, Greenwillow, 1985.
King Island Christmas, Greenwillow, 1985.

SIDELIGHTS: Jean Rogers told *CA:* "My writing is definitely an outgrowth of my lifelong pleasure in reading. I am honored to be described as a children's book author. A great deal of very fine writing is done in that field, and it has long been a keen interest of mine."

* * *

ROGERS, Vincent R(obert) 1926-

BRIEF ENTRY: Born December 9, 1926, in New York, N.Y. American educator, editor, and author. Rogers taught at Syracuse University, the University of Massachusetts, and the University of Minnesota, before he was appointed professor of education at the University of Connecticut in 1967. A Fulbright scholar in England in 1965, he has also worked in Kenya and Italy. Rogers edited *A Sourcebook for Social Studies* (Macmillan, 1969), *Teaching in the British Primary School* (Macmillan, 1970), and *Teaching Social Studies in the Urban Classroom* (Addison-Wesley, 1972). He collaborated on writing and editing *Open Education: Critique and Assessment* (Association for Curriculum and Development, 1975). *Address:* Department of Education, University of Connecticut, Storrs, Conn. 06268.

BIOGRAPHICAL/CRITICAL SOURCES:

PERIODICALS

New York Times Book Review, September 10, 1970.

* * *

ROGERSON, J(ohn) W(illiam) 1935-
 (John Rogerson)

PERSONAL: Born May 16, 1935, in London, England; son of George W. H. (a carpenter and joiner) and Fanny (Page) Rogerson; married Rosalind Ann Fulford, September 11, 1965. *Education:* University of Manchester, B.D., 1961, D.D., 1975; University of Oxford, B.A., 1963, M.A., 1967. *Religion:* Christian.

ADDRESSES: Office—University of Sheffield, Sheffield S10 2TN, England.

CAREER: University of Durham, Durham, England, lecturer, 1964-75, senior lecturer in theology, 1975-79; University of Sheffield, Sheffield, England, professor of biblical studies and chairman of department, 1979—. *Military service:* Royal Air Force, 1953-55.

MEMBER: Society for Old Testament Study (home secretary, 1972-77).

WRITINGS:

Myth in Old Testament Interpretation, De Gruyter, 1974.

(With J. W. McKay) *Psalms: Cambridge Old Testament Commentaries,* Cambridge University Press, 1977.
Anthropology and the Old Testament, Blackwell/John Knox, 1978.

Contributor to theological and anthropological journals, including *Journal of Theological Studies, Churchman, Theology, Journal of the Anthropological Society of Oxford,* and *Modern Churchman.*

UNDER NAME JOHN ROGERSON

The Supernatural in the Old Testament, Lutterworth, 1976.
(Editor) *Beginning Old Testament Study,* Westminster, 1983.
Old Testament Criticism in the Nineteenth Century, Fortress, 1984.
The New Atlas of the Bible, Macdonalds, 1985.

WORK IN PROGRESS: Researching the history of Old Testament criticism; writing the Old Testament portion of a history of the use of the Old Testament in the Christian Church; a critical biography of Wilhelm Leberecht de Wette, one of the founders of Old Testament criticism.

SIDELIGHTS: John Rogerson describes his book, *Beginning Old Testament Study,* as "a guide to how to approach the academic study of the Old Testament." In it he explores Old Testament and Israelite history, the world view of the Old Testament, the history of Old Testament scholarship, and the application of the texts to social and moral issues. Anthony Phillips, writing in the *Times Literary Supplement,* determined that *Beginning Old Testament Study* should appear on the "first reading list" of Old Testament students. The critic added: "Conscious of the different spiritual backgrounds from which students come, [Rogerson] exhibits throughout a gentle pastoral touch which in no way blunts the sharpness of his essays."

Rogerson told *CA:* "I hold some competence in French, German, Hebrew, and Arabic; I make frequent journeys to Germany and Israel's West Bank. I am convinced that the history of a discipline is a fundamental part of its critical self-awareness."

BIOGRAPHICAL/CRITICAL SOURCES:

PERIODICALS

Times Literary Supplement, July 1, 1983.

*   *   *

ROGERSON, John
See ROGERSON, J(ohn) W(illiam)

*   *   *

ROMPKEY, Ronald (George)   1943-

PERSONAL: Born February 10, 1943, in St. John's, Newfoundland, Canada; son of William H., Sr., and Margaret (Fudge) Rompkey; married Noreen Golfman (a university professor), August 5, 1983. *Education:* Memorial University of Newfoundland, B.A., 1965, B.Ed., 1966, M.A., 1968; King's College, London, Ph.D., 1972.

ADDRESSES: Office—Department of English Language and Literature, Memorial University of Newfoundland, St. John's, Newfoundland, Canada A1C 5S7.

CAREER: University of Alberta, Edmonton, lecturer in English, 1976-77; University of Saskatchewan, Saskatoon, as-

sistant professor of English, 1977-79; University of Alberta, lecturer in English, 1979-82; University of Lethbridge, Lethbridge, Alberta, assistant professor of English, 1982-83; University of Maine at Orono, visiting professor of English, 1983-84; Memorial University of Newfoundland, St. John's, assistant professor of English, 1984—. *Aide de camp* to Governor-General of Canada, 1984—. *Military service:* Canadian Naval Reserve, 1961—, commanding officer of HMCS *Cabot,* 1984—; present rank, commander.

MEMBER: Association of Canadian University Teachers of English, American Society for Eighteenth-Century Studies, Modern Language Association of America, Royal Society of Arts (fellow), Royal Historical Society (fellow).

WRITINGS:

(Editor and author of introduction and notes) *Expeditions of Honour: The Journal of John Salusbury in Halifax, Nova Scotia, 1749-1753,* University of Delaware Press, 1982.
Soame Jenyns, Twayne, 1984.

WORK IN PROGRESS: Edward Gibbon: An Annotated Bibliography, publication by Garland expected in 1987; *Sir Wilfred Grenfell: A Biography,* publication expected in 1988; research on eighteenth-century British literature.

SIDELIGHTS: Ronald Rompkey told *CA:* "My writing is concerned with the life and literature of the eighteenth century, particularly the activities surrounding the life of Samuel Johnson. In *Expeditions of Honour,* I first set out to establish biographical details for John Salusbury (1707-1762), the father of Mrs. Hester Thrale (later Piozzi), close friend and biographer of Johnson. I then wanted to publish Salusbury's observations about the founding of Halifax, Nova Scotia, since they are the only private, unofficial observations of these events known.

"In the case of *Soame Jenyns,* I was interested in setting straight the life of an individual with a long political career in England and a considerable publication record. Even though Jenyns wrote poetry as well as prose works on politics, economics, and religion, his reputation had been determined by a crushing review—written by Johnson and published in *Literary Magazine*—of his tract *A Free Inquiry Into the Nature and Origin of Evil* (1757). My intention was to show that this event overshadowed much of what he accomplished as a writer and a public figure.

"The projected biography of Sir Wilfred Grenfell is an assessment of Grenfell's life as a medical missionary in Newfoundland and Labrador. This study will fill the need for a more accurate evaluation of Grenfell's work than any found in more than twenty-five biographical works already in print, works that hold Grenfell too much in awe and neglect of the ample primary sources available. This bibliography is intended as a guide to scholars interested in criticism of Grenfell's works."

*   *   *

ROOSEVELT, Theodore   1858-1919

BRIEF ENTRY: Born October 27, 1858, in New York, N.Y.; died January 6, 1919, near Oyster Bay, Long Island, N.Y. American politician, conservationist, big-game hunter, and author of historical works. Roosevelt became the twenty-sixth president of the United States on September 14, 1901, following the assassination of President William McKinley, for whom Roosevelt was serving as vice-president. Roosevelt, fondly known as "Teddy" by Americans, remained president following the 1904 election and served until 1909, gaining a reputation for his use of executive action and promotion of legislation to protect labor and consumers against big business abuses, his sponsorship of efforts to conserve and reclaim wildlife and natural resources through legislation and the creation of national preserves, and his foreign policies characterized by imperialism and military strength. In foreign affairs Roosevelt lived by the motto "Speak softly and carry a big stick," viewing himself and his country as the leading force of the Western Hemisphere. In this capacity, Roosevelt's administration assumed responsibility for Latin American nations' debts and supported the secession of Panama from Colombia, then assumed control of that part of the new country designated for construction of the Panama Canal. In addition, Roosevelt mediated negotiations that ended the Russo-Japanese War, a service for which Roosevelt won the 1906 Nobel Peace Prize.

Prior to his tenure in the White House, Roosevelt held various governmental posts, including those of New York State legislator, U.S. Civil Service commissioner, president of the New York City Board of Police Commissioners, and assistant secretary of the navy. Appointed to his naval office in 1897, he resigned the following year to volunteer for service in the Spanish-American War. He became commander of the 1st U.S. Volunteer Cavalry, popularly known as the "Rough Riders," and led them on their famous charge up Kettle Hill—often referred to as San Juan Hill—in Cuba. He returned to the United States a war hero and in 1899 was elected governor of New York, a post he held until running for vice-president in 1900.

Following the completion of his first elected term as president of the United States, Roosevelt declined to run for reelection, having served as chief executive for nearly eight years. Instead, he went to Africa on a big-game safari, followed by a tour of Europe during which he met with many national leaders. In 1912 Roosevelt again ran for president, this time as the Progressive or "Bull Moose" party candidate. He succeeded only in splitting the Republican party, which allowed Democrat Woodrow Wilson to win the election. Among his numerous books, based on history and personal experience, are *Hunting Trips of a Ranch Man* (1885), the four-volume *Winning of the West* (1889-1896), *Rough Riders* (1899), *Progressive Principles* (1913), *America and the World War* (1915), an autobiography, and two biographies, one of Thomas Hart Benton and the other of Gouverneur Morris. *Address:* Sagamore Hill, near Oyster Bay, Long Island, N.Y.

BIOGRAPHICAL/CRITICAL SOURCES:

BOOKS

Beale, Howard Kennedy, *Theodore Roosevelt and the Rise of America to World Power,* Johns Hopkins Press, 1956.
Burton, David H., *Theodore Roosevelt: Confident Imperialist,* University of Pennsylvania Press, 1968.
Harbaugh, William Henry, *Power and Responsibility: The Life and Times of Theodore Roosevelt,* 1963.
Morison, Elting E., and others, *Letters,* eight volumes, Harvard University Press, 1951-54.
Putnam, Carleton, *Theodore Roosevelt: A Biography,* Volume 1: *The Formative Years,* Scribner's, 1958.

*   *   *

ROSE, Kenneth Jon   1954-

PERSONAL: Born June 23, 1954, in New York, N.Y.; son of

Leo (an engineer) and Barbara (a literary agent and writer; maiden name, Berson) Rose. *Education:* University of Connecticut, B.A., 1976; studied at Marine Biological Laboratory, Woods Hole, Mass., 1977; graduate study at New York University, 1980—.

ADDRESSES: Agent—Barbara Bova Literary Agency, 32 Gramercy Park S., New York, N.Y. 10003.

CAREER: Woods Hole Oceanographic Institution, Woods Hole, Mass., research assistant, 1976-78; free-lance science writer, 1978—.

MEMBER: American Association for the Advancement of Science, National Space Institute, New York Academy of Sciences.

AWARDS, HONORS: Distinguished technical communication award from International Audiovisual Competition and Silver Cindy Award from International Film Producers Association, both 1982, for "The Chemistry of Life: Hormones and the Endocrine System."

WRITINGS:

Classification of the Animal Kingdom, McKay, 1980.

Contributor to magazines, including *Omni, Travel and Leisure, Boys' Life, Natural History, Analog,* and *Futurific.*

WORK IN PROGRESS: Research on the effects of certain hormones secreted by the brain on the aging nervous and muscular system; an audiovisual production on cell division and growth.

SIDELIGHTS: Kenneth Jon Rose told *CA:* "I always enjoyed writing, but didn't start to do it professionally until I had the great fortune to study sharks at Woods Hole. I felt the experience had to be shared. After I had exhausted the subject (some four or five articles later), I left for New York, where the magazine editors there gave me plenty of work.

"As a writer, I have traveled to mummy digs in Chile, remote villages in Peru, met with Nobel Prize laureates, senators, astronauts, corporate executives, and television celebrities. I recommend it."

*   *   *

ROSEN, Edward   1906-1985

OBITUARY NOTICE—See index for *CA* sketch: Born December 12, 1906, in New York, N.Y.; died of congestive heart failure, March 28, 1985, in New York, N.Y. Educator, historian, translator, editor, and author. Rosen taught the history of science at City College of New York (now City College of the City University of New York) from 1926 to 1977. He was an authority on the great astronomer Nicholas Copernicus and edited the scientist's complete works. Rosen's translations include *Three Copernican Treatises,* Vasco Ronchi's *Optics, the Science of Vision* and Johann Kepler's *Somnium.* Rosen was also both translator and editor of *Kepler's Conversation With Galileo's Sidereal Messenger.* He wrote *The Naming of the Telescope.*

OBITUARIES AND OTHER SOURCES:

BOOKS

Directory of American Scholars, Volume I: *History,* 8th edition, Bowker, 1982.
The Writers Directory: 1984-1986, St. James Press, 1983.

PERIODICALS

New York Times, March 30, 1985.

* * *

ROSENBERG, Joel 1954-

PERSONAL: Born May 1, 1954, in Winnipeg, Manitoba, Canada; came to the United States in 1955; son of Mervin E (an American physician) and Irene (a housewife; maiden name, Yamron) Rosenberg; married Felicia Gail Herman, October 23, 1978. *Education:* Attended University of Connecticut, 1972-76. *Politics:* "Idiosyncratic." *Religion:* Jewish.

ADDRESSES: Home and office—New Haven, Conn. *Agent*—Richard Curtis, Richard Curtis Associates, Inc., 164 East 64th St., Suite 1, New York, N.Y. 10021.

CAREER: Writer.

MEMBER: Science Fiction Writers of America, Haven (writer's workshop).

WRITINGS:

The Sleeping Dragon (novel), New American Library, 1983.
The Sword and the Chain (novel), New American Library, 1984.
(With Kevin O'Donnell, Jr., Mark J. McGarry, Mary Kittredge, and Ester Friesner-Stutzman) *The Electronic Money Machine* (nonfiction), Avon, 1984.
Ties of Blood and Silver (novel), New American Library, 1984.
The Silver Crown (novel), New American Library, 1985.
Emile and the Dutchman (novel), New American Library, 1985.

Work represented in anthologies, including *Perpetual Light* and *Men of War.* Contributor to magazines, including *Isaac Asimov's Science Fiction, Amazing Stories, The Dragon,* and *Writer's Digest.* Past contributing editor of *Gameplay.*

WORK IN PROGRESS: The Heir Apparent, for New American Library; *Writing Fantasy Fiction,* with Darrell Schweitzer, for New American Library; *The Kindred* (tentative title), a murder mystery.

SIDELIGHTS: Joel Rosenberg commented on the circumstances that led to his writing career: "Part of it is straightforward: Like H. G. Wells, I became a writer out of necessity. Due to an injury, for a long time I was unable to do anything more strenuous than sit at a typewriter keyboard.

"So: I write because I like eating, having a roof over my head and clothes on my back.

"But . . . there's quite a bit more to it than that. The field of science fiction was, in more ways than one, my first love; it's always been a faithful one.

"For more than twenty years, it has been evident to me that the grandest thing one can be is a science fiction writer. Others might aspire to becoming president of the United States, a heart surgeon, Rogerian psychotherapist, oil billionaire, or whatever. That doesn't bother me; I'm perfectly willing to let them have the lesser professions.

"So. Here I am, not only a published science fiction writer, but at age thirty, finding that I can support myself increasingly well by doing what I love best.

"There's an old saying: 'Be careful what you wish for—you may get it.' That's remarkably irrelevant to my life. Each year is better than the preceding; I'm enjoying both the practice and the rewards of my chosen profession more and more all the time.

"The only negative side to it all is that I've become almost intolerably smug. People who don't like that are invited to hold their hands over their ears so that my chuckling won't bother them."

Rosenberg described some of his novels: "*Emile and the Dutchman* is a short story cycle somewhat in the spirit of Paul Anderson's chronologically early 'Flandry' stories.

"*Guardians of the Flame*—the story which began in *The Sleeping Dragon* and has been continued in *The Sword and the Chain, The Silver Crown,* and will be continued in *The Heir Apparent*—is a longish one that will probably go nine books before I reach the end. Among other things, it's an attempt to reconstruct heroic fantasy from the ground up, as well as a love letter to the industrial revolution.

"The 'Thousand Worlds Cycle' includes *Ties of Blood and Silver,* which is the first of these related-but-not-series-per-se stories. They will span approximately a thousand years and more than two hundred billion cubic light-years. *Emile and the Dutchman* is the second book in the cycle. Obviously a stage this large has room for a great variety.

"It's unlikely that I'm going to restrict myself as a writer, beyond the limitations of my abilities and interests. I plan to write at least one murder mystery, as well as science fiction novels outside of the 'Thousand Worlds Cycle,' though I'm unlikely to tackle a major fantasy project once *Guardians of the Flame* is complete. My primary orientation is toward science fiction."

The author concluded: "I have worked as a short order cook, truck driver, mental retardation aide, gambler, bookkeeper, motel desk-clerk, gas pumper, and door-to-door encyclopedia salesman. I like writing better. *Much* better."

* * *

ROSENFELD, Jeffrey P(hilip) 1946-

PERSONAL: Born August 15, 1946, in New York, N.Y.; son of Harry (a lawyer) and Sylvia (Aretsky) Rosenfeld; married Susan Rodin (in sales promotion), August 30, 1970; children: Jordan Heath. *Education:* University of Rhode Island, A.B. (cum laude), 1968; University of Massachusetts at Amherst, M.A., 1970; State University of New York at Stony Brook, Ph.D., 1977.

ADDRESSES: Home—Bayside, N.Y. 11361. *Office*—Department of Sociology, Nassau Community College of the State University of New York, Stewart Ave., Garden City, N.Y. 11530.

CAREER: Nassau Community College of the State University of New York, Garden City, associate professor of sociology, 1973—. Principal of PlanWise, Inc. Visiting scientist at Tavistock Centre, London, England, 1980.

MEMBER: American Sociological Association, Eastern Sociological Society (chairman of Committee on Undergraduate Education, 1982-84, and Committee on Employment, 1984—).

AWARDS, HONORS: Fulbright scholar, 1977-78; grant from the National Institute of Mental Health.

WRITINGS:

The Legacy of Aging: Inheritance and Disinheritance in Social Perspective, Ablex Publishing, 1979.

Relationships, Random House, 1980.

Contributor to *American Demographics* and *Psychology Today.*

WORK IN PROGRESS: Continuing research on inheritance patterns in the United States today, focusing on reasons why parents disinherit their children; research on will contests; software for estate planners.

SIDELIGHTS: Jeffrey P. Rosenfeld told CA: "A disinheritance in my own family first got me interested in that topic. The result has been ongoing research, writing, expert testimony in will contests, and software development. My research starts from the premise that disinheritance is a legal decision with social and emotional consequences. For this reason I've spent a great deal of time studying why parents disinherit their children, and I have more recently been researching the impact of disinheritance on the survivors in a family.

"*The Legacy of Aging,* my first book on this topic, focused on ways that disinheritance is socially structured. I read wills that had been written by older people who were about the same in terms of wealth but whose last years were spent in different social settings. Specifically, I read wills written by elderly people who had lived with or near their childen, in long-term nursing homes, and in retirement communities. I found a dramatic increase in disinheritance with residents of nursing homes and retirement communities, which led me to conclude that this behavior becomes more common as traditional ties between elders and their families are broken.

"I have also examined will contests, in part with the help of a grant from the National Institute of Mental Health for a study called 'Kinship, Conflict, and Contested Wills.' The research revealed that the public is becoming ever more litigious. Once only 2 percent of all wills were ever contested but now, in some states, contests are as high as 10 percent. The percentage would be higher still except that many families settle their objections out of court before the case technically becomes a will contest. I have concluded that the family once had the role of mediator when its members were dissatisfied with a will, but the American family has since changed significantly and has lost the mediating function. The result is a surge in will contests that will probably continue increasing for years to come.

"My research goals are twofold: I hope to learn even more about motives for disinheritance and about social settings in which this behavior occurs, and I want to develop more accurate tools for predicting the caseload of will contests that will burden probate courts across the nation in the very near future.

"Now more than ever I appreciate what the Roman poet Martial said centuries ago: 'If you want them to mourn, you had best leave them nothing.'

"*Relationships* is a book of readings about marriage and family in the United States today. It takes a life cycle approach and examines the strains and contradictions that must be resolved as we go through courtship, marriage, parenthood, midlife, and old age."

*   *   *

ROSENSTIEL, Annette   1911-

PERSONAL: Born June 29, 1911, in Jersey City, N.J.; daughter of Julius I. (a doctor) and Rose (Altshul) Bitterman; married Raymond Rosenstiel; children: Leonie. *Education:* Attended Sorbonne, University of Paris, 1933; Hunter College (now of the City University of New York), A.B., 1936; New York University, M.A., 1941; Columbia University, M.Phil., 1952, Ph.D., 1953.

ADDRESSES: *Home*—4 Old Mill Rd., Manhasset, N.Y. 11030. *Office*—R & A Associates, P.O. Box 704, Manhasset, N.Y. 11030. *Agent*—Author Aid Associates, 340 East 52nd St., New York, N.Y. 10022.

CAREER: High school teacher of modern languages and social studies in New York City, 1936-37, Jersey City, N.J., 1937-40, and Ardsley, N.Y., 1940-43; full-time writer, 1943-48; Hunter College (now of the City University of New York), New York City, assistant professor of anthropology, 1953-54; New York University, New York City, assistant professor of anthropology and sociology, 1955-59; Mills College of Education, New York City, professor of behavioral sciences and language and head of division, 1959-72; William Paterson College of New Jersey, Wayne, professor of anthropology and sociology and chairman of department, 1972-81; full-time writer and researcher, 1981-84; R & A Associates, Manhasset, N.Y., president, 1984—. Adjunct professor at Queens College of the City University of New York and Rutgers University, 1955-81; consultant to UNESCO and Ford Foundation. *Military service:* U.S. Army, Women's Army Corps, 1943-46; became captain; served in Papua, New Guinea.

MEMBER: Authors Guild, American Anthropological Association (fellow), American Association for the Advancement of Science (fellow), Ethnological Society, Council on Anthropology and Education, Academy of Political and Social Science, Royal Anthropological Institute of Great Britain and Ireland (fellow), New York Academy of Sciences.

AWARDS, HONORS: Teaching award from American Association of Teachers of French, 1940; New York State Scholar in International Affairs, 1966; grant from Columbia University for Latin America, 1967; grant from State of New York for research in Alaska, 1968.

WRITINGS:

Auditory and Reading Comprehension in French, College Entrance Book Co., 1965.
French Omnibus, College Entrance Book Co., 1969.
Education and Anthropology, Garland Publishing, 1977.
Red and White: Indian Views of the White Man, 1492-1982, Universe Books, 1983.

Author of plays in French for WCDA-Radio.

Contributor to magazines, including *Journal of Negro Education, Oceania, School and Society, Human Organization, Arctic and Alpine Research, Science Digest, Practical Anthropology,* and *Man* (journal of the Royal Anthropological Institute of Great Britain and Ireland).

WORK IN PROGRESS: *Changing Images of the American Indian; The Queen's Lover,* a novel of eighteenth-century Spain.

SIDELIGHTS: Annette Rosenstiel told CA: "I believe that every life experience leaves a permanent imprint. Writing has been a consistent thread in my life ever since my great uncle Joshua presented me with a brass inkwell as a gift. When I was twelve I wrote my first novel. It was a highly personal experience, and I refused to share it, so I destroyed the novel. Since then I have written poems, articles in English, French, and Spanish, radio plays in French and English, and books.

Some have been published; some have been destroyed; and some remain as partially developed ideas that I still hope to complete. A historical novel I wrote, which was highly praised by Andre Maurois, is as yet unpublished.

"My experiences as a WAC in Papua, New Guinea, during World War II led to my becoming an anthropologist, and to the publication of many articles in scientific journals, as well as to my books. After the war, I joined the Authors Workshop, and worked with such well-known writers as Oscar Schisgall.

"I am currently working on a book about changing images of the American Indian, and I am revising my historical novel. Writing continues to be the ongoing expression of a challenging inner compulsion.

"My interest in the American Indian was first sparked by my desire to find out what had happened to the Indians of New Jersey, where I had lived as a child. My interest was expanded during my graduate studies at Columbia University. Professors such as Julian Steward, Alfred Kroeber, William Duncan Strong, and Charles Wagley gave a new dimension to my understanding of the history and current status of the Indians in both North and South America.

"Continuing research resulted in the compilation of a great deal of data on Indian-white relations and eventually led to my book *Red and White*. What emerged was a vivid portrait of both the consistent disregard by whites for Indians as human beings and the shocked reactions of the Indians, who lacked the technology to defend themselves physically and whose philosophy of life made it difficult—if not impossible—for them to accept the diametrically opposed point of view of the white man. Even more striking was the verbal power of the Indians. They used the only tool at their command: a beautiful, moving eloquence that gathered force through the centuries but that unfortunately, until now, has proven inadequate against the technological and social weapons with which they have been attacked.

"As the Indians have acquired greater mastery over the English language, as well as an understanding—though not an acceptance—of the white man's philosophy of life, they have become increasingly capable of presenting their point of view to the white man. And they have been able to change their image from one of passive acceptance to one of active, sometimes forceful, resistance."

*   *   *

ROSS, Gary 1948-

PERSONAL: Born October 16, 1948, in Toronto, Ontario, Canada; son of Walter S. and Mary Leila (Walker) Ross. *Education:* University of Toronto, B.A., 1970.

ADDRESSES: Office—*Saturday Night*, 70 Bond St., Toronto, Ontario, Canada.

CAREER: Weekend Magazine, Toronto, Ontario, senior editor, 1977-79; *Saturday Night,* Toronto, senior editor, 1980—.

MEMBER: Writers Union of Canada.

AWARDS, HONORS: E. J. Pratt medal for poetry, 1968, Norma Epstein Award, 1968, Frederic Davidson Prize for fiction, 1969, all from University of Toronto; National Magazine Award for Fiction from National Magazine Awards Foundation of Canada, 1981, for "Blueberries."

WRITINGS:

Always Tip the Dealer (novel), McClelland & Stewart, 1981, Bantam, 1982.

Also author of *Tears of the Moon* (novel), 1985.

WORK IN PROGRESS: Oh Gorgeous Girls, a collection of short stories.

SIDELIGHTS: Gary Ross told *CA:* "I divide my time between Toronto and Venice, Italy, where I write fiction while on leave of absence from my duties as senior editor of *Saturday Night* magazine."

*   *   *

ROSS, J. H.
See LAWRENCE, T(homas) E(dward)

*   *   *

ROSS, Mary Adelaide Eden
See PHILLPOTTS, (Mary) Adelaide Eden

*   *   *

ROSSI, Philip Joseph 1943-

PERSONAL: Born April 30, 1943, in Mount Vernon, N.Y.; son of Philip J. and Mary (Scola) Rossi. *Education:* Fordham University, A.B., 1967; Woodstock College, B.D., 1971; University of Texas at Austin, Ph.D., 1975.

ADDRESSES: Office—Department of Theology, Coughlin Hall, Marquette University, Milwaukee, Wis. 53233.

CAREER: Entered Society of Jesus (Jesuits), 1962; ordained Jesuit priest, 1971. Marquette University, Milwaukee, Wis., assistant professor, 1975-82, associate professor of theology, 1982—, chairperson of department, 1985—. Visiting scholar at Woodstock Theological Center, 1979-80.

MEMBER: American Catholic Philosophical Association, American Academy of Religion, Western American Philosophical Association, Society of Christian Ethics, College Theology Society, Society of Christian Philosophers.

WRITINGS:

(Contributor) Alfred Hennelly and John Langan, editors, *Human Rights in the Americas: The Struggle for Consensus,* Georgetown University Press, 1982.
Together Toward Hope: A Journey to Moral Theology, University of Notre Dame Press, 1983.

Contributor to religious studies and philosophy journals.

WORK IN PROGRESS: The Moral and Religious Philosophy of Immanuel Kant, completion expected in 1989.

SIDELIGHTS: Philip Joseph Rossi told *CA:* "*Together Toward Hope: A Journey to Moral Theology* analyzes four basic ideas—freedom, imagination, community, and hope—as the basis of moral life and as the fundamental concepts for the discipline of ethics. It is intended for advanced students of philosophical and religious ethics."

*   *   *

ROSSKAM, Edwin 1903(?)-1985

OBITUARY NOTICE: Born c. 1903 in Munich, Germany (now

West Germany); died February 25, 1985, in Roosevelt, N.J. Photographer and author. In the 1940's Rosskam worked as a photographer for the Standard Oil Company of New Jersey. *Towboat River,* his book about life on the Ohio and Mississippi Rivers, was compiled in collaboration with his wife, Louise. In the early 1950's, the photographer worked in a rural education program in Puerto Rico. Rosskam's experiences there led to his novel *The Alien.*

OBITUARIES AND OTHER SOURCES:

PERIODICALS

New York Times, March 6, 1985.

*   *   *

ROSTAND, Robert
See HOPKINS, Robert S(ydney)

*   *   *

ROTELLA, Guy Louis   1947-

PERSONAL: Born October 18, 1947, in Rutland, Vt.; son of Guido (a barber) and Laura (a homemaker; maiden name, Bottomley) Rotella; married Mary Jane Marro (a teacher), August 15, 1970. *Education:* Siena College, B.A., 1969; Northeastern University, M.A., 1972; Boston College, Chestnut Hill, Mass., Ph.D., 1976.

ADDRESSES: Home—3 Gilmore Rd., Belmont, Mass. 02178. *Office*—Department of English, Northeastern University, Boston, Mass. 02115.

CAREER: Northeastern University, Boston, Mass., instructor, 1974-76, assistant professor, 1976-79, associate professor of English, 1979—.

MEMBER: Modern Language Association of America.

WRITINGS:

E. E. Cummings: A Reference Guide, G. K. Hall, 1979.
(Contributor) Earl J. Wilcox, editor, *Robert Frost: The Man and the Poet,* Winthrop Publishing, 1981.
(Editor with Francis C. Blessington, and contributor) *The Motive for Metaphor: Essays on Modern Poetry,* Northeastern University Press, 1983.
Three Contemporary Poets of New England: William Meredith, Philip Booth, and Peter Davison, G. K. Hall, 1983.
(Editor and contributor) *Critical Essays on E. E. Cummings,* G. K. Hall, 1984.

Work represented in anthologies, including *Anthology of Magazine Verse and Yearbook of American Poetry.* Contributor of articles and poems to literature journals.

WORK IN PROGRESS: A book on the uses of nature in twentieth-century American poetry; research on modern and contemporary poetry.

SIDELIGHTS: Guy Louis Rotella told *CA:* "My literary criticism and poetry are both based on a continuing interest in the relationships of man and nature, as thoughts and feelings about those relationships inform and are reflected in the history of ideas and in the languages and concepts of poetry and other arts, and as they are involved in our efforts to know ourselves and the world. I suppose this interest to some extent accounts for the poets I've chosen to write about and for the approach I've taken to their work."

ROTHENBERG, Diane Brodatz   1932-

PERSONAL: Born March 20, 1932, in New York, N.Y.; daughter of Murray (in the garment industry) and Pauline (a legal secretary; maiden name, Altman) Brodatz; married Jerome Rothenberg, December 25, 1952; children: Matthew. *Education:* Queens College of the City of New York (now of the City University of New York), A.B. (with honors), 1953; attended University of Michigan, 1953; graduate study at Columbia University, 1953-54, City College of the City University of New York, 1956-63, and Hunter College of the City University of New York, 1968-69; Graduate School and University Center of the City University of New York, Ph.D., 1976. *Religion:* Jewish.

ADDRESSES: Home—1026 San Abella Dr., Encinitas, Calif. 92024.

CAREER: Teacher of English and remedial reading at public junior high school in Bronx, N.Y., 1956-64; Queens College of the City University of New York, Flushing, N.Y., instructor in anthropology, 1971-72; conducted anthropological field work at Allegheny Seneca Reservation in Cattaraugus County, N.Y., 1972-74; University of Wisconsin—Milwaukee, instructor in anthropology, 1975-76; University of Southern California, Los Angeles, instructor in anthropology, 1979-81. Consultant to Manpower Demonstration Research Corp. and to Cultural Systems Research, Inc., 1981—. Member of faculty at Palomar Community College, 1979-80. Co-host of International Summer Solstice Radio Festival, 1984.

MEMBER: American Anthropological Association, American Ethnological Society, Society for Ethnohistory, Mingei International Museum of Folk Art.

WRITINGS:

(Contributor) Eleanor Leacock and Mona Etienne, editors, *Women and History: Studies in the Colonization of Pre-Capitalist Societies,* Praeger, 1980.
(Contributor) Carolyn Rhodes and other editors, *First Person Female American: A Selected and Annotated Bibliography of the Autobiographies of American Women Living After 1960,* Whitston, 1980.
(Editor with husband, Jerome Rothenberg) *Symposium of the Whole: A Range of Discourse Toward an Ethnopoetics,* University of California Press, 1983.

Contributor to anthropology journals.

WORK IN PROGRESS: Research on anthropological approaches to performance art, issues of aging and creativity, aging and feminism, and institutional flexibility in a changing world, with publications expected to result.

SIDELIGHTS: Diane Brodatz Rothenberg told *CA:* "What attracted me to anthropology from the first was the holistic approach to human behavior, which saw any manifestation of that behavior as fair game for study. My current interest in performance art is a subcategory of a larger concern with ethnopoetics, itself an interdisciplinary combination of anthropology and poetics. But it is not the exotic and aberrant that most excites me. Within a discipline that addresses both similarities and differences among humans, I am compelled by the power of the places, by the unity of humankind, and the possibility of understanding that process of being human through innovative investigation."

ROTHENBERG, Marc 1949-

PERSONAL: Born October 13, 1949, in Philadelphia, Pa.; son of William David (a teacher) and Marcella (a teacher; maiden name, Paul) Rothenberg. *Education:* Villanova University, B.A., 1970; Bryn Mawr College, Ph.D., 1974.

ADDRESSES: Home—410 11th St. N.E., Washington, D.C. 20002. *Office*—Smithsonian Institution, SI-149, Washington, D.C. 20560.

CAREER: Academy of Natural Sciences, Philadelphia, Pa., research associate, 1974-75; Smithsonian Institution, Washington, D.C., historian, 1975—. Visiting assistant professor at University of Maryland at College Park. Member of council of Folger TheatreWorks, 1978—; consultant to American Museum of Natural History.

MEMBER: History of Science Society, Society for the History of Technology, American Studies Association, Organization of American Historians.

WRITINGS:

(Editor with Nathan Reingold and others) *The Papers of Joseph Henry,* Smithsonian Institution Press, Volume III: *1836-1837: The Princeton Years,* 1979, Volume IV: *1838-1840: The Princeton Years,* 1981.
(Editor with Arthur P. Molella and others) *A Scientist in American Life: Essays and Lectures of Joseph Henry,* Smithsonian Institution Press, 1980.
The History of Science and Technology in the United States: A Critical and Selective Bibliography, Garland Publishing, 1982.

Contributor to scientific journals.

WORK IN PROGRESS: Historical and bibliographic research on American astronomy.

SIDELIGHTS: Marc Rothenberg told *CA:* "It is one of the contradictions of our technological age that most Americans are ignorant of the history of the science and technology that surround them. Because they do not know the past, they do not understand the present. In publishing the letters, laboratory notebooks, diaries, and other manuscripts of one of the founders of the American scientific community and outstanding researchers in the field of electro-magnetism, I hope not only to increase public knowledge of the history of American science, but to also reveal Joseph Henry as an intricate part of mid-nineteenth-century American culture."

*   *   *

ROUBICZEK, Paul (Anton) 1898-1972
(Paul A. Robert)

OBITUARY NOTICE: Born September 28, 1898, in Prague, Austria-Hungary (now Czechoslovakia); died July 26, 1972. Philosopher, educator, publisher, and author. Roubiczek began his career as a publisher in Berlin, while at the same time pursuing his interests in philosophy and literature by contributing articles to scholarly journals. When Adolf Hitler came to power in 1933, Roubiczek fled Germany and founded an anti-Nazi publishing firm in Paris. He worked as a publisher and writer in Prague and Vienna from 1935 until 1939, when the Nazi occupation of these areas once again forced Roubiczek to escape. Settling in England, he took a teaching position

with Cambridge University's Board of Extra-Mural Studies. There Roubiczek's lectures on philosophy, science, and religion were so popular that students reportedly waited in lines to get seats. The educator was named a fellow of Cambridge University's Clare College in 1961.

In 1934 Roubiczek published his first book, *Der Missbrauchte Mensch,* which was written under the pseudonym Paul A. Roberts. His 1952 publication of *Thinking in Opposites* contributed to the author's reputation, garnering him wider recognition as a philosopher. It was followed by four more books, *Thinking Towards Religion, Existentialism: For and Against, Ethical Values in the Age of Science,* and *Across the Abyss.* Roubiczek was completing the final draft of another book, *The Necessity of Contradictions,* at the time of his death. (Date of death provided by B. Powell, secretary to the master, Clare College, Cambridge University.)

*   *   *

ROWE, Frank 1921-1985

OBITUARY NOTICE: Born December 19, 1921, in Portland, Ore.; died of cardiac arrest, March 23 (one source says March 24), 1985, in Walnut Creek, Calif. Artist, educator, and author. Rowe was a first-year art instructor at San Francisco State College (now University) in 1950 when he and eight other faculty members were dismissed for refusing to sign the California State loyalty oath, which was required for employment. Barred from teaching until 1967, when the Supreme Court declared the loyalty oath unconstitutional, Rowe joined the faculty of Laney College in 1968 as an instructor in graphics; he served at that school until the time of death. Rowe recounted his experiences as an opponent of the loyalty oath in his self-illustrated book *The Enemy Among Us: A Story of Witch-Hunting in the McCarthy Era.* The book won the California Federation of Teachers Civil Liberties Union Award, the United Professors of California Academic Freedom Award, and the Hugh M. Hefner First Amendment Award. Rowe's other publications include *The Treasure of Neahkanie Mountain* and *Display Fundamental: A Basic Display Manual.*

OBITUARIES AND OTHER SOURCES:

PERIODICALS

Contra Costa Times (Walnut Creek, Calif.), March 28, 1985.
Los Angeles Times, March 30, 1985.

*   *   *

ROZMAN, Deborah 1949-

PERSONAL: Born November 8, 1949, in Minneapolis, Minn.; daughter of David (an accountant) and Celia (a teacher; maiden name, Friedell) Rozman. *Education:* Attended University of Chicago, 1967-69; University of California, Santa Cruz, B.A., 1970; University of the Trees, M.A., 1977, Ph.D., 1979.

ADDRESSES: Home and office—P.O. Box 867, Boulder Creek, Calif. 95006.

CAREER: University of the Trees Press, Boulder Creek, Calif., editor, 1975-81; Microalgae International Sales Corp., Santa Cruz, Calif., vice-president, 1981—. Director of Evergreen School, 1979—; member of Santa Cruz Chamber of Commerce; educational consultant.

WRITINGS:

Meditating With Children, University of the Trees Press, 1975.

Meditation for Children, Celestial Arts, 1976.
(With Christopher Hills) *Exploring Inner Space,* University of the Trees Press, 1978.
Holistic Education, University of the Trees Press, 1985.

EDITOR

Christopher Hills, *Nuclear Evolution,* University of the Trees Press, 1977.
Hills, *Rise of the Phoenix,* University of the Trees Press, 1979.
Hills, *Golden Egg,* University of the Trees Press, 1979.
Hills, *Creative Conflict,* University of the Trees Press, 1980.

Contributor to magazines.

SIDELIGHTS: Deborah Rozman told *CA:* "My work is 'several-fold.' I have had inner realizations illuminating the inner light of consciousness and penetrating the soul. Seeing that as the highest of human experience, I have dedicated my life to exploring the higher reaches of consciousness and learning to practically manifest them in the world. This extends to writing and to teaching both adults and children. Through teaching and writing, more penetrating insights come to me as to the essence of our spiritual nature.

"In 1979 I founded a children's school dedicated to developing seven levels of consciousness in children—physical/sensory awareness, social awareness (communication skills and creative conflict), intellectual awareness (Socratic approach), emotional awareness (trust building), mental awareness (mind and memory development), intuitive awareness (telepathy, intuition, insight), and imaginative awareness (visualization and dissolving ego barriers to feel oneness with all). These compose holistic education; and all human experience can be seen in one or more of these levels. All levels are trainable and constitute an important part of education. My books on meditation for children go into these levels of consciousness and are non-denominational spiritual lessons for unfolding potential and feeling one with all life.

"I teach a simple five-step meditation to children that includes relaxation, getting in touch with feelings through rhythmic breathing, focusing, expansion of awareness, and grounding the energy into creative activity. Results have often been dramatic, with children feeling better about themselves, being more aware of others' feelings and needs, being more able to handle themselves in difficult situations, and achieving more creativity and better academic test scores. Stephanie Herzog used my techniques in a public school classroom for three years with phenomenal success, which is detailed in her book *Joy in the Classroom,* published by University of the Trees Press in 1981.

"I have worked closely with Christopher Hills for the past ten years—as a student and as an editor of many of his books. Hills developed the typology of the seven levels of consciousness based upon scientific and philosophical research into the nature of light and consciousness. His book *Nuclear Evolution* links physics and psychology and spiritual awareness by showing that light and consciousness literally are identical. They become modified by filters which create frequency, whether in the atmosphere or in the human mind. Meditation is essential to learning how to perceive on subtle levels of consciousness, to tuning our awareness to the finer frequencies of light both within our brain and in our environment.

"Much of Christopher Hills's research and writing is on the leading edge of human thought and has great implications for the future manifestation of human achievement. His work is still relatively little known, but his books *Rise of the Phoenix* and *Nuclear Evolution* show the link between light, consciousness, and the seven unfolding centers of awareness as they relate to the human brain and to human activity in the world. One of the areas that has most impressed me is Hills's view that the true 'laboratory for democracy' is the human brain and that our brain potential and awareness is directly reflected in how we lead our lives and govern ourselves. In 1973 Hills founded a community of writers and thinkers called University of the Trees, where over forty people have gathered to work together to develop this research and these teachings and to make a difference in the world. University of the Trees is a consciousness research school that grants mostly graduate-level degrees in consciousness-related studies. Several businesses evolved from the community, including Microalgae International, where I also work. Microalgae International researches and markets edible algae—which contains the highest concentration of protein available in the world—as a potential mass food source to solve the world hunger problem."

*   *   *

RUBENSON, Sven (Abel)   1921-

PERSONAL: Born October 20, 1921, in Faringtofta, Sweden; son of Ruben Bengtsson and Eva Persson; married Britta Maria Berglund (a nurse), June 23, 1946; children: Birgitta, Kerstin Rex, Inger Nilsson, Samuel, Daniel. *Education:* University of Lund, Sweden, B.Phil., 1946, L.Phil., 1954, D.Phil., 1976.

ADDRESSES: Home—Tordoensvaegen 4K, Lund, Sweden S-22227. *Office*—Department of History, Magle Lilla Kyrkogata 9A, Lund, Sweden S-22351.

CAREER: Swedish Evangelical Mission Schools, Addis Ababa and Adwa, Ethiopia, missionary, teacher, and headmaster, 1947-52; University of Lund, Lund, Sweden, assistant at Historical Institution, 1953-54; Ethiopian Evangelical College, Debre Zeyt, director, 1955-58; Ethio-Swedish Institute of Building Technology, Addis Ababa, dean of students, 1958-60; University College, Addis Ababa, assistant professor of history, 1960-62; Haile Sellassie I University (now Addis Ababa University), Addis Ababa, associate professor, 1962-66, professor of history, 1966-77, head of department, 1962-66 and 1967-68, associate dean of faculty of arts, 1967-68, dean of faculty of arts, 1968-70; University of Lund, associate professor of history, 1977—. Visiting professor of history at School of International Affairs, Columbia University, 1967. Researcher with Swedish Agency for Research Cooperation With Developing Countries, Stockholm, 1977—.

MEMBER: International Conferences of Ethiopian Studies (member of organizing committee), Societe francaise d'etude ethiopien, Historielaerarnas Foerening (Sweden).

WRITINGS:

Wichale XVII: The Attempt to Establish a Protectorate Over Ethiopia, Haile Sellassie I University, 1964.
King of Kings, Tewodros of Ethiopia, Haile Sellassie I University/Oxford University Press (Nairobi), 1966.
The Survival of Ethiopian Independence, Heinemann Educational, 1976.

Editor of *Proceedings of the Seventh International Conference of Ethiopian Studies,* 1984. Contributor to journals, including *Journal of African History, Journal of Ethiopian Studies, English History Review, Kyrkohistorisk aarskrift,* and *Ethnos.*

WORK IN PROGRESS: Translating and annotating *Acta Ae-thipica,* Volume 1, a collection of Ethiopian correspondence, treaties, and related writings; researching the nineteenth- and twentieth-century history of the Horn of Africa.

SIDELIGHTS: Sven Rubenson's *The Survival of Ethiopian Independence* chronicles Ethiopia's struggle to remain autonomous during the turbulent nineteenth century. Edward Ullendorff, reviewing the work in *Times Literary Supplement,* described it as a "massive achievement that may have as durable qualities of survival as the Ethiopian independence to which Professor Rubenson alludes in the title of his book."

Rubenson told *CA:* "My research and writing has throughout been concerned with Ethiopian affairs, historical and contemporary. As a teenager I was introduced to international politics by Fascist Italy's attack on Ethiopia fifty years ago. As a historian I became fascinated with the long and unique history of the country and above all with the question of how Ethiopia managed to survive as an independent nation when all the rest of Africa succumbed to European colonialism in the era of the 'scramble for Africa.' In my research I have been motivated by a desire to correct the kinds of misunderstandings and misinterpretations which were all too common in earlier scholarship due to the Euro-centered approach to African history which prevailed until after World War II. Though Swedish is my mother tongue, I write almost exclusively in English."

BIOGRAPHICAL/CRITICAL SOURCES:

PERIODICALS

Times Literary Supplement, December 31, 1976.
West Africa, October 25, 1976.

*   *   *

RUBIN, Vera (Dourmashkin)   1911-1985

OBITUARY NOTICE: Born August 6, 1911, in Moscow, Russia (now U.S.S.R.); died February 7, 1985, in New York, N.Y. Anthropologist, educator, editor, and author. A specialist in Caribbean cultures, Rubin is remembered for her role as co-director of a major 1970's research project focusing on marijuana use in Jamaica. Earlier in her career, Rubin, who had studied with noted anthropologists Ruth Benedict and Margaret Meade and had earned her doctorate at Columbia University in 1952, also served as research director of a program studying man in the tropics. In 1955 she became the director of the Research Institute for the Study of Man, the position she held thereafter. At the time of Rubin's death the institute was involved in a joint study on longevity and aging with the Soviet Academy of Science.

During her career Rubin was associated with the teaching staff of such schools as Columbia University, New York University, Brandeis University, Hunter College, and Cornell University Medical School. In addition, she served as president of the Society for Applied Anthropology and as director of the American Orthopsychiatric Association. Rubin was the author of *Fifty Years in Rootville* and co-author of *We Wish to Be Looked Upon: A Study of the Aspirations of Youth in the Developing Society.* Among the books she edited were *Caribbean Studies: A Symposium, Social and Cultural Pluralism in the Caribbean,* and *Culture, Society, and Health.*

OBITUARIES AND OTHER SOURCES:

BOOKS

Who's Who of American Women, 3rd edition, Marquis, 1964.

PERIODICALS

New York Times, February 8, 1985.

*   *   *

RUBINSTEIN, H(arold) F(rederick)   1891-1975

OBITUARY NOTICE: Born March 18, 1891; died June 12, 1975. Attorney, editor, and author. Rubinstein, who was best known as a playwright, was a partner and solicitor with the London firm of Rubinstein Nash & Company. He wrote more than twenty plays, including "Churchill," "All Things Are Possible," "The House," "The Deacon and the Jewess," and "The Dickens of Gray's Inn." Rubinstein was also author of *The English Drama* and of three volumes of one-act plays. In addition, he edited *Great English Plays.*

OBITUARIES AND OTHER SOURCES:

BOOKS

Who's Who in the Theatre: A Biographical Record of the Contemporary Stage, 16th edition, Pitman, 1977.

*   *   *

RUSH, Alison   1951-

PERSONAL: Born March 30, 1951, in Birmingham, England; daughter of George Logan (an engineer) and Jean (a nurse; maiden name, Finlayson) Smith; married Malcolm John Rush (a librarian), March 6, 1981. *Education:* University of Durham, B.A. (with honors), 1973. *Politics:* Labour.

ADDRESSES: Home—8 Stonebridge, Orton Malborne, Peterborough, England.

CAREER: Nature Conservancy Council (government agency), London, England, executive officer, 1979—.

WRITINGS:

The Last of Danu's Children (young adult novel), Houghton, 1982.

WORK IN PROGRESS: A second novel, *Undry;* research for a third novel about Morgan Le Fay and the Arthurian legend.

SIDELIGHTS: Alison Rush told *CA:* "When I want to describe the background to what I write, I cannot approach it in a direct way. I was brought up in a very ordinary part of rural Lancashire, the immediate landscape being a drained marsh, flat, criss-crossed by ditches and hedges, dotted by clumps of trees like islands. There was also an estuary full of migratory birds in winter. This sort of landscape has no ready charm; both the marsh and the estuary are unexpansive and tamed, yet at the same time repellingly bleak—more akin to the nearby industrial landscapes than to the usual idea of the English countryside.

"I never really felt at home in this environment. While you walk on the beach or in the fields, the landscape withdraws into itself, rejects you. It has a very strong character of its own, but that character is without friendliness. It will work for man, but it will not smile on him. I used to read of children whose native countryside was a friend, a welcoming playmate; but my countryside would not anthropomorphize in this way. It was not actively hostile, but it ignored one. I could not relate to the natural environment except when on holiday, in less exacting and more compliant landscapes.

"This did not suit me. It meant always being rootless, unattached, but at last I came to grips with my landscape by reading up on the local folklore and history. Not the very recent history, but more distant accounts of how the area was once a real marsh, inhabited by a tribe called the *Setantii*. It was an inhospitable district. Time and again the tradition emerges of a disastrous flood which destroyed a forest, engulfed a church, swept away a village. The river goddess survives in local lore as a horrible sprite who claims a human life once every seven years. It became clear that this tamed landscape had once been a grim, dangerous place where people had lived with great difficulty.

"This did not endear my countryside to me, but I now understand it and, magically, with understanding came belonging. I no longer live there, but when I visit it is with a genuine sense of coming home.

"This has been fundamental to the writing I have done so far. My landscape would mean nothing to me without its past, the ghosts, so to speak, of the forest and marshland which no longer exist and the ever-changing coastline. In the same way, human beings mean nothing without their background of thought, history, and mythology. I found that what interested me most in books was the attempt a few authors had made to toe the line between real life and imagination, to examine how fantasy and reality flow into and feed each other. I like pure fantasy (such as Tolkien) but I want reality to enter too, in an active way, meaning something in the context of the fantasy—and vice versa. So like many people, I tried to write the kind of story I would have liked to read.

"I went to the University of Durham, which is located in a beautiful city. With its castle, cathedral, and river, there was no need to struggle in order to understand its loveliness; most of its history is there on the surface. My time there was spent on Latin and Greek. Thereafter I worked at various office jobs, and joined the Nature Conservancy Council (NCC) in 1979. This is a government agency charged with the furthering of nature conservation in Great Britain. In 1981 I married the NCC's deputy librarian."

* * *

RUSH, Elizabeth 1918-

PERSONAL: Born March 20, 1918. *Education:* California State College, B.A. *Religion:* "Eclectic."

ADDRESSES: Office—1060 India St., San Diego, Calif. 92101.

CAREER: Writer.

WRITINGS:

The House at the End of the Lane, Green Tiger, 1982.

WORK IN PROGRESS: A sequel to *The House at the End of the Lane.*

AVOCATIONAL INTERESTS: Reading, birdwatching, gardening.

* * *

RUSHFORD, Patricia H(elen) 1943-

PERSONAL: Born December 4, 1943, in Rugby, N.D.; daughter of Hjalmar and Dagny (a homemaker; maiden name, Olsen) Anderson; married Ronald G. Rushford (a self-employed investor), 1963; children: David W., Caryl E. *Education:* Clark College, Vancouver, Wash., A.A.S., 1972. *Religion:* Christian.

ADDRESSES: Home and office—3600 Edgewood Dr., Vancouver, Wash. 98661.

CAREER: Registered nurse; bookkeeper and secretary, 1961-70; registered nurse, 1972; Veterans Administration Hospital, Vancouver, Wash., medical/surgical nurse, 1972-75; Bess Kaiser Urgency Care Clinic, Portland, Ore., pediatric nurse, 1975—, part-time nurse, 1978—. Member of board of directors of Speakers and Writers, Ink; guest on radio and television programs in the United States and Canada; teacher at writers' conferences.

MEMBER: National Speakers Association, Pacific Northwest Writers, Oregon Christian Writers Association.

AWARDS, HONORS: Writer of the Year Award from Mount Hermon Christian Writer's Conference, 1983; Writer of the Year Award in Christian Parenting from Warner Pacific Writer's Conference, 1984, for *Have You Hugged Your Teenager Today?* and *The Care and Feeding of Sick Kids.*

WRITINGS:

Have You Hugged Your Teenager Today?, Fleming Revell, 1982.
The Care and Feeding of Sick Kids, Ronald N. Haynes, 1983, revised as *Caring for Your Sick Child,* Fleming Revell, in press.
From Money Mess to Money Management, Fleming Revell, 1984.
The Help, Hope, and Cope Book for People With Aging Parents, Fleming Revell, 1985.
Cracked Pots and Broken People, Fleming Revell, in press.
The Final Event (teen novel), Augsburg, in press.

Contributing editor of *PRN,* newsletter of Nurses for Laughter.

WORK IN PROGRESS: How Do I Love Me, on self-esteem.

SIDELIGHTS: "I began writing in 1980," Patricia H. Rushford commented, "never having thought about it as a career. My first writings included poetry and writing about mothering teenagers. Each book I write deals with real human hurts and concerns. My style is conversational. I take difficult subjects, write in an informative, easy to understand way, injecting humor in moderate doses. I've come to love writing and accept it as a part of myself."

Rushford described her background. "I was born a farm girl in North Dakota, and I remain a homespun, down-home, country girl at heart. I'm not too keen on picking up a plow, but it's nostalgic. My family headed west in 1955 and settled in Longview, Washington. I adjusted well to city life and graduated from high school there. My parents temporarily destoyed my life when they pulled up roots again and moved to the Vancouver area. Then at age nineteen, just about the time I'd declared myself single forever, this handsome, blue-eyed fellow named Ron came along and married me. Now, twenty years and two teenagers later, we're still married, still in love, and still living in Vancouver, Washington.

"If there ever was a born Christian," she added, "it would be me. I never knew a time without Christ. However, until the age of thirty, I was a 'dud.' Either nobody ever lit my fuse or I didn't have one. After years of playing the part of a perfect person, I finally gave up, went to a hospital for repairs, and, while I was there, God lit my fuse. Today I love to blow people away with the exciting things God accomplishes in my life. I share hope with people who suffer from depression, cancer, and other health problems, problem teenagers, and money messes. I draw my hope from personal experience and commitment to God, who continually salvages me.''

* * *

RUSKIN, Ronald 1944-

PERSONAL: Born October 16, 1944, in Toronto, Ontario, Canada; son of David John and Rita (Freeman) Ruskin; married Marilyn Zaidman (a social worker); children: Danielle, Natalie, Joelle. *Education:* Queen's University, Kingston, Ontario, M.D., 1970; attended University of Aix-Marseille, 1970-71; McGill University, Diploma in Psychiatry, 1975.

ADDRESSES: Home—223 A St. Clair Ave. W., Toronto, Ontario, Canada M4V 1R3.

CAREER: University of Toronto, Toronto, Ontario, assistant professor of psychiatry, 1978—. Director of outpatient psychiatry at Wellesley Hospital, Toronto, 1978-83.

MEMBER: Writers Union of Canada, Canadian Medical Association, Canadian Psychiatric Association, American Board of Psychiatry and Neurology (diplomate), Amnesty International.

WRITINGS:

The Last Panic (novel), Bantam, 1979.

Contributor of poems to magazines, including *Quarry* and *Canadian Forum.*

WORK IN PROGRESS: ''Dadabar,'' a two-act play ''about a young boy and his family and their attempts to understand the nightmare the boy has had each night for two years''; *Duck Lake,* a novel about a family living in Toronto one hundred years ago.

SIDELIGHTS: Ronald Ruskin told *CA:* ''I wanted to write and become a doctor. While I was studying medicine I worked as a journalist. I wrote poems and short stories. Finally, after a year of trying, my first poems were accepted for literary magazines. I was looking for a vision of the world to write about, and I felt I would find it in the south of France. I was twenty-five when I went there and wrote my first novel. It was terrible. Later I realized that great visions come from inside oneself. My search continued.

''Being a psychiatrist and studying psychoanalysis has made me more objective about myself and more subjective in my experience of others.

''*The Last Panic* is a story of the growing violence in the world as exemplified in terrorism and senseless aggression. The story centers around a group of scientists in the United States and Europe who begin to study group violence and find to their surprise that there is a syndrome of paranoia-aggression that is reaching epidemic proportions. The story is a metaphor for the unsettled and changing nature of our world, which is in a precarious state of transition.

''My play in progress was prompted by my work with young children in families. Children are the most vulnerable and defenseless creatures of all; they are dependent on the outside world for their survival and on their parents for their inner

early nourishment and being. The play, about a young child, is really about the potential—or struggle for potential—in the child in all of us. This child of course never grows up; it remains inside of us in various stages of life or death. In the play the child of Dadabar, Badabar, gets perilously close to his own inner death. His family cannot understand his nightmare, but they really are not able to understand him.''

* * *

RZHEVSKY, Nicholas 1943-

PERSONAL: Born November 8, 1943, in Linz, Austria; immigrated to United States in 1949, naturalized citizen, 1961; son of Jaroslaw (an architect) and Sofia (a housewife; maiden name, Karsanova) Rzhevsky; married Tatiana Goncharenko (a teacher), November 6, 1966; childen: Natalie, Kyra. *Education:* Rutgers University, B.A. (with highest honors), 1964; Princeton University, M.A., 1968, Ph.D., 1972. *Politics:* Independent.

ADDRESSES: Home—10 Three Village Lane, Setauket, N.Y. 11733. *Office*—Department of German and Slavic Languages, State University of New York at Stony Brook, Stony Brook, N.Y. 11733.

CAREER: University of Illinois at Urbana-Champaign, Urbana, assistant professor of Russian, 1976-81; State University of New York at Stony Brook, assistant professor of Russian, 1982—.

MEMBER: American Association of Teachers of Slavic and East European Languages, American Association for the Advancement of Slavic Studies, Phi Beta Kappa.

AWARDS, HONORS: Fulbright fellow in London and Paris, 1969-70, and in U.S.S.R., 1977-78 and 1982-83; National Endowment for the Humanities summer grant, 1982; American Philosophical Society grant, 1985.

WRITINGS:

Russian Literature and Ideology: Herzen, Dostoevsky, Leontiev, Tolstoy, Fadeyev, University of Illinois Press, 1983.
(Adapter and translator) ''Crime and Punishment'' (two-act play; based on novel of the same title by Fedor Dostoevsky), first produced in London, England, at Lyric Theatre, September 5, 1983.

Also adapter and translator of ''House of the Dead'' (two-act play based on Dostoevsky's novel *The House of Death*), as yet unpublished and unproduced.

WORK IN PROGRESS: Russian Literary Theatre, publication expected in 1985; adapting additional works by Dostoevsky; explicating the literary texts of Dostoevsky and other Russian authors.

SIDELIGHTS: Nicholas Rzhevsky told *CA:* ''I am a literary scholar by vocation, who has turned increasingly to theatre in recent times. A major preoccupation has been the transgression of conventional boundaries between literature and theatre, both as a theoretical matter and a craft. My training is in modern critical theory and the history of Russian literature; on the whole, I have found it to provide healthy impulses for such theatrical involvements. I continue, however, to write on literary texts and to value the critical endeavor in its own right.''

S

SACHDEV, Paul

PERSONAL: Born in Hafizabad, India. *Education:* Punjab University, B.A., 1956; University of Baroda, M.S.W., 1959; Institute of Social Studies, The Hague, Netherlands, Diploma in Social Welfare Policy, 1963; University of Illinois at Chicago Circle, M.S.W., 1968; University of Wisconsin—Madison, Ph.D., 1975.

ADDRESSES: Home—46 Tupper St., St. John's, Newfoundland, Canada A1A 2T8. *Office*—School of Social Work, Memorial University of Newfoundland, St. John's, Newfoundland, Canada A1B 3X8.

CAREER: Regional leprosy welfare officer with the government of Madhya Pradesh Department of Social Services in India, 1959-62; New Delhi Family Planning Association, New Delhi, India, research officer, 1963-65; Children's Aid Society, Kirkland Lake, Ontario, social worker, 1965-66; Children's Aid Society of York County, Newmarket, Ontario, social worker, 1966-67; Cook County Hospital, Chicago, Ill., psychiatric social worker, 1967-68; Memorial University of Newfoundland, St. Johns, assistant professor, 1973-76, associate professor of social work, 1976—. Part-time caseworker at Methodist Youth Services, Chicago, 1967-68; group leader of discussion groups for single parents, Mental Health Association of Newfoundland, 1975; Canadian delegate to Congress on Adoption, Eilat, Israel, 1982; Canadian vice-president of Symposium on Reproductive Health Care, 1982; guest on Canadian radio and television programs.

MEMBER: International Association of Schools of Social Work, Canadian Association of Schools of Social Work (member of accreditation board, 1983—), Canadian Association of University Teachers, Child Welfare League of America, British Agencies for Adoption and Fostering, Council on Social Work Education, Parent Finders Incorporated, Friends of India Association (president, 1977-78).

AWARDS, HONORS: Grants from International Development Research Centre, New Delhi, India, 1975-76, Health and Welfare of Canada, 1976-77, 1980, 1981-83, and Social Science and Humanities Research Council of Canada, 1980, 1981, 1982.

WRITINGS:

(Contributor) Cenovia Addy, editor, *Family Planning and Social Work,* National Health and Welfare, 1977.

(Contributor) *Childhood and Sexuality,* Editions Etudes Vivantes, 1980.

(Editor) *Abortion: Readings and Research,* Butterworth, 1981.

(Editor) *Adoption: Current Issues and Trends,* Butterworth, 1984.

(Editor) *Perspectives on Abortion,* Scarecrow, 1984.

Abortion and After: Unmarried Women's Personal and Emotional Experiences, Greenwood Press, 1985.

(Editor) *International Handbook on Abortion,* Greenwood Press, 1985.

Also author of *In Search of Roots.*

Contributor of articles and reviews to social work journals and newspapers in India and Canada. Editor of *Harmony,* 1954-56; editor of child abuse and domestic violence section of *Medicine and Law,* 1983—.

WORK IN PROGRESS: A Study of Adoption Record Disclosure to Adoptees and Their Birth Parents; Sexual Knowledge, Attitudes, and Behavior of Memorial University Students.

* * *

SACHS, Margaret 1948-

BRIEF ENTRY: Born March 21, 1948, in Hamburg, West Germany. Researcher and author. Sachs is a field investigator for the Aerial Phenomena Research Organization. She collaborated with Ernest Jahn on *Celestial Passengers: UFO's and Space Travel* (Penguin, 1977), and she wrote *The UFO Encyclopedia* (Putnam, 1980).

* * *

SACHS, Michael L(eo) 1951-

PERSONAL: Born September 7, 1951, in New York, N.Y.; son of George (a company president) and Eva (an artist) Sachs; married Fay Ades (a public health nutritionist), August 22, 1981. *Education:* Union College, Schenectady, N.Y., B.S. (cum laude), 1973; Hollins College, M.A., 1975; Florida State University, Ph.D., 1980. *Politics:* Democrat. *Religion:* Jewish.

ADDRESSES: Home—P.O. Box 213, Reisterstown, Md. 21136. *Office*—Department of Pediatrics, School of Medicine, University of Maryland at Baltimore, WPCC, 630 West Fayette St., Baltimore, Md. 21201.

CAREER: Universite du Quebec a Trois-Rivieres, assistant professor of sport psychology, 1980-83; University of Maryland at Baltimore, research project coordinator in department of pediatrics, 1983—.

MEMBER: American Association on Mental Deficiency; American Alliance for Health, Physical Education, Recreation, and Dance; Association for the Advancement of Behavior Therapy; Society for the Advancement of Social Psychology; Running Psychologists; Psi Chi; Phi Kappa Phi.

AWARDS, HONORS: Certificate of Merit from Florida Association for Health, Physical Education, and Recreation, 1976 and 1977; outstanding dissertation award from the Sport Psychology Academy of the National Association for Sport and Physical Education, 1981.

WRITINGS:

(Associate editor and contributor) *Psychology of Running,* Human Kinetics, 1981.
(Editor with Gary W. Buffone, and contributor) *Running as Therapy: An Integrated Approach,* University of Nebraska Press, 1984.

CONTRIBUTOR

Robert C. Cantu, editor, *The Exercising Adult,* Collamore, 1982.
Cantu and William J. Gillespie, editors, *Sports Medicine, Sports Sciences: Bridging the Gap,* Collamore, 1982.
Terry Orlick, John T. Partington, and John H. Salmela, editors, *Mental Training for Coaches and Athletes,* Coaching Association of Canada, 1982.
Partington, Orlick, and Salmela, editors, *Sport in Perspective,* Coaching Association of Canada, 1982.
John M. Silva and Robert Weinberg, editors, *Psychological Foundations of Sport and Exercise,* Human Kinetics, 1984.

OTHER

Contributor of more than thirty articles and reviews to physical education journals and sport magazines, including *Journal of Sport Behavior, Journal of Physical Education and Recreation, Runner's World,* and *Racing South.* Editor of "Sport Psychology," a column in *Contemporary Social Psychology;* editor of *Running Psychologist,* 1979-83, and *Sport Sociology Academy Newsletter,* 1980-82; co-editor of bulletin of Canadian Society for Psychomotor Learning and Sport Psychology, 1982-83; member of editorial advisory board of *Wellness Perspectives;* member of sports medicine editorial board of F. A. Davis Co. (publishers).

WORK IN PROGRESS: Research on psychology of running, particularly addiction to running, the "runner's high," and cognitive strategies used during running.

SIDELIGHTS: Michael L. Sachs told *CA:* "My interests in exercise/sport psychology in general, and the use of running in particular, date back to 1973, when I discovered that I could integrate my academic interests in psychology with my participant interest in sports. I started reading and doing research in the area, and went on to get my Ph.D. in the field. I began running in 1975, and I have enjoyed it ever since. It has proven to be effective for me, as well as for many other individuals, in coping with stress and enhancing the quality of life (and perhaps the quantity as well).

"The field of exercise psychology offers many exciting avenues, in teaching, research, and practice, and anyone interested in integrating psychology with exercise and sport should be encouraged to pursue his or her interests. At the very least, one finds many personal rewards from regular participation in sport and physical activity."

AVOCATIONAL INTERESTS: Going to movies.

* * *

SALAZAR, Ruben 1928-1970

OBITUARY NOTICE: Born March 3, 1928, in Chihuahua, Mexico; died August 29, 1970; buried at Pacific View Memorial Park, Newport Beach, Calif. Journalist. Salazar came to the United States in 1929, becoming a naturalized citizen in 1949. He began his journalism career in 1952 as a staff member with the *El Paso Herald-Post,* and in the next seven years held consecutive positions with the *Santa Rosa Press Democrat* and the *San Francisco News.* Salazar joined the staff of the *Los Angeles Times* in 1959. He served the *Times* as a correspondent in Vietnam from 1965 to 1966, after which he was named bureau chief in Mexico City; he became a columnist in 1969. In addition to his newspaper work, Salazar was news director of the Los Angeles television station KMEX until 1970.

OBITUARIES AND OTHER SOURCES:

BOOKS

Martinez, Al, *Rising Voices,* New American Library, 1974.
Who Was Who in America, With World Notables, Volume V: *1969-1973,* Marquis, 1973.

PERIODICALS

Newsweek, June 22, 1970, September 14, 1970.

* * *

SALINGER, Margaretta 1908(?)-1985

OBITUARY NOTICE: Born c. 1908; died after a long illness, March 8, 1985, in New Britain, Conn.; buried in Bloomfield, N.J. Museum curator and author. Salinger joined the Metropolitan Museum of Art as a cataloger in 1928. During the next forty years she lectured frequently and wrote articles for museum publications. In 1970 she was named curator of the department of European paintings, and she retired two years later as curator emeritus. Salinger's writings include *Michelangelo's "The Last Judgment", Early Flemish, Dutch, and German Painting in the Metropolitan Museum of Art,* and *French Painting of the Nineteenth and Twentieth Centuries in the Metropolitan Museum of Art.*

OBITUARIES:

PERIODICALS

New York Times, March 14, 1985.

* * *

SALISBURY-JONES, Guy 1896-1985

OBITUARY NOTICE: Born July 4, 1896, in London, England; died February 8, 1985. Military officer, diplomat, vintner, and author. Salisbury-Jones studied at the French Military Academy at St. Cyr, where he met and developed a life-long friendship with his military history tutor, Charles de Gaulle. Following his graduation from the academy, Salisbury-Jones began a twenty-five-year career with the British Army. He served in Syria, Italian Somaliland, Greece, and Crete, becoming head of the military mission to South Africa in 1941. From 1946 until 1949 Salisbury-Jones was a military attache in Paris. He received the Croix de Guerre in 1946 and was named a commander of the British Empire. In 1950 he retired from military service with the rank of major-general, and for the next eleven years he served as marshal of the Diplomatic Corps. Later in life, Salisbury-Jones also achieved success as a wine grower by steadily increasing a small crop at his home in Hampshire, England, until it was a productive, seven-and-one-half-acre vineyard. By 1981 he was producing enough white wine to export to the United States and Europe. In addition, he was author of a book titled *So Full of Glory: A Life of Marshal de Lattre de Tassigny.*

OBITUARIES AND OTHER SOURCES:

BOOKS

International Authors and Writers Who's Who, 7th edition, Melrose, 1976.

PERIODICALS

Times (London), February 15, 1985.

* * *

SALTER, Stefan 1908(?)-1985

OBITUARY NOTICE: Born c. 1908 in Berlin, Germany; died January 11, 1985, in Columbia, Mo. Designer of books and author. Salter began his career in Hollywood as a prop designer and poster artist. He became a free-lance book designer in 1947, and it has been estimated that he may have designed more than three thousand books for as many as one hundred different publishers. His *Publishers Weekly* column "Designer's Corner" led to Salter's book *From Cover to Cover: The Occasional Papers of a Book Designer.* The author was also a member of the faculty of Yale University and the University of Missouri at Columbia, and he once headed the American Institute of Graphic Arts.

OBITUARIES:

PERIODICALS

Publishers Weekly, February 8, 1985.

* * *

SALTZGABER, Jan M. 1933-

PERSONAL: Born July 27, 1933, in Chicago, Ill.; son of M. A. (a psychologist) and Ann (a social caseworker; maiden name, Collier) Saltzgaber; married Jo Muller, March 25, 1953 (divorced); children: Dirk, Lisa, Erik. *Education:* Wayne State University, B.A., 1959, M.A., 1964; attended McGill University, 1966; Syracuse University, Ph.D., 1970.

ADDRESSES: Home—38 Meadowlark Dr., Ithaca, N.Y. 14850. *Office*—Department of History, Ithaca College, Danby Rd., Ithaca, N.Y. 14850.

CAREER: Ithaca College, Ithaca, N.Y., instructor, 1965-67, assistant professor, 1970-72, associate professor of history, 1972—. *Military service:* U.S. Army, Airborne Infantry, 1953-60; became captain.

MEMBER: Organization of American Historians, American Historical Association, American Association of University Professors, Phi Alpha Theta.

WRITINGS:

(With Glenn C. Altschuler) *Revivalism, Social Conscience, and Community in the Burned-Over District: The Trial of Rhoda Bement,* Cornell University Press, 1983.

Contributor to *The Journal of Social History.*

WORK IN PROGRESS: Research on American social history, social welfare history, and poverty in postbellum rural America.

SIDELIGHTS: Jan M. Saltzgaber told *CA:* "I was trained as a Russian historian, but a fortuitous grant from the National Endowment for the Humanities led to a three-year stint as the director of a center for research in early religious studies of antebellum New York State. The experience proved irresistible, and I have been caught up in the study of American social history ever since. Largely by accident a colleague and I discovered the fascinating community of Seneca Falls, New York, and a sufficiency of primary sources on the village to make possible a long-term study of the many facets of community life and culture. Our work to date is part of a projected series of books and articles relating the history of Seneca Falls to the larger issue of *communitas* in America. As with most historians, I suspect, the end of our scholarly journey is distant indeed. But the journey itself is an endless delight."

* * *

SANSONE, Sam J(ohn) 1915-

PERSONAL: Surname is pronounced in two syllables, San-sone; born January 29, 1915, in Milwaukee, Wis.; son of Michael J. (a laborer) and Rose T. (a housewife; maiden name, Glorioso) Sansone; married Katherine Tomaro (a beauty operator), September 3, 1938 (died April 23, 1982); children: Rosanne H. *Education:* John Carroll University, Ph.B., 1937; attended Kent State University, 1937-38; Institute of Applied Science, Chicago, Ill., Diploma as Fingerprint Expert, 1946; Heidelberg College, B.S., 1976; attended Syracuse University, 1976.

ADDRESSES: Home—180 College Park, Apt. F-10, Elyria, Ohio 44035. *Office*—Department of Police Science and Photography, Lorain County Community College, 1005 North Abbe Rd., Elyria, Ohio 44035.

CAREER: Restaurant owner, 1938-41; Ravenna Arsenal, Ravenna, Ohio, in security, 1941-43; Cleveland Graphite Bronze, Cleveland, Ohio, in security, 1943-44; Shaker Heights Police Department, Shaker Heights, Ohio, patrolman, 1944-49, detective, 1949-65, detective sergeant, 1965-69; Lorain County Community College, Elyria, Ohio, assistant professor of police science and photography, 1967—. Member of Cleveland Crime Clinic; president of Cuyahoga County Crime Bureau, 1955.

MEMBER: International Association of Identification (member of board of directors, 1964), Evidentiary Photography International Council (fellow), Professional Photographers of America, Fraternal Order of Police (president), Ohio Identification Officers (president, 1957).

WRITINGS:

Modern Photography for Police and Firemen, Anderson Publishing, 1971.

Police Photography: Law Enforcement Handbook, Anderson Publishing, 1977.

Contributor to magazines.

WORK IN PROGRESS: A new book on police photography for Anderson Publishing.

SIDELIGHTS: Sam J. Sansone told *CA:* "When I began teaching the subject of police photography, there was no book to use as a text, so I wrote *Modern Photography for Police and Firemen.* Police photography is a difficult subject and one that is very dear to my heart. Teaching the subject requires not only the experience in police work, but also the ability to put it into words.

"I first became involved with photography in 1938. I took a course in photography at Kent State University. In 1949, the Shaker Heights Police Department promoted me to detective and I was put in charge of the record, identification, and photographic bureaus. I also learned police photography from a home study course I took from the Institute of Applied Science. I tried to learn as much as I could about photography by joining several photography clubs. It was just a matter of applying photography to the many different situations applying to the police. Once you understand the basics of photography, it is easy to apply it to whatever field you go into. I think police photography is the most difficult, because a policeman has to shoot film in all kinds of outdoor weather, every day of the year, night and day, and most crimes occur at night, making it very difficult for the policeman to get photos at night, outdoors, when it is dark.

"In the future I expect police to use many of the newer cameras and materials that are coming out today. There are so many good products produced but the average policeman does not know they exist. A policeman gets involved with his own department but he has to go out and see what other departments and schools are doing. Today there are many schools where a policeman can go to broaden education in the field. When I was a policeman, all these different schools and books did not exist. I do hope that future policemen will strive to get better at taking photos so they can present them properly in court to help them win their cases."

*   *   *

SANTAYANA, George   1863-1952

BRIEF ENTRY: Name originally Jorge Augustin Nicolas de Santayana; born December 16, 1863, in Madrid, Spain; died September 26, 1952, in Rome, Italy. Educator, philosopher, poet, and novelist. Santayana was one of the most prominent proponents of critical realism, a philosophical school which postulates that, since reality cannot be grasped directly through perception or thought, knowledge is essentially an act of faith. His first important work, *The Sense of Beauty* (1896), outlines a theory of aesthetics that argues that the experience of beauty cannot be rationally analyzed. In *The Life of Reason* (five volumes; 1905-06), Santayana traces the development of the mind in the context of physical reality.

Santayana wrote both *The Sense of Beauty* and *The Life of Reason* while teaching at Harvard University. In 1912 he left the school upon inheriting a legacy and began traveling in Europe. During the late 1920's Santayana completed *The Realm of Essence* (1927), the first of four volumes collectively titled *The Realms of Being.* In this work he discusses essence, matter, truth, and spirit—what he considers four fundamental modes

of being—from the standpoint of critical realism. In 1936 Santayana wrote *The Last Puritan,* a novel about an American youth preoccupied with his spiritual salvation. Santayana's last major work was *Domination and Powers* (1949), in which society is defined as an aristocratic hierarchy.

BIOGRPHICAL/CRITICAL SOURCES:

BOOKS

Arnett, Willard E., *George Santayana,* Washington Square Press, 1968.
Sprigge, Timothy L.S., *Santayana: An Examination of His Philosophy,* Routledge & Kegan Paul, 1974.

*   *   *

SAPIEYEVSKI, Anne Lindbergh   1940-
(Anne Lindbergh Feydy, Anne Lindbergh)

PERSONAL: Born October 2, 1940, in New York, N.Y.; daughter of Charles Augustus (an aviator) and Anne (a writer; maiden name, Morrow) Lindbergh; married Julien Feydy (divorced); married Jerzy Sapieyevski (a composer and conductor), January, 1978; children: (first marriage) Charles, Constance; (second marriage) Marek (son). *Education:* Attended Radcliffe College and Sorbonne, University of Paris.

ADDRESSES: Home—Washington, D.C. *Agent*—Harriet Wasserman, 230 East 48th St., New York, N.Y. 10017.

CAREER: Writer.

WRITINGS:

BOOKS FOR CHILDREN

(Under name Anne Lindbergh Feydy) *Osprey Island,* illustrated by Maggie Kaufman Smith, Houghton, 1974.
(Under name Anne Lindbergh) *The People in Pineapple Place,* Harcourt, 1982.
(Under name Anne Lindbergh) *Nobody's Orphan,* Harcourt, 1983.
(Under name Anne Lindbergh) *Bailey's Window,* Harcourt, 1984.

Contributor of short stories to periodicals, including *Vogue* and *Redbook.*

WORK IN PROGRESS: The Worry Week, for Harcourt; *Sidney Sitter; The Hunky Dory Diary; Otherwhere.*

SIDELIGHTS: Anne Lindbergh Sapieyevski, the daughter of aviator Charles Lindbergh and writer Anne Morrow Lindbergh, told Jean F. Mercer of *Publishers Weekly* how her parents had influenced her writing. "I would willingly hand anything over to my mother, and she would willingly read it," Sapieyevski recalled. "But, you know, she's too much of a mother. She would offer support rather than suggestions: 'It's very nice, dear,' no direct literary criticism. . . . My father was much more helpful." According to Sapieyevski, Charles Lindbergh "never stopped trying to perfect his own work," and he was similarly scrupulous about editing his daughter's manuscripts. "He visited me in Paris, the year before he died, and spent days going over my first manuscript and saying things like, 'This is repetitive; this is too long.' I was just dizzy from the comments! But *he* was right too. He was absolutely able to take a book apart and find all the weak spots."

For her book *Nobody's Orphan,* Sapieyevski created an elderly, loquacious character named Amory, whom she based partly on her father. "Amory quotes nonstop from Calvin

Coolidge and Robert Service,'' she explained to Mercer, ''the way my father used to, at home.'' When Sapieyevski's editor advised her to check the accuracy of Amory's quotations, however, she discovered that Coolidge and Service ''had never said any such things. My father had made up all those 'quotes' himself.''

Sapieyevski told *CA:* ''I began to write for children after a friend asked me why on earth I didn't stop tormenting myself and start writing the sort of thing I like to read.

''People often say, 'How you must love children!' I don't, particularly; at least, it depends on who they are, as with adults. Whoever says to a writer for adults, 'How you must love grownups!' However, I enjoy talking with children and, having recently talked with many groups of children in schools, think this is probably due to a child's capacity to challenge and/or accept, in both cases unpredictably. A child is quite likely to challenge the logical and accept the fantastic.

''I write very quickly, but the writing comes only at the end of a long process of 'walking out' the book. A basic idea comes first, along with one or two central characters. It then takes me several months to 'learn' my characters. During this time I wander around outside a lot, while the characters become clear and real to the point where I begin to imagine how they would react in whatever circumstances come up in my everyday life. The action of the completed book is, in a way, only an incident in the lives of my characters.

''Once the characters are ready, I work out the plot. I try to avoid any note-taking, as this tends to confuse me later; I do not allow myself to sit down and write until each chapter is totally thought through. Then I scribble. The reason for all the walking is that if I stay home, I am willingly distracted by the slightest temptation unless the story is really ready to go down on paper.

''I enjoy writing and, in the case of children's books, would rather be writing than not writing, but to write at all I need enormous amounts of space. I don't necessarily mean physical space. For years I made the mistake of shutting myself up in a special room at a special time to write. This didn't work. It was boring and unproductive, and made me feel guilty. Then I learned that the time and place I write don't really matter. When something is ready to be written I *always* get it down on paper somehow. The important thing is the time and place I *don't* write: hours alone in my house or outside, emptying out all formulated thoughts, leaving my mind free to fill up with what I didn't know I knew. Of course there are drawbacks to this state of mind. This is the period when I throw ice cubes into the wastepaper basket rather than the sink because they are apparently solid, and forget to feed the children dinner (which they don't mind) and dye all the laundry green (which they do). But without this space, I don't think I could write at all.''

AVOCATIONAL INTERESTS: Reading, walking (''preferably alone''), swimming, and listening to music.

BIOGRAPHICAL/CRITICAL SOURCES:

PERIODICALS

Publishers Weekly, July 27, 1984.
Washington Dossier, December, 1982.
Washington Post, March 18, 1983.
Washington Post Magazine, February 6, 1983.

SAUNDERS, B(ernard) C(harles)   1903-1983

OBITUARY NOTICE: Born May 30, 1903, in Birmingham, England; died December 14, 1983, in Sherbourne, England. Chemist and author. At the beginning of World War I Saunders, who had become known for his experiments with amino acids, directed a group of chemists and biologists in developing a lethal gas to be used for military purposes; the assignment was in response to reports that a similar gas had been formulated in Germany. The team came up with a compound of organic fluorine and phosphorus that could be inhaled or absorbed through the skin to produce immediate convulsions and fatal paralysis. Though the gas was never used for warfare, Saunder's continuing research and experimentation proved that in miniscule amounts the compound could be effective in the treatment of such diseases as myasthenia gravis and glaucoma.

In 1931 Saunders began an association with Cambridge University that lasted for nearly fifty years. He served as director of the faculty of medicine from 1966 until 1973, as president of Magdalene College from 1967 until 1973, and as fellow and prelector thereafter. An adviser on civil defense in the United Kingdom beginning in 1950, Saunders was also active in Great Britain's Misuse of Drugs Council. He was the author of books, many of which were aimed at a young adult audience. Among them were *Order and Chaos in the World of Atoms,* which he co-authored, and *Atoms and Molecules Simply Explained.* Saunders also wrote, *Qualitative Analysis, Phosphorus and Fluorine: The Chemistry and Toxic Action,* and *Peroxidase.* In addition, he contributed more than one hundred articles to professional journals.

OBITUARIES AND OTHER SOURCES:

BOOKS

Annual Orbituary 1983, St. James Press, 1984.
Who's Who in the World, 5th edition, Marquis, 1980.

*   *   *

SAVAGE, Minot Judson   1841-1918

BRIEF ENTRY: Born June 10, 1841, in Norridgewock, Me.; died May 22, 1918, in Boston, Mass. Clergyman and author. Ordained a Congregational minister in 1864 after graduating from Bangor Theological Seminary, Savage spent nine years as a missionary and pastor for the Congregational church. But by 1873 Savage found himself at variance with the orthodox views of Congregationalism because of his acceptance of the then-new theories of evolution. Having adapted his religious beliefs to incorporate these theories, he decided to end his affiliation with the Congregational church, and he accepted a pastoral post with the Third Unitarian Church of Chicago, which did not object to his sermons reconciling Christianity with evolutionary theory. After a year in Chicago, Savage transferred to the Church of Unity in Boston, where he served as pastor from 1874 until 1896, after which time he became pastor of New York's Church of the Messiah. Savage remained in this last capacity until retiring in 1906. Known as an effective, engaging speaker, he also wrote a number of books on his religious and scientific convictions, including *Christianity, the Science of Manhood* (1873), *Religion of Evolution* (1876), *Morals of Evolution* (1880) and *The Passing and the Permanent in Religion* (1901). Among Savage's other works are *Can Telepathy Explain?* (1902) and *Immortality* (1906), which reflect his belief in life after death and his interest in psychic phenomena. He also wrote two poetry volumes, edited a book of Unitarian catechism, wrote several books on human relationships, problems, and questions, and co-edited a volume of sacred songs. Many of his sermons and lectures have been published in book form.

BIOGRAPHICAL/CRITICAL SOURCES:

BOOKS

Biographical Dictionary of Parapsychology, With Directory and Glossary: 1964-1966, Garret Publications, 1964.
Encyclopedia of Occultism and Parapsychology, 2nd printing with revisions, Gale, 1979.
The National Cyclopaedia of American Biography, Volume 1, James T. White, 1892.
Who Was Who in America, Volume I: *1897-1942,* Marquis, 1943.

*   *   *

SAWYER, Diane K.   1946(?)-

PERSONAL: Born December 22, c. 1946, in Glasgow, Ky.; daughter of E. P. (a county judge) and Jean W. (a schoolteacher; maiden name, Dunagan) Sawyer. *Education:* Wellesley College, B.A., 1967.

ADDRESSES: Office—CBS-News, 524 West 57th St., New York, N.Y. 10019.

CAREER/WRITINGS: WLKY-TV, Louisville, Ky., 1967-70, began as weathercaster, became reporter; served as assistant to White House Press Secretary Ron Ziegler, 1970-74; researcher for Richard M. Nixon's *Memoirs,* 1974-78; CBS-News, New York, N.Y., general assignment reporter and State Department correspondent, 1978-81, co-anchor of "CBS Morning News," 1981-84, correspondent for news program "60 Minutes," 1984—.

MEMBER: Council on Foreign Relations.

AWARDS, HONORS: Selected America's Junior Miss, 1963.

SIDELIGHTS: Characterized in a *Newsweek* profile as "the fastest-rising star in television news and its most intriguing personality," Diane Sawyer has been given much of the credit for helping the "CBS Morning News" achieve ratings parity with its early-morning competitors for the first time since the program aired in 1957. The show's perennially anemic ratings had persisted despite the efforts of previous anchors, including Walter Cronkite, Hughes Rudd, Lesley Stahl, Charles Kuralt, and even Dick Van Dyke.

Sawyer first gained public recognition in 1963 when she was named America's Junior Miss. Following her graduation from Wellesley College four years later, she landed a job with WLKY-TV in Louisville, Kentucky, where she began her on-air career as a weathercaster, and eventually became a reporter. By 1970 "I felt sort of nonspecifically undernourished," Sawyer later recalled in a *New York Times* article.

Sawyer interviewed with several Capitol Hill members' staffs seeking a job as a press aide and, with the help of family friend Lamar Alexander (later to become governor of Tennessee), secured an interview with Ron Ziegler, President Richard M. Nixon's press secretary. Ziegler hired Sawyer to write press releases, and her work soon caught the attention of Nixon, who referred to her as "the smart girl."

Later, as the Watergate scandal unfolded, Sawyer devoted increasingly more time to her work: "I was so convinced there

was a rational way of confronting Watergate," she told Ted Bent of *People.* "I would get in at 5:45 a.m. and usually leave around 10 p.m. I acquired a sort of computer compendium of Watergate information." When Nixon resigned in 1974 he asked Sawyer to accompany him to San Clemente, California, to assist him in the writing of his memoirs. Sawyer accepted the offer to serve as the Watergate expert on Nixon's research team, viewing it as "something that honor demanded" as well as an educational experience.

Following the book's completion in 1978 Sawyer was offered a position as a general assignment reporter by CBS-News despite initial concern voiced by some newsmen (including Robert Pierpoint and Dan Rather) that her close association with partisan politics might taint her objectivity. Sawyer silenced the skeptics and earned the respect of her colleagues with her reportage of such stories as the return of bodies to Dover Air Force Base following the Jonestown massacre and her coverage, as State Department correspondent, of the Iranian hostage crisis.

In the fall of 1981 Sawyer was selected to co-anchor "Morning" (now "CBS Morning News") with Charles Kuralt. Her on-air presence was initially described as "stiff" and "cool," but after a brief adjustment period Sawyer began to impress critics and guests alike with her relaxed, professional manner. One guest, former Secretary of State Alexander Haig, noted that Sawyer's persistence while conducting interviews "badgers you in such a professional way, with no thought of self-aggrandizement, that you have to respect it." Sawyer's success on the morning news broadcast led to her being assigned to join the investigative team of correspondents on "60 Minutes" in the fall of 1984.

CA INTERVIEW

CA interviewed Diane Sawyer by telephone at her office in New York City on April 2, 1984.

CA: What inspired you to apply for work at WKLY-TV in Louisville?

SAWYER: My inspiration was lack of any other inspiration at the time. I came home from college uncertain of what I wanted to do, and decided that the most adventurous thing was to be a woman on television, because in those days in Louisville there were no women doing hard news. So it seemed to me a terrifically pioneering and enterprising job. Also, I wanted to write, and at the time television was the most untested of the two media, print or broadcast journalism.

CA: Did the station give you a job reporting hard news or did they make you the weatherlady?

SAWYER: They started me out doing weather and part-time news. The weather was their extortion for my getting to do part-time news, but I was a calamity doing the weather. After about a year, or maybe less, I was moved onto full-time news.

CA: You've said that you made a few faux pas *on the air at that stage of your career. Do you remember any of them?*

SAWYER: First of all, I was very nearsighted, and I couldn't stand on the East Coast side of the map and see the West Coast side, so I was forever reeling forward and backward trying to focus my little astigmatic eyes on the temperatures out in San

Francisco, and, consequently, reading them wrong and getting flummoxed and flustered.

One day, in utter obliviousness, I signed off the air by saying the high temperature for the day was sixty-three degrees and the current temperature was sixty-nine degrees. It never occurred to me there was a discrepancy.

I also signed off one day saying "It's going to be cooler and warmer tomorrow," and it wasn't until an editor mentioned it to me after the broadcast, shaking her head in dismay, that I realized what I had done.

CA: Even at this late date, people may be interested in what problems you had as a woman in a field that a few years ago was mostly male.

SAWYER: I think the discrimination era is over, although people still make distinctions. I think it's no accident that we have a male and a female on "CBS Morning News" right now, so I can't say that everyone's completely sex-blind. At the same time, I've never felt there were obstacles put in my way because of my sex. I've never felt there were stories I couldn't get to because of my sex. I've never felt that my competence was questioned, or less was assumed of me or expected of me because of my sex. To the contrary, I think that I've been treated as a full correspondent, in every sense of the word, from the beginning. At the same time, I know discrimination has been there in the past, and I know that I owe my progress and progression to people like [broadcaster] Barbara Walters, who made it possible for me to have such an easy road.

CA: [CBS-TV Diplomatic Correspondent] Robert Pierpoint once said people talked to you more, or more easily, because you're a woman. He also said, perhaps jokingly, that that was reverse sexism. Does that make any sense to you?

SAWYER: When I was covering the State Department, because it was fairly unusual to have a female network correspondent there, it's possible that my calls were returned a little more quickly, but only because my name was easier to remember since there were so few women correspondents there. But had my questions not been serious ones, and had my approach not been tenacious, it wouldn't have made any difference after the first phone call was returned.

CA: What was the most challenging part of your job in the White House press relations office?

SAWYER: Endurance. Those jobs require more physical stamina than any job I'd done before—because of the hours and the unrelenting nature of the work. You're forever reacting to world events, and rarely in control of your day, or your life, or your words, for that matter.

And, for me, it was a process of stretching and growing in a number of ways. First of all, it was my foray away from home; secondly, it was a complete education in politics. I had experienced politics on a local and state level at home, through my father, but not until you've been in a position where everything that you do can reverberate across the nation do you understand the full implications of a political move.

CA: Did you learn any political lessons in the Nixon White House?

SAWYER: I learned charity toward one's opponents, and toward one's colleagues as well, if that can be considered a political lesson.

CA: What were your actual tasks in helping to prepare President Nixon's memoirs?

SAWYER: I was assigned Watergate, starting with July, 1972, and everything thereafter that dealt with Watergate or the final days of Nixon's presidency. What I did was compile the research and work with the President on the draft itself. Some of it he dictated cold, while some I did preliminary work on and then wrote and rewrote.

CA: Did you criticize the drafts that he wrote?

SAWYER: "Criticize" might be a little adventurous.

CA: Edit, maybe?

SAWYER: Yes. If he had written something or dictated something he'd send it to me and I would make notes on it, either factual or contextual.

CA: Did he bridle at any of the changes you suggested?

SAWYER: Let me put it this way: Because I was working on the Watergate section, I think it's fair to assume that it was not an easy or congenial exercise for him. But as anyone who has worked with him on this kind of project will tell you, he is amazingly unresistant to new ideas or to someone else's ideas. He's not jealous of either his prose or his approach and he's interested in hearing what you have to say. I don't want to leave the impression that it was an arm wrestle.

CA: Did you have any particular system for doing the research? For instance, did you start by going over the news clippings?

SAWYER: I went over everything. I went over the newspaper clippings. I read every book extant on Watergate, and books written by any of the participants. I reread all of the [U.S. Senator Sam] Ervin Committee hearing books. I cross-referenced everything. I had the definitive cross-reference dictionary of Watergate. Everything that I could think of, everything that was on the public record, I read through and reorganized in a cross-referenced, chronological book of my own.

CA: Did you ever think of getting that book published separately?

SAWYER: I don't think it would make intoxicating reading, but it was useful for me.

CA: Do you think you provided President Nixon with any new insights into Watergate?

SAWYER: I think that rereading all of the material in its chronological context and seeing the simultaneity of things gave him some additional insight. There were passages that he would read and say, "I didn't know that," or "I didn't realize that," because I included everything, even peripheral events, and I don't think he had at all a sense of the rapidity with which some things had happened and the sequence of some of the events.

CA: Assuming you can evaluate President Nixon's memoirs objectively, what do you think of them as a work of nonfiction?

SAWYER: I think they're compelling. I think they're fascinating. I don't know of any memoir—and I've read President [Jimmy] Carter's, for instance—in which the diaries are as Melvillian and complicated and interesting as his.

CA: Did you have any problems going back to reporting after working in the White House and then for President Nixon?

SAWYER: I didn't have personal inhibitions that I felt I had to overcome. Because I think appearances are important, though, I wanted an unwritten understanding with the network that I wouldn't do Nixon stories. Once that was agreed on, I didn't feel there was any particular constraint I had to deal with. I did have trouble getting the rhythm of the writing down again, though. Broadcast writing is quite different from the kind of writing that I'd been doing in San Clemente, and that took a while to get used to. The first time I sat down to do a radio script, it took me about two hours to write thirty seconds of copy, I was so traumatized.

CA: Did you, as a reporter, have a different perspective on White House public relations people after having been one yourself?

SAWYER: Oh, sure. Primarily, you understand that the mistakes that are made are human errors more often than not and not the result of some grand calculation, so you tend to believe the simpler explanations.

CA: You worked in Washington covering the State Department, and you and your show do many Washington stories. Is there a way that TV coverage of Washington could be improved?

SAWYER: I think CBS has begun to improve it in one way. It's important to cover the stories out in the country, not to cover a dry hearing but instead to go out and explain to people, for example, what the impact of a law will be after Congress passes it. But public policy stories—stories about the Medicare question, the health cost question—are still the most difficult stories to do. We continue to grapple with ways to do those. Someday we'll find a way to do them well, and, when we do, that will be the biggest service that we will perform. We can deal with small vignettes, but we still struggle when we try to present the kind of story that you can do in a newspaper in, say, a three-part series, with graphics that people can study and linger over.

CA: Is the problem the need to dramatize the story with pictures?

SAWYER: I think the problem is presenting it in a way that can be absorbed. It's so difficult to assimilate figures when they're being hurled at you from the television screen. Even if a graphic is shown, it can only stay on the screen a short time. In a newspaper, the reader can linger until he has absorbed the information.

I would also like to see us cover the news a little more humanistically. I think there are a lot of good people in Washington who work very long hours with fine motives who really believe in what they're doing. And I'm not sure that we don't, occasionally, simply relegate everyone to stereotypes. It's good to tell the stories of those people who care and who count.

CA: That would be relatively easy to do, wouldn't it?

SAWYER: Well, we did one the other day I liked very much: the Senate Chaplain. It was a beautiful story—Phil Jones did it for us—and I think it captured just that quality. Here is a man who takes his job very seriously and who works on the prayers that he gives in the morning. He believes they influence the course of events. It was a chance to show someone whose spirit we could remember as well as his name.

CA: Which do you prefer: reporting, anchoring, or press relations?

SAWYER: I'm home now. I'm where I belong right now.

CA: In anchoring?

SAWYER: Well, what I do is not just anchoring, because I go out and do stories. I'm doing stories for "The American Parade," and I do stories for "CBS Morning News" all the time, so I have the combination. Anchoring is something that I do from 7 to 9 A.M. The rest of the day I'm a reporter.

CA: What makes your show better than its two morning competitors?

SAWYER: I don't know that I want to be comparative. I'll let someone else do that. But I will say that our ambition in the morning is to be eclectic and intelligent and tough where we should be tough and provocative on all other occasions, so that when the viewer leaves in the morning he really feels he has been in the presence of interesting friends and people, and that he has learned something he's just burning to tell someone about at lunch.

CA: What's your eventual goal in TV news?

SAWYER: On the most basic level, I enjoy learning about things and telling people about them and I can do that on any number of different shows. I can do pieces for the evening news; I can do pieces for Sunday morning. I'm fairly easy to please because I love the basic craft, which is getting a story and telling it.

CA: Do you have a burning desire to get to the evening slot, because of the larger audiences at that time of day?

SAWYER: Not really. I admire what "CBS Evening News" anchorman Dan Rather does and, heaven knows, I would love to do it too, but I don't have a single-minded ambition that way, because you pay a price in each case. The price for anchoring an evening-news broadcast is that you don't get to go out and travel as much as I do.

CA: You seem very well-read, and you love literature. Have you thought of doing any creative writing yourself?

SAWYER: I guess we all feel we have a major work in us struggling to get out. I'm not sure what mine is or would be, but I'd love to do some writing some day. I'd also like to do some teaching about books and literature some day.

CA: You don't secretly wish to write a novel?

SAWYER: No, I'm not sure that I could ever write fiction. I'd really like to do one of those definitive and captivating biographies like the Judith Thurman biography of Isak Dinesen. I'd love to bring someone to life with a biography.

BIOGRAPHICAL/CRITICAL SOURCES:

PERIODICALS

Detroit News, March 25, 1984.
Ms., December, 1984.
Newsweek, March 14, 1983.
New York Times, September 30, 1981.
People, November 9, 1981.
Playboy, March, 1985.

—*Interview by Peter Benjaminson*

*   *   *

SCARBOROUGH, Ruth   1904-

PERSONAL: Born March 25, 1904, in Pineview, Ga.; daughter of Robert Lee and Georgia (a homemaker; maiden name, Turner) Scarborough. *Education:* Bessie Tift College (now Tift College), A.B., 1923; Mercer University, M.A., 1927; George Peabody College for Teachers (now Vanderbilt University), Ph.D., 1932.

ADDRESSES: Home—Shepherdstown, W.Va. 25443.

CAREER: Shepherd College, Shepherdstown, W.Va., professor of history, 1936-66; Tift College, Forsyth, Ga., professor of history, 1966—.

MEMBER: American Association of University Women.

WRITINGS:

Oppositions to Slavery in Georgia Before the Civil War, Peabody Press, 1927, reprinted, Greenwood Press, 1968.
Belle Boyd: Siren of the South, Mercer University Press, 1983.

WORK IN PROGRESS: Life on a Georgia Plantation in the Twentieth Century.

*   *   *

SCHEIER, Michael   1943-

PERSONAL: Born May 1, 1943, in New York, N.Y.; son of Murray (a professor) and Celia (a library clerk; maiden name, Lieberman) Scheier; married Julie Frankel (an author and illustrator), 1977. *Education:* New York University, B.S. (with honors), 1966; received master's degree from Teachers College, Columbia University, 1985.

ADDRESSES: Home—Putnam Valley, N.Y. *Office*—P.O. Box 694, Putnam Valley, N.Y. 10579.

CAREER: Teacher. Creator of jigsaw puzzles.

MEMBER: Authors' Guild, Society of Children's Book Writers.

AWARDS, HONORS: Readers Choice Award for *Ridiculous World Records,* and for *Digging for My Roots;* Children's Choice Award from International Reading Association, 1979, for *The Whole Mirth Catalog: A Super Complete Collection of Things.*

WRITINGS:

WITH WIFE, JULIE FRANKEL; ALL JUVENILE

Ridiculous World Records, Scholastic Book Services, 1976.
Digging for My Roots, Scholastic Book Services, 1977.

The Whole Mirth Catalog: A Super Complete Collection of Things, illustrated by Frankel, F. Watts, 1978.
What to Do With the Rocks in Your Head: Things to Make and Do Alone, With Friends, With Family, Inside, and Outside, F. Watts, 1980.
Me by Me, Scholastic Book Services, 1982.

Also contributor of cartoons to *Animals, Animals, Animals* (cartoon collection), edited by George Booth and others, Harper, 1979, and to *Cosmopolitan, Audubon,* and *Runner.*

WORK IN PROGRESS: "Books relating to puns, imaginative activities, fill-in formats, adoption, and humor relating to birds, plants, and wildlife, all with elaborate illustrations."

*   *   *

SCHER, Paula   1948-

PERSONAL: Surname is pronounced "share"; born October 6, 1948, in Washington, D.C.; daughter of Marvin B. (an engineer) and Gladys (a teacher; maiden name, Schecter) Scher; married Seymour Chwast, October 14, 1973 (divorced, 1980). *Education:* Temple University, B.F.A., 1980. *Politics:* "Left." *Religion:* None.

ADDRESSES: Home—141 East 33rd St., New York, N.Y. 10016. *Office*—Koppel & Scher, 40 West 27th St., New York, N.Y. 10001.

CAREER: Atlantic Records, New York City, associate art director, 1974-76; Columbia Broadcasting System, CBS Records, New York City, art director, 1976-82; Time, Inc., New York City, art director in magazine development, 1982-83; Koppel & Scher (graphic design firm), New York City, partner and president, 1984—. Professor at School of Visual Arts and Cooper Union; book designer.

MEMBER: American Institute of Graphic Arts (member of board of directors), Art Director's Club (New York).

AWARDS, HONORS: Awards for graphic design; American Book Award nominations for best book design, and for best compilation of written and graphic material, both 1981, both for *The Honeymoon Book: A Tribute to the Last Ritual of Sexual Innocence.*

WRITINGS:

The Brownstone (juvenile novel; Junior Literary Guild selection), Pantheon, 1973.
The Honeymoon Book: A Tribute to the Last Ritual of Sexual Innocence (adult), M. Evans, 1981.

Contributor to *Push Pin Graphic* and the journal of the American Institute of Graphic Arts.

WORK IN PROGRESS: A novel, tentatively titled *The Art Director;* a book on derivatives of expression.

SIDELIGHTS: Paula Scher told *CA:* "Writing comes easily to me but it is a 'second career.' I am primarily a graphic designer, and I write when I have a good idea or a strong opinion to express. Both *The Brownstone* and *The Honeymoon Book* were purely naked attempts to make money that both failed. Occasionally, I have screenplay ideas or magazine article ideas. At the moment I am so involved in running my new business that I only write for graphics periodicals, often as a result of requests.

"I am considered to be a witty, articulate writer who is highly opinionated. In fact, I'm a rank amateur."

BIOGRAPHICAL/CRITICAL SOURCES:

BOOKS

Thorgerson, Storm, and others, editors, *Album Cover Album: The Second Volume*, A & W Visual Library, 1982.

PERIODICALS

Graphis, July, 1982.
Novum Grabrausgraphic, June, 1982.

*   *   *

SCHEUER, Philip K(atz)   1902-1985

OBITUARY NOTICE: Born March 24, 1902, in Newark, N.J.; died following a heart attack, February 18, 1985, in Hollywood, Calif. Lecturer, newspaper editor, and critic. A reviewer of both silent and sound movies, Scheuer was a drama and film critic for the *Los Angeles Times* from 1927 until his retirement forty years later. In 1958 he became motion picture editor for the paper and was named outstanding film critic of the year by the Screen Directors Guild. Scheuer also reviewed movies for *Family Circle* and *Pictureplay* magazines and contributed articles to such publications as *Collier's* and the *Saturday Evening Post*. He lectured frequently at university film classes.

OBITUARIES AND OTHER SOURCES:

BOOKS

Biographical Encyclopaedia and Who's Who of the American Theatre, James Heineman, 1966.
International Motion Picture Almanac, Quigley, 1975.

PERIODICALS

Los Angeles Times, February 19, 1985, February 23, 1985.

*   *   *

SCHIMMELS, Cliff   1937-

PERSONAL: Born May 11, 1937, in Arapaho, Okla.; son of Claude S. (a farmer) and Ina (a farmer; maiden name, Smith) Schimmels; married Mary Wade (an office manager), June 6, 1958; children: Paula Schimmels Hampton, Larry, Kristina. *Education:* Oklahoma Baptist University, A.B., 1959; Southwestern State College (now Southwestern Oklahoma State University), M.A.T., 1964; University of Oklahoma, Ph.D., 1974. *Politics:* Independent. *Religion:* Baptist.

ADDRESSES: Home—910 Webster, Wheaton, Ill. 60187. *Office*—Department of Education, Wheaton College, 501 East Seminary Ave., Wheaton, Ill. 60187. *Agent*—Paul Mouw, 688 Euclid, Glen Ellyn, Ill. 60137.

CAREER: Teacher and athletic coach at public schools in Clinton, Okla., Watonga, Okla., Syracuse, Kan., Pittsburg, Kan., and Hale Center, Tex., 1959-69; *Catoosa Times Herald*, Catoosa, Okla., editor, 1969-70; Deer Creek School, Edmond, Okla., teacher and principal, 1970-74; Wheaton College, Wheaton, Ill., professor of education, 1974—. Interim pastor of Baptist church in Wheaton, 1982.

MEMBER: Southwest Philosophy of Education Society, Phi Delta Kappa.

WRITINGS:

How to Help Your Child Survive and Thrive in Public Schools, Fleming Revell, 1982.

How to Survive and Thrive in College, Fleming Revell, 1983.
When Junior High Invades Your Home, Fleming Revell, 1984.
Their First Three Years in School, Fleming Revell, 1984.
Sports and Your Child: What Every Parent Must Know, Oliver Nelson, 1985.
I Was a High School Drop-In, Fleming Revell, 1985.
Wheatheart Chronicles (series of novels), Victor Books, in press.

SIDELIGHTS: Cliff Schimmels told *CA:* "Several years ago, I woke up one morning with the realization that I had a strong affinity for the smell of new denim and the beauty of yellow vehicles. Presto! I became a teacher and I shall always be one. Now, through my writing, I have just enlarged my classroom.

"I get to tell the same country stories and I get to make the same point: that teachers and parents are partners in the awesome task of helping children grow to adulthood. Since those partners need to understand each other, since I am both a parent and a teacher, and since I am comfortable looking at the world through an adolescent perspective anyway, maybe I can say something worthwhile to everyone involved.

"In the meantime, I enjoy the research. I visit about two hundred classrooms a year; in the fall of 1984, I spent six weeks as a fully-participating high school freshman; and I have suffered both the frustrations and joys of parenthood."

*   *   *

SCHMITT, Heinrich   1894-1976
(Frank Arnau)

OBITUARY NOTICE: Born March 9, 1894, in Geneva, Switzerland (one source says Vienna, Austria); died February 11, 1976, in Munich, West Germany. Intelligence adviser, journalist, and author. Schmitt is probably best known for his numerous detective novels written under the pseudonym Frank Arnau. He first worked as a police and court reporter while a teenager. When World War II began he fled Europe and settled in Brazil, where he eventually worked at British and West German embassies; he returned to West Germany in 1955. Schmitt's writings include *The Hungarian Revolution: An Eye Witness's Account of the First Five Days*. Under the Arnau pseudonym he wrote *The Art of the Faker*, which concerned art forgeries, *Panik vor Torschluss, Lexicon der Philatelie,* and *Das Ratsel der Monstranz.*

OBITUARIES AND OTHER SOURCES:

PERIODICALS

AB Bookman's Weekly, April 19, 1976.
New York Times, February 12, 1976.

*   *   *

SCHMITTER, Phillipe Charles   1936-

PERSONAL: Born November 19, 1936, in Washington, D.C.; son of Lyle Lester (a government economist) and Laure (an insurance administrator; maiden name, Babut) Schmitter; divorced; children: Monika Anne, Marc Emile. *Education:* Attended Universidad Nacional Autonoma de Mexico, 1957-58; Dartmouth College, B.A. (cum laude), 1959; University of Geneva, Lic. es Sciences Politiques, 1961; University of California, Berkeley, Ph.D., 1968.

ADDRESSES: Home—Via Vecchia Fiesolana 48, San Domenico di Fiesole, Italy. *Office*—European University Institute, Badia Fiesolana, 50016 San Domenico di Fiesole, Italy.

CAREER: University of Brazil, Institute of Human Sciences, Rio de Janeiro, visiting professor of political science, 1965-66; University of California, Berkeley, research political scientist at Institute of International Studies, 1966-67; University of Chicago, Chicago, Ill., assistant professor, 1967-71, associate professor, 1971-75, professor of political science, 1975-84, chairman of committee on Latin American studies, 1970-73, 1974-76, chairman of committee on Western Europe, 1974-77; European University Institute, Florence, Italy, professor, 1982—, chairman of department of political and social sciences, 1984—. Lecturer at California State University, Sacramento, 1967; visiting professor at Instituto Para la Integracion de America Latina, Buenos Aires, Argentina, 1969, University of Geneva, 1973-74, University of Paris I, 1976, University of Munich, 1977-78, University of Zurich, 1978, and University of Barcelona, 1984; visiting lecturer at Harvard University and research associate at the university's Center for International Affairs, 1970. Conducted field research in Mexico, Costa Rica, Nicaragua, Honduras, El Salvador, and Guatemala, 1967. Member of grants selection committee of Carnegie Endowment for International Peace, 1968-71; member of academic council of Latin American program at Woodrow Wilson International Center for Scholars, 1977-82; founding member of Committee on Southern Europe, 1977—; chairman of Social Science Research Council-American Council of Learned Societies Joint Committee on Western Europe, 1982—.

MEMBER: International Sociological Association, American Political Science Association (vice-president, 1983-84), Social Science History Association, Conference Group on Contemporary Portugal (founding member), Council for European Studies, Conference Group on Italian Politics, Societe Tocqueville, Association Francaise de Science Politique, Schweizerische Vereinigung fuer Politische Wissenschaft, Societa Italiana di Scienza Politica, Deutsche Vereinigung fuer Politische Wissenschaft.

AWARDS, HONORS: Grant from Institut des Hautes Etudes Internationales for University of Geneva, 1960-61; Rockefeller Foundation fellow in Brazil, 1964-65; grant from Social Science Research Council and American Council of Learned Societies for Argentina, 1969; grant from Social Science Research Council for Portugal, 1971; international fellow of Council on Foreign Relations, 1972-73; Alexander von Humboldt fellow, 1977; Guggenheim fellow, 1978; National Science Foundation grant, 1977-80; grant from Stiftung Volkswagen, 1981-83.

WRITINGS:

(With Ernst B. Haas) *The Politics of Economics in Latin American Regionalism* (monograph), Institute of Social Studies, University of Denver, 1965.
Interest Conflict and Political Change in Brazil, Stanford University Press, 1971.
Autonomy or Dependence as Regional Integration Outcomes: Central America, Institute of International Studies, University of California, Berkeley, 1972.
(Editor and contributor) *Military Rule in Latin America: Functions, Consequences, and Prospectives*, Sage Publications, 1973.
Corporatism and Public Policy in Authoritarian Portugal, Sage Publications, 1975.
(Editor with Gerhard Lehmbruch) *Trends Toward Corporatist Intermediation*, Sage Publications, 1981.
(Editor with Lehmbruch) *Patterns of Corporatist Policy-Making*, Sage Publications, 1982.

(Editor with Lehmbruch, and contributor) *La politica degli interessi nei paesi industrializzati* (title means "The Politics of Interests in Industrialized Countries"), Il Mulino, 1984.
(With Guillermo O'Donnell) *Political Life After Authoritarian Rule: Tentative Conclusions About Uncertain Transitions*, Johns Hopkins University Press, 1985.
(Editor with O'Donnell) *The Demise of Authoritarian Rule and the Rise of Democracy in Latin America and Southern Europe*, Johns Hopkins University Press, 1985.
(With Wolfgang Streeck) *Private Interest Governments*, Sage Publications, 1985.
(With Claus Iffe) *Neo-Corporatist Practice and Democratic Theory*, Sage Publications, in press.

CONTRIBUTOR

International Political Communities, Anchor Books, 1966.
M. Janowitz and J. van Doorn, editors, *On Military Intervention*, 1971.
D. Chalmers, editor, *Changing Latin America*, 1972.
Alfred Stepan, editor, *Authoritarian Brazil: Origins, Policies, and Future*, Yale University Press, 1983.
F. B. Pike and T. Stritch, editors, *The New Corporatism*, University of Notre Dame Press, 1974.
H. Biener and D. Morrell, editors, *Political Participation Under Military Regimes*, Sage Publications, 1976.
E. Gil and others, editors, *Chile, 1970-1973*, Editorial Tecnos, 1977.
G. Hermet, R. Rose, and A. Rouquie, editors, *Elections Without Choice*, Macmillan, 1978.
K. Jowitt, editor, *Social Change in Romania, 1860-1940*, Institute of International Studies, University of California, Berkeley, 1978.
Gil and others, editors, *Chile at the Turning Point: Lessons of the Socialist Years, 1970-1974*, Institute for the Study of Human Issues, 1979.
U. von Alemann and R. G. Heinze, editors, *Verbaende und Staat* (title means "Associations and the State"), Westdeutscher Verlag, 1979.
L. S. Graham and H. M. Makler, editors, *Contemporary Portugal*, University of Texas Press, 1979.
S. Berger, editor, *Organizing Interests in Western Europe*, Cambridge University Press, 1981.
Mario Telo, editor, *Sindacato, politica, e corporativismo in Europa, 1970-1980* (title means "Unions, Politics, and Corporatism in Europe"), Franco Angeli, 1983.
Gianfranco Pasquino, editor, *Le societa complesse* (title means "Complex Societies"), Il Mulino, 1983.

Contributor to political science journals. Member of editorial board of *P.S.*, 1969-71, *Comparative Political Studies*, 1974-77, *Papers: Revista de Scoiologia*, 1976-82, *Politics and Society*, 1982—, and *Stato e mercato*, 1983—; member of editorial advisory board of *Armed Forces and Society*, 1976-80.

WORK IN PROGRESS: *Historical Change, Interest Intermediation, and the Governability of Advanced Industrial/Capitalist Societies*, publication expected in 1986; *The Organization of Business Interests*, with Wolfgang Streeck.

*   *   *

SCHORSCH, Ismar 1935-

BRIEF ENTRY: Born November 3, 1935, in Hanover, Germany (now West Germany). American rabbi, historian, educator, and author. After eight years at the Jewish Theological

Seminary, Schorsch was named Rabbi Herman Abramovitz Professor of Jewish History in 1980. He has received grants from the Foundation for Jewish Culutre and the National Foundation for the Humanities and has served as a member of the executive committee at the Leo Baeck Institute. Schorsch is the author of *Jewish Reactions to German Anti-Semitism, 1870-1914* (Columbia University Press, 1972). He edited and translated *The Structure of Jewish History, and Other Essays* (Jewish Theological Seminary, 1975). *Address:* 5430 Netherland Ave., New York, N.Y. 10471; and Department of Jewish History, Jewish Theological Seminary, New York, N.Y. 10027.

BIOGRAPHICAL/CRITICAL SOURCES:

BOOKS

Who's Who in American Jewry, Standard Who's Who, 1980.

* * *

SCHULMERICH, Alma   1902(?)-1985

OBITUARY NOTICE: Born c. 1902 in Oregon; died of a heart ailment on or shortly before January 28, 1985, in Washington, D.C. Civil servant, sculptor, and author. At the time of her retirement in 1971, Schulmerich was an administrative assistant for the Internal Revenue Service. She had become a government employee in the nation's capital in 1917. She spent World War I and World War II as a secretary in the War Department, and she worked for the Department of the Interior in the 1950's. Actively involved in the arts, Schulmerich made sculpture busts of many American presidents, beginning with Herbert Hoover. She also wrote two books, *Washington, D.C.: A Walk Through* and a biography, *Josie Pearl.*

OBITUARIES:

PERIODICALS

Washington Post, February 4, 1985.

* * *

SCHULZ, Bruno   1892(?)-1942

BRIEF ENTRY: Born in 1892 (one source says 1893) in Drohobycz, Poland (now Drogobych, U.S.S.R.); died from a gunshot wound in 1942, in Drohobycz, Poland. Polish art teacher, translator, and author. Schulz is best known for his fiction combining realism and fantasy. He wrote while working as an art teacher in his hometown of Drohobycz. Encouraged by Debora Vogel, a literary editor with whom he had corresponded, Schulz finally sought publication in the early 1930's. The result was *Sklepy cynamonowe* (1934; translated as *The Street of Crocodiles,* 1963), a loosely structured, autobiographical novel about one man's often hallucinatory experiences in provincial Poland. For this work, which elicited comparisons to the writings of Franz Kafka and Marcel Proust, Schulz received a golden laurel from the Polish Academy of Art. In 1936 he completed a Polish translation of Kafka's novel *The Trial,* and the following year he finished his second original work, *Sanatorium pod klepsydra* (translated as *Sanatorium Under the Sign of the Hourglass,* 1978), a collection of bizarre, yet realistic, tales that sometimes recall Kafka's stories. Schulz, a Jew, remained in Drohobycz even after Germany conquered Poland in 1939. He was killed there three years later by Nazi occupation troops. His final work, the novel *Mesjaz,* was lost.

BIOGRAPHICAL/CRITICAL SOURCES:

BOOKS

Milosz, Czeslaw, *The History of Polish Literature,* Macmillan, 1969.
Twentieth-Century Literary Criticism, Volume 5, Gale, 1981.

* * *

SCHWARZKOPF, LeRoy C(arl)   1920-

PERSONAL: Born December 9, 1920, in Sebewaing, Mich.; son of Hugo T. and Clara (Sting) Schwarzkopf. *Education:* Yale University, B.A., 1943; University of Michigan, M.A., 1951; Rutgers University, M.L.S., 1967.

ADDRESSES: Home—8429 Greenbelt Rd., Greenbelt, Md. 20770. *Office*—P.O. Box 232, Greenbelt, Md. 20770.

CAREER: Career officer in the U.S. Army, 1944-49 and 1951-66; served in the United States, Japan, Korea, and France; retired as lieutenant colonel. University of Maryland at College Park, government documents librarian, 1967-77, head of Documents/Maps Room, 1977-83; free-lance writer and consultant, 1983—.

MEMBER: American Library Association (charter member of Government Documents Round Table, 1972—), Special Libraries Association (Geography and Map Division), American Association of Law Libraries, Society of American Archivists, Beta Phi Mu.

AWARDS, HONORS: Documents to the People Award from American Library Association's Government Documents Round Table, 1981.

WRITINGS:

Government Reference Books 82/83: A Biennial Guide to U.S. Government Publications; 8th Biennial Volume, Libraries Unlimited, 1984.
Popular Guide to U.S. Government Publications, Libraries Unlimited, 1985.

Author of "U.S. Government Publications," a monthly column in *Booklist,* 1972—; author of "Government Publications and Depository System," an annual article in *ALA Yearbook of Library and Information Services,* 1978; author of "News from Washington," a bimonthly column in *Government Publications Review,* 1983—.

Editor of *Documents to the People* and author of its bimonthly column "Unclassified News From Washington," 1978-82; contributing editor for government documents, *American Reference Books Annual,* 1976—.

Contributor to library journals.

SIDELIGHTS: LeRoy C. Schwarzkopf told *CA:* "My career as a government documents librarian and author has been guided by the theme 'Documents to the People,' which is the motto of the American Library Association's Government Documents Round Table (GODORT) and is also the title of the GODORT official bimonthly publication. This motto seeks to increase awareness by the general public of the thousands of useful and interesting publications that are issued annually by government agencies (primarily in the federal government) and are available through the federal depository library program. My writings consist of annotated bibliographies of U.S. government publications and of current news and historical analysis of federal government printing and publishing, as well as information collection and dissemination activities and policies.

"I find that the chore of writing and revising manuscripts has been greatly reduced by the use of a computer with a word processing and file management program. I began with a Kaypro II and have upgraded to an IBM PC compatible but continue to use the Perfect Writer and Perfect Filer programs that came packed with both computers."

* * *

SCOTT, Robert F(alcon) 1868-1912

BRIEF ENTRY: Born June 6, 1868, near Devonport, England; died in 1912 on the Ross Ice Shelf near One Ton Depot, Antarctica. British explorer, naval officer, and author of reports on his expeditions. Scott entered the naval training program of the H.M.S. *Brittania* when he was thirteen years old and attained the rank of midshipman by 1883. He then served as such on board the *Boadicea, Lion, Monarch,* and *Rover* before being promoted to lieutenant-commander in 1897. In 1900 Scott was named commander of the British National Antarctic Expedition that commenced on board the *Discovery* in August, 1901, with the aim of exploring the region of Antarctica south of New Zealand called Victoria Land. This expedition, which lasted until 1904, resulted in the discovery of King Edward VII Land and in a sledge trip led by Scott that reached the southernmost latitude gained up to that time. Scott wrote an account of this first expedition titled *The Voyage of the "Discovery"* (1905) and was promoted to the rank of captain upon his return to England.

After the *Discovery* voyage, Scott commanded three warships before being named naval assistant of the British Admiralty in 1909 and heading another Antarctic expedition the following year. The trip, whose purpose was to reach the as yet unattained South Pole, began in June, 1910, when Scott and his crew set forth in the *Terra Nova,* and gained intensity when Scott learned enroute that a Norwegian party led by Roald Amundsen was also journeying toward the South Pole. On November 1, 1911, after reaching the Ross Ice Shelf and setting up headquarters at Cape Evans, Scott set off on a sledge trip, determined to get to the South Pole before Amundsen. But the journey proved disastrous. After traveling 1842 miles by pony, motor sledge, and foot, Scott and his companions discovered that Amundsen's party had been to the South Pole five weeks earlier. The Britons then headed back toward Cape Evans, but died from exhaustion, exposure, and lack of food some eight hundred miles into the trip—only eleven miles from the base camp. Scott, who kept a journal of his experiences, entered his last journal notation on March 29, 1912, and he and his party were found dead eight months later in a tent containing their diaries, papers, and geological samples. Scott's death prompted the founding of the Scott Polar Research Institute in Cambridge, England, and the information gathered on his journey to the South Pole was published as *British Antarctic Expedition ("Terra Nova"), 1910-13: Scientific Results* (1914). An account of the expedition based on Scott's journal was also published posthumously and titled *Scott's Last Expedition: From the Personal Journals of Captain R. F. Scott* (1964).

BIOGRAPHICAL/CRITICAL SOURCES:

BOOKS

Evans, Edward R.G.R., *South With Scott,* W. Collins Sons & Company, 1921.

Gwynn, Stephen, *Captain Scott,* Harper, 1930.
Lindsay, Martin, *The Epic of Captain Scott,* Heinemann, 1962.
Ludlam, Harry, *"Captain" Scott: The Full Story,* Foulsham, 1965.
Pound, Reginald, *Scott of the Antarctic,* Cassell, 1966.

* * *

SCRIVER, Bob
See SCRIVER, Robert MacFie

* * *

SCRIVER, Robert MacFie 1914-
(Bob Scriver)

PERSONAL: Born August 15, 1914, in Browning, Mont.; son of Thaddeus E. (a merchant) and Ellison (a housewife; maiden name, MacFie) Scriver. *Education:* VanderCook School (now College) of Music, B.Mus., 1936; graduate study at Northwestern University; University of Washington, Seattle, M.Mus., 1950. *Religion:* "Native American."

ADDRESSES: Home and office—P.O. Box 172, Browning, Mont. 59417.

CAREER: Museum of Montana Wildlife, Browning, Mont., owner and curator, 1956—. Sculptor, with work on display at Glenbow Foundation, Whitney Gallery of Western Art, and Panhandle Plains Museum; exhibited in group and solo shows throughout the West and at Grand Central Art Gallery, New York, N.Y. Member of national advisory board of Charles M. Russell Museum. Past president of local Chamber of Commerce; justice of the peace; city magistrate. *Military service:* U.S. Army Air Forces, lead trumpet player in band, 1940-45; served abroad; became sergeant.

MEMBER: International Art Guild, National Sculpture Society, Cowboy Artists of America, National Academy of Western Art, Society of Animal Artists, Salmagundi Club.

AWARDS, HONORS: Cowboy Artists of America, gold medal from 1970 exhibit for "An Honest Try," gold medal from 1971 exhibit for "Paywindow," and silver medal from 1972 exhibit for "Not for Glory"; silver medal from National Academy of Western Art, 1973, for "Layin' the Trap"; Ph.D. from Carroll College, Helena, Mont., 1976.

WRITINGS:

(Under name Bob Scriver) *An Honest Try* (nonfiction), Lowell Press, 1975.
(Under name Bob Scriver) *No More Buffalo* (nonfiction), Lowell Press, 1982.

Contributor to history journals.

WORK IN PROGRESS: Eternal Vigilance, a book on North American animals, publication by Lowell Press expected in 1987.

SIDELIGHTS: Robert MacFie Scriver told *CA:* "I have lived amongst the rodeo cowboys all my life; therefore I write about rodeos. I have lived amongst the Indians all my life; therefore I write about Indians. All the information I gathered for my books came from firsthand knowledge. I am an observer of the transitional period of the Blackfeet Indian."

BIOGRAPHICAL/CRITICAL SOURCES:

BOOKS

Broder, Patricia Janis, *Bronzes of the American West*, Abrams, 1974.
McDowell, Bart, *The American Cowboy in Life and Legend*, National Geographic Society, 1972.
McDowell, Bart, *The World of the American Indian*, National Geographic Society, 1974.
Snyder, Gerald S., *In the Footsteps of Lewis and Clark*, National Geographic Society, 1970.

*   *   *

SEABURY, Paul 1923-

BRIEF ENTRY: Born May 6, 1923, in Hempstead, N.Y. American political scientist, educator, and author. Seabury began teaching political science and government at the University of California, Berkeley, in 1953 and became a full professor ten years later. He has conducted research at the Center for International Affairs at Harvard University, the Royal Institute of International Affairs in London, England, and the Hoover Institution on War, Revolution, and Peace. Seabury has also been associated with the University Centers for Rational Alternatives, the International Council on the Future of the University, and the League for Industrial Democracy.

His research has resulted in such books as *Power, Freedom, and Diplomacy: The Foreign Policy of the United States of America* (Random House, 1963), which was awarded Columbia University's Bancroft Prize, and *The Rise and Decline of the Cold War* (Basic Books, 1967), which traces the history of American-Soviet relations from the Truman Doctrine issued in 1947. Seabury also wrote *The Balance of Power* (Chandler Publishing, 1965), *The Great Detente Disaster: Oil and the Decline of American Foreign Policy* (Basic Books, 1975), and *America's Stake in the Pacific* (Ethics and Public Policy Center, 1981). He edited *Bureaucrats and Brainpower: Government Regulation of Universities* (Institute for Contemporary Studies, 1977). *Address:* 600 Alvarado Rd., Berkeley, Calif. 94705.

BIOGRAPHICAL/CRITICAL SOURCES:

BOOKS

The Writers Directory: 1984-1986, St. James Press, 1983.

PERIODICALS

Nation, April 15, 1968.

*   *   *

SECKLER, David William 1935-

PERSONAL: Born February 18, 1935, in Sterling, Colo.; married; children: four. *Education:* University of Denver, B.A., 1957, M.A., 1958; London School of Economics and Political Science, London, Ph.D., 1961.

ADDRESSES: Office—Department of Economics, Colorado State University, Fort Collins, Colo. 80521.

CAREER: Colorado State University, Fort Collins, assistant professor, 1963-67, associate professor of economics, 1967-68; University of California, Berkeley, acting associate professor of agricultural economics, 1968-70; Colorado State University, professor of economics, 1970—. Program officer of Ford Foundation in New Delhi, India, 1978-83; senior devel-

opment policy adviser to U.S. Agency for International Development in Djakarta, Indonesia, 1983—; consultant.

MEMBER: American Economic Association.

AWARDS, HONORS: Awards from American Agricultural Economics Association, 1977, for article "Mechanized Agriculture and Social Welfare," 1979, for article "Economic and Policy Implications of the 160-Acre Limitation in Federal Reclamation Law," and 1982, for "Publication of Enduring Quality" (named best article of the decade).

WRITINGS:

(With Paul C. Huszar and D. D. Rohdy) *Economics of Irrigation System Consolidation*, Experiment Station, Colorado State University, 1969.
(Editor) *California Water: A Study in Resource Management*, University of California Press, 1971.
(With Paul W. Barkley) *Economic Growth and Environmental Decay: The Solution Becomes the Problem*, Harcourt, 1972.
Thorstein Veblen and the Institutionalists: A Study in the Philosophy of Economics, Colorado Associated Universities Press, 1975.

Contributor to economics journals.

WORK IN PROGRESS: Resource Management in India.

BIOGRAPHICAL/CRITICAL SOURCES:

PERIODICALS

Times Literary Supplement, July 25, 1975.

*   *   *

SEGERBERG, Osborn, Jr. 1924-

PERSONAL: Born February 18, 1924, in New York, N.Y.; son of Osborn Carl (an artist) and Elsie (Kregler) Segerberg; married Nancy Reutti (an interior designer), May 7, 1955; children: Margaret, Paul, Katherine. *Education:* Brown University, A.B., 1947.

ADDRESSES: Home and office—Kinderhook, N.Y.

CAREER: United Press International, New York City, writer and editor, 1949-55; free-lance journalist for news services, including Hearst Metrotone News, 1955-60; WNEW-Radio, New York City, news writer and reporter, 1960-61; United Press Movietone, New York City, writer, reporter, and editor, 1962-63; WCBS-TV News, New York City, producer and writer, 1963-69; free-lance writer, 1969—. Writer for national television news programs, including "NBC News," "Today," "ABC News," "20/20," and "CBS News." Film producer and writer for New York State Department of Education and United Nations Television. *Military service:* U.S. Army Air Forces, 1943-46; fighter pilot; became first lieutenant.

MEMBER: Writers Guild of America East, Authors Guild, New York Academy of Sciences.

AWARDS, HONORS: National Safety Council Public Service Award, 1966, for producing a series on Ralph Nader for WCBS-TV news; award from New York Associated Press, 1969, for producing "DDT/SOS" for WCBS-TV news; "The Limits to Growth" was a finalist in the American Film Festival, 1973; *Living With Death* was selected as an outstanding book in 1976 by the *New York Times Book Review*.

WRITINGS:

Where Have All the Flowers, Fishes, Birds, Trees, Water, and Air Gone?: What Ecology Is All About, McKay, 1971.
The Immortality Factor, Dutton, 1974.
Living With Death, Dutton, 1976.
Living To Be One Hundred, Scribner, 1982.

Author of works for television, including "DDT/SOS," CBS-TV News, 1969; and "The Limits to Growth," United Nations Television, 1973. Contributor of articles to periodicals, including *New York* and *Esquire.*

SIDELIGHTS: Among Osborn Segerberg, Jr.'s books is *Living With Death,* which, according to Morton Hunt in the *New York Times Book Review,* is "a work of breadth and scholarship" that "covers virtually everything related to the topic of death. . . . Mr. Segerberg's reportage is thorough, his outlook rational and honest." Vivian J. Scheinmann, writing in the *Washington Post Book World,* noted that *Living With Death,* which is directed at an adolescent audience, is the "*sine qua non*" for high school death-education courses.

In a *New York Times* article, Jane Brody described Segerberg's next book, *Living to Be One Hundred,* as "very revealing." Brody further commented that the book's "account of the secrets of longevity is at once encouraging and discouraging: encouraging because it puts the emphasis on living habits and attitudes, rather than on genetics, thereby (at least theoretically) giving us some control of our destiny; and discouraging because the habits and outlooks it singles out are antithetical to the demands of the highly mechanized go-getting civilization in which we now live."

Segerberg told *CA:* "The central discovery of extensive research on American centenarians is that these very long-lived people learned how to neutralize and cope with harmful stress and to promote what the founder of stress theory, Hans Selye, called eustress or good stress—what we recognize as positive emotions and good feelings."

BIOGRAPHICAL/CRITICAL SOURCES:

PERIODICALS

Library Journal, February 15, 1982.
New York Times, February 2, 1982.
New York Times Book Review, August 15, 1976.
Washington Post Book World, February 17, 1974, November 7, 1976.

*   *   *

SELLERS, Ronnie 1948-

PERSONAL: Born September 20, 1948, in Philadelphia, Pa.; son of Ronald W., Sr. (in retail piano business) and Barbara Anne Louise (an assistant manager in family business; maiden name, Wake) Sellers; married Lois Eileen Wagner, March 17, 1967 (divorced June, 1980); married Jeanne Marie Herringshaw (a singer), August 22, 1982; children: Devin Lee (daughter), Dixie Lee (daughter), Lindsey Lee (son). *Education:* University of Pennsylvania, B.A., 1970.

ADDRESSES: Home—2 Essex St., Sanford, Maine 04073. *Office*—Renaissance Greeting Cards, P.O. Box 126, Springvale, Maine 04083. *Agent*—Joan Brandt, Sterling Lord Agency, Inc., 660 Madison Ave., New York, N.Y. 10021.

CAREER: Wheatfield Recording Studios, Turner Falls, Mass., producer and manager, 1970-77; Ronnie Sellers Management

& Production, owner, manager, and producer, 1977-80; Renaissance Greeting Cards, Springvale, Maine, founder, co-owner, and marketing director, 1980—.

WRITINGS:

If Christmas Were a Poem (juvenile), Caedmon, 1983.
When Springtime Comes (juvenile), Caedmon, 1984.
My First Day of School (juvenile), Caedmon, 1985.

Radio writer, including work for public service radio; television writer.

Contributor to magazines.

WORK IN PROGRESS: The Kennebunkport Stories (tentative title), a collection of children's stories, publication expected in 1986; short stories for adults.

SIDELIGHTS: Ronnie Sellers told *CA:* "I began reading and writing poetry when I was thirteen years old. I wrote poetry exclusively until my sophomore year of college. Then I was fortunate enough to enroll in a fiction writing class taught by John Edgar Wideman. In his patient and gentle way, this gifted teacher taught me how to go about the business of writing.

"I began writing children's books in 1981. I met an artist named Peggy Jo Ackley during that year, and I wrote my first book to give us an opportunity to collaborate. She has continued to illustrate my books.

"Writing children's books is as rewarding an occupation as I could expect to find. It is remedial to spend time talking with children when working on a book, and children's authors are also able to *act* like children from time to time with legitimacy.

"In my children's books I try to remember that children are not only interested in learning about the way things are; they also love to spend time fantasizing about how things could be.

"My first three books are about events: the celebration of Christmas, the arrival of spring, and the first day of school. My intent was to create books that would help children appreciate those special occasions more. In so doing, I hoped to introduce them to the concept of reading for the sake of pleasure. As adults, we read in order to appreciate the experience of life more, and this can add much pleasure to our lives.

"The book I'm presently working on, *The Kennebunkport Stories,* chronicles the day-to-day adventures of a little girl, Jenny Lee, and her imaginary friends. I call it 'fiction for children.' As such, it depicts a world that is moved by forces both real and imaginary.

"As a writer I'm fascinated by the way children use their imaginations to construct worlds of their own. I try to appeal to the child's sense of 'how things could be' when I write, knowing that those little ones who imagine will someday be the ones who create!"

*   *   *

SENN, Frank C(olvin) 1943-

PERSONAL: Born April 22, 1943, in Buffalo, N.Y.; son of Max Frank (a laundry worker) and Katherine (a housekeeper; maiden name, Lichtenberger) Senn; married Mary Elizabeth Langford (a social worker), May 15, 1976; children: Andrew Martin, Nicholas John. *Education:* Hartwick College, B.A., 1965; Lutheran School of Theology at Chicago, M.Div., 1969; University of Notre Dame, Ph.D., 1979.

ADDRESSES: Home—401 East 32nd St. No. 1915, Chicago, Ill. 60616. *Office*—Christ the Mediator Lutheran Church, 3100 South Calumet Ave., Chicago, Ill. 60616.

CAREER: Ordained Lutheran minister, 1969; Gloria Dei Lutheran Church, South Bend, Ind., assistant pastor, 1969-74; Christ Seminary-Seminex, St. Louis, Mo., visiting instructor in liturgy, 1975; Fenner Memorial Lutheran Church, Louisville, Ky., pastor, 1975-77; Lutheran School of Theology at Chicago, assistant professor of liturgy and church history, 1977-81; Christ the Mediator Lutheran Church, Chicago, pastor, 1981—. Lecturer at University of Chicago Divinity School. Vice-president of Greater Chicago Neighborhoods; member of board of directors of Ancona Montessori School.

MEMBER: North American Academy of Liturgy, Societas Liturgica.

WRITINGS:

The Pastor as Worship Leader, Augsburg, 1977.
Christian Worship and Its Cultural Setting, Fortress, 1982.
(Editor) *Protestant Spiritual Traditions,* Paulist Press, 1985.

Contributor to liturgy and theology journals; member of editorial board of *Dialog.*

WORK IN PROGRESS: A textbook on Lutheran liturgics, with Philip Pfatteicher, publication by Fortress expected in 1988.

SIDELIGHTS: Frank C. Senn told *CA:* "I write because I am vitally interested in the issues I address in books and articles, and putting words on paper is a way in which I have the possibility of expressing myself clearly. The overriding concern I have addressed in my writings is the renewal of the church in its calling to celebrate and anticipate the divine kingdom, principally through the medium of its liturgy or 'public work.'

Increasingly I have found instructive parallels between Christian worship and theories of human ritual, particularly Victor Turner's concept of 'liminality' as a mode for expressing the church's eschatological vocation. Ritual has a 'liminal' or 'betwixt and between' character. It takes place between stages and states in life. Christian worship takes place between this world and the life of the world to come. In *Christian Worship and Its Cultural Setting* I demonstrate that Christian worship is essentially a counter-cultural activity that also serves the purpose of transforming culture. The worship leaders have to be sensitive not only to the needs of the worshipers, but also to the theological tradition that is transmitted and adapted in worship from one generation to another. It is equally important to know the forms and content of the liturgy and the character of the local worshiping community.

"I hope to carry forward these two themes—know the tradition, and know the worshiping community—in the projected textbook on which I am working with Philip Pfatteicher. It will be a commentary on the *Lutheran Book of Worship* with considerable attention to the historical and theological foundations of Christian worship done by Lutherans."

*   *   *

SERVICE, Robert
See SERVICE, Robert W(illiam)

SERVICE, Robert W(illiam)   1874(?)-1958
(Robert Service)

BRIEF ENTRY: Born January 16, 1874 (some sources say 1876), in Preston, England; died September 11, 1958, in France. British-born Canadian journalist, poet, and novelist. Service enjoyed success in the early twentieth century for his works about life in northern Canada. He arrived there from his native England in 1894 and traveled along the Pacific coast. In 1902 he joined the Canadian Bank of Commerce, which transferred him from Vancouver to the Yukon in 1904. This wild country, with its miners and lumberjacks, proved inspirational to Service, who turned to poetry to express his frequently melodramatic vision. His verse was collected in *Songs of a Sourdough* (1907; also published as *The Spell of the Yukon*) which earned Service a reputation as the Canadian Rudyard Kipling. The book contains many of Service's most popular poems, including "The Shooting of Dan McGrew," which details the violent demise of a rough miner. A second collection, *Ballads of a Cheechako* (1909), proved equally popular and enabled Service to abandon banking. He retired to a wilderness cabin and wrote *The Trail of Ninety-Eight* (1912), a novel about a courageous drifter's hardships in the Canadian North.

After moving to Europe Service completed a second novel, *The Pretender: A Story of the Latin Quarter* (1914), which concerns Parisian bohemians. When World War I began Service worked as a war correspondent and ambulance driver before becoming an intelligence officer for the Canadian Army. He wrote of his war experiences in *Rhymes of a Red Cross Man* (1916), a volume that some critics consider a departure from the melodramatic narratives of earlier collections. After the war Service settled in France. He completed one more book, *Ballads of a Bohemian* (1921), before withdrawing from the literary world for nearly twenty years. In 1940, when he resumed publication with *Bar-Room Blues,* Service fled from France during the German invasion. He returned to Canada, then moved to Hollywood, California, where he wrote *Ploughman of the Moon* (1945), the first of two autobiographical volumes. The second work, *Harper of Heaven,* appeared in 1948. Service moved back to France after World War II. He continued writing in the 1950's, but his later verses—with their political and social commentary—were less popular than his earlier poems of the Yukon.

BIOGRAPHICAL/CRITICAL SOURCES:

BOOKS

Everyman's Dictionary of Literary Biography, English and American, revised edition, Dutton, 1960.
Longman Companion to Twentieth Century Literature, Longman, 1970.
The Reader's Encyclopedia of American Literature, Crowell, 1962.
Twentieth-Century Literary Criticism, Gale, Volume 15, 1985.

*   *   *

SESSIONS, Roger Huntington   1896-1985

OBITUARY NOTICE—See index for *CA* sketch: Born December 28, 1896, in Brooklyn, N.Y.; died following a stroke and pneumonia, March 16, 1985, in Princeton, N.J. Educator, composer, and author. Sessions received a Pulitzer Special Citation for music in 1974 for his accomplishments as a composer and a second Pulitzer Prize for music in 1982. He began his career by fashioning chromatic, fairly accessible works such as "The Black Maskers," but eventually adopted the neoclassical style pioneered by Igor Stravinsky. In the early 1930's Sessions began writing serial music derived from specific series of tones. This technique, also practiced by Stravinsky and, more rigidly, by Arnold Schoenberg, marked most of Sessions' subsequent music. Among his many works in this exacting form are the "Concerto for Violin," which some violinists consider unplayable, the opera *Montezuma,* which sparked violence at its premier in 1964, the "Concerto for Orchestra," which earned Sessions his 1982 Pulitzer Prize for music, and several other symphonic chamber works. In addition to composing, Sessions taught music at several institutions, including Princeton University and the Juilliard School of Music. Among his writings are *The Musical Experience of Composer, Performer, Listener* and *Reflections on the Musical Life in the United States.* He also participated in a series of interviews published as *The Reminiscences of Roger Sessions.*

OBITUARIES AND OTHER SOURCES:

BOOKS

The International Who's Who, 48th edition, Europa, 1984.
Who's Who in American Music, Bowker, 1983.

PERIODICALS

Chicago Tribune, March 19, 1985.
Los Angeles Times, March 18, 1985.
Time, April 1, 1985.
Times (London), March 20, 1985.

*   *   *

SETH, Ronald (Sydney)   1911-1985
   (Robert Chartham)

OBITUARY NOTICE—See index for *CA* sketch: Born in 1911 in Ely, Cambridgeshire, England; died February 1, 1985. Educator, wartime spy, translator, and author. Seth is remembered for his writings on espionage and for his exploits as a spy and prisoner-of-war during World War II. After teaching at the University of Tallinn and working in intelligence for the British Broadcasting Corporation, Seth joined British intelligence and became an officer with the Royal Air Force. During World War II Seth parachuted into Estonia and was captured by Germans. He endured lengthy interrogation and torture before escaping execution by agreeing to spy for his captors. In 1945, on orders from Nazi official Heinrich Himmler, Seth was sent to England to negotiate a peace settlement. For Seth, who had merely connived to obtain Himmler's confidence, the return to England ended three years of anguish. After the war Seth began writing. Among his numerous books are *Spies at Work: A History of Espionage, Forty Years of Soviet Spying, The Spy Who Wasn't Caught: The Story of Julius Silber,* and the autobiographical *A Spy Has No Friends.* His other writings include military history and travel books for children and, under the pseudonym Robert Chartham, sex guides.

OBITUARIES AND OTHER SOURCES:

PERIODICALS

Times (London), February 5, 1985.

*   *   *

SHACKLEY, Myra (Lesley)   1949-

PERSONAL: Born March 5, 1949, in London, England. Ed-ucation: University of Southampton, B.A. (with honors), 1970, Ph.D., 1973.

ADDRESSES: Home—Leicester, England. *Office*—Department of Archaeology, University of Leicester, Leicester LE1 7RH, England. *Agent*—Curtis Brown Ltd., 162-8 Regent St., London W1R 5TA, England.

CAREER: Department of the Environment, London, England, excavated paleolithic site on Isle of Wight, 1971; University of Southampton, Southampton, England, joint organizer of international conference "Sediments in Archaeology," 1973; Oxford University Institute of Archaeology, Oxford, England, head of laboratory, 1974; University of Leicester, Leicester, England, lecturer in archaeology, 1978—. Lecturer at Society of American Archaeologists, 1980, and University of Arizona, 1982.

AWARDS, HONORS: Grant from Centre National de la Recherche Scientifique for University of Bordeaux and visits to French cave sites, 1972; Strakosch travel fellowship from Oxford University for South Africa, Namibia, Lesotho, and Swaziland, 1976; Swan Fund grant from Oxford University and Suzette Taylor fellowship from Lady Margaret Hall, Oxford, for Namibia, 1977; honorary research associate at University of Cape Town, 1978; British Council exchange scholar in South Africa, 1978, and at University of Ulan Bator, 1979; grant from Royal Society, 1982.

WRITINGS:

Archaeological Sediments, Butterworth, 1975.
(Editor with D. A. Davidson, and contributor) *Geoarchaeology: Earth Science and the Past,* Butterworth, 1976.
Rocks and Man (Book Club choice), Allen & Unwin, 1977.
Neanderthal Man, Duckworth, 1980.
Environmental Archaeology, Allen & Unwin, 1981.
Still Living?: Yeti, Sasquatch, and the Neanderthal Enigma, Thames & Hudson, 1983.
Using Environmental Archaeology (Book Club choice), Batsford, 1985.

Contributor to scientific journals in archaeology and anthropology and to popular magazines, including *Geographical, Country Life,* and *Nature.*

WORK IN PROGRESS: A long-term research project on the archaeology of the central Namib Desert of Namibia; research on environmental archaeology and on early communities.

SIDELIGHTS: In 1974 Myra Shackley visited Australia at the invitation of the Western Australian Museum. While there she lectured at universities, worked on sediments from Devils Lair Cave, and visited several archaeological sites and museums. In 1975 she participated in British excavations at Carthage, and in 1978 the archaeologist directed the excavation of Equus Cave in Bophutatswana and made field trips in the Negev and Sinai Deserts of Israel. One year later Shackley conducted a three-month solo expedition to Outer Mongolia to live with the nomadic tribesmen of the Gobi Desert and to examine the distribution of paleolithic sites in the area. She worked at the Museum of Natural History in New York in 1982 and conducted field work in the American Southwest.

Since her first visit to Namibia in 1976, however, Shackley has concentrated her research on the Namib Desert. She has spent a total of more than nine months in the desert since 1978, conducting field surveys of archaeological sites that represent resource exploitation events from 340,000 years ago up to the present.

Shackley commented: "I love deserts, and I like multi-level work, ranging from detailed research to extensive general broadcasting. I believe in (relatively) low-level synthesis as a good way of getting people interested in a subject."

AVOCATIONAL INTERESTS: Travel (including the U.S.S.R., Italy, West Germany, Mexico, and Syria), books, log fires, fast cars, fitness and exercise, fashion, martial arts, contemporary dance.

*   *   *

SHAW, T. E.
See LAWRENCE, T(homas) E(dward)

*   *   *

SHELLY, Judith A(llen)   1944-

PERSONAL: Born July 8, 1944, in Washington, D.C.; daughter of Hugh Arthur, Jr. (in the U.S. Army) and Anne (a secretary; maiden name, Croft) Allen; married James Alfred Shelly (a Lutheran pastor), May 15, 1976; children: Janell MaRee, Jonathan Michael. *Education:* Medical College of Virginia (now Virginia Commonwealth University), B.S.N., 1966; Lutheran Theological Seminary at Philadelphia, M.A.R., 1976. *Religion:* Lutheran.

ADDRESSES: Home and office—P.O. Box 306, Frederick, Pa. 19435.

CAREER: Mercy Medical Center, Springfield, Ohio, staff nurse, 1966-67; family practice nurse in Springfield, 1967-70; Nurses Christian Fellowship, Madison, Wis., member of campus staff, 1970-74; Lankenau Hospital, Philadelphia, Pa., staff nurse, 1974-76; Nurses Christian Fellowship, Madison, materials developer, 1976-82, associate director of resources, 1982-84; writer.

WRITINGS:

(With Sharon Fish) *Spiritual Care: The Nurse's Role,* with workbook, Inter-Varsity Press, 1978, revised edition, 1983.
Caring in Crisis, Inter-Varsity Press, 1979.
Dilemma: A Nurse's Guide for Making Ethical Decisions, Inter-Varsity Press, 1980.
(Editor and contributor) *The Spiritual Needs of Children,* Inter-Varsity Press, 1982.
(Editor and contributor) *Spiritual Dimensions of Mental Health,* Inter-Varsity Press, 1983.
Not Just a Job: Serving Christ in Your Work, Inter-Varsity Press, 1985.
(Editor) *Teaching Spiritual Care: A Resource Book for Nursing Faculty,* Nurses Christian Fellowship, 1985.

Contributor to *Critical Care Update.*

SIDELIGHTS: Judith A. Shelly's books have been translated into Korean, German, Mandarin Chinese, and Norwegian. She told *CA:* "While working as a nurse I found a vast difference between the quality of technical physical care and the spiritual care that we offered patients. The importance of spiritual care glared at me as I watched patients who were physically doing well lose hope and die for lack of meaningful relationships or purpose in life. As I offered spiritual care—a willingness to discuss spiritual concerns, prayer, encouragement from the Scriptures—I saw a striking improvement in patients' attitudes and physical health. My books are drawn from my own experience and the experiences of my nursing colleagues."

BIOGRAPHICAL/CRITICAL SOURCES:

PERIODICALS

Partnership, March/April, 1984.

*   *   *

SHEPARD, Richard F.   1922-

PERSONAL: Born December 31, 1922, in Bronx, N.Y.; son of Benjamin (a lawyer) and Anna (a lecturer and author) Shepard; married Gertrude Ellenberg (a librarian), February 18, 1951; children: Robert B., Daniel J. *Education:* Attended City College of New York.

ADDRESSES: Home—Fresh Meadows, N.Y. *Office—New York Times,* 229 West 43rd St., New York, N.Y. 10036. *Agent*—Arthur Pine, 1776 Broadway, New York, N.Y. 10019.

CAREER: New York Times, New York, N.Y., copyboy, 1946-53, reporter, 1953—, cultural news editor, 1969-71, served as columnist at various times during the 1970's. *Military service:* U.S. Merchant Marine, 1942-46; became radio officer.

WRITINGS:

Going Out in New York: A Guide for the Curious, Quadrangle, 1974.
(With Vicki Gold Levi) *Live and Be Well: A Celebration of Yiddish Culture in America From the First Immigrants to the Second World War,* Ballantine, 1982.

SIDELIGHTS: In *Live and Be Well* Richard Shepard and Vicki Gold Levi take a look at the rich cultural heritage of European Jews who immigrated to America in the early 1900's. Included are a catalogue of Yiddishisms, personality profiles, and a look at cultural institutions ranging from unions to grandmothers.

BIOGRAPHICAL/CRITICAL SOURCES:

PERIODICALS

New York Times, December 2, 1982.
New York Times Book Review, November 21, 1982.

*   *   *

SHERCLIFF, Jose   1902(?)-1985

OBITUARY NOTICE: Born c. 1902 in Burton-on-Trent, England; died January 21, 1985, in Cascais, Portugal. Journalist. Shercliff is best remembered for her long career as a news correspondent in Lisbon, Portugal. She had been living in Paris and working for the *Daily Herald* and the *News Chronicle* at the outset of World War II. After making her way back to her native England, the journalist was given an assignment in the United States. While enroute, an unexpected delay left the reporter stranded in Lisbon. She became enchanted with the country and its people and spent the rest of her life in Portugal. For several years Shercliff wrote for the Associated Press. In 1961 she became the Lisbon correspondent for the *Times* of London, and she held that post for twenty years. During the 1930's Shercliff wrote a book about the French cabaret performer Jane Avril.

OBITUARIES:

PERIODICALS

Times (London), January 24, 1985.

SHERROD, Jane
See SINGER, Jane Sherrod

*   *   *

SHIELD, Renee Rose   1948-

PERSONAL: Born April 2, 1948, in New York, N.Y.; daughter of Gilbert Jacob (a physician) and Anne (a writer; maiden name, Kaufman) Rose; married Paul Harold Shield (a physician), May 21, 1972; children: Sonja Eve, Aaron Michael, David Charles. *Education:* Pembroke College (now Brown University), B.A., 1970; University of Texas at Austin, M.A., 1973; Brown University, Ph.D., 1984.

ADDRESSES: Home—Seekonk, Mass. *Agent*—Sidney B. Kramer, Mews Books Ltd., 20 Bluewater Hill, Westport, Conn. 06880.

CAREER: Brown University, Providence, R.I., postdoctoral research associate, 1984—.

MEMBER: American Anthropological Association, Society for Medical Anthropology, Association for Anthropology and Gerontology, National Association for Practicing Anthropology.

WRITINGS:

Making Babies in the Eighties: Common Sense for New Parents, Harvard Common, 1983.

WORK IN PROGRESS: The Living End: Liminality in an American Nursing Home.

SIDELIGHTS: Renee Rose Shield told *CA:* "My academic and personal interests are combined in a deep involvement in both ends of the life cycle: raising children and a cross-cultural interest in old age.

"I wrote *Making Babies* in reaction against the current trend of highly educated, older new parents to overprepare for their new babies as if proper study ensures excellent pregnancies, ecstatic labor and deliveries, and exemplary, super-IQ children. I think that, despite the choices available today, there is a prescribed set of 'right' things that parents are supposed to do, such as breathe the 'natural childbirth' way, avoid analgesics, have the father in the labor and delivery rooms, breastfeed, and seek 'quality time' and 'bonding.' Sometimes these 'supposed to's' are more paralyzing than freeing. I wanted to suggest to couples that there are no necessarily right ways to go about pregnancy and having babies. And I wish to support the individual couple's right to making personal decisions based on their own informed judgments.

"My book offers *anti*-advice. It's reassuring and funny. I am of the opinion that things mess up and things go well despite the best intentions and the most zealous preparations. The book, written right after my third child was born, is based on my own experiences and viewpoints as observer and participant in the child and parent scene.

"*The Living End* is the result of fourteen months of anthropological research at a nursing home. In it I try to answer the basic question 'What is it like to live in this home?' I studied both the staff and the residents, and I investigated the native (i.e. staff's) belief that old people are just like children. I suggest reasons for this perception and conclude that the equation is often the result of dependency-inducing behaviors of the nursing home. I also compare nursing home life to rites of passage events elsewhere in the world. In this nursing home,

existence is 'liminal'—neither here nor there, in between productive life as a capable adult in the community and death; people wait. I suggest that it need not necessarily be so. I became interested in the academic study of old age after I became a parent and realized that it was aging me!'"

*   *   *

SHIFLETT, Lee
See SHIFLETT, Orvin Lee

*   *   *

SHIFLETT, Orvin Lee   1947-
(Lee Shiflett)

PERSONAL: Born August 1, 1947, in Melbourne, Fla.; son of James W. and Elsie (a housewife; maiden name, Davis) Shiflett; married Marisol Zapater-Ferra, December 20, 1979 (divorced April 28, 1982). *Education:* University of Florida, B.A.E., 1969; Rutgers University, M.L.S., 1971; Florida State University, Ph.D., 1979. *Politics:* Democrat.

ADDRESSES: Home—Route 2, Box 903, St. Gabriel, La. 70776. *Office*—School of Library and Information Science, Louisiana State University, Baton Rouge, La. 70803.

CAREER: University of Wisconsin—La Crosse, collection development librarian, 1971-74, coordinator of technical services, 1976-78; Louisiana State University, Baton Rouge, assistant professor, 1979-83, associate professor of library and information science, 1983—.

MEMBER: American Library Association (chairman of Library History Round Table, 1984), Association of American Library Schools, Association of Records Managers and Administrators, Association for Library and Information Science Education, Louisiana Library Association, Beta Phi Mu.

WRITINGS:

The Origins of American Academic Librarianship, Ablex Publishing, 1981.

Editor of "Dissertation Reviews," a column in *Library and Information Science Research.*

Contributor, sometimes under name Lee Shiflett, to library journals. Associate editor of *Library and Information Science Research.*

WORK IN PROGRESS: Louis Shores and the Search for an Academic Profession (tentative title), a biographical study, completion expected in 1986.

SIDELIGHTS: Orvin Lee Shiflett told *CA:* "Trying to discover a motive for writing is impossible. Even the mandate for academics to publish is, as many have found, insufficient. Perishing is much easier. My own motive for writing *Origins* came out of my need to understand the peculiar hobby of academic librarianship. The actual writing came as a process of organizing my thoughts. The book on Louis Shores is a continuation of the work into the twentieth century. Shores's work was, from the 1930's on, influential in the development of the perceived educational function of academic librarianship.

"Aside from this, my time is spent rebuilding an old house on the Mississippi levee, maintaining my collection of Confederate imprints, and finding time to throw pots."

SHILTS, Randy 1952(?)-

BRIEF ENTRY: Born c. 1952. American journalist, radio and television reporter, and author. Often called the Gay Reporter, Shilts first became known in the 1970's for his media coverage of the San Francisco area homosexual community. The journalist gained national renown with his 1982 biography, *The Mayor of Castro Street: The Life and Times of Harvey Milk* (St. Martin's), which examines the political climate surrounding the death of the homosexual activist and San Francisco supervisor who was assassinated in 1978 by a frustrated political opponent. Described in the *Washington Post* as "a comprehensive history of the homosexual movement in San Francisco," Shilts's book drew high praise from critics and readers, both within and outside the homosexual community. Shilts has also contributed articles to newspapers and periodicals, including the *Washington Post, Christopher Street, Village Voice,* and *Columbia Journalism Review.*

BIOGRAPHICAL/CRITICAL SOURCES:

PERIODICALS

Chicago Tribune, February 13, 1983.
Los Angeles Times, March 25, 1982.
Los Angeles Times Book Review, March 7, 1982.
Village Voice, March 23, 1982.
Washington Post, April 2, 1982.

*   *   *

SHINGLETON, John D.

PERSONAL: Education—Michigan State University, B.A., 1948.

ADDRESSES: Office—Office of Placement Services, Michigan State University, East Lansing, Mich. 48824.

CAREER: Employed by Wyandotte Chemical Corp. as a lathe operator, by Ford Motor Co., Dearborn, Mich., as an accountant, and by Detroit Edison Co., Detroit, Mich., as a personnel interviewer; Michigan State University, East Lansing, served as assistant director of personnel, assistant director of placement, administrative officer of engineering project in Madras and Poona, India, assistant to secretary of board of trustees, director of placement, 1963—, acting director of intercollegiate athletics, 1975-76, and as member of university development council. Member of board of governors of College Placement Council; member of College-Industry Personnel Group. Member of Lansing Tri-County Area Manpower Planning Council, Michigan Department of Education *ad hoc* committee on placement, and board of directors of Michigan governor's Executive Corps. Guest on television programs, including the "Today Show." Member of board of governors of National Fresh Water Fishing Hall of Fame. *Military service:* U.S. Army Air Forces, pilot.

MEMBER: Association for School, College, and University Staffing, Great Lakes Association for School, College, and University Staffing, Michigan College Placement Association, Michigan College and University Placement Association.

WRITINGS:

(With Phil Frank) *The Trout, the Whole Trout, and Nothing but the Trout,* Winchester Press, 1974.

(Co-author) *How to Increase Your Net Value,* Winchester Press, 1975.
College to Career: Finding Yourself in the Job Market, McGraw, 1977.
(With Patrick Scheetz) *Recruiting Trends, 1981-1982,* Placement Services, Michigan State University, 1981.

Also co-author of *Which Niche?,* 1969. Contributor to magazines, including *Parade, Business World, Michigan Challenge, Graduate,* and *American Youth.*

AVOCATIONAL INTERESTS: Sports (especially tennis).

*   *   *

SHIVELY, Donald H(oward) 1921-

BRIEF ENTRY: Born May 11, 1921, in Kyoto, Japan. American historian, educator, and author. Shively, who has taught Oriental languages at Stanford University and at the University of California, Berkeley, became a professor of Japanese history and literature at Harvard University in 1964. He has also served as director of the school's Language and Area Center for East Asian Studies, and, in 1975, he was appointed executive director of the Japan Institute and editor of the *Harvard Journal of Asiatic Studies.* In addition, the educator has been involved with the U.S. National Commission for the United Nations Educational, Scientific, and Cultural Organization and the Committee for United States-Japan Cultural and Educational Interchange.

Shively is the co-author of *Studies in Kabuki: Its Acting, Music, and Historical Context* (University Press of Hawaii, 1978). He edited *Personality in Japanese History* (University of California Press, 1970) and *Tradition and Modernization in Japanese Culture* (Princeton University Press, 1971). *Address:* 2 Divinity Ave., Cambridge, Mass. 02138; and Japan Institute, Harvard University, Cambridge, Mass. 02138.

BIOGRAPHICAL/CRITICAL SOURCES:

BOOKS

Directory of American Scholars, Volume I: *History,* 8th edition, Bowker, 1982.

*   *   *

SHKLOVSKY, Iosif Samuilovitch 1916-1985

OBITUARY NOTICE: Given name also transliterated as Iosef or Josef; surname also transliterated as Shklovskii; born July 1, 1916, in Glukhov, Russia (now U.S.S.R); died March 3, 1985, in Moscow, U.S.S.R. Astrophysicist, educator, and author. Shklovsky was internationally known for his contributions in the field of astrophysics and for his promotion of the search for intelligent extraterrestrial life. Head of the department of radio astronomy at the Soviet Union's Shternberg Astronomical Institute in Moscow beginning in 1938, Shklovsky was also professor at Moscow University and was associated for nearly twenty years with the Soviet Institute of Space Research. In 1953 he proposed a theory to explain puzzling light emissions from supernovas and over the course of his career contributed to the understanding of planetary physics, quasars, the solar corona, neutron stars, and exploding galaxies. Influential in the Soviet Union's unmanned planetary space program, Shklovsky received the Lenin Prize in 1960.

Shklovsky's book on the search for intelligent extraterrestrial life appeared in 1962; in 1966 the manuscript was translated into English and published, with extensive annotations by American astronomer Carl Sagan, as *Intelligent Life in the Universe.* This collaborative effort—which provides fundamental discussion of such topics as astronomy, physics, biology, chemistry, and the origin of life—is widely used as a basic textbook in introductory general science courses. Another of Shklovsky's works appeared in English in 1978 under the title *Stars: Their Birth, Life, and Death.* His other writings treat such subjects as the solar corona, cosmic rays, the Crab Nebula, the planet Venus, and radio astronomy.

OBITUARIES AND OTHER SOURCES:

BOOKS

The International Who's Who, 47th edition, Europa, 1983.

PERIODICALS

Los Angeles Times, March 8, 1985.
New York Times, March 6, 1985.
Time, March 18, 1985.
Washington Post, March 7, 1985.

*   *   *

SHNEIDERMAN, Ben A.   1947-

PERSONAL: Born August 21, 1947, in New York, N.Y.; son of Samuel L. and Eileen Shneiderman; married, March 25, 1973; children: Sara, Anna. *Education:* City College of the City University of New York, B.S., 1968; State University of New York at Stony Brook, M.S., 1972, Ph.D., 1973.

ADDRESSES: Office—Department of Computer Science, University of Maryland at College Park, College Park, Md. 20742.

CAREER: Indiana University—Bloomington, assistant professor of computer science, 1973-76; University of Maryland at College Park, associate professor of computer science, 1976—.

MEMBER: Association of Computing Machinery, American Society for Information Science, Institute of Electrical and Electronic Engineers, Software Psychology Society.

WRITINGS:

Software Psychology: Human Factors in Computer and Information Systems, Winthrop, 1980.
(Editor with Albert Nasib Badre) *Directions in Human/Computer Interaction,* Ablex Publishing, 1982.
Let's Learn BASIC, Little, Brown, 1984.

Contributor of articles to computer journals.

*   *   *

SHOEMAKER, William Lee   1931-
(Willie Shoemaker)

BRIEF ENTRY: Born August 19, 1931, in Fabens, Tex. American jockey and author. Shoemaker began racing horses in 1949 and, despite several serious injuries, managed a long career. He won the Kentucky Derby three times, the Belmont Stakes four times, and the Preakness twice. He has ridden to more than eight thousand wins, and his success has made him a millionaire. Shoemaker's books include *The Shoe: Willie Shoemaker's Illustrated Book of Racing* (Rand McNally, 1976).

BIOGRAPHICAL/CRITICAL SOURCES:

BOOKS

1000 Makers of the Twentieth Century, David & Charles, 1971.

SHOEMAKER, Willie
See SHOEMAKER, William Lee

*   *   *

SHRIMPTON, Gordon Spencer   1941-

PERSONAL: Born October 12, 1941, in Kenilworth, England; son of George Douglas (a quality control specialist) and Freda (a homemaker; maiden name, Lloyd) Shrimpton; married Grace Mary Edith Crawford (a homemaker), May 8, 1965; children: Paul Douglas, Karen Jayne. *Education:* University of British Columbia, B.A. (with first class honors), 1963, M.A., 1965; Stanford University, Ph.D., 1970.

ADDRESSES: Home—1753 Blair Ave., Victoria, British Columbia, Canada V8N 1M6. *Office*—Department of Classics, University of Victoria, Box 1700, Victoria, British Columbia, Canada V8W 2Y2.

CAREER: University of Victoria, Victoria, British Columbia, instructor, 1967-70, assistant professor, 1970-76, associate professor of classics, 1976—.

MEMBER: Classical Association of Canada, Archaeological Institute of America, Classical Association of the Pacific Northwest, Confederation of University Faculty Associations of British Columbia (president, 1984—), University of Victoria Faculty Association (president, 1982-84).

WRITINGS:

(Editor with David Joseph McCarger, and contributor) *Classical Contributions: Studies in Honour of Malcolm Francis McGregor,* J. J. Augustin, 1981.
(Contributor) Warren Magnusson and others, editors, *The New Reality: The Politics of Restraint in British Columbia,* New Star Books, 1984.

Contributor to journals, including *Classical Philology, Phoenix,* and *Symbolae Osloenses.*

WORK IN PROGRESS: Research for a book on Theopompus and the fourth century.

SIDELIGHTS: Gordon Spencer Shrimpton told *CA:* "The research I do in ancient history has all the excitement of detective work. I like to take difficult problems and try to find new evidence or new ways of looking at existing data. Even well-ploughed fields yield new secrets.

"My interest in antiquity began at a very early age. A fascination with languages and the excitement of a seventh-grade course on ancient history created in me the determination to go to university and study ancient languages and culture. At the University of British Columbia the only department that offered courses of interest to me was that of classics. There, exposure to two stimulating teachers, C. W. J. Eliot and M. F. McGregor, hooked me on classical Greek history.

"I made my first discovery as a scholar when I turned to the study of the lost history of the age of Philip (father of Alexander the Great) by the fourth-century historian Theopompus. This work is studied through several hundred surviving quotations called fragments. In antiquity Theopompus had a reputation for taking sides on every issue, and there had been a debate among modern critics over whether he admired Philip or detested him. I discovered that a number of Philip's friends and allies were mentioned in the fragments and that they were generally attacked with greater vehemence the more friendly they were to him. By contrast, Philip's enemies were criticized for ineptitude. The conclusion that Theopompus was generally hostile to Philip seemed inescapable.

"My next major essay focused on the famous battle of Marathon in the fifth century, B.C. Scholars always believed that the Athenians had won the battle because the Persians had foolishly withdrawn their cavalry too early, permitting the Greeks to attack an exposed infantry. I was able to show a great deal of evidence to prove that the Persian cavalry was actually in the battle and, further, that the evidence used to disprove its presence was bogus.

"My most recent discovery is new evidence that the world of Homer—the Mycenaean Age—was brought to its end by a prolonged drought. The report on this research will be soon offered for publication."

*   *   *

SHRIVER, Rosalia (Oliver)   1927-

PERSONAL: Given name is pronounced Ro-sa-lee-ah; born October 14, 1927, in Baltimore, Md.; daughter of Mark Owings, Jr. (a lawyer) and Rosalia (Oliver) Shriver. Education: Alliance Francaise, Paris, France, Diplome de la Langue, 1952; College of Notre Dame of Maryland, B.A., 1967; Drexel University, M.S., 1971. Religion: Roman Catholic.

ADDRESSES: Home—1101 St. Paul St., Baltimore, Md. 21202. Office—Enoch Pratt Free Library, 400 Cathedral St., Baltimore, Md. 21201.

CAREER: John C. Legg & Co. (investment bankers), Baltimore, Md., clerk, 1953-65; Enoch Pratt Free Library, Baltimore, Md., librarian, 1967-69, 1970—.

MEMBER: National Association of American Pen Women.

AWARDS, HONORS: Marjorie Davies Roller Nonfiction Award from National Association of American Pen Women, 1983, for Fish in Art.

WRITINGS:

Rosa Bonheur, With a Checklist of Works in American Collections, Art Alliance, 1982.
Also author of Fish in Art.

SIDELIGHTS: Rosalia Shriver told CA: "Much of my time at the library is spent in answering reference questions. One day we were asked about Rosa Bonheur, and, in trying to answer the question, I discovered that very little had been published about her since 1911. What I did find convinced me that she was a very interesting person, who deserved some current attention. France and the French language are major areas of interest, so the fact that she was a French artist was a further inducement to write the book.

"Bonheur was a pioneer feminist who defied convention. She insisted on being an artist even though it 'wasn't done' by women. In an era when unmarried women were expected to stay with their families, she bought her own house and lived in it with a woman friend. She liked to wear men's clothing because, she said, it facilitated her work. She seemed to have been a woman who would win sympathy in the last part of this twentieth century."

SHUFFELTON, Frank   1940-

PERSONAL: Born March 10, 1940, in St. Marys, Ohio; son of Frank B. (a postmaster) and Dorothy (a registered nurse; maiden name, Axe) Shuffelton; married Jane Ballou Weiss (a teacher), April 20, 1963; children: Amy Ballou, George Gordon. Education: Harvard University, B.A., 1962; Stanford University, M.A., 1968, Ph.D., 1972.

ADDRESSES: Home—51 Fair Oaks Ave., Rochester, N.Y. 14618. Office—Department of English, University of Rochester, Rochester, N.Y. 14627.

CAREER: University of Rochester, Rochester, N.Y., instructor, 1969-72, assistant professor, 1972-77, associate professor of English, 1977—. Military service: U.S. Coast Guard, 1962-66; became lieutenant.

MEMBER: Modern Language Association of America, Melville Society, Thoreau Society, American Society for Eighteenth-Century Studies, Northeastern American Society for Eighteenth-Century Studies.

AWARDS, HONORS: Mellon faculty fellow, University of Rochester, 1977.

WRITINGS:

Thomas Hooker, 1586-1647, Princeton University Press, 1977.
Thomas Jefferson: A Comprehensive Bibliography of Writings About Him, Garland Publishing, 1983.

Contributor to scholarly journals.

WORK IN PROGRESS: Thomas Jefferson and the Republic of Letters.

SIDELIGHTS: Frank Shuffelton told CA: "I have always been interested in the role that writing plays in the lives of writers and readers, and my own writing has been an attempt to understand the power literature has to order wide ranges of idea and experience. Thomas Hooker and a congregation of Puritan settlers in New England organized a community held together by the power of words, or, as they would have had it, by the power of God's Word.

"I am at the moment particularly interested in the cultural history and literature of the United States in the last half of the eighteenth century. Our founding fathers included among their number a group of remarkable writers. In their political essays, their private letters, and the Declaration of Independence and the Constitution they projected a vision of an American society that was echoed, and sometimes vociferously criticized, by contemporary poets, novelists, and dramatists.

"Because I am concerned about the possible disintegration or vulgarization of national community in our own time, I am most drawn to thinkers who forcefully attempted in their writings to clarify and create audiences of engaged citizens."

BIOGRAPHICAL/CRITICAL SOURCES:

PERIODICALS

New England Quarterly, December, 1977.

*   *   *

SHYNE, Ann W(entworth)   1914-

PERSONAL: Born July 10, 1914, in Troy, N.Y.; daughter of William Thomas (a contractor) and Mary E. (a housewife; maiden name, Cluett) Shyne. Education: Vassar College, B.A.,

1935; Bryn Mawr College, M.A., 1937, Ph.D., 1943. *Politics:* "Democrat—a liberal one, at that." *Religion:* None.

ADDRESSES: Home—Brooklands 3, Bronxville, N.Y. 10708.

CAREER: Austen Riggs Foundation, Stockbridge, Mass., research assistant, 1937-39; Community Service Bureau, Belleville, N.J., caseworker, 1941-42; Riggs Clinic, Pittsfield, Mass., psychiatric social worker, 1942-44; Bryn Mawr College, Bryn Mawr, Pa., senior research associate, 1944, instructor in social economy, 1944-45; Family Service Association of America, New York City, research consultant, 1945-55; Community Service Society of New York, New York City, research associate at Institute of Welfare Research, 1955-62, director of Center for Social Caseworker Research, 1962-65, director of Institute of Welfare Research, 1963-68; Child Welfare League of America, New York City, director of research, 1968-76; writer, 1976—. Consultant to Westat, Inc., Council on Social Work Education.

MEMBER: National Association of Social Workers.

WRITINGS:

(Editor) *Use of Judgments as Data in Social Work Research*, National Association of Social Workers, 1959.

(With William J. Reid) *Brief and Extended Casework*, Columbia University Press, 1969.

(With Michael H. Phillips, Edmund A. Sherman, and Barbara L. Haring) *Factors Associated With Placement Decisions in Child Welfare*, Child Welfare League of America, 1971.

(With Phillips and Haring) *A Model for Intake Decisions in Child Welfare*, Child Welfare League of America, 1972.

(With Phillips, Haring, and Sherman) *Service to Children in Their Own Homes*, Child Welfare League of America, 1973.

(With Sherman and Renee Neuman) *Children Adrift in Foster Care*, Child Welfare League of America, 1973.

(With Neuman and Mary Ann Jones) *A Second Chance for Families: Evaluation of a Program to Reduce Foster Care*, Child Welfare League of America, 1976.

Salary Study 1977, Child Welfare League of America, 1977.

Statistics on Social Work Education in the United States: 1976, Council on Social Work Education, 1977.

(With Anita G. Schroeder) *National Study of Social Services to Children: An Overview*, Children's Bureau, U.S. Department of Health, Education, and Welfare, 1978.

(Editor) *Child Welfare Perspectives: Selected Papers by Joseph H. Reid*, Child Welfare League of America, 1978.

(With Schroeder) *National Study of Social Serivces to Children and Their Families*, Children's Bureau, U.S. Department of Health, Education, and Welfare, 1978.

CWLA Voluntary Member Agency Income, 1977-1978, Child Welfare League of America, 1978.

(With Eva M. Russo) *Coping With Disruptive Behavior in Group Care*, Child Welfare League of America, 1980.

CONTRIBUTOR

Leonard S. Kogan, editor, *Social Science Theory and Social Work Research*, National Association of Social Workers, 1960.

Norman Polansky, editor, *Social Work Research*, University of Chicago Press, 1960, revised edition, 1975.

Catherine S. Chilman, editor, *Approaches to the Measurement of Family Change*, Division of Research, Welfare Administration, U.S. Department of Health, Education, and Welfare, 1966.

Donnell M. Pappenfort and others, editors, *Child Caring: Social Policy and the Institution*, Aldine, 1973.

Contributor to *Encyclopedia of Social Work;* contributor of about twenty articles to social work journals.

OTHER

Associate editor of *Children and Youth Services Review;* member of editorial advisory coimttee of *Social Casework;* member of editorial committee of *Social Work Research and Abstracts*.

SIDELIGHTS: Ann W. Shyne told *CA:* "A bifocal interest in people and in science led to my career in social work research. I have always been concerned with practical questions about what kinds of social work services are needed and what works in which circumstances. I am also concerned that my research writing communicates to professionals who are not themselves researchers.

"Research takes patience on the part of the doer and user, and it's slow and usually deals with only small pieces of large problems. One thing my fellow writers and I have learned through our research is that many personal and interpersonal problems yield as well or better to time-limited, narrowly focused counseling than to open-ended, wide-ranging treatment, but it is a mistake to look for quick results in the case of a person or a family with multiple problems developed over a lifetime. We have learned that understanding, respect, and emotional support are extremely important ingredients of any service, but they do not suffice in dealing with practical problems like financial, job, training, or health needs.

"The nation has long since taken for granted Social Security, a system created barely half a century ago, but there is still reluctance on the part of some people to accept the fact that public social services are also essential to the well-being of the community, even if social service can't and shouldn't be expected to solve all the problems of society."

*   *   *

SICINSKI, Andrzej   1924-

PERSONAL: Born May 20, 1924, in Warsaw, Poland; son of Antoni (a civil engineer) and Stanislawa Sicinski; married Barbara Laczkowska (an editor), 1959; children: Jacek Stebnicki (stepson), Marcin. *Education:* Warsaw Polytechnic Institute, Civil Engineer, 1952; University of Warsaw, M.A., 1952, Ph.D., 1961.

ADDRESSES: Home—Klaudyny 16-160, 01-684 Warsaw, Poland. *Office*—Division of Lifestyles Studies, Institute of Philosophy and Sociology, Polish Academy of Sciences, Nowy Swiat 72, 00-330 Warsaw, Poland.

CAREER: Public Opinion Research Center, Warsaw, Poland, deputy director, 1958-64; Polish Academy of Sciences, Warsaw, head of Division of Lifestyles Studies at Institute of Philosophy and Sociology and professor of sociology, 1965—, scientific secretary of committee, Poland 2000, 1979—. *Military service:* Polish Underground Army (AK), 1940-44.

MEMBER: International Sociological Association (vice-president of Future Research Committee), World Future Studies Federation (member of council), Polish Sociological Association, Polish Philosophical Association.

AWARDS, HONORS: Ford Foundation grant, 1968; Award of the Secretary of the Polish Academy of Sciences, 1971, for study "Polish Simulation Model of Development of Schooling System."

WRITINGS:

(Editor with Helmut Ornauer, Hakan Wiberg, and Johan Galtung; and contributor) *Images of the World in the Year 2000: A Comparative Ten-Nation Study,* Humanities, 1976.

(Contributor) Ian Miles and John Irvine, editors, *The Poverty of Progress,* Pergamon, 1982.

(Contributor) Eleonora Masini, editor, *Visions of Desirable Societies,* Pergamon, 1983.

(Editor with Monica Wemegah, and contributor) *Alternative Ways of Life in Contemporary Europe,* United Nations University, 1983.

(Editor with Rolf Homann and Masini, and contributor) *Changing Lifestyles as Indicators of New and Cultural Values,* World Future Studies Federation, 1984.

IN POLISH

Literaci polscy (title means "Polish Writers"), Ossolinskich, 1971.

Technika a spoleczenstwe: Antologia (title means "Technology and Society: A Reader"), Instytut, 1974.

Dzis i jutre kultury polskiej (title means "Today and Tomorrow of Polish Culutre"), Ksiazka i Wiedza, 1975.

Mledzi o roku 2000 (title means "Youth About the Year Two Thousand"), Centralnej Rady Zwiazkow Zawodowych, 1975.

(Editor and contributor) *Styl zycia: Koncepcje i propozycje* (title means "Style of Life: Concepts and Proposals"), PWN, 1976.

(Editor and contributor) *Styl zycia: Przemiany we wspolczesnej Polsce* (title means "Style of Life: Transformations in Contemporary Poland"), PWN, 1978.

Editor in chief of *Polska 2000* (magazine; title means "Poland 2000"); co-editor of *Kultura i Spoleczenstwe* (quarterly magazine; title means "Culture and Society").

WORK IN PROGRESS: The Year 2000 Revisited: A Midterm Review, with Hakan Wiberg and Johan Galtung, completion expected in 1986; *Styles of Life in Finland and Poland,* with J. P. Roos, publication expected in 1986.

SIDELIGHTS: Andrzej Sicinski told *CA:* "It is bad luck but also a privilege to live in the dramatic and fascinating social laboratory called Poland. How can an individual use his or her personal and national experience to understand what is going on in the world? That is the question.

"Despite my being a social scientist, I am interested more in social reality—or, in more general terms, in human existence and its sense—than in any social theory. This, I believe, explains the 'future orientation' of many of my studies. From that point of view, both the present and the past are important. But, perhaps above all, the future is important, the future that to some extent could be shaped by us.

"I don't overestimate our influence on what is going on in our personal lives, in the lives of our countries, or, all the more, our influence on what is happening on a larger scale. I do appreciate, however, not only actual influence, but also any human efforts aiming at exerting such an influence, given many restraints.

"In my recent studies, the crucial idea is a concept of the human making the choice. Our present choice, directed toward the future, is also coloring the meaning of our past. In fact,

culture and styles of life—the main subjects of my studies—are both manifestations and results of choices being made, consciously or unconsciously, by individuals, groups, and societies.

"I am concerned above all with 'social reality,' its means, and with social practice. However, I want to stress that social sciences can contribute to that practice better through developing people's wisdom rather than trying to be directly 'useful' in decision-making processes."

＊　　＊　　＊

SIEGEL-GORELICK, Bryna   1954-

PERSONAL: Born April 21, 1954, in Quincy, Mass.; daughter of David H. and Hilda L. Siegel; children: Alyssa Lea. *Education:* University of South Florida, B.A., 1974; Stanford University, M.A., 1977, Ph.D., 1980. *Politics:* Democrat. *Religion:* Jewish.

ADDRESSES: Home—465 Wellington Dr., San Carlos, Calif. 94070. *Office*—Division of Child Psychiatry and Child Development, School of Medicine, Stanford University, 600 Willow Rd., Palo Alto, Calif. 94304. *Agent*—Raphael Sagalyn, Inc., 2813 Bellevue Ter. N.W., Washington, D.C. 20007.

CAREER: Stanford University, School of Medicine, Palo Alto, Calif., research associate in psychiatry, 1984—.

MEMBER: Society for Research in Child Development, National Association for Young Children, American Psychological Association, Sigma Xi.

WRITINGS:

The Working Parents' Guide to Child Care, Little, Brown, 1983.

WORK IN PROGRESS: A study of professional women who return to work before their babies are six months old; research on patterns of disability and etiology in infantile autism; research on parents of children with autism.

SIDELIGHTS: Bryna Siegel-Gorelick told *CA:* "I spent years doing research on day care in an academically-based research project. The project took much from its subjects and gave back little. Statistically-based research on groups is of little day-to-day use for most people, so I wrote my book to share real experiences, ideas, solutions, and alternatives about child care. I feel that the quality of child care today will be reflected in the discontent of personal lives in our growing generations."

＊　　＊　　＊

SIEPMANN, Charles Arthur   1899-1985

OBITUARY NOTICE—See index for *CA* sketch: Born March 10, 1899, in Bristol, England; died of a heart attack, March 19, 1985, in London, England. Educator, broadcaster, and author. Siepmann was an authority in communications. He entered the field as a director for the British Broadcasting Corporation (BBC) in 1927. After twelve years Siepmann left the BBC to teach at Harvard University. He remained at Harvard for three years before working for the Office of Information during World War II. In 1946 Siepmann became professor of communications in education at New York University (NYU). That same year he helped draft the controversial Federal Communications Commission publication *Public Service Responsibilities of Broadcast Licensees,* delineating broadcaster responsibilities and criticizing the industry for its public irresponsibility and excessive advertising. He taught at NYU for the next twenty-two years, retiring as chairman of his department. Siepmann's writings in communications include *Radio's Second Chance; Radio, TV, and Society; TV and Our School Crisis;* and articles in several periodicals.

OBITUARIES AND OTHER SOURCES:

BOOKS

Who's Who, 136th edition, St. Martin's, 1984.

PERIODICALS

New York Times, March 22, 1985.
Television Digest, March 25, 1985.

*   *   *

SIERRA, Gregorio Martinez
See MARTINEZ SIERRA, Gregorio

*   *   *

SIERRA, Maria (de la O'LeJarraga) Martinez
See MARTINEZ SIERRA, Maria (de la O'LeJarraga)

*   *   *

SIKORA, Frank J(oseph)   1936-

PERSONAL: Born March 19, 1936, in Byesville, Ohio; son of John George (a grocer) and Josephine Anne (a housewife; maiden name, Jurcak) Sikora; married Mildred Helms (a nurse), October 4, 1958; children: Deborah Sikora Carpenter, Victor, Frank J., Jr., Terry, Jan, Michelle. *Education:* Attended Ohio State University. *Politics:* Democrat. *Religion:* Roman Catholic.

ADDRESSES: Home—8137 Rugby Ave., Birmingham, Ala. 35202. *Office—Birmingham News,* P.O. Box 2553, Birmingham, Ala. 35206. *Agent*—Diane Cleaver, Sanford J. Greenburger Associates, Inc., 825 Third Ave., New York, N.Y. 10022.

CAREER: Associated with the *Gadsden Times,* Gadsden, Ala., 1964-67; *Birmingham News,* Birmingham, Ala., reporter, 1967—. *Military service:* U.S. Army, 1954-56.

AWARDS, HONORS: Award from Associated Press, 1977, for stories on black land loss in the South; award from U.S. Conference of Christians and Jews, 1980, Author of the Year Award from Alabama Library Association, 1980, and award from American Library Association, 1981, all for *Selma, Lord, Selma.*

WRITINGS:

(With Sheyann Webb and Rachel West Nelson) *Selma, Lord, Selma: Girlhood Memories of the Civil-Rights Days,* University of Alabama Press, 1980.

Contributor to magazines, including *Ebony, Time, Newsweek,* and *Parade.*

WORK IN PROGRESS: "An autobiography of a little-known black schoolteacher who tells of growing up in the segregated South and his early days of teaching in the 1950's"; research for collaboration on the autobiography of U.S. Judge Frank M. Johnson, Jr., who heard major civil rights cases in Alabama.

SIDELIGHTS: Frank J. Sikora told *CA:* "As a news reporter in Alabama I covered some of the civil rights activities of the sixties. Following up on these stories has been my prime interest.

"I have always felt that there is too much 'shock value' in today's writing and thus I try to stay away from brutality and shock that is written for impact in and of itself. I would prefer something that, if it does anything at all—in addition to telling a story—would tend to inspire a reader. Coming from Ohio, I found that one of the things that struck me about the Deep South is that the people in rural areas have some inner sense of determination that defies poverty and past repressions—that through the worst of times they have a spirit that seems to prevail. Some of this has come out in *Selma, Lord, Selma;* it's an innocence that goes with childhood but also reaches into the lives of most of the people. In researching the work on Judge Frank M. Johnson, Jr., I found this same human spirit in the people who came to him for redress of grievances.

"Of Johnson himself, I think I've found the most truly American hero since Abraham Lincoln, for in many ways Judge Johnson is like Lincoln: One freed the people from slavery, the other from segregation. The book on Judge Johnson, still in its research phase, will not be put into a final manuscript until he retires. He is sixty-six, and currently on the U.S. Eleventh Court of Appeals. A number of publishers, including Scribner's and Harper & Row, have written the judge about an autobiography.

"The other book currently in the works is another biography about an obscure black educator in Greene County, Alabama. It recounts growing up in a segregated society, facing the violence of the Ku Klux Klan, and finding the challenge of trying to educate black children when the only teaching aids he receives are an eraser, 144 pieces of chalk, and a register book.

"Since I have only had one book published, I'm certainly not an authority on the subject of writing. I've seen people in their early twenties who get books published. I never had a desire to write a book. It wasn't until I was nearly thirty-eight years old that the impulse suddenly hit me. I knew I had to do it when I first met Sheyann Webb, and later, Rachel West Nelson, and heard about their part in the civil rights movement of Selma, Alabama. I came home that evening and told my wife I was going to write a book. When I couldn't go to sleep that night, I knew that I was really going to. To me it was the most important thing I could be working on. I think anybody writing a book has to feel that way about the work—that it's the most important thing."

*   *   *

SILKO, Leslie Marmon   1948-

BRIEF ENTRY: Born in 1948 in Laguna, N.M. American educator and author. Silko's first novel, *Ceremony* (Viking, 1977), draws on the author's childhood on a Luguna Pueblo Indian reservation in New Mexico, as well as on her knowledge of Indian ritual and lore. Her other books include *Luguna Woman: Poems* (Greenfield Review Press, 1974) and *Storyteller* (Seaver, 1981), a collection of short fiction. In 1981 Silko received a grant from the John D. and Catherine T. MacArthur Foundation, which conducts annual searches for men and women of genius and high intellectual potential. The author was, at that time, an assistant professor of English at the University of Arizona. *Address:* Department of English, University of New Mexico, Albuquerque, N.M. 87131.

BIOGRAPHICAL/CRITICAL SOURCES:

BOOKS

Contemporary Literary Criticism, Volume 23, Gale, 1983.

PERIODICALS

Christian Science Monitor, August 24, 1977.
Ms., July, 1981.
New York Review of Books, June 12, 1977.
Saturday Review, May, 1981, June, 1981.

*　　*　　*

SILVA, Julian 1927-

PERSONAL: Born June 1, 1927, in San Lorenzo, Calif.; son of Claude Thomas (a professor of history) and Olive (a housewife; maiden name, Smith) Silva. *Education:* Attended St. Mary's College of California, 1944-45, and San Francisco Junior College (now City College), 1947; University of San Francisco, B.S., 1949; graduate study at University of California, Berkeley, 1950. *Politics:* Liberal. *Religion:* None.

ADDRESSES: Home—2106 Divisadero St., San Francisco, Calif. 94115. *Agent*—Teresa Chris, Thompson & Chris, 3926 Sacramento St., San Francisco, Calif. 94115.

CAREER: San Francisco Unified School District, San Francisco, Calif., English teacher at public high schools, 1953—, head of English department at Galileo High School, 1973-80. *Military service:* U.S. Naval Reserve, active duty as pharmacist's mate in Medical Corps, 1945-47.

MEMBER: Authors Guild, California Teachers Association.

WRITINGS:

The Gunnysack Castle (novel), Ohio University Press, 1983.

Contributor of stories to magazines, including *Writers Forum* and *Cosmopolitan.*

WORK IN PROGRESS: Two novels.

*　　*　　*

SIMMIE, James Martin 1941-

PERSONAL: Born July 18, 1941, in Oxford, England; son of Walter (an engineer) and Millicent (a fashion buyer; maiden name, Martin) Simmie. *Education:* University of London, B.Sc., 1964, Ph.D., 1979; University of Southampton, M.Phil., 1969.

ADDRESSES: Office—University College, University of London, Gower St., London W.C.1, England.

CAREER: Oxford Polytechnic, Oxford, England, lecturer, 1965-67, senior lecturer in sociology, 1967-70; University of London, University College, London, England, lecturer in urban sociology, 1970—. Lecturer at University of California, Berkeley, summer, 1970.

MEMBER: Policy Studies Association.

WRITINGS:

The Sociology of Internal Migration, Centre for Environmental Studies, 1972.
Citizens in Conflict, Hutchinson, 1974.
(Editor) *Sociology, Politics, and Cities, Macmillan, 1976.*
Power, Property, and Corporatism, Macmillan, 1981.

(Contributor) W. Grant, editor, *The Political Economy of Corporatism,* Macmillan, 1985.

Contributor to various journals, including the *International Journal of Urban and Regional Research.*

SIDELIGHTS: James Martin Simmie told *CA:* "I am a confirmed Californiaphile, and much of my work has been sparked by frequent visits there. I first visited Berkeley in the summer of 1970 and was struck by the differences between the more pluralistic political atmosphere in local government there than in the United Kingdom. Subsequently, I have developed specific interests in the ways that changes in production, finance, and government policies affect events at the local level. In general I feel that the United Kingdom tends to be dominated by large corporations that not only have more clout with government at all levels, which I regard as potentially corporatist, but also are mainly responsible for the changing spatial division of labor."

AVOCATIONAL INTERESTS: Boating, rugby, squash, tennis, M.G. sports cars, and "my vintage Thames River cruiser."

*　　*　　*

SIMON, Kate (Grobsmith)

BRIEF ENTRY: Born in Warsaw, Poland. American book reviewer, editor, and author. Simon, who came to the United States when she was four years old, is the author of numerous travel books, including the best-selling *New York Places and Pleasures: An Uncommon Guidebook* (Meridian Books, 1959). Her books have been termed "classics" and have been used by universities as sociology texts. Prior to her career as an author, Simon wrote book reviews for *New Republic* and *Nation* and served as a free-lance editor for Knopf.

Her autobiographical *Bronx Primitive: Portraits in a Childhood* (Viking, 1982) was nominated for a National Book Critics Circle Award. Among her other writings are *Mexico: Places and Pleasures* (Doubleday, 1963), *Italy: The Places in Between* (Harper, 1970), and *England's Green and Pleasant Land* (Knopf, 1974). She also wrote *Fifth Avenue: A Very Social Story* (Harcourt, 1978), a social history of Manhattan.

BIOGRAPHICAL/CRITICAL SOURCES:

BOOKS

Who's Who of American Women, 8th edition, Marquis, 1974.

PERIODICALS

New Yorker, July 28, 1962.
New York Times, May 24, 1982.
Publishers Weekly, May 14, 1982.

*　　*　　*

SINGER, Jane Sherrod 1917-1985
(Jane Sherrod)

OBITUARY NOTICE—See index for *CA* sketch: Born May 26, 1917, in Wichita Falls, Tex.; died after a long illness, January 26, 1985, in Fullerton, Calif. Educator, publisher, columnist, editor, and author. Singer taught at the University of California, Berkeley, and San Francisco State College (now University) in the 1940's. With her husband, Kurt Singer, she founded B. P. Singer Features, serving as managing editor and president. Among her writings are *Cooking With the Stars, What You Should Know About Yourself, Positive: Self Analy-*

sis, and the popular syndicated columns "Pathways to Success" and "Test Yourself." Under her former name, Jane Sherrod, she also collaborated with her husband on several juvenile works.

OBITUARIES AND OTHER SOURCES:

BOOKS

Who's Who in the West, 16th edition, Marquis, 1978.

PERIODICALS

Editor and Publisher, March 30, 1985.

*   *   *

SINGING NUN, The
  See DECKERS, Jeanine

*   *   *

SISK, Frank A., Jr.   1915-1985

OBITUARY NOTICE: Born October 6, 1915; died April 23, 1985, in Essex, Conn. Author. During his lifetime, Sisk wrote more than two hundred magazine articles and short stories, notably mystery stories for such periodicals as Alfred Hitchcock's Mystery Magazine, Ellery Queen's Mystery Magazine, the Saturday Evening Post, and New Yorker. In 1981 he won a first place award from the Third Crime Writers International Congress for the story "A Visit With Montezuma." His work has also been chosen for inclusion in the Anthology of Best Detective Stories of the Year. Early in his career, Sisk worked as a newspaper reporter in Bridgeport, Connecticut. He then spent twenty-five years with the Minnesota Mining and Manufacturing Company, from which he retired in 1971.

OBITUARIES:

PERIODICALS

Chicago Tribune, April 28, 1985.
Philadelphia Inquirer, April 28, 1985.

*   *   *

SISTER LUC-GABRIELLE
  See DECKERS, Jeanine

*   *   *

SISTER SMILE
  See DECKERS, Jeanine

*   *   *

SLADE, Madeleine   1892-1982
  (Mirabehn)

OBITUARY NOTICE: Born in 1892; died of heart disease July 20, 1982, outside Vienna, Austria. Disciple and co-worker of Mahatma Gandhi and author. Slade gave up an aristocratic British background, and her name, to devote her life to Gandhi's nonviolent struggle for India's independence and the unification of all Indians. Her earliest commitment, as intense as that to Gandhi would later be, was to the nineteenth-centry German composer Ludwig van Beethoven. At a time when Britain's sentiment against Germans and Austrians was great, Slade was responsible for bringing Beethoven's music to provincial British audiences. Her discovery of Romain Rolland's

epic novel about the composer eventually led to a visit with the French author, during which he mentioned Gandhi and the book about him that he was writing at the time. Immediately and wholeheartedly attracted to Gandhi and his cause, Slade proceeded to dedicate the next year to training for the rigorous life she knew awaited her in Gandhi's ashram, or religious community. Slade left for India in October, 1925 and, upon her arrival, was met by Gandhi himself, who welcomed her as his daughter and named her Mirabehn. For the next twenty-three years, until Gandhi was assassinated in 1948, she was one of his closest helpers and disciples. After his death Slade traveled throughout northern India working on agricultural and forestation projects. Faithful in her commitment to Gandhi's precepts to the end of her life, she left India in 1959 and moved to a peasant's cottage outside Vienna, returning to the natural surroundings that inspired the only other passion of her life, Beethoven and his music. In the last year of her life she was awarded the Padma Vibhushan, India's second highest civilian medal of honor. Her writings include an autobiography, The Spirit's Pilgrimage, and a study of Beethoven's life and work.

OBITUARIES AND OTHER SOURCES:

BOOKS

Gandhi, Mohandas Karamchand, Letters to a Disciple, Harper, 1950.
Stern, Gertrude, The Women in Gandhi's Life, Dodd, 1953.

PERIODICALS

New York Times Magazine, November 14, 1982.
Globe and Mail (Toronto), August 11, 1984.

*   *   *

SLOANE, Eric   1910(?)-1985

OBITUARY NOTICE—See index for CA sketch: Name originally Everard Jean Hinrichs; name changed c. 1930; born February 27, 1910 (some sources say 1905), in New York, N.Y.; died of a heart attack, March 6, 1985, in New York, N.Y. Meteorologist, artist, and author. Noted for his expertise on Americana and for his collection of Early American tools, Sloane was probably best known for his paintings of old barns, covered bridges, and skyscapes. He worked as a sign painter in the 1920's and then worked at an airport painting serial numbers on planes. While working at the airport Sloane became interested in cloud formations and meteorology. He eventually studied the subject at the Massachusetts Institute of Technology and began lecturing on his observations. Among his numerous self-illustrated volumes are American Barns and Covered Bridges, Our Vanishing Landscape, How You Can Forecast the Weather, Folklore of American Weather, and the autobiography I Remember America. Sloane also wrote the syndicated column "It Makes You Think" and contributed to periodicals.

OBITUARIES AND OTHER SOURCES:

PERIODICALS

Los Angeles Times, March 9, 1985.
Newsday, March 8, 1985.
New York Times, March 8, 1985.

*   *   *

SMALLWOOD, James (Milton)   1944-

PERSONAL: Born July 10, 1944, in Terrell, Tex.; son of

Elmer M. (an executive) and Martha M. (in sales; maiden name, Turner) Smallwood; married Victoria Ann Seitz (a professor), January 8, 1985; children: (from previous marriage) Martha, James Milton, Jr. *Education:* East Texas State University, B.S., 1967, M.A., 1969; Texas Tech University, Ph.D. (with honors), 1974. *Politics:* Democrat. *Religion:* Christian.

ADDRESSES: Home—1112 South Gray, Stillwater, Okla. 74074. *Office*—Department of History, Oklahoma State University, Stillwater, Okla. 74074. *Agent*—Nat Sobel Associates, Inc., 146 East 19th St., New York, N.Y. 10003.

CAREER: East Texas State University, Commerce, instructor in history, 1967-69; Southeastern State College (now Southeastern Oklahoma State University), Durant, visiting assistant professor of history, 1969-70; Texas Tech University, Lubbock, instructor in history, 1970-74; Oklahoma State University, Stillwater, assistant professor, 1975-80, associate professor of history, 1980—, director of Will Rogers Research Project, 1976-81. Executive director of Morton Museum and Cooke County Bicentennial Commission, 1974-75; guest on media programs; guest lecturer at Oklahoma Institute, summers, 1977-78; public speaker. Consultant to Oklahoma Humanities Council and Center for Political Economic Research, Riverside, Calif.

MEMBER: American Historical Association, Organization of American Historians, Southern Historical Association, Western History Association, Mid-America Historical Association, Southern Conference on Afro-American Studies, Texas Historical Association, Oklahoma Historical Society, Red River Valley Historical Association, East Texas Historical Association.

AWARDS, HONORS: Citation from governor of Oklahoma, 1979, for work on Will Rogers Centennial Commission; Coral P. Tullis Award from Texas Historical Association, 1982, for *Time of Hope, Time of Despair.*

WRITINGS:

A History of the United States From 1865 to the Present, Oklahoma State University Press, 1976.
Urban Builder: The Life and Times of Stanley Draper, University of Oklahoma Press, 1977.
A History of the United States From the Era of Discovery to 1877, Oklahoma State University Press, 1977.
(With Joe Stout) *Five Frontiers in Oklahoma,* Frontier Press (Stillwater, Okla.), 1978.
Genealogical Research, Oklahoma State University Press, 1978.
An Oklahoma Adventure: Of Banks and Bankers, University of Oklahoma Press, 1979.
Time of Hope, Time of Despair: Black Texans During Reconstruction, Kennikat, 1981.
Blacks in Oklahoma, Oklahoma State University Press, 1981.
(With Edwin Derrick) *Highways of Adventure: Transportation Frontiers in Oklahoma,* University of Oklahoma Press, 1982.
The Struggle Upward: Blacks in Texas, American Press, 1983.
The Great Recovery: The New Deal in Texas, American Press, 1983.
A Problem in American Diplomacy: The Mexican Zona Libre, 1858-1905, Texas Western Press, 1983.
(With Samuel Bell) *Readings in Texas History,* American Press, 1984.
Genealogical Research and Family History, Oklahoma State University Press, 1984.

EDITOR

Studies in History, Texas Tech Press, 1973.
And Gladly Teach: Reminiscences of Teachers From Frontier Dugout to Modern Module, University of Oklahoma Press, 1976.
Daily Telegrams of Will Rogers, Oklahoma State University Press, Volume I: *The Coolidge Years, 1926-1929,* 1978, Volume II: *The Hoover Years, 1929-1931,* 1978, Volume III: *The Hoover Years, 1931-1933,* 1979, Volume IV: *The Roosevelt Years, 1933-1935,* 1980.
North American Indian Cultures, Oklahoma State University Press, 1978.
The Weekly Articles of Will Rogers, Oklahoma State University Press, Volume I: *The Harding/Coolidge Years, 1922-1925,* 1980, Volume II: *The Coolidge Years, 1925-1927,* 1980, Volume III: *The Coolidge Years, 1927-1929,* 1981, Volume IV: *The Hoover Years, 1929-1931,* 1982, Volume V: *The Hoover Years, 1931-1933,* 1982, Volume VI: *The Roosevelt Years, 1933-1935,* 1983.
Digital Electronics, Oklahoma State University Press, 1981.

CONTRIBUTOR

Arrell Gibson, editor, *Will Rogers: A Centennial Tribute,* Oklahoma Historical Society, 1979.
Howard Suggs, editor, *Black Newspapers in the South,* Greenwood Press, 1983.
Donald Wisenhunt, editor, *A History of Texas,* Eakins, 1984.
Terrence J. Barragy and Harry R. Heubel, editors, *From Colony to Republic,* D. Armstrong, 1984.

Contributor to *Handbook of Texas, West Texas Yearbook, Biographical Encyclopedia of the World, Biographical Directory of the Governors of the United States, 1789-1976,* and *Encyclopedia USA.* Contributor of more than a hundred articles and reviews to history journals.

OTHER

Editor of *Studies in History,* 1971-74; member of editorial board of East Texas Historical Association and Southern Conference on Afro-American Studies.

WORK IN PROGRESS: Lyndon B. Johnson and Civil Rights; Shaka and the Zulu Nation, a novel; ''The Christmas Gift,'' a short story.

SIDELIGHTS: James Smallwood, an American of Cherokee Indian descent, told *CA:* ''Looking back from the age of forty, I realize I have accomplished many of my goals, which included teaching at the university level and pursuing research and writing. I have had eighteen years of college teaching and have written or edited more than twenty books.

''I am now moving from history to fiction and am enjoying the transition. Generally, though, I find fiction harder to deal with than history. With all my history projects, the 'facts' always dictated the story line. However, so much in the area of fiction must be pulled from the mind—and from research notes.''

Smallwood added: ''As a liberal Democrat, I am alarmed at trends in national politics. I grew into political awareness in the 1960's and today, politicians are elected to office (our president, for example) that we once considered too reactionary even to be taken seriously (Goldwater in 1964). I lament that I live in reactionary times.

''I also believe that education is in serious trouble today. Here in Oklahoma, there are now budget struggles every year, usually resulting in college budget *cuts* of six to twelve percent each year. Our administration is now pressed tremendously.''

AVOCATIONAL INTERESTS: Sailing, swimming, chess, bridge, spectator sports (such as football and basketball).

* * *

SMITH, Charles Merrill   ?-1985

OBITUARY NOTICE: Died February 23, 1985, in Bloomington, Ill. Clergyman and author. A United Methodist minister, Smith wrote the 1965 best-selling satire *How to Become a Bishop Without Being Religious* as well as a number of other religious books and several mystery novels. His writings include *How to Talk to God When You Aren't Feeling Religious, When the Saints Go Marching Out, The Case of a Middle Class Christian,* and *Reverend Randollph and the Wages of Sin.* Smith also collaborated with his son on the autobiographical *Different Drums: How a Father and Son Bridged Generations With Love and Understanding.*

OBITUARIES AND OTHER SOURCES:

PERIODICALS

Michigan Christian Advocate, March 11, 1985.
New York Times, March 2, 1965.

* * *

SMITH, Frederick William Robin   1936-1985
(Robin Furneaux)

OBITUARY NOTICE: Born April 17, 1936; died of an apparent heart attack, February 16, 1985, in Royal Leamington Spa, Warwickshire, England. Historian and author. Born into a literary family, Smith was the son of British biographer Frederick Winston Furneaux Smith, whom he succeeded as earl of Birkenhead. His former title, viscount Furneaux, was combined with one of his middle names to form the pseudonym Robin Furneaux, under which Smith wrote *The Amazon.* The book, which was based upon the author's travels in South America, was well received by critics. Smith also published *William Wilberforce* under the Furneaux pen name. A biography of the celebrated British crusader against slavery, the volume earned Smith the 1975 Heinemann Award. A book about Winston Churchill was left unfinished at the author's death.

OBITUARIES AND OTHER SOURCES:

BOOKS

Who's Who, 126th edition, St. Martin's, 1974.

PERIODICALS

Chicago Tribune, February 19, 1985.
Detroit Free Press, February 18, 1985.
New York Times, February 18, 1985.
Times (London), February 19, 1985.

* * *

SMITH, Jim   1920-

BRIEF ENTRY: British shop owner, illustrator, and author. Smith is known primarily for his ''Frog Band'' books, a series for children published by Little, Brown that includes *The Frog Band and the Onion Seller* (1976), *The Frog Band and Dorrington Mouse* (1978), *The Frog Band and the Mystery of Lion*

Castle (1978), and *The Frog Band and the Owlnapper* (1981). In addition to these, the author has written and illustrated three other picture books for children, including *Alphonse and the Stonehenge Mystery* (Little, Brown, 1980), *Nimbus and the Crown Jewels* (Little, Brown, 1982), and *Nimbus the Explorer* (Little, Brown, 1982). Smith, who first won acclaim for his drawings while he was a Japanese prisoner of war during World War II, has been the proprietor of a curio shop in Salisbury, England.

* * *

SMITH, John Coventry   1903-1984

PERSONAL: Born June 10, 1903, in Stamford, Ontario, Canada; died January 15, 1984; buried in Grove City, Pa.; son of a United Presbyterian minister; married Floy Oressa Bauder, June 20, 1928 (died, 1980); children: John Coventry, Jr., Louise Adelle Smith Woodruff. *Education:* Muskingum College, A.B., 1925; Pittsburgh-Xenia Seminary (now Pittsburgh Theological Seminary), B.D., 1928, Th.M., 1936; Hartford Seminary, M.A., 1936.

CAREER: Ordained United Presbyterian minister, 1928; pastor of United Presbyterian churches near Beaver, Pa., 1928-29; United Presbyterian missionary in Japan, 1929-43, prisoner of war, 1943; assistant pastor of Presbyterian church in Pittsburgh, Pa., 1943-44; pastor of United Presbyterian church in Mount Lebanon, Pa., 1944-48; Presbyterian Church of the U.S.A., Board of Foreign Missions, secretary for the Far East, 1948-58, associate general secretary for Japan, Korea, the Philippines, and Thailand, Commission on Ecumenical Mission and Relations, 1958-59, general secretary of commission, 1959-70, moderator of General Assembly, 1968. World Council of Churches, member of Central Committee, beginning in 1961, president, 1968-75, vice-chairman of Division on World Mission and Evangelism; National Council of Churches, chairman of Theological Education Fund Committee, vice-president and chairman of Division of Overseas Ministries; cofounder and member of executive committee of Japan International Christian University, vice-president of Japan International Christian University Foundation; member of administrative committee of International Missionary Council.

AWARDS, HONORS: D.D. from Muskingum College and Tokyo Union Theological Seminary; LL.D. from Yonsei University, Tarkio College, and Grove City College; D.H.L. from International Christian University, Tokyo, Japan.

WRITINGS:

From Colonialism to World Community: The Church's Pilgrimage (autobiography), Westminster, 1982.

OBITUARIES:

PERIODICALS

Philadelphia Inquirer, January 17, 1984.*

* * *

SMITH, Marilyn Cochran
See COCHRAN-SMITH, Marilyn

* * *

SMITH, Ralph B.   1894(?)-1985

OBITUARY NOTICE: Born c. 1894 in Newburgh, N.Y.; died

February 11, 1985, in Neshanic, N.J. Publishing executive and editor. A contributor to the early growth of *Business Week,* Smith worked for such publications as the *New York Herald Tribune,* the *New York Sun,* and *Popular Science* before joining the McGraw-Hill magazine in 1929. He was promoted to managing editor in 1931 and became chief editor in 1937. Smith was appointed editorial director of McGraw-Hill in 1950 and became a vice-president of the company in 1952. He received the Columbia Journalism Alumni Award in 1958, the year before he retired from McGraw-Hill.

OBITUARIES:

PERIODICALS

New York Times, February 19, 1985.

* * *

SMITH, Winsome   1935-

PERSONAL: Born April 7, 1935, in Sydney, Australia; daughter of Rupert Harold (a clergyman) and Willa (a bookkeeper; maiden name, Russell) Hayes; married Henry George Smith (an investor), June 26, 1954 (divorced); children: Lynette Smith Rennie, Joanne, Sharon Smith Manton. *Education:* Macquarie University, B.A.; University of New England, Diploma in Education; Southern Australian College of Advanced Education, Diploma in Reading and Language Education.

ADDRESSES: Home—2/15 Balo St., Moree, New South Wales 2400, Australia. *Office*—Moree Technical College, Frome St., Moree, New South Wales 2400, Australia.

CAREER: Worked as teacher of English and history at high schools; became adult literacy officer at Moree Technical College, Moree, New South Wales, Australia.

MEMBER: Australian Society of Authors, Fellowship of Australian Writers, Toastmistresses International.

WRITINGS:

CHILDREN'S BOOKS

Somewhere to Go, Something to Do, McGraw, 1976.
Joy Ride, McGraw, 1976.
Does Anyone Care?, Macmillan, 1977.
Breakthrough, Holt-Saunders, 1978.
Elephant in the Kitchen, Scholastic Book Services, 1980.
The Half-Dolls, Ashton Scholastic, 1982.

OTHER

Work represented in anthologies, including *The Blindfold Horse and Other Stories,* Australian Association for the Teaching of English, 1975; *The Kids' Own Book of Stories and Things to Do,* Thomas Nelson, 1978; *More Stuff and Nonsense* (poems) edited by M. Dugan, Collins, 1980. Writer for radio program "Kindergarten of the Air."

WORK IN PROGRESS: The Gate-House.

SIDELIGHTS: Winsome Smith told *CA:* "I grew up in country parsonages, as my father was a Methodist minister. Ours was a very strict and restricted home, but we did have lots of books—and everyone did a lot of talking. My mother was an avid reader and, now at the age of seventy-one, still reads at least six books a week. My father was a great storyteller and raconteur. Every night he would tell us children a story, often one he had made up himself. He also told us Bible stories, Aesop's fables, and Greek and Roman legends.

"I left school at fourteen and went to work at the local telephone exchange. My weekly wage was one pound sixteen shillings ($3.60). I loved my job so much that I often went to work on my day off.

"I got married at nineteen and subsequently had three daughters. When my youngest girl was five I went back to school. I eventually graduated from Macquarie University and became a teacher.

"My first jobs were teaching English and history in high schools. Then I became interested in remedial reading because I discovered that many high school students could not read. I am now an adult literacy officer with the Department of Technical and Further Education, teaching adults to read.

"My first writing was stories for 'Kindergarten of the Air.' I think I began writing for children because my own children were young at the time.

"Although I write children's books, I do not read children's books, as I do not want to be influenced by them. I want all my ideas to be original. *Elephant in the Kitchen* was first told to my own children. During the long summer holidays we would sit around the breakfast table every morning and I would tell them a new episode every day. Sometimes we sat there till nearly lunchtime. My favorite author is Charles Dickens and my three favorite books are *Pride and Prejudice, The Great Gatsby,* and *The Catcher in the Rye.*

"At present I am living in Moree, a small town on the great northwest plains of New South Wales. This is wheat and cotton growing country. It is also the home of large mobs of kangaroos and emus. It is the Australian outback. Life here is very interesting, but I am looking forward to going back to Sydney, to the theaters, the Opera House, the beautiful harbor, and, mostly, my family."

AVOCATIONAL INTERESTS: Theater, ballet, art exhibitions, movies, photography, public speaking, cryptic crosswords.

* * *

SMOLL, Frank L(ouis)   1941-

PERSONAL: Surname is pronounced like "small"; born July 2, 1941, in Chicago, Ill.; son of Frank L. and Elizabeth (Schinagel) Smoll; married; children: James Allen, Jeffrey Michael. *Education:* Ripon College, B.A. (cum laude), 1963; University of Wisconsin—Madison, M.S., 1966, Ph.D., 1970.

ADDRESSES: Home—5535 Lake Washington Blvd. N.E., No. 207, Kirkland, Wash. 98033. *Office*—Department of Psychology, NI-25, University of Washington, Seattle, Wash. 98195.

CAREER: University of Wisconsin—Madison, information specialist at Educational Resources Information Center Clearinghouse on Educational Facilities, 1969-70; University of Washington, Seattle, assistant professor, 1970-76, associate professor of kinesiology, 1976-84, adjunct associate professor, 1977-84, associate professor of psychology, 1984—. Conference moderator; workshop coordinator; guest on radio and television programs; youth sport consultant; educational sport psychologist.

MEMBER: North American Society for the Psychology of Sport and Physical Activity, American Alliance for Health, Physical Education, Recreation, and Dance (fellow of Research Consortium), Western Psychological Association.

AWARDS, HONORS: Grants from National Institutes of Health, 1972-73, National Institute of Mental Health, 1975-79, British Columbia Ministry of Labour, 1977, Safeco Insurance Co., 1979-80, and Seattle Catholic Youth Organization, 1981-83.

WRITINGS:

Areas and Facilities for Physical Education and Recreation, Educational Resources Information Center Clearinghouse on Educational Facilities, University of Wisconsin—Madison, 1970.
(Editor with R. A. Magill and M. J. Ash, and contributor) *Children in Sport: A Contemporary Anthology,* Human Kinetics, 1978, 2nd edition, 1982.
(Editor with Ronald E. Smith, and contributor) *Psychological Perspectives in Youth Sports,* Hemisphere Publishing, 1978.
(With R. E. Smith) *Improving Relationship Skills in Youth Sport Coaches,* Institute for the Study of Youth Sports, Michigan State University, 1979.
(With N. J. Smith and R. E. Smith) *Kidsports: A Survival Guide for Parents,* Addison-Wesley, 1983.
(With J. J. Stapleton) *Introduction to Coaching: Communicating With Parents,* Coaching Association of Canada, 1985.

CONTRIBUTOR

J. R. Thomas, editor, *Youth Sports Guide for Coaches and Parents,* American Alliance for Health, Physical Education, Recreation, and Dance, 1977.
G. C. Roberts and K. M. Newell, editors, *Psychology of Motor Behavior and Sport, 1978,* Human Kinetics, 1979.
Newell, Roberts, and others, editors, *Psychology of Motor Behavior and Sports, 1979,* Human Kinetics, 1980.
J.A.S. Kelso and J. E. Clark, editors, *The Development of Movement Control and Co-ordination,* Wiley, 1981.
N. J. Smith, editor, *Sports Medicine: Health Care for Young Athletes,* American Academy of Pediatrics, 1983.
Thomas, editor, *Motor Development During Childhood and Adolescence,* Burgess Publishing, 1984.
J. M. Silva and R. S. Weinberg, editors, *Psychological Foundations of Sport,* Human Kinetics, 1984.

OTHER

Contributor of about forty articles to scientific journals and popular magazines, including *Woman's Day.* Member of editorial board of *Journal of Sport Psychology,* 1981.

WORK IN PROGRESS: An article, "Inventories and Norms for Children's Attitudes Toward Physical Activity," with R. W. Schutz, F. A. Carre, and R. E. Mosher, for publication in *Research Quarterly for Exercise and Sport.*

*   *   *

SNELLGROVE, David L(lewellyn) 1920-

BRIEF ENTRY: Born June 29, 1920, in Portsmouth, England. British educator, administrator, and author. Snellgrove made several expeditions to India and the Himalayas between 1953 and 1967. He is the co-founder and director of the Institute of Tibetan Studies, which was created in 1966. Snellgrove became a member of the faculty of the University of London in 1960 and was appointed professor of Tibetan in 1974. His writings include *Himalayan Pilgrimage: A study of Tibetan Religion* (Cassirer, 1961), *A Cultural History of Tibet* (Praeger, 1968), and *The Cultural Heritage of Ladakh* (Aris & Phillips, 1977-80). Snellgrove edited *Four Lamas of Dolpo: Tibetan Biographies* (Cassirer, 1967) and *The Image of the*

Buddha (Serindia Publications, 1978). *Address:* 113 Cross Oak Rd., Berkhamsted, Hertfordshire, England; and Institute of Tibetan Studies, Tring, Hertfordshire, England.

BIOGRAPHICAL/CRITICAL SOURCES:

BOOKS

Who's Who, 134th edition, St. Martin's, 1982.

PERIODICALS

New York Times Book Review, January 26, 1969.

*   *   *

SNYDER, Bernadette McCarver 1930-

PERSONAL: Born December 6, 1930, in Long Island, N.Y.; daughter of William C. (in private business) and Hazel (a housewife; maiden name, Davids) McCarver; married John William Snyder (in U.S. Civil Service), September 28, 1963; children: Matthew Joseph. *Education:* Attended private school in Nashville, Tenn. *Religion:* Roman Catholic.

ADDRESSES: Home—Creve Coeur, Mo. *Office*—Liguori Publications, Liguori Dr., Liguori, Mo. 63057.

CAREER: Speight Agency, Nashville, Tenn., advertising copywriter, 1950's; Gardner Advertising, St. Louis, Mo., advertising copywriter, 1960's; homemaker and free-lance writer, 1965-77; Liguori Publications, Liguori, Mo., director of special advertising, 1977—.

MEMBER: Advertising Federation of St. Louis.

WRITINGS:

Hoorays and Hosannas: An Everyday-Anyday Book of Family Ideas and Activities, Ave Maria Press, 1980.
Graham Crackers, Galoshes, and God: Laughs From Everyday Life, Prayers for Everyday Problems, Liguori Publications, 1982.
Dear God, I Have This Terrible Problem: A Housewife's Secret Letters, Liguori Publications, 1983.
(With sister, Hazelmai McCarver Terry) *Decorations for Forty-four Parish Celebrations,* Twenty-Third, 1983.
The Kitchen Sink Prayer Book, Liguori Publications, 1984.
Everyday Prayers for Everyday People, Our Sunday Visitor, 1984.
Heavenly Hash (collected columns), Our Sunday Visitor, 1985.
Goulash, Goldfish, and God (tentative title), Liguori Publications, 1985.

Author of "A Mother's Meditation," a weekly column in *Our Sunday Visitor.*

SIDELIGHTS: Bernadette McCarver Snyder told *CA:* "I always wanted to become a writer—and I'm still trying to 'become' one. I started writing in school and continued taking writing classes and collecting rejection slips for several years but got sidetracked when I started getting paid real money for writing television commercials and other advertising. When I married and 'retired' to raise a family, I thought I'd have more time for writing—but actually had less than ever. However, I continued doing free-lance advertising and did sell some humor articles.

"I never thought I would have the stick-to-itiveness to write a whole book but in 1977, I started working in the advertising department of a publisher of religious books. As I worked with others' manuscripts, I thought 'why not?' And since I had had success writing humor articles, I thought 'why not a humorous religious book?' My first book was accepted by the second publisher I sent it to—and after that, the company where I was working noticed I was an 'author' and published my next one. Now I have actually had a publisher ask me to write a book for them—a nice contrast to my collection of rejection slips!

''There aren't too many religious humor books on the market so maybe that's why mine have sold well. But I think of God as a good friend, rather than a judge sitting on a cloud watching to see if I make a mistake—and I don't think he minds my laughing about and rejoicing in all the funny and delightful things in his world. In fact, I think he often laughs along with me—because he's the one who gave me the crazy kind of mind that would associate God with such things as graham crackers, goulash, galoshes, heavenly hash, and kitchen sinks!''

*   *   *

SOBIN, Gustaf 1935-

PERSONAL: Born November 15, 1935, in Boston, Mass. *Education:* Brown University, A.B., 1958.

ADDRESSES: Home—New York, N.Y.

CAREER: Writer.

WRITINGS:

The Tale of the Yellow Triangle (juvenile), Braziller, 1973.
(Translator) Henri Michaux, *Ideograms in China,* New Directions Publishing, 1984.

BOOKS OF POEMS

Wind Chrysalid's Rattle, Montemora Foundation, 1980.
Celebration of the Sound Through, Montemora Foundation, 1982.
The Earth as Air, New Directions Publishing, 1984.

BOOKLETS OF POEMS

Telegrams, privately printed, 1963.
Ascension, Ribaute-les-Taverne, 1964.
Caesurae: Midsummer, Shearsman Books, 1981.
Ten Sham Haikus, Grenfell Press, 1983.
Carnets, Shearsman Books, 1984.
Nile, Shearsman Books, 1984.

Contributor to literary journals, including *Conjunctions, Ironwood, Kayak, Montemora, New Directions Anthology, Pequod, Sulfur,* and *2Plus2.*

SIDELIGHTS: Gustaf Sobin told *CA:* ''I write in order to extend sense past myself. For me, an accomplished poem is one utterly released, given, offered up to its ever-sought-after 'other.' It's the poem that touches, not the poet. It's the poem that confers.

''In doing so, the poem frees itself of the tyranny of the personal pronoun: of the self, that is, as central, as the mandatory pivot around which all expression must, by debased usage, rotate.

''In the poem, power is redistributed. The center shifts. The poem, in its ongoing movement, extends the significant, reflects it *forward.*''

BIOGRAPHICAL/CRITICAL SOURCES:

BOOKS

Crick, Philip, *Evolving the Idol: The Poetry of Gustaf Sobin,* Shearsman Books, 1984.

PERIODICALS

Parnassus, spring/summer/fall/winter, 1980.
Village Voice Literary Supplement, June, 1984.

*   *   *

SOEUR SOURIRE
See DECKERS, Jeanine

*   *   *

SOMERS, Albert B(ingham) 1939-

PERSONAL: Born March 11, 1939, in Wilkesboro, N.C.; son of Albert Bingham (in insurance) and Margaret (a teacher; maiden name, Pritchard) Somers; divorced; children: Susannah Kathleen. *Education:* University of North Carolina at Chapel Hill, B.A., 1961, M.Ed., 1962; Florida State University, Ph.D., 1972.

ADDRESSES: Home—55 Westview Ave., Greenville, S.C. 29609. *Office*—Department of Education, Furman University, Greenville, S.C. 29613.

CAREER: Furman University, Greenville, S.C., assistant professor of English and education, 1973-81, associate professor of education, 1981—, chairman of department, 1978—. College representative for South Carolina Council of Teachers of English, 1973-75.

MEMBER: National Council of Teachers of English, Conference on English Education, Adolescent Literature Association, South Carolina Council of Teachers of English.

WRITINGS:

(With Janet Evans Worthington) *Response Guides for Teaching Children's Books,* National Council of Teachers of English, 1979.
(With Worthington) *Candles and Mirrors: Response Guides for Teaching Novels and Plays in Grades Six Through Twelve,* Libraries Unlimited, 1984.

Editor of *Harbinger* (newsletter of the South Carolina Council of Teachers of English), 1975-79.

SIDELIGHTS: Albert B. Somers told *CA:* ''I am mostly interested in helping teachers help students to become lifetime readers of literature. We presently do a fairly poor job of this. We do a good job turning out nonreaders or people who go on to read books by Harold Robbins and Harlequin romance novels.''

*   *   *

SONG, C(hoan-)S(eng) 1929-

PERSONAL: Born October 19, 1929, in Tainan, Taiwan; son of Chui-Khim and Chin-ti (Wu) Song; married Mei-Man Chen (a pianist), August 10, 1962; children: Ju-Ping, Ju-Ying (daughters). *Education:* Taiwan National University, B.A., 1954; University of Edinburgh, B.D., 1958; attended University of Basel; Union Theological Seminary, New York, N.Y. Ph.D., 1965.

ADDRESSES: Home—17E Chemin des Prejins, 1218 Grand-Saconnex, Geneva, Switzerland. *Office*—World Alliance of Reformed Churches, 150 Route de Fernby, 1211 Geneva 20, Switzerland.

CAREER: Ordained Presbyterian minister, 1960; Tainan Theological College, Tainan, Taiwan, lecturer in Old Testament,

1960-62, professor of systematic theology and principal of college, 1965-70; Reformed Church of America, New York, N.Y., secretary for Asian Ministries, 1970-73; World Council of Churches, Geneva, Switzerland, associate director of Commission on Faith and Order, 1973-82; professor of theology at South East Asia Graduate School of Theology, 1982—; World Alliance of Reformed Churches, Geneva, Switzerland, coordinator of study "Called to Witness to the Gospel Today," 1983—; Pacific School of Religion, Berkeley, Calif., professor of theology and Asian cultures, 1985—. Visiting professor at Princeton Theological Seminary, 1976-77; Joseph Cook Memorial Lecturer of United Presbyterian Church in the U.S.A. and East Asian Christian Conference, 1972; Thatcher Lecturer at United Theological College, Sydney, Australia, 1984; Birks Lecturer at McGill University, 1984; Johnson Lecturer at Toronto School of Theology, 1984; regional professor at South East Asia Graduate School of Theology. Member of archaeological team that excavated El Jib (the biblical Gibeon), 1959.

MEMBER: North East Asia Association of Theological Schools (past member of executive committee), South East Asia Association of Theological Schools (past member of executive committee).

WRITINGS:

(With Gayraud Wilmore) *Asians and Blacks: Theological Challenges,* East Asia Christian Conference, 1972.
Christian Mission in Reconstruction, Orbis, 1975.
Third Eye Theology: Theology in Formation in Asian Settings, Orbis, 1979.
The Tears of Lady Meng: A Parable of People's Political Theology, Orbis, 1981.
The Compassionate God, Orbis, 1982.
Tell Us Our Names: Story Theology From an Asian Perspective, Orbis, 1984.
Theology From the Womb of Asia, Orbis, 1985.

IN CHINESE

Sin Chi-Yuan te Ch'ien-chou (title means "Prelude to the New Era"), Taiwan Church Press, 1966.
Chiau-hoe te Shu-Min yu Chang-wan (title means "The Church: Its Task and Responsibility"), Taiwan Church Press, 1968.
Jen-t'ong yu Ho-yi (title means "Theology and Practice of Church Unity"), Christian Literature Council (Hong Kong), 1978.

EDITOR

Giving Account of Salvation Today, World Council of Churches, 1975.
Giving Account of Hope in These Testing Times, World Council of Churches, 1976.
Giving Account of Hope Today, World Council of Churches, 1976.
Doing Theology Today, Christian Literature Society (Madras, India), 1976.
Giving Account of Hope Together, World Council of Churches, 1978.
Growing Together Into Unity, Christian Literature Society (Madras, India), 1978.
Confessing Our Faith Around the World, World Council of Churches, 1980.
Testimonies of Faith: Letters and Poems From Prison in Taiwan, World Alliance of Reformed Churches, 1984.

OTHER

Contributor to theology journals.

SIDELIGHTS: C. S. Song told *CA:* "Many of my writings focus on the area of interactions between the Christian faith and contemporary social-political and cultural-religious situations, especially those of Asia.

"I have also developed story theology—a theology empowered by stories, for there is something deep in folktales and fairy stories, something culturally and spiritually deep. Portrayed in them are children, women, and men who are puzzled by the mystery of the universe, bewildered by riddles of life, victimized by injustices in the world, and hard pressed by evil socio-political forces. These are stories of despair and hope, tales of doubt and faith, and accounts of the search for the moral power that will enable persons to live in the world. It is a world in which meaning and purpose are terribly twisted to serve the whims of the powerful, the cunning, and the unscrupulous. The tales, are, in a true sense, parables of human lives. In them we find popular theology at its most unsophisticated and yet at its most profound, at its simplest and yet at its deepest, at its most unadorned and yet at its most moving."

*   *   *

SOUR, Robert B(andler) 1905-1985

OBITUARY NOTICE: Born October 31, 1905, in New York, N.Y.; died after a brief illness, March 6, 1985, in New York, N.Y. Music company executive and lyricist. Sour became a full-time lyricist in 1929 and wrote or collaborated on the words to many songs, including "Body and Soul," "Practice Makes Perfect," "Walking by the River," "We Could Make Such Beautiful Music Together," and "I See a Million People." He became associated with Broadcast Music Incorporated (BMI) in 1940, was named the company's president in 1966, and held that position until 1968. In 1970 Sour became vice-chairman of the company's board of directors. He also assisted in the establishment of BMI's Musical Theatre Workshop.

OBITUARIES AND OTHER SOURCES:

BOOKS

Biographical Dictionary of American Music, Parker Publishing, 1973.
Who's Who in America, 41st edition, Marquis, 1980.

PERIODICALS

New York Times, March 8, 1985.

*   *   *

SPARKES, Ivan G(eorge) 1930-

PERSONAL: Born April 2, 1930, in Stratton St. Margaret, England; son of Albert William (a butcher) and Gladys Emma (a housewife; maiden name, Price) Sparkes; married Joyce Andrews; children: Geraldine, Elizabeth, Timothy, David. *Education:* Attended technical college and art school in Swindon, Wiltshire, England.

ADDRESSES: Home—124 Green Hill, High Wycombe, Buckinghamshire, England. *Office*—High Wycombe Central Library, Queen Victoria Rd., High Wycombe, Buckinghamshire HP11 1BD, England.

CAREER: Swindon Public Libraries, Swindon, Wiltshire, England, librarian, 1947-53; Thurrock Public Libraries, Thurrock, England, librarian, 1953-65; London Borough of Havering, London, England, reference librarian, 1965-69; Penzance Public Libraries, Penzance, England, borough librarian, 1969-

71; High Wycombe Borough Library, High Wycombe, Buckinghamshire, England, borough librarian, 1971-74; High Wycombe Central Library, High Wycombe, librarian, 1974—. Curator of Wycombe Chair Musuem, 1971—; member of staff at Buckinghamshire County Library Service; presents lectures and slide shows on libraries and local history, High Wycombe and its history, the furniture industry, stagecoaches, and Egypt. Town Clerk, High Wycombe Charter Trustees, 1983—.

MEMBER: Library Association (fellow), Royal Historical Society (associate member).

AWARDS, HONORS: Sir Evelyn Wrench fellowship; 1965; grant for the United States from English-Speaking Union, 1965; Senior Librarian's Award from Library Association, 1974, for *Resources of Country Chair History.*

WRITINGS:

The English Country Chair, Spur Publications, 1973, revised edition, 1977.
A Dictionary of Group Terms and Collective Nouns, White Lion, 1974, revised edition, Gale, 1985.
The Windsor Chair, Spur Publications, 1975.
Stagecoaches and Carriages, Spur Publications, 1975.
(With Margaret Lawson) *Victorian and Edwardian Buckinghamshire From Old Photographs,* Batsford, 1976.
Old Horseshoes, Shire Publications, 1976.
High Wycombe as It Was, Hendon Press, 1977.
Woodland Craftsmen, Shire Publications, 1977.
The Book of Wycombe, Barracuda Books, 1979, revised edition, 1984.
English Domestic Furniture, Spur Publications, 1980.
The English Windsor Chair, Shire Publications, 1981.
Yesterday's Town: High Wycombe, Barracuda Books, 1983.
High Wycombe in Old Postcards, European Press, 1983.
Collective Nouns, Gale, 1985.

Author of "Local History Series," thirteen books, self-published, 1963-69. Contributor to magazines.

WORK IN PROGRESS: Research for *A Bibliography of Furniture History* and *Handbook of Animal Terminology.*

SIDELIGHTS: Ivan G. Sparkes told *CA* that he spent a year in Egypt from 1949 to 1950, which gave him a lasting interest in the country's history and antiquities. He also mentioned the value of his trip to the United States in 1965.

*   *   *

SPEED, (Herbert) Keith   1934-

PERSONAL: Born March 11, 1934, in Evesham, England; son of Herbert Victor (a director) and Dorothy Barbara (Mumford) Speed; married Peggy Voss Clarke, 1961; children: Mark, Crispin (deceased), Nicholas, Emma. *Education:* Attended Royal Naval College, Dartmouth, England, 1947-51, and Royal Naval College, Greenwich, England, 1953. *Religion:* Church of England.

ADDRESSES: Home—Strood House, Rolvenden, Cranbrook, Kent, England. *Office*—House of Commons, London S.W.1, England.

CAREER: Amos Ltd. (electronics firm), Buckingham, England, sales manager, 1957-60; Plysu Products Ltd., Milton Keynes, England, marketing manager, 1960-65; Conservative Research Department, London, England, officer, 1965-68; Conservative member of Parliament for Meriden, England,

1968-74, assistant government whip, 1970-71, lord commissioner of Her Majesty's Treasury, 1971-72, parliamentary undersecretary of state for Department of the Environment, 1972-74; Conservative member of Parliament for Ashford, England, 1974—, opposition spokesman on local government, 1976-77, and home affairs, 1977-79, parliamentary undersecretary of state for defense for Royal Navy, 1979-81. Chairman of Westminster Communications Ltd. *Military service:* Royal Navy, 1947-56; became lieutenant. Royal Naval Reserve, 1956—; present rank, lieutenant commander.

MEMBER: U.S. Naval Institute.

WRITINGS:

Blueprint for Britain, Conservative Political Centre, 1965.
Sea Change: The Battle for the Falklands and the Future of Britain's Navy, Ashgrove, 1982.

Contributor to military and political science journals.

WORK IN PROGRESS: "Sketches taking place in a contemporary novel with a military/international background."

SIDELIGHTS: Keith Speed told *CA:* "*Sea Change* is a descriptive account of the run-down by politicians of Britain's maritime power over the past twenty years, culminating in the battle of the Falklands and the lessons to be drawn from it. The book includes chapters on the U.S. Navy over the same period of time, and the Soviet Navy, and it was written following my dismissal by Prime Minister Thatcher for opposing major cuts in the Royal Navy. I was the last Navy Minister of the United Kingdom; the cuts were never fully implemented and have now been restored.

"The chapters in *Sea Change* highlight the massive increase in Soviet maritime power from 1956 to 1982 under Admiral Sergei Gorshkov's leadership. They also highlight the dramatic run-down of the U.S. fleet after Vietnam and up to 1980—a run-down that is only now being reversed. In this the U.S. Navy and the Royal Navy both suffered under shortsighted politicians. The British fleet's run-down has been diminished but Britain's acquisition of the Trident missile threatens all her conventional forces because of inadequate resources in years to come.

"The lesson of the Falklands conflict between Argentina and Great Britain was the need for a balanced fleet above, on, and under the waves. This is a lesson equally applicable in the North Atlantic and one the Soviets have learned well."

*   *   *

SPENCE, (James) Lewis (Thomas Chalmers)   1874-1955

BRIEF ENTRY: Born November 25 (one source says November 23), 1874, in Broughty Ferry (one source says Forfarshire), near Dundee, Scotland; died after a short illness, March 3, 1955, in Edinburgh, Scotland. Scottish editor, folklorist, and poet. Spence began his career in journalism, working as subeditor of the *Scotsman,* then as editor of *Edinburgh Magazine* and subeditor of *British Weekly.* He soon turned to the study of Mexican and Central American mythology, folklore, and religion, however, and is best remembered as an authority in those fields. Among his notable books are *The Gods of Mexico* (1923), *An Encyclopaedia of Occultism: A Compendium of Information of the Occult Sciences, Occult Personalities, Psychic Science, Magic, Demonology, Spiritism, Mysticism and Metaphysics* (1920), *A Dictionary of Mythology*

(1910), and a series on Atlantis, including *The History of Atlantis* (1926) and *The Occult Sciences in Atlantis* (1943). Spence was also a poet of English and Scottish verse and in the latter capacity dedicated himself to re-establishing the Scottish language as a poetic medium; he received a royal pension for services to literature in 1951 and published his *Collected Poems* in 1953. Spence is additionally remembered as a pioneer of Scottish nationalism. As one of the Scottish Nationalist party's first candidates for public office, he ran unsuccessfully for the division of North Midlothian in 1929.

BIOGRAPHICAL/CRITICAL SOURCES:

BOOKS

Encyclopedia of Occultism and Parapsychology, Gale, 1978.
Twentieth-Century Authors: A Biographical Dictionary of Modern Literature, 1st supplement, H. W. Wilson, 1955.

PERIODICALS

New York Times, March 4, 1955.
Times (London), March 4, 1955.

*   *   *

SPENCER, (Charles) Bernard   1909-1963

OBITUARY NOTICE: Born November 30, 1909, in Madras, British India (now India); died September 12, 1963, in Vienna, Austria. Lecturer, educator, editor, poet, and author. An English poet born in India, Spencer was considered particularly skilled in evoking the inward character of places and situations. During the 1930's he worked as a teacher, as a scriptwriter, and in an advertising agency. He was also a reviewer for the London *Morning Post,* a columnist for the *Oxford Mail,* and a British Broadcasting Corporation (BBC) radio commentator on the arts. In 1940 Spencer joined the British Council and was sent to Greece. When events during World War II forced him out of Greece he went to Egypt, where he joined noted poet and novelist Lawrence Durrell in publishing the magazine *Personal Landscape,* which featured the works of other expatriate writers. After the war Spencer became the British Council's director of studies in Madrid, and then for several years he traveled widely, lecturing in Greece, England, Turkey, Spain, and Austria. Among his collections of poetry are *Aegean Islands, The Twist in the Plotting,* and a posthumous volume, *With Luck Lasting.* His *Collected Poems* were published in 1965. Spencer also contributed to poetry magazines, including *New Verse,* which he helped to edit.

OBITUARIES AND OTHER SOURCES:

BOOKS

A Dictionary of Literature in the English Language: From 1940 to 1970, Pergamon, 1978.
World Authors: 1950-1970, H. W. Wilson, 1975.

*   *   *

SPIGELGASS, Leonard   1908-1985

OBITUARY NOTICE—See index for *CA* sketch: Born November 26, 1908, in Brooklyn, N.Y.; died after a long illness, February 15 (one source says February 14), 1985, in Los Angeles, Calif. Author. An award-winning screenwriter, Spigelgass earned Academy Award nominations for "Mystery Street" and "Butch Minds the Baby" and received Writers Guild Awards for such screenplays as "I Was a Male War Bride," "Gypsy," and "A Majority of One," which he adapted from

his successful Broadway play of the same title. His other screenwriting credits include "Million Dollar Baby," "The Big Street," and "The Youngest Profession." Among his play titles are "Dear Me, the Sky Is Falling," "The Playgirls," and "Look to the Lillies." In addition, Spigelgass wrote for television, providing material for "Playhouse 90," "Climax," and eleven Academy Award programs. Spigelgass wrote books as well, collaborating with Allen Rivkin on *I Wasn't Born Yesterday* and with Edward G. Robinson on *All My Yesterdays,* the actor's autobiography. An active member of the Writers Guild, Spigelgass was the recipient of the Morgan Cox Award for service to the guild and the Valentine Davies Award for service to the community at large.

OBITUARIES AND OTHER SOURCES:

BOOKS

International Motion Picture Almanac, Quigley, 1985.

PERIODICALS

New York Times, February 16, 1985.
Variety, February 20, 1985.

*   *   *

SPITZ, Mark (Andrew)   1950-

BRIEF ENTRY: Born February 10, 1950, in Modesto, Calif. American amateur athlete, businessman, broadcaster, and author. Spitz achieved international fame in 1972 when he won gold medals in seven swimming competitions during the Olympic Games in Munich, West Germany. The athlete broke existing world records in each of the seven events as well as established a new record for total gold medals won by an individual during a single Olympics. Spitz, who had garnered two gold medals during the 1968 Olympics, retired from swimming in 1972. Since then his public appearances have declined substantially, though he occasionally appears on television as a commentator for American Broadcasting Companies (ABC-TV) sports programs. Spitz collaborated with Alan LeMond on writing *The Mark Spitz Complete Book of Swimming* (Crowell, 1976).

BIOGRAPHICAL/CRITICAL SOURCES:

BOOKS

Current Biography, Wilson, 1972.
Stambler, Irwin, *Speed Kings,* Doubleday, 1973.

PERIODICALS

New York Times, October 28, 1982.
Sports Illustrated, July 5, 1976.

*   *   *

SPIVEY, Richard L.   1937-

PERSONAL: Born April 2, 1937, in San Jose, Calif.; son of Thomas S. (a restaurateur) and Sylvia (a housewife; maiden name, Rhoten) Spivey; married Leora Scattini, August, 1963 (divorced, 1970); married Lynne Plant (a housewife), November 24, 1978. *Education:* Stanford University, B.A. 1958.

ADDRESSES: Home and office—Carmel, Calif.

CAREER: Spivey's Coffee Shops, San Jose, Calif., general manager, 1959-62, president, 1962-69; Indian Trader (dealers in Pueblo pottery), Santa Fe, N.M., owner, 1969-81; American Indian art consultant and farmer, 1981—. Judge of Pueblo

Indian pottery for Southwestern Association on Indian Affairs, Heard Museum, and Gallup Inter-Tribal Indian Ceremonial; Wheelwright Museum of the American Indian, vice-president of board of trustees, guest curator, 1980. *Military service:* U.S. Army Reserve, 1959-65.

MEMBER: Southwestern Association on Indian Affairs (past president), California State Restaurant Association (member of board of directors), Old Santa Fe Association (member of board of directors).

WRITINGS:

(Contributor) Clara Lee Tanner, editor, *Arizona Highways: Indian Arts and Crafts,* Arizona Highways, 1976.
Maria, Northland Press, 1979, revised edition, 1981.
(Author of foreword) Susan Brown McGreevy, *Maria: The Legend, the Legacy,* Sunstone Press, 1982.

Contributor to *American Craft* and *El Palacio.* Member of editorial advisory board of *American Indian Art.*

WORK IN PROGRESS: Pueblo Indian Potters: A Biographical Reference Book (tentative title), publication expected in 1987.

SIDELIGHTS: Richard L. Spivey told *CA:* "In regard to my career with Pueblo Indian pottery, I have to give considerable credit to Popovi Da, the son of Maria Martinez, who was my mentor until his death in 1971. Without his guidance and support, it would have been difficult to obtain the depth of knowledge and the degree of success that I achieved in this field. Popovi Da provided a compelling reason for writing the book on Maria.

"A subject of vital importance to Pueblo Indian pottery is the disturbing recent and growing use of nontraditional methods and materials in the manufacture of what is represented as traditionally made pottery. I will deal with this subject in my forthcoming book on Pueblo potters.

"I have a broad interest in ceramics in general, but especially (other than Pueblo Indian pottery) I am interested in early Japanese and Chinese wares, and the contemporary folk-craft pottery wares of Japan."

BIOGRAPHICAL/CRITICAL SOURCES:

PERIODICALS

Arizona Highways, May, 1974.
Arizona Republic, March 12, 1972.
Los Angeles Times, October 5, 1971.
Santa Fean, December, 1973-January, 1974.
Santa Fe Reporter, August 14, 1980.

*   *   *

SPRINGER, Nelson P(aul)   1915-

PERSONAL: Born August 15, 1915, in Minier, Ill.; son of Ben (a farmer and minister) and Clara (a homemaker; maiden name, Hieser) Springer; married Betty Weber (an office clerk), August 18, 1951; children: Ken, Beth Springer Farrand, Joseph, Christina. *Education:* Goshen College, B.A., 1941, graduate study, 1947-49; University of Illinois at Urbana-Champaign, M.S., 1953. *Religion:* Mennonite.

ADDRESSES: Home—1806 Mayflower Pl., Goshen, Ind. 46526.

CAREER: Goshen College, Goshen, Ind., bookstore manager, 1941-47, assistant librarian at Mennonite Historical Library,

1949-54, curator of library, beginning 1954, editor of *Alumni Newsletter,* 1955-56; Bethel College, North Newton, Kan., consultant to Mennonite Library and Archives. Archives of Mennonite Church, archivist, 1949-54, custodian, 1955-57; librarian at Mennonitische Forschungsstelle, Weierhof, West Germany, 1975-76.

MEMBER: Mennonite Historical Society (member of board of directors), Mennonitischer Geschichtsverein, Schweizerischer Verein fuer Taeufergeschichte.

WRITINGS:

(Editor with A. J. Klassen) *Mennonite Bibliography,* two volumes, Herald Press, 1977.

Member of editorial staff of *Mennonite Quarterly Review,* 1969—.

SIDELIGHTS: Nelson P. Springer told *CA:* "I have had the privilege of being the first full-time manager of the Goshen College Bookstore, the first full-time curator of the Mennonite Historical Library, and the first trained archivist in the archives of the Mennonite Church. My language specialities are German and Dutch; my professional concentration during my final years before retirement was cataloging rare books. I am currently serving as consultant to the Mennonite Library and Archives, Bethel College, in relation to their three-year grant from the National Endowment for the Humanities for cataloging their holdings."

*   *   *

STALEY, Allen   1935-

BRIEF ENTRY: Born June 4, 1935, in St. Louis, Mo. American art historian, educator, and author. Staley began teaching art history at Columbia University in 1969; he became a full professor in 1976. He has also been a member of the curatorial staff at the Philadelphia Museum of Art. Staley wrote *Romantic Art in Britain: Paintings and Drawings, 1760-1860* (Praeger, 1968) and *The Pre-Raphaelite Landscape* (Clarendon Press, 1973). *Address:* Department of Art History, Columbia University, Broadway and West 116th, New York, N.Y. 10027.

BIOGRAPHICAL/CRITICAL SOURCES:

BOOKS

Who's Who in American Art, 15th edition, Bowker, 1982.

PERIODICALS

New York Times Book Review, December 2, 1973.
Observer, December 9, 1973.
Yale Review, December 2, 1973.

*   *   *

STAM, Robert   1941-

PERSONAL: Born October 29, 1941, in Paterson, N.J.; son of Jacob (a lawyer) and Deana (a legal assistant; maiden name, Bowman) Stam; married Gilda Penteado, January, 1971 (divorced); children: Gilberto. *Education:* Indiana University-Bloomington, M.A., 1966; Sorbonne, University of Paris, Diplome Semestriel, 1968, 1969; University of California, Berkeley, Ph.D., 1976.

ADDRESSES: Home—37 Spring St., New York, N.Y. 10012. *Office*—Department of Cinema Studies, South Building, New York University, New York, N.Y. 10003.

CAREER: University of California, Berkeley, lecturer in cinema studies, 1975-77; New York University, New York, N.Y., assistant professor, 1977-83, associate professor of cinema studies, 1983—. Fulbright lecturer in Brazil, 1985-86.

AWARDS, HONORS: Woodrow Wilson fellow, 1963-64; presidential fellowship from New York University, NDEA fellowship.

WRITINGS:

O espetaculo interrompido (title means "The Interrupted Spectacle"), Paz e Terra, 1981.
(With Randal Johnson) *Brazilian Cinema,* Associated University Presses, 1982.
Reflexive Pleasures, UMI Research Press, 1985.
Blacks in Brazilian Cinema, Brasiliense, 1985.
Film Semiotics: A Conceptual Dictionary, Redgrave, 1986.

Member of editorial board of *Jump Cut, Critical Arts,* and *Journal of the University Film and Video Association.*

WORK IN PROGRESS: The Cinema After Babel, on translation in the cinema, for *Screen; Third World Cinema.*

SIDELIGHTS: Robert Stam attributed his motivation to his origins in "a family of seven, five of whom have doctorates. It was a family in which ideas were taken seriously, but also handled playfully, and one of which I am very proud."

*   *   *

STANFORD, Alfred (Boller)   1900-1985

OBITUARY NOTICE—See index for *CA* sketch: Born February 12, 1900, in East Orange, N.J.; died after a long illness, February 8, 1985, in Milford, Conn. Newspaper executive, publisher, editor, and author. Stanford worked as editor and publisher of *Boats* and as second vice-president and advertising director of the *New York Herald Tribune* in the early years of his career. In 1954 he began a long stint as publisher of the *Milford Citizen;* after retiring as publisher he wrote a weekly column for the paper. His books include *Groundswell, A City Out of the Sea, Invitation to Danger, Pleasures of Sailing,* and *Mission in Sparrow Bush Lane.* He also contributed articles and short stories to periodicals.

OBITUARIES AND OTHER SOURCES:

BOOKS

Who's Who in America, 40th edition, Marquis, 1978.

PERIODICALS

Chicago Tribune, February 15, 1985.

*   *   *

STANFORD, William Bedell   1910-1984

OBITUARY NOTICE—See index for *CA* sketch: Born January 16, 1910, in Belfast, Ireland (now Northern Ireland); died December 30, 1984, in Dublin, Ireland. Educator, Greek scholar, editor, and author. Stanford was Regius Professor of Greek at the University of Dublin from 1940 to 1980. Among his writings on Greek classicism are *Ambiguity in Greek Literature, Aeschylus in His Style,* and *The Ulysses Theme.* Stanford served as the editor of works by Aristophanes, Sophocles, and Aeschylus, and he also edited the publication *Hermathena* from 1942 to 1962.

OBITUARIES AND OTHER SOURCES:

BOOKS

The Writers Directory: 1984-1986, St. James Press, 1983.

PERIODICALS

AB Bookman's Weekly, February 11, 1985.
Times (London), January 10, 1985.

*   *   *

STANLEY, David   1944-

PERSONAL: Born September 11, 1944, in Toronto, Ontario, Canada; son of Robert A. (an accountant) and Emily (Hesp) Stanley. *Education:* Universidad de Barcelona, Diploma de Estudios Hispanicos, 1971; University of Guelph, B.A. (with honors), 1972. *Politics:* "Ecologist."

ADDRESSES: Home—Bracebridge, Ontario, Canada. *Office*—Moon Publications, P.O. Box 1696, Chico, Calif. 95927.

CAREER: Unitours (Canada) Ltd., Toronto, Ontario, tour representative, 1975-80; Moon Publications, Chico, Calif., staff travel writer, 1980—.

MEMBER: Canadian Hosteling Association (life member), Greenpeace Foundation (life member), Sierra Club.

WRITINGS:

South Pacific Handbook, Moon Publications, 1st edition (with Bill Dalton), 1979, 2nd edition (sole author), 1982, 3rd edition, 1985.
Alaska-Yukon Handbook: A Gypsy Guide to the Inside Passage and Beyond, Moon Publications, 1983.
Finding Fiji, Moon Publications, 1985.

SIDELIGHTS: David Stanley told *CA:* "I write about travel because that is what I enjoy doing most. To date I have visited 103 countries on every continent and hope to make it 175 before I retire in the 1990's, probably to a small Pacific island. I try to make my travel writing helpful to residents of the areas covered, that is, to subject them to as little disruption from tourists as possible. I do this by educating tourists about local customs and suggesting patterns of behavior which will benefit the local people by patronizing local businesses, purchasing local products, and so on. This is the only way I can justify writing about places it is often better that most Westerners know nothing about."

BIOGRAPHICAL/CRITICAL SOURCES:

PERIODICALS

Pacific Islands Monthly, September, 1983.

*   *   *

STANTON, William, J(ohn, Jr.)   1919-

BRIEF ENTRY: Born December 15, 1919, in Chicago, Ill. American educator and author. Stanton became a professor of marketing at the University of Colorado in 1955. His theories on business, marketing, and management have been published in *Management of the Sales Force* (Irwin, 1959) and *Fundamentals of Marketing* (McGraw, 1964). *Address:* Department of Marketing, University of Colorado, 1100 14th St., Denver, Colo. 80202.

BIOGRAPHICAL/CRITICAL SOURCES:

BOOKS

Who's Who in America, 42nd edition, Marquis, 1982.

*   *   *

STANWOOD, Brooks
See KAMINSKY, Susan Stanwood

*   *   *

STARKE, J(oseph) G(abriel)   1911-

PERSONAL: Born November 16, 1911, in Perth, Australia; son of Phillip (a merchant) and Gertrude (a businesswoman; maiden name, Bernstein) Starke; married Irma Myslis (a community worker), June 1, 1943; children: Sanchia Starke Glaskin. *Education:* University of Western Australia, B.A., 1930, LL.B. (with first class honors), 1932; Oxford University, B.C.L. (with first class honors), 1934; attended University of Geneva and Post-Graduate Institute of International Studies, Geneva, Switzerland, 1934-35.

ADDRESSES: Home—Unit 63, Argyle Sq., 1 Allambee St., Reid, Canberra, Australian Capital Territory 2601, Australia.

CAREER: League of Nations, Geneva, Switzerland, member of Secretariat, 1935-40; barrister at law in Sydney and Canberra, Australia, 1940—. Appointed Queen's Counsel, 1961. Professor at International Institute of Humanitarian Law, San Remo, Italy, 1975—. Member of panel of international arbitrators, International Court of Justice, 1969—; consultant to Australian Law Reform Commission. *Military service:* Australian Army, 1943-44. Royal Australian Air Force, 1944-45; became flight lieutenant.

MEMBER: National Press Club, Peace Institute of Australia (honorary member), New South Wales Bar Association.

AWARDS, HONORS: Rhodes scholar at Oxford University, 1932.

WRITINGS:

Introduction to International Law, Butterworth, 1947, 9th edition, 1984.
Studies in International Law, Butterworth, 1965.
The ANZUS Treaty Alliance, Cambridge University Press, 1965.
Law of Town and Country Planning in New South Wales, Butterworth (Sydney), 1966.
(With P.F.P. Higgins) *Cheshire and Fifoot on Contract,* Australian edition, Butterworth (Sydney), 1966, 4th Australian edition, 1981.
(Editor) *Protection and Encouragement of Private Foreign Investment,* Butterworth (Sydney), 1966.
Introduction to the Science of Peace: Irenology, Sijthoff, 1968.
Assignment of Choses in Action in Australia, Butterworth (Sydney), 1972.
The Validity of Psycho-Analysis, Angus & Robertson, 1973.
Contributions to Irenology in the Writings of Leonard Nelson, Felix Meiner Verlag, 1974.
(With Higgins and J. P. Swanton) *Casebook on the Law of Contract,* Butterworth (Sydney), 1975.

General editor of *Australian Law Journal,* 1974—; founder and editor of *Australian Yearbook of International Law,* 1965-67.

WORK IN PROGRESS: Felix Frankfurter at Oxford, publication expected in 1986; *The Last Six Years of the League of Nations,* completion expected in 1988.

SIDELIGHTS: J. G. Starke told *CA:* "I came to be interested in international law and irenology through five years of service in the League of Nations Secretariat in Geneva, 1935 to 1940, which provided me with practical insights into both subjects. As to irenology in particular, I found that there was no comprehensive textbook on the subject and accordingly decided that when I had time, I would write one. As visiting professor at the University of Paris in January, 1967, I delivered a course of lectures on the science of peace, and these lectures formed the basis of my book, published in 1968, which still remains the only comprehensive book on irenology.

"The two fields of international law and irenology have changed to some extent over the past fifteen years. The content of international law is now largely contained in international treaties and conventions, codifying and clarifying the former rules which were mainly of a customary nature. As regards irenology—the fields of arms control and nuclear disarmament have assumed greater importance in the past ten years. I am fairly optimistic about progress in both these disciplines, although with respect to irenology, writers and lecturers on peace studies seem to avoid a comprehensive approach to the subject, preferring to deal piecemeal with different topics—sociology of peace, disarmament, etc.—instead of looking at it as a general science, such as economics.

"The most considerable influence of my writing generally was that of Professor Geoffrey Cheshire and Justice Felix Frankfurter. I was Frankfurter's pupil at Oxford in 1933 and 1934, while he was Eastman Visiting Professor. Both men motivated me to write books, and to write clearly, avoiding verbosity. I found, actually, that I was able to write only on subjects with which I had had practical experience. My five years in Geneva, with experience in French writing, also highlighted the importance of writing with clarity."

*   *   *

STEELE, Alan   1905-1985

OBITUARY NOTICE: Born in May, 1905; died January 4, 1985. Bookseller, printer, and publisher. Steele is remembered as the treasurer of the exclusive Society of Bookmen and as an expert on all aspects of the British book trade. He opened his first bookshop in 1924 and soon became a director of the bookselling firm of William Jackson Limited. Steele, who served as manager of the *Times* Book Club, was also the founder of the publishing company of Joiner & Steele. In addition, he spent nearly forty years with the printing company of Butler & Tanner, where he was appointed chairman in 1970. At the time of his death at the age of seventy-nine, Steele was the chairman of the High Hill Bookshop, located in the Camden borough of Hampstead.

OBITUARIES:

PERIODICALS

Times (London), February 7, 1985.

*   *   *

STEELE, Curtis
See DAVIS, Frederick C(lyde)

STEELE, James B(ruce, Jr.) 1943-

PERSONAL: Born January 3, 1943, in Hutchinson, Kan.; son of James Bruce and Mary (Peoples) Steele; married Nancy Saunders, June 25, 1966; children: Allison. *Education:* University of Missouri at Kansas City, B.A., 1967.

ADDRESSES: Home—Philadelphia, Pa. *Office*—*Philadelphia Inquirer*, P.O. Box 8263, Philadelphia, Pa. 19101.

CAREER: Kansas City Times, Kansas City, Mo., copyboy, 1962, reporter, 1962-67; Laborers' International Union of North America, Washington, D.C., director of information, 1968-70; *Philadelphia Inquirer*, Philadelphia, Pa., investigative reporter, 1970—.

AWARDS, HONORS: American Political Science Association award for distinguished reporting of public affairs, 1971, for a series on abandoned housing; George Polk Memorial Award for metropolitan reporting and Sigma Delta Chi Distinguished Service in Journalism award, 1971, for newspaper series on the Federal Housing Administration; George Polk Memorial Award for special reporting, Heywood Broun Award for public interest reporting, and Sidney Hillman Foundation Award, 1973, for newspaper series "Crime and Injustice"; Gavel award from the American Bar Association, John Hancock Award for business reporting, and Business Journalism award from the University of Missouri at Columbia for newspaper series "Oil: The Created Crisis," all 1973; Pulitzer Prize for national reporting, 1975, for newspaper series "Auditing the IRS"; Distinguished Service in Journalism award from University of Missouri, 1983.

WRITINGS:

(With Donald L. Barlett) *Oil: The Created Crisis* (pamphlet), Philadelphia Inquirer, 1973.
(With Barlett) *Empire: The Life, Legend, and Madness of Howard Hughes*, Norton, 1979.
(With Barlett) *Forevermore: Nuclear Waste in America*, Norton, 1985.

Contributor to periodicals, including *New Republic* and *Nation*.

WORK IN PROGRESS: With Barlett, a book on income tax, publication by Norton expected in 1986.

SIDELIGHTS: Prize-winning reporters for the *Philadelphia Inquirer* since the early 1970's, Donald L. Barlett and James B. Steele, declared James H. Dygert in *The Investigative Reporter*, are "perhaps the most systematic and thorough investigative reporting team in the U.S. today." Together they have uncovered fraud in the Federal Housing Administration's (FHA) subsidy program for rehabilitating and selling slum houses, disclosed inequities in Philadelphia's criminal courts, and, in a Pulitzer Prize-winning series of articles, demonstrated that the Internal Revenue Service enforces tax laws more stringently on middle-income and poor taxpayers than on the wealthy. The team's most ambitious project of the seventies was a biography, *Empire: The Life, Legend, and Madness of Howard Hughes.* The book was well received and, like all of Barlett and Steele's work, is notable, appraised a *Newsweek* reporter, for its "impressive use of documents."

Prior to collaborating with Barlett at the *Inquirer*, Steele worked as a reporter for the *Kansas City Times* (Missouri) and then as an information director of a labor union in Washington, D.C., jobs which taught him the skills needed by investigative journalists. At the *Times,* reported Leonard Downie, Jr., in

The New Muckrakers, Steele was, in his own words, "schooled in the use of records to verify facts for stories like obituaries [and] taught respect for facts and shown how they could be found in records of all kinds." The lessons of his early training were reinforced during his tenure in Washington, D.C., where, according to Downie, "he learned in detail just where information could be found in the federal bureaucracy."

The two men began working at the *Inquirer* on the same day in 1970, and since their first joint assignment (documenting abuses in the FHA subsidy program) reliance on the facts has been their trademark. They are among a "new breed of muckraker," contended Downie, who rely on the public record for evidence rather than solely on stories from informants. According to Steele, "the challenge is to gather, marshal, and organize vast amounts of data already in the public domain and see what it adds up to." He insists that investigative reporters must be systematic and review their assumptions as they go; they must constantly evaluate the evidence they turn up and determine if it is adequate to prove their thesis.

Overall, Steele takes satisfaction, he told Downie, in "spending months on a subject and having it all come together at the end. . . . No matter how much you know, there is always more to find out." One of his favorite projects was investigating Howard Hughes's dealings with the U.S. Government. After months of reviewing contracts, trial records, partnership agreements, financial statements, and the like, Barlett and Steele had amassed ten thousand pages of notes and documents. They published their initial findings in a series of articles for the *Inquirer* in 1975, but when more material became available after Hughes's death, the reporters took the opportunity to collaborate on their first book, *Empire: The Life, Legend, and Madness of Howard Hughes.* It is "the best big business-big government biography of 1979, maybe of the decade," declared a *Washington Post Book World* reviewer, while a critic for the *New York Times Book Review* opined: "Of all the books written about Howard Hughes, 'Empire' is easily the best. . . . From the mountain of subpoenaed files and depositions, and from interviews, the authors have assembled the first fully documented, cradle-to-grave account of a unique American life."

More recently, Steele and Barlett have received praise for their 1985 work, *Forevermore: Nuclear Waste in America.* Evolving from their 1983 investigative series for the *Inquirer*, the book discusses failed attempts to safely store nuclear waste. According to Victor Gilinsky's critique in the *Los Angeles Times Book Review,* "the authors have dug up interesting material" for their "important" story.

The two-man team attributes much of their success to the support they receive from the *Inquirer.* They are free to investigate whatever subject seems pertinent to them, have open-ended work schedules, can travel if necessary, and have access to computers and other resources. In addition, the paper has never yet killed one of their stories under pressure, even when it has meant losing advertisements. This being the case, Downie reported that Steele claims not to tire of his work. And regarding the future Steele has said: "There are always more records and more in them to find out. . . . The work is never done."

See also *BARLETT, Donald L(eon)*

CA INTERVIEW

CA interviewed James B. Steele by telephone at his office at the *Philadelphia Inquirer* on June 10, 1983.

CA: Modern government provides you with many of the records that undergird your investigations. Yet a number of your investigations reveal government mistakes or corruption. Does this give you an ambivalent attitude toward government as a whole?

STEELE: Not really. The government keeps the records for a variety of reasons. It doesn't keep them to make our work easier. We can vouch for that, because sometimes it's very difficult to locate some of the material that's kept for a number of bureaucratic reasons.

Besides, the whole process of documentation and record keeping is really a very, very ancient one. I read a lot of history, and I never cease to be amazed at how far back documents can be traced. Record keeping is built into civilization and certainly predates us. We're just the most current generation to make use of some of the records.

CA: You prefer stories based on documents to stories based on sources. Why?

STEELE: I wouldn't phrase it as one versus the other. Interviewing at some point is extremely important. But we [Steele and his investigative reporting partner, Donald Barlett] feel it's very important before you do anything to have a documentary basis for the things you're looking for. Also, if you develop something sensitive or important in an interview, you should try to get some additional confirmation of it. We feel better doing that than simply taking somebody's word for something. Memory is fragile.

But the general thrust of your question is accurate: over the years we have dealt more with documents than with interviews as such. It's a question of emphasis. Let me go back to my first days in this business for an illustration. At that time, if you had a question like, "I wonder who owns this land next to the new school that's being built" or "I wonder who owns the land where that highway's going through" or "This fellow running for mayor: how wealthy a family did he come from?" your first instinct was to reach for a phone and try to get an answer by interviewing. It didn't occur to me until later that there's very often another way, and sometimes a more accurate way, to get that information, which is through public records and documents.

CA: Some people would say that some of your work involves an invasion of privacy of the people you're investigating. What's your response to that?

STEELE: I'm not sure that that particular criticism has been directed at us, although I have seen it directed at others. I feel in general that with most public officials, and most people on the periphery of public life, certain things about them are open to scrutiny.

The whole privacy issue is an interesting one, though, because the whole country has gotten obsessed with it in recent years. There's a fear that computers will divulge all types of information about us. A number of lawmakers have made very expert use of this obsession by using the privacy act to help frustrate some of the intentions of the Freedom of Information Act. The government itself doesn't care that much about privacy, of course, but it has become very convenient for them to say, "That's an invasion of privacy. We can't release those documents." We have encountered an awful lot of that in the past three or four years. Such an objection was literally unheard of five or six or ten years ago.

CA: Were you allowed to do investigative reporting at the Kansas City Times?

STEELE: No, but I trace some of my interest in long-range reporting from that period. I was in a *Times* suburban bureau for quite a few years and was constantly coming face to face with very complex issues like, "Does the city really need this new sewer line?" Or I'd cover some debate on the question of whether one school district should be merged with another, and the charges would fly. And I'd sit there wondering, "Who's telling the truth here?" or "Is anybody telling the truth here?" or "What is the story here?" My interest in long-range independent reporting stemmed from that because we'd print all sides of the story, but we weren't always able to figure out exactly what the story was.

CA: You were in union public relations a while. Why did you take that job and why did you leave it?

STEELE: It may appear to have been a public relations job, but actually it was a job doing all kinds of writing internally for a union. The union was moving into a different area, and I was impressed by some of the things they were doing, so I took the job and stayed there about two and one-half years. It was a fascinating job because I was able to observe how Washington works: how congressional committees work, how the Washington press corps works, how lobbying is done. I didn't personally do any of the lobbying, but I was around enough of those people to see how it was done. I could have gotten a similar view of Washington by working for a newspaper there, but not that easily or that quickly. But after I'd been out of the newspaper business for more than two years, I really wanted to return to newspapers, and did.

CA: You and Donald Barlett come from very different backgrounds, yet you work very well together. Why?

STEELE: There are certain things we have in common: we like to spend time on large subjects, we enjoy the excitement of reporting, and we both pay a lot of attention to detail. We agree on how much work you have to do—a great deal of work—before a story is ready to be written. Neither one of us particularly enjoyed working with other people in the past, but when we found one whose work habits were similar and realized we could get along, we were struck by how much two people could do. That's what's exciting.

CA: Why can't other reporters work together?

STEELE: The ego thing is the biggest problem other reporters who try to work together have. "Who does this?" and "Who does that?" and "My stuff is better than your stuff": that kind of thing. We've never had those problems because we're so similar and because we've always had an agreed-upon goal in each case.

Also, some reportorial teams will have one person doing the reporting and one the writing. But we split everything up: we both do the reporting, and we both do the writing. That's important in our relationship; it's an equal partnership in terms of who does the work.

CA: Many of your stories seemed aimed at proving unequal treatment of people who should be treated equally: oil customers, defendants, taxpayers. Is unequal treatment what interests you most?

STEELE: That's what bothers me the most, emotionally, when I see various systems malfunctioning. It's not so much that that motivates me to investigate something, but once I start looking at a system, that's often what strikes me about it. For instance, we did this series years ago on the IRS and ran across an audit in which the IRS told a big company, "You owe $500 million in back taxes on your Middle East operations" and then settled for about $250 million. So our questions were how often does that happen, and can the average taxpayer work out the same kind of arrangement with the government?

CA: Which story of yours is your favorite?

STEELE: The two different series we did on oil, in 1973 and in 1979-80, both were immensely exciting and probably had as much impact, in terms of how widely they were distributed, as anything we've ever done.

As a sheer single challenge, though, the Hughes book has got to be way up there too, partly because we were dealing with an unbelievable volume of documents and an incredible number of incidents you don't normally encounter in a biography. Also, we were dealing with Hughes's bizarre behavior in combination with his huge private empire that was and is influencing national policy and being influenced by it. There was a great deal of work involved in researching all of the Hughes material, which was in six principal locations scattered around the U.S. In fact, our private joke was, if we ever do another biography, it's going to be of a Philadelphian who has been dead for a hundred years, so everything is nearby, in the same place, and easily accessible.

The major challenge with Hughes, though, was trying to unravel the mystery that surrounded him and determine what about him was true and what was not true. A great deal of mythology had built up about him, created both by those who despised him and those who revered him. This is true of any well-known figure, but it was even more true of Hughes because of the veil of secrecy protecting him. We were trying to penetrate that veil and not sensationalize what we found when we did so, and, when we discovered astonishing documents, trying to assess whether they were true or fake.

CA: Do you think it's true that your stories would have more impact if you were working in New York rather than in Philadelphia?

STEELE: The answer to that question really depends on what you mean by impact. Something is revealed in the *New York Times* or the *Washington Post* and there's a sort of outraged rippling through Congress, a somewhat superficial response that's known as impact. But I think as time has gone on that the people who are interested in the areas we write about pay as much attention to our stuff as if we were writing it for the *Times* or the *Post.*

Another problem with thinking of things in terms of impact is that often there's no traditional, simple response to a problem we may bring to light. You can't just introduce a bill or indict someone as a way of solving the problem. It's usually a much more complex problem that we write about, so our work has a much more subtle sort of impact.

Also, we're glad to be working for the *Inquirer* because it gives us very free access to a number of agencies that might be a little more concerned if we represented some other paper and were prowling around their records. And time is given here in a way it isn't given anywhere else, so we're able to look at a subject with a scope and scale that's just not possible elsewhere.

CA: Do you worry about how many people will read what you write?

STEELE: Anyone likes to see what they've written read by ten million people. But, having said that, in all honesty although you may want a great many people to read what you write, there are so many things you can't control that the only thing you can do is deal with the material right before you each day and get that done and be satisfied with it yourself.

CA: Are you bothered when things don't change permanently as a result of a story you write?

STEELE: A lot of people get very disenchanted with the whole investigative process when some problem continues to exist even though they've brought it to light. It doesn't bother me, though. If you've shown some enterprise and revealed the existence of some problem, it's out of your ballpark at that point. I'm pleased if we've brought some material together and drawn a picture showing X number of people something they didn't even know existed before. That's satisfying. If anything changes, so much the better, but I don't consider it a failure if nothing changes. Anyway, with many of the things we write about, if change occurs, it does so over such a long period of time that it's very hard for us to sense the change occurring.

CA: Many reporters burn out after a few investigative stories. Why not you?

STEELE: Part of the reason is the basic support this paper gives to the whole concept. It's almost nonexistent at a lot of other newspapers. Also, we've gotten a great deal of recognition here and elsewhere for what we've been doing, and that spurs us on. And we've gotten seasoned: we know what these things are like when we begin, we know what they're like in the middle, and we know what they're like at the end. For many years after I started in this business, I couldn't have spent as much time as I now do on a subject. I would have had too many anxieties about getting in the paper. But once you've gone through it a few times, you have faith that it's all going to be okay in the end. You develop a certain kind of patience, a sense that everything will work out. But many people go through so much torment every time they do one of these long-range projects—they run into the normal obstacles, they're overwhelmed with anxiety, and they get no support— that they begin to think, "Life is too short to endure this kind of difficulty. I think I'll try something else."

CA: Did you have any trouble switching from newspaper writing to book writing?

STEELE: One problem was pace: the amount of information you want to discharge right away. When we started writing book chapters, we tended to tell everything very quickly and then start going back over the story, adding detail in the retelling, as if we were writing a newspaper story. But a book is a much more leisurely approach to telling a story: you can tell everything about one thing before you go on to the next thing.

CA: Do you prefer book writing to magazine and newspaper writing?

STEELE: No, what we prefer is in-depth and long-range reporting and subjects we can look at a while. It doesn't matter whether we do such work for newspapers or for books, but some subjects lend themselves much more to this sort of reporting than other subjects do.

CA: How's your book on taxes coming?

STEELE: It's coming along, and we're very happy with it, but it presents a much different sort of writing problem than a biography does. A person's life is a unifying theme you can always wander away from and come back to, but with straight nonfiction you don't have that structure, and to erect one, obviously, is harder than having one ready-made.

BIOGRAPHICAL/CRITICAL SOURCES:

BOOKS

Downie, Leonard, Jr., *The New Muckrakers*, New Republic Books, 1976.
Dygert, James H., *The Investigative Journalist*, Prentice-Hall, 1976.

PERIODICALS

Christian Science Monitor, May 21, 1979.
Los Angeles Times Book Review, March 24, 1985.
Maclean's Magazine, June 4, 1979.
Nation, May 5, 1979.
National Review, April 27, 1979.
Newsweek, December 30, 1974, April 23, 1979.
New West, May 21, 1979.
New York, May 7, 1979.
New York Review of Books, May 31, 1979.
New York Times Book Review, May 6, 1979, November 25, 1979, March 22, 1981.
Publishers Weekly, April 26, 1976.
Washington Monthly, April, 1979.
Washington Post Book World, December 2, 1979.
West Coast Review of Books, July, 1979.

—*Sketch by Nancy H. Evans*

—*Interview by Peter Benjaminson*

*   *   *

STEINBERG, Fannie 1899-

PERSONAL: Born February 6, 1899, in Russia (now U.S.S.R.); immigrated to United States c. 1903; daughter of Maierchaim (a scholar) and Mindel (Rubinstein) Karshmey; married David Steinberg (a realtor; deceased); children: Marvin E. *Education:* Rutgers University, B.A., 1931, M.A., 1947, graduate study, 1976. *Religion:* Jewish.

ADDRESSES: Home—212 South First Ave., Highland Park, N.J. 08904.

CAREER: Teacher at public elementary schools in New Brunswick, N.J., 1920-50; manager of a real estate/insurance business; writer.

MEMBER: B'nai B'rith Women (past president of Simcha chapter), Middlesex County Women's Democratic Organization (past president).

WRITINGS:

Birthday in Kishinev (juvenile fiction), Jewish Publication Society, 1979.

Contributor to political journals and *U.S. Congressional Record.*

WORK IN PROGRESS: To the Golden Door, a sequel to *Birthday in Kishinev; Grandma and Heidi.*

SIDELIGHTS: Fannie Steinberg described herself to *CA* as "a potential Grandma Moses." Most of her life was spent teaching elementary school; upon her retirement, she managed her husband's real estate and insurance business. In 1976, at the age of seventy-seven, she returned to her alma mater to take a course in creative writing. Her study resulted in *Birthday in Kishinev*, a fictionalized account of Steinberg's survival of the anti-Jewish pogrom which took place in Kishinev on her twelfth birthday. She is currently working on a sequel, *To the Golden Door*, which chronicles her family's escape from Russia to the United States.

*   *   *

STEINER, Barry R(aymond)

PERSONAL: Son of George and Ann (Goldstein) Steiner; married Faye Saxon, August 6, 1972; children: David, Lauri, Miriam, Marci.

ADDRESSES: Home—8386 Shadow Wood Blvd., Coral Springs, Fl. 33065. *Office*—1211 West Farwell, Chicago, Ill. 60626. *Agent*—Dominick Abel Literary Agency Inc., 498 West End Ave., New York, N.Y. 10024.

CAREER: Worked for the Internal Revenue Service, 1964-65; certified public accountant, 1964—. Gives radio and television interviews.

WRITINGS:

"PAY LESS TAX LEGALLY" SERIES

Pay Less Tax—Legally!, edited by Sander P. Stagman, [Chicago], 1972.
Pay Less Tax Legally: The Tax Preparation Guide, Regnery, 1974, revised edition, 1975.
Pay Less Tax Legally: The Tax Preparation Guide to the Latest Laws and Loopholes, New American Library, 1976, revised edition, 1978.
Pay Less Tax Legally, New American Library, 1980, revised editions, 1981 and 1985.

OTHER

(With David W. Kennedy) *Perfectly Legal: 275 Foolproof Methods for Paying Less Taxes*, Wiley, 1982.
Also author of *The Teacher's Taxman, The Talking Taxman, Dial-a-Deduction*, and *Pay Less Tax: The Computer Program.*

SIDELIGHTS: Former Internal Revenue Service agent Barry R. Steiner is most notable as author of the best-seller *Pay Less Tax Legally.* Updated numerous times since it was first published in 1972, the book provides a step-by-step guide for taxpayers with incomes ranging from fifteen to one hundred thousand dollars a year. Part one, "Save Money Now," includes information on such topics as capital gains and losses, adjustments to income, itemizing deductions, and preparing for an audit, while part two, "Save Money Later," focuses on tax-planning opportunities that will save the taxpayer money later on. Issues dealt with in the second section include the alternative minimum tax and how to avoid it, the audit lottery, college costs, volunteer work, divorce, and energy tax credits.

BIOGRAPHICAL/CRITICAL SOURCES:

PERIODICALS

Christian Science Monitor, February 9, 1981.
Consumer Reports, February, 1985.
National Observer, March 5, 1977.
West Coast Review of Books, April, 1982.

* * *

STEINER, Gilbert Y(ale) 1924-

BRIEF ENTRY: Born May 11, 1924, in Brooklyn, N.Y. American political scientist, educator, administrator, and author. Until 1966 Steiner was a professor at the University of Illinois at Urbana-Champaign and director of the university's Institute for Government and Public Affairs. He then became a senior fellow of the Brookings Institution. Steiner wrote *Social Insecurity: The Politics of Welfare* (Rand McNally, 1966), *The State of Welfare* (Brookings Institution, 1971), *The Children's Cause* (Brookings Institution, 1976), and *The Futility of Family Policy* (Brookings Institution, 1981). He edited *The Abortion Dispute and the American System* (Brookings Institution, 1983). *Address:* 5408 Center St., Chevy Chase, Md. 20015; and Brookings Institution, 1775 Massachusetts Ave. N.W., Washington, D.C. 20036.

BIOGRAPHICAL/CRITICAL SOURCES:

PERIODICALS

Commonweal, December 3, 1971.
New York Times Book Review, July 18, 1971, February 20, 1977.
Washington Post Book World, April 24, 1977.

* * *

STEINER, Susan Clemmer 1947-

PERSONAL: Born April 22, 1947, in Sellersville, Pa.; daughter of Lester M. (in business) and Martha (a homemaker; maiden name, Derstine) Clemmer; married Samuel Jay Steiner (a librarian), August 2, 1969. *Education:* Goshen College, B.A., 1969; Associated Mennonite Biblical Seminaries, M.Div., 1982. *Religion:* Mennonite.

ADDRESSES: Home—3-87 Westmount N., Waterloo, Ontario, Canada N2L 5G5.

CAREER: Provident Bookstores, book buyer in Kitchener, Ontario, 1969-79, and in London, Ontario, 1974-79; Mennonite Conference of Ontario and Quebec, Waterloo, Ontario, youth minister, 1982-85; religion teacher, 1982—. Member of Mennonite Board of Education, 1983—.

WRITINGS:

Joining the Army That Sheds No Blood, Herald Press, 1982.
How to Teach Peace to Youth, Herald Press, 1986.

Also author of Mennonite church school curriculum material. Editor of ''Women's Concerns Report'' of Mennonite Central Committee, 1982-84.

STERN, Rudi 1936-

BRIEF ENTRY: Born November 30, 1936, in New Haven, Conn. American artist, educator, business director, and author. Stern is often described as a kinetic light artist. His neon creations have been widely exhibited throughout the United States. A co-founder of the Global Village Video Resource Center, he serves as co-director of the enterprise. He established the Let There Be Neon Workshop in 1972. Stern's artistic work has been funded by the Rockefeller Foundation, the John D. Rockefeller III Fund, and the National Endowment for the Arts. Stern wrote *Let There Be Neon* (Abrams, 1977). *Address:* c/o Let There Be Neon Workshop, 451 West Broadway, New York, N.Y. 10012.

BIOGRAPHICAL/CRITICAL SOURCES:

BOOKS

Acton, Jay, *Mug Shots: Who's Who in the New Earth,* World Publishing, 1972.

PERIODICALS

New York Times Book Review, June 24, 1979.

* * *

STEVENSON, Ian (Pretyman) 1918-

BRIEF ENTRY: Born October 31, 1918, in Montreal, Quebec, Canada. American psychiatrist, educator, and author. Stevenson became a professor of psychiatry at the University of Virginia in 1957; he was named Carlson Professor in 1967. He has also been president of the Parapsychological Association and has studied reincarnation, out-of-body experiences, and precognition. Stevenson wrote *Twenty Cases Suggestive of Reincarnation* (American Society for Psychical Research, 1966), *The Psychiatric Examination* (Little, Brown, 1969), *Telepathic Impressions: A Review and Report of Thirty-Five New Cases* (University Press of Virginia, 1970), and *Unlearned Language: New Studies in Xenoglossy* (University Press of Virginia, 1984). *Address:* Wintergreen, Old Lynchburg R.S., Charlottesville, Va.; and Division of Parapsychology, Medical Center, University of Virginia, Box 152, Charlottesville, Va. 22901.

BIOGRAPHICAL/CRITICAL SOURCES:

BOOKS

American Men and Women of Science: The Physical and Biological Sciences, 15th edition, Bowker, 1982.
Encyclopedia of Occultism and Parapsychology, Gale, 1978.

* * *

STEVENSON, James 1929(?)-

PERSONAL: Born c. 1929 in New York, N.Y.; children: nine. *Education:* Graduated from Yale University.

ADDRESSES: Home—Connecticut. *Agent*—c/o Greenwillow Books, 105 Madison Ave., New York, N.Y. 10016.

CAREER: Life Magazine, New York City, reporter, until 1955; *New Yorker,* New York City, cartoonist and writer for ''Talk of the Town,'' 1956-63; illustrator and writer. *Military service:* Served in U.S. Marine Corps.

AWARDS, HONORS: New York Times Book Review named *Could Be Worse!* an outstanding book of the year in 1977;

School Library Journal named *Could Be Worse!* a best book for spring in 1977 and *Monty* a best book for spring in 1979; *New York Times* named *Howard* one of the best illustrated books of 1980.

WRITINGS:

Do Yourself a Favor, Kid (fiction), Macmillan, 1962.
(Illustrator) William K. Zinsser, *Weekend Guests: From "We're So Glad You Could Come" to "We're So Sorry You Have to Go," and Vice-Versa* (adult satire), Harper, 1963.
Sorry, Lady, This Beach Is Private (cartoons), Macmillan, 1963.
The Summer Houses (novel), Macmillan, 1963.
Sometimes, But Not Always (novel), Little, Brown, 1967.
Something Marvelous Is About to Happen (drawings), Harper, 1971.
(Illustrator) Sara G. Gilbert, *What's a Father For?: A Father's Guide to the Pleasures and Problems of Parenthood With Advice From the Experts*, Parents Magazine Press, 1975.
Let's Boogie (cartoons), Dodd, 1978.
Uptown Local, Downtown Express (vignettes), Viking, 1983.

SELF-ILLUSTRATED CHILDREN'S BOOKS

Walker, the Witch, and the Striped Flying Saucer, Little, Brown, 1969.
The Bear Who Had No Place to Go, Harper, 1972.
Here Comes Herb's Hurricane, Harper, 1973.
Cool Jack and the Beanstalk: A James Stevenson Production, Penguin, 1976.
Could Be Worse!, Greenwillow, 1977.
Wilfred the Rat, Greenwillow, 1977.
(With Edwina Stevenson) *"Help!" Yelled Maxwell*, Greenwillow, 1978.
The Sea View Hotel, Greenwillow, 1978.
The Worst Person in the World, Greenwillow, 1978.
Monty, Greenwillow, 1978.
Winston, Newton, Elton, and Ed (stories), Greenwillow, 1978.
Fast Friends: Two Stories (contains "Murray and Fred" and "Thomas and Clem"), Greenwillow, 1979.
Clams Can't Sing, Greenwillow, 1980.
Howard, Greenwillow, 1980.
That Terrible Halloween Night, Greenwillow, 1980.
The Night After Christmas, Greenwillow, 1981, also published as *The Night After Christmas: Story and Pictures*, Morrow, 1981.
The Wish Card Ran Out!, Greenwillow, 1981.
Oliver, Clarence, and Violet, Greenwillow, 1982.
We Can't Sleep, Greenwillow, 1982.
Barbara's Birthday, Greenwillow, 1983.
Grandpa's Great City Tour, Greenwillow, 1983.
The Great Big Especially Beautiful Easter Egg, Greenwillow, 1983.
What's Under My Bed?, Greenwillow, 1983.
Worse Than Willy!, Greenwillow, 1984.

ILLUSTRATOR OF CHILDREN'S BOOKS

James Walker Stevenson, *If I Owned a Candy Factory*, Little, Brown, 1968.
Eric Stevenson, *Tony and the Toll Collector*, Little, Brown, 1969.
Lavinia Ross, *Alec's Sand Castle*, Harper, 1972.
Alan Arkin, *Tony's Hard Work Day*, Harper, 1972.
John Donovan, *Good Old James*, Harper, 1975.
Janet Schulman, *Jack the Bum and the Haunted House*, Greenwillow, 1977.

Schulman, *Jack the Bum and the Halloween Handout*, Greenwillow, 1977.
Schulman, *Jack the Bum and the UFO*, Greenwillow, 1978.
Charlotte Zolotow, *Say It!*, Greenwillow, 1980.
Jack Prelutsky, *The Baby Uggs Are Hatching*, Greenwillow, 1982.
Gage Wilson (pseudonym of Mary Q. Steele) *Cully Cully and the Bear*, Greenwillow, 1983.
Louis Phillips, *How Do You Get a Horse Out of the Bathtub?: Profound Answers to Preposterous Questions*, Viking, 1983.

Also author of syndicated political comic strip.

SIDELIGHTS: A noted humorist and children's author, James Stevenson began primarily as a suburban satirist, expanding his subjects to include social criticism, nostalgia, and children's problems. Stevenson's early novels and cartoons explored suburban lifestyles. For example, one cartoon during the 1960's pictured an elderly commuter in a business suit sitting on a railroad bench in his living room. The commuter's wife explains: "He retired last January, but he's been tapering off gradually." After considering this cartoon and similar works, one *Newsweek* writer indicated that Stevenson's "understated and gentle humor exploited incongruity and anachronisms to penetrate facades and assumptions" of suburbia.

Likewise, other critics found that Stevenson's autobiographical novel *Sometimes, But Not Always* shows the ludicrousness of contemporary life through suburbanite Joe Roberts, a laboring gag writer plagued by financial stress. Roberts works several jobs to attain financial security for his harried wife and many children, but he nevertheless suffers with a recurring nightmare that a banker forecloses on his home and family. Roberts eventually becomes the idea man for "So What Else Is New?," a television series affectionately known as "SWEIN." In this role he persuades Rosco Ritz, a has-been vaudevillian, to appear on a show in which the song-and-dance man is cruelly humiliated. When Ritz dies, Roberts is beset by guilt. He flees to the town dump where he decides amid the junk that everyone is "obsolete" and disposable. After reading *Sometimes, But Not Always*, a *Time* reviewer commented that "author Stevenson has combined a sardonic view of showbiz with verbal cartooning that veers into wild hallucination."

By the late 1960's Stevenson moved from covering suburbanites to lampooning national problems, and a *Newsweek* reporter observed that "his political art, like his suburban drawings, remains humorous and even playful." One of Stevenson's first social commentaries was a six-page *New Yorker* cartoon spread that satirized the U.S. military. Titled "The ABCs of Your ABM: A Public Service Pamphlet From Your Defense Department," the feature advocated disarmament and parodied Pentagonese. Similarly, part of Stevenson's 1971 book *Something Marvelous Is About to Happen* satirized government investigative panels by scrutinizing the credentials of a Professor Lamberti, a cult hero and xylophonist. The outcome of the inquiry is of course vague, for as S. K. Oberbeck explained in *Newsweek*, "That's Stevenson's world." "In one flourish," Oberbeck continued, "he captures the frustration and befuddlement of modern man awash in government's and media's programed inconclusiveness." However delighted Oberbeck was with Stevenson's political satire, the reviewer still maintained that the humorist's "forays into nostalgia are really his forte." For example, in *Something Marvelous Is About to Happen* Stevenson doodles a portrait of his early life, including a disclosure that his brother's hidden diary was boring.

In addition to recalling his childhood, Stevenson explores the predicaments of most children in his many juvenile books, particularly those featuring Mary Ann, Louie, and their grandfather. For example, *Worse Than Willy* confronts the problem of sibling rivalry. Mary Ann and Louie quickly become jealous of their parents' doting on their new brother Willy. They complain to Grandpa, who tells them of his similar dilemma years ago when his brother Wainwright was born. Grandpa felt ignored while Wainwright was hugged and kissed. So he threw blocks at his brother, ruined the baby's toys and books, and always received full blame, for his parents never found fault with Wainwright. Mary Ann and Louie finally concede that Wainwright was ''worse than Willy,'' so Grandpa tells them an elaborate tale of adventure in which young Wainwright saves his life.

Elizabeth Crow, for one, praised *Worse Than Willy* in the *New York Times Book Review* for putting a child's problem into perspective. ''This is a terrific book for little children,'' she remarked, ''good-humored, hysterically funny and true about sibling rivalry.... Mr. Stevenson understands that this too shall pass, and that it'll pass a lot quicker if you make up a funny story about it.''

An earlier Mary Ann and Louie story, *That Terrible Halloween Night*, has the children attempting to frighten Grandpa because he is apparently unimpressed by the holiday. They disguise themselves and the dog, but Grandpa remains collected; rather than being scared, he frightens them with a spooky story of his adventures as a youth in a ''strange'' house. According to a *Washington Post Book World* reviewer, in *That Terrible Halloween Night* ''Stevenson, as always, manages to convey an entire world—its style, its atmosphere, and the emotions of its inhabitants—through a few strokes of his pen.'' Karla Kuski expressed a similar sentiment about Stevenson's work in general. Writing in the *New York Times Book Review*, she maintained that ''whether writing or drawing, Mr. Stevenson understands perfectly the strength of a simple understated line and a quiet laugh.''

BIOGRAPHICAL/CRITICAL SOURCES:

PERIODICALS

Atlantic, July, 1963.
Best Sellers, August 15, 1967.
Chicago Tribune Book World, October 5, 1980, April 10, 1983.
Christian Science Monitor, November 6, 1969, November 10, 1980.
Commonweal, November 11, 1977.
Los Angeles Times Book Review, August 14, 1983.
National Observer, July 24, 1967.
Newsweek, April 8, 1963, July 14, 1969, December 20, 1971, December 11, 1978, December 18, 1978, December 7, 1981.
New Yorker, July 20, 1963, August 5, 1967, December 11, 1971, December 2, 1972, December 6, 1982.
New York Times, August 4, 1972.
New York Times Book Review, July 23, 1967, August 7, 1977, November 13, 1977, April 30, 1978, June 17, 1979, October 7, 1979, April 27, 1980, October 26, 1980, April 26, 1981, November 15, 1981, April 25, 1982, November 14, 1982, March 27, 1983, April 24, 1983, May 20, 1984.

Saturday Review/World, December 4, 1973.
Spectator, November 13, 1971.
Time, April 12, 1963, August 4, 1967, December 4, 1978.
Times Educational Supplement, December 14, 1979, January 18, 1980, June 5, 1981, February 18, 1983.
Times Literary Supplement, October 21, 1977, December 14, 1979, March 27, 1981.
Village Voice, December 11, 1978.
Washington Post Book World, October 26, 1969, April 13, 1980, October 12, 1980, December 13, 1981, May 13, 1984.*

—*Sketch by Charity Anne Dorgan*

*   *   *

STINNETT, Tim Moore   1901-1985

OBITUARY NOTICE—See index for *CA* sketch: Born May 2, 1901, in Junction City, Ark.; died April 5, 1985. Educator, editor, and author. A respected authority on education, Stinnett served the National Education Association in executive capacities from 1948 to 1966, when he ended five years as assistant executive secretary for professional development and welfare. He also taught at Texas A & M University in the late 1960's. Stinnett wrote many volumes on education, including *The Teacher and Professional Organizations, Teachers in Politics: The Larger Roles, Turmoil in Teaching,* and, with Kenneth T. Henson, *America's Public Schools in Transition: Future Trends and Issues.* He also edited works such as *The Teacher Dropout* and *Unfinished Business of the Teaching Profession in the 1970's.*

OBITUARIES AND OTHER SOURCES:

PERIODICALS

Little Rock Gazette (Arkansas), April 7, 1985.

*   *   *

STOKES, Doris   1919-

BRIEF ENTRY: Born in 1919 in Grantham, Lincolnshire, England. British psychic and author. A spiritualist for more than thirty-five years, Stokes has been endorsed as a bona fide clairaudient by the Spiritualists National Union. In her book *Voices in My Ear: The Autobiography of a Medium* (A. Ellis, 1980) Stokes wrote that she first became aware of her psychic abilities while still in her teens. She did nothing, however, to develop her mediumship until after the death of her infant son many years later. According to Stokes, she had been warned of the child's death by her deceased father, who had appeared to her in a vision. Since then she has developed an international reputation as a psychic medium and is particularly known for her ability to hear spirit voices. Stokes has appeared before large audiences in Britain and on popular radio and television programs in the United States, Australia, and New Zealand. A second autobiographical volume, *More Voices in My Ear* (A. Ellis), was published in 1981.

BIOGRAPHICAL/CRITICAL SOURCES:

BOOKS

Encyclopedia of Occultism and Parapsychology, Supplement, Gale, 1982.

STONE, Louis   1910(?)-1985

OBITUARY NOTICE: Born c. 1910 in New York, N.Y.; died of heart and kidney failure, March 16, 1985, in New York, N.Y. Financial executive, investment analyst, publisher, and financial writer. Stone founded the influential *Louis Stone Monthly Investment Letter* in 1953 and published it until his death. He also contributed to the *Boston Globe* and wrote for *Investment Dealers Digest.* A vice-president of Shearson Lehman Brothers, Stone was associated with a number of major investment companies during his fifty-year career on Wall Street. He served under General Dwight D. Eisenhower during World War II as a financial officer in the Supreme Headquarters of the Allied Expeditionary Force.

OBITUARIES AND OTHER SOURCES:

PERIODICALS

New York Times, March 19, 1985.

*   *   *

STONEMAN, Paul   1947-

PERSONAL: Born July 12, 1947, in Hoddesdon, England; son of L. H. and V. E. (Gillman) Stoneman; married Catherine A. Watkinson (a computer programmer), September 20, 1969; children: Alex Paul, Madeline Grace. *Education:* University of Warwick, B.A., 1968; London School of Economics and Political Science, London, M.Sc., 1969; Cambridge University, Ph.D., 1974.

ADDRESSES: Home—30 Cannon Park Rd., Coventry CV4 7AY, England. *Office*—Department of Economics, University of Warwick, Coventry CV4 7AL, England.

CAREER: University of Warwick, Coventry, England, lecturer, 1973-80, senior lecturer, 1980-84, reader in economics, 1984—. Associate managing editor of *International Journal of Industrial Organisation.*

WRITINGS:

Technological Diffusion and the Computer Revolution, Cambridge University Press, 1976.
(With Keith G. Cowling and others) *Mergers and Economic Performance,* Cambridge University Press, 1979.
The Economic Analysis of Technological Change, Oxford University Press, 1983.

Contributor to economic journals.

WORK IN PROGRESS: The Economic Analysis of Technology Policy, publication expected in 1986; research on technological change.

*   *   *

STOPES, M. C.
See STOPES, Marie (Charlotte) Carmichael

*   *   *

STOPES, Marie C.
See STOPES, Marie (Charlotte) Carmichael

*   *   *

STOPES, Marie (Charlotte) Carmichael   1880-1958
(Erica Fay, M. C. Stopes, Marie C. Stopes)

BRIEF ENTRY: Born in 1880 in Surrey, England (one source

says Edinburgh, Scotland); died October 2, 1958, in Dorking, Surrey, England. British scientist and author. Best known as a birth control pioneer, Stopes, with her second husband, H. V. Roe, founded Britain's first birth control clinic in 1921. Her landmark books on marriage and contraception, noted for their candor, were forerunners to a multitude of books on sex technique appearing in the twentieth century and included two best sellers, *Married Love* and *Wise Parenthood,* both published in 1918. Stopes's views on contraception incurred the ire of the Catholic Church, and throughout her life she found herself embroiled in public and religious controversy.

Before embarking on her birth control work, Stopes took university degrees in botany and geology and became the first female scientist to join the faculty of Manchester University. She wrote many scientific papers as well as several science books, including *The Study of Plant Life* (1910), under the name M. C. Stopes. Stopes's literary pursuits involved writing poems, plays, and fiction, sometimes using the pseudonym Erica Fay. Publications credited to the Fay pseudonym include a book of verse, *Kings and Heroes* (1937), and a book of fairy tales, *A Road to Fairyland* (1926). Writings under the name Marie C. Stopes include *A Japanese Mediaevel Drama* (1909). *Address:* Dorking, Surrey, England.

BIOGRAPHICAL/CRITICAL SOURCES:

BOOKS

Longman Companion to English Literature, 2nd edition, Longman, 1977.
Makers of Modern Culture, Facts on File, 1981.
1000 Makers of the Twentieth Century, David & Charles, 1971.

PERIODICALS

Times (London), October 3, 1958.

*   *   *

STOTZ, Charles Morse   1898-1985

OBITUARY NOTICE: Born August 1, 1898, in Pittsburgh, Pa.; died March 5, 1985, in Fort Myers, Fla. Architect and author. A specialist in architectural restoration, Stotz was among the first architects in the United States to practice in that field. During his career he directed the restoration of such nineteenth-century Pennsylvania buildings as Old Economy near Ambridge and the original engine house and derrick of Drake's Oil Well in Titusville. Stotz wrote books on Pennsylvania's architecture and history, including *The Early Architecture of Western Pennsylvania, The Architectural Heritage of Early Western Pennsylvania,* and *Point of Empire: Conflict at the Forks of the Ohio.*

OBITUARIES AND OTHER SOURCES:

BOOKS

American Architects Directory, 3rd edition, Bowker, 1970.
Who's Who in America, 39th edition, Marquis, 1976.

PERIODICALS

New York Times, March 9, 1985.

*   *   *

STRATTON, Rebecca
(Lucy Gillen)

BRIEF ENTRY: British civil servant and author. Stratton worked at the Coventry county courthouse from 1957 until 1967, when she became a full-time writer. She has produced more than eighty romance novels, including *The Black Invader* (Mills & Boon, 1981), *Black Enigma* (Mills & Boon, 1981), and *The Silken Cage* (Mills & Boon, 1981). Her most traditional romances appear under the pseudonym Lucy Gillen; among them are *Heron's Point* (Harlequin, 1978), *Hepburn's Quay* (Mills & Boon, 1979), and *The Storm Eagle* (Mills & Boon, 1980). *Address:* c/o Mills & Boon Ltd., 15-16 Brooks Mews, London W1A 1DR, England.

BIOGRAPHICAL/CRITICAL SOURCES:

BOOKS

The Writers Directory: 1984-1986, St. James Press, 1983.

*   *   *

STRINGFELLOW, (Frank) William   1928-1985

OBITUARY NOTICE—See index for *CA* sketch: Born April 26, 1928, in Johnston, R.I.; died of a metabolic disorder, March 2, 1985, in Providence, R.I. Lawyer, educator, lay theologian, activist, and author. Stringfellow was an adamant supporter of equal rights. His work as an attorney was marked by the continued defense of poor people, drug users, and homosexuals. Stringfellow also advocated priesthood for Episcopalian women and racial integration for Christian churches. In 1970 he was arrested for harboring a fugitive, the Reverend Daniel Berrigan, who had been convicted of destroying military draft records. The charges against Stringfellow were eventually dismissed, and his experiences were documented in his *Suspect Tenderness: The Ethics of the Berrigan Witness.* Among Stringfellow's other books are *A Private and Public Faith, Instead of Death, Dissenter in a Great Society: A Christian View of America in Crisis,* and, with Anthony Towne, two volumes on controversial church reformer and mystic Bishop James A. Pike, including *The Death and Life of Bishop Pike.*

OBITUARIES AND OTHER SOURCES:

BOOKS

The Writers Directory: 1984-1986, St. James Press, 1983.

PERIODICALS

Chicago Tribune, March 5, 1985.
Los Angeles Times, March 10, 1985.
Michigan Christian Advocate, March 18, 1985.
New York Times, March 4, 1985.
Washington Post, March 4, 1985.
Washington Times, March 4, 1985.

*   *   *

STRONG, Harrington
See McCULLEY, Johnston

*   *   *

STRUTT, Malcolm   1936-

PERSONAL: Born October 18, 1936, in Hull, England; son of Henry (a builder) and Selena (a hairdresser; maiden name, Gadie) Strutt. *Education:* Attended University of Warwick, beginning in 1983.

ADDRESSES: Home—Yew Tree Cottage, Spinfield Lane W., Marlow, Buckinghamshire SL7 2DB, England.

CAREER: British Broadcasting Corp., London, England, studio technician, 1958-70; yoga teacher in England and Ireland, 1972—. Director of Centre for Conscious Living; gives seminars and lectures on yoga; moderator for yoga teachers of Irish Yoga Association, 1977—.

WRITINGS:

A Stage One Course in Yoga, L. N. Fowler & Co., 1973.
A Stage Two Course in Yoga, L. N. Fowler & Co., 1973.
A Stage Three Course in Yoga, L. N. Fowler & Co., 1973.
Wholistic Health and Living Yoga, University of the Trees Press, 1976.

WORK IN PROGRESS: With Danielle Lessware, *Yoga Teachers Manual.*

SIDELIGHTS: Malcolm Strutt studied yoga with Paramahansa Yogananda's Self-Realization Fellowship, with B.K.S. Iyengar, and with Christopher Hills of California. Strutt told *CA:* "I was drawn into yoga after a long search for the way in which one might not only aspire to but also systematically work towards the stature of the great masters of the holy books. It was after reading the *Autobiography of a Yogi* by Paramahansa Yogananda, loaned to me by a friend at work, that a sudden internal change of values took place. I realized the end of my search and the start of a new way of life—how to practice the art and science of yoga."

*   *   *

STUART, Douglas (Keith)   1943-

PERSONAL: Born February 8, 1943, in Concord, Mass.; son of Streeter S. (in business) and Merle M. (in business; maiden name, Dierolf) Stuart; married Gayle J. Johnson (a teacher), June 26, 1971; children: Joanna, Eliza, Eden, Holly. *Education:* Harvard University, B.A., 1964, Ph.D., 1971; attended Yale University, 1964-66. *Religion:* Conservative Baptist.

ADDRESSES: Home—132 Old Topsfield Rd., Boxford, Mass. 01921. *Office*—Gordon-Conwell Theological Seminary, 130 Essex St., South Hamilton, Mass. 01982.

CAREER: Ordained Baptist minister, 1976; Gordon College, Wenham, Mass., instructor in Near Eastern history, 1968-69; Gordon-Conwell Theological Seminary, South Hamilton, Mass., assistant professor, 1971-77, associate professor, 1978-81, professor of Old Testament, 1981—. Co-chairman of Old Testament Colloquium at Boston Theological Institute; president of Boston area chapter of Huxley Institute for Biosocial Research, 1974—. Pastor in Lynn, Mass. and Haverhill, Mass., 1980-84.

MEMBER: American Schools of Oriental Research, Evangelical Theological Society, Society of Biblical Literature, Biblical Archaeological Society, Massachusetts Bible Society (member of board of trustees, 1980—), Boston Orthomolecular Society (president, 1976—).

WRITINGS:

Studies in Early Hebrew Meter, Harvard University Press, 1976.
Old Testament Exegesis: A Primer for Students and Pastors, Westminster, 1980, 2nd edition, 1984.
(Contributor) J. R. Michaels and Roger Nicole, editors, *Inerrancy and Common Sense,* Baker Book, 1980.
(With G. D. Fee) *How to Read the Bible for All Its Worth,* Zondervan, 1982.
Everybody's Favorite Bible Passages: Commentary, Westminster, 1985.

Hosea, Joel, Obadiah, Jonah, Nahum (commentaries), Word Books, in press.

Contributor to scholarly journals.

WORK IN PROGRESS: Ezekiel, a commentary, publication expected in 1987.

SIDELIGHTS: Douglas Stuart told *CA:* "I have tried to produce a balance of quite technical books and articles with quite popular books and articles, all from an evangelical Christian viewpoint. My greatest challenge in writing technical works is to synthesize accurately, to capture the essence of what a lot of scholars and their data add up to. But in popular writing, the greatest challenge is to clarify, to make things genuinely understandable for people who don't have the time and expertise to understand them otherwise, but who still want to understand them."

His views have been enhanced by studies in the Hebrew, Aramaic, Syriac, Akkadian, Ugaritic, Sumerian, and Egyptian languages.

He added: "As a conservative evangelical Christian, I hold to the belief that the Bible is fully accurate—inerrant, and this perspective means that most of what I write must always be measured for its consistency with the only body of literature that does its job perfectly. Even though I am writing about the Bible, it is the Bible itself that provides the objective standard for my work."

*   *   *

SUGITA, Yutaka   1930-

PERSONAL: Born July 13, 1930, in Ohmiya City, Japan; son of Aisaburo and Toshiko Sugita; married wife, Sadako, November 12, 1954; children: Takumi, Itaru. *Education:* Tokyo University of Education, B.A., 1953.

ADDRESSES: Home—1-42 Azuma-cho, Ohmiya City, Saitama Prefecture, Japan 330. *Office*—Atelier Sugita, 245 Tokyu Apt. 4-15-29 Mita, Minato-ku, Tokyo, Japan 108.

CAREER: Worked as a designer at Gakko Tosho Education Publishing Co., and as an art designer at Tosho Printing Co.; currently professor at Tsukuba National University; artist and in advertising.

WRITINGS:

SELF-ILLUSTRATED PICTURE BOOKS FOR CHILDREN

Minnano Onegai, Shiko-sha, 1965, published as *When We Dream,* with text by Kit Reed, Hawthorn, 1966.
Dobutsu AIUEO (title means "Animals ABC"), Kaisei-sha, 1977.
Oyasuminasai Ichi Nii San, Shiko-sha, 1971, published as *Goodnight, One, Two, Three,* Scroll Press, 1971, published in England as *One to Eleven,* Evans, 1971.
Minna Genkidesu, Shiko-sha, 1972, published as *The Flower Family,* McGraw, 1975.
Bokuwa Sensei, Shiko-sha, 1972, published as *My Friend Little John and Me,* McGraw, 1973.
Kabawa Kaba, Shiko-sha, 1973, published as *Helena the Unhappy Hippopotamus,* McGraw, 1973.
Monomane Kurochan, Shiko-sha, 1974, published as *Blackie, the Bird Who Could,* McGraw, 1974.
Kurochan to Ohmu, Shiko-sha, 1974, adaptation by Robin Hyman and Inge Hyman published as *Casper and the*

Rainbow Bird, Evans, 1975, translation from the Japanese by Hisako Aoki published by Barron, 1978.
Inemuri Robakun (title means "A Sleepy Donkey"), Kodansha, 1975.
Bokuno Wanage, Shiko-sha, 1976, translation by H. Aoki published as *Fly Hoops, Fly!,* Barron, 1979 (published in England as *Whoops, Hoops!,* Dent, 1980).
Yorimichishita Tenshi, Shiko-sha, 1977, published as *Angel,* Celestial Arts, 1979.
Ohkii Ishi Chiisai Ishi (title means "Hippo and Turtle"), Shiko-sha, 1978, adaptation by R. Hyman and I. Hyman published as *The Greatest Explorers in the World,* Evans, 1978.
Nezumi no Gochiso, Kodansha, 1978, published as *The Mouse's Feast,* Barron, 1980, Takaramono, 1979, adaptation by R. Hyman and I. Hyman published as *The Treasure Box,* Evans, 1980.
Ureshii Hi (title means "My Happy Day"), Shiko-sha, 1979.
Shiawaseno Isu (title means "The Happy Chair"), Shiko-sha, 1980.
Bokuwa Tobitai, Kodansha, 1981.
Kappino Booken, Kodansha, 1982.
Kakurenbo, Shiko-sha, 1982, adaptation by R. Hyman and I. Hyman published as *Peter's Magic Hide-and-Seek,* Evans, 1982.
Kurochan no Hirune (title means "Blackie and His Siesta"), Shiko-sha, 1983.

ILLUSTRATOR OF BOOKS FOR CHILDREN

Chizuko Kuratomi, *Okaasanwa Doko?,* Shiko-sha, 1966, adaptation by Anne Maley published as *Have You Seen My Mother?,* Carolrhoda Books, 1969.
Yasoo Takeichi and C. Kuratomi, *Boku Hanataroo,* Shiko-sha, 1967, adaptation by Robert Allen published as *Jamie and the Leopard,* Platt & Munk, 1969.
Kuratomi, *Ohayoo,* Shiko-sha, 1969, published as *Run, Run Chase the Sun,* Evans, 1969, adaptation by Stewart Beach published as *Good Morning, Sun's Up,* Scroll Press, 1970.
Yakeichi, *Hoshiwa Mitano,* Shiko-sha, 1970, published as *Wake Up, Wake Up, Little Tree,* Thomas Nelson, 1970.
Hans Christian Andersen, *The Little Match Girl,* Sekai Bunka-sha, 1971.
Andersen, *The Snow Queen,* Sekai Bunka-sha, 1971.
Nankichi Niimi, *Gacho no Tanjobi* (title means "Goose's Birthday"), Dai-Nihon Tosho, 1973.
Takeshi Sakuma, *Bokumo Ittemiyoo* (title means "The Joyful Journey"), Shiko-sha, 1982.

Also illustrator of *Chikaramochi no Hanashi* (title means "A Story of a Strong Man"), by Hisashi Inoue, Japan Reader's Digest.

*   *   *

SUK, Julie

PERSONAL: Born in Mobile, Ala.; daughter of Samuel Palmer, Jr. (an attorney) and Florence (Hollingsworth) Gaillard; married William Joseph Suk; children: Julie Florence, William Gaillard, Palmer Gaillard. *Education:* Attended Stephens College and University of Alabama.

ADDRESSES: Home—845 Greentree Dr., Charlotte, N.C. 28211.

CAREER: Charlotte Nature Museum, Charlotte, N.C., teacher and program coordinator, 1967-78; *Southern Poetry Review,* Charlotte, N.C., associate editor and business manager, 1978-

79. Creative writing teacher in adult education program at Queen's College, Charlotte.

WRITINGS:

(Editor with Anne Newman; and contributor) *Bear Crossings* (poems), New South Co., 1978.
The Medicine Woman (poems), St. Andrews Press, 1980.

Contributor of poems to magazines, including *Poetry Now, Carolina Quarterly,* and *Shenandoah.*

WORK IN PROGRESS: Point of Departure, poems.

SIDELIGHTS: Julie Suk told *CA:* "When Anne Newman and I initially began collecting work for *Bear Crossings,* we deliberately avoided any move toward organization. Instead, we let the poems decree their own categories as they fell into place thematically. Even after we became more selective, choice was often arbitrary as we found bears contrary critters, adaptable to more than one of the six sections of the book. Consequently, the short prose quotations, which introduce each group of poems, not only emphasize the various aspects of 'bearness' in man, but also the rich variety of imaginative representation in subject, tone, and technique. Anne wrote the foreword and I contributed with an introductory poem. Now in its second printing, *Bear Crossings* was a labor of love, and we are more than grateful that *Library Journal* described it as 'the best small press book of this year or any year.'

"As for my own work, the more I write the more humbled I am by the process, and find it difficult to describe poetic views and methods without repeating what others have said better. Perhaps it is best to quote the artist Yves Tanguy: 'It amuses me to imagine what is beyond a hill. I want so much to represent those things I will never see.' I understand that to mean those presences around and within the tangibles of this world, an energy that is our privilege to transform."

*   *   *

SULLIVAN, Edward A(nthony)   1936-

PERSONAL: Born January 1, 1936, in Arlington, Mass.; son of Edward A. (a police officer) and Helen (a homemaker) Sullivan; married Rose L. Saia (a teacher), November 16, 1963; children: Edward, Paul, Mary Rose, Joseph, John. *Education:* Boston College, B.S., 1956; Boston State College, M.Ed., 1958; Michigan State University, Ph.D., 1969.

ADDRESSES: Home—20 Larchwood Dr., Cumberland, R.I. 02864. *Office*—Department of Education, Providence College, Eaton St. and River Ave., Providence, R.I. 02918.

CAREER: High school teacher of chemistry in Wilmington, Mass., 1956-65; intern at Mott Foundation, Flint, Mich., 1965-66; South Kingston Junior High School, South Kingston, R.I., principal, 1966-68; Michigan State University, East Lansing, Mich., instructor in education, 1968-69; Providence College, Providence, R.I., associate professor of education, 1969—.

MEMBER: Rhode Island Association of Teacher Educators, Phi Delta Kappa.

AWARDS, HONORS: National Science Foundation fellowships, 1959, 1961, and 1963.

WRITINGS:

The Future: Human Ecology and Education, ETC Publications, 1975.

Contributor of articles to education periodicals, including *Phi Delta Kappan, School Board Journal,* and *Community School Journal.*

WORK IN PROGRESS: Identification of Tasks in Teacher Evaluation, publication expected in 1985.

SIDELIGHTS: Edward A. Sullivan told *CA:* "My writing has been motivated by my interests. If I am interested in a subject, I research it and then write about it."

*   *   *

SULLIVAN, Elizabeth L.   1904(?)-1985

OBITUARY NOTICE: Born c. 1904; died in 1985 in Boston, Mass. Critic. Sullivan spent forty-five years at the *Boston Globe,* retiring in 1971 from her career as a television and radio critic.

OBITUARIES:

PERIODICALS

Detroit Free Press, April 3, 1985.

*   *   *

SULLIVAN, Jerry   1938-

PERSONAL: Born November 3, 1938, in Chicago, Ill.; married Glenda Daniel (a writer), April 11, 1974; children: Eleanor. *Education:* Attended University of Illinois; received B.A. from University of Illinois at Chicago Circle. *Politics:* "Yes."

ADDRESSES: Home and office—4422 North Malden, Chicago, Ill. 60640.

CAREER: Writer. *Military service:* U.S. Marine Corps, 1956-58.

MEMBER: National Audobon Society, Sierra Club, American Society of Journalists and Authors, Chicago Audobon Society (member of board of directors).

WRITINGS:

(With wife, Glenda Daniel) *Hiking Trails in the Midwest,* Contemporary Books, 1974, revised edition, 1980.
(With Daniel) *Hiking Trails in the Southern Mountains,* Contemporary Books, 1975.
(With Daniel) *A Naturalist's Guide to the North Woods,* Sierra Books, 1981.
(With Daniel) *National Parks of the Great Lakes,* Chicago Review Press, 1984.

Author of "Media," an occasional column in *Playboy.* Editor of newsletter of Chicago Audubon Society.

*   *   *

SULLIVAN, Richard E(ugene)   1921-

BRIEF ENTRY: Born March 27, 1921, in Doniphan, Neb. American historian, educator, and author. Sullivan has been a professor of medieval history at Michigan State University since 1954. He was a Fulbright fellow in Belgium and a Guggenheim fellow, both in 1961. Sullivan's writings include *A Short History of Western Civilization* (Knopf, 1960), *Heirs of the Roman Empire* (Cornell University Press, 1960), *Aix-la-Chapelle in the Age of Charlemagne* (University of Oklahoma Press, 1963), *Critical Issues in History* (Heath, 1966), and *Essays on Medieval Civilizaion* (University of Texas Press, 1978). *Address:* 1182 Bryant Dr., East Lansing, Mich. 48823;

and College of Arts and Sciences, Michigan State University, East Lansing, Mich. 48224.

BIOGRAPHICAL/CRITICAL SOURCES:

BOOKS

Directory of American Scholars, Volume I: *History,* 8th edition, Bowker, 1982.

* * *

SUTTON, Carol   1933-1985

OBITUARY NOTICE: Born June 29, 1933, in St. Louis, Mo.; died of cancer, February 19, 1985, in Louisville, Ky. Journalist. Sutton became the first woman ever to head the news operation of a major U.S. daily newspaper when she was named managing editor of the Louisville *Courier-Journal* in 1974. After initially serving the *Courier-Journal* as a secretary in 1955, Sutton was promoted to reporter. In 1963 she was named women's editor, a post she held until becoming managing editor. She later acted as senior editor of the jointly operated *Courier-Journal* and *Louisville Times* and served as assistant to the publisher of the two newspapers. In 1973 she wrote a series of award-winning articles on New York clothing manufacturers' gifts to out-of-town fashion reporters. Under Sutton's direction, the *Courier-Journal* won a 1975 Pulitzer Prize for its photographic coverage of events relating to school desegregation. *Time* magazine named Sutton one of its twelve Women of the Year in 1976.

OBITUARIES AND OTHER SOURCES:

BOOKS

Who's Who of American Women, 10th edition, Marquis, 1977.

PERIODICALS

Chicago Tribune, February 21, 1985.
Newsweek, September 2, 1974.
New York Times, February 20, 1985.
Time, January 5, 1976.
Washington Post, February 20, 1985.

* * *

SWIFT, Joan   1926-

PERSONAL: Born November 2, 1926, in Rochester, N.Y.; daughter of Elbert (a newspaper writer) and Lorraine Angevine; married Wayne Swift (a manager), February 14, 1953; children: Lauren Margaret, Lisa Andrea. *Education:* Duke University, A.B., 1948; University of Washington, Seattle, M.A., 1965.

ADDRESSES: Home—18520 Sound View Pl., Edmonds, Wash. 98020.

CAREER: Storm Advertising, Rochester, N.Y., copywriter, 1950-54; poet and author. Teacher of adult workshops at public schools in Edmonds, Wash., 1966-68; teacher of adult poetry workshops at Snoline Young Men's Christian Association, 1976-78; teacher of poetry workshops for gifted junior high school students in Edmonds, 1977, 1981; gives poetry readings at colleges, universities, libraries, and poetry festivals. Member of Edmonds Arts Commission, 1976-81.

MEMBER: Poetry Society of America, Phi Beta Kappa.

AWARDS, HONORS: Award from Academy of American Poets, 1965, for poems "Lost," "Earthquakes," and "Vancouver Island"; Lucille Medwick Memorial Award from Poetry Society of America, 1982, for "The Alphabet of Coal"; fellow of National Endowment for the Arts, 1982; resident poet at the Ossabaw Foundation, Ossabaw Island, Ga., 1982, and Yaddo, Saratoga Springs, N.Y., 1984.

WRITINGS:

This Element (poems), Alan Swallow, 1965.
Brackett's Landing: A History of Early Edmonds, Washington State American Revolution Bicentennial Commission, 1975.
Parts of Speech (poems), Confluence, 1978.
The Dark Path of Our Names (poems), Dragon Gate, 1985.

WORK IN ANTHOLOGIES

Fifty Contemporary Poets: The Creative Process, McKay, 1977.
Extended Outlooks: The Iowa Review Collection of Contemporary Women Writers, Macmillan, 1982.
Rain in the Forest, Light in the Trees: Contemporary Poetry From the Northwest, Owl Creek Press, 1983.

OTHER

Contributor of more than one hundred poems, articles, and reviews to magazines, including *Nation, Yankee, Saturday Review, Atlantic, New Yorker,* and *Poetry Northwest,* and newspapers.

SIDELIGHTS: Joan Swift told *CA:* "I write many of my poems as a way of explaining things to myself, of getting matters straight. Others are written to distill the experience and rid it of whatever clutter that accompanied it, or to recreate the experience in a new light. I hope to transmit to the reader the emotion of the experience so that the reader can feel what I felt, and can know what he or she feels too. I think I write best about people, but I have a strong attachment for the natural world as well."

* * *

SZYMANSKI, Albert (John)   1942(?)-1985

OBITUARY NOTICE: Born c. 1942; died of a self-inflicted gunshot wound c. March 1, 1985, in Eugene, Ore. Sociologist, educator, and author. Szymanski joined the faculty of the University of Oregon in 1970 and became a full professor in 1984. His books include *The Capitalist State and the Politics of Class, Class Struggles in Socialist Poland,* and *Human Rights in the Soviet Union.*

OBITUARIES:

PERIODICALS

Register-Guard (Eugene, Ore.), March 12, 1985.

T

TABACK, Simms 1932-

BRIEF ENTRY: Born February 13, 1932, in New York, N.Y. American artist, educator, illustrator, and author. Taback graduated with a degree in art from Cooper Union and attended the School of Visual Arts in New York City, where he later served as an instructor in illustration and design. He wrote and illustrated *Joseph Had a Little Overcoat* (Random House, 1977), a children's book based on a Far Eastern European folk song. Taback has illustrated several children's books by other authors, including *Please Share That Peanut!* (Harcourt, 1967)— a work designated one of ten best illustrated books of the year by the *New York Times*—as well as *Too Much Noise* (Houghton, 1967), *Jabberwocky and Other Frabjous Nonsense* (Crown, 1967), *Amazing Maze* (Dutton, 1969), *Euphonia and the Flood* (Parent's Magazine Press, 1976), and *Laughing Together* (Four Winds Press, 1977). *Address:* 38 East 21st St., New York, N.Y. 10010.

BIOGRAPHICAL/CRITICAL SOURCES:

BOOKS

Who's Who in American Art, 16th edition, Bowker, 1984.

* * *

TANAKA, Beatrice 1932-

PERSONAL: Born March 1, 1932, in Cernauti, Romania (now Chernovtsy, U.S.S.R.); daughter of Paul (a lawyer) and Clara (Spitzer) Lauder; married Flavio-Shiro Tanaka (a painter under name Flavio-Shiro), July 13, 1955; children: Josue, Noemi. *Education:* Attended Guiguard School of Art, 1947-50, Ecole Paul Colin, Atelier d'Essai des Decorateurs-Maquettistes, 1951-54, and Universite du Theatre des Nations, 1961-62.

ADDRESSES: Home—Paris, France.

CAREER: Set and costume designer for Brazilian and French theatres, 1954—, including work for Escola de Samba Portela, in Rio de Janeiro, Brazil, University of Bahia, Festival de Liege, Comedie de la Loire, and Festival de Hammamet. Freelance advertising designer in Brazil and France, 1959-61. Teacher of crafts classes for children and puppetry classes for the elderly; organizer of exhibits of drawings by children of Third World countries.

MEMBER: Sociedade Brasileira de Autores de Teatro, Societe des Auteurs et Compositeurs Dramatiques, Societe des Gens de Lettres, Illustrators Union, Writers Union, Set Designers Union.

AWARDS, HONORS: Prize for best costumes at Sao Paulo International Art Biennial, 1961, and Novi Sad Triennial, 1972; sets and costume awards from Universite du Theatre des Nations, 1962, for "Don Perlimplin"; Prix Leon Chancerel from Association Theatre Enfance Jeunesse, 1968, for children's play "Equipee bizarre au Cirque Basile"; Diplome from organization Loisires Jeunes, 1971, for "Le Tresor de l'Homme," 1972, for "La Savane enchantee," and 1976, for "La Montagne aux trois questions"; Best of the Best Award from International Jugendbibliothek, 1971, for "Le Tresor de l'Homme."

WRITINGS:

(With Francoise Douvaines and Pierre Marchand) *Tresores de la plage* (children's craft book), Edicope, 1971, translation by Halina Tunikowska published as *Seaside Treasures,* Mills & Boon, 1971.
(Author of adaptation) *The Tortoise and the Sword: A Vietnamese Legend* (self-illustrated children's book), Lothrop, 1972.
(Contributor) Marianne Carus and Clifton Fadiman, editors, *Cricket's Choice,* Open Court, 1974.
(With Marie-Francoise Heron and Michele Rivol) *Joyeux Papiers* (children's craft book), Gallimard, 1975, translation published as *Fun With Paper,* Collins & World (London), 1975.
Aktionsbuch (children's book), Otto Maier Verlag, 1982, translation by Anthea Bell published as *Disguise Workshop,* Pepper Press, 1982.
(And illustrator) *Kantjil's Tigerwar* (picture book with cassette), Vif Argent, 1984.
(And illustrator) *Savitri,* Editions La Farandole, 1984.
Beans, Beef, and Bang (picture-book), Edicoes Antares, 1984.
(And illustrator) *Tales in F,* Editions La Farandole, 1985.

ILLUSTRATOR

Andree Clair and Boubou Hama, *La Savane enchantee: Contes d'Afrique,* Editions La Farandole, 1972, translation by Olive Jones published as *The Enchanted Savannah: Tales From West Africa,* Methuen, 1974.

Boubou Hama, *Ize-Gani,* Presence Africaine, 1985.

OTHER

Author and/or illustrator of more than thirty books published in French and German, including adaptations of folktales, craft books, poems, novels, plays, and translations. Contributor to magazines, including *Jeunes Annees, Puffin Post,* and *Cricket.* Editor of children's magazines.

WORK IN PROGRESS: A series of folktale picture-books with cassettes of traditional music, for Vif Argent; "a story about mass media entering a traditional village society"; collecting stories about teenagers in various countries; "a folktale picture-book about the sun, moon, and stars."

SIDELIGHTS: Beatrice Tanaka wrote: "I was born in a place that changed country, language, and government three times in a generation, twice during my childhood. By the age of fifteen I had had a taste of absolute monarchy and Stalinist communism, of Nazi and colonial rule, of racism, bombs, and the black market, and had learned that history, written by the winner, reads quite differently when one sits at the loser's place. My education was a patchwork quilt stitched in half a dozen languages, and if I was pretty bad in math, I seemed an expert in applied relativity, with an allergy to dogma and a passion for traveling and meeting people.

"By age seventeen, now in Brazil, I hesitated between drawing, theatre, and journalism. Then, discovering that one could draw for theatre, I went to study theatre-design in Paris. As this work generally fed its men rather badly and its women even worse, I decided to do graphic arts, too. At the time, Paris's gray walls were ablaze with the best posters ever. By the time I finished school, got married, and had two babies, advertising had changed altogether. It had been mostly cultural but was now commercial, and I felt no interest in imitating Kodachromes to tell people to smoke that masculine cigarette.

"As I found very few books I really enjoyed for my children, I tried to write them myself. Publishers told me not to: since grandparents mostly bought the books, I should draw them the way they'd please the grandparents! Happily I fell across the editor of a children's paper who had enough ideas and courage for a dozen people. He gave me some illustrations to do, and then texts, too. And so I finally did do some sort of journalism, after all, while drawing and of course working for theatre whenever possible (which makes a crazy quilt of professional life, too). So is life: a mixture, not a specialization. So is our little planet, with its varieties of landscapes and cultures—even if the last century did its best to standardize crops and thoughts alike and killed off more species and cultures combined than all the historical periods that preceded it.

"This maybe explains or rationalizes why I love working with traditional tales that have something to tell us here and now (and since there are so many of them risking oblivion, why I only found time for one original novel, though there are at least two other half-finished ones in my head). It explains why I like experimenting with new techniques, drawing, painting, lino- and papercuts, even embroidery, or doing crafts, explaining different 'how-to's'; and why I don't agree with people who generally say I write for children. Where does one stop being a child? When? How? Folktales and crafts never were intended for any special age-group, nor were stories or poems. When books did not exist, the storyteller (or shadow-puppeteer) just sat down under a tree, and whoever wanted to look and listen came near, and nobody asked their ages. If more children stop, maybe it's simply because they are more eager to look and listen."

Tanaka speaks fluent French, English, Portuguese (Brazilian), and German, as well as some Italian, Spanish, Hebrew, and Romanian. She has traveled to several countries, including Greece, Yugoslavia, Israel, Morocco, Tunisia, Indonesia, Japan, and Senegal.

AVOCATIONAL INTERESTS: "Bible studies and mythologies (not only Greek!), folktales and poetry, folk arts, non-European theatre, puppetry, music (only listening), ecology, ethnography, anthropology, painting, sculpture, cooking (even worked on a Vietnamese cookbook!), and history (mostly the history of those who didn't write—or rewrite—it: American Indians, African peoples, Southeast Asians, women and children, and plain people, instead of kings and generals."

*   *   *

TANNENBAUM, D(onald) Leb 1948-

PERSONAL: Born April 8, 1948, in Orange, N.J.; son of Gustave (a contractor) and Estelle (a secretary; maiden name, Lax) Tannenbaum; married Cheryl Ramette (a quilter), May 15, 1977; children: Nathan, Jonas, Abram. *Education:* Ithaca College, B.A., 1970; Oregon State University, Certificate of Elementary Education, 1975.

ADDRESSES: Home—604 North East 61st Ave., Portland, Ore. 97213. *Agent*—Bertha Klausner, Bertha Klausner International Literary Agency, Inc., 71 Park Ave., New York, N.Y. 10016. *Office*—Educational Computer Systems Corp., 10818 North East Coxley Dr., Suite E, Vancouver, Wash. 98662.

CAREER: Catlin Gabel School, Portland, Ore., team teacher of preschool children, 1978—, school printer, 1980—; writer. Director of workshop "Writing the Children's Book Within You"; volunteer worker on Hunger Project.

MEMBER: Children, Inc., Society of Children's Book Writers, Willamette Writers Group.

AWARDS, HONORS: Getting Ready for Baby was included in *American Bookseller*'s "Pick of the Lists" selection, 1982.

WRITINGS:

CHILDREN'S BOOKS

Baby Talk, Avon, 1981.
A Visit to the Doctor, Simon & Schuster, 1981.
Getting Ready for Baby, Simon & Schuster, 1982.
Duck Tales, Educational Computer Systems, 1984.

OTHER

Author of column "Upstarts," in *Young American,* a newspaper supplement for children.

WORK IN PROGRESS: The Musician, a picture book "about being what you love"; *The Sad Blob,* self-illustrated; volume six in an eighteen-part series of integrated, educational software programs, for Educational Computer Systems.

SIDELIGHTS: D. Leb Tannenbaum informed *CA:* "A near trip to Iran sparked my writing career. I wrote three manuscripts while waiting in Portland, Oregon, to take my hired post as director of a multilingual preschool. My family and I never left the states! One of these three manuscripts, *Baby Talk,* was purchased by Avon/Camelot on a trip I made to

New York City the spring after the fall of the Shah's government.

"As a man teaching preschool children for approximately ten years now, it dawned on me one day that many of the books I read daily to children were within the range of writing that seemed no different than the writing I was currently toying with. More simply, I realized that authors were people like myself and that I was capable and qualified. I began to write consistently in late 1979 and sold *Baby Talk* to Avon/Camelot in March 1980. I felt just like the children I spend so much time with—excited!

"I now consider writing vital to my existence. I love to write and grow from the experience of writing. Writing for children is confronting. It demands the truth. Confronting the truth is not always easy, yet it is rewarding. I lean towards transformation in writing lately. I find that books for children that really move me, move children, have transformational qualities. A great book may transform one's thinking, one's point of view, or, more simply, the moment in the room. I love reading out loud to children and adults as well.

"Paul Hagard's book, *Men, Children, and Books*, has had a great effect on me. He places children's literature in a historical perspective that is meaningful and enlightening. My summer workshop with Uri Schulevitz in upstate New York has also had a powerful effect on me and my writing. Uri's visual approach to writing is powerful. Uri himself is an excellent teacher as well as skilled craftsperson. I plan to return to New York with my entire family to pick up studying with Uri again someday. I am scared about taking my wife, our five- and two- year-old sons, *and* a new baby on this adventure east to pursue my dreams. They are all supportive, so watch out, New York!

"I have always been fascinated by books. I have poems I wrote and saved from the fourth grade. Books and writing have always been with me. I wrote a strong poem when President Kennedy was killed. Another poem followed my first experience of a funeral. I have written my way through experiences of love, hate, joy, and sadness for as long as I can remember. In college I wrote for our newspaper. I also wrote record reviews at Oregon State University. I've been storytelling with children for about ten years. Reading out loud always gives me a lift. At the Catlin Gabel School, a very well-regarded private school in the West, I picked up printing on an offset press. My fascination with the art of putting thoughts on paper led me into this field. The printing process is involved and requires skill. Learning printing techniques has helped me visualize the illustrative side of my writing. I think the printer's name and/or company should be included in the byline of a book's credit. Printers are skilled artists who are an integral part of the creation of a good book. My hat is off to all you skilled printers out there!

"We all have a children's book within us. I am convinced of this. The thrill of self-expression in this form is well worth the effort put out. From Harper & Row to the book made by a caring individual for one special person in their world, the completed project is equally exciting. As Aleksandr Solzhenitsyn said, 'One word of truth outweighs the whole world.' I love it!"

BIOGRAPHICAL/CRITICAL SOURCES:

PERIODICALS

Oregonian, December 4, 1982.

TATTERSALL, Ian (Michael) 1945-

PERSONAL: Born May 10, 1945, in Paignton, Devon, England; immigrated to United States in 1967. *Education:* Cambridge University, B.A., 1967, M.A., 1970; Yale University, M.Phil., 1970, Ph.D., 1971.

ADDRESSES: Office—Department of Anthropology, American Museum of Natural History, Central Park at 79th St., New York, N.Y. 10024.

CAREER: New School for Social Research, New York City, visiting lecturer, 1971-72; Lehman College, City University of New York, New York City, adjunct assistant professor, 1971-74; American Museum of Natural History, New York City, assistant curator, 1971-76, associate curator, 1976-81, curator of physical anthropology, 1981—.

MEMBER: American Association for the Advancement of Science, American Anthropological Association, American Association of Physical Anthropologists, Society of Systematic Zoology, Society of Vertebrate Paleontology.

WRITINGS:

Man's Ancestors: An Introduction to Primate and Human Evolution, Murray, 1970.
(Editor with R. W. Sussman) *Lemur Biology*, Plenum, 1975.
The Primates of Madagascar, Columbia University Pess, 1982.
(With Niles Eldredge) *The Myths of Human Evolution*, Columbia University Press, 1982.

Contributor to numerous scientific journals and popular magazines.

SIDELIGHTS: English paleontologist Ian Tattersall believes that scientists are influenced by their culture. A case in point, according to Tattersall, is nineteenth-century British naturalist Charles Darwin's theory that evolution is a slow, gradual process. Darwin's "gradualism," as Tattersall and co-author Niles Eldredge point out in their 1982 book *The Myths of Human Evolution*, is one of the "myths" that became incorporated into the theory of evolution in spite of insufficient evidence. The authors themselves are proponents of "punctuationism," a hypothesis that the life of species consists of long periods of stagnation interrupted by brusque transformations, and, as J. R. Durant recounted in the *Times Literary Supplement*, Tattersall and Eldredge "attribute the general tendency among Darwinian biologists to explain evolution in terms of constant, adaptive change to the pernicious influence of the Victorian idea of social progress." While critics found the argument for punctuationism convincing, they were skeptical about the authors' attempt to apply this hypothesis to social history. As David Graber of the *Los Angeles Times* asserted, this approach may be valid, "but it's hardly a new idea." However, Graber praised *The Myths of Human Evolution* as "better balanced" than other books on the same topic, such as Richard E. Leakey's *The Making of Mankind* or Donald C. Johanson and Maitland A. Edey's *Lucy*.

In *The Myths of Human Evolution*, Tattersall and Eldredge also challenge the notion of creationism, a religious explanation of natural history. According to the book's authors, creationism is another "myth of human evolution," and should be approached as a cultural phenomenon, an "aspect of American populism." *Washington Post Book World*'s Edwin M. Yoder, Jr., concurred with this analysis of creationism, observing that "the validity of a scientific proposition cannot be tested by majority opinion or vote." Furthermore, critics maintained that the book's discussion of myths, both within and outside the realm of science, dispels much of the confusion surrounding the conflict between creationists and the scientific community. As Yoder concluded, Tattersall and Eldredge show "that the creationist controversy is as much a social and pedagogical crisis as a crisis in science."

BIOGRAPHICAL/CRITICAL SOURCES:

PERIODICALS:

Los Angeles Times, December 26, 1982.
Times Literary Supplement, February 18, 1983.
Washington Post Book World, December 26, 1982.

*   *   *

TAYLOR, Hugh A(lexander) 1920-

PERSONAL: Born January 22, 1920, in Chelmsford, England; son of Hugh Lambert and Enid Essex (Horrocks) Taylor; married, July, 1919; children: Hugh Alexander. *Education:* Oxford University, B.A., 1949, M.A., 1953; University of Liverpool, Diploma in Archival Administration, 1951.

ADDRESSES: Home—P.O. Box 1421, Wolfville, Nova Scotia, Canada B0P 1X0.

CAREER: Leeds Public Libraries, Leeds, England, archivist, 1951-54; Liverpool Public Libraries, Liverpool, England, archivist, 1954-58; Northumberland County Records Office, Newcastle upon Tyne, England, county archivist, 1958-65; Provincial Archives of Alberta, Edmonton, provincial archivist, 1965-67; Provincial Archives of New Brunswick, Fredericton, provincial archivist, 1967-71; Public Archives of Canada, Ottawa, Ontario, director of archives branch, 1971-77; Public Archives of Nova Scotia, Halifax, provincial archivist, 1978-82; consulting archivist, 1982—. Adjunct professor at University of British Columbia, 1983—. *Military service:* Royal Air Force, 1939-46; became flight lieutenant.

MEMBER: Society of Archivists (England; member of council, 1963-65), Canadian Historical Association (chairman of archives section, 1967-68), Association of Canadian Archivists, Society of American Archivists (president, 1978-79).

WRITINGS:

Northumberland History: A Brief Guide to Records and Aids, Northumberland County Council, 1963.
New Brunswick History: A Checklist of Secondary Sources, Government of New Brunswick, 1971.
The Arrangement and Description of Archival Materials, Volume II, Gale, 1980.
Archival Services and the Concept of the User: A RAMP Study, UNESCO, 1984.

Contributor to archival journals.

WORK IN PROGRESS: Society and the Documentary Record: The Impact of Records on Human Communication and Organisation, publication expected in 1987.

SIDELIGHTS: Hugh A. Taylor told *CA:* "An archivist selects, reads, and makes available records and documents in all 'media of record' that are of permanent value to society. This work is closely allied to that of modern paperwork and other records manufactured in institutions, but in addition there is a far-reaching cultural responsibility that involves pre-visionary

society to some extent, as well as learning to 'read' the codes of all media of record so that the appropriate records will be preserved into the future mythopoeiac age."

*   *   *

TAYLOR, Jerry D(uncan) 1938-

PERSONAL: Born June 5, 1938, in Plumerville, Ark.; son of William Sherman (an ironworker) and Edna Faye (a homemaker; maiden name, Duncan) Taylor; married Louise Todd (a teacher), December 18, 1964; children: Todd, Joshua, Nathan. *Education:* Arkansas State Teachers College (now University of Central Arkansas), B.A., 1960; University of Arkansas, M.S., 1964; Florida State University, Ph.D., 1969. *Politics:* Democrat. *Religion:* Southern Baptist.

ADDRESSES: Home—P.O. Box 396, Buies Creek, N.C. 27506. *Office*—Mathematics Department, Campbell University, Buies Creek, N.C. 27506.

CAREER: Campbell University, Buies Creek, N.C., assistant professor, 1961-66, associate professor, 1969-83, professor, 1984—.

MEMBER: National Council of Teachers of Mathematics.

WRITINGS:

(With Ellen N. Griesbach, Beverly Henderson West, and wife, Louise Todd Taylor) *The Prentice-Hall Encyclopedia of Mathematics,* Prentice-Hall, 1982.

Contributor to *Christian Science Monitor* and *Mathematics Teacher.*

SIDELIGHTS: "Books that whetted my interest in the history of math were *Men of Mathematics,* by E. T. Bell, and *What Is Mathematics?,* by Courant and Robbins. My goals are to learn to speak a little Spanish and to play a little Chopin. The things I like doing best are playing bridge and chess. I dream of spending a summer or two touring Spain, Italy, France, Germany, and Switzerland."

*   *   *

TAYLOR, Louise Todd 1939-

PERSONAL: Born February 6, 1939, in Mt. Vernon, Ohio; daughter of W. Thurman (a lawyer) and Dove (a homemaker; maiden name, Jessee) Todd; married Jerry Duncan Taylor (a teacher), December 18, 1964; children: Todd, Joshua, Nathan. *Education:* Swarthmore College, B.A., 1961; Duke University, M.A.T., 1962; Florida State University, Ph.D., 1969. *Politics:* Democrat. *Religion:* Southern Baptist.

ADDRESSES: Home—P.O. Box 396, Buies Creek, N.C. 27506. *Office*—Department of English, Meredith College, Raleigh, N.C. 27611.

CAREER: Teacher at junior high school in Raleigh, N.C., 1961-64, and at Campbell College, Buies Creek, N.C., 1969-74; Meredith College, Raleigh, N.C., assistant professor of English, 1978—.

MEMBER: National Council of Teachers of English.

WRITINGS:

(With Beverly Henderson West, Ellen N. Griesbach, and husband, Jerry D. Taylor) *The Prentice-Hall Encyclopedia of Mathematics* (young adult), Prentice-Hall, 1982.

PLAYS:

"Lucy and Glenda" (one act), 1981.
"Pay Attention to Elmer" (one act), 1982.

OTHER

Contributor to language arts textbooks, including *Holt English.* Contributor to magazines and newspapers, including *Christian Science Monitor, Home Life, Tar Heel,* and *NRTA Journal.*

SIDELIGHTS: Louise Taylor told *CA:* "Letters! It took me a long time to appreciate the importance of letters. I had written letters, lots of letters, in fact. I've always preferred making carbons of my letters to journal writing as a way of keeping track of my life. But I had never thought of letters as writing. Letters were easy, natural, and fun, whereas real writing, whatever that was, was serious, important, and above all hard. When I sat down to do real writing, I felt like Emily Dickinson: 'This is my letter to the world that never wrote to me.' With the whole world as an audience, I had to write something deeply significant, something august. As a result, when I managed to write at all under such constraints, I produced bombast that nobody in the whole world would have enjoyed, not even my mother. And although I sent some of the stuff to editors, who sent it right back, I would never have sent it to my friends with whom I corresponded. I would have been too embarrassed.

"Then I came upon a passage in John Holt's book *What Do I Do Monday?* that changed my attitude toward letters and my writing. In talking about the variety of writing students should do, Holt said: 'Letters are a very natural and important kind of writing, and one of the best kinds of training for writers. I wrote millions of words in letters before I ever thought of writing for any other purpose, and my first book and part of my second were first written only as letters. We would be wise to let students use school time—class, study hall, whatever—to write letters if they wanted.'

"I had never thought of letters like that before. For the first time I realized that I probably had more to say and said it better in the letters I wrote my friends than in the articles I addressed to the whole world. I was more concrete, more concise, and a whole lot less preachy. (To people who know you, you can't pretend to be an expert.) After reading Holt, I began to rehearse ideas for articles in letters to friends, and a few of those letters were turned into articles that editors actually bought."

AVOCATIONAL INTERESTS: Theatre, reading Mark Twain and Dr. Seuss, playing piano, baseball.

*   *   *

TAYLOR, Richard S(helley) 1912-

PERSONAL: Born March 30, 1912, in Cornelius, Ore.; son of Ernest E. (a minister) and Luzena (a writer; maiden name, Shelley) Taylor; married Amy Overby, September 9, 1931 (died January 10, 1983); married Bertha Syverson Gordon (a homemaker), September 12, 1983; children: David Richard, Paul Wesley. *Education:* Cascade College, Th.B., 1943; George Fox College, A.B., 1944; Pasadena College (now Point Loma College), M.A., 1945; Boston University, Th.D., 1953.

ADDRESSES: Home—4415 Northeast 41st Ave., Portland, Ore. 97211.

CAREER: Ordained minister of Church of the Nazarene, 1934; pastor of Nazarene churches in Washington, 1931-41, Oregon, 1941-49, and Massachusetts, 1949-51, and in Australia, 1954-60; Nazarene Theological Seminary, Kansas City, Mo., associate professor, 1961-64, professor of theology and missions, 1965-77, professor emeritus, 1977—. Associate director of Church of the Nazarene Department of Education and Ministry, 1974-77. Professor at Cascade College, 1944-46; president of Nazarene Bible College, Sydney, Australia, 1952-60; visiting professor at Church of the Nazarene Seminary in Japan, 1966-67; interim principal of European Nazarene Bible College in Switzerland, 1969-70.

MEMBER: Evangelical Theological Society, Wesleyan Theological Society (president, 1968-69).

AWARDS, HONORS: Holiness Exponent of the Year Award from Christian Holiness Association, 1978, for *God, Man, and Salvation.*

WRITINGS:

A Right Conception of Sin, 1939, revised edition, Nazarene Publishing, 1945.
Talks by the Way, Better Book and Bible House, 1942.
Our Pacific Outposts, Nazarene Publishing, 1956.
The Disciplined Life, Beacon Hill Press of Kansas City, 1962.
Joy for Dark Days, Beacon Hill Press of Kansas City, 1964, revised edition published as *Miracle of Joy,* Beacon Hill Press of Kansas City, 1975.
Life in the Spirit, Beacon Hill Press of Kansas City, 1966.
(Contributor) Albert Harper and Ralph Earl, editors, *Beacon Bible Commentary,* Volume X, Beacon Hill Press of Kansas City, 1967.
Preaching Holiness Today, Beacon Hill Press of Kansas City, 1968.
Tongues: Their Purpose and Meaning, Beacon Hill Press of Kansas City, 1973.
(Editor) *Timely Sermon Outlines,* Baker Book, 1973.
A Return to Christian Culture, Beacon Hill Press of Kansas City, 1973, published as *The Disciplined Life-Style,* Bethany House, 1980.
The Shape of Things to Come, Beacon Hill Press of Kansas City, 1975, revised edition published as *End Times,* Wesleyan Press, 1976.
(With W. T. Purkiser and Willard H. Taylor) *God, Man, and Salvation,* Beacon Hill Press of Kansas City, 1977.
Biblical Authority and Christian Faith, Beacon Hill Press of Kansas City, 1980.
(Editor) *Beacon Dictionary of Theology,* Beacon Hill Press of Kansas City, 1983.
Exploring Christian Holiness, Volume III, Beacon Hill Press of Kansas City, 1985.
(Editor) *Great Holiness Classics,* Volume III: *Leading Wesleyan Thinkers,* Beacon Hill Press of Kansas City, 1985.

CONTRIBUTOR

K. Geiger, editor, *Further Insights Into Holiness,* Beacon Hill Press of Kansas City, 1963.
Geiger, editor, *The Word and the Doctrine,* Beacon Hill Press of Kansas City, 1965.
M. Boyd and M. A. Harris, editors, *Projecting Our Heritage,* Beacon Hill Press of Kansas City, 1969.
E. S. Phillips, editor, *Ministering to the Millions,* Beacon Hill Press of Kansas City, 1971.
James McGraw, editor, *The Holiness of the Pulpit,* Beacon Hill Press of Kansas City, 1974.

J. B. Nelson, editor, *Family Love in All Dimensions*, Beacon Hill Press of Kansas City, 1976.

Contributor to theology journals.

OTHER

Editor of *Nazarene Pastor*, 1964-72.

SIDELIGHTS: Richard S. Taylor commented: "I have been motivated by the conviction that all truth is ultimately theological in nature, and that such truth centers in Jesus Christ, and in the religion which bears his name. A further conviction has been that Christ, as a living and risen lord, is adequate as a savior from sin, here and now. Therefore my writing has focused on this available salvation. I have endeavored to expound, as simply and helpfully as possible, its doctrinal, experiential, and practical aspects."

*   *   *

TEBELAK, John-Michael   1949(?)-1985

OBITUARY NOTICE: Born c. 1949; died of a heart attack, April 2, 1985, in New York, N.Y. Stage director and playwright. Tebelak is best remembered as writer and director of the religious rock musical "Godspell." The play, written by Tebelak as a master's thesis at Carnegie-Mellon University in Pittsburgh, was first produced Off-Broadway. It eventually played on Broadway and became a 1973 motion picture. Tebelak also directed several other plays, including "Elizabeth I" and "The Glorious Age," and was drama director at the Cathedral Church of St. John the Divine in New York City.

OBITUARIES AND OTHER SOURCES:

PERIODICALS

Chicago Tribune, April 4, 1985.
Detroit News, April 3, 1985.
New York Times, April 3, 1985.
People, December 15, 1980.
Washington Post, April 5, 1985.

*   *   *

TEFFETELLER, Gordon Lamar   1931-

PERSONAL: Born September 12, 1931, in Maryville, Tenn.; son of Lamar G. (a welder) and Ethel (a teacher; maiden name, Birchfield) Teffeteller; married Elaine Gilliland (a teacher), December 28, 1950; children Sherri Teffeteller Horonjeff, Philip, Steven, Barry. *Education:* Valdosta State College, B.A., 1959; Duke University, M.A., 1963; Florida State University, Ph.D., 1969.

ADDRESSES: Home—2205 Park Lane, Valdosta, Ga. 31602. *Office*—Department of History, Valdosta State College, Valdosta, Ga. 31698.

CAREER: Valdosta State College, Valdosta, Ga., assistant professor, 1969-72, associate professor, 1972-76, professor of nineteenth-century European history, 1976—, chairman of department of history, 1974-81.

MEMBER: American Historical Association, National Council for the Social Studies, American Association of University Professors (president, 1982-84), Society for Army Historical Research, Southern Historical Association, Georgia Association of Historians (president, 1984-85), Kiwanis International.

AWARDS, HONORS: Calouste Gulbenkian Foundation fellow in Portugal, 1972; grants from Ministry of National Education for Portugal, 1972 and 1982.

WRITINGS:

The Surpriser: The Life of Rowland, Lord Hill, University of Delaware Press, 1982.

Contributor to history and social studies journals.

WORK IN PROGRESS: A biography of Percy Smythe, Sixth Viscount Strangford.

*   *   *

TENNEY, Merrill C(hapin)   1904-1985

OBITUARY NOTICE—See index for *CA* sketch: Born April 16, 1904, in Chelsea, Mass.; died March 18, 1985, in Winfield, Ill. Educator, theologian, editor, and author. Tenney taught at Gordon College of Theology and Missions (now Gordon College) from 1930 to 1943, when he became professor of Bible and theology at Wheaton College. Tenney remained at Wheaton for more than thirty years, serving as dean of the Graduate School from 1947 to 1971. He continued to teach at the college thereafter, and at the time of his death he was professor emeritus of theological studies. He wrote such books as *John: The Gospel of Belief, The New Testament: An Historical and Analytic Survey, Interpreting Revelation,* and *New Testament Times.* Tenney also edited several works, including *The Word for This Century* and *The Pictorial Bible Encyclopedia,* which was named 1975's best book by the Catholic Press Association and Associated Church Press.

OBITUARIES AND OTHER SOURCES:

BOOKS

Directory of American Scholars, Volume IV: *Philosophy, Religion, and Law,* 8th edition, 1982.
Who's Who in America, 42nd edition, Marquis, 1982.
The Writer's Directory: 1984-1986, St. James Press, 1983.

PERIODICALS

Chicago Tribune, March 20, 1985.

*   *   *

TERKEL, Susan N(eiburg)   1948-

PERSONAL: Born April 7, 1948, in Philadelphia, Pa.; daughter of Sidney A. (in life insurance) and Deborah (a homemaker; maiden name, Burstein) Neiburg; married Lawrence Arthur Terkel (a business executive); children: Ari, Marni, David. *Education:* Cornell University, B.S., 1970.

ADDRESSES: Home—44 West Case Dr., Hudson, Ohio 44236. *Agent*—Andrea Brown, 199 President St., Brooklyn, N.Y. 11231.

CAREER: Teacher, 1971-72; writer. Coordinator of Northeast Ohio chapter of Gillain Barre Syndrome Support Group; codirector of Spiritual Life Society and Hudson Yoga Center.

MEMBER: Authors Guild, Society of Children's Book Writers; Woman's Action for Nuclear Disarmament.

WRITINGS:

FOR YOUNG PEOPLE

Yoga Is for Me, Lerner Publications, 1982.

(With Janice E. Rench) *Feeling Safe, Feeling Strong: How to Avoid Sexual Abuse and What to Do If It Happens to You*, Lerner Publications, 1984.

Contributor of poems and articles to magazines and newspapers.

WORK IN PROGRESS: Alexander Johnson, a juvenile novel; research for a children's book on the nuclear arms race.

SIDELIGHTS: Susan N. Terkel told *CA:* "I can still recall the thrill I got when, at the age of six, I completed the last line of my first story. I told myself, 'Susan, you're a writer now.' That conviction has never wavered.

"I love writing because of the chance I get to create my own world, to rewrite my own past, or to share my views about the real world with others, especially with children. Moreover, I like the work conditions that go along with being a writer—working at home, on my own schedule, never having to face retirement.

"There is a great responsibility, particularly when one is writing for our young people today. While I discovered the truth in writing, especially in fiction, that you cannot manipulate your characters into doing things that they wouldn't do if they were real, I also discovered that it is quite possible to infuse in your characters a sense of hope or sense of despair. I hope my work is evidence that I chose to infuse a sense of hope about the world, whether my book is about sexual abuse survivors or about fantasy. I write to tell each child, each reader, that he or she *can* make a difference in the world."

* * *

TERRY, Luther L(eonidas) 1911-1985

OBITUARY NOTICE—See index for *CA* sketch: Born September 15, 1911, in Red Level, Ala.; died of heart failure, March 29, 1985, in Philadelphia, Pa. Physician, educator, administrator, and author. A cardiologist, Terry was instrumental in focusing public attention on cigarets as a health hazard during his term as U.S. surgeon general in the early 1960's. His report to President Kennedy linked smoking to cancer and heart disease and led to the inclusion of a health warning on cigaret packs. Prior to his work as surgeon general Terry practiced medicine at hospitals and other medical institutions throughout the midwestern and southern United States. His many positions included chief of general medicine and experimental therapeutics at the National Heart Institute from 1950 to 1958 and assistant director of the institute from 1958 to 1961. After his service as surgeon general ended in 1965 Terry became an administrator and professor of medicine at the University of Pennsylvania, where he remained until 1980. Among his notable achievements during this time was his successful campaign to outlaw cigaret advertisements from radio and television. Terry's writings include *To Smoke or Not to Smoke*, written with Daniel Horn, and contributions to books such as Lewis Herker's *Crisis in Our Cities*, Seymour Tilson's *Toward Environments Fit for Men*, and Gerald Leinwand's *Air and Water Pollution*.

OBITUARIES AND OTHER SOURCES:

BOOKS

The International Who's Who, 48th edition, Europa, 1984.
Who's Who in the World, 6th edition, Marquis, 1982.

PERIODICALS

Chicago Tribune, April 1, 1985.
Los Angeles Times, March 31, 1985.
New York Times, March 31, 1985.
Washington Post, March 31, 1985.

* * *

THOMAS, Dave 1949(?)-
(Doug McKenzie)

BRIEF ENTRY: Born c. 1949 in St. Catherines, Ontario, Canada. Canadian comedian, actor, film director, copywriter, comedy writer, and screenwriter. Thomas is best known for his portrayal of Doug McKenzie, one of the McKenzie brothers, two fictional Canadian talk show hosts. He created the duo with his partner Rick Moranis (Bob McKenzie), and they became popular through their regular appearances on "Second City Television" (SCTV). Before becoming a founding member of SCTV Thomas worked briefly as a copywriter and was a member of the Second City comedy troupe.

In 1981 Thomas and Moranis recorded an album as the McKenzies, *Great White North*, and it became a best-seller in the United States and Canada. "Take Off," a cut from the album, became a number one single. This success was followed by "Strange Brew," a 1983 film based on the McKenzie brothers and written by Thomas, Moranis, and Steven De Jarnatt. Thomas and Moranis co-directed and starred in the movie. In addition to "Strange Brew," Thomas has written several unproduced screenplays, including some with fellow Second City alumnus Dan Aykroyd. Bob and Doug McKenzie were nominated for the Order of Canada, that nation's highest civilian honor.

BIOGRAPHICAL/CRITICAL SOURCES:

PERIODICALS

Chicago Tribune, August 28, 1983.
Maclean's Magazine, January 11, 1982.
Newsweek, July 19, 1982.
Rolling Stone, February 4, 1982.

* * *

THOMPSON, (Richard) Ernest 1950(?)-

BRIEF ENTRY: Born c. 1950 in Vermont. American actor, playwright, and screenwriter. Thompson is best known for his Academy Award-winning screenplay for the 1981 film "On Golden Pond." The script was adapted from his Broadway play of the same name which was first produced in 1978 and published in 1979 by Dodd. Thompson's screenplay also earned him a Writers Guild Award in 1982 for best dramatic adaptation.

Before turning to writing in 1977 Thompson starred in the television soap opera "Somerset," in a number of network dramas, and on stage. Among the other plays he has written are *The West Side Waltz: A Play in Three Quarter Time* (Dodd, 1982; first produced in 1981) and "A Sense of Humor" (1983).

BIOGRAPHICAL/CRITICAL SOURCES:

PERIODICALS

Time, April 12, 1982.
Washington Post, October 1, 1978, March 19, 1982.
Writer's Digest, July, 1982.

THOMPSON, Ernest Trice   1894-1985

OBITUARY NOTICE—See index for CA sketch: Born July 2, 1894, in Texarkana, Tex.; died March 29, 1985, in Richmond, Va. Clergyman, educator, historian, theologian, editor, and author. Thompson was a key figure in the 1983 reunion of the Southern and Northern denominations of the Presbyterian Church that had separated during the Civil War. As an influential member of the Southern Presbyterian church—once officially known as the Presbyterian Church in the United States—he helped direct the church away from its extreme Calvinism and towards more moderate positions. Thompson was professor of church history at Union Theological Seminary from 1922 to 1964. He wrote books such as *Presbyterian Missions in the Southern United States, Changing Emphasis in American Preaching, Tomorrow's Church—Tomorrow's World, The Spirituality of the Church,* and *Through the Ages: A History of the Christian Church.* He also edited the magazine *Presbyterian Outlook.*

OBITUARIES AND OTHER SOURCES:

BOOKS

Directory of American Scholars, Volume I: *History,* 8th edition, Bowker, 1982.
Who's Who in America, 39th edition, Marquis, 1976.

PERIODICALS

Chicago Tribune, April 1, 1985.
Los Angeles Times, March 31, 1985.
Washington Post, March 31, 1985.

* * *

THORNING, Joseph F(rancis)   1896-1985

OBITUARY NOTICE—See index for CA sketch: Born April 25, 1896, in Milwaukee, Wis.; died of a heart ailment, March 8, 1985, in Baltimore, Md. Clergyman, educator, sociologist, administrator, editor, and author. Thorning was ordained a Roman Catholic priest in 1928 and taught at Loyola and Georgetown universities in the 1920's and 1930's. Beginning in 1937 he taught sociology and Latin American history at Mount St. Mary's College and eventually established himself as an authority on Latin American affairs. He participated in seminars in Peru, Cuba, and Mexico, and taught Latin American history at Marymount College. For his work Thorning received many citations from Latin American nations, including the Cross of Boyaca from Colombia and the National Order of Merit from Ecuador. Thorning's writings include *Religious Liberty in Transition, A Primer of Social Justice, Builders of the Social Order,* and *Miranda: World Citizen.* He also wrote numerous pamphlets on Latin American and religious subjects and was an associate editor of publications such as *Thought* and *World Affairs.* He was Washington correspondent for *America* in the mid-1930's.

OBITUARIES AND OTHER SOURCES:

BOOKS

American Catholic Who's Who, Volume 23, *1980-1981,* National Catholic News Service, 1979.
Who's Who in America, 40th edition, Marquis, 1978.

PERIODICALS

Baltimore Sun, March 14, 1985.

New York Times, March 12, 1985.
Washington Post, March 13, 1985.

* * *

TOMASI, Silvano M(ario)   1940-

PERSONAL: Born October 12, 1940, in Vicenza, Italy; immigrated to the United States in 1961, naturalized citizen, 1978; son of Giuseppe and Amabile (Bordignon) Tomasi. *Education:* Collegio Scalabrini-O'Brien, B.A., 1960; Fordham University, M.A., 1967, Ph.D., 1972.

ADDRESSES: Office—Center for Migration Studies of New York, Inc., 209 Flagg Pl., Staten Island, N.Y. 10304.

CAREER: Center for Migration Studies of New York, Inc., New York, N.Y., director, 1966-76, president, 1976—. Richmond College of the City University of New York, instructor, 1970-72, adjunct assistant professor, 1972; lecturer at New School for Social Research, 1972 and 1974, and at Fordham University, 1972; adjunct associate professor at City College of the City University of New York, 1973. Director of U.S. Catholic Conference program on Pastoral Care for Migrants and Refugees, 1983—. Member of board of directors of Congress of Italian American Organizations, 1968-72, and American Immigration and Citizenship Conference, 1970-75; vice-president of National Coordinating Assembly of Ethnic Studies, 1972-73; U.S. member of Consiglio Consultivo degli Italiani all'Estero (advisory council of Italians abroad) of Italy's Foreign Ministry, 1972-75. Member of national advisory board of University of Minnesota's Immigration History Research Center in St. Paul, 1974-75; conference coordinator.

MEMBER: International Sociological Association (vice-president of research committee on migration, 1974-75, 1978-82), American Italian Historical Association (member of executive council, 1971-74, 1980), Population Association of America, Organization of American Historians, American Sociological Association.

AWARDS, HONORS: Howard R. Marraro Award from American Catholic Historical Association, 1975, for *Piety and Power.*

WRITINGS:

Piety and Power: The Role of Italian Parishes in the New York Metropolitan Area, 1880-1930, Center for Migration Studies, 1975.
(With Charles B. Keely) *Whom Have We Welcomed? The Adequacy and Quality of United States Immigration Data for Policy Analysis and Evaluation,* Center for Migration Studies, 1975.
(With Edward C. Stibili) *Italian-Americans and Religion: An Annotated Bibliography,* Center for Migration Studies, 1978.
National Directory of Research Centers, Repositories, and Organizations of Italian Culture in the United States, Fondazione Giovanni Agnelli, 1980.

EDITOR

(With Madeline H. Engel) *The Italian Experience in the United States,* Center for Migration Studies, 1970.
(With Michael G. Wenk and Geno Baroni) *Pieces of a Dream: The Ethnic Workers Crisis With America,* Center for Migration Studies, 1972.
The Religious Experience of Italian Americans, American Italian Historical Association, 1975.

(With Francesco Cordasco, Salvatore Mondello, and others) *The Italian American Experience,* thirty-nine volumes, Arno, 1975.

Perspectives in Italian Immigration and Ethnicity, Center for Migration Studies, 1976.

Images: A Pictorial History of Italian Americans, Center for Migration Studies, 1981.

(With Mary M. Kritz and C. B. Kelly, and contributor) *Global Trends in Migration: Theory and Research in International Population Movements,* Center for Migration Studies, 1981.

OTHER

Contributor of more than twenty-five articles and reviews to academic journals and newspapers in the United States and Italy. Editor of *International Migration Review,* 1965—; advisory editor of *Studi Emigrazione,* 1966—.

* * *

TORGOVNICK, Marianna 1949-

PERSONAL: Surname is pronounced Tore-*guv*-nick; born August 31, 1949, in Brooklyn, N.Y.; daughter of Salvatore (a clerk) and Rose (a garment worker; maiden name, Cozzitorto) DeMarco; married Stuart Torgovnick (an investment counselor), December 22, 1968; children: Kate Meredith, Elizabeth Victoria. *Education:* New York University, B.A., 1970; Columbia University, M.A., 1971, Ph.D., 1975.

ADDRESSES: Home—Durham, N.C. *Office*—Department of English, 325 Allen, Duke University, Durham, N.C. 27706.

CAREER: Williams College, Williamstown, Mass., assistant professor of English, 1975-81; Duke University, Durham, N.C., assistant professor, 1981-85, associate professor of English, 1985—.

MEMBER: International Society for the Study of Time, Modern Language Association of America, Northeast Modern Language Association (chairman of Genre Criticism Section, 1979, and Literature and Visual Arts Section, 1984).

AWARDS, HONORS: National Endowment for the Humanities grant, summer, 1977; Guggenheim fellow, 1981.

WRITINGS:

Closure in the Novel, Princeton University Press, 1981.
The Visual Arts, Pictorialism, and the Novel: James, Lawrence, and Woolf, Princeton University Press, 1985.

Contributor to literature journals and literary magazines, including *South Atlantic Quarterly.*

WORK IN PROGRESS: Visualizing Novels, on visual elements in novels, and on history and cultural implications of the novel's collaboration with visual media, completion expected in 1988; *Mirror, Mirror: The Career and Implications of a Figure for the Novel,* a study of the constraints and supports provided for various trends in the development of the novel by dominant metaphors for fiction, especially the various forms taken by the metaphor of novel as mirror.

SIDELIGHTS: Marianna Torgovnick's *Closure in the Novel* is an analysis of methods and means by which novels are concluded. Peter Kemp, reviewing the book in *Times Literary Supplement,* described it as "briskly sensible as well as unusually percipient." Kemp added that Torgovnick "restores your faith in present-day criticism."

Torgovnick told *CA:* "As in my teaching, my basic motivation for writing is a desire to enhance my own and others' responses to literature, to make those responses more informed, more resonant, more life-enhancing. I feel my work is successful if I make readers better able to understand the books I have discussed, better equipped to re-read them in the future. In my own future projects, I hope to reach not just a scholarly audience, but a more general one as well—something not always easy in an academic career, but very important, I think, for the state of our culture.

"In the sixties and part of the seventies, literary criticism was a harmless, sometimes enlightening, but usually self-contained activity. In the eighties, that has changed, in part because of new interdisciplinary emphases (from which my latest work arises), in part because of new views of history as influenced by women as well as men, by popular as well as official culture. Literary criticism today is an exciting field, very much influenced by and—what is new—influencing other fields. I see two major dangers: that in-fighting and proliferating jargon will once again render literary criticism a relatively harmless but isolated activity, or that literary criticism will become second-rate history, or anthropology, or philosophy.

"My own work repeatedly investigates the ways that art imitates/influences life and life imitates/influences art. *Closure in the Novel* asserts that endings, while difficult and 'unnatural,' are crucial to the artfulness of narrative and defamiliarize (make new) aspects of both literary form and life experiences. *Visual Arts* investigates how modern novelists interpreted, internalized, and translated into fictional terms theories and developments in the visual arts. My new work, when it comes, will, I hope, address issues engaged with life and culture but illuminating of texts—the real business, as I see it, of literary criticism."

BIOGRAPHICAL/CRITICAL SOURCES:

PERIODICALS

Modern Fiction Studies, summer, 1982.
Times Literary Supplement, November 13, 1981.
World Literature Today, spring, 1982.

* * *

TOUSSAINT, Stanley D. 1928-

PERSONAL: Born April 23, 1928, in Prinsburg, Minn.; son of Harry (a retailer) and Agnes (a housewife; maiden name, Roelofs) Toussaint; married I. Maxine Calvert (a housewife), June 30, 1950; children: Douglas, Mark. *Education:* Attended Northwestern Bible School (now College), Roseville, Minn., 1947-48; Augsburg College, B.A., 1951; Dallas Theological Seminary, Th.M., Th.D., 1957.

ADDRESSES: Office—Department of Bible Exposition, Dallas Theological Seminary, 3909 Swiss Ave., Dallas, Tex. 75204.

CAREER: Ordained Baptist minister; Northwestern College, Roseville, Minn., professor, 1957-60; Dallas Theological Seminary, Dallas, Tex., professor of Bible exposition, 1960-68; Western Bible Institute, Denver, Colo., president, 1968-69; pastor of Baptist church in Richmond, Va., 1969-73; Dallas Theological Seminary, professor of Bible exposition and chairman of department, 1973—. Host of radio program "Dallas Today."

WRITINGS:

Behold the King: A Study of Matthew, Multnomah, 1982.

TREMAINE, Jennie
   See CHESNEY, Marion

*   *   *

TREVELYAN, Humphrey   1905-1985

OBITUARY NOTICE—See index for *CA* sketch: Surname is pronounced Tre-*vill*-ian; born November 27, 1905, in Hindhead, England; died February 8, 1985. Diplomat, administrator, and author. Trevelyan entered the Indian Civil Service in 1929, joining the Political Department in 1932 as an undersecretary. He remained in India until 1944, when he became secretary to the Indian agent general in Washington, D.C. After India achieved independence in 1947 Trevelyan joined the British Diplomatic Service. In 1955 he was appointed British ambassador to Egypt. During his tenure he dealt with Egyptian President Gamal Abdel Nasser's nationalization of the Suez Canal. Trevelyan eventually left Egypt for an appointment with the United Nations, where he served until 1958. Four years later he became British ambassador to the Soviet Union. He left the diplomatic corps in 1965 and assumed the directorship of companies such as British Petroleum and the British Bank of the Middle East. Trevelyan was created a life peer in 1968. He wrote such books as *The Middle East in Revolution, Worlds Apart,* and *The India We Left.*

OBITUARIES AND OTHER SOURCES:

BOOKS

International Authors and Writers Who's Who, 9th edition, [and] *International Who's Who in Poetry,* 6th edition, Melrose, 1982.
The International Who's Who, 48th edition, Europa, 1984.

PERIODICALS

Times (London), February 12, 1985.

*   *   *

TRIBICH, Susan   1945(?)-1985
   (Susan Blumenthal)

OBITUARY NOTICE: Born c. 1945; died of cancer, February 10, 1985, in New York. Journalist and author. Tribich was a letters correspondent for *Time* magazine. She wrote a guidebook, *Bright Continent: A Shoestring Guide to Sub-Saharan Africa,* published in 1974 under the name Susan Blumenthal.

OBITUARIES AND OTHER SOURCES:

PERIODICALS

New York Times, February 12, 1985.

*   *   *

TROGDON, William (Lewis)   1939-
   (William Least Heat Moon)

BRIEF ENTRY: Born August 27, 1939, in Kansas City, Mo. Native American teacher and author. Trogdon, whose pen name—William Least Heat Moon—is derived from his Sioux ancestry, achieved both critical and commercial success with his first book, *Blue Highways: A Journey Into America* (Little, Brown, 1982). In 1978, when Trogdon found himself separated from his wife and laid off from his job as a teacher of

English at a small Missouri college, he packed his van with a few belongings and headed east. Shunning the interstates in favor of the "blue highways"—the back roads that used to be colored blue on gas-station road maps—he journeyed across the United States, seeking out towns with curious names for the next three months. He then spent four years converting his observations of the people and places of rural America into the book that would quickly top the *New York Times* bestseller list. Compared favorably to the "road literature" of Herman Melville, John Steinbeck, and Jack Kerouac, *Blue Highways* sold over one million copies, was named a notable book of 1983 by the *New York Times* and one of the top five best nonfiction books of 1983 by *Time* magazine, and received a Books-Across-the-Sea Award and a Christopher Award. Under the pseudonym William Least Heat Moon, Trogdon also wrote *The Red Couch* (Alfred Van der Marck, 1984).

Address: 8 Arlington St., Boston, Mass. 02116; and c/o Lois Wallace, 177 East 70th St., New York, N.Y. 10021.

BIOGRAPHICAL/CRITICAL SOURCES:

BOOKS

Contemporary Literary Criticism, Volume 29, Gale, 1984.

PERIODICALS

America, April 9, 1983.
New Yorker, May 2, 1983.
New York Times Book Review, February 6, 1983.
Times Literary Supplement, August 26, 1983.
Washington Post Book World, December 16, 1982.

*   *   *

TROY, Katherine
   See BUXTON, Anne (Arundel)

*   *   *

TROY, Nancy J.   1952-

PERSONAL: Born December 27, 1952, in New York, N.Y.; daughter of William B. (a business executive) and Joanne (Joslin) Troy; married Wim de Wit. *Education:* Wesleyan University, Middletown, Conn., B.A. (magna cum laude), 1974; Yale University, M.A., 1976, Ph.D., 1979.

ADDRESSES: Home—521 West Roscoe St., Chicago, Ill. 60657. *Office*— Department of Art History, Northwestern University, Evanston, Ill. 60201.

CAREER: Johns Hopkins University, Baltimore, Md., assistant professor of history of art, 1979-83; Northwestern University, Evanston, Ill., assistant professor of art history, 1983—. Solomon R. Guggenheim Museum, museum training intern, summer, 1972, curatorial and research assistant, summer, 1973, curatorial coordinator, summer, 1974; gallery assistant at Waddington Galleries, London, England, 1973; assistant to curator of French paintings at National Gallery of Art, summer, 1975; guest curator at Art Gallery, Yale University, 1979. Member of Maryland Council on the Arts, 1981-82; consultant to Art Institute of Chicago and Walker Art Center.

MEMBER: College Art Association of America, Society of Architectural Historians.

AWARDS, HONORS: Kress Foundation travel grants, 1976, 1977; Fulbright fellow in the Netherlands, 1977-78, 1978; fellow of American Council of Learned Societies, 1981, 1982-

83, and National Endowment for the Humanities, 1982-83; grant from Graham Foundation for Advanced Studies in the Fine Arts, 1982; fellow of Lilly Endowment, 1984-85.

WRITINGS:

The De Stijl Environment, MIT Press, 1983.

CONTRIBUTOR

Theodore Stebbins, editor, *The Hudson River School: Nineteenth-Century American Landscapes in the Wadsworth Atheneum,* Wadsworth Atheneum, 1976.
Yve-Alain Bois, editor, *L'Atelier de Mondrian: Recherches et dessins* (title means "The Studio of Mondrian: Research and Drawings"), Macula, 1982.
Mildred Friedman, editor, *De Stijl, 1917-1931: Visions of Utopia,* Abbeville Press, 1982.
Robert L. Herbert and others, editors, *The Societe Anonyme and the Dreier Bequest at Yale University: A Catalogue Raisonne,* Yale University Press, 1984.

OTHER

Contributor of articles and reviews to art and museum journals. Contributing editor of *Design Issues,* 1984—.

WORK IN PROGRESS: The Decorative Arts in France, 1895-1925.

*   *   *

TRUCH, Stephen   1947-

PERSONAL: Surname is pronounced Troosh; born January 25, 1947, in Coleman, Alberta, Canada; son of Peter (a coal miner) and Anne (a housewife; maiden name, Galaza) Truch; married Jacqueline Sue Hall (a housewife), June 28, 1968; children: Kama Elizabeth, Alita Cathryn. *Education:* University of Calgary, B.A., 1969, B.Ed., 1970, M.Sc., 1976, Ph.D., 1978.

ADDRESSES: Home—13027 Lake Twintree Rd. S.E., Calgary, Alberta, Canada T2J 2X2.

CAREER: Teacher at Canadian Forces Base school in Cold Lake, Alberta, 1970-72; County of Mountain View, Didsbury, Alberta, assistant superintendent of schools, 1978-80; consulting psychologist in Calgary, Alberta, 1980—. Director of Foothills Educational Services, 1978-80. Girls' softball coach, 1981—.

MEMBER: Psychologists Association of Alberta, Alberta Association of School Psychologists (president), Alberta Speaker's Association, Calgary Association for Students and Adults With Learning Disabilities (member of board of directors, 1976-78).

WRITINGS:

The TM Technique and the Art of Learning, Little, Brown, 1977.
Teacher Burnout and What to Do About It, Academic Therapy Publications, 1980.

WORK IN PROGRESS: A revision of *Teacher Burnout and What to Do About It,* tentatively titled *Teacher Burnout Revisited; R.E.A.D. for Your Life: Personal Stress Management* (tentative title).

SIDELIGHTS: Stephen Truch told *CA:* "I've been passionately interested in the topic of stress management since 1970, when I first started transcendental meditation (TM). Meditation is a process of deep relaxation that seems to clear both my mind and body, making it more receptive to learning. I found the benefits to be so profound in fact (and stress-relieving) that I naturally wanted to know more about stress in general and how TM and other deep relaxation/meditation techniques affect us physiologically and psychologically. Pursuing those interests led me to graduate school and the 'research trail.'

"I discovered in my research and reading over the years that personal stress management is a matter of balancing activities from four major categories, each of which is research-based. I coined the acronym R.E.A.D. to help people remember them as (1) Deep Relaxation (2) Exercise (3) Attitude and (4) Diet. I first introduced these principles in my book *Teacher Burnout and What to Do About It* in 1980. Contrary to expectations, the topic of teacher stress has not proven to be faddish. If anything, I find teachers more interested than ever in stress and burnout. So I find myself doing many presentations and workshops on stress management for educators and business people. As well, I found in a recent literature search that hundreds more studies on teacher stress have been done since the publication of my book. This has prompted me to work on another book on the topic, tentatively called *Teacher Burnout Revisited.* The need is great.

"I have plenty of stressors in my life, so I try to live by my own advice and strive for the 'balanced life.' My family is my highest priority. I love my wife and children dearly. I meditate twice a day for twenty minutes. My life is full of challenges, and I like to meet them with integrity and commitment. I know I can relax. Leisure time means a lot to me. My family and I like spending our summers at our cabin on Shuswap Lake in British Columbia. My highest priority there is just having fun.

"I would like to be wealthy enough to semi-retire and have more time for fun and writing."

AVOCATIONAL INTERESTS: Swimming, jogging, skiing, tennis, squash, travel.

*   *   *

TSADICK, Marta Gabre
See GABRE-TSADICK, Marta

*   *   *

TUCHOCK, Wanda   1898(?)-1985

OBITUARY NOTICE: Born c. 1898 in Pueblo, Colo.; died February 10, 1985, in Woodland Hills, Calif. Director of motion pictures and screenwriter. Tuchock worked in the entertainment industry for forty-six years beginning in 1927. Her screenwriting credits include "Nob Hill," "The Foxes of Harrow," "The Homestretch," and the 1930 version of "Billy the Kid." She also co-directed "Finishing School" with George Nicholls, Jr., in 1934. Tuchock was a lifetime member of the Motion Picture and Television Fund's board of trustees.

OBITUARIES AND OTHER SOURCES:

BOOKS

International Motion Picture Almanac, Quigley, 1985.
Women Who Make Movies, Hopkinson & Blade, 1975.

PERIODICALS

Chicago Tribune, February 14, 1985.
Los Angeles Times, February 14, 1985.

TUMA, Elias H. 1928-

BRIEF ENTRY: Born November 12, 1928, in Kafr-Yasif, Palestine (now Israel). American economist, educator, and author. Tuma became a professor of economics at the University of California, Davis, in 1971. He has also been a fellow of the Near Eastern Center at the University of California, Los Angeles, and a special consultant to the United Nations. The educator's research interests range from international politics to agrarian reform. His books include *Twenty-Six Centuries of Agrarian Reform: A Comparative Analysis* (University of California Press, 1965), *Economic History and the Social Sciences: Problems of Methodology* (University of California Press, 1971), *Euroepan Economic History, Tenth Century to the Present: Theory and History of Economic Change* (Harper, 1971), *Peacemaking and the Immoral War: Arabs and Jews in the Middle East* (Harper, 1972), and *The Economic Case for Palestine* (St. Martin's, 1978). Tuma edited *Food and Population in the Middle East* (Institute of Middle Eastern and North African Affairs, 1976). *Address:* Department of Economics, University of California, Davis, Calif. 95616.

* * *

TURNER, Bryan S(tanley) 1945-

PERSONAL: Born January 14, 1945, in Birmingham, England; son of Stanley (a waiter) and Joan (a waitress; maiden name, Brookes) Turner; married Lesley Cawley (a public servant), 1965 (divorced); children: Nicolas D. W. *Education:* University of Leeds, B.A., 1966, Ph.D., 1970. *Politics:* Centralist.

ADDRESSES: Home—3 Lowan Ave., Glenalta, South Australia, Australia. *Office*—Department of Sociology, Flinders University of South Australia, Bedford Park, South Australia 5052, Australia.

CAREER: University of Aberdeen, Aberdeen, Scotland, lecturer, 1969-74; University of Lancaster, Lancaster, England, lecturer, 1974-78; University of Aberdeen, senior lecturer, 1978-80, reader, 1980-82; Flinders University of South Australia, Bedford Park, professor of sociology, 1982—.

MEMBER: Australian and New Zealand Sociological Association (vice-president, 1983).

AWARDS, HONORS: Morris Ginsberg fellow (London School of Economics and Political Science), 1981.

WRITINGS:

Weber and Islam: A Critical Study, Routledge & Kegan Paul, 1974.
Marx and the End of Orientalism, Allen & Unwin, 1978.
(With Nicholas Abercrombie and Stephen Hill) *The Dominant Ideology Thesis,* Allen & Unwin, 1980.
For Weber: Essays on the Sociology of Fate, Routledge & Kegan Paul, 1981.
(With Mike Hepworth) *Confession: Studies in Deviance and Religion,* Routledge & Kegan Paul, 1982.
Religion and Social Theory: A Materialist Perspective, Heinemann, 1983.
(With Abercrombie and Hill) *Penguin Dictionary of Sociology,* Penguin, 1984.
Capitalism and Class in the Middle East, Heinemann, 1984.

The Body and Society: Explorations in Social Theory, Basil Blackwell, 1984.
Capitalism and Individualism, Allen & Unwin, in press.
Talcott Parsons and the Sociological Paradigm, Routledge & Kegan Paul, in press.
Max Weber and the Sociology of Capitalism, Routledge & Kegan Paul, in press.
Citizenship and Capitalism, Allen & Unwin, in press.

SIDELIGHTS: In *Confession: Studies in Deviance and Religion* Bryan S. Turner and Mike Hepworth investigate the characteristics of the act of confession in Western society, perceiving it both as an exercise in individual conscience and as a form of social coercion that validates social norms and authority. Barbara Goodwin, writing in the *Times Literary Supplement,* observed that ''the book's main virtue is that it reveals the uniqueness of confession in Western society . . . [where] Christianity has propagated a special, individualistic conception of confession as a result of the doctrine of free will and responsibility, a conception which fashions both our religious and our legal institutions.'' The critic added that while Turner and Hepworth explicate the private-public tensions inherent in confession they ''neglect confession as a normal form of communication, integral to an individualistic culture.'' ''A study of confession in its broadest sense as a cultural and linguistic practice would make a useful companion volume to their fascinating but specialized study,'' Goodwin concluded.

Turner told *CA:* ''As a working-class child, my aim was to be as powerful and succesful as possible in an academic field. My aim is to write at least one major book per year for the next twenty years. My central interest is the development of sociology at university level. My main political belief is the moral value of the maximum degree of democratic citizenship.

''While originally concerned with the problem of religion in modern societies, my work has moved towards an analysis of the conditions of individual and collective resistance to social control. This interest has led to the study of the history and origins of individualism.''

AVOCATIONAL INTERESTS: Bush-walking, jogging, collecting antiques, exploring southeast Asia (''having migrated to Australia in 1982'').

BIOGRAPHICAL/CRITICAL SOURCES:

PERIODICALS

Los Angeles Times Book Review, December 20, 1981.
Times Literary Supplement, September 11, 1981, December 17, 1982, June 1, 1984.

* * *

TWEDT, Dik Warren 1920-1985

OBITUARY NOTICE—See index for *CA* sketch: Born December 30, 1920, in Minneapolis, Minn.; died March 17, 1985, in St. Louis, Mo. Educator, psychologist, market researcher, businessman, administrator, and author. Twedt taught marketing and psychology at the University of Missouri—St. Louis from 1972 until his death. He held several important business posts, including president of Faison & Twedt, a marketing and consulting company, from 1960 to 1962, and director of marketing planning for Oscar Mayer & Company from 1963 to 1971. Twedt also worked for advertising companies, such as the Chicago-based Leo Burnett Company, and served the American Marketing Association in various administrative capacities, including national vice-president in 1962. Among his books are *Essentials of the Promotional Mix,* which he wrote with Harry Deane Wolfe, *Modern Marketing, Personality and Marketing,* and *Survey of Marketing Research.* Twedt also contributed to several marketing and psychology journals, including *Harvard Business Review* and *Journal of Applied Psychology.*

OBITUARIES AND OTHER SOURCES:

PERIODICALS

Marketing News, April 12, 1985.

*   *   *

TYLER, W. T.
   See HAMRICK, Samuel J., Jr.

*   *   *

TYRMAND, Leopold   1920-1985

OBITUARY NOTICE—See index for *CA* sketch: Born May 16, 1920, in Warsaw, Poland; died of a heart attack, March 19, 1985, in Rockford, Ill. (one source says Fort Meyers, Fla.). Editor and author. Tyrmand was an outspoken opponent of liberalism and communism. A member of the Polish underground during the German and Russian occupations of Poland, Tyrmand was imprisoned by the Russians during the early 1940's for his anti-Stalinist activities. He, nevertheless, maintained his anti-regime position, and in 1953 the weekly newspaper where he worked as a writer was shut down for refusing to print a Stalin eulogy. After immigrating to the United States in 1966 Tyrmand co-founded and served as vice-president of the Rockford Institute, a foundation dedicated to conservatism in American literature. Among Tyrmand's most important works are the novels *Zly* and *The Seven Long Voyages* and the collected essays *Notebooks of a Dilettante.* Tyrmand also edited volumes such as *Explorations in Freedom: Prose, Narrative and Poetry From Kultura* and *Kultura Essays.* He contributed articles to periodicals, including the *New Yorker* and *Reporter,* and served as editor of *Chronicles of Culture* and *Rockford Papers.*

OBITUARIES AND OTHER SOURCES:

PERIODICALS

Chicago Tribune, March 22, 1985.
New York Times, March 22, 1985.

U

UNCLE GORDON
    See ROE, F(rederic) Gordon

*   *   *

UNDERWOOD, Ted Leroy 1935-

PERSONAL: Born July 22, 1935, in Agra, Kan.; son of Theodore R. (a salesman) and Dora (a homemaker; maiden name, Hassler) Underwood; married Judith Roberts (an educational specialist), June 14, 1958; children: Tamara Lyn, Mark Andrew. *Education:* University of California, Berkeley, B.A., 1959; Berkeley Baptist Divinity School, B.D., 1962; University of London, Ph.D., 1965.

ADDRESSES: Home—3524 Beard Ave. N., Minneapolis, Minn. 55422. *Office*—Department of History, Social Science Division, University of Minnesota, Morris, Minn. 56267.

CAREER: Bishop College, Dallas, Tex., assistant professor of ecclesiastical history, 1965-67; University of Minnesota, Morris, assistant professor, 1967-68, associate professor, 1968-73, professor of history, 1973—, chairman of Social Science Division, 1978—. Co-director of West Central Minnesota Historical Research Center, 1972-74. Member of board of directors of Morris Centennial Celebration, 1970-71.

MEMBER: American Society of Church History, Friends Historical Society, Conference on British Studies.

AWARDS, HONORS: Morse-AMOCO Foundation Award for Outstanding Contributions to Undergraduate Education, 1975; Bush Foundation fellow, 1985.

WRITINGS:

(Contributor) Peter Toon, editor, *Puritans, the Millennium, and the Future of Israel,* James Clarke, 1970.
(Editor with Roger Sharrack) *The Miscellaneous Works of John Bunyan,* Volume I: *Some Gospel Truths Opened, a Vindication of Some Gospel Truths Opened, and A Few Sighs From Hell,* Oxford University Press, 1980.

Contributor to scholarly journals.

WORK IN PROGRESS: Editing *The Miscellaneous Works of John Bunyan,* Volume IV, publication by Oxford University Press expected in 1989.

SIDELIGHTS: Ted Leroy Underwood told *CA:* "The University of Minnesota, Morris, is a small, undergraduate, residential liberal arts college, but one of the few in the United States to be also a part of a large public university system. It provides for students a high quality small college experience which is affordable. For faculty, it offers the attractiveness of undergraduate teaching, as well as the challenge and support of a major research institution. In my case, it has made possible, among other things, participation in the editorial project, 'The Miscellaneous Works of John Bunyan.' When the project is completed, all of Bunyan's works will be available in modern Oxford editions, providing for scholars and others easy access to the insights, attitudes, and creative imagination of this influential seventeenth-century nonconformist preacher and writer. The project reflects my broader interest in helping illuminate the history of the lower class as well as the more radical religious elements in seventeenth-century English society. I have been inspired in this effort by Dr. Geoffrey F. Nuttal of the University of London, among others."

*   *   *

UNDY, R(oger) 1938-

PERSONAL: Born November 2, 1938, in Nottingham, England; son of Harold (a fitter) and Harriet (a housewife; maiden name, Holmes) Undy; married Kathleen Claire Stevenson (a librarian's assistant), September 19, 1959; children: Kim Undy-Burden, Ruth. *Education:* Ruskin College, Oxford, Diploma, 1969; Wadham College, Oxford, M.A., 1972.

ADDRESSES: Office—Templeton College, Kennington, Oxford OX1 5NY, England.

CAREER: Boots Pure Drug Co., Nottingham, England, fitter, 1954-67; Oxford University, Oxford Centre for Management Studies (now Templeton College), Oxford, England, research associate, 1972-75, research fellow, 1975-77, fellow in industrial relations, 1977-80, senior tutor, 1980-83, fellow in industrial relations, 1983—. Engineering union shop steward, 1965-67; Labour party candidate for Parliament for Bridgewater, England, 1974.

WRITINGS:

(With Valerie Ellis, William E. J. McCarthy, and A. M. Halmos) *Change in Trade Unions,* Hutchinson, 1981.

(With McCarthy and Cyril Jennings) *The Identification of Training Needs,* Manpower Services Commission, 1983.

(With Roderick Martin) *Ballots and Trade Union Democracy,* Basil Blackwell, 1984.

(With Martin) *Technological Development and Its Impact on Shiftwork in the Newspaper Industry: The United Kingdom,* European Foundation for the Improvement of Living and Working Conditions, 1984.

(Contributor) Christopher Clegg, Karen Legge, and Nigel Kemp, editors, *Case Studies in Organization Behavior,* Harper, 1985.

Contributor to industrial relations journals.

WORK IN PROGRESS: The Line Management of Industrial Relations, publication expected in 1987; *The Management of Change in Industrial Relations,* publication expected in 1988.

SIDELIGHTS: R. Undy told *CA:* "My transition from fitter to academic and author, studying and researching in industrial relations, was most influenced by my father's interest in, and enthusiasm for, both education and the trade union movement and by my own experiences as a shop steward. Given this background I won a trade union scholarship and re-entered full-time education at the age of twenty-nine. From that point on it was probably a case of being in the right place (Oxford) at the right time.

"My main work on trade unions attempts to show the diversity and complexity of British trade unions. In what is a highly contentious and politically sensitive field of work, the research on union ballots and democracy examines and questions the value of legislating for a particular form of union democracy when faced by widely differing forms of union organization. It also discusses the role of independent trade unions in maintaining a liberal democracy.

"Too often in industrial relations politicians, trade union leaders, and managers know a lot about their own part of the system but little about the world of their colleagues and adversaries. It is hoped that the research and writing so far completed, and that still in progress, will help the practitioner and student better appreciate the contexts in which trade unionists and managers work and interact."

* * *

UNGER, Walter P(eter)   1939-

BRIEF ENTRY: Born April 8, 1939, in Toronto, Ontario, Canada. Canadian dermatologist, educator, and author. Unger has been a practicing dermatologist since 1968. In 1973 he became chief of dermatology at Toronto's Wellesley Hospital and assistant professor at University of Toronto. Unger has been president of Dermatologists Administrative Services Limited since 1970. His books include *The Intelligent Man's Guide to Hair Transplants and Other Methods of Hair Replacement* (Contemporary Books, 1979) and *Hair Transplantation* (Dekker, 1979). *Address:* 26 Alexandra Wood, Toronto, Ontario, Canada M5N 2S1; and 2156 Yonge St., Toronto, Ontario, Canada M4S 2A5.

URQUHART, Colin   1940-

PERSONAL: Born January 26, 1940, in Twickenham, England; son of Kenneth Hector (an architect) and Lilian Rosida (Batten) Urquhart; married Caroline Josephine May (a housewife and author), October 24, 1964; children: Claire, Clive Ross, Andrea. *Education:* King's College, London, Associate, 1963.

ADDRESSES: Office—Bethany Fellowship, The Hyde, Handcross, Haywards Heath, West Sussex RH17 6EX, England. *Agent*—Edward England Books, Crowton House, The Broadway, Crowborough, East Sussex TN6 1AB, England.

CAREER: Ordained Anglican priest, 1963; Anglican curate in Cheshunt, England, 1963-67; priest in charge of Anglican church in Letchworth, England, 1967-70; vicar of Anglican church in Luton, England, 1970-76; Bethany Fellowship, Haywards Heath, England, director, 1976—.

WRITINGS:

When the Spirit Comes (autobiography), Hodder & Stoughtonj, 1974, Bethany Fellowship (United States), 1975.
My Father Is the Gardener, Hodder & Stoughton, 1977.
Anything You Ask, Hodder & Stoughton, 1978.
In Christ Jesus, Hodder & Stoughton, 1981.
Faith for the Future (autobiography), Hodder & Stoughton, 1982.
Holy Fire, Hodder & Stoughton, 1984.
The Positive Kingdom, Hodder & Stoughton, 1985.
Receive Your Healing, Hodder & Stoughton, in press.

Contributor to Christian magazines.

WORK IN PROGRESS: Preparation for a book on revival.

SIDELIGHTS: Colin Urquhart described his work as "the teaching of the Bible in the power of the Holy Spirit, and ministry to individuals at the corporate church in his power. I am concerned with evangelism and revival."

He added: "My writing began out of an experience of revival in the church where I was pastor and in the movement of the Holy Spirit that brought many to new life, the empowering of the Holy Spirit and to healing in the name of Jesus. My present ministry has been an extension of that local ministry traveling to many nations encouraging renewal and revival. Each of the books that has been written has come out of personal experience of the word being lived out in practice. Most are simple biblical expositions but related very much for everyday life and to how it is possible for us to live according to the Word and in the power of the Holy Spirit.

"There has always been a ready market for the books here because of the extent of the ministry in this country and beyond. This is a great responsibility but it is also a tremendous opportunity. There are so many today who are discovering the experience of the Holy Spirit but without their lives getting deeply rooted in the word of God. They need to know how to live victoriously, overcoming all the difficulties of the world, the flesh, and the devil. So each of the books is written very much from a faith perspective, that Jesus means us to take his promises seriously. We are able to do the same things as he has done and greater things still. We are to anticipate that God will answer our prayers of faith, doing as he promised, anything we ask in the name of Jesus. Obviously such promises can only be fulfilled in the power of the Holy Spirit. Therefore it is important for every Christian to know a true baptism in the Holy Spirit where the life and power of God's spirit is released throughout their whole being.''

BIOGRAPHICAL/CRITICAL SOURCES:

BOOKS

Urquhart, Caroline, *His God, My God,* Hodder & Stoughton, 1983.

V

van BEECK, Frans Jozef 1930-

PERSONAL: Born June 11, 1930, in Helmond, the Netherlands; son of L. W. M. (a postmaster) and J. H. (Mennen) van Beeck. *Education:* Collegium Berchmanianum, Nijmegen, Netherlands, Ph.L., 1954; University of Amsterdam, Ph.D., 1961; Collegium Maximum Canisianum, Maastricht, Netherlands, S.T.L., 1964.

ADDRESSES: Office—Department of Theology, Boston College, Chestnut Hill, Mass. 02167.

CAREER: Entered Society of Jesus (Jesuits), 1948, ordained Roman Catholic priest, 1963; St. Ignatius College, Amsterdam, Netherlands, teacher of English (junior), 1957-59; Veldeke College, Maastricht, Netherlands, teacher of English (senior), 1961-64; St. Ignatius College, teacher of English (senior), 1965-67; prefect of studies for Jesuit Dutch province, 1965-68; Boston College, Chestnut Hill, Mass., assistant professor, 1968-74, associate professor, 1974-82, professor of theology, 1982-85; Loyola University of Chicago, Chicago, Ill., John Cardinal Cody Professor, 1985—. Professional member of National Training Laboratories Institute of Applied Behavioral Science (NTLI), 1970-72; visiting professor of theology at Weston School of Theology, Cambridge, Mass., 1977-78; elected delegate to General Congregation XXXIII of the Society of Jesus, Rome, 1983.

MEMBER: North American Academy of Ecumenists, American Theological Society, American Academy of Religion, Catholic Theological Society of America.

WRITINGS:

The Poems and Translations of Sir Edward Sherburne, 1616-1702: Introduced and Annotated, Van Gorcum (Assen, Netherlands), 1961.
Christ Proclaimed: Christology as Rhetoric, Paulist Press, 1979.
Meditations in Glass, St. John's Bangor, 1981.
Grounded in Love, University Press of America, 1981.

Contributor to theology journals, including *Journal of Ecumenical Studies* and *Theological Studies.*

WORK IN PROGRESS: Admirable Exchange, a two-volume systematic theology, publication expected in 1990.

SIDELIGHTS: In *Commonweal* John Shea wrote that Frans Jozef van Beeck's *Christ Proclaimed: Christology as Rhetoric*

"is a sustained and brilliant argument for the neglected emphasis of the presence of Christ in the spirit, worship, and witness in Christology." The author examines the thinking of such philosopher-theologians as Paul Tillich, Friedrich Schleiermacher, and Martin Buber, using it to clarify his own thoughts concerning a Christological rhetoric that sustains Christological logic. Shea concluded: "*Christ Proclaimed* is a landmark work. Van Beeck's erudition is vast. . . . Rarely has a theological work used previous thinking so creatively. . . . This book takes some pondering; but it is well worth it."

Van Beeck told *CA* that he has taught, given retreats, and traveled in Canada, England, and Indonesia. He has done some training at the National Training Laboratories in Bethel, Maine. He added: "I like to combine disciplines, experiences, etc. The whole world asks to be appreciated, treasured, and understood: It is God's creation."

BIOGRAPHICAL/CRITICAL SOURCES:

PERIODICALS

America, November 15, 1980.
Commonweal, January 30, 1981.

* * *

Van DEVENTER, David E(arl) 1937-

BRIEF ENTRY: Born May 31, 1937, in Syracuse, N.Y. American historian, educator, and author. In 1965 Van Deventer moved from Kent State University to California State University where he has been a professor of American history since 1980. He wrote *The Emergence of Provincial New Hampshire, 1623-1741* (Johns Hopkins University Press, 1976). *Address:* Department of History, California State University, 800 North State College Blvd., Fullerton, Calif. 92634.

BIOGRAPHICAL/CRITICAL SOURCES:

PERIODICALS

American Historical Review, April, 1977.

* * *

Van DINE, S. S.
See WRIGHT, Willard Huntington

VAN HORN, William 1939-

PERSONAL: Born February 15, 1939, in Oakland, Calif.; son of William Jennings and Virginia Ruth (Hygelund) Van Horn; married Frances Elaine Dixon (an operating room nurse), July 29, 1966; children: Noel Charles, Tish Johanna. *Education:* California College of Arts and Crafts, B.F.A., 1961.

ADDRESSES: Home and office—4562 Ranger Ave., North Vancouver, British Columbia, Canada V7R 3L7.

CAREER: Imagination, Inc., San Francisco, Calif., inking and background artist, 1961; Moulin Studios, San Francisco, layout and background artist, 1961-62; The Smith Company, San Francisco, designer, illustrator and layout artist, 1964; Walter Landor Associates, San Francisco, artist in motion picture department, 1965-67; Davidson Films, San Francisco, art director of animation department, 1967-75; Aesop Films, Inc., San Francisco, co-owner and art director, 1975-77; free-lance artist and writer. Illustrator, designer, and author of metric system posters, California State Department of Education, 1975, and of metric system study prints, Encyclopaedia Britannica Corporation, 1976. *Military service:* U.S. Army, artist, 1962-64. U.S. Army Reserve, 1964-66; became sergeant.

AWARDS, HONORS: Numerous international and national film awards, including five CINE Golden Eagle certificates from the Council on International Nontheatrical Events, 1970-75; two silver medals at Venice Children's Film Festival; first prize at both Columbus and Atlanta Film Festivals, 1971; best of festival citation at National Educational Film Festival, and certificate of merit at Chicago International Film Festival, both 1971, both for "The Weird Number"; Notable Film Award from Calvin Workshop, 1972, and Blue Ribbon from New York Educational Film Festival, 1973, both for "The Weird Number"; West Coast Emmy nomination, 1981, for "The Reluctant Robot."

WRITINGS:

SELF-ILLUSTRATED CHILDREN'S BOOKS

Harry Hoyle's Giant Jumping Bean (Junior Literary Guild selection), Atheneum, 1978.
Twitchtoe, the Beastfinder, Atheneum, 1978.
Harry Hoyle's Slippery Shadow, Scholastic Book Services, 1980.
The Very Special Birthday Present, Atheneum, 1982.
The Wiggly Wobbly Boat Ride (first volume of a series), Scholastic Book Services, 1982.
A Picnic With Bert (second volume of a series), Scholastic Book Services, 1983.
The Big Sneeze (third volume of a series), Scholastic Book Services, 1985.

ANIMATED CHILDREN'S FILM SCRIPTS

(And producer) "Whatever Is Fun," Audio Brandon Films, 1973.
(And producer) "The Truth About Horsefeathers," Xerox Films, 1974.
(And producer) "Idiom's Delight," Xerox Films, 1974.
(And producer) "If You're a Horse," Xerox Films, 1974.
(And producer) "Where Did Leonard Harry Go?," Xerox Films, 1974.
(And producer) "The Telescope," Encyclopaedia Britannica Educational Corp., 1976.
(And producer) "Zenith," Encyclopaedia Britannica Educational Corp., 1977.

(Co-author and producer) "The Reluctant Robot," released for television by Field Communications Group, 1981.

WORK IN PROGRESS: The Great Blue Earthquake, the fourth volume in a series, for Scholastic Book Services; *The Mouse With the Very Long Legs; Uncle Conrad.*

SIDELIGHTS: William Van Horn told *CA:* "I once wrote an autobiographical sketch for the Junior Literary Guild which, written in the third person, was intended to be a bit tongue-in-cheek. They liked it, but to my horror, put it into the first person and made me sound like a complete idiot. I shall try to be a bit more serious this time.

"I began to draw when I was very young, five or six. I drew mostly war scenes and pictures of Mickey Mouse. Later I tried my hand at Dick Tracy and the Lone Ranger. I really wasn't very good at any of them, but was mercifully too young to realize it. I was very interested in astronomy at one point, and spent quite a bit of time trying to draw a decent picture of the planet Saturn. When that didn't work out, I switched to dinosaurs. Drawing dinosaurs was much more satisfying somehow, and to this day I've had a love affair with the things. The characters in my latest books are two little dinosaurs named Charlie and Fred.

"From around 1954, I was determined that I would work someday in the animation business. In college I did my own films (or tried to) and gained just enough practical experience to land a job with an animation studio upon graduation. It was during my years in the animation business that I began to write. It was out of sheer necessity. We often received scripts for animated films (all for children, by the way) that were so lifeless and pedantic that something had to be done. With my partner, Mitchell Rose, I learned to put one word after another in a reasonably entertaining way. We must have done something right because many of our films went on to win awards.

"Later I began to write my own scripts, seven of which were sold to distributors. I then produced the films, and a couple of them won awards.

"The first children's book I wrote was *Harry Hoyle's Giant Jumping Bean.* It sold on its first submission, and believe me, that was absolutely the last time it was ever so easy. Every book since then has involved an uphill fight. I really think that a children's book is the most difficult thing to write, although many friends are under the impression that if the book can be read in ten minutes, it can't therefore have taken more than twenty minutes to write.

"I was born and raised in Oakland, California, and lived for many years in San Francisco. I moved (in 1980) with my family to Vancouver, British Columbia. My wife Elaine is a Canadian citizen, so she was able to get the rest of us in. The children and myself are landed immigrants."

*   *   *

VAN NIEL, Cornelius B(ernardus) 1897-1985

OBITUARY NOTICE: Born November 4, 1897, in Haarlem, Netherlands; died March 10, 1985, in Carmel, Calif. Microbiologist, educator, and author. Van Niel, a professor of microbiology at Stanford University's Hopkins Marine Station for thirty-four years, was the first person to explain the chemical basis for photosynthesis. He received a number of awards for his work in microbiology, including the National Medal of Science in 1964 and the Rumford Medal of the American

Academy of Arts and Sciences in 1967. Van Niel co-authored *The Microbe's Contribution to Biology* with A. J. Kluyver in 1956.

OBITUARIES AND OTHER SOURCES:

BOOKS

American Men and Women of Science: The Physical and Biological Sciences, 15th edition, Bowker, 1982.
McGraw-Hill Modern Scientists and Engineers, McGraw, 1980.
Who's Who in America, 39th edition, Marquis, 1976.

PERIODICALS

New York Times, January 14, 1964, March 14, 1985.

*   *   *

VAN SETERS, John   1935-

PERSONAL: Born May 2, 1935, in Hamilton, Ontario, Canada; son of Hugo and Anne (a homemaker; maiden name, Hubert) Van Seters; married Elizabeth Marie Malmberg (a homemaker), June 11, 1960; children: Peter John, Deborah Elizabeth. *Education:* University of Toronto, B.A., 1958; Yale University, M.A., 1959, Ph.D., 1965; Princeton Theological Seminary, B.D., 1962. *Religion:* Presbyterian.

ADDRESSES: Home—303 Hoot Owl Lane, Chapel Hill, N.C. 27514. *Office*—Department of Religion, 101 Saunders Hall, University of North Carolina at Chapel Hill, Chapel Hill, N.C. 27514.

CAREER: Waterloo Lutheran University, Waterloo, Ontario, assistant professor of Near Eastern studies, 1965-67; Andover Newton Theological School, Newton Centre, Mass., associate professor of Old Testament studies, 1967-70; University of Toronto, Toronto, Ontario, associate professor, 1970-76, profesor of Near Eastern studies, 1976-77; University of North Carolina at Chapel Hill, James A. Gray Professor of Biblical Literature, 1977—, chairman of department of religion, 1980-85.

MEMBER: American Oriental Society, American Association of University Professors, American Schools of Oriental Research, Society of Biblical Literature, Society for the Study of Egyptian Antiquities.

AWARDS, HONORS: Woodrow Wilson fellow, 1958; J. J. Obermann fellow, 1962-64; Agusta Hazard fellow, 1964-65; Canada Council research grantee, 1973; Guggenheim fellow, 1979-80; National Endowment for the Humanities research fellow, 1985-86.

WRITINGS:

The Hyksos: A New Investigation, Yale University Press, 1966.
Abraham in History and Tradition, Yale University Press, 1975.
In Search of History: Historiography in the Ancient World and the Origins of Biblical History, Yale University Pess, 1983.

Contributor to journals, including *Journal of Biblical Literature, Orientalia, Biblica, Vetus Testamentum,* and *Zeitschrift fur die alttestamentliche Wissenschaft.*

WORK IN PROGRESS: "A study of the nature of historiography in the Pentateuch as a sequel to *In Search of History.* The authors of the Pentateuch will be viewed as belonging to the intellectual tradition of ancient history writing—as the best way to understand the diversity of their materials, the ways in which they brought them together, and their motivation for writing."

SIDELIGHTS: In *The Hyksos: A New Investigation* John Van Seters examines the kings who ruled Egypt during most of the Second Intermediate Period and about whom few facts are actually known; he employs long-existing information, recently-discovered textual evidence, and new archaeological finds from western Asia in determining who these Hyksos rulers were and what they achieved. In a *Times Literary Supplement* critique one reviewer wrote that Van Seters presents his investigation with "great confidence. The study is useful in the overall freshness of the approach and especially in the emphasis given to archaeological evidence." While the critic noted that the author "is inclined to assume the possession of too much knowledge by his readers" and his book displays "the terseness of argument proper to" a doctoral dissertation, he nonetheless called *The Hyksos: A New Investigation* "the best general study of the Hyksos to have appeared for many years. It properly emphasizes certain conclusions now generally accepted by Egyptologists, but often ignored by historians of western Asia and by popular writers on the ancient world."

Van Seters told *CA:* "The historical criticism of the Old Testament stands in great need of revitalization. Many have grown weary of its complexity and rigor as a discipline of learning and have become preoccupied with a plethora of simple methodological fads. What is needed is another inspiring genius like Julius Wellhausen. While there is none like him on the scene today, it may still be possible—and it is my modest ambition—to rekindle an interest in the discipline of historical criticism."

BIOGRAPHICAL/CRITICAL SOURCES:

PERIODICALS

Times Literary Supplement, April 20, 1967.

*   *   *

VAUGHAN WILLIAMS, Ralph   1872-1958

BRIEF ENTRY: Born October 12, 1872, in Down Ampney, Gloucestershire, England; died August 26, 1958, in London, England. British composer, musician, and author. Regarded as one of the twentieth century's finest British composers, Vaughan Williams wrote orchestral and chamber music, stage music, songs, and film scores. Vaughan Williams took his first music instruction as a youth, then went on to study music both at Cambridge and the Royal College of Music. After completing his studies he worked as an organist in London but before long took the opportunity to study with Max Bruch in Berlin; he also practiced orchestration with Maurice Ravel in Paris and studied the music of Edward Elgar, identifying all three composers as having major influences on his music. Vaughan Williams's important works include *Fantasia on a Theme by Thomas Tallis* (1909), for double stringed orchestra and string quartet; *A Sea Symphony* (1910); *A London Symphony* (1914), which earned him international recognition; the opera *Sir John in Love* (1929), based on Shakespeare's *Merry Wives of Windsor;* and *The Pilgrim's Progress* (1949), which the composer himself identified as "a morality."

Vaughan Willliams was often described in the British press as "the grand old man of Englsih music" and was regarded as instrumental in fostering national pride in Britain's native music. The composer began the study of the English folk song early in his career, and some critics contend that his compositions exhibit an English character deriving from folk roots. Throughout his life Vaughan Williams was associated with the English Folksong and Dance Society. He also wrote the books

National Music (1934) and *The Making of Music* (1955). *Heirs and Rebels*, a collection of letters between Vaughan Williams and his lifelong friend musician Gustav Holst, was published posthumously in 1959. *Address:* London, England.

BIOGRAPHICAL/CRITICAL SOURCES:

BOOKS

Current Biography, Wilson, 1953, November, 1958.
1000 Makers of the Twentieth Century, David & Charles, 1971.
The Oxford Companion to Music, 10th edition, Oxford University Press, 1974.
The Reader's Encyclopedia, 2nd edition, Crowell, 1965.

PERIODICALS

New York Times, August 26, 1958.

*   *   *

VEBLEN, Thorstein (Bunde)   1857-1929

BRIEF ENTRY: Born July 30, 1857, in Valders, Wis.; died August 3, 1929, in Menlo Park, Calif. American social scientist, economist, educator, and author. Occasionally called "the American Marx," Veblen was considered an outstanding and influential social scientist by his peers. Many of his ideas and insights have become an integral part of American sociological analysis; among the many terms he coined are "conspicuous consumption," "the leisure class," "cultural lag," "waste," and "sense of workmanship." His best known work, *The Theory of the Leisure Class* (1899), defined idleness, wastefulness, and excessive consumption among the wealthy as symbols of social status. Veblen's other works, still considered relevant today, include *The Theory of Business Enterprise* (1904), *Imperial Germany and the Industrial Revolution* (1915), *The Higher Learning in America: A Memorandum on the Conduct of Universities by Business Men* (1918), *Absentee Ownership and Business Enterprise in Recent Times: The Case of America* (1923), and his posthumously published *Essays on Our Changing Order* (1934).

BIOGRAPHICAL/CRITICAL SOURCES:

BOOKS

Encyclopedia of American Biography, Harper, 1974.
McGraw-Hill Encyclopedia of World Biography, McGraw, 1973.
The Oxford Companion to American Literature, 4th edition, Oxford University Press, 1966.
The Reader's Encyclopedia, 2nd edition, Crowell, 1965.
Webster's New World Companion to English and American Literature, World Publishing, 1973.

*   *   *

VEDDER, Richard K(ent)   1940-

PERSONAL: Born November 5, 1940, in Urbana, Ill.; son of Byron C. (a newspaper publisher) and Kathleen (a housewife; maiden name, Fry) Vedder; married Karen Pirosko (a teacher), June 18, 1968; children: Virin Kent, Vanette Kelly. *Education:* Northwestern University, B.A., 1962; University of Illinois at Urbana-Champaign, A.M., 1963, Ph.D., 1965. *Politics:* Republican. *Religion:* Presbyterian.

ADDRESSES: Home—295 Beechwood Dr., Athens, Ohio 45701. *Office*—Department of Economics, Ohio University, Athens, Ohio 45701.

CAREER: Ohio University, Athens, assistant professor, 1965-69, associate professor, 1969-74, professor of economics, 1974—, chairman of department, 1980-81. Visiting professor at Claremont Men's College (now Claremont McKenna College), 1979-80, and University of Colorado at Boulder, 1979, 1980. Economist for Joint Economic Committee of Congress, 1981-82; member of board of trustees of Business History Conference.

MEMBER: American Economic Association, Economic History Association, Rotary.

AWARDS, HONORS: Grant from Rockefeller Foundation and Ford Foundation, 1974-75; fellow of Earhart Foundation, 1963-70, and Pacific Institute for Public Policy Research, 1984.

WRITINGS:

(Editor with David C. Klingaman) *Essays in Nineteenth Century Economic History: The Old Northwest*, Ohio University Press, 1975.
The American Economy in Historical Perspective, Wadsworth, 1976.
(Editor with Bruce Dalgaard) *Variations in Business and Economic History*, JAI Press, 1982.

Author of column in *Ohio Conservative Review*. Member of editorial board of *Journal of Austrian Economics*.

WORK IN PROGRESS: Principles of Economics, with Robert Clower, Philip Graves, and Robert Sexton, publication by Harcourt expected in 1987; a monograph on the twentieth-century United States.

SIDELIGHTS: Richard K. Vedder told *CA:* "The first great book on economics, Adam Smith's *Wealth of Nations*, was also the best, for it illustrated so clearly how individual self-interest could work for the public good and how highly decentralized decision making in a market environment is often superior to highly centralized decision making. In my works I attempt to demonstrate the essential correctness of Smith's proposition that the 'invisible hand' of the market serves the public as well as private interests. Our scarce resources are allocated relatively efficiently by the market mechanism to secure more goods and services than they are where market forces are not allowed to operate."

*   *   *

VEIT, Lawrence A.   1938-

BRIEF ENTRY: Born in 1938, in New York, N.Y. American economist and author. Veit has worked as a representative of the U.S. Treasury Department in India, as an economist for the U.S. Department of State and the National Industrial Conference Board, and as a research fellow for the Council on Foreign Relations. He is the author of *U.S. Production Abroad and the Balance of Payments: A Survey of Corporate Investment Experience* (National Industrial Conference Board, 1966), *India's Second Revolution: The Dimensions of Development* (McGraw, 1976), and *Economic Adjustment to an Energy-Short World: A View From the United States* (Allanheld, Osmun, 1979).

BIOGRAPHICAL/CRITICAL SOURCES:

PERIODICALS

New York Times Book Review, July 25, 1976.
New York Times, January 28, 1977.

VERHOEVEN, Paul 1901-1975

OBITUARY NOTICE: Born in 1901 in Unna/Westfalen, Germany (now West Germany); died of a heart attack, March 22, 1975, in Munich, West Germany. Actor, director, and screenwriter. A stage and screen actor, Verhoeven appeared in "Menschen im Netz" (released in the United States as "The Unwilling Agent") and a 1968 version of "Hamlet." His writings include the screenplay for the 1979 film "Soldier of Orange."

OBITUARIES AND OTHER SOURCES:

BOOKS

Who Was Who on Screen, 2nd edition, Bowker, 1977.

* * *

VERISSIMO, Erico (Lopes) 1905-1975

OBITUARY NOTICE: Born December 17, 1905, in Cruz Alta, Rio Grande do Sul, Brazil; died November 28, 1975, in Porto Alegre, Brazil. Lecturer, editor, and author. Regarded as one of Brazil's major twentieth-century authors, Verissimo was still in his teens when, influenced by the works of Portuguese novelist Eca de Queiroz, he decided to become a writer. The would-be author had to leave high school to help support his family, but he managed to find time to write short fiction while holding a variety of odd jobs. Eventually he moved to the capital city of Porto Alegre, where he served as editorial consultant to the publishing house O Globo and as editor of the firm's magazine. During the 1940's, after achieving success as a writer, Verissimo was a guest lecturer at the Berkeley campus of the University of California, and from 1953 to 1956 he served as director of the Department of Cultural Affairs of the Pan-American Union in Washington, D.C.

Verissimo first achieved critical success with *Caminhos cruzados,* winner of the Graca Aranha Prize from the Brazilian Academy of Letters. Translated as *Crossroads,* the novel has been compared to works by Aldous Huxley. Verissimo's first commercial success was the best-seller *Olhai os lirios do campo,* which was later translated as *Consider the Lilies of the Field.* The trilogy *O tempo e o vento,* considered the most ambitious of Verissimo's works, was published in English as *Time and the Wind.* Tracing the fortunes of a Rio Grande do Sul family from the eighteenth to the twentieth century, the trilogy covers a period of radical political and social unrest in Brazil. Other novels by Verissimo in English translation include *Clarissa* and *The Rest Is Silence.* He also wrote short stories, two volumes of impressions of the United States, a biography of Joan of Arc, and several books for children.

OBITUARIES AND OTHER SOURCES:

BOOKS

Encyclopedia of Latin America, McGraw, 1974.
International Authors and Writers Who's Who, 8th edition, Melrose, 1977.
The International Who's Who, 40th edition, Europa, 1976.
The Penguin Companion to American Literature, McGraw, 1971.
World Authors: 1950-1970, H. W. Wilson, 1975.

* * *

VERYAN, Patricia
See BANNISTER, Patricia V.

VESPER, Karl H(ampton) 1932-

PERSONAL: Born August 12, 1932, in San Marino, Calif.; son of Karl C. and Roxie (Armstrong) Vesper; married Joan Frantz (a lecturer), June, 1964; children: Karen, Linda, Holly, Nancy. *Education:* Stanford University, B.S.M.E., 1955, M.S.M.E., 1966, Ph.D., 1969; Harvard University, B.M.A., 1960.

ADDRESSES: Office—Department of Business Administration, University of Washington, Seattle, Wash. 98195.

CAREER: Marine Advisers, Inc., La Jolla, Calif., business manager, 1961-62; Stanford University, Stanford, Calif., research associate, lecturer in engineering, director of case development, 1963-69; University of Washington, Seattle, began as associate professor, became professor of business administration, mechanical engineering, and marine studies, 1974—, chairman of department of management and organization. Director of summer institutes on case method in engineering at Rensselaer Polytechnic Institute and University of Illinois at Urbana-Champaign, 1966-67; Joseph F. Schoen Visiting Professor of Entrepreneurship at Baylor University, 1980; Paul T. Babson Visiting Professor of Entrepreneurship at Babson College, 1981. Director of Hosmer Machine Co., 1966-69; member of board of directors of Washington Research Foundation; member of advisory board of Center for Entrepreneurial Management, Stanford University's Institute for Entrepreneurship, and Syracuse University's Center for Innovation; consultant to U.S. Department of State.

MEMBER: Sigma Xi.

AWARDS, HONORS: Grants from National Science Foundation and National Oceanic and Atmospheric Administration.

WRITINGS:

Engineers at Work, Houghton, 1975.
(With LaRue T. Hosmer and Arnold C. Cooper) *The Entrepreneurial Function,* with instructor's manual, Prentice-Hall, 1977.
(Editor and contributor) *Small Business and Entrepreneurship in the Pacific Northwest,* University of Oregon Books, 1979.
New Venture Strategies, Prentice-Hall, 1980.
Entrepreneurship Education, Babson Center for Entrepreneurial Studies, revised edition, 1980.
Frontiers of Entrepreneurship Research, Babson Center for Entrepreneurial Studies, 1981.
(Co-author) *Encyclopedia of Entrepreneurship,* Prentice-Hall, 1982.
Entrepreneurship and National Policy, Heller Institute for Small Business, 1983.

CONTRIBUTOR

W. A. Hosmer, F. L. Tucker, and A. C. Cooper, editors, *Small Business Management,* Irwin, 1966.
D. V. DeSimone, editor, *Education for Innovation,* Pergamon, 1968.
Ralph Smith, editor, *Engineering as a Career,* McGraw, 1969.
Technical Entrepreneurship, Center for Venture Management, 1972.
Ten Cases in Engineering, Longman, 1973.
Entrepreneurship and Enterprise Development: A Worldwide Perspective, Center for Venture Management, 1975.

D. Cunningham, J. Craig, and T. Schlie, editors, *Technological Innovation*, Westview, 1977.
Don E. Schendel and Charles W. Hofer, editors, *Strategic Management*, Little, Brown, 1979.
Donald L. Sexton and Philip M. Van Auken, editors, *Entrepreneurship Education, 1981*, Baylor University Press, 1981.
Suzanne K. Gray, editor, *Lectures for Inventors*, Boston Public Library, 1983.

OTHER

Editor of "Mechanical Engineering Series," McGraw, 1966-74. Contributor of more than a dozen articles to management and engineering journals.

WORK IN PROGRESS: New Venture Mechanics for Prentice-Hall.

SIDELIGHTS: Karl H. Vesper told *CA:* "My central interest is in helping individuals take initiative in constructive ways to control their own destinies, and in innovation per se."

* * *

VIDICH, Arthur J. 1922-

PERSONAL: Born May 30, 1922, in Minnesota; son of Joseph and Pauline (Pesjak) Vidich; maried Mary Rudolph; children: Charles, Paul, Andrew, Joseph, Rosalind (Mrs. Max Gregoric). *Education:* Attended University of Wisconsin—Madison, 1940-42, M.A., 1948; University of Michigan, B.A., 1943; Harvard University, Ph.D., 1953.

ADDRESSES: Home—37 South Oxford St., Brooklyn, N.Y. 11217. *Office*—Department of Sociology, New School for Social Research, 65 Fifth Ave., New York, N.Y. 10003.

CAREER: Cornell University, Ithaca, N.Y., assistant professor of sociology and resident field director, 1951-54; University of Puerto Rico, Rio Piedras Campus, associate professor of social sciences, 1954-57; University of Connecticut, Storrs, assistant profesor of sociology and anthropology, 1957-60; New School for Social Research, New York, N.Y., professor of sociology and anthropology, 1960—, chairman of department, 1964-69, 1978—. Visiting associate at Florence Heller Graduate School for Advanced Studies in Social Welfare, Brandeis University, 1960-66; visiting professor at Clark University, spring, 1963, 1964-66, Universidad Nacional de Bogota, 1964, University of South Florida, 1969-70, and University of California, San Diego, 1977; senior Fulbright lecturer at University of Zagreb, 1973-74; distinguished lecturer in Kyoto, Japan, summer, 1978; Breman Professor of Social Relations at University of North Carolina at Asheville, 1979; distinguished visiting professor at State University of New York College at New Paltz, 1981. Member of advisory board of Small Towns Institute. *Military service:* U.S. Marine Corps, 1942-46; served in Guam, Saipan, and Japan.

MEMBER: American Sociological Association (fellow; chairman of community section, 1980-82), American Anthropological Association (fellow), Latin American Studies Association, Slavic Studies Association, American Studies Association, Caribbean Studies Association, Fulbright Alumni Association, Eastern Sociological Society, Inter-University Seminar on the Armed Forces and Society (fellow).

AWARDS, HONORS: Peter Gelman Award from Eastern Sociological Society, 1975.

WRITINGS:

(With Joseph Bensman) *Small Town in Mass Society: Class, Power, and Religion in a Rural Community*, Princeton University Press, 1958, revised edition, 1968.
(With Maurice Robert Stein) *Sociology on Trial*, Prentice-Hall, 1963.
(With Bensman and Stein) *Reflections on Community Studies*, Wiley, 1964.
(Editor and author of introduction) Paul Radin, *The Method and Theory of Ethnology*, Basic Books, 1966.
(With Bensman) *The New American Society*, Quadrangle, 1971.
(Compiler with Bensman) *Metropolitan Communities: New Forms of Urban Sub-Communities*, F. Watts, 1975.
(Editor with Robert M. Glassman) *Conflict and Control: Legitimacy Problems of Modern Government*, Sage Publications, 1979.
The Political Impact of Colonial Administration, Arno, 1980.
(Contributor) Art Gallaher, Jr., and Harland Padfield, editors, *The Dying Community*, University of New Mexico Press, 1980.
(Editor with Hans Heinrich Gerth, and author of introduction) *Politics, Character, and Culture: Perspectives From Hans Gerth*, Greenwood Press, 1982.
(With S. M. Lyman) *American Sociology: Worldly Rejections of Religion and Their Directions*, Yale University Press, 1984.

Also co-author of *Identity and Anxiety*, Free Press, 1960, and author of *Ideological Themes in American Anthropology*.

OTHER

Editor of series "Viewpoints in Sociology," Praeger, 1974-77.

Contributor of articles and reviews to sociology journals. Associate editor of *Current Perspectives in Social Theory;* member of editorial board of *Social Research* and *Journal of Political and Military Sociology*.

WORK IN PROGRESS: Not the Same Nation, selected essays on American society; *On the Public Philosophy: Selected Essays by Herbert Blumer on the Process and Order of Race Relations, Industrialization, Collective Behavior, and Mass Society*, with S. M. Lyman; research on the problems of capitalism and industrial society; research on intellectuals and public policy; research on Yugoslavia.

* * *

von FRISCH, Karl (Ritter)
See FRISCH, Karl (Ritter) von

* * *

VO NGUYEN Giap 1912(?)-

BRIEF ENTRY: Surname listed in some sources as Giap; born September 1, 1912 (one source says 1910), in Quangbinh Province, French Indochina (now Vietnam). Vietnamese military officer and author. Vo Nguyen Giap was organizing communist guerrillas in Vietnam as early as World War II. He commanded the guerrilla army of Ho Chi Minh until 1954, when his victory over the French at Dien Bien Phu established his reputation as a military leader. In 1976 he was appointed vice-premier of the Vietnamese Council of Ministers, and he also served from 1976 to 1980 as commander in chief of the armed forces and minister of national defense of the Socialist

Republic of Vietnam. Vo Nguyen Giap's writings include *To Arm the Revolutionary Masses to Build the People's Army* and *Unforgettable Days,* both published by Foreign Languages Publishing House (Hanoi) in 1975, and *How We Won the War* (Recon, 1976). *Address:* Dang Cong San Vietnam, 1C Bd. Hoang Van Thu, Ho Chi Minh City, Vietnam.

BIOGRAPHICAL/CRITICAL SOURCES:

BOOKS

Current Biography, Wilson, 1969.
International Who's Who, 46th edition, Europa, 1982.
O'Neill, Robert J., *General Giap: Politician and Strategist,* Cassell, 1969.

*   *   *

VOSE, Clement E(llery)   1923-1985

OBITUARY NOTICE—See index for *CA* sketch: Born March 18, 1923, in Caribou, Me.; died of a stroke, January 28, 1985, in San Juan, Puerto Rico. Educator, administrator, archivist, and author. Vose was John E. Andrus Professor of Government at Wesleyan University from 1965 to his death. Considered an authority on constitutional law and civil rights litigation, he was also a respected archivist, and in 1977 he helped convince the Supreme Court that President Nixon's presidential papers were government property and should be available for public inspection. Among Vose's writings are *Caucasians Only: The Supreme Court, the NAACP, and the Restrictive Covenant Cases, Constitutional Change: Amendment Politics and Supreme Court Litigation Since 1900,* and the monograph *A Guide to Library Sources in Political Science: American Government.*

OBITUARIES AND OTHER SOURCES:

BOOKS

Who's Who in America, 43rd edition, Marquis, 1984.

PERIODICALS

Hartford Courant, January 29, 1985.
New York Times, February 8, 1985.

W

WACHTEL, Paul L(awrence)   1940-

PERSONAL: Born July 28, 1940, in New York, N.Y.; son of Nathan and Estelle (Sollow) Wachtel; married Ellen Finer (a psychologist), December 22, 1966; children: Kenneth Yale, Karen Jamie. *Education:* Columbia University, B.A., 1961; Yale University, M.S., 1963, Ph.D., 1965; New York University, Certificate in Psychoanalysis and Psychotherapy, 1971.

ADDRESSES: Home—79 West 12th St., New York, N.Y. 10011. *Office*—Department of Psychology, City College of the City University of New York, 138th and Convent Ave., New York, N.Y. 10031.

CAREER: State University of New York Downstate Medical Center, Brooklyn, instructor in psychiatry, 1965-69; New York University, New York City, research assistant professor of psychology, 1969-72; City College of the City University of New York, New York City, associate professor, 1972-77, professor of psychology, 1977—, associate director of clinical doctoral program, 1975—.

MEMBER: American Psychological Association, Association for the Advancement of Behavior Therapy, Society for the Exploration of Psychotherapy Integration.

WRITINGS:

Psychoanalysis and Behavior Therapy: Toward an Integration, Basic Books, 1977.
(Editor) *Resistance: Psychodynamic and Behavioral Approaches,* Plenum, 1982.
The Poverty of Affluence: A Psychological Portrait of the American Way of Life, Free Press, 1983.
(With wife, E. F. Wachtel) *Lessons From Family Therapy: Insights for the Individual Therapist,* Guilford, 1985.
Action and Insight, Guilford, in press.

Contributor to psychology journals and popular magazines. Member of editorial board of *Contemporary Psychology, Journal of Marital and Family Therapy,* and *Journal of Personal and Social Relationships.*

WORK IN PROGRESS: Research on psychotherapy and the social implications of psychological ideas.

SIDELIGHTS: Paul L. Wachtel told *CA:* ''I am committed to questioning time-worn assumptions and hollow pieties. I try to cut across theoretical and disciplinary lines. I believe most of us can lead richer, fuller lives than we now do. I also believe that our current emphasis on the market and on careerist, materialistic pursuits is a dead end.''

AVOCATIONAL INTERESTS: Movies, professional basketball, playing tennis, good conversation.

*   *   *

WALLACE, (Richard Horatio) Edgar   1875-1932

BRIEF ENTRY: Born April 1, 1875, in Greenwich, London, England; died February 10, 1932. British journalist, editor, film director, and author. Known as the ''King of Thrillers,'' Wallace wrote nearly 175 books, more than half of them thrillers. His first and most famous mystery novel, *The Four Just Men,* was published in 1905 by Wallace's own Tallis Press— a venture founded after he was unable to secure a publisher for the book. Wallace followed that first book with a number of sequels and by the 1920's and 1930's was so prolific and popular that rumors estimated one quarter of all books read in England were written by him. *The Tom of Ts'in* (1916), *The Green Archer* (1923), *The Fellowship of the Frog* (1925), and *The Hand of Power* (1927) are considered among Wallace's best books. The widespread appeal of Wallace's books also led to the creation of hundreds of films based on his work. In the late 1950's, in fact, films adapted from Wallace's work became the rage in Germany, prompting a decade-long ''Wallace mania.'' During the 1960's the British film industry enjoyed a similar resurgence, with a series of short screen adaptations being produced for British and American television as the Edgar Wallace Mystery Theatre.

In addition to writing crime and mystery novels, Wallace established himself as a money-making playwright with the production of ''On the Spot'' in 1930. It was the first of approximately seventeen of his plays produced within a six-year period, although not all were as successful as the first. Films and paperback editions of his thrillers were lucrative, however, the latter continuing to sell more than one million copies a year long after his death. Wallace, who began his career writing and editing for newspapers, also wrote science fiction, screenplays, short stories, poetry, and nonfiction.

BIOGRAPHICAL/CRITICAL SOURCES:

BOOKS

Encyclopedia of Mystery and Detection, McGraw, 1976.

Lane, Margaret, *Edgar Wallace: The Biography of a Phenomenon*, Heineman, 1938.

Longman Companion to Twentieth Century Literature, Longman, 1970.

The Oxford Companion to English Literature, Oxford University Press, 1967.

Science Fiction Writers: Critical Studies From the Early Nineteenth Century to the Present Day, Scribner, 1982.

Twentieth-Century Crime and Mystery Writers, St. Martin's, 1980.

*   *   *

WALLOP, (John) Douglass III   1920-1985

OBITUARY NOTICE—See index for *CA* sketch: Born March 8, 1920, in Washington, D.C.; died of a heart ailment, April 2 (one source says April 1), 1985, in Washington, D.C. Journalist and author. Wallop is best known for *The Year the Yankees Lost the Pennant*, his novel about a middle-aged baseball fan who trades his soul to the devil for restored youth and the opportunity to lead the Washington Senators to the pennant. The book was adapted as the popular stage musical and motion picture "Damn Yankees." Wallop's other writings include the novels *The Sunken Garden, Ocean Front, So This Is What Happened to Charlie Moe,* and *The Mermaid in the Swimming Pool,* and the nonfiction work *Baseball: An Informal History.* Early in his career Wallop wrote for United Press International and the Associated Press.

OBITUARIES AND OTHER SOURCES:

PERIODICALS

Chicago Tribune, April 7, 1985.
New York Times, April 5, 1985.
Washington Post, April 4, 1985.

*   *   *

WALSDORF, John J(oseph)   1941-

PERSONAL: Born June 19, 1941, in Sheboygan, Wis.; son of Isadore A. (a veterinarian) and Johanna (a homemaker; maiden name, Wollner) Walsdorf; married Karen Wendt, June 13, 1964 (divorced May, 1979); married Bonnie Allen (a librarian), December 5, 1981; children: (first marriage) John Joseph II. *Education:* Wisconsin State University—Oshkosh, B.S., 1963; University of Wisconsin—Madison, M.L.S., 1964. *Politics:* Democrat. *Religion:* Roman Catholic.

ADDRESSES: Home—18820 Northwest Astoria Dr., Portland, Ore. 97229. *Office*—c/o Blackwell North America, Inc., 6024 Southwest Jean Rd., Bldg. G, Lake Oswego, Ore. 97034.

CAREER: Milwaukee Public Library, Milwaukee, Wis., government documents and reference librarian, 1964-66; Oxford City Library, Oxford, England, senior lending librarian, 1966-67; B. H. Blackwell Ltd., Oxford, England, senior library service adviser, 1967—; Blackwell North America, Inc., Lake Oswego, Ore., vice-president, operations, 1983—. Council of the Friends of the University of Iowa, chairperson, 1983-84; Northwest Conservation Center, Portland, Ore., board member, 1984—.

MEMBER: American Library Association, William Morris Society, Private Libraries Association, Book Club of California, Oregon Library Association, Book Club of Washington, Grolier Club.

WRITINGS:

(Editor) *Men of Printing: Anglo-American Profiles,* Pennyroyal, 1976.

(Editor) *A Collector's Choice,* University of Wisconsin Press, 1976.

(Editor) *Printers on Morris,* Beaverdam, 1981.

William Morris in Private Press and Limited Editions, Oryx, 1983.

Contributor to library journals.

WORK IN PROGRESS: Annotated Bibliography of the Works of Julian Symons, completion expected in 1986; *The Kroiker Affair: A Biblio-Mystery,* completion expected in 1986-87.

SIDELIGHTS: John J. Walsdorf told *CA:* "I grew up in a very small Wisconsin village near Lake Michigan, a village of some two hundred people with a three-room school, three taverns, a church, and little else. Books were not a vital part of my life, and I can't remember reading a novel until my sophomore year in high school. I had hoped for a college football career at the University of Notre Dame (the dream of most Midwestern Catholic boys in the 1950's) and then a stint with the Green Bay Packers. My high school days were filled with sports, and some of my early claims to fame were as a fullback who gained 117 yards in a game, who was the high scorer for the next year, and was chosen as the all-conference tackle for the Eastern Wisconsin League.

"But my lack of size (5'11", 190 lbs.) brought me not to Notre Dame, but to Wisconsin State University—Oshkosh. It was at Oshkosh, after a single, frustrating week of college football, that I decided that football was not my forte after all. I turned my attention to reading and writing and won local awards for short stories; I eventually became editor of the student newspaper, the *Oshkosh Advance.* Under my editorship, the *Advance* was granted a national award for excellence.

"While attending the University of Wisconsin—Madison, I became interested in book collecting as a hobby. After being granted an M.L.S. I worked for two years at the Milwaukee Public Library and was then accepted for a library exchange program by the Oxford, England, Public Library. My year in England brought me in contact with a vast number of inexpensive books, and I returned from England with the start of a number of collections, one of which has proven valuable to me as an author.

"My interest in collecting books by English authors started with the famous poet and printer William Morris. The collection itself grew to nearly nine hundred items and resulted in three books and three exhibition catalogues. Parts of my collection of Morris have been on display at such geographically diverse institutions as George Washington University, the University of California at Los Angeles, the University of Victoria in British Columbia, Louisiana State University, the University of Miami, and the University of Western Ontario. My collecting and the display of my collection has also resulted in speaking invitations at the University of Missouri, the University of Illinois, Washington State University, the University of Arizona, and Arizona State University.

"Besides Morris, my principal collecting interests are Julian Symons, T. J. Cobden-Sanderson, T. J. Wise, books about books, biblio-mystery novels, August Derleth, Elbert Hubbard, and the Roycroft movement. In most cases, my collecting interests have directly led to my publishing achievements. The first book I edited, *Men of Printing,* is now highly collected, not because of my involvement, but because the illustrations were done by Barry Moser of Pennyroyal Press.

"My writing is very much in the background of my everyday life. Although my job is fairly time consuming and energy draining, I find that collecting, reading, and then writing are good outlets for my creative desires. Given a choice, my free time usually is consumed in one of these three activities, with book collecting my first choice."

* * *

WALSH, Sheila 1928-
(Sophie Leyton)

PERSONAL: Born October 10, 1928, in Birmingham, England; daughter of Wilfred (a civil servant) and Margaret (a housewife; maiden name, Moran) O'Nions; married Desmond Walsh (a retail jeweler), April 22, 1950; children: Frances Mary Gregson, Teresa. *Education:* Attended Southport College of Art, 1945-48. *Religion:* Roman Catholic.

ADDRESSES: Home and office—35 Coudray Rd., Southport, Merseyside PR9 9NL, England. *Agent*—Mary Irvine, 11 Upland Park Rd., Oxford OX2 7RU, England.

CAREER: Writer, 1975—.

MEMBER: Romantic Novelists Association (chairman, 1985), Soroptimist International of Southport (press officer), Southport Writer's Club (vice-president; past chairman).

AWARDS, HONORS: Named Romantic Novelist of the Year by Romantic Novelists Association, 1983-84, for *A Highly Respectable Marriage.*

WRITINGS:

ROMANCE NOVELS

The Golden Songbird, Hutchinson, 1975, New American Library, 1975.
Madalena, Hutchinson, 1976, New American Library, 1977.
The Sergeant Major's Daughter, Hutchinson, 1977, New American Library, 1977.
A Fine Silk Purse, Hutchinson, 1978, published in the United States as *Lord Gilmore's Bride,* New American Library, 1979.
(Under pseudonym Sophie Leyton) *Lady Cecily's Dilemma,* Sundial, 1980, published in the United States, under name Sheila Walsh, as *The Pink Parasol,* New American Library, 1985.
The Incomparable Miss Brady, Hutchinson, 1980.
The Rose Domino, Hutchinson, 1981.
A Highly Respectable Marriage, Hutchinson, 1982, New American Library, 1982.
The Runaway Bride, Hutchinson, 1983, New American Library, 1983.
The Diamond Waterfall, New American Library, 1984.
The Incorrigible Rake, New American Library, 1984.
The Wary Widow, New American Library, 1985.

WORK IN PROGRESS: Research for a book (or books) about Liverpool from the late 1800's to the 1930's.

SIDELIGHTS: Sheila Walsh told *CA:* "I find that writing becomes more difficult as time goes by, perhaps because I am afraid of getting stale or repeating myself—a particular hazard when writing within a genre. I hate talking about current projects or ones that I am about to begin. The same goes for writing synopses or plotting ideas on paper, rather than in my

head. The moment it is down in black and white, the idea goes cold on me.

"Research is most important. With regard to historical research I believe that you can only achieve absolute authenticity if you immerse yourself totally in your chosen period until you feel at home there, so you can tell your story without the research showing. This applies just as much to a light romantic novel as to a more serious work.

"I very much enjoy contact with other writers and publishers, and I find the exchange of ideas and trends stimulating. I also get great satisfaction from encouraging novice writers. These needs are largely filled by my involvement with the Romantic Novelists Association and with my local writers' group.

"I have a love-hate relationship with writing, but the love always wins."

* * *

WARD, Charlotte
See CHESNEY, Marion

* * *

WARRACK, Graeme Matthew 1913-1985

OBITUARY NOTICE: Born June 27, 1913; died January 13, 1985. Military officer and author. Warrick became a colonel in the Royal Army Medical Corps during World War II. He participated in the Battle of Arnhem in 1944 as the assistant director of medical services and was taken prisoner with the rest of his staff. Warrack's escape, with the aid of the Dutch Resistance, was detailed in his book *Travel by Dark.* The book was adapted for television and broadcast by the British Broadcasting Corporation under the title "Arnhem: The Story of an Escape." Warrack remained in military service and was appointed local brigadier in 1960. He also served as president of the Royal Odonto-Chirurgical Society of Scotland and as chairman of the Royal British Legion in Scotland. He was named a commander of the Order of the British Empire and honored with the Distinguished Service Order.

OBITUARIES:

PERIODICALS

Times (London), January 18, 1985.

* * *

WARREN, Frank A. III 1933-

BRIEF ENTRY: Born August 3, 1933, in Cortland, N.Y. American historian, educator, and author. Warren joined the faculty of Queens College of the City University of New York in 1962; he became a professor of history in 1975. He wrote *Liberals and Communism: The "Red Decade" Revisited* (Indiana University Press, 1966) and *An Alternative Vision: The Socialist Party in the 1930's* (Indiana University Press, 1974). Warren co-edited *The New Deal: An Anthology* (Crowell, 1968). *Address:* Department of History, Queens College of the City University of New York, 65-30 Kissena Blvd., Flushing, N.Y. 11367.

* * *

WASSERSTROM, (Jacob) William 1922-1985

OBITUARY NOTICE—See index for CA sketch: Born October

14, 1922, in Brooklyn, N.Y.; died of cancer, February 7, 1985, in DeWitt, N.Y. Educator, editor, and author. Wasserstrom taught English at Syracuse University from 1960 to his death. He wrote such books as *Heiress of All the Ages: Sex and Sentiment in the Genteel Tradition, The Genius of American Fiction,* and *The Legacy of Van Wyck Brooks: A Study of Maladies and Motives,* and edited such volumes as *The Time of the Dial* and *A Dial Miscellany.* Wasserstrom contributed to several journals and was a member of the editorial boards of *Literature and Psychology* and *Hartford Studies in Literature.*

OBITUARIES AND OTHER SOURCES:

BOOKS

Directory of American Scholars, Volume II: *English, Speech, and Drama,* 8th edition, Bowker, 1982.

PERIODICALS

Syracuse Post-Standard, February 11, 1985.

* * *

WATSON, Elaine 1921-

PERSONAL: Born October 13, 1921, in Jackson, Mich.; daughter of William J. (a farmer) and Elsie (a teacher and housewife; maiden name, Feldkamp) Reno; married William J. Watson (a teacher), April 16, 1949; children: David, Douglas, Diane Watson Calloway. *Education:* University of Michigan, A.B., 1943, M.A., 1949; also attended Michigan State University, Wayne State University, and Eastern Michigan University.

ADDRESSES: Home—Ann Arbor, Mich. *Office*—Department of English, Henry Ford Community College, 5101 Evergreen Rd., Dearborn, Mich. 48128.

CAREER: High school English teacher in Milan, Mich., 1943-46, and Dearborn, Mich., 1946-56; Henry Ford Community College, Dearborn, Mich., part-time instructor in English, 1967—.

MEMBER: Women's International League for Peace and Freedom, Michigan Poetry Society, Washtenaw County Genealogical Society, Detroit Women Writers.

WRITINGS:

(Editor) *Echoes From the Moon* (poems), Hot Apple Press, 1976.
Anna's Rocking Chair (historical novel), Zondervan, 1984.
To Dwell in the Land (historical novel), Zondervan, 1985.

Contributor of articles and poems to magazines and newspapers.

WORK IN PROGRESS: A contemporary mystery novel.

SIDELIGHTS: Elaine Watson told *CA:* "I have written verse since childhood, for therapy and to get my reactions down so I could examine them. Then I wrote articles, for the same reason. I've always played a little music and done some painting, but I've been in love with letters. I feel a novelist can make use of historical facts to illuminate the lives of people whose dreams and fears and joys might otherwise be lost.

"I also love to explore the myths that people live by. Some of my better verse has grown out of my travels and visits to museums. Afterward I read contemporary letters and books until I begin to share, as much as I can, another person's

myths, to breathe the same kind of air, and to comtemplate the same horizons. Sometimes these myths are much like my own. Sometimes, as I found in China, they are not. However, the characters in my historical novels have a midwestern German heritage, like mine."

AVOCATIONAL INTERESTS: Travel (including Europe, the U.S.S.R., the People's Republic of China).

* * *

WAUGH, Albert E(dmund) 1902-1985

OBITUARY NOTICE—See index for *CA* sketch: Born September 28, 1902, in Amherst, Mass.; died after a long illness, March 6, 1985, in Boston, Mass. Educator, administrator, economist, statistician, and author. Waugh distinguished himself as an expert in agricultural economics and statistics while working as a professor of economics at the University of Connecticut from 1937 to 1965. He was also dean of the college of arts and sciences from 1945 to 1950 and provost and academic vice-president from 1950 to 1965. His writings include *Elements of Statistical Method, Statistical Tables and Problems, Principles of Economics, Samuel Huntington: A Biography,* and *Sundials.*

OBITUARIES AND OTHER SOURCES:

BOOKS

The Author's and Writer's Who's Who, 6th edition, Burke's Peerage, 1971.

PERIODICALS

Hartford Courant, March 8, 1985.
New York Times, March 8, 1985.

* * *

WAY, Peter (Howard) 1936-

BRIEF ENTRY: British historian, publisher, magazine editor, and author. Way was appointed feature editor at the London office of *Reader's Digest* in 1962. In 1968 he became the editor of *Mind Alive.* Way's poems were collected in *The Pieces of a Game* (Allison & Busby, 1969). His novels include *A Perfect State of Health* (Allison & Busby, 1969), *Dirty Tricks* (St. Martin's, 1977), and *Super-Celeste* (Gollancz, 1977). Way also wrote *Codes and Ciphers* (Aldus Books, 1977) and *Icarus* (Coward, 1980). *Address:* 5 Egerton Dr., London S.E.10, England.

BIOGRAPHICAL/CRITICAL SOURCES:

PERIODICALS

Listener, June 4, 1970, June 30, 1977, November 1, 1979, August 14, 1980.
New York Times Book Review, May 28, 1972, January 8, 1978.

* * *

WEATHERWAX, Rudd (B.) 1908(?)-1985

OBITUARY NOTICE: Born c. 1908; died of cardiac arrest, February 25, 1985, in Mission Hills, Calif. Animal trainer and author. Weatherwax is best remembered as the trainer of Lassie, the heroic dog who starred in films and television. Lassie was played by seven generations of collies, all trained by Weatherwax. Beginning with the 1943 movie "Lassie Come

Home,'' the Lassie character instituted a Hollywood career that spanned nearly thirty years, including a television series that ran from 1954 until 1971. Weatherwax trained hundreds of animals during his career and wrote *The Lassie Method: Raising and Training Your Dog With Patience, Firmness and Love.* He co-authored *The Story of Lassie: His Discovery and Training From Puppyhood to Stardom* with John H. Rothwell.

OBITUARIES AND OTHER SOURCES:

PERIODICALS

Chicago Tribune, February 28, 1985.

*   *   *

WEBER, Ronald   1934-

PERSONAL: Born September 21, 1934, in Mason City, Iowa; son of Harley George and Anne M. (McCauley) Weber; married Patricia Jean Carroll, December 27, 1957; children: Elizabeth, Andrea, Kathryn. *Education:* University of Notre Dame, B.A., 1957; University of Iowa, M.F.A., 1960; University of Minnesota—Twin Cities, Ph.D., 1967.

ADDRESSES: Home—52513 Gumwood Rd., Granger, Ind. 46530. *Office*—Department of American Studies, University of Notre Dame, Notre Dame, Ind. 46556.

CAREER: Loras College, Dubuque, Iowa, instructor in English, 1960-62; University of Notre Dame, Notre Dame, Ind., assistant professor, 1963-67, associate professor, 1967-76, professor of American studies, 1976—, chairman of department, 1970-77, chairman of Graduate Program in Communication Arts, 1972-79. University of Coimbra, Fulbright lecturer, 1968-69, senior Fulbright lecturer 1982.

MEMBER: American Studies Association, Great Lakes American Studies Association (president, 1980-82).

AWARDS, HONORS: Fellow of National Endowment for the Humanities, 1972-73; *The Literature of Fact* was included on *Choice*'s "Outstanding Academic Book" list, 1981-82; Gannett fellow at Columbia University, 1985-86.

WRITINGS:

O Romance Americano (study of the American novel), Livraria Almedina (Coimbra, Portugal), 1969.
(Editor and contributor) *America in Change: Reflections on the Sixties and Seventies,* University of Notre Dame Press, 1972.
(Editor and contributor) *The Reporter as Artist: A Look at the New Journalism Controversy,* Hastings House, 1974.
(Contributor) Marshall Fishwick, editor, *The New Journalism,* Bowling Green University, 1975.
(Editor with Walter Nicgorski, and contributor) *An Almost Chosen People: The Moral Aspirations of Americans,* University of Notre Dame Press, 1976.
The Literature of Fact: Literary Nonfiction in American Writing, Ohio University Press, 1980.
Seeing Earth: Space Exploration in American Writing, Ohio University Press, 1984.

Contributor of more than thirty articles to magazines, including *Cimarron Review, Virginia Quarterly Review, Sewanee Review, South Atlantic Quarterly, Journal of Popular Culture,* and *Review of Politics.*

WORK IN PROGRESS: Research on the impact of journalism on American literature.

WEINGAND, Darlene E.   1937-

PERSONAL: Born August 13, 1937, in Oak Park, Ill.; daughter of Edward E. (a manufacturer's representative) and Erna I. (a homemaker; maiden name, Heidenway) Weingand; married Wayne Weston, September 7, 1957 (divorced, 1976); married James Elberling, May 28, 1977 (divorced, 1980); married Roger P. Couture (an industrial mechanic), April 7, 1984; children: (first marriage) Kathleen, Lynda Weston Foster, Judith, B. Jeanne Weston Lisse. *Education:* Elmhurst College, B.A., 1972; Rosary College, M.A.L.S., 1973; attended Mankato State University, 1976-77; University of Minnesota—Twin Cities, Ph.D., 1980. *Religion:* Unitarian.

ADDRESSES: Office—Extension Communication Programs and Madison School of Library and Information Studies, University of Wisconsin—Madison, Madison, Wis. 53706.

CAREER: Minneapolis Public Library, Minneapolis, Minn., community librarian, 1973-80; Derby Associates (consulting firm), Madison, Wis., president, 1980-81; University of Wisconsin—Madison, assistant professor of library science, 1981—. Member of *ad hoc* faculty at Metropolitan State University, 1975-80, and University of Minnesota—Twin Cities, 1980-81. Member of board of trustees of Madison Public Library.

MEMBER: World Future Society, American Library Association, American Association for Adult and Continuing Education, Public Library Association, Library Administration and Management Association, Association for Library and Information Science, Continuing Library Education Network and Exchange, Wisconsin Library Association, Wisconsin Association for Adult and Continuing Education, Beta Phi Mu, Phi Delta Kappa.

WRITINGS:

Reflections of Tomorrow: Lifelong Learning and the Public Library, Derby Associates, 1980.
(Editor) *Women and Library Management,* Pierian, 1982.
The Organic Public Library, Libraries Unlimited, 1984.
(Editor) *Marketing for Libraries and Information Agencies,* Ablex Publishing, 1984.

Editor of "Continuing Education," a column in *Journal of Education for Library and Information Science.* Contributor to library journals. Associate editor of *Library and Information Science Research Quarterly.*

WORK IN PROGRESS: A book tentatively titled *Planning/Marketing Information Services,* publication by Libraries Unlimited expected in 1987; research on marketing, library futures, and fee-based interloan arrangements.

SIDELIGHTS: Darlene E. Weingand told *CA:* "The American public library is definitely an 'organic' organization, alive with the opportunity for proactive growth and development. The library today exists in the midst of a rapidly changing society, with technological development bombarding it from every direction. The library can no longer afford to be viewed by its public as a warehouse or storehouse for books; it must assume its rightful place as the nerve center of its community, serving as the switching point between citizens and their information needs. This opportunity must be seized if the public library is to endure—and prevail—in the information age.

"Public libraries across the nation have recognized that their role must change with the times; many have altered their names to include some variation of 'Library and Information Center' in an attempt to reflect the new role for libraries. It is important, however, to recognize that a long and illustrious history can be written for libraries in the development of American culture. The challenge facing libraries is to build upon this foundation.

"With the rapid rate of change and technological development causing society to virtually spin upon its axis, it is imperative that there be some focal point to serve as a frame of reference. This is an appropriate role for the public library. In addition, many of the new technologies have a cost factor that puts them out of reach of a significant portion of the population. It is here that the crucial issues of intellectual freedom and access to information become paramount. The public library has the responsibility and continued challenge to provide information and access to that information on all sides of issues for the benefit of the entire community. Without this opportunity for equality of access, the gap between the information-rich and information-poor will join the other gaps facing society.

"The future for the public library can be bright indeed if both the library and the community change perceptions regarding the library's role. If the library can rightfully be viewed as the linkage between citizen and information, as the channel through which equality of access and First Amendment rights is maintained, then society will have gained a major victory. It is imperative that the public library function in this manner, that it be regarded as an essential—if not the *most* essential—community service and be funded accordingly."

* * *

WELCH, William 1917-

BRIEF ENTRY: Born September 11, 1917, in New Haven, Conn. American political scientist, educator, and author. Welch taught at Hamilton College for four years, then worked as a research analyst for the United States Government. In 1961 he joined the political science faculty of the University of Colorado at Boulder; he became a full professor in 1968. Welch wrote *American Images of Soviet Foreign Policy: An Inquiry Into Recent Appraisals From the Academic Community* (Yale University Press, 1970) and *The Art of Political Thinking: Government and Common Sense* (Littlefield, Adams, 1981). *Address:* Department of Political Science, University of Colorado at Boulder, 1200 University Ave., Boulder, Colo. 80309.

* * *

WELDON, John 1890(?)-1963
(Brinsley MacNamara)

OBITUARY NOTICE: Professionally known as Brinsley MacNamara; born September 6, 1890 (some sources say 1891), in Hiskenstown, Westmeath, Ireland; died after an illness, February 4, 1963, in Dublin, Ireland; buried in Dean's Grange Cemetery, Dublin, Ireland. Actor, drama critic, playwright, and author. As a youth MacNamara, feeling alienated from provincial society and motivated by an avid interest in drama, left his hometown to experience the literary and theatrical life of Dublin, Ireland. There he joined the Abbey Theatre, adopted his professional pseudonym, and before long toured the United States with the theatre's company of players. Returning to his hometown in 1913 MacNamara separated from the Abbey troupe and began writing. His portrayal of regional life, the 1918 novel *The Valley of the Squinting Windows,* caused considerable bitterness among his neighbors and in turn made Mac-

Namara more determined to write in the realist style. His literary output increased over the next few years as he again turned to playwriting to express his criticism of the rural lifestyle.

By the 1920's MacNamara had begun writing comedies of romantic intrigue. This new approach produced the successful plays "Look at the Heffernans!," "The Master," "Margaret Gillan," and others. MacNamara's novels, which have earned him recognition as the pioneer of a new school of Irish realism, include *The Clanking of Chains, In Clay and in Bronze,* and *Some Curious People.* The playwright also compiled the chronicle *Abbey Plays: 1899-1948* and served as drama critic for the *Irish Times.*

OBITUARIES AND OTHER SOURCES:

BOOKS

Dictionary of Literary Biography, Volume 10: *Modern British Dramatists, 1940-1945,* Gale, 1982.
McGraw-Hill Encyclopedia of World Drama, 2nd edition, McGraw, 1984.
The Oxford Companion to the Theatre, 3rd edition, Oxford University Press, 1967.

* * *

WELLES, Margery Miller 1923-1985
(Margery Miller)

OBITUARY NOTICE: Born July 19, 1923, in Springfield, Vt.; died of cancer, February 24, 1985, in Charlotte, N.C. Journalist and author. Welles, who wrote under the name Margery Miller, was the first female reporter allowed in the dressing room of professional boxer Joe Louis. She began her career as a sportswriter for King Features Syndicate in New York City and later wrote for the *Christian Science Monitor.* After editing trade books for A. S. Barnes, Welles became an original staff member of *Sports Illustrated.* A boxing expert, she wrote *Joe Louis: American* in 1945.

OBITUARIES AND OTHER SOURCES:

BOOKS

Who's Who of American Women, 4th edition, Marquis, 1966.

PERIODICALS

Chicago Tribune, February 28, 1985.
Detroit Free Press, February 27, 1985.
New York Times, February 26, 1985.

* * *

WELS, Alena 1938(?)-1985

OBITUARY NOTICE: Born c. 1938; died of cancer, March 26, 1985, in New York, N.Y. Journalist. Wels worked as the banking editor of the *Journal of Commerce* until her 1981 promotion to chief editorial writer. She was regarded as an expert on international issues connected with banking and monetary systems.

OBITUARIES:

PERIODICALS

New York Times, March 28, 1985.

WESTIN, Richard A(xel)   1945-

PERSONAL: Born July 8, 1945, in London, England; came to United States, 1952; son of Gosta Victor (a diplomat) and Muriel Yalden (a veterinarian; maiden name, Thomson) Westin; married Elizabeth J. Cook (an optometrist), June 13, 1981; children: Monica Jean. *Education:* Columbia University, B.A., 1967, M.B.A., 1968; University of Pennsylvania, J.D., 1972.

ADDRESSES: Home—2210 Dorrington, Houston, Tex. 77030. *Office*—Law Center, University of Houston, Houston, Tex. 77004.

CAREER: Dewey, Ballantine, Bushby, Palmer & Wood (law firm), New York, N.Y., associate, 1972-75; Vermont Life Insurance Co., Montpelier, tax counsel, 1975-79; Illinois Institute of Technology, Chicago-Kent College of Law, Chicago, associate professor of law, 1979-83; University of Tennessee, Knoxville, associate professor of law, 1983-84; University of Houston, Houston, Tex., professor of law, 1984—. Director of Millenium Leasing Corp.; former consultant to World Bank.

MEMBER: American Bar Association (leader of Task Force on Liquidation and Reincorporation), Vermont Bar Association, California Bar Association.

WRITINGS:

Middle Income Tax Planning and Shelters, McGraw, 1982.
(With Alan H. Neff) *Tax, Attacks, and Counterattacks: Your Indispensable Guide to Long-Range Tax Strategy,* Harcourt, 1983.
Lexicon of Tax Terminology, Wiley, 1984.

Contributor to law journals.

WORK IN PROGRESS: Research on federal taxation of natural resources.

SIDELIGHTS: Richard A. Westin told *CA:* "Alan Neff and I decided to write a joint book in which we could bowdlerize the rather severe material written for and published by Shepard's, McGraw-Hill. The book wound up being a good product in that it really does tell people how to *think* about tax planning in the most general terms, after which annual variations in the details of tax planning become comprehensible. Unfortunately, while the book enjoyed fine reviews, its sales were modest—evidently because the public wants the boldest and most venal formats, it seems. Alan Neff has since tried his hand, with some success, at writing a mystery thriller. I am writing a technical book on the taxation of natural resources."

*   *   *

WESTRUP, J(ack) A(llan)   1904-1975

OBITUARY NOTICE: Born July 26, 1904, in London, England; died April 21, 1975, in Hampshire, England. Musicologist, educator, operatic producer, lecturer, editor, music critic, and author. Westrup's name first became prominent in the music world during the mid-1920's when he staged celebrated productions of Claudio Monteverdi's operas for Oxford University's Opera Club. During his career he served as editor of *Monthly Musical Record* and *Music and Letters,* and he was music critic for the *Daily Telegraphy.* In 1947, Westrup began his twenty-four year tenure as Heather Professor of Music at Oxford and fellow of Oxford's Wadham College. He also lectured at the Royal Academy of Music and acted as president of the Royal Musical Association. Knighted in 1961, Westrup was described in the London *Times* as "one of the finest musical scholars of his day." He wrote many books on music, including *Purcell, Sharps and Flats,* and *An Introduction to Musical History.* In addition, he co-authored *Collins Music Encyclopedia* and *The New College Encyclopedia of Music.* Westrup also revised several musical books, among them Ernest Walker's *History of Music in England.*

OBITUARIES AND OTHER SOURCES:

BOOKS

Baker's Biographical Dictionary of Musicians, 6th edition, Schirmer, 1978.
International Who's Who, 38th edition, Europa, 1974.
The Oxford Companion to Music, 10th edition, Oxford University Press, 1974.
Who's Who, 126th edition, St. Martin's, 1974.

PERIODICALS

Music and Letters, July, 1975.
Times (London), April 23, 1975.

*   *   *

WEXLEY, John   1907-1985

OBITUARY NOTICE: Born September 14, 1907, in New York, N.Y.; died of a heart attack, February 4, 1985, in Doylestown, Pa. Screenwriter, playwright, and author of nonfiction and short stories. Wexley is best remembered for "The Last Mile," the Broadway play that launched actor Spencer Tracy to star status. The play, a prison drama, was first produced in 1930 and was twice adapted for the screen, in 1932 and 1959. Another of Wexley's plays, "They Shall Not Die," sparked controversy in 1934 with its dramatization of the 1931 Scottsboro, Alabama, court case in which nine black youths were charged with raping two white schoolgirls. Wexley also wrote several screenplays, including "Angels With Dirty Faces," "The Amazing Dr. Clitterhouse," "The Long Night," "Confessions of a Nazi Spy," and "Hangmen Also Die." His films starred such actors as Humphrey Bogart, James Cagney, and Edward G. Robinson. One of Wexley's short stories was included in a 1934 collection of award-winning fiction. Wexley also wrote *The Judgement of Julius and Ethel Rosenberg,* a 1955 book about the couple executed in 1953 for giving U.S. atomic secrets to the Soviet Union.

OBITUARIES AND OTHER SOURCES:

BOOKS

Contemporary American Authors: A Critical Survey and 219 Bio-Bibliographies, AMS Press, 1970.
Modern World Drama: An Encyclopedia, Dutton, 1972.
The Oxford Companion to American Literature, 4th edition, Oxford University Press, 1965.
The Reader's Encylcopedia of American Literature, Crowell, 1962.

PERIODICALS

Chicago Tribune, February 8, 1985.
Los Angeles Times, February 14, 1985.
Newsweek, February 18, 1985.
New York Times, February 6, 1985.
Washington Post, February 11, 1985.

WHEATLEY, Ronald   1923(?)-1985

OBITUARY NOTICE: Born c. 1923; died January 15, 1985. Historian, administrator, and author. Wheatley joined the British Cabinet Office in 1948 to work on German military documents captured during World War II. *Operation Sea Lion* is his highly regarded account of German plans for an invasion of England during the early years of the war. In 1960 Wheatley transferred to the Foreign Office, where he was appointed United Kingdom editor of *Documents on German Foreign Policy, 1918 to 1945.* Three years later he was promoted to editor in chief. At the time of his death Wheatley was head of the Historical Branch of the Foreign and Commonwealth Office.

OBITUARIES:

PERIODICALS

Times (London), January 29, 1985.

*   *   *

WHISLER, Thomas Lee   1920-

BRIEF ENTRY: Born February 12, 1920, in Dayton, Ohio. American educator and author. Whisler joined the business faculty of the University of Chicago in 1953. He became a professor of industrial relations in 1968 and a professor of business policy in 1975. The educator has taught at the Management Development Institute in Cairo and served as a consultant to the Center for Productivity Study and Research at the State University of Ghent. Whisler's books include *Performance Appraisal: Research and Practice* (Holt, 1962), *Information Technology and Organizational Change* (Wadsworth, 1970), *The Impact of Computers on Organizations* (Praeger, 1970), and *Rules of the Game: Inside the Corporate Boardroom* (Dow Jones-Irwin, 1983). *Address:* 9 Wilson Court, Park Forest, Ill. 60466; and Graduate School of Business, University of Chicago, 5801 Ellis Ave., Chicago,Ill. 60637.

BIOGRAPHICAL/CRITICAL SOURCES:

PERIODICALS

Times Literary Supplement, May 21, 1971.

*   *   *

WHITE, James L.   ?-1981

OBITUARY NOTICE: Poet. White's posthumously published fourth book, *The Salt Ecstasies,* is thought to be an artistic parallel of the poet's own life experiences. Written while White was dying, the collection of poems has been likened to a confessional dealing with love, loneliness, and death.

OBITUARIES AND OTHER SOURCES:

PERIODICALS

Library Journal, December 15, 1982.

*   *   *

WHITE, Lawrence   1942-

PERSONAL: Born January 21, 1942, in Detroit, Mich.; married wife, E. Jane; children: Rebecca Sundwell, Samuel Brady. *Education:* Sonoma State College (now Sonoma State University), B.A., 1969; Catholic University of America, J.D., 1975.

ADDRESSES: Agent—Diane Cleaver, 825 Third Ave., New York, N.Y. 10022.

CAREER: Workers' compensation attorney in California; writer.

WRITINGS:

Human Debris: The Injured Worker in America, Seaview, 1983.

*   *   *

WHITE, Lee A.   1886-1971

OBITUARY NOTICE: Born November 23, 1886, in Flint, Mich.; died September 29, 1971. Business executive, educator, journalist, editor, and author. White worked for the *Detroit News* in many capacities from 1911 to 1914, when he became an assistant professor of journalism at the University of Washington. He later acted as head of the journalism department at that school. White rejoined the editorial staff of the *Detroit News* in 1917 and remained there for thirty-five years, serving as public relations director for the last sixteen. In addition to his newspaper duties, White was president of La Choy Food Products from 1922 to 1941 and director of the Cranbook School in Bloomfield Hills, Michigan, for twenty years beginning in 1926. He wrote *The Detroit News, 1873-1917: A Record of Progress* and co-authored *Cranbook Institute of Science: A History of Its Founding and First Twenty-Five Years.* White also edited *Poems of Harold Brian Steele* and Ilhan New's *When I Was a Boy in Korea.*

OBITUARIES AND OTHER SOURCES:

BOOKS

American Authors and Books: 1640 to the Present Day, 3rd revised edition, Crown, 1962.
Who Was Who in America, With World Notables, Volume V: *1969-1973,* Marquis, 1973.
Who Was Who in Journalism, 1925-1928, Gale, 1978.

*   *   *

WHITE, Margaret B(lackburn)   1936-

PERSONAL: Born January 11, 1936, in Dandridge, Tenn.; daughter of Benjamin A. (a teacher and in business) and Mary Ruth (a teacher; maiden name, Marston) Blackburn; married Herbert D. White, 1955 (divorced, 1972); children: David Eric, Susan Katherine. *Education:* Maryville College, Maryville, Tenn., B.A., 1956; graduate study at State University of New York at Buffalo, 1960-64; University of Rochester, M.A., 1966, Ph.D., 1968.

ADDRESSES: Home—50 Golf Ct., Teaneck, N.J. 07666. *Agent*—Sandra Elkin, Electronic Media Associates, 161 West 15th St., New York, N.Y. 10011.

CAREER: University of Maryland, U.S. Eighth Army Program, Seoul, Korea, English teacher, 1968-70; Ateneo de Manila University, Graduate School, Quezon City, Philippines, instructor in English, 1970-72; Goddard College, Plainfield, Vt., faculty member and director of regional graduate program, 1972-81; Vermont College of Norwich University, Montpelier, assistant professor, 1981-83, associate professor of alternative education, 1983—, regional director of graduate program, 1981—. Fulbright lecturer at Yonsei University and Sogang Jesuit University, 1968-70; member of workshop faculty at Taechon University, summer, 1971. Teacher of television awareness training at Media Action Research Center, New York, N.Y., 1976-78; director of Non-Traditional Education and Information Service, 1977-78; guest on television and radio programs; member of board of trustees of Child Development Research Center, Sands Point, N.Y., 1979-82; member of Teaneck Citizens for a Nuclear Freeze; consultant to Firman Associates; research associate for Elsie Y. Cross Associates, 1983—.

MEMBER: American Society for Training and Development, American Association for Higher Education, Modern Language Association of America (chairperson of New Developments in Education Section, 1975), Family Mediation Association, Academy of Independent Scholars, Northeast Modern Language Association, Alliance of Alternative Higher Education Institutions, *Nation* Associates, Writers Union.

AWARDS, HONORS: Fiction award from the New Jersey State Council on the Arts, 1984, for *Vangie.*

WRITINGS:

(With Herbert D. White) *The Power of People,* East Asia Christian Conference, 1973.
(Editor with Robert N. Quigley) *How the Other Third Lives: An Anthology of Third World Literature,* Orbis, 1977.
Sharing Caring: The Art of Raising Kids in Two-Career Families, Prentice-Hall, 1982.
(Editor with Edgar Bottome) *The "1984" Syndrome: Myth or Reality?,* Norwich University Press, 1985.

Also author of novel *Vangie.* Contributor to literary journals in Korea and the United States.

SIDELIGHTS: Margaret B. White told *CA:* "Whenever I sit down to write—or for that matter whenever I sit with a student or in a committee meeting—only one thing seems to be important to me: how can we help ourselves and each other make this experience we call life as pain-free and ecstatic as possible? This means to me trying to be honest, trying to be fair, acting as though we believe each human being is as worthwhile and important as every other human being. So I end up writing about men and women trying to figure out how to be fair to each other in the two most important adult tasks: love and work. Or, I write or teach about members of different races or political persuasions trying to see each other clearly—really *see* each other, not just look at each other. My perceptions have been formed through the process of living my own life, which has taken me along many unexpected paths: from a childhood in a loving but narrowly homogeneous southern community; through a decade and half of living in four very different American cities (New York, Baltimore, Buffalo, and Rochester) and two still more different foreign countries (Korea and the Philippines); to another ten years plus spent in writing and in directing the graduate programs of adult students who are interested in everything from the protection of the elephant to the current revival of interest in ancient witchcraft.

"I have become out of necessity a kind of cultural translator. In my writing, my teaching, and my life I am trying to listen to people and help them communicate to other people what they care about and what their hopes and fears are. I know—really know—this: *all our hopes and fears are very much alike.* None of us wants to go hungry or be homeless, to be blown up by a little bomb or a big bomb, to be out of work or unable to do something useful and exciting with our lives. We get greedy and take too much of what is available (whether as individuals or as nations or as political 'blocs') because we are always, obsessively, compulsively afraid there will not be 'enough.'

"But there is. There is enough, of everything. Except maybe the confidence that that is true."

AVOCATIONAL INTERESTS: Folk dancing, folk singing, travel, camping.

*   *   *

WHITE, Walter (Francis)   1893-1955

BRIEF ENTRY: Born July 1, 1893, in Atlanta, Ga.; died March 21, 1955, in New York, N.Y. American activist, consultant, and author. White was executive secretary of the National Association for the Advancement of Colored People (NAACP) from 1931 until his death in 1955. He joined the organization in the late 1910's after working as an insurance salesman in the South. White was named assistant secretary of the NAACP in 1918 and held that post until 1930, when he became acting secretary. He served in the latter position only briefly before becoming executive secretary. As executive secretary White became known for his vigorous opposition to racism and for his efforts to promote black activities. In 1931 he helped block the appointment of segregationist John J. Parker to the U.S. Supreme Court, and in 1938 he unsuccessfully campaigned for passage of a federal antilynching bill. For his work White received the Spingarn Medal from the NAACP.

In addition to his civil-rights activities White wrote six books. His novels *Fire in the Flint* (1924) and *Flight* (1926) both deal with problems of minorities in the South. *Fire in the Flint* is the story of a black doctor who gradually realizes the futility of his nonconfrontational behavior towards racism. *Flight* tells of a mulatto woman's infiltration of white society. White's other writings include *Rope and Faggot: A Biography of Judge Lynch* (1929), *A Rising Wind* (1945), a collection of essays on the international implications of American racism, *A Man Called White* (1948), an autobiography, and *How Far the Promised Land* (1955), an account of the NAACP and its effect on America.

BIOGRAPHICAL/CRITICAL SOURCES:

BOOKS

Cannon, Poppy, *A Gentle Knight: My Husband, Walter White,* Rinehart, 1958.
Twentieth-Century Literary Criticism, Gale, Volume 15, 1985.
Waldron, Edward E., *Walter White and the Harlem Renaissance,* Kennikat, 1978.

*   *   *

WHITMONT, Edward C.   1912-

PERSONAL: Born December 5, 1912, in Vienna, Austria. *Education:* University of Vienna, M.D., 1936.

ADDRESSES: Office—185 East 85th St., New York, N.Y. 10028.

CAREER: C. G. Jung Institute, New York, N.Y., president, 1979—; private practice of analytical psychology; writer.

WRITINGS:

The Symbolic Quest: Basic Concepts of Analytical Psychology, Princeton University Press, 1978.
Psyche and Substance: Essays on Homeopathy in the Light of Jungian Psychology, North Atlantic Books, 1980.
The Return of the Goddess, Crossroad Publishing, 1982.

Contributor to psychology journals.

WIENER, Jon
See WIENER, Jonathan M.

*   *   *

WIENER, Jonathan M. 1944-
(Jon Wiener)

PERSONAL: Born May 16, 1944, in St. Paul, Minn.; son of Daniel N. (a psychologist) Wiener and Gladys (a housewife; maiden name, Aronsohn) Spratt. *Education:* Princeton University, B.A., 1966; Harvard University, Ph.D., 1972.

ADDRESSES: Home—Los Angeles, Calif. *Office*—Department of History, University of California, Irvine, Calif. 92717. *Agent*—Elaine Markson Literary Agency Inc., 44 Greenwich Ave., New York, N.Y. 10011.

CAREER: University of California, Santa Cruz, lecturer in politics, 1973; University of California, Los Angeles, acting assistant professor of sociology, 1973-74; University of California, Irvine, assistant professor, 1974-78, associate professor, 1979-83, professor of history, 1984—.

MEMBER: Organization of American Historians, National Writers Union, Authors Guild.

AWARDS, HONORS: American Council of Learned Societies fellowship, 1979; Ford fellowship, 1985-86; Rockefeller Humanities fellowship, 1980.

WRITINGS:

Social Origins of the New South: Alabama, 1860-1885, Louisiana State University Press, 1978.
(Under name Jon Wiener) *Come Together: John Lennon in His Time,* Random House, 1984.

Contributor to periodicals and scholarly journals, including *Nation, New York Times Book Review, Vanity Fair, New Republic, American Historical Review, American Journal of Sociology, Alabama Review, Village Voice,* and *Socialist Review.*

WORK IN PROGRESS: A study of how politics changed the writing of history.

SIDELIGHTS: When Jon Wiener, a social historian concerned with the relationship between popular culture and politics, became interested in John Lennon's involvement in the anti-war movement of the Vietnam years, he requested all of the information on the rock star that had been compiled by the Federal Bureau of Investigation (FBI) and immigration authorities. "Wiener's fishing expedition," according to Chet Flippo of *People* magazine, "netted a whopping initial catch." The first of the Lennon files released under the Freedom of Information Act—twenty-six pounds of documents originating in the Immigration and Naturalization Service (INS)—along with subsequent releases from the FBI confirmed widespread government surveillance of Lennon and his wife Yoko Ono, especially preceding the 1972 Republican Convention in Miami. The documents also indicated the lengths to which both FBI chief J. Edgar Hoover and the Nixon administration had gone in the attempt to discredit and deport Lennon.

Wiener's requisition and study of the government files, as well as his additional research of the music and politics of John Lennon, resulted in *Come Together: John Lennon in His Time.* In his book Wiener addresses Lennon's career as artist, husband, and father, but his main focus is on the people, events,

and music associated with the ex-Beatle's various political commitments. Most of the book chronicles the causes that Lennon espoused during his last ten years of life and the music he made in order to broadcast his anti-war message. Additionally, Wiener contends that the government harassment Lennon endured for so long "played a large role in his artistic and personal deterioration between '72 and '75." Flippo concurred, assessing that "although [Lennon] managed to outlast the FBI's interest and beat the INS at its deportation game, no one may have understood, until now, the cost of his victory."

In his Toronto *Globe and Mail* review of *Come Together,* Paul McGrath complimented Wiener for granting the politics and music of Lennon "the kind of critical attention" usually reserved for "those 'serious' arts which affect, by comparison, an infinitely smaller group of people." McGrath further lauded Wiener's book for "establishing a fairly convincing thread of consistency in all of Lennon's politics, an anti-authoritarian bias that fed his associations with the Black Panthers, the peace movement, the inmates of Attica Prison and the rioters in Berkeley's People Park" and concluded that "what Wiener has saved for posterity are those parts of Lennon's life that are likely to be overlooked in the biographies that will be written about the musical Lennon."

Wiener told *CA:* "In addition to writing about politics and music, I also have a career as a historian of the American South. My book *Social Origins of the New South* argued that the planter class survived the Civil War and dominated the region's post-war economy and society. It generated wide controversy among historians and was the subject of more than forty reviews."

BIOGRAPHICAL/CRITICAL SOURCES:

PERIODICALS

Globe and Mail (Toronto), July 21, 1984.
Los Angeles Times, March 22, 1983, March 13, 1984, June 23, 1984.
New York Post, March 22, 1983, March 12, 1984.
New York Times, March 12, 1984, June 26, 1984.
People, June 18, 1984.
Time, April 4, 1983.
Washington Post, March 23, 1983.
Washington Post Book World, July 31, 1984.

*   *   *

WIERZYNSKI, Kazimierz 1894-1969

OBITUARY NOTICE: Born August 27 (one source says August 26), 1894, in Drohobycz, Austria-Hungary (now Drogobych, U.S.S.R.); died February 13, 1969, in London, England. Poet, critic, biographer, essayist, and author of short stories. As a youth Wierzynski engaged in activities devoted to the liberation of Poland and, when Poland gained independence after World War I, Wierzynski entered Polish literary circles in Warsaw. While there he contributed poetry to literary magazines and published several volumes of poems, the first in 1919. His 1927 poem *Laur olimpijski* won first prize in the literary contest for the ninth Olympic Games in Amsterdam, Netherlands. Wierzynski, who continued to produce poetry as well as short stories throughout the 1930's, left Poland in 1939 at the outbreak of World War II. His emigre writings appeared from France, Portugal, and Brazil before Wierzynski settled, in 1941, in the United States. From his self-imposed exile Wierzynski produced several more volumes of poetry as well as works of prose. He wrote the 1949 biography *The Life and*

Death of Chopin in English; his *Selected Poems* was published in 1959. Wierzynski also wrote essays and literary criticism.

OBITUARIES AND OTHER SOURCES:

BOOKS

Cassell's Encyclopaedia of World Literature, revised edition, Morrow, 1973.
Columbia Dictionary of Modern European Literature, 2nd revised edition, Columbia University Press, 1980.
Encyclopedia of World Literature in the Twentieth Century, updated edition, Ungar, 1967.

PERIODICALS

New York Times, February 15, 1969.

* * *

WIGG, George (Edward Cecil)   1900-1983

OBITUARY NOTICE: Born November 28, 1900; died of myasthenia gravis, August 11, 1983, in London, England. Politician and author. A Labour party member of the British Parliament from 1945 to 1967, Wigg is best remembered for his role in breaking the 1963 sex-and-spying scandal involving British Secretary of State for War John Profumo. Wigg gathered evidence that Profumo was having an affair with Christine Keeler, a woman who was also seeing Yevgeni Ivanov, the Soviet Union's naval attache in London at the time. Many feared that the Soviets would learn British defense secrets through this association. After first denying the accusations, Profumo admitted that he had lied and resigned from office. The scandal rocked the Conservative government of Prime Minister Harold Macmillan and paved the way for Harold Wilson's Labour party to gain control of Parliament in 1964. Wigg was then appointed paymaster general, a post he held until 1967. Upon leaving Parliament that same year, Wigg was given a life peerage as baron of the Borough of Dudley. He wrote the autobiographical *George Wigg,* which was published in 1972.

OBITUARIES AND OTHER SOURCES:

BOOKS

Blue Book: Leaders of the English-Speaking World, St. Martin's, 1976.
The International Who's Who, 47th edition, Europa, 1983.
Who's Who, 135th edition, St. Martin's, 1983.

PERIODICALS

New York Times, August 13, 1983.
Annual Obituary 1983, St. James Press, 1984.

* * *

WILCOX, Francis (Orlando)   1908-1985

OBITUARY NOTICE—See index for *CA* sketch: Born April 9, 1908, in Columbus Junction, Iowa; died after a heart attack, February 20, 1985, in Washington, D.C. Educator, political scientist, public servant, administrator, editor, and author. Wilcox was professor of political science and dean of the School of Advanced International Studies at Johns Hopkins University from 1961 to 1973. He also held several government posts during his career, including chief of staff of the Senate Foreign Relations Committee from 1947 to 1955 and U.S. assistant secretary of state from 1955 to 1961. He participated in United Nations conferences and served on President Nixon's Com-

mission to the United Nations in the early 1970's. Beginning in 1975, Wilcox was director general of the Atlantic Council, an organization promoting close ties among NATO nations. Among Wilcox's writings are *Some Aspects of the Financial Administration of Johnson County, Iowa,* and, with Carl Milton Marcy, *Congress and the United Nations* and *Proposals for Change in the United Nations.* Wilcox also co-edited volumes such as *The United States and the United Nations* and *The Atlantic Community: Progress and Prospects* and contributed to several other works and periodicals.

OBITUARIES AND OTHER SOURCES:

BOOKS

Current Biography, Wilson, 1962, April, 1985.
Who's Who in America, 43rd edition, Marquis, 1984.

PERIODICALS

Washington Post, February 23, 1985.

* * *

WILLIAMS, Ralph Vaughan
   See VAUGHAN WILLIAMS, Ralph

* * *

WILSON, August   1945-

BRIEF ENTRY: Born in 1945 in Pittsburgh, Pa. American poet and playwright. Wilson won critical acclaim with his first Broadway play, *Ma Rainey's Black Bottom* (Plume, 1985; first produced in 1984). Staged within the framework of a mythical 1927 recording session with the legendary blues singer Gertrude "Ma" Rainey, Wilson's drama depicts black Americans caught up in a racist society that forces them to express their anger and frustration through their music. Earlier in his career Wilson contributed poems to small magazines, mostly black publications such as *Black World* and *Black Lines,* and founded and directed the Black Horizons Theatre Company in St. Paul, Minnesota.

BIOGRAPHICAL/CRITICAL SOURCES:

BOOKS

Black American Writers Past and Present: A Biographical and Bibliographical Dictionary, Scarecrow, 1975.

PERIODICALS

Ebony, January, 1985.
New Yorker, October 22, 1984.
New York Times, April 13, 1984, October 12, 1984, October 22, 1984.

* * *

WILSON, Derek (Alan)   1935-

BRIEF ENTRY: Born October 10, 1935, in Colchester, England. British historian and author noted for his works about England's Tudor period. His titles include *A Tudor Tapestry: Men, Women and Society in Reformation England* (Heinemann, 1972), *The World Encompassed: Francis Drake and His Great Voyage* (Harper, 1977), *England in the Age of Thomas More* (Hart-Davis, 1978), and *Sweet Robin: A Biography of Robert Dudley, Earl of Leicester, 1533-1588* (Hamish Hamilton, 1981). Among Wilson's other books are *A History of South and Central Africa* (Cambridge University Press, 1975),

and *The World Atlas of Treasure* (Collins, 1981). *Address:*
Winnibrook House, Carhampton, Somerset, England; and c/o
John Parker, Campbell Thomson & McLaughlin Ltd., 31
Newington Green, London N16 9PU, England.

BIOGRAPHICAL/CRITICAL SOURCES:

PERIODICALS

American Historical Review, February, 1974.
New Yorker, February 27, 1978.
New York Times Book Review, February 12, 1978, April 24,
     1978, August 16, 1981.
Times Literary Supplement, September 4, 1981, January 1,
     1982.

*   *   *

WINDLE, William Frederick   1898-1985

OBITUARY NOTICE—See index for *CA* sketch: Born October
10, 1898, in Huntington, Ind.; died of Parkinson's disease,
February 20, 1985, in Granville, Ohio. Educator, scientist,
editor, and author. Windle taught anatomy at several institutions, including Northwestern University from 1923 to 1946
and the University of Pennsylvania from 1947 to 1951. In 1954
he began a nine year association with the National Institute of
Neurological Diseases and Blindness, first serving as chief of
the Laboratory of Neuroanatomical Sciences throughout the
1950's, then becoming assistant director in 1960 and chief of
the Laboratory of Perinatal Physiology in 1961. After leaving
the institute Windle became a research director and professor
at New York University, where he stayed until 1971. Windle
also served as a visiting professor and guest lecturer at other
universities. In 1968 he received the prestigious Lasker Award
for his work on neonatal asphyxia and newborn infants. His
writings include *Textbook of Histology,* which he wrote with
Jose Fernandez Nonidez, *Physiology of the Fetus: Relation to
Brain Damage in the Perinatal Period,* and *The Pioneering
Role of clarence Luther Herrick in American Neuroscience.*
Windle also edited such volumes as *The Spinal Cord and Its
Reaction to Traumatic Injury* and *Stephen Walter Ranson:
Groundbreaking Neuroscientist.* He founded and edited the
"Experimental Neurology" series for Academic Press.

OBITUARIES AND OTHER SOURCES:

PERIODICALS

Washington Post, February 24, 1985.

*   *   *

WODHAMS, (Herbert) Jack   1931-

PERSONAL: Born September 3, 1931, in Dagenham, Essex,
England; immigrated to Australia, 1955, naturalized citizen,
1978; son of Herbert Victor (a police officer) and Rose (a
maid; maiden name, Pitman) Wodhams. *Education:* Educated
in England.

ADDRESSES: Home—P.O. Box 48, Caboolture, Queensland
4510, Australia.

CAREER: Worked as salesman, scalemaker and repairman,
bartender, and welder; Australian Post Office, Brisbane, driver,
1975—; writer.

WRITINGS:

SCIENCE FICTION NOVELS

The Authentic Touch, Curtiss, 1971.

Looking for Bluecher, Cory & Collins, 1980.
Ryn, Cory & Collins, 1982.
Future War, Cory & Collins, 1982.

OTHER

Contributor of short stories to science fiction periodicals, including *Analog.*

WORK IN PROGRESS: Pumfenpuffenwagen, a whimsical novel
set in the late nineteenth century.

SIDELIGHTS: Jack Wodhams told *CA:* "My writing career
was kicked off by the late, great John W. Campbell, the editor
who in 1966 bought my 'Crooked Man' story for *Analog.*
Since that time I have seen uncounted tens rather than hundreds
of my short stories, mostly science fiction, in print.

"My work in progress could be anything at any time, from
fooling to carpenter furniture in experimental designs, to simply planting trees. *Pumfenpuffenwagen* may or may not get
written during 1985. I write only if I feel like it, not because
I have to. From personal insight I exalt not writers, who ever
and always appear to be less bold, less noble, less great, less
lovable, and altogether much shorter in either vice or virtue,
than their creations.

"She who would aspire to gain applause by the pen self-inflects
a burdensome yoke upon herself. A writer should never blame
anybody but herself for her presumption. She asks for pity,
when all she has to do is shut up. Writing is for bums. I am
most suited."

*   *   *

WOHL, Paul   1901(?)-1985

OBITUARY NOTICE: Born c. 1901 in Berlin, Germany; died
April 2, 1985, in New York, N.Y. Journalist. Wohl arrived
in the United States in 1938 as a correspondent for Czech
newspapers. He joined the *Christian Science Monitor* in 1941
and remained there until his retirement in 1979. As a special
correspondent Wohl covered Soviet affairs, and he sometimes
wrote for other publications, including the *New York Herald
Tribune, Commonweal,* and *Nation.*

OBITUARIES:

PERIODICALS

New York Times, April 4, 1985.

*   *   *

WOLF, Adolf Hungry
See HUNGRY WOLF, Adolf

*   *   *

WOLF, Bernard   1930-

BRIEF ENTRY: Born in 1930 in New York, N.Y. American
interior designer, photographer, and author. A former interior
designer for furniture manufacturers, Wolf has worked as a
travel photographer in such locations as Thailand, Greece, and
the Madeira Islands of Portugal. Magazines featuring his work
include *Travel and Camera, House Beautiful, Fortune,* and
Camera 35. Wolf has also written children's books, including
Don't Feel Sorry for Paul (Lippincott, 1974), *Connie's New
Eyes* (Lippincott, 1976), and *Anne's Silent World* (Lippincott,
1977)—all of which focus on handicapped characters—as well

as *The Little Weaver of Agato: A Visit With an Indian Boy Living in the Andes Mountains of Ecuador* (Cowles Book Co., 1969), *Tinker and the Medicine Man: The Story of a Navajo Boy of Monument Valley* (Random House, 1973), and *Firehouse* (Morrow, 1983). His 1978 book *Adam Smith Goes to School* (Lippincott), was named Notable Children's Trade Book by the National Council for the Social Studies and the Children's Book Council. *Address:* New York, N.Y.

BIOGRAPHICAL/CRITICAL SOURCES:

BOOKS

Fifth Book of Junior Authors and Illustrators, H. W. Wilson, 1983.

PERIODICALS

Washington Post Book World, September 11, 1983.

*   *   *

WOLF, Fred Alan   1934-

PERSONAL: Born December 3, 1934, in Chicago, Ill.; son of Maurice (an artist) and Emma (a homemaker; maiden name, Stern) Wolf; married Elaine Davis, April 7, 1957 (divorced June, 1972); married Judith Anderson (an artist), December 31, 1977; children: (first marriage) Leslie, Michael, Jacqueline, Anthony; Shawn (stepdaughter). *Education:* University of Illinois, B.S., 1957; University of California, Los Angeles, M.S., 1959, Ph.D., 1963.

ADDRESSES: Home and office—La Jolla, Calif. *Agent*—John Brockman Associates, Inc., 2307 Broadway, New York, N.Y. 10024.

CAREER: Lawrence Radiation Laboratory, Livermore, Calif., staff physicist, 1961-62; San Diego State College (now University), San Diego, Calif. assistant professor, 1964-68, associate professor, 1968-71, professor of physics, 1971-77; Global Marine Development Corporation, Newport Beach, Calif., systems analyst consultant, 1978-79; Alta Technology, San Diego, systems analyst consultant, 1978-79, systems analyst consultant and senior physicist, 1980-81, 1983; writer and lecturer, 1983—. Visiting professor at Hahn-Meitner Institut fuer Kernforschung, Berlin, West Germany, 1971, at Hebrew University of Jerusalem, Israel, 1971, and at Laboratoire de Physico-Chimie des Rayonnements, Orsay, France, 1971; associate professor of physics at University of Paris, Orsay, 1973-74. President, Youniverse Seminars, Inc., La Jolla, Calif., 1977—. Consulting physicist for U.S. Navy Eletronic Laboratory, San Diego, 1966-68, for Aerospace Research Lab., Wright Patterson Air Force Base, Ohio, 1969, and for Quantum Systems, Inc., Albuquerque, N.M., 1971. Technical staff member at General Atomic/General Dynamics, San Diego, 1964-68; Laser Consultant for Avco-Everett Corp., Everett, Mass., 1966-68. Lecturer in Europe, India, and Japan, 1965-75. Guest on radio and television programs. *Military service:* U.S. Air Force, first lieutenant reserve officer, 1957-62.

AWARDS, HONORS: Howard Hughes Master of Science Fellow, 1957-59; honorary research fellow at University of London, Birkbeck College, 1972, 1973, and 1974; American Book Award for best science paperback, 1982, for *Taking the Quantum Leap: The New Physics for Nonscientists; Taking the Quantum Leap* named to *Library Journal*'s "One Hundred Outstanding Sci-Tech Books of the Year" list.

WRITINGS:

(With Bob Toben and Jack Sarfatti) *Space-Time and Beyond: Toward an Explanation of the Unexplainable,* Dutton, 1975, new edition, with scientific commentary by Wolf, Dutton, 1982.
Taking the Quantum Leap: The New Physics for Nonscientists, (Science Book-of-the-Month Club selection) Harper, 1981.
Star-Wave: Mind, Consciousness, and Quantum Physics, Macmillan, 1984.
Mind and the New Physics, Heinemann, 1985.
The Body Quantum: The Quantum Physics of Body, Mind, and Health, Macmillan, in press.

Also author of *Der Quantensprung ist Keine Hexerei: Die neue Physik fuer Einsteiger* (title means "The Quantum Jump Is Not Witchcraft: The New Physics for Beginners"), Birkhauser Verlag.

Contributor to professional journals, including *Bulletin of the American Physical Society, Physical Review,* and *Journal of Chemical Physics.*

WORK IN PROGRESS: Planning a book titled *The Physics of Love and Sex.*

SIDELIGHTS: Fred Alan Wolf is best known for writing the award-winning science paperback *Taking the Quantum Leap: The New Physics for Nonscientists.* The book provides overviews of both classical and modern physics. Paul Stuewe, reviewing for *Quill & Quire,* found that Wolf's history and explanation of quantum mechanics constituted "a readable and informative work of scientific popularization" and provided "a good practical understanding of ideas that are going to be the basis of any future breakthrough in theoretical physics."

In his 1985 book, *Star-Wave,* Wolf contends that quantum physics provides the best means for understanding the mind-brain relationship and for understanding the nature of reality. Richard M. Restak praised the book in the *New York Times Book Review* as "a brilliant, original leap into the future rather than a restatement of the challenges of the past in the terminology of present-day neuroscience."

Wolf told *CA:* "I feel I am on a brink between the complementary ways we have of viewing the world. That brink is symbolized by the slash, '/'. I am a writer/scientist. I think/feel that the world needs/wants a new view of reality/illusion: the quantum physical view. I sense/intuit that the world is not explainable without the feelings of the heart as well as the thoughts of the intellect. I believe that I am on the right track to finding that view: a merger of heart and mind through the enriching understanding of our quantum world."

BIOGRAPHICAL/CRITICAL SOURCES:

PERIODICALS

Bloomsbury Review, March, 1985.
Choice, February, 1982.
East West Journal, April, 1982.
Library Journal, November 15, 1981, March 1, 1982.
New Realities, Volume IV, number 4, 1982.
New Scientist, July 1, 1982.
New York Times Book Review, January 20, 1985.
Omega Science Digest (New Zealand), May/June, 1982.
Quill & Quire, February, 1982.
ReVISION, spring, 1982.
Science Digest, December, 1981, February, 1982.
VOYA, June, 1982.

WOLKOFF, Judie (Edwards)

BRIEF ENTRY: Born in Montana. American educator and author. Wolkoff, a graduate of the University of Utah, has been a teacher at elementary schools in California and New York. Among her books are *Wally* (Bradbury, 1977), a children's book about a young boy who attempts to harbor a chuckwalla in his closet. Wolkoff has also written fiction for young adults, including *Where the Elf King Sings* (Bradbury, 1980) and *Ace Hits the Big Time* (Delacorte, 1981). *Residence:* Chappaqua, N.Y.

*   *   *

WOOLSEY, Sarah Chauncy   1835(?)-1905
(Susan Coolidge)

BRIEF ENTRY: Born January 29, 1835 (some sources say 1845) in Cleveland, Ohio; died April 9, 1905, in Newport, R.I. American editor, poet, and author. Woolsey is best remembered as a writer for children, first gaining popularity for her "Katy Did" series. Written under the pseudonym Susan Coolidge and begun in 1872, the series—a greater literary influence in England than in the United States—has since been recognized as a precursor to the popular British girls' school stories that proliferated in the twentieth century. Books in the series include *What Katy Did* (1873), *What Katy Did at School* (1874), and *What Katy Did Next* (1887). Woolsey also contributed both prose and poetry to periodicals, published several books of verse for adults, and edited the two-volume *Autobiography and Correspondence of Mrs. Delany* (1879), the two-volume *Diary and Letters of Frances Burney, Mrs. D'Arblay* (1880), and the *Letters of Jane Austen* (1892). *Address:* Newport, R.I.

BIOGRAPHICAL/CRITICAL SOURCES:

BOOKS

The National Cyclopaedia of American Biography, Volume 11, James T. White, 1967.
Twentieth-Century Children's Writers, St. Martin's, 1978.
Who Was Who in America, Volume 1: *1897-1942,* Marquis, 1943.

*   *   *

WORTHINGTON, Janet Evans   1942-

PERSONAL: Born January 30, 1942, in Springfield, Ill.; daughter of Orville Ray and Helen (Tuxhorn) Evans; married Gary H. Worthington (a writer and editor); children: Rachael, Evan, Adam Nicholas Karl. *Education:* Attended Blackburn College, 1960-62; University of Chicago, B.A., 1965; University of Iowa, M.A., 1969; Florida State University, Ph.D., 1977.

ADDRESSES: Home—118 Clark St., Fayetteville, W.Va. 25840. *Office*—Department of English, West Virginia Institute of Technology, Montgomery, W.Va. 25136.

CAREER: Teacher in Lone Tree, Iowa, 1965; teacher of high school English in Lena, Ill., 1965-67; William Rainey Harper College, Palatine, Ill., teacher of freshman English, 1969-70; Piedmont Schools Project, Greer, S.C., language arts resource coordinator, 1973-76; high school teacher in Beckley, W.Va., 1976-77; West Virginia Institute of Technology, Montgomery,

reading instructor and adjunct instructor in English, 1977-78, assistant professor, 1978-82, associate professor of English, 1983—, reading instructor in Upward Bound program, summers, 1980-84, coordinator of the Technical Communications Project at the Community and Technical College, 1983—. Adjunct instructor at College of Graduate Studies, Institute, W.Va., spring, 1981 and 1983.

MEMBER: National Council of Teachers of English, Society for Technical Communications, West Virginia Community College Association.

AWARDS, HONORS: Grants from West Virginia Humanities Foundation, 1979 and 1983.

WRITINGS:

(Contributor) Dwight L. Burton and others, editors, *Teaching English Today,* Houghton, 1975.
(With Albert B. Somers) *Response Guides for Teaching Children's Books,* National Council of Teachers of English, 1979.
(With Somers) *Candles and Mirrors: Response Guides for Teaching Novels and Plays in Grades Six Through Twelve,* Libraries Unlimited, 1984.
(With William C. Burns, Jr.) *Introduction to Industrial Robotic Components Technology,* Reston, 1985.

Contributor to magazines.

SIDELIGHTS: Janet Evans Worthington told *CA:* "Co-authoring books is especially rewarding. When two people work together, one writer can provide support and enthusiasm when the other feels discouraged. In the end, the shared trials and joys make the finished book a special thrill."

*   *   *

WRIGHT, Cobina   ?-1970

OBITUARY NOTICE: Name originally Elaine Cobb; born on September 20, in Lakeview, Ore.; died following a stroke, April 9, 1970, in Hollywood, Calif. Singer, columnist, and author. A wealthy socialite, Wright made her debut as an opera singer at the age of sixteen in Mainz, Germany. After singing throughout Europe, she first performed in the United States at Carnegie Hall in 1924 and went on to sing with orchestras in the United States and Canada. When the stock market crashed in 1929, Wright and her husband, William M. Wright, lost millions of dollars. She then began singing in supper clubs and later wrote a society column for Hearst Newspapers. Wright's autobiography, *I Never Grew Up,* was published in 1952.

OBITUARIES AND OTHER SOURCES:

BOOKS

Obituaries on File, Facts on File, 1979.
Who Was Who in America, With World Notables, Volume V: *1969-1973,* Marquis, 1973.

PERIODICALS

Newsweek, April 20, 1970.
New York Times, April 11, 1970.
Time, February 18, 1952.

*   *   *

WRIGHT, Olgivanna Lloyd   1900(?)-1985

OBITUARY NOTICE: Born c. 1900 in Cetinje, Montenegro

(now Yugoslavia); died of a heart attack, March 1, 1985, in Scottsdale, Ariz. School administrator, composer, and author. Educated in Russia and France, Wright was married to renowned architect Frank Lloyd Wright. With her husband she co-founded a colony, Taliesin West, in Scottsdale, Arizona, which served as both an architectural firm and a school for aspiring architects. After her husband's death in 1959, Wright became president of the Frank Lloyd Wright Foundation, the Frank Lloyd Wright School of Architecture and Taliesin. She also composed chamber and orchestral music for Taliesin festivals of music and dance. Wright wrote books about her husband, including *Our House, The Shining Brow: Frank Lloyd Wright, The Roots of Life*, and *Frank Lloyd Wright: His Life, His Work, His Words*. She was also author of *The Struggle Within*.

OBITUARIES AND OTHER SOURCES:

BOOKS

Who's Who in America, 42nd edition, Marquis, 1982.

PERIODICALS

Life, June 11, 1971.
Newsweek, March 11, 1985.
New York Times, February 24, 1972, March 3, 1985.
People, January 31, 1983.

*   *   *

WRIGHT, Willard Huntington   1888-1939
   (S. S. Van Dine)

BRIEF ENTRY: Born in 1888 in Charlottesville, Va.; died April 11, 1939. American critic, editor, and author. Under the pseudonym S. S. Van Dine, Wright gained fame as the author of a series of detective novels featuring the sleuth Philo Vance. The best-selling novels, which include *The Benson Murder Case* (1926), *The Scarab Murder Case* (1930), and the *Kidnap Murder Case* (1936), also earned Wright credit for inaugurating the Golden Age in American detective fiction. The author, who began to read detective fiction and study criminology while convalescing from overwork, eventually developed his own theory of detective fiction, set forth in his now well-known ''Twenty Rules for Writing Detective Stories''; they first appeared in the September, 1928, issue of *American Magazine*.

Prior to the 1925 illness that launched his detective writing career, Wright had worked as an art, music, and literary critic for periodicals. He had also worked as an editor and as such served *Smart Set* magazine from 1912 to 1914. Wright collaborated with H. L. Mencken and George Jean Nathan on *Europe After 8:15* (1914) and wrote a number of other books, including *What Nietzsche Taught* (1915) and *The Future of Painting* (1923).

BIOGRAPHICAL/CRITICAL SOURCES:

BOOKS

Longman Companion to Twentieth Century Literature, Longman, 1970.
The Oxford Companion to American Literature, 4th edition, Oxford University Press, 1965.
Twentieth-Century Crime and Mystery Writers, St. Martin's, 1980.
Who Was Who in America, Volume I: *1897-1942*, Marquis, 1943.

WYATT, Richard Jed   1939-

PERSONAL: Born June 5, 1939, in Los Angeles, Calif. *Education:* Johns Hopkins University, B.A., 1961, M.D., 1964.

ADDRESSES: Office—National Institute of Mental Health, W.A.W. Bldg., Rm. 536, Saint Elizabeth's Hospital, Washington, D.C. 20032.

CAREER: Western (now Case Western) Reserve University, Cleveland, Ohio, pediatric intern at University Hospital, 1964-65; Massachusetts Mental Health Center, Boston, resident in psychiatry, 1965-67; National Institute of Mental Health, Bethesda, Md., clinical associate of Laboratory of Clinical Psychobiology, 1967-69, research psychiatrist at Laboratory of Clinical Psychopharmacology, 1967-71, chief of Intramural Research Program, Neuropsychiatry Branch, 1972—. Private practice of psychiatry in Washington, D.C., 1968—; associate director for research at Saint Elizabeth's Hospital, 1977—. Instructor at Foundation for Advanced Education in the Sciences, National Institutes of Health, 1971—, and Washington School of Psychiatry, 1971—; consulting associate professor at Stanford Medical Center, Palo Alto, Calif., 1973-74; clinical professor at Duke University, 1975—; adjunct professor at Uniformed Services University of the Health Sciences, 1980—. Organizer of psychiatric services for Resurrection City, Washington, D.C., 1970; Foundations' Fund for Research in Psychiatry, member of board of directors, 1976-81, chairman of board, 1977-79; member of scientific advisory council of Paralysis Cure Foundation, 1980-83; member of stress and illness panel, Institute of Medicine, 1980-81; president of Assembly of Scientists of National Institute of Neurological and Communicative Disorders and Stroke and National Institute of Mental Health, 1983-84.

MEMBER: International Psychogeriatric Association, American Association for Geriatric Psychiatry, American College of Neuropsychopharmacology (fellow), American Medical Association, American Narcolepsy Association (member of medical board, 1975—), American Psychiatric Association (fellow; chairman of advertising committee, 1984-86), Psychiatric Research Society, Society for Biological Psychiatry, Society for Neuroscience, Society for Psychophysiological Study of Sleep, Washington Geriatric Association, Washington Psychiatric Society.

AWARDS, HONORS: Harry Solomon Research Award from Massachusetts Mental Health Center and Harvard University, 1968; A. E. Bennett Award in Clinical Psychiatric Research from Society for Biological Psychiatry, 1971; Psychopharmacological Award from American Psychological Association, 1971; Administrators Award for Meritorious Achievement from Alcohol, Drug Abuse, and Mental Health Administration, 1977; M.D. from Universidad Central de Venezuela, 1977; Superior Achievement Award from U.S. Public Health Service, 1980; Stanley R. Dean Research Award from American College of Psychiatrists, 1982; named a Future Leader of Washington by *Washingtonian*, 1982; Daniel Efron Award from American College of Neuropsychopharmacology, 1983; Outstanding Performance Award from Senior Executive Service and Senior Scientific Service, 1983; Tri-Services Award, 1985.

WRITINGS:

(With A. E. Slaby) *Dementia in the Presenium*, C. C. Thomas, 1974.

(With W. B. Mendelson and J. C. Gillin) *Human Sleep and Its Disorders*, Plenum, 1977.

(With D. V. Jeste) *Understanding and Treating Tardive Dyskinesia*, Guilford, 1982.

(Editor with Jeste) *Neuropsychiatric Movement Disorders*, American Psychiatric Press, 1984.

After Middle Age: A Physician's Guide to Staying Healthy While Growing Older, McGraw, 1985.

Editor of series "Foundations of Modern Psychiatry," Guilford, 1982—. Contributor of about four hundred articles to medical journals. Member of executive editorial board of *Sleep Reviews*, 1972-73, and *Neuropharmacology*, 1974—; member of editorial board of *Schizophrenia Bulletin*, 1976—, *Communications in Psychopharmacology*, 1978-81, *Psychiatry Research*, 1979—, *Journal of Clinical Psychopharmacology*, 1980—, *Journal of Clinical Psychiatry*, 1980—, *International Review of Neurobiology*, 1980—, *Experimental Neurology*, 1981—, *Psychiatry Briefs*, 1984—, *Psychiatry*, 1985—, and *Journal of Nervous and Mental Disease;* editor of *Schizophrenia Newsletter*, 1980-81.

SIDELIGHTS: Richard Wyatt told *CA:* "*After Middle Age* is a book derived from my notes on questions that were asked me by my family and friends beginning in medical school. It was clear that most people have little knowledge about how to approach the second half century of life, how to make their life more comfortable and safer, and what they should do when something does goes wrong. *After Middle Age* does not substitute for a physician or other community resources. It does, however, provide information about how to make best use of the resources that are available. It tells older people and family members who worry about them how to be in control and, when that is impossible, how to compromise. It especially gives useful advice about planning ahead. A great deal can be done to make growing older easy, pleasant, and graceful. One reviewer has commented that what Doctor Spock has become to the under-twelve set, *After Middle Age* will become for those already over fifty, or who someday aspire to be."

BIOGRAPHICAL/CRITICAL SOURCES:

PERIODICALS

Psychology Today, August, 1983.

*　　　*　　　*

WYMAN, Oliver
    See HOLMES, Olive

Y-Z

YELLIN, David G(ilmer) 1916-

BRIEF ENTRY: Born April 3, 1916, in Philadelphia, Pa. American television producer, broadcaster, educator, and author. Yellin joined the faculty of Memphis State University in 1964. He was a professor of broadcasting and film until 1981, when he was named professor emeritus. In 1969 he began producing and moderating the television program "Face to Face." Yellin wrote *Special: Fred Freed and the Television Documentary* (Macmillan, 1973). *Address:* Department of Speech and Drama, Memphis State University, Memphis, Tenn. 38152.

*   *   *

ZEND, Robert 1929-

PERSONAL: Born December 2, 1929, in Budapest, Hungary; son of Henrik and Stephanie Zend; married wife, Janine; children: Aniko, Natalie. *Education:* Peter Pazmany Science University, B.A., 1953; University of Toronto, M.A., 1969.

ADDRESSES: Home—82 Hillcrest Dr., Toronto, Ontario, Canada M6G 2E6.

CAREER: Free-lance children's writer, 1952-56; CBC-Radio, Toronto, Ontario, editor, producer, director, and author of more than a hundred programs for series "FM—Ideas," 1958-77; free-lance writer and poet, 1978—. Writer in residence at universities; member of poetry performance group Three Roberts.

MEMBER: League of Canadian Poets.

AWARDS, HONORS: Grants from Ontario Arts Council and Canada Council.

WRITINGS:

(And translator from the Hungarian with John R. Columbo) *From Zero to One* (poems), Sono Nis Press, 1973.
(Editor) Peter Singer, *Ariel and Caliban: Selected Poems,* Aya Press, 1980.
My Friend, Jeronimo, Omnibooks, 1982.
Arbormundi: Sixteen Selected Typescapes, blewointmentpress, 1982.
Beyond Labels (self-illustrated), Hounslow Press, 1982.
OAB, Exile Editions, 1982.

Work represented in anthologies, including *The Poets of Canada; To Say the Least;* and *Sound of Time.* Contributor to magazines, including *Tamarack Review, Malahat Review, Exile,* and *Canadian Forum.*

WORK IN PROGRESS: OAB, Volume II.

SIDELIGHTS: Robert Zend told *CA:* "My most often used themes are creation, death, the cosmic view, concepts of God, bureaucracy and the state, and mystical topics. I have created radio programs with Marcel Marceau, Jorge Luis Borges, Immanual Velikovsky, and others. I have also translated from Latin, German, Hungarian, Italian, and Spanish."

*   *   *

ZIMMERMAN, Paul D.

CAREER: Writer.

WRITINGS:

NONFICTION

(With Burt Goldblatt) *The Marx Brothers at the Movies,* Putnam, 1968.
(With Dick Schaap) *The Year the Mets Lost Last Place,* World Publishing, 1970.

SCREENPLAYS

"The King of Comedy," Twentieth Century-Fox, 1983.

OTHER

Contributor to periodicals, including *Newsweek* and *Time.*

SIDELIGHTS: Paul D. Zimmerman's *The Marx Brothers at the Movies,* which he wrote with Burt Goldblatt, offers extensive information, including production credits and plot synopses, about every Marx Brothers film. Jack Kroll, reviewing the book in *Newsweek,* called it an "evocative, richly illustrated book that all lovers of the great, mad brothers will have to read." A *Time* reviewer remarked that, aside from the films, "this book is the best possible way to meet the Marx Brothers when they had all their energy, all their laughs and all their feet."

Zimmerman's *The Year the Mets Lost Last Place,* written with sportswriter Dick Schaap, is an account of nine crucial days during the New York Mets' 1969 season. During these nine days, in which the Mets played the division-leading Chicago Cubs six times, they proved to their fans everywhere that they were no longer the bunglers of years past. With several victories over the Cubs, including a near perfect game by Met pitcher Tom Seaver, the Mets established themselves as legitimate contenders for the National League's Eastern Division title. The Mets eventually won not only their division in 1969 but also the National League championship series and the World Series. Pete Axthelm, in his review of *The Year the Mets Lost Last Place* for *Newsweek*, wrote that Zimmerman and Schaap "have reproduced the most important fact of Met life—the fun that was had by all."

Zimmerman is also author of the screenplay for "The King of Comedy," a 1983 film directed by Martin Scorsese. It is the story of Rupert Pupkin, an obnoxious, aspiring comedian who imposes himself on popular talk-show host and comedian Jerry Langford. The men meet when Pupkin rescues the celebrity from a mob of fans. Langford thanks Pupkin, who interprets the comedian's few words as intimations of comradery. Inspired, Pupkin eventually barges into Langford's home only to receive a humiliating dismissal. Pupkin then kidnaps Langford and holds him hostage in an attempt to obtain an appearance on Langford's show. The *Chicago Tribune*'s Gene Siskel found "The King of Comedy" a "most unhappy film" and added that it was "disturbing and conventionally unsatisfying." The *Washington Post*'s Gary Arnold agreed, deeming the film a "distasteful study of delusional behavior."

BIOGRAPHICAL/CRITICAL SOURCES:

PERIODICALS

Chicago Tribune, March 18, 1983.
Los Angeles Times, February 28, 1983.
Newsweek, November 25, 1968, December 8, 1969.
New Yorker, January 25, 1969.
New York Times, February 20, 1983.
Time, March 28, 1969.
Washington Post, April 15, 1983.*

* * *

ZORN, Robert L. 1938-

PERSONAL: Born March 22, 1938, in Youngstown, Ohio; married Joan M. Wilkos (a director of nursing), April 26, 1957; children: Deborah Zorn Becherer, Patricia Zorn Kelley. *Education:* Kent State University, B.S.Ed., 1959; Westminster College, New Wilmington, Pa., M.Ed., 1964; University of Pittsburgh, Ph.D., 1970; postdoctoral study at National Academy for School Executives, 1984. *Politics:* Republican. *Religion:* United Methodist.

ADDRESSES: Home—7386 North Lima Rd., Poland, Ohio 44514. *Office*—Poland School District, 53 College St., Poland, Ohio 44514.

CAREER: Teacher at public school in Beloit, Ohio, 1961-62; elementary school principal in Poland, Ohio, 1962-67; high school unit principal at public schools in Boardman, Ohio, 1967-70; assistant superintendent of schools in Mahoning County, Ohio, 1970-76; Poland School District, Poland, Ohio, superintendent of schools, 1976—. Adjunct professor at Youngstown State University, 1971—. Chairman of Ohio State Advisory Committee for Division of Guidance and Testing, 1979-80; member of board of directors of Industrial Infor-

mation Institute, 1980—. *Military service:* U.S. Air Force, Strategic Air Command, 1959-61; became lieutenant.

MEMBER: American Association of School Administrators, William McGuffey National Historical Society (member of board of directors, 1978—; chairman of National Educators Hall of Fame), Doctoral Association of Educators of University of Pittsburgh, Poland Business and Professional Association (member of board of directors, 1983—), Phi Delta Kappa.

WRITINGS:

(With Edward E. Ford) *Why Marriage?*, Argus, 1974.
(With Ford) *Why Be Lonely?*, Argus, 1975.
(With Richard P. Hartzell) *The Average Finder*, Mafex, 1977.
(Contributor) Glenn Saltzman, editor, *Counseling Midshipmen*, Department of Education and Training, U.S. Navy, 1977.
Speed Reading, Harper, 1980.

Contributor to education journals. Editor of *The Chalkboard*, 1973-76.

WORK IN PROGRESS: Research on education and on human growth, development, and motivation.

* * *

ZOSHCHENKO, Mikhail (Mikhailovich) 1895-1958

BRIEF ENTRY: Born August 10, 1895, in Poltava, Ukraine, Russia (now U.S.S.R.); died of heart disease, July 22, 1958, in Leningrad, U.S.S.R. Russian worker and author. Zoshchenko is known for his humorous—and sometimes controversial—tales of life in the Soviet Union. His early years were marked by a failed suicide attempt and several brief occupations, including gambler, detective, shoemaker, and clerk-typist. In the early 1920's, after he had already begun writing short stories, Zoshchenko joined a literary group that supported the independence of art from politics. Zoshchenko's first collection of short fiction, *Rasskazy Nazara Il'icha, gospodina Sinebryukhova* (1922; title means "Stories of Nazar Ilyich, Mr. Bluebelly"), proved immensely popular with Soviet readers. Many of the tales in this volume are written in the *skaz*—oral—tradition of Russian storytelling as evolved from Gogol and Leskov. The tales, which usually center on an absurd situation as recounted by an equally bizarre narrator, featured such stylistic devices as slang and idiomatic speech in portraying life in the Soviet working class.

In subsequent years Zoshchenko wrote hundreds of short stories depicting the absurdities of life in a Marxist state. Among his best known tales is "Banya" (title means "The Bathhouse"), which details the hardships of a man who lives in a public bathhouse. Many of Zoshchenko's stoires are available in English translation in such collections as *The Woman Who Could Not Read, and Other Tales* (1940), *Scenes From the Bathhouse, and Other Tales of Communist Russia* (1961), and *Nervous People, and Other Satires* (1963). In the mid-1940's Zoshchenko ran afoul of the Stalin regime for his often critical stories and his supposedly "self-indulgent" autobiographical work, *Pered voskhodom solntsa* (1943). He was expelled from the Writers Union in 1946 and afterwards wrote little. His autobiography was published with the fragment *Povest' o razume* (1972) in English translation as *Before Sunrise* in 1974.

BIOGRAPHICAL/CRITICAL SOURCES:

BOOKS

Alexandrova, Vera, *A History of Soviet Literature*, Doubleday, 1963.

Hingley, Ronald, *Russian Writers and Soviet Society, 1917-1918*, Random Hosue, 1979.
Struve, Gleb, *Russian Literature Under Lenin and Stalin*, University of Oklahoma Press, 1971.
Twentieth-Century Literary Criticism, Volume 15, Gale, 1985.

*   *   *

ZUGSMITH, Leane   1903-1969

OBITUARY NOTICE: Born January 18, 1903, in Louisville, Ky.; died October 13, 1969, in Madison, Conn. Journalist and author. Best remembered for her novels, Zugsmith began her career as a journalist, working as a copy editor for such publications as *Detective Stories* and *Western Story Magazine*. A contributor to *New Yorker, Atlantic,* and other magazines, Zugsmith served in the early 1940's as a special feature writer for *PM*, a New York newspaper. Among the several novels to her credit are *Never Enough, The Reckoning,* and *A Time to Remember.* She collaborated with her husband, Carl Randau, on *The Visitor,* which was adapted as a Broadwar play in 1944, and *The Setting Sun of Japan.* A collection of Zugsmith's short stories, *Home is Where You Hang Your Childhood,* was published in 1937.

OBITUARIES AND OTHER SOURCES:

BOOKS

American Women Writers: A Critical Reference Guide From Colonial Times to the Present, Ungar, 1979-82.
Contemporary American Authors: A Critical Survey and 219 Bio-Bibliographies, AMS Press, 1970.
The Oxford Companion to American Literature, 4th edition, Oxford University Press, 1965.
Twentieth-Century Authors: A Biographical Dictionary of Modern Literature, H. W. Wilson, 1942, 1st supplement, H. W. Wilson, 1955.

PERIODICALS

New York Times, October 14, 1969.
Publishers Weekly, November 3, 1969.

*   *   *

ZWEIG, Arnold   1887-1968

OBITUARY NOTICE: Born November 10, 1887, in Gross-Glogau, Germany (now Glogow, Poland); died after a long illness, November 26, 1968, in East Berlin, Germany. Public official, journalist, editor, translator, playwright, and author of fiction and nonfiction. Zweig is best known for his highly acclaimed antiwar novels. He began writing short stories in 1909 and completed his first novel in 1912. He turned to playwriting in the early 1910's and completed two tragedies before World War I. Zweig enlisted in the German Army and fought on the Russian front. When he was discharged, he suffered from an eye disease that impaired his vision and rendered him unable to read by 1915. After the war Zweig settled in Berlin and concentrated on a literary career. He wrote more plays, including two comedies, and published several sympathetic essays on the plight of European Jews. In 1927 he completed *The Case of Sergeant Grischa,* a novel about a Russian prisoner of war who assumes the identity of a German deserter and is ultimately executed for the German's crime.

Zweig enjoyed immense popularity with *The Case of Sergeant Grischa,* and he returned to its characters and the theme of injustice in subsequent works. In 1931 he wrote *Young Woman of 1914,* which concerns a wartime romance between one of Grischa's friends and a German woman. Zweig finished the Grischa cycle with two more novels, *Education Before Verdun,* which features the male protagonist of *Young Woman of 1914,* and *The Crowning of a King,* which details the effect of Grischa's execution on his fellow soldiers. Aside from the Grischa tetralogy Zweig distinguished himself for his many short stories, literary criticism, and pro-Zionist writings. Among his many later works is *Insulted and Exiled: The Truth About the German Jews.* Such publications prompted the Nazis to expel Zweig from Germany in 1933. He moved to Palestine (now Israel) and remained there until 1948, when he removed to East Germany. There he eventually served in Parliament and as president of the Academy of Arts. For his achievements, Zweig received many decorations, including the Soviet Union's Lenin Peace Prize and East Germany's National Prize. Zweig was a friend of pioneering psychoanalyst Sigmund Freud in the 1920's; their correspondence was published in English translation in 1970.

OBITUARIES AND OTHER SOURCES:

BOOKS

The Reader's Encyclopedia, 2nd edition, Crowell, 1965.
Twentieth-Century Authors: A Biographical Dictionary of Modern Literature, H. W. Wilson, 1942, 1st supplement, 1955.

PERIODICALS

Newsweek, November 27, 1968.
New York Times, November 27, 1968.
Time, December 6, 1968.
Times, (London), November 27, 1968.